IN THE MAKING OF EUROPE

IN THE MAKING OF EUROPE

DONALD F. LACH and EDWIN J. VAN KLEY

VOLUME

III

A
Century of
Advance

BOOK FOUR: EAST ASIA

THE UNIVERSITY OF CHICAGO PRESS

CHICAGO AND LONDON

DONALD F. LACH is the Bernadotte E. Schmitt Professor of Modern History, Emeritus, at the University of Chicago.

EDWIN J. VAN KLEY is Professor of History at Calvin College.

THE UNIVERSITY OF CHICAGO PRESS, CHICAGO 60637
The University of Chicago Press, Ltd., London

©1993 by The University of Chicago
All rights reserved. Published 1993
Printed in the United States of America
98 97 96 95 94 93   5 4 3 2 1

Library of Congress Cataloging-in-Publication Data
(Revised for volume 3)

Lach, Donald F. (Donald Frederick), 1917–
    Asia in the making of Europe.

    Vol. 3–   by Donald F. Lach and Edwin J. Van Kley.
    Includes bibliographies and indexes.
    Contents: v. 1. The century of discovery.   2 v.—
v. 2. A century of wonder.   Book 1. The visual arts.
Book 2. The literary arts.   Book 3. The scholarly dis-
ciplines.   3 v. — v. 3. A century of advance. Book 1.
Trade, missions, literature. Book 2. South Asia.
Book 3. Southeast Asia. Book 4. East Asia. 4. v.
    1. Europe—Civilization—Oriental influences.
2. Asia—History.   3. Asia—Discovery and exploration.
I. Van Kley, Edwin J.   II. Title.
CB203.L32   303.48'2405'0903   64-19848
ISBN 0-226-46753-8 (v. 3. bk. 1)
ISBN 0-226-46754-6 (v. 3. bk. 2)
ISBN 0-226-46755-4 (v. 3. bk. 3)
ISBN 0-226-46756-2 (v. 3. bk. 4)
ISBN 0-226-46757-0 (v. 3 : set)

This publication has been supported by a grant
from the National Endowment for the Humanities,
an independent federal agency.

This book is printed on acid-free paper.

Endpaper: Chinese ladies. From Athanasius Kircher,
La chine illustrée (Amsterdam, 1670).

Contents

Contents

(*Contents of other books in Volume III*)

BOOK ONE

PART I

The Continuing Expansion in the East

Contents

Contents

BOOK TWO

PART III

The European Images of Asia

Contents

BOOK THREE

(PART III CONTINUED)

Contents

Abbreviations

AHSI   *Archivum Historicum Societatis Iesu*

Annales.   *Annales: Economies, sociétés, civilisations; revue trimestrielle*
E.S.C.

Asia   Earlier volumes of this work: D. Lach, *Asia in the Making of Europe,* Vols. I and II (Chicago, 1965–77)

BR   Blair, Emma H., and Robertson, James A. (eds.), *The Philippine Islands, 1493–1898* (55 vols., Cleveland, 1903–9)

BTLV   *Bijdragen tot de taal-, land- en volkenkunde van Nederlandsch-Indië*

BV   [Commelin, Isaac (ed.)], *Begin ende voortgangh van de Vereenighde Nederlantsche Geoctroyeerde Oost-Indische Compagnie* . . . ([Amsterdam], 1646). (First edition published 1645. Facsimile edition published in Amsterdam, 1969. The facsimile edition has volumes numbered I, II, III, and IV, corresponding to vols. Ia, Ib, IIa, and IIb of the 1646 edition.)

CV   [Churchill, Awnsham and John (eds.)], *A Collection of Voyages and Travels, Some Now First Printed from Original Manuscripts* . . . (4 vols.; London, 1704)

"HS"   "Works Issued by the Hakluyt Society"

JRAS   *Journal of the Royal Asiatic Society*

Abbreviations

NR   L'Honoré Naber, Samuel Pierre (ed.), *Reisebeschreibungen von deutschen Beamten und Kriegsleuten im Dienst der Niederländischen West- und Ost-Indischen Kompagnien, 1602–1797* (The Hague, 1930–32)

NZM   *Neue Zeitschrift für Missionswissenschaft*

PP   Purchas, Samuel, *Hakluytus Posthumus, or Purchas His Pilgrimes:* . . . (20 vols.; Glasgow, 1905–7. Originally published 1625.)

SCPFMR   *Sacrae Congregationis de Propaganda Fide Memoria Rerum* (Freiburg, 1971)

Streit   R. Streit, *Bibliotheca Missionum* (30 vols.; Münster and Aachen, 1916–75)

Ternaux-   H. Ternaux-Compans, *Bibliothèque asiatique et africaine*
Compans   (Amsterdam, 1968; reprint of Paris, 1841–42 ed.)

TR   Thévenot, Melchisédech, *Relations de divers voyages curieux qui n'ont point esté publiées, ou qui ont esté traduites d'Hacluyt, de Purchas & d'autres voyageurs anglois, hollandois, portugais, allemands, espagnols; et de quelques Persans, Arabes, et autres auteurs orientaux* (4 vols.; Paris, 1663–96)

"WLV"   "Werken uitgegeven door de Linschoten Vereeniging"

ZMR   *Zeitschrift für Missionswissenschaft und Religionswissenschaft*

A Note to the Illustrations

Study of the illustrations of Asia published in seventeenth-century Europe shows that the artists and illustrators tried in most cases to depict reality when they had the sources, such as sketches from the men in the field or the portable objects brought to Europe—plants, animals, costumes, paintings, porcelains, and so on. Many of the engravings based on sketches and paintings are convincing in their reality, such as the depiction of the Potala palace in Lhasa (pl. 384), the portrait of the "Old Viceroy" of Kwangtung (pl. 323), and the drawings of Siamese and Chinese boats. A number of Asian objects—Chinese scroll paintings, a Buddhist prayer wheel, and small animals—appeared in European engravings and paintings for the first time. Asians, like the Siamese emissaries to France, were sketched from life in Europe and their portraits engraved.

When sources were lacking, the illustrators and artists filled in the gaps in their knowledge by following literary texts, or by producing imaginary depictions, including maps. The illustrations of Japan, for example, are far more fantastic than those depicting other places, perhaps because Japan so stringently limited intercourse over much of the century. Printing-house engravers frequently "borrowed" illustrations from earlier editions and often "improved" upon them by adding their own touches which had the effect of Europeanizing them.

Illustrations were "translated" along with texts in various ways. If the publisher of a translation had close relations with the original publisher or printer he might borrow the original copperplate engravings or have the original publisher pull prints from the original plates to be bound with the translated pages. Engraved captions could be rubbed out of the plate and redone in the new language, although many printers did not bother to do so. Lacking the cooperation of the original printers, new engravings could still be made from a print. The simplest method was to place the print face down on the varnished and waxed copper plate to be engraved and then to rub the back of the print causing the ink from the print to adhere to the waxed surface of the plate. The resulting image was then used to engrave, or etch with nitric acid, the new plate, and being reversed it would print exactly as the original version printed. If the engraver wanted to avoid damaging the print, however, which he might well need to finish the engraving, he would use a thin sheet of paper dusted with black lead or black chalk to transfer the image from the print to the new copper plate. He might further protect the print by putting oiled paper on top of it while he traced the picture. This procedure worked whether the print was face down or face up against the plate. In fact it was easier to trace the picture if the print were face up, in which case the new plate would be etched in reverse of the original plate. For a seventeenth-century description of the ways in which new plates could be etched from prints see William Faithorne, *The Art of Graveing and Etching* (New York, 1970), pp. 41–44 (first edition, London, 1662). See also Coolie Verner, "Copperplate Printing," in David Woodward (ed.), *Five Centuries of Map Printing* (Chicago, 1975), p. 53. We have included a number of illustrations that were "borrowed" by one printer from another: see, for example, plates 113 and 114; 117, 118, 121; 174; 312 and 313; 412 and 413; 419–21.

Most of the following illustrations were taken from seventeenth-century books held in the Department of Special Collections in the Regenstein Library at the University of Chicago. Others have been obtained from libraries and archives in Europe and the United States, which have kindly granted us permission to reproduce them. Wherever possible, efforts are made in the captions to analyze the illustrations and to provide relevant collateral information whenever such was available.

Almost all of the four hundred or so illustrations were reproduced from the photographs taken (or retaken) by Alma Lach, an inveterate photographer and cookbook author. We were also aided and abetted by the personnel of the Special Collections department—especially the late Robert Rosenthal, Daniel Meyer, and Kim Coventry—in locating the illustrations and in preparing them for photography. Father Harrie A. Vanderstappen, professor emeritus of Far Eastern art at the University of Chicago and a man endowed with marvelous sight and insight, helped us to analyze the illustrations relating to East Asia. C. M. Naim of the Department of South Asian Languages at the University of Chicago likewise contributed generously of his skills, particularly with reference to the Mughul seals (pls. 117, 118, and 121) here depicted. The China illustrations have benefited from the contributions of Ma Tai-loi and Tai Wen-pai of the East Asian Collection of the Regenstein Library and of Zhijia Shen who generously gave freely of her time and knowledge. The captions for the Japan illustrations have been improved by the gracious efforts of Yoko Kuki of the East Asian Collection of the Regenstein Library. Tetsuo Najita of Chicago's History Department lent a hand in the preparation of the caption for pl. 432. Ann Adams and Francis Dowley of Chicago's Art Department helped us to analyze some of the engravings, especially those prepared by Dutch illustrators.

To all of these generous scholars we express our sincere gratitude for their contributions to the illustration program.

Illustrations

[xvii]

66. Portrait of Alvarez Semedo
67. Portrait of Jean de Thévenot
68. Frontispiece, Olfert Dapper, *Asia,* 1681
69. Frontispiece, Johann Nieuhof, *Gesandtschafft,* 1666
70. Frontispiece, J. T. and J. I. De Bry, *India orientalis,* 1601
71. Frontispiece, Johann von der Behr, *Diarium,* 1669
72. Title page of *Regni Chinensis descriptio,* with Chinese landscape painting, 1639
73. Title page, Edward Terry, *Voyage to East India,* 1655
74. Title page, Johan van Twist, *Generale beschrijvinge van Indien,* 1648
75. Title page, Johan Albrecht von Mandelslo, *Ein Schreiben,* 1645
76. Title page, Philippe de Sainte-Trinité, *Orientalische Reisebeschreibung,* 1671
77. Frontispiece, *ibid.*
78. Title page, Giuseppe di Santa Maria Sebastiani, *Seconde speditione,* 1672
79. Title page, Giovanni Filippo Marini, *Historia,* 1665
80. Title page, Louis Le Compte, *Memoirs and Observations,* 1697
81. Title page, Robert Knox, *Historical Relation of the Island ceylon,* 1681
82. Title page, Adam Olearius, *Offt begehrte Beschreibung der cewen orientalischen Reise,* 1647
83. Title page, Bernhard Varen, *Descriptio Regni Japoniae et Siam,* 1673
84. Title page, Simon de La Loubère, *Du royaume de Siam,* 1691
85. Title page, Gabriel Dellon, *History of the Inquisition at Goa,* 1688
86. Title page, Athanasius Kircher, *China illustrata,* 1667
87. Portrait of Athanasius Kircher
88. Title page, Johann Jacob Saar, *Ost-Indianische funfzehen-jährige Kriegs-Dienste,* 1672
89. Title page, Abbé Carré, *Voyage des Indes Orientales,* 1699
90. Title page, Pietro Della Valle, *Travels,* 1665
91. Title page, Johann von der Behr, *Diarium, oder Tage-Buch,* 1668
92. Title page, Gotthard Arthus, *Historia Indiae Orientalis,* 1668
93. Title page, David Haex, *Dictionarium Malaico-Latinum et Latino-Malaicum,* 1631
94. Title page, Nicolaas Witsen, *Noord en Oost Tartarye,* 1692
95. Title page, Thomas Herbert, *Some Yeares Travels,* 1638
96. Title page, A. and J. Churchill, *Collection of Voyages and Travels,* 1744
97. Frontispiece, Arnoldus Montanus, *Die Gesantschaften an die Keiser van Japan,* 1669
98. Title page, Willem Lodewyckszoon, *Premier livre,* 1609
99. Malay-Latin phrases from Haex's *Dictionarium*
100. Malay-Latin wordlist (*ibid.*)
101. German-Malay wordlist from Dapper's *Beschreibung,* 1681
102. Portrait of Edward Terry

BOOK THREE

FOLLOWING PAGE 1380

Illustrations

BOOK FOUR

FOLLOWING PAGE 1730

Maps

CHAPTER XX

China: The Late Ming Dynasty

The Ming (1368–1644) was a native, or Han, Chinese dynasty which stood chronologically between the foreign Mongol (Yüan, 1280–1368) and Manchu (Ch'ing, 1644–1912) dynasties. The twenty-first of the official dynasties, the Ming had reached its apogee by the time the Europeans became active in the mid-sixteenth century off China's southeastern coast. In its last hundred years the Ming dynasty declined precipitously, particularly after 1620. The empire's foreign trade, especially its silver imports, was cut severely by the worldwide trading depression of 1620 to 1660. Internally it suffered from inflation, extreme cold weather in the north, and droughts, floods, and famines in the south. Under these severe conditions the empire's population fell off abruptly and the rich became richer and the poor more impoverished. As class lines and economic divisions sharpened, unrest and criticism of the government grew apace. At Peking, the Ming capital since 1421, and at Nanking, its second capital, an underpaid officialdom became more lethargic and restive.

The last two Ming emperors supported an elaborate court hierarchy dominated by a horde of eunuchs, who were masters of the harem and the powerful arm of the emperors in managing the palace bureaucracy and the imperial treasury. As their influence and numbers mounted, the eunuchs arrogated broad police powers to themselves while isolating the emperor from important affairs of state. Strategically located between the ministries and the throne, the eunuchs of the palace transmitted the memorials to the emperor and drafted the imperial responses. Under these conditions corruption and factionalism tore the bureaucracy apart and public services collapsed. Distressed by the deterioration of the dynasty, conscientious bureaucrats, literati, and soldiers organized into groups demanding reform.

China and Its Periphery

TARIM BASIN

Lop Nor

Turfan

Hami

Aksu

Kashgar

Yarkand

MO

K

Su-chou

A

Ch'inghai Lake

Hsi-ning

CHINGHAI

C

Srinagar

Leh

Chini

Simla

Tsaparang

Toling

Mana Pass

Hardwar

Badrinath

Delhi

TIBET

Lhasa

SZE

Mt. Everest

Katmandu

Brahmaputra R.

YUNNA

Indus R.

Sutlej R.

Ganges R.

Yangtze R.

BAY OF BENGAL

Scale

0   100 200 300 400

Kilometers

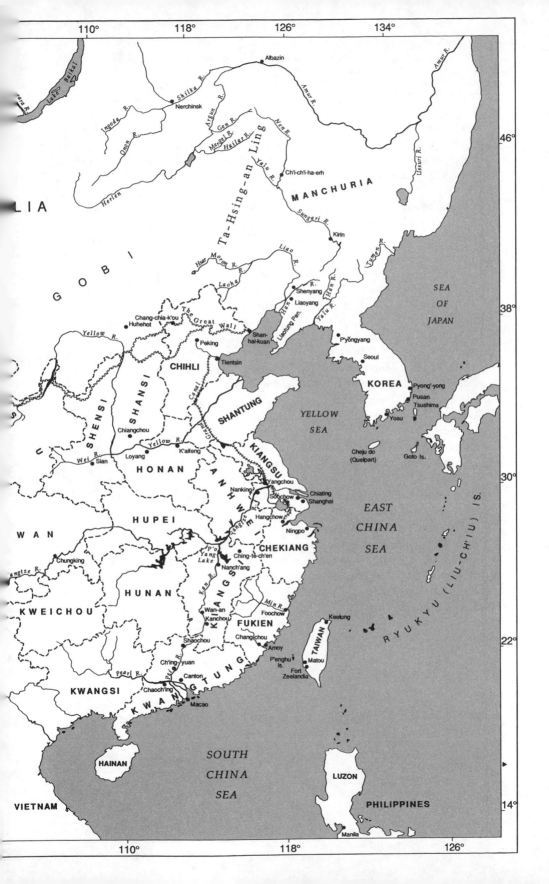

Some disillusioned and disgruntled officials and military leaders collaborated with the Manchus who had begun around 1620 to attack the northern marches of the empire. By 1644 the last of the Ming emperors had committed suicide and the Forbidden City was occupied by the Ch'ing dynasts.[1]

The new Manchu rulers, insecure in their legitimacy and in their control over Chinese society, instituted a literary censorship that lasted until the end of the eighteenth century. The *Ming shih,* or the official history of the Ming dynasty, first appeared in print only in 1739. Study of Ming history by critical scholars remained suspect as surreptitious criticism of the Ch'ing until the nineteenth century. As a consequence, prudent Chinese scholars preferred until near the end of the nineteenth century to confine themselves to study of the Confucian classics or to the history of earlier dynasties. The Ch'ing rulers, perhaps because of their foreign origin, were inclined even more than the Ming to encourage Confucian studies. Late in the Ch'ing dynasty, scholars finally began the systematic collection of Ming documents and the reconstruction of Ming history. It was not until the middle years of the twentieth century that Chinese and foreign scholars were able to produce a rounded history of the Ming from domestic and alien sources. For the study of the second half of the Ming dynasty, the European accounts neatly supplement the Chinese documents, particularly because the observations of the European missionaries and merchants contain descriptions and comments on everyday matters taken for granted by the Chinese writers.[2]

Unlike India, China was a single integrated state and, although massive in size and complexity, permitted much more generalization on the part of seventeenth-century observers than did India. Throughout the century, the Jesuits provided the overwhelming bulk of information about China, in contrast to India where there was greater variety among the Europeans who visited there. The Jesuit reports, although voluminous and detailed, are also somewhat more repetitious than the more variegated European reports of India. Consequently, although by the end of the century China was probably better known to European readers than any other part of Asia, the image of China that emerges from the seventeenth-century reports can be described in somewhat less space than that of the several parts of India.

I

JESUIT LETTERBOOKS, ETHNOHISTORIES, AND TRAVELOGUES

Europe's store of information about China increased very rapidly during the first half of the seventeenth century. The Jesuit missionaries, by the turn of

[1] Based on F. Wakeman, Jr., *The Great Enterprise* (2 vols.; Berkeley, 1985), I, 1–18.
[2] Based on A. Chan, S.J., *The Glory and Fall of the Ming Dynasty* (Norman, Okla., 1982), pp. xvi–xxiii.

the century securely ensconced in Peking, continued to provide the most perceptive as well as the most numerous reports. Their letters were regularly published, and reports from China occupied a large and growing place in them. Some were widely distributed. Niccolò Longobardo's *Breve relatione del regno della Cina,* first published in 1601, for example, was translated into French, Latin, and German, was regularly cited in other descriptions of China, and included in collections of Jesuit letters.[3] Longobardo's letter optimistically describes the state of the Jesuit mission in China, translates a letter from a Chinese convert, "Thaiso," to Matteo Ricci, and lists ten characteristics of China that he thinks will facilitate the spread of the gospel. Some description accompanies the ten characteristics, most of it laudatory.

Equally popular and far more perceptive is Diego de Pantoja's letter of 1602, first published as the *Relación de la entrade de algunos padres de la Compania de Iesus en la China* in 1605.[4] Pantoja's account is far less adulatory of China than Longobardo's or than Juan Gonzáles de Mendoza's sixteenth-century account;[5] for example, he lashes out sharply against the immorality and covetousness of the emperor, the eunuchs, and the military. He gives good detail on the gifts presented by the Jesuits—clocks, books, maps, and oil paintings—and of the wonder they produced among the Chinese. He asserts repeatedly that the Cathay of Marco Polo is the same as China. He is disdainful of the Chinese ignorance of the outside world, of their architecture, of their mathematics, and of their religions. Like Ricci and other Europeans, he is impressed by China's size, teeming population, immense cities, low food prices, high standards of civility, and moral learning.

China also figures prominently in the five volumes of Fernão Guerreiro's *Relaçam annual* (1603–11) which was based on a very large collection of Jesuit missionary letters.[6] A similar work, which drew from Guerreiro's compilation as well as from other Jesuit publications and letters, was published in Bordeaux by Pierre Du Jarric between 1608 and 1614.[7] Together these works provide a comprehensive account of the origin and progress of the Jesuit mission in China along with a substantial amount of descriptive material.

Jesuit authors also published several major descriptions of China during the first half of the seventeenth century which were probably even more influential in shaping Europe's image of China than were their letterbooks. The most important of these, Nicolas Trigault's *De christiana expeditione apud Sinas* (1615), Alvarez Semedo's *Imperio de la China* (1642), and Martino Martini's *Novus atlas sinensis* (1655), provided European readers with more

---

[3] See above, pp. 371–72.
[4] See above, pp. 319–20, for bibliographic details.
[5] For Mendoza's account see *Asia,* I, 742–94.
[6] See above, pp. 315–18, for details.
[7] *Histoire des choses plus memorable advenues tant ez Indes Orientales* . . . (3 vols.). For details see above, p. 396.

comprehensive and better organized information about China than ever before.[8]

Trigault's and Semedo's works resemble Mendoza's in format. Each contains a long comprehensive description of China divided into topical sections such as "names, location, and size," "fertility and products," "mechanical arts," "the liberal arts," "sciences and academic degrees," "administration," "customs," and so forth. Part two of each work is a history of the Christian mission in China from its beginnings. Trigault brings the story down to the death of Matteo Ricci in 1610; Semedo to 1638. Much of the history of the mission as told by Trigault and Semedo would have been familiar to readers of the Annual Letters. Stories are retold, and many of the same events or incidents are reported.

The general description of China in Martini's *Atlas* is similar to that of Trigault and Semedo, but much shorter. It is followed not by a history of the mission but by a detailed description of China's provinces, each accompanied by a provincial map. These and the accompanying descriptions eliminated several erroneous notions about internal geography and clarified Europe's cartographical image of China. The maps were not superseded during the remainder of the century. While better organized, these general descriptions produced a more static image of China than that based on the more haphazard reports of events and characteristics contained in the Jesuit letters. Readers who depended on the ethnohistories and on Mendoza's sixteenth-century description would probably see China as relatively changeless and seemingly devoid of living dynamic leaders and changing events.

The image of China projected through both the ethnohistories and the Jesuit letters becomes progressively more adulatory. Trigault and Pantoja, while they admired much that they found in China, also described many aspects of Chinese life which they judged to be inferior to European practice. For all his admiration for Chinese philosophical attainments, Trigault remained convinced of Europe's scientific and technological superiority. Nor did he excessively praise the natural morality of the Chinese. In his history of the mission one meets "imposters" from all ranks of society, and he frequently deplores the blind superstitions of the heathen Chinese. Semedo was somewhat more laudatory. He finds, for example, that the Chinese are naturally inclined to virtue—especially to humility, virginity, chastity, and filial piety—and he berates Europeans who consider the Chinese to be barbarians.[9] Semedo, writing shortly before 1642, was concerned to defend the Jesuits' position and practice in China against competition and criticism from rival orders—a concern which had arisen since Trigault and Pantoja

[8] For bibliographic details on these three works see above, pp. 512–13, 349, 479–82. Note especially the discrepancies between the modern English translation of Trigault's classic by Louis Gallagher and the Latin and Italian originals; see above, p. 512, n. 34. See our pls. 55, 295, and 388. For portraits of Trigault and Semedo, see our pls. 53 and 66.

[9] *The History of the Great and Renowned Monarchy of China* (London, 1655), p. 26.

wrote. It shows up most clearly in part two of Semedo's book, where he tends to exaggerate the success of the mission and to defend the Jesuit policy of cultural accommodation by extolling the sincerity and constancy of Chinese Christians during the persecutions. Rites Controversy considerations show up even more clearly in Martini's description. Whether because of this or because he relied more heavily than the others on Chinese sources, he appears to be more enthusiastic about China and occasionally to idealize and exaggerate Chinese virtues. Still, in contrast to some later Jesuit writings, none of these descriptions appears to be seriously distorted by the developing polemic in Europe and Asia over Jesuit practices in China.

Less important and for the most part secondary descriptions of China were produced by Don Francisco de Herrera Maldonado in 1621 [10] and by Michel Baudier in 1624. [11] Maldonado's is another comprehensive description based on Jesuit letters, on Trigault, and on sixteenth-century authors such as Gaspar da Cruz, Martin de Rada, Bernardino de Escalante, and Mendoza. What he describes is available elsewhere in firsthand accounts. His *Epitome,* however, is important as the earliest printed description of the death and burial ceremonies of the empress dowager and for his large bibliography of books on China and Asia. [12] Semedo also describes the death of the empress—the Wan-li emperor's mother—but his account appeared later. Baudier's description of China also is entirely based on other printed accounts. He claims to have learned much from hearing Trigault tell Louis XIII about China in 1616, but his descriptions seem to be almost entirely based on Mendoza. Baudier is less critical and more enthusiastic about China than either Mendoza or Trigault.

Although not published until 1663, the volume devoted to China in Daniello Bartoli's official history of the Jesuit mission is essentially an ethnohistory of the Ming dynasty. [13] All of Bartoli's descriptions, even his extensive account of Chinese government, relate to the Ming period. We can find only two brief and vague references to the Manchu Conquest. [14] The one, for example, refers to it as the "last inundation of Tartars when she [China] stood in great part at the mercy of a vile traitor." [15] Bartoli's *La Cina* appears to follow Trigault more closely than any other source, although parts of the volume obviously come from the works of other Jesuit writers; he cites Rho, Ruggiero, Schall, and Martini. Most likely some of what he reports came from the many unpublished letters and official Jesuit docu-

---

[10] *Epitome historial del reyno de la China* (Madrid). See above, pp. 334–35, for bibliographical details.

[11] *Histoire de la cour du roy de la Chine* (Paris). See above, p. 402, for bibliographical details.

[12] On the mistake in his dating of the empress' death see below, p. 1627.

[13] *Dell' istoria della Compagnia de Gesù; la Cina* (Rome, 1663). For bibliographic details see above, p. 381. On Bartoli's work see J. J. Renaldo, *Daniello Bartoli. A Letterato of the Seicento* (Naples, 1979); and Bartoli, *La Cina,* ed. Bice Garavelli Mortara (Milan, 1975), pp. 1–22.

[14] Mortara (ed.), *op. cit.* (n. 13), pp. 33 and 217.

[15] *Ibid.,* p. 217.

ments at his disposal. This makes Bartoli's work somewhat more important as a source of information about China than if it were merely a compilation from already published accounts. Rites Controversy considerations also affect Bartoli's description more seriously than they did Trigault's or Semedo's. His admiration for China is less restrained, he treats Confucianism as an ethical system compatible with Christianity, and he explicitly argues the Jesuit case for cultural accommodation and for the use of traditional Chinese terms for God.[16]

The chapters on China in Faria y Sousa's *Asia portuguesa,* published in 1666, also form an ethnohistory of the Ming. They are in fact a condensation of Semedo's description which Faria had earlier translated from the Portuguese.[17] His history of the Portuguese in Asia ends in 1640, and no books on China published after Semedo's are mentioned in his bibliography.

Far less perceptive than the information about China from Jesuit sources were the reports of European merchants and seamen who encountered the Chinese in the East Indies or along the China coast. Unlike the missionaries, the authors of the travelogues usually knew no Chinese language and nothing of Confucian ethics or Buddhist theology, saw only the haziest outlines of the empire's grand political edifice, and had no notion of how it was supposed to work. They usually displayed little admiration for the inhabitants of the Celestial Empire, whom they tended to describe as avaricious, crafty, and deceitful at best. Their general lack of appreciation for China and the Chinese no doubt partly resulted from their unfamiliarity with Chinese language and culture. They were frequently describing phenomena which they did not understand and crudely evaluating what they saw, as travelers often do still, by the standards of their own land and people. On the other hand, their lack of appreciation also may have been engendered by the kind of Chinese they encountered. They usually met merchants and sailors, often the dregs of Chinese society. Of the officials they generally met only the lowest echelons. Quite often these people indeed were avaricious, did lie and cheat, and were simply not very good examples of Confucian morality. The crude idolatry of the Chinese frequently depicted by European travelers was probably a fairly accurate picture of the religious beliefs of the people with whom they came in contact—Chinese who themselves did not understand the subtleties of Confucian ethics or Buddhist theology. Consequently, despite their flaws, the travelogues contributed an important dimension to Europe's image of China. They added the shadows to the frequently over-idealized picture painted by the Jesuits. They frequently described the lower strata of Chinese society—if not peasants, at least merchants—people

---

[16] *Ibid.,* pp. 152–55, 225–38.
[17] See above, pp. 354–55. The descriptive chapters of *Asia portuguesa* are in Vol. II; see John Stevens (trans.), *The Portuguese Asia* (3 vols.; London, 1695), II, 448–99. Volume III contains some chapters on the history of the Jesuit mission in China, also condensed from Semedo, *op. cit.* (n. 9), pp. 78–91, 174–80.

largely absent from the Jesuit accounts. They also provided some very useful materials on provincial government in action. Many of the travelers confronted the Chinese bureaucracy at the local level, negotiated with local and provincial officials, and waited long for responses from higher officials or from Peking. Some described formal receptions by provincial officials. Finally, the travel accounts also introduced European readers to the overseas Chinese communities and thus conveyed another dimension of the predominance of China in Asia.

Bartolomé Leonardo de Argensola's *Conquista de las islas Malucas* (1609), for example, includes a considerable discussion of China and the overseas Chinese.[18] The Spanish in Manila continually worried about possible Chinese intervention in the Moluccas, and after the 1603 rebellion and massacre of the Chinese in Manila, they feared imperial reprisals. Argensola includes an exchange of letters between the Spanish governor in Manila and a Fukienese official whom he called the "Visitor of Chincheo" (Chang-chou) concerning the rebellion.[19] Implicit in Argensola's discussion is an appreciation of the size, extent, and influence of the Chinese overseas community in Southeast Asia and the Spaniards' fear of what they mistakenly saw as a close relationship between the overseas Chinese and their homeland. Argensola also includes some general description of China, but this seems to come primarily from Mendoza and his other sixteenth-century Spanish sources.[20]

Jean Mocquet never traveled to China, but he apparently met Chinese merchants in Goa and heard stories about China from the Portuguese there. His very popular *Voyages*, first published in 1617, contains some descriptions of Chinese people.[21] Mocquet's opinion of them was not very favorable. He describes them as clever, greedy, and superb cheats.[22] As an example he tells the story of a Portuguese in Canton who bought a roast duck only to find its skin stuffed with paper and wood when he attempted to eat it.[23] Still, he reports that the Portuguese in Goa prefer Chinese servants because of their loyalty and industry.[24] Mocquet claims to have visited and eaten with Chinese in Goa. Their houses are sumptuous, he reports, but they are gluttons and eat "with ill grace." They eat much rice and little bread, and they eat dog flesh. Mocquet also describes how they use chopsticks.[25]

Sir Thomas Herbert's *A Relation of Some Yeares Travaile*, first published in

---

[18] *Conquista de las islas Malucas* (Madrid, 1609). See above, pp. 310–12, for bibliographical details and for a discussion of Argensola's work.

[19] Argensola, *op. cit.* (n. 18), pp. 336–40. An abridged translation of these letters is included in *PP*, XII, 218–22.

[20] Argensola, *op. cit.* (n. 18), pp. 158–62.

[21] See above, pp. 397–98, for bibliography.

[22] *Voyages en Afrique, Asie, Indes Orientales, & Occidentales* (Rouen, 1665), p. 341.

[23] *Ibid.*, pp. 340–41.

[24] *Ibid.*, p. 342.

[25] *Ibid.*, pp. 346–47.

1634, contains some remarks about China although he had never been there. Herbert was impressed by the reports of the size, wealth, and power of the empire. He mentions the Great Wall, printing, and gunpowder as major Chinese achievements. But the Chinese themselves he says are "subtle and cowardly," worship idols, have very spare beards, are inveterate gamblers, and are "given to Epicureanism." [26]

Seyger van Rechteren never visited China, but his *Journael* (1635) contains a rather large description which shows no dependence on the standard Jesuit literature. He claims to have culled his information from shipboard conversations with some Dutch officials who had been imprisoned in China for five years. [27] More likely he took it from the official papers relating to the Reijersen expedition to the Pescadores in 1622–24. In any case, his is a sailors' and merchants' view of the Middle Kingdom, from the coastal periphery rather than from the capital. Van Rechteren, too, admires the empire for its wealth and power, but he regards it with hostility—a land whose pagan and superstitious people are clever and dishonest and despise all foreigners. Compared with Jesuit descriptions, Van Rechteren's is superficial and in places misleading. His account of imperial government, for example, is confused and inadequate. He says nothing about the scholarly attainments of the officials nor, for that matter, about learning and education at all. Confucius is not mentioned. Furthermore, he makes some geographical blunders as, for example, when he describes the Chiu-lung River at Chang-chou as "the largest and the most famous for navigation and commerce in the whole empire of China." [28] On the other hand, even Van Rechteren's error regarding the Chiu-lung River illustrates the impressive commercial activity of the Chang-chou district, and his detailed descriptions of the provincial governor's formal reception of a foreigner and of the difficulties encountered by foreigners in dealing with local or provincial officials are useful additions to Europe's image of China's periphery, where the ideals of the imperial system were most seriously compromised. Much more information of this sort is included in the detailed account of the Reijersen expedition appended to Van Rechteren's *Journael* as it was published in the *Begin ende voortgangh* in 1646. [29] News about the Reijersen expedition and the establishment of the Dutch fort on Formosa had been reported earlier in Nicolaes van Wassenaer's Amsterdam newsheet. [30]

The *Begin ende voortgangh* also contains other descriptions of China and

---

[26] *A Relation of Some Yeares Travaile, Begunne Anno 1626* . . . (London, 1634), pp. 206–7. For bibliographical details and a discussion of Herbert's book see above, pp. 571–72.

[27] Van Rechteren, "Journael ghehouden op de reyse ende weder-komste van Oost-Indien . . . ," *BV*, IIb, p. 41. For bibliographic details see above, pp. 453–55.

[28] Van Rechteren, *loc. cit.* (n. 27), p. 44.

[29] *Ibid.*, pp. 45–53. On the Reijersen expedition see above, pp. 52, 453–54.

[30] *Historisch verhael alder ghedenck-weerdichste geschiedenisse* . . . (Amsterdam, 1621–32), IV (Oct., 1623), 31–32; VII (June, 1624), 63–70; XI (June, 1626), 94a–96b.

the Chinese. The Dutch travelers whose accounts are included in it frequently describe the overseas Chinese whom they met in Java and other places in Southeast Asia. Descriptions of China itself, or at least its coastal regions, are included in the journals of Cornelis Matelief, Roelof Roelofszoon, and Wybrand van Warwijck. Roelofszoon describes the misadventures of Jacob van Neck's seamen off Macao in 1601.[31] Van Warwijck's journal contains an interesting description of his negotiations with local Chinese officials in the Pescadores in 1604.[32] Matelief, too, tried to negotiate trade in 1607 with Chinese officials at Nan-ao and at Lan-tao islands on the Kwangtung coast. His account as published in the *Begin ende voortgangh* contains some very perceptive description of the negotiations and of the people, villages, and temples he visited on the islands. The editor, Isaac Commelin, appended a much larger description of China to Matelief's account taken from Pierre d'Avity's *Les estats, empires, et principautez du monde,* which in turn was a condensation of Mendoza.[33]

Willem Ysbrantszoon Bontekoe's immensely popular *Journael* was also first published in 1646, and it, too, contains descriptions of the Chinese and of their ships and villages which Bontekoe encountered along the Fukien coast in 1622 when he commanded one of the Reijersen's warships.[34] To Bontekoe, also, the Chinese were a sinister and dangerous folk. He found little about them to admire. Fewer references to China are found in Vincent Le Blanc's popular *Les voyages fameux,* first published in 1648.[35] He seems less hostile to the Chinese than some of the other travelers, although he, too, reports that the Chinese in Bantam worship the devil. He marvels at the arrogance of the Chinese who reportedly presume their empire to be at the center of the earth.[36]

2

GEOGRAPHY, CLIMATE, AND NAMES

Europe's knowledge of China's geography improved considerably during the first half of the seventeenth century, primarily because the Jesuits who wrote the major descriptions during those years were no longer confined to the south coast, but traveled all over China along its roads, rivers, and canals, and lived in the capital as well as in provincial towns and villages. Fur-

[31] See above, pp. 463–64.
[32] See above, p. 466.
[33] For a discussion of the *Begin ende voortgangh,* its contents, and its various editions see above, pp. 461–73.
[34] See above, pp. 474–75.
[35] See above, pp. 406–7, for details on Le Blanc.
[36] Le Blanc, *The World Surveyed . . .* (London, 1660), pp. 99, 162.

thermore, they had access to and were able to read Chinese descriptions of the empire which augmented their personal observations and provided a larger context for them.[37] Their accounts, therefore, contain geographic information about the northern provinces as well as the south, the interior as well as the coast; about the capital, other great inland cities, and small towns and villages; and about peripheral areas such as Tibet and Mongolia. By 1655, with the publication of Martini's *Atlas,* Europe's image of Chinese geography was quite complete, not to be appreciably altered during the next two centuries.

All European observers during the first half of the seventeenth century seem awed by China's vast size and population. Trigault in 1615 quoted a 1579 Chinese "Description of the Chinese Empire":

"In the Chinese Empire there are two regal provinces [metropolitan provinces]—Nankin, the southern kingdom, and Pekin, the northern kingdom. Besides these two there are thirteen other provinces. These fifteen provinces"—which might very well be called kingdoms—"are further divided into one hundred fifty-eight departments or small provinces," which the Chinese call Fu and most of which contain twelve to fifteen large cities, besides smaller towns, fortresses, villages, and farms. "In these regions two hundred forty seven large cities are designated by the title, Cheu [*chou*], although for the most part these are differentiated from other large cities by their dignity and importance rather than by their size. Then there are eleven hundred and fifty-two common cities which are called Hien [*hsien*]."[38]

Pantoja already in 1605 had referred to the same Chinese publication and regarding the size of China's provinces and cities, added helplessly: "to believe their greatness it is necessary to see them."[39] Most of Trigault's successors repeat or summarize his description of the fifteen provinces and their subdivisions with minor variations. Many writers name the provinces, sometimes dividing them into northern and southern groups. Semedo includes a brief description of each province.[40] Martini's provincial descriptions are, of course, the most detailed. (See pls. 286, 302, 318.) For each of

---

[37] The Jesuits probably used the imperially compiled treatise on administrative geography, the late Ming *Fu-i Ch'üan-shu.* Cf. Ho Ping-ti, *Studies on the Population of China* (Cambridge, Mass., 1959), chaps. ii, vi.

[38] L. J. Gallagher, S.J. (trans.), *China in the Sixteenth Century: The Journals of Matthew Ricci: 1583–1610* (New York, 1953), p. 9. Gallagher's work is a translation of Trigault's *De Christiana expeditione . . . ex P. Matthaei Ricci . . commentariis.* For the differences between Gallagher's translation of Trigault's *De expeditione* and Ricci's original journals, see above, pp. 511–12. Trigault's "Description of the Chinese Empire" is most likely the *Kuang-yü t'u* ("Map of the Broad World") originally compiled by Chu Ssu-pen in 1312. See Walter Fuchs, *The "Mongol Atlas" of Chu Ssu-pen and the Kuang-yü t'u* ("Monumenta Serica," Monograph VIII; Peiping, 1946). According to Fuchs, p. 11, the *Kuang-yü t'u* also formed the foundation for Martini's *Atlas.* See Min-sun Chen, "Geographical Works by Jesuits in Chinese, 1584–1672" (M.A. diss., University of Chicago, 1959), pp. 1–7, esp. nn. 5, 12. For examples of the maps see our pls. 286 and 325.

[39] Pantoja, "A Letter of Father Diego de Pantoja . . . ," *PP,* XII, 364.

[40] Semedo, *op. cit.* (n. 9), pp. 8–22.

the fifteen provinces his *Atlas* contains a double-spread, folio-sized map, a description of the province's location and borders, its climate, population, and tax revenues. Following the general description of each province, Martini describes each of its major cities (*fu*) and names the towns, districts, and fortified places subordinate to it. Both for the province generally and for each *fu* he describes the rivers, mountains, roads, and bridges, as well as the unique features of the landscape, its fertility, products, and something of its history. These provincial descriptions range from six to twelve folio-sized pages as additions to the maps. It would have been difficult to find comparably detailed descriptions of many parts of Europe during the seventeenth century.

What amazed seventeenth-century Europeans even more than China's vast size was its awesomely dense population. No one failed to comment on it. There were so many large cities. "For your Worship will hardly believe," writes Pantoja about his journey to Peking, "that wee spent two or three houres in sayling still by the walls of one Citie. After which there still followed many Townes and Villages, one within sight of another."[41] Peking, he reports, had 200,000 houses—more populous than any four major European cities combined.[42] After having lived in China for twenty-two years, Semedo claimed to be still as amazed by the throngs of people as when he had first arrived.[43] Martini writes that China was so heavily populated and so intensively cultivated that he often thought of it, surrounded as it was by the Great Wall and the seas, as one enormous city.[44] Several of the Jesuits made estimates of the population based on the tax rolls of the empire. The number of men registered is well over 58,000,000. Trigault says 58,550,801; Semedo says 58,055,180.[45] Martini, writing shortly after a new registration, records 58,914,284.[46] But these figures, as the writers point out, included only taxpayers; they did not include women, children, royal relatives, government officials, soldiers, eunuchs, and priests—an almost innumerable host, according to Martini. Estimates of China's real population based on these figures went as high as 200,000,000.[47]

Most early seventeenth-century writers describe China as being almost square in shape. Longobardo, in 1602, talked about its "diameter" of 550 leagues: 550 leagues from south to north (from 19° to 50° north latitude) and

[41]Pantoja, *loc. cit.* (n. 39), p. 364.

[42]*Ibid.*, p. 365. Note that being called a city in the administrative hierarchy does not necessarily indicate position in the economic hierarchy accurately. A township outside the walled "city" might be economically much more important than the latter if it were located at the junction of rivers or of important roads.

[43]Semedo, *op. cit.* (n. 9), p. 3.

[44]*Novus atlas sinensis,* Vol. XI of Johan Blaeu, *Le grand atlas* (Amsterdam, 1663), p. 6.

[45]Trigault in Gallagher (trans.), *op. cit.* (n. 38), p. 9; Semedo, *op. cit.* (n. 9), p. 3; those two figures are so similar that one suspects the difference is simply a typographical error.

[46]*Op. cit.* (n. 44), p. 6.

[47]*Ibid. Cf.* Ho, *op. cit.* (n. 37), pp. 3–23 and 277. Ho estimates the population of China to have reached 150,000,000 by 1600.

about the same from east to west.[48] Most subsequent writers disagree with Longobardo about the location of China's northern border. Pantoja contends that Peking was at 40° north and the wall not further north than 42°. He also thought Hainan Island in the south was at 17° or 18°.[49] Trigault locates China between 19° and 42° north latitude and between 112° and 132° longitude.[50] Semedo places the northern frontier at 43° and has nothing to say about longitude.[51] Martini places Peking at 39°59' and the northern frontier at 42°.[52] He locates the southern tip of Hainan Island, taken by most European writers to be China's southern extremity, at 18°. From east to west China spans thirty degrees, according to Martini,[53] and his maps show Ningpo, the eastern extremity, at about 152°, which would place the western frontier at about 122°—considerably different from Trigault's estimate, and from modern maps which locate the eastern tip of Chekiang Province at 122° and western Kansu at about 94°. Martini's latitudinal calculations, however, are very close to those shown on modern maps. He also includes a table of longitudes and latitudes for each of the cities and towns mentioned in the *Atlas*. For these tables he calculated longitude in degrees east or west of Peking, whose longitude he took as his base meridian.[54]

China also enjoys naturally protected frontiers, which most writers describe in very similar terms. To the east and south lies a sea whose treacherous coastline protects China's maritime approaches; in the west, high mountains separate China from the rest of Asia, and in the north and northwest lie inhospitable deserts and the Great Wall, built to protect the empire where nature's barriers seemed inadequate.[55] Several writers describe the various lands on China's frontiers; none so thoroughly as Martini, whose *Atlas* contains fairly detailed descriptions of Manchuria, Hokkaido, Mongolia, Chinese Turkestan, Tibet, Laos, northern Cambodia, and Vietnam.[56]

Most European writers report that China lies in the temperate zone and in general enjoys a temperate climate, but with much more variation than one

---

[48]*Nouveaux advis du grand royaume de la Chine, . . .* (Paris, 1602), pp. 9–10.

[49]Pantoja, *loc. cit.* (n. 39), pp. 361–62.

[50]Gallagher (trans.), *op. cit.* (n. 38), pp. 7–8. For some early seventeenth-century maps of China see pls. 284 and 288.

[51]*Op. cit.* (n. 9), p. 1. For the maps accompanying Semedo's book see our pls. 287 and 288.

[52]*Op. cit.* (n. 44), pp. 2, 4.

[53]*Ibid.*, p. 2.

[54]*Ibid.*, pp. 213–32. On the calculation of latitude and longitude in Martini's *Atlas* see David E. Mungello, *Curious Land: Jesuit Accommodation and the Origins of Sinology* (Stuttgart, 1985), pp. 122–23. See also pls. 286, 290, and 291 for Martini's general map of China and other maps based on it.

[55]For example, see Pantoja, *loc. cit.* (n. 39), p. 364; Gallagher (trans.), *op. cit.* (n. 38), p. 9; Martini, *op. cit.* (n. 44), pp. 2–3. *Cf.* A. Waldron, "The Great Wall Myth: Its Origins and Role in Modern China," *Yale Journal of Criticism*, Vol. II, No. 1 (1988), pp. 76–77. See pls. 300 and 289.

[56]Martini, *op. cit.* (n. 44), pp. 23–33. On China's periphery see below, chap. xxii.

would expect to find between 18° and 42° north latitude. Semedo, for example, complains that Peking winters are very cold for 40° north latitude; rivers and lakes freeze over and people use stoves to heat their homes.[57] Martini, too, thinks Peking surprisingly cold. Rivers are frozen over for four months at a stretch, with ice thick enough to support chariots and horses. Thaws do not set in before the month of March.[58] On the other hand, some parts of China lie in the torrid zone; Fukien he describes as warm, but healthy; it never snows in Kwangtung, where the trees are green all year, while Kwangsi and Yunnan are usually very hot.[59] In his description of Hangchow he tells of the prodigiously strong tides which occur each year on the eighteenth of October. The whole city turns out to watch them. Martini reports that tides are always strong in the Ch'ien T'ang River and speculates that the unusually strong October tide was related to the transition from autumn to winter, during which the sea took on a more sinister aspect.[60]

A more spectacular development in Europe's geographic knowledge was the convincing identification of China with Marco Polo's Cathay. Martin de Rada in the late sixteenth century had already suggested that China and Cathay were but two names for the same place.[61] The Jesuit missionaries who got inside the empire soon became convinced that Marco Polo had really visited China. Pantoja, after talking with central Asian merchants in Peking, was certain of the identity:

> Wee asked these men certaine questions: and one was this of Catayo, enquiring of them, How they called this Kingdome of China in their Countrey? They answered, Catayo, and that in all the Countries of Mogor, Persia, and other parts, it had none other name, and that they knew none other Kingdome that was called so. Wee asked them how they called this Citie of Paquin? They said Cambalu, which, as I have said, is that which our men set down for the head Citie of Catayo.[62]

A controversy developed between the missionaries in China and those at the court of the Mughul emperor (Akbar); the latter still insisted that Cathay was an empire or a region distinct from China. The Jesuits, concerned about the large number of Christians supposedly living in Cathay, finally arranged an expedition to settle the question. In 1603 a lay brother of the society,

[57] *Op. cit.* (n. 9), pp. 20–21.

[58] *Op. cit.* (n. 44), pp. 34–35. China was in a cold cycle and the seventeenth was the coldest century in modern times. See Shen Wen-hsiung, "Changes in China's Climate," *Bulletin of the American Meteorological Society*, LV (1974), 1350; and Wakeman, *op. cit.* (n. 1), I, 7. For Martini's map of Pei Chih-li (Peking metropolitan province) see pl. 302.

[59] *Op. cit.* (n. 44), pp. 148–61, 174, and 191.

[60] *Op. cit.* (n. 44), p. 137. The autumn bore on the Ch'ien T'ang was one of Hangchow's celebrated sights. See, for example, the Sung dynasty painter Li Sung's well-known "The Hangchow Bore in Moonlight" (ca. 1210).

[61] See *Asia*, I, 752.

[62] Pantoja, *loc. cit.* (n. 39), p. 363.

Bento de Goes, was sent from Delhi over the caravan routes to Cambaluc, the capital of Marco Polo's Cathay. Trigault records the story of Brother Bento's travels; how he journeyed with Saracen caravans headed for Cambaluc, finally arriving at Su-chou in western Shensi late in 1605.[63] Goes died in Su-chou, but not before he had exchanged letters with Matteo Ricci in Peking and had become convinced that the Cambaluc towards which he was traveling and the Peking in which Ricci lived were one and the same place and that Cathay was simply the Saracen name for China.[64]

Despite Trigault's convincing discussion, many Europeans were still not persuaded that China and Cathay were identical. Purchas, for example, who in 1625 published both Pantoja's letter and large parts of Trigault's book, was still inclined "to believe some greater Prince or Can with his Cambalu or Court in the more Northerly parts of Asia, than the Jesuits could learne of; which the China jealousie, admitting no entercourse of Strangers, and the many quarrelling Tartar Princes in the way have concealed from us hitherto."[65] Perhaps the main difficulty was the reputed existence of large numbers of Christians in Cathay, whereas no Christian community had been found in China. Trigault tries to show that there had been Christians in China at an earlier date, and that traces of their existence can still be found.[66] He also suggests that the reports concerning the large numbers, mostly originating with Muslim observers, might have been exaggerated or that these observers might have confused Chinese Buddhism with Christianity.[67] A letter of Gaspar Luís published in a 1628 Jesuit letterbook brought new evidence for the early presence of Christianity in China with his description of the Nestorian monument found in Sian.[68] The monument was again described by Semedo.[69] Since Marco Polo had visited China during the Mongol dynasty, it was also possible that China had acquired the name Cathay from some contiguous land during the period in which the Great Khan had ruled all of these lands.

Such doubts were prevalent enough to induce Martini to treat the problem at length in his *Atlas* and to offer still more evidence for the identification of Cathay with China. Nonetheless, the Blaeu *Atlas major* volume which includes Martini's *Atlas* also contains the description of a separate "Kingdom of Cathay." Martini contends that Cathay was simply a Mongol

[63] Gallagher (trans.), *op. cit.* (n. 38), pp. 499–521. Goes' journey was first reported in 1603 by Guerreiro. See Artur Viegas (ed.), *Relação annual das coisas que fizerâm os padres da Companhia de Jesus nas suas missões . . .* (3 vols.; Coimbra, 1930–42), I, 285–314 (Pt. II, ch. ii).

[64] Actually Cathay is a Mongol designation for China, but Saracen traders who came to China by the overland route still used the term in the seventeenth century.

[65] *PP*, XII, 478.

[66] Gallagher (trans.), *op. cit.* (n. 38), pp. 106–14.

[67] *Ibid.*, p. 500.

[68] *Advis certain, d'une plus ample descourverte du royaume de Cataï, . . . & de l'antiquité de la foy chrestienne dans la Chine . . . .* (Paris, 1628), pp. 12–28. Bound with the letter of François Godin (or Francisco Godinho) from Tibet.

[69] *Op. cit.* (n. 9), pp. 157–65.

name for the six northern provinces, while Marco Polo's "Mangin" was their name for the southern provinces.[70] He repeats Trigault or Ricci's conversations with Muslim merchants in Peking, and he retells the story of Bento de Goes' travels.[71] Tartars, he reports, still called Peking "Cambalu," and he observes that Polo's description of "Cambalu" fits the Peking he knows.[72] In many other places Martini compares Polo's descriptions with his observations, usually attesting to the general accuracy of Polo's story. For example, Polo's "Quiang" was the Yangtze, his "Singui" was Soochow, his "Quinsai" was Hangchow, his "Fugui" was Foochow, which name he applied to the whole of Fukien province, and his "Zarte"—not a Chinese name, according to Martini—was Chang-chou, in which were found many vestiges of Christianity.[73]

The most intriguing proof for the identity of Cathay and China was that presented by the Dutch orientalist, Jacob Golius (1596–1667), in an "Additamentum" to Martini's *Atlas*.[74] Golius had long been interested in China and had entertained the same doubts concerning the identification of China with Cathay as did many other European scholars. Often he had come across references to Cathay in his study of Persian literature. He had in his possession astronomical tables written by the thirteenth-century Persian philosopher, Nasirodin, which described the way in which the Cathayans kept time—the divisions of the year down to the divisions of the day. Golius had also collected a few Chinese books, but could not read them. When he learned in 1654 that Father Martini, who reputedly knew Chinese well, would be passing through Leyden, Golius hurried to meet him. His primary concern was to establish definitely whether China was indeed Cathay or whether some other people to the north had given their name to China during Mongol times. Upon meeting Martini, Golius began to recite the names of the twelve hours into which Nasirodin had said the Cathayans divided the day. He pronounced the first three names and Martini easily completed the list. Next he tried the twenty-four parts into which Nasirodin had said the people of Cathay divided the year, and again Martini finished. Golius was convinced. He knew not a word of Chinese and Martini knew no Persian; still they were obviously talking about the same people. The people of Cathay whose divisions of time Golius had learned from Nasirodin were obviously Chinese, who still told time in the same way. Some time after their first brief meeting in Leyden, Martini and Golius talked at greater length in Antwerp and amassed still more convincing proof for the identification of China with Cathay. After the publication of Martini's *Atlas* with Golius' "Additamentum," most European scholars seem to have been convinced of the identification.

[70] *Op. cit.* (n. 44), p. 53.
[71] *Ibid.*, pp. 35–36.
[72] *Ibid.*, p. 37.
[73] *Ibid.*, pp. 115–16, 122, 133–35, 140, 147, 152.
[74] *Ibid.*, pp. i–xvi, following p. 232.

The problem of whether or not China was the same place as Cathay grew, in part, out of the great variety of names commonly assigned to the empire. Trigault and most subsequent writers prefaced their descriptions of China with a discussion of the names by which it was known. Ptolemy, said Trigault, had called it "Sina," and in ancient times it was also known as the land of the "Hippophagi" and as "Serica regio." The people on China's borders all gave different names to the empire; those living in Indochina, the East Indies, and India, for example, called it "China" or "Cina"—the Portuguese learned it here—and the people to the west called it "Cathay," just as they did in Marco Polo's time. Most European reporters went on to list other names by which China was known to her neighbors—names unknown to the Chinese themselves. One reason for all this confusion was the Chinese custom of changing the empire's name with each new dynasty. Thus in the first half of the seventeenth century the empire was known to its inhabitants as the empire of Ta Ming. Formerly it had been known as "Than" (T'ang), "Yu" (Yü), "Hia" (Hsia), "Sciam" (Shang), "Cheu" (Chou), and Han, following Trigault's list.[75] Martini added the "C'in" (Ch'in), from which he thought derived the name, China, the "Ijue" (Yüan), and the "C'ing" (Ch'ing), the title of the new Manchu dynasty.[76] The ancient Chinese tradition of referring to their land as Chung-kuo or Chung-hua, the Middle Kingdom or Garden, was also known to most European writers. In illustration Trigault describes the disbelief evidenced by the Chinese when they first saw Ricci's world map showing China at its eastern edge rather than at the center.[77] The story was repeated again and again during the remainder of the century.

The general geographic information and the name issue contained in the seventeenth-century European reports unfortunately overshadow the detailed feel for the Chinese landscape which European readers could have obtained from them. Included are vivid descriptions of hundreds of Chinese villages and cities—scores written about Peking alone; of the sights along the roads, rivers, and canals over which the Jesuits traveled; of majestic mountains in the west, terraced hillsides, verdant paddies, and the dusty loess plateau; of the coves and inlets along the coast visited by Dutch and English merchant ships. In short, European readers were treated to thousands of specific impressions of the Middle Kingdom's landscape while they read about Reijersen's raids along the Fukien coast, Bento de Goes' long trek from Agra to Su-chou, and the missionaries' many journeys between Peking and their widely separated outposts. The provincial descriptions in Martini's *Atlas* are likewise packed with details about specific mountains, valleys, streams, roads, and villages.

[75] Gallagher (trans.), *op. cit.* (n. 38), p. 6.
[76] *Op. cit.* (n. 44), p. 2.
[77] Gallagher (trans.), *op. cit.* (n. 38), p. 7.

3

GOVERNMENT AND ADMINISTRATION

No aspect of Chinese society was so uniformly admired by seventeenth-century Europeans as its government and administration. Already in the sixteenth century Mendoza had suggested that China was the best-governed land on earth. Thereafter no one essayed to describe China without devoting an almost disproportionately large share of space to government and administration. Consequently seventeenth-century Europeans accumulated voluminous and reasonably accurate notes on Chinese government. Most of this information originated, as might be expected, with those Europeans who had lived in China for long periods of time—the Jesuit missionaries. Their descriptions found their way into the works of many other writers and were also supplemented by the observations of merchants and seamen.

The pinnacle of Chinese government is the emperor, and his absolute power apparently fascinates European writers, who indulge in elaborate but fairly accurate characterizations of this imposing ruler. For example, almost all European writers discuss the emperor's various names and titles. He is called, they report, *T'ien-tzu,* Son of Heaven, because he has received his throne by the Mandate of Heaven. He is also commonly called *Huang-ti* or Yellow Emperor, after the third sage emperor of Chinese legend. Martini compares the Chinese emperor's use of *Huang-ti* to the Roman use of *Caesar.*[78] The succession of Chinese emperors was from fathers to sons, although Trigault reports that some ancient sage emperors had given the throne to others.[79] Semedo declares that if the empress has no son, the first son born to any of the emperor's concubines becomes the heir. The emperor, he asserts, is not free to change the succession, and he describes the Wan-li (r. 1573–1620) emperor's unsuccessful attempt to do so as proof.[80] Semedo lists thirteen actions taken by a new emperor upon his accession. Among them, he receives a new name and also designates a name for the period of his reign (reign title). Time is counted from the New Year's Day following his accession, and new money is coined in his name. The new emperor also makes offerings on the altars to Heaven and to Earth, gives generous alms to the poor, and sets many prisoners free. All officials in the empire come to the court to pledge allegiance to the new monarch, where they are lavishly entertained at the emperor's expense. All the former em-

---

[78] *Op. cit.* (n. 44), p. 15. The character *huang* (皇) as used in *Huang-ti* (皇帝) is a homophone of *huang* (黃), meaning yellow. *Huang-ti* (皇帝) means simply August One or emperor.

[79] Gallagher (trans.), *op. cit.* (n. 38), p. 42.

[80] Semedo, *op. cit.* (n. 9), pp. 113–14. See also Pantoja, *loc. cit.* (n. 39), pp. 388–89. *Cf.* Ray Huang, *1587, A Year of No Significance: The Ming Dynasty in Decline* (New Haven: 1981), pp. 86–106, on the succession issue.

peror's concubines are sent away, and new concubines are selected from all over the kingdom.[81] Considerable detail concerning the emperor's dress, his daily routine, his wives and concubines, and the eunuchs who serve his court can be found in the seventeenth-century descriptions. Pantoja describes the imperial palaces and grounds; Semedo adds considerably more detail.[82] The common people never see the emperor. Indeed, the Wan-li emperor is almost never seen by anyone except his women and the eunuchs who serve him.[83] Such complete seclusion, however, is exceptional. At court the women and eunuchs constitute a multitude. Chinese emperors marry one empress, but keep thousands of concubines.[84] All of the women are chosen solely for their beauty. Unlike European monarchs, Chinese emperors do not marry daughters of neighboring kings or of great noble families.[85] Thousands of eunuchs are employed to serve the emperor and his harem. Pantoja describes them and how they are selected; he has little good to say for them and reports that there were over sixteen thousand eunuchs in royal service.[86] Semedo reckons twelve thousand eunuchs in 1626 and describes the occupations, grades, and organization of the eunuchs in considerable detail.[87] When favored by an emperor they could become insolent and rapacious; no one was safe from their abuse of power.

Semedo also recounts the honors and ceremonies due this powerful monarch: once each month officials in every city gather to do him reverence. They perform similar ceremonies on his birthday. Once each year every province sends a high official to the imperial court to venerate the emperor on behalf of the province, and all high officials come to Peking for that purpose every third year. No one may pass the palace gate on horseback or in a sedan chair, and no one in mourning may enter the palace gate. Foreign ambassadors and others rehearse the ceremonies before an empty throne in preparation for imperial audiences. In the emperor's presence, all kneel and hold flat pieces of ivory before their mouths when speaking.[88] Semedo thinks the honors shown the emperor are excessive, more appropriate for God than for any human.[89]

[81] Semedo, *op. cit.* (n. 9), pp. 108–10.

[82] Pantoja, *loc. cit.* (n. 39), pp. 407–9; Semedo, *op. cit.* (n. 9), pp. 110–17. *Cf.* pls. 23, 306, and 314.

[83] Pantoja, *op. cit.* (n. 39), p. 406; Semedo, *op. cit.* (n. 9), p. 110. On the Wan-li emperor and his seclusion see Huang, *op. cit.* (n. 80), pp. 1–41.

[84] Most of the palace women were attendants; only a few dozen became concubines. See Huang, *op. cit.* (n. 80), pp. 28–30.

[85] For example, see Pantoja, *op. cit.* (n. 39), p. 404, and Semedo, *op. cit.* (n. 9), pp. 110–13.

[86] Pantoja, *op. cit.* (n. 39), pp. 404–6.

[87] Semedo, *op. cit.* (n. 9), pp. 114–17. On their number and functions see Wakeman, *op. cit.* (n. 1), I, 11–13, and Huang, *op. cit.* (n. 80), pp. 13, 19–21. On the grave problem of growing eunuch control during the Ming see P. M. Torbert, "The Ch'ing Imperial Household Department: A Study of Its Organization and Principal Functions" (Ph.D. diss., Dept. of History, University of Chicago, 1973), pp. 10–23.

[88] Semedo, *op. cit.* (n. 9), pp. 117–19.

[89] *Ibid.*, p. 110.

The Jesuits report that China had always been a monarchy; Trigault contends that even the names of other forms of government are unknown in China.[90] Most Europeans seem surprised to learn that there is no hereditary nobility in China to share political power with the emperor. Trigault correctly reports that there had been a nobility which held titles like duke, marquis, and count in China's early history, but that these had become defunct at least eighteen hundred years earlier.[91] Relatives of the emperor and descendants of those who performed outstanding service in the establishment of the dynasty hold hereditary titles—usually king (*wang*)—and government stipends, but these, Trigault notes, hold no office or authority and are subject to the civil magistrates just like any other Chinese.[92] They, in fact, may not hold office or reside in either of the capitals. Trigault claims that each of these families possesses a royal token which grants its holder pardon for any crime except treason. It can be used, however, only three times.[93] Semedo, writing around 1642, reports that royal relatives have but recently been allowed to take the examinations.[94] Pantoja, however, in 1605, reports that he knew one of the royal relatives who was studying for the examinations.[95]

While greatly impressed with the emperor's absolute power, most of the Jesuit writers sense the limitations placed on this power by the civil bureaucracy. Trigault, for example, observes that China, although a monarchy, is "to some extent an aristocracy" in that the emperor makes "no final decision in important matters of state without consulting with the magistrates or considering their advice." He states it strongly—perhaps too strongly: "I can assert the following as certain because I have made a thorough investigation of it, namely: that the King has no power to increase a monetary grant to anyone, or to confer a magistracy upon anyone, or to increase the power thereof, except on request of one of the magistrates."[96] The emperor, of course, could reward anyone from his private fortune, but he might not dispose of public tax and tribute income as he pleased. The budgets of all de-

---

[90] Gallagher (trans.), *op. cit.* (n. 38), p. 41.

[91] *Ibid.*, pp. 41–42. In 127 B.C. the Former Han ordered that the land of each principality be divided after the death of the prince (vassal king), but that the vassal king's title be inherited by only one son. This amounts to the abolition of primogeniture, in fact, but not to the noble ranks and titles, which usually passed on to the eldest son of the legitimate wife.

[92] *Ibid.*, pp. 43–44. The principalities after 1402 were brought under increasing supervision by provincial authorities, even though some princes remained powerful.

[93] *Ibid.*, p. 44.

[94] Semedo, *op. cit.* (n. 9), p. 108. On the Ming royal relatives and hereditary nobility see Charles O. Hucker, *The Traditional Chinese State in Ming Times, 1368–1644* (Tucson, 1961), pp. 12–14, 41–42; Ho Ping-ti, *The Ladder of Success in Imperial China* (New York, 1962), pp. 21–24; and Lynn A. Struve, *The Southern Ming, 1644–1662* (New Haven, 1984), pp. 11–13. These studies confirm the seventeenth-century Europeans' picture of the condition of the royal relatives and nobility.

[95] *Loc. cit.* (n. 39), p. 409.

[96] Gallagher (trans.), *op. cit.* (n. 38), p. 45. "Aristocracy" is not the right word to apply to the bureaucracy. It was never a hereditary estate.

partments, indeed the allowance for the emperor himself, are all established and regulated by the appropriate administrators and bureaus.[97] Semedo dubs the scholar-officials—even the students—a nobility, but a nobility raised by their learning rather than a hereditary caste.[98] The admiration for China's learned governors on the part of many European observers was unbounded. Trigault, for example, reports:

Only such as have earned a doctor's degree or that of licentiate are admitted to take part in the government of the kingdom, and due to the interest of the magistrates and of the King himself there is no lack of such candidates. Every public office is therefore fortified with and dependent upon the attested science, prudence, and diplomacy of the person assigned to it, whether he be taking office for the first time or is already experienced in the conduct of civil life.[99]

Athanasius Kircher later writes: "this state is governed by the learned in the manner of the Platonists, and according to the desire of the divine philosopher; in which I consider this kingdom happy, which has a king who is able to philosophize or who at least allows a philosopher to govern it and guide him."[100] Martini's sentiments are expressed in similar tones.[101]

   At the apex of the central administration in Peking were the six boards, "courts" or "councils" described by all the Jesuits from Pantoja to Martini.[102] The functions of most of the administrative boards are evident from their titles: the Hu-pu, or Board of Finance; the Hsing-pu, or Board of Punishments; the Ping-pu, or Board of War; and the Kung-pu, or Board of Public Works. Two of the boards, however, performed functions unique to China and these attracted more attention from the seventeenth-century European writers than the others—the Li-pu, or Board of Civil Office, and the Board of Rites, also called Li-pu, although the character *li* in this case differs from that used for the Board of Civil Office.[103] All agree that the Board of Civil Office is the most important of the six boards. It keeps records on all officials and on all the empire's qualified candidates for civil office. Nominations for administrative posts are made to the emperor by this board. The Board of Civil Office also reviews the records of each official every third year and makes recommendations for promotion and demotion. The Board of Rites has responsibility for the court's elaborate ceremonial. It also supervises the maintenance of temples and shrines and exercises authority over

[97] *Ibid.*, p. 46.
[98] Semedo, *op. cit.* (n. 9), pp. 121–22.
[99] Gallagher (trans.), *op. cit.* (n. 38), pp. 44–45. Not all those appointed to the bureaucracy had earned degrees. For some exceptions see Ho, *op. cit.* (n. 94), pp. 21–41.
[100] *La Chine illustrée de plusieurs monuments tant sacrés que profanes, et de quantité de recherchés de la nature et de l'art* . . . , trans. F. S. Dalquié (Amsterdam, 1670), p. 226.
[101] *Op. cit.* (n. 44), p. 15.
[102] The romanization of the Chinese names for the offices varies greatly in Europe from writer to writer. Wherever possible we have converted them to Wade-Giles romanizations.
[103] Board of Civil Office (吏部); Board of Rites (禮部).

priests and monks. A more important function of the Board of Rites is the administration of the governmental school system, the examinations, and the granting of the academic degrees by which scholars qualify for civil office. The reception of tribute missions and the supervision of foreign visitors, such as the Jesuit missionaries, are also the responsibility of the Board of Rites. Semedo observes, too, that the members of the Board of Rites are always appointed from the scholars of the prestigious "Royal Colledge" or Han-lin Yüan and frequently were also appointed Grand Secretaries (*ko-lao*) which he judges to be "the chiefest dignity in China." [104] Each board has a president (*shang-shu*) and two assistants (*shih-lang*) called the Assessor on the Right and the Assessor on the Left. There are ten other members on each board. [105]

Another important body in seventeenth-century Chinese government—and another which had no western counterpart—was the Censorate. It was consequently described by all the Jesuits. Pantoja and Martini call the censors "visitors." [106] As described by the Jesuits, the censors watch over the conduct of government both in the capital and in the provinces and memorialize the emperor when there is any sort of misconduct on the part of an official. Trigault admires them: "sixty or more chosen philosophers, all prudent men and tried"; "keepers of the public conscience," he calls them. "No one is spared from their scrutiny, even the highest magistrates, as they do not hesitate to speak, even though it concerns the king himself or his household." [107] Trigault provides two contemporary examples in which the censors reproved the emperor himself, as well as a Grand Secretary. [108] Semedo, on the other hand, while he considers the Censorate potentially beneficial, asserts that the censors' power is seldom properly used. Any official, if he is diligent in his duties, makes some enemies. If any of these enemies has any connection or influence with one of the censors, however, memorials are written against the official, and he rarely escapes complete ruin. [109] By the time Semedo wrote, the Jesuit mission had had some difficulty with the Censorate. In several instances, opponents of the missionaries had complained to the censors about local officials who were friendly to the foreigners and had allowed them to reside in their jurisdiction. Persecutions resulted, and many officials became more fearful about allowing the missionaries to stay. [110] Trigault and Semedo are somewhat imprecise in their accounts of the structure of the Censorate. They refer to two varieties of

---

[104] Semedo, *op. cit.* (n. 9), p. 124.
[105] Gallagher (trans.), *op. cit.* (n. 38), p. 48; Semedo, *op. cit.* (n. 9), p. 124. *Ko-lao* was an unofficial term for a Grand Secretary; see C. O. Hucker, *A Dictionary of Official Titles in Imperial China* (Stanford, 1985), pp. 278–79.
[106] Pantoja, *loc. cit.* (n. 39), p. 392; Martini, *op. cit.* (n. 44), p. 15.
[107] Gallagher (trans.), *op. cit.* (n. 38), p. 49.
[108] *Ibid.*, p. 50.
[109] Semedo, *op. cit.* (n. 9), pp. 126–27.
[110] For example, see Gallagher (trans.), *op. cit.* (n. 38), pp. 461–63.

censors, K'o-li and Tao-li; each has a separate sphere of activity. Nowhere do they delineate the jurisdictions of the two groups. The K'o-li appear to have been *chi-shih-chung* (supervising secretaries), whose function it was to inspect the activities of the administrative boards and even to admonish the emperor, while the Tao-li may have been the *chien-ch'a yü-shih* (investigating censors), who were regularly sent to investigate the conduct of officials in the provinces.[111] The operation of the Censorate, however, they describe in considerable detail. When a censor detects any mismanagement of government affairs, he sends a memorial to the emperor naming the official involved and describing his misconduct. The content of the censor's memorial is also published so that the official involved may write a memorial in his own defense and suspend his official functions until the emperor replies to his memorial. According to Trigault, any citizen may memorialize the throne, but memorials from the censors carry the most prestige and influence.[112] Their memorials also do not have to pass through the Office of Transmission as do all others.

One of the most prestigious bodies in Peking is the Han-lin Yüan, or Imperial Academy, a group of the most illustrious scholars who have nothing to do with the everyday conduct of government. These scholars have the official duties of recording the emperor's daily acts, writing imperial correspondence, and drafting imperial laws and edicts. Members of the Han-lin Yüan also serve as tutors for the imperial family. Actually the purpose of the Han-lin Yüan seems primarily to have been that of providing a training ground for top-rank *chin-shih* scholars. Its members are also chosen for some of the highest offices of the empire. Semedo observes that most of the members of the Board of Rites have been members of the Han-lin Yüan.[113]

Chosen from among high officials who had formerly been members of the Han-lin Yüan are the Grand Secretaries, the highest officials of the realm. There are usually three or four Grand Secretaries, sometimes as many as six. The emperor rarely sees any other officials.[114] Their actual duties, however, are ambiguously described. Trigault reports: "their particular obligation is the general safety of the kingdom; a secret service to the throne."[115] Describing the relationship between the Grand Secretaries and the Wan-li emperor (1573–1620), he writes: "As the King does not now take part, in a public way, in discussing the business of the realm with the

[111] Chan, *op. cit.* (n. 2), pp. 23–25. See C. O. Hucker, *The Censorial System of Ming China* (Stanford, 1966), pp. 47–57, for the general organization of the Ming Censorate. *K'o-li* and *Tao-li* appear to be popular terms that neither Chan nor Hucker uses. See also Hucker, *op. cit.* (n. 105), pp. 133, 145–46.

[112] Gallagher (trans.), *op. cit.* (n. 38), p. 49.

[113] Semedo, *op. cit.* (n. 9), p. 124. See also Gallagher (trans.), *op. cit.* (n. 38), pp. 50–51.

[114] Gallagher (trans.), *op. cit.* (n. 38), pp. 48–49; Semedo, *op. cit.* (n. 9), p. 127; Martini, *op. cit.* (n. 44), p. 14.

[115] Gallagher (trans.), *op. cit.* (n. 38), p. 48.

'Colao' [ko-lao, Grand Secretaries], as was formerly the custom, they remain in the palace during the whole day and answer the numerous petitions made to the king."[116] The vague descriptions of the Grand Secretaries made by the Jesuits reflect the actual ambiguity of their position in the imperial administration. They had gradually come into existence during the last half of the Ming dynasty after the Hung-wu emperor (r. 1368–98) had abolished the offices of prime minister and secretariat. The role of the Grand Secretaries and their relationship to the rest of the administration, therefore, remained in fact poorly defined.[117]

Semedo also describes nine other ministries in Peking which he identifies as belonging to the imperial household—probably what others call the "service agencies."[118] Among them were such offices as the "High Steward of the King's Household," the "Chief Master of the Horse," the "Master of Ceremonies and Complements of the Court," and the court of "Rites in more particular matters."[119] Semedo's list, however, also includes the "Great Chancery of the Kingdom," whose functions seem to indicate that he is referring to the Grand Court of Revision, and the "Chancery of Requests," obviously the Office of Transmission, which handled all non-censorial correspondence to and from the provinces.[120] Trigault notes that all the Peking bureaus, except for the Grand Secretaries, are duplicated in Nanking.[121]

Concerning the administration in Peking, seventeenth-century merchants and seamen had little to say. Most of them had no contact with the central bureaucracy. The general description of China included in Commelin's edition of Matelief's journal—based ultimately on Mendoza—notes the absolute power of the emperor and the absence of an hereditary aristocracy. It describes a royal council of twelve men who were astrologers as well as philosophers.[122] Van Rechteren's comments concerning the central government are even more confusing:

The ordinary council of the monarch is composed of eight persons who meet with the emperor twice a year in front of the palace, except that whoever rides beside him, remains with the head of his horse, slightly behind the King.

Under this council is another, lower council which is not permitted to meet with

[116] Ibid., pp. 48–49.

[117] Hucker, op. cit. (n. 111), pp. 40–41; Huang, op. cit. (n. 80), pp. 18–19, 42–129.

[118] Hucker, op. cit. (n. 111), p. 37. On these offices see Min-sun Chen, "Three Contemporary Western Sources on the History of the Late Ming and the Manchu Conquest of China" (Ph.D. diss., Dept. of History, University of Chicago, 1971), p. 101.

[119] Semedo, op. cit. (n. 9), pp. 125–26.

[120] Ibid. Cf. Hucker, op. cit. (n. 111), pp. 36 and 39, and Chen, loc. cit. (n. 118), pp. 101–2. The heads of the Grand Court of Revision and the Office of Transmission were also, with the presidents of the six boards and the chief censor, frequently called the Nine Chief Ministers. See Ch'ien Mu, Traditional Government in Imperial China, trans. Chün-tu Hsüeh and George O. Totten (Hong Kong, 1982), p. 92.

[121] Gallagher (trans.), op. cit. (n. 38), p. 51. On the dual capital system see E. L. Farmer, Early Ming Government: The Evolution of Dual Capitals (Cambridge, Mass., 1976), chap. v.

[122] Matelief, "Historische verhael . . . ," BV, IIa, 108–9.

the King, but if they have any request must present it to the higher council; just like the governors over each province, who are called by them Mandarins, and who serve in office for three years.[123]

According to the Jesuits, Peking sent two supreme officials to each of the thirteen provincial capitals. One of these is variously called a governor-general or viceroy by the Europeans—*tu-t'ang* or *chün-men* in Chinese—and appointed for three years.[124] The other (*ch'a-yüan*), called a "Visitor" in Jesuit writings, is a provincial inspector sent out from Peking each year.[125] Below these two Peking-appointed officials the Jesuits describe the regular provincial government; the *pu-cheng-ssu,* in charge of revenue and finances, and the *an-ch'a-ssu,* chief judicial officer, were its most prominent officials.[126] The provinces are further divided into *fu* (prefectures), *chou* (departments), and *hsien* (districts). Each of these has a commanding official called the *chih-fu, chih-chou,* and *chih-hsien,* respectively. As described by the Jesuits, each of these provincial officials has staffs of advisers and subordinates.[127] Semedo even describes the ten-family groupings in the countryside:

But it must be observed that both the greater and the lesser officers have not so much authority as ours in *Europe.* Besides, every Hamlet (whereof there are almost Infinite in China . . .) hath a Head or Tithing-man called *Licham* [*li-chia*]. The houses are divided by tens, like Tithings or Decuries, with a Head or Tithing-man belonging to each, by which meanes the Government becometh more easie, and the contributions which is exacted, more certaine.[128]

On the whole, the Jesuit picture of provincial and local government is fairly accurate. Perhaps the most serious inadequacy is the failure to distinguish between the governor of a province (*hsün-fu* or Grand Coordinator) and the viceroy (*tsung-tu* or Supreme Commander), who was ordinarily a civil and military commander over two provinces.[129] That the Jesuits knew the difference, however, seems clear from passages like Trigault's description of the "Viceroy of the Province of Canton" who had jurisdiction over both Kwangtung and Kwangsi provinces and whose seat was in Chaoch'ing on the border between the two provinces.[130]

Something of the complexity of provincial and local government comes

[123] Van Rechteren, *loc. cit.* (n. 27), pp. 41–42.
[124] The governor-general or *tsung-tu* was vulgarly referred to as *tu-t'ang* or *chün-men.*
[125] Gallagher (trans.), *op. cit.* (n. 38), pp. 52–53; Semedo, *op. cit.* (n. 9), pp. 128–29. See Chen, *loc. cit.* (n. 118), pp. 104–5, on provincial government. See also Hucker, *op. cit.* (n. 105), p. 543, on the interchangeability of the terms *tu-t'ang* and *tu ch'a-yuan; chün-men* is an unofficial term for a provincial military commander (*ibid.,* p. 202).
[126] Gallagher (trans.), *op. cit.* (n. 38), p. 51; Semedo, *op. cit.* (n. 9), pp. 129–30.
[127] Gallagher (trans.), *op. cit.* (n. 38), p. 52; Semedo, *op. cit.* (n. 9), p. 131.
[128] Semedo, *op. cit.* (n. 9), p. 131.
[129] See Hucker, *op. cit.* (n. 111), pp. 37–39. Hucker also notes (pp. 51–52) that by the late Ming, Grand Coordinators and Supreme Commanders were usually given concurrent censorial titles. See also Hucker, *op. cit.* (n. 105), p. 543.
[130] Gallagher (trans.), *op. cit.* (n. 38), p. 136.

out more clearly in the writings of the Dutch travelers and in the histories of the Jesuit missions. These discuss a host of lesser officials not mentioned in the neatly organized general descriptions. Many are impossible to identify, especially from the titles given them by the Dutch writers. The terms governor, magistrate, and mandarin were used to describe an extremely broad range of dignitaries. Some, however, emerge with considerable clarity. In the Amoy area, for example, the official with whom most of the Dutch negotiations were conducted was the military commander of Fukien and Chekiang provinces, called the *tu-tu*. Dealing with foreigners was apparently his responsibility. In Canton relations with foreigners, including the Portuguese at Macao, were handled by a similar official called the *hai-tao*, or Grand Admiral.

The military hierarchy which paralleled the civil administration was less adequately described by both Jesuits and travelers. Occasionally regional commanders like the *tu-tu* are mentioned, but no one describes their position in an overarching hierarchy. Although the Board of War is always mentioned, no one discusses the central military command at Peking. Perhaps this is the result of a lack of interest in military affairs on the part of the Jesuits, who had the best opportunity to observe military organization in its general aspects. Pantoja observes that while China has many soldiers, they are poorly paid, ill treated, and inadequately armed. He thinks long years of peace have made them soft and disinterested, although he speculates that they might show valor enough if the occasion demanded it.[131] Trigault agrees and adds that the whole military establishment is subject to civilian control. Soldiers are despised, distrusted, often given menial tasks, and publicly demeaned and beaten by civil officials. Soldiers on guard duty, for example, are always watched by other sentinels for fear that they might revolt; military commanders are never entrusted with large numbers of troops.[132] Semedo's description of the military is the most complete.[133] He notes that although there are imperial troops at the wall and on the coast, each province has its own militia which can be called out by the viceroy. Their numbers are large: 40,000 in Nanking, 80,000 in Peking, perhaps 594,000 in all the villages and cities, not counting the coastal defense forces, and another 682,888 on the wall. The militia is regularly mustered in the towns and villages, and maneuvers held each year. Semedo sees these war games as "the most ridiculous thing in the world."[134] Military officers, he writes, are granted the same degrees as the literati after having passed examinations which combine practical achievements, such as shooting arrows from horseback, with written questions on military strategy. These examinations are

[131] Pantoja, *loc. cit.* (n. 39), p. 383.
[132] Gallagher (trans.), *op. cit.* (n. 38), pp. 89–90.
[133] *Op. cit.* (n. 9), pp. 96–100.
[134] *Ibid.*, p. 99. These militia figures are suspect, according to Ho Ping-ti (personal communication). See also Chan, *op. cit.* (n. 2), pp. 188–89.

considerably easier than those for the literary degrees, however, and far fewer people take them. A career in the Chinese military is simply not very prestigious, and the common soldier has very little chance of rising in rank.

Still Semedo notes that the knowledge of war is very old among the Chinese, and that their historical annals show that they were once "a valiant and warlike nation" which conquered many famous kingdoms.[135] What is more, they used gunpowder in ancient times and there are very old cannons still standing at the gates of Nanking. But in his day Semedo observes that the most commonly used weapons of the Chinese army are bows and arrows, lances, and scimitars, that such guns as they have are very small and cannot be aimed very well, and that they use more powder for fireworks in one year than they use for military purposes in five. Semedo lists what he thinks are the major reasons for the decline of China's military: the empire has been too long at peace; the high esteem in which learning is held dissuades able young men from military careers; choosing officers by examination rather than demonstrated ability and valor produces poor field commanders; and the shabby treatment accorded soldiers insures that only the poor, uneducated, and uncourageous will enlist. Furthermore, Chinese generals never lead their troops but try to direct battles from positions too far from the action to be effective. Finally, he thinks it deplorable that there are no soldiers on the Board of War which controls the whole militia.[136] Semedo illustrates the consequences of China's military lassitude in his account of their poor showing against the Manchu incursions of 1618 to 1622.

In traditional China the legal system was not distinct from the regular civil administration. The local magistrate served as prosecutor, judge, and jury, and the higher administrative officials functioned as courts of appeal.[137] While no seventeenth-century European writers specifically make this connection, it is nevertheless implicit in what most of them say about Chinese law and administration. Their opinions differ, however, concerning the basic law of the empire. Longobardo, for example, thinks the Chinese have good laws and government.[138] Pantoja, on the other hand, notes the absence of abstract legal codes and the heavy reliance on the wisdom of individual officials, so characteristic of traditional China.

There is no great store of Lawes, but commonly they decide Controversies in their owne heads, and make Lawes in their Jurisdiction after their pleasure, every one diverse. And heere your Worship may imagine, that the Government in the practise cannot bee very just, since every one that can tell how to make a good theame or exercise, are not sufficient to bee Law-makers.[139]

---

[135] *Op. cit.* (n. 9), pp. 96–97.
[136] *Ibid.*, p. 99. On the decline of the military in late Ming see Chan, *op. cit.* (n. 2), pp. 187–210.
[137] See Hucker, *op. cit.* (n. 94), pp. 70–71.
[138] *Op. cit.* (n. 48), p. 11.
[139] Pantoja, *loc. cit.* (n. 39), p. 389.

Trigault, too, avers that there are no ancient laws in China comparable to the Roman Twelve Tables, but that each dynasty establishes its own. The basic laws of China in the first half of the seventeenth century, therefore, go back no farther than 1368—to the founding of the Ming dynasty.[140] Perhaps Semedo's analysis is the most accurate. The dynasty's laws and the decisions of its officials are based on an ancient moral and political philosophy—on the five virtues and the five relationships as taught in the Confucian classics. Accepting the traditional Confucian account, he describes an antique past during which men lived in accord with the Confucian virtues, when scholars refused to govern under a bad monarch and took no personal joy in governing. In those days there were few laws. Since then, however, ambition and avarice have crept in, and as virtue decreased the number of laws increased.[141] Still those who live virtuously without recourse to the law or courts are honored. Semedo quotes the old proverb, "The man who hath never seen a Mandarine is a precious stone."[142]

European writers also differed widely in their general evaluations of China's judicial system. Some thought Chinese justice horribly cruel; others found it lax. Van Rechteren contends, for example, that for serious crimes not only is the criminal executed but also his entire family to the second or third generation.[143] Trigault, on the other hand, thinks the punishments for theft are too lenient. He seems surprised that capital punishment is never imposed. As a consequence he reports that "thieves are numerous everywhere, especially among the lower classes," and while "thousands of night watchmen in the cities roam the streets sounding a gong at regular intervals" and the "streets are closed with iron bars and locks, . . . it frequently happens that houses are . . . ransacked by night marauders . . . probably . . . because the watchmen themselves are robbers or are in league with the robbers."[144]

Concerning the details of Chinese judicial practice there was more agreement among the European observers. The Jesuits report that most officials are reluctant to impose death sentences for fear of gaining a reputation for cruelty—a reputation which might cost an official his office. Semedo reports that only counterfeiting, murder, and highway robbery bring death sentences (by hanging, strangulation, or decapitation).[145] Thieves are often branded, and sentences for other crimes include banishment, towing barges and boats along the rivers and canals, and the wearing of the "Kian Hao" (Cantonese, *k'ang-giai,* cangue), a large, heavy board locked around the

---

[140] Gallagher (trans.), *op. cit.* (n. 38), p. 43. No two dynasties had exactly the same laws, but the dynastic codes were based at all times on the Confucian ideology with respect to family and the class system. See T. T. Chü, *Law and Society in Traditional China* (Paris, 1961), intro.

[141] Semedo, *op. cit.* (n. 9), pp. 148–49.

[142] *Ibid.,* p. 151.

[143] Van Rechteren, *loc. cit.* (n. 27), p. 43.

[144] Gallagher (trans.), *op. cit.* (n. 38), pp. 81–82.

[145] *Op. cit.* (n. 9), p. 140.

neck on which the bearer's crime is written.[146] Everyone reports that by far the most frequent punishment is a beating across the bared thighs and buttocks with a stout bamboo cane. It is inflicted in court, in the jails, and on the streets. Even when they travel, officials are accompanied by men with canes. Convicted criminals are beaten, but so are suspected malefactors, to induce them to confess, and reluctant witnesses. Officers use canes on their soldiers and schoolmasters on their students.[147] By all reports, a great many people not formally sentenced to death die from these beatings.[148] Semedo also includes a lengthy description of Chinese prisons; he had been in them during the persecutions of 1616–17. They are not pleasant places, but he thought them "more commodious and spacious than ours."[149] They are all built around a courtyard from which the individual cells are separated by wooden grates. During the day prisoners are free to walk about the courtyard, visit each other's rooms, or pray in the small chapels. More dangerous prisoners are kept in what Semedo calls a "close prison" where they sleep with their feet in stocks and their hands manacled. He is amazed by the number of services for which prisoners have to pay: for the trip to the prison, for having their names registered in the prison book, for having their cells cleaned, for more comfortable manacles, and for sacrifices at the shrines. Visitors, too, he learns, always bring food and money for the prisoners, without which life in jail would be grim indeed. The prisoners are visited once a month by an official. Should a prisoner die in jail, his body is thrown out through a small hole in the courtyard rather than carried through the door.[150]

Some features of Chinese governmental practice evoke general admiration from the Jesuits.[151] No official, for example, may hold office in his native province; this practice, known as the Law of Avoidance, is intended to prevent the possibility of favoritism being shown toward an official's family and relatives. To prevent officials from becoming too friendly with the citizens under their jurisdiction, no one is permitted to serve more than three years in the same office unless specifically reappointed to it by the emperor.[152] They report that a rigorous general review of the conduct of officials is held every third year. Those who have acquitted themselves well are promoted at this time and those found guilty of misdemeanors are punished

---

[146] *Ibid.*, p. 141. The Cantonese and ultimately the Mandarin word was probably derived from Portuguese *canga*, "ox-yoke." See H. Yule and A. C. Burnell, *Hobson-Jobson* (rev. ed., edited by W. Crooke; London, 1968), p. 156.

[147] On punishments, *cf.* J. D. Ball, *Things Chinese* (5th rev. ed.; London, 1926), pp. 331–33.

[148] For example, see Pantoja, *loc. cit.* (n. 39), p. 391; Gallagher (trans.), *op. cit.* (n. 38), pp. 87–88; Semedo, *op. cit.* (n. 9), pp. 141–43.

[149] *Op. cit.* (n. 9), p. 134. On sixteenth-century Chinese prisons see *Asia*, I, 762–63.

[150] Semedo, *op. cit.* (n. 9), pp. 135–40.

[151] For example see *ibid.*, pp. 144–51, and Trigault in Gallagher (trans.), *op. cit.* (n. 38), pp. 54–59.

[152] Hucker, *op. cit.* (n. 94), p. 17, says the limit was nine years.

and demoted. Both Trigault and Semedo list the misdemeanors for which officials can be punished and the appropriate punishments.[153] Officials do all their judging in open public sessions, usually in a crowded courtroom. The family and servants of the accused are sequestered during official sessions to prevent bribery. That China is governed by learned men results in a de-emphasis on the military and produces the empire's peaceful foreign policy. Also, only soldiers are permitted to bear arms, and no one is permitted to do so inside the cities, with the consequence that there is very little violence among the people.

According to the Jesuits, all the officials in the empire, military and civil, are ranked in nine orders.[154] Their names, addresses, and ranks are recorded in five or six large books which are constantly being revised.[155] All officials of the same grade receive the same salary, paid monthly, either in money or in rice. The salaries are small in comparison to the dignity of their offices. Trigault reports that none exceeds a thousand gold pieces per year.[156] Never-theless they live well, not on their salaries but on what could be called the perquisites of office. As Trigault describes it, "they receive far more than their official pay from other than government sources. We make no mention here of what they receive from extra-official industry, by their business acu-men, or from inheritance and gifts accruing from their particular positions, which at times may add up to a considerable fortune."[157] Semedo reports that officials always travel at the emperor's expense and are lodged in gov-ernment buildings. In fact he believes that even their palaces, furniture, and servants are provided by the government.[158] Everyone describes the great pomp and dignity of Chinese officials, their distinctive robes, their magnifi-cent courts, the elaborate processions attending them when they travel through the streets, and the honor and respect shown them by the common people. They are all called *kuan-fu* (Commander), *lao-yeh* or *lao-tieh* (sir, or Your Honor), Trigault reports. And they all wear distinctive black hats with two wings [*fu-t'ou*] which "fall off very easily . . . to guarantee that the one wearing the hat will walk upright and modestly, without . . . bending the head."[159] Semedo writes an entire chapter on the dress, insignia, dignity, and manners of the officials, including a detailed description of the governor of Kwangtung's court and the procedures followed in his official public sessions.[160]

---

[153] *Ta-fu,* or officials, were not subject to physical punishment but were punished by censure, demotion, and ridicule. See Chü, *op. cit.* (n. 140), pp. 172–73.

[154] Actually there were nine grades with two subdivisions within each grade. See Hucker, *op. cit.* (n. 94), p. 14.

[155] Trigault in Gallagher (trans.), *op. cit.* (n. 38), p. 46.

[156] *Ibid.*, p. 53. See also Pantoja, *loc. cit.* (n. 39), p. 391.

[157] Gallagher (trans.), *op. cit.* (n. 38), p. 53.

[158] *Op. cit.* (n. 9), p. 144.

[159] Gallagher (trans.), *op. cit.* (n. 38), pp. 45, 53.

[160] *Op. cit.* (n. 9), pp. 132–35. For an official's procession see our pl. 360.

In their general descriptions of China, the Jesuits tend to depict the ideals of Chinese government rather than its less savory reality. Pantoja, Trigault, Semedo, and their colleagues are not as uncritical in their admiration for China as were later seventeenth-century Jesuits,[161] but they still emphasize China's uniqueness and describe Chinese government as it was supposed to work. In fact, however, the reality and the ideal of Chinese administration were often poles apart, particularly during the last decades of the Ming dynasty. European readers were able to glimpse this less orderly and less attractive reality also in the histories of the Jesuit mission and in the writings of the Dutch travelers. Here they met insufferably pompous district magistrates, arbitrary and vindictive officials, timid and indecisive officials, officials who took bribes, greedy and exploitive eunuchs, and the frustrating complexity and slowness of the bureaucracy as well as its factionalism. These differences between the ideal and the real often confused the missionaries and made administrative decisions appear arbitrary. Matteo Ricci, for example, was detained for weeks at Tientsin by the infamous eunuch Ma T'ang who was hoping to extort some exotic or expensive gift from the missionaries.[162] When he finally escaped Ma T'ang's clutches and was allowed to proceed to Peking, he discovered that the Board of Rites opposed allowing him to reside in Peking because they thought he had been sent to court by the eunuch.[163] The Jesuits frequently saw memorials made on their behalf arbitrarily held up by the Office of Transmission. The regular transfer of higher officials caused them no end of confusion and occasionally deprived them of a valuable protector. Fear of the censors made many officials afraid to help the Jesuits. Sometimes, however, they benefited from official arbitrariness, such as when the district magistrate of Chaoch'ing administered an impromptu beating to a man who brought unfounded charges against the missionaries.[164] Van Rechteren thought the Law of Avoidance added to the harshness of local government, the people always being governed by outsiders.[165] All the Dutch writers—Roelofszoon, Matelief, Warwijck, and Van Rechteren—report that no negotiations with local officials were possible without generous bribes. The account of the Reijersen expedition appended to Commelin's edition of Van Rechteren's journal also illustrates the frustrations which attended any negotiations with local officials—and the dangers, for example when the *tu-tu* of Amoy invited a Dutch commander and his assistants to his residence ostensibly to sign a trade agreement but actually to poison them and set fire to their ships.[166] All

---

[161] This may also reflect the fact that the government of the K'ang-hsi era was less arbitrary and tyrannical than that of the late Ming period.

[162] Trigault in Gallagher (trans.), *op. cit.* (n. 38), pp. 359–69.

[163] *Ibid.*, pp. 379–88.

[164] *Ibid.*, pp. 163–65.

[165] Van Rechteren, *loc. cit.* (n. 27), p. 43.

[166] *Ibid.*, pp. 50–51.

of this adds a useful corrective to the more systematic general descriptions of the Jesuits. From all this material, taken together, European readers of the early seventeenth century could have formed a remarkably accurate image of the ideals, sophistication, complexity, and reality of Chinese government during the late Ming dynasty. [167]

4

ECONOMIC LIFE

Unlike modern observers, seventeenth-century Europeans usually understood China's enormous population to indicate strength and wealth rather than hopeless poverty. The general impression conveyed by their writings is that China's natural resources could have sustained even a much larger population. Their usual reaction to the fertility of the land and the diversity of its products was one of amazement. China produces everything necessary for human life and thus does not need foreign trade. [168] Trigault, in a statement frequently repeated during the remainder of the century, writes:

Generally speaking, it may be said with truth that all these writers are correct when they say that everything which the people need for their well-being and sustenance, whether it be for food or clothing or even delicacies and superfluities, is abundantly produced within the borders of the kingdom and not imported from foreign climes. I would even venture to say that practically everything which is grown in Europe is likewise found in China. If not, then what is missing here is abundantly supplied by various other products unknown to Europeans. [169]

Long lists of agricultural products are included in the works of almost all the seventeenth-century writers. China, they report, produces all the cereal grains—wheat, barley, millet, maize [170]—in abundance; they raise and eat much more rice than Europeans. Rice is the staple in the south, while wheat and barley are common in the north. Of fruits and vegetables, too, China produces a superabundance. Apart from olives and almonds, "all the prin-

---

[167] On the tension between Confucian ideals and the day-to-day practice of government during the Ming dynasty see Huang, *op. cit.* (n. 80), pp. 130–53.

[168] Pantoja, *loc. cit.* (n. 39), p. 370.

[169] Gallagher (trans.), *op. cit.* (n. 38), pp. 10–11. See also Van Rechteren, *loc. cit.* (n. 27), p. 44; Semedo, *op. cit.* (n. 9), p. 4; Martini, *op. cit.* (n. 44), p. 3; Faria y Sousa in Stevens (trans.), *op. cit.* (n. 17), II, 450, for other examples.

[170] Maize was introduced to southwestern China in the first half of the sixteenth century; it probably came via the overland route. The likelihood is that its cultivation did not spread rapidly to other regions and that it was not as abundant in the seventeenth century as the Europeans seem to indicate. See Ho Ping-ti, "The Introduction of American Food Plants into China," *American Anthropologist,* Vol. LVII, Pt. 1 (April, 1955), pp. 194–97. On maize in Siam see above, p. 1198.

cipal fruits known in Europe grow also in China."[171] In Kwangtung and other southern provinces tropical fruits are common, all "in a larger variety and possessing a finer flavor than the same fruits grown in other countries." Much the same can be said "of the variety and quality of table vegetables, all of which the Chinese use in far greater quantity than is common among the people of Europe."[172] Martini, as might be expected, describes the crops peculiar to each province. The lists are somewhat repetitious, but he reports, for example, that the best grapes come from Shansi (although the Chinese do not make wine from them), and good rhubarb grows in Shensi. Honan and Szechwan are exceedingly fertile, Hukuang (Hupei and Hunan) is called "the granary of China," large amounts of silk are produced in Chekiang, and all sorts of citrus fruits are cultivated in Kwangtung.[173] Several other writers declare Kwangtung sweet oranges to be the best in the world.[174]

Special attention was given to the fruits, plants, and trees unknown to Europe. Some, such as rhubarb, *li-chih* (litchi), *lung-yen* or dragon's eye, bamboo, ginseng, and, of course, tea, are described in considerable detail. Others are less frequently described, or described in less detail, but the catalog of exotic Chinese flora available to seventeenth-century readers from all sources was substantial. For example, Trigault describes what he calls ironwood, harder and more durable than oak.[175] Both he and Martini write about an excellent candlewax produced by small worms bred in certain trees.[176] Martini describes "Quei," an herb which banishes sorrow, and a tree (sago palm) which produces flour.[177] He describes many exotic flowers in his provincial descriptions, among them the "meutan" (*mu-tan,* peony) which grows on a shrubby tree resembling the elder, the lotus, and a "Chinese rose" in Kwangtung Province which changes color twice a day.[178] Semedo observes that "Flowers are in singular esteeme with these people."[179]

Not only was the empire seen as a veritable garden of Eden, but its inhabitants were credited with making the most of their natural heritage. European writers invariably express admiration for the Chinese peasants. Being extremely diligent, they leave hardly a square foot of arable land untilled. Even the mountains are terraced and cultivated. The farmers replenish the soil by judicious fertilization, nothing which can be used for nutrients being

[171] Gallagher (trans.), *op. cit.* (n. 38), p. 11.

[172] *Ibid.* In Chinese dishes the main constituents are the vegetables. Meats are generally employed as garnishes.

[173] Martini, *op. cit.* (n. 44), pp. 40, 54, 73, 80, 91, 132, and 161.

[174] Chinese oranges and tangerines were exported to Iberia and America in the seventeenth century. See pls. 365, 368, 369, 370.

[175] Trigault in Gallagher (trans.), *op. cit.* (n. 38), p. 15. "Ironwood" is a common name given to many heavy, hard woods.

[176] *Ibid.*, p. 16; Martini, *op. cit.* (n. 44), pp. 94 and 140.

[177] *Op. cit.* (n. 44), pp. 57 and 178.

[178] *Ibid.*, pp. 63, 103–4, and 163.

[179] *Op. cit.* (n. 9), p. 6.

wasted. In dry areas the Chinese ingeniously irrigate the land. In much of China, two and sometimes three crops per year are grown on the same land, one crop sometimes being planted before the other is harvested.[180] Farming techniques were also commonly admired by the Europeans. Semedo, for example, describes a method of plowing and sowing in a single operation:

As I passed by *Honum* [Honam], I saw one plowing with a plow of 3 irons, or plough-sheares, so that at one bout he made 3 furrowes: and because the ground was good for the seed which we here call *Feazols* or Kidny-beanes; this seed was put, as it were, in a bushel, or square dish fastened upon the upper part of the plough, in such manner, that with the motion thereof the Beanes were gently scattered upon the earth as some falleth upon a Milstone, at the moving of the Mill-hopper; so at the same time the land is plowed and sown with hopes of a future crop.[181]

In animal husbandry the Chinese are no less skilled than in soil cultivation. They raise a wide variety of animals for food, including some, like dogs, mules, and horses, normally not eaten by Europeans. Pork and poultry appear to be the most common meats. Martini reports that almost all Chinese families keep a pig, that pork is available all year, and that it is unusually delicious.[182] Oxen are commonly used as draft animals in north China; water buffalo in the south. Most Europeans agree that the Chinese remain far behind them in horsemanship and in the breeding of fine horses.[183] Most seventeenth-century writers describe the making of musk, in part apparently to correct the errors of Mendoza, who thought the little pouches of musk which were bought from the Chinese were made by beating little animals called "muske cats" to death, allowing their flesh and blood to putrify, and finally sewing the putrified flesh of the animals into small pouches made from their skins.[184] The Jesuits observe that the little sack containing the musk grows naturally on the abdomen of a certain species of deer.[185] Martini reports that the small, antlerless musk deer are plen-

[180] For examples see Wassenaer, *op. cit.* (n. 30), VII (June, 1624), 67; Semedo, *op. cit.* (n. 9), p. 23; Martini, *op. cit.* (n. 44), pp. 7, 17, and 147. Multiple crops were produced mainly in south China. For a contemporary discussion of land utilization and food production see Ho, *op. cit.* (n. 37), pp. 169–95. See also our pl. 361.

[181] Semedo, *op. cit.* (n. 9), p. 23. Cast-iron plowshares in China date from about the sixth through the fifth centuries B.C. See Joseph Needham, *Science and Civilisation in China* (6 vols.; Cambridge, 1956–86), Vol. IV, Pt. 2, p. 65. For a Chinese seed-drill plough with hopper see the engraving in Sung Ying-hsing, *Tien-Kung K'ai-Wu. Chinese Technology in the Seventeenth Century,* trans. E-tu Zen Sun and Shiou-chuan Sun (University Park, Pa., 1966), p. 26.

[182] *Op. cit.* (n. 44), p. 4.

[183] Regarding domesticated animals see, for example, Trigault in Gallagher (trans.), *op. cit.* (n. 38), p. 12; Semedo, *op. cit.* (n. 9), pp. 4–5; Martini, *op. cit.* (n. 44), p. 4.

[184] Juan González de Mendoza, *The History of the Great and Mighty Kingdom of China. . . . ,* reprinted from the translation of R. Parke; edited by Sir George T. Staunton (2 vols.; "HS," o.s., XIV, XV; London, 1853–54), I, 16.

[185] For example, see Pantoja, *loc. cit.* (n. 39), pp. 363–64; Semedo, *op. cit.* (n. 9), p. 16; Martini, *op. cit.* (n. 44), pp. 54–55.

tiful in Shansi Province and that the Chinese eat the deer's flesh as well. Merchants frequently adulterate the musk with blood and flesh so that what is purchased is not always pure musk.[186] The raising of ducks aboard ships by allowing them to feed ashore during the day and calling them back again in the evening by means of a horn also fascinates European observers.[187]

Game, especially deer and rabbits, is also readily available and inexpensive.[188] Semedo, however, thinks that the Chinese eat less game than the Europeans.[189] Still, everyone reports that China abounds in wild animals: tigers, bears, wolves, and foxes, but no lions. Martini describes a large number of exotic animals in his provincial descriptions: for example, the long-eared white cats of Peking, huge bats in Shensi Province whose flesh tastes as good as chicken, a brightly colored bird of Szechwan called the "Tunghoafung" which is born of a flower,[190] white tortoises on an island in the Yangtze River in Hukuang, a fish that emerges from the water to attack domestic cows in Kwangtung whose horns wither if it remains too long on land, a fish with four eyes and six feet, and an exceedingly fast, one-horned cow also found in Kwangtung.[191] Kwangsi, Kweichou, and Yunnan seem to be particularly rich in exotic fauna. Elephants are found in Nan-ning prefecture in Kweichou and in Yunnan.[192]

Chinese rivers, lakes, and coastal waters teem with every imaginable kind of fish. Martini itemizes the fish or crustaceans native to the provinces and cities particularly well known as centers of fishing. Trigault reports that stocked fishponds are very common, and that while they are heavily fished "a fisherman never casts a line without making a catch."[193] The large number of people who earn their livelihood from fishing, many living continuously in their boats, invariably draws comments from the Europeans. Trigault said he could understand why one writer thought as many Chinese lived on water as on land.[194] Pantoja marvels at the birds (cormorants) which Chinese fishermen train to dive into the water for fish and bring them back to their boats.[195] Martini notes that fishermen pay an imperial tax on each cormorant owned.[196]

Seventeenth-century writers, especially the Jesuits, also assure their readers that China is rich in all kinds of minerals. Trigault flatly observes that

[186] Martini, *op. cit.* (n. 44), pp. 54–55.
[187] For example, see Jean Mocquet, *Voyages en Afrique, Asie, Indes Orientales, & Occidentales* (Rouen, 1665), pp. 340–41; Martini, *op. cit.* (n. 44), pp. 162–63.
[188] Trigault in Gallagher (trans.), *op. cit.* (n. 38), p. 12.
[189] *Op. cit.* (n. 9), p. 4.
[190] Possibly the Szechwan hill partridge (*Arboraphila rufipectus*).
[191] Martini, *op. cit.* (n. 44), pp. 36, 56–57, 82, 95, 169, and 170–71.
[192] *Ibid.*, pp. 180–91. Wild elephants are still found in southwestern Yunnan.
[193] Gallagher (trans.), *op. cit.* (n. 38), p. 13. China still leads the world in fish culture.
[194] *Ibid.*, p. 12. See also Martini, *op. cit.* (n. 44), p. 6. See our pl. 328 for a floating village.
[195] Pantoja, *loc. cit.* (n. 39), pp. 367–68. See our pl. 367.
[196] *Op. cit.* (n. 44), pp. 7–8.

"All the known metals without exception are to be found in China."[197] Semedo and Martini list the products of China's "infinity of mines": quicksilver, iron, tin, copper, brass, vermilion, vitriol, saltpeter, and a wide variety of precious stones.[198] Martini provides the most detailed information regarding the provenance of particular minerals and gems: for example, gold, silver, and jasper are found in Shensi Province; azure in Honan; salt, iron, amber, tin, lead, and loadstone in Szechwan; gold, silver, tin, iron, and lead in Kiangsi; and gold, amber, rubies, sapphires, agates, cat-eyes, marble, sulphur, and benzoin in Yunnan.[199] Trigault observes that coal is plentiful in north China.[200] Gold and silver are abundant, the richest deposits being in the northwest, especially in Shensi.[201] Nevertheless very little mining is apparently done by the Chinese. Semedo and Martini assert that the emperor prohibits mining because of the danger to human life involved in it.[202] Most of the gold taken from Shensi and Yunnan is panned from streams and rivers.

Chinese artisans and craftsmen are judged to be very ingenious and industrious, and most Western descriptions include sizable sections devoted to the arts and crafts. As Trigault puts it, "They have all sorts of raw material and they are endowed by nature with a talent for trading, both of which are potent factors in bringing about a high development of the mechanical arts."[203] Martini enthusiastically describes some of the products of their industry: silk, porcelain, gilt cabinets, glue, and "perfectly" carved ebony, ivory, coral, amber, jasper, marble, and other precious stones.[204] But the Europeans did not indiscriminately praise Chinese accomplishments in the crafts. Trigault, for example, detects a lack of polished perfection in the works of Chinese artisans:

It should be noted that because these people are accustomed to live sparingly, the Chinese craftsman does not strive to reach a perfection of workmanship in the object he creates, with a view to obtaining a higher price for it. His labor is guided rather by the demand of the purchaser who is usually satisfied with a less finished product. Consequently they frequently sacrifice quality in their productions, and rest content with a superficial finish intended to catch the eye of the purchaser. This seems to be particularly noticeable when they toil for the magistrates who pay the craftsmen according to their own whims without any regard to the real value of what they buy.

---

[197] Gallagher (trans.), *op. cit.* (n. 38), p. 14. On metals see Sung, *op. cit.* (n. 181), chap. xiv.
[198] Semedo, *op. cit.* (n. 9), p. 7; Martini, *op. cit.* (n. 44), p. 6. On gems see Sung, *op. cit.* (n. 181), pp. 299–300.
[199] Martini, *op. cit.* (n. 44), pp. 53–54, 78, 80–81, 102, 191, 194.
[200] Gallagher (trans.), *op. cit.* (n. 38), pp. 15–16. *Cf.* Sung, *op. cit.* (n. 181), pp. 205–6.
[201] Martini, *op. cit.* (n. 44), p. 53.
[202] Semedo, *op.cit.* (n. 9), p. 6; Martini, *op. cit.* (n. 44), p. 5. Gold mining was carried on in southwest China. See Sung, *op. cit.* (n. 181), p. 236.
[203] Gallagher (trans.), *op. cit.* (n. 38), p. 19.
[204] *Op. cit.* (n. 44), p. 7.

At times, too, they compel the artisans to design things for which they have no genius or aptitude.[205]

The writers consider many European achievements superior to those of the Chinese and evince a fairly balanced appreciation for the relative achievements of both Chinese and Europeans in the arts and crafts.

Almost all Western writers credit the Chinese with the very early invention of printing, papermaking, and gunpowder. But while the Chinese had known about gunpowder much longer than Europeans they remain quite inexpert in its military uses. They use it primarily in the manufacture of ornamental fireworks; lavish pyrotechnic displays accompany the celebration of most festive occasions in China. Trigault calculates that a New Year's celebration which he witnessed in Nanking "consumed enough powder to carry on a sizable war for a number of years."[206] The Jesuits occasionally use this information to demonstrate the peaceable character of the Chinese.

Europeans realized that the celebrated art of printing had also existed much longer in China than in Europe. Trigault thinks it dates back to about 50 B.C.[207] The Chinese technique of printing differs significantly from that of the Europeans. Instead of composing plates from movable type, the Chinese printer pastes the page which he wishes to reproduce face down on a wooden block. Then he cuts away the unwanted portions of the block, the characters being left to stand out in relief. From this wooden plate a Chinese printer can print as many as fifteen hundred copies in a day—a speed Trigault considers incredible.[208] Most of the European writers recognize that the Chinese method of printing was better adapted to the numerous and complex Chinese characters than was the movable-type process. Nor do they consider the Chinese process less efficient; they believe that a Chinese engraver can prepare a wooden block almost as rapidly as a European compositor can set up the type for a similar page. Furthermore there are some distinct advantages to the Chinese method: the plates can easily be preserved for future editions of a book, thus avoiding the necessity of printing an excessively large first edition. Trigault also contends that the Chinese method is very inexpensive, to which he attributes the large number of books in circulation in China.[209]

[205] Gallagher (trans.), *op. cit.* (n. 38), p. 19. See also Pantoja, *loc. cit.* (n. 39), p. 376.
[206] Gallagher (trans.), *op. cit.* (n. 38), p. 18. See also Martini, *op. cit.* (n. 44), p. 7.
[207] Gallagher (trans.), *op. cit.* (n. 38), p. 20. Block printing was invented in the seventh and eighth centuries A.D. Movable type was invented in the late eleventh century but was never widely used. See T. H. Tsien, *Paper and Printing* (Vol. V, Pt. 1 of Needham, *op. cit.* [n. 181]), pp. 1, 201. T. C. Carter and L. F. Goodrich (*The Invention of Printing in China and Its Spread Westward* [New York, 1955], p. x) say printing began in China about A.D. 950.
[208] Gallagher (trans.), *op. cit.* (n. 38), p. 20.
[209] *Ibid.*, p. 21. By the end of the fifteenth century, China had probably produced more books than all other countries combined. See T. H. Tsien, *Written on Bamboo and Silk* (Chicago, 1962), p. 2.

Paper was also reported to be abundant, cheap, and of very ancient use in China. As with printing, Chinese paper was judged to be different from that produced in Europe, but not necessarily better. Trigault describes it quite accurately:

The use of paper is much more common in China than elsewhere, and its methods of production more diversified. Yet the best variety produced here is inferior to many of our own brands. It cannot be printed or written upon both sides, so that one of our sheets is equivalent to two of theirs. Moreover, it tears easily and does not stand up well against time . . . the kind they manufacture from cotton fiber is as white as the best paper found in the West.[210]

Painting, too, had been anciently practiced in China and was still held in high esteem, but most early seventeenth-century European writers show little appreciation for Chinese painting. Pantoja bluntly asserts that the Chinese painters "have no Art, nor paint the things with shadowes, and know not how to paint in Oile."[211] Trigault agrees: "it seems to me that the Chinese, who in other respects are so ingenious, and by nature in no way inferior to any other people on earth, are very primitive in the use of these latter arts [painting and sculpture]." Like Pantoja, he complains that they do not use oils, shading, or perspective in their paintings, "with the result that their productions are likely to resemble the dead rather than the living." In sculpture they follow "rules of symmetry determined by the eye only," which results "in illusions and causes glaring defects in their works of larger proportions."[212] Semedo concurs, but he also observes that "trees, flowers, birds, and such like things they paint very much to the life."[213]

The earliest Western observers, such as Mendoza, had expressed great admiration for Chinese architecture. They described stone buildings which had stood for centuries; Mendoza, in fact, refers to "buildings verie sumptuous which endure to this day, built by the first emperor."[214] During the seventeenth century, Europeans continue to be impressed by bridges, temples, pagodas, and some public buildings. But their general estimation

[210]Gallagher (trans.), *op. cit.* (n. 38), p. 16. Paper made of plant fibers was used in China beginning in the second century A.D. See Tsien, *op. cit.* (n. 209), pp. 135–37.

[211]Pantoja, *loc. cit.* (n. 39), p. 387.

[212]Gallagher (trans.), *op. cit.* (n. 38), p. 22.

[213]*Op. cit.* (n. 9), p. 56. Despite their lack of appreciation for Chinese paintings, the Jesuits apparently carried some landscape scrolls back to Europe. One was reproduced as the frontispiece to the *Regni chinensis descriptio ex varijs authoribus* (Leyden, 1639), which is very likely the earliest depiction of a Chinese landscape painting printed in the West. See our pl. 72. Another was published in Athanasius Kircher's *China illustrata* (Amsterdam, 1667). See our pl. 316. On linear perspective as a Western cultural symbol and the difficulties experienced by seventeenth-century Chinese and Westerners in understanding each other's art see the three-part article by Richard M. Swiderski, "The Dragon and the Straightedge," *Semiotica*, Vol. LXXXI, Nos. 1–2 (1990), pp. 1–41; Vol. LXXXII, Nos. 1–2 (1990), pp. 43–136; Vol. LXXXII, Nos. 3–4 (1990), pp. 211–268.

[214]*Op. cit.* (n. 184), I, 70.

of Chinese architectural achievements declines as more precise information becomes available. Trigault, for example, declares that "Chinese architecture is in every way inferior to that of Europe with respect to the style and the durability of the buildings." The Chinese, he reports, do not dig deeply into the ground to lay foundations for their buildings; usually they simply place large stones on the unbroken surface of the ground. They seem unconcerned that their buildings will not last beyond their own lifetimes. They build "for themselves rather than for posterity."[215] When the Jesuits describe European buildings which have stood securely for several centuries, the Chinese will scarcely believe it. Most Chinese buildings are built of wood, and even those of masonry have wooden pillars to support the roof so that the walls may be easily repaired without affecting the stability of the roof.[216]

Most of the other seventeenth-century writers agree with Trigault's evaluation of Chinese architecture.[217] Semedo, however, while admitting that Chinese homes are not as sumptuous or durable as European structures, insists that they are pleasanter and more convenient within—and always cleaner and neater.[218] He particularly admires the gardens in the houses of wealthier people with their carefully chosen trees, artificial mountains, fishponds, birds, and animals. He and several other European writers also comment on the extensive use of varnish or lacquer in Chinese buildings. It has "the appearance of milk but the consistency of glue," and is "pressed from the trunk of a certain tree." Wood finished with it has a high gloss and becomes exceedingly durable. The Chinese, in fact, are able to eat at tables without table cloths and still not endanger the finish of the table with spills.[219] Semedo is also intrigued by the use of coal stoves to heat homes in north China:

They make use of stoves, that are more convenient than ours, and waste not so much fewell, conveighing the heate by pipes laid underground; and so within doores enjoy a pleasant spring in the heart of winter. The same heate supplieth also the absence of the sun, and by means thereof the trees are clothed with leaves and flowers before their time.[220]

Trigault reports that coal is so abundant that even the poorest people use it.[221] He also describes the typical north Chinese *k'ang* or heated bed:

[215] Gallagher (trans.), *op. cit.* (n. 38), p. 19.
[216] *Ibid.*, p. 20. *Cf.* Needham, *op. cit.* (n. 181), Vol. IV, Pt. 3, pp. 58–144, on traditional Chinese building technology.
[217] For example, see Pantoja, *loc. cit.* (n. 39), p. 450; Semedo, *op. cit.* (n. 9), p. 3; Martini, *op. cit.* (n. 44), p. 8; Faria y Sousa in Stevens (trans.), *op. cit.* (n. 17), p. 450.
[218] *Op. cit.* (n. 9), p. 3.
[219] Trigault in Gallagher (trans.), *op. cit.* (n. 38), pp. 17–18. See also Pantoja, *loc. cit.* (n. 39), pp. 342–43; Semedo, *op. cit.* (n. 9), p. 3; and Faria y Sousa in Stevens (trans.), *op. cit.* (n. 17), p. 449.
[220] *Op. cit.* (n. 9), p. 21.
[221] Gallagher (trans.), *op. cit.* (n. 38), pp. 15–16.

The beds here are built up with bricks, with a hollow space underneath, through which pipes from a fireplace are passed, creating a heat chamber beneath the bed. One does not have to keep the heat on during the night because the chamber stays hot for a long time. This kind of bed is in common use through all the northern provinces.[222]

Public buildings, walled cities, triumphal arches, bridges, and temples continually fascinated European observers. The imperial palace in Peking is repeatedly described. Pantoja, while impressed with its size, judges its architecture to be inferior to that of great European palaces. Its walls, he reports, embrace an area comparable to that of a good-sized city. He is much taken with its yellow-tiled roofs gleaming like gold from a distance, and with the artificial mountains, the long avenues of stairs, the rivers, and the ornate marble bridges in the palace grounds.[223] Martini's description of the palace differs very little from Pantoja's, but he apparently is more favorably impressed with it. "If you consider its grandeur and embellishments," he writes, "it completely surpasses the magnificence of ours."[224] The palaces and temples in Nanking are occasionally described in the European reports, as were the palaces of great provincial officials. Martini, for example, includes a rather thorough description of a typical provincial "governor's" official residence: At the entrance are three doors—the largest of which is in the middle—flanked by marble lions. Inside, near the entrance, is a courtyard surrounded by a trellis and containing two small towers for musicians. Quarters for lesser officers are located off the courtyard, as are the two great halls for receiving guests. Scholars are received in the left hall, "those who carry the sword" in the right. Beyond these halls are three more doors which open into the hall where the governor holds court. The lodgings of his permanent staff, those who remain when the governor is transferred, are on either side of this hall. Next is an inner hall where the governor entertains friends. Domestic servants have their quarters around it, and a large door separates it from his personal quarters. From his private quarters he has access to his gardens, with their forests and lakes. There are fifteen to twenty such palaces in each provincial capital, four in middle-sized cities, all built and furnished by the emperor.[225] Semedo describes the mansion of the viceroy of Canton.[226] The Dutch admirals who attempted to trade in the Amoy and Canton areas comment on the residences of some of the officials with whom they had contact, and the *Begin ende voortgangh* edition of Matelief's journal contains a sketch of the magistrate of Lan-tao's palace.[227]

[222] *Ibid.*, p. 311.

[223] Pantoja, *loc. cit.* (n. 39), pp. 407–9.

[224] *Op. cit.* (n. 44), pp. 38–39. Later visitors provided sketches of the imperial palace; see our pls. 23, 306, and 314.

[225] Martini, *op. cit.* (n. 44), pp. 13–14.

[226] *Op. cit.* (n. 9), pp. 134–35.

[227] Matelief, *loc. cit.* (n. 122), facing page 84.

Martini, as might be expected, discourses more than anyone else on temples, palaces, towers, triumphal arches, and bridges. For example, he describes the beautiful stone bridges which cross the Wei River near Sian; an octagonal porcelain tower eight stories high in Tung-chung, Shantung Province; a floating bridge in Kiangsi built on 130 pontoons; an iron tower in Chin-chiang, Kiangnan Province (present-day Anhwei and Kiangsu); a stone bridge at Lo-yang, Fukien Province, 360 rods long, 1½ rods wide, built in the shape of a great ship; a suspension bridge hung on iron chains over a mountain stream in Kweichou; and another similar bridge, twelve rods long in Yunnan.[228] No structure, however, attracts as much attention as the Great Wall. It is described as one of the wonders of the world by nearly every writer. Its dimensions are recorded, as are its history and the details of its construction. But Semedo scoffs: the wall has "more reputation than effect"; it is far too long to be adequately defended, and the Tartars regularly cross and wreck it.[229] Semedo's realism, however, does not dampen the enthusiasm of Martini, who, writing after the Manchu conquest, still includes a lengthy description and history of the wall.[230]

Porcelain and silk were perhaps the two Chinese products most sought by the Europeans, and most of the early seventeenth-century writers describe both. They were much more concerned with porcelain than with silk, possibly because true porcelain could not then be produced in Europe. Pantoja merely reports that the Chinese make "the best Porcelane that hitherto hath beene found," and that it is plentiful and inexpensive.[231] Trigault discusses it in more detail: among its properties he lists its ability to hold hot foods without breaking and notes that a broken piece can be so successfully mended with a brass wire that it can hold liquids without leaking. He also observes that the best pieces are made from clay in Kiangsi Province.[232] Neither Pantoja nor Trigault describes porcelain manufacture, although some sixteenth-century writers had circulated some rather fanciful descriptions of its manufacture. Semedo includes a brief account of porcelain in his description of Kiangsi Province:

It [Kiangsi] is famous . . . for the *porcellane* dishes (indeed the only work in the world of this kind) which are made only in one of its Townes: So that all that is used in the Kingdom, and dispersed through the whole world, are brought from this place: although the earth, whereof they are made commeth from another place: but there only is the water, wherewith precisely they are to be wrought to come to their perfection, for if they be wrought with other water the worke will not have so much

---

[228] *Op. cit.* (n. 44), pp. 56, 69–70, 113, 125, 151–52, 189, and 197. Iron-chain suspension bridges date back to A.D. 580. See Sung, *op. cit.* (n. 181), p. 366. *Cf.* our pl. 299 for an example of a Chinese bridge.

[229] *Op. cit.* (n. 9), pp. 121–22.

[230] *Op. cit.* (n. 44), pp. 19–20. *Cf.* our pls. 300 and 308.

[231] *Loc. cit.* (n. 39), pp. 374–75.

[232] Gallagher (trans.), *op. cit.* (n. 38), pp. 14–15.

glosse and luster. In this worke there are not those mysteries that are reported of it here, neither is the matter, the form, nor the manner of working; they are made absolutely of earth, but of a neate and excellent quality. They are made in the same time and in the same manner, as our earthen vessels; only they make them with more diligence and accuratenesse. The Blew, wherewith they paint the Porcellane is Anill, whereof they have abundance, some do paint them with Vermilion, and (for the King) with yellow.[233]

Martini repeats most of what Trigault and Semedo had written but locates the center of porcelain manufacture in Fou-liang, Kiangsi Province.[234] He ridicules the fanciful stories circulating in Europe about its manufacture— that it was made of eggshells or seashells and that its manufacture was a closely guarded secret. He thinks that the clay, which comes from Hui-chou prefecture in Kiangnan Province, was the most important ingredient. This clay, he reports, was not thick or greasy, "but very clear and shiny like fine sand." It is thrown into water to temper it and then molded. Shattered dishes, he reports, are ground up, tempered, and remolded in the same manner.[235]

Most writers mention silk. Pantoja and Trigault are impressed with the enormous quantities produced and the low price, but not with its quality. "They know not how to dresse it," claims Pantoja.[236] Trigault judges European silk to be finer; he reports that the Chinese are imitating it.[237] Semedo and Martini both locate the center of Chinese silk production in Chekiang Province.[238] Martini asserts that as much silk is produced there as in the rest of the world combined.[239] The Chinese, he reports, knew sericulture as early as 2080 B.C.; all other peoples learned it from the Chinese.[240] Unlike Pantoja and Trigault, Martini thinks Chinese silk is superior to European silk, as well as much less expensive. Silkworms are hatched twice a year, he reports, and those hatched in the spring produce finer thread than those of the fall.[241]

Silk was not the only textile produced by Chinese weavers in the early seventeenth century. According to European reports, the Chinese produce no linen and very little wool, but cotton is becoming very common. Trig-

[233] *Op. cit.* (n. 9), p. 12.

[234] In fact the Ming royal porcelain works were in the nearby village of Ching-te-chen.

[235] *Op. cit.* (n. 44), pp. 106–7. On porcelain manufacture see Sung, *op. cit.* (n. 181), pp. 146–57. Sung (p. 146) lists six widely scattered places from which the white clay for porcelain comes.

[236] Pantoja, *loc. cit.* (n. 39), p. 375.

[237] Gallagher (trans.), *op. cit.* (n. 38), p. 13.

[238] Semedo, *op. cit.* (n. 9), p. 13; Martini, *op. cit.* (n. 44), pp. 5 and 132. Cf. Sung, *op. cit.* (n. 181), p. 36.

[239] *Op. cit.* (n. 44), p. 5.

[240] Sericulture originated in north China during the Shang dynasty (*ca.* 1766–*ca.* 1027 B.C.). The center of silk production shifted to the Yangtze valley only after the eleventh century A.D. See Tsien, *op. cit.* (n. 209), pp. 114–16.

[241] *Op. cit.* (n. 44), pp. 5 and 132. On the differences between early and late silkworms see Sung, *op. cit.* (n. 181), p. 37.

ault reports in 1615 that cotton is a new product, introduced to China only forty years earlier.[242] It grows so well, however, that Trigault thinks China will eventually be able to supply it to the whole world.[243] Semedo, writing shortly before 1642, reports that two hundred thousand looms produce cotton cloth in the Shanghai district of Kiangnan Province. He also reports that most of the work is done by women.[244] In his general introduction Martini repeats Trigault's statement, and notes that cotton seed was introduced to China about five hundred years earlier.[245] Both Semedo and Martini report that fine felt tapestries and hats are produced from goat and horse hair in Shensi.[246]

A great many other products of Chinese artisans and craftsmen were described during the first half of the seventeenth century, some known to Europeans and some unique to China. The Chinese, for example, make a great variety of cast-iron products, use brass and copper extensively, and also produce a very useful imitation silver alloy which costs no more than brass.[247] China has glassblowers, but their work is judged to be far inferior to that of Europeans.[248] Trigault particularly admires Chinese fans; their manufacture involves many more workmen than in any other country. Men and women of all classes carry them on cool days as well as hot; "it would be considered a lack of taste to appear in public without a fan." Carried "more for ornamental display than for any necessity," they are made in a great variety of shapes and from many different materials:

Ordinarily they consist of ribs of reed, wood, ivory, or ebony, covered with paper or perhaps with cotton and at times even with a sweet-scented straw. Some are round, some oval, and some square. Those used by the upper classes are generally made of bright paper decorated with a design, beautifully traced in gold, and they are carried either spread out or folded up. Sometimes, too, these fans are inscribed with certain maxims or even with whole poems. The gift most frequently exchanged as a sign of friendship and esteem is a fan.[249]

---

[242] It was probably grown in China as early as the second century A.D., but grown for its fiber only since the twelfth century. See Sung, *op. cit.* (n. 181), pp. 71–72, n. 14. On its manufacture in China, see *ibid.*, pp. 60–64. *Cf.* also Nishijima Sadao, "The Formation of the Early Chinese Cotton Industry," in Linda Grove and Christian Daniels (eds.), *Japanese Perspectives on Ming-Qing Social and Economic History* (Tokyo, 1984), pp. 17–77.

[243] Gallagher (trans.), *op. cit.* (n. 38), p. 13.

[244] *Op. cit.* (n. 9), p. 14. Nishijima (*op. cit.* [n. 242], pp. 63–64) sees no reason to doubt Semedo's report.

[245] *Op. cit.* (n. 44), p. 5. Sung (*op. cit.* [n. 181], p. 60) observes that cotton in two varieties had been used in China since antiquity.

[246] Semedo, *op. cit.* (n. 9), p. 16; Martini, *op. cit.* (n. 44), p. 5.

[247] Trigault in Gallagher (trans.), *op. cit.* (n. 38), p. 14; Martini, *op. cit.* (n. 44), p. 6; Semedo, *op. cit.* (n. 9), p. 7. Semedo calls it "Tomnaga," which appears to be tutenag, or "white copper," an alloy of copper, zinc, and nickel, still used. *Cf.* Chen, *loc. cit.* (n. 118), p. 36.

[248] Trigault in Gallagher (trans.), *op. cit.* (n. 38), p. 15; Martini, *op. cit.* (n. 44), p. 7. Little is known about Chinese glass manufacture, although it appears that the Chinese made glass since Chou times (1122–255 B.C.) and may have blown glass since the Latter Han (A.D. 25–220). See Needham, *op. cit.* (n. 181), Vol. IV, Pt. 1, pp. 99–111.

[249] Gallagher (trans.), *op. cit.* (n. 38), pp. 24–25.

Another trade peculiar to China is the manufacture of the seals used to affix a person's name in red ink to letters, paintings, official documents, and for many other purposes. The seals usually contain only the owner's name, carved in characters of a very old form, although some authors have seals containing their degrees and titles as well; and since most Chinese have more than one name, a scholar's desk may contain a cabinet full of seals. Seals are made of rare wood, brass, marble, ivory, red coral, or semi-precious stones, and much care is taken in their carving. Many skilled workmen—Trigault says they are considered artists—are employed in making them. Craftsmen who make writing ink and those who make the often beautifully carved stones on which the solid ink is mixed with water for writing are also considered artists. Trigault was less impressed with Chinese timepieces. He somewhat vaguely mentions clocks which employed waterpots, those which used fire, and those which used sand. All of these and even Chinese sundials are far inferior to European clocks.[250]

The Europeans were most impressed by the enormous number of Chinese craftsmen, by the quantity and variety of their products, and by the general preoccupation with trade.

They [the Chinese] are naturally inclined to be Merchants, and it is incredible, the Traffick which they make, not only from one Province to another, with very great profit (So that they which transport Porsellane within their own Kingdom, although they sell it but from one Province to another, gain thirty *per cent,* twice a Year) but even in the same City: For almost whatever is found in the shopps, is sold in the streets in lesser quantity; employing in this trade even to little children, as far as they are able, as selling fruits, herbs, wash balls, and such like things.[251]

The merchants might have occupied the lowest rung on the social ladder according to Confucian theory, but as a general rule, the European observers agree, they lived somewhat better and seemingly had more fun than their theoretical social superiors, the peasants.[252] The Western writers, furthermore, convey the impression of a very large merchant class. Their books are filled with descriptions of the crowded streets lined with shops, hucksters selling their wares on street corners and on the waterfronts, and rivers virtually choked with trading vessels. Several such accounts were written by Dutch merchants, themselves representatives of one of the most bustling commercial communities in Europe.

European traders also had a healthy respect for the ability of their Chinese counterparts. They invariably describe Chinese merchants as "quick and subtle," aware of the value of products, and unusually adept at driving a

[250] *Ibid.*, pp. 23–24. Also see below, p. 1693, on timepieces.

[251] Semedo, *op. cit.* (n. 9), p. 23.

[252] Hucker (*op. cit.* [n. 94], p. 33) reports that "mercantile wealth became steadily more esteemed during the Ming Period and that customs became increasingly extravagant, to the detriment of the rather puritanical agrarian values espoused by the government." Indeed, many sons of rich merchants obtained the *chin-shih,* or doctor's degree.

hard bargain. From their first contacts with Chinese merchants until the end of the century, both in China and overseas, Europeans habitually compared them to the Jews in Europe. The Dutch, for example, first encountered the Chinese in Bantam, where they virtually controlled the economic life of the land. They were the middlemen in the pepper trade, Java's main commercial enterprise. They bought the pepper from the growers, stored it, and sold it to merchants from China and elsewhere who came each year to Javan ports. The Chinese apparently dominated Java's financial life also; the Dutch observed that Chinese copper cash served as the predominant monetary medium for all of Java and the surrounding islands. Admiral Matelief in his advice to the VOC directors asserts that no people on earth are more assiduously devoted to material profit than the Chinese.[253] Nor, if we may believe the European writers, were Chinese merchants overly scrupulous about the means employed in making a profit; they apparently had an international reputation for deceit and fraud. Dutch travel accounts and VOC records are full of complaints about Chinese merchants who adulterated products, misrepresented goods, cheated in monetary exchanges, and formed price-fixing syndicates. The French traveler Jean Mocquet voices an almost universally accepted judgment when he writes: "The people of China are very crafty and great cheats."[254] Even Semedo, who is somewhat reluctant to criticize the Chinese, admits that "the nature of the people and the inclination of the whole nation, as well those who sell, as those who buy, is much inclined to guile and deceit, which they put into execution with admirable subtiletie." He includes some examples of Chinese craftiness: partridges cleverly stuffed with wood and bones, their meat having been removed, wooden hams or bacon, and old horses fattened and even artfully painted to make them appear young.[255]

Apart from taxes and a monopoly on the sale of salt, the Western observers do not remark on any appreciable degree of governmental control of, or interference in, the internal commercial life of the empire. Although despised by Confucian officials, merchants were apparently free to go on making money as they saw fit. In the many large walled cities—whose very existence implies a vital middle class—the merchants seem to have occupied a fairly distinct quarter. Many Western accounts asserted that all persons engaged in the same trade would be found on the same street.[256] Much commercial activity, however, was carried on outside the city walls in the crowded suburbs, and many writers refer to the large number of peddlers plying the streets and roadways. In addition to the normal commercial routine of the towns, the Western observers often described regular fairs which

[253] Matelief, "Discours op de handelinghe, die men in O.I. soude mogen drijven," as quoted in W. P. Groeneveldt, "De Nederlanders in China," *BTLV*, XLVIII (1898), 39.

[254] *Op. cit.* (n. 187), p. 341.

[255] Semedo, *op. cit.* (n. 9), p. 24.

[256] For example see Van Rechteren, *loc. cit.* (n. 27), p. 43.

were held in some Chinese cities; the biennial fairs in Canton, which the Portuguese from Macao were permitted to attend, were most frequently mentioned.[257]

The cities themselves were a source of constant amazement to European observers—so densely populated, and so many of them. Still, they detected an astonishing amount of uniformity. All Chinese cities are surrounded by thick stone or brick walls with watch towers at regular intervals. Entrance to the city is usually through double gates with soldiers stationed between the first and second gates. In addition, the outer walls are frequently girdled by canals or moats, with bridges providing access to the gates. Outside the gates lie bustling suburbs which frequently house as many people as the cities themselves. The main streets of the cities are usually paved. Typically two broad straight streets cross each other at right angles and terminate at the city's four gates. Whatever other monuments and public buildings they contain, most cities also boast a tower where the time of day is kept and publicly displayed or announced and from which watchmen look out for fires. Usually a temple dedicated to the city's tutelary deity stands nearby. In fact Pantoja comes close to saying of Chinese cities that when you've seen one, you've seen them all: "For the Chinese are so like, and so uniforme in all naturall and artificiall things, that he that hath seene one of the principall Cities, findeth no new thing to bee seene in the others."[258] This uniformity, however, does not prevent the early seventeenth-century writers from describing particular cities. Almost everyone describes Peking and Nanking, sometimes in considerable detail. Nanking is one of the grandest and most beautiful cities in the world, with long, broad, paved avenues and many magnificent stone bridges, towers, and palaces, and a nine-story porcelain pagoda. It is surrounded by three circular walls; the main wall containing twelve gates and the inner wall encircling the imperial palace. Trigault writes: "There is probably no king in the world with a palace surpassing this one."[259] It is also an exceedingly large city. With minor variations everyone repeats the story of how two horsemen riding the circuit of the city wall, galloping in opposite directions from the same gate early in the morning, would not meet each other until nightfall. Nanking is also commercially important. The Yangtze washes its walls and its canals allow even large boats to enter the city.[260]

[257] For example, see Gallagher (trans.), *op. cit.* (n. 38), p. 132; Martini, *op. cit.* (n. 44), pp. 163–64.

[258] Pantoja, *loc. cit.* (n. 39), p. 366. For general descriptions of Chinese cities see also Van Rechteren, *loc. cit.* (n. 27), p. 143; Matelief, *loc. cit.* (n. 122), p. 93; Martini, *op. cit.* (n. 44), pp. 15–16.

[259] Gallagher (trans.), *op. cit.* (n. 38), p. 269. On Ming-dynasty Nanking see Barry Till, *In Search of Old Nanking* (Hong Kong, 1982), pp. 99–165. For a city plan see F. W. Mote and D. Twichett (eds.), *The Cambridge History of China*, VII (Cambridge, 1988), 110. For a vista of Nanking see our pl. 319.

[260] Pantoja, *loc. cit.* (n. 39), pp. 365–66; Trigault in Gallagher (trans.), *op. cit.* (n. 38),

In size and grandeur Peking is not as impressive as Nanking; but its population is larger and its throngs of officials and soldiers provide the northern capital with an aura of prestige and power. Peking is protected by two high, thick walls on the south, a single wall on the north, and a large garrison, "as numerous as if a war were raging," in Trigault's estimation.[261] The emperor's palace grounds extend through the center of the city from the southern wall, which contains its main gate, to the northern wall. While "not as wide as the palace at Nankin," Trigault claims that "the grace and beauty of its [the Peking palace's] architecture are emphasized by its slender lines."[262] Peking also has twelve gates through which pass "an incredible abundance of all things." Martini also attests to the truth of the popular proverb "that nothing grows in Peking, nevertheless nothing is lacking there."[263] Tolls are collected at Peking's gates by palace eunuchs, something not done in any other Chinese city.[264] Living in Peking with its cold winters is less comfortable than in Nanking. It is also a dirtier city. Few of its streets are paved, and between the mud in winter and the dust in summer it is rarely comfortable to walk about in the city. Dust swirls in everywhere and soils everything. People wear long veils over their faces against the dust, which practice has the side benefit of rendering the wearer anonymous and thus obviating the frequent greetings and salutes otherwise required in this protocol-ridden capital.[265]

Seventeenth-century writers describe many other Chinese cities. Hangchow and Soochow are favorites; "earthly paradises," the Chinese call them. Hangchow is Marco Polo's Quinsay, with its "infinity of bridges," high towers, burgeoning commerce, and idyllic West Lake.[266] Soochow's streets are canals, choked with boats, along which its houses are built on wooden pilings. Known for its delicious food and gracious living, it reminds the missionaries of Venice, except that Soochow's canals are fresh and clear.[267] Canton, too, is frequently described, and of course Martini's *Atlas* contains descriptions of scores of provincial cities, among them Tient-

---

pp. 268–69; Martini, *op. cit.* (n. 44), pp. 117–20; Semedo, *op. cit.* (n. 9), pp. 14–15. Nanking's wall was 33.4 kilometers long, probably the longest city wall in the world. About two-thirds of it still stands. Little remains of the imperial palace. The porcelain pagoda was destroyed in 1856. See Till, *op. cit.* (n. 259), pp. 108–17, 127–31. For the pagoda see our pl. 321. For a Nanking street scene see our pl. 320.

[261] Gallagher (trans.), *op. cit.* (n. 38), p. 309. See our pl. 304.

[262] Gallagher (trans.), *op. cit.* (n. 38), p. 309. Later seventeenth-century writers included engravings. See our pls. 305, 306, and 314.

[263] *Op. cit.* (n. 44), p. 37. For a later seventeenth-century view of Peking see our pl. 303.

[264] Trigault in Gallagher (trans.), *op. cit.* (n. 38), p. 309.

[265] *Ibid.*, p. 310; Martini, *op. cit.* (n. 44), p. 38.

[266] Pantoja, *loc. cit.* (n. 39), p. 366; Gallagher (trans.), *op. cit.* (n. 38), pp. 316–17; Martini, *op. cit.* (n. 44), pp. 133–37.

[267] Pantoja, *loc. cit.* (n. 39), p. 366; Gallagher (trans.), *op. cit.* (n. 38), p. 317; Martini, *op. cit.* (n. 44), pp. 121–22.

sin, Chungking, Nanch'ang, Ningpo, Foochow, Chang-chou, Canton, and Macao.[268]

Macao, Martini reports, is one of the most famous ports in all of the Indies, but since it has been so frequently described in earlier European reports he will be very brief. The city is located on a small peninsula connected to a large island northward by a narrow tongue of land. On the other three sides, the surrounding sea is shallow, except for a commodious harbor, which is protected by a strong bulwark with many large cannons. Two forts protect the city, and on the landside the terrain is open and barren. The Portuguese were allowed to settle here because the peninsula was uninhabited and uncultivated. An "idol" called "Ama" once stood near the harbor, hence the name "Amacao" or Macao. In a very short time the Portuguese built a magnificent, populous, and prosperous city; prosperous not only because of its trade, but also because from Macao, Christian missionaries are sent to China, Japan, Tongking, Cochin-China, Cambodia, and many other places, all supported by the Portuguese merchants of the city. Macao boasts many fine churches and monasteries and a large number of priests. Because of its piety, the Portuguese king has given it the episcopal dignity.[269]

Indeed, a great many of the missionaries who passed through Macao during the first half of the century described the city, and many of these descriptions appeared in the published letterbooks. Perhaps the best of the early descriptions, however, was that written by an otherwise unknown Italian named Marco d'Avalo in approximately 1638 but not published until 1645 when it appeared as an appendix to Van Rechteren's voyage in the *Begin ende voortgangh*.[270]

D'Avalo describes the terrain much as Martini had, but he fixes Macao's latitude at 20.5° north.[271] The Chinese have built a stone wall with a gate in it across the strip of land connecting the city with the coast. Here they collect duties on everything that passes through. Chinese carry the goods and provisions back and forth; Portuguese are not permitted to pass through the gate. D'Avalo describes the city's walls and forts in much more detail than does Martini. There are three hills with forts on them which form a sort of triangle. The strongest of these is called "St. Paulo," where Macao's first captain-general, António de Mascarenhas, lived. It has thirty-four large bronze cannons. The second fort is called "Nostra Seignora de la Penna de Francia." The third, "Nostra Seignora de Guyll," is on a higher hill outside

---

[268] Martini, *op. cit.* (n. 44), pp. 48, 84–85, 105–6, 143–44, 149, 152–53, 163–64, 164–65.

[269] *Ibid.*, pp. 164–65.

[270] *BV*, IIb, 78–86. D'Avalo's description is translated in C. R. Boxer (ed.), *Seventeenth Century Macau in Contemporary Documents and Illustrations* (Hong Kong, Kuala Lumpur, and Singapore, 1984), pp. 69–80. Apparently nothing is known about the author, not even whether his original account was written in Italian or Portuguese.

[271] On Macao's location (22.2° north and 113.6° east), surface geography, climate, and vegetation, see Antonio Costa, *Macau, imagens e numeros* (2 vols.; Lisbon, 1981–82), Vol. I.

the city and overlooks the others. From it, watchmen alert the city of incoming ships by ringing bells. Four bulwarks protect the city on the ground, three on the seasides and one on the landside. The strongest of these, "Santiago de la Barra," guards the harbor. All ships must pass under its sixteen heavy guns to enter or leave the harbor. The Portuguese have blocked all other channels. Near the second bulwark, called "Nostra Seignora del Bon Patto," stands a gunpowder mill. Macao also has a gun foundry which makes fine brass and iron cannons.[272]

Macao has five religious houses: one each for the Jesuits, Dominicans, Franciscans, and Augustinians; and the convent of "St. Clara" (Franciscan), established in 1631 by nuns brought over from Manila. There are three churches within the city: the cathedral, "St. Lorensio," and "St. Antonio"; and one, "St. Lasaro," outside the walls.[273]

Prior to the unsuccessful Dutch attack on Macao in 1622 it had no walls and was governed as a republic by its oldest councillors. After the Dutch attack, the walls and fortifications were built and the viceroy at Goa was asked to send three hundred soldiers and a governor to be maintained at the city's expense. The viceroy responded quickly to this opportunity to establish royal authority over Macao, and sent Mascarenhas to be the first governor (captain-general). Mascarenhas, however, was not well received by the independent-minded citizens until after he seized control over the Jesuit fort "St. Paulo" by subterfuge. D'Avalo recounts the popular story describing these events.[274] In addition to the captain-general, D'Avalo reports, Macao has a bishop, a sergeant-major, a captain of artillery, and three captains of infantry.[275]

Macao's trade occupies a prominent place in D'Avalo's account. Three or four Chinese junks leave Macao for Manila each April carrying silk goods, raw silk, cotton, hemp, porcelain, vermilion, quicksilver, zinc, "tentenago" (tutenag or white copper), other metals and minerals, and a variety of *objets d'art*. They usually return in October. The Japan ships, usually four to six Portuguese galliots, leave from Macao laden with similar Chinese goods in the middle of July and return in November with cargoes of silver bullion. Prior to 1630 the Japan voyages were undertaken by the Senate of Macao and the profits were used to support the garrison and to maintain the for-

[272] Boxer (ed.), *op. cit.* (n. 270), pp. 72–74.

[273] *Ibid.*, p. 74. D'Avalo's account also contains a full-page copperplate engraving of Macao. See our pls. 24 and 332.

[274] Boxer (ed.), *op. cit.* (n. 270), pp. 74–76. A detailed contemporary report of the Dutch attack on Macao is included in the appendices to Van Rechteren's voyage as publsihed in the *Begin ende voortgangh;* see *BV,* IIb, 45–53. For a modern account see Boxer, *Fidalgos in the Far East, 1550–1770* (The Hague, 1948), pp. 72–92.

[275] Boxer (ed.), *op. cit.* (n. 270), p. 76. Boxer reports that the episcopal see was vacant when D'Avalo visited Macao. The last bishop of China had died in 1633, and the first bishop of Macao (as distinct from the bishops of Japan or China who lived in Macao) took office in 1692.

tifications. Since then individuals bid for the right to command the lucrative Japan voyage. D'Avalo describes how Lopes Carmiente Carravallo first negotiated this privilege with the viceroy at Goa.[276] Trade with Southeast Asian places such as Tongking, Champa, Cambodia, Makassar, Solor, and Timor are open to any Portuguese merchant. An attempt made in 1631 to allow the highest bidder to monopolize trade with Makassar, Solor, and Timor failed.[277]

Chinese officials levy anchorage fees on each ship which comes to Macao but no duties on their cargoes. Trade between Macao and Canton, however, is anything but free. A few Portuguese merchants are permitted to attend the biennial fairs in Canton, during which they order Chinese goods for themselves and for others. They sometimes stay as long as four or five months in Canton, living in their boats to avoid the numerous difficulties and disputes which attend living ashore. Large presents must be given to local and provincial officials in order to obtain permission to trade, licenses allowing Chinese merchants to come to the fairs, and permission to return to Macao. Dues are levied on the boats during the downriver trip. Each day some small Chinese boats bring raw silk and gold to Macao without official permission. Should they be caught, their crews would be killed without mercy.[278]

Macao has some fine Chinese shops and a large number of Chinese peddlers who go from house to house. They are sometimes so aggressive that they must be forcefully driven away. D'Avalo concludes that Macao "may justly be considered as the best, strongest and most profitable of the Portuguese possessions in the Indies." To illustrate its trade he appends a list of the cargo carried by the Japan voyage of 1637, in total value about 2,141,468 taels of silver.[279]

By the time D'Avalo's description was published in 1645, Macao was no longer as strong and profitable as it had appeared when he visited there in 1637 or 1638. The Portuguese were finally excluded from Japan in 1639, and the embassy sent in 1640 to revive the trade was executed by the Japanese. The Dutch captured Malacca in 1641, seriously impeding Macao's direct contacts with Goa and with Southeast Asian ports. The restoration of Portugal's independence from Spain also had the initial effect of threatening Macao's trade with Manila. Europeans could learn about Macao's problems both from published letterbooks and from the several publications which

---

[276] *Ibid.*, pp. 76–77. The text of Boxer's translation is defective at this pont; see *BV*, IIb, 81. On the Japan voyages see Boxer, *The Great Ship from Amacon; Annals of Macao and the Old Japan Trade, 1555–1640* (Lisbon, 1959).

[277] Boxer (ed.), *op. cit.* (n. 270), pp. 77–78.

[278] *Ibid.*, pp. 78–80.

[279] *Ibid.*, p. 80. The list is not included in Boxer's translation; for it see *BV*, IIb, 83–86. Cf. ship's manifest of 1648 as summarized on p. 68, above.

describe how the Macanese celebrated the restoration when the news of it arrived in 1642.[280]

At first the Macanese seem to doubt the news which Antonio Fialho Ferreira brought from Lisbon. Then they worry about possible invasion from Manila and hope they can persuade the Dutch in Batavia to cease their depredations while newly independent Portugal negotiates a treaty with the United Provinces. Nevertheless the news of the restoration seems a tonic to them, depressed as they were by recent events.[281] As Dom João Marquez Moreira somewhat extravagantly put it: "All evils vanished, and the city became as if it had returned to its former condition when many millions came over the bar each year, and when at the height of its wealth and glory, supplied by channels of gold and rivers of silver."[282] And celebrate they did; Moreira describes in close detail the public oaths of allegiance, the bonfires and illuminations, the bullfights, horse races, masquerades, parades, military salutes, and solemn masses which took place between May 30, 1642, when Fialho Ferreira arrived with the news, and August 20, when slaves from the city and St. Anthony's parish staged the last parade costumed as Negroes, Bengalis, Malabars, Bugis, and the like. Each religious foundation, school, civic organization, military unit, social class, and ethnic group seems to have participated. Even torrential rains seemed unable to dampen their spirits.[283] Moreira concludes:

The Christians rejoiced, the heathen rejoiced, the nobleman, the knight, the squire and the plebian, all and each as one who considers himself safely freed from the attacks and violence which Portuguese subjects in India and its dependencies had suffered. For as they had no King they were taken as captives and prisoners, not only by European nations but even by Oriental races, losing the best and wealthiest places which had been taken by those famous early conquerors, and which in the golden days of India's prosperity yielded such store of wealth and treasure as sufficed to make Portugal the richest country in Europe. This is the reason why the stream of wealth was diverted to other foreign Kingdoms, leaving [Portuguese] India so weak and exhausted that in the opinion of the best judges it could not last another three years.[284]

Many Portuguese apparently shared Moreira's judgment that Portugal's decline in Asia was a consequence of Spanish rule. The restoration of Portuguese independence, however, did not cure Macao's ills. Despite the cele-

---

[280] The most important published accounts of the celebrations in Macao are Antonio Fialho Ferreria, *Relaçam da viagem, que por ordem de S. Mg. de fez António Fialho Ferreira deste reyno à cidade de Macau na China:* . . . (Lisbon, 1643), and Dom João Marques Moreira, *Relação da magestosa, misteriosa, e notavel acclamaçam, que se fez a magestade d'El Rey Dom Ioam o IV nosso senhor na cidade do nome de Deos do grande imperio da China* . . . (Lisbon, 1644). Both of these and other accounts of the celebrations are translated in Boxer (ed.), *op. cit.* (n. 270).
[281] For example, see Fialho Ferreira in Boxer (ed.), *op. cit.* (n. 270), pp. 95–103.
[282] Boxer (ed.), *op. cit.* (n. 270), p. 148.
[283] *Ibid.*, pp. 150–71.
[284] *Ibid.*, p. 171.

brations of 1642, Macao's trade continued to languish, and under the Ch'ing, Macao faced more severe crises than ever before.[285]

Western observers during the seventeenth century were always intrigued by China's monetary system. The Chinese, they report, coin neither gold nor silver. In fact, although it is highly valued as a commodity, gold is never used as a medium of exchange. Unminted silver is the most commonly used form of money. Merchants cut it from bars and dispense it by weight. Clippings collected during a day's business are melted down into bars.[286] Merchants had to be equipped to cut and weigh the silver, and they also had to be able to assay its purity. Semedo avers that impure silver or an alloy of silver can be used for small transactions.[287] Most commonly, however, copper or brass coins called "cash" or "caxa" were used for small purchases. These were of little value individually. Usually one thousand of the coins were strung together and used in that form. Dutch merchants report that strings of cash were the most common form of money on Java and in many other parts of the East Indies. Both Semedo and Martini describe the Chinese decimal-based system of weights and measures, and provide some European equivalents.[288]

The Chinese apparently had developed banking practices such as loans and bills of exchange by the seventeenth century, but the Europeans write little about them. The Jesuit missionaries had some experience with bills of exchange, but if the two examples mentioned by Trigault are at all typical, their acceptability was not routine in China. On both occasions the bills of exchange were not honored.[289] About one of these incidents he writes, "this way of doing business is frowned upon by Chinese tradesmen, and is not a common practice anywhere in the kingdom."[290] The Jesuits also allude to loans, for they occasionally had to borrow money. Interest rates are described as being almost prohibitively high.

The bustling economic life of the empire presupposed a rather efficient system of transportation. Most impressive to Europeans was the ease with which one could travel about the empire by boat. Trigault, for example, writes that China is "so thoroughly covered by an intersecting network of rivers and canals that it is possible to travel almost anywhere by water."[291] Martini contends that there was hardly a city or town that could not be reached by boat. For example, one could travel from Macao to Peking, a distance of seven hundred leagues from south to north with only one day's

[285] See below, pp. 1697–1700.
[286] See, for example, Pantoja, *loc. cit.* (n. 39), p. 374; Trigault in Gallagher (trans.), *op. cit.* (n. 38), p. 14; Van Rechteren, *loc. cit.* (n. 27), p. 44; Semedo, *op. cit.* (n. 9), pp. 52–53.
[287] *Op. cit.* (n. 9), p. 53.
[288] *Ibid.*, pp. 52–53; Martini, *op. cit.* (n. 44), p. 21. See also Van Rechteren, *loc. cit.* (n. 27), p. 75.
[289] Gallagher (trans.), *op. cit.* (n. 38), pp. 314 and 351.
[290] *Ibid.*, p. 314.
[291] *Ibid.*, p. 12. True mainly for the Pearl River delta and the Yangtze region.

travel on land. Similarly one could travel from Chekiang Province on the east coast to Szechwan in the far west entirely by boat.[292] The missionaries all recount long journeys undertaken entirely or predominantly by water. Several missionaries describe China's rivers, especially the Yangtze and the Yellow River. Martini, for example, traces the course of each of them from its source to the sea.[293] The missionaries also describe the canals, especially the Grand Canal which connects Hangchow with Peking. Pantoja, Trigault, and Martini had all traveled on it, and each described it. Martini's account of its route, its locks, and the way it was constructed is probably the most complete.[294]

Not only was travel by water possible to many parts of the realm, but an incredible number of Chinese seemed always to be traveling. All the Western writers are astonished at the number of vessels daily plying the rivers and canals. Trigault thought "it might be said with greater truth and without fear of exaggeration that there are as many boats in this kingdom as can be counted in all the rest of the world."[295] Semedo, standing on the bank of the Yangtze River near Nanking, counts three hundred small ships sailing upstream in one hour.[296] The major rivers are also alive with fishing boats, houseboats, the sumptuous lacquered barges of officials (sometimes with musicians playing on deck), rafts made from lumber lashed together hauling wood from the western forests to the eastern cities (see pl. 328), and the ubiquitous government barges hauling tax grain from the Yangtze valley to the capital. Ten thousand imperial grain barges are in regular service between Peking and the Yangtze.[297] At the entrances to the canals or at the locks, traffic may be backed up for days while government barges, especially those carrying perishable foods kept cool with ice, and the boats of high officials in order of their rank, are given precedence. Semedo writes that he "stayed eight days for a passage through that wonderful concourse of vessels."[298] Passengers can rent vacant cabins on commercial boats, even on the government barges. With all this traffic it is easy to believe the missionaries when they report that bamboo which grows only in the south is used all over China, that coal mined in the north is also widely available, that most Chinese silk is produced in Chekiang, or that the porcelain found in

[292] *Op. cit.* (n. 44), p. 5.

[293] *Ibid.*, pp. 17–19.

[294] *Ibid.*, pp. 66–67. See also Pantoja, *loc. cit.* (n. 39), pp. 369–70; and Gallagher (trans.), *op. cit.* (n. 38), pp. 306–7. See Needham, *op. cit.* (n. 181), Vol. IV, Pt. 3, pp. 306–20, on the Grand Canal. On the logistic importance of the canal in Ming times see Mark Elvin, *The Pattern of the Chinese Past* (Stanford, 1973), pp. 102–6.

[295] Gallagher (trans.), *op. cit.* (n. 38), p. 13.

[296] *Op. cit.* (n. 9), p. 2.

[297] Pantoja, *loc. cit.* (n. 39), p. 396; Gallagher (trans.), *op. cit.* (n. 38), p. 305. Huang, *op. cit.* (n. 80), p. 161, reports twelve thousand grain boats on the Grand Canal.

[298] *Op. cit.* (n. 9), p. 2. See our pls. 327 and 330 for pictures of Chinese boats, all taken from later seventeenth-century publications.

most Chinese homes and shipped overseas all comes from one small village in Kiangsi.

Several writers also describe the varieties of Chinese sailing vessels and a few even discuss their construction. They are most impressed with the ornate colorful boats of high officials, with their beautiful carvings, paintings, and galleries. Martini claims that they resemble multi-storied houses.[299] Both Pantoja and Trigault describe the eunuch Ma T'ang's sumptuous barge.[300] The Europeans are not so unanimously impressed with Chinese seagoing junks as they are with river transportation. Trigault, for example, considers Chinese sailing vessels inferior to those of Europe both in number and quality.[301] And he seems to have endorsed the prevalent judgment that the Chinese are not comfortable at sea, and therefore spend great sums maintaining inland waterways. Regarding the traffic jam on the Grand Canal, he writes:

All this may seem strange to Europeans who may judge from maps that one could take a shorter and less expensive route to Peking by sea. This may be true enough, but the fear of the sea and the pirates who infest the seacoast has so penetrated the Chinese mind that they believe the sea route would be more hazardous for conveying provisions to the royal court.[302]

The Dutch, however, who met them more frequently, hold Chinese ocean-going junks in somewhat greater esteem, especially their maneuverability. Van Rechteren reports that "their junks always cruise close to the wind because all their rigging is flat and close together, of the sort that ours is not able to follow. They sail well, tack and retack with ease."[303] Matelief's journal also contains a good sketch of Chinese seagoing junks.[304]

Occasionally European writers also stressed the superiority of Chinese roads. Nothing in Europe approaches them, according to Martini; in fact, he claims that they challenge the grandeur of Roman roads. Many are paved, he reports, even to the tops of mountains. Runners are stationed at regular intervals on them to relay official messages, and government hostels are built about one day's journey apart to accommodate traveling officials.[305]

[299] *Op. cit.* (n. 44), p. 13.

[300] Pantoja, *loc. cit.* (n. 39), pp. 342–43; Gallagher (trans.), *op. cit.* (n. 38), p. 36. On grain barges and official boats see Sung, *op. cit.* (n. 181), pp. 172–76.

[301] Gallagher (trans.), *op. cit.* (n. 38), p. 13. It should be recalled that the eunuch-admiral Cheng Ho had junks two hundred feet in length when he explored the Indian Ocean in the early fifteenth century. On seagoing vessels of the seventeenth century see Sung, *op. cit.* (n. 181), pp. 176–77. See also Needham, *op. cit.* (n. 181), Vol. IV, Pt. 3, pp. 379–695, on Chinese nautical technology.

[302] Trigault in Gallagher (trans.), *op. cit.* (n. 38), p. 306.

[303] Van Rechteren, *loc. cit.* (n. 27), p. 46.

[304] *Loc. cit.* (n. 122), facing p. 82.

[305] Martini, *op. cit.* (n. 44), pp. 12–13. Huang, *op. cit.* (n. 80), p. 132, reports that local districts bore the expenses for the official hostels. On ancient Chinese roads and the post-station system see Needham, *op. cit.* (n. 181), Vol. IV, Pt. 3, pp. 1–37.

On these roads the missionaries encounter the various means of land transport used by the Chinese: horses and horse-drawn carts or carriages for cargo and lower-class passengers, sedan chairs for persons of rank. Ricci once traveled from Hangchow to Soochow on a three-seated wheelbarrow, which Trigault claims was faster than sailing on the traffic-clogged canal.[306] Martini is particularly intrigued by the practice of carrying heavy burdens on poles laid across the porters' shoulders.[307] Europeans, especially the Dutch, are fascinated by what they call sailing chariots—carts equipped with sails which enable them to travel across flat plains or beaches by means of wind.[308] Mendoza had described them earlier and the Dutch mathematician Simon Stevin had constructed a similar wind-driven cart in 1600.[309]

No aspect of Chinese economic organization received as much attention as the persistent refusal of the Chinese to allow foreigners to trade freely with them. When the Dutch first came to the Chinese coast they were simply baffled by it, especially when they saw the Portuguese not only trading regularly at Canton but also residing in nearby Macao. For the following half century they continually badgered the Chinese to allow them regular trade and residence on the coast similar to that enjoyed by the Portuguese. Gradually and painfully, however, they came to understand the Ming tributary system. Admiral Matelief succinctly described the situation as early as 1607, although it took nearly twenty-five more years before the Dutch resigned themselves to operating within the system.[310]

Foreign commerce with China is thought to be almost impossible because of a general imperial prohibition against contact with any foreigners, either within or without the empire. Foreigners are not permitted to trade in China, and subjects of the emperor are not allowed to travel outside the empire. The only exceptions to this rule are the carefully regulated numbers of merchants permitted to enter the empire with the regular tribute missions, some staying in the port of entry and some accompanying the ambassadors to the capital. Even these, Western observers agree, are treated more like dangerous criminals than honorable ambassadors from friendly monarchs. They are carefully guarded during their journey, seldom permitted to enter cities, and often housed in circumstances more appropriate to cattle than humans.[311] Chinese disdain for foreigners is so profound that the Chinese refer to them with terms ordinarily reserved for beasts or demons. When a for-

---

[306] Gallagher (trans.), *op. cit.* (n. 38), p. 317.

[307] *Op. cit.* (n. 44), p. 154.

[308] For example, see Matelief, *loc. cit.* (n. 122), p. 98; Martini, *op. cit.* (n. 44), p. 35. In China sailing carriages had been in use since A.D. 552.

[309] See *Asia*, Vol. II, Bk. 3, pp. 402–3.

[310] *Loc. cit.* (n. 122), p. 119. For a sketch of the Ming tributary system see John E. Wills, Jr., *Embassies and Illusions: Dutch and Portuguese Envoys to K'ang-hsi, 1666–1687* (Cambridge, Mass., 1984), pp. 13–25.

[311] For example, see Pantoja, *loc. cit.* (n. 39), pp. 406–7; Trigault in Gallagher (trans.), *op. cit.* (n. 38), pp. 89, 569–70.

eign ship anchors off the China coast, it is immediately surrounded by junks so that the foreigners cannot trade, buy provisions, or talk with anyone. If somehow a foreigner steals ashore he is informed by the first official he meets that no contact may be made without the governor's approval; and he is also told that it is against the law for him to contact the governor! If the foreigners ask to petition the emperor they are told by local officials that they dare not allow it for fear of their lives.[312]

Despite all the indignities suffered by members of the tribute missions, foreigners still come regularly and offer their gifts and obeisance to the Celestial Emperor. The Jesuits assert that the foreigners keep coming because it is financially profitable. Their stay within the empire is at the emperor's expense, and the emperor's return gifts to the ambassadors are always more valuable than the tributary gifts. Furthermore, a limited amount of trade is allowed the tribute missions. For these reasons many people come regularly to Peking from neighboring lands, claiming to be ambassadors of nonexistent kings and princes.[313]

Despite the strong Chinese antipathy toward foreigners, seventeenth-century Europeans report three places in which foreign trade outside the tributary system is permitted: Macao, Chang-chou in Fukien Province, and Su-chou in western Shensi (present-day Kansu) Province. Although circumscribed by numerous restrictions, the Portuguese in Macao are allowed continuous residence there with the privilege of attending the biennial fairs in Canton. Perhaps other Europeans could have lived and traded there along with the Portuguese if the Portuguese had allowed it. The Portuguese, however, were understandably reluctant to share the benefits of their unique position in China.[314]

A situation somewhat similar to that of the Portuguese community in Macao existed in Su-chou, where Muslim merchants were permanently established in a distinct quarter of the inland city. Europeans first became aware of this "third gate," as they called it, as a result of Bento de Goes' overland travels from India to China. Trigault, comparing it to Macao, was the first to describe the Muslim colony in Su-chou.

The Chinese, whom the Saracens call Cathayans, live in one part of Soceu [Su-chou], and the Saracens, who have come here to trade, from the kingdom of Cascar [Kashgar] and other western countries, inhabit the other section. Many of the merchants have taken wives here and brought up families; hence they are looked upon as natives who will never return to their own lands. They are like the Portuguese who have settled in Macao in the Province of Canton, save that the Portuguese make

---

[312] Van Rechteren, *loc. cit.* (n. 27), p. 45.

[313] Trigault in Gallagher (trans.), *op. cit.* (n. 38), pp. 569–70. See our pls. 314, 315, 374, and 377.

[314] On the exceptions to the Ming tribute system see C. W. MacSherry, "Impairment of the Ming Tribute System as Exhibited in Trade through Fukien" (Ph.D. diss., University of California, Berkeley, 1956).

their own laws and have their own judges, while the Saracens are governed by the Chinese. Every night they are shut in behind the walls of their part of the city, but otherwise they are treated as natives and are subject in all things to the Chinese magistrates. According to law, anyone who lives here for nine years is not allowed to return to his own country.[315]

The third anomaly within the Chinese foreign trade system was the port of Chang-chou in Fukien Province. No foreigners were allowed to trade here, but from this port licensed Chinese merchants were permitted to trade overseas. The earliest Western observers, such as Mendoza, had been under the impression that Fukienese merchants traded abroad illegally with the connivance of local officials.[316] Seventeenth-century writers—Matelief was one of the first—shortly came to recognize that the merchants from the Chang-chou area had official permission to trade beyond the empire's borders. Chinese merchants from Chang-chou had long traded with the Spanish at Manila and after 1624 with the Dutch at Fort Zeelandia on Formosa. Some illicit trade took place along the Fukien coast as well. Van Rechteren, for example, reports that whenever the ships being laden at Fort Zeelandia for the annual voyage to Japan or Batavia were short of Chinese goods, the Dutch simply dispatched two or three yachts directly to Amoy to buy what they needed.[317] It was also from this area in Fukien Province that most of the Chinese overseas communities in insular Southeast Asia and the Philippines were populated. That some official concern for the overseas communities may have continued despite the general understanding that Chinese who lived abroad were disloyal to the emperor is suggested by an exchange of letters between the "Visitor of Chincheo" and the Spanish governor of the Philippines published by Leonardo de Argensola after the 1603 massacre of Chinese in Manila. The Chinese letter inquired about the cause of the massacre and contained veiled threats of possible retaliation.[318]

China is depicted by the Europeans as a most favored part of the world with an exceedingly sophisticated economy. Again and again the Jesuits list China's provinces and major cities and estimate its population, armed forces, and imperial tax income, almost as if to reassure themselves that their impressions are really accurate. Martini gives these figures in detail for each province of the empire. The Jesuits regularly report, however, that despite this wealth and abundance, the Chinese are habitually frugal and that

---

[315] Trigault in Gallagher (trans.), *op. cit.* (n. 38), pp. 514–15. See also Semedo, *op. cit.* (n. 9), pp. 16–17. *Cf.* D. D. Leslie, "Assimilation and Survival of Muslims in China," *Actes du IIIe Colloque International de Sinologie* (Paris, 1983), pp. 116–26.

[316] *Op. cit.* (n. 184), I, 95.

[317] *Loc. cit.* (n. 27), p. 75.

[318] Argensola, *op. cit.* (n. 18), pp. 336–40. The "Visitor of Chincheo" was probably the Grand Coordinator or Supreme Commander of Fukien Province, who also had a censorial title. See Hucker, *op. cit.* (n. 111), pp. 51–52.

compared to Europeans, few Chinese are very rich and few very poor. Semedo, writing around 1642, thought this augured well for China's future:

In all this abundant riches of the Country, industry of the inhabitants, Arts and
means of gaining a living to an excessive plenty, they doe not let passe any other
thing, that can bring them any profit; and notwithstanding the sight of so great
afluence of noble commodities, they make a profit of their beef-bones, Hogges-
Haires, and the smallest ragge, which is thrown into the streets. There raigneth
among them that only pledge and surety of the duration of Empires; that is that the
public is rich, and no particulars.[319]

5

SOCIETY AND CUSTOMS

About the physical appearance of the Chinese there is little disagreement.
All the Europeans comment on their full round faces, small flat noses, black
hair, black eyes, and sparse beards. Pantoja reports that his grey eyes were a
curiosity to the Chinese, and that they thought men with heavy beards,
large eyes, and large noses were "ill favored."[320] Trigault claims the Chinese
hate red hair; Martini agrees and adds blond hair.[321] The Europeans describe
Chinese skin color as white or nearly white, although some writers observe
variations in pigmentation between the northerners and the darker southerners. Martini also describes minority groups living within the empire
whose appearance and social customs differ appreciably from those of the
Chinese. The mountain people of Kiangsi Province, for example, had not
even submitted to imperial authority.[322] Some report that the people of
Kwangtung and Kwangsi commonly have two nails on their small toe.
Trigault thinks they might at one time have had six toes on each foot.[323]
Both men and women let their hair grow long; only children below age fifteen have it cut. Buddhist priests are shaven. The Chinese lavish much attention on their hair, combing it frequently, plaiting it, and coiling it into
knots on their heads. The Chinese captives on Bontekoe's ship in 1622
spend almost all day on deck cleaning and combing their hair. When loose,
their hair hangs down to the calves of their legs.[324] Europeans who have
been inside China also invariably comment on the seclusion of women and

[319]*Op. cit.* (n. 9), p. 7.
[320]Pantoja, *loc. cit.* (n. 39), p. 376.
[321]Gallagher (trans.), *op. cit.* (n. 38), p. 77; Martini, *op. cit.* (n. 44), p. 9.
[322]*Op. cit.* (n. 44), p. 103. See also Semedo, *op. cit.* (n. 9), p. 13.
[323]Gallagher (trans.), *op. cit.* (n. 38), p. 77.
[324]G. J. Hoogewerff (ed.), *Journalen van de gedenkwaerdige reizen van Willem Ijzbrantsz. Bontekoe, 1618–1625* ("WLV," LIV; The Hague, 1952), p. 86.

on the practice of footbinding. Small feet are considered beautiful. Martini speculates that the Chinese would have judged Helen of Troy ugly because of her large feet.[325] Footbinding was probably encouraged by Chinese men in order to keep the women secluded by making it difficult for them to walk. Semedo, however, thinks the practice had become popular in imitation of an ancient Chinese empress who bound her poorly shaped feet in hopes of improving them.[326]

Both men and women wear long robes down to their toes, with large wide sleeves in which they hide their hands. Men's robes are double-breasted and fasten under the left shoulder with the overlap attached under the right shoulder. Women's robes fasten down the front. Only a simple white undergarment is worn against the skin. Dutch travelers usually comment that it is difficult to tell men from women, since both wear long hair and long gowns. The Jesuits admire the modest simplicity of Chinese dress, and frequently note that, in contrast to European practices, the styles never change. Semedo, however, correctly observes that clothing styles are set by imperial decree. He reports that in 200 B.C. the Chinese wore short-sleeved gowns like the Japanese, but that during the reign of the emperor "Hoan" about A.D. 400, they adopted the style of robe still in use.[327] Gowns are changed for seasonal wear and for formal and informal occasions; gown types and colors vary for different classes and ranks of people. Semedo devotes most of a chapter to the public dress and insignia of officials. All officials, except for the "Colais" (Grand Secretaries), wear caps of black silk, "lined with a certaine stiffe & strong stuffe" (the *fu-t'ou*). (See pl. 52.) Each also wears a square patch of material on the breast "richly embroidered round about, in the middle whereof is the device of their offices and dignitie." Civil officials are distinguished by different sorts of birds on these badges (see pl. 50), military officials by animals. Officials' girdles are about four fingers wide and festooned in front with large buckles. There are nine sets of buckles: "of *Bufalo,* of *Rhinoceros* horne, of *Ivory,* of *Tortoise-shell,* of *Lighum aguile,* of *Calamba,* of Silver, Gold, and precious stones," each denoting the wearer's office. They wear certain kinds of boots ("cloud toe" or court shoes), and they wear a large loose vest or *gamon* over their ordinary robes. These marks of rank are worn only in public, not in their homes or

[325] *Op. cit.* (n. 44), p. 9.

[326] *Op. cit.* (n. 9), p. 30. The practice of footbinding apparently began during the late T'ang dynasty or soon thereafter among court dancers. It became increasingly popular among all classes and from Sung times onward was often justified as a means of keeping women secluded. See Howard S. Levy, *Chinese Footbinding: The History of a Curious Erotic Custom* (New York, 1966), pp. 23–63.

[327] *Op. cit.* (n. 9), p. 29. New styles were decreed by each new dynasty. Ming styles, decreed in 1393, were patterned after those of the Chou and Han and those of the T'ang and Sung. See Xun Zhou and Chunming Gao, *Five Thousand Years of Chinese Costumes* (San Francisco, 1987), pp. 146–69. Semedo's costume change of A.D. 400 probably refers to the reforms of the emperor Hsiao Wen of the northern Wei; see Zhou and Gao, p. 54. See our pl. 52. For examples from later seventeenth-century publications see our pls. 340, 341, and 382.

when they are at leisure.[328] Young men wear a variety of colors; older men dress more modestly, although at feasts officials often wear red. Wealthy people change outer garments four times a year while commoners usually change only twice and usually wear black. Sometimes they pawn the previous season's garments to finance the new ones.[329] Everyone comments on the widespread use of silk in dress, although cotton is also common and wool occasionally used.

The Chinese pay as much attention to their headdress as to their hair. Men sometimes wear a sort of hair net made of horsehair or even steel wire through which their hair is coiled.[330] Women, however, secure their top-knots with gold or silver pins and ornaments and often decorate them with flowers. Men's hats display considerable variety and elegance, and also indicate the rank of the wearer. They are made from horsehair, felt, silk, or cotton. In general, scholars and officials wear square hats, common people round. Pantoja claims that it was considered discourteous for a man to appear without a hat.[331]

Chinese footwear also attracts considerable attention; the writers describe not only women's bound feet, but also men's shoes. Only the lowest classes have leather shoes. Others wear silk or cotton shoes. The soles are made from many layers of tightly sewn cloth and the upper parts decorated with embroidered flowers; Trigault claims that men's shoes are more highly decorated than those of European women. He also describes long "bandages" wound around men's feet and shins which look like loose-fitting stockings. Finally, he reports, one's costume is never complete without a parasol.[332]

While there was much agreement among seventeenth-century Europeans concerning the physical appearance of the Chinese, there was less concerning their non-physical characteristics. European merchants and sailors invariably judge the inhabitants of the Celestial Empire to be greedy, shrewd, and dishonest. Those who had dealings with Chinese officials found them polite and friendly, but apparently always willing to make promises which they had no intention of keeping in order to extort gifts from the foreigners. Indeed, Europeans often report that without bribes and gifts nothing could be accomplished in China. Dutch travelers, whose observations were based primarily on their contact with the Chinese in Java, frequently comment on what they consider the despicable morals of the Chinese. They are extremely lecherous and addicted to sodomy; and they are reckless gamblers, sometimes gambling away their homes, wives, children, and personal free-

---

[328] Semedo, *op. cit.* (n. 9), pp. 132–35. Semedo's account is quite accurate; *cf.* Zhou and Gao, *op. cit.* (n. 327), pp. 146–47, 152–60.

[329] Semedo, *op. cit.* (n. 9), p. 29.

[330] Trigault in Gallagher (trans.), *op. cit.* (n. 38), p. 78.

[331] Pantoja, *loc. cit.* (n. 39), pp. 375–76. On the etiquette regarding hats see Ball, *op. cit.* (n. 147), p. 220.

[332] Gallagher (trans.), *op. cit.* (n. 38), p. 78. *Cf.* Ball, *op. cit.* (n. 147), pp. 195–98, on Chinese dress.

dom in a single evening.[333] Those who fought against the Chinese in battle also found little to admire. The Chinese, the Dutchmen assert, are devoid of courage, usually running away from the fray unless they possess an obvious advantage. On the other hand, the Chinese prove to be exceedingly cruel towards vanquished opponents.

The Jesuits, however, paint a very different picture of Chinese morality. Semedo finds them to be naturally inclined toward virtue, especially toward humility, virginity, and chastity. They also magnify the virtues of others while deprecating their own.[334] Longobardo describes them as disciplined, gentle and benign, and habitually restrained in passions; Chinese women are all as virtuous as nuns.[335] Faria y Sousa documents this assertion from the experience of some shipwrecked Portuguese sailors who were cared for by Chinese women.

For tho' they were beautiful, and Beauty be inclined to Wantonness, and though our men were long among them and familiarly entertained, yet they could never by any means prevail with any of them to yield to their Desires.[336]

In social relations the Chinese are extremely polite and courteous, although too much given to ceremony. The missionaries laud Chinese industry and ingenuity and point to the intensive cultivation of the land as an example. They also praise Chinese respect for authority and learning. The missionaries were aware of the differences between the people with whom they associated and the merchants of the seaports. Semedo admits that Chinese merchants are frequently shrewd and deceitful. Nevertheless he admonishes his readers not to form general opinions about the Chinese on the basis of the behavior of despised merchants. But the Jesuits also provide other evidence of the darker side of Chinese behavior. Trigault, for example, describes the sale of small children, the drowning of infant daughters, the castration of young boys, and the prevalence of suicide among China's poor.[337]

Modern scholars almost invariably identify the Chinese family system as unique and as the most characteristic and fundamental institution of Chinese society. They frequently credit the family with the preservation of Chinese culture through its long history. Certainly it has traditionally performed a host of social services and governmental functions which in European societies have usually been performed by governments, churches, and chari-

---

[333] On the Dutch image of the Chinese in Java see above, pp. 1318–21. On games of chance *cf.* Ball, *op. cit.* (n. 147), pp. 524–30.

[334] *Op. cit.* (n. 9), p. 26.

[335] Longobardo, *op. cit.* (n. 48), pp. 11, 14.

[336] Stevens (trans.), *op. cit.* (n. 17), III, 195.

[337] Gallagher (trans.), *op. cit.* (n. 38), pp. 86–87. On suicide *cf.* Ball, *op. cit.* (n. 147), pp. 622–27.

table organizations. The Chinese family with its emphasis on filial piety has been the training school and bulwark of the Confucian moral code. Of the five relationships which form the core of Confucian ethics, three are familial. Indeed, the family has traditionally been used as the model for the government of the empire itself. None of the seventeenth-century European sources actually discusses the Chinese family and its importance as a separate topic; nevertheless something of its structure can be seen in the descriptions of social customs, especially marriages and funerals.

Chinese marriages are all arranged by the parents. Chinese tend to marry early—between fifteen and twenty years of age—according to Pantoja.[338] Often children are betrothed when very young—sometimes even before birth—and the arrangements made by the parents are usually kept. A third party always acts as an intermediary in the conclusion of a marriage contract, even when the families are close friends. Chinese practice concerning consanguinity also differs greatly from Europe's. No one may marry a paternal relative or a person with the same family name however distantly related they might actually be. Trigault reports that since there are only about one thousand surnames in all of China, this constitutes a serious limitation.[339] On the other hand, few restrictions are placed on marriage with members of the mother's family. Courtship, which begins with the arranged betrothal, follows a rigidly formal pattern. Gifts of a prescribed nature are given at regular intervals and many other formalities are observed. The betrothed couple, however, usually do not see each other until the bride is ceremoniously conducted to the groom's home on her wedding day. Several European writers assert that the Chinese buy their wives; that before the wedding day the groom must send a sizable gift to his bride which she in turn gives to her father. Trigault claims that this was so among the lower classes.[340] Semedo, however, disagrees. There are no dowries, he reports, and among the common people the groom merely gives the bride's father money to buy garments and household goods for the bride, from which the notion of buying brides may have arisen. Among the wealthy, however, the father of the bride supplies these necessities from his own purse. Once married, the bride becomes part of the groom's family. Upon her arrival at the groom's home, she and her husband pay reverence to the pictures of his ancestors and bow before his parents. The bride is then taken to the women's quarters by her mother-in-law. A month later the couple returns to the bride's home for a visit, but afterwards she lives with her husband's family.[341]

[338] *Loc. cit.* (n. 39), p. 378.

[339] Gallagher (trans.), *op. cit.* (n. 38), p. 76. On the surname question see J. G. Cormack, *Chinese Birthday, Wedding, Funeral, and Other Customs* (Peking, 1923), p. 36.

[340] Gallagher (trans.), *op. cit.* (n. 38), p. 75.

[341] Semedo, *op. cit.* (n. 9), pp. 71–72.

Most Western observers note that the Chinese have only one lawful wife, but as many concubines as can be afforded. Concubines are definitely considered to be of a lower social order than the wife. They eat separately, are sometimes housed separately, and are often regarded as servants of the wife. Concubines may be sent away easily. Sometimes a man takes a concubine solely for the purpose of producing a son and sends her away as soon as the boy is born. The children of concubines honor only their father's true wife as mother, and are not required to mourn when their natural mother dies.[342] Most European writers claim that concubines were bought and sold; Semedo reports that many girls were raised just for that purpose.[343] Traveling merchants often maintain concubines in the cities in which they do business. The earliest Dutch travelers were probably describing a variation of this practice when they reported the strange marriage customs of the Chinese in Java. Chinese merchants, they write, buy wives in Java, whom they leave behind when they return to China with the children.[344] According to Semedo, all the sons receive an equal share of the inheritance, whether or not they are children of their father's legal wife. Some families, however, give a larger share to the oldest son.[345]

Chinese women are never seen in the streets unless carried in closed sedan chairs. Even at home they are kept from the view of visitors. Semedo reports that no man other than the husband, not even the husband's father, may enter a woman's room.[346] On the other hand, he also reports having seen ordinary women walking out-of-doors in some parts of China.[347] Although widows are permitted to remarry, most of them remain unmarried, even when still young and without children. Such loyalty to the dead husband is greatly honored by the Chinese, often by the construction of a memorial arch.[348] Van Rechteren mentions young girls who, when their betrothed dies before the marriage has been consummated, cut off their hair, renounce marriage, and retire to a sort of nunnery.[349]

Imperial marriage customs especially fascinate the Europeans, particularly the procedures followed in selecting a spouse for a future emperor. Like his subjects, the emperor has only one true wife, who is styled em-

---

[342] All children were considered to be legitimate. Funerals of concubines, at which the children mourned their natural mother, were much simpler, according to Ho Ping-ti (personal communication).

[343] *Op. cit.* (n. 9), p. 70.

[344] See, for example, Willem Lodewyckszoon's *D'Erste Boek* (1598), in G. P. Rouffaer and J. W. Ijzerman (eds.), *De eerste schipvaart der Nederlanders naar Oost-Indië onder Cornelis de Houtman, 1595–1597* (3 vols.; "WLV," VII, XXV, XXXII; The Hague, 1915–29), I, 121–22.

[345] *Op. cit.* (n. 9), p. 72.

[346] *Ibid.*, pp. 31 and 72.

[347] *Ibid.*, p. 31.

[348] *Ibid.*, p. 26. For a picture of such an honorary arch or portal see J. Doolittle, *Social Life of the Chinese* (2 vols.; New York, 1867), I, 111.

[349] Van Rechteren, *loc. cit.* (n. 27), p. 44. On marriage customs *cf.* Ball, *op. cit.* (n. 147), pp. 367–76.

press. She is chosen from among the populace with no concern for her family or social status.[350] In addition to the empress, the emperor is reported to have nine other wives called queens and about thirty more who are still considered wives. Mendoza had called these thirty women concubines,[351] but seventeenth-century writers refer to a large number of concubines in addition to the thirty. Semedo estimates their number at three thousand.[352]

Mendoza had also described a peculiar marriage custom which he said was practiced by the Tartars and by the Chinese in some of the northern provinces. Each year all marriageable young people met with officials in a designated city. The officials then divided the men into three classes according to their wealth and the women into three groups according to their physical beauty. They were then paired off, the wealthiest men with the comeliest women, after which they were all married in a single ceremony.[353] Mendoza's rather fanciful description is included in Matelief's journal and with some variations is repeated by Mocquet.[354] None of the later travelers or Jesuits mention it.

Funeral practices, too, reveal much about family life and the filial piety so admired by European writers. Children are extremely scrupulous about the details of the funeral and the mourning period for their parents. To insure that they overlook nothing they consult a large volume on funeral rites. Immediately after death they wash the body, dress it in its finest clothes, and place it in a coffin. The coffin may have been ready for years; the Chinese usually see to the preparation of their own coffins, on which they spare no effort or expense.[355] Matelief, following Mendoza, claims that they first place the deceased in a chair before which relatives and friends ceremoniously bid it farewell.[356] All the other sources state that the body is sealed in the coffin and placed in the largest room of the house. A picture of the deceased stands upon the coffin. Here friends and relatives come to pay their last respects, and the family remains in attendance to receive the mourners. Every detail follows a prescribed pattern. The guests bow before the coffin, and the children bow to the guests, after which the guests are taken to another room and given refreshments of tea and dried fruits. After relatives and friends have paid their respects to the departed, the oldest son returns the visit to each, although he sometimes fulfills this obligation by leaving a calling card at the door of the house to be visited.

The interment of the dead takes place any time after the reception of the

---

[350] Hucker (*op. cit.* [n. 94], p. 43) substantiates this. While this was true in Ming times, it was not a practice followed by the Ch'ing.

[351] *Op. cit.* (n. 184), I, 65.

[352] *Op. cit.* (n. 9), p. 113. Many of those called concubines by the Jesuits were probably palace attendants and servants.

[353] *Op. cit.* (n. 184), I, 63–64.

[354] Matelief, *loc. cit.* (n. 122), p. 100; Mocquet, *op. cit.* (n. 187), p. 342.

[355] For a good description of coffins see Pantoja, *loc. cit.* (n. 39), p. 380.

[356] Mendoza, *op. cit.* (n. 184), I, 63–64; Matelief, *loc. cit.* (n. 122), p. 101.

mourners is completed. Sometimes it is deferred for a long time. During this interval the coffin is kept in one of the best rooms of the house, and the mourning children visit it each day to perform obeisances before it, burn incense, and set out food.[357] According to Semedo the burial is sometimes deferred because the family has exhausted its funds.[358] On the day of the burial, friends and relatives are summoned to join the procession from the house to the sepulchre outside the town. The place of burial has been carefully selected, usually with the help of an expert in the spirits of the winds and waters (*feng shui*). Trigault describes the typical family tomb, often built of white marble and embellished with carvings and statuary.[359] Both Buddhist and Taoist priests usually attend the funeral procession, reciting prayers and playing music. The children follow the bier, walking as if exhausted from grief.[360] At the grave, incense, paper or silk representations of people and animals, and messages written in gilt characters are burned. Food is set out before the tomb just as it had been set out before the coffin each day while it had remained at home.

Regulations for mourning are also carefully prescribed. During the period of mourning, coarse white garments are worn; white rather than black is the customary color of mourning in China. The mourners sleep on straw mats instead of beds, abstain from meats and certain other foods, and absent themselves from public gatherings. Mourners sometimes sit on low stools instead of chairs, use special stationery, and always refer to themselves with self-demeaning phrases implying disobedience.[361] The period of mourning for parents is three full years; shorter periods are prescribed for other relatives. If the father or mother of an official dies, he resigns his office and returns to his home to mourn for three years. The stipulated periods for mourning are rigidly followed, even if the mourning official happens to be a Grand Secretary. Trigault, for example, describes how the celebrated convert and future Grand Secretary, Hsü Kuang-chi, then a member of the Han-lin Yüan, resigned his office upon the death of his father in 1607 and retired to Shanghai for three years.[362] The regular mourning period for a deceased emperor or empress is also three years, which, according to Trigault, is reduced to one month by making each day stand for a month. Semedo, for example, reports that in his will the Wan-li emperor requested that instead of "twenty-seven months as is the usual custome" mourning "should only last for as many days." Semedo includes descriptions of two imperial funerals in his account, those of the Wan-li emperor, who died in

---

[357] Pantoja, *loc. cit.* (n. 39), p. 379.
[358] *Op. cit.* (n. 9), p. 74.
[359] Gallagher (trans.), *op. cit.* (n. 38), p. 74. *Cf.* our pl. 339.
[360] Gallagher (trans.), *op. cit.* (n. 38), p. 74.
[361] Pantoja, *loc. cit.* (n. 39), p. 379.
[362] Gallagher (trans.), *op. cit.* (n. 38), pp. 477–78.

1620, and of his mother, the empress dowager who died in 1614.[363] Herrera Maldonado had earlier printed an account of the empress dowager's death and funeral although he incorrectly dated it in 1617.[364]

Almost all the European writers admire the loyalty and respect which the Chinese show to their parents, and most seem to approve of the seclusion of Chinese women as well. Not every aspect of Chinese family life is admired, however. Most deplore polygamy and agree with Martini who thought "the condition of women was unfortunate in this regard."[365] Pantoja thinks the attraction of monogamous marriage might induce Chinese women to embrace Christianity and to persuade their husbands to do so as well.[366] Some writers describe how poor parents often sell their children, especially their daughters, into slavery, concubinage, or prostitution. In the northern provinces, it is reported, many parents have their sons castrated in order to make them eligible for palace service.[367] Still worse in the eyes of most Europeans is the practice of drowning infant daughters. As described by Trigault, impoverished parents often condone the drowning of infants out of belief in the transmigration of souls; they think they are doing the child a favor by releasing it from the poverty of the family into which it was born.[368]

All the writers comment on the absence of a hereditary aristocracy comparable to that of most European countries. China's upper class was composed of those who had become scholars, had passed the examinations, and were eligible to hold public office. Nevertheless the scholarly class displayed many of the characteristics of an aristocracy. The entire family of a successful scholar rose in wealth and prestige when he passed his examinations. Furthermore, the children of official families had the benefits of private tutors and years of leisure in which to prepare for the examinations—luxuries which most Chinese could not afford. The successful scholars, therefore, were very often from families of scholars who frequently had certain of its members in the administration. In this way the official class somewhat resembled a hereditary aristocracy, and the Jesuits often described it as such, seemingly forgetting the basic differences between these Chinese aristocrats and their European counterparts.[369] The Jesuits also report on the existence

[363] *Ibid.*, p. 72; Semedo, *op. cit.* (n. 9), pp. 78–86.

[364] Don Francisco de Herrera Maldonado, *Epitome historial del Reyno de la China, muerta de su Reyna . . .* (Madrid), pp. 91–120. On death, burial, and mourning customs, *cf.* Doolittle, *op. cit.* (n. 348), Vol. I, chaps. vi–vii.

[365] *Op. cit.* (n. 44), p. 11.

[366] *Loc. cit.* (n. 39), pp. 399–400.

[367] Self-castration, however, was illegal during the Ming dynasty. See Hucker, *op. cit.* (n. 94), pp. 11–12.

[368] Gallagher (trans.), *op. cit.* (n. 38), pp. 86–87.

[369] In some respects the Jesuits were correct in regarding the official families as a hereditary aristocracy. The sons of the first three grades of civil officials could receive hereditary entrance into officialdom—the *yin* privilege. But the *yin* was very limited in scope. Most scholars of the

of a genuine hereditary aristocracy, the imperial relatives. This was a small group, however, and according to the Jesuits, without political power. Trigault judges them to be an idle, insolent class of sixty thousand persons who constitute a serious drain on public funds.[370]

The Jesuits, from whose writings most of the accurate information concerning Ming Chinese government and society comes, associated almost exclusively with the official class and consequently supplied less information about the other levels of society. Even their descriptions of marriage and funeral customs are more applicable to the literati than to the peasants. Still, the Jesuits report that farming is considered the most important work in the empire and that peasants are held in high social esteem.[371] Aside from this, however, virtually nothing was written about the social conditions of the peasants. Concerning tradesmen and merchants, several writers observe that sons almost invariably follow their father's trades, although Pantoja insists that every man is free to choose whatever trade he wishes.[372] Everyone notes that labor is cheap. The Jesuits insist that the merchants are the lowest and most despised class in the land, a comment which accords well with Confucian ideals. Nevertheless they frequently refer to wealthy and prosperous merchants and to officials who seem to be involved in commerce. Soldiers and Buddhist monks are also extremely low on the social scale, while lower still are beggars and vagabonds. Matelief, following Mendoza, reports that there are no beggars on the streets of China. He describes an official whose sole duty is to see that the poor are maintained by their own families, that the handicapped are taught some trade, and that those who are unable to work and those with no family are cared for by the state.[373] Longobardo observes that there are few vagabonds in China,[374] but the other Jesuit writers neither confirm nor deny Mendoza's report. At the bottom of the social scale are the slaves. European observers assert that Chinese slaves are neither a separate race nor captives taken in wars; they are instead native Chinese whose parents have sold them into slavery or individuals who have sold themselves. As a result of this traffic in human life, writes Trigault, "the whole country is virtually filled with slaves; not such as are captured in war or brought in from abroad, but slaves born in the country and even in the same city or village in which they live."[375] Some of

---

lower grades were poor. In fact, many official families could not "perpetuate" their successes in the examinations. See Ho, *op. cit.* (n. 94), chap. i, and pp. 107–11, 149–53.

[370] Gallagher (trans.), *op. cit.* (n. 38), p. 88. Hucker (*op. cit.* [n. 94], p. 10) estimates that by 1644 there were approximately one hundred thousand royal relatives.

[371] For example, see Martini, *op. cit.* (n. 44), p. 7.

[372] Pantoja, *loc. cit.* (n. 39), p. 376.

[373] Mendoza, *op. cit.* (n. 184), I, 66–68; Matelief, *loc. cit.* (n. 122), p. 114. Also *cf. Asia* I, 741, 775–76.

[374] Longobardo, *op. cit.* (n. 48), pp. 12–14.

[375] Gallagher (trans.), *op. cit.* (n. 38), p. 86. On domestic slavery *cf.* Doolittle, *op. cit.* (n. 348), II, 209–13.

these are taken out of China by the Portuguese and Spanish at Macao. Mocquet claims that his Chinese hostess in Goa had been kidnapped in Canton and sold to the Portuguese when she was eight years old. The Portuguese, he reports, prefer Chinese slaves because they are so faithful and industrious.[376] Although he deplores slavery, Trigault admits that most Chinese are lenient masters and that slaves can buy their freedom at any time for the same price that had been originally paid for them.[377]

The European observers, Jesuits and secular travelers alike, were deeply impressed by the ceremonial character of social relations. To merchants and seamen, Chinese formality appeared very odd and attracted their attention primarily because it was so different from European practice. As Van Rechteren puts it, they are "the very most ceremonious people in the world."[378] To the Jesuits the understanding and observance of formal manners was a necessity to win the acceptance of the Chinese. They therefore studied manners and ceremonies seriously and frequently recorded their observations. Virtually no one in the seventeenth century wrote about China without including long and tedious descriptions of formal manners. They describe the postures and bows which were employed in greeting one another, varying from a slight nod and the raising of clasped hands when greetings equals, to an abject prostration on the knees when addressing a great official. The ritual involved in meeting an acquaintance in the street— getting out of one's sedan chair and exchanging bows—is often remarked upon. The punctilious regulations concerning visiting and the exchange of gifts are carefully related, even to the garments appropriate to various occasions. Some writers provide lengthy accounts of the various kinds of calling cards used in sending invitations, announcing visits, and accepting or declining presents. The ritual followed in serving tea, an important part of every visit, is repeatedly described. Not only the Jesuits, for whom ritual became a part of everyday life, but also the merchants and seamen, write in detail about the formalities involved in meeting with Chinese officials. The reader of all these minute descriptions is inclined to agree with Semedo: "In a word they are excessive in their civilities and good manners, which seems rather more proper for divine worship, than civall respect."[379] In general, the portrayal of Chinese manners is accurate, and the importance of ceremonial to scholar-officials is not exaggerated. Ceremony, or *li,* is clearly an important aspect of Confucian ethics. Again Semedo states it succinctly:

To be courteous and outwardly well composed, to do things with maturity, circumspection, gravity, and eavennesse, they account among their chiefest vertues: all

[376] *Op. cit.* (n. 187), p. 342.
[377] Gallagher (trans.), *op. cit.* (n. 38), p. 86. On slavery see Joseph McDermott, "Bondservants in the T'ai-hu Basin during the Late Ming: A Case of Mistaken Identities," *Journal of Asian Studies,* Vol. XL, No. 4 (August, 1981), pp. 675–701.
[378] *Loc. cit.* (n. 27), p. 42.
[379] *Op. cit.* (n. 9), p. 60.

of which are expressed in this word *Li;* in which they comprehend also the circumstances of time, and habit; and the *Thie* [calling card], with which they are performed.[380]

Even the names by which one refers to friends and acquaintances are provided by *li.* Trigault and Semedo describe the situation in considerable detail.[381] In addition to family names, boys are given a personal name by their parents which no one other than parents and older relatives use. All others call them by the number which designates the order of their birth. Girls and women, in fact, receive no name other than this sequential number. Boys, however, receive increasingly more dignified names at important junctures in their lives: for example, upon entering school, achieving manhood or marrying, attaining an important dignity or office, joining a religious sect or literary society, and becoming middle-aged. It is an important part of manners, the Jesuits report, to use the proper name for the occasion and for one's relationship to the person involved.

From the bewildering detail of formal manners a general principle emerges which shows the unmistakable mark of Confucian ethics: in all areas of social intercourse a gentleman seeks to deprecate himself while heaping exaggerated praise on his host or guest. The seat of honor, according to the Jesuits, is on the left in north China but on the right in the southern provinces. He who is offered the seat of honor invariably declines it and can never be induced to take it without considerable urging. When conversing with one another, Chinese gentlemen never use "you" or "me," but always refer to themselves in derogatory language while using flattering titles to refer to those with whom they are speaking. A son talking with his father, for example, refers to himself as "the youngest son," even if he is the oldest. Before a magistrate even a plaintiff or a witness will style himself "the offender." The same principle applies to the language used in referring to the possessions of others. This is carried so far, according to Semedo, that a man asking about the health of an ailing friend will refer to his "noble indisposition."[382] Semedo, in illustration of this concern for saving the public respect of others, tells the story of a provincial inspector whose official seal was stolen—a bit of negligence which might have cost him his office—and who suspected an old enemy who was also a local official. Instead of accusing the suspect outright, the censor caused the outer court of his own palace to be set ablaze and called on city officials for help. When he saw the suspect in the crowd, he called aloud to him, consigning to his safekeeping the locked cabinet in which the seal was usually kept. In this way the inspec-

---

[380] *Ibid.* Three classical Chinese books deal with the subject of *li,* or ceremonial: the *I-li,* the *Chou-li,* and the *Li-chi.*

[381] Gallagher (trans.), *op. cit.* (n. 38), pp. 78–79; Semedo, *op. cit.* (n. 9), pp. 63–64.

[382] *Op. cit.* (n. 9), p. 63.

tor meant to give the suspect an opportunity to replace the seal if he had stolen it; if not he would be able to accuse the suspect of negligence and thus lay the blame on him anyway. On the morning after the fire, the cabinet was returned to the inspector with the seal safely inside; no accusations were made, each concealed the fault of the other.[383]

Most of the European writers had attended formal Chinese banquets, and they recount their gustatory experiences with delight. Again the formality of these affairs impressed them. Everything is conducted in accord with punctilious etiquette: the invitations, the seating of guests, the drinking of wine, the courses of food, and the farewells. The Chinese, they report, never touch food with their hands, nor do they use a fork and knife to cut food into bite-sized pieces. The food is brought to the table already cut into small pieces so that everything may be eaten with chopsticks. The seating arrangements also intrigue the Europeans. The Chinese always use small tables and never seat more than four people at a table. At a very important banquet there might be one or even two tables for each guest.

The Jesuits rave about Chinese cooking. The Chinese eat most of the foods regularly served in Europe and many others besides. They dine on the flesh of dogs and horses, in addition to the meats common in the West, and they are especially fond of pork. Lacking olives and olive oil, the Chinese cook with sesame-seed oil, which Trigault finds pleasing but which to Pantoja smells bad.[384] The Chinese drink all their beverages hot from very small cups. They make wines from rice rather than grapes. Most of the Europeans prefer their own wines. The Jesuits report that the Chinese eat much more rice than Europeans, but little bread. While the quantity of food served at banquets and dinners is not impressive, the variety is overwhelming and the preparation exquisite. Pantoja claims there is more tasting than eating at a Chinese banquet and complains that "they spend five or sixe houres at a Banquet, and goe home an hungered."[385] Considerable quantities of wine are consumed at banquets, but the Jesuits insist that no one is urged to drink beyond his capacity and that drunkenness is rare. In general the Chinese are moderate both in eating and drinking.

Semedo distinguishes between northern and southern banquets. Southerners drink at the beginning of a feast and continue to drink as they taste the variety of dishes set before them. There is more conversation and tasting than eating and drinking. When the guests insist that they have had enough wine, the glasses are put aside and rice is brought in. In the north the dishes are fewer and larger. When a banquet begins, everyone eats his fill from the dishes without drinking anything. Then the dishes are removed and the guests talk with each other for about an hour, after which more dishes—

---

[383] *Ibid.*, p. 28.
[384] Gallagher (trans.), *op. cit.* (n. 38), p. 12; Pantoja, *loc. cit.* (n. 39), pp. 373–74.
[385] Pantoja, *loc. cit.* (n. 39), p. 397.

"salt meats" and "gammons of bacon," for example, called "guides"—are brought in. Then they begin to drink. Semedo notes that while the Chinese use many sauces, they never have salt or pepper on their tables. They serve meat and fish cooked in several ways at the same banquet. They serve many kinds of soup, but never without meat, fish, or noodles in it.[386]

Almost any occasion provides an excuse for a formal banquet: a birthday, wedding, festival day, or even a journey out of town. Pantoja claims that they spend half of their lives at such functions.[387] Frequently there is no other motive for a banquet than that of "Let us eat and drink for tomorrow we die." Semedo describes the organization of "brotherhood of the month" fraternities in which thirty people eat at one another's houses by turns. The banquets, usually held at night, sometimes last until the small hours of the next morning. Sometimes they are held at public houses, of which there are many. If the host does not wish to trouble his family, he can order the entire banquet to be delivered to his home.[388]

Visiting and banqueting are especially popular during festival days. While the Chinese observe no regular day of rest like the Christian Sunday, their year is broken up by several important festivals. The most important and the most frequently described is, of course, the New Year. It begins with the new moon in late January or early February and involves several days of feasting, visiting, and celebration. Shortly after the New Year, on the fifteenth day of the first moon, is the Feast of Lanterns, during which houses and streets are all illuminated and joyous parades held in the streets. Semedo presents a list of the major Chinese festivals.[389] In addition to the New Year festival and the Feast of Lanterns, he describes Ch'ing Ming, the chief spring festival, held on the third day of the third moon, at which people clean up graves and ancestral tablets and place oblations before them;[390] the Dragon Boat Festival on the fifth day of the fifth moon called "Toune" (Tuan Yang); a festival on the seventh day of the seventh moon; and finally one on the ninth day of the ninth moon. The last two festivals on Semedo's list are poorly described. His account of the seventh day of the seventh moon states only that at this time the Chinese "begg abilitie and power of the moone."[391] Semedo includes no description of the festival on the ninth day of the ninth moon; he simply mentions the date.[392] Some of the festivals, especially that of the New Year, are occasions for dramas, singing, masquerade parades, and fireworks.

---

[386] *Op. cit.* (n. 9), pp. 65–67.
[387] Pantoja, *loc. cit.* (n. 39), p. 397.
[388] *Op. cit.* (n. 9), p. 65.
[389] *Ibid.*, pp. 61–62.
[390] The Festival of the Tombs is celebrated throughout China on this date.
[391] On this day they worship the stars rather than the moon, primarily on behalf of women. See Doolittle, *op. cit.* (n. 348), II, 60–61.
[392] This is the kite-flying festival. See Ball, *op. cit.* (n. 147), p. 312.

At banquets and dinners the guests amuse themselves with conversation, drinking games, and music, or are entertained by professionals.[393] Drama is the most popular form of entertainment at banquets. According to Trigault, the plays are performed by professional troupes, some resident in larger cities, some itinerant. They give public as well as private performances and are in great demand. "Without question this is a curse in the empire, and so much so that it would be difficult to discover any other activity which is more prone to vice." Some of the actors were purchased by the troupes as young children and raised in the profession. Most of the plays are of ancient origin and well known to the spectators; few new plays are produced any longer. When performing at a banquet, the actors must be prepared to perform any play chosen by the host or one of his guests. Sometimes they perform all evening; when one play is concluded they begin another. The texts are sung; spoken lines are rare.[394] Also in demand at festivals are jugglers, acrobats, and magicians, many of whom travel from place to place (see pl. 364).

The more routine amusements and recreations of the Chinese also attract attention. The Dutch see the Chinese in Java as incorrigible gamblers who sometimes stake their personal freedom or that of their families. The Jesuits also report that the common people gamble much, using both cards and dice. The upper classes play a game very similar to European chess; several Jesuits describe the differences. Another game is played on a board of three hundred spaces, probably *wei-ch'i* (Japanese *go*) or "blockade chess."[395] All classes enjoy cockfighting, quail fighting, and cricket fighting. Semedo contends that students are not allowed to play games and that it is possible for them to be imprisoned "for spending too much time at play."[396]

In describing the social customs of the Chinese, the Jesuits again provide much more information in a more highly organized form than other European travelers in East Asia. The qualitative differences between the two sources of information, however, are not as great as in the areas of government, education, and religion. The secular travelers occasionally generalized on the basis of too few observations, but their descriptions of what they saw often supplied valuable illustrative information which supplements the Jesuit accounts: for example, the Dutch accounts of their reception by various provincial dignitaries in Canton and Fukien and their descriptions of the Chinese communities in Java. Furthermore, there are few instances of disagreement between the two types of sources; far fewer than in the areas of Chinese religion, for example. The European readers of the first half of the seventeenth century, therefore, had at their disposal a substantial

[393] Semedo, *op. cit.* (n. 9), pp. 67–68.
[394] Gallagher (trans.), *op. cit.* (n. 38), pp. 23–24. See our pl. 363.
[395] See Ball, *op. cit.* (n. 147), p. 112.
[396] *Op. cit.* (n. 9), p. 69.

amount of reliable information concerning the social life and customs of Ming China.

6

INTELLECTUAL LIFE

Since most early seventeenth-century European writers agreed that success in the examinations was the key to political power and social prominence in China, they devoted considerable space in their books to Chinese literature and education, including the civil service examinations. Once again, most of the information on these subjects came from Jesuit missionaries—from Pantoja, Trigault, Semedo, and Martini—who had lived in China long enough to write knowledgeably about language and learning.

The language was itself one of the most immediately intriguing aspects of Chinese intellectual life. A language more different from those of Europe could hardly have been imagined by seventeenth-century writers. They describe again and again how the Chinese use symbols or characters which, like Egyptian hieroglyphs, represent entire words or thoughts rather than syllables or letters. Chinese, therefore, is completely uninflected and employs neither alphabet nor grammar. Semedo, for example, observes that the same character may frequently serve as verb, noun, adjective, or adverb.[397] Chinese is written, the Jesuits report, in lines running from the top of the page to the bottom, moving from right to left across the page.[398]

Spoken Chinese, the Jesuits discovered, differs greatly from the written form, not so much in vocabulary but in that the spoken language contains many explicatives and phrases unnecessary in writing. The reason for this is the paucity of sounds in the Chinese language. Each word—each character—is pronounced as a single syllable; there are no polysyllabic words. Semedo, for example, estimates that there are only 336 monosyllables in the official dialect and that the variations of tone and aspiration only increase the number to 1,228.[399] He reports that there are 60,000 characters, and that many of them are pronounced identically, although their meanings are very different.[400] Indeed, as Trigault reports, a book could never be written from dictation or properly understood if read aloud.[401] Even the spoken language is adjudged by the Europeans to be the most equivocal in all the world. Am-

[397] *Ibid.*, p. 31. But *cf.* our pl. 352.
[398] On the order and arrangement of Chinese writing see Tsien, *op. cit.* (n. 209), pp. 183–84. For example, see our pl. 344.
[399] *Op. cit.* (n. 9), p. 31. Note that there is a difference between a "character" and a "word." There are many bisyllabic words, especially in the spoken language.
[400] *Ibid.*, p. 33.
[401] Gallagher (trans.), *op. cit.* (n. 38), p. 27.

biguities are reduced somewhat by the practice of pronouncing in different tones words that are otherwise identical. The Jesuits detect four or five tones.[402] Despite tonal variations, however, educated Chinese often clarify conversations by drawing the characters as they talk. The Jesuits allege that the Chinese, for this reason, much prefer to communicate in writing, and that friends living in the same city write messages to one another rather than meet for conversation.[403] The spoken language varies greatly from one locale to another. The dialect problem is greatly alleviated, however, by the existence of an official spoken language, the "Quonhoa" (*kuan-hua*), which is common to all the provinces and in which all official business is conducted. It is used by all cultured people; in fact, it is so widely used that even tradesmen, women, and children, who normally speak a dialect, can understand it.[404] The Jesuits, however, may have somewhat exaggerated the widespread intelligibility of the *kuan-hua* in order to justify to their European superiors their concentration on the language of the learned. The written characters are, of course, understood in all the provinces of the empire, even though their pronunciation varies greatly from one place to another. Not only are they understood in all parts of the empire, but they are even used in neighboring lands. The Japanese, Koreans, and Indochinese use the same Chinese characters for their books and for much of their writing, although they pronounce them very differently from the Chinese. The characters, therefore, serve as an international literary language for most of eastern Asia, a fact which made the missionaries eager to translate Christian literature into Chinese.[405]

Semedo made some fairly sophisticated analyses of the characters themselves.[406] He was aware that changes had occurred in the form of the characters from ancient times to his own day and he traces the evolution of a character. He also describes the formation of complex characters by the combination of simpler characters, and he provides some examples. Semedo discusses the various calligraphic styles as well. The characters, he asserts, are very old—thirty-seven hundred years old, in fact. He ascribes their invention to the legendary sage emperor Fu Hsi.[407] Semedo was one of the

---

[402] For example see *ibid.*, pp. 27–28.

[403] *Ibid.*, p. 28.

[404] *Ibid.*, pp. 28–29. For a sample page from a Chinese-French dictionary see our pl. 353.

[405] See Longobardo, *op. cit.* (n. 48), p. 20; Semedo, *op. cit.* (n. 9), p. 33.

[406] For a thorough and critical discussion of Semedo's presentation of the Chinese language see Mungello, *op. cit.* (n. 54), pp. 76–79.

[407] *Op. cit.* (n. 9), pp. 32–34. Ts'ang Chieh, who flourished in about 2700 B.C., is traditionally credited wth the invention of characters. Fu Hsi was the legendary inventor of the trigrams and hexagrams. For a discussion of the evolution of the Chinese language see H. G. Creel, Chang Tsung-ch'ien, and R. Rudolph (eds.), *Literary Chinese by the Inductive Method* (3 vols.; Chicago, 1948), I, 1–33. See also Knud Lundbaek, *The Traditional History of the Chinese Script from a Seventeenth-Century Jesuit Manuscript* (Aarhus, 1988). See our pl. 350 for Martini's examples of the evolution of characters from the depiction of natural objects.

earliest European writers to analyze the composition and trace the evolution of the characters. Later in the century Martini and Kircher would carry this analysis significantly further.[408]

The task of learning to read Chinese appears formidable to most of the Jesuits. The sparseness of grammar and the absence of inflections, they think, places too heavy a burden on memory. The sheer number of characters is frightening; the Jesuits estimate that there are between forty thousand and eighty thousand of them, and that to read and write, one has to know about ten thousand.[409] To become educated, therefore, a Chinese student must spend a large part of his lifetime learning the characters, thereby consuming a great amount of time that might have been more profitably spent on other studies.[410] Pantoja reports that children begin memorizing characters at age seven.[411] Trigault sees some moral benefit from all this labor—it keeps Chinese youth from waywardness by occupying most of their time in study.[412] Semedo does not share his colleagues' judgment about the difficulty of learning Chinese. He claims that it is easier to learn than Latin, in which the student spends so much time mastering the complex grammar. In Semedo's words, Chinese is a "very narrow language," and "so sweet, that it exceedeth almost all the others that I know."[413] Despite the excessive number of characters, Longobardo reports, almost everyone except a few merchants, artisans, and laborers is literate. Even the very poor, he thinks, are able to read and write a little.[414]

Not only is learning the characters a formidable task, great pains are expended on writing the characters, as well. The Chinese value good calligraphy more highly than good painting. Indeed, painting and calligraphy are similar arts to the Chinese, for they write with brushes much like those used in painting. The Jesuits are also impressed by the almost reverent attitude toward the written word in China. It is even offensive to leave paper with writing on it lying on the streets. Such literate litter is collected and ceremoniously burned at local schools.[415] The large volume of printed literature in China also looks impressive. Printing and papermaking were anciently

---

[408] See below, pp. 1717–19.

[409] Pantoja, *loc. cit.* (n. 39), p. 385; Trigault in Gallagher (trans.), *op. cit.* (n. 38), p. 27; Semedo, *op. cit.* (n. 9), p. 33. The Jesuits' figures are exaggerated; the dictionary compiled during the K'ang-hsi reign, the *K'ang-hsi Tzu-tien*, contains about forty-nine thousand characters. To read and write Chinese, one must know considerably fewer than ten thousand characters.

[410] Trigault in Gallagher (trans.), *op. cit.* (n. 38), p. 29.

[411] Pantoja, *loc. cit.* (n. 39), p. 385.

[412] Gallagher (trans.), *op. cit.* (n. 38), p. 20.

[413] *Op. cit.* (n. 9), p. 32.

[414] Longobardo, *op. cit.* (n. 48), p. 11. See also Semedo, *op. cit.* (n. 9), p. 33. Most peasants were illiterate, as were many merchants. On the extent of popular literacy before Ch'ing times see E. S. Rawski, *Education and Popular Literacy in Ch'ing China* (Ann Arbor, Mich., 1979), pp. 4–8.

[415] Semedo, *op. cit.* (n. 9), p. 34. *Cf.* Ball, *op. cit.* (n. 147), pp. 721–22, and T. H. Tsien in Needham, *op. cit.* (n. 181), Vol. V, Pt. 1, p. 109. For a detailed discussion of the reverence for lettered paper see Doolittle, *op. cit.* (n. 348), II, 167–70.

practiced, Semedo claims for sixteen hundred years.[416] He also comments on the low cost of printing and the complete lack of censorship, all of which encourages the publication and wide distribution of books.

Longobardo, like Mendoza in the sixteenth century, describes what he calls public schools and universities in China.[417] Subsequent Jesuit writers all repudiate this notion, asserting that there are no state-supported schools in China but only local or private education. Semedo intimates that the earlier writers may have been misled by the elaborate buildings in the provincial capitals in which the examinations were given.[418] In any case, the picture of Chinese education which prevails is primarily that of private education. Each family, whenever possible, hires a tutor for its children. The tutor usually lives with the family and accompanies his pupils wherever they go. In many places there are also village schools for poor children, but these depend for their existence on local initiative. Older students often pool their resources to hire a master. Those who have won the first degree no longer hire teachers, but form academies in which they regularly meet to practice writing and to criticize one another's work.[419] Apparently there is no dearth of teachers, many of whom are unsuccessful candidates for the literary degrees. Wealthy families, however, hire only those who have passed the first examinations as tutors for their children. The Jesuits report that all teachers, whether or not degree holders, are held in high esteem.

Education for Chinese children begins rather early, around age seven.[420] Elementary pupils immediately start memorizing characters and reading books. Their first readers are books on manners and morals, especially filial piety. Soon they are at work on the Confucian classics, memorizing the texts and the commentaries on them. Semedo tells of students who turn their backs to their books and recite the texts for their tutors.[421] Beginning students also spend part of each day practicing calligraphy. At first they trace through thin paper the characters drawn by their teachers. Later they work at reproducing the characters freehand. Once a reasonable number of characters has been learned and some proficiency attained in writing them, the students begin to study the rules of composition. Chinese education is rigorous, and many of the Jesuits comment on the diligence of the students. School days are long, and family tutors usually accompany their charges at meals and even during visits, constantly correcting their conduct and manners. Nor might Chinese students look forward to long summer vacations

---

[416]*Op. cit.* (n. 9), p. 35. Paper was invented in the first century A.D., but block printing dates back only to around A.D. 700. See Tsien, *op. cit.* (n. 209), pp. 1, 135–37.

[417]Longobardo, *op. cit.* (n. 48), p. 11.

[418]*Op. cit.* (n. 9), p. 30. Hucker, *op. cit.* (n. 94), p. 14, however, describes the establishment of a system of government-supported schools early in the dynasty. See also Ho, *op. cit.* (n. 94), pp. 194–97, on community and clan schools during the late Ming.

[419]On literary societies for the *sheng-yüan* see Ho, *op. cit.* (n. 94), p. 278.

[420]Pantoja, *loc. cit.* (n. 39), p. 385. *Cf.* Rawski, *op. cit.* (n. 414), pp. 36–38.

[421]*Op. cit.* (n. 9), p. 36.

like their European counterparts. They enjoy very few holidays and only one annual fifteen-day vacation at the beginning of the new year.[422]

The content of traditional education was dominated by the nine books comprising the Confucian canon. The first group, called the Five Classics, was supposedly compiled or written by Confucius himself: the *I Ching,* or *Classic of Changes;* the *Shu Ching,* or *Classic of History* (Semedo calls it the Book of Instructions); the *Shih Ching,* or *Classic of Poetry;* the *Li Chi,* or *Record of Rites;* and the *Ch'un Ch'iu,* or *Spring and Autumn Annals.* Following Chinese tradition, the Jesuits believe that the first four classics were compiled by Confucius from the writings of all the ancient philosophers, and that the *Ch'un Ch'iu* had actually been written by Confucius himself.[423] Modern scholars, however, usually reject Confucius' association with any of the Five Classics and show, in fact, that most of them were written long after his death.[424] The remaining four volumes of the Confucian canon are, according to the Jesuits, collections of the teachings of Confucius, of his prominent disciples, and of Mencius. These texts, called the Four Books, contain precepts for virtuous living and just government. None of the early seventeenth-century writers mentions the names of the Four Books, but they obviously were referring to the *Lun Yü,* or *Analects;* the *Ta Hsüeh,* or *Great Learning;* the *Chung Yung,* or *Doctrine of the Mean;* and the *Meng-tzu,* or *Mencius.* To be considered learned, a Chinese scholar must be able to discourse on any small point—indeed, on any word—contained in the Four Books. Students consequently memorize them in their entirety. "In these nine books," writes Semedo, "is contained all the naturall and morall philosophy."[425]

The goal of traditional Chinese education is to prepare students for the state examinations. These are the portals through which one enters the class of the literati to win positions in the civil administration, the most coveted of all careers in China. The examinations lead to three degrees which the Jesuits consider equivalent to the baccalaureate, licentiate, and doctorate of the European universities. Most of the Jesuits describe the examinations, but Trigault's and Semedo's accounts are the most detailed.[426]

The lowest degree is called *hsiu-ts'ai* (or *sheng-yüan*) and the examinations for this degree are held periodically in the larger cities (actually only in the prefectural capitals).[427] Candidates for the *hsiu-ts'ai* go through three elimi-

---

[422] On education, see especially *ibid.,* pp. 35–38.

[423] For example, Trigault in Gallagher (trans.), *op. cit.* (n. 38), p. 33, and Semedo, *op. cit.* (n. 9), p. 49.

[424] For example, see H. G. Creel, *Confucius and the Chinese Way* (New York, 1960), pp. 95–108, and Mungello, *op. cit.* (n. 54), pp. 58–59.

[425] *Op. cit.* (n. 9), p. 49. For the title page of the 1687 translation of the *Chung Yung* see our pl. 355.

[426] Gallagher (trans.), *op. cit.* (n. 38), pp. 34–41; Semedo, *op. cit.* (n. 9), pp. 40–47.

[427] *Hsiu-ts'ai* means "budding genius." This was a term inherited from the T'ang dynasty (618–907). By Ming times they were scholar-commoners called *sheng-yüan.* See Ho, *op. cit.* (n. 94), pp. 12, 35–36.

nation stages, each of which lasts one day and involves the writing of an essay. The first elimination is made by the local *hsiu-ts'ai,* the second by prefectural officials, and the third by the *ti-hsiao* (or *ti-hsüeh*), the provincial superintendent of education.[428] Only a small minority of the candidates for the *hsiu-ts'ai* actually receive the degree; Trigault estimates that of the four or five thousand candidates in a single prefecture only two hundred are eligible for the final test, and only twenty to thirty are awarded degrees.[429] Those who are successful immediately become members of the literati, wear the distinctive garb of their class, and receive certain civil privileges and immunities. The successful *hsiu-ts'ai,* however, are not permitted to rest on their laurels. They are periodically examined by the *ti-hsiao* to see if they diligently continue their studies. The diligent are rewarded; the slothful are punished and sometimes even lose their degrees.[430]

The *hsiu-ts'ai* degree seldom entitles its holder to an official position, but it allows him to compete in the examinations for the next higher degree—the *chü-jen.*[431] These examinations are held in the provincial capitals once every three years during the eighth month (September–October). They are given in large buildings which house the candidates and the imperially appointed examiners. The candidates are locked in small cells from dawn until sunset on the days designated for writing—the ninth, twelfth, and fifteenth of the month. Elaborate precautions are taken to avoid cheating; the candidates are searched as they enter the compound, the examiners are not permitted to speak to anyone, the buildings and cells are under constant guard. According to Trigault, the candidates write seven essays on the first day of testing, three on passages selected from the Four Books and four on topics related to any one of the Five Classics.[432] Semedo reports that four essays from the Four Books and three from one of the classics are required.[433] Only three essays are assigned for the second session. These are on topics of past or present governmental policy cast in the form of advice to the emperor. On the third day the candidates write three essays arguing a position on topics of government planning or policy, according to Trigault. Semedo merely reports that these essays concern "the lawes and statutes of the realme."[434]

[428] Trigault in Gallagher (trans.), *op. cit.* (n. 38), p. 34, calls him the "Tihio," or chancellor. Semedo, *op. cit.* (n. 9), p. 41, calls him the "chancellor." *Ti-hsüeh* was the vulgar term for the provincial educational commissioner.

[429] Gallagher (trans.), *op. cit.* (n. 38), p. 34.

[430] *Ibid.,* pp. 34–35; Semedo, *op. cit.* (n. 9), p. 41.

[431] *Chü-jen* means a "recommended man," or one who is permitted to take the metropolitan examination. See Ch'ien, *op. cit.* (n. 120), p. 110.

[432] Gallagher (trans.), *op. cit.* (n. 38), pp. 36–37.

[433] *Op. cit.* (n. 9), p. 42. Both Trigault and Semedo are correct, according to Chen, *loc. cit.* (n. 118), p. 75. There was a change in practice between the writing of their accounts.

[434] Gallagher (trans.), *op. cit.* (n. 38), p. 37; Semedo, *op. cit.* (n. 9), p. 45. Miyazaki Ichisada, *China's Examination Hell,* trans. Conrad Shirokauer (New York and Tokyo, 1976), pp. 45, 50–51, describes only three essays from the Four Books on the first day, five questions on the Five Classics during the second day, and one "essay involving a broad critique of certain past or

All of the essays are written in triplicate, only one copy bearing the name of the candidate along with his father's and grandfather's names. Even the open copies are recopied by clerks before being submitted to the examiners in order to prevent a possible recognition of the candidate's calligraphy.[435] Some students are disqualified after each session because of poor calligraphy or other formal errors.[436] After the third day of examination the judges are sequestered for fifteen days, during which time they select the best essays. Familiarity with the classics and literary style rank high as criteria for evaluation, although some attention is given to the candidates' response to practical governmental problems. The pedantry sometimes characteristic of the exams is conveyed by Semedo's description of the candidate who was turned down because he wrote the character *ma* [馬] (horse) with a line replacing the four points at the bottom of the character.[437]

After the essays have been evaluated, the names of the successful candidates are announced with great fanfare. Semedo estimates that about fifteen hundred *chü-jen* degrees are awarded every three years. In larger provinces as many as seventeen hundred students take the exams.[438] Certain provincial offices are open to the *chü-jen,* but most of them seem to prepare themselves for the third and final examination. Semedo is puzzled by the sudden improvement in the financial condition of the successful candidates and their families, a phenomenon which may be partially explained by the fact that most of the *chü-jen* could enter the bureaucracy, usually, in the eighth or seventh ranks.[439]

Examinations for the highest degree, that of *chin-shih,* are held in Peking during the third month of the year following the *chü-jen* examinations. These are conducted by the Grand Secretaries and members of the Han-lin Yüan; in other respects they are similar to the *chü-jen* examinations. Every three years about three hundred candidates are awarded the *chin-shih* degree;[440] these degree-holders are esteemed as the empire's nobility and, according to the Jesuits, given immediate employment in the administration.[441] The successful candidates, in full regalia, also take another examination in the imperial pal-

present government policies on the third day." Miyazaki's description, however, is of the examinations in the late Ch'ing dynasty. For a description and evaluation of the examinations during the Sung dynasty see John W. Chaffee, *The Thorny Gates of Learning in Sung China: A Social History of Examinations* (Cambridge, 1985).

[435] Gallagher (trans.), *op. cit.* (n. 38), p. 37.

[436] Semedo, *op. cit.* (n. 9), p. 43.

[437] *Ibid.* Neither Trigault nor Semedo explains how or when the students' calligraphy was judged when presumably the examiners only read copies of their essays; nor does Miyazaki or Chaffee clarify the matter.

[438] Semedo, *op. cit.* (n. 9), pp. 41 and 45.

[439] *Cf.* Ho, *op. cit.* (n. 94), pp. 27 and 43–44.

[440] Trigault (in Gallagher [trans.], *op. cit.* [n. 38], p. 39) claims 300; Semedo (*op. cit.* [n. 9], p. 46) says 350.

[441] In the ninety exams given during the Ming dynasty, 24,874 *chin-shih* degrees were awarded—an average of 276 per exam. The smallest number awarded at one time was 32; the largest, 472. See Hucker, *op. cit.* (n. 94), p. 16.

ace—formerly conducted by the emperor—at which the three best graduates are given singular honors. They were also given immediate employment in the Han-lin Yüan, but none of the Jesuits actually says so. Semedo describes still another examination, in which thirty of the new *chin-shih* are chosen for the Han-lin Yüan, five being admitted each year.[442]

Without doubt, the study of literature and moral philosophy with the intention of passing the examinations was the most respected type of education in China. Most Chinese, however, never attempted the examinations. The vast majority of students went to school for only one or two years—long enough to learn a sufficient number of characters for the conduct of trade. From the Jesuits, however, one gets the impression that almost everyone in the empire was an aspirant for the degrees or at least spent long years at traditional literary studies. Martini, for example, writes "there is almost no one among them, not even the peasants, who had not studied up to fifteen years; there is scarcely a man found who does not know how to write."[443] Actually, much education in China took place outside the traditional system leading to the examination stall. The Buddhist monasteries provided education for their novitiates—a rather large number—and often for village children as well. Trade guilds provided practical education for their apprentices, a training which often included the study of a limited number of characters. Elementary education was also provided by clan schools and by free government-supported schools. Even more informal education was afforded by peasants for their sons and mothers for their daughters. The Jesuits rarely mention any of these opportunities for learning and they say nothing at all about education for women.[444] The training of physicians, however, is frequently discussed. The Jesuits report that there are no schools for the study of medicine; aspiring physicians simply learn from someone already skilled in the craft. Examinations for degrees in medicine could be taken in both Nanking and Peking, but the holder of a medical degree had no particular advantage over a physician without a degree. No one is prohibited from practicing medicine.[445] The Jesuits also discuss the system of military examinations and degrees, which exactly paralleled those in the regular studies. They judge the military examinations not to be very rigorous, however, and the degrees to be of little significance or advantage. Trigault observes that the examinations in medicine and military science are even administered and judged by those who hold regular civil service degrees.[446]

According to Semedo, the Chinese divide all learning into three general

[442]*Op. cit.* (n. 9), p. 46.
[443]*Op. cit.* (n. 44), p. 11. Clearly an exaggeration.
[444]For a discussion of popular education during the Ch'ing dynasty, with considerable relevance to the Ming, see Rawski, *op. cit.* (n. 414), pp. 1–53; on female literacy see pp. 6–8. On the Ming see also Ho, *op. cit.* (n. 94), pp. 194–97.
[445]For example, see Trigault in Gallagher (trans.), *op. cit.* (n. 38), p. 32.
[446]*Ibid.*, pp. 40–41, and above, pp. 1587–88.

"sciences": the science of the heavens, that of the earth, and that of man. The "science of the heavens" includes astronomy and astrology and is also concerned with the creation of the universe, the generation and corruption of the myriad things, the elements, and the seasons. The "science of earth" includes agriculture, the study of the seasons, geography, surveying, and geomancy (*feng-shui*). All of ethics, political philosophy, and the study of rites and manners—in short, all of Confucian thought—is considered part of the "science of man." This, as Semedo and the other Jesuits correctly perceive, was by far the most important area of learning to the Chinese and it was the area in which Chinese accomplishments were most admired by the Europeans.[447]

While Semedo seems to realize that the Chinese divide the world of learning into different categories than do Europeans, he and the other Jesuits nevertheless use Western categories—the traditional liberal arts and sciences—with which to discuss and evaluate Chinese achievements. Consequently their admiration for Chinese thought has distinct limits. While impressed with Confucian moral and political philosophy, they find other areas of intellectual endeavor in which the Chinese have made little or no progress. Trigault, for example, notes that moral philosophy was "the only one of the higher philosophical sciences with which the Chinese have become acquainted."[448] Semedo writes that in many of the liberal arts and sciences the Chinese had produced nothing at all.[449] They have little use for grammar and "for Logick they have no other rules but what are dictated to them by the light of nature." They are very skilled in rhetoric, Semedo decides, but in this, too, they use no rules; they learn through imitation. Arithmetic, he writes, the Chinese had "in perfection," but no algebra.[450] They had a "sufficient knowledge" of geometry. Even in ancient times the land had been carefully surveyed and divided, which Semedo illustrates by referring to the Mencian well-field system.[451] Semedo discovers that the Chinese love mathematics and are quick to learn what the Jesuits teach them, but that they have as yet made little progress in it. Trigault reports that

---

[447] Semedo, *op. cit.* (n. 9), p. 50.

[448] Gallagher (trans.), *op. cit.* (n. 38), p. 30.

[449] *Op. cit.* (n. 9), p. 47.

[450] *Ibid.*, p. 51. In fact, the Chinese had invented an algebra independently, but it was not like its Western counterpart. The common people, as in Europe, had no knowledge of algebra. On the Chinese form of algebra see Needham, *op. cit.* (n. 181), III, 112–15.

[451] *Op. cit.* (n. 9), pp. 51, 53. See also Martini, *op. cit.* (n. 44), p. 8. The "well-field" system seems to have been practiced during the early Chou period (1122–771 B.C.), and it was championed by Mencius (371–289 B.C.) as the equitable way to finance the government. In it, all land was to be divided into large squares which in turn were divided into nine smaller squares. Each of the eight outer squares would be farmed by a single family. The central square or "public field" (*kung t'ien*) was to be cultivated by the eight families together, its produce going to the lord or ruler. See Fung Yu-lan, *A History of Chinese Philosophy*, trans. Derk Bodde (2 vols.; Princeton, 1952), I, 10–13, 117–19.

much more was known about mathematics during the Mongol period, but even then it was not based on a reliable system of proofs.[452] Both Trigault and Semedo report high interest in astronomy among Chinese scholars. They describe the way in which the Chinese divide the heavens, and observe that Chinese astronomers identify fully four hundred more stars than do Europeans. They describe the two official astronomical bureaus in Peking and the ancient instruments of the Peking and Nanking observatories (see pl. 307). In this connection Semedo also discusses the Chinese calendar. Both thought the ancient instruments indicated that ancient Chinese astronomers were superior to their Ming descendants. Ming astronomers were far too interested in astrology and did not understand the regularity and system of planetary and stellar movements.[453] Perhaps Trigault most clearly reflects seventeenth-century European scientific thought when he complains that "Chinese astronomers take no pains whatever to reduce the phenomena of celestial bodies to the discipline of mathematics."[454]

The Jesuits report that music is highly esteemed by the Chinese. Semedo notes that Confucius had taught it, but that the Chinese admit that the true rules have since been lost.[455] He discusses the twelve tones, the absence of harmony, and Buddhist chants (which he thought sounded like plainsong). He mentions most traditional Chinese musical instruments, which he classifies according to Chinese categories (metal, stone, skin, silk, and wood). Semedo is not favorably impressed with Chinese music; it is, he thinks, "pleasing only to those of their own country." Still, he acknowledges that when all the Chinese instruments are played together the results are sometimes pleasing.[456] Trigault is far more critical: the Chinese have no keyboard instruments and apparently fail to realize that gut could be used for strings. As he puts it:

The whole art of Chinese music seems to consist in producing a monotonous rhythmic beat as they know nothing of the variations and harmony that can be produced by combining different musical notes. However they themselves are highly flattered by their own music which to the ear of a stranger represents nothing but a discordant jangle.[457]

---

[452]Gallagher (trans.), *op. cit.* (n. 38), p. 31. On traditional Chinese mathematics see Needham, *op. cit.* (n. 181), Vol. III, *Mathematics and the Sciences of the Heavens and the Earth,* pp. 1–168.

[453]Gallagher (trans.), op. cit. (n. 38), pp. 30–32; Semedo, *op. cit.* (n. 9), pp. 53–54.

[454]Gallagher (trans.), *op. cit.* (n. 38), p. 31. *Cf.* Needham, *op. cit.* (n. 181), III, 171–461, on traditional Chinese astronomy; see especially pp. 437–58 for his criticisms of the Jesuits' understanding of Chinese astronomy.

[455]*Op. cit.* (n. 9), p. 54.

[456]*Ibid.*, pp. 54–55. *Cf.* William P. Malm, *Music Cultures of the Pacific, the Near East, and Asia* (2d ed.; Englewood Cliffs, N.J., 1977), pp. 144–67. Malm (pp. 149–52) lists eight classes of Chinese instruments: earth, stone, metal, skin, wood, bamboo, gourds, and silk. Stringed instruments are classified as silk.

[457]Gallagher (trans.), *op. cit.* (n. 38), p. 22.

Of the early seventeenth-century missionaries only Pantoja professes to enjoy Chinese music.[458]

Semedo is the only one of these European writers to comment on Chinese poetry. He reports that it was highly esteemed in ancient times already and is still very popular among the upper classes. He thinks the form of most Chinese poetry is similar to that of European vernacular sonnets or ditties and not at all like Latin verses. He describes in some detail the rhyme scheme and correspondence pattern of the popular eight-verse poems. He is particularly impressed by the high moral tone of Chinese poetry.[459]

Most of the Jesuits write favorably about Chinese medicine. They report that while there are many books on medicine, some of which are very old, Chinese physicians are weak on theory. In the practice of medicine, however, the Jesuits judge them to be very good. They do not let blood or use cupping glasses, cautery, syrups, or pills. They use simple remedies made from herbs, roots, seeds, fruits, and so forth, of which there are many. Semedo reports that whole fairs are devoted to the sale of medicines. Chinese physicians are also exceedingly skilled at diagnosing ailments by taking the pulse. They never ask their patients where the pain is located. Good physicians are rarely wrong in either their diagnoses or prescriptions.[460] Not all Chinese physicians are good, however. In Trigault's view medicine and all other forms of Chinese intellectual endeavor suffer from the primacy given to the field of moral philosophy.

It is evident to everyone here that no one will labor to attain proficiency in mathematics or in medicine who has any hope of becoming prominent in the field of philosophy. The result is that scarcely anyone devotes himself to those studies, unless he is deterred from the pursuit of what are considered to be the higher studies, either by reason of family affairs or by mediocrity of talent. The study of mathematics and that of medicine are held in low esteem, because they are not fostered by honors as is the study of philosophy, to which students are attracted by the hope of glory and the rewards attached to it. This may readily be seen in the interest taken in the study of moral philosophy. The man who is promoted to the higher degrees in this field prides himself on the fact that he has in truth attained to the pinnacle of Chinese happiness.[461]

Many of the European descriptions of China allude to the traditional concern for history among Chinese scholars and their claims to a very high antiquity for the empire.[462] Bartoli, for example, describes the regular ap-

[458]Pantoja, *loc. cit.* (n. 39), p. 387.

[459]*Op. cit.* (n. 9), pp. 55–56.

[460]*Ibid.*, pp. 56–57. For illustrations from later seventeenth-century books on Chinese medicine and the diagnostic use of the pulse see our pls. 356, 357, and 358.

[461]Gallagher (trans.), *op. cit.* (n. 38), pp. 32–33. For Chinese philosophy see below pp. 1651–54.

[462]For example, see Pantoja, *loc. cit.* (n. 39), pp. 400–401; and Bartoli, in Mortara (ed.), *op. cit.* (n. 13), pp. 74–75.

pointment of court historians and the uninterrupted series of official dynastic histories.[463] During the first half of the seventeenth century no observer of the Chinese scene attempts to relate systematically the history of the Middle Kingdom. This does not mean, however, that information concerning Chinese history was not available. Almost all the writers relate isolated incidents from China's past which, if collected in one place, would have comprised an interesting, although very uneven, sketch of Chinese history. Mendoza, writing in 1584, includes a "Genealogy of the Kings of China" in his description, which dates the first Chinese monarch at 2550 or 2600 B.C.—long before the generally accepted date for the universal flood described in Genesis.[464] Mendoza presents only a list of obscurely romanized names with little convincing detail to support them, but Pantoja worries about how Chinese ancient history might be reconciled with traditional, biblically based Western chronology.[465] In their discussions of the names for the empire, most European writers observe that the Chinese change the official name for the empire with each new dynasty. Semedo enumerates the dynasties—twenty-two of them—and names some of them and some of the individual emperors. Although generally impressed with Chinese historical writing, he apparently distrusts what the Chinese write about their earliest history because these accounts conflict with the accepted biblical chronologies.[466] Martini's *Atlas* also contains a simplified sketch of the dynasties, and Bartoli includes a rather sophisticated discussion of the chronological problems.[467] Whatever reservations they may have had about the historicity of the sage emperors of China's most distant past, several writers mention one or more of them. Semedo, for example, credits Fu Hsi incorrectly with the invention of the characters. Martini notes that the title translated as "emperor" is from the name of the sage emperor Huang-ti, and both Pantoja and Semedo report that some of the sage emperors chose worthy successors in place of their sons.[468]

Few aspects of ancient Chinese history are so widely reported in Europe as the life and teachings of Confucius. Trigault's report is brief: Confucius was born, he says, in 551 B.C., and he encouraged people to live virtuously by his teaching, writings, and example. He thinks Confucius wrote most of the classics.[469] Semedo adds that he held high office in several kingdoms, in-

---

[463] Mortara (ed.), *op. cit.* (n. 13), p. 140.

[464] *Op. cit.* (n. 184), II, 69–76.

[465] *Loc. cit.* (n. 39), pp. 400–401.

[466] *Op. cit.* (n. 9), pp. 106–7.

[467] Martini, *op. cit.* (n. 44), pp. 20–21; Mortara (ed.), *op. cit.* (n. 13), pp. 140–42. For a discussion of the chronological problem see E. Van Kley, "Europe's 'Discovery' of China and the Writing of World History," *American Historical Review,* LXXVI (1971), 358–85.

[468] Semedo, *op. cit.* (n. 9), pp. 33–34, 106–7; Martini, *op. cit.* (n. 44), p. 15; Pantoja, *loc. cit.* (n. 39), p. 401. According to Chinese tradition, the model Confucian sage emperors Yao and Shun both chose as their successors virtuous men other than their own sons. Yao chose Shun and Shun chose Yü, who founded the Hsia dynasty.

[469] Gallagher (trans.), *op. cit.* (n. 38), pp. 30 and 33.

troduced new customs, and taught many disciples. His descendants still live in Shantung Province and are regarded as nobility.[470] Trigault also introduces Lao Tzu as an older contemporary of Confucius. Both he and Semedo relate the traditional story of Lao Tzu's eighty-year gestation period.[471]

Martini's *Atlas* contains a description of the building of the Great Wall during the Ch'in dynasty—an account which found its way into almost every subsequent seventeenth-century description. Trigault, Semedo, and Martini all repeat some of the moral stories told about ancient Chinese emperors. Trigault, for example, describes how Han Wu-ti's loyal minister snatched a vial of life-prolonging elixir from a Taoist "imposter" and drank it down before it could be given to the emperor. As he was about to be killed for his effrontery, the good Confucian minister brought the emperor to his senses by shouting that if the elixir were effective he couldn't be killed, but that if indeed he could be dispatched he would have cheated the emperor of nothing save a foolish act.[472] Both Trigault and Semedo describe the introduction of Buddhism into China during the later Han dynasty. Semedo is the first to tell the story of Emperor Ming Ti's dream and its consequences: In A.D. 64 Ming Ti supposedly was commanded in a dream to seek the true law in the west. He sent ambassadors to India, who after three years returned with Buddhist teachings and books which were quickly translated into Chinese. Trigault mentions nothing about the dream but suggests that the ambassadors were probably sent to India because the Chinese had heard reports about Christianity. Both Saint Thomas and Saint Bartholomew were preaching in India at the time.[473] In any case, the Chinese received Buddhism rather than Christianity. Semedo relates one of the Buddha birth stories along with some events from Gautama's life. Trigault reports that Buddhism spread rapidly in China, even influencing Confucian scholarship during the Sung period.[474]

Trigault, Martini, and Semedo all mention evidences for an earlier planting of Christianity in China. In 1623 or 1625 a stele was unearthed near Sian at the site of the T'ang capital of Ch'ang-an which indicates that there had been a Nestorian Christian church in China as early as A.D. 636. Trigault and Semedo saw it soon after it was discovered. Europe first learned about it from Gaspar Luís' letter which was published in a Jesuit letterbook of 1628.[475] Both Semedo and Martini also describe the Nestorian monument,

[470] *Op. cit.* (n. 9), pp. 48–49. See also Martini, *op. cit.* (n. 44), p. 68.

[471] For example, Gallagher (trans.), *op. cit.* (n. 38), p. 102; Semedo, *op. cit.* (n. 9), p. 87. The English translation of Semedo has eight rather than eighty years.

[472] Gallagher (trans.), *op. cit.* (n. 38), p. 92. See also Semedo, *op. cit.* (n. 9), pp. 109–10.

[473] Trigault in Gallagher (trans.), *op. cit.* (n. 38), pp. 98–99; Semedo, *op. cit.* (n. 9), p. 89. On Ming-ti's dream see Kenneth Ch'en, *Buddhism in China: A Historical Survey* (Princeton, 1974), pp. 29–31.

[474] Gallagher (trans.), *op. cit.* (n. 38), p. 95.

[475] *Op. cit.* (n. 68), pp. 12–28.

Semedo in some detail.[476] Trigault and Semedo, however, believe that Christianity had been preached in China centuries earlier by Saint Thomas.[477] Evidence for these visitations, however, came from the traditions and records of the Malabar church in India rather than from the Nestorian Monument or any other Chinese source.

In his description of Hangchow, Martini discusses its establishment as the capital of the southern Sung dynasty after China's northern provinces had been lost to the Tartars.[478] Almost everyone reports something about the thirteenth-century Mongol conquest.[479] Many also mention Marco Polo and his visit to China during the Mongol period. Trigault, for example, took pains to demonstrate that Polo's Cathay was indeed China.[480] Martini did even more. In his *Atlas* he repeatedly compares Polo's description with his own observations in attesting to the general accuracy of Polo's story.[481] The Jesuits also note that the impressive astronomical instruments in the Nanking observatory had been made by Mongol astronomers.[482]

As might be expected, early seventeenth-century descriptions of China contain considerable information about the early history of the Ming dynasty. The story of the Ming founder Chu Yüan-chang's revolt against the Mongols in 1368 is included in most descriptions. He is usually described as wise and valiant, of obscure parentage—he was an orphan—and a former Buddhist monk.[483] Semedo reports that the new Hung-wu emperor (r. 1368–98) drove the Mongols far beyond the Wall, conquered large parts of their homeland, and forced the eastern Tartars, the Manchus, to pay tribute to him.[484] Most writers credit Hung-wu with the establishment of a uniquely wise government in which political power was placed in the hands

[476]Semedo, *op. cit.* (n. 9), pp. 157–64; Martini, *op. cit.* (n. 44), p. 55. It is today still on display at Sian in the *pei-lin* (Forest of Stone Tablets). For a new translation of the Nestorian monument see Alois Bürke, S.M.B., "Das Nestorianer-Denkmal von Si-an-fu, Versuch einer Neuübersetzung," *NZM*, Supplementa XVII (1971), 125–41. On p. 127, n. 10, Bürke notes that Trigault made a Latin translation in 1625 and Terenz a French translation from the Syriac in 1629. In 1631 the text of the stele was translated into Italian; see *Dichiaratione di una pietra antica scritta e scolpita con l'infrascritte lettere, ritrouata nel regno della Cina* (Rome, 1631). We have not seen these translations. See also Henri Havret, *La stèle chrétienne de Si-ngnan-fou* (Shanghai, 1895, reprint 1902).

[477]Trigault in Gallagher (trans.), *op. cit.* (n. 38), p. 113; Semedo, *op. cit.* (n. 9), pp. 154–55, 164.

[478]*Op. cit.* (n. 44), pp. 133–37. North China was overrun in the early twelfth century by Tungusic tribes known as the Jürchen.

[479]Pantoja, *loc. cit.* (n. 39), p. 384; Trigault in Gallagher (trans.), *op. cit.* (n. 38), p. 42; Semedo, *op. cit.* (n. 9), p. 107; Martini, *op. cit.* (n. 44), pp. 21, 37, 116–17.

[480]Gallagher (trans.), *op. cit.* (n. 38), pp. 311–12, 499–522.

[481]See above, pp. 1576–77.

[482]Pantoja, *loc. cit.* (n. 39), p. 401; Trigault in Gallagher (trans.), *op. cit.* (n. 38), pp. 329–31; Martini, *op. cit.* (n. 44), p. 118.

[483]Pantoja, *loc. cit.* (n. 39), pp. 401–2; Trigault in Gallagher (trans.), *op. cit.* (n. 38), p. 107; Martini, *op. cit.* (n. 44), p. 120.

[484]*Op. cit.* (n. 9), pp. 100, 107.

of degree-holders rather than the nobility, generals, or members of the royal family.[485] Considerable historical detail about the late Ming dynasty can also be gleaned from the Jesuit letters and histories; these report the events that affected the Christian mission, whose history and activities are their main concern. The Tartars are a continuing part of the story. Soon after the establishment of the Ming dynasty they escape Chinese control to again trouble the empire. During the Wan-li era (1573–1620) problems with the Manchus reach the crisis point. Semedo describes these developments in some detail. To his readers, the reports of the Manchu Conquest which arrived in Europe at mid-century could not have been completely surprising.[486]

Much more could be said about the historical information presented piecemeal in the early seventeenth-century descriptions of China. Every city, mountain, bridge, temple, institution, festival, or custom in China had its history or semi-historical legends. Martini's *Atlas* is a particularly rich storehouse of such information as, to a lesser degree, were Trigault's and Semedo's histories of the Christian mission. In short, even before the publication in the second half of the seventeenth century of continuous accounts of Chinese history in Western languages, European readers could have gleaned much historical information from the Jesuit literature on Ming China.

7

RELIGION AND PHILOSOPHY

Europeans first confronted Chinese religious practices in the overseas Chinese communities—in places like Bantam on Java, for example—and they described these practices as the most benighted kind of idolatry. According to the Dutch travelers who visited Bantam in the last years of the sixteenth century, the Chinese actually worshipped the devil, although they recognized the existence of a supreme being who had created all things. They believed that this God-creator was a benign spirit who would not harm anyone. The devil, on the other hand, had to be appeased with worship and sacrifice or he most certainly would harm men.[487] The image which De Houtman and his men called the devil could have been any of several popular Chinese deities: the Buddhist Lord of Hell, the Taoist Stove (or Fireplace) God, or the Soil God, for examples. The Dutch, however, report that

---

[485] See Pantoja, *loc. cit.* (n. 39), p. 401; Trigault in Gallagher (trans.), *op. cit.* (n. 38), p. 107.
[486] *Op. cit.* (n. 9), pp. 100–130. Also see below, pp. 1662–76.
[487] See pl. 253; see also Rouffaer and Ijzerman (eds.), *op. cit.* (n. 344), I, 124–25, and II, 25–26.

the Chinese called him "Joosie."[488] These early Western observers are also intrigued by the way in which the Chinese worshipped their idols. Europeans were familiar with some aspects of their worship—the burning of candles or incense, and bowing before the images. But the Chinese, they observe, set food before the idols, often exquisitely cooked dishes.

Almost all of the early descriptions of China and most of the travel accounts mention the apparent devil worship of the Chinese. But Mendoza and his sources, Gaspar da Cruz and Martin de Rada, record many other aspects of Chinese religion as well.[489] They report that the Chinese, in addition to worshipping the devil, also worship the sun and moon, making especially elaborate sacrifices during eclipses. Mendoza also reports that they believe in the immortality of the soul and in rewards and punishments after death. He and his sources talk about the vast number of images found in Chinese temples, pagodas, houses, and wayside shrines, and they describe many of them. Various methods of fortune-telling and divination are described, as well as the rough and sacrilegious way the Chinese treat their idols. If after compliments and pleadings the god does not return the desired answer, the irate suppliant might kick the image, douse it with water, or scorch it with fire in order to coerce the recalcitrant deity into rendering a more favorable verdict.[490] They describe priests and monks and are aware of two varieties of clergy, those who shave their heads and those who let their hair grow long. Mendoza detects vestiges of Christianity in many Chinese religious practices. He describes an image with three heads for example, which he thought might have been an attempted representation of the Trinity, and he talks about pictures and tales which suggested that the Chinese also revere an image of a virgin holding a child.[491] The oblations and ceremonies made before the graves of ancestors, Mendoza thinks, are prayers offered to assist the dead in passing through a place of purging, which was a prelude to heaven.

Descriptions of Chinese religion by European travelers during the first half of the seventeenth century varied little from that of the sixteenth-century writers. Indeed, Mendoza's description is frequently borrowed by the writers of later travel tales; lengthy condensations of it, for example, found their way

[488] Apparently a Dutch corruption of *Deos*. See ch. xviii, n. 111 above, and Yule and Burnell, *op. cit.* (n. 146), p. 353. The Stove God (Tsao Chün) and the Soil God (T'u Ti Kung) were the two most important deities at the local level. They were really demons, spies of the Jade Emperor, and sacrifices were made to appease them. In contrast, sacrifices were not made to the Jade Emperor. See Arthur P. Wolf, "Gods, Ghosts, and Ancestors," in Arthur P. Wolf (ed.), *Religion and Ritual in Chinese Society* (Stanford, 1974), pp. 133–45.

[489] Staunton (ed.), *op. cit.* (n. 184), I, 36–49. See *Asia*, I, 783–86.

[490] Staunton (ed.), *op. cit.* (n. 184), I, 47. The gods of the stove or fireplace and of the soil were often taken out of doors to "feel" the heat during a drought or to get wet during undesirably heavy rains.

[491] *Ibid.*, pp. 36–37. Most likely Kuan Yin, the Buddhist Bodhisattva of Mercy, often pictured with a child in her arms.

into Jan Huygen van Linschoten's *Itinerario,* Pierre d'Avity's popular survey of the world's states, and the *Begin ende voortgangh* collection as part of Cornelis Matelief's journal.[492] Baudier's comments on Chinese religion also appear to have come entirely from Mendoza.[493] While seventeenth-century writers continue to describe new "idols" and new ceremonial practices as they become aware of them, the general picture of Chinese religion painted by Mendoza and the early travelers remains relatively unchanged. Matelief, for example, describes his visit to a pagoda on Nan-ao Island in ways that would have seemed familiar to readers of Mendoza.[494] None of the travelers distinguishes between Buddhism, Taoism, and Confucianism. They apparently think they are describing a general Chinese pantheon of gods. They are aware of the existence of a priesthood, most members of which live celibately and shave their heads. Obviously they are describing Buddhist monks, but they seem unaware of Buddhism as a religion distinct from other varieties of Chinese religious expression. European merchants and seamen never penetrate below the surface manifestations of Chinese religious life. In large measure, however, their failure to discriminate between the various Chinese religions resulted from a similar lack of discrimination of the part of the Chinese whom they encountered. Popular Chinese religion was a hodgepodge of Buddhist, Taoist, and traditional animist beliefs, undergirded by Confucian ethics. The European sailors and traders could hardly have been expected to reduce this bewildering panorama of gods and beliefs to a rational system.[495]

Some general aspects of Chinese religion, however, became discernible to the travelers during the first half of the century. Beneath the profusion of gods, incense, and oblations, they detect a general belief on the part of the Chinese in a supreme spirit, far superior to the deities found in homes and temples. Usually the Europeans describe this god as too sublime to be concerned with, or affected by, the affairs of men, and as having left terrestrial government to lesser spirits. The Europeans also report a fairly consistent belief in the immortality of the soul and in future recompense for one's actions during this life. Van Rechteren, who probably did not borrow from Mendoza, was nevertheless typical of many of the travelers in his discussion of the general tenets of Chinese religion:

[492] H. Terpstra (ed.), *Itinerario, voyage ofte schipvaert van Jan Huygen van Linschoten naer Oost ofte Portugaels Indien, 1579–1592* (3 vols.; "WLV," LVII, LVIII, and LX; 2d ed.; The Hague, 1955–57), I, 93–112; D'Avity, *The Estates, Empires and Principalities of the World. . . .* (London, 1615), pp. 714–44; Matelief, *loc. cit.* (n. 122), pp. 91–118.

[493] Baudier, *op. cit.* (n. 11), pp. 41–43, 94–105.

[494] Matelief, *loc. cit.* (n. 122), pp. 78–79. *Cf.* our pl. 338.

[495] On Chinese popular religion see C. K. Yang, *Religion in Chinese Society* (Berkeley and Los Angeles, 1961); Arthur P. Wolf (ed.), *op. cit.* (n. 488); Laurence G. Thompson, *Chinese Religion, An Introduction* (Belmont, Cal., 1979); David K. Jordan, *Gods, Ghosts, and Ancestors: Folk Religion in a Taiwanese Village* (Berkeley and Los Angeles, 1972); and Daniel I. Overmeyer, *Folk Buddhist Religion: Dissenting Sects in Late Traditional China* (Stanford, 1976).

Those who have had some conversation with the Dutch prisoners, who were merchants, painters, and other reasonable people, who had some education, held, on the point of the knowledge of God, that there is only one all-powerful God who is in the heavens, but who is a being too sublime to concern himself with the affairs of earth. They pretend that he has given this commission to a holy personage named Comichicho,[496] who has been down here in the world and who must return there; that it is he who punishes men every day, and who sends to them the misfortunes that they have merited; that one day they will come to life again and live in complete repose with their fathers and mothers, or wives and children without having any other chief or sovereign than him. His statue is that which they honor most in their pagodas, and which they invoke with the most ardor, in order that he may not treat them rigorously.[497]

Van Rechteren was most likely describing Buddhist beliefs, but the main lines of his presentation seem to have been held by most of the Chinese whom the Europeans encountered.

If the travel accounts fail to distinguish between the various religious groups in China, the Jesuit accounts perhaps make the distinctions too clearly. They, like the Chinese themselves, discuss three religious "sects": the Confucians, the Buddhists, and the Taoists.

Of the three, the Jesuits unanimously prefer Confucianism, or the "sect of the Literati," as they call it. This sect, they assert, is the most ancient and highly esteemed in the empire. Indeed, only Confucians can aspire to public office. As Trigault puts it: "Individually the Chinese do not choose this sect: they rather imbibe the doctrine of it in the study of letters."[498] Most of the Jesuit writers correctly doubt that Confucianism can properly be considered a religion; its followers worship no idols or images, it has no priesthood or common ceremony of worship, and lays down no rigid commandments from which it would be sinful to depart. The Jesuit writers aver that most of the Confucians believe in a single supreme deity, although contemporary Confucians do not worship him or even discuss him extensively. Trigault, for example, is convinced that the ancient Chinese knew and worshipped a supreme being whom they called "King of Heaven." Nor was this pristine monotheism corrupted in ancient times as it was among the Greeks, Romans, and Egyptians. "Of all the pagan sects known to Europe," he writes, "I know of no people who fell into fewer errors in the early ages of their antiquity than did the Chinese."[499] He is confident that many of the ancient Chinese found salvation by following the law of nature. The Jesuits believe that some remnants of this primitive monotheism still remain among the

[496] Perhaps the Buddha, Amitàbha (*O-mi-t'o-fo*), who presides over the Western Paradise. In China this god was a favorite object of popular devotion.

[497] *Op. cit.* (n. 27), pp. 43–44.

[498] Gallagher (trans.), *op. cit.* (n. 38), p. 94. See our pl. 355.

[499] Gallagher (trans.), *op. cit.* (n. 38), p. 93. See also Semedo, *op. cit.* (n. 9), p. 86, and Martini, *op. cit.* (n. 44), p. 9.

literati of the seventeenth century. While the literati themselves do not worship the one God, the Jesuits decide that the emperor still does when he makes the regular sacrifices on the altars of Heaven and Earth in the capital cities. But it seems that the ancient beliefs are dying out. The Jesuit writers still find a belief in rewards and punishments among the Confucians, but it apparently is confined to this life only. Many of the literati are convinced that the soul dies with the body, and consequently deny the existence of heaven or hell. While the Confucians have kept themselves free from idolatry, many of them have fallen into the more serious error of atheism.[500] Longobardo and Pantoja simply report that most educated Chinese are atheists.[501]

The Jesuits have only the highest praise for the ethical teachings of Confucius and his followers. It is a moral code, they report, designed to produce personal virtue and peace, as well as stability in the government of the empire. The Jesuits list the five cardinal virtues taught by Confucius and his followers: "Gin" (*jen*), "Y" (*i*), "Li" (*li*), "Chi" (*chih*), and "Sin" (*hsin*), which Semedo translates as "pietie, justice, prudence, policie, and fidelity." They note that Confucius taught the application of these virtues to the five human relationships: those between father and son, husband and wife, master and servants, older and younger brothers, and friends of equal status. In addition, the Jesuits observe that the Confucians subscribe to a negatively formulated Golden Rule: "Do not do unto others what you would not wish others to do unto you."[502] Nor do the Confucians teach and practice these virtues merely in the hope of some reward in this life or in heaven. They insist that Confucius and his true followers taught that virtue was its own reward and enjoined virtuous living without any hope of reward.

The Jesuits' portrayal of Confucius and his teachings early led them to distinguish between the "real" or "true" literati of Ming China and those whose religious ideas departed from the Jesuit image of Confucius. Trigault is the first to make this distinction—a distinction which is greatly exaggerated by Jesuit writers during the second half of the century.[503] The "real" literati, according to Trigault and most other Jesuits, confine their teachings and conduct to Confucius' moral system and do not concern themselves with metaphysical speculations. In making this distinction, the Jesuits apparently considered many of the orthodox Confucians of the seventeenth century to have been false literati because they had developed a rather elaborate meta-

---

[500] Trigault in Gallagher (trans.), *op. cit.* (n. 38), pp. 93–94.

[501] Longobardo, *op. cit.* (n. 48), p. 16; Pantoja, *loc. cit.* (n. 39), p. 357.

[502] Trigault in Gallagher (trans.), *op. cit.* (n. 38), p. 97. See also Semedo, *op. cit.* (n. 9), pp. 50, 86–87, 149, and Martini, *op. cit.* (n. 44), pp. 9–10. The Confucian five virtues are usually translated as humanity, righteousness, decorum, wisdom, and fidelity, although Semedo's translations are fairly accurate.

[503] Gallagher (trans.), *op. cit.* (n. 38), p. 94.

physics and certainly did not confine themselves to moral philosophy.[504] Despite their disapproval of the Confucians' metaphysical speculations, the Jesuits relate some aspects of that metaphysics to Europeans in their books. Semedo reports the Chinese division of all philosophy into three spheres: the study of heaven, the study of earth, and the study of man. The three are inextricably related, and the moral philosophy which the Jesuits so admire comprises only the third sphere.[505] The Jesuits correctly recognize Buddhist and Taoist influences in the Confucian metaphysics. Trigault, for example, describes a kind of pantheism which he calls the most common metaphysical teaching of the literati of his day, and in so doing he correctly identifies its Buddhist origin:

The doctrine most commonly held among the Literati at present seems to me to have been taken from the sect of idols, as promulgated about five centuries ago. This doctrine asserts that the entire universe is composed of a common substance; that the creator of the universe is one in a continuous body, a corpus continuum as it were, together with heaven and earth, men and beasts, trees and plants, and the four elements, and that each individual thing is member of this body. From this unity of substance they reason to the love that should unite the individual constituents and also that man can become like unto God because he is created one with God. This philosophy we endeavor to refute, not only from reason but also from the testimony of their own ancient philosophers to whom they are indebted for all the philosophy they have.[506]

Despite their preference for the literati and the moral teachings of the Confucians, the Jesuits also describe aspects of Confucianism which look suspiciously like pagan superstition. The scholar-officials, who were, of course, all Confucians, offer sacrifices to spirits of all kinds. While the emperor alone or his appointed delegate might sacrifice on the altars to Heaven and Earth, the highest officials and they alone are permitted to sacrifice to the spirits of the mountains, rivers, and the four quarters of the universe. The Jesuits observe, too, that the literati also sacrifice to the tutelary spirits of cities and towns, to Confucius, and to their ancestors. All Chinese sacrifice to their ancestors and are encouraged to do so by the literati. The Jesuits usually insist that these ceremonies are not superstitious or even religious.

[504] On the types of Neo-Confucian orthodoxy prevailing in Ming China see W. T. de Bary, *Neo-Confucian Orthodoxy and the Learning of the Mind-and-Heart* (New York, 1981), pp. 188–89.
[505] Semedo, *op. cit.* (n. 9), p. 50.
[506] Gallagher (trans.), *op. cit.* (n. 38), p. 95. *Cf.* K. Lundbaek, "Notes sur l'image du Néo-Confucianism dans la littérature européene du XVIIIe à la fin de XIXe siècle," in *Actes du IIIe Colloque International de Sinologie (Chantilly, 1980)* (Paris, 1983), pp. 133–34. On Ricci's attempts to distinguish between ancient Confucianism and Neo-Confucianism see John D. Young, "Original Confucianism Versus Neo-Confucianism: Matteo Ricci's Chinese Writings," *Actes du XXIXe Congrés International des Orientalistes, Paris, Juillet 1973* (Paris, 1977), pp. 372–77.

The Chinese, they allege, do not pray to the dead or expect anything from them. Setting food out is simply a means of honoring their departed ancestors and is practiced primarily out of filial piety and as an example to children and unlearned adults. The ceremonies in honor of Confucius, held each month in temples built for that purpose in each major city, are similarly explained by the Jesuits as simply a way of showing honor and gratitude to the man whose teachings they follow, and not worship of, or prayer to, him.[507] All this is correct, but it is not the whole story. While the inculcation of social and ethical values may have been the primary goal of the sacrifices for many Ming scholar-officials, most Chinese and many literati as well still believed that spirits existed and could aid or harm the living in relation to their diligence in performing the sacrifices at the regularly appointed times.

While the image of Confucianism presented by the Jesuits is somewhat biased and in places confusing, it is in general surprisingly accurate. Try as they may to make Confucianism appear a rational moral philosophy, they are nevertheless forced to admit the existence of a speculative metaphysics and a rather elaborate program of religious sacrifices to a host of spirits and ancestors. Intentionally or not, the Jesuits' image of the literati reveals the unmistakably religious aspects of Confucianism. They correctly observe that most Chinese conceive of Heaven (*t'ien*) as a personal power, despite the efforts of many scholars to make it an impersonal force. They also detect the non-Confucian source of some Neo-Confucian metaphysical doctrines, and they recognize the importance of sacrifice to the spirits in the Confucian system even while they attempt to minimize its spiritual significance by stressing its social and ethical purposes. Jesuit writers during the latter half of the century would provide European readers with much more detail about Confucius and Confucianism, but the growing concern for defending their position in the Rites Controversy would also produce some distortions not seriously present in works written during the first half of the century.

While the Jesuits tried to minimize the religious and superstitious practices of the Confucians, they, in contrast, sought to maximize the image of the Buddhists as benighted idolators. A striking change in vocabulary occurs in the Jesuit literature when the authors finish with the Confucians and turn to the Buddhists. Almost invariably they refer to the Buddhists as idolators and seldom speak of them except in derogatory terms. Introducing his remarks on Buddhism in the *Atlas,* for example, Martini writes: "The second sect is that of the idolators, which they call xekiao [*shih chia*]: this plague and contagion contaminated China a few years after the birth of Christ."[508]

---

[507] For example see Trigault in Gallagher (trans.), *op. cit.* (n. 38), pp. 96–97, and Semedo, *op. cit.* (n. 9), pp. 86–87. See our pl. 309.

[508] *Op. cit.* (n. 44), p. 10.

As indicated by Martini's statement, the Jesuits were aware of the Indian origin of Buddhism; they date its entrance into China in A.D. 63 or 65.[509] Trigault concludes that Buddhism had borrowed many of its tenets from the West and perhaps even from Christianity. He observes that the Chinese envoys were sent to India during the time of St. Thomas' and St. Bartholomew's Christian mission there. Perhaps the Chinese had heard reports about the Christian gospel, only to have their legates return with a false and idolatrous distortion instead of the true gospel. Buddhists, he reports, recognize only four elements, like the ancient Western philosophers and unlike the Chinese. He thinks their belief in the transmigration of souls resembles Pythagorean notions. He refers to the same three-headed image earlier mentioned by Mendoza as a possible depiction of the Christian Trinity. Buddhists, he notes, believe in heaven and hell. The celibate Buddhist clergy also suggests Christian antecedents to Trigault, and he observes that some Buddhist rites and ceremonies appear to be similar to those of his own church.[510] Most of the Jesuits are convinced that Buddhism's popularity in China is continuously declining, although Trigault seems to detect a resurgence in his day.[511]

The Jesuits' presentation of Chinese Buddhist thought is more confusing than their portrayal of Confucian teachings. They fail to distinguish properly between the various Buddhist sects and instead present a conglomeration of Buddhist mythology, popular religious practices, and serious Buddhist philosophy. A few important aspects of Buddhist thought, however, emerge from this mélange. Semedo, for example, distinguishes between what he calls an "exterior way" and an "interior way."[512] Most Buddhists follow the "exterior way," and most of what Longobardo, Pantoja, Trigault, and the others write was descriptive of that sort of Buddhism. Crucial to this "exterior way" is the belief that one's actions will be rewarded or punished after death and a belief in the transmigration of souls. Semedo reports the teaching that the soul after death passes to one of the many Buddhist hells to be purged of its sins. After traveling through a series

[509] For example, Semedo, *op. cit.* (n. 9), p. 88.

[510] Gallagher (trans.), *op. cit.* (n. 38), pp. 98–99.

[511] *Ibid.*, pp. 99–100, 101. On the condition of Buddhism under the Ming see C. Eliot, *Hinduism and Buddhism* (3 vols.; London, 1954), III, 274–79. The Wan-li emperor (r. 1573–1620) declared that Buddhism and Confucianism are like the two wings of a bird, each is useless without the other. See also Ch'en, *op. cit.* (n. 473), pp. 434–49.

[512] *Op. cit.* (n. 9), pp. 88–91. "Exterior" may refer vaguely to popular Mahayana Buddhism and "interior" to the earlier Hinayana form imported into China from India. In south China the Buddhists generally followed the Hinayana with its emphasis on wisdom and learning; in the north the Buddhists stressed faith and external worship. See K. K. S. Ch'en, *Buddhism: The Light of Asia* (Woodbury, N.Y., 1968), chap. vii. Or it may be that the Jesuits are merely distinguishing between the ("exterior") Buddhism of the populace and that of learned priests and monks. See H. de Lubac, *La rencontre du Bouddhisme et de l'Occident* (Paris, 1954), p. 84. Again, "exterior" may refer to the popular Pure Land sect and "interior" to Ch'an or Meditation sect Buddhism.

of nine hells it is reborn in this world, its condition depending on the virtue accumulated during its previous existence.[513] Pantoja describes some of the Chinese pictures of the Buddhist hells.[514] Trigault mentions "many worlds" in which the souls of the dead are reborn.[515] The Jesuits have little to say about Buddhist ethics beyond observing that followers eat no flesh and drink no wine. Trigault thinks these rules are very poorly kept, and that infractions are easily atoned for by almsgiving.[516]

The wiser Buddhists, Semedo asserts, follow an "interior way." They believe that the entire universe is composed of a single substance which is molded into the many particular existing things; like wax, it may be given many different shapes. The goal of a devout Buddhist, therefore, is to contemplate this first principle. Practitioners of the "interior way" divide all men into ten classes according to the degree of enlightenment they have attained. Four classes are good; six are evil, and for each of these there is a hell characterized by a specific sin. Rebirth, either in one of the hells or in some other condition, happens in this world only. Men who choose to live in such a way that they are ethically indistinguishable from animals have, in short, been reborn as animals.[517]

Buddhism had an established and celibate priesthood, which the Christian priests describe in unflattering detail. The Buddhist priests, called "bonzes" or "osciami" (*ho-shang-men*) by the Chinese, are, according to the Jesuits, recruited from the dregs of Chinese society. Most of them grew up in monasteries into which they had been sold as slaves by their parents. "Not a single one of them," writes Trigault, "could ever have elected of his own will to join this vile class of cenobites as a means of leading a holy life."[518] Consequently, the Jesuits assert, the Buddhist priests are indolent and unlearned. Most of them live in monasteries, although some are hermits who live in the mountains where they subject themselves to all manner of privations and hardships. Many monks, whom the Jesuits call vagabonds and thieves, also roam the countryside begging for their sustenance. The monks shave their heads and beards, wear distinctive clothing, abstain from eating flesh, and live celibately. The Jesuits assert, however, that even the extremely severe punishments inflicted upon them for fornication fail to keep them chaste. Of the early Jesuit writers, only Semedo manages to say a good word for them. Despite their many failings, he writes, "the greater part of these . . . *Sectaries,* is not scandalous; but very patient, meek, and humble; whether it is from the habit, which humbleth them; or from the little esteem that is made of them, which keepeth them under." Although

[513] *Op. cit.* (n. 9), p. 90.
[514] Pantoja, *loc. cit.* (n. 39), p. 381. *Cf.* our pl. 333.
[515] Gallagher (trans.), *op. cit.* (n. 38), p. 99.
[516] *Ibid.*
[517] *Op. cit.* (n. 9), pp. 90–91.
[518] Gallagher (trans.), *op. cit.* (n. 38), p. 100.

the Chinese frequently discuss the low morals of the Buddhist monks, Semedo says that he heard only two bad reports about them during his twenty-two years in China.[519]

The Jesuits report that each monastery is ruled by a single governor, who at death passes on his position to a previously chosen protégé. Aside from these governors there is no hierarchy. Semedo further notes that the Buddhists are under the jurisdiction of the Board of Rites and receive imperial subsidies.[520] Each monastery has its own temple. The monks usually rent rooms to travelers and to people interested in studying Buddhist beliefs. As a result, writes Trigault, the monasteries "look more like large and noisy hotels, where people convene to spend time in idol worship or in learning the doctrines of this iniquitous cult."[521] The monks also conduct ritualistic services and at stated occasions pray for the dead or for deliverance from fires, storms, and other misfortunes. Some of the services are sung very much like the Gregorian chants of European churches. While most of the Jesuits insist that only eunuchs, women, and the very lowest classes pay serious attention to the Buddhists, they nevertheless admit that Chinese of all classes hire the monks for funerals. While the Jesuits did not generally attempt to distinguish among the various Buddhist sects, Semedo includes a brief discussion of the "Pe Lien Kiao" (*Pai-lien-chiao*), or the notorious White Lotus Society. This, he reports, is a proscribed sect because of its political purposes, among them the overthrow of the dynasty. He briefly sketches the 1622 White Lotus uprising in Shantung Province and its suppression, adding that the society still retains many adherents.[522]

The Taoists, or as some Europeans called them, the "Epicureans," are the third sect described by the Jesuits. They receive even less attention than the Buddhists. During the first half of the seventeenth century only Trigault, Semedo, and Martini effectively distinguish Taoism from Buddhism or from a more generalized popular religion. Many of the same accusations hurled against Buddhist monks are repeated against the Taoists: they are described as ignorant, as immoral, and as having been sold as slaves into the Taoist temples. Trigault observes that Taoist priests let their hair grow long like other Chinese and that they wear a distinctive wooden skull cap.[523] Hermits and those who live in temples remain unmarried, but many Taoist priests marry and live with their families. Other Taoist priests pretend to be magicians and fortune-tellers. Cleansing homes and buildings of evil spirits,

---

[519] *Op. cit.* (n. 9), pp. 89–90. Semedo calls the monks "bonzes," as do many other Jesuit writers. See our pls. 336 and 337.

[520] Semedo, *op. cit.* (n. 9), pp. 88–89. See also Yang, *op. cit.* (n. 495), pp. 281–82.

[521] Gallagher (trans.), *op. cit.* (n. 38), p. 101. For a typical temple and pagoda see our pl. 338.

[522] *Op. cit.* (n. 9), pp. 91–92. The White Lotus Society originated in the first half of the twelfth century as an offshoot of T'ien-t'ai Buddhism. It remained a center of political protest until well into the nineteenth century. *Cf.* Overmeyer, *op. cit.* (n. 495), p. 103.

[523] Gallagher (trans.), *op. cit.* (n. 38), p. 102.

calling down rain, and conducting funerals seem to be their most important functions. Unlike the Buddhists, the Taoists are said to have a national organization, at the head of which stands a hereditary high priest maintained in Peking by the emperor. This high priest is much honored by the emperor and has access to the private apartments of the palace in order to drive demons from them.[524] The Jesuits observe that Taoist priests also live at the temples to Heaven and Earth and assist the emperor in his sacrifices there.

Among the host of idols which the Taoists worship, they honor most one who is the supreme god, called the Lord of Heaven, whom they envision in corporeal form. Trigault claims that they also call him "Ciam." He relates a story of how "Ciam" usurped the heavenly throne from "Leu," his predecessor, by inviting him to dinner and stealing off on "Leu's" white dragon while his guest was dining. In Trigault's words: "And so these poor people now admit that they are venerating a false lord, a usurper, and a tyrant."[525] Next in dignity below the Lord of Heaven is a trinity of gods, one of which was the reputed founder of the sect, Lao Tzu, supposedly a contemporary of Confucius. His eighty-year gestation period is in many of the European accounts. Taoists, according to the Jesuit writers, also believe in a heaven and hell where punishment and reward are meted out to the deceased in accord with their merits. This and many other aspects of Taoism demonstrate the influence of Buddhism on Taoist thought. On the other hand, most of the Jesuit writers report that the highest good to the Taoists is pleasure, and that they seek, therefore, to prolong this life as long as possible because there is no pleasure after death—hence the epithet Epicurean. The Jesuits nowhere attempt to resolve the apparent contradiction between the search for pleasure in this life and the belief in heaven and hell. They report, however, that the Taoist heaven is a place in which people enjoy physical pleasure and to which they ascend in both body and soul. Taoist temples contain the images of many saints who had been taken directly from this life into heaven. Trigault mentions the use of certain exercises, postures, prayers, and medicines to prolong life or to attain heaven.[526]

In addition to the native Chinese religions and Buddhism, which they

---

[524] "The so-called Taoist pope, Chang T'ien-shih, may have high religious or magical prestige derived from assumed ability, for example, to make rain or to harness evil spirits, but he commands no organizational subordination from Taoists or Taoist temples in different parts of the country" (Yang, *op. cit.* [n. 495], p. 281).

[525] Gallagher (trans.), *op. cit.* (n. 38), p. 102. The story related here seems to be a popularized version of the rivalry between two famous Taoists, Liu Yüan-jan (1350–1432) and Chang Yü-ch'u (1361–1410). Chang was the forty-third Taoist Master of Heaven, a position hereditary in the Chang family. Liu is the family name of the Han emperors. See Giuliano Bertuccioli, "Matteo Ricci and Taoism," *International Symposium on Chinese-Western Cultural Interchange in Commemoration of the Four Hundredth Anniversary of the Arrival of Matteo Ricci, S.J., in China* (Taipei, 1983), pp. 41–49.

[526] Gallagher (trans.), *op. cit.* (n. 38), p. 103. Also see Semedo, *op. cit.* (n. 9), pp. 87–88; and Martini, *op. cit.* (n. 44), p. 10. Cf. J. Dehergne, S.J., "Les historiens jésuites du Taoisme," in *Actes du Colloque International de Sinologie (Chantilly, 1974)* (Paris, 1976), pp. 59–67.

recognize as being of foreign origin, the Jesuits also report the existence of Jewish and Muslim communities in China and advance evidence for an earlier Christian presence. Muslims remain quite numerous, according to Trigault, but are still regarded as outsiders by the Chinese. Apart from not eating pork, they remember little of Islamic doctrine and practice. They usually renounce their faith if they pass the civil service examinations.[527] Semedo adds that they do not intermarry with Chinese and that educated Muslims usually stop at the *chü-jen* degree. He dates their entrance into China at about A.D. 940 when they were invited in by an emperor to help suppress a rebellion.[528] Both Trigault and Semedo comment on the Jesuits' contacts with Chinese Jews.[529] Trigault describes Ricci's visit with a Jew in Peking, and Semedo reports on Father Giulio Aleni's visit with the Jews of K'aifeng.[530] Both report that Judaism is no longer clearly understood or faithfully practiced by its adherents in China. In addition to Luís' and Semedo's descriptions of the Nestorian monument and everyone's discussion of St. Thomas' reported mission to the Chinese, there are several accounts by the Jesuits of other evidences for an earlier Christian presence in China: the number ten (a cross [+]) on tombstones, and people reputedly crossing themselves without knowing why.[531] Several writers also mention Marco Polo's claim that there were many Christians in China during the Mongol period.[532] Martini, for example, found abundant evidence of a Christian presence in Chang-chou, Fukien Province.[533]

The Jesuits realize that the three Chinese religious groups (*san-chiao*) do not make exclusive claims for themselves or work for one another's destruction. They understand that the emperors maintain each of them with public funds and that each is under the jurisdiction of the Board of Rites. The Chinese do not consider the three sects mutually exclusive or even contradictory; they select elements from each to suit their convenience. The Jesuits note that the Confucian literati almost always have Buddhist and Taoist priests at their funerals. In fact, most Chinese consider the three cults to be complementary. Semedo states this most clearly:

> The *Litterati* of the first *Sect,* imitating Heaven and Earth, apply all to the government of the Kingdome; of their families; and of their persons; only in this life; and

[527] Gallagher (trans.), *op. cit.* (n. 38), pp. 106–7.

[528] *Op. cit.* (n. 9), pp. 152–53. The T'ang rulers recruited Muslim soldiers during the An Lushan rebellion (753–63). See Chen, *op. cit.* (n. 118), pp. 97–98, and Samuel Couling, *The Encyclopedia Sinica* (London, 1917), pp. 378–79.

[529] Gallagher (trans.), *op. cit.* (n. 38), pp. 107–10; Semedo, *op. cit.* (n. 9), pp. 153–54.

[530] Cf. J. Dehergne and D. D. Leslie, *Juifs du Chine à travers la correspondance inédite des Jesuites du dix-huitième siècle* (Rome and Paris, 1980), pp. 11–13, 38–39.

[531] See, for example, Trigault in Gallagher (trans.), *op. cit.* (n. 38), pp. 110–14, and Semedo, *op. cit.* (n. 9), pp. 154–65.

[532] On the Christians of China in Marco Polo's book, see L. Olschki, *Marco Polo's Asia* (Berkeley, 1960), pp. 223–32.

[533] *Op. cit.* (n. 44), pp. 152–53.

after that pretend to nothing. The *Tausi* [Taoists] of the second *Sect,* without any regard to their families or the government, treate only of the body. The disciples of *Xaca* [Buddhists] of the third *Sect,* without any regard to the body, treate only of the Spirit, internal peace, and quiet of conscience.[534]

Although oversimplified, Semedo's statement succinctly reflects the eclectic nature of Chinese religion.

Trigault suggests that the attempt to believe in all three sects inevitably leads to atheism: "In believing that they can honor all three laws at the same time, they find themselves without any law at all, because they do not sincerely follow any one of them."[535] Among the common people, however, the attempt to follow all three ways certainly did not result in atheism. It produced instead a conglomeration of gods and beliefs not unlike that described by the European travelers. The Jesuits are aghast at the proliferation of idols among the people: not only in temples, but in houses, shops, streets, and ships. The people blindly follow a multitude of superstitious rites. In addition to practicing ancestor worship and spirit worship, they believe in the existence of demons that have to be periodically driven out of their homes and public buildings. They are addicted to fortune-telling, and the Jesuits describe many ways in which divination was accomplished. Extremely prevalent is the belief in lucky and unlucky days. The Chinese consult almanacs to determine the appropriate day for marriages, funerals, building homes, beginning journeys, and almost every imaginable undertaking. And the empire abounds with magicians, astrologers, fortune-tellers, and the like, who, for a fee, will perform the necessary rituals and supply the desired information or forecast future events. Before erecting public buildings or houses, "geologists" are consulted who determine whether or not the site is fortunate, which directions the doors or windows should face, and where trees should be planted or walls raised. Two superstitious practices are a virtual mania among the Chinese, affecting all classes of society. These are the search for a chemical to turn base metals into silver and the search for a potion of immortality. Fortunes are squandered in search of these, and imposters, who claim to have found the secrets, never lack an audience.

In fact, the popular religion of the Chinese was a combination of beliefs taken from each of the three authorized cults and from the traditional animism of the distant past. No one of the cults remained untainted; many doctrines of the Buddhists and Taoists had infiltrated the orthodox Confucianism of the seventeenth century, and Confucian ethics in return permeated both Taoism and Buddhism. Buddhism and Taoism also borrowed heavily from each other. The sharp distinctions which the Jesuits would have liked to make, therefore, especially between the Confucians and the other two sects,

[534] *Op. cit.* (n. 9), p. 91. On the *san-chiao* tradition see Overmeyer, *op. cit.* (n. 495), pp. 133–34. *Cf.* our pl. 333.
[535] Gallagher (trans.), *op. cit.* (n. 38), p. 105.

simply did not exist. The Jesuits were obliged to note what they called superstitious rites in Confucianism, and the presence of the Confucian ethic in the other despised sects. Despite their efforts to distinguish between the cults, therefore, the image of Chinese religion and philosophy developed by the Jesuits, while inaccurate in some details and certainly biased in favor of the literati, nevertheless approximated actual conditions in seventeenth-century China.

CHAPTER XXI

China: The Early Ch'ing Dynasty

Founded early in the seventeenth century, contemporary with the Thirty Years' War in Europe, the Ch'ing dynasty ruled China from 1644 to 1911. The Manchu Conquest and the subsequent civil wars tore China apart from the early 1640's to 1683. The establishment subsequently of domestic peace and internal unity led to a century of economic prosperity and sustained population growth. As the last phase of China's *ancien régime,* the Ch'ing period included both the zenith and the nadir of the traditional Chinese imperial system. While acting as jealous guardians of China's established institutions and values, by 1800 the Manchus had laboriously extended China's effective jurisdiction over a geographical area far larger than it controlled at any earlier (or later) period. From Peking the Manchus painstakingly welded the peoples of China's internal frontiers to the imperial standard and to the Chinese way of life. After adopting intact the Ming system, the Manchus undertook a systematic program of sinicization for themselves and the other non–Han peoples of their extensive empire.

The new rulers endorsed the social and political relationships of the Chinese past and elevated to official orthodoxy the teachings of the Later Sung school of Neo-Confucianism. While preserving and inculcating a few traits and customs of their own Manchu heritage, the Ch'ing dynasts honored Confucianism and cultivated traditional Chinese literature, calligraphy, painting, and social practices. From K'ang-hsi's majority (1667) onward the political hierarchy was increasingly dominated by key Chinese officials and scholars. Established Chinese economic and social institutions likewise matured with the benevolent tutelage of the court and through the interregional cooperation and economic integration encouraged by the Ch'ing. While Peking remained the official center of government, voluntary associations of merchants and craftsmen brought new life and stimulation to the major cities and prospering towns of central China. In the favorable climate of a rising standard of living, material culture and education leisurely advanced, along with a broader range of intellectual and artistic activities that were cultivated especially by the merchant-princes of the lower Yangtze.[1]

To the Europeans, the China ruled by the Ch'ing continued in many ways to be but a more rational and better administered edition of the Ming. Since some of the missionaries personally experienced the dynastic change, they and their successors were constantly on the lookout for portents which might encourage or hinder their own activities. The conquest itself is a separate subject in the European literature. But much of what the Europeans later report concentrates on the early Ch'ing as a continuation of or as a departure from the Ming system, and duplicates or merely extends or modifies the remarks of the earlier observers—in a reflection of what was actually taking place in China itself. As a consequence there is a current quality about the later reports that is not so prevalent in those of the first half of the century.

I

THE MANCHU CONQUEST

When news about the Manchu Conquest arrived in Europe at mid-century, earlier images of China as a remote and changeless empire were at least partially replaced by those of a more dynamic China which was enduring a most disruptive revolution—a China from which countless innovations and new personalities would soon emerge. The reports of the Manchu Conquest seemed dramatically to move China into the European awareness, and for a time, informed Europeans seemed conscious of living in the same world with the Chinese.[2] Announcements of the Manchu invasions of north China began to appear in print in Europe during the 1620's, or shortly after their commencement. Semedo also reported mounting troubles on China's northern frontier. Some brief notices of the conquest also appeared in the annual Jesuit letters and in the reports of trading companies. The *Hollandtsche mercurius* on July 22, 1650, carried a brief note "confirming the calamities of the ingenious China," and in November, 1653, observed that "the Tartar [Manchu] still holds the once-splendid China partially under his power."[3]

---

[1] Based on Ho Ping-ti, "The Significance of the Ch'ing Period in Chinese History," *Journal of Asian Studies*, XXVI (1967), 189–95.

[2] For a more detailed discussion of the reporting of the conquest in Europe see E. Van Kley, "News from China: Seventeenth-Century European Notices of the Manchu Conquest," *Journal of Modern History*, XLV, No. 4 (December, 1973), pp. 561–82.

[3] *Hollandtsche mercurius*, I, 25, and IV, 94.

The Polish Jesuit Michael Boym arrived at Venice in 1652 carrying an appeal from the Ming empress for European aid against the Manchus. She and several members of her family and of the Southern Ming court had accepted Christianity.[4] In 1653 Boym's book was published. It describes the Jesuit mission in China and the most recent Christian successes at the Ming pretender's court.[5] It also contains a brief history of the conquest, although for the most part it ignores the Manchus. Boym apparently assumed that the Ming refugee Chu Yu-lang (1623–62; reign title: Yung-li) was indeed still emperor of China and would perpetuate the Ming line.

More detailed information about the Manchu Conquest arrived in 1654 with Father Martino Martini, who had been sent to Rome by the Jesuits in China to persuade the pope to reverse his 1654 condemnation of certain Jesuit accommodation practices. He wrote his *De bello tartarico* during the homeward voyage and arranged for its publication soon after his arrival in Europe in August, 1653.[6] The conquest was also mentioned in a German newssheet called *Zeiting auss der newen Welt* (Augsburg, 1654); it reported Martini's arrival and the state of the Jesuit mission in China. The *Hollandtsche mercurius* of August, 1654, carried a much longer account of the conquest that appears to have come primarily from Martini, although some parts of it also owe a debt to Boym's report.

The *De bello tartarico* became the most authoritative and best-known description of the conquest. In it Martini traces the background of hostility between the Chinese and the tribes north of the Great Wall: the thirteenth-century Mongol conquest and the resulting Yuan dynasty, the Ming restoration of 1368, and the late Ming's growing difficulty with the Manchus. He also discusses the Manchu people, as well as their customs, government, and military techniques. He traces the growth of Manchu power in the northeast and the careers of its leaders—Nurhachi (1559–1626), Abahai (1592–1643), and Dorgon (1612–50). Then Martini analyzes the internal problems of the late Ming: oppressive taxation, corruption, arbitrary misuse of power by court eunuchs, and the personal weakness and avarice of the Ch'ung-chen emperor (1628–44). Imperial greediness and mismanagement

[4] *Ibid.*, IV, 4. See also Robert Chabrié, *Michel Boym, Jésuite Polonais et la fin des Ming en Chine (1646–1662)* (Paris, 1933), pp. 90–114.

[5] *Sehr wehrte und angenehme newe Zeitung von der Bekehrung zum catholischen Glauben desz. jungen Königs in China und anderer furstl. Personen und von der Legation desz. Ehrw. P. Michaelis Bouyn der Societet Jesu Priestern polnischer Nation zu ihrer Päbstl. Heyligkeit nach Rohm . . .* (Augsburg, 1653). We have used the enlarged French edition of 1654: *Briefe relation de la notable conversion des personnes royales & de l'estat de la religion Chrestienne en la Chine . . .* (Paris, 1654). See Streit, V, 793–95, for bibliography. For a discussion of Boym's works see B. Szczesniak, "The Writings of Michael Boym," *Monumenta Serica*, XIV (1949–55), 481–538. Also see above, pp. 526, 538–39. On the conversion episode in the context of late Ming resistance see Lynn A. Struve, *The Southern Ming* (New Haven, 1984), pp. 139–66 and especially n. 17, pp. 241–42.

[6] For Martini's publications see above, pp. 379–81, 525–27. On Martini's activities in Europe and the *De bello tartarico* see D. Mungello, *Curious Land: Jesuit Accommodation and the Origins of Sinology* (Stuttgart, 1985), pp. 106–16.

of public affairs, he explains, alienated Manchu chieftains as well as Chinese officials and subjects.[7] The results were both unrest on the frontier and rebellion at home. Rebels led by Li Tzu-ch'eng (1605[?]–45) finally topple the dynasty.[8] As Li's army, aided by traitors within the capital, enters Peking, the emperor, according to Martini, stabs to death his young daughter, writes a letter in his own blood accusing high officials of treason, and then hangs himself with his garter from a plum tree in the palace garden. The empress, several imperial concubines, and loyal officials follow suit.[9] The victorious Li Tzu-ch'eng then crowns himself emperor and attempts to gain the submission of the remaining Ming military forces. Wu San-kuei (1612–78), however, who commanded the largest Chinese army on the northern frontier, refuses to submit despite the fact that his father is a hostage in Li's court.[10] Whether motivated by loyalty and a desire to revenge the Ming emperor's death or by personal enmity toward Li, Wu makes a pact with the Manchus, who then march on Peking. Li flees to the northwest; the Manchus stay and establish a new dynasty. Martini describes the conquest of the rest of China, city by city and province by province, up to 1651, in which year he left the country.

Martini obviously thought the Manchu Conquest was an event of world-historical significance, and he conveyed to his readers a deep sense of the tragedy involved in the event. In contrast to Boym, he insists that the Ch'ung-chen emperor was the last Ming ruler because he was the last to govern all of China.[11] About Wu San-kuei's pact with the Manchus, Martini says: "Wu San-kuei, eager for revenge, admitted all they desired, unaware, as the Chinese say, that he let tigers into the empire to drive out the dogs."[12]

---

[7] *De bello tartarico historia: in qua, quo pacto tartari hac nostra aetate sinicum imperium invaserint, ac fere totum occuparint narratur: eorumque mores breviter describuntur* (Antwerp, 1654), pp. 24–25, 51–56. On the Ming-Manchu confrontation *cf.* F. Wakeman, *The Great Enterprise* (2 vols.; Berkeley, 1985), I, chaps. i–iii.

[8] For a history of Li Tzu-ch'eng and other Chinese rebels see J. B. Parsons, *The Peasant Rebellions of the Late Ming Dynasty* (Tucson, 1970), chaps. iv–v.

[9] *Op. cit.* (n. 7), pp. 70–71. Martini's description of the details surrounding the fall of Peking is not entirely accurate. There were so many conflicting stories and rumors circulating at the time that it was probably impossible for Martini to learn the truth. It appears, however, that the emperor did not kill his fifteen-year-old daughter, although he intended to do so. He lost heart after cutting off her left arm; she survived until 1645. The emperor's last letter was not written in his own blood. It was, however, presumably written on the sleeves of his gown. Martini appears to have accurately described the general content of the letter. According to Martini, Li later had the emperor's body cut into small pieces. In fact, however, it appears that Li had the emperor and empress ceremonially buried in their imperial robes. See A. W. Hummel (ed.), *Eminent Chinese of the Ch'ing Period (1644–1912)* (Washington, D.C., 1943), p. 192; Min-sun Chen, "Three Contemporary Western Sources on the History of the Late Ming and the Manchu Conquest of China" (Ph.D. diss., Dept. of History, University of Chicago, 1971), pp. 186–87; and Wakeman, *op. cit.* (n. 7), I, 257–66. Wakeman avers (p. 266) that the emperor did not leave the suicide note to which many contemporary annalists make reference.

[10] On Li's efforts to use Wu Hsiang to exert pressure on his son see Parsons, *op. cit.* (n. 8), pp. 138–40.

[11] *Op. cit.* (n. 7), p. 71.

[12] *Ibid.*, p. 75. *Cf.* Parsons, *op. cit.* (n. 8), pp. 140–41.

Martini depicts the conquest as the tragic fall of the Chinese empire to foreign conquerors. He does not, however, consider it the fall of civilization to barbarism as did some of his contemporaries in Europe. True, he describes some barbarous Manchu customs—for example, the burning of wives, servants, and animals with the body of a deceased prince—but he quickly adds that they relinquished this custom once they ruled China.[13] He provides abundant evidence for the sinicization of the Manchus prior to the conquest. As Martini sees it, the Manchus at the time of the conquest were no longer barbarians.

His description of Manchu rule, once it is established in Peking, makes the Ch'ing appear like a traditional Chinese dynasty. He reports that they justify their continued presence in China on the grounds that there are still rebels to be driven out of the empire; Li Tzu-ch'eng is still alive![14] He recounts the six-year-old Shun-chih emperor's (r. 1644–61) speech from the throne in 1644 and the inauguration of Manchu government in adulatory terms. The whole court, he asserts, was astounded by the young emperor's moderation and wisdom, while his uncle Dorgon's humane government impressed Chinese officials and induced many of them to support the new dynasty.[15]

Not that the Manchu armies were so gentle. Martini provides ample evidence for the destruction and slaughter that accompanied the conquest. The plundering of Canton after its capture in 1650, for example, he describes as an act of barbarous cruelty: "On the next day (November 24) they really began to plunder the city, and the ravaging continued until the fifth of December, in which children, women, and anyone in the way were most cruelly slain; and only one cry was heard, 'Kill, kill these barbarous rebels.'"[16] But where cruelty in battle was concerned, the Manchus had plenty of company. Li Tzu-ch'eng's seizure of Peking in 1644 was as bloody and destructive as any Manchu victory. For wanton cruelty and slaughter no one in Martini's account compares with Li's fellow rebel, Chang Hsien-chung (1605–47), who tyrannized Szechwan between 1644 and 1647. His career seems an almost continuous succession of mass murders, culminating in the slaughter of six hundred thousand inhabitants at Cheng-tu in 1646.[17] The Ch'ung-chen emperor, too, could be callously inhumane. Martini reports that he personally ordered the dikes above K'aifeng breached in order to disrupt Li Tzu-ch'eng's siege of the city in 1641. The siege was lifted and Li's

[13]*Op. cit.* (n. 7), p. 26.
[14]*Ibid.*, pp. 77–78.
[15]*Ibid.*, pp. 83–84.
[16]*Ibid.*, pp. 134–35. Cf. the Manchu sack of Chiating in August, 1645, as described in J. Dennerline, *The Chia-ting Loyalists: Confucian Leadership and Social Change in Seventeenth-Century China* (New Haven, 1981), pp. 1–2.
[17]Martini, *op. cit.* (n. 7), pp. 139–53. For Gabriel de Magalhães' unpublished account of Chang's efforts to establish a regime of his own in Szechwan see Parsons, *op. cit.* (n. 8), pp. 170–71.

troops were routed, but most of K'aifeng's already starving residents were drowned.[18]

Massive, disruptive changes such as the Manchu Conquest naturally cry out for explanation. Martini, like most others who have written about it, tried to find reasons for Ming failure and Manchu success. His analysis is generally perceptive and accurate, although it echoes his familiarity with traditional Chinese explanations. As Martini describes it, a significant increase in Manchu strength and restiveness along the frontier in the early years of the century coincided with the Wan-li court's general mismanagement of Mongol and Manchu relations. A series of injustices against the Manchus ensued, which provoked their first raid south of the wall in 1616, their seizure of Liaoyang, and their assumption of the imperial title in 1618.[19] According to Martini, the court frequently treated Chinese officials and generals as shabbily as it treated the Manchus. Many were alienated and during the Ch'ung-chen period threw in their lot with the growing number of bandit or rebel gangs in the empire. Famine further swelled their numbers. Martini concludes that the emperor's personal greediness and his heavy taxes aggravated the situation.[20] But far more important than the emperor's personal failings as a source of governmental mismanagement is the almost unrestrained power held by the court eunuchs.[21] All these factors, Martini argues, fanned popular discontent, swelled the ranks of rebel bands such as those led by Li Tzu-ch'eng and Chang Hsien-chung, and alienated the treasonous officials who opened Peking to Li's army in 1644.

Despite his apparent debt to official historiography, Martini, the Christian missionary, posits still another interpretation of the Manchu triumph. He thinks it significant that the Manchu prince Nurhachi invaded the Liaotung Peninsula and assumed the imperial title in the same year, 1618, in which the Wan-li emperor (1573–1620) began to persecute Christian missionaries:

I should like, nevertheless, briefly to touch on it here, so that we may admire Divine Providence, who raised sharp war against China at the time when they were neglecting Christian peace; and in the same year permitted the Tartars to sink their roots in the Chinese empire, from which they later grew so great that they uprooted the Ming family and subjugated almost the entire Chinese empire, while otherwise the Chinese thought utterly to uproot Christian truth: but as it ordinarily does, the Christian cause has through such persecution grown to so great a state that the church rejoices in it; and the Chinese, unless God comes to aid their distressed condition, have lost possession of their empire.[22]

[18] *Op. cit.* (n. 7), pp. 60–61. Recent scholarship avers that both sides were responsible for cutting the dikes. See Parsons, *op. cit.* (n. 8), pp. 162–63, and, on the numbers drowned in K'aifeng, pp. 103–4.

[19] *Op. cit.* (n. 7), pp. 24–29.

[20] *Ibid.*, pp. 51–57.

[21] *Ibid.*, pp. 63–66.

[22] *Ibid.*, p. 30.

The Manchu Conquest, then, was God's punishment for the Wan-li emperor's persecution of Jesuit missionaries.

While Martini could not resist looking for God's purposes in the Manchu Conquest, he probably enjoyed a degree of detachment from the events not possible for a Chinese observer. However much he thinks the Chinese may have deserved it, Martini is obviously saddened by Ch'ung-chen's death and the fall of the Ming dynasty. He describes it as a catastrophe. On the other hand, he extolls the intelligent and humane government of the new Manchu rulers, and especially their gracious treatment of the missionaries. He foresees exciting possibilities in the new dynasty: "And perhaps God opened China to the Tartars in order to throw open for the Christian religion a way into furthest Tartary, hitherto unknown and inaccessible to us." [23]

Martini provided European readers with generally accurate details and with a remarkably balanced interpretation of the Manchu Conquest. [24] Later writers, whether they wished to emphasize the destructive war and the tragic collapse of the Ming dynasty or the vigorous and enlightened Manchu rulers, could find most of the necessary details in the *De bello tartarico*. It was also a very popular book. The Latin text went through seven editions, and it was translated into nine other European languages. Altogether at least twenty-five editions and translations appeared before the end of the century. [25] Some of the changes in these editions reflect the emphases of the publishers or editors: Gillis Janszoon Valckenier's 1660 Dutch edition, for example, is entitled *China Devastated by the Barbarous Tartar: Including the Dreadful Ruinous War Begun by the Tartars in the Empire of China*. [26] His 1661 Latin edition was entitled *An Elegant Exposition of the Empire of China Tyrannically Devastated and Ravaged by the Tartars*. [27] Valckenier faithfully reproduced the original text in his Latin edition, and his Dutch edition is an accurate translation of it. Only the titles and illustrations are new. Half of the plates in each edition depict destruction and bloodshed. [28] Three of the eleven, for example, illustrate the seventeen-page career of Chang Hsienchung. The poem which follows the title page of the Dutch edition adds to the impression of carnage and bloodshed; it is called "The Destruction of China by the Tartars."

Johann Nieuhof's 1665 account of the first Dutch embassy to the Manchu

[23] *Ibid.*, p. 137.

[24] For a detailed examination of the accuracy of the *De bello tartarico* see Chen, *op. cit.* (n. 9), pp. 146–230.

[25] For most of the editions, see Henri Cordier, *Bibliotheca sinica: Dictionnaire bibliographique des ouvrages relatifs a l'empire chinoise* (2d ed.; 5 vols.; New York, 1968), I, 623–27. See also Streit, V, 797–800, and above, pp. 525–26.

[26] *Het verwoest Sina, door den wreeden Tartar: vervaatende de schrickelijcke landt-verdervende oorlogh by de Tartar in't rijck van Sina aangevangen* (Amsterdam, 1660).

[27] *Regni sinensis a Tartaris tyrannice evastati depopulatique concinna enarratio* (Amsterdam, 1661).

[28] For an informative discussion of one of these engravings and its possible debt to a famous European prototype see Mungello, *op. cit.* (n. 6), pp. 110–14.

court in 1655–57 tends to reinforce the image of carnage and destruction.[29] The first part of Nieuhof's book recounts the embassy's journey from Canton to Peking and back; it conveys the impression that they were traveling through a devastated countryside. Nieuhof repeatedly describes the former grandeur of towns and cities that had been depopulated and reduced to rubble when he saw them. Concerning "Sanyuum" (Ch'ing-yuan) on the Pei River, for example, he reports:

In the recent war the Tartars, that rough people, miserably wrecked and demolished this town and almost reduced it to a rubble heap. This fate, to have been so pitiably and profanely devastated and demolished, like a second Troy, fell the lot of almost all excellent but small towns and their inhabitants, who did not accept the irresistible might of the Tartars.[30]

Again, describing "Vannungam" (Wan-an) on the Kan River, he writes: "The furious Tartar raged so dreadfully against this city in the recent war, and so pitiably mutilated it with the razing, destruction, and the burning of almost all of the prominent buildings, that it has retained little or nothing of its former ancient splendor whole and intact."[31] Even the people, Nieuhof concludes, showed scars of humiliation and conquest. He describes the coolies who pulled his boat upriver as pathetic slaves to the conquerors: "Here we saw, alas! to what a miserable and piteous condition the Chinese were reduced by the recent war: for in this towing they must serve the least Tartars as servile slaves; and without distinction between young and old, people must strain on the towline harder than beasts to pull their vessel against the current of the river."[32] In all of human history, he believes, few conquerors have been as ruthless as the Manchus: "The ancient Greeks and haughty Romans, who formerly subdued so much of the world, never injured their defeated and subjugated peoples with so much misery and cast down their eyes with such unbearable sorrows as these cruel and merciless Tartars."[33] Nevertheless, Nieuhof's firsthand description of the way the Manchu overlords shared power with Chinese officials in Peking does not depict the Chinese as helpless slaves. From his report it seems that the Chinese members of the Board of Rites were more influential than the Manchus in handling the Dutch request for frequent tributary missions and regular trade in Canton.[34] In other words, Nieuhof, like Martini, provides evidence for considerable continuity between the two dynasties. He in fact adds an

---

[29] *Het gezantschap der Neêrlandtsche Oost-Indische Compagnie aan den grooten tartarischen cham, den tegenwoordigen keizer van China . . .* (2 vols. in 1; Amsterdam, 1665). For bibliographic detail see above, pp. 483–84. For a further discussion of the book in this chapter, see below, p. 1685.

[30] Nieuhof, *op. cit.* (n. 29), I, 59.

[31] *Ibid.*, p. 78.

[32] *Ibid.*, p. 57.

[33] *Ibid.*, p. 58.

[34] *Ibid.*, pp. 165–67.

eyewitness account of how the new government operated. Nevertheless, he made the conquest in the Chinese countryside appear more destructive and oppressive than Martini had.

The second part of Nieuhof's book is a description of China based primarily on the works of Trigault, Semedo, and Martini but augmented by his personal observations. It contains a lengthy description of the Manchu Conquest which follows Martini's *De bello tartarico* very closely but which also contains some geographic descriptions taken primarily from Martini's *Atlas*.[35] Nieuhof, a Protestant, also omits the role of the Jesuits during the conquest as well as Martini's interpretation of the conquest as God's judgment on the Ming for its persecution of Christian missionaries.

Another major account of the Manchu Conquest appeared in 1670, this one by Juan Palafox y Mendoza, who held bishoprics in both Spain and Mexico and briefly served as viceroy of New Spain.[36] Palafox wrote his history of the conquest in Mexico from information sent to him from the Philippines. He never visited China. Nor does he appear to have borrowed from Martini; there are far too many differences in details and in emphases between the two. Palafox, for example, begins his account with the rebellion of Li Tzu-ch'eng and Chang Hsien-chung in 1640. He includes none of the background to the revolt related by Martini. He devotes more space than Martini, however, to the conquest of south China, especially to the campaigns against the Ming partisan and pirate Cheng Chih-lung (known to Europeans as Nicholas Iquan) (1604–61) and his son Cheng Ch'eng-kung (Koxinga) (1624–62). Finally he includes chapters on Manchu government, religion, customs, dress, military techniques, and manners. Palafox's account is considerably less reliable and accurate than Martini's.[37]

Palafox, too, considered the fall of the Ming dynasty an exceedingly important event—far more serious than a simple change in dynasties. He uses phrases such as "the destruction of this empire," "the Chinese empire has perished," and "the ruin of the whole state of China."[38] He thought the Ch'ung-chen emperor was one of the best ever to have governed China,

[35] *Ibid.*, II, pp. 181–253.

[36] We cite from the 1732 French edition, Juan Palafox y Mendoça, *Histoire de la conqueste de la Chine par les Tartares: contenant plusieurs choses remarquables touchant la religion les moeurs, & les coûtomes de ces deux nations* (Amsterdam, 1732), p. i. The first edition was entitled *Historia de la conquista de la China por el Tartaro, escrita por el Illustrissimo Senor Don Juan de Palafox y Mendoça, siendo Obispo de la Puebla de los Angeles, y Virrey de la Nueva-Espana y a su muerte Obispo de Osma* (Paris, 1670). Palafox's history was first translated into French in 1670, then into English in 1671. Each translation was reissued twice; see Cordier, *op. cit.* (n. 25), I, 627–28. See also above, pp. 356–57.

[37] For a discussion of the sources and an evaluation of Palafox's account, see Chen, *op. cit.* (n. 9), pp. 231–52. Koxinga is the latinized form of the Amoy-area pronunciation of Kuo-hsing yeh, or "Master of the [imperial] surname." The Ming emperor gave Cheng Ch'eng-kung the dynastic surname as an honor to Ch'eng-kung's father, Cheng Chih-lung.

[38] *Op. cit.* (n. 36), pp. 32, 33, 43.

even though he was served by corrupt and self-interested officials.[39] The popularity of rebels like Li and Chang, he suggests, resulted from the cruelty and mismanagement of these officials. Nevertheless he moralizes about how it is never permissible for subjects to rebel against their sovereign.[40]

Palafox's description of the Ch'ung-chen emperor's suicide is heavily dramatic—and long. What Martini describes in less than two small pages takes Palafox eight.[41] Martini describes the emperor's bloody letter to Li Tzu-ch'eng in eight lines; Boym summarizes it in two sentences. Palafox expands it to almost two pages of melodramatic monologue.[42] His final comments on the emperor's death exemplify the mood:

The emperor of China remained thus hanging from a tree. This prince who had been the idol of his people, at whose name alone so many millions of subjects trembled, the sovereign of more than a hundred million subjects, the monarch of a kingdom as large as all of Europe, he who counted his soldiers by millions and his tribute by hundreds of millions; finally the great emperor of China is hanged from a tree, and the empress his wife from another close by him. What a sight on those two tree trunks![43]

A great tragedy, surely not deserved by the Ch'ung-chen emperor. Nor, according to Palafox, was it God's judgment on the Ming for its mistreatment of Christian missionaries. Rather it was the result of slow deterioration and neglect:

For many years already, all the symptoms of mortal illness in the body of this great empire were recognized. But through a lax and too-imprudent negligence, which only served better to show the weakness of the government, the ailment was perceived only sufficiently to fear it; and it was not perceived sufficiently to bring forth remedies for it. . . . In short, the empire of China did not perish because of an ailment which was completely incurable, but solely because of an ailment which had not been treated.[44]

Palafox has no good words for Li Tzu-ch'eng. Still, like Martini, he seems to think that even Li's usurpation would have been better than the takeover by the Manchus. "It is true," he writes, "that the usurper had already become extremely powerful; but at least he was of Chinese birth, and all his soldiers were likewise Chinese."[45] Unlike Martini, he shows no sympathy for Wu San-kuei.

---

[39] *Ibid.*, pp. 2 and 28.
[40] *Ibid.*, p. 7.
[41] *Ibid.*, pp. 23–31.
[42] *Ibid.*, pp. 29–30; Martini, *op. cit.* (n. 7), p. 70; Boym, *op. cit.* (n. 5), p. 47.
[43] Palafox, *op. cit.* (n. 36), pp. 30–31.
[44] *Ibid.*
[45] *Ibid.*, p. 44.

If Palafox deplores the "fall of the Chinese empire," he nevertheless describes the Manchu successor state in very favorable terms. The conquerors certainly do not appear to be rapacious barbarians. He avers that the Manchu ruler, saddened by Ch'ung-chen's death, displays righteous anger against Li Tzu-ch'eng.[46] Like Martini, Palafox seems to admire the young Shun-chih emperor and the moderate character of the new Manchu government.[47] He also emphasizes the political and administrative continuity between the two dynasties.[48] Although he refers to such events as the pillage of Canton, Palafox's book probably contains less material on Manchu cruelty and destruction than Martini's; certainly less than Nieuhof's, although the Spaniard believed cruelty in battle to be the Manchus' most serious failing. To Palafox the most oppressive aspect of Manchu rule seems to have been the requirement that all Chinese cut their hair and wear the queue.[49]

When Palafox compares the Manchus to the Chinese, he seems to prefer the Manchus; they are not as effete or formal as the Chinese, and they are less hostile to foreigners. They are, he believes, more like Europeans, or like the ancient Romans.[50] He finds the Roman conquest of Carthage a more apt historical parallel to the Manchu Conquest than the burning of Troy or the barbarian invasions of the Roman Empire.[51] In short, Palafox thought the Chinese empire had been destroyed, but the Manchu empire that replaced it was just as good and perhaps better.

Brief descriptions of the conquest are also included in many of the Jesuit reports about the mission under the new dynasty, particularly in those published after 1647.[52] Most of these seem to have been based on Martini's account of the conquest, and they usually stress the continuity between the two dynasties. Johann Adam Schall's account (1665) is particularly interesting because it describes his personal experiences in Peking during Li Tzu-ch'eng's capture of the city, during the looting and burning when Li's armies fled, and during the first days of Manchu occupation.[53] His general interpretation of the events, however, does not differ significantly from Martini's. If anything, Schall seems more favorably inclined toward the Manchus, who were so kind to the Christian mission and who raised him to such high honor and influence.[54] His report appears to confirm Martini's optimism regarding the future of the mission under Manchu rule.

[46] *Ibid.*, pp. 38–42.
[47] *Ibid.*, pp. 66–69.
[48] For examples see *ibid.*, pp. 71, 367, 377–79.
[49] *Ibid.*, pp. 72–74 and 369. Almost everyone who wrote about the Manchu Conquest, from Martini on, described the fierce Chinese resistance to wearing the queue.
[50] *Ibid.*, pp. 222 and 331.
[51] *Ibid.*, pp. 352–56.
[52] See below, pp. 1676–84.
[53] *Historica narratio de initio et progressu missionis Societatis Jesu apud Chinensis* . . . (Vienna, 1665). For bibliography see above, p. 528.
[54] Schall, *Historica relatio de ortu et progressu fidei orthodoxae in regno chinensi per missionarios Societatis Jesu . . . 1581–1669* . . . (Ratisbon, 1672). pp. 178–96, 345–52.

Olfert Dapper's general description of China (1670) also contains an account of the Manchu Conquest.[55] It is primarily a condensation of Martini with some additions taken from Schall. Dapper also emphasizes the continuity between the Ming and the Ch'ing; the China of 1670 is essentially the same as that described earlier by Trigault and Semedo. In his historical sketch Dapper simply lists the Ch'ing ("Taising," or Great Ch'ing) as the latest Chinese dynasty.

The Dominican missionary Domingo Fernández Navarrete, writing in 1676, uses similar language; he calls the inhabitants of the Ch'ing empire "Tartar-Chinese."[56] His account of the conquest, however, includes a great deal more violence than that of Dapper. He describes, for example, how the Ming pretender offered his life to the Manchu general whose troops were besieging Hangchow if only the innocent citizens and soldiers could be spared. A grand gesture, thinks Navarrete:

What an opportunity this was for the *Tartar* to have shown a Noble Soul! How well the King and his Subjects would come off, had he met with an Alexander or a Caesar. He lighted among barbarous and cruel People, who were not satisfy'd with destroying the King, but butcher'd all his Army. Those who fled, which were very numerous, were drown'd in the River that washes the Walls, only the unarm'd Multitude was spar'd.[57]

In another context, however, Navarrete argues at some length that Asian peoples—Chinese, Tartars, and Japanese—are as civilized as Europeans and should not be called barbarians. Here he makes no distinctions between the three peoples.[58] Nor are all the barbarous deeds in Navarrete's account perpetrated by the Manchus. Li Tzu-ch'eng's mutilation of Ch'ung-chen's corpse he calls "Horrid barbarity!" and he depicts Chang Hsien-chung as being "more cruel than Nero, or all the Tyrants that ever were."[59] The Manchus, in short, are no more cruel or barbarous than the Chinese.

Still Navarrete regarded the conquest a tragic disaster for China. Much of what he wrote belies the possibility of continuity between the dynasties. The carnage attending Li's seizure of Peking was so great, he contends, that it was impossible to reconstruct the details of the emperor's last days from the conflicting reports. Navarrete thinks Ch'ung-chen's greed and seclusion precipitated the rebellion, but he in no way condones Li's usurpation. He

---

[55] Olfert Dapper, *Gedenkwaerdig bedryf der Nederlandsch Oost-indische Maetschappye, op de kuste en in het keizerrijk van Taising of Sina . . .* (2 vols. in 1; Amsterdam, 1670), II, 26–36. Vol. II has a separate title page: *Beschryving des keizerryks van Taising of Sina. . . .* For bibliography see above, pp. 490–91. For a further discussion of his book in this chapter, see below, p. 1685.

[56] Domingo Fernández Navarrete, "An Account of the Empire of China . . . ," *CV* (1704), I, 27. The first edition of Navarrete's book was *Tratados, historicos, politicos, ethicos y religiosos de la monarchia de China . . .* (Madrid, 1676). For bibliographical details see above, pp. 358–60.

[57] Navarrete, *CV*, I, 338.

[58] *Ibid.*, pp. 14–15.

[59] *Ibid.*, pp. 336–37.

sympathizes with Wu San-kuei's refusal to serve Li but thinks inviting the Manchus in to be worse still.[60] He also condemns Manchu perfidy in refusing to withdraw after Li's defeat and in usurping the crown for themselves. Even while describing the collapse of Ming resistance in south China and the young "Constantine's" flight to Pegu, Navarrete seems to be hoping for a restoration. "Perhaps God," he wrote, "may preserve *Constantine* for his greater Glory; for Nothing that is violent is lasting; no one ever long held a violent Command, that which is moderate is lasting."[61] Nevertheless, when later pondering whether missionaries might baptize soldiers and officials who had served the illegal Manchu emperor, Navarrete concludes affirmatively. They might even baptize the Manchu emperor. The Roman Constantine, he observes, had "tyrannically usurp'd the Empire, and yet S. Sylvester baptis'd him."[62]

One of the appendices to Navarrete's description of China contains his notes on Martini's *De bello tartarico*.[63] He makes little effort here to hide his antagonism toward Martini. He seems almost surprised whenever he finds something in the *De bello tartarico* with which to agree. His criticism of Martini, however, is largely personal or trivial. He questions, for example, Martini's competence in the Chinese language. He disagrees with Martini over when the Manchus left off burning the wives and servants of dead men and over how many cannons there were in Peking at the time of Li Tzu-ch'eng's entry. His most serious criticisms pertain to Martini's account of his personal experiences during the conquest and to anything Martini wrote that touched on the Rites Controversy.

Time was on the side of continuity, so far as European interpretations of the Manchu Conquest are concerned. They increasingly depicted the Manchus as the creators of a new but an essentially Chinese dynasty despite their foreign origin. This is also true for most of the descriptions of the conquest included in the Rites Controversy literature published during the last decades of the seventeenth century. In these later writings the images of cruelty and destruction seem to fade from view. Gabriel de Magalhães, for example, included an almost bloodless account of the conquest in his *New History of China*, even though he had witnessed some of the bloodiest episodes while a hostage at Chang Hsien-chung's court in Szechwan.[64] He treats the Ch'ing as simply the last in the long series of Chinese dynasties.[65]

---

[60] *Ibid.*

[61] *Ibid.*, p. 339. Constantine was the name given to Chu Tz'u-hsüan, the young son of the Ming Pretender Chu Yu-lang, at his Christian baptism. See Hummel, *op. cit.* (n. 9), p. 195.

[62] Navarrete, *CV*, I, 398.

[63] *Ibid.*, pp. 366–71.

[64] Magalhães' book was written in Portuguese in 1668. It was first published in French translation in Paris, 1688. See above, p. 424.

[65] Gabriel de Magalhães, *A New History of China, Containing a Description of the Most Considerable Particulars of that Vast Empire* (London, 1688), pp. 252–53.

Andreas Müller, the German sinologist, did the same.[66] Joachim Bouvet's treatise of 1697 is almost entirely a panegyric to the K'ang-hsi emperor. His legitimacy is unquestioned. Bouvet pictures Chinese learning and Manchu military vigor as being happily wedded in the K'ang-hsi reign to produce a balanced ideal.[67]

One last major description of the Manchu Conquest appeared in 1688, the Jesuit Pierre Joseph d'Orléans' *History of the Two Tartar Conquerors of China.* Based primarily on Martini and Schall, it, too, underscores the continuity between the Ming and the Ch'ing. Orléans conveys a sense of high tragedy in the passages that describe Li Tzu-ch'eng's seizure of Peking and the death of the Ch'ung-chen emperor, but he also accepts Martini's view that the Ming deserved God's wrath. He makes no effort to hide his preference for the Manchus in the post-1644 portions of the story, repeatedly contrasting Chinese effeminacy and exclusiveness with Manchu vigor and openness. Concerning the Shun-chih emperor's relationship with Adam Schall, for example, he writes: "He excited the admiration of all those who recollected the haughty and exclusive manners of the late Chinese sovereigns, by his easy familiarity with this foreigner."[68] Orléans' attitude can perhaps best be summarized with his observation about the Great Wall: "After all, the monarch who, in our days, has reunited the Chinese and the Tartars under the same dominion, has done things more advantageous for the safety of China than the Chinese emperor who built this long wall."[69]

Nevertheless, occasional glimpses of disjuncture remain, even in late seventeenth-century histories. Magalhães, for example, provides abundant evidence for the continuity between Ming and Ch'ing governments, but in a description of the Board of Rites (*Li-pu*) he asserts:

When the *Chineses* were Masters of their own Countrey, none but Docteurs, and those too onely such as were of the most repute for their knowledge and merit were admitted into this Tribunal. So that they were the most esteem'd, and such as stood the fairest for preferment; for out of their number it was that the King made choice of the *Colao* [Grand Secretary] and his Counsellors of State. But now *Tartars* are put in, who dispose of all things at their own pleasure, while the *Mandarins* signify no more among them than onely dumb Statues: and so it is in the rest of the Tribunals. So truly may we believe it to have been the will of God, to chastise and bring down the incredible pride of this Nation, by subduing and subjecting them to a small

[66] Andreas Müller, *Hebdomas observationum de rebus sinicis* . . . (Cologne, 1674).

[67] Joachim Bouvet, *Portrait historique de l'empereur de la Chine, presentée au roy* . . . (Paris, 1697), p. 14.

[68] Pierre Joseph d'Orléans, *History of the Two Tartar Conquerors of China, including the Two Journeys into Tartary of Ferdinand Verbiest, in the Suite of the Emperor K'ang-hsi.* . . , ed. Earl of Ellesmere ("HS," o.s., XVII; London, 1854), p. 38; we will cite this edition throughout this chapter. The first edition was entitled *Histoire des deux conquerans Tartares qui ont subjugué la Chine* . . . (Paris, 1688). For further bibliography see above, p. 424.

[69] D'Orléans, *op. cit.* (n. 68), p. 83.

handfull of poor, ignorant, rustick *Barbarians;* as if God for the punishment of *Europe,* should deliver it over into the power of the *Cafers* of *Angola* or *Mozambique.*[70]

For seventeenth-century Europe the reports of the Manchu Conquest engendered and appreciably increased familiarity with China and its recent history. During the half-century after the conquest an impressive amount of new information about China poured into Europe. It became popular and seems to have been widely read. In fact, it inspired plays, novels, and poems.[71] Furthermore, there seems to have been a new dynamism about much of this literature. It made China and its people a little more believable and more obviously a part of the world of those who read it.

2

THE POST-CONQUEST LITERATURE

Jesuit missionaries continued to contribute the lion's share of the new information about China which appeared in print during the second half of the seventeenth century. Their newsletters continued and, in fact, the number of Jesuit publications increased as the century wore on. But these later publications focused more and more on the defense of the Jesuit position in the Rites Controversy. While readers could still learn about China from them, the topics they treated were fewer and the information they conveyed more biased and less reliable. Much the same can be said about the anti-Jesuit letters, pamphlets, and books which swelled in number and size as the Rites Controversy heated up.[72]

The missionaries' larger descriptions of China were similarly affected by controversy. Nevertheless, the rites issue, along with the Manchu Con-

---

[70] Magalhães, *op. cit.* (n. 65), p. 208.

[71] For examples see E. Van Kley, "An Alternative Muse: The Manchu Conquest of China in the Literature of Seventeenth-Century Northern Europe," *European Studies Review,* VI (1976), 21–43.

[72] Among the major Rites Controversy pieces published during the second half of the seventeenth century were: Domingo Fernándes Navarrete, *Tratados historicos, politicos, ethicos, y religiosos de la monarchia de China* (Madrid, 1676); Vol. II of A. Arnauld, *La morale pratique de Jesuites . . .* (Paris, 1683); Michel Le Tellier, *Defense des nouveaux chrestienes et des missionaires de la Chine, du Japon, et des Indes, contre deux livres intitulez La morale pratique des Jesuites et l'esprit de M. Arnauld* (Paris, 1687); Philippe Couplet, *Histoire d'une dame chrétienne de la Chine, ou par occasion les usages de ces peuple, l'établissement de la religion, les maximes des missionaires, et les exercises de piété des nouveaux chrétiens sont expliquez* (Paris, 1688); Louis Le Comte, *Nouveaux mémoires sur l'état present de la Chine* (Paris, 1696); Joseph Suarez, *La libertad de la ley de Dios en el imperio de la China* (Lisbon, 1696); Charles Le Gobien, *Histoire de l'edit de l'empereur de la Chine en faveur de la religion chrestienne. Avec un eclaircissement sur les honneurs que le chinois rendent à Confucius aux morts* (Paris, 1698); [Noel Alexandre], *Apologie des dominicains missionaires de la Chine. Ou réponse au livre du Père le Tellier, Jesuite, intitulé Défense des nouveaux chrétiens; et à l'éclaircissement du P. Gobien . . .* (Cologne, 1699). For a more complete bibliography see Streit, V, 803–961; VII, 1–44; and above, pp. 423–24, 428–30.

quest, engendered writings about China that greatly increased the volume of information available to European readers. The new literature was also more dynamic and current than the ethnohistories of Trigault and Semedo or even than Martini's report on the Manchu Conquest and his *Atlas*. The Jesuits report on contemporary events in China generally, as well as on the state and progress of the Christian mission. Their writings are also more narrowly focused and more frequently deal with limited topics or time periods. Adam Schall's *Historica narratio* (1665), for example, is essentially an account of the mission in Peking and of the author's experiences at court; the expanded second edition of 1672 brings the story down to 1669.[73] It does not pretend to be a general description of China or even of the Ch'ing dynasty, although much can be learned from it about society and learning, about the Manchu Conquest, and especially about the workings of government and life in Peking under the first Ch'ing emperors.

News about the early Ch'ing could be extracted from Palafox y Mendoza's history of the Manchu Conquest and from Francisco Garcia's account of the 1664–68 persecutions.[74] But neither was an eyewitness account. The Jesuit missionary Adrien Greslon's *Histoire de la Chine sous la domination des Tartares* (1671) was perhaps the first description of China devoted entirely to the Ch'ing.[75] While it is primarily a history of the Christian mission in China from 1651 to 1669, it nevertheless contains some useful descriptive passages and considerable detail about politics during the Shun-chih period (1644–61) and the Oboi Regency (1661–69). To describe the missionaries' troubles during the regency, Greslon presents a wealth of detailed information about Chinese law and administration at all levels. Several important Chinese persons emerge from Greslon's story accurately and in their full complexity: the Shun-chih emperor, for example, Yang Kuang-hsien (1597–1669), the Jesuits' main antagonist, some of the regents, and the young K'ang-hsi emperor.

The *Historia tartaro-sinica nova* of the Jesuit François de Rougemont was published in Latin in 1673 but had already been translated into Spanish during the preceding year. It is in many ways similar to Greslon's *Histoire*.[76] Part II of Rougemont's work treats events at the Ch'ing court during the Shun-chih period and also describes the fate of the Ming pretenders' court in the south. Part III recounts the story of the Oboi regency with primary emphasis on the trials and persecutions of the missionaries. It ends with the K'ang-hsi emperor's formal assumption of power, which Rougemont dates on August 25, 1666.[77] Rougemont's description of these events is very similar

---

[73] For a bibliography see above, p. 528.
[74] For Palafox see above, pp. 356–57. For Garcia see above, pp. 357–58.
[75] For bibliography see above, pp. 414–15.
[76] See above, p. 358, for bibliographical details.
[77] The personal rule of K'ang-hsi officially began on August 25, 1667, although the regent, Oboi, remained a major influence at court until K'ang-hsi had him imprisoned in June, 1669. See Hummel, *op. cit.* (n. 9), p. 328.

to Greslon's, except that Greslon is more precise about Chinese terms, and names more individuals than Rougemont. Rougemont's Part I, however, contains a detailed description of the Manchu consolidation of power in the south, including the career of Cheng Chih-lung and his son Cheng Ch'eng-kung (Koxinga) and the Manchu campaigns against the latter. The events described by Schall, Greslon, and Rougemont were recounted once more in 1672 by another Jesuit missionary, Prospero Intorcetta.[78] Intended as a report to the Congregation for the Propagation of the Faith in Rome, Intorcetta's account is much more narrowly focused on the mission than the other Jesuit accounts, and it therefore contains less information about Chinese life and institutions.

The Dominican friar Domingo Fernández Navarrete's *Tratados historicos, politicos, ethicos y religiosos de la monarchia de China,* published in 1676, was perhaps the most important single anti-Jesuit piece of Rites Controversy literature. It is, however, much more than an anti-Jesuit polemic. While Navarrete's hostility to the Jesuits is apparent throughout the work and sometimes colors and distorts his descriptions, the seven treatises which comprise the *Tratados* nevertheless contain a wealth of information about China. Some of it is explicitly critical of earlier Jesuit descriptions; much, however, agrees with Jesuit observations. Most of the *Tratados* are based on Navarrete's personal ten years' experience in China and treat topics irrelevant to the Rites Controversy—indeed he digresses lengthily on a wide variety of subjects. His long description of Confucian thought and religious beliefs is illustrated with hundreds of quotations and paraphrases from the classics, histories, and Neo-Confucian writings. Book IV, entitled "Concerning Chinese Moral Doctrine," is a translation of the "Ming Sin Pao Kien" (*Ming-hsin pao-chien*), "i.e. The precious mirror of the soul; or The precious mirror that enlightens and diffuses a brightness into the heart," with Navarrete's gloss. Navarrete was not as impressed with Confucian thought as were the Jesuits, and he pays much more attention to Buddhism. He was convinced that Confucius and most of his followers were atheists. His critical stance was obviously motivated by Rites Controversy issues; nevertheless, his description provides a useful contrast to the adulatory Jesuit image.

Fresh information about the rehabilitation of the Jesuit mission under the K'ang-hsi emperor arrived with Ferdinand Verbiest's letters during the early 1680's. A French translation of his 1678 letter appeared in 1681 and the letters describing his hunting trips with the emperor were published in 1685. Verbiest's description of his work in the Calendrical Bureau of Peking and of his efforts to tutor the emperor in Western mathematics, science, mu-

---

[78] *Compendiosa narratione dello stato della missione cinese . . . dall' ano 1581 fino al 1669 . . .* (Rome, 1672). It was translated into Latin in the same year. See Streit, V, 849, 851.

sic, and painting were reported in his *Astronomia europaea sub imperatore tartaro-sinico Cám Hý apellato,* which was published in 1687.[79] Apart from his descriptions of the imperial hunting expeditions north of the Wall there is little new description of the Chinese and their land in Verbiest's writings. Some insights into the character of the K'ang-hsi emperor could be gleaned from them, however. Appended to Verbiest's *Astronomia* is a list of Jesuits who had served in China from the death of Matteo Ricci until 1681. Verbiest had first published the list in Chinese; Philippe Couplet translated it into Latin under the title *Catalogus patrum Societatis Jesu* (1686).

The two letters which describe Verbiest's travels into Tartary with the K'ang-hsi emperor were also appended to Pierre Joseph d'Orléans' account of the Manchu Conquest, published in 1688.[80] These contain information about the emperor, the Manchus, and the regions beyond the Wall through which they traveled. D'Orléans' book also traces the events of the Shun-chih reign, the Oboi regency, the Manchu conquest of the south, the campaigns against Koxinga (Cheng Ch'eng-kung), and the fate of the several Ming pretenders and their heirs. He was not a witness to these events; his information came from the writings of the Jesuits Martini, Schall, Rougemont, Verbiest, and Greslon.[81]

The most comprehensive and accurate general description of China published during the second half of the seventeenth century was the *Nouvelle relation de la Chine* written by the Portuguese Jesuit Gabriel de Magalhães. Magalhães' Portuguese manuscript was carried back to Europe by Philippe Couplet in 1682, translated into French by Abbé Claude Bernou, and published in Paris in 1688. An English translation appeared during the same year.[82] Unlike other Jesuit accounts of the second half of the century, which were primarily histories of or apologies for the mission, Magalhães' work is a major ethnohistory in the tradition of Trigault and Semedo. Rites Controversy considerations occasionally intrude into his description, and he unblushingly judges the Jesuits to have written the best earlier descriptions of China. Nevertheless Magalhães' description is remarkably balanced, and he occasionally criticizes the works of his Jesuit predecessors. Nor is he uncritical of Chinese customs and institutions. In short, Magalhães' *Nouvelle relation* is perhaps the best single source to amplify and supplement the image of China sketched out earlier by Mendoza, Trigault, Semedo, and Martini.

Louis Le Comte's *Nouveaux mémoires sur l'état present de la Chine* (1696) also contains much accurate information about Chinese history, religion, and culture, and about life and government under the new dynasty. It was

---

[79] See above, pp. 419 and 539, for bibliographic details on Verbiest's publications.
[80] See above, p. 424.
[81] D'Orléans, *op. cit.* (n. 68), pp. iv–v.
[82] For bibliographical details see above, p. 424. Also see Mungello, *op. cit.* (n. 6), pp. 91–96.

also, however, so obviously intended to bolster the Jesuit position in the Rites Controversy that it quickly became a focus of dispute. Refutations were written by the Jesuits' opponents and the book was eventually censored. Nevertheless, it was translated into several other languages and frequently reprinted.[83] Despite Le Comte's biases and his excessive enthusiasm for much of Chinese civilization, the *Nouveaux mémoires* probably shaped the European view of China more definitively than many other more accurate descriptions.

While relatively free of Rites Controversy polemics, Joachim Bouvet's *Portrait historique de l'empéreur de la Chine* (1697) is a panegyric to the K'ang-hsi emperor as a replacement in the Jesuit galaxy for Confucius. Bouvet describes the emperor as an absolute but wise and humane ruler, a superb administrator, a valiant soldier and avid hunter, a brilliant intellect, a diligent scholar, a paragon of personal morality, and the protector of the Jesuits, who hoped for his conversion. K'ang-hsi was, in short, very much like Louis XIV, to whom Bouvet dedicated the *Portrait,* and to whom the Jesuits also looked for continued support.[84]

Near the end of his *Portrait* Bouvet discusses K'ang-hsi's edict of toleration for Christianity in China (1692) and the conversion of several high officials.[85] He presents the edict as the culmination of the Jesuits' tireless and courageous efforts to preach the gospel in China and as the dawning of a new era in which "Christian China" and the conversion of the emperor have become distinctly possible.[86] Similar descriptions of the edict were published by Joseph Suarez (1696) and by Charles Le Gobien (1698).[87] These, however, are very much a part of the Rites Controversy literature which became increasingly abundant and intemperate during the late 1690's. Little new information about China can be found in this literature, and much of it is seriously distorted. Nevertheless the polemic certainly contributed to the higher visibility and the wider availability in Europe of printed information about China.

Europe's perception of China was also sharpened appreciably by more specialized publications and by the translation of some Chinese texts into Western languages. Michele Ruggiero, one of the Jesuit pioneers, had apparently translated the Confucian Four Books into Latin before he left China in 1588. Of Ruggiero's translations only a part of the *Ta Hsüeh,* or *Great Learning,* was ever published. It appeared in Antonio Possevino's *Bibliotheca selecta*

---

[83] See above, pp. 427–28; see also Mungello, *op. cit.* (n. 6), pp. 329–31.

[84] See Mungello, *op. cit.* (n. 6), p. 17. The *Portrait historique* does not do Bouvet's Chinese scholarship justice, and his substantive Chinese works were suppressed because of the Rites Controversy; see D. Mungello, "Unearthing the Manuscripts of Bouvet's *Gujin* after Nearly Three Centuries," *China Mission Studies (1550–1800) Bulletin,* X (1988), 34–61. See also Claudia von Collani, *P. Joachim Bouvet, S.J., sein Leben und sein Werk* (Nettetal, 1985).

[85] *Op. cit.* (n. 67), pp. 242–45.

[86] How far from reality these hopes were may be seen in Jonathan Spence, *Emperor of China: Self-Portrait of K'ang-hsi* (New York, 1975), pp. 72–85.

[87] For Suarez see above, p. 363; for Le Gobien see above, p. 429.

in 1593.[88] In 1672 Prospero Intorcetta's translation of the *Chung Yung,* or *Doctrine of the Mean,* appeared in Latin;[89] a French translation of it was published during the following year.[90] In 1687 the China Jesuits brought out their *Confucius sinarum philosophus,* a Latin translation of three of the Four Books: the *Chung Yung, Ta Hsüeh,* and the *Lun Yü,* or *Analects.* Four names—Prospero Intorcetta, Christian Herdtrich, Francesco (François) Rougemont, and Philippe Couplet—appear on its title page, but it appears to have been a cooperative project involving many other China Jesuits over a long period of time. Couplet functioned as its editor.[91] A long "Proëmialis declaratio" describes the Five Classics and the Four Books, ancient Chinese religion, and the development of China's three religions, and sketches the life of Confucius.[92] Jean de La Brune published a condensation of the introduction and a précis of the text of the *Confucius sinarum philosophus* in French in 1688.[93] It became quite popular and was frequently reissued. Finally in 1696 Christian Mentzel, physician to the elector of Brandenburg, claimed to have translated the *Hsiao-erh lun,* or *Small Child's Discourse,* into German along with his comments.[94]

The Polish Jesuit Michael Boym contributed two important special studies: *Flora sinensis* (1656), in which he described and illustrated plants and a few animals from south China, and a collection of treatises on Chinese medicine: *Specimen medicinae sinicae* (1682).[95] Both were influential works frequently cited or used by others who wrote about China. The *Flora sinensis* not only accurately describes some of the plants native to south China and Southeast Asia, but also indicates that several plants which had been brought over from America during the preceding century had acclimated to south China.[96]

[88] Antonio Possevino, *Bibliotheca selecta qua agitur de ratione studiorum in historia, in disciplinis, in salute omnium procuranda* (Rome, 1593), IX, 583. See K. Lundbaek, "The First Translation from the Confucian Classics in Europe," *China Mission Studies Bulletin,* I (1979), 2–11.

[89] *Sinarum scientia politico-moralis, sive scientiae sinicae liber inter Confucii libros secundus* (Paris).

[90] *La science des Chinois ou le livre de Cum fu-çu traduit mot pour mot de la langue chinois par le P. Intorcetta* (Paris, 1673).

[91] *Confucius sinarum philosophus, sive scientia sinensis, latine exposita . . .* (Paris, 1687). For a detailed analysis of its authorship and content see Mungello, *op. cit.* (n. 6), chap. viii.

[92] See K. Lundbaek, "The Image of Neo-Confucianism in *Confucius sinarum philosophus,*" *Journal of the History of Ideas,* XLIV (1983), 19–30.

[93] *La morale de Confucius, philosophe de la Chine* (Amsterdam, 1688).

[94] Christian Mentzel, *Kurtze chinesische Chronologia oder Zeit-Register aller chinesischen Kayser . . . gezogen aus der chineser kinder Lehre Siao ul hio oder lun genandt . . .* (Berlin, 1696). It is extremely doubtful that Mentzel knew enough Chinese to translate a Chinese text. His chronology appears to have come from Couplet's *Tabula chronologica monarchiae Sinicae,* which Mentzel seems to have thought came from the *Hsiao-erh lun.* The *Hsiao-erh lun,* however, is not a chronology, but a four-page hypothetical dialogue between Confucius and a boy. On the beginnings of Sinology in Germany see F. R. Merkel, "Deutsche Chinaforscher," *Archiv für Kulturgeschichte,* XXXIV (1951–52), 81–106; and Mungello, *op. cit.* (n. 6), chaps. vi–vii. See Mungello, pp. 238–41, for a detailed analysis of Mentzel's possible sources.

[95] See above, pp. 526, 538–39.

[96] See Hartmut Walravens, "Eine Anmerkung zu Michael Boyms Flora Sinensis (1656)— einer wichtigen naturhistorischen Quelle," *China Mission Studies Bulletin,* I (1979), 16–20.

In 1658 Martino Martini published Europe's first work on general Chinese history, the *Sinicae historiae*.[97] It contains a chapter on each emperor from the legendary Fu Hsi through the Former Han dynasty (206 B.C.–A.D. 8). Derived from the Confucian classics and official histories, it contains a wealth of detailed information about the sage emperors, chronology, and the ancient dynasties: the Hsia, Shang, Chou, Ch'in, and Former Han. It is essentially a court chronicle, containing details about the lives of emperors and ministers, relations between the various states and the barbarians on the fringes of the Chinese world, the unification of China under the Ch'in, and the consolidation of the imperial system under the Han. Martini's description of court affairs also includes details about religion and philosophy, the lives and thoughts of the great thinkers of the Hundred-Schools Era (5th–3rd centuries B.C.), and the further development of Confucianism and Taoism during Ch'in and Han times. Martini used both Chinese sixty-year cycles and the Christian calendar to date the emperors' reigns. For other events he frequently used the year of the reigning emperor as well as Western dates. In sum, Martini provided European readers with a rather complete account of traditional Chinese dynastic history from its beginning to the birth of Christ.

Martini's intended continuation of the *Sinicae historiae decas prima* was apparently never published, although the manuscript of a "decas secunda" seems to have existed.[98] He included a very brief outline of the post-Han dynasties in his *Atlas*.[99] Melchisédech Thévenot produced a complete Chinese chronology from Fu Hsi to the fifteenth century, which provided detailed coverage of the post-Han dynasties comparable to Martini's coverage of the earlier era.[100] Thévenot claims to have used a Persian manuscript in its preparation, but the post–Former Han part of his "Synopsis" is entitled "Historiae sinicae decas secunda," which sounds suspiciously like Martini's promised manuscript. He also once refers to the Jesuit order as "Societas nostra," although Thévenot was not a Jesuit. In the following line, however, he names Martini along with Trigault, Semedo, and Magalhães in his list of Jesuits who brought accurate information about China to Europe.[101]

Like Martini's *Sinicae historiae,* Thévenot's "Synopsis" is essentially a

---

[97] *Sinicae historiae decas prima, . . .* (Munich, 1658), For bibliographic details see above, pp. 526–27.

[98] H. Cordier, *op. cit.* (n. 25), I, 580.

[99] Martini, *Novus atlas sinensis,* Vol. XI of Johan Blaeu, *Le grand atlas* (Amsterdam, 1663), pp. 20–21.

[100] "Synopsis chronologica monarchiae sinicae . . . ," *TR,* Vol. II, Pt. 4 (Paris, 1672?). The earliest edition of part 4 is dated 1672, but there is no way of knowing whether or not the "Synopsis" was part of it, since many pieces of part 4 were separately published and only later bound together as a single volume. The "Synopsis" could have appeared at any time between 1672 and 1696. It should be noted, however, that Magalhães' manuscript was brought back to Europe in 1682 and was published only in 1688, thus suggesting that Thévenot's "Synopsis" was not published before 1682. On Thévenot's collection see above, pp. 410–11.

[101] Thévenot, *loc. cit.* (n. 100), p. 65.

court chronicle. The first part retraces Martini's ground, but in far less detail. Thévenot also employed a system of romanization different from that Martini used, included variant names for the emperors, and occasionally referred to events in Hebrew or classical history contemporary with those he was describing. Apart from these differences this part of his "Synopsis" reads like a condensation of Martini. The second part of Thévenot's "Synopsis," the "Decas secunda," on the other hand, is more richly detailed. It describes the rise and fall of the dynasties from Han to Ming, China's relations with other peoples—especially with the Mongol and Manchu tribes—the reception of tribute missions, the character and deeds of emperors and high officials, the role of court eunuchs, Confucian scholars, and consort families, the introduction and progress of Buddhism, and the development of learning and scholarship. Like Martini's *Decas prima,* it includes a host of illustrative stories and conversations. A chapter is devoted to each dynasty. Within the chapters he, like Martini, names, dates, and describes the reign of each emperor. Thévenot's sketch of the interdynastic periods is incomplete. Through the Three Kingdoms epoch (A.D. 221–65) he follows the Shu Han kingdom, treating the Wu and Wei kingdoms only as they related to the Shu Han.[102] He then chronicles the Western and Eastern Chin dynasties as a single house, although he reports the move to Loyang in A.D. 317.[103] Following the demise of the Eastern Chin, Thévenot chronicles only the southern dynasties—the Liu Sung, Southern Ch'i, Liang, and Ch'en—writing very little about the Sixteen Kingdoms, the Northern, Western, and Eastern Wei states, the Northern Chou, or the Northern Ch'i.[104] His treatment of the Five Dynasties period (A.D. 907–79) is briefer still. He names each emperor in each dynasty but includes only enough detail to illustrate that it indeed was a time of "war, rebellion, slaughter, and parricide."[105] Thévenot's "Decas secunda" ends with the Ming dynasty's Hung-hsi emperor, who reigned but for a single year in 1425, thus providing European readers with a proper continuation of the story begun by Martini if, indeed, it is not itself Martini's work.

In 1686 Philippe Couplet produced a complete Chinese chronology from the beginning of the reign of Huang Ti, the third sage emperor (2697 B.C.), to the K'ang-hsi reign, or A.D. 1683.[106] It is a detailed chronological table; it is not divided into chapters on individual emperors like Martini's *Decas prima* or even on dynasties, as was Thévenot's "Decas secunda." The divisions in Couplet's *Tabula* are those which mark the beginning of sixty-year cycles, and it is primarily at these junctures that Western dates are provided. In content, however, apart from the material on the late Ming and early

[102] *Ibid.,* pp. 27–28.
[103] *Ibid.,* pp. 30–31.
[104] *Ibid.,* pp. 34–40.
[105] *Ibid.,* pp. 53–56.
[106] *Tabula chronologica monarchiae sinicae* (Paris, 1686). See above, pp. 423–24.

Ch'ing, Couplet's *Tabula* appears to be a condensation of the "Decas secunda" in Thévenot. At least half of Couplet's sentences appear to come directly from the "Decas secunda." Perhaps, like the translation of the Four
Books, the Jesuit history of China was a cooperative project.[107]

Taken together, Martini, the "Decas secunda," and Couplet provided
their readers with a substantial, comprehensive account of Chinese court
history and legendary pre-history derived from the Chinese classics, especially the *Shu Ching* (*Classic of History*), from the works of the Han dynasty
historian Ssu-ma Ch'ien and the Sung scholars Ssu-ma Kuang and Chu Hsi,
and perhaps from official dynastic histories—the sources on which the
Jesuits apparently relied either directly or in a simpler, popularized form.
Martini and the "Decas secunda" mention the *Shu Ching* frequently. Martini may also have used the *Ch'un Ch'iu* (*Spring and Autumn Annals*), the *Lun
Yü* (*Analects*), the *Meng-tzu* (*Mencius*), and the *Shih-chi* (*Historical Records*) of
Ssu-ma Ch'ien. The "Decas secunda" mentions both Ssu-ma Kuang and
Chu Hsi.[108] Even if Thévenot's "Persian manuscript" was Fadl Allah Rasid
ad-Din's thirteenth-century *Universal History* or some other Muslim history,
it, too, would have been based on the same standard Chinese sources.[109]

Finally, among the specialized studies produced by the Jesuits during the
last half of the seventeenth century was Athanasius Kircher's influential
China illustrata.[110] Ostensibly the Jesuit Kircher's purpose was to demonstrate the authenticity of the Nestorian monument unearthed at Sian in 1625
or shortly before and reported to Europe soon after. To that end he reproduced the original Chinese and Syriac inscriptions with his translations
and commentary—their first printing in Europe.[111] Kircher's thesis is much
grander, however: he sought to locate the seventh-century planting of
Christianity in China as well as the more recent Jesuit mission within the
universal spread of idolatry from its origin in ancient Egypt and God's
counterattack—the spread of Christianity since the first century. To illustrate this vision, and in digressions from his thesis, Kircher presents much

[107] See above, pp. 1680–81.

[108] *Op. cit.* (n. 100), pp. 61, 63. Ma Yong, a present-day Chinese scholar, contends that most
of Martini's *Sinicae historiae* was taken from the *T'ung-chien kang-mu* ("The Outlines and Details
of the Comprehensive Mirror"), a popular history composed by Chu Hsi and his students; see
K. Lundbaek's report of the "Convegno internazionale su Martino Martini (Trento 1614–
Hangzhou 1661): geografo-cartagrafo-storico-teologo," Trent, October 9–10, 1981, in *China
Mission Studies Bulletin*, IV (1982), 39.

[109] See Franz Rosenthal, *A History of Muslim Historiography* (Leyden, 1968), pp. 147–48.

[110] *China monumentis qua sacris qua profanis, nec non variis naturae & artis spectaculis, aliarumque
rerum memorabilium argumentis illustrata . . . .* (Amsterdam, 1667). For bibliography see above,
pp. 485–86. For a complete analysis of this encyclopedic work see Mungello, *op. cit.* (n. 6),
chap. v. We have used the 1670 French translation: *La Chine illustrée de plusieurs monuments tant
sacrés que profanes, et de quantité de recherchés de la nature & de l'art . . . ,* trans. F. S. Dalquié
(Amsterdam, 1670). See also the new English translation of the *China illustrata* by Charles D.
Van Tuyl (Muskogee, Okla., 1987).

[111] Alois Bürke, S.M.B., "Das Nestorianer-Denkmal von Si-an-fu, Versuch einer Neuübersetzung," *NZM*, Supplementa XVII (1971), 127, n. 10. See above, ch. xx, n. 476.

information about China and its history, especially its religious history. Most of it can be found in other Jesuit writings, but some of it came from reports and conversations which had never before been published.

The VOC embassies to the Ch'ing court in 1655 and 1666, Koxinga's seizure of Formosa in 1661, and the joint Manchu-Dutch campaigns against him produced two huge, lavishly illustrated descriptions of China: *Het gezantschap der Neerlandtsche Oost-Indische Compagnie aan den grooten Tartarischen cham,* written by the embassy's secretary, Johann Nieuhof, in 1665, and the *Gedenkwaerdig bedryf der Nederlandsch Oost-Indische Maatschappye, op de kust en in het keizzerrijk van Taising of Sina,* compiled by the Amsterdam clergyman Olfert Dapper in 1670. Both are encyclopedic works, largely drawn from the standard Jesuit sources—Trigault, Semedo, and Martini (and for Dapper, Kircher). Each also contains, however, fresh, eyewitness reports by people who had traveled with the Dutch embassies from Canton or Fukien to Peking, negotiated with officials in the provinces and in the capital, and were received by the emperor in formal audiences. They are thus amalgams of Jesuit description and secular travel reports. Nieuhof's book went through many editions and was translated into French, German, English, and Latin. Dapper's, while not as popular as Nieuhof's, nevertheless was translated into German and English.[112]

Both texts are profusely illustrated. Nieuhof's contains 150 prints, many of them two-page spreads and most of them based on Nieuhof's own sketches. Some exotic elements were introduced either by the engravers or by Nieuhof himself. Nevertheless they provided European readers with relatively accurate visual images of Chinese landscapes, cityscapes, and people. Many of the prints were also used in Dapper's book. In fact, they were frequently copied during the remainder of the century and probably contributed to the chinoiserie of the next.[113]

Two travel reports published during the 1670's contain small amounts of information about China. A Dutch pamphlet describing the loss of Formosa to Koxinga, *'t Verwaerloosde Formosa* (1675), contains some information about China, the Manchu consolidation of the south, and the Chinese who accompanied Koxinga to Formosa.[114] Frederick Bolling, a Dane in VOC service, provided a brief but intriguing description of his experiences on an island near Macao where he worked as a bookkeeper for a private Batavian merchant in 1672.[115]

The last decade of the century saw the publication of the accounts of several overland travelers to China and their descriptions of China's inner-Asian neighbors. The story of the Jesuit Philippe Avril's attempt to establish

[112] Nieuhof, *op. cit.* (n. 29); Dapper, *op. cit.* (n. 55).
[113] For an analysis of the illustrations see Leonard Blussé and R. Falkenburg, *Johan Nieuhof's beelden van een chinareis* (Middelburg, 1987).
[114] See above, pp. 495–96, and below, pp. 1818–23.
[115] Frederick Bolling, *Oost-Indiske Reise-bog* (Copenhagen, 1678). See above, pp. 535–36.

a land route across Russia for the safer passage of missionaries to China appeared in 1692 and includes descriptions of both the routes from Moscow to China and the peoples on China's frontiers. Avril, himself, however, did not travel beyond Moscow, and his descriptions therefore are not the result of his own observations.[116] Nicolaas Witsen published *Noord en Oost Tartarye,* also in 1692. He, too, had never traveled east of Moscow and his descriptions of Tartar tribes also were drawn primarily from other writers, although some of them derived from his interviews with people who had accompanied Fedor Baikov from Moscow to Peking in 1653. Baikov's journal was included in the second edition of *Noord en Oost Tartarye* (1705).[117] In 1698 Adam Brand published an account of his overland journey of 1693 to China in the company of Evert Ysbrandszoon Ides, the tsar's ambassador. Brand's accounts of the Great Wall, the Chinese frontier towns, and the embassy's reception in Peking are particularly vivid. Ides' own account of the embassy appeared in Dutch in 1704, and his descriptions of inner-Asian tribes and of north China are, if anything, better still than Brand's. Ides appended a general description of China to his account, supposedly written by a Chinese Christian, which shows obvious Jesuit influences.[118]

The Italian traveler Francesco Gemelli Careri also visited China. His experiences there as described in his *Giro del mondo* (1700) make fascinating reading, although questions have been raised regarding their veracity.[119] His description of China was largely cribbed from Magalhães. As a consequence, many of the Jesuits in the eighteenth century questioned whether he had ever visited China personally. It is now conceded that he probably was received in Peking as he claimed.[120] Nikolaas de Graaf's *Reisen* also contains a brief description of China taken from Nieuhof. But he also traded in Canton, visited Macao in 1684, and wrote an eyewitness account of the nontributary trade there and of his contacts with the Chinese and with the Portuguese in Macao.[121]

For the most part, with the notable exceptions of the encyclopedic works of Nieuhof and Dapper, travel literature published during the second half of the seventeenth century supplemented the much more impressive Jesuit literature by describing the fringes of the empire: the sea campaigns against Cheng Ch'eng-kung (Koxinga), the sometimes illicit trade along the

---

[116] *Voyage de divers états d'Europe, et d'Asie, entrepris pour découvrir un nouveau chemin à la Chine* . . . (Paris, 1692). For bibliography see above, p. 428.

[117] See above, pp. 501–2.

[118] See above, pp. 503–4, 543.

[119] On Gemelli Careri see above, pp. 386–87.

[120] See P. de Vargas, "Le 'Giro del Mondo' de Gemelli Careri, en particulier le récit du séjour en Chine, roman ou verité?" *Schweizerische Zeitschrift für Geschichte,* V (1955), 417–51.

[121] Nikolaas de Graaf, *Reisen* (Hoorn, 1701), pp. 174–81. See also above, pp. 505–6. When the K'ang-hsi emperor ended the maritime trade ban along the southeastern coast in 1684 after the Cheng rebels on Taiwan had been subdued, he allowed foreign merchants to trade independently of tributary missions in several ports, Macao and Canton among them. See Lawrence D. Kessler, *K'ang-hsi and the Consolidation of Ch'ing Rule, 1661–1684* (Chicago, 1976), pp. 95–97.

Kwangtung coast, the inner-Asian tribes, and the frontier settlements along the Great Wall. They do not provide, as one might hope, an unbiased view of matters too much colored by the Rites Controversy. Even the Dutch observers, who traveled through much of China and participated in court receptions and negotiations, turned to the Jesuit works to flesh out their general descriptions of China.

3

THE LAND AND ITS PEOPLE

No basic alterations were made in Europe's image of Chinese geography during the second half of the seventeenth century. Most writers follow Martini's *Atlas* for their general descriptions of the empire and its provinces. Nieuhof and Dapper, for example, each include slightly abridged versions of Martini's provincial descriptions. China's size, population, and the number of its cities and towns continue to amaze Europeans. Most observers persist in listing the number of *fu, chou, hsien,* fortified places, and the like. The numbers vary little from Trigault's original report. Navarrete's, for example, is slightly lower than Trigault's or Martini's; Magalhães' is higher, but he apparently includes Liaotung, the Manchu homeland, in his tally.[122] Dapper adds that the Chinese built many forts and military towns near the coast of Fukien during the campaigns against Koxinga.[123] Population figures also vary little from Martini's. The same is true for the estimates of China's size. Magalhães produces the most elaborate figures on China's dimensions, reporting them in degrees of latitude and longitude, Chinese *li,* Spanish leagues, French leagues, German miles, and Italian miles.[124] Avril and Le Comte both contend that China is about five hundred leagues closer to Europe than was formerly thought.[125]

Most writers still name all the Chinese provinces. Following Martini's *Sinicae historiae,* some also report that the sage emperor Shun first divided China into twelve provinces and that his successor Yü divided it into nine.[126] Navarrete thought each province had once been a separate kingdom.[127] Several writers also report that Liaotung, the Manchu homeland, is now a part of China, although it is not listed with the fifteen provinces. Verbiest reports

[122] Navarrete, *CV* I, 6–7; Magalhães, *op. cit.* (n. 65), pp. 34–38. Official Chinese compilations were not readily available. The *Ta-ch'ing i-t'ung-chih,* the gigantic Ch'ing imperial topographic treatise, was not published until 1812.

[123] Dapper, *op. cit.* (n. 55), II, 11.

[124] Magalhães, *op. cit.* (n. 65), pp. 32–33.

[125] Avril, *op. cit.* (n. 116), pp. 107–9; Le Comte, *Memoirs and Remarks . . . Made in Above Ten Years Travels Through the Empire at China . . .* (London, 1738), pp. 15–17.

[126] For example, see Dapper, *op. cit.* (n. 55), II, 8–11.

[127] Navarrette, *CV,* I, 5.

that "all the towns and villages, of which in Leuton [Liaotung] I saw many, are completely ruined. One meets continually with remnants of walls and heaps of rubbish." Some new houses are being built out of the rubble of the old buildings.[128]

The various names of China continue to fascinate Europeans during the second half of the century. Most accounts still begin with a rather long discussion of the problem. Navarrete and Magalhães write the most thorough discussions of it.[129] They all add the Ch'ing to the list of dynastic appellations, which probably indicates that they accept the Manchus as having established a traditional Chinese dynasty. Europeans continue to speculate about the origin of the term China—for example, that it was a foreigners' mispronunciation of the much-used word *ch'ing* (please), or that it derived from "Cincheu" (Chang-chou), from which town most overseas Chinese merchants came. Most Europeans, however, accept Martini's explanation, found in his *Sinicae historiae,* that it came from the Ch'in dynasty.[130] They usually explain the term Cathay as having originated during the late Sung period, when China was divided, or during the Mongol period, when Marco Polo visited China. From Moscow, Avril reports that the Russians call all the territory east of the Ob River "Kitay" (Cathay), but that they call China, "Kitay-Kitay."[131] Navarrete discusses the etymologies of several foreign names for China or for Chinese cities, the most bizarre being the Philippine term for Chinese, "Sangley," which he says derives from the Spaniards' misunderstanding of "Xang-lai, we come to trade."[132] Navarrete thinks the identification of China with Cathay is still uncertain, possibly because the Jesuits are so certain about it.[133] Everyone else seems to be as convinced as the Jesuits, although all of the writers, Jesuits as well as secular travelers, include long demonstrations of the identification. Dapper's discussion of it is the most thorough; he presents not only Trigault's, Semedo's, Martini's, and Golius' evidence, but also gleans support from William of Rubruquis, John of Plano-Carpini, Marco Polo, Hayton of Armenia, and several Arab, Persian, Greek, and Latin writers, and from Nieuhof's report that the Russians and Muslims he met in Peking during the 1655 tribute mission called the capital by its Mongol name, "Cambalu."[134]

The European literature of the second half of the century contains even more vivid descriptions of the Chinese landscape than did the earlier writ-

---

[128] "Translation of Father Verbiest's first letter from the Dutch," in D'Orléans, *op. cit.* (n. 68), p. 105.

[129] Navarrete, *CV,* I, 1–3; Magalhães, *op. cit.* (n. 65), 1–18.

[130] *Op. cit.* (n. 97), p. 195.

[131] Avril, *op. cit.* (n. 116), pp. 161–62. "Kitay" seems to derive from the Khitans, a Mongol tribe which founded an empire in parts of north China and in Manchuria (the Liao dynasty, 947–1199).

[132] Navarrete, *CV,* I, 2. Also *cf.* above, p. 1509, on the derivation of "Sangley."

[133] Navarrete, *CV,* I, 2–3.

[134] Dapper, *op. cit.* (n. 55), II, 12–19.

ings. Martini's provincial descriptions were repeated by Nieuhof, Dapper, and others, but even more impressive are the eyewitness accounts of thousands of places in China written by missionaries who were shuttled around the empire during the conquest and the persecutions, by Admiral Bort's men during the campaigns against Koxinga along the Fukien coast, or by the Dutch embassies to the Ch'ing court. Nieuhof's account is particularly rich in detailed descriptions of the rivers, towns, and countryside between Canton and Peking. He traveled with the Dutch ambassadors up the Pei River from Canton to "Xaocheu" (Shao-kuan) at the confluence of the Pei, Wu, and Chen Rivers, then up the Chen to "Nanhung" (Nan-hsiung), near the Kwangtung-Kiangsi border. From here they traveled overland across Mei-kuang Pass to "Nangan" (Nan-an) on the Chang River. Just south of "Kancheu" (Kanchou) they joined the Kan River on which they traveled, past Nanch'ang, until it flows into the P'oyang Lake. Across the lake at "Hukeu" (Hu-k'ou) they entered the Yangtze River. On the Yangtze they visited several cities, the most important of which was Nanking, which Nieuhof extensively describes. Near "Jamcefu or Yancheu" (Yangchou), known for its beautiful women, they entered the Grand Canal, which they followed all the way to "Tiencienwey" (Tientsin). From Tientsin they moved up the Pei River to "Sansianwey" near "Tongsiou" (Tung-hsien), about four miles north of Peking. The final four miles were made on foot.[135] In northern Kwangtung Province, Nieuhof describes what must be karst formations: mountains along the river and deep inland rising straight up from the plain. They appear so orderly and elegant that one would think they were man-made and artistically placed. "Kancheu" (Kanchou) in southern Kiangsi is a bustling commercial center on the river "Kan" (Kan) near where it is joined by the river "Chang" (Chang). The city is square with high strong walls and numerous apertures decorated with fierce-looking lions' heads. There are four gates. Nieuhof climbs up the broad stone steps from the river, past two beautiful stone arches, to the west gate, where he enters the city. Inside, the streets are neat and clean, mostly paved with large stone slabs. On the east side of the city Nieuhof finds a striking nine-story pagoda. From its top he enjoys a splendid view of the city, the surrounding countryside, and the river. The city boasts many temples; Nieuhof visits several of them. One has bedrooms for travelers. At one, across the river from the city, travelers bring offerings to the river god in hopes of a safe journey. "Xiexui or Kissuwen" (Chi-shui) on the Kan River is small—only a half hour around—ringed by pleasant hills and mountains, but nevertheless surrounded by a fifteen-foot wall with four strong gates.

---

[135] Nieuhof, *op. cit.* (n. 29), I, 54–158. For a careful analysis of Nieuhof's journey through Kwangtung Province see C. Imbault Huart, "Le voyage de l'ambassade hollandaise de 1656 a travers la province de Canton," *JRAS, North China Branch*, n.s., Vol. XXX, No. 1 (1895–96), pp. 1–73.

Its buildings are very old, giving the town an antique appearance. In addition to its elegant but time-worn houses and temples, it boasts three graceful memorial arches.[136] Not only was Nieuhof a perceptive observer, but his many beautiful sketches add impressive visual images to his account.

Dapper's account of the Van Hoorn embassy, while not as vividly descriptive as Nieuhof's, contains some good eyewitness accounts and some beautiful illustrations of the route and places along it. Starting from Foochow, Van Hoorn sailed up the Min River to "Jenping" (Nan-p'ing), where they turned north on what is today called the Chien. At "Poutchin" (P'u-ch'eng) in northern Fukien Province, they debarked and crossed the mountains into Chekiang Province, presumably over the Feng-ling Pass, although Dapper does not identify it. He does, however, name all the villages through which they passed. At "Pinhoea" or "Puchoea" (?) on the "Chang" (Kang-shan) River they reembark, following the course of what by the time they pass "Fojang" or "Fuyang" (Fu-ch'un-chiang) Dapper calls the "Che River" to "Hangcheu" (Hangchow). He notes that in Hangchow the river is called the "Cientang" (Ch'ien-t'ang). At Hangchow the embassy enters the Grand Canal, although Dapper does not name it. They follow it northwards past "Sucheu" (Soochow) and Lake T'ai, crossing the Yangtze at "Sinckian" or "Chinkiang" (Chen-chiang?), after which their route is identical to Nieuhof's.[137]

Finally, there were the impressions of Brand and Ides as they approached China in 1693 from the Siberian steppes. Little imagination is needed to recreate their excitement:

The nearer we approached the *Chinese* Wall, the more populous we found the Country. For three days together before we came in sight of it, we travelled over Rocks and Precipices, through which there was cut a safe Road for the convenience of Travellers . . .

On the 27th of *October,* towards *Evening,* we came in sight of the famous *Chinese* Wall, which is four Fathoms high, and of such thickness that eight Persons may ride upon it a-breast. . . . At the first Gate we entered, the Wall appear'd to be much decay'd, but at the Musketshot from thence we passed through another Gate, which resembled a high Bastion. We were conducted through two more, and these three last enclosed a large place with their Walls, the three Gates serving for as many Bastions.[138]

Once inside it was as if they had entered an entirely new world. Brand and Ides feverishly tried to record it all: the dignified officials, their many receptions, the crowds of people, and the sights along the road to Peking.

Most later seventeenth-century observers were as impressed with China's natural resources and industry as were the earlier writers. They continued to

---

[136] Nieuhof, *op. cit.* (n. 29), I, 67–68, 75–78, 83–84.
[137] Dapper, *op. cit.* (n. 55), I, 282–47.
[138] Brand, *A Journal of an Embassy* . . . (London, 1698), p. 28.

describe the Middle Kingdom's wealth, products, crafts, and commerce in superlative terms, often repeating earlier descriptions. They added much detail, however, and frequently noted changes that had resulted from the change in dynasties. Its abundant resources still made China appear to be the most favored land on earth. Michael Boym, for example, thought China was "an epitome of the world because it contains all that which is the most beautiful in the rest of the inhabited earth."[139] Kircher puzzles over why God gave an earthly paradise to the idolatrous Chinese.[140] European writers continue to describe China's natural wealth and wonders in specific as well as general terms. Nieuhof and Dapper, for example, write chapters on China's trees, flowers, plants, fruit, animals, minerals, and so forth. Their information comes primarily from Martini's provincial descriptions, augmented somewhat by what the Dutch saw during their embassies. Boym, however, provides scientific descriptions and sketches of twenty-one plants and eight animals from south China. Not all of them were new to European readers, and some were also native to Southeast Asia. Dapper includes in his account most of Boym's descriptions and about half of his sketches. Although scientifically less exact, Navarrete describes many of the plants and animals he has seen or heard about in China, and while most of them had been reported on before, many of his descriptions display the earthy perceptions of a man more familiar with rural life and agriculture than were most of the Jesuits. He is not enthralled by tigers: they kill large numbers of people each year.[141] He, like everyone else, reports that the Chinese eat dogs, horses, buffaloes, cats, and mice. He claims, however, to have tried and savored most of them. His account of the butcher carrying live dogs to his shop followed by a street full of barking dogs is realistic.[142] But Navarrete sometimes believes too much. He describes an animal called the "jang," which has no mouth and lives on air; crabs on Hainan that turn into stones when taken from the water; a lizard from which an ointment is made which emperors rub on their concubines' wrists—it disappears only after the concubine has been with a man. Navarrete also reports that when pursued by hunters the musk deer sometimes bites off its musk sack to avoid capture—to no avail, for it always dies soon after.[143]

European writers also continue to profess admiration for China's diligent peasants. Navarrete, who seems to have spent more time with them, provides some realistic details and insights into their lives. "The husbandmen of China," he reports, "are mighty numerous and as to rank are prefer'd before merchants and mechanics." They deserve to be, he thought; they work hard. If they were not so industrious, China's vast population could

---

[139] Boym, "Flora sinesis," TR, II, 17.
[140] Op. cit. (n. 110), p. 225.
[141] CV, I, 37–38.
[142] Ibid., pp. 59–60.
[143] Ibid., pp. 38–39.

not be fed. "There is not a foot of waste land in all of China; and if it were not tilled, the product would not suffice to maintain such multitudes."[144] Neither the peasants nor the land are ever idle. They often raise three crops per year on the same fields. Chinese farmers maintain that high productivity not by allowing the land to lie fallow, but by intensive fertilization. They buy human dung in the towns, cities, monasteries, and even prisons, and cart it off to the fields. They also gather all sorts of other waste, burn it, and use the ashes for fertilizer. He reports that six thousand "country men" come into Hangchow each day to carry out the dung.[145] Navarrete also describes some of the farm work, especially rice culture. For all their diligence and hard work, he observes, most Chinese peasants remain poor. Landlords usually pay all the taxes on the land in return for half of the crop. The peasants retain the other half for their labor.[146] As a consequence of peasant diligence, Chinese cities are abundantly supplied with inexpensive foodstuffs and the streets are kept clean. Navarrete reports, for example, that Hangchow

is so well stor'd (and there is none but what is so) that 70,000 Soldiers coming to it in my time, they all liv'd upon what was then actually in the shops, and sold about the streets, without raising the Price of any thing, or causing the least scarcity in the City, no more than if twenty men had come to it.[147]

The ingenuity and productivity of Chinese artisans and craftsmen also continued to evoke admiration. Magalhães was impressed with their frugality. They discard nothing, and he thought they used far fewer tools than their European counterparts.[148] Navarrete stresses their ability to imitate. "In the Province of Canton they have counterfeited several things so exactly that they sell them inland for goods brought from Europe."[149] Not only do Chinese craftsmen copy European products, they also imitate one another. For example, artisans in Fukien were counterfeiting the porcelain produced at the imperial porcelain factories in Kiangsi Province until the emperor ordered them to stop.[150] The quantity and variety of products continue to

[144] *Ibid.*, pp. 52–53. Navarrete here seems to be voicing traditional Confucian judgments about the moral superiority of peasants to merchants and artisans and about their practical importance in society.

[145] J. S. Cummins (ed.), *The Travels and Controversies of Friar Domingo Navarrete, 1618–1686* (2 vols.; "HS," 2d ser., CXVIII–CXIX; Cambridge, 1962), II, 204. Cummins' edition is a translation of only the autobiographical sixth book of Navarrete's *Tratados;* see *ibid.*, pp. cxix–cxx.

[146] Navarrete, *CV*, I, 53.

[147] Cummins (ed.), *op. cit.* (n. 145), II, 204.

[148] *Op. cit.* (n. 65), p. 121.

[149] Navarrete, *CV*, I, 53.

[150] *Ibid.*, p. 54. Porcelain was manufactured in Te-hua, Ch'üan-chou prefecture, in Fukien Province during the seventeenth century. See Sung Ying-hsing, *T'ien-kung k'ai-wu. Chinese Technology in the Seventeenth Century,* trans. E-tu Zen Sun and Shiou-chuan Sun (University Park, Pa., 1966), p. 146.

amaze European observers. Navarrete thought there were at least four gal-
leons full of "Curiosities and toys" on the store shelves in either Nanking,
Hangchow, or Soochow.[151] Despite the large number of descriptions, however, and the occasional description of a new craft or product, there were no
major changes in Europe's view of Chinese arts and crafts. In fact, products
such as silk, porcelain, paper, gunpowder, printing, architecture, temples,
palaces, and the Great Wall were described again and again in language similar to that of Trigault, Semedo, and Martini. Some new descriptions of
buildings and bridges appeared. Navarrete, for example, describes a bridge
cut from a single stone in Kweichou Province,[152] and Magalhães identifies
the magnificent bridge west of Peking which Marco Polo had described.[153]
Magalhães also tells of coiled ropes made from powdered wood which
burned at a regular rate and thus served as timepieces. The Chinese, he reports, also use them as alarm clocks by hanging a small weight on the coil
which falls into a copper pan when the rope burns to that point. He thinks
these timepieces are much cheaper than European clocks and watches.[154]
Navarrete sees wind-devices for raising water into irrigation ditches near
Nanking, and speculates that Mendoza's story about sailing chariots came
from them.[155] Everyone reports the measurements and weight of a massive
bell in Peking which they thought might be the largest in the world.[156] All of
the Jesuits and Navarrete describe the observatory in Peking. (See pl.
307.) Nieuhof and Dapper depict in words and sketches many buildings
and bridges which the Dutch ambassadors saw during their tribute missions.[157] Nieuhof writes about ordinary merchants' houses in Nanking:
They are poor, built without comfort or convenience. Most of them are one
story high. Each has but one door and a single room for both eating and
sleeping. Along the street a large rectangular opening serves as a window,
its shutter as a counter on which merchandise is displayed. The opening is
covered with straw mats. The roofs are of white tile and the walls are white-
washed. In front of each store is a well-finished board displaying the mer-

[151] Cummins (ed.), *op. cit.* (n. 145), I, 154–55.
[152] *CV*, I, 29.
[153] *Op. cit.* (n. 65), pp. 11–15.
[154] *Ibid.*, pp. 124–26. The Jesuits, who prided themselves on introducing mechanical clocks to
China, usually tend to deprecate the more primitive Chinese timepieces based on fire or water.
For the history of Chinese measures of time, including mechanical clockworks, see J.
Needham, *Science and Civilization in China* (6 vols.; Cambridge, 1954–84), Vol. IV, Pt. 2,
pp. 437–40, 509.
[155] Navarrete, *CV*, I, 30. These were probably the same type of horizontal windmills observed and commented upon by Nieuhof in 1656, which he saw along the Grand Canal and of
which he made sketches. On these windmills see Needham, *op. cit.* (n. 154), Vol. IV, Pt. 2,
p. 5.
[156] For example, Magalhães, *op. cit.* (n. 65), pp. 123–24; Navarrete, *CV*, I, 13.
[157] For examples see pls. 320, 334, 338, and 339. See also Kircher's picture of the Flying
Bridge in Shensi Province (pl. 299) and Nieuhof's depiction of the porcelain pagoda of Nanking (pl. 321).

chant's name and business. Many have high poles standing next to the signboard from which fly pennants or flags.[158]

Many writers—for example, Schall, Nieuhof, Dapper, Navarrete, Magalhães, and Le Comte—describe the imperial palace; some of them in great detail, with the consequence that much more was known about it than in the first half of the century. Schall and Magalhães had been inside the palace and had personally seen much of what they describe. Nieuhof had accompanied the Dutch ambassadors to their formal audience with the emperor; he both describes and sketches what he saw. Two of his sketches—one of the imperial audience and a ground plan of the palace enclosure—were engraved and printed with his book.[159] For the rest, Nieuhof relies on Trigault's and Martini's descriptions. Dapper uses Martini's, Schall's, and Nieuhof's descriptions, quoting passages from each of them.[160] Magalhães' description of the palace is by far the most detailed; it also differs in several respects from Nieuhof's.[161] The Portuguese Jesuit conducts his readers through the double gate on the north side of the "Cham gan Kiai" (Chang-an chieh, Street of Perpetual Repose) and from there through the nine courts and twenty "apartments" that stretch to the northern gate. He also describes the river than runs through the large area between the inner and outer walls on the east side, and the lake on the west side. Then he names and describes many separate palaces and temples inside the inner enclosure and several imperial temples in the city outside the palace grounds, the Altars of Heaven and of Earth among them. Magalhães is obviously awed by the grandeur of the imperial palace, by the red-lacquered walls and yellow-tiled roofs, by the ornate carvings of dragons and the other decorations on all the buildings, by the beautiful marble bridges and stairs, by the ornate roofs whose ridges usually terminate in the heads of tigers, lions, or dragons. Wherever he can, Magalhães provides measurements so that his readers may appreciate the sizes of the buildings. Le Comte is far less impressed with it all. He dislikes Chinese architecture and continually judges Chinese buildings deficient by contemporary French standards. The great number of halls, the grand marble stairs and arches and the yellow glazed roofs are indeed dazzling, but in their design, he thinks, the Chinese committed many "unpardonable faults": "The apartments are all ill contrived, the ornaments irregular, there wants that uniformity in which consists the beauty and convenience of our palaces." They "must needs offend any one that has the least notion of true architecture."[162] The enthusiasm of other missionaries, the Frenchman thought, resulted either from their never having seen really

[158] *Op. cit.* (n. 29), I, 104–5. See our pl. 320.
[159] *Op. cit.* (n. 29), I, 172–73, 166–77. See our pls. 305 and 314.
[160] *Op. cit.* (n. 55), II, 23–25.
[161] Magalhães, *op. cit.* (n. 65), pp. 268–314.
[162] Le Comte, *op. cit.* (n. 125), pp. 59–60.

good architecture or from having lived in China for so long that their standards had deteriorated.[163]

The second half of the century saw many more eyewitness accounts of Chinese cities and thus much more accurate detail about them. Jesuit writers describe the towns they visited on their involuntary travels during the Oboi regency; Navarrete, who distrusted Jesuit reports, writes only about the cities he actually visited; and Nieuhof carefully describes each village and town through which the Dutch embassy passed, frequently sketching them as well.[164] Not only were more cities described in greater detail, but changes were reported as well. Nieuhof, for example, repeatedly describes ruined cities, casualties of the Manchu Conquest, which he is told were stately and populous before the civil war. Dapper, Navarrete, and Magalhães, on the other hand, frequently describe rebuilt towns.

Everyone wrote about Peking; more details became known, some earlier misinformation was corrected, and the changes resulting from the conquest introduced. Magalhães, Navarrete, and Le Comte, for example, describe what they call a new city with separate walls adjoining the old city on its southern side. Most of the Chinese live there; the northern city has become known as the Tartar city.[165] Both cities are square with straight streets intersecting at right angles. Out of deference to the emperor the houses are built low, unlike those in other Chinese cities. Magalhães writes that the northern city has nine gates rather than Martini's twelve, and that the new Chinese city has seven. Large suburbs have grown up outside each gate.[166] The streets are still not paved and the dust is as bad as ever. Upon entering the capital, Ides' embassy, writes Brand, "raised such a dust that we could scarce see one another."[167] Still much of Peking's vibrant commercial life takes place in those streets. Reports Magalhães, "there is every thing to be sold at your Door for entertainment, subsistence or pleasure . . . the throng is everywhere as great that there is nothing to compare with it but the Fairs and Processions of Europe."[168] Many trades are practiced in the streets: shoemakers, tailors, smiths, and those who repair broken porcelain all carry their tools with them and perform their services in doorways or on the street, or whereever they find a customer. So do manicurists, who use little chisels to cut finger- and toenails, and barbers. Navarrete thinks barbering is a new trade, having grown up since the conquest and the queue. Barbers ply the streets, carrying stool, basin, water, and fire on their backs and beating a

---

[163] *Ibid.*, p. 60.

[164] For examples see pls. 303, 319, 324, 326, and 329.

[165] For example, see Navarrete, *CV*, I, 11; Magalhães, *op. cit.* (n. 65), pp. 265–66; Le Comte, *op. cit.* (n. 125), pp. 54–57. For Magalhães' plan of Peking see our pl. 304.

[166] Magalhães, *op. cit.* (n. 65), pp. 265–66. This is essentially correct; see Nigel Cameron and Brian Blake, *Peking; A Tale of Three Cities* (New York, 1965), p. 40.

[167] *Op. cit.* (n. 138), p. 83.

[168] *Op. cit.* (n. 65), pp. 267–68.

distinctive sort of drum; they shave heads, clean ears, and massage backs.[169]
To transport people and the goods they have purchased, beasts of burden
can be hired at virtually every street corner, bridge, or city gate. They are as
cheap as they are numerous. Navarrete says that fifty or a hundred can be
delivered to your door on short notice. To find their way around, people
carry little books which contain the name and location of every street or
alley in the city. Restaurants are numerous and good. According to Navarrete, "There is meat ready dressed to be had at any time of the day, and at all
rates, in every city or town, or even in the villages that lie on any frequented
road."[170] In summer, he reports, cartloads of ice stand at every Peking street
corner, where hot and dusty pedestrians buy it to cool a bowl of drinking
water. Just to see them is refreshing.[171]

Other cities are described in similar detail, especially Nanking, Hangchow, Soochow, Foochow, and Canton. So are the roads, rivers, and canals
on which the writers travel from city to city and the boats on which they
ride. The Grand Canal continues to amaze Europeans, as do the number of
boats on it. The emperor is reported to employ 9,999 boats to carry tax
grain to the capital. Magalhães thinks the number of grain barges was determined by the Chinese affection for the number nine; Navarrete says the emperor ordered 10,000 but had one burned to see how much iron was in it.[172]
According to Magalhães it takes half a day to sail clear of the boats that
crowd around any Chinese city. "A man may say," he observes, "that there
are two Empires in *China,* the one upon the Water, and the other upon the
Land; and as many Venice's as there are Cities."[173] Many more details about
China's cities, commerce, roads, and waterways can be found in the literature of the second half of the century, but they do not appreciably alter the
image painted by Trigault, Semedo, and Martini. Occasionally Navarrete or
Magalhães questions an earlier report. Navarrete, for example, refuses to
believe that Chinese junks could have sailed to India, Madagascar, and East
Africa centuries earlier. He believes Chinese ships or navigation were not
good enough, and he finds no substantial reason why they should go
there.[174] Magalhães disbelieves Marco Polo's report about the use of paper
money during the Mongol period. He supposes that Marco Polo was misled
by the paper imitations of copper cash or silver bars sold for funeral fires.[175]
Both corrections are wrong. Magalhães also observes that Marco Polo and
Martini exaggerated the number of bridges in Hangchow; he counts only

[169] Navarrete, *CV,* I, 23.
[170] *Ibid.,* p. 54.
[171] *Ibid.,* p. 22.
[172] Magalhães, *op. cit.* (n. 65), pp. 129–31; Navarrete, *CV,* I, 22.
[173] Magalhães, *op. cit.* (n. 65), p. 129. For Nieuhof's sketch of a "floating village" see our pl.
328.
[174] Navarrete, *CV,* I, 6.
[175] Magalhães, *op. cit.* (n. 65), pp. 136–38.

five major bridges, not twelve thousand.[176] Nonetheless he is as impressed with Hangchow's beauty and bustling commercial life as was Marco Polo or any of the early seventeenth-century writers.

In addition to Chinese cities, Europeans continued to describe the Portuguese city of Macao. As Alexandre de Rhodes observed, "The town isn't large, but it is beautiful and built in the style of Europe, where building is much better done than in China." Rhodes also noted the decline in Macao's trade and prosperity.[177] Both Nieuhof and Dapper included descriptions of Macao; they seem to have been taken almost entirely from Martini's *Atlas*, omitting, however, what Martini said about Macao's importance for Christian missions. Neither says anything about Macao's decline in the 1640's.[178]

The restoration of Portuguese independence in 1640 did not revive Macao's sixteenth-century prosperity; nevertheless the city survived. Trade with Manila continued despite the separation of Portugal from Spain, and a vigorous trade developed with Makassar and Timor.[179] The Macanese supplied China with Timor sandalwood, and, through Portuguese ports in India, supplied the Indian brass industry with Chinese tutenag. Despite initial worries about the consequences of the Manchu Conquest for their city, the Macanese established amicable relations with the local and provincial Ch'ing officials, including the feudatory Shang K'o-hsi (see pl. 323).

In 1662, however, new threats to Macao appeared. In an effort to deprive the anti-Ch'ing rebels led by Koxinga of local support, the Ch'ing rulers in 1660 ordered the evacuation of all the people and the burning of all the villages in a ten-mile strip along the Fukien coast. In 1662 the coastal evacuation program was extended to the rest of the south coast, including Kwangtung Province. When the order was posted in Macao all the Chinese residents hurried to obey, leaving the city without most of its work force. Trade was banned, and even food supplies were reduced to a small trickle. Local Chinese officials were bribed to allow some illicit trade and to use their influence to obtain an exemption from the coastal evacuation policy for Macao. The Jesuits in Peking, led by Father Adam Schall, tried to help, but in 1665 they were put on trial as a result of Yang Kuang-hsien's accusations against them. Elsewhere in China all the churches were closed and the missionaries were all detained in Canton. Negotiations continued, as did bribes and smuggling. The Portuguese organized an embassy to the Ch'ing court led by Manoel de Saldanha, which finally left Canton for Peking in

[176] *Ibid.*, p. 18.

[177] Solange Hertz (trans.), *Rhodes of Viet Nam; The Travels and Missions of Father Alexander de Rhodes in China and Other Kingdoms of the Orient* (Westminster, Md., 1966), p. 37.

[178] Nieuhof, *op. cit.* (n. 29), I, 34; Dapper, *op. cit.* (n. 55), II, 76. For Martini's description see above, p. 1609.

[179] On the trade with Makassar and Timor see C. R. Boxer, *Francisco de Figueiredo: A Portuguese Merchant-Adventurer in South East Asia, 1624–1667* ("Verhandelingen van het Koninklijk Instituut voor Taal-, Land-, en Volkenkunde," LII; The Hague, 1967).

1670. Not until 1668, after the K'ang-hsi emperor proclaimed his majority, was the evacuation order rescinded, allowing Macao to begin its rehabilitation.[180]

The story of Macao's troubles during the 1660's was relayed to Europe in the Jesuit letterbooks and histories as well as in some Dutch reports. Greslon (1671) provided one of the most complete accounts.[181] From it one can learn not only about the events in Macao, but also about the workings of the new administration in Canton. After the death of "Chunchy" (Shun-chih) the "Tartars" (Manchus) place a garrison and artillery at the wall which separates Macao from China, with orders to open the gate only on certain days. All of Macao's food and necessities come through that gate. Apart from a few herb gardens there is no arable land in Macao. At one point in the crisis the gate remains closed for three months. Macao is also besieged by a small navy, and thus cannot receive food by land or sea. Some food is smuggled in, but at an excessive price that only the rich can afford. Meanwhile merchants cannot sell their goods; they are forced to give it to local mandarins at a very low price in return for smuggled food. Ships which try to trade at Macao, unaware of the imperial prohibition, are seized and their cargoes confiscated. Five or six ships of the smugglers are also seized. The Macanese are not even permitted to place a sloop in the water to obtain firewood from neighboring islands. Next they are ordered to abandon the city and move inland. In turn they ask that they be allowed to leave China if trade cannot be restored. The "mandarins of the provinces" want to restore Macao's trade because of the wealth they receive from the trade. Greslon estimates that they are losing "more than four million [taels?] in gold each year" that Macao remains closed. The Tartars, however, are willing to endure that loss because they fear the loss of the empire if foreigners are allowed freely to trade in China. Still, they hesitate to send the Portuguese away for fear that they will be decried by foreigners for driving the Europeans out of a port they have peacefully held for more than a century. The "tsumto" of Canton (*tsung-tu* or governor-general, probably Lu Hsing-tu) offers to obtain freedom of trade and navigation for Macao in return for 500,000 ecus. The Macanese agree, but receive in return only permission to remain in Macao. The "tsumto" allows some illegal trade so that the Macanese will have the means to pay the bribe; also forty percent of this trade must go to the "tsumto." More bribes are solicited; the Macanese argue that they should not have to pay the entire sum because trade was not restored. Finally imperial officials come down to investigate. Merchants are arrested, and the "tsumto" is put in prison, where he commits suicide. The "viceroy" (actually the governor of Kwangtung, Wang Lai-jen) was also brought to trial,

---

[180] See John E. Wills, Jr., *Embassies and Illusions: Dutch and Portuguese Envoys to K'ang-hsi, 1666–1687* (Cambridge, Mass., 1984), pp. 83–101. On the De Saldanha embassy see *ibid.*, pp. 101–26.

[181] Adrien Greslon, *Histoire de la Chine sous la domination des Tartares. . . .* (Paris, 1671).

but died during the investigation. He left behind a memorial recommending clemency and the restoration of trade for the sake of the poor people who had suffered so much.[182]

François de Rougemont, in a book published one year after Greslon's, also described Macao's troubles during the 1660's. He says relatively little about the situation in the city itself and about the negotiations with local and provincial officials. He concentrates on the efforts of the Jesuits in Peking to help Macao, especially those of Father Jacques Le Favre who traveled from Kwangtung to Peking and back again to carry messages to Adam Schall and the others in Peking and to negotiate on their behalf with officials in Kwangtung.[183]

Navarrete visited Macao twice: once in 1658, before the evacuation edict, and again in 1670 after the crisis had passed. Accounts of both visits are included in his *Tratados,* published in 1676. Navarrete's contempt for the Jesuits and the Portuguese strongly flavors his account; in the main, however, it is accurate.[184] The Portuguese are not masters of Macao. "Tartar soldiers . . . uncover Women's faces as they go along the Streets, and even in [religious] Processions, and there is no body can hinder them, tho in China they look upon it as a heinous offence for a Man to look upon a Woman." After some Manchu soldiers were treated brusquely by the priests when they were viewing the Jesuit church, they respond by beating up two Jesuit priests on the streets later during the day. Several Jesuit lay brothers in turn attack the soldiers, who report the incident to Cantonese authorities. Arrests are made, the Jesuits are imprisoned for several months, and the Society is fined three thousand ducats. More offensive still, a minor Chinese official organizes a "Festival to his Idols" in imitation of Portuguese religious processions. No one dares interfere. Says Navarrete: "I was an eyewitness to it, woe is me, and bewail'd the miserable condition of that place." Everyone in Macao, churchman as well as layman, pays ground rent to the Chinese on their houses and churches. The Jesuits refuse to pay, citing a fourteenth-century papal bull as justification. The Portuguese magistrates who collect the ground rent must therefore pay the Jesuits' share from city funds.[185]

In connection with his 1670 visit to Macao, Navarrete briefly describes the city's geography, buildings, and history; he adds little to what was written by earlier visitors. He retells the old story about Macao's origins: that local Chinese authorities allowed the Portuguese to settle there because they had driven out some troublesome pirates. Macao's existence is against China's ancient laws, but Cantonese mandarins connive to allow the Por-

[182] *Ibid.*, pp. 303–13. Greslon's account is fairly accurate; *cf.* Wills, *loc. cit.* (n. 180).
[183] *Historia Tartaro-Sinica nova* . . . (Louvain, 1673), pp. 72–83. (First Portuguese edition, Lisbon, 1672.)
[184] Wills, *op. cit.* (n. 180), p. 96, n. 56.
[185] Cummins (ed.), *op. cit.* (n. 145), I, 131–36.

tuguese to continue there because of the personal gain they receive from Macao. Macao prospered from the trade with Japan and Manila, but even in its heyday it should never be compared with Manila: "for the People [Spanish] of Manila are free, and those of Macao slaves [to the Chinese]." The Macanese have always paid ground rent to the Chinese for their houses and churches and anchorage fees for their ships.[186]

Since the failure of the trade with Japan and Manila the city has become quite poor. Navarrete is told that at one time twenty-four monks were supported by the Dominican monastery in Macao, whereas now with great difficulty it maintains three in poverty. Under the Manchus, the Portuguese in Macao are even less free than they were under the Ming:

When the City has any business, they go in a Body with Rods in their hands to the Mandarine who resides a League from thence and they petition him on their Knees. The Mandarine in his Answer writes thus: "This barbarous and brutal People desires such and such a thing, let it be granted," or "refus'd them". Thus they return in great state to their City, and their Fidalgos or Noblemen with the Badg of the Knighthood of the Order of Christ hanging at their Breasts, have gone upon these Errands; . . . If their King knew these things, it is almost incredible that he should allow of them.[187]

Navarrete briefly describes the crisis of the sixties in Macao and the negotiations between the city and the Chinese authorities. He includes far less detail than did Greslon, and he is far less sympathetic to the plight of the Macanese than was Greslon. Nevertheless their stories essentially agree. During the long months when the gate to Macao was closed or when it was opened only twice a month, many poor people in Macao starved to death. According to Navarrete, Macao has always enjoyed an unsavory reputation: "It would take up much time and paper to write but a small Epitome of the Broils, Uproars, Quarrels and Extravagancies there have been in Macao." He includes only a couple of examples. But then, he observes, the Portuguese lower the moral tone of every place they visit or settle. Their present sufferings he judges to be God's scourging.[188]

Regarding China's foreign commerce, some changes were reported. China's traditional aversion to foreigners continued to be noted, but the exceptions or changes under the Manchus must have been obvious to many readers. All the missionaries describe Adam Schall's close relationship with the Shun-chih emperor and with important officials in Peking, as well as the role of Jesuits such as Verbiest, Magalhães, and Gerbillon during the K'ang-hsi reign. The Dutch heard rumors that the Manchus intended to permit free trade, but their three embassies during the last half of the seventeenth

[186] *Ibid.*, II, 260–64.
[187] *Ibid.*, pp. 263–69.
[188] *Ibid.*, pp. 264–75.

century were still treated as tribute missions, and they received no permission to trade outside their infrequent official tribute missions. Nevertheless Dapper describes trade along the Fukien coast during Bort's campaigns against Koxinga. Some non-tributary trade seems to have been available in the Canton area as well. Frederick Bolling, for example, describes an apparently illicit trade at sea and on the coastal islands between Cantonese and Batavian private merchants.[189] Nikolaas de Graaf describes his VOC ship's officially permitted trade off Canton during the winter of 1684–85. Not only did Cantonese officials negotiate with the Dutch and allow the trade, but the Chinese entertained the Dutch with banquets and fireworks. De Graaf does not describe these events as if they were in any way unusual.[190] Ides and Brand discuss the treaties between Russia and China and the trade along the northern frontier.

The physical appearance and dress of the Chinese were described in great detail. Nieuhof and Dapper provide sketches of officials, soldiers, merchants, farmers, beggars, entertainers, and prisoners of both sexes.[191] Both depend heavily on Trigault, Semedo, and Martini for their descriptions. Many of the illustrations depict people in Ming rather than in Ch'ing costume. Dapper devotes an entire chapter to clothing and to the insignia of civil and military officials. He first rehearses what Trigault, Semedo, and Martini had written and then describes the various kinds of flags, pennants, ceremonial weapons, belts, footwear, and hats worn by officials. Four full-page engravings illustrate each item. Depending heavily on Martini's *Sinicae historiae,* Dapper also describes the processions of great "mandarins" through Chinese cities and towns. They are carried in elegant, often beautifully carved, open sedan chairs accompanied by a large entourage of soldiers and servants, some of whom carry flags and pennants indicating the office and dignity of the official. One carries a large elaborate parasol; others, "executioners," carry the ubiquitous bamboo canes with which they inflict summary punishments. The number of bearers and the size of the entourage vary with the rank of the official. Lesser officials ride on horseback, as do almost all officials in Peking, where they travel with far less pomp than in the provinces.[192] Le Comte also uses many pages to describe Chinese clothing and the kinds of cloth from which it was made.[193] Kircher provides some beautiful illustrations of Chinese dress but little other description.[194] All the Jesuits emphasize the modesty of Chinese dress, and the admirable

[189] Bolling, "Oost-Indische reisboek, bevattende zijne reis naar Oost-Indië . . ." *BTLV,* LXVIII (1913), pp. 366–71.

[190] *Op. cit.* (n. 121), pp. 174–81. The K'ang-hsi emperor permitted non-tributary trade in several ports, Canton among them, in 1684. See above, n. 121, and Kessler, *op. cit.* (n. 121), pp. 95–97.

[191] For examples see pls. 337, 341, 361–64, 381, and 382.

[192] *Op. cit.* (n. 55), I, 453–66.

[193] *Op. cit.* (n. 125), pp. 124–46.

[194] See pls. 316, 317, and 340.

fact that the styles never change.¹⁹⁵ Women, for example, never allow even their hands to show in public, and according to Magalhães, are offended by the naked hands and feet in the pictures of Christian saints.¹⁹⁶ Nevertheless, the Chinese lavish considerable attention on their clothing and are always careful to wear robes appropriate to the occasion. Even the poor, Magalhães reports, wear new or newly cleaned clothes on New Year's Day.¹⁹⁷ Le Comte reports that Chinese women spend much time on their dress and appearance despite their seclusion.¹⁹⁸ He also claims that common workmen, especially in the south, are anything but modest, going about the streets clad in a single pair of drawers.¹⁹⁹ All Europeans report one major style change since the Manchu Conquest—the new hair style. Before the conquest all Chinese wore their hair long and lavished much time and attention on combing, coiling, and dressing it. Since the conquest, men are required to shave their pates and wear the queue. Europeans are amazed at the intensity with which some Chinese resist the newly imposed style, and noted that many overseas Chinese would not wear it at all. Some also report that the Manchus at first tried to discourage footbinding but that the custom persists nonetheless and that the Manchus seem to have given up trying to change it.

European impressions about the character of the Chinese also changed little as the century wore on. The Jesuits tend to stress their natural virtues, the depiction of which is further enhanced by references to the constancy of Chinese converts under persecution. Nevertheless, they frequently agree with the European merchants and travelers about Chinese greed and guile. Le Comte, for example, describes not only crafty merchants, but thieves so clever they could steal the furniture and even the bed covers from a sleeping man's room without awakening him.²⁰⁰ Concerning their propensity to gamble for high stakes, he remarks: "There is no degree of extravagance to which the desire of lucre and riches will not carry a Chinese."²⁰¹ Less appears to have been said about the antipathy of the Chinese toward foreigners. In fact, some writers include hospitality and graciousness toward foreigners among their admirable characteristics. Several writers portray graciousness toward foreigners as a Manchu rather than a Chinese trait. Nieuhof, for example, was convinced that the Manchu members of the

---

¹⁹⁵ Actually new clothing styles, especially for men, were decreed by each new dynasty. On Ch'ing costumes see Xun Zhou and Chunming Gao, *Five Thousand Years of Chinese Costumes* (San Francisco, 1987), pp. 172–211.

¹⁹⁶ *Op. cit.* (n. 65), p. 103. The narrow sleeves of Ch'ing robes ("horseshoe sleeves") ended in a cuff which hid the hands but which also could be folded up. Horseshoe sleeves, however, were worn by men as well as women. See Zhou and Gao, *op. cit.* (n. 195), pp. 172–73, 182–83, 188–89.

¹⁹⁷ *Op. cit.* (n. 65), p. 102.

¹⁹⁸ *Op. cit.* (n. 125), p. 125.

¹⁹⁹ *Ibid.*, p. 138.

²⁰⁰ *Ibid.*, pp. 242–43.

²⁰¹ *Ibid.*, p. 299

Board of Rites would have permitted the Dutch to trade more freely in China but were blocked by the Chinese members. By the end of the century, however, few European writers distinguish any longer between Manchus and Chinese.

Chinese marriage customs continued to attract considerable attention. Despite opinions to the contrary, Le Comte insists that Chinese men buy their wives. They buy them sight unseen, and as a consequence some brides are sent back home by their prospective grooms when the carriage door is opened and the couple see each other for the first time. Brides, of course, have to accept the grooms whether or not they are pleased, because they have been purchased.[202] Le Comte thinks husbands may not divorce their wives except for adultery; they can, however, be sold to another.[203] Navarrete lists many other reasons for divorce in China: talkativeness, disobedience to father or mother-in-law, theft, leprosy, barrenness, or jealousy. He concludes that no Chinese marriages are valid in the Catholic sense.[204] He also describes the occasional marriage of two dead young people, by which the families become related as if the couple had lived.[205] Everyone comments on the seclusion of women. Navarrete, for example, traveled from one end of Hangchow to the other without seeing a single woman.[206] Apparently Manchu women were not so closely kept: Navarrete reports that while modestly dressed, they wore boots and rode astride in public like men.[207] Nieuhof reports seeing and talking with several Manchu women, the wives of officials. In Nanking one descended from her sedan chair on the street to look at Ambassador De Keizer's side arm and to try on his hat. She then invited the Dutchmen to her home, introduced them to her twenty-year-old daughter, and served them tea.[208]

Funerals were described as frequently as marriages. Navarrete stresses the religious aspects of Chinese funerals. For example, he reports that the son of a deceased person would commonly take one of his father's garments to the rooftop and there call for the soul to return. The children would then wait three days before laying the corpse in his casket.[209] Several Jesuit writers and Dapper describe specific royal funerals: that of the Shun-chih emperor, his favorite wife, and the K'ang-hsi emperor's mother. Martini had earlier reported that the Manchus frequently burned wives, servants, and animals on the funeral pyre of a deceased prince. He assured his readers, however, that

[202] *Ibid.*, pp. 299–300.

[203] *Ibid.*, p. 302.

[204] *CV*, I, 66–67.

[205] *Ibid.*, p. 69. On posthumous marriages in the twentieth century see J. G. Cormack, *Chinese Birthday, Wedding, Funeral, and Other Customs* (Peking, 1923), p. 57.

[206] *CV*, I, 17.

[207] *Ibid.*, p. 22.

[208] *Op. cit.* (n. 29), pp. 52, 102, 107.

[209] *CV*, I, 71.

after the conquest they abandoned that barbarous custom and conformed to Chinese funeral practices.[210] There were lapses, however. The Shun-chih emperor had twenty ladies and eunuchs commit suicide to accompany his wife into the other world.[211] Navarrete reports that in 1668 the family of a seventeen-year-old concubine petitioned the emperor to prevent her having to hang herself at her husband's funeral. The K'ang-hsi emperor then abolished the custom.[212]

The change from Ming to Ch'ing seems to have clarified the status of China's hereditary aristocracy for European observers. The relatives of the Ming emperors described by earlier writers as living royally on provincial estates did not survive the conquest. To Magalhães, for example, it became clear that China had very few aristocratic families and that none endured beyond the life of a single dynasty, at the longest, three hundred years.[213] The only exception to this rule was the family of Confucius, who still lived in Shantung Province, and had been granted a hereditary title and tax exemption.[214] The scholar-official families who comprised what looked like an aristocracy—Magalhães calls them "gown nobles"—were even shorter-lived. None, he reports, ever remained prominent for the duration of a dynasty.[215] About other strata of Chinese society, European writers of the late seventeenth century provided more details but few new insights. Navarrete wrote more about peasants than anyone else, and several observers described the people at the bottom of the social scale: the poor, actors, jugglers, acrobats, and beggars. Nieuhof, for example, describes beggars so brazen that they grabbed the clothing of passers-by. They were frequently deformed as a consequence of self-inflicted injuries to elicit pity. Worse still, Nieuhof thought, they maimed and disfigured their children to make them more effective beggars.[216] There were apparently many poor. Nieuhof reports that he met them everywhere; Navarrete agrees. The emperor makes a yearly gift, Navarrete reports, which "exceeds four million [taels?]," for the maintenance of the poor. Many more survive by begging, praying, or doing tricks with dogs or snakes; he thinks them

proud, troublesome, and saucy, and not satisfied with any thing. They have their judge that is their protector in every city and town, and they all pay him a contribution out of their gettings. Whensoever any of them is brought before a court, this man appears, protects, defends, and pleads for them; and it is strange to see that

[210] *Op. cit.* (n. 7), p. 26.
[211] For example, see Greslon, *op. cit.* (n. 181), pp. 47–49. *Cf.* Hummel (ed.), *op. cit.* (n. 9), p. 302, which reports that some eunuchs and ladies-in-waiting were indeed ordered to commit suicide when the empress Hsiao-hsien died, and that the practice, known as *hsün-tsang,* continued through the Shun-chih reign.
[212] *CV,* I, 70.
[213] *Op. cit.* (n. 65), p. 146.
[214] *Ibid.,* p. 147.
[215] *Ibid.,* p. 146. See also Le Comte, *op. cit.* (n. 125), p. 289.
[216] *Op. cit.* (n. 29), II, 31–35.

judgment is always given for the poor, which makes people stand in awe of them; no body dares so much as give them an ill word, but rather will let them have anything they ask for.[217]

Ceremony in social relations continues to be discussed at length. Most of the observers describe formal visits, banquets, official receptions, and the important audiences which they had attended. Many note that the Manchus were much more open and less formal in their social relations than the Chinese. The several accounts of Schall's friendship with the Shun-chih emperor, Verbiest's account of K'ang-hsi's hunting expeditions, and even Nieuhof's and Dapper's descriptions of the entertainment of the Dutch tribute missions, en route and in the capital, seem to support that observation. Nevertheless the importance of *li* in the eyes of European writers and the space they devote to it is in no way diminished. A thorough knowledge of *li* remained indispensable to the missionaries. Le Comte observes that newcomers frequently make awful blunders;[218] most writers provide some amusing examples. Even Navarrete, usually so critical of the Jesuits, defends the time and effort devoted to ceremony and civility as "absolutely necessary."[219] He contends that the knowledge and consistent practice of *li* affects all levels of Chinese society and all places in the empire, as if it were "all a mere court, and its inhabitants all courtiers."

I have often seen it, that a child of eight years of age performs all points of civility as nicely as a man of fifty, . . . The mechanicks, plough-men, and porters, are all men of fashion, for they are all very full of civility, and express themselves in the same words as they do in the capital cities.[220]

During the persecutions, Navarrete observed, even prisoners follow the rules of courtesy and civility among themselves and toward foreign prisoners.[221] On the other hand, Magalhães, after a long and detailed description of manners and civility, notes that lesser officials do not always perform the ceremonies properly.[222]

Everyone describes banquets, the food served, and the entertainments that accompanied them. Nieuhof's descriptions are particularly vivid. Apart from the additional eyewitness illustrations, the late seventeenth-century accounts agree with those of Trigault, Semedo, and Martini. Some writers note peculiar Manchu customs. Navarrete, for example, reports that while Manchus use chopsticks like the Chinese they prefer to sit on cushions at

[217] Navarrete, *CV*, I, 25–26. On the begging system and its operation *cf*. J. D. Ball, *Things Chinese* (5th rev. ed.; London, 1926), pp. 379–82.
[218] *Op. cit.* (n. 125), p. 280.
[219] *CV*, I, 64.
[220] *Ibid.*, p. 65.
[221] *Ibid.*, p. 16.
[222] *Op. cit.* (n. 65), p. 102.

low tables like the Japanese.[223] Nieuhof reports that the Manchu host of a banquet given for foreign ambassadors in Peking sat cross-legged like a tailor on a wide, elevated bench.[224] Generally the missionaries profess to like Chinese food. Navarrete seems to have been more adventurous than most; he sampled everything and enjoyed it all. Nieuhof, on the other hand, was less adventurous. He occasionally complains about the food served to the Dutch during the 1655 tribute mission. At one of the banquets given them by the Board of Rites in Peking, Nieuhof thought the meat "looked so grey and dirty that one had reason to question what it had been cooked in."[225] Perhaps the difference between northern and southern cooking, or between Chinese and Manchu cooking, had something to do with Nieuhof's impressions. Most of the dinners which elicit complaints from him were given in Peking. After the second Dutch tribute mission, Dapper also comments on the differences in manners and eating habits between north and south. Southerners, he thought, were more refined and ceremonious than northerners. In the south, he reports, smaller portions of food were served, but with more variety and better preparation.[226] Nieuhof, too, comments favorably on a banquet given the Dutch ambassadors in Canton.[227] He also reports that the Chinese, north and south, commonly drink tea mixed with milk and a little salt. The Dutch called it bean broth.[228] Any description of Chinese food and banquets includes a description of chopsticks, how they were used and of what they were made. Navarrete reports that in addition to those made of wood, silver, ebony, and ivory, glass chopsticks were much esteemed; the Dutch, he said, had invented them, but the Chinese had learned to make them in curious designs.[229]

Chinese festivals and entertainments are described with few changes from the earlier literature, apart from eyewitness accounts of particular festivals. The Feast of Lanterns was the most frequently described festival. The Europeans were fascinated by its elaborate paper lanterns and describe them in great detail. Le Comte claims to have seen one large enough to dine, dance, or enact plays in.[230] Several writers, Navarrete, Magalhães, and Le Comte among them, tell stories about the festival's origin. According to one popular tradition, it began centuries ago when a well-loved official lost his daughter along the river bank and the people of his district came out with lanterns to help him search for her. Others thought the festival celebrated the demise of Chieh, the last despotic and debauched emperor of the Hsia

---

[223] *CV*, I, 13.
[224] *Op. cit.* (n. 29), I, 179–80.
[225] *Ibid.*, p. 180.
[226] *Op. cit.* (n. 55), I, 398.
[227] *Op. cit.* (n. 29), I, 45–57.
[228] *Ibid.*, pp. 40, 107. Is this a description of congee, or boiled rice water? It is most doubtful that the Chinese added milk and salt to tea.
[229] *CV*, I, 13.
[230] *Op. cit.* (n. 125), p. 162.

dynasty (1766 B.C.), who complained to his favorite concubine about the succession of days and nights and of the seasons, which daily reminded him that his pleasures and debaucheries would some day end. At her suggestion he built a palace without doors or windows, lit entirely by lanterns where they could surrender themselves to their pleasures without noticing the passage of time.[231] Magalhães also tells the story of the Taoist emperor who visited the Feast of Lanterns in Hangchow on a throne of white clouds drawn by white swans.[232] Navarrete describes a celebration of the Dragon Boat Festival which he had seen and explains that it was thought to have originated from a virtuous official who had drowned himself after the emperor rejected his memorial.[233]

European descriptions published after the Manchu Conquest generally depict the Chinese people, their society, customs, commerce, land, and natural resources in language that would have been familiar to readers of Trigault, Semedo, or Martini's *Atlas*. There was, in fact, much repetition. Changes resulting from the conquest were reported, but these affected China's social and economic life very little and its geography not at all. Perhaps the most conspicuous change from the ethnohistories of the first half of the century is the current quality of the new literature. It contains more illustrations, more eyewitness reports of specific events and places, and relatively fewer unqualified generalizations.

4

GOVERNMENT AND ADMINISTRATION

Obviously the Manchu Conquest affected China's government and administration perhaps more than any other aspect of life. Despite the changes reported by post-conquest European observers, however, Ch'ing government is portrayed as still essentially Chinese, structurally continuous with that of the Ming, and unmistakably imbued with traditional Chinese attitudes toward politics.

Several of the late seventeenth-century writers emphasize the special importance attached to Confucian teaching in guiding Ch'ing government. Navarrete, for example, admires its familial nature: "all is so excellently ordered that the whole empire looks like one well-governed family."[234] As

---

[231] For example, see Martini, *op. cit.* (n. 97), pp. 54–55; Magalhães, *op. cit.* (n. 65), pp. 104–12.

[232] Magalhães, *op. cit.* (n. 65), p. 112. Traditionally the Feast of Lanterns was celebrated in the middle of the first month. For a later description of these festivals see J. Doolittle, *Social Life of the Chinese* (2 vols.; New York, 1867), II, 34–38.

[233] *CV*, I, 46. This is a reference to Ch'ü Yüan (d. 265 B.C.), the famous writer of *Ch'u-tz'u* ("The Elegies of Ch'u"). For Nieuhof's illustration of a dragon boat see our pl. 330.

[234] *CV*, I, 48.

he sees it, the moral basis for Chinese government is in the Confucian Five Relationships, which he explains in some detail.[235] He thought the emperors took Confucian teachings very seriously; not only did their high officials remind them of their duty, but the emperors were obliged to study diligently, if only to understand the memorials submitted, because of the many figures of speech, allusions, and other rhetorical devices employed by their authors.[236] He relates scores of sayings and pious stories about emperors and great officials to illustrate Confucian ethics in government.[237] The only defect in the structure and philosophy of Chinese government and society in Navarrete's view was the absence of any definite and prestigious place for the military.[238] Magalhães also emphasizes the Confucian basis for government. He lists nine qualities of a virtuous monarch taken from the *Doctrine of the Mean* and describes how each of them would produce good government and render the emperor a fit example for his subjects.[239] Le Comte stresses the role of the emperor as the virtuous example. If he were not above corruption, immorality and double-dealing would spread to the entire administration; the people would be oppressed by immoral officials and would very likely revolt.[240] As Le Comte sees it, the "unbounded authority which the laws give the emperor, and a necessity which the same laws lay upon him to use that authority with moderation and discretion, are the two props which have for so many ages supported this great fabric of the Chinese monarchy."[241] For example, although the emperor taxes everyone at any rate he pleases, he always reduces the taxes for provinces which have experienced floods or bad harvests. While he is acknowledged to be sovereign over the bureaucracy and able to appoint or dismiss at will, he is nevertheless morally obliged to consult with his officials, each of whom has the right to tell him his faults.[242] Martini's *Sinicae historiae* is also full of examples which illustrate the importance of the emperor's moral authority.

As described by Europeans, the first emperors of the Ch'ing were indeed virtuous and exemplary. What is more, they were visible and describable. Unlike Trigault's Wan-li emperor (r. 1573–1620), the Shun-chih emperor

---

[235] *Ibid.*, p. 57. On the Five Relationships see above, p. 1652.

[236] *CV*, I, 99.

[237] See *ibid.*, pp. 83–110.

[238] *Ibid.*, p. 48. On the contrary, marquisates and earldoms were earned only through distinguished military service. On the upward mobility of the military see Ho Ping-ti, *The Ladder of Success in Imperial China* (New York, 1962), pp. 217–19.

[239] Magalhães, *op. cit.* (n. 65), pp. 193–94.

[240] *Op. cit.* (n. 125), p. 262.

[241] *Ibid.*, p. 249.

[242] *Ibid.*, pp. 254–55, 259. This is an exaggerated estimate of the role of court officials in advising the emperor. The censors were the only officials who regularly informed and petitioned the emperors about deficiencies in administration at all levels. But only a Grand Secretary or a favorite would have had the temerity to question the emperor's decisions or to admonish him. On K'ang-hsi's key officials see Kessler, *op. cit.* (n. 121), pp. 112–17.

(r. 1644–61) and the K'ang-hsi emperor (r. 1661–1723) appeared in public, held frequent audiences, received tribute missions, traveled outside the Forbidden City, and conversed on almost familiar terms with the Jesuits. According to Greslon, for example, Schall claimed that the Shun-chih emperor visited him twenty-four times in 1656 and 1657, frequently talking with him late into the night.[243] Verbiest saw the K'ang-hsi emperor frequently and tutored him in astronomy, mathematics, painting, and music. Twice he accompanied the emperor on hunting expeditions in Manchuria, during which he was almost continuously at the emperor's side, talking with him each day and frequently receiving food from his table. Once he sat with the emperor and about five others on the bank of a mountain stream to look at the stars. In Verbiest's words:

As the night was fair, and the Heavens very clear; he willed me to Name in the *Chinese* and *European* Languages, all the Constellations that then appeared above the Horizon, and he himself first named all these he already knew; then unfolding a small Map of the Heavens, which I had some years since presented him, he put himself upon inquiring the Hour of the Night, by the Stars in the Meridian: Pleasing himself to show to all the Knowledge he had acquired in all these Sciences.[244]

When he arrived in Peking, Le Comte was received by the emperor in a small bare audience room because K'ang-hsi was still in mourning for the death of the empress dowager. Nieuhof describes the Shun-chih emperor as he appeared in full regalia during the reception of the Dutch tribute mission of 1656, admittedly from a considerable distance.[245] Dapper similarly reports K'ang-hsi's reception of the 1667 Dutch mission.[246] To European readers the Ch'ing emperors must have appeared immensely powerful and rich. Available were many detailed descriptions of Shun-chih or K'ang-hsi on the throne, at dawn in the full splendor of a formal audience, or carried through the streets in a palanquin by twenty-four bearers surrounded by an enormous retinue of Manchu princes, Grand Secretaries, high officials, musicians, soldiers, fan and umbrella carriers, and pages. The emperor's annual revenues and the numbers of his soldiers, horses, elephants, and concubines were regularly rehearsed. But European readers could also have known the emperors as human beings in a way quite closed off to their Chinese subjects. They could have known Shun-chih as an impulsive young man, curious about Western science and religion, struggling not too successfully to restrict the delights of the harem, superstitious, and at heart still a Lamaist. They could have seen him act irrationally, broken with grief at the death of

[243] Greslon, *op. cit.* (n. 181), p. 5.
[244] D'Orléans, *op. cit.* (n. 68), p. 79. Quotation from *Philosophical Transactions,* XVI (1686–87), 49.
[245] Le Comte, *op. cit.* (n. 125), p. 39; Nieuhof, *op. cit.* (n. 29), I, 174–75.
[246] Dapper, *op. cit.* (n. 55), I, 354–56.

his favorite wife. Kircher provided a full-length portrait of Shun-chih at about eighteen years of age.[247] European readers could have seen K'ang-hsi not only as an exceedingly vigorous and sagacious monarch, but also as the bright and curious student of Chinese and Western learning, studying Confucius and Euclid, learning to calculate time by the positions of the stars, trying his hand at Western painting and music, lightheartedly enjoying the rigors of the hunt, angry with the duplicity and factionalism of the bureaucracy, concerned about the education of his sons and the effects of the Chinese good life on Manchu military vigor. They also knew what he looked like. In Le Comte's words, for example:

He was something above the middle stature, more corpulent than what in Europe we reckon handsome; yet somewhat more slender than a Chinese would wish to be: full visaged, disfigured with the small pox, had a broad forehead, little eyes, and a small nose after the Chinese fashion: his mouth was well made, and the lower part of his face very agreeable.[248]

Bouvet's *Portrait historique* depicts K'ang-hsi as the quintessence of the wise and virtuous monarch, a model even for Louis XIV. While too uncritical, Bouvet provided European readers with an astonishingly well-rounded sketch of an able and fascinating ruler. Both Le Comte's and Bouvet's books contain engraved likenesses of the K'ang-hsi emperor.[249]

Many traditional aspects of Chinese court life coninued to flourish under the Manchus. There were still eunuchs and concubines. Navarrete reports that the Shun-chih emperor expelled six thousand eunuchs and as many concubines when he became emperor.[250] Soon, however, he chose his own concubines. Eunuchs, too, appear regularly in later descriptions. The missionaries, however, report less about them and about imperial concubines than did earlier writers. They emphasize Shun-chih's, and especially K'ang-hsi's, restraint and their avoidance of the voluptuous habits of the later Ming emperors.[251] Also prominent in the early Ch'ing court were royal relatives and Manchu nobles. Unlike the Ming royal relatives, who had resided in the provinces, these newcomers seem to have remained at court. Their relationship to the emperor and to the bureaucracy was not clearly defined. Magalhães, for example, reports that "at present the Kindred of the King of

[247] *Cf.* Schall's estimate of this emperor as summarized in G. H. Dunne, S.J., *Generation of Giants* (Notre Dame, 1962), pp. 349–52. For Shun-chih's portrait see our pl. 311.

[248] *Op. cit.* (n. 125), pp. 40–41.

[249] See pls. 312 and 313. Compare the Jesuits' descriptions of K'ang-hsi with that drawn from the emperor's own writings in Spence, *op. cit.* (n. 86).

[250] *CV*, I, 12. On the elimination and control of the Ming eunuchs as preparation for the reestablishment of the Imperial Household Department (*nei-wu-fu*) in 1662 see P. M. Torbert, "The Ch'ing Imperial Household Department: A Study of Its Organization and Principal Functions, 1662–1796," (Ph.D. diss., Dept. of History, University of Chicago, 1973), pp. 37–38, 65.

[251] See especially Bouvet, *op. cit.* (n. 67), pp. 178–81.

Tartary that now reigns are all great Lords and live at Court."[252] Navarrete describes them as twenty-four kings, but adds, "they are only titular, and have no subjects" and "they are generals in the army."[253] They seem always to be near to the emperor in audiences and processions. Sometimes they are described as close imperial advisers, standing above the bureaucracy. Le Comte, for example, mentions an "extraordinary council," composed exclusively of "princes of the blood" in addition to the "council in ordinary," composed of the Grand Secretaries (*ko-lao*).[254] Magalhães comments on a "Tribunal of the Grandees," whose president was styled king and which saw to the pensions of the royal relatives.[255] That the Manchu princes were not rivals for imperial power is suggested by Le Comte's story about a "prince of the blood" who was deprived of his title and stipend because he spent too much time at cockfighting.[256]

The most obvious change in the central bureaucracy was the addition of Manchu members to all of the metropolitan boards. Almost everyone reports that under the Ch'ing each board had two presidents, four assistants or assessors, and twice as many members as under the Ming; in each case half were Manchus and half Chinese. Greslon, for example, reports that after the conquest, the Manchus recognized that they did not have the experience to govern China by themselves and therefore simply added Manchu members to the old Chinese boards and bureaus. He observes, however, that they were becoming wiser about Chinese government and were taking control more forcefully.[257] Dapper also reports in 1670 that under K'ang-hsi the Manchus shut out the Chinese wherever possible and tried to monopolize the government posts for themselves.[258] Greslon, however, reports on arguments between the Manchu and Chinese members of the Board of Rites over the frequency of Dutch tribute missions; in these debates the Chinese members seem to have been more influential.[259] Magalhães also suggests that by the time he wrote, the Manchus dominated the central government.[260]

Another major change in the central administration under the Ch'ing em-

[252] *Op. cit.* (n. 65), p. 238. On the Manchu aristocracy during the regency and the Shun-chih reign see Wakeman, *op. cit.* (n. 7), II, 881–86, 925–31.

[253] *CV*, I, 12.

[254] *Op. cit.* (n. 125), p. 263. This is probably a reference to the Assembly of Princes, a deliberative council of Manchu princes. See Wakeman, *op. cit.* (n. 7), II, 850–56.

[255] Magalhães, *op. cit.* (n. 65), pp. 237–38.

[256] *Op. cit.* (n. 125), pp. 251–52.

[257] *Op. cit.* (n. 181), p. 96.

[258] *Op. cit.* (n. 55), I, 439.

[259] *Op. cit.* (n. 181), pp. 16–17.

[260] Magalhães, *op. cit.* (n. 65), p. 208. *Cf.* Kessler, *op. cit.* (n. 121), pp. 112–36, who concludes that K'ang-hsi increasingly appointed non-banner Chinese to the highest posts in the bureaucracy. At the time of the conquest the Manchu military was organized under twenty-four banners, distinguished by the colors of their flags. There were eight Manchu, eight Mongol, and eight Chinese banners. In the first years after the conquest most of the Chinese appointed to high offices were Chinese bannermen, who had served the Manchus even before the conquest.

perors was the reestablishment of the Grand Secretariat. Magalhães and Navarrete call it the Council of State.[261] As they describe it, the Grand Secretariat (*nei-ko*) was composed of fourteen members, half of whom were Manchus;[262] it met regularly to supervise the work of the Six Boards and to consider petitions, submitting their recommendations in writing to the emperor. Navarrete claims the Grand Secretaries never took vacations.

Legal reform and rationalization was one of the major concerns of the early Ch'ing rulers. Magalhães mentions a bureau called the "San Fan Su" (*san fa-ssu*, or three branches of the judiciary) or "Council of Conscience," which examined what the emperor considered questionable death sentences. Perhaps it was not a new body: Magalhães also describes it as a joint meeting of the Board of Punishments, the Grand Court of Revision (*tai li su*), and the metropolitan censorate.[263] Magalhães also remarks on a body called the "Him gin su" (*hsing-jen ssu*, or Messenger Office), composed of officials "of the seventh Order," whose "employment is to be sent abroad, either as Envoys or Ambassadors." "Abroad" means inside the empire as well as to foreign lands. For example, it supplies the emissaries charged with carrying the emperor's honors to the family of an officer killed in battle; other members were sent to confirm the king of Korea in his office.[264] Several post-conquest writers report that the Ch'ing emperors dismantled the central governmental apparatus in Nanking; Kiangsu and Anhwei provinces were made into the double province of Chiang-nan of which Nanking, renamed Chiang-ning, was the capital. According to Dapper even the imperial palace in Nanking was destroyed.[265] Le Comte reports that the Censorate was purged under the Manchus: "but since the Tartars have been masters of China, these officers have been laid aside; inasmuch as some of them abused their commission, enriching themselves by taking money of the guilty to conceal their faults, and of the innocent whom they threatened to accuse as criminal."[266] He thinks that the censorial function is at least in part replaced by the K'ang-hsi emperor's personal visits to the provinces. He relates some examples of the emperor's accessibility on these visits and his summary punishment of despotic local officials. Also according to Le Comte, officials are periodically required to confess their secret and public faults to the emperor in what sounds like a Ch'ing antecedent to recent

---

[261] Magalhães, *op. cit.* (n. 65), pp. 197–98; Navarrete, *CV*, I, 18.

[262] The Grand Secretariat, as reorganized in 1658, included an indefinite number of Manchu and Chinese councillors. See Kessler, *op. cit.* (n. 121), p. 29.

[263] Magalhães, *op. cit.* (n. 65), pp. 228–29.

[264] *Ibid.*, p. 228. The *hsing-jen ssu* was a subordinate office of the Board of Rites. See Hucker, "Governmental Organization of the Ming Dynasty," *Harvard Journal of Asiatic Studies*, XXI (1958), p. 34.

[265] *Op. cit.* (n. 55), I, 444–45. See also Magalhães, *op. cit.* (n. 65), p. 206. On the fall of Nanking and its renaming see Lynn A. Struve, *op. cit.* (n. 5), pp. 57–60.

[266] *Op. cit.* (n. 125), p. 267. On the reform of the Censorate under the early Manchus see Wakeman, *op. cit.* (n. 7), II, 922–25.

"struggle and criticism" sessions.[267] Other European observers describe the Ch'ing censorate in terms similar to Trigault's and Semedo's description of the Ming censorate. Magalhães adds considerably more detail and distinguishes its various functions more clearly than had Trigault and Semedo. He describes the function of the Six Offices of Scrutiny, for example, although he does not call them by that name. He also correctly notes that despite their power, censors usually come from the lower ranks of the civil-service scale—the seventh grade, he reports. While he admires the ideal embodied in the Censorate, Magalhães thinks the censors commonly abuse their powers. They usually return from provincial inspection tours laden with bribes. "Generally," he reports, "they never impeach anyone of the *Mandarins* but such whose injustice and tyrannies are so publick that it is impossible to conceal them, or such who through their virtue or their poverty are not able to gratifie their avarice."[268]

Most other organs of the central bureaucracy are described much as Trigault, Semedo, and Martini had reported on them, except that the post-conquest Jesuit writers add many more details about their structure and operation. For example, the several bureaus subordinate to the Board of Rites, including the Calendrical Bureau, are prominent in the Jesuit accounts. The Jesuits also comment on the workings of government in great detail: how issues come before one of the metropolitan boards and how they are resolved, the effects of factionalism on the bureaucracy, how none of the Six Boards functions independently of the others, how if the emperor is dissatisfied with a decision he sends it back for reconsideration again and again if necessary. The missionaries' problems and trials during the Oboi regency and their return to favor during the early K'ang-hsi years made them expert observers of such matters and provided them with a large store of concrete examples. The persecutions seem to have soured Magalhães' perceptions of Chinese government. While he admires its ethical basis and structure, he depicts a wide gap between theory and practice. Although K'ang-hsi is wise and virtuous, his officials are frequently corrupt and hypocritical: "it is a rare thing," Magalhães writes, "to meet with a Mandarin that is free from avarice and corruption."[269] Almost no case is tried according to reason and justice. He that "gives money is always in the Right, till another gives more."[270]

Provincial government, according to the Europeans, changed little with the change of dynasties. The distinction between viceroys or governors-general (*tsung-tu*), with civil and military authority over two or more provinces, and provincial governors (*hsün-fu*) is somewhat clarified.[271]

---

[267] *Op. cit.* (n. 125), pp. 267–69.
[268] Magalhães, *op. cit.* (n. 65), pp. 221–28; quotation on p. 222.
[269] *Ibid.*, p. 204.
[270] *Ibid.*, p. 210.
[271] For example, see Navarrete, *CV*, I, 14, and Magalhães, *op. cit.* (n. 65), p. 241.

Magalhães' description of the structure of provincial government is the most complete. He describes each office from viceroy down to district magistrate, including several not mentioned by Trigault, Semedo, or Martini. In each case he describes the office-holder's rank in the civil-service hierarchy, over what affairs he has jurisdiction, how many assistants he employs, and so on. Altogether, with his usual love for exact figures, he declares that there are 13,647 civil and 18,525 military officials in China.[272] Most writers describe the general policies of the administration, such as the Law of Avoidance (*hui-pi*) and the triennial assize, usually in approving terms. Magalhães reports that when district magistrates are reassigned every three years, members of the Board of Civil Office draw the names of cities and towns from a bowl and that worried officials often bribe board members to obtain desired assignments.[273] In its provincial government, too, Magalhães concludes that "no Kingdom in the world could be better governed or more happy if the Conduct and Probity of the Officers were but answerable to the Institutions of the Government."[274]

Most provincial posts during the early Ch'ing were filled by Chinese. Greslon thought there were simply too few Manchus to go around.[275] Several European writers report that until 1673 large areas of south and southwest China were ruled almost independently by great feudal lords who had cooperated with the Manchus during the conquest: Wu San-kuei in Yunnan, Shang Chih-hsin in Kwangtung, and Keng Ching-chung in Fukien.[276] Nieuhof's account of the first Dutch embassy provides eyewitness details about the rule of Shang Chih-hsin and his aged father, Shang K'o-hsi, in Kwangtung, while Dapper's account of Admiral Bort's campaigns against Koxinga along the Fukien coast contains considerable detail about Keng Ching-chung and his independent powers. These three feudatories rebelled in 1673 and were subdued in a destructive civil war which lasted until 1681.[277]

As they do with other aspects of Ch'ing government, the late seventeenth-century Europeans provide an enormous amount of detail about the conduct of provincial government. Processions of high officials and their retinues are frequently described, as well as official sessions of a district magistrate's or a governor's court. Navarrete's account is particularly rich in such details. "The supreme governor of *Canton*," he reports, "without all

[272] Magalhães, *op. cit.* (n. 65), pp. 241–50.

[273] *Ibid.*, pp. 245–47.

[274] *Ibid.*, p. 249.

[275] *Op. cit.* (n. 181), pp. 96–97. On the prominence of ethnic Chinese in early Ch'ing government see Kessler, *op. cit.* (n. 121), pp. 117–24. In the years immediately following the conquest, most of the high provincial offices were filled by Chinese bannermen.

[276] For example, see Navarrete, *CV*, I, 14.

[277] On the outbreak of the rebellion of the three feudatories see Wakeman, *op. cit.* (n. 7), II, 1099–1105. Nieuhof included a portrait of Shang K'o-hsi and a sketch of the banquet given by the "viceroys" of Canton for the Dutch in September, 1655. See our pls. 322 and 323.

doubt, goes abroad in more state than any king in Europe."[278] The greater the official the less frequently he holds court. District magistrates hold open sessions in their official residences every morning and evening; governors and viceroys only two or three times per month.[279] Navarrete is also impressed by the rapid communication within the bureaucracy and the speed with which orders from Peking are implemented in the provinces. The emperor, for example, might issue an order for a thorough search for a criminal and within two months it would have passed down from the appropriate metropolitan board to the viceroys, governors, district magistrates, and heads of ten-family groupings; homes would have been searched, and reports sent back to the capital. That is how the missionaries were rounded up all over China during the persecutions.[280] When the Dutch arrived at Fukien in 1663 officials in Canton knew about it almost immediately.[281]

Navarrete and the Jesuit writers also provide firsthand information about Chinese law and justice. For the most part they agree with Semedo about Chinese laws, trials, punishments, and jails, adding their personal experiences and observations for illustration. Greslon, for example, depicts old Adam Schall, seriously impaired by a recent stroke, kneeling uncomfortably for four or five hours at a time during his trial. Schall was finally sentenced to the lingering "death by ten-thousand cuts," although the sentence was never carried out.[282] Magalhães reports that decapitation is the most shameful punishment because it shows the criminal to have been unfilial for having caused such awful mutilation of the body which he had received from his parents. If the emperor wished to be gracious to a condemned official he would send a piece of silken cord with which the condemned man might hang himself. Sometimes, according to Magalhães, relatives of a decapitated criminal would bribe the executioner for the dead man's remains in order to stitch head and body together before burial.[283] Navarrete, who spent some time in a Hangchow jail, thinks Chinese prisons are better than those of Europe. Chinese jails are cleaner, more orderly, and quieter, and the prisoners in them do not victimize one another. But prisons are sometimes overcrowded: Navarrete slept for eight nights under the cane bed in which slept two of his fellow missionaries, fearing all the while what might happen to him if the bed should fall. Finally the Europeans rented one of the private rooms in the jail for more space and comfort.[284] Everyone describes the ubiquitous beating with bamboo canes as the most common punishment in China. Many people die from the beatings, they report, although

---

[278] *CV,* I, 63.
[279] *Ibid.,* p. 61.
[280] *Ibid.,* p. 59.
[281] *Ibid.,* p. 60.
[282] *Op. cit.* (n. 181), p. 165.
[283] Magalhães, *op. cit.* (n. 65), pp. 211–12. See also Greslon, *op. cit.* (n. 181), pp. 175–76.
[284] *CV,* I, 15–16.

wealthier lawbreakers can sometimes bribe the executioners to lay the strokes on gently or hire a stand-in to take the punishment for them.[285] Le Comte tells that Yang Kuang-hsien, the missionaries' archenemy during the persecutions, hired a stand-in to take his punishment. Yang was sentenced to death, however, and the unfortunate stand-in, expecting only a beating, died in Yang's place.[286] The other missionaries, however, merely report that Yang was finally disgraced and condemned to die, but allowed to return to his home because of his age and poor health.[287]

After the many detailed descriptions of the Manchu Conquest, later writers have surprisingly little to say about the Ch'ing military establishment. Magalhães lists the various military tribunals in the capital and again emphasizes that the whole military establishment is under civilian control.[288] Greslon briefly describes the Manchu Banners, eight of them, each commanded by one of the princes of the blood. He believes most of the civil officials also are grouped under the banners.[289] Navarrete mentions what he calls major generals or "Cusan" (Manchu, *kushan*) at court, who are secretly sent out two or three at a time on military missions. Their soldiers, he claims, are always ready. Perhaps they were the commanders of the Manchu Banners.[290] No one clarifies the relationship of the Banner forces to the rest of the Chinese military, which makes it difficult to know which soldiers are meant when they discuss military affairs in general terms. Verbiest reports that K'ang-hsi's Manchurian hunting expeditions had a military purpose: to exercise the Manchu army and to keep their Mongol allies loyal.[291] Bouvet also reports the emperor's worry that his soldiers would become corrupted by the good life in China.[292] According to many post-conquest writers, K'ang-hsi's fears were justified. Many of them describe Ch'ing soldiers exactly as their predecessors described Ming soldiers. Navarrete praises them for their decency and civility, but not for their valor. They are better behaved and better disciplined than European soldiers. And they are numerous, everyone agrees; Navarrete estimates that they are two million strong. If only the Chinese soldiers would seriously apply themselves to the study of war, no one on earth would be able to oppose them.[293] But as Le Comte puts it:

---

[285] For examples, see *ibid.*, p. 61; Le Comte, *op. cit.* (n. 125), pp. 291–92; Greslon, *op. cit.* (n. 181), p. 176.

[286] Le Comte, *op. cit.* (n. 125), p. 293.

[287] *Ibid.*, p. 371. Actually Yang Kuang-hsien was condemned to banishment. See Hummel, *op. cit.* (n. 9), p. 891.

[288] Magalhães, *op. cit.* (n. 65), pp. 215–18.

[289] *Op. cit.* (n. 181), pp. 118–19. Chinese bannermen were prominent in provincial administration. See Kessler, *op. cit.* (n. 121), p. 117.

[290] *CV*, I, 12.

[291] D'Orléans, *op. cit.* (n. 68), pp. 121–23. Cf. Kessler, *op. cit.* (n. 121), pp. 105–7.

[292] *Op. cit.* (n. 67), pp. 97–107.

[293] Navarrete, *CV*, I, 26–27.

Their soldiers are very graceful, and pretty well disciplin'd, for the Tartars have almost degenerated into Chinese, and the Chinese continue as they always were, soft, effeminate, enemies of labour, better at making a handsome figure at muster or in a march, than at behaving themselves gallantly in an action.[294]

K'ang-hsi himself was supposed to have said, "They are good soldiers when opposed to bad ones, but bad when opposed to good ones."[295] The Mongols deride them saying, "the neighing of a Tartary horse is enough to rout all the Chinese cavalry."[296] Nor were the Dutch who fought with Ch'ing armies against Koxinga much impressed with their valor or expertise. Dapper's account is full of derogatory remarks about their timidity, unreliability, and cowardice. Still, most of the European writers report their victory over the intrepid Koxinga and their successful suppression of the revolt of the three feudatories. By 1683 K'ang-hsi's empire was at peace, thanks to its soldiery.

While the changes in China's governmental structure and practice were amply reported to European readers by the post-conquest writers, the elements of continuity loomed larger than the changes. Survivals and stable conditions were also described in detail, often differing little from accounts written during the first half of the century. Perhaps what made the most important difference between the image of Chinese government presented by later seventeenth-century Europeans and that sketched by Trigault, Semedo, and Martini was the dynamic quality and the wealth of eyewitness evidence found in the later accounts.

5

INTELLECTUAL LIFE

Major changes in European depictions of China's intellectual life resulted after 1650 not from the Manchu Conquest but from the missionaries' deeper familiarity with Chinese culture, especially with history and Confucian philosophy. The language, of course, remained the same, and most European descriptions of it repeat what Trigault, Semedo, and others had written earlier. Everyone reports that the sage emperor Fu Hsi was supposed to have invented the first characters. Kircher, however, claims they had been brought from Egypt by the biblical Ham and his sons when they migrated to China.[297] Magalhães insists that the characters antedate the Egyptian hi-

[294] *Op. cit.* (n. 125), p. 290.
[295] *Ibid.*
[296] *Ibid.*, p. 312–13.
[297] *Op. cit.* (n. 110), p. 303. The China Jesuits persist in incorrectly attributing the invention of the characters to Fu Hsi. Fu Hsi was regarded as the inventor of writing through his creation of the trigrams.

eroglyphs.[298] Kircher lists and sketches sixteen forms of written characters with their modern equivalents, most of them ascribed to one of the ancient sage emperors.[299] Several writers describe and illustrate the evolution of modern characters from their ancient forms.[300] Navarrete observes that the modern forms date from the Han dynasty.[301] Kircher and Magalhães also give clear, illustrated accounts of how complex characters had been developed by adding to a simple root or signific.[302]

The large number of written characters, in contrast to the phonetic poverty of spoken Chinese, continues to fascinate Europeans during the second half of the century. Several of them write clearer and more perceptive descriptions of Chinese phonetics and of the tones with which words are pronounced than were earlier produced in Europe. Le Comte, for example, constructs a table listing the 326 monosyllables which he thinks exhausts Chinese sounds. By means of the five tones these could be expanded to 1,665 spoken words.[303] Magalhães also distinguishes between aspirated and unaspirated words and as an example lists eleven different meanings for the sound "Po" depending on its tone and whether or not it is aspirated when pronounced.[304] Still he contends, contrary to many earlier writers, that the use of tones comes quite naturally to the Chinese, that they do not sing out their words or carry tablets around their necks on which to write, and that they indeed can whisper and be understood.[305] In contrast to Navarrete and Le Comte, who stress the difficulty of the language, Magalhães thinks it easier to learn than Latin or Greek, or for that matter the language of any other country in which the Jesuits have missionaries. It usually takes only one year for a new missionary to understand and speak it. After two years most Jesuits can preach, read, and write fluently, despite their having begun to study it as adults. As evidence he produces the long catalogue of Jesuit writings in Chinese. Finally, as an example, he reproduces the first charac-

[298] *Op. cit.* (n. 65), p. 68.

[299] *Op. cit.* (n. 110), pp. 305–10. Dapper, *op. cit.* (n. 55), II, 258–59, repeated the list without the illustrations. Some of it seems to have been culled from Martini, *op. cit.* (n. 97), pp. 12–40. For further detail and commentary see Mungello, *op. cit.* (n. 6), pp. 101–2, 130–31, 143–57.

[300] For example, Martini, *op. cit.* (n. 97), p. 12; Kircher, *op. cit.* (n. 110), pp. 304–5; Magalhães, *op. cit.* (n. 65), p. 69; Le Comte, *op. cit.* (n. 125), p. 182. For Martini's examples see our pl. 350.

[301] *CV*, I, 130. The *k'ai-shu* or "model script," still used in the twentieth century, was indeed developed during the Han dynasty, although it was derived from the *li-shu* style of the Ch'in dynasty. The first Chinese etymological dictionary of over nine thousand characters was compiled in the Later Han dynasty (*ca.* A.D. 100). See T. H. Tsien, *Written on Bamboo and Silk* (Chicago, 1962), p. 183.

[302] Kircher, *op. cit.* (n. 110), pp. 310–13; Magalhães, *op. cit.* (n. 65), pp. 68–75. See also Navarrete, *CV*, I, 130–33, and Le Comte, *op. cit.* (n. 125), p. 182.

[303] Le Comte, *op. cit.* (n. 125), pp. 176–77. He listed 326 monosyllables in his table, but on page 176 said there were "not more than 330," and on page 177 said there were 333. Cf. Mungello, *op. cit.* (n. 6), pp. 340–43.

[304] *Op. cit.* (n. 65), p. 73.

[305] *Ibid.*, p. 77.

ters of his commentary on Confucius, gives the pronunciation and meaning of each character, explicates the text, and describes how the missionaries used it.[306]

About Chinese learning and education outside the areas of history, philosophy, and religion, the later European writers add little to what was presented earlier by Trigault, Semedo, and Martini. In fact, apart from the encyclopedic works of Nieuhof and Dapper, who repeated most of what the earlier writers had said, less appeared in the new literature about some important topics—about the examinations, for example. Not that post-1650 European writers were less impressed with Chinese learning and education. No other land on earth, asserts Magalhães, could boast so many educated men or such widespread literacy.[307] Navarrete thinks the Chinese are "addicted to learning" and "inclined to reading." He reports that officials and wealthy men commonly read books as they are carried through the streets in their sedan chairs. Shopkeepers read behind their counters while waiting for customers. Children are motivated by stories such as that of the cowherd who read all day as he rode, using his cow's horns as a desk, or of poor students who, lacking money for candles, gathered fireflies in summer or read outside in winter by light reflected from the snow.[308] It is also commonly agreed that no other people published as many books as the Chinese. Le Comte reports numerous libraries, some containing more than forty thousand volumes.[309] Magalhães lists the types of Chinese publications: historical chronicles, mathematics, natural sciences, military science, medicine, agriculture, eloquent discourses, filial piety stories, loyalty tales, romances, poems, tragedies, and comedies.[310]

Almost all the European writers talk about the Five Classics and the Four Books; almost all in much more detail than had the pre-1650 writers. By the end of the century, European readers could have known that the *I Ching* with its trigrams was reputed to be China's oldest book, and that it was written by the sage emperor Fu Hsi, although Magalhães suspects that parts of it were written later. They could have known that the *Shu Ching* was the oldest historical text, that it related historical events from the sage emperor Yao (2356–2225 B.C.) to the middle of the Chou dynasty, and that much of it was supposedly written by the duke of Chou (d. 1105 B.C.). Certainly they could have read quotations from it. They might have learned about the

---

[306] *Ibid.*, pp. 77–86. See pl. 344. For a careful analysis of Magalhães' presentation of the Chinese language see Mungello, *op. cit.* (n. 6), pp. 96–102.

[307] *Op. cit.* (n. 65), p. 88.

[308] Navarrete, *CV*, I, 99.

[309] *Op. cit.* (n. 125), p. 192.

[310] *Op. cit.* (n. 65), pp. 88–89. In all probability more books and printed pages were produced in Chinese by 1700 than in the entire West. See T. H. Tsien, *Paper and Printing,* Vol. V, Pt. I, of Needham, *op. cit.* (n. 154), p. 377. See also Evelyn S. Rawski, *Education and Popular Literacy in Ch'ing China* (Ann Arbor, 1979), pp. 109–24.

types and the content of the poetry found in the *Shih Ching,* that the *Li Ch'i* was a record of ceremonies and rituals, and that the *Ch'un Ch'iu* was a court chronicle of the state of Lu, supposedly compiled by Confucius.[311] They would not only have known the names and general content of the Four Books, but they had a translation of the first three and several detailed descriptions of the *Mencius,* which had not been translated.[312] They would also have known that the Four Books were the basis for the civil service examinations, that most students memorized them entirely, and that only the Sung dynasty commentaries of the Ch'eng brothers and Chu Hsi were officially endorsed.[313]

European judgments about Chinese medicine did not change during the latter half of the seventeenth century, but a great deal more was written about it, especially about the way in which Chinese physicians diagnosed ailments by taking the pulse and about the various herbs and cures they used. Michael Boym, in fact, translated a major Chinese treatise on the diagnostic use of the pulse which was published twice before the end of the century.[314] Several missionaries related stories of their personal experiences with Chinese physicians. In general, the missionaries praised their diagnostic acumen, but noted that Chinese medicine lacked scientific foundations. Physicians, they report, rely on experience and practice rather than theory, and while some are very good, others are very poor.[315]

European descriptions of the last half of the century also contain considerably more information about mathematics and astronomy than did earlier publications. The Jesuits judge the Chinese to be quick to understand and master Western geometry and algebra; traditional Chinese mathematics they consider to be far inferior to that of Europe, despite its great antiquity. The Europeans assert that Chinese mathematics, like Chinese medicine, lacks precise rules and basic principles. Le Comte writes, for example:

> Their geometry is very superficial, it is restrained to a very few propositions, and to some problems in algebra, which they resolve without elements or principles, and that only by induction.[316]

[311] For example, see Magalhães, *op. cit.* (n. 65), pp. 89–98; Le Comte, *op. cit.* (n. 125), pp. 189–92; Dapper, *op. cit.* (n. 55), II, 93–94; *Confucius sinarum philosophus* (n. 91), pp. xv–xxi; and De La Brune, *op. cit.* (n. 93), pp. 6–12. For the hexagrams from the *I Ching* see our pls. 348 and 349.

[312] On Mencius see Martini, *op. cit.* (n. 97), pp. 155–60; Dapper, *op. cit.* (n. 55), II, 101–4; Magalhães, *op. cit.* (n. 65), pp. 98–99. See pl. 355.

[313] On the special status of the Sung commentaries see *Confucius sinarum philosophus* (n. 91), pp. liii–lx. The Ch'eng-Chu school of Neo-Confucianism became the official state teaching in the Ming dynasty; it emphasized study of the Four Books for civil servants. See Fung Yu-lan, *A Short History of Chinese Philosophy* (New York, 1959), pp. 319–21.

[314] See above, pp. 538–39, and our pls. 356–58.

[315] For example, see Le Comte, *op. cit.* (n. 125), pp. 215–29.

[316] *Ibid.,* p. 214. On traditional Chinese mathematics see Needham, *op. cit.* (n. 154), III, 1–53.

The Chinese are reported, however, to be very facile at arithmetic. Martini describes and pictures the Chinese abacus in common use, which he claims was invented during the sage emperor Huang-ti's reign (2697–2597 B.C.).[317] Most subsequent European writers also comment on it. The Jesuits praise China's traditional astronomy and the accuracy of the ancient observations recorded in the classics and the histories which helped to date important reigns or acts. Martini describes many of these celestial events. Almost everyone admiringly comments on the antique instruments in the Peking observatory; several books contain plates picturing them.[318] For the missionaries, however, there was no doubt about the superiority of European astronomy. Their reformation of the Chinese calendar and their accurate predictions of eclipses and planetary conjunctions had earned them their prestigious place in the Chinese court. All the accounts of the Jesuits' calendrical and astronomical work in Peking contain descriptions of the deficiencies of traditional Chinese astronomy, of superstitions regarding eclipses and conjunctions, and the absence of sound astronomical theory. Under Verbiest's direction even the ancient instruments in the Peking observatory were replaced with new, more accurate ones patterned after those of Europe.[319] Le Comte puts it more cynically than most:

If China hath been deficient in excellent mathematicians, they have at least had perfect astrologers; because, for the well succeeding in judicial astrology it sufficeth to be an able deceiver, and to have a knack of lying handsomely, which no nation can dispute with China.[320]

How the Chinese kept time was described by many of the missionaries, who accurately named the ten heavenly stems and the twelve earthly branches and told how these functioned in timekeeping. Making use of their accounts, especially Martini's, Dapper includes in his book one of the largest and most detailed descriptions of Chinese timekeeping. The day, the period of light and darkness which Europeans divide into twenty-four hours, the Chinese divide into twelve, so that one Chinese hour equals two European hours. They do not designate the hours by numbers as westerners do, but by characters: "Cu" (*tzu*), "Ch'eu" (*ch'ou*), "Yin" (*yin*), "Mao" (*mao*), "Xin" (*ch'en*), "Su" (*ssu*), "U" (*wu*), "Vi" (*wei*), "Xin" (*shen*), "Yeu" (*yu*), "Sio" (*hsü*), and "Hai" (*hai*)—the twelve branches. While the Chinese com-

[317] *Op. cit.* (n. 97), p. 16. The abacus, in one form or another, was probably developed independently and came into common use in Europe and China from the eleventh to thirteenth centuries. Nothing very definitive has so far appeared on the origins of this practical calculating instrument. See Needham, *op. cit.* (n. 154), III, 74–80.

[318] For example, see Le Comte, *op. cit.* (n. 125), pp. 63–71. See our pl. 307.

[319] *Ibid.*, p. 65.

[320] *Ibid.*, p. 215. For an evaluation of the Jesuits' comments on Chinese astronomy and of their contributions see Needham, *op. cit.* (n. 154), III, 437–58. On traditional Chinese astronomy see Needham, III, 182–461, and especially the summary on pp. 458–61.

monly use the year of the reigning monarch to date events, they also use a sexegenary cycle formed by combining each of the twelve branches with one of the ten stems: "Kia" (*chia*), "Yi" (*i*), "Ping" (*ping*), "Ting" (*ting*), "Vu" (*mou*), "Ki" (*chi*), "Ken" (*keng*), "Sin" (*hsin*), "Giu" (*jen*), and "Quei" (*kuei*). The first year of a cycle would thus be "Kia-cu" (*chia-tzu*), the second "Yi-ch'eu" (*i-ch'ou*), and the sixtieth year would be "Quei-hai" (*kuei-hai*), after which a new cycle would begin. Dapper lists the years of an entire cycle. Each of the ten stems corresponds to one of the five planets and to one of the five elements, thus making the cycle an integral part of the order of nature. Further, each of the twelve branches is associated with a specific animal which is thought to characterize the hour or day so designated. Sexegenary cycles themselves are designated upper, middle, or lower, thus producing a grand cycle of 180 years. Still larger numbers of years are designated in terms of the character "van" (*wan*), or ten thousand. Each year is divided into twelve "moons," half of which contain 30 days and half of which contain 29 days, thus producing a year of 354 days. To every third year—"leap year"—another moon of 30 days is added, making that year 384 days. Each new year begins when the sun enters the fifteenth degree of Aquarius (near February 15) which day also marks the beginning of spring. Like westerners, the Chinese divide the year into four seasons, but they also divide each season into six parts. Dapper lists the twenty-four parts of the year thus produced.[321]

According to Magalhães and Le Comte, Chinese astronomy, indeed all of Chinese science, was handicapped by Chinese smugness—by their distrust of any knowledge originating outside the empire—and by an uncritical reverence for antiquity and a reluctance to challenge ancient ideas and practices.[322] Still, China's concern for the past, evinced in the number and quality of its historical writings, was nonetheless one of the most admired aspects of Chinese learning. Martini's *Sinicae historiae* and its sequels published by Thévenot and Couplet made available to late seventeenth-century European readers a continuous, detailed account of traditional Chinese history from the legendary sage emperors to the K'ang-hsi reign. Most other writers include some pieces of China's history, frequently derived from Martini but sometimes reflecting the writers' particular interests or emphases. All in all, Europe's knowledge of Chinese history was greatly increased over what was available during the first half of the century.

Martini's *Sinicae historiae* begins with Fu Hsi, the first legendary sage emperor, whose reign Martini calculated began in 2952 B.C. He dismisses as myth the long dynasties of heavenly, earthly, and human sovereigns who were supposed to have reigned before Fu Hsi, observing that most Chinese scholars did the same. He does not, however, question the authenticity of

---

[321] Dapper, *op. cit.* (n. 55), I, 496–501. See also Martini, *op. cit.* (n. 97), pp. 3–13.
[322] Magalhães, *op. cit.* (n. 65), p. 63; Le Comte, *op. cit.* (n. 125), p. 69.

Fu Hsi and his successors. Martini's first book contains a chapter on each of the sage emperors—Fu Hsi, Shen Nung, Huang Ti, Shao Hao, Chuan Hu, Ku, Yao, and Shun—which recounts their achievements and the outstanding events of their reigns. It also contains a discussion of ancient Chinese mathematics and astronomy, the sixty-year cycles, and the great flood during Yao's reign, which Martini supposed was the biblical deluge.[323] Most subsequent writers accept Martini's judgment about the beginning of Chinese history, although some point out that the *Shu Ching* begins with Yao (2356–2255 B.C.) and several speculate about how the ancient Chinese chronology could be reconciled with Genesis.[324] Magalhães, for example, observes that most learned Chinese considered it probable that Fu Hsi was the first emperor. No one would dare question the authenticity of Yao. The Jesuits in China, therefore, used the Septuagint version of the Old Testament for their chronologies, making it somewhat easier to reconcile ancient Chinese chronology with that derived from the Old Testament.[325]

Martini's account of the sage emperors and of the ancient dynasties—the Hsia, Shang, and Chou—reflects the semi-mythological and heavily moralistic character of the classics and the Confucian histories. Each dynasty, for example, was allegedly founded by a pious emperor who acted as Heaven's (*t'ien*) instrument in deposing tyrants and in relieving the oppressed people. Martini recounts stories from the classics to illustrate the piety of Yao, Shun, Yü (the founder of the Hsia dynasty), T'ang (the founder of the Shang dynasty), Wen Wang, and Chou Kung (the duke of Chou).[326] While each dynasty was founded by a pious recipient of Heaven's mandate, each ended with an impious, debauched tyrant. About the tyrants, too, Martini provides illustrative stories.[327] Of the emperors who ruled between the virtuous founders and the vicious forfeiters of Heaven's mandate, Martini reports very little. His account of the Chou dynasty is much more detailed—over one hundred pages long.[328] Soon after applauding the wise and virtuous administration of Wu Wang and the duke of Chou, Martini tells of disloyalty to the emperors, intrigues, assassinations, and wars between the feudal lords. His description of the Warring States Period (403–221 B.C.) especially depicts the alliances, battles, and intrigues that resulted in the ex-

---

[323] *Op. cit.* (n. 97), pp. 1–34.

[324] For a discussion of the chronological problems and the attempts of European scholars to solve them see E. Van Kley, "Europe's 'Discovery' of China and the Writing of World History," *American Historical Review,* LXXVI (1971), pp. 358–85.

[325] Magalhães, *op. cit.* (n. 65), pp. 59–61, 251–53. See also Mungello, *op. cit.* (n. 6), pp. 102–3. Ancient chronology derived from the Hebrew Masoretic texts of the Old Testament or from the Vulgate date the Creation at 4004 B.C., and the universal flood at 2349 B.C. Chronologies derived from the Greek Septuagint text date the creation at *ca.* 5200 B.C., and the flood at 2957 B.C.

[326] *Op. cit.* (n. 97), pp. 34–36, 58–61, 87–92.

[327] *Ibid.,* pp. 54–55, 77–86.

[328] *Ibid.,* pp. 87–193.

pansion of the outlying states of Ch'u, Ch'i, and Ch'in; he gives the names of kings, generals, ministers, and philosophers, their conversations as well as their deeds. Edifying anecdotes about emperors, ministers, and philosophers creep into many other European descriptions of China. Martini's history and its continuation in Thévenot seem to be the sources for most of them, although some obviously derive from elsewhere. Navarrete devotes several chapters to such stories.[329] Some of them were repeated often enough before the end of the century to have become quite familiar to European readers.

Late seventeenth-century writers—Martini, Nieuhof, Dapper, Navarrete, Couplet *et al.,* and Le Comte—provide much more information about Confucius than could have been learned from Trigault and Semedo.[330] He was born, they report, in 551 B.C., married at age nineteen, fathered one son, and held high office in his native state of Lu. In just three months' time he affected astounding reforms in morals and government only to see it all undone when the envious duke of Ch'i sent a beautiful woman to corrupt the duke of Lu. Confucius resigned when his duke neglected government for the lady. "Raro enim virtus et Venus sociantur," observes Martini.[331] Thereafter Confucius traveled, advised several other princes, taught, and wrote. He reportedly taught three thousand students, seventy-two of whom were outstanding, and twelve of whom became philosophers. The Jesuits name the outstanding students.[332] And, of course, he edited or wrote each of the Five Classics and three of the Four Books. Navarrete and the *Confucius sinarum philosophus* report on his miraculous birth and its attendant portents (according to the *Confucius sinarum philosophus* the Shang emperors were his ancestors). Both describe him as fully mature at age six.[333] Basing their statements on the *Ch'un Ch'iu,* Martini and the authors of the *Confucius sinarum philosophus* declare that Confucius had foretold the coming of Christ and of Christianity to China.[334] The Jesuit compilers and Le Comte hold that Confucius' prophecy was partially fulfilled by the Han emperor Ming Ti's dream, which because of an ambassador's error brought Buddhism rather than Christianity to China.[335] Navarrete, however, contends

---

[329] *CV,* I, 83–100.

[330] Martini, *op. cit.* (n. 97), pp. 120, 123, 125–33; Nieuhof, *op. cit.* (n. 29), II, 19–21; Dapper, *op. cit.* (n. 55), II, 90–94; Navarrete, *CV,* I, 111–14; *Confucius sinarum philosophus* (n. 91), pp. cxvii–cxxiv; Le Comte, *op. cit.* (n. 125), pp. 194–201. See our pl. 309 for a representation of Confucius taken from the *Confucius sinarum philosophus.*

[331] "For virtue and Venus seldom go together"; *op. cit.* (n. 97), p. 126.

[332] *Confucius sinarum philosophus* (n. 91), p. cxix.

[333] Navarrete, *CV,* I, 111–12; *Confucius sinarum philosophus* (n. 91), p. cxvii.

[334] Martini, *op. cit.* (n. 97), pp. 131–32; *Confucius sinarum philosophus* (n. 91), p. cxx. See also Dapper, *op. cit.* (n. 55), II, 98, and Le Comte, *op. cit.* (n. 125), p. 200.

[335] *Confucius sinarum philosophus* (n. 91), p. cxx; Le Comte, *op. cit.* (n. 125), p. 200. Ming-ti's dream, dated around A.D. 67, is a traditional story. Buddhism was already a recognized form of temple worship by this time. See Wing-tsit Chan, *Religious Trends in Modern China* (New York, 1953), pp. 136–37. On Ming-ti's dream see Kenneth Ch'en, *Buddhism in China: A Historical Survey* (Princeton, 1974), pp. 29–31.

that Confucius was an atheist and reports nothing about the prophecy.[336] Most European writers discuss some aspects of Confucius' teaching and the classics which he supposedly edited or wrote. Many quote aphorisms apparently taken from the *Lun Yü*. Still more important, three of the Four Books, those containing the essence of Confucian thought, were translated into Latin by Couplet and his colleagues, and paraphrased in French by Jean de La Brune.[337] Modern scholarship has painted a very different picture of Confucius. Much of what was related to Europeans during the seventeenth century now appears to be the hagiography of late Confucians.[338] Apart from the miracles attending Confucius' birth, however, seventeenth-century Europeans did not question the story; consequently they furnished their readers with an accurate replica of the traditional Chinese portrait of the sage, to which they added their own Christian myth.

The missionaries were far more critical of what they learned about Lao Tzu, probably because they learned it from hostile Confucians. Trigault had already introduced him as a contemporary of Confucius.[339] Martini gives 605 B.C. as his birth date.[340] All European writers repeat the fable of his eighty-year gestation period which made him old and wise at birth. Most of them also include some, usually unsympathetic, account of Taoist beliefs and practices. The Taoists are frequently called Epicureans because of their search for physical immortality through elixirs or exercises and the attempts to change base metals into gold, which were reported by Martini and others as the major preoccupations of popular Taoism. Le Comte thinks Taoism began to corrupt ancient Chinese monotheism, a process temporarily arrested by Confucius and his followers but later completed by Buddhism.[341]

Martini also describes the career and teaching of Mencius and of some philosophers with whom Mencius had debated.[342] The only other westerners who wrote about Mencius were Dapper, who repeats Martini's account, and Navarrete, who relates a few stories from the *Meng-tzu* to demonstrate that Mencius had no knowledge of the true God.[343]

Martini's account of the Ch'in and the Former Han is also richly detailed, and quite faithfully transmits the official Confucian historiography of his sources. He carefully charts China's unification under the Ch'in and the new empire's expansion to areas never before considered part of China. He also describes the rigor and cruelty of Ch'in rule which eventually drove many Chinese to live as rebels and outlaws—Liu Pang among them. He relates General Meng T'ien's construction of the Great Wall which, he reports, en-

[336] *CV*, I, 113.
[337] *Op. cit.* (n. 93).
[338] For example, see Herrlee Creel, *Confucius and the Chinese Way* (New York, 1960), chap. i.
[339] See above, p. 1658.
[340] Martini, *op. cit.* (n. 97), p. 117. See also Dapper, *op. cit.* (n. 55), II, 134.
[341] *Op. cit.* (n. 125), pp. 324–26.
[342] *Op. cit.* (n. 97), pp. 155–61, 170–71.
[343] Dapper, *op. cit.* (n. 55), II, 101–4; Navarrete, *CV*, I, 138–41.

tailed the conscription of one-third of China's work force.[344] Li Ssu's infamous burning of the books in 213 B.C., the persecution of Confucian scholars, and the imaginative ways in which people preserved the ancient books are also recounted. The most detailed, apart from Martini's, were those accounts written by Dapper and Le Comte.[345] Martini's history of the Ch'in ends with the first emperor's death, the subsequent intrigues of Li Ssu and the eunuch Chao Kao, and the rebellions which overthrew the dynasty.[346]

After describing the attempts to restore the pre-Ch'in states and the long rivalry between Liu Pang, Hsiang Yu, and other rebels, Martini devotes a chapter to each emperor of the Former Han dynasty. The longest are naturally those which treat of Kao Tsu (Liu Pang), the founder (206–195 B.C.), and Wu Ti (141–87 B.C.). Martini's coverage is thorough and accurate. It includes not only conquests, rebellions, and relations with the Tartars, but also the revival of Confucianism, the recovery of the classics, the power and intrigues of consort families, and the influence of popular Taoism. He depicts the rise of the Wang family but does not report on Wang Mang's usurpation of the throne in A.D. 9. Martini's account ends with the death of the twelfth emperor in A.D. 1.[347] Apart from a few morally edifying tales about virtuous emperors and loyal officials, little of Martini's richly detailed history of the Former Han appeared in other European accounts.

The most commonly reported incident from the history of the Later Han dynasty was the introduction of Buddhism. Almost everyone tells the story of Emperor Ming Ti's dream and its consequences.[348] Several writers also recount Gautama's life and teachings and discuss some of the varieties of Buddhism.[349] Kircher treats Buddhism as another variety of the idolatry that slowly spread from ancient Egypt to the rest of the world, arriving rather late in China and Japan.[350] Couplet and his colleagues correctly suspect that Buddhism influenced even the Neo-Confucian philosophy of the Sung dynasty, which was still regarded as being the officially correct interpretation during the early Ch'ing.[351] Navarrete recounts some Buddhist birth stories and suggests that the Confucians in their antagonism towards Buddhist "idolatry" fell instead into the error of atheism.[352]

Despite Ming Ti's part in bringing Buddhist idolatry to China, the "Decas secunda" of Thévenot judges him to have been a good emperor—

[344] *Op. cit.* (n. 97), p. 208.
[345] *Ibid.*, pp. 209–11; Dapper, *op. cit.* (n. 55), II, 104–6; Le Comte, *op. cit.* (n. 125), pp. 192–93; *Confucius sinarum philosophus,* (n. 91), pp. xxii–xxiii.
[346] *Op. cit.* (n. 97), pp. 215–29.
[347] *Ibid.*, p. 362.
[348] See above, p. 1646.
[349] For example, Dapper, *op. cit.* (n. 55), II, 106–13; *Confucius sinarum philosophus* (n. 91), pp. xxii–xxxiv; Le Comte, *op. cit.* (n. 125), p. 326.
[350] Kircher, *op. cit.* (n. 110), pp. 173–223. For further detail see Mungello, *op. cit.* (n. 6), pp. 160–62.
[351] *Confucius sinarum philosophus* (n. 91), pp. lx–lxii.
[352] *CV,* I, 78, 91–92.

"prudent, wise, and clement"—unlike most of his successors.[353] It also traces the rapid growth of both Buddhism and popular Taoism during the Later Han and gives a rather complete account of politics and court affairs from Wang Mang's usurpation (A.D. 9–23) to the fall of the dynasty in A.D. 220.[354]

To European observers the most important event of the glorious T'ang dynasty (618–907) was the coming of Christianity to China. A stele which had been erected by the Nestorians in the T'ang capital of Ch'ang-an was unearthed in 1623 or 1625. Semedo saw it in 1625 and described it in his 1642 description of China.[355] Most subsequent writers also comment on the stele and the Christian mission which had produced it. Kircher's *China illustrata* (1667) contains the most complete discussion of it, together with the text of its inscription in Chinese and Syriac, and a Latin translation. The inscription describes the advent of Christianity at Ch'ang-an in 636, summarizes the basic Nestorian beliefs, and lists the bishops and priests who had served the church in Ch'ang-an and the emperors who had patronized it. The stele itself had been erected only in 781. In Kircher's work, the planting of Christianity in China became part of the global spread of the gospel just as Buddhism was part of the global spread of idolatry. Although the missionaries continued to believe that Saint Thomas had preached Christianity in China during the first century, neither the stele nor any other Chinese source supported them. Navarrete, in fact, complains that Chinese historians even fail to mention the seventh-century Christian church.[356]

Apart from edifying stories about the emperor T'ai Tsung (618–26) related by Navarrete,[357] nothing else about the T'ang as depicted by Chinese scholars appears in European publications before Thévenot's "Decas secunda." That work contains a detailed and balanced sketch of the T'ang. There are pious stories about T'ai Tsung and other emperors, but in addition to the affairs of rulers, the "Decas secunda" traces the fortunes of Christianity—especially its persecution under the empress Wu (684–710)— the influence of Buddhism, the revival of Confucianism under Hsuan Tsung (712–56), and An Lu-shan's rebellion (755). In the period of rapid decline after Hsuan Tsung's death, the "Decas secunda" reports, most of the emperors were Buddhists chosen by the palace eunuchs.[358] Buddhism's popularity, deplored by the writer and his Confucian sources, was further attested by the elaborate court reception put on in 803 for the bone of Buddha.[359]

Apart from its treatment in the "Decas secunda" the Sung dynasty was

[353] *Loc. cit.* (n. 100), pp. 22–23.
[354] *Ibid.*, pp. 21–27.
[355] See above, pp. 1646–47.
[356] Kircher, *op. cit.* (n. 110), pp. 1–62; Navarrete, *CV,* I, 74.
[357] *CV,* I, 93–95.
[358] *Loc. cit.* (n. 100), pp. 42–53.
[359] *Ibid.*, p. 51. This miracle-working bone was brought in state to the imperial palace in 819

similarly slighted by those who described China to Europe during the latter seventeenth century. Martini and some others notice that Hangchow, the Southern Sung capital, was the city Marco Polo called "Quinsai." The tenth Sung emperor had moved there, Martini reports, after the northern provinces had been lost to the Tartars.[360] Navarrete writes more about Sung than most. It was a time, he claims, "when learning flourished most," and when the number of schools and degree holders increased. He lists the numbers and categories of "bachelors" alloted to each town, city, and metropolis.[361] Navarrete observed, too, that the Sung commentaries on the classics were the officially established homework for the examinations.[362] In his catalog of exemplary deeds and sayings of emperors and officials, a disproportionate number come from the Sung period, although he does not identify them as such.[363]

The "Decas secunda" provides considerable detail to support the general impression that Confucian morality and scholarship flourished during the Sung. It bristles with the names and accomplishments of scholars such as Ssu-ma Kuang, Wang An-shih, Cheng I, and Chu Hsi, and is replete with stories exemplifying Confucian virtues. Nevertheless, along with the virtuous deeds of Sung emperors, Emperor Jen Tsung's homosexuality and its popularity in his court are reported, as are the moral decline of the last emperors and the dynasty's continuous inability to control the Mongols.[364]

Much more was reported in European publications about the fall of Sung to the Mongols and about the Yüan dynasty which the intruders established. The Manchu Conquest of 1644 obviously provoked curiosity about China's earlier relations with the Tartars and about the Mongol period when, as the European writers understood it, the Tartars had ruled all of China. Martini reports that the hostility between the Chinese and Tartar tribes was millennia old; the first Tartar invasion reported by Chinese historians occurred during the reign of the sage emperor Shun in the third millennium B.C.[365] Martini's *Sinicae historiae* and the "Decas secunda" in Thévenot's compilation contain hundreds of reports about Tartar raids or wars and about Chinese efforts to control the Tartars diplomatically or militarily. Almost everyone, from Pantoja in the beginning of the century to Ides at the end, reports something about the Mongol Conquest, if only to observe that the Tartars had once before conquered all of China. Several writers—Martini, the author of the "Decas secunda," D'Orléans, and

---

by Emperor Hsien Tsung despite the protests of some of his Confucian officials. See C. Eliot, *Hinduism and Buddhism* (3 vols.; London, 1954), III, 265–67.

[360] *Op. cit.* (n. 99), pp. 133–37.

[361] Navarrete, *CV*, I, 49.

[362] *Ibid.*, p. 198. See also *Confucius sinarum philosophus* (n. 91), pp. xxxiv–xxxix.

[363] *CV*, I, 96–102.

[364] *Loc. cit.* (n. 100), pp. 56–66.

[365] *Op. cit.* (n. 97), p. 32.

Magalhães, for example—describe the Mongol effort in some detail.[366] They usually distinguish between the Eastern Tartars or Manchus, who had established the Chin state in north China in 1126, and the Western Tartars or Mongols, who had been invited by the Southern Sung emperor to drive out the Chin in 1206. As D'Orléans saw it, the emperor had "called in the aid of a powerful enemy to drive out a weaker one."[367] The Mongols indeed subdued the Chin and then turned on the Southern Sung, although it took over seventy years to end Sung resistance. D'Orléans describes how the dynasty died in 1279 when the defeated Sung general took the child-emperor in his arms and plunged into the sea.[368]

In 1271 Khublai Khan (Shih-tsu) established the dynasty called Yüan after having moved his court in 1264 to Peking—Marco Polo's "Cambaluc." Post-1650 European writers continue to comment on Marco Polo's visit to China during the Yüan, to demonstrate the identity of Polo's Cathay with China, and to note the general accuracy of his story. Magalhães, however, thinks Polo had erred in reporting the use of paper money during the Yüan, but in this, too, Marco Polo was correct.[369] D'Orléans reports that Khublai became popular with his Chinese subjects and is still considered "holy."[370] In the "Decas secunda," too, he is described as pious, perspicacious, prudent, magnanimous, and a patron of letters.[371] Martini observes that the Mongols brought almost seventy years of peace to China, during which time they lost their former vigor and martial spirit.[372] Nor was the Yüan devoid of peaceful achievements: the Grand Canal and the much-admired astronomical instruments in the imperial observatory are credited to the Mongols.[373]

Late seventeenth-century writers continue to describe Chu Yüan-chang's revolt and the consequent establishment of the native Ming dynasty in 1368.[374] They sometimes add additional details and insights to the story, but in general they report it much as had Pantoja, Trigault, and Semedo earlier in the century.[375] That an orphan, former monk, and bandit could have successfully led the revolt which toppled the Yüan dynasty fascinates European

---

[366] Martini, *De bello tartarico* (n. 7), pp. 255–57, and *Atlas* (n. 99), pp. 116–17; "Synopsis chronologica" (n. 100), pp. 64–66; D'Orléans, *op. cit.* (n. 68), pp. 2–5; Magalhães, *op. cit.* (n. 65), pp. 19–21.

[367] *Op. cit.* (n. 68), p. 3.

[368] *Ibid.*, p. 4. See also "Synopsis chronologica" (n. 100), p. 66.

[369] *Op. cit.* (n. 65), pp. 136–37.

[370] *Op. cit.* (n. 68), p. 4.

[371] *Loc. cit.* (n. 100), p. 67.

[372] *Op. cit.* (n. 7), p. 256.

[373] See above, p. 1643; "Synopsis chronologica" (n. 100), p. 67; Magalhães, *op. cit.* (n. 65), pp. 114–15, 118.

[374] For examples see Martini, *op. cit.* (n. 7), p. 256; Nieuhof, *op. cit.* (n. 29), II, 251–52; "Synopsis chronologica" (n. 100), pp. 70, 72; Magalhães, *op. cit.* (n. 65), pp. 253–54; D'Orléans, *op. cit.* (n. 68), p. 5.

[375] See above, pp. 1647–48.

observers. Chu, of course, claimed the "Mandate of Heaven" to free China from Mongol tyranny. Magalhães observes that all rebels in Chinese history claimed as much and hoped to found new dynasties. That hope, he speculates, probably accounts for the many rebellions in Chinese history.[376] Once the Mongols were defeated and the new dynasty secured, Chu, the Hung-wu emperor, turned to more peaceful pursuits. He established new laws, as did all founders of Chinese dynasties, and as reported in the "Decas secunda," he collected books and received tribute missions.[377] Several writers describe the Yung-lo emperor's usurpation of the crown and removal of the court from Nanking to Peking in 1421. Some also mention the wide-ranging maritime expeditions of his reign, but other Europeans doubt the accuracy of those reports.[378] Late seventeenth-century writers, especially those who report on the Manchu Conquest, also give increased attention to Ming relations with the Tartars and the persistent ineptitude of late Ming government, all of which appeared as antecedents to the 1644 conquest.

Post-1650 European descriptions of China naturally contain countless details about the last years of the Ming dynasty, the Manchu Conquest, and the early Ch'ing. Many of these derived from the writers' own observations rather than from traditional Chinese scholarship. Seventeenth-century readers, however, no doubt considered this information news rather than history. They may also have seen it as the working out of long-term trends in Chinese history or the dynamic play between the ancient, great traditions sketched by Martini and the disruptive events of the mid-seventeenth century.

An industrious seventeenth-century reader could have learned a great deal about China's history. Some of it was systematically, indeed chronologically, organized for him—by Martini, Thévenot, and Couplet, for example. Some of it was tucked away in the descriptions of China's people, institutions, customs, and landscape. Some parts of it were frequently repeated. If it was somewhat slanted, the bias was primarily that of its Confucian sources. But an interpretive bias need not necessarily produce inaccurate history, and apart from obviously mythological stories about the sage emperors, the ancient dynasties, and the hagiographic life of Confucius, the story of China's past presented to seventeenth-century Europeans was fairly reliable. No better information became available in the West—or in China, for that matter—for the next two and one-half centuries. If he or she were reasonably diligent, therefore, our seventeenth-century European reader could have learned as much about Chinese history as "all the schoolboys in China know," to steal Navarrete's phrase,[379] and considerably more than most twentieth-century university graduates in the West.

[376] *Op. cit.* (n. 65), pp. 253–54.
[377] "Synopsis chronologica" (n. 100), pp. 72–74.
[378] For example, see Le Comte, *op. cit.* (n. 125), p. 231; Navarrete, *CV*, I, 6.
[379] *CV*, I, 7.

The European depiction of China, unlike the mapping
of India, owes a heavy debt to the native cartographic
tradition. Beginning early in the century the Europeans
began to collect and imitate the maps prepared by the
Chinese themselves. On these outlines they placed romanizations of the names of provinces, cities, rivers,
mountains, lakes, and seas. To the Chinese maps they
added conventions and physical features taken from
earlier European maps and written descriptions, or
they added new Chinese materials to earlier European
prototypes. In the latter half of the century the Jesuits
acquired more and better Chinese maps, which they
relayed to Europe along with new geographical information. By century's end certain of the Jesuits had
begun to cooperate with the Chinese in the geographical survey of the empire. For a succinct history of the
beginnings of the Jesuit cartography of China see T. N.
Foss, "A Jesuit Encyclopedia for China. A Guide to
Jean-Baptiste Du Halde's *Description . . . de la Chine*
(1735)" (Ph.D. diss.; 2 vols.; Committee on History of
Culture, University of Chicago, 1979), Vol. I, chap. ii;
and H. Wallis, "Missionary Cartographers to China,"
Geographical Magazine, XLVII (1975), 751–59.

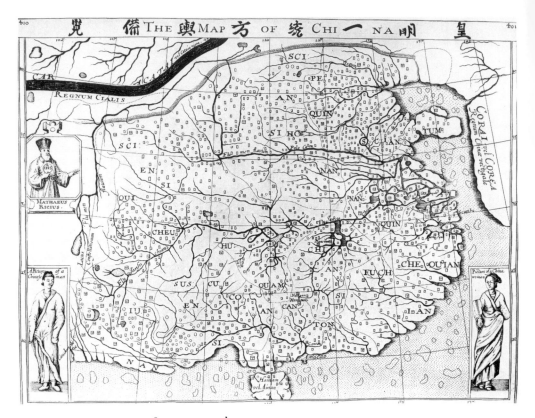

284. PURCHAS' MAP OF CHINA

From Samuel Purchas, *Hakluytus Posthumus* (Glasgow, 1906), XII, between pp. 480 and 481.

"The originall Map, whence this present was taken and contracted, was by Captaine [John] Saris . . . gotten at Bantam of a Chinese, in taking a distresse of debts owing to the English merchants; who seeing him carefull to convey away a Boxe, was the more carefull to apprehend it and therein found this Map, which another Chinese lodged at his house, lately come from China, had brought with him. . . . Master Hakluyt procured it of the Captaine, . . . and Master Hakluyt following, this Map came to my hand, who sought to express my love to the publike in communicating what I could thereof. For it being in China Characters (which I thinke, none in England, if any in Europe, understands) I could not wholly give it, when I give it; no man being able to receive, what he can no way conceive" (p. 470).

Purchas dropped the characters off this map, which was "above foure foot one way, and almost five foot the other" (p. 471). He filled in the names of the provinces from his study of the Jesuit relations. Notice that Korea appears here as an overly large peninsula, that is extended much too far to the south.

The characters at the top of the map, reading from right to left, are *huang-ming i-tung fang-yü pei-lan;* they mean: "Map of the Whole of China under the Ming emperor." The European, probably missionary, calligrapher has written several of the characters incorrectly.

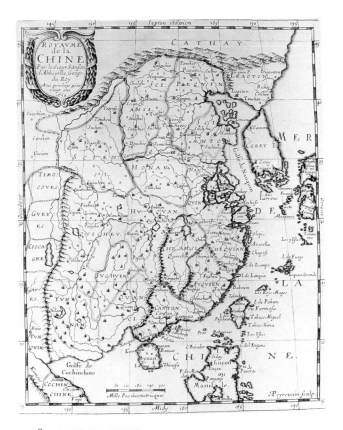

285. MAP OF CHINA
AND ITS EASTERN PERIPHERY

From Nicolas Sanson d'Abbeville, *L'Asie en plusieurs
cartes* (Paris, 1652), n.p. Pls. 372 and 390 are also from
this book.

Engraved by A. Peyrounin.

This outline is possibly based on one of Purchas'
maps but with many changes, omissions, and modifica-
tions. See B. Szcześniak, "The Seventeenth Century
Maps of China. An Inquiry into the Compilations of
European Cartographers," *Imago mundi*, XIII (1956),
118–23. Notice that the longitude of China is much too
far to the east.

According to the text, Sanson gathered his information from the works of Juan González de Mendoza and
from Diego de Pantoja in Purchas as well as from the
available Jesuit letterbooks. His materials on Annam
were probably derived from Rhodes and other Jesuits.
Korea is here shown as an island. Perhaps Sanson
copied this mistake from the Japan map (*ca.* 1650) of
Philippe Briet, a Jesuit teacher of geography in Paris.
The confusion over Korea as an island or peninsula
goes back at least to the maps prepared for Abraham
Ortelius' *Theatrum orbis terrarum* (1580). A few earlier
maps, such as the Lopo Homem planisphere (1554),
correctly depicted Korea as a peninsula.

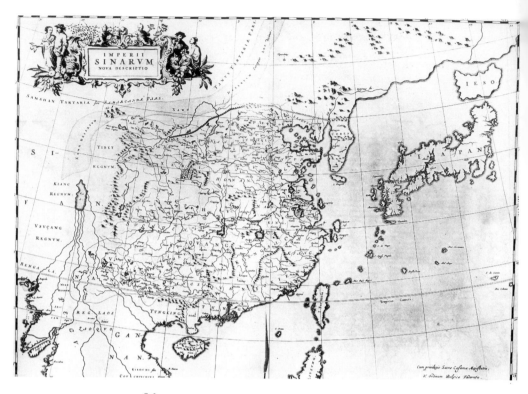

286. MAP OF CHINA AND ITS PERIPHERY

From Johan Blaeu, *Atlas maior, Asia* (Amsterdam, 1662), Vol. X, Bk. 2, frontispiece. Pls. 294, 295, 297, 302, and 318 are also from this book.

This is Martino Martini's general map of China. It is essentially a Latin version of Chu Ssu-pen's work entitled *Yü ti t'u* (printed 1311–12) as it appeared in the revised version by Lo Hung-hsien (1504–64) entitled *Kuang yü t'u*. It was first published separately in Martini's *Novus atlas sinensis* (Amsterdam, 1655) issued by the Blaeu printing house. Notice that Korea is clearly depicted as a peninsula even though misshapen. To the west Martini retains the European map convention of the imaginary lake in which the rivers of Southeast Asia were supposed to originate. Yezo is shown as an island north of Japan. Japan itself, as well as Formosa and part of Luzon, are within Martini's delineation of the Chinese empire.

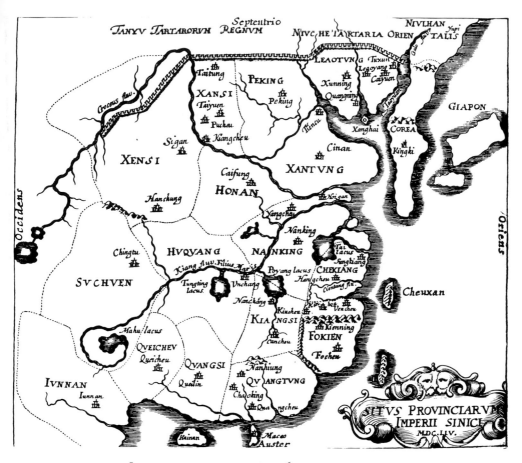

Map labels (clockwise / as positioned):

Septentrio REGNVM · TANYV TARTARORVM · NIVCHE TARTARIA ORIENTALIS · NIVLHAN · Yupi · LEAOTVNG · Tuxun · Legoyang · Caiyuen · Taitung · PEKING · Xunning · Quangnin · GIAPON · XANSI · Peking · Taiyuun · Pincu · Puchau · Xanghai · COREA · Kiangcheu · Cinan · Kingki · Croceus fluu. · Sigan · Occidens · XENSI · Caifung · XANTVNG · HONAN · Hoigan · Hanchung · Yangcheu · Nanking · NANKING · Tai lacus · Sunghiang · HVQVANG · Kiang fluu.Filius Maris · Poyang lacus · CHEKIANG · Chingtu · Vnchang · Hanjcheu · Cientung fluu · Tungting lacus · Nanchang · Kiucheu · Cheuxan · SVCHVEN · KIANGSI · Vencheu · Kinning · Oriens · Mahu lacus · Cancheu · FOKIEN · QVEICHEV · Quicheu · QVANGSI · Nanhiung · Focheu · IVNNAN · Quelin · QVANGTVNG · Iunnan · Chaoking · Quangcheu · Hainan · Macao Auster · SITVS PROVINCIARVM IMPERII SINICI MDC.LIV.

287. MAP OF CHINA DATED 1654

From the English translation of Martino Martini's *Bellum Tartaricum* appended to Alvarez Semedo, *The History of That Great and Renowned Monarchy of China* (London, 1655), facing p. 255. Pls. 288, 342, and 388 are also from this edition of Semedo.

This is known as Martini's "little map," according to B. Szcześniak, *loc. cit.* (pl. 285), p. 125, pl. 6. The same map is found in Adrien Greslon's *Histoire de la Chine* (Paris, 1671).

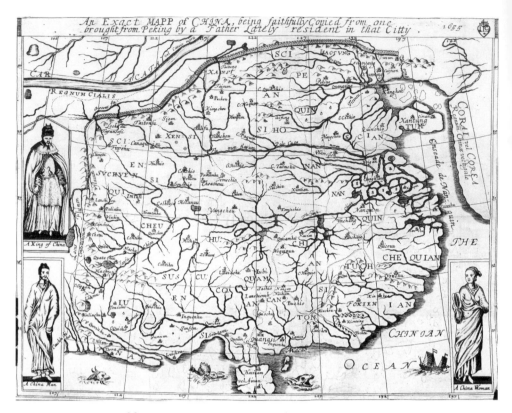

288. MAP OF CHINA DATED 1655

From Semedo, *op. cit.* (pl. 287), facing p. 1.

This is closely related to the Purchas map (pl. 284) in proportions, nomenclature, and illustrations. Ricci's portrait on the Purchas map is replaced here with a depiction of "A King of China."

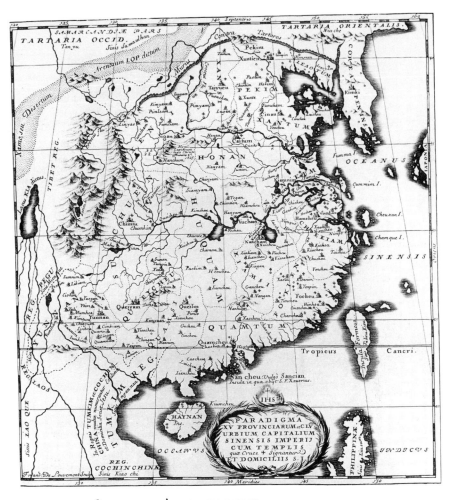

289. COUPLET'S MAP OF CHINA

From Philippe Couplet *et al.*, *Confucius sinarum philosophus* (Paris, 1687), section on Couplet's *Tabula chronologica monarchiae sinicae* (Paris, 1686), facing p. 108.
Pls. 309, 345, 349, 352, 354, and 355 are also from this
book.

This map shows the 15 provinces and 150 major
cities of the Chinese empire. The Christian churches
and Jesuit residences, marked by a cross, number
around 200. Notice the mythical lake "Kia" to the
west. Korea is shown correctly as a peninsula, but it is
still placed incorrectly. The Great Wall erroneously en-
closes Liaotung.

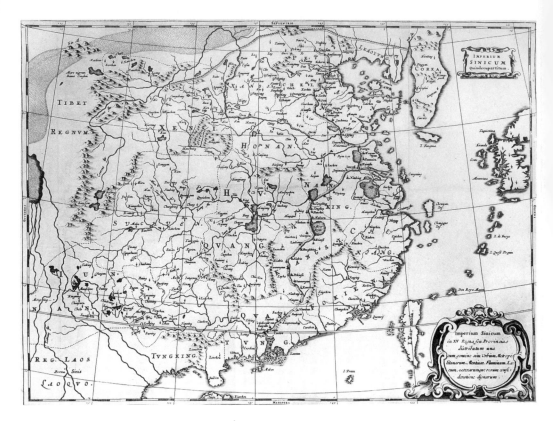

290. KIRCHER'S MAP OF CHINA

From Athanasius Kircher, *La Chine illustrée* (Amsterdam, 1670), between pp. 4 and 5. Pls. 296, 299, 300, 308, 311, 316, 317, 333, 340, 353, 375, 383–87, and 410 are also from this book. See also pl. 376.

This is based on the general map of China in Martini's *Atlas* (see our pl. 286). It omits much of the Japan and Yezo shown on Martini's map, but it does depict Korea as a peninsula. It also omits Luzon, Cochin-China, and materials to the west of the imaginary lake, but is otherwise a close copy of the Martini map.

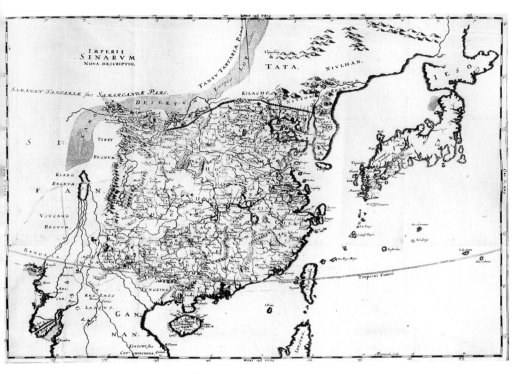

291. NIEUHOF'S MAP OF CHINA

From Johann Nieuhof, *Ambassade des Hollandois à la Chine . . . traduits sur deux manuscrits Hollandois* (Paris, 1666), end of vol.

This is Martini's map, taken from the Blaeu atlas. It shows better than most the peripheral states of China.

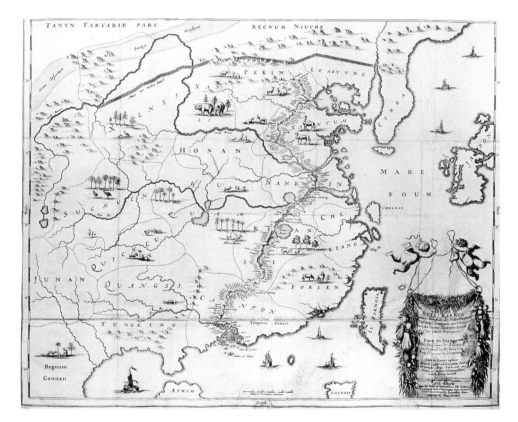

292. ROUTE TAKEN BY DUTCH EMBASSY FROM CANTON TO PEKING IN 1655–56

From Johann Nieuhof, *Die Gesandtschafft* . . . (Amsterdam, 1666), facing p. 444. Pls. 301, 303, 305, 314, 315, 319–24, 326, 328–30, 334, 335, 337–39, 341, 351, 360–64, 367, 374, 377, 381, and 382 are also from this book.

Evidently drawn and prepared by Nieuhof himself, according to the caption on the map. But the map still owes a heavy debt to the Martini map. Lists almost every town on the route from Canton to Peking, to give the viewer a vivid impression of China's crowded landscape. For identifications of the towns and showplaces of Kwangtung see C. Imbault Huart, "Le voyage de l'ambassade hollandaise de 1656 à travers la province de Canton," *JRAS (China Branch)*, n.s., Vol. XXX, No. 1 (1895–96), pp. 1–73.

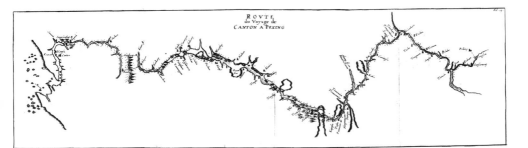

293. ROUTE OF THE DUTCH EMBASSY
From Nieuhof, *op. cit.* (pl. 291), facing p. 68.

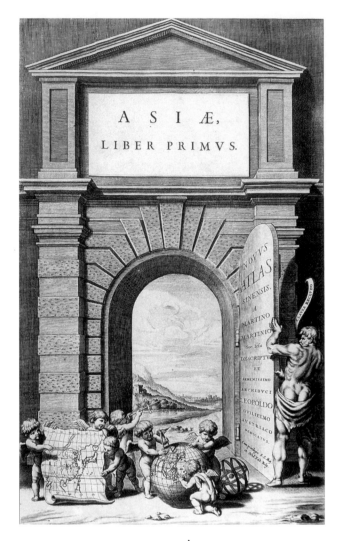

294. FRONTISPIECE, BLAEU'S
ATLAS MAJOR, X (1662).

This is the volume that contains Martini's *Novus atlas sinensis. Cf.* to close-up engravings of door, opener, cupids, globes, etc., in the frontispiece to Martini's work itself (pl. 295).

295. FRONTISPIECE,
MARTINI'S *NOVUS ATLAS SINENSIS*
From Vol. X of Blaeu's *Atlas major.*

LA
CHINE
D'ATHANASE KIRCHERE
De la Compagnie de JESUS,
ILLUSTRÉE
De plusieurs
MONUMENTS
Tant Sacrés que Profanes,
Et de quantité de Recherchés
DE LA
NATURE & de l'ART.
A
Quoy on à adjousté de nouveau les questions curieuses que le Serenissime
GRAND DUC de TOSCANE a fait depuis peu au P. Jean Grubere touchant ce
grand Empire.

Avec un Dictionaire Chinois & François, lequel est tres-rare, & qui n'a pas encores
paru au jour.

Traduit par F. S. DALQUIE'

A AMSTERDAM,
Chés *Jean Janffon à Waesberge*, & les *Heritiers d'Elizée Weyerstraet*,
l'An clɔlɔc lxx. Avec Privilege.

296.

ASIA,
QVÆ EST
GEOGRAPHIÆ
BLAVIANÆ
PARS QVARTA,
LIBRI DVO.
VOLVMEN DECIMVM.

INDEFESSVS AGENDO

AMSTELÆDAMI,
Labore & Sumptibus
IOANNIS BLAEV,
M DC LXII.

297.

The Effigies of M.r Jn Nieuhoff.

298. PORTRAIT OF JOHANN NIEUHOF
From *CV* (3rd ed.; 1744), Vol. II, frontispiece.

299. THE MYSTERIOUS FLYING BRIDGE OF SHENSI

From Kircher, *op. cit.* (pl. 290), a fold-out inserted between pp. 288 and 289.

Kircher identifies this as a representation of a bridge in Shensi Province near "Chogan" on the river Fi. It connects two mountains "by one extended arc which is forty Chinese perches (400 feet) . . . and the distance down to the Yellow River beneath the bridge is said to be fifty perches (500 feet), so the Chinese call this the Flying Bridge."[1]

Kircher took this information directly from Martini's *Novus atlas sinensis* (1655).[2] Martini, but not Kircher, identifies "Chegan" as being near Ninghsia, but we have not been able to locate it on Martini's map of Shensi or on modern maps. Joseph Needham, who was also unable to locate "Chogan," speculates that Kircher misunderstood the meaning of Martini's description, particularly in the use of *Fi*. Martini wrote: "propre Chegan ad ripam, Fi pons de monte ad montem unico exstructus arcu." Kircher rendered it as follows: "propre Chogan [notice difference in spelling] ad ripam Fi, spectatus [notice difference in the placement of the comma]." Needham believes that the "Fi pons" of Martini stands for "fei chiao" (the Chinese for "Flying Bridge" or suspension bridge). Kircher, in Needham's view, was also misled by "unico exstructus arcu" into concluding that Martini was describing a semicircular arched bridge of the type shown in the illustration.[3] To support Needham's conclusion it should be noted that Martini said the bridge spanned the Yellow River and not the "Fi."

Nothing tells us about the provenance of this copper-engraving itself or its caption. Kircher cryptically remarks: "Here we placed a picture which will easily show its [the bridge's] arrangement." The caption on the engraving reads: "Flying Bridge in Shensi province, in one arch from mountain to mountain. Length 400 cubits. Height 50." If we take the cubit to be approximately 20 inches, the length is about 666 feet and the height 83 feet, a height that is well within reason.[4] In the text Kircher compares this Chinese bridge to Le Pont du Gardon, a Roman bridge which he had seen near Nimes in France. But nowhere does he indicate where he obtained the copper engraving of the alleged Shensi bridge.

It may be a Western bridge to which the caption was added, for in the text Kircher refers the reader to his own work on the structure of bridges to understand how such a bridge was constructed and how it was kept up during the building.[5] It certainly could also be a copper engraving based on a sketch of a genuine Chinese bridge. Unlike most of the illustrations in Kircher's book, only this and one other are not printed on the page but are inserted and folded into the book like a map—perhaps as an afterthought. Kircher, certainly because he tried to do too much, was not always careful and circumspect in his use of the mass of materials which passed into his hands from Jesuits in the field.[6] Johann Grueber wrote to him in 1669: "There are certain points in *China illustrata* that need correction, especially the drawings, but it is better to leave things as they are though I shall send you the emendations for insertion in case the work should be reprinted."[7]

[1] Charles Van Tuyl, *China Illustrata by Kircher. Translated by Dr. Charles Van Tuyl from the 1677* [*sic*] *Original Latin Edition* (Muskogee, Okla., 1987), p. 205.

[2] See the anastatic edition published at Trent in 1981, p. 52.

[3] See Needham, *Science and Civilization in China* (5 vols.; Cambridge, 1971), Vol. IV, Bk. 3, p. 189.

[4] These differ from Needham's figures. His calculation uses the "Chinese perch" (10 ft.), a unit of measurement given in the text but not in the caption. *Ibid.* While semicircular arched bridges were common in both Europe and China in the seventeenth century, the longest surviving Roman arch of this type spans only 117 ft. Very few later bridges span more than 150 ft. *Ibid.*, p. 168. Based on these figures this was a very high bridge indeed.

[5] So far we have not located a work by Kircher dealing with bridge construction.

[6] See C. Wessels, S.J., *Early Jesuit Travellers in Central Asia, 1603–1721* (The Hague, 1924), pp. 58, 59, 167, 196.

[7] As quoted in *ibid.*, p. 168. When it was reprinted in French translation in 1670, Grueber's corrections of the pictures were not added as far as we can determine. That the French text had errors of its own can be demonstrated by noting that Shensi became Shansi province in the text but not in the caption. The English translation of Van Tuyl does not reproduce this engraving at all.

Pons volans in Provincia Xensi unico arcu
à Monte ad Montem long: 400 cub: altitud: 50

300. THE GREAT WALL MYTH
Frontispiece from Kircher, *op. cit.* (pl. 290).

The map of East Asia is here held up to view by Father Adam Schall (on the left) and Father Matteo Ricci. Notice how the Great Wall runs uninterruptedly between northern China and Tartary. The Ming wall system was completed by mid-century; this mythical depiction of a continuous wall was amplified by other Jesuits, like Martino Martini in his *Atlas* (1665), who probably generalized about the whole wall on the basis of observations made in the capital region. See A. Waldron, "The Great Wall Myth: Its Origins and Role in Modern China," *The Yale Journal of Criticism,* II (1988), 77. But not all the walls shown in European depictions run uninterruptedly across northern China (for example, see pl. 289).

VYF PAARDS HOOFDEN
LES MONTS DES CINQ TESTES DE CHEVAUX.

301. MOUNTAINS OF THE FIVE HORSES' HEADS

From Nieuhof, *op. cit.* (pl. 292), p. 79, text on p. 80.

The Tartars (Manchus), according to Nieuhof, call these "wondrous mountains" the "heads of five horses" because of their strange shapes.

These heights along the Pei River, known to the Chinese as *Wu-ma t'ou* (Five Horses' Heads), belong to the group of red sandstone mountains called *Wu-ma kuei ts'ao-shan* (The Five Horses Who Return Here to Eat). This is a "peculiar group of hills that change their appearance continually as observed from different points of view, until we come directly behind them, when they stand out like mighty colossal steeds, arranged as the equestrian guards of the land." From B. O. Henry, *Ling-Nam or Interior Views of Southern China* (London, 1886), p. 97. For identifications see Huart, *loc. cit.* (pl. 292), pp. 54–55.

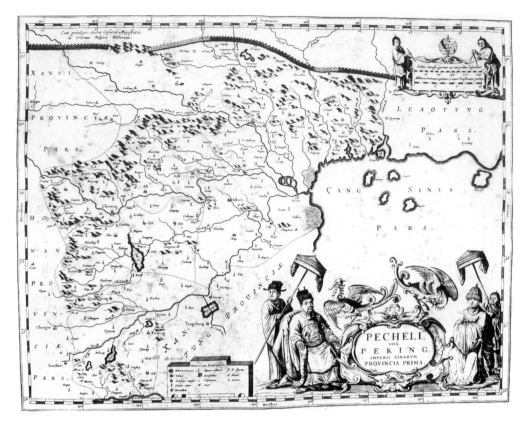

302. MAP OF THE METROPOLITAN PROVINCE, "PECHELI" OR PEKING

From Martini's *Atlas,* in Blaeu, *op. cit.* (pl. 286), Vol. X, between pp. 26 and 27.

This, like the original Martini atlas, was founded on a printed version of the revised Mongol atlas of the fourteenth century. Blaeu had the seventeen maps in his atlas of China engraved after Martini's manuscript maps. But Blaeu's maps are richer in detail which suggests that he must have followed another model as well. See I. C. Koeman, *Joan Blaeu and His Grand Atlas* (Amsterdam, 1970), pp. 84–88.

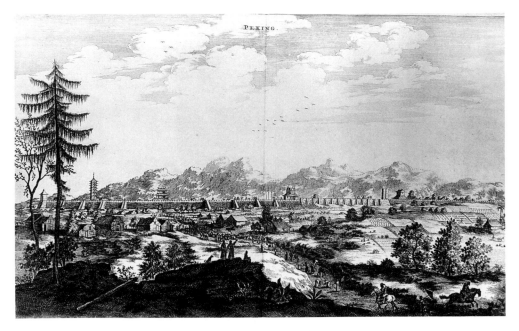

303. PEKING WITH THE GREAT WALL
IN THE DISTANCE
From Nieuhof, *op. cit.* (pl. 292), between pp. 176–77.

304. PLAN OF PEKING

From Gabriel Magaillans (Magalhães), *A New History of China* (London, 1688), frontispiece. Pl. 344 is also from this book.

Peking was one of the world's largest cities in the seventeenth century and was rivaled in Asia only by Agra, Delhi, Kyoto, and Constantinople. The Europeans of the time, as is illustrated here, were most impressed by its planned character as an administrative and imperial capital.

The city, built on an axial pattern in the Ming dynasty, is correctly shown here as a series of concentric rectangles. Its outer walls, faced with bricks, measured more than fourteen miles around and enclosed an area of about twenty-four square miles. Within this spacious rectangle, interior walls enclosed the imperial city (*huang ch'eng*), the administrative center of about 1,480 acres. The palace city, commonly called the "Forbidden City," occupied hardly more than 250 acres within the imperial city. It was here that Nieuhof and other foreigners were formally received.

A feeling of monumentality was conveyed by the city as a whole rather than by spectacular buildings or other architectural creations, although temples were numerous. Unlike Versailles, then being built in Louis XIV's France, the Chinese imperial city did not present great vistas or wide-open spaces. North-south and east-west thoroughfares divided the outer city into small blocks where the people lived and worked in what were generally seen to be uncrowded conditions. The city, then as now, had many one-story houses with enclosed gardens. Within the city there were more trees than in the surrounding countryside. For further description see Andrew Boyd, *Chinese Architecture and Town Planning, 1500 B.C.–A.D. 1911* (Chicago, 1962), pp. 62–74; and A. F. Wright, "The Cosmology of the Chinese City," in G. W. Skinner (ed.), *The City in Late Imperial China* (Stanford, 1977), pp. 66–77.

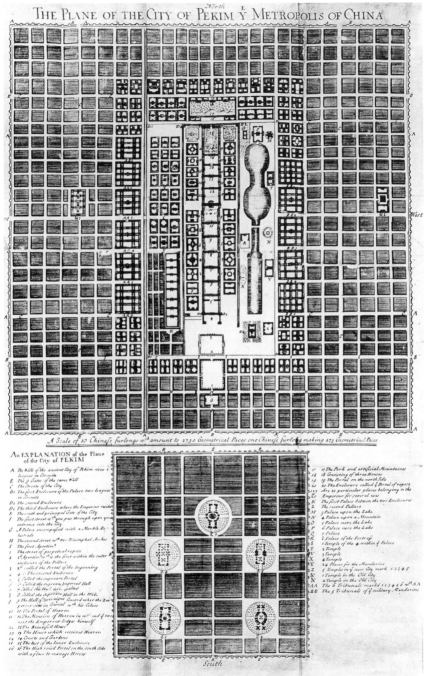

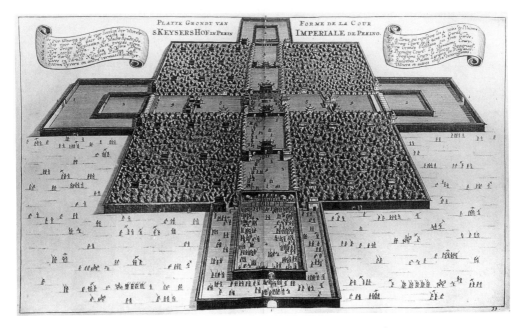

305. PROSPECT OF THE IMPERIAL CITY
(*HUANG CH'ENG*) AT PEKING
From Nieuhof, *op. cit.* (pl. 292), between pp. 194
and 195.

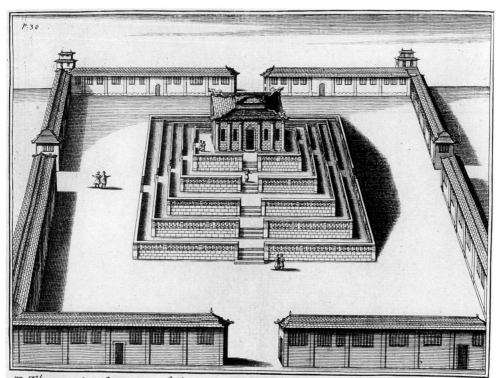

The Throne of the Emperour of China, Scituated, in the Middle of the Greatest Court of his Pallace , and raised vpon five bases of White Marble.

306. THE IMPERIAL THRONE IN PEKING

From Louis Le Comte, *Memoirs and Observations . . . Made in a Late Journey through China* (London, 1698), between pp. 38 and 39. Pls. 307 and 312 are also from this book.

"In the midst of one of those great Courts stands a square Basis or solid Building, of an extraordinary bigness, whose top is adorned with a Balustrade, much after our fashion; this supports another like unto it, but framed Taper-wise, over which is placed three more, still loosing in bulk as they gain in height. Upon the uppermost is built a large Hall, whose Roof being covered with gilt Tiles, is born by the four Walls, and as many rows of Varnished Pillars, between which is seated the Throne.

These vast Bases, with their Balustrades made of white Marble, and thus disposed Amphitheater-wise, when the sun shines, dazzle the Eyes of the Beholder with Lustre and Splendor of the Gold and Varnish, and afford a most beautiful Prospect, especially since they are placed in the midst of a spacious Court, and surrounded by four stately rows of Buildings" (pp. 38–39).

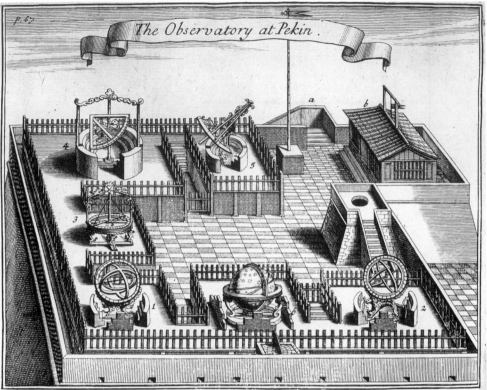

307. THE OBSERVATORY AT PEKING

From Le Comte, *op. cit.* (pl. 306), between pp. 66 and 67.

"This Observatory, of little worth, as to its ancient Machines, and less as to its Situation and Building, is now enriched with several Brazen Instruments which Father [Ferdinand] Verbiest has set up. They are large, well cast, imbellished with Figures of Dragons, and very well disposed to the use they are designed for" (p. 64).

Portiuncula Muri Sinensis; qua structura ejus exprimitur.

12. Cubit.

30 Cubit.

Porta Tartarica.

Croceus fluvius.

308. TARTAR GATE IN THE GREAT WALL NEAR HSI-NING

From Kircher, *op. cit.* (pl. 290), p. 292.

This was drawn by the Jesuit fathers Albert D'Orville and Johann Grueber as exactly "as the nature of the place allowed them." At this point six horsemen may ride abreast atop the wall "without hindering one another." The people of Hsi-ning climb on top of the wall "to enjoy the pleasant and unobstructed view on all sides." The distance to the next gate (apparently the westernmost) is "so great that one can scarcely travel it in eighteen days" (quotations from Van Tuyl [trans.], *op. cit.* [pl. 299], p. 61). The elephant and the horsemen seem to indicate that it was at this "Tartar Gate" that traders had to await permission to enter China. The "Yellow River" which is shown running through the watergate may be the Hsi-ning ho, one of its tributaries.

Today no part of the Great Wall is to be seen near Hsi-ning. But it is not to be concluded therefore that a wall did not stand nearby in 1661. Certainly traces of numerous ancient walls and towers have been discovered in the vicinity of Hsi-ning (see Wessels, *op. cit.* [pl. 299], pp. 179–82). Joseph Needham comments on "a very mysterious extension of the Great Wall in . . . the neighbourhood of Lanchow (Lan-chou). Originating from the western junction of the Lanchow Loop with the Outer Wall, it passes south-westerly in an arc enclosing Hsi-ning and . . . crosses the Yellow River and returns in a curve to the neighbourhood of Lanchow" (*Science and Civilization in China* [5 vols.; Cambridge, 1971], Vol. IV, Pt. 3, p. 49). This wall appears to date from the fourth century A.D.

309. A REPRESENTATION OF CONFUCIUS IN THE *KUO HSÜEH* (IMPERIAL ACADEMY)

From Couplet *et al.*, *op. cit.* (pl. 289), p. cxvi.

Engraved in Paris at Chez Nolin.

Confucius is here referred to in the caption to the picture by his given name (*Chung-ni*, romanized here as Chum Nhij) and the characters in the picture call him the "great teacher of China" (*T'ien hsia hsien-shih*). In his hands Confucius holds a *hu*, a votive tablet held before the chest by officials at an imperial audience. Behind him three members of the academy are shown working in a library lined with copies of the Confucian classics. The decorative dragons at the top are both five-clawed imperial dragons.

R.P.IOANNES ADAMVS SCHALL, GERMANVS
è Societate IESV: Pequini Supremi ac Regij Mathe,
matum Tribunalis Præses; indefels9 pro Conuersi,
one gentiū in Chinis Operarig ab aūis 50. ætat: suæ 77.

G.H.Wolfgang. f:

310. FATHER JOHANN ADAM SCHALL
IN MANDARIN DRESS
From Schall, *Historica relatio de ortu et progressu fidei*
(Ratisbon, 1672), frontispiece. Engraving by G. H.
Wolfgang.

311. THE FIRST MANCHU EMPEROR, SHUN-CHIH (R. 1644–61), AT ABOUT EIGHTEEN YEARS OF AGE

From Kircher, *op. cit.* (pl. 290), facing p. 152.

Copper engraving possibly based upon a drawing by an anonymous artist. The portrait is Europeanized: it might be the work of a Jesuit artist or it might have been "improved upon" by the engraver. At any rate it is not very Chinese; the drapery at the left is an obvious European addition.

According to Kircher, "the royal dress is decorated with dragons, bird feathers, and many priceless gems and pearls."[1] The emperor's costume is contrasted in Kircher's text to that of Father Schall, who is shown in the dress of a mandarin of the first class (see pl. 310). Schall was very close to the young emperor between 1652 and 1657; both portraits were probably drawn near the end of this period.

The robe of the emperor actually displays a bird of uncertain identity. This is particularly strange since the Ch'ing first adopted mandarin squares decorated with dragons for the imperial dress in 1652.[2]

Father Grueber in a letter of 1670 to Kircher "gives his correspondent to understand that the portrait of the Emperor of China carrying a stick and accompanied by a dog will be taken as an insult in that country. The Emperor should be represented standing or sitting at a table covered with books and mathematical instruments."[3]

Akbar (pl. 112) is likewise shown in the company of a dog—probably a symbol of the "Excellent Prince".[4] A stylized portrait called "Der Sinesische Käyser Xunchi," obviously based on the engraving shown here, appears without the stick and the dog that Grueber complains about, in E. W. Happel's *Thesaurus exoticorum* (Hamburg, 1688). For a reproduction see H. Walravens, *China illustrata. Das europäische Chinaverständnis im Spiegel des 16. bis 18. Jahrhunderts* (Wolfenbüttel, 1987), p. 100.

[1] Van Tuyl (trans.), *op. cit.* (pl. 299), p. 100.

[2] See S. Cammann, *China's Dragon Robes* (New York, 1952), p. 25.

[3] From Wessels, *op. cit.* (pl. 299), p. 169. Indeed the young emperor was very much interested in what he could learn from Schall about Western civilization.

[4] Guy de Tervanent, *Attributes et symboles dans l'art profane, 1450–1600* (Geneva, 1958), p. 94.

312. PORTRAIT OF THE K'ANG-HSI EMPEROR AT AGE THIRTY-TWO

Frontispiece, Le Comte, *op. cit.* (pl. 306).

Engraved in Europe by M. van der Gucht.

This portrait of K'ang-hsi, born in 1654, was done in or around 1686. It was probably painted by one of the European missionaries who then worked in the Ju-i-kuan, the hall in the imperial palace where the Westerners painted, engraved, and repaired mechanical devices.

Notice the dragon decor and dragon robe. The dragon robe (*lung-p'ao*) was bright yellow, a costume for ceremonial occasions. K'ang-hsi wears a winter hat that complements his dragon robe. The dragon on the robe and elsewhere in the picture is the five-clawed dragon reserved to imperial use. See Cammann, *op. cit.* (pl. 311), pp. 25–26. The dragons on the frame are encircled by clouds, possibly to indicate the emperor's celestial character.

This portrait appeared originally in J. Bouvet, *Portrait historique de l'Empereur de la Chine* (Paris, 1697). It was shortly thereafter reproduced with decorative additions and an extended caption in the English edition of Le Comte reproduced here. An engraving closer to the original was included as a frontispiece to the second edition (1699) of Leibniz' *Novissima Sinica*. Another (pl. 313), similar to the Le Comte engraving, was published as the frontispiece to the Italian translation of Bouvet. Also see J. J. Heeren, "Father Bouvet's Picture of Emperor K'ang-hsi (with Appendices)" *Asia Major,* VII (1932), 556–72.

Le Comte recalls that in 1689, when he saw the K'ang-hsi emperor for the first time, "he was something above the middle stature, more corpulent than an European Beau, yet somewhat more Slender than a Chinese would wish to be; full Visaged, Disfigured with the Small Pox, had a broad Forehead, little Eyes, and a small Nose after the Chinese fashion; his Mouth was well made, and the lower part of his Face very agreeable. In fine, tho' he bears no great Majesty in his Looks, yet they shew abundance of Good Nature, and his Ways and Action have something of the Prince in them, and shew him to be such" (p. 41 of the English edition).

CAM-HY
Emperor of China &
the Eastern Tartary
Aged 41 years, Drawn
when he was but 32.

313. K'ANG-HSI: ANOTHER VER-
SION OF THE SAME PORTRAIT
Frontispiece to Italian translation made
by Franco Cisnocilio, of J. Bovet
(Bouvet), *Istoria de l'imperador de la
Cina* (Padua, 1710).

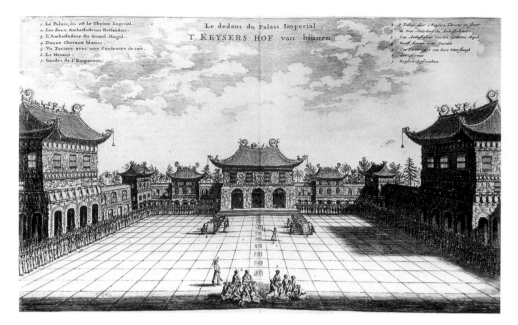

Le dedans du Palais Imperial.

'T KEYSERS HOF van binnen

314. RECEPTION OF EMISSARIES AT THE IMPERIAL COURT

From Nieuhof, *op. cit.* (pl. 292), between pp. 192 and 193 (and between pp. 172 and 173 of Dutch edition).

This depicts the official reception of the Dutch, Mughul, and Tartar emissaries at the imperial court of Peking, October 2, 1656. *Cf.* our pl. 23 (in bk. 1).

MOGOLSCHE *gezant.*

315. ENVOYS FROM MUGHUL INDIA TO PEKING (OCTOBER, 1656)

From Nieuhof, *op. cit.* (pl. 292), p. 189.

According to Nieuhof, the Mughul emissary wore leather boots and a blue silk robe decorated all over with dragons. We can find no other record of a Mughul embassy of 1656 to Peking.

The costumes of the envoys are of the Persian and Central Asian types so popular at the Mughul court. Notice especially the turbans and the boots.

Nieuhof's report of a Mughul embassy to Peking was taken at face value by C. B. K. Roa Sahib, "Shah Jehan's Embassy to China, 1656 A.D.," *Quarterly Journal of the Mythic Society,* Silver Jubilee Number XXV (1934–35), 117–21. By examination of the Chinese sources, Luciano Petech concluded that Nieuhof was mistaken in this identification. He argues, quite convincingly, that these were probably emissaries from Turfan in central Asia. See Petech, "La pretesa ambascita di Shah Jahan alla Cina," *Rivista degli studi orientali,* XXVI (1951), 124–27.

316, 317. TWO CHINESE NOBLE LADIES

From Kircher, *op. cit.* (pl. 290), between pp. 154 and 155, Copper-plate engravings.

"If the reader wishes to examine the dress of the palace noblewomen more closely, I have attached a drawing sent to me by the fathers from China."[1] This probably means that this pair of drawings was executed in Peking by a Jesuit artist who certainly added touches of his own.[2] The engraver in Europe might also have provided embellishments.

Chinese and Western elements are here fused together. Essentially Chinese are the robes and stance of the ladies, the copper and porcelain vases full of flowering branches, the straight lines and sharp angles of the rectangular tables, the landscape scroll,[3] the stringed musical instruments, the Buddha on the wall, and the decorative characters, which mean "beautiful ladies." Essentially Western are the faces of the ladies, the invented interiors with draped windows which look to the out-of-doors, the positioning of the women standing by the tables, and the ornate picture frames enclosing the characters.[4]

The birds, Kircher alleges, keep the ladies company and divert them while they remain secluded in their apartments.

[1] Van Tuyl (trans.), *op. cit.* (pl. 299), p. 102.

[2] Michael Sullivan, *The Meeting of Eastern and Western Art* (London, 1973), p. 93, thinks the ladies themselves were "certainly taken from a Chinese painting."

[3] The scroll is shown draped "in a way that would horrify a Chinese connoisseur" (*ibid.*). Sullivan also suggests that this is "the earliest representation of a Chinese landscape painting in European art" (*ibid.*). But *cf.* our pl. 72. The scroll depicted here does not have a wooden roll at the base of the scroll as it normally would.

[4] *Cf.* catalog of the exhibition of 1973 held at the Schloss Charlottenburg (Berlin) issued by the Verwaltung der staatlichen Schlösser und Gärten, *China und Europa: Chinaverständnis und Chinamode im 17. und 18. Jahrhundert,* p. 157.

318. NANKING PROVINCE

From Blaeu, *op. cit.* (pl. 286), Vol. X, Bk. 2, between pp. 94 and 95.

This is a Blaeu engraving based upon Martini's manuscript map. It shows clearly the Yellow and Yangtze rivers and their tributaries, and the routes by which these two major rivers flowed to the coast. It also shows how the Grand Canal linked the two deltas and then proceeded from the Yellow River northward. It highlights the province's many lakes and coastal islands. For a key to its cities see the *Notarum Explicatio* in the left-hand corner.

In Manchu times Nanking, no longer the second imperial capital, was known as "Kiangnan" (Chiangning), the capital of a newly created double province.

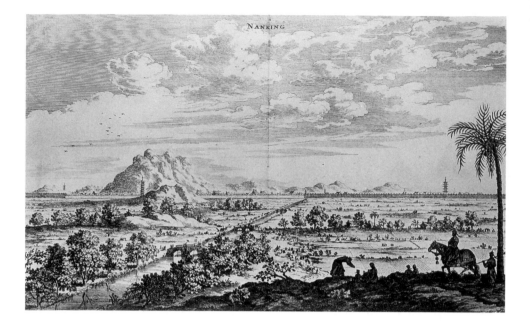

319. VISTA OF NANKING

From Nieuhof, *op. cit.* (pl. 292), between pp. 116 and 117.

Notice the canal and bridges. The high mountain is either the "purple mountain" or "stone city," two of the most striking physical features of Nanking.

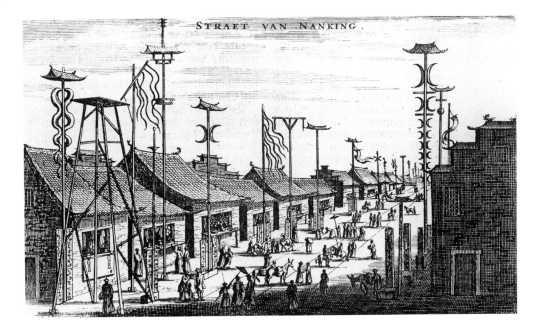

320. STREET OF NANKING (1656)

From Nieuhof, *op. cit.,* p. 119; text, pp. 118–20.

According to Nieuhof, Nanking's most important streets were twenty-eight paces wide, paved in the middle with rectangular blue stone slabs, and lined on both sides with gravel. Every hundred paces or so there was a gate that was closed at night and each such enclosed neighborhood was guarded by a night watchman.

In front of the establishments of the streets' most distinguished merchants stood a signboard bearing the name of the merchant and his business written in golden characters. Next to the signboard a pole was erected, extending higher than the houses; to this a distinctive flag or banner was attached which indicated what each place had for sale. Nieuhof compares these banners to the shop signs or business symbols common in European towns.

La Tour de PORCELLYNE PORCELAINE TOOREN.

321. THE PORCELAIN PAGODA OF NANKING

From Nieuhof, *op. cit.* (pl. 292), between pp. 124 and 125.

Located outside the south gate of Nanking, the porcelain pagoda belonged to the Bao En Buddhist temple. The pagoda had been built between 1415 and 1430 by the Yung-lo emperor to honor his mother. Nine stories and 261 feet in height, it was octagonal in shape and encased in white glazed brick. The overhanging eaves which covered the balconies on each level were covered with green glazed tiles. It was topped by a gilded spiral that pointed to the sky. More than one hundred bells hanging from the corners of its turned-up eaves tinkled in the wind. At night at least 140 lighted lamps were placed in its windows and at the corners of the eaves.

In 1856 the pagoda was completely destroyed by the Taiping rebels. Little remains of it today except for a few stone relics in Nanking and a number of its glazed tiles. In the West a few of the glazed tiles are preserved in the Metropolitan and in the Victoria and Albert museums. See Barry Till, *In Search of Old Nanking* (Hong Kong, 1982), pp. 127–31. Also see J. D. Ball, *Things Chinese* (5th ed.; London, 1926), pp. 441, 444, 506. Nieuhof's portrait of the porcelain pagoda resembles closely the replica of the pagoda now kept in Nanking. See Till, *op. cit.,* p. 128.

On the confused etymology of the Western word "pagoda" or "pagode" see H. Yule and A. C. Burnell, *Hobson-Jobson* (London, 1968), pp. 652–57.

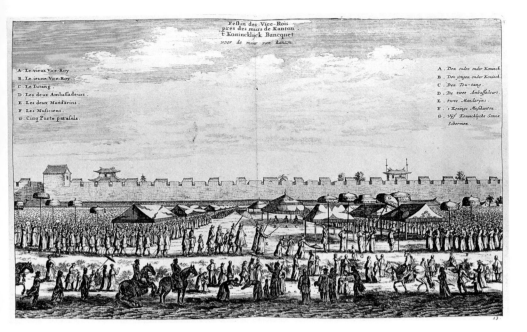

Feſtin des Vice-Rois
pres des murs de Kanton.
t Koninclijck Bancquet
voor de muur van kanton.

A . Le vieux Vice-Roy
B . Le ieune Vice-Roy
C . Le Tutang .
D . Les deux Ambaſſadeurs .
E . Les deux Mandarins .
F . Les Muſiciens .
G . Cinq Porte paraſols .

A . Den ouden onder Koninck
B . Den jongen onder Koninck
C . Den Tou-tang .
D . De twee Ambaſſadeurs .
E . twee Mandarijns .
F . 's Konings Muſikanten .
G . Vyf Koninklycke Sonne
   Schermen .

322. BANQUET IN HONOR OF THE DUTCH EMISSARIES

From Nieuhof, *op. cit.*, between pp. 56 and 57.

A depiction of the banquet given by the "Viceroys" of Kwangtung before the walls of Canton in honor of the Dutch emissaries in September, 1655.

During the 1650's Kwangtung continued to be caught up periodically in the wars between the Ming loyalists and the Ch'ing supporters. In the latter half of the 1640's both sides had appointed governor-generals of the province. Tu Yung-ho, the last Ming appointee, technically ruled Kwangtung from 1649 to 1652. He was replaced by Li Shuai-t'ai (d. 1666), the Ch'ing governor-general, who nominally ruled the province from 1653 to 1656.

When the Dutch arrived in Kwangtung in September, 1655, its actual rulers were Shang K'o-hsi (d. 1676) and Kêng Chi-mao (d. 1671), the so-called feudatory princes. Shang was known as the "pignowan" (*p'ing-nan wang*, the Prince who pacifies the south) and Kêng as the "Synowa" (possibly *ching-nan wang*, his hereditary title). These two military overlords were known to the Dutch respectively as the "old and new kings or viceroys" of the province. It was evidently they who presented the banquet depicted here. See A. W. Hummel (ed.), *Eminent Chinese of the Ch'ing Period (1644–1912)* (2d ed., Washington, D.C., 1967), pp. 415, 484, 635. For the Chinese sources on the Dutch in Canton see L. Petech, "L'ambasciata olandese del 1655–57 nei documenti cinesi," *Revista degli studi orientali*, XXV (1950), 79–80.

Umbrellas like those shown here were usually given as honors to officials. They were circular canopies made in the Ch'ing period of scarlet silk with the name of the donor embroidered on the deep borders. See Ball, *op. cit.* (pl. 321), p. 175.

't Conterfeytfel vande OUDE ONDER-KONING

**323. PORTRAIT OF THE "OLD VICEROY" OF
KWANGTUNG (1655)**
From Nieuhof, *op. cit.* (pl. 292), p. 64.
This realistic portrait of Shang K'o-hsi (1604–1676),
known to the Dutch as the "Old Viceroy," and his staff
was evidently made from a sketch done by Nieuhof
himself. Shang K'o-hsi was the feudatory prince of
Kwangtung who gave the Dutch a written permission
to trade in this province.

324. XAOCHEU, OR SUCHEU

From Nieuhof, *op. cit.*, between pp. 78 and 79; text, pp. 78–79.

"Xaocheu" (Shao-chou), second city of Kwangtung, was commonly known as "Sucheu" (Shao-kuan), which means the "toll barrier of Shao." Situated on a point where the Pei divides into two other rivers, it was a center of the internal transit trade in the northern section of Kwangtung. When the Dutch emissaries passed through, the city had not yet fully recovered from the depredations left by the civil wars. The pagoda shown here stood on a small elevated island near the bifurcation of the river. See Huart, *loc. cit.* (pl. 292), pp. 42–48.

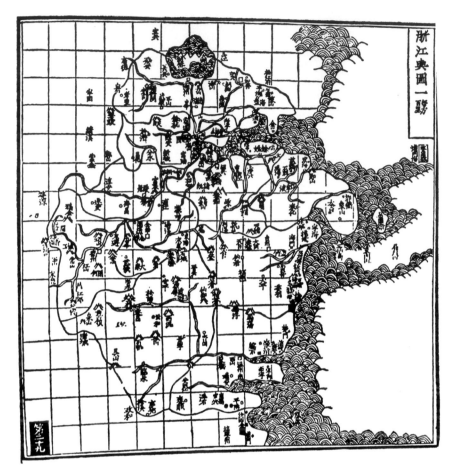

325. CHINESE MAP OF CHEKIANG PROVINCE

From a Chinese atlas presented to Nicholas Witsen by
Philippe Couplet when the latter was in Amsterdam
some time between 1683 to 1692, the years of his trip
in Europe. The Chinese atlas is now in the Museum
Meermano-Westreenianum at The Hague (115 B1). An
annotation in the atlas is in Witsen's handwriting and
dated 1684. These maps, according to Witsen's note,
are newer and better than those presented by Martini in
his *Atlas* (1655). See Koeman, *op. cit.* (pl. 302), p. 85.

The Hague Atlas is the first edition of the *Ku'ang-
yu-t'u* by Lo Hung-hsien (1504–64) of 1555–58. Martini's *Atlas* was based on a smaller Chinese atlas, the
Ku'ang-yu-chi of 1600 by Lu Ying-yang. See M.
Destombes, "A Rare Chinese Atlas," *Quaerendo,* IV
(1974), 336–37.

326. "NANGAN" (NAN-AN) IN KIANGSI
PROVINCE

From Nieuhof, *op. cit.* (pl. 292), between pp. 86
and 87.

In April, 1656, the Dutch embassy stopped for four
days at Nan-an, the southernmost of Kiangsi's thirteen
main cities. This city, according to Nieuhof, was divided into northern and southern parts by the Kan
River. This north-flowing river empties into the P'o-
yang Lake and from thence into the Yangtze River. An
exchange center of north-south trade, Nan-an was
heavily damaged in China's mid-century civil wars.

327. DIFFERENT TYPES OF CHINESE VESSELS
From TR, III, between pp. 68 and 69. Pls. 336 and 380
are also from this book.

The French engraver evidently put together this collection from Nieuhof and perhaps others.

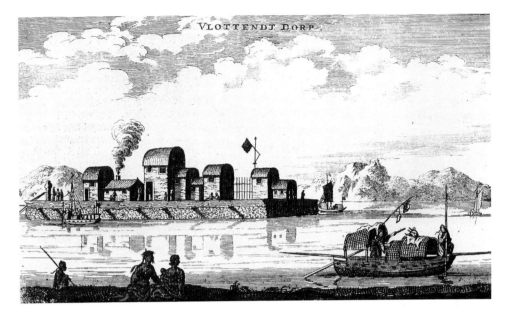

328. A FLOATING VILLAGE

From Nieuhof, *op. cit.* (pl. 292), p. 141.

Produced from a sketch by Nieuhof. According to the text, these were huge rafts of bamboo logs tied together with reeds and overlaid with heavy boards. The houses on them were built of light wooden materials. The largest rafts had space for two hundred families.

This is probably a "timber raft" or *mu p'ai,* the largest of which appear to be "floating villages." See G. R. G. Worcester, *The Junks and Sampans of the Yangtze* (Annapolis, Md., 1971), p. 374. Probably they were assembled at the mouth of the Han River by lashing together many small rafts. Some of the greater "floating villages" were two to three hundred meters in length and carried 150 to 200 persons and their habitations. They went downstream with their cargoes to the cities at the mouth of the Yangtze. For a modern discussion and depiction of these rafts see L. Audemare, *Les jonques chinoises* in "Publicaties van het Museum voor Land- en Volkenkunde," No. 4 (Rotterdam, 1962), p. 18; No. 6 (Rotterdam, 1965), pp. 74–76, pls. 77–79.

This engraving from Nieuhof's work was later reproduced in J. B. du Halde's famous *Description . . . de la Chine* (Paris, 1735). See Theodore N. Foss, "A Jesuit Encyclopedia for China. A Guide to Jean-Baptiste Du Halde's *Description . . . de la Chine* (1735)," (Ph.D. diss.; 2 vols.; Committee on History of Culture, University of Chicago, 1979), II, 577.

329. (TOP) "TONGLOU" (DONG-LIU), A YANGTZE TOWN

From Nieuhof, *op. cit.* (pl. 292), between pp. 112 and 113.

The Dutch embassy landed here in April, 1656, on the south side of the Yangtze. According to Nieuhof, this walled town was heavily damaged by China's civil wars of mid-century.

330. (BOTTOM) A DRAGON BOAT

From Nieuhof, *op. cit.*, p. 132; text, pp. 131–32.

Nieuhof reports that these boats are called "Long chou" (*Lung-chou*) by the Chinese. He also wrote: "I thought it good to make a draught thereof which you have in the annexed cut."

For Nieuhof's sketch see L. Blussé and R. Falkenburg, *Johan Nieuhofs beelden van een chinareis, 1655–1657* (Middelburg, 1987), pl. 109.

Nieuhof's textual description is called "ingenious" by Worcester, *op. cit.* (pl. 328), p. 333.

331. (FACING PAGE, TOP) DUTCH FORT ZEELANDIA ON TAIWAN (1632)

BV (facsimile ed., Amsterdam, 1969) IV, *Journael, Seyger van Rechteren,* facing p. 54.

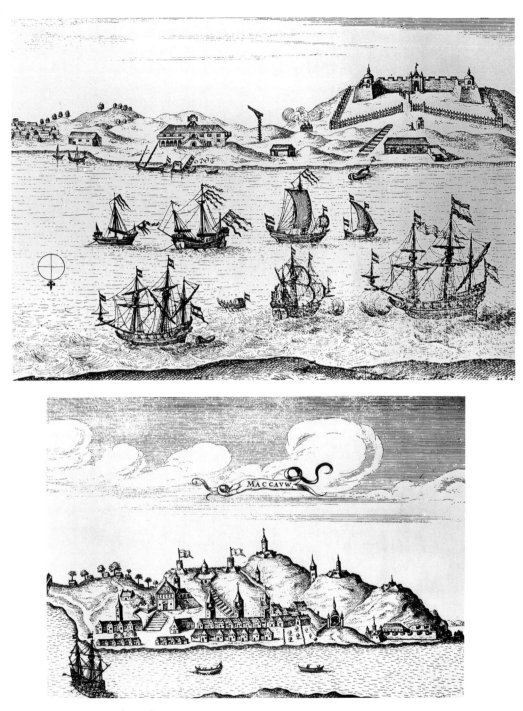

332. MACAO (1632)

BV (facsimile) IV, *Journael, Seyger van Rechteren,* facing
p. 78.

    Sketched by the Italian, Marcus d'Avalo.

333. THE CELESTIAL, TERRESTRIAL, AND INFERNAL GODS OF THE CHINESE

From Kircher, *op. cit.* (pl. 290), facing p. 184.

A close copy of a Chinese woodcut brought back by Johann Grueber to Kircher for his museum. It is possibly a Buddhist book illustration.

The engraving is divided into three parts. In the upper region, (A) is Fo (Buddha), the divinity known as Lord of Heaven "whose hands are covered to show that his power in this world is invisible." At his right sits (B), "who is the deified Confucius." To his left sits (C) Lao-tze, "whom the Chinese call the Old Philosopher, apotheosized and adorned with divine honor as the founder of the Chinese religion (Taoism)." At (D), above, are "the other philosophers . . . who share, as they say, in the Divine illumination." At the right is (E), "the great lotus-born military leader and defender of the Chinese empire (possibly Ch'in Shih Huang-ti, the 'first emperor')." (G) and (H), below Fo, are depictions of lesser divinities (bodhisattvas), and the deities of the third order are the water and fire spirits "who are in charge of the elements of the world" (Van Tuyl [trans.], *op. cit.* [pl. 299], pp. 126–27).

Each of the three main gods wears a nimbus (*yüankuang*), a common religious symbol in Chinese Buddhist art. Most striking, but not unusual, is the admission of Confucius and Lao-tze to the Buddhist pantheon. Buddha, it should be noticed, sits at a somewhat more elevated position than the other two. The infernal spirits at the bottom of the illustration figure prominently in Chinese Buddhism as the damned who were saved by Buddha's grace.

334. TEMPLE OF "SANG-WON-HAB"
From Nieuhof, *op. cit.* (pl. 292), p 72.

In the gorge called "Sang-won-hab" (Mandarin, *Ch'ing-yüan Hsia*) in "Sanyvum" (a bad transcription of *Ch'ing-yüan*), a county north of Canton, is the celebrated Buddhist monastery *Fei-lai ssŭ* dating from the sixth century A.D. It is situated on a rocky outcropping overlooking the Pei River. For these identifications and later descriptions of this region and the monastery see Huart, *op. cit.* (pl. 292), pp. 32–36.

335. CHINESE IDOLS
From Nieuhof, *op. cit.*, p. 316.

The large idol in the center is Chin-kang, a Buddhist god known for his physical strength. The idol on the left is Shou hsing, who, like the crane and deer behind him, is a symbol of long life or immortality in popular Chinese religion. The god on the right called Ninifo appears to be a combination of *Mi-lo Fo* (the future Buddha), and a god of good fortune. Notice joss sticks burning before the idol in the background.

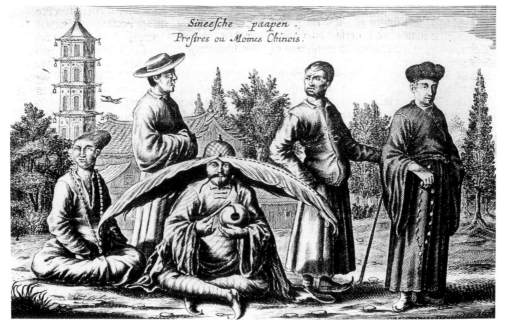

Sineesche paapen.
Prestres ou Moines Chinois.

PAGODE *le dedans du* TEMPLE.
van binnen.

338. (ABOVE) CHINESE TEMPLE AND PAGODA
From Nieuhof, *op. cit.*, between pp. 318 and 319.
   Nieuhof claims (p. 318) to have seen this temple in the outskirts of a Chinese city
during his tour northward. His text describes the temple's interior in some detail. It
presumably housed the gods of the nearby city. Many Buddhist temples and monasteries had pagodas (*pao-t'a*, the precious tower) nearby to commemorate one of the
great Buddhas and to house relics.

336. (FACING PAGE, TOP) CHINESE PRIESTS OF VARIOUS TYPES
From TR, III, following p. 67 at the end of the *Voyage des Hollandois*. For Thévenot's
explication of each figure see p. 67, nos. 8–11.
   The mendicant on the left with the strange hat is holding a *mu yü* (wooden fish), a
gourdlike wooden bell that he sounds when praying. The man next to him is a
clearly recognizable Buddhist priest. The priest on the right exhibits the headgear of
a Mongol lama—although the illustrator seems to have thought it was the shape of
his head! What the other two are we do not know—probably Buddhist monks (*cf.*
pls. 337 and 374).

337. (FACING PAGE, BOTTOM) CHINESE PRIESTS OR MONKS
From Nieuhof, *op. cit.* (pl. 292), p. 309.

339. A CHINESE SEPULCHRE

From Nieuhof, *op. cit.* (pl. 292), p. 285.

The typical Chinese grave site was a mound or artificially constructed hill usually located outside the city wall. The mound and its interior room were large or small according to the importance of the family.

340. CHINESE COSTUMES

From Kircher, *op. cit.* (pl. 290), between pp. 152 and 153.

Top left, Jesuit in Chinese dress; top right, scholar of Nanking Province; center left, woman of Chekiang; center right, woman of Fukien; bottom left, soldier of "Quamsi" (Kwangsi); bottom right, soldier of "Quicheu" (Kweichou).

The woman of Chekiang and the soldier of Kwangsi were copied directly from the figures on the provincial maps in Martini's *Atlas* (1655). The scholar of Nanking and the woman of Fukien were possibly adapted from figures on Martini's provincial maps.

The Nanking scholar appears to be wearing the "straight dress" of the Ming dynasty. His small round skullcap, known as a "six-in-one cap, was a patchwork of six scraps of gauze mostly worn by commoners."

The Chekiang woman appears to be wearing a hairstyle "which involved combing the hair high, lacing it up with gold and silver strings and decorating it with pearls and emeralds. Seen from a distance, it looked like a man's gauze cap" (quotations from Zhou Xun *et al., Five Thousand Years of Chinese Costume* [Hong Kong, 1987], pp. 146–47).

Most of the other features in these costumes are Europeanized to the point that they no longer even look Chinese. The faces of the figures except for the mustaches also look more European than Chinese.

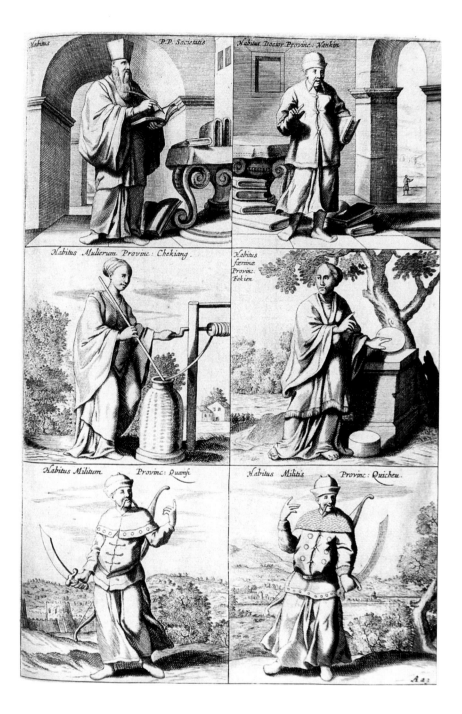

Habitus P.P. Societatis   Habitus Doctor Provinc: Nankin

Habitus Mulierum Provinc: Chekiang.   Habitus fœminæ Provinc: Fokien

Habitus Militum Provinc: Quansi   Habitus Militis Provinc: Quicheu.

A 43

SINEESE VROUWEN.
Femmes Chinoises.

341. CHINESE LADIES
From Nieuhof, *op. cit.* (pl. 292), p. 288.

Judging by their costumes and hair styles, these seem to be Han women. Female dress underwent less change than male costume after the establishment of Manchu rule. Thus the costumes shown here, particularly the wide sleeves and circular collars, are strongly reminiscent of Ming times. *cf.* Zhou Xun *et al., op. cit.* (pl. 340), p. 173.

The true Portraiture of a Mandarine or Governour in China, and of the Lady his Wife. being exactly copied from two statues brought from Macao by Capt: William Bradbent.

342. A "PORCELAIN" COUPLE
From Semedo, *op. cit.* (pl. 287), facing p. 29.

F. Cross, engraver.

Captain William Bradbent (or Broadbent), a ship's commander for the East India Company, brought these figurines back to England.

This is an early example of what would later be called "Chinoiserie" in Europe.

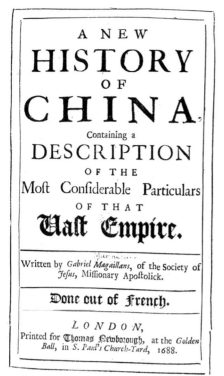

343.

345.

344. MAGALHÃES' CHINESE COMMENTARY ON CONFUCIUS

From Magaillans (Magalhães), *A New History of China* p. 83.

This is the first paragraph of the first article of Magalhães' *Commentary on the Works of Confucius*. It was a device contrived for the use of Jesuits beginning the study of the Chinese language; the translation was to be read according to the numbers.

Magalhães based this upon the commentaries of Chu Hsi and of a scholar named "Cham Kui Chim" (Chang Chücheng, 1525–82), an interpreter of the Classics whose commentaries the Jesuits in China relied upon. See D. E. Mungello, "The Jesuits' Use of Chang Chücheng's Commentary in Their Translation of the Confucian Four Books (1687)," *China Mission Studies (1550–1800) Bulletin*, III (1981), 16.

MARTINI MARTINII
TRIDENTINI
E SOCIETATE JESU
SINICÆ HISTORIÆ
DECAS PRIMA
Res à gentis origine ad Chriſtum natum in extremâ
Aſiâ, five Magno Sinarum Imperio ge-
ſtas complexa.

MONACHII
Typis LUCÆ STRAUBII,
Impenſis JOANNIS WAGNERI CIVIS
& Bibliopolæ Monacenſis,
Cum Privilegio Cæſareo.
Anno CIƆ. IƆ. CLVIII.

MARTINI MARTINII,
TRIDENTINI,
E SOCIETATE IESV,
SINICÆ
HISTORIÆ
DECAS PRIMA,
Res à gentis origine ad Chriſtum natum
in extrema Aſia, five Magno Sinarum
Imperio geſtas complexa.

AMSTELÆDAMI,
Apud JOANNEM BLAEV.
M. DC. LIX.

346. TITLE PAGE OF THE OFFICIAL
JESUIT VERSION OF MARTINI'S
DECAS PRIMA (MUNICH, 1658)

347. TITLE PAGE OF THE BLAEU
VERSION (AMSTERDAM, 1659)

348. HEXAGRAMS OF THE *I CHING*, CLASSIC OF CHANGES
From Martini (pl. 346), p. 6.
    Possibly the earliest (1658) depiction to appear in Europe of the sixty-four
hexagrams.

Tabula fexaginta quatuor Figurarum,
feu Liber mutationum *Ye kim* dictus.

No.	(upper)	(lower)	No.	(upper)	(lower)
1.	Cælum.	Cælum.	2	Terra.	Terra.
3	Aqua.	Tonitrua.	4	Montes.	Aqua.
5	Aqua.	Cælum.	6	Cælum.	Aqua.
7	Terra.	Aqua.	8	Aqua.	Terra.
9.	Venti.	Cælum.	10	Cælum.	Aquæ m.
11	Terra.	Cælum.	12	Cælum.	Terra.
13	Cælum.	Ignis.	14	Ignis.	Cælum.
15	Terra.	Montes.	16	Tonitrua.	Terra.
17.	Aquæ m.	Tonitrua.	18	Montes.	Venti.
19	Terra.	Aquæ m.	20	Venti.	Terra.
21	Ignis.	Tonitrua.	22	Montes.	Ignis.
23	Montes.	Terra.	24	Terra.	Tonitrua.
25.	Cælum.	Tonitrua.	26	Montes.	Cælum.
27	Montes.	Tonitrua.	28	Aquæ m.	Venti.
29	Aqua.	Aqua.	30	Ignis.	Ignis.
31	Aquæ m.	Montes.	32	Tonitrua.	Venti.
33.	Cælum.	Montes.	34	Tonitrua.	Cælum.
35	Ignis.	Terra.	36	Terra.	Ignis.
37	Venti.	Ignis.	38	Ignis.	Aquæ m.
39	Aqua.	Montes.	40	Tonitrua.	Aqua.
41	Montes.	Aquæ m.	42	Venti.	Tonitrua.
43	Aquæ m.	Cælum.	44	Cælum.	Venti.
45	Aquæ m.	Terra.	46	Terra.	Venti.
47	Aquæ m.	Aqua.	48	Aqua.	Venti.
49	Aquæ m.	Ignis.	50	Ignis.	Venti.
51	Tonitrua.	Tonitrua.	52	Montes.	Montes.
53	Venti.	Montes.	54	Tonitrua.	Aquæ m.
55	Tonitrua.	Ignis.	56	Ignis.	Montes.
57	Venti.	Venti.	58	Aquæ m.	Aquæ m.
59	Venti.	Aqua.	60	Aqua.	Aquæ m.
61	Venti.	Aquæ m.	62	Tonitrua.	Montes.
63	Aqua.	Ignis.	64	Ignis.	Aqua.

Has

349. THE SIXTY-FOUR HEXAGRAMS

From Couplet *et al., op. cit.* (pl. 289), p. xliv.

This is a representation of the empirical hexagram order commonly used by diviners.

350. "LETTERS" INVENTED BY
FU-HSI, THE FIRST EMPEROR,
ACCORDING TO CHINESE
TRADITIONAL SCHOLARSHIP

From Martini, *Sinicae historiae decas prima* (Amsterdam, 1659), p. 23 (p. 12 in Munich, 1658, ed.).

This is an effort to show how Chinese characters derived from pictures of natural objects. The fantastic pictographs on the left supposedly evolved into the characters on the right. For details see D. E. Mungello, *Curious Land* (Stuttgart, 1985), pp. 130–31.

Modern scholars trace the pictographic origins of the characters back to the inscriptions on oracle bones and bronzes. The only one of the above that is confirmed is the circle with a dot in the middle (no. 3) that evolved into *jih,* the word for sun.

In our opinion Martini here reproduces a popular etymology of the sort still sold today by street vendors in Taiwan (*cf.* Mungello, p. 149.) Characters "1" and "2" should be shown in reverse, for "2" is the picture and "1" can be regarded as the character (*cf.* pl. 351). Several of the pictures are much too realistic to qualify as traditional Chinese pictographs, according to Ma Tai-loi, curator of the East Asian collection of the University of Chicago Library (personal communication).

351. (FACING PAGE, TOP) EXAMPLES FROM THE CHINESE WRITING SYSTEM
From Nieuhof, *op. cit.* (pl. 292), p. 246.

This compilation apparently derives in large part, as does the text (pp. 244–48), from Jesuit materials brought back to Europe. The pictographs in the center obviously hark back to Martini's pictographs (pl. 350), though the first two are here given in the correct order. On the left the illustrations explaining the formation of Chinese characters ultimately derive from Alvaro Semedo's discussion in his *Relatione* (Rome, 1643), pp. 45–56. The trigrams from the *I Ching* at the bottom of the page likewise derive from Martini (pl. 348). The only thing new in this presentation is the seal (M) which Nieuhof reportedly copied from the title to the "Dragon book" of Fu Hsi, a work which we have not been able to identify, although it may be an oblique reference to the *I Ching,* the oldest Chinese book extant. See Mungello, *op. cit.* (pl. 350), p. 147. Another of Nieuhof's sources was possibly A. Kircher, *Oedipus Aegyptiacus* (3 vols., Rome, 1653), III, 11–21, where the Chinese pictographs and characters are compared to Egyptian hieroglyphs.

352. AN ATTEMPT TO ALPHABETIZE CHINESE
From Couplet *et al.*, *op. cit.* (pl. 289), following the *Viaggio del P. Giovanni Grueber* near the end of the volume.

353. SAMPLE PAGE FROM A CHINESE-FRENCH DICTIONARY

From Kircher, *op. cit.* (pl. 290), p. 328.

Notice that the French still use "cha" rather than "thee" in 1670 (lines 2–6 in left column). "Cha," the Mandarin and Cantonese word, was brought into Europe by the Portuguese from Macao. "Thee" and "tea" are derived from *t'i,* the word in the Amoy dialect of Chinese, brought into Europe by the Dutch, probably as a result of their activities in Fukien and Formosa where the Amoy dialect was current.

354. (BELOW, LEFT) TITLE PAGE OF COUPLET'S *TABULA CHRONOLOGICA*

From the reprint in Couplet *et al., op. cit.* (pl. 289).

This is the most comprehensive of the seventeenth-century Jesuit chronologies, based almost exclusively upon Chinese sources.

355. (BELOW, RIGHT) *CHUNG YUNG,* OR *DOCTRINE OF THE MEAN*

From the reprint in Couplet *et al., op. cit.* (pl. 289).

Title page to the Latin translation of the *Chung Yung,* one of the Four Books which constituted the core of Chinese education in the seventeenth century.

---

328   DICTIONAIRE CHINOIS.

Yèu chă ti	frid dans l'huyle.
Čhă	un vase ou pot de chă.
Piùm chă	porter du chă au marché.
Tièn chă chă / Yù cièn chă / Tum cô chă	trois differences de fin chă.
Chă	manquer, faillir, cesser.
Chă tĕ yvèn	deffaut, manquement, disette. / grande elevation, grande felicité.
Chă	fourche ou fourchette.
Hò chă	pincettes.
C'hăm	croistre, augmenter, aggrandir.
Xèu chăm	la paulme de la main.
Chăm yn	(ment.
Pă chăm	soufflet, ou bien soufflement.
Chăm chir.ă	grand, qui a beaucoup creu.
Chăm pièn	estable à chevaux.
Kiă chăm	don d'embarquement.
Hoéi chăm	la teste, le chef, le premier ou principal.
C'hăm	la moitié des.
Chăm fŭ	le mary, l'espoux, l'homme de la femme.
Sùon chăm	faire compte, supputer.
Chăm çă	tomber ou il tomboit.
Pĭ chăm	camper dresser les tentes du camp.
Tăo chăm	cacher les debtes ou ce qu'on doit.
Mĭmĭ chăm	crochet ou tout autre instrument qui accroche ou qui prend.
Cù chăm	hydropique.
Chăm	long.
Chăm sù	chose ordinaire.
Y' chăm tĭ tú	extraordinaire.
Chŏ chăm	entrer & sortir.
Cùi chăm / Chăm	gouster ce qu'on doit manger, ou qui peut estre mengé.
Chăm pù kièu.	à chasque pas, à tout moment, & à toute rencontre.

Chăm tuòn	long & court.
Gè chăm	bien & mal.
Fi chăm nèm	n'avoir pas le pouvoir ordinaire.
Cìe chăm	augmenter accroistre, amplifier de plus en plus.
Chăm fŭ	putain, femme qui court & qui est abandonnée.
Chăm	chanter.
Xù chăm	celuy-cy est couvert, couvé, fomenté ou bien estouffé.
Pù xù chăm	relasché descouvert, ou joyeux.
Tăn chăm	toucher, chanter.
Cô chăm	chanter des chansons ou des hymnes.
Yèu chán	une journée de 60 ou 80 lieuës.
Chaò	appeller en faisant signe des mains.
Caò pim	lever des soldats, faire des troupes, & des levées.
Chaò paĭ	enseigne de boutiques.
Chĭm chaò	dire ses fautes, advoüer ses pechés, & confesser ses crimes.
Chào	ongles ou griffes d'oyseau ou de passerau.
Chào tèŭ	marque, signe, indice, caractere, enseigne.
Chào xù	lettre, missive, epistre, du Roy ou edits de sa Majesté.
Chĕ chaò	certitude, assurance, infaillibilité.
Iem chaò	une piece qui desrobe la veuë de la chandele, laquelle est faite à dessein pour n'estre pas incommodé de sa clarté.
Hăo chaò	bonne marque, bon pronostiq, bonne conjecture.
Chĭò	visiter le Roy, faire sa cour, la mer.
Chĭò hŏ	congratuler le Roy, feliciter sa Majesté.

T.im

TABULA
CHRONOLOGICA
Monarchiæ Sinicæ
JUXTA CYCLOS ANNORUM LX.
Ab anno ante Christum 2952. ad annum post Christum 1683.
Auctore R. P. Philippo Couplet Belgâ, Soc. Jesu, Sinensis Missionis in Urbem Procuratore.
Nunc primùm in lucem prodit
è BIBLIOTHECA REGIA.

PARISIIS,
M. DC. LXXXVI.
CUM PRIVILEGIO REGIS.

SINARVM
SCIENTIA
POLITICO-MORALIS,
SIVE
SCIENTIÆ SINICÆ LIBER
INTER
CONFVCII LIBROS SECVNDVS,
A P. PROSPERO INTORCETTA SICVLO SOC. IESV
E SINENSI LINGVA IN LATINAM VERSAS

Chŭm 中 Medium

Yvm 庸 Constanter Tenendum

PARISIIS,
M. DC. LXXII.

356, 357, 358. PARTS OF THE BODY, PULSES, AND ACU-POINTS IN CHINESE MEDICINE

From Michael Boym, *Clavis medica ad chinarum doctrinam de pulsibus,* ed. Andreas Cleyer, as published in the appendix to the *Miscellanea curiosa* of the Academia Caesareo-Leopoldina Naturae Curiosorum (Nuremberg, 1686); illustrations follow p. 142 of Boym.

These illustrations to Boym's *Clavis* (see p. 142) are taken in turn from Cleyer's *Specimen medicinae Sinicae* (Frankfurt, 1682). Plate 356 shows the three coctive regions (*shang chiao, chung chiao,* and *hsia chiao*), "cavities," and pulses, giving for each a Chinese name in romanization, a translation, and a description of the location, and for some, the diagnostic use. Lu Guei-djen and Joseph Needham reproduce this illustration in *Celestial Lancets. A History and Rationale of Acupuncture and Moxa* (Cambridge, 1980), p. 278; they know of no Chinese original on which this depiction is based. Boym's *Clavis* was probably a translation of some version of the sixteenth-century *Mo chüeh* (the secrets of the pulse) (Lu and Needham, p. 285).

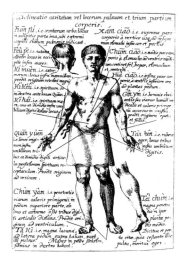

CLAVIS
MEDICA
ad
Chinarum Doctrinam
DE
PULSIBUS,
AUTORE
R. P. MICHAELE BOYMO, è Soc.
JESU, & in China Missionario.
Hujus operis ultra viginti annos jam sepulti fragmenta,
hinc indè dispersa, collegit & in gratiam Medicæ Facultatis
in lucem Europæam produxit
CL. DN. ANDREAS CLEYERUS,
M. D. & Societatis Batavo - Orientalis
PROTO-MEDICUS.
A quo
Nunc demum mittitur
Totius Operis Exemplar, è China recens allatum,
& à mendis purgatum,
Procuratore
R. P. PHILIPPO COPLETIO,
Belgâ, è Soc. JESU, Chinensis missionis
Romam misso.
ANNO cɔ ɔc LXXXVI.

359.

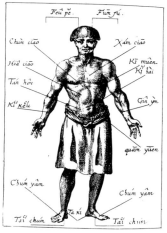

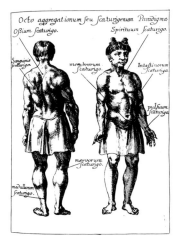

360. (TOP) *DRAAG ZETEL* OR PALANQUIN

From Nieuhof, *op. cit.* (pl. 292), p. 208.

    According to the text, this shows a mandarin moving from place to place on what they call a "Palakyn." In the background there appears to be a place of execution.

361. (BOTTOM) CHINESE FARMERS

From Nieuhof, *op. cit.*, p. 290.

    Notice the queues on the men. The one on the man to the right is badly placed on his head. The feet of the farm woman are bound. The furrows in the field and the donkey suggest north China, but the palm trees would indicate a south China location. This may be just another instance of the use of palm trees to produce an exotic effect.

362. (TOP) THE RUFFIAN AND HIS PRIZE
From Nieuhof, *op. cit.*, p. 265.

The ruffian, an old word for a guardian of prostitutes, scours the Chinese countryside to buy young girls from their impoverished parents. Here the girl with her face veiled is being taken elsewhere to be sold or rented to a brothel keeper, according to Nieuhof's text (p. 265).

363. (BOTTOM) CHINESE ACTORS IN COSTUME
From Nieuhof, *op. cit.*, p. 262.

According to the text, many of the plays enacted are historical dramas that go on for hours while the spectators eat and drink. The entire performance includes more singing than speaking. When one play is ended, another begins.

These are obviously performers in what today we call Chinese opera. Notice the stage at the far left, where a play is in progress.

364. POPULAR PERFORMERS

From Nieuhof, *op. cit.* (pl. 292), p. 263.

According to the text, most of these Chinese players are young people who travel about the country putting on performances. Some show off dancing mice or rats. Others stand one-footed on a bamboo pole held by an associate in his girdle. Still others put a fellow into a bamboo basket through which they push swords. After much moaning and gushing of "blood," the "victim" emerges unscathed from the basket. The man in the middle appears to be forcing sticks up his nose, and the one on the left is playing a tambourine-like instrument.

365. THE MANGO

From Michael Boym's *Briefve Relation de la Chine*, printed in TR, II, between pp. 22 and 23. Pls. 366, 368, 369, and 370 are also from this work.

The word "Mango" is derived from Tamil, *mān-kāy* or Malay, *maygā*. The Chinese word is *mang kuo*.

Boym (1612–59), a Polish Jesuit and a cartographer of China, was particularly interested in the empire's physical and natural aspects.

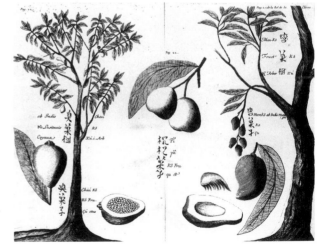

Auis Regia.

Mas. 凰 Fùm

Fem. 凰 Bôam

緑 LôVindium.
毛 mâe alarum
龜 quey testudo.

Gallina Syluestris.

野 Yé
鷄 Xí

Rhabarbarum.

太 Tay
黃 huàm

366. "FUM–HOAM" (*FENGHUANG*) OR "ROYAL BIRD" AND THE "FOREST"
(OR WILD) CHICKEN

From Boym, *op. cit.*, between pp. 26 and 27.

    The *Fenghuang* is the phoenix, a mythical bird. The male bird is often called *Feng*, the female *Huang*. Reputedly a native of Liaotung, it is usually depicted to look like a wild chicken or a pheasant. Its parts are symbols to Chinese poets: the back is virtue, the wings equal justice, the sides are obedience, and the whole body is fidelity. The magistrates have their gowns ornamented in golden figures of this bird.

    The "Ye-ki" (*Yeh chi*) is a large wild chicken with a beautiful plumage. The tortoise (*Lü-mao kuei*), like the female unicorn, the male phoenix, and the dragon, is one of the four supernatural or spiritually endowed creatures, according to the Chinese. The rhubarb plant (*Tai huang*) is the *Rheum undulatum* of Linnaeus, commonly known as the rheum of China. Its roots were widely used as medicine.

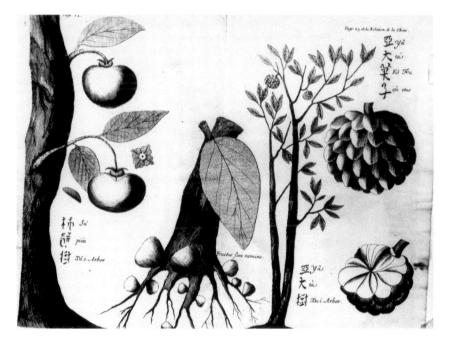

367. (TOP) CORMORANT, OR FISHING BIRD

From Nieuhof, *op. cit.* (pl. 292), p. 148; text, pp. 147–48.

Notice the fishing sampans in the background.

"Louwa" (on the plate) probably derives from *lu-tz'u* (Cantonese, *lo-ts'z*), the Chinese word for the fishing cormorant.

Fishing with domesticated cormorants was practiced in China for a long time before the seventeenth century; for instance, Tu Fu (A.D. 712–70) mentions it in one of his poems. Friar Odoric of Pordenone (1286–1331) also writes of this "strange" mode of fishing in China. Cormorant fishing was also practiced in England and France by the seventeenth century. (*Cf. Asia*, I, 766, n. 173.)

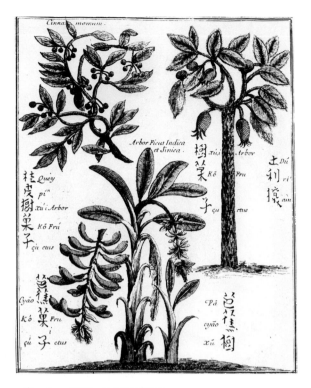

369. CHINESE FRUIT TREES

From Boym, *op. cit.* (pl. 365), between pp. 26 and 27.

The fruit of the *Cinnamomum cassia* on the left is known to the Chinese as *Kui-pi Shu kuo-tzu*. On the right is the durian with its fruit, known as the *Tu li-yüan* (du-ri-an). At the bottom is the small plantain or banana tree called *Pa-chiao shu*.

368. (FACING PAGE, BOTTOM) CHINESE FRUIT TREES

From Boym, *op. cit.* (pl. 365), between pp. 25 and 26.

On the left is the persimmon tree (*shih-ping shu*) and its fruit. The characters in the engraving refer, in today's usage, to dried or sugared persimmons. On the right is the custard apple tree (*Annona squamosa,* Linn.) and its fruit (*Ya-ta kuo-tzu* in Chinese). The fruit in the middle is without a name (*sine nomine*) according to the engraving.

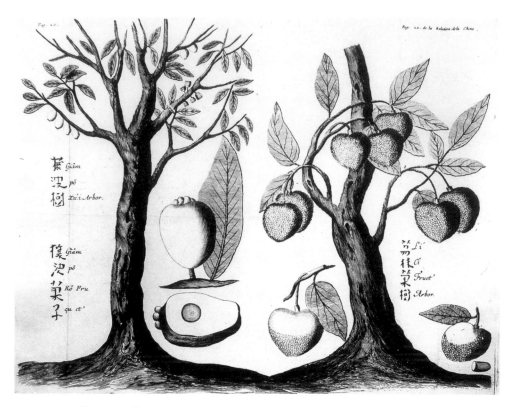

370. "GIAMBO" AND LITCHI TREES AND FRUITS
From Boym, *op. cit.* (pl. 365), between pp. 20 and 21.

The "Giambo" is the rose apple (*Eugenia jambos*), a highly scented fruit. Its name derives from Sanskrit, *jambū*, and it is often referred to by Westerners as the "Giambo d'India" and also the "Giambo di China." See Yule and Burnell, *op. cit.* (pl. 321), pp. 448–49.

There are two types of "litchi" (*Li-chi kuo-tzu*), one whose fruit is red or white which comes from the Indies, and one which is more nearly yellow that looks and smells like a rose. The latter came from Malacca to Macao and Hainan, according to Boym.

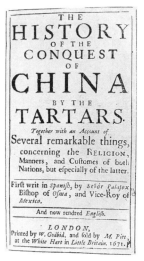

THE
HISTORY
OF THE
CONQUEST
OF
CHINA
BY THE
TARTARS.

Together with an Account of
Several remarkable things,
concerning the RELIGION,
Manners, and Customes of both
Nations, but especially of the latter.

First writ in *Spanish*, by *Señór Palafox*
Bishop of *Osma*, and Vice-Roy of
Mexico.

And now rendred *English*.

LONDON,
Printed by *W. Godbid*, and sold by *M. Pitt*,
at the *White Hart* in *Little Britain*. 1671.

371.

372. GREAT TARTARY FROM THE VOLGA TO THE STRAIT OF "IESSU" (YEZO)
From Sanson d'Abbeville, *op. cit.* (pl. 285), n.p.

Based on the Jesuit relations of 1624, 1626, 1650, 1651. Sanson mentions the 1618 Manchu invasion of China in the text.

373. TITLE PAGE, *RELATION . . . DE MUSCOVIE*, BY FOY DE LA NEUVILLE

Foy de la Neuville was a French diplomatic agent sent to Moscow in 1689 by the Marquis de Bethune, Louis XIV's ambassador to Poland. The French were anxious to learn more about Russia's trade and expansion on its eastern frontiers. While in Moscow Foy de la Neuville was attended by "Spaturus" (Nikolai Spathary), who had undertaken a mission to Peking (1675–77) on Russia's behalf. The last section of this work contains a summary of conversations with Spathary about Russia's overland commerce with eastern Siberia and China, a relation marred by numerous inaccuracies.

This work was first published at Paris in 1698. Its authorship is usually attributed to Adrien Baillet (1649–1706), a native of Neuville, a scholarly priest, a gadfly of the Jesuits, and the longtime librarian of Lamoignon. It was probably reissued at The Hague so quickly because of the profound interest of the Dutch in trading with Russia.

RELATION
CURIEUSE
ET NOUVELLE
DE
MOSCOVIE.
CONTENANT

L'état present de cet Empire. Les Expeditions des Moscovites en Crimée, en
1689. Les causes des dernieres Revolutions. Leurs Mœurs, & leur Religion. Le Recit d'un Voyage de Spata-
rus, par terre, à la Chine.

Foy de la Neuville

A LA HAYE,
Chez MEYNDERT UYTWERF,
Marchand Libraire près de la Cour.

M. DC. XCIX.

gezant vande
LAMMAS

374. EMISSARY OF THE LAMAS

From Nieuhof, *op. cit.* (pl. 292), p. 191.

Nieuhof's text (p. 190) tells us that the envoy (probably the man in the middle) is dressed in a yellow robe and wears a hat like that commonly worn by a Roman cardinal. This was an envoy of the Fifth Dalai Lama of Tibet; he and his attendants were well received in Peking in January, 1656. See Z. Ahmad, *Sino-Tibetan Relations in the Seventeenth Century* (Rome, 1970), p. 187. (*Cf.* to our pls. 336 and 337.)

By a Chinese law of 1655 the most important lamas of Tibet and Mongolia were granted the right to wear yellow robes. See Cammann, *op. cit.* (pl. 311), p. 172.

375. KALMUKS AND THEIR HABITATIONS

From Kircher, *op. cit.* (pl. 290), p. 93; text, p. 92.

Fig. I: a lama wearing a red head covering, a white throw-back cape, a red belt, and a tunic of pale yellow. He stands next to a prayer wheel (fig. IV), probably the first to be depicted in European illustration; fig. II (on extreme right): a male in a leather dress with a pale yellow jacket; fig. III (in middle): a woman in a garment of red and green leather. Her necklace supposedly cures or prevents illnesses.

Kalmuks (sometimes also called Eleuths) are western Mongols from the region of Ili in Chinese Turkestan. According to Kircher, "these people dwell in yurt camps, which could be called mobile cities. . . . Since fathers [D'Orville and Grueber] often came upon their dwellings scattered across the desert, they drew the dress of a few of them" (Van Tuyl [trans.], *op. cit.* [pl. 299], pp. 62–63).

Their tents or yurts in the background are "made on the inside of small, pliable twigs woven together, and on the outside of a rough material which is a certain kind of wool bound with cords" (*ibid.*). Notice how they stand in contrast to the structure of Chinese design in the middle.

376. TANGUTS

From Kircher, *China illustrata* (Amsterdam, 1667), p. 71. See also pl. 290.

Two men in the common dress of the Tanguts, seminomadic natives of the frontier zone between China and Tibet, that is, more particularly, from western Szechwan and the Kansu corridor.

The small boy is a "buth" (possibly Tibetan for boy) or *bu,* a boy "executioner," whom the fathers drew "exactly as they had seen him while they were staying there" (Van Tuyl [trans.], *op. cit.* [pl. 299], p. 64). He is reputedly armed and divinely authorized to kill other humans on certain days of the year. People killed by him, it is believed, will be honored eternally. On the role of murder in Tibetan Lamaism see G. Tucci, *The Religions of Tibet* (Berkeley, 1980), p. 19.

The Habitts of the Ostiacken & Kerrgieſen people.

The Habitts of the Tunguſen and Dauriſchn people.

378. COSTUME OF A TARTAR ARCHER

From frontispiece, Adam Brand, *A Journal of the Embassy from their Majesties . . . Over Land into China . . .* (London, 1698).

Notice the yurts in the background.

379. COSTUME OF TUNGUSIC WARRIOR

From frontispiece, Brand, *op. cit.*

In the background the sledges on the ice are being drawn by what appear to be dogs.

377. (FACING PAGE, BOTTOM) EMISSARIES FROM SOUTH TARTARY TO PEKING

From Nieuhof, *op. cit.* (pl. 292), p. 188.

The figures, dress, and weapons were sketched from life, according to the text. For a detailed description of their dress see pp. 188–89.

380. A TARTAR CAVALIER AND
A TARTAR WOMAN

From TR, III (Paris, 1666), following p. 67 at the end
of the "Voyage des Hollandois"; text, p. 68, nos. 3–4.

A Manchu soldier with his wife behind him, a position to which "these women are accustomed,"
according to the "explication." This Ch'ing warrior
wears the jacket, helmet, and boots of the Manchu
bowmen. *Cf.* Zhou Xun *et al.*, *op. cit.* (pl. 340),
pp. 200–201. Manchu women, unlike the Han women,
did not bind the feet. The cocoapalm is once again out
of place in this depiction.

381. (TOP) TARTAR (MANCHU) WOMEN
From Nieuhof, *op. cit.* (pl. 292), p. 394.
    Manchu women wear black clothes, sometimes of silk. Common women wear cotton. They dress their hair in two long braids. Contrast to the Han women in pl. 341.

382. (BOTTOM) TARTAR (MANCHU) MEN
From Nieuhof, *op. cit.* (pl. 292), p. 393.
    Notice the armor on the soldier on the right. *Cf.* this warrior to the one in pl. 380.
    The man in the center, possibly a civil official, has ornaments hanging from his waistband following Ch'ing custom. See Zhou Xun *et al., op. cit.* (pl. 340), p. 173.

383. FRONT AND BACK VIEW OF A WOMAN IN
THE DRESS OF NORTHERN TARTARY

From Kircher, *op. cit.* (pl. 290), p. 95.

Sketched by Grueber, this is a portrait of a woman
at the court of the king of Tangut, whom they called a
"Deva" (*s-De-pa*), or a regent, in Tibetan. According
to Kircher, "she wore her hair braided like ropes, and
she had seashells on her head and on her belt" (Van
Tuyl [trans.], *op. cit.* [pl. 299], p. 63).

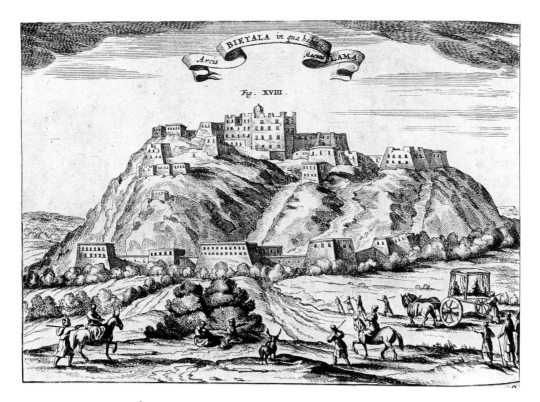

384. THE POTALA

From Kircher, *op. cit.*, p. 100.

The famous lamasery and citadel of "Bietala" (*Po-ta-la*) in "Barantola" (Lhasa) as sketched by Johann Grueber in 1661. "Barantola," according to Grueber, was the Tartar name for Lhasa (Kircher, p. 318). This structure reminded Grueber of the castle architecture of Europe.

Named after the hill on which it stands, this palace-citadel was built by the Fifth Dalai Lama between 1645 and 1694. In Grueber's sketch, only the main buildings, a few smaller structures, and the ramparts are completed. The Dutch engraver, in all probability, added the two-wheeled carriage in the foreground, because wheeled carriages, it is now believed, were not then known in Tibet (Wessels, *op. cit.* [pl. 299], p. 190). In the West this remained the only available depiction of the Potala until a photograph of it was published in 1901: the first photograph was taken by a Kalmuk cameraman and it was published in *La géographie,* IV (1901), 242.

XIX. Le pourtrait du grand *Lama*,
c'est à dire le Pere eternel.

XX. *Han* defunt Roy de *Tanguth*, à qui l'on
rend des honneurs divins.

385. THE DALAI LAMA AND "HAN," THE
DECEASED AND REVERED KING OF TANGUT

From Kircher, *op. cit.* (pl. 290), facing p. 99.

On the left is the portrait of Ngawang Labsang
Gyatso (1617–82), the Fifth Dalai Lama, as executed
by Johann Grueber, S.J., in 1661. Since Grueber could
not see him in person, the Jesuit copied an effigy of the
Dalai Lama set out in the vestibule of his palace. The
prostrate Tibetans are making their obeisances before
the representation as if it were the living Dalai Lama
himself.

The bust labeled "Han, the Dead King of Tangut" is
probably a representation of Gushi Khan, a powerful
Kalmuk ruler who pacified Tangut, presumably the region between Koko Nor and Tibet.[1] In 1640 he helped
the Dalai Lama take control over Lhasa where Gushi
managed secular affairs until his death in 1655. As a
reward for his efforts Gushi Khan was awarded the title
of "Han."[2] After his death the successors of "Han"
continued to wield a degree of secular power and were
similarly awarded titles by the Dalai Lama.[3]

[1] See Wessels, *op. cit.* (pl. 299), pp. 187–88.
[2] See the quotation from the Jesuit cartographer Jean-Baptiste Régis as
given in Ahmad, *op. cit.* (pl. 374), p. 145.
[3] *Ibid.*, p. 146. Kircher concludes from this that all the secular rulers of
Tibet were descended from "the Tartars of Tangut."

P'XVII. Marque l'Idole de *Manipe* dans la Ville de
Barantola, du Royaume de *Laſſa*.

P'XXI. Un autre Idole de
Manipe.

386. THE IDOL "MANIPE" IN LHASA

From Kircher, *op. cit.*, p. 98.

"Manipe rises to a great height and has a nine-fold division of heads in a cone shape" (Van Tuyl [trans.], *op. cit.* [pl. 299], p. 64). "Our fathers, to illustrate the blind folly of those nations worthy of the pity of lamentation, drew the idol in the form they saw it. However, they also sent it to me in another form" (p. 65).

"Manipe" is not the name of the idol shown but is, as Kircher also realized, a garbled version of the mantra *om ma ni pad me hum,* which is an appeal to Avalokitésvara, a Tantric deity in Tibetan Buddhism. The idol on the left is probably the eleven-headed Avalokitésvara with the two backward-facing heads not showing.

Kircher believed that the many-headed idols of Asia were copied from similar idols of Egypt.

Pagodes In.Iorum Numen

387. "PAGODES," DEITY OF THE INDIANS, WITH "MANIPE"

From Kircher, *op. cit.* (pl. 290), p. 177.

"Pagodes," in this case a European word for an idol of India, is applied here to a deity that resembles no figure in the Hindu pantheon. (See P. Mitter, *Much Maligned Monsters* [Oxford, 1977], p. 60.) Apparently it is supposed to be a deity of the "wicked sect" of Buddhism. The six heads perhaps reflect a comment in a Spanish letter by Trigault, which Kircher had seen, to the effect that "there exists in the province of Paguin [Peking] a certain idol which has a man's body but three heads which look at each other" (Van Tuyl [trans.], *op. cit.* [pl. 299], p. 122).

Or do the heads merely represent "Manipe" (see pl. 386) as the Tibetan form of the Buddha, who was originally the god of the Indians, and whose teachings spread to Tibet? This surmise is reinforced by the illustration in Kircher of a Japanese three-headed god who is shown in the company of Amida Buddha (see pl. 410). Certainly Kircher at this point in the *China illustrata* was endeavoring to show that Buddhism had spread from India to Central and East Asia.

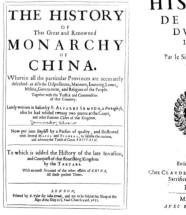

THE HISTORY
OF
That Great and Renowned
MONARCHY
OF
CHINA.

VVherein all the particular Provinces are accurately described : as also the Dispositions, Manners, Learning,Laws, Militia,Government, and Religion of the People.
Together with the Traffick and Commodities of that Countrey.

Lately written in Italian by F. ALVAREZ SEMEDO, a Portughess, after he had refided twenty two yeares at the Court, and other Famous Cities of that Kingdom.

Now put into English by a Perfon of quality, and illuftrated with feveral MAPPS and FIGURES, to fatisfie the curious, and advance the Trade of Great BRITTAIN.

To which is added the Hiftory of the late Invafion, and Conqueft of that flourifhing Kingdom by the TARTARS.
With an exact Account of the other affairs of CHINA, till thefe prefent Times.

LONDON,
Printed by E. Tyler for John Crook, and are to be fold at his Shop at the Sign of the Ship in S. Pauls Church-yard. 1655.

388.

HISTOIRE
DE LA COVR
DV ROY DE
LA CHINE.

Par le Sieur MICHEL BAVDIER
de Languedoc.

A PARIS.
En la boutique de l'Angelier.
Chez CLAVDE CRAMOISY, rue S.Iacques, au Sacrifice d'Abel, & à l'Aigle d'or,
proche S. Benoift.

M. DC XXXI.
AVEC PRIVILEGE DV ROY.

389.

390. MAP OF JAPAN

From Sanson d'Abbeville, *op. cit.* (pl. 285), n.p.

Text derived from the Jesuit letterbooks and the work of Pinto, Cardim, Varenius, and Caron. Sanson gives a long list of cultural contrasts reminiscent of the earlier Jesuit writers on Japan. He divides the Japanese state into seven principal parts or provinces. Text includes materials on Yezo, which is barely shown on the map.

The map itself was based closely on the map (*ca.* 1650) of Father Philippe Briet (1601–68), Sanson's countryman and a teacher of geography at the Jesuit college of Louis-le-Grand in Paris. For a reproduction of Briet's map see Hugh Cortazzi, *Isles of Gold, Antique Maps of Japan* (New York and Tokyo, 1983), pl. 67. Later editions of Sanson's map include a much larger Yezo. The Sanson maps are more realistic in their depiction of Kyushu than were Briet's maps.

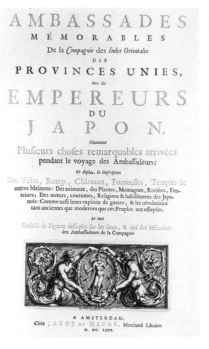

391, 392. TITLE PAGE AND FRONTISPIECE,
MONTANUS' *AMBASSADES MEMORABLES . . .*
VERS LES EMPEREURS DU JAPON
(AMSTERDAM, 1680).
Pls. 393, 397, 400, 401, 413, and 414 are also from this
book. See also pl. 395.

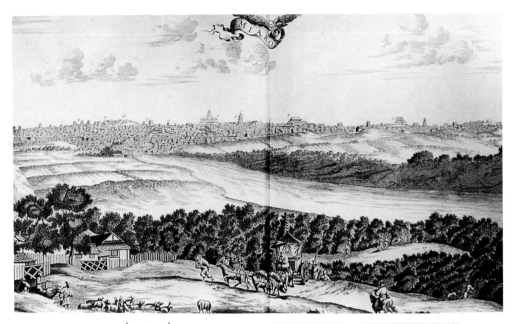

393. MIYAKO (KYOTO)

From Montanus, *op. cit.*, between pp. 72 and 73.

Shows the Kamo River running through the eastern part of the city. The wall and fortifications were built following the orders of Hideyoshi of 1591.

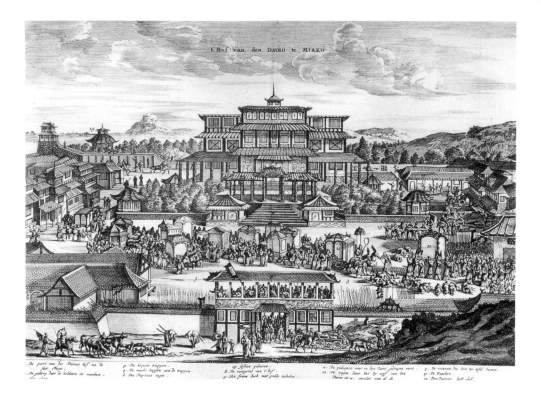

t Hof van den DAYRO te MIAKO

395. IMPERIAL PALACE AT MIYAKO

From Montanus, *Denckwürdige Gesandtschafften* (Amsterdam, 1669), between pp. 130 and 131; textual description, pp. 130–32. Pls. 396, 398, 399, 402, 405–9, 411, 412, 417, 419, 420, 422–27, 429–31, and 433 are also from this book. See also pl. 391.

According to the text, the shogun visits the emperor every six years. The journey from Edo takes twenty-eight days. One year before this event, its coming is announced and the road is cleaned. There are twenty large forts along the road from Edo to Miyako.

396. DAIBUTSU TEMPLE AND ITS IDOL (MIYAKO)
From Montanus, *op. cit.*, between pp. 240 and 241; description, pp. 240–41.

According to the text, the statue is made of wood and covered with plaster and decorated with copper. Very few temples are larger or more beautiful in Japan.

Notice that the Buddha is surrounded by a flame halo and by what appear to be *apsarases* (nymphs). The pillars of the temple are very much Westernized.

Built originally by Hideyoshi in 1588, this temple housed a large image of Roshana Butsu, the Buddhist god of light. After the original temple was destroyed by an earthquake in 1596, it and the image were reconstructed by 1614 through the dedicated work of Hideyori and his mother. This is the temple reputedly shown here. Temple and image were both destroyed by an earthquake in 1662. The Daibutsu, or the large statue of Buddha *Dainichi-Nyorai*, seen in Kyoto today was erected in 1801.

For the history of this temple and its idol see B. H. Chamberlain and W. B. Mason, *A Handbook for Travellers in Japan* (5th rev. ed.; London, 1899), pp. 369–70.

TEMPEL met Duyfend BEELDEN.

**397. BUDDHIST TEMPLE OF A THOUSAND IMAGES
(NEAR KYOTO)**

From Montanus, *op. cit.* (pl. 391), between pp. 102
and 103.

Temple dedicated to "Canon" (Kannon). Engraving
based on text.

This is supposedly the San-jū-san-gen-dō, a temple
founded in the twelfth century. Rebuilt in 1266, it
houses one thousand statues of Kannon, the goddess of
mercy, which surround a larger image of the same god.
It stands in the Shirakawa area of Kyoto.

See Chamberlain and Mason, *op. cit.* (pl. 396),
p. 368; and H. E. Plutschow, *Historical Kyoto* (Tokyo,
1983), p. 73.

398. IDOL AT "DUBO" NEAR MIYAKO (KYOTO)
From Montanus, *op. cit.* (pl. 395), p. 71; text,
pp. 71–72.

According to the text, this idol was in a temple built
by Oda Nobunaga (1534–82). The idol sits on a round
metal placque made in the form of a shell. "Dubo" is
here referred to as a suburb of Miyako.

This possibly relates to the Honnō-ji, a temple rebuilt by Nobunaga with merchant support. Nobunaga
committed suicide here when enemy forces surrounded
his headquarters. The temple was burned down only to
be rebuilt by Hideyoshi in Nobunaga's memory. See
Plutschow, *op. cit.* (pl. 397), pp. 127–28.

399. RICH CARRIAGE OF A TAIKŌSAMA (COURT) LADY-IN-WAITING

From Montanus, *op. cit.* (pl. 395), p. 161.

The lady sits cross-legged on a rug in her covered carriage that is pushed by a young male servant.

To the modern eye this is a depiction whose authenticity is highly questionable, especially the conveyance. We also wonder if a Dutchman would have been permitted to see a court lady, much less be allowed to sketch her.

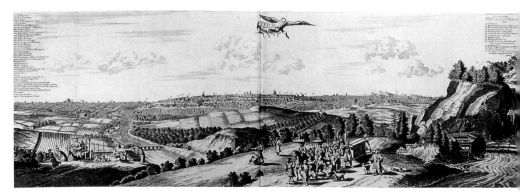

400. EDO (TOKYO)

From Montanus, *op. cit.* (pl. 391), between pp. 98 and 99.

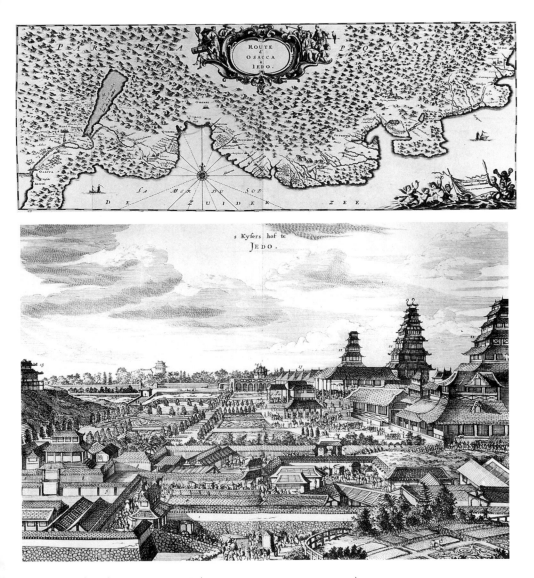

401. (TOP) THE TŌKAIDŌ (ROAD FROM OSAKA TO EDO)

Facing preface in Montanus, *op. cit.* (pl. 391).

Map of the "Great Eastern Sea Road" traversed by the daimyos of the western provinces when going to pay their visits of respect to the shogun in Edo. This was one of the world's busiest highways in the seventeenth century. Its travelers were carried in palanquins, rode horses, or went on foot; wheeled vehicles were not permitted. The road was lined on either side by rows of fir trees to guide the travelers and to provide them shelter from the elements. See C. J. Dunn, *Everyday Life in Traditional Japan* (Tokyo, 1969), pp. 24–26. For an impressionistic view of life along this road see Oliver Statler, *Japanese Inn* (New York, 1961), especially pp. 116–32.

402. (BOTTOM) SHOGUN'S CASTLE AT EDO

From Montanus, *op. cit.* (pl. 395), between pp. 110 and 111.

There is a long written description of the castle on pp. 115–17.

403. PART OF THE IMPERIAL (SHOGUNAL) CASTLE

From [Jean Crasset], *Histoire de l'eglise du Japon* (2 vols.; Paris, 1689), II, facing p. 23. Pls. 415, 416, 418, and 421 are also from this book.

Cf. to Montanus' depiction, pl. 402.

Tome II. pag. 23.

Partie du Palais de l'Empereur.

404. IMPERIAL (SHOGUNAL) AUDIENCE IN JAPAN

From Caron's *Relation* printed in TR, II (Paris, 1666), p. 30.

Western authors usually refer in this period to the shogun as the emperor because he was in fact the temporal ruler. The engraving reproduced here was copied with but a few changes from the original in the Dutch edition (1661) of Caron's work. For a reproduction of the 1661 engraving and for an explanation of what is represented in it see C. R. Boxer (ed.), *A True Description of the Mighty Kingdoms of Japan and Siam by François Caron and Joost Schouten Reprinted from the English Edition of 1663* (London, 1935), between pp. 56 and 57.

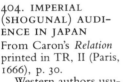

Palais de L'empereur du Japon, et sa maniere de donner audience.

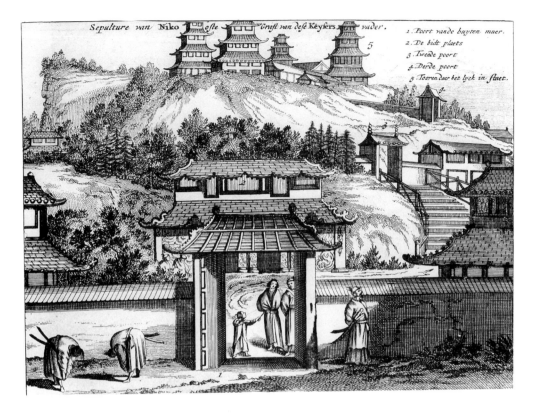

Sepulture van Niko efte Gruft van defe Keyfers vader.

5

1. Poort vande buyten muer.
2. De bidt plaets
3. Tweede poort
4. Derde poort
5. Tooren daer het lyck in ftaet.

405. SEPULCHRE AT NIKKO, GRAVE OF TOKUGAWA IEYASU

From Montanus, *op. cit.* (pl. 395), p. 118; text, p. 117.

Nikko, "four days' journey" north of Edo, was located on a high hill surrounded by a strong wall. The tomb is lighted by 150 lamps that burn constantly. The "emperor" (shogun) goes there to sacrifice for his father. In the chapel where he worships stands the thirty-branch copper candelabra that the Dutch Company presented through François Caron in 1635. The Japanese considered this gift to be a symbol of the tributary status of the VOC.

406. THE TEMPLE OF THE GOLDEN AMIDA
IN EDO

From Montanus, *op. cit.* (pl. 395), p. 107; text,
pp. 107–8.

According to the text, this was one of the most superb temples of Edo. Its idol is Amida riding a seven-
headed horse. Each head of the horse symbolizes a
thousand centuries. Amida is one of the most powerful
of their gods and these people hope to obtain life eternal by frequently repeating the name of Amida. Amida
is represented in many different forms, sometimes as
here with the head of a dog sitting on a horse.

Horses are sometimes associated with Buddhist
deities.

The image of Kannon, the goddess of mercy, sometimes has a horse's head set above it, or in place of the
human head, to indicate that Kannon is the protectress
of horses. See C. Eliot, *Japanese Buddhism* (London,
1964), pp. 140–41.

The inscription on the base of the statue is illegible.

407. SHAKA (BUDDHA) IN AN EDO TEMPLE
From Montanus, *op. cit.,* p. 111; text, p. 110.
    According to the text, this temple was erected by
the widow of Hideyoshi: it is said to be comparable to
the Shaka temple in Miyako.

408. JAPANESE BUDDHIST PRIEST

From Montanus, *op. cit.* (pl. 395), p. 78.

According to the text this priest belongs to the "Saccibonsiens" (Shaka bonzes?) or devotees of "Mia" (Mida or Amida). In his girdle he carries books and tablets, especially on ceremonial occasions. In his right hand he carries a copper bowl-shaped gong around which several Japanese idols are engraved. In his left hand he carries a knotted rope with which to hit the copper gong to call the worshippers to service in the street.

409. A BONZE PREACHING

From Montanus, *op. cit.*, p. 256.

This Buddhist priest, probably of the Nichiren sect, holds in his right hand a fan of gold thread and his head is covered with a parasol of multicolored silk. He rings a bell and then reads a text from the book called "Foquequium" (*Hokke-kyō* or the *Lotus Sutra*). Then he preaches eloquently. More of the audience is devoted to Amida than to Kannon or Shaka.

On Nichiren see G. B. Sansom's essay in Eliot, *op. cit.* (pl. 406), chap. xviii.

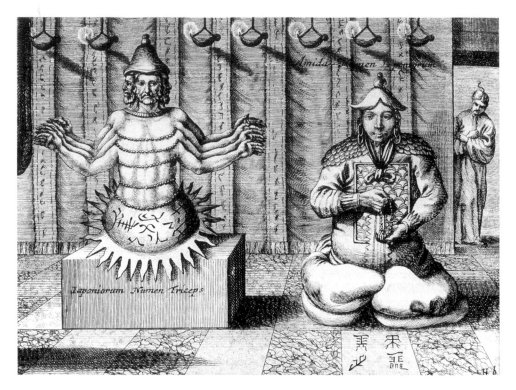

410. JAPANESE GOD WITH THREE HEADS AND BUDDHA AMIDA

From Kircher, *op. cit.* (pl. 290), p. 188.

Luis de Guzman in his *Historia de las missiones* (2 vols.; Alcalà de Henares, 1601) in Bk. V, chap. ix, discussed how the Japanese venerated a many-armed, three-headed god. This picture of such a god with Buddha Amida was sent to Kircher from Portugal and he reproduced it to satisfy the curious. It also supported Kircher's thesis that the many-headed gods of Asia were copied from those of the Egyptians, and he reports that Grueber saw such a deity in Nepal.

The Japanese, according to Kircher, depict the deity known as Amida or "Fombum" sitting on a rose or on a lotus and surrounded by rays. Notice the prayer beads held in the hands of Buddha Amida. The characters are illegible.

411. WANDERING BUDDHIST PRIESTS

From Montanus, *op. cit.* (pl. 395), p. 262; text,
pp. 262–63.

The Dutch met these priests on the road near Osaka.
They always travel in twos, wear torn clothing, and
do not cut their hair or beards—so they look like
wild men.

They carry a rosary and a gourd-shaped water
bottle.

On their heads they wear a six-cornered cap and are
always highly regarded by the laymen because they
pray with the sick and for the dead.

Sometimes these priests carry the dead to the grave.
They are often called "bad monks" because they are
accused of all sorts of crimes.

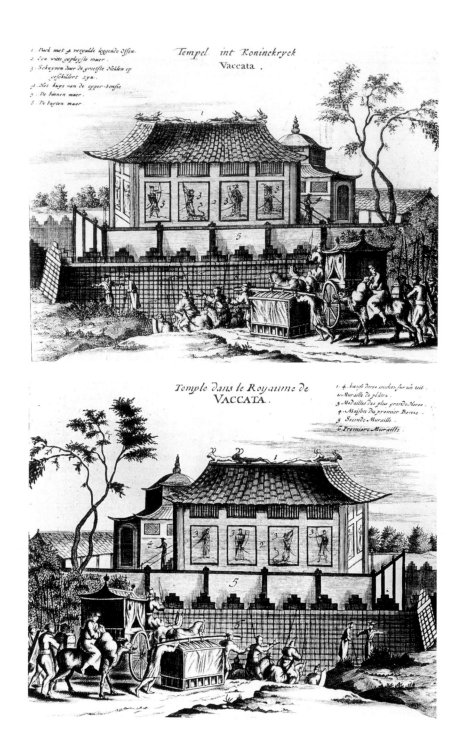

Tempel int Koninckryck
Vaccata.

1 Dack met 4 vergulde leggende Ossen.
2 Een witte gepleystte muer.
3 Schuyren daer de grootste Nobelen op geschildert zyn.
4 Het huys van de opper-bonsie.
5 De binnen muer.
6 De buyten muer.

Temple dans le Royaume de
VACCATA.

1 4. boeufs dorez couchez sur un toit.
2 Muraille de plâtre.
3 Medailles des plus grands Heros.
4 Maison du premier Bonze.
5 Seconde Muraille.
6 Premiere Muraille.

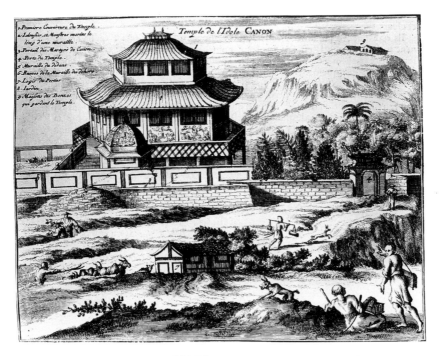

414. TEMPLE OF KANNON IN OSAKA

From Montanus, *op. cit.* (pl. 391), p. 66; text, pp. 65–67.

The temple housed Kannon, the Buddhist goddess of mercy who dominates the waters and the fish. This is possibly an effort to depict the Tennōji, a temple founded by Shōtoku Taishi around A.D. 600.

412, 413. (TOP AND BOTTOM, FACING PAGE) TEMPLE OF "VACCATA" (HAKATA) IN KYUSHU

From Montanus, *Denckwürdige Gesandtschafften* (see pl. 395), p. 101, and *Ambassades memorables . . .* (see pl. 391), p. 96.

Plate 412, with its Dutch caption, seems to be the original, since Montanus' book was first published in Dutch. Plate 413 is reversed and the caption has been translated into French. On the techniques employed in copying engravings from publisher to publisher, see our Note to the Illustrations (following the Table of Contents). Curiously, both these books were published by Meurs.

This is probably a Shinto shrine. According to Montanus, it was dedicated to "Toranga," a hunter from Korea, who defeated eight tyrannical kings and brought peace to Japan. As god of the Japanese armies (Hachiman?), he is represented as having eight arms, each of which defeated one of the tyrants. On the outside of the temple are four murals, portraits of the four heroes of Japan whose deeds the poor chant when begging for alms. On its roof lie four decorated statues of oxen. The shrine is enclosed by inner and outer walls and to its side stands the residence of its chief priest.

Hakata is the port of Fukuoka, the two practically forming one city. Is this supposed to be the celebrated Shinto shrine in Fukuoka known as Hakozaki Hachiman-gu?

415. CHATEAU AND PLEASURE HOUSE NEAR FISEN (HIZEN)
From Crasset, *op. cit.* (pl. 403), I, between pp. 14 and 15.
    Hizen is a peninsular region and province of northwestern Kyushu in the vicinity of Nagasaki.

416. A JAPANESE CROSS
From Crasset, *op. cit.*, II, 53.
    Notice how it differs from ours.

417. COSTUMES OF JAPANESE WOMEN IN EDO
From Montanus, *op. cit.* (pl. 395), p. 401; text,
pp. 401–2.

According to the text, they wash their hair everyday
with egg whites and water to make it lustrous. Girls
are distinguished by the tuft they wear on the top of
the head. Women of the first rank sometimes cover
their heads with shawl-like bonnets. Robes are long
and colorful. Notice the tea service on the table and
the fans.

To the modern eye these women look like commoners. The little dog being teased by the women is
certainly a touch added by the European engraver.

Tome I. pag. 10.

Figure d'vne Dame de qualité. — Autre d'vne Dame en dueil

Procure[...] de [...] de qualité

418. DRESS OF WOMEN OF QUALITY

From Crasset, *op. cit.* (pl. 403), II, facing p. 10.

The woman in the center is in undecorated mourning clothes. The lady on the right is walking under a parasol of oiled paper carried by a servant.

The lady of quality on the left exhibits the traditional coiffure with big hairpins and is dressed in a gay kimono with a white underkimono. In the seventeenth century white linings and undergarments were commonly worn by the noble classes. See H. B. Minnich, *Japanese Costume and the Makers of Its Elegant Tradition* (Tokyo, 1964), p. 341.

419. URBAN COSTUME OF "SURINGA" (SURUGA)
From Montanus, *op. cit.* (pl. 395), p. 185.

Suruga, now in Shizuoka-ken, was one of the fifteen provinces of the Tōkaidō, or the region of the Eastern Ocean. Tokugawa Ieyasu retired in 1605 to the castle of Sumpu in Suruga where a number of Europeans visited him and his successors.

This gentleman wears a three-quarter-length kimono-like coat. Like his contemporaries he had the front half of his head shaved and allowed the hair on the back half to grow into a queue that he turned up into a knot and decorated with a ribbon. In his obi he wears two swords as an indication of his samurai status. *Cf.* Minnich, *op. cit.* (pl. 418), pp. 347–48.

420. DAIMYO AND WIFE

From Montanus, *op. cit.* (pl. 395), p. 57; text, p. 58.

The underneath robe of the daimyo is so wide and
long that he walks on it, according to the text. His
outer garment appears to be the big-sleeved *hitatare*
often worn by noblemen.

Habillemens de deux personnes de qualité   *Figure d'un Bourgeois*

421. JAPANESE CLOTHING

From Crasset, *op. cit.* (pl. 403), I, facing p. 9.

On the left stand a couple of high social status, and on the right a middle-class city dweller, possibly a samurai-merchant. All three wear the *obi* (sash or belt), an accessory of Japanese dress that enjoyed great popular favor with both men and women during the Tokugawa era. The bougeois wears *geta,* or wooden clogs for the out-of-doors.

According to Crasset (pp. 8–9), the principal exercise of the Japanese is that of arms, which they carry beginning at twelve years of age. Women of distinction wear a number of robes over one another. Bourgeois males have gowns which end just below the knees.

This is really a composite of two illustrations taken from Montanus. See the two preceding plates.

424. SEPPUKU—RITUAL SUICIDE IN JAPAN

From Montanus, *op. cit.* (pl. 395), p. 84; text, pp. 83–84.

This is the brother of the king who took the throne in 1629 (1620 in French text), against whom the king had a grudge and so ordered him to commit suicide.

Possibly a reference to Tokugawa Tadanaga (1605–33), the brother of Iemitsu, the shogun. Tadanaga was accused of plotting against Iemitsu; after this, Iemitsu invited him to commit hara-kiri or *seppuku*. See E. Papinot, *Historical and Geographical Dictionary of Japan* (2 vols.; New York, 1968), II, 670.

422. (FACING PAGE, TOP) A NOBLE JAPANESE WOMAN
AND HER ENTOURAGE

From Montanus, *op. cit.* (pl. 395), p. 326.

The Japanese noblewoman appears to be wearing the *uchikake* (Edo name), an overkimono worn over the regular kimono and obi.

423. (FACING PAGE, BOTTOM) JAPANESE MEN OF SUBSTANCE

From Montanus, *op. cit.* (pl. 395), p. 396; detailed description, p. 395.

One of the servants holds a parasol over his master, who is wearing a *haori* (top-coat) and *hakamo* (wide trousers). Another servant carries a little case slung over his shoulder holding the writing instruments and the slippers of the master. Both servants wear short robes. The long-robed figures show the front and back of the samurai's costume.

425. "FAISENA," A JAPANESE PLEASURE YACHT OR FLYBOAT

From Montanus, *op. cit.* (pl. 395), p. 61.

This vessel, according to the text, is ordinarily propelled by forty rowers, twenty on each side. It has a Portuguese-style rudder and a prow in the shape of an elephant's head. It makes the long voyage from Osaka to Nagasaki in twelve days.

"Faisena" is possibly a transcription of *kaisen,* a trading or carrying vessel. *Cf.* the Tokugawa pennants flying from this vessel to those in pl. 426.

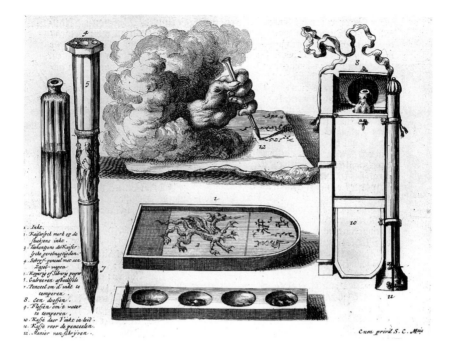

427. JAPANESE WRITING INSTRUMENTS

From Montanus, *op. cit.*, p. 323.

This is not an entirely decipherable depiction, and is a far from ordinary collection of writing materials.

Item *1* is presumably the stone where the ink stick and water are mixed. But it looks more like the cover for the stone, since it is decorated with what is alleged to be the imperial insignia (*2*) and seal (*3*). Below it reposes a board with holes in which to mix the ink.

The brush (*4,5,6,7*) is made of metal rather than bamboo or reed and is decorated in the middle with engraved portraits. Next to it is an item which appears to be its cover.

On the right-hand side of the picture is a case (*8,9,10*) for carrying a bottle of plain water, the ink stick, and the ink-stone. To its right is a case for carrying the brush.

In the background is shown, certainly incorrectly, the manner of writing with a brush. It is here held in the left hand, and certainly not in the usual way of grasping a brush. The characters are illegible.

426. (FACING PAGE) JAPANESE EMBLEMS AND DECORATIONS

From Montanus, *op. cit.*, p. 333; text, p. 334.

1, Seal of Yedo; *2*, seal of Osaka; *3*, seal of Miyako (Kyoto); *4*, seal of "Quano" (Kanto or Kwanto); *5*, a pennant with the "emperor's" arms; *6*, a great flag.

No. *5* is a ship's pennant with the Tokugawa seal on it, three heliotrope leaves (*mitsu-aoi*).

No. *6* is probably a pennant of a trading ship of the type called *Go-shuin-sen*, private merchant vessels authorized by the government to trade overseas. Their heyday was from 1589 to the adoption of Japan's national policy of isolation in 1636. For a similar pennant *cf.* the ship portrait in *Kokushi daijiten* (Tokyo, 1986), VII, between pp. 252 and 253, no. 4.

We have been unable to verify the city seals shown here (*1–4*).

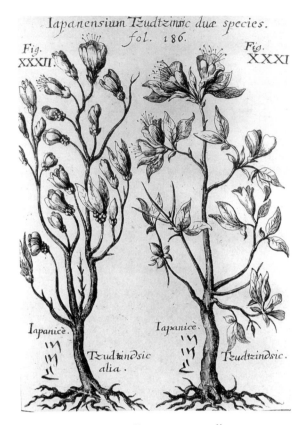

Iapanensium Tzudtzinsic duæ species.
fol. 186.

Fig. XXXII.   Fig. XXXI

Iapanicè.   Iapanicè.

Tzudtzindsic alia.   Tzudtzindsic.

428. TWO TYPES OF "TZUDTZINSIC" (*TSU-TSUJI*) TREE

Drawing sent by Andreas Cleyer in a letter to Christian Mentzel. Published in *Miscellanea curiosa sive Ephemeridum medico-physicarum germanicarum . . .* of the Academia Caesareo-Leopoldina Naturae Curiosorum (Nuremberg, 1686), facing p. 186.

Cleyer's letter in Latin describes these as flowering trees or shrubs which are often planted in porcelain vases for exhibition.

Tsutsuji is the general term for the evergreen and deciduous azaleas of the ericaceous genus *Rhododendron*. In the Tokugawa era, azaleas were particularly popular as ornamental flowers. The flowering shrubs above appear to be two types of wild rhododendron native to the hilly and mountainous areas of Japan, especially Kyushu.

429. JAPANESE PROSTITUTES OF A PLEASURE QUARTER

From Montanus, *op. cit.* (pl. 395), p. 310.

Notice the storage jars and the exposure of the breasts in a low-cut kimono.

The Tokugawa government controlled prostitutes by setting up special brothel districts in or near the great cities or at the post stations on the main roads. Most of the girls were the daughters of farmers who were sold by their fathers when in dire need of money. In 1617 the "pleasure girls" were confined to specific areas by law. Over time these pleasure quarters developed into centers of theatre (*Kabuki*), art, and literature, as well as prostitution. These quarters were most frequented by the Japanese merchants. See Dunn, *op. cit.* (pl. 401), pp. 75–76, 181–86; and Plutschow, *op. cit.* (pl. 397), pp. 164–67.

"Pleasure girls" from the Maruyama quarter of Nagasaki visited the Dutch merchants on Deshima. See Plutschow, pp. 85–94.

430. WANDERING PLAYERS

From Montanus, *op. cit.* (pl. 395), p. 290.

These are portraits of women and men who entertain at celebrations. The seated woman is holding *shaku-byoshi* (wooden clappers). Her strange hat is possibly a kind of *kanmuri,* a black hat usually worn by nobles to house the queue. The man on the right is carrying a drum that is hit by the stick held in his right hand. The other man's instrument makes a singing sound when he pulls the string taut between the two sticks.

The company was usually owned by one person (possibly the veiled figure seated to the right?). Wandering entertainers were considered to be little better than beggars.

431. JAPANESE FISHERMAN AND WIFE

From Montanus, *op. cit.*, p. 271.

    He carries water in tanks suspended from his shoulders to bring his fish living to market. Others carry their tanks on poles carried by two persons.

432. PRIVILEGES GRANTED THE ENGLISH IN 1613 BY "OGASHOSAMA, EMPEROUR OF JAPAN"

From *PP*, III, p. 466; translation given on pp. 467–68.

This writing is printed sideways; the edge to the reader's left should be on top. The document is not what Purchas alleges it to be: Tokugawa Ieyesu's grant of trading privileges to the English in 1613, brought back to England by Captain John Saris. In fact, it is the Japanese version of an abridgment of Saris' petition for such privileges. Purchas' "translation" is a summary of the original petition. Saris indeed returned to England with a document containing the privileges with Ieyasu's seal affixed; it is in the Bodleian Library, Oxford (MS JAP b.2 [R]). The Purchas "charter" is the first example of Japanese writing printed in England. See Derek Massarella, *A World Elsewhere; Europe's Encounter with Japan in the Sixteenth and Seventeenth Centuries* (New Haven, Conn., 1990), p. 392, n. 84.

"Ogashosama" is possibly a reference to Ieyasu as shogun; *sama* is an honorific. See Ernest M. Satow (ed.), *The Voyage of Captain John Saris to Japan, 1613*, "H.S.," 2d ser., V (London, 1900), p. lxxviii. Professor Tetsuo Najita, of the University of Chicago, suggests that "Ogashosama" might mean "emperor," since the imperial household in Kyoto is called *gosho*. Prefixed by O and followed by *sama*, this could mean the chief honorable person of the *gosho*.

For further detail on this and related documents see Murakawa Kengo *et al.*, *Saris Nihon tokōki Wilman Nihon taizaiki* [*The Voyage of Captain John Saris to Japan, 1613, and Wilman's Stay in Japan*] (Tokyo, 1970), pp. 402–11.

The Japonian Charter, the lines to be read down-
wards, beginning at the right hand.

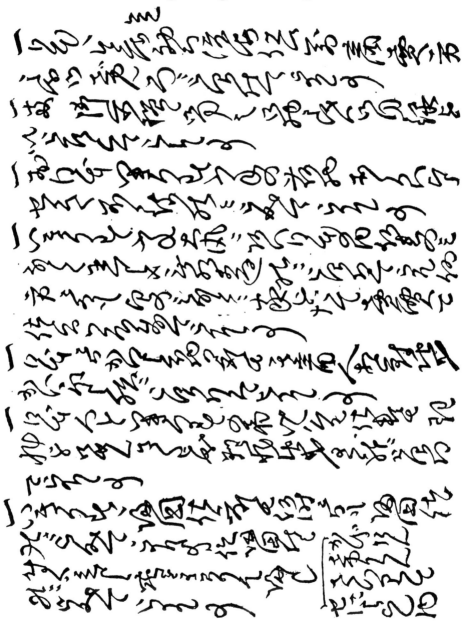

This last is the Seale.

433. JAPANESE BEGGARS OF THE ROAD

From Montanus, *op. cit.* (pl. 395), p. 75; text, p. 74.

According to the text, many women beggars are on
the roads everywhere in Japan. They bring their children with them. The mother carries a water flask
suspended from her girdle as well as a beggar's bag.
The children carry a little wooden box for alms. Sometimes whole families, as in the back of the picture, take
to the roads. They sing songs about ancient Japanese
heroes as they go from house to house asking alms.

These may have been *eta* (outcast) or *hinin* (non-
human) women.

6

RELIGION AND PHILOSOPHY

Information about Chinese religion and philosophy became much more abundant and detailed during the latter half of the seventeenth century. Not only did the missionaries, who reported most of it, learn more through the study of Chinese history, but the Rites Controversy provoked still more study of and writing about Chinese religion and philosophy—especially Confucianism—on the part of all parties to the quarrel. Europeans who read the works of both the Jesuits and their opponents may have become confused about some aspects of Confucian thought, but they surely became familiar with it. By the end of the century the names of several Chinese philosophers could have become household words to European readers. Furthermore, some of the texts attributed to Confucius were available in European languages along with many long quotations from the classics and from other Chinese books.

The Jesuits of the second half of the seventeenth century contend, as Trigault and Semedo had earlier, that the ancient Chinese had worshipped the one true God, the creator of the universe, whom they had called Shang-ti (Ruler on High) or T'ien-chu (Lord of Heaven).[380] The Jesuits found what they thought to be ample evidence of this ancient monotheism in the history of the sage emperors and of the good emperors of the three ancient dynasties. Fu Hsi, for example, was supposed to have sacrificed to the "supreme spirit of heaven and earth," Huang Ti built a temple to the Lord of Heaven, and during a long drought T'ang of the Shang dynasty left his palace, barefooted and dressed in skins, imploring heaven to punish him for his sins, rather than the innocent people. Many more examples are preferred to demonstrate that the pristine knowledge of God was preserved longer in ancient China than anywhere else.[381] Not only did the pious ancient emperors personally worship God and thus set admirable examples for their subjects, but realizing that God rewarded virtue and punished vice, they also maintained exceedingly high standards of morality. The *Shu Ching,* from which many of the pious stories were taken, is described as a "tissue of moral maxims," praising virtue, blaming vice, and giving counsel to rulers that would have been appropriate for any Christian prince.[382] True, the Jesuits report

[380] The Chinese, in fact, used *t'ien* (Heaven) as another name for the deity. Because of the vague character of this term, the Jesuits (*i.e.,* Ricci) invented the term *t'ien-chu,* the "master of heaven," as a more precise term for the Christian "God." Protestant missionaries later were to accept *shang-ti* as a satisfactory term.

[381] For examples, see Martini, *op. cit.* (n. 97), pp. 1–89; Le Gobien, *op. cit.* (n. 72), preface; Le Comte, *op. cit.* (n. 125), pp. 317–22; Kircher, *op. cit.* (n. 110), p. 176; *Confucius sinarum philosophus* (n. 91), pp. xv–xvi, lxxvii–lxxxii; De La Brune, *op. cit.* (n. 93), preface, pp. 5–6; Dapper, *op. cit.* (n. 55), II, 81–87.

[382] For example, see De La Brune, *op. cit.* (n. 93), pp. 6–7.

that the ancient Chinese also offered sacrifices to various tutelary spirits, but these, they contend, were infinitely less important than the sacrifices and prayers to Shang-ti.

Idolatry first threatened ancient Chinese monotheism with the coming of Lao Tzu and his followers, according to the Jesuits. The malignant effects of Taoism, however, were largely offset by the teachings and influence of Confucius. He opposed idolatry, enjoined rulers to follow the will of Heaven, and to choose men of virtue and talent as advisers and ministers. He encouraged personal morality as the first step towards a moral and harmonious society, both by his actions and his writings. Laudatory discussions of the Five Virtues and the Five Relationships found space in almost all post-1650 writings about China in almost all European languages. As the Jesuits present it, the heart of Confucian ethics was that each man should, through study, contemplation, and right practice, clarify the light of nature within him, follow it, and help others—all of society—to do the same.[383] The Jesuits also report that Confucius claimed to have introduced no new doctrine, but to have revived and reorganized the teachings of the sage emperors and the pious founders of the three ancient dynasties.[384] Not only did Confucius adore the true God—Le Comte asserts that he never ate without first offering his food to the "Supreme Lord of Heaven"[385]—but the Jesuits were convinced that he had also prophesied the coming of Christ and the advent of Christianity in China.[386]

A much more serious threat to China's pristine monotheism came from Buddhism during the first century A.D. As described by the Jesuits, it spread rapidly, resulting in the ubiquitous idols, temples, monks, magicians, and charlatans so characteristic of Chinese popular religion ever since. During the Sung dynasty, however, Confucianism was revived. Emperors again supported it, and philosophers such as the Cheng brothers and Chu Hsi refuted Buddhism and wrote learned commentaries on the Confucian classics. The Sung philosophers, however, did not restore Confucianism to its ancient purity. The long centuries of Buddhist popularity had taken their toll. Sung Neo-Confucianism consequently retained some Buddhist and Taoist elements. Furthermore, in their anti-Buddhist zeal, many Neo-Confucians had slipped from the error of idolatry into one still worse—atheism. Nevertheless, the Ming dynasty's Yung-lo emperor pronounced the Four Books and Chu Hsi's commentaries on them officially correct for the civil service examinations.[387] Most educated Chinese, the missionaries report, subscribed to this official Neo-Confucianism.

[383] For example, see Dapper, *op. cit.* (n. 55), II, 95–97.
[384] For example, see *Confucius sinarum philosophus* (n. 91), p. xiv.
[385] *Op. cit.* (n. 125), p. 194.
[386] For example, see Martini, *op. cit.* (n. 97), pp. 131–32; Dapper, *op. cit.* (n. 55), II, 97–98; *Confucius sinarum philosophus* (n. 91), p. cxx; De La Brune, *op. cit.* (n. 93), p. 16; Le Comte, *op. cit.* (n. 125), p. 200.
[387] *Confucius sinarum philosophus* (n. 91), p. xxxvi.

Taken all together, the missionaries' account of Neo-Confucianism is quite accurate. The universe and all things in it, they report, are composed of *li* (principle) and *ch'i* (material force), originating in *t'ai-chi* ("the Supreme Ultimate") which they also seem to identify with *li*. *Li* they define as the "pure and most perfect principle," the "source and essence of all things," the "first principle," the "great vacuum," "singular unity," or "the nature of things." *Li* is infinite, eternal, pure, without shape, changeless; it contains all perfections, but cannot exist apart from the *ch'i*. *Ch'i* they describe as "more material" and changeable. *Ch'i* produces the universe and all things, moral and physical, through the action of the two primeval forces, *yin* and *yang*—some writers call them the two *ch'i*—and the five elements: earth, metal, wood, fire, and water. These, of course, had been known in ancient times. *Yang* is perfect, complete, male, sun, hot, hard, motion, *etc.*; *yin* is imperfect, incomplete, female, moon, cold, soft, rest, *etc.* The five elements also correspond to the five directions, the five parts of the earth, the five planets, and the five tastes. How *yin* and *yang* through the five elements produce heaven, earth, and man is supposed to be explained by the sets of broken and unbroken lines (trigrams and hexagrams) in the *I Ching*, supposedly written by Fu Hsi.[388] Chu Hsi apparently used this ancient tradition to explain how the *ch'i* produced the myriad things.[389] The missionaries seem to realize that the Neo-Confucians' primary concern is still ethical rather than metaphysical, their good is still the public good. Piety meant bringing one's thoughts and actions into conformity with "right reason" or human "nature"—one's *li,* in short. This was achieved through study, meditation, and the restraint of passions. Rulers and officials who followed this course would be able to govern well and make the people happy.[390]

The missionaries also realize that if all things are composed of *li* and *ch'i,* there can be no God or spirits who existed before and who will endure after the *li*. Nor can there be immortal souls, life after death, or even an eternal moral code. Only *li* is immortal, and at death the immaterial part of a person simply rejoins the *li*. In practical terms, therefore, the Neo-Confucians cannot really worship their ancestors, Confucius, or the other spirits to which they offer sacrifices. On the other hand, it seems to make them atheists. Most of the Jesuits admit this. Their mission tactic, therefore, is to distinguish clearly between the ancient, God-worshipping Confucians and the modern Neo-Confucians, usually by emphasizing the foreign, Buddhist

---

[388] See Martini, *op. cit.* (n. 97), pp. 5–9; *Confucius sinarum philosophus* (n. 91), pp. xxxix–liv; Dapper, *op. cit.* (n. 55), II, 82–85. On *t'ai-chi* see Mungello, *op. cit.* (n. 6), pp. 266–67.

[389] On Neo-Confucianism see *Confucius sinarum philosophus* (n. 91), pp. liv–lxiii; Navarrete, *CV,* I, 165–201; Le Comte, *op. cit.* (n. 125), pp. 340–46; Le Gobien, *op. cit.* (n. 72), preface. *Cf.* Fung, *op. cit.* (n. 313), pp. 296–301. For an analysis of the Jesuits' account of Neo-Confucianism in the *Confucius sinarum philosophus* see Mungello, *op. cit.* (n. 6), pp. 260–71.

[390] See, for example, Le Gobien, *op. cit.* (n. 72), preface.

elements in Neo-Confucian thought. Confucius and the sage emperors, they contend, were closer to the truth and, of course, closer to Christianity.[391]

The Dominican and Franciscan opponents of the Jesuits contend that the distinction between the "true" Confucians of ancient times and the Neo-Confucians is artificial. Navarrete, for example, does not believe that the ancient Chinese worshipped the true God. On the one hand, he finds ample evidence for idolatry in ancient times;[392] on the other, he is convinced that when the ancient Chinese called the emperor Son of Heaven or talked about the Mandate of Heaven they meant the material heavens. They believed, he writes, that "heaven punishes the wicked and rewards the good; gives crowns and takes them away, not through any intellectual virtue it has, but naturally and of necessity."[393] Nor was atheism merely the fruit of Sung Neo-Confucianism. While he admires Confucius' moral philosophy and translates many of the finest aphorisms of the *Lun Yü,* Navarrete also finds texts in which Confucius seemed to take the spirits seriously as well as some which suggested disbelief in their existence.[394] Confucius' and Mencius' talk of "the rule of reason" and "heaven," he thinks, meant rational instinct or conscience.[395] Surely they understood rewards and punishments to be imposed in this life only.[396] Navarrete quotes the early Jesuit missionary Niccolò Longobardo to show that Confucius had encouraged a public religion for the masses, while he and his disciples were in fact atheists. He scorns the idea that Confucius was a prophet.[397] Navarrete has no doubts at all about the atheism of the Neo-Confucians. He quotes, with comments, Longobardo's perceptive unpublished treatise on Neo-Confucianism to prove it and also to show that it could not be blamed solely on the Sung philosophers.[398] Much of their work, he argues, was consistent with the teachings of Confucius and the classics. Confucius himself had written commentaries on the *I Ching.* Furthermore, he points out, Chinese scholars all accept the Sung Neo-Confucians as the only valid interpreters of the classics.[399] After interviewing several of them, Navarrete concludes that most Christian Chinese scholars also accept most of Neo-Confucian thought.[400]

---

[391] For example, see *Confucius sinarum philosophus* (n. 91), pp. lxiii–lxix.

[392] *CV,* I, 82–84.

[393] *Ibid.,* p. 20.

[394] *Ibid.,* pp. 111–28.

[395] *Ibid.,* pp. 140–41.

[396] *Ibid.,* p. 138.

[397] *Ibid.,* pp. 174–76, 178–88, 113.

[398] *Ibid.,* pp. 165–201. Longobardo's Latin treatise was written during the 1620's and remained in manuscript until it was translated into Spanish and published by Navarrete in his *Tratados* (1676). It was later published in French: *Traité sur quelques points de la religion des Chinois* (Paris, 1701).

[399] *CV,* I, 171.

[400] *Ibid.,* pp. 198–202.

Despite its polemical intent, Longobardo's treatise, as quoted and amplified by Navarrete, is one of the clearer European discussions of Neo-Confucianism to emerge during the seventeenth century.

Alhough it was far less vital to them than Confucianism, the post-1650 missionaries considerably expanded Europe's knowledge of Buddhism. The Rites Controversy seems to have had little effect on these descriptions; Jesuits and anti-Jesuits were about equally critical of Buddhist idolatry and priestcraft. The coming of Buddhism to China is regularly rehearsed, as is Gautama's birth and life. Most missionaries tell how the Buddha's mother, supposedly impregnated by dreaming of a white elephant, gave birth to him from her left side, and then died in labor. Immediately after birth, Gautama was supposed to have taken seven steps, pointed up and down, and announced that in heaven and earth, only he was holy: blasphemy, judge the missionaries! Some believe he was devil-possessed. The missionaries also report that the historic Buddha married three wives when he was seventeen years old, fathered one son, became a hermit at age nineteen, was enlightened at thirty, and preached until his death at seventy-nine. On his deathbed he was supposed to have revealed to his ten closest disciples a new teaching which the missionaries called the "interior way," thus repudiating his earlier teaching.[401] Couplet calls the new doctrine atheism. Gautama's disciples cremated his body and distributed his remains. The king of Ceylon, the missionaries report, received a tooth. Some list the many miracles attributed to the Buddha as well as his many reincarnations.[402]

Semedo's earlier description of the "interior way" is frequently repeated by the missionary-writers of the second half of the century, but with more detail and a clearer conception of its underlying philosophy. The Buddhists who follow the "interior way" regard the world as an illusion, a constant purposeless flux of which metempsychosis is one important aspect. Salvation for the Buddhists is to escape the ceaseless change and reincarnations by becoming one with ultimate reality, variously called the first principle, nothingness, emptiness, the vacuum, or chaos, which is the same as becoming one with the Buddha, called "Fo" or "Foe." Metaphors such as that of

---

[401] *Cf.* above, pp. 1655–56, on the "exterior" and the "interior" ways. Mahayana Buddhism in China celebrates particularly the Buddha type (bodhisattva) known as Amitabha (O-mi-t'o Fo in Chinese). This deity, most popular with the Pure Land School, is not mentioned by Hinayana Buddhists or the writers of Vedic literature. See K. L. Reichelt, *Truth and Tradition in Chinese Buddhism* (Shanghai, 1928), pp. 38–39. Most of what follows relates to Mahayana Buddhism in which artifacts from the earlier Hinayana variety still reposed. The "interior doctrine," at this point, may refer to the Ch'an school, or meditative Buddhists, who seek to develop techniques of concentration and intuition to discover one's own internal Buddha nature. As one of the few Buddhist schools to survive the persecution of A.D. 845, it subsequently greatly influenced Neo-Confucianism and continued into recent times, as did the Pure Land School, as a dominant force in Chinese Buddhism. See Chan, *op. cit.* (n. 335), pp. 94–95.

[402] *Confucius sinarum philosophus* (n. 91), pp. xxviii–xxxiv; Navarrete, *CV*, I, 78–79; Dapper, *op. cit.* (n. 55), II, 112–13; Le Comte, *op. cit.* (n. 125), pp. 326–28.

water taking the shape of various containers but still remaining water, or the moon reflected in streams, ponds, and looking glasses while still remaining the moon are used to illustrate the relationship between ultimate reality and the things of this world. One achieves identification with ultimate reality—nirvana, although no seventeenth-century European writers on China use the term—by extinguishing human desire and contemplating ultimate reality or the first principle.[403]

Some writers describe the various stages of existence and of enlightenment. Navarrete, for example, provides a fairly understandable description of the "six objects or ways," presumably the six stages of existence: that of kings and princes, which he calls "Tien" (*t'ien*, or heaven); that of men, which he calls "Jin Tao" (*jen-tao*), characterized by "the uneasiness of compliments and the customs of the world"; that of "angry devils" who are passionate and quarrelsome—"Sieu Lo" (*asuras*); that of "Cho Seng" (*chou-sheng, tirisan*) or brute beasts; that of hungry devils—"Ngo Kuei" (*o-kuei*); and that of those who dwell in hells, called "San To" (*san-tao*) because of the three passions of anger, covetousness, and ignorance which characterize them. Navarrete seems to understand that Buddhists desire to escape all of these stages. To accomplish that requires four steps. In the first stage the beginner learns "that all things are nothing." Learners in the second stage are called "Lo Haon" (*lo-han, arhats*), whose "business is reflection and meditation." Those of the third stage called "Pu Sa" (*p'u-sa,* bodhisattvas) are "perfect" and "can advance no further," but compassionately devote themselves to instructing others. They are almost equal to "Xe Kia" (Shih-chia, Gautama). Finally those of the fourth stage, called "Foe" (*fo,* Buddhas), are "in all respects like the first principle, absolutely perfect, which state is being in paradise, united with the *vacuum,* or nothing, or with the refined, thin, and imperceptible air, and become one and the same thing with it."[404] Navarrete mentions "Ta Mo" (Bodhidharma), the Ch'an patriarch who reputedly meditated with his face to the wall for nine years.[405] He also sees similarities between the Buddhist first principle, the Taoist *tao,* and the Neo-Confucian *li* and *ch'i.*[406] Le Gobien notes that Confucians re-

[403] See especially Navarrete, *CV,* I, 78–80; Le Gobien, *op. cit.* (n. 72), preface; Le Comte, *op. cit.* (n. 125), pp. 326–28; *Confucius sinarum philosophus* (n. 91), pp. xxvii–xxxiv; Dapper, *op. cit.* (n. 55), II, 114–20. Dapper's long and somewhat confusing discussion of Buddhism comes largely from Giovanni Filippo de Marini, *Delle missioni de' padri della Compagnia de Giesu nella povincia del Giappone e particolarmente de quella de Tunkina* (Venice, 1663). On the first mention of nirvana in European literature see the chapter on Siam, above, p. 1241.

[404] Navarrete, *CV,* I, 81. Mahayana teaches that the bodhisattva and Buddha steps are the top two rungs on the ladder of salvation. For the six stages of existence see K. L. Reichelt, *Religion in Chinese Garment,* trans. J. Tetlie (London, 1951).

[405] Navarrete, *CV,* I, 79. *Ta-mo* is an abbreviation for P'u-t'i-ta-mo, the famous Bodhidharma who came to China from India in A.D. 527. He was the founder of Ch'an Tsung or the Meditation School. See Reichelt, *op. cit.* (n. 401), pp. 46–48.

[406] Navarrete, *CV,* I, 80. On the relationship of Buddhism to general Chinese religious ideas

gard Buddhism of the "interior way" immoral and antisocial, because it disregards the Five Relationships.[407]

Still more was written during the second half of the century about the "exterior way," which everyone agrees was the most popular form of Buddhism in China.[408] The later missionaries do not distinguish between the various sects, but unlike Trigault and Semedo, they explain the role of the bodhisattva in Mahayana Buddhism and thus make the ubiquitous "idols" more understandable to their readers. A careful reader of late seventeenth-century reports could have learned that most of the statues were of bodhisattvas who, having achieved nirvana for themselves, compassionately remained in the world to aid others.[409] The pantheon of Buddhas and bodhisattvas—always called idols—and their temples nevertheless dominate the descriptions. The two idols most frequently described, however, are O-mi-t'o-fo (Amitabha), who rules the Western Paradise, and Kuan-yin, usually called simply "Pussa" (*p'u-sa*), the popular Chinese term for bodhisattva. Dapper, for example, describes Kuan-yin's miraculous birth and her role as the merciful goddess of nature. He also prints four beautiful folio-sized pictures of Kuan-yin surrounded by other deities as well as by Confucius, Mencius, and Lao Tzu, each of which is explained in detail. The pictures are obviously of Chinese origin.[410] Curiously, Dapper identifies "Pussa" with the beliefs of the learned. Later he briefly refers to Kuan Yin but does not identify her with "Pussa." Kircher includes two plates depicting Kuan-yin, one of which shows her with eighteen arms.[411] Both Kircher and Dapper identify Kuan-yin with the Greek Cybele and the Egyptian Isis. Navarrete reports that a prominent Chinese Christian believed her to be a corrupt form of the Virgin Mary.[412] Regarding O-mi-t'o-fo, Navarrete reports that the Chinese call on him incessantly, believing that they will be saved from their sins and reborn in paradise thereby. He decides that the Chinese were more devoted to O-mi-t'o-fo than were most Christians to God, Christ, or

---

see W. Pachow, *Chinese Buddhism: Aspects of Interaction and Reinterpretation* (Lanham, Md., 1980), chap. vi.

[407] *Op. cit.* (n. 72), preface.

[408] This refers almost certainly to the Pure Land School, which stresses faith and is probably the oldest of the existing Buddhist sects. Its influence on Chinese literature, drama, and art has given it great mass appeal and popularity. In practice it is long on personal faith and short on dogma and elaborate rituals. Emphasis is on the worship and invocation of the name of Buddha. See Reichelt, *op. cit.* (n. 401), chap. v.

[409] For example, see Navarrete, *CV,* I, 79.

[410] Dapper, *op. cit.* (n. 55), II, 106–10. The woodcuts and paintings were probably brought back by Johann Grueber from whom Kircher received those which he used in his *China illustrata* (1667). See our pls. 316 and 317. *Cf.* Michael Sullivan, *The Meeting of Eastern and Western Art* (New York, 1973), p. 93. One edition of Kircher was published by Jacob van Meurs in 1667. Meurs published Dapper's *Gedenkwaerdig bedryf* in 1670.

[411] *Op. cit.* (n. 110), between pp. 184 and 85, 190 and 91.

[412] *CV,* I, 79.

the Virgin.[413] Dapper's descriptions of deities and practices are particularly detailed, but taken as they were from a variety of sources, including Marini's account of Buddhism in Tongking, they are repetitious and somewhat confused.[414]

The missionaries accurately describe a Buddhist moral code for laymen which includes five prohibitions and six works of mercy. The believers are commanded not to kill any living thing, not to steal, not to fornicate, not to lie, and not to drink wine. They are enjoined to support the monks, because they pray for the people, to build temples for the images, to erect cloisters for the monks, to invoke the name of the bodhisattvas frequently, to bury the dead, and to burn paper money and the like for the dead.[415] The missionaries add little that was new about the Buddhist clergy or public worship, although they give it considerable space. Greslon, for example, reports an "infinity of bonzes" in the empire, most of whose lives are "criminal" and subject to "great impurities." These priests do not scruple "to use the most violent means to hide their crimes." He tells how some monks in Canton tried to kill a soldier who had caught them with a woman.[416] Most of the missionaries agree with Greslon's judgment, perhaps because the Buddhist monks had so actively supported the Christian persecutions of 1664–68. Navarrete reports that the Chinese do not respect monks and nuns as much as did the people of neighboring Buddhist countries.[417] Le Comte tells about a man in Nanking who brought formal charges against an "idol" for having failed to cure his daughter despite his prayers, offerings, sacrifices, and the promises of the monks. The suit was heard by local officials, the provincial governor, the viceroy, and even the Board of Punishments in Peking; it was sent back for final decision to the viceroy who banished the idol, dismantled its temple, and punished the monks.[418] Le Comte relates several other stories illustrating how monks prey on people's superstitions to extort money from them.[419] Greslon thinks the Lamas from Tibet are the worst of the Buddhist clergy. Many members of the Manchu court were devotees of Lamaism and consequently many Lamas have moved to the capital. To the Jesuits' deep chagrin they exercised a dominant influence on the Shun-chih emperor during the last years of his life. According to Greslon the emperor wanted publicly to prostrate himself before the Dalai Lama when he visited Peking but was dissuaded by Adam Schall.[420] Shun-chih nevertheless built a new temple

---

[413] *Ibid.*

[414] *Op. cit.* (n. 55), II, 106–25.

[415] For example, see Navarrete, *CV*, I, 79; Dapper, *op. cit.* (n. 55), II, 113–14; Le Comte, *op. cit.* (n. 125), pp. 332–33.

[416] Greslon, *op. cit.* (n. 181), pp. 31–32.

[417] *CV*, I, 77.

[418] *Op. cit.* (n. 125), pp. 329–31.

[419] *Ibid.*, pp. 333–39; see also Dapper, *op. cit.* (n. 55), II, 126–33.

[420] On Schall's disillusionment as the Shun-chih emperor after 1658 increasingly turned to court eunuchs and Buddhist monks and became interested in Ch'an Buddhism, see Dunne, *op. cit.* (n. 247), pp. 351–53.

for the Lamas inside the Forbidden City.[421] Navarrete calls the Dalai Lama the Buddhist pope and reports that even his excrements are prized as holy relics. Nor did Navarrete believe that Schall talked the emperor out of bowing to the Dalai Lama in Peking.[422]

Much less was written about Taoism than about Buddhism, and most of what appeared in print repeated what had already been reported by Trigault—in fact, he is frequently cited. Everyone calls the Taoists Epicureans and emphasizes the various practices of popular Taoism: the search for physical immortality through alchemy and exercises, demon chasing, and rainmaking. Martini and the many others who quote him put Taoism in historical context as the first onslaught of idolatry against primitive Chinese monotheism.[423] Martini also includes a quotation, presumably from the *Tao-te-ching* (*The Way and Power Classic*), traditionally attributed to Lao Tzu, which suggests something more of Taoism's philosophic content than was usually reported:

> *Tao,* or great reason, has no name. He created heaven and earth; is without form; moves the stars; is himself immovable. Because I do not know his name I will call him *Tao,* or highest reason without form.[424]

Le Comte also quotes from the *Tao-te-ching* or the *Lao-tzu* on the "foundation of true wisdom": "Eternal Reason [*tao*] produced one, one produced two, two produced three, and three produced all things." Le Comte thinks this statement suggests that Lao Tzu had had some knowledge of the trinity.[425] Le Gobien reports that the Taoist sage sought repose and tranquility and tried to avoid ambition and greed. Even the Taoist search after pleasure was moderate, according to Le Gobien; pleasures which might carry sorrow or anxiety in their train are avoided. The popular search for the secret of immortality, Le Gobien thinks, stems from the realization that the anticipation of death diminishes the pleasure of living.[426]

The post-1650 writers, like Trigault and Semedo before them, also report that all three religions (*san-chiao*) in China are officially tolerated and supported by the government and that most Chinese practice all three. In fact, some missionaries—Navarrete in particular—think their philosophical foundations are all identical. Quoting Longobardo, Navarrete contends that

---

[421] Greslon, *op. cit.* (n. 181), pp. 33–34. The Manchu emperors cultivated Lamaism as a powerful instrument for gaining and retaining control over Tibet and Mongolia. See below, p. 1770.

[422] *CV,* I, 76.

[423] Martini, *op. cit.* (n. 97), pp. 117–18. See also Kircher, *op. cit.* (n. 110), pp. 179–80, and *Confucius sinarum philosophus* (n. 91), pp. xxiv–xxvii.

[424] *Op. cit.* (n. 97), p. 117. See also Dapper, *op. cit.* (n. 55), II, 134, and *Confucius sinarum philosophus* (n. 91), p. xxiv.

[425] *Op. cit.* (n. 125), p. 324. See *Tao-te-ching,* 42, in W. T. De Bary *et al.* (eds.), *Sources of Chinese Tradition* (New York, 1960), I, 59.

[426] *Op. cit.* (n. 72), preface.

all three sects follow the practice of the ancient Egyptians, teaching two doctrines: one secret which they consider true, the other a public idolatrous worship with which they control the common people.[427] In fact, he thinks the *li* of the Confucians, the *tao* of the Taoists, and the "first principle" or "nothingness" of the Buddhists are identical.[428]

Perhaps the clearest picture of eclectic Chinese popular religion published during the entire century is that in Dapper's *Gedenkwaerdig bedryf* describing the religion of the Chinese on Taiwan; it is attributed to a Scotchman named David Wright.[429] In Wright's detailed description, the supernatural bureaucracy of Chinese popular religion emerges with some clarity. At the top is the supreme God, creator and sustainer of the earth, heavens, seas, stars, and planets, whom Wright simply calls "Ty" (Ti). The Chinese make sacrifices to him, a live pig burned in sandalwood, once each year. Subordinate to him are four gods: "Tien Sho Joch Koung Shanch Tee" (T'ien Shang Yü Kung Shang Ti, the Jade Emperor), who governs the earth, "Jok Tee" (?), "Quanoung" (Kuan-ti?), and "Jamoungh" (Yang Hou Wang?). The last three mentioned were unusually wise and upright humans who were taken up to heaven. The Jade Emperor is also served by three spirits who respectively govern the rain, men, and all other living things, and the sea and whatever is in or on it: "Heuoung" (?); "Teoung" (?); and "Tsuy Zyen Tei Oung" (?). Residing with these four gods and three spirits are twenty-eight heavenly councillors who also govern the stars. These were formerly great and wise philosophers. Beneath these heavenly deities are thirty-six gods who reside on earth but who go to heaven each year to report the misdeeds of humans. Wright names each of these gods, relates traditional stories about some of them, describes their powers and the festivals in which they are worshipped. Some are wise and upright officials who became gods after they died, some are deified war heroes, some are credited with the discovery of things like cooking, fire, marriage, medicine, and military skills. Some are of Buddhist origin, some are Taoist, some are local Fukienese or Taiwanese deities. Several are giants. Among the more important of them are "Pot Sou" (*p'u-sa*, the Chinese abbreviation for bodhisattva, meaning Kuan-yin), often depicted as a goddess with a child in her arms; the goddess "Quaniem" (Kuan-yin?), mentioned already by Marco Polo and Mendoza; "Nioma or Matzou" (Ma-tsu, also called T'ien fei, the "imperial concubine of Heaven"), who is described as the daughter of a high official who lived a pious life on P'eng-hu (the Pescadores) and whose aid is especially sought by fishermen and sailors; "Sikjaa" (Shih-chia, or Sakyamuni); and "Quantecong" (Kuan Ti Kung?), called "Vitie" by Mendoza and described as the

[427] *CV,* I, 174–75.

[428] *Ibid.*, pp. 80, 179, 197, 200–201. See also Le Gobien, *op. cit.* (n. 72), preface.

[429] Dapper, *op. cit.* (n. 55), I, 42–51; Wright apparently lived on Formosa sometime during the 1650's. See William Campbell, *Formosa under the Dutch* (London, 1903; reprinted, Taipei, 1967), p. 551.

first Chinese emperor, a gigantic and heroic warrior who also invented clothing and architecture and regulated trades.[430] Finally, in addition to these seventy-two gods, Wright briefly describes "Ty Tsoequi" (Ti Ts'ang Kuei?), the "Prince of the Devils" (Lord of Hell), his two councillors, and twelve subordinate spirits.[431]

During the seventeenth century, Europe's tantalizing glimpse into the Middle Kingdom opened to reveal an expansive and detailed vista. Jesuit missionaries, established in Peking at the turn of the century, provided the most numerous and perceptive reports. Their published letterbooks appeared regularly, were usually translated into several European languages, and were widely circulated. Dozens of them were published during the course of the century. While they primarily described the experience of the missionaries in China so as to elicit support for the mission, they also included substantial and perceptive descriptions of China and the Chinese. Even more influential than the letterbooks were the ethnohistories of Nicolas Trigault (1615), Alvaro Semedo (1642), and Martino Martini's *Atlas* (1655). From these, Europe's image of China emerged more clearly and in more detail than ever before. Martini's maps and descriptions clarified Europe's cartographical image of China and were not superseded during the next century.

While much less perceptive and appreciative of the Chinese and of Chinese culture than the Jesuits, secular European travelers nevertheless added useful and accurate details to the Jesuits' image. Their descriptions of Chinese merchants and lower-level officials along the coast were usually uninformed by any understanding of the structure and ideals of Chinese government. Nor did any appreciation of China's "three religions" or of Confucian ethics color their descriptions of the "idolatry" they observed in the many overseas Chinese communities of Southeast Asia or of the shrewd and frequently dishonest Chinese merchants with whom they had to trade. The secular travel accounts introduced European readers to the Southeast Asian Chinese communities and to the behavior and customs of the people in them and along the China coast, often ignored in the better organized and sometimes more idealized descriptions of the Jesuits.

The major descriptions of China published during the first half of the seventeenth century—general descriptions, in contrast to letterbooks and his-

---

[430] For an example of the metamorphosis of a human, in this case the warrior hero Kuan Ti, into a god with specified powers, see Prasenjit Duara, "Superscribing Symbols: The Myth of Guandi, Chinese God of War," *The Journal of Asian Studies,* XLVII (1988), 778–95.

[431] It is difficult to identify all of the deities named by Wright in his romanizations of Hokkien, Cantonese, and Mandarin words. For a brief account of the supernatural bureaucracy see A. P. Wolf, "Gods, Ghosts, and Ancestors," in A. P. Wolf (ed.), *Religion and Ritual in Chinese Society* (Stanford, 1974), pp. 131–82. See also Reichelt, *op. cit.* (n. 404), pp. 94–100, and Laurence G. Thompson, *Chinese Religion: An Introduction* (Encino, Cal., and Belmont, Cal., 1975), pp. 56–62. For Chinese popular religion see above, pp. 1649–51. See also pl. 335.

tories of the mission—depicted China as being impressively stable, almost changeless. The important and widely circulated ethnohistories of Trigault, Semedo, and Martini generalized about Chinese government, society, religion, learning, and customs, but rarely reported current events. When at mid-century, however, news of the 1644 Manchu Conquest arrived in Europe, the image of China as a remote and changeless empire was largely replaced by that of a dynamic China experiencing a most disruptive revolution. Some early, brief notices of the conquest appeared in the annual Jesuit letterbooks and in newssheets, but Martini's *De bello tartarico historia,* reissued or translated at least twenty-five times before the century's end, became the authoritative description of the conquest. It was not the only account. Between 1650 and 1688, sixteen full-scale histories of the Manchu Conquest appeared in Europe. Two Dutch tragedies, one English play, and two German novels were written about the conquest. References to it could also be found in a wide variety of other pieces.

Subsequent Chinese events continued to be reported in Europe, and at first the Jesuits provided most of the new publications. Their books and published letters were rivaled after mid-century by those of Dominicans and Franciscans critical of the Jesuits' policy of accommodation in China in what became known as the Rites Controversy. Publications on both sides of the issue became increasingly biased and in some ways less reliable. Nevertheless the Rites Controversy, like the Manchu Conquest, engendered much writing about China and thus greatly increased the store of information readily available in Europe. While the Rites Controversy also affected the Jesuits' larger descriptions of China, many of these provided richly detailed information on the early Ch'ing dynasty as well as additional detail and new insights on topics which had been treated earlier. The most informative of these accounts were written by Adam Schall, Adrien Greslon, François de Rougemont, Prospero Intorcetta, Ferdinand Verbiest, Gabriel de Magalhães, and Joachim Bouvet. All of these, except that of Magalhães, were more narrowly focused than were the ethnohistories of Trigault or Semedo, or Martini's *Atlas.* Magalhães' work, however, is a major comprehensive description of China in the tradition of Mendoza, Trigault, Semedo, and Martini.

Europe's knowledge was further enhanced by more specialized publications and by the issuance of some translated Chinese texts. By the end of the century, three of the Confucian Four Books, the *Chung Yung,* or *Doctrine of the Mean,* the *Ta Hsüeh,* or *Great Learning,* and the *Lun Yü,* or *Analects,* were translated into Latin and French, along with descriptions of the Five Classics and a life of Confucius. Michael Boym contributed influential studies of Chinese botany and medicine. Three major accounts of Chinese history appeared, drawn from the official histories and from the classics. Martini's *Sinicae historiae decas prima* (1658) was a detailed account of Chinese history from the legendary sage emperor Fu Hsi, thought to have begun his reign in

2952 B.C., to the end of the Former Han dynasty or the beginning of the Christian era. What serves as a continuation of Martini's work appeared as the "Synopsis chronologica monarchiae sinicae," in Thévenot's collection of voyages. The "Synopsis" briefly retraced the periods covered by Martini's *Decas prima* and then in what Thévenot called "Decas secunda" provided a detailed account of Chinese history from the fall of the Former Han into the seventeenth century. In 1686 Philippe Couplet published a chronological survey of Chinese history extending from Huang-ti, the third sage emperor, to 1683. Finally, Athanasius Kircher's popular and often-quoted *China illustrata* (1667) was intended to prove the authenticity of the Nestorian monument by reproducing and translating its inscriptions. It contains much interesting collateral information about China's religions, geography, writing, natural wonders, and the like.

The massive, profusely illustrated volumes of Johann Nieuhof (1665) and Olfert Dapper (1670) are virtual encyclopedias of things Chinese. In each of them the firsthand experiences and observations of writers who accompanied the Dutch embassies to the Ch'ing court were augmented by information taken from most of the major published Jesuit works. The illustrations in these volumes, many of which were based on Nieuhof's own sketches, provided more, and more reliable, visual images of China than Europe had ever seen before. Even these expensive tomes were frequently reissued and translated.

In the last decade of the century, several accounts of overland journeys to China appeared which also contained descriptions of Peking, north China, the Great Wall, and the peoples of China's land frontiers. The most informative of these were written by Nicolaas Witsen, who interviewed people who had accompanied the Russian ambassador Fedor Baikov from Moscow to Peking in 1653, and by Evert Ysbrandszoon Ides and Adam Brand, members of the Russian embassy of 1693.

Altogether more than fifty major independent accounts of China were published during the century, not counting those found in general descriptions of Asia, those whose authors had never been to China, most Jesuit letterbooks, and accounts which added nothing new to previously published information even if their authors had traveled to China. When all of this literature in its various editions, translations, repetitions, and incorporation into collections is taken together it constitutes a massive corpus of information in almost every European language. It seems unlikely that many readers could have missed all of it.

The image of China's geography which emerged from this literature was surprisingly detailed and complete, particularly with respect to size, location, and climate. Convincing proofs were also advanced for China's identification with Marco Polo's Cathay, the most impressive of which was probably the account of the Jesuit lay brother Bento Goes' journey from Delhi with a Muslim caravan headed for Cambaluc, the capital of Cathay, which in the end he found to be Peking. Names and locations, even the co-ordinates, of hundreds of Chinese cities, towns, counties, and prefectures became available in Europe. Martini's *Atlas* identified what each jurisdiction was best known for, and discussed its population, taxes, military forces, and the names of its rivers, lakes, important mountains, and even important historical residents. This information was repeated by Nieuhof and Dapper as well as by other writers and augmented by new eyewitness descriptions of scores of China's cities and towns, some of which had been ruined in the civil wars. Rivers and canals were repeatedly described and the facility with which one could travel for long distances by water was much admired. Nieuhof and Dapper, for example, provided vividly detailed descriptions of the arteries along which the Dutch tribute missions traveled on their way from south China to the capital. Nieuhof's book contained many beautiful prints of scenes engraved from his personal sketches; Dapper reprinted many of them. Missionaries who frequently journeyed from city to city provided similar descriptions. Writers such as Schall, Nieuhof, Dapper, Navarrete, Magalhães, and Le Comte described the imperial palace buildings, and many more depicted the capital city in colorful detail. Brand and Ides, who journeyed overland from Moscow to Peking, described China's frontiers, far northern and western landscapes, and the peoples who lived on the empire's periphery. European visitors then as now were awed by the Great Wall. Many of them described it and recounted its history.

Everyone was impressed with China's huge population, and several European writers provided fairly accurate estimates of its size. Seventeenth-century European visitors described huge cities which stood within sight of one another. Peking's population, Diego de Pantoja concluded, was greater than that of any four major European cities combined. Martini wrote that China's population was so dense and its land so intensively cultivated that he often imagined it to be a single gigantic city.

Many seventeenth-century European writers itemized China's natural resources: plants, animals, minerals, products, wealth, and commerce. They reported that China was extremely well endowed. Michael Boym, for example, thought China was "an epitome of the world because it contains all that which is most beautiful in the rest of the inhabited earth." Boym's *Flora sinensis* and Martini's *Atlas* provided the most accurate and numerous descriptions and sketches of Chinese plants, animals, and products. Their works were repeatedly and extensively mined by later writers, especially by Kircher, Nieuhof, and Dapper.

Within the general geographic descriptions there were often included detailed impressions of the Chinese landscape. Detailed descriptions and sketches appeared in print of hundreds of Chinese cities and villages—scores written about Peking alone; of what travelers saw along the roads, rivers, and canals; of majestic mountains, verdant rice fields, terraced hillsides, and the dusty loess plateau. Dutch and English merchants provided glimpses of the islands, coves, and inlets along the coast. Overland travelers recounted their first impressions of the Great Wall snaking its way over the hills of north China and of the imposing gates, uniformed guards, dignified officials, and throngs of people they met as they entered the empire. In sum, European readers encountered hundreds of vivid pictures of China's physical environment in the accounts of Ides's embassy from Moscow, D'Andrade's or Grueber's journeys to Tibet, Cornelis Reijersen's or Balthasar Bort's raids along the Fukien coast, Nieuhof's riverine voyage from Canton to Peking, Bento Goes' long trek from Delhi to Su-chou, and the missionaries' journeys across almost all parts of the Middle Kingdom. Martini's provincial descriptions are particularly rich in details about China's landscape.

European writers generally agreed about the physical appearance of the Chinese: they had full round faces, small feet, tiny flat noses, black hair, black eyes, and very sparse beards. Most Europeans judged Chinese skin color to be white or nearly so. While some noted differences in color between northerners and southerners, Martini also described minority groups whose appearance and customs were quite different from those of the Chinese. Dress was repeatedly described, frequently with the comment that it was difficult to tell men from women since both wore long robes with wide sleeves. The Jesuits admired the modest simplicity of Chinese dress and reported approvingly that in China, as opposed to Europe, clothing styles never changed. Everyone commented on the widespread use of silk, and several described the dress and insignia of officials in elaborate detail.

One style which changed drastically at mid-century was the standard Chinese coiffure. After the Manchu Conquest, Chinese men were no longer permitted to let their hair grow long; they shaved their heads allowing only the queue to grow.

Assessments of Chinese character differed widely. European merchants and mariners usually judged the Chinese to be shrewd, greedy, dishonest, cowardly, frequently immoral, and addicted to gambling. The Jesuits, however, painted a startlingly different picture, probably because they associated primarily with better-educated Chinese. They used adjectives such as humble, courteous, gentle, disciplined, chaste, restrained, industrious, and ingenious to depict what they thought to be essential in Chinese national character. A few thought the scholars suffered from parochialism and smugness and that both of these characteristics contributed to their unwillingness to learn from outsiders. The Jesuits admitted that Chinese merchants were frequently shrewd and deceitful—some provided amusing examples—but cautioned their readers not to judge the other Chinese by the behavior of the despised merchants. Nevertheless the Jesuits also provided evidence for the darker side of Chinese social behavior: the sale of small children, slavery, prostitution, the drowning of infant daughters, the castration of young boys, and the prevalence of suicide among China's poor. Most Jesuit writers described footbinding and the possible reasons for it, but never with the sense of moral outrage characteristic of later European descriptions.

Like modern scholars, seventeenth-century Europeans sensed and admired the importance of the Chinese family. They described it and its attendant social customs in elaborate detail. Chinese marriage customs were remarked upon, from the betrothal of infants and the role of go-betweens, through the details of the wedding day. Marriages were regarded as arrangements between families in which the bride literally became a member of her husband's family. Concubinage, which the Jesuits disliked, and the seclusion of women were touched upon. Remarks on the importance of filial piety, which the Jesuits admired, were accompanied by discussions of inheritance laws, divorce, and countless details about funerals, the selection of grave sites, mourning practices, tombs, subsequent visitations, and ancestor veneration.

Missionaries and merchants alike thought the Chinese were excessively formal, and both groups described the ceremonial character of social relations in abundant and often tedious detail. Merchants seemed fascinated but also exasperated by ceremony when it complicated their negotiations with provincial officials. For the Jesuits, familiarity with formal manners and customs was a practical necessity if they were to be accepted by the upper-class Chinese. They studied and reported on the intricacies of forms of address and greeting, the protocol involved in visiting or receiving guests, gift exchanges, the use of calling cards, seating arrangements at banquets, drinking toasts, the order of dishes at a banquet, the use of chopsticks, the entertainments at banquets, and the ritual of serving tea. Their portrayal of Chinese manners was accurate, and the importance of ceremonial not exaggerated. In addition, the Jesuits learned countless details about Chinese homes and food, about the giving of names, and about festivals and entertainments. One rule seemed to apply to almost all social situations: a Chinese gentleman always deprecated himself while praising his guest or host, always praised others' virtues while overlooking their faults.

The main lines of social stratification also intrigued European observers. Most noted the absence of a hereditary aristocracy and described the examinations whereby one entered the scholarly class. Nevertheless they wrote about the scholar-officials as if they comprised an aristocracy. The Jesuits associated almost exclusively with the official class and consequently wrote much less about other levels of society. They realized, however, that agriculture was considered the most important work in the empire and that peasants were highly regarded. They reported that merchants and soldiers were among the lowest and most despised groups, as were the Buddhist monks. Lower still were beggars, vagabonds, and slaves. Nevertheless European writers frequently mentioned very prosperous merchants as well as officials who seemed to be involved in trade.

Chinese peasants were seen to be extremely diligent, clever, and frugal.

Scarcely a square foot of land was left untilled, the soil was reinvigorated by judicious fertilization, and in dry areas the land was irrigated. In many parts of China two or three crops per year were grown on the same land. Navarrete provided more details about agriculture than most other seventeenth-century writers.

The Europeans were equally impressed with Chinese crafts and industry. Among the most frequently admired products of their ingenuity were printing, paper, gunpowder (for fireworks), porcelain, silk, lacquerware, architecture, bridges, and brass; some were discussed in extensive detail. The commercial vitality of Chinese cities continued to amaze European visitors. They repeatedly described canals and rivers near the cities choked with boats and grain barges, and urban streets lined with shops and teeming with people. Artisans who plied their trades in streets, beasts of burden for rent at almost every corner, the numerous restaurants, ice to cool drinking water in summer, and coal to heat homes in winter were among the urban amenities which fascinated the Europeans.

China's government was perhaps the most uniformly admired aspect of the Chinese world and almost no Europeans attempted to describe the empire without allocating a large space to government and administration. The emperor, his various names and titles, his absolute power, his public ceremonies and routines, his dress, wives, and concubines were all remarked upon again and again, especially by those who wrote during the Ch'ing period, when the emperors were publicly visible. European observers were awed by the emperor's wealth, and they repeatedly listed his revenues and the numbers of his soldiers, province by province. They found it almost unbelievable that so large and populous an empire was united under a single ruler. But while they usually described the emperor's power as absolute, most European writers also observed that his power was limited by the civil bureaucracy. Even more impressive than the emperor's power was the fact that the bureaucracy which advised him and helped him govern was an aristocracy of talent. In Kircher's words, "this state is governed by the learned in the manner of the Platonists, and according to the divine philosopher."

Most of seventeenth-century Europe's information about the civil bureaucracy came from the Jesuits. They described the six metropolitan boards and the composition and function of each of them. Most judged the Board of Civil Office to be the most important, although they all wrote extensively about the Board of Rites and accurately listed its varied responsibilities, including the reception of tribute missions. Some noted that its members were usually appointed from the prestigious Imperial Academy (Han-lin Yüan). They concisely and accurately described the Han-lin Yüan and ambiguously commented on the Grand Secretaries, thus accurately reflecting the ambiguity of the position of these officers in the late Ming administration. The Jesuits delineated several other "courts" and imperial household offices in Peking but were particularly fascinated by the Censorate. They disagreed with one another, however, about its benefits. Trigault, for example, admired the Censorate as an effective restraint on the abuse of power by the bureaucracy. Semedo, on the other hand, thought the censors' power was rarely used properly. Semedo and many other Jesuits as well seem to have understood the role of factions in the bureaucracy.

The Jesuits described China's provincial government from the viceroys and governors to the district magistrates. Semedo even described the ten-family groupings at the local level. On the whole, their picture of provincial and local government was fairly accurate, although they failed to distinguish clearly between the governor of a province and a viceroy or supreme commander. The complexity of the workings of provincial and local government emerged most clearly in the writings of the Dutch travelers and in the Jesuits' mission histories.

China's military, both in its late Ming and early Ch'ing forms, was often described. But it does not receive high marks, not even after the successful Manchu Conquest. Despite evidence of past military glory, Chinese soldiers were usually described as poor, uneducated, and low in public regard.

Much was written about Chinese law. The Europeans were suprised to learn that actual law codes went back no further than the founding of a dynasty, but realized that the codes of each dynasty were based on ancient Confucian principles. They provided rich detail about the implementation of justice: about courts, prisons, punishments, and the like. Some thought Chinese justice exceedingly harsh; some thought it lax. Many of those who commented had firsthand experience with it.

Most of the Jesuits writing during the late Ming admired Chinese government and in their general descriptions tended to show how closely it conformed to Confucian ideals rather than how far it departed from them. Ample evidence for the imperial government's less admirable qualities—corruption, factionalism, arbitrariness, and inefficiency—however, could easily be found in the secular travel accounts and in the histories of the mission. From all of this a perceptive reader could have fashioned a fairly accurate image of late Ming political structure and practice.

Although most Europeans who reported on China's government after the Manchu Conquest emphasized the continuity between the Ming and Ch'ing, they also described the changes made by the new rulers. Perhaps the most frequently reported of the Ch'ing innovations was the doubling in size of the six metropolitan boards by adding a Manchu counterpart for each Chinese officer or member. They also reported the reestablishment of the Grand Secretariat or Council of State, as some writers called it, to supervise the work of the six boards and to advise the emperor on memorials. Most European observers noted that the Ch'ing emperors, to create a new political image, dismantled the duplicate central government in Nanking, destroyed its imperial palace, and changed the name of the city. Le Comte erroneously reported that the Censorate was abolished, replaced, he thought, by the K'ang-hsi emperor's visits to the provinces. Other late seventeenth-century writers described the Censorate in terms similar to those used by Trigault and Semedo. Magalhães' account was the most detailed and perceptive produced in the century.

For the rest, the various organs of the central government and of provincial governments were described by post-conquest writers much as Trigault, Semedo, and Martini had reported them, except that the later writers added many more details about structure and operation. In short, the Manchus altered China's central government in several important ways. European writers detailed these changes. Nevertheless, they reported far more governmental continuity between the two dynasties than change. Their descriptions of Chinese government carry abundant experiential detail; they read more like news from the contemporary world than descriptions of a remote empire, and thus produce a more dynamic image of Chinese government than that sketched by Trigault, Semedo, and Martini.

Most European commentators, especially the missionaries, wrote extensively about Chinese language, learning, and the examinations. That study and passing the examinations was the road to wealth and power in China proved endlessly fascinating to them. From the beginning to the end of the century they noted the obvious peculiarities of the language: that the characters represented words or thoughts rather than sounds, that it was uninflected and largely devoid of grammar, that it was written in vertical lines and read from right to left, that the vernacular differed greatly from written Chinese, that each character was pronounced as a monosyllable, and that tones distinguished between words that were otherwise identical in sound. It was not long, however, before European writers were reproducing characters in their books and describing the formation of complex characters from simpler ones. By the end of the century, Europeans could have read about the evolution of modern characters from their ancient forms, about the various calligraphic styles, about Chinese dictionaries, and about many details of Chinese phonetics, from the tones to aspirated and unaspirated sounds.

The task of learning Chinese appeared daunting to some Jesuit writers, although others thought the absence of grammar made it easier to master than Latin. All agreed that it placed a heavy burden on the student's memory and most described how Chinese students spent long years memorizing characters, practicing calligraphy, and then reading, even memorizing, the classics. Mendoza in the sixteenth century had described what he thought were public schools and universities, but almost all seventeenth-century writers saw Chinese education as essentially private instruction leading to the examinations. The examinations, as might be expected, were described in close detail: their frequency, the elaborate precautions to prevent cheating, the stalls in which candidates for degrees were locked, the kinds of essays written on each day of examination, the numbers of successful candidates and their sudden prosperity, the palace examination, and the appointment of the top *chin-shih* to the Han-lin Yüan.

Preparation for the exams included the mastery of the Confucian classics. European readers could have learned the names and a great deal about the content of each of the Five Classics from published reports. They could have read excerpts from some of the classics, complete translations of three of the Four Books, and detailed biographical sketches drawn from traditional Chinese accounts on Confucius and Mencius. They could also have read about the officially orthodox commentaries on the classics written by the Sung Neo-Confucians.

Because of—or in spite of—the rigors of Chinese education more people could read, more were educated, and more books were published in China than anywhere else. Among the categories of Chinese books, Magalhães listed history, mathematics, natural sciences, military science, medicine, agriculture, eloquent discourses, filial piety stories, loyalty tales, romances, poems, tragedies, and comedies. Many examples of these books and the sciences they represented were discussed by seventeenth-century European writers. In general, Europeans judged themselves superior to the Chinese in mathematics, astronomy, and other natural sciences, although they reported that these subjects had been studied by the Chinese since ancient times. They were somewhat more impressed by Chinese medicine, especially by the use of the pulse in diagnosis and by the variety of herbal medicines. Michael Boym, for example, translated a major Chinese treatise on the diagnostic use of the pulse. Nevertheless, European observers generally judged that Chinese medicine lacked scientific foundations; a judgment they made about most other Chinese science as well.

In contrast to their disdain for Chinese science, the missionaries praised Chinese historical writings. They consequently presented their readers with an impressive amount of information about history. By the end of the century, European scholars had, in the historical works of Martini, Thévenot, and Couplet, a richly detailed sketch of Chinese history, from earliest times to their present, drawn from the classics and the official histories. Later writers regularly borrowed from these Jesuit scholars for the historical material in their descriptions, but they also obtained historical information independently. Martini's *Atlas* and Navarrete's *Tratados,* for example, contain a great many historic or legendary details about particular places, institutions, and customs in seventeenth-century China. Most writers included some information about Chinese history, and much of this information was frequently repeated. Seventeenth-century readers, therefore, could have become quite well informed about Chinese history; and while much of what they read reflected the Confucian bias of the original Chinese sources, it was still quite reliable. It would be a couple of centuries at least before much better information became available.

In their descriptions of Chinese religion and philosophy the Jesuits distinguished three sects: Confucians, whom they called the "Sect of the Learned"; Buddhists, or "idolaters"; and Taoists, epitomized as "Epicureans." Of the three they much preferred Confucianism, which they considered to have been a pristine monotheism in ancient times, somewhat corrupted through the centuries by the idolatries of Taoism and Buddhism. They described Confucius, his life, and his teachings, and found evidence in the classics for ancient monotheism. The orthodox Neo-Confucianism of the seventeenth century, they correctly deduced, had been pervaded by Buddhism and Taoism, although they stressed its ethical teachings and practice and judged it far less corrupted by idolatry than any other pagan system of thought. Despite their attempts to present Confucianism as a theistic, rational, moral philosophy, the pre-conquest Jesuits dutifully described religious sacrifices in which the Confucians participated and a speculative metaphysics which most Confucians accepted. In doing so they may have conveyed to Europe a more accurate image of Confucianism than they realized.

Whether Confucianism was—or ever had been—a pagan religion, a theistic moral philosophy compatible with Christianity, or an atheistic philosophy became a major issue in the Rites Controversy during the second half of the century. However confusing to European readers, the quarrel made available to them many more writings on Confucianism and on Chinese religion and philosophy generally than ever before. Not all of it was narrowly polemic. The Jesuits published translations of several major philosophic texts. They and their opponents wrote perceptive and detailed analyses of Neo-Confucian metaphysics, quoted liberally from the classics, and introduced European readers to several important Chinese philosophers.

In contrast to their portrayal of the Confucians, the seventeenth-century Jesuits usually depicted Chinese Buddhists as simple idolators. What they wrote about Buddhism often lacks the clarity found in their discussions of Confucianism. The earlier writers, especially, seemed content to describe temples, images, priests, some myths, and rituals without attempting to understand Buddhist thought or even to distinguish between sects. In part the missionaries were reflecting Confucian attitudes toward Buddhism. Nevertheless, by the end of the century European readers could have learned much about Chinese Buddhism. The traditional stories about Gautama's birth and life were repeatedly told, basic differences between Ch'an and the other Mahayana sects were accurately described, as was the role of the bodhisattvas and several of their names. European readers could have quite clearly understood the Buddhist view of reality, reincarnations, the hope of nirvana, and the various stages of enlightenment. They could have read countless details, however unflattering, about Buddhist priests, their ethical teachings, and the rituals they performed.

Much less still was written about the Taoists. The Jesuits called them Epicureans because of their attempts to prolong life, reported Lao Tzu's reputed eighty-year gestation, and described some popular practices. They described Taoist priests and hermits and a much-honored high priest who lived at the imperial court. They commented on some Taoist deities. Few, however, wrote about Taoist thought.

Most Europeans reported that all three religions were officially maintained by the government and that most Chinese seemed to believe in all three of them. The Jesuits noted that even Confucian scholars almost always had Buddhist and Taoist priests at their funerals. They usually described Chinese popular religion as a confusing hodgepodge of deities and beliefs taken from all three. So did the European merchants and seamen who confronted Chinese religion in the overseas Chinese communities and in the villages along the China coast. Nevertheless, their descriptions of popular religion were surprisingly accurate. David Wright seems to have glimpsed the order underlying the myriad popular deities. His account in Dapper's book depicts more than seventy gods as part of a supernatural bureaucracy.

Certain stereotypes about China appeared in the European accounts from Mendoza to Careri. Writer after writer discussed in awe the extent, the vast population, and the wealth of China; in its size, numbers, and riches they compared the Middle Kingdom to Europe as a whole. China was endowed with a rational government under emperors who either follow the rule of Heaven in governing or face popular revolt and a change of dynasty. The ruler and the bureaucracy were themselves governed by Confucian ethics, an admirable set of moral prescriptions inherited from antiquity. Weak emperors were surrounded by a corps of corrupt and conscienceless eunuchs. China's mandarins formed an aristocracy of talent and merit recruited through state examinations from all parts and from all classes of the country. The Chinese, unlike the Indians, were seen to be industrious and efficient farmers, or, in the cities, able and shrewd merchants. Persons of all classes were literate, and literacy was more universal in China than anywhere else in the world. In the arts of war and in individual bravery in battle the Chinese were thought to be most backward. They were also thought to be duped by idolatrous Buddhists and Taoist priests and bogged down in a mire of superstitious beliefs and rites. While technically advanced, the Chinese were limited in science by their lack of theory in mathematics, astronomy, medicine, and other natural studies. In the fine arts, especially in household architecture, they had no tradition of building for posterity, and in painting had no ability to produce perspective.

While these stereotypes contributed a particular cast and color to the European image of China, it would be simplistic to assume that they went unchallenged or unmodified by contemporaries. While it was hard to question the figures on China's area and population, the Jesuits and others pointed out repeatedly that China's government was not as rational in practice as it was in theory. Others were forced to adjust their views of the effectiveness of China's soldiery as they recounted the lengthy civil wars and the takeover of Formosa from the Dutch by Koxinga and his Chinese troops. Ideas about the revolutionary character of dynastic change had to be adjusted to account for the continuities between the Ming and the Ch'ing. Although enthralled by the humanistic Confucianism of China's ruling class, a few of the Europeans strove to understand the attractiveness of Buddhism and Taoism to the populace at large and to evaluate the contributions of Buddhism to the evolution of Neo-Confucianism. While deprecating household and temple architecture, the Europeans never ceased to marvel at the Great Wall and at the imperial palaces. Even the reputed morality of the Confucianists was called into question when the Europeans commented on the eunuchs and the addiction of the Chinese for gambling—in what might be called a clash between stereotypes.

Much of what Europeans wrote about China during the seventeenth century certainly appeared as current news to European readers. Countless details were reported about the political problems of the late Ming dynasty and the increasingly frequent incursions by the Manchus along the northern frontier. Martini and several others provided a virtually blow-by-blow description of Li Tzu-ch'eng's rebellion and the Manchu Conquest. His successors—Schall, Greslon, Rougemont, Intorcetta, Verbiest, and Magalhães—and the Dutchmen Nieuhof and Dapper, produced comparably detailed descriptions of the Manchus' consolidation of control, the new Ch'ing emperors, the Oboi regency, the campaigns against Koxinga, the revolt of the Three Feudatories, and the K'ang-hsi reign. Readers of those accounts could have become extremely knowledgeable about the events surrounding the change in dynasties. They would have known, for example, a large number of Chinese contemporaries, known the names, characters, and deeds of three emperors, of the Manchu regents, of many generals and high officials, and of a large number of less important people. They would probably have known more about the Shun-chih and K'ang-hsi emperors than almost any of their subjects knew. Seventeenth-century European readers, in short, could have been quite conscious of living in the same world as the Chinese and very likely puzzled over the world significance of the important events taking place at the other end of the Eurasian continent. The European accounts were weakest in their appreciation and understanding of China's creations in literature, drama, painting, and the related arts. Still, most twentieth-century students of China, perhaps even the most expert of them, could discover in this literature thousands of details and insights about Chinese history, culture, society, government, religion, and philosophy with which they are unfamiliar.

CHAPTER XXII

China's Periphery

East Asian civilization was already fitted to the Chinese pattern when the Europeans first arrived upon the scene. The Sinic world outside China proper had been known to the Europeans of the sixteenth century only through medieval traditions, a few firsthand reports, and accounts gathered by Europeans in the field from Chinese and Japanese written materials and from oral reports. By 1700 the Europeans had learned that the agricultural civilizations of China and India had been checked in their advances towards Central Asia by forbidding mountains, endless steppes, windblown deserts, and high plateaus which could support only a pastoral economy. Chinese agricultural development was possible outside the Great Wall only on the riverine plains of Manchuria, in a few border regions of Inner Mongolia, around the oases in Chinese Turkestan, and in the valleys of eastern Tibet. The pastoral peoples in Inner Asia and the mountaineers of Tibet had therefore managed because of geography and climate to stave off the advances of their great agricultural neighbors and to develop distinctive civilizations of their own. Still, the borderland cultures of Manchuria, Mongolia, Central Asia, and Tibet had intermittently received religious and cultural infusions from both India and China as well as from Persia and Turkey to their west. Historically, Inner Asia was most important for the intermediary role it played between the great sedentary civilizations on its borders.[1]

Climate and topography did not impede to the same degree the advance of Chinese civilization to the south and east. Vietnam, like the Yangtze region and southern China, had been deeply penetrated by the culture that originated in the Yellow River valley. Politically, as well as culturally, Viet-

---

[1] See D. Sinor, *Inner Asia and Its Contacts with Medieval Europe* (London, 1977), p. 104.

nam had gradually developed independently of China beginning in the tenth century, a story that has already been related in chapter xvi. Like China and Vietnam, Korea to the east was basically an economy and a society based on intensive rice cultivation. Throughout its history Korea owed much to China for its political institutions, its ethical and religious ideas, and its arts, sciences, and letters. Still, Korea, like Japan, had always managed to retain a separate political identity and distinctive cultural attributes. Its language, like Japanese, contrasts sharply to that of China in being an agglutinative tongue. Historically Korea acted as a geographical bridge between China and Japan. But its land connection to China had guaranteed that over time Korea should fall definitively into the world dominated by China.

The island of Taiwan (Formosa), like Korea, had become a pawn in the East Asian contests of China and Japan. Populated originally by aborigines who spoke an Austronesian language, Taiwan acted as a strategic trading station for both Chinese and Japanese merchants before Europeans first appeared on its shores. The Dutch in the seventeenth century were the first to establish a political and military hegemony over Taiwan. By the end of the century, the Ch'ing rulers of China controlled Taiwan politically and rapidly converted it into a Chinese colony. From 1895 to 1945 the Japanese added Taiwan to their East Asian empire and in 1910 annexed Korea. Today both Taiwan and Korea remain outside the political control of China, while Manchuria, Inner Mongolia, and Tibet have fallen under Peking's jurisdiction. The modern Chinese, like their ancestors of the seventeenth century, face the hard task of establishing permanent lines of demarcation in Inner Asia between the Russian area of control and their own.

I

INNER ASIA

The regions lying between China and Russia form what modern scholars refer to as Inner Asia. Most of those who described China for European readers before and during the seventeenth century mentioned the "Tartars" to the north who had so frequently troubled the Chinese empire. Before the middle of the century no one tried to distinguish between the various tribes on China's inland frontiers. For example, Marco Polo and the other medieval travelers, most of whose accounts were reprinted during the seventeenth century, naturally described China's Mongol rulers and the overland routes which brought them to China.[2] Fernão Mendes Pinto claimed to

[2] For example, see *PP*, Vol. XI; *Markus Paulus Venetus reizen* . . . (Amsterdam, 1664); Sir John Mandeville, *The Voyages and Travels* . . . (London, 1612); Mandeville, *De wonderlijke reyse* . . . (Amsterdam, 1659); Heer van Kirchus Haithon van Armenien, *Historie der oostersche lantschappen* . . . (Amsterdam, 1664).

have been captured by a Tartar king—perhaps the Mongol Altan (or Altine) Khan (1507–82)—whom he said was besieging Peking in 1544. He describes outlandishly the king's army and military tactics, and also a city full of skulls which he calls the lamas' "Rome" (Lhasa?), and a lama's sermons.[3] Most of the Jesuit authors of the first half of the century mention tribute missions to China from the Tartars. Bento de Goes had traveled from Delhi to Su-chou in western China along the caravan route, but the account of his journey in Trigault's *De christiana expeditione* (1615) contains little description of the lands through which he passed or of the people he met along the way.[4]

The first half of the seventeenth century also saw the Russians move eastward across Siberia, led mostly by free-lance Cossacks in search of sable and other furs. They established trading posts, forts, and finally towns on the rivers, usually obtaining the submission of the local tribes and then collecting tribute from them. Tobolsk on the Irtysh River, for example, was founded in 1587, Surgut on the Ob in 1593, Tomsk in 1604, Irkutsk on Lake Baikal in 1652, Albazin in 1651, and Nerchinsk in 1658. Albazin and Nerchinsk, located in the Amur River valley, had been the homeland of native tribes who were the subjects or allies of the Manchus, although the Russians did not at first realize it. After their pacification of China, the Manchu emperors began to reassert their supremacy in Inner Asia. Several Russian embassies were sent to China during the seventeenth century, beginning with that of Ivan Petlin and Andrei Mundoff in 1618. Finally in 1689 the Russians and the Ch'ing agreed on a boundary at the Argun River between their empires by the treaty concluded at Nerchinsk. Many of the Russian envoys to China and those who traded in eastern Siberia describe the territory and the peoples, but no Russian accounts of either China or Inner Asia appear to have been published during the century.[5]

[3] For an evaluation of Pinto's report see John F. Baddeley (ed.), *Russia, Mongolia, China. Being Some Record of the Relations between Them from the Beginning of the Seventeenth Century to the Death of the Tsar Alexei Mikhailovitch, A.D. 1602–1676* . . . (2 vols.; London, 1919), I, lxi–lxv. He finds a great many problems in Pinto's account, for example, that he traveled from the Great Wall to Cochin-China, stopping at Lhasa, entirely by water and sailing downstream all the way. Nevertheless Baddeley detects a substratum of truth in Pinto's story. Altan Khan attacked the environs of Peking in 1550.

[4] Louis J. Gallagher (trans.), *China in the Sixteenth Century: The Journals of Matthew Ricci: 1583–1610* (New York, 1953), pp. 499–521; *PP*, IV, 222–39. See above, chap. xx, n. 38.

[5] For Russian expansion in Siberia and its relations with China see especially Baddeley, *op. cit.* (n. 3); Basil Dmytryshyn, E. A. P. Crownhart-Vaughan, and Thomas Vaughan (eds. and trans.), *Russia's Conquest of Siberia, 1558–1700,* Vol. I (Portland, Oregon, 1985); Joseph Sebes, *The Jesuits and the Sino-Russian Treaty of Nerchinsk (1689); The Diary of Thomas Pereira, S.J.* (Rome, 1961); Mark Mancall, *Russia and China: Their Diplomatic Relations to 1728* (Cambridge, Mass., 1971); and Eric Widmer, *The Russian Ecclesiastical Mission in Peking* (Cambridge, Mass., 1976). The Russian chronicles from this period were not published until the nineteenth and twentieth centuries. See T. Armstrong (ed.), *Yermak's Campaign in Siberia* ("HS," 2d ser., CXLV; London, 1975), pp. 24–29. For a summary account from the Soviet point of view of Russia's eastward expansion in the seventeenth century see E. M. Murzaev, *Die mongolische Volksrepublik. Physisch-geographische Beschreibung,* trans. from Russian by F. Tutenberg (Gotha,

A very few Russian descriptions of Inner Asia, however, were translated into European languages and published in western Europe during the seventeenth century. The earliest of these was written by Isaac Massa (1587–1635), a Dutch merchant who lived in Moscow from 1609 to 1612.[6] Using Russian reports, Massa describes Russian travels to the Yenisey (Enisei) River, the Tungusic tribes who lived along its banks, and several expeditions still further east to the river "Pisida," where they met a strange people who repeated the words "om om," who sailed ships with square sails like those of India, and from whose land across the river they heard bells and horses. Massa thought the "Pisida" might have been the frontier of Cathay.[7] Massa's account was first published in 1612 with Hessel Gerritszoon's edition of Henry Hudson's voyage to the Northeast, and was included in all its subsequent editions and translations.[8]

The English collector Samuel Purchas includes three brief translated pieces describing Russian expansion into Siberia: one brought back by John Mericke,[9] another in the account of Josias Logan's voyage,[10] and the third in the observations of William Pursglove.[11] These are very brief, but they all mention the Tungusic tribes and the Yenisey River, and vaguely refer to the borders of Cathay. Pursglove also mentions the river "Pisida" and reports that people from the Altan Khan and from Cathay traded at Surgut.[12]

Purchas also published the first account of Petlin and Mundoff's 1618 mission from Russia to China.[13] In addition to providing some good description of China and the Great Wall, Petlin also describes what he called "Mongal Land," apparently the area between Turfan and the Great Wall, Bukhara or Eastern Turkistan to the sea, commenting on its divisions,

---

1954), pp. 76–82. See Eric Widmer, "'Kitai' and the Ch'ing Empire in Seventeenth Century Russian Documents on China," *Ch'ing-shih Wen-t'i*, Vol. II, No. 4 (Nov., 1970), pp. 21–39, for a summary of Russia's confused understanding of China and the Manchus during the seventeenth century. For a convenient map of the Russian expansion see M. Rossabi, *China and Inner Asia from 1368 to the Present Day* (London, 1975), p. 86. For the Soviet view of the discovery and occupation of Siberia, see also the work originally published in 1956 by the Russian Academy of Science and edited by M. G. Levin and L. P. Potapv, which was translated into English by Stephen Dunn and entitled *The Peoples of Siberia* (Chicago, 1964), pp. 105–34.

[6]"Een cort verhael van de weghen ende rivieren uyt Moscovia oostwaerts end oost ten noorden aen te landewaert, . . ." *BV*, Ia, 60–67; "A Brief Description of the Wayes and Rivers, Leading out of Moscovia towards the East and Northeast . . . ," *PP*, XIII, 180–93. Allegedly Massa published a map of Russia, including Siberia, on his return to Holland. See Levin and Potapv (eds.), *op. cit.* (n. 5), p. 119.

[7]Baddeley thinks the "Pisida" may have been the Lena River, Lake Baikal, the Amur, or even the gulf of Pei chih-li; *op. cit.* (n. 3), II, 1–15. Pp. 1–12 contain a translation of Massa's account; on pp. 13–15 is Baddeley's evaluation of it.

[8]Hessel Gerritszoon, *Beschryvinghe vander Samoyeden Landt in Tartarien . . .* (Amsterdam). For bibliographical information see above, p. 445.

[9]"A Note on the Travels of the Russes over Land . . . ," *PP*, XIII, 193–94.

[10]"Extrakts Taken out of Two Letters of Josias Logan," *ibid.*, pp. 236–38.

[11]"Other Observations of the Sayd William Pursglove," *ibid.*, pp. 249–55.

[12]*Ibid.*, pp. 252–53.

[13]"A Relation of Two Russe Cossacks Travailes out of Siberia to Cathay and Other Countries Adjoining Thereto," *ibid.*, XIV, 272–85.

products, and religion.[14] An account of Fedor Baikov's 1653–57 embassy to Peking first appeared in Thévenot's *Recueil de voyages* (Paris, 1681).[15] It contains some interesting details about the route followed by the embassy, but little description of the land or the people.

The Manchus catapulted into Europe's consciousness in 1644 when they toppled the Ming dynasty and then conquered all of China. By this time Europeans who wrote about China usually distinguish between the eastern Tartars (the Manchus) and the western Tartars (the Mongols). They frequently observe that the eastern Tartars had controlled most of north China during the thirteenth century but were driven out by the western Tartars, who went on to subjugate all of China in 1279.[16] The western Tartars in turn were driven out and defeated by Chu Yüan-chang, who established the Ming dynasty in 1368. What little is said about the Tartars and their homelands by the Europeans working in China reflects Chinese prejudices. Beyond the Wall, Trigault and Semedo report, there is nothing but waste and desolate spaces and roving bands of Tartar barbarians. The Manchu Conquest, however, began to change that image. Martini, for example, describes the Manchus briefly in his account of the conquest and in more detail in his *Novus atlas sinensis*. In fact, he records some typical Chinese stereotypes of the Manchus and comments on their inaccuracy. Although he had himself never been to Tartary, Martini realized, for example, that the Manchus did not live in caves as the Chinese insisted, but in tents.[17] All of the Jesuits, as well as the Dutch ambassadors, met Manchus in China after the conquest and found them not at all uncivilized or barbaric. Everyone who wrote about China after the conquest includes some description of China's new rulers and their armies. One of the Jesuits, Ferdinand Verbiest, traveled to Manchuria in 1682 and to Mongolia in 1683 with K'ang-hsi's hunting expeditions. His reports, first published in 1685, included some eyewitness descriptions of the landscape and the people.[18]

[14] *Ibid.*, pp. 276–79; cf. Baddeley, *op. cit.* (n. 3), II, 75–78.

[15] What seems to be an earlier edition is found in some copies of Thevenot's *Relations*. Baddeley, *op. cit.* (n. 3), II, 130, complains that it is a very corrupt translation, as is the German version published by Andreas Müller in 1689: *Abdullae Beidavaei historia sinensis persicè è gemino manuscripto edita, latinè quoque reddita ab Andrea Mullero Greiffenhagio, Berolini . . . MDCLXXVII expressa, nunc verò una cum additamentis edita ab Auctoris filio Quodvultdeo Abraham Mullero* (Jena, 1689). Dutch translations appeared in Witsen's *Noord en Oost Tartarye* (Amsterdam, 1692) and in Peter vander Aa's *Naaukeurige versameling* (1707). An English translation can be found in *CV*, II, 549–51. See Baddeley, *op. cit.* (n. 3), II, 130–66, for bibliographical details, a translation of the Russian manuscript, and other information about the embassy.

[16] On the Chinese border empires see L. Kwanten, *Imperial Nomads* (Philadelphia, 1979), chapter v.

[17] *Novus atlas sinensis*, Vol. XI of Johan Blaeu, *Le grand atlas* (Amsterdam, 1663), p. 24.

[18] Ferdinand Verbiest, *Voyages de l'empereur de la Chine dans la Tartarie . .* (Paris, 1685). See above, p. 419, for bibliography. Verbiest's letters were also included in Pierre Joseph d'Orléans, *Histoire des deux conquerans Tartares qui ont subjugué la Chine . . .* (Paris, 1688), and Witsen, *op. cit.* (n. 15), and were translated into English, in the Royal Society's *Philosophical Transactions*, XVI (1686–87), 35–78.

Meanwhile in 1661 Johann Grueber and Albert d'Orville, in search of a land route to China, traveled from Peking to Lhasa by way of Kokonor (Mongol, Köke nayur; Chinese, Ch'ing-hai hu; Blue Lake or Sea), crossing parts of present-day Inner Mongolia, Kansu, and Ch'inghai. Grueber's report, which contains some description of the countryside and of the various peoples they met along the way, was first published in Athanasius Kircher's *China illustrata* in 1667.[19] The search for land routes out of the range of Dutch ships also led the Society of Jesus to seek the cooperation of the Russian tsar in hopes of reaching China more quickly and safely across Siberia. Philippe Avril was sent to investigate, and in 1692 he published a description of the routes used by the Russians to travel from Moscow to China, a map of northern Asia, and references to its peoples.[20] While Avril used the published accounts of Marco Polo, Grueber, Bento de Goes, and Verbiest, much of his information appears to have come from Russian sources. He did not himself travel east of Moscow.

Nicolaas Witsen's *Noord en Oost Tartarye* was also published in 1692. Like Avril's *Voyages* it is a composite work. Witsen apparently used and cited everyone who ever wrote anything about northeast Asia. He also incorporated information he received through interviews with returning travelers and through his vast correspondence. Witsen's book contains little new, firsthand information, but it nevertheless provided European readers with a voluminous collection of chaotically organized material on northeast Asian geography and ethnography.[21]

At the end of the century, new, firsthand reports arrived in Europe from Inner Asia: two accounts of Evert Ysbrandszoon Ides' embassy from the Russian tsar to the Chinese emperor of 1692–95. The first, written in German by Adam Brand, the embassy's secretary, appeared in 1698. Within a year it had been translated into Dutch, English, and French. Ides' own account appeared in 1704.[22] These works contain the most detailed and accurate descriptions of Inner Asia up to that time. As the seventeenth century ended, therefore, a much clearer and more reliable image of the lands and peoples on China's inland frontiers was emerging from European reports.

A. MANCHURIA, INNER MONGOLIA, AND EASTERN SIBERIA

From a Chinese viewpoint, Manchuria is a vast "cut-off region." It has more than twice the area of Japan and includes a variety of landforms. In the

---

[19] See above, pp. 485–86, for bibliographical details.

[20] Philippe Avril, *Voyages en divers états d'Europe et d'Asie, entrepris pour découvrir un nouveau chemin à la Chine* (Paris, 1692). See above, p. 428, for bibliographical details. For a reproduction of Avril's map see Baddeley, *op. cit.* (n. 3), II, facing p. 216.

[21] See above, pp. 501–2, for bibliographical details.

[22] See above, pp. 503–4, 543, for bibliographical details.

central area and the south lie the rich agricultural lands of the Sungari and the Liao river valleys and the Liaotung peninsula; in the west the steppes are continuous with those of Mongolia, and in the north and east grow dense forests. The name Manchuria itself is of recent and Western origin. The peoples who lived in the area during the seventeenth century were just as varied as the landscape. The agricultural lands of the lower Liao Valley and Liaotung had been settled by Chinese since the third century B.C. and were usually considered to be the part of the empire called the Chinese Pale.[23]

Martini erroneously places the Chinese Pale inside the Great Wall on his map. In reality it was separated from intramural China and was thus vulnerable to barbarian attacks. To the west and northwest of the Chinese Pale lived steppe nomads, usually of Mongol origin. The forests to the north, northeast, and east, however, were thinly populated by a variety of Tungusic tribes and clans. Most were hunting, fishing, and pastoral tribes, some were agriculturalists, and in the far north, where the forests gave way to tundra, some herded reindeer.[24] The tribes along the frontiers of the Chinese Pale—at the willow palisade or wall—sometimes formed states, built forts and towns, and from time to time conquered the Chinese Pale. Control of the rich agricultural Chinese Pale was crucial to the success of any state in Manchuria. Frequently leaders of such states attracted Chinese collaborators, and sometimes they moved from the south Manchurian base into north China. Both the Liao (947–1125) and the Chin (1122–1234) dynasties of China began in this way.

The Manchus also subdued the Chinese Pale in 1621, long before they moved across the Great Wall. The term Manchu (*manju*) is apparently an old clan name which came to be used in the seventeenth century as a designation for the whole confederacy which invaded China.[25] Martini calls the area to the north and east of Liaotung "Eastern Tartarie," or the Kingdom of "Niuche" (Jürchen). The "Niuche," he reports, used to be called "kin" (Chin; the Chin dynasty, 1122–1234), and they once had controlled north China—all of which describes the tribal group of the Manchu prince Nurhachi.[26] According to the Chinese these people lived in caves, ate raw meat, dressed in animal skins, approved of rape and plunder, and took great

---

[23] Owen Lattimore, *Inner Asian Frontiers of China* (Boston, 1962), pp. 103–5; Franz Michael, *The Origin of Manchu Rule in China* (New York, 1972), pp. 12–13.

[24] Lattimore, *op. cit.* (n. 23), pp. 110–15; Michael, *op. cit.* (n. 23), pp. 15–16.

[25] R. B. Oxnam, *Ruling from Horseback* (Chicago, 1975), p. 35, reports that Abahai (1592–1643) called his people Manchu (*man-chou*) to cut them off from their Jürchen past. F. Wakeman, Jr., *The Great Enterprise. The Manchu Reconstruction of Imperial Order in Seventeenth Century China* (2 vols.; Berkeley, 1985), I, 42n, notes that the term "Manchu" first appeared in records in 1613 but was not officially adopted until 1635. James Bosson of the University of California, Berkeley, notes in a private communication that the term is not so obscure as it once was, thanks to the work of the noted Russian scholar of Tungusic languages, Vera Tsintsius, who has identified it with a clan name meaning "belonging to or connected with the Amur River."

[26] See O. Lattimore, *Manchuria, Cradle of Conflict* (New York, 1932), p. 44n.

pride in their strength.[27] Martini had never been to Manchuria, but he distrusts the Chinese image of these frontier people. Those whom he met after the conquest did not fulfill the Chinese stereotypes relayed to him. He reports that they do not live in caves but in pavilions or tents, and that while they often wear skins they also have silk and cotton clothes very much like the Chinese. Some live in cities and forts. They sit on the floor around low tables like most Asians other than the Chinese. He describes their clothing in some detail: long robes, a large girdle with a handkerchief on each side, two purses (one for tobacco), low round hats rimmed by a band of fur with which to cover the ears and foreheads in cold weather. They wear shoes of silk or leather. They shave their heads and beards, leaving only a mustache and queue. The Manchus are white-skinned and look much like the Chinese except that their noses are not as flat or their eyes as small. They are vigorous and strong, good horsemen and hunters. They eat meat not raw but only half-cooked—perhaps medium rare. Martini thinks they are somewhat taciturn and talk little, but are friendly to strangers. Concerning their religion he reports that they have priests called lamas, hate Islam, and burn the wives, servants, horses, and weapons of their dead. He thinks they believe in the immortality of the soul.[28] The Manchu language, Martini reports, resembles Persian and is easy to learn. Their written characters, however, are more like Arabic, except that the Manchus write from the top to the bottom of the page and from right to left like the Chinese.[29] Martini knew the term Manchu ("Muoncheu"); he thought it referred to a large city because when asked who they were, most Tartars responded with "Muoncheu."[30]

Ferdinand Verbiest, who traveled in Manchuria with the K'ang-hsi emperor in 1682, provides a firsthand account of some of its geography. For example, he correctly describes the location of Shan-hai-kuan, where the Great Wall meets the sea separating Liaotung from Pei-chih-li.[31] He calculates the latitude of Shenyang (Mukden), the capital of Liaotung, as 41°56' and that of "Ula" on the Sungari River near Chi-lin as 44°20'.[32] Nevertheless his description of the eleven-hundred-mile journey from Peking to "Ula" and back is disappointingly thin. He writes about mountains whose eastern

---

[27] Martini, *op. cit.* (n. 17), pp. 23–24.

[28] *Ibid.*; *Bellum tartaricum, or the Conquest of the Great and renowned Empire of China, by the Invasion of the Tartars*, . . . (London, 1654), pp. 262–63.

[29] Martini, *op. cit.* (n. 17), p. 26. Erdini (ca. 1623), the originator of the script and Nurhachi's adviser, based the written Manchu language on a modified form of the Mongol alphabet. James Bosson observes that while the Manchu language in no way resembles the Persian language, it is true that the script resembles Arabic in so far as the Mongolian script, on which is was formed, eventually goes back to Aramaic script (personal communication).

[30] *Op. cit.* (n. 17), p. 24. *Cf.* our pls. 381, 382.

[31] *Philosophical Transactions*, XVI, 44.

[32] *Ibid.*, pp. 41–42. He is correct on Shenyang, but seemingly places the land of "Ula" too far to the north. "Mukden" means origin; it was the original capital of the Manchu empire. "Ula," meaning large river, was the capital of the Ula clan, one of the members of the Manchu confederacy.

slopes are covered with "great Oaks and old Forests," and about deep valleys. And he also describes the land beyond Liaotung as "exceeding desert." He reports seeing many ruined, uninhabited towns in Liaotung on whose edges a few structures are being rebuilt. The road to Shenyang is ten feet wide and as smooth as a threshing floor; it is the route along which the imperial entourage travels. It passes through no towns or villages capable of feeding or housing the procession; therefore the imperials carry all their provisions and encamp in tents. Local people keep the road cleanly swept ahead of the emperor's party.[33] Verbiest comments little about the trip between Shenyang and Chi-lin other than to note that it was four hundred miles long and that they hunted en route. At Chi-lin, according to Verbiest, the emperor kowtowed to the Sungari River and was shown great affection by the populace. He locates the source of the Sungari in the Ch'ang-pai-shan or the Long White Mountains, and observes that the people of Chi-lin keep a large number of boats in order to repel the Russians, who frequently come up the river in search of pearls.

"Ula," Verbiest reports, is about thirty-two miles downstream from Chi-lin. The emperor intended to fish there, but the unusually heavy rains and high waters prevented it.[34] The swollen streams and mud continued to plague the imperial party on its homeward journey. Verbiest's account contains no descriptions of Manchuria's peoples.

Writing at the end of the century, Brand and Ides not only describe the landscape on their journey through the northwestern and western parts of Manchuria but also some of the people they encountered. They traveled across Siberia by way of the Ob, Yenisey, and Angara rivers to Lake Baikal and from there to Nerchinsk by way of the Ingoda and Shilka rivers. Ides calls the area between Lake Baikal and the Argun River the province of Daur. Its landscape is barren, with no trees, no agriculture, and not even many fish in the streams. Mongols from the south, he reports, raid the area for horses each summer.[35] According to Ides and Brand the people of Daur are Tungus of several different sorts, all subjects of the Russian tsar. Specifically mentioned are the "Konni Tunguzians," who were obliged to protect the Russian settlement at Nerchinsk on horseback and the "Olenni Tunguzians" who had to do so as foot soldiers. The chief of the Konni is described as having come from "Niuche" (Jürchen); he was a former Chinese vassal who had fallen out of favor. When he came over to the Russians he also converted to Orthodox Christianity.[36] Brand also mentions a third Tungusic

---

[33] *Ibid.*, pp. 41–43.

[34] *Ibid.*, pp. 54–57.

[35] Evert Ijsbrantszoon Ides, *Three Years Travels from Moscow Overland to China* (London, 1706), pp. 40–42. On the Daurians or the Daghors, mixed Mongol-Tungusic tribes, see Lattimore, *op. cit.* (n. 26), pp. 34–35.

[36] Ides, *op. cit.* (n. 35), p. 43. *Konni* and *olenni* are the Russian words for "equestrian" and "reindeer," which terms were used to distinguish two different groups of Tungus.

group, the "Soboltzy" (Russian for sable-men, or sable-hunters), who live more like dogs than men.[37] The Tungus graze cattle, hunt during the spring and autumn, and trap black sable to sell or give as tribute to the Russians. Near Nerchinsk along the Shilka the Russians do some farming. The Tungus, a strong and warlike people, are more than a match for the Mongols. Both men and women are excellent horsemen and skilled with the bow and arrow. They even fish with them. Ides describes arrows that produce a whistling sound in flight. According to Brand and Ides the Tungus wear sheepskin clothes and fur-trimmed caps in winter. In summer, however, they dress in Chinese blue cotton or calico and go hatless. Men wear the queue, "like the Chinese"; women fix their hair in two long braids, tied with silver or tin rings, which hang over their breasts. (See pl. 381.) Apart from hair styles, the women dress like the men. They preserve meat by drying it, grind meal for bread from yellow lily bulbs, and boil tea leaves in mare's milk. They also make a sort of brandy (kumiss) from fermented mare's milk which is quite intoxicating. Even women and young girls become drunk on it. They never use cow's milk. Ides contends that Tungusic cows never permit themselves to be milked. The Tungus are polygamous; they buy wives from one another. Both Brand and Ides report that the Tungus swear oaths by drinking the blood from a freshly killed dog.[38] Their reports about Tungusic religion, or shamanism, however, are contradictory and somewhat confused. Ides writes that the Tungus recognize a "God in Heaven," but that they do not worship or pray to him. However, "in the Night they apply themselves to Sutkur or Saitan, by beating of Drums and performing of Exorcisms, especially when they are going on a Hunting or upon any Robbing Design, to inquire whither they are to expect good or ill success."[39] Brand, on the other hand, describes wooden idols representing tutelary gods which are sometimes thrown out of doors if they fail to answer prayers.[40] Both authors also describe the Tungus who lived along the banks of the Yenisey River far to the west. These are hunting and fishing tribes, who ply the river in birch-bark canoes propelled by double-bladed paddles. They stitch geometric designs into their cheeks with black thread

[37] Adam Brand, *A Journal of an Embassy from their Majesties John and Peter Alexowits, Emperors of Moscovy . . . into China . . .* (London, 1698), p. 49. On the names of the frontier Tungusic clans see R. H. G. Lee, *The Manchurian Frontier in Ch'ing History* (Cambridge, 1970), pp. 14–15.

[38] The description of the Tungus is found in Brand, *op. cit.* (n. 37), pp. 48–50, and Ides, *op. cit.* (n. 35), pp. 43–45, 101–3. For a summary of contemporary Chinese accounts of Manchu society and customs see R. H. G. Lee, *op. cit.* (n. 37), pp. 9–14.

[39] Ides, *op. cit.* (n. 35), p. 102. *Cf.* Brand's description of shamanic divination in J. P. Roux, "Le chaman altaïque d'après les voyageurs européens des XVIIe et XVIIIe siècles," *Anthropos,* LVI (1961), 445–46. On the role of drums in shamanic ceremonies see M. Eliade, *Shamanism, Archaic Techniques of Ecstasy* (New York, 1964), pp. 168–76. "Sutkur" is a distortion of the Mongol word *sidkür* (evil spirit, or devil). "Saitan" (*saitan, seitan*) is the word for devil used in many Turkic languages.

[40] *Op. cit.* (n. 37), pp. 49–50.

and seem to have an amazing ability to endure cold: "For no sooner are their children come into the World, but they lay them in the Summer in cold Water, in the Winter in the Snow, by which means they are so accustomed to Cold, that they are the hardiest People in the World."[41] They expose their dead in trees and have no priests but conjurers.[42]

Ides' description of the trip from Nerchinsk to "Xixigar" (Ch'i-ch'i-ha-erh or Tsitsihar) is particularly vivid. The land between Nerchinsk and the Argun River is high and mountainous, but still abounds with flowers, grass, tall cedars, and birches. It is also quite populous. Here and there stand ruined castles, built in times past to protect the "Niuche" from the Mongols.[43] Across the river, however, in what is today northern Inner Mongolia, begins what Ides calls an uninhabited wilderness. The Argun, he understood, divides the Russian empire from that of the Chinese. Even in August, water would freeze overnight. The passage across the "Gan" (Gen River) is particularly difficult, but as they climb higher into the "Jalischian" (Ta-hsing-an Ling mountains) the streams become shallower. They ford the "Mergeen" (Mergel) and the "Kailar" (Hailar) rivers without difficulty. On the south slopes of the mountains the landscape changes abruptly. The descent is more rapid than the climb had been. Ides delights in the green grass, the oak and lime trees, and the hazelnut bushes. He describes the Yalu valley through which they traveled down to Ch'i-ch'i-ha-erh as

A Paradise, as consisting of beautiful Pasture Grounds, Silver Streams, and the pleasantest Woods in the World; and the delicious entertainment of the Eye is not a little improved by the prospect of the rising Ground and beautiful towering Hills, which offer themselves to our view at about a Mile and a half distance on each side, and are a perfect Warren or Park of Wild Game;[44]

Of the game Ides seems most fascinated by what might have been one of the common pheasants so numerous in northeastern Asia: "a particular sort of extraordinary beautiful Partridges, whose feathers are of several colours, their tails about an Ell long, which prove very delicate, being in taste as well as size and shape like Pheasants."[45]

The people on the south side of the mountains Ides calls "Targazinians," by which he probably means Daurians or Daghors, because elsewhere he observes that the "Tungusi Konni . . . believe themselves to be Descendants of the Targasinians of Daorzi."[46] They are broad-faced like Mongols and

[41] *Ibid.* p. 49.

[42] *Ibid.*, pp. 48–49; Ides, *op. cit.* (n. 35), pp. 30–32.

[43] Ides, *op. cit.* (n. 35), pp. 46–51.

[44] *Ibid.*, pp. 50–51.

[45] *Ibid.*, p. 51. On the common pheasant (*Phasianus calchicus*) see R. M. de Schauensee, *The Birds of China* (Washington, 1984), pp. 195–96. Pheasant casserole was made from birds which had fed on pine nuts in the forests of Manchuria. See Su Chung (Lucille Davis), *Court Dishes of China. The Cuisine of the Ch'ing Dynasty* (Rutland, Vt., 1970), p. 179.

[46] Ides, *op. cit.* (n. 35), p. 103. Also see Sebes, *op. cit.* (n. 5), pp. 18, 47.

live on the Chinese side of the Argun River. Their language is like that of the other Tungus. They live in huts of bamboo or reeds, and they dress much like the Tungus. Unlike the Tungus on the Russian side of the Argun, the Daurians are farmers, raising mostly barley, oats, and millet. They keep cattle as well. Ides claims that they are "an Infidel Heathen Nation, which worship the Devil."[47]

Ch'i-ch'i-ha-erh, according to Brand and Ides, stands on the border of China. Here they first met Chinese officials and were entertained in Chinese fashion. The area around Ch'i-ch'i-ha-erh in the Nen River valley they also call Daur or Old Daur. These Daurians, or "Naunschian Tartars," as Ides also calls them, are agriculturists. On these rich lands they grow a variety of garden crops. Their main crop, however, seems to be tobacco.[48]

They live in houses of clay or earth with square, papered windows[49] and roofs of reeds or small bamboos. They remind Ides of European peasants' thatched cottages. The houses are simple structures, not divided into rooms. In the center of each stands a pillar on which there is hung a small bow and arrows or other weapons wound about with the entrails of animals; the Daurians seem to worship this. Around the interior walls of a Daurian house runs a wide bench under which passes a heating flue—obviously a version of the north Chinese *k'ang*. According to Ides the Daurians keep the corpses of their relatives in their homes for three days, after which they are buried in a raised grave. For several weeks thereafter relatives bring food and drink to the grave, conveying it to the corpse's mouth through a hole left open for that purpose. Later the corpse will be buried deeper. The Daurians, Ides reports, practice a diabolical religion—they conjure up the devil:

Several neighbors of both Sexes, frequently assemble together about Midnight; one of them lies with his Body extended on the Earth, and the by-standers with united and exalted Voices make a dismal howl: others beat a sort of Drums; which ceasing for a small interval, the howl is renewed, and sometimes lasts for two Hours, until he that lies on the Earth, seems returned to his Senses, and after a tedious howling, rises up and relates where he has been, and what he hath seen and heard; after which whatever any of the Company are desirous to be informed of concerning future events, or other particulars, is proposed to him; and while I stayed there, no Night passed without this hideous howling of these Diabolical Ministers.[50]

Daurians of both sexes dress just like the Manchus in China. The women are unusually well shaped. Ides claims that officials and secretaries of offi-

---

[47] *Op. cit.* (n. 35), p. 50.

[48] Brand, *op. cit.* (n. 37), p. 70; Ides, *op. cit.* (n. 35), p. 54.

[49] Windows were pasted over with Korean paper. See Lee, *op. cit.* (n. 37), p. 10.

[50] Ides, *op. cit.* (n. 35), pp. 54–55. Possibly refers to the shamanistic dance called *t'iao-shen* in Chinese. See Lee, *op. cit.* (n. 37), pp. 11–12. Also *cf.* Roux, *loc. cit.* (n. 39), pp. 445–46.

cials have the right to use any woman, married or not, for their pleasure, and that their men do not seem to mind.[51]

The route from Ch'i-ch'i-ha-erh to Peking took the Russian embassy away from the Nen valley back into the steppes of western Manchuria and Inner Mongolia.[52] Here the land is dry, mountainous, sandy, and unpopulated. They note several ruined and abandoned cities along the way, built in Chinese fashion—square, with earthen walls and four gates.[53] In one of them Brand and Ides see closed octagonal brick towers containing impressive, life-size carvings of kings, queens, warriors, servants, and the like. In the town they also find large statues of people, idols, lions, and tortoises lying in the streets. Their Chinese guides inform them that the city had been the home of a Tartar king called "Utaichan" (?) who had been defeated by the Chinese centuries earlier. Another of the ruined cities Ides calls "Burgan Koton or Idol City" (Mongolian, Burqan Qota or Buddha City); reportedly it was formerly inhabited only by lamas. An octagonal stone tower in its center still holds bells which chime in the wind as well as thousands of Buddhist statues. Nearby is a village in which a great many lamas live and a sacred hill whose trees are festooned with articles of clothing hung there by travelers hoping for safe journeys. Ides supposes many of the octagonal brick towers are mausoleums. Across the "Schara Murin" (Mongolian, Shar Märön, Yellow River) and the "Logaa" (Laoha) rivers the land is rocky, but spotted also with thickets of trees, grass, and many more villages. Ides believes that the area is very dangerous at night because of tigers. All the horses, cows, camels, and other domesticated animals wear bells around their necks to frighten the tigers away. According to Ides, the Manchu emperor hunts tigers in the area each August. As they near Chang-chia-k'ou (Kalgan) at the Great Wall, the country becomes more populous. Ides and Brand describe the trees, flowers, birds, abandoned temples, and the landscape, but give nothing about the people.[54]

Ides' and Brand's accounts of their travels through Manchuria and Inner Mongolia opened up a hitherto unknown part of Asia for European readers. Their descriptions seem accurate and convey colorful impressions of the frontier, of the Chinese and Russian officials who served there, of the vari-

---

[51] *Op. cit.* (n. 35), p. 55.

[52] Inner Mongolia lies between Outer Mongolia and the Gobi desert on the north, Kansu Province on the west, China proper on the south, and Manchuria on the east. Its capital, Köke-qota—later named Kuei-hua on Chinese maps—was founded in the sixteenth century by Altan Khan outside the Great Wall to the northwest of Ta-t'ung. It is usually called Huhehot on contemporary maps, but officially is once again named Kökeqota. Since the seventeenth century, Inner Mongolia has belonged to the Chinese state system. For a full geographical description see T. R. Tregear, *A Geography of China* (Chicago, 1965), pp. 294–97; and for impressions as of 1945 see S. Cammann, *The Land of the Camel. Tents and Temples in Inner Mongolia* (New York, 1951).

[53] On the rise and fall of cities north of the Great Wall see O. Lattimore, *The Mongols of Manchuria* (New York, 1934), pp. 63–69.

[54] Ides, *op. cit.* (n. 35), pp. 56–60; Brand, *op. cit.* (n. 37), pp. 73–76.

ous Tungusic tribes, of the fluid nature of these tribes' loyalties, and of the landscape. They provide their readers with an on-the-spot glimpse of the confrontation between the expanding Chinese and Russian empires of the late seventeenth century, and its effects on the peoples of the area.

Although he had not seen them personally, Ides mentions tribes on the coast far north of Manchuria: the "Xuxi" (Chukchis) and the "Koeliki" (Koryaks), who, he reports, live in caves, dress in sealskins, eat raw fish and meat, and wash themselves in urine. Reputedly a treacherous people, they arm themselves with slings. Their language is totally different from those of the Mongols and Tungus.[55] About the "Jugogayers" (Yukaghirs), who also lived in northeastern Siberia, Ides reports only that they cut the flesh from the skeletons of their dead, dry the skeletons, decorate them with colored beads, and carry them around to their huts to be worshipped.[56] Finally, among the peoples of the far northeast, Ides briefly describes the "Jakutisians" (Yakuts) of the Lena River basin. They dress in furs, worship a "God in Heaven," are polygamous, and bury their wives or closest relatives with their dead. They both ride and harness reindeer, and they ply the river and the Arctic coast in leather boats. Ides reports that "about one-half of their languages agrees very well with that of the *Mohometan Tartars* near *Tobolskoy* which is derived from the *Bulgarian.*"[57]

B. MONGOLIA AND CENTRAL ASIA

The vast area north and northwest of the Great Wall and west of the upper Yellow River—present-day Mongolia, Ch'inghai, and Sinkiang—was called by a variety of names during the seventeenth century. Martini, for example, lists several "kingdoms" in the area: "Tanyu, Samahania, and Sifan." His brief descriptions, based on Chinese sources, are not very informative. "Tanyu" (Tangut), he reports, had been called "Tangu" by Marco Polo.[58] Its people are frequently mentioned in old Chinese histories, which

[55]Ides, *op. cit.* (n. 35), p. 104. He was correct. The Chukchis and the Koryaks are of the Paleo-Siberian language group and still live in enclaves along the coast of Kamchatka and along the Bering Sea. To the south the neighbors of the Koryaks are the Kamchadals, to the west the Yukaghirs, and to the southwest the Tungus. For a listing of the Palaeo-Siberian tribes see M. A. Czaplicka, *Aboriginal Siberia. A Study in Social Anthropology* (Oxford, 1914), pp. 18–19.

[56]Ides, *op. cit.* (n. 35), p. 106. *Cf.* Czaplicka, *op. cit.* (n. 55), p. 145.

[57]Ides, *op. cit.* (n. 35), pp. 105–6. See also Avril, *op. cit.* (n. 20), p. 195. In fact, the language of the Yakuts is Turkic; see W. Jochelson, "The Yakut,"in *Anthropological Papers of the American Museum of Natural History,* Vol. XXXIII, Pt. 2 (1983), p. 90. But Ides' connection of Yakut to Bulgarian is not as far-fetched as it seems. The ancient Volga Bolgar kingdom was a Turkic state. Fragmentary remnants of their language have survived, and Chuvash is most likely their linguistic descendant. In fact, the Slavic Bulgarians probably got their ethnonym from these Bolgars. See Jean Deny, et al. (eds.), *Philologiae turcicae fundamenta* (2 vols.; Wiesbaden, 1959–64), I, 685–95.

[58]On the Tanguts or northern Tibetans see Lattimore, *op. cit.* (n. 23), p. 227.

makes them seem a little more human than the eastern Tartars. They ruled all of China during the Yüan dynasty.[59] The peoples of "Tanyu," Martini relates, are nomads constantly moving in search of water and pasture for their herds. When angry, they spare neither fathers nor brothers. Some tribes burn their dead; others hang corpses in the trees for three years, after which they burn the bones. Martini reports that these western Tartars raise fast and brave horses, large sheep whose meat is tasty, and many camels. "Samahania" lies to the west of "Tanyu" in what Martini also calls "old Tartary." He thought it might be the same as Samarkand. The Chinese report fine cities and wealthy kings in "Samahania." Martini's description is vague, but he associates "Samahania" with Tamerlane.[60] West of China lies the kingdom of "Sifan" (Chinese, Hsi-fan, Western Fan, Fan being a Chinese name for Tibetans), which Martini sees as being divided into three countries: "Usucang" (Chinese, Wu-ssu-tsang; Tibetan, dBus gTsang, eastern and western provinces of united Tibet), "Kiang" (Ch'iang, or shepherd people in Chinese), and Tibet.[61] The Chinese report many different peoples, excellent laws, and fortified cities. Martini suggests that "Sifan" might have been the land of Prester John, but most of the people, he reports, are Buddhists. He also describes the lake "Kia" which was supposed to be the source for the Ganges and several other major rivers.[62]

Long before Martini's *Atlas* was published, Bento de Goes actually traveled from Delhi to Su-chou on China's far western border by way of Kabul, Yarkand (So-ch'e), Aksu (A-k'o-su), Turfan (T'u-lu-fan), and Hami (Hami). He thus crossed present-day Sinkiang by following the northern branch of the silk road around the Tarim Basin to western Kansu.[63] As relayed by Trigault in 1615, Bento's description of the area is limited to a single paragraph:

The district lying between Cialis [a kingdom east of Kashgar] and the Chinese borderlands is dangerous country, being wide open to the raiding Tartars, and this part of the journey is made by merchants in fear and in trepidation. They send exploring parties into the neighboring hills to see if the Tartars are moving; and if the

[59] The Tanguts and the Mongols should not be confused. The Tanguts became vassals of the Mongols. In fact, the Mongol conqueror Jenghis Khan died during a punitive expedition against the Tanguts. The Mongols, not the Tanguts, ruled all of China during the Yüan dynasty.

[60] *Op. cit.* (n. 17), pp. 27–29.

[61] The Ch'iang, a Tibeto-Burman people, began to be mentioned in the Chinese sources around 1400 B.C. Groups of Ch'iang still survive today in the mountainous borderlands between China and Tibet. See R. A. Stein, *Tibetan Civilization,* trans. from French by J. E. Stapleton Driver (Stanford, 1972), pp. 29, 31. For excellent maps of Tibet see those at the beginning of G. Tucci, *The Religions of Tibet,* trans. from German and Italian by G. Samuel (Berkeley, 1980).

[62] *Op. cit.* (n. 17), p. 30. Possibly the imaginary "Lago do chiamay" (chieng-mai) of the European cartographers or perhaps Nam-tsho phyug-mo ("Chumo"). *Cf.* above, pp. 1203–4, but also see below, p. 1776.

[63] For Bento's journey see above, p. 147.

roads are clear, they travel at night and quietly. Bento's party came across the bodies of several Saracens who had been bold enough to travel alone and were cruelly murdered. The Tartars seldom slay the natives. They call them their slaves and their shepherds, and they keep themselves supplied from their flocks and their herds. These Tartars never eat wheat or rice or any kind of vegetable. They say, all that is food for beasts, not for men. They eat nothing but flesh meat, including that of horses and camels, and they are said to be a long-lived people, some of them surviving to more than a hundred years. The Saracens on the Chinese frontier are not a warlike people. They could very easily be conquered by the Chinese, if the Chinese were interested in subjugating other nations.[64]

Johann Grueber and Albert d'Orville's 1661 journey from Peking to Lhasa took them across modern Ch'ing-hai rather than Sinkiang. They followed the Yellow River to "Sinung" (Hsi-ning) near Kokonor (Ch'ing-hai Lake) before crossing the mountains and deserts into Tibet. In his account as published in Kircher's *China illustrata,* Grueber depicts the Yellow River valley outside the Great Wall as pleasant country, well populated, and green during parts of the year. He enjoys the clear streams, fresh fish and game, and invigorating air. The mountains and deserts between Hsi-ning and Lhasa, however, are anything but pleasant. It takes three difficult months to cross them.[65] Grueber lists the names by which the desert is called: Lop, Belgian, Samo, Kalmuk, or Caracathai; names also frequently attributed to the Gobi by seventeenth-century writers.[66] According to Grueber the area between Hsi-ning and Lhasa is largely uninhabited, containing no arable land whatever.[67] Grueber understands Tibet to be part of a larger kingdom of Tangut and describes its rulers and people as Kalmuk Tartars. Kircher's account of Grueber and D'Orville's journey contains sketches as well as brief descriptions of their clothing and tents.[68]

In 1683 Ferdinand Verbiest accompanied the emperor's seventy-day hunting expedition into Mongolia, or Western Tartary, as he calls it in his published account. It is difficult to determine precisely where they traveled; Verbiest mentions no specific places. Nevertheless he clearly depicts the

[64] Gallagher (trans.), *op. cit.* (n. 4), p. 513.

[65] Kircher, *La Chine illustrée de plusieurs monuments tant sacrés que profanes, et de quantité de recherches de la nature & de l'art . . .*, (Amsterdam, 1670), pp. 91–92. For further details on Grueber's route see C. Wessels, "New Documents Relating to the Journey of Fr. John Grueber," *AHSI*, IX (1940), p. 192; and J. MacGregor, *Tibet. A Chronicle of Exploration* (New York, 1970), p. 52. For an illustration from Kircher of the Great Wall at Hsi-ning see pl. 308.

[66] Kircher, *op. cit.* (n. 65), pp. 88–89. "Gobi" is not the name of a geographical area, but a common expression used by Mongols to indicate a definite set of geographical features. What is called the Gobi desert stretches for thirty-six hundred miles from the Pamirs to the borders of Manchuria.

[67] *Ibid.*, p. 318.

[68] *Ibid.*, pp. 92–93. "Kalmuk" is the name for only one portion of the western Mongols and is probably Turkic in origin. "Oirat" is the common name for the western Mongols, which, after passing through Chinese and Manchu forms became the "Eleuth" of the European writers. See Baddeley (ed.), *op. cit.* (n. 3), I, xli–xlvii. For their clothing and habitations see our pl. 375.

sharp contrast between the Mongolian and the Chinese landscapes. Mongolia is barren, "nothing . . . but mountains, Rocks, and Valleys, there are neither Cities, Towns, nor Villages, nor so much as any Houses. The Inhabitants Lodge under Tents, pitched on all sides in the open Fields." Because of Mongolia's high elevation, which Verbiest calculates to be three thousand geometrical paces above sea level, the air is always cool. Even in July and August they need thick coats and furs at night. As Verbiest describes them, the Mongols are true nomads. They do not farm or raise any of the animals associated with settled agriculture, such as hogs and poultry. They graze cattle, horses, and camels, and move with them in search of grass and water. They spend their days hunting or loafing. Their diet consists primarily of milk, cheese, and meat. "In short," Verbiest concludes, "they care for nought from Morning to Night, but to Drink and Eat; like the Beasts, and Droves which they feed." [69]

Some glimpse of the changes in Mongol life brought by the Manchus can be detected in Verbiest's report. One reason for K'ang-hsi's massive and pompous expedition was to intimidate and maintain control over the Mongols as part of his program to pacify and control China proper. Verbiest decides that if the Mongols ever united they could still conquer China. K'ang-hsi, however, had divided Mongolia into forty-eight tributary provinces. He assigned specific lands and pastures to the nomadic Mongols, keeping the stronger tribes far from the Chinese frontier. According to Verbiest, the emperor governs the Mongol tribes personally, not through the Chinese bureaucracy. [70] K'ang-hsi also patronizes Lamaism for political purposes, according to Verbiest. He thinks the Mongols are singularly and unswervingly devoted to the lamas who could be used by the emperor to control his Mongol subjects. [71]

While Brand and Ides did not travel through Mongolia or the central Asian oases on their way to Nerchinsk, they, like Avril and Witsen, nevertheless describe some of the Mongol tribes who roamed China's borderlands. The danger of Mongol raiding parties from the south seems to have been an almost continuous concern to Ides' embassy as it traveled eastward. East of Lake Baikal, for example, they drew their wagons up into a defensive circle each night. [72] Ides traces the boundaries of what he calls "Mongalia" territories, roughly corresponding to those of present-day Mongolia. The Mongols, he reports, are ruled by three khans, two of which had accepted Chinese protection for fear of the Kalmuks. [73]

[69] *Philosophical Transactions*, XVI, 53.
[70] *Ibid.*, pp. 56–57. On Manchu policies towards the Mongols see Lattimore, *op. cit.* (n. 23), pp. 89–92; and Rossabi, *op. cit.* (n. 5), pp. 149–52.
[71] *Op. cit.* (n. 18), p. 56. The lamas were actually confronted in Mongolia itself by a revival of shamanism and nativism.
[72] Brand, *op. cit.* (n. 37), p. 56.
[73] Ides, *op. cit.* (n. 35), p. 101. See also Avril, *op. cit.* (n. 20), pp. 178–80; Petlin, *op. cit.* (n. 9), pp. 276–79; and Baddeley, *op. cit.* (n. 3), II, 75–78.

The Kalmuks were reported to control the territory between the borders of Mongolia and the Volga River. They are frequently mentioned by Ides and Brand, but are not described in very much detail. Avril thinks the Kalmuks are divided into "an infinity of hordes," each having its own khan, one of whom claims to be a descendant of Tamerlane. Most of the Kalmuks, he reports, are Lamaists, although the westernmost hordes seem to be Muslims. They live in tents, have no cities or fixed habitation, move often and rapidly.[74] Witsen describes a Kalmuk prince whom he met in Moscow in 1665 as an uncouth, awkward man whose speech sounded like a turkey's. He had long black hair, a flat face, and a high forehead. His tan-yellow skin was rough and full of pimples like the skin of a plucked goose.[75] Some Kalmuk hordes raid the Russian settlements.[76] Some, like the "Barabinsy" Kalmuks of the Upper Irtysh valley, pay tribute to the Russians. These Ides describes as agriculturalists who live in wooden houses but are nevertheless "an insolent villanous sort of people." Their common food is a hard barley bread or dried lily bulbs boiled with milk. They drink black tea or a brandy (kumiss) made from mare's milk. They raise horses, cows, camels, and sheep, but not hogs. Ides claims they are polygamous. They carry rough wooden idols called "Saitans" with them on their hunts on which they hang rich furs in gratitude when the hunt is successful.[77]

In the Lake Baikal region the Ides-Brand delegation met Buryat Mongols or "Burattians," tribes who also paid tribute to the Russians.[78] The Buryats practice no agriculture, but neither are they nomads. They live in villages of low wooden houses covered with earth and having holes in the roof for smoke to escape. They hunt deer, dry the meat in the sun to preserve it, and raise cattle and camels. They barter their especially large camels to people making the trip to China. According to Ides, the Buryats mount large hunts in the spring and fall in which hunters on horseback encircle a large area and then gradually tighten the ring while killing the encircled game with bows and arrows. Occasionally the hunters also shoot one another. Ides describes the Buryats as large handsome people who dress in sheepskins during the winter. They look like devils, however, because they never wash their bodies or cut their nails. Young girls wear their hair stuck together into knots, standing on end. Ides thought they looked like the European artists' stereotype of Envy. Women wear two braids hanging down on either side of their faces. Apparently the Buryats were not Lamaists. Ides claims they worship dead deer and sheep impaled on poles in front of their houses. They also have priests whom they sometimes kill, then bury with clothes and

[74] Avril, *op. cit.* (n. 20), pp. 181–82. In fact the Kalmuks were not Muslims.
[75] Witsen, *op. cit.* (n. 15), p. 194; Baddeley, *op. cit.* (n. 3), II, 159.
[76] For example, see Ides, *op. cit.* (n. 35), p. 10.
[77] *Ibid.*, pp. 98–99.
[78] Around 1652 the Russians pacified the Buryats and constructed the town of Irkutsk in their territory.

money, thus sending them ahead to pray for the people. Ides does not explain where the Buryats thought they were sending their priests.[79]

Both Ides and Brand describe their trip across Lake Baikal on sleds and both relate the legends about how dangerous it was to cross if you referred to it as a lake ("Ozero") rather than a sea. The lake reputedly avenged such insolence with violent storms. Ides tested the legend; he stopped in the middle, called for a large glass of sherry, and drank a toast to all good Christians and to his friends in Europe, calling upon the lake ("Ozero")—not the sea—as witness. He then finished the crossing in clear calm weather.[80]

Ides also briefly comments on the "Kirgizens" (Kirghiz), a warlike Turkish group which harassed Russian settlements in the Upper Yenisey valley. Ides decides they look like Kalmuks and share much of the Kalmuk language, although they also use words common to the Crimean Tartars which the Turks could understand.[81] Avril mentions another Turkic group, the "Yousbecs" (Uzbeks), but does not describe them.[82]

By the end of the century, the lands and peoples beyond China's inland frontiers were no longer unknown to European readers. Chinese and even some Russian descriptions were available, and still more important, several firsthand accounts by European travelers had been published. European readers initially may have been struck by the number and variety of peoples described in these accounts, but they may also have discerned many characteristics common to most of them. The many Tungusic forest tribes, for example, often far removed from one another, shared a remarkable number of characteristics and beliefs. Their means of livelihood, houses, diet, clothing, and even religion displayed many similarities. The same can be said for the even wider-ranging Mongols. Yurts seem to have been everywhere the same, as was their nomadism, dress, and food. The widespread acceptance of Tibetan Buddhism is particularly striking, as is its encouragement by the Manchu rulers of China. The most impressive differences between the peoples of Inner Asia are those between the tribes who lived near the Chinese frontier, and were thus heavily influenced by the Chinese, and the outlying tribes.

The seventeenth-century European travel accounts also provided eyewitness evidence for the spread of Russian power and influence across Siberia. By the end of the century the Russians controlled the major rivers, were settling on their banks, had built forts, trading posts, and towns, and were subjugating the native peoples. But the European reports show that China's

[79] *Op. cit.* (n. 35), pp. 32–34. See also Brand, *op. cit.* (n. 37), pp. 53–54. On the Buryats see Sebes, *op. cit.* (n. 5), pp. 15–17. This is perhaps a reference to the celestial ascent of the shamans, a belief common to shamanism. See Eliade, *op. cit.* (n. 39), p. 235.

[80] Ides, *op. cit.* (n. 35), pp. 36–38; Brand, *op. cit.* (n. 37), pp. 53–54. The natives on the shores call it the "Holy Sea" and make sacrifices to calm its waters. See Czaplicka, *op. cit.* (n. 55), p. 10.

[81] *Op. cit.* (n. 35), p. 100. The Kirghiz speak a Turkic language.

[82] *Op. cit.* (n. 20), p. 181.

new Manchu rulers were doing similar things in Manchuria, Mongolia, and Central Asia. At Nerchinsk in 1689 the two empires had to negotiate their differences and establish a frontier.

The effects of Chinese and Russian empire building can also be seen in the seventeenth-century European accounts. While 1700 is obviously too early to pronounce the death of steppe and forest nomadism, the impression conveyed by the late seventeenth-century accounts is that there were few Mongol or Tungusic tribes who were not claimed as vassals of either the Chinese emperor or the Russian tsar. Ides and Brand also describe some tribal chieftains who changed allegiances—as if they were forced to choose between overlords. To remain independent of both empires was apparently becoming very difficult and very rare.

2

TIBET

Tibet was still largely unknown to Europeans when the seventeenth century began. Apart from the fourteenth-century mention of it by Odoric of Podernone, the only description of Tibet published in Europe was Father Antonio Monserrate's brief account as summarized in Giovanni Battista Peruschi's *Informatione del regno et stato del Gran Re di Mogor* (Rome, 1597).[83] Among the Jesuits in the Mughul Empire Tibet was still identified with Marco Polo's Cathay, as was China, and it was to clarify this confusion that Bento de Goes was sent overland from India to China in 1603–7.[84] Even after it was clear to the Jesuits at the Mughul court that Cathay was China, the belief lingered that there had once been large Christian communities in Tibet. It was primarily to establish contact with these trans-Himalayan Christians that Father Antonio de Andrade journeyed across the mountains to Tsaparang on the upper Sutlej in western Tibet during 1624. He thus became the first European to visit Tibet, and the account of his journey, *Novo descobrimento do Gram Cathayo, ou reinos de Tibet* was published at Lisbon in 1626.[85] From the "King of Guge" in his capital of Tsaparang, Andrade received permission to establish a Christian mission providing he would return the following year. Andrade subsequently established a mission station in 1625 that endured for the next fifteen years. He and the other Jesuits who

---

[83] See *Asia,* I, 454–55.

[84] *Ibid.,* p. 278. See also E. Maclagan, *The Jesuits and the Great Mogul* (New York, 1972), pp. 335–42.

[85] For bibliographical details see above, pp. 338–39. For Andrade's journeys see Maclagan, *op. cit.* (n. 84), pp. 342–46; Giuseppe M. Toscano, *La prima missione cattolica nel Tibet* (Parma, 1951), pp. 41–48; and C. Wessels, *Early Jesuit Travellers in Central Asia, 1603–1721* (The Hague, 1924), pp. 43–68. For a swift survey of the missionaries in seventeenth-century Tibet see L. Petech (ed.), *I missionari italiani nel Tibet e nel Nepal* (7 vols.; Rome, 1952–56), I, xxiii–viii.

occasionally served there sent reports back to Europe, a few of which were published in letterbooks and with later editions of Andrade's original letter.[86]

Even after the mission in Tsaparang was closed, Jesuits from their station at Srinagar in Garhwal, on the route to Mana Pass, seem to have made occasional visits to Tibet. The Srinagar post, however, was closed in 1656. Meanwhile, from Bengal the Jesuits made several attempts to penetrate southern Tibet during the twenties and thirties, without much success.[87] No published descriptions of Tibet resulted from their efforts. In October, 1661, however, the Jesuits Johann Grueber and Albert d'Orville arrived in Lhasa, having traveled from Peking by way of Kokonor. They had been sent to explore the overland route between Peking and Agra in response to the increasing dangers from the Dutch along the sea routes. Grueber and D'Orville were probably the first Europeans to visit Lhasa and surely the first to describe it. They stayed only one month before moving on to Katmandu and Agra. D'Orville died at Agra in April, 1662; Grueber, accompanied by Heinrich Roth, a German Jesuit, continued the overland journey to Rome. They arrived in 1664. Grueber's report of his journey and his description of Tibet first appeared in Athanasius Kircher's *China illustrata* in 1667 and, somewhat expanded, in its French translation of 1670. In 1672 it appeared in Melchisédech Thévenot's collection of travels.[88]

Tibet, Andrade reports in his second published letter, embraces several separate kingdoms: "Cogue" (Guge or Guje), "Ladak" (Ladakh), "Mariul" (Maryul), "Rudok" (Rudoc), "Utsang" (U-Tsang), and two others to the east.[89] All these kingdoms, along with the Kingdom of "Sopo" (Sog-po, or Mongolia) which borders on China to the east and Muscovy to the West, comprise what Andrade calls "Grand Tartary." Despite the misleading title of his first published letter, *Novo descobrimento do Gram Cathayo, ou reinos de Tibet,* Andrade did not identify Tibet with Cathay. He thought, however, that Cathay was a great city near the Chinese border and subject to the King

---

[86] See above, p. 147. For translations of some of the Jesuit letters about Tibet not published in the seventeenth century see the appendices to Wessels, *op. cit.* (n. 85); H. Hosten (ed.), "A Letter of Father Francisco Godinho, S.J., from Western Tibet (Tsaparang, August 16, 1626)," *The Journal of the Asiatic Society of Bengal,* n.s., XXI (1925), pp. 49–73. For the history of the mission see Maclagan, *op. cit.* (n. 84), pp. 346–55, and Toscano, *op. cit.* (n. 85), who translated into Italian all the published reprints of Andrade and Godinho (Godin).

[87] Maclagan, *op. cit.* (n. 84), pp. 355–57. On the efforts of the Portuguese missionaries Estevão Casella and João Cabral see Wessels, *op. cit.* (n. 85), chap. v.

[88] See above, pp. 485–86. For Grueber's and D'Orville's journey see Maclagan, *op. cit.* (n. 84), pp. 357–58; Bruno Zimmel, "Der erste Bericht uber Tibets Hauptstadt Lhasa aus dem Jahre 1661," *Biblios* (Vienna), II (1953), 127–45; MacGregor, *op. cit.* (n. 65), chap. ii; Wessels, *loc. cit.* (n. 65).

[89] Toscano, *op. cit.* (n. 85), p. 104; F. M. E. Pereira (ed.), *O descobrimento do Tibet. Pelo . . . da Companhia de Iesu, 1624, narrado em duas cartas . . .* (Coimbra, 1921), p. 80. Toscano thinks the other two "kingdoms" were probably Khams and Amdo.

of "Sopo" (Mongolia).[90] Father Francisco Godinho (or François Godin) (1583–1633) distinguished Andrade's Tibet, which he called "Grand Tibet," from "Little Tibet," by which he probably meant Baltistan and other parts of Kashmir. He reports that "Little Tibet" had recently accepted Islam.[91] Grueber's romanizations vary; Guge is called Guge Chaparang, after the town of Tsaparang, and U-Tsang, Barantola or Lhasa, but he agrees with Andrade and Godinho that all of these provinces belong to Tibet.[92]

Andrade visited Tsaparang in the kingdom of Guge, which he describes as independent but frequently at war in Garhwal with Ladakh and with the raja of Srinagar. In fact, Guge had been a strong, independent kingdom during the eleventh century but had since that time usually been tributary to Ladakh. During the reigns of weak Ladakhi monarchs, however, Guge would sometimes rebel and reestablish its independence. One such time of independence lasted from 1560 until 1630, at the end of which period Andrade came to Tsaparang.[93] Grueber, in 1661, correctly reported that Guge again had become subordinate to Ladakh.[94]

Grueber and D'Orville did not visit Guge or Tsaparang; they traveled through U-Tsang and stayed for a month in Lhasa, which Grueber claims was governed by a Tartar king called the "Deva" (*sDe-pa,* regent). The "Grand Lama" (Dalai Lama), who lived secluded in his vast palace, was adored like a god; he had nothing to do with secular offices, although all the kings of Tartary were his subjects.[95] Elsewhere Grueber notes that Barantola or Lhasa was part of the great kingdom of "Tanguth" (Tangut) and subject to its ruler. He describes a former king of Tangut called "Han" who was so revered by the Tibetans that he was declared a saint after his death and was still worshipped like a god. Kircher also printed Grueber's sketch of the king's bust.[96] Grueber's king of Tangut was apparently a powerful Qŏsot ruler from the Kokonor region, named Gušri-Khan, who in 1640 militarily aided the Dalai Lama and thus gained political control over Lhasa and other parts of Tibet. He symbolically returned power to the Dalai Lama but exer-

[90] Toscano, *op. cit.* (n. 85), p. 105; Pereira (ed.), *op. cit.* (n. 89), p. 80. The publisher in Lisbon inserted Cathay into the title. For a modern map showing these kingdoms in relation to India see J. E. Schwartzberg (ed.), *A Historical Atlas of South Asia* (Chicago, 1978), p. 46, pl. VI.A.3.

[91] Toscano, *op. cit.* (n. 85), p. 151; Hosten, *loc. cit.* (n. 86), p. 65. Also see above, p. 403. The rulers of Ladakh did not accept Islam before 1665.

[92] Kircher, *op. cit.* (n. 65), p. 319.

[93] Toscano, *op. cit.* (n. 85), pp. 77–95. On the expansion of Ladakh in the seventeenth century see L. Petech, *The Kingdom of Ladakh, c. 950–1842 A.D.* (Rome, 1977), chap. v.

[94] Kircher, *op. cit.* (n. 65), p. 319. For Ladakh's efforts to remain independent of the Tibet-Mongol forces and the Mughuls see P. N. Chopra, *Ladakh* (New Delhi, 1980), pp. 26–28.

[95] Kircher, *op. cit.* (n. 65), pp. 70, 97, 100. The Dalai or "All-Embracing" Lama received his title around 1580 from Altan Khan, the Mongol prince. Grueber here refers to Ngowang Labzang Gyatso, the Great Fifth Dalai Lama, whom he calls "Lama Kongji." See MacGregor, *op. cit.* (n. 65), p. 53.

[96] Kircher, *op. cit.* (n. 65), pp. 93–95. See our pl. 385.

cised political control through a regent called the *sDe-pa*. Gušri-Khan died in 1654.[97]

The seventeenth-century travelers to Tibet were as awed by the beauty and dangers of the Himalayas as are modern visitors. Andrade's account of his first trip in 1624 is the most vivid. He seems to have felt some kinship with the pilgrims with whom he traveled up the Ganges, drinking in the beauty of the snowy peaks above them and of the river plunging over the falls below the trail, of clear waters and little flowers close by, and chanting "Ye Badrynateye ye" (*Jaya Bhadranātha jaya jaya,* or Hail, o Badrinath, hail, hail!).[98] Above Srinagar they crossed the river on a rope bridge—very difficult, Andrade reports—and at Badrinath he saw pilgrims at this Hindu shrine from all over India bathing in its hot and cold springs.[99] The climb from Badrinath over the Mana Pass which separates India from Tibet was much more difficult; on it he endured snowstorm and thirst and suffered from fatigue, snow blindness, frostbite, and probably altitude sickness. Still, he was able to observe the lake from which the Ganges originates and to enjoy the splendid view of the Tibetan plateau from the north side of the pass—the first European to have seen these things.[100] The description of Godinho's trip two years later is much briefer. He too describes the peaks and precipices, the foaming river, the snow, the many streams and rivulets, and the beautiful flowers which appeared wherever the snow had melted. Godinho, however, seems to have traveled another route: from Delhi to Simla and over Niti Pass to Chini on the Sutlej and from there upstream to Tsaparang. He does not mention the temples and springs of Badrinath; nor does he seem to have suffered from the excessive fatigue experienced by Andrade. Instead he reports many marshes and a rocky path along the river sometimes scarcely visible above its waters—features not mentioned by Andrade. That he called the river Ganges, however, is confusing, although later Europeans also thought the Sutlej was a branch of the Ganges.[101] Grueber and D'Orville traveled through Tibet by entirely different routes. From Peking they traveled by way of Sian to Hsi-ning, twice crossing the Yellow River. Grueber depicts the river valley beyond the Great Wall as pleasant country, green during parts of the year, and well populated. Crossing the desert to Tibet was another matter. Here there are only sterile mountains and dry sandy plains. The desert is vast, Grueber reports, and

[97] Zimmel, *loc. cit.* (n. 88), pp. 137–39; R. Grousset, *The Empire of the Steppes,* trans. N. Walford (New Brunswick, N.J., 1970), pp. 522–25.

[98] Pereira (ed.), *op. cit.* (n. 89), p. 48; Toscano, *op. cit.* (n. 85), pp. 51.

[99] Pereira (ed.), *op. cit.* (n. 89), pp. 51–54; Toscano, *op. cit.* (n. 85), pp. 54–57.

[100] Pereira (ed.), *op. cit.* (n. 89), pp. 54–58; Toscano, *op. cit.* (n. 85), pp. 58–63. Andrade is correct. This is the large glacial pool from which the Ganges originates. According to Father Heinrich Roth, as reported by Kircher, there was a large lake in Tibet which gave rise to several of Asia's greatest rivers: the Ganges, the Ravi, and the Atech. See Kircher, *op. cit.* (n. 65), p. 67.

[101] Toscano, *op. cit.* (n. 85), pp. 148–49; Hosten, *loc. cit.* (n. 86), pp. 62–64.

called by many names.[102] About the southward journey from Lhasa across the Himalayas to Katmandu, Grueber reports disappointingly little, even though his route must have taken him near Mount Everest and through some of the world's most spectacular scenery. It took four days from Lhasa for them to reach the foot of the mountains and a month to reach the first Nepalese village. All he reports is that the mountains are so high that it is difficult to breathe on their heights because the air is too thin. Worse still, the winded climbers dared not rest much because of the venomous plants which exhale a dangerous odor. South of the pass, however, they enjoy clear streams and springs and an abundance of fresh fish.[103]

Grueber reports nothing about the geography or climate of Lhasa and its environs, but Andrade describes that of Guge and Tsaparang in adequate detail. Tibet, the Portuguese claims, produces plenty of fruits, rice, and other grains, but the region around Tsaparang is the most sterile part of the country. It is treeless and barren, except where the land is watered by a stream or springs. A little grain grows near the river, and the people raise sheep, goats, and horses, but no melons, fruits, vegetables, or poultry. There are many clear streams and springs, however, because of the heavy winter snows and frequent summer showers. Life is hard; the people of Tsaparang commonly remark that they live on the edge of disaster.[104] Although Tsaparang stands at 31° or 32° of latitude (actually 31°29′) it is nonetheless very cold, Andrade reports, because of the altitude.[105] In the winter months, for example, the communion wine has to be warmed before pouring it into the chalice to prevent it from freezing. The people butcher their livestock around the first of November because there is no forage for the animals during the winter. Meat can be preserved without smoking or salting because it becomes so solidly frozen.[106] Many necessities of life must be brought in from India or China. Caravans from India arrive every year—the missionaries frequently travel with them—and also from China. Andrade reports meeting twelve Chinese merchants on his first visit to Tsaparang.[107]

Upon his arrival at Tsaparang in 1624 Andrade is received by the king of Guge. After some initial difficulties in explaining his mission, apparently aggravated by a Muslim interpreter, he is amicably and generously treated by the king and queen and by the people of Tsaparang. He, in turn, finds the Tibetans "good natured" and "inclined to things of the spirit." He also describes them as brave, well trained for war, and with a strong aversion to Islam. They wear woolen clothes and well-made leather boots. Their hats

---

[102] Kircher, *op. cit.* (n. 65), pp. 88–89, 91–92. Also see text at note 66, above.
[103] Kircher, *op. cit.* (n. 65), p. 89. On the route see n. 65, above, and Zimmel, *loc. cit.* (n. 88), p. 144.
[104] Pereira (ed.), *op. cit.* (n. 89), pp. 69–70; Toscano, *op. cit.* (n. 85), pp. 70–71.
[105] This is about the latitude of El Paso, Texas.
[106] Pereira (ed.), *op. cit.* (n. 89), p. 91; Toscano, *op. cit.* (n. 85), p. 120.
[107] Pereira (ed.), *op. cit.* (n. 89), p. 72; Toscano, *op. cit.* (n. 85), p. 76.

are like those worn by Portuguese soldiers.[108] Andrade sees no great difference between the people of the various kingdoms or provinces of Tibet. Their languages are similar and they are devoted to the same religion.[109] But the Tibetans are certainly different from their southern neighbors. Godinho, for example, describes the people of Chamdo as scarcely human. They are, he asserts, ugly, misshapen, filthy, monsters of vice; they eat raw animals and have no notion of God or any superior being. They are kind to travelers, however.[110] Grueber considers the women of Nepal to be so ugly that they resemble the devil. They never wash in water because of their religion, but use a strong-smelling oil which disfigures them and gives off a foul odor. They also abandon their terminally ill in fields or ditches.[111]

To the Jesuits the most important distinguishing characteristic of the Tibetan people was their piety and devotion to religion. Most of Andrade's published report has to do with religion, and it occupies a large place in Grueber's account as well. Probably because they were convinced that Tibet had once been Christian, the Jesuits' description of Tibetan Buddhism (Lamaism) was much more perceptive and sympathetic than anything their confreres wrote about Chinese Buddhism. They readily saw traces of Christianity in Tibetan beliefs and worship. Andrade, for example, thought their reverence for the three precious things—the Buddha, the Doctrine, and the community of monks—was reminiscent of the Christian trinity: God the Father, the Son or Eternal Word, and the Holy Spirit which dwells with the church. One statue, probably of Prajñaparamita or of Tara, was called the Mother of God—obviously the Virgin Mary.[112] Another of an angel (*lha,* a god of the sky) wearing a breastplate, carrying a sword, and threatening a devil under his feet, Andrade thought must be Saint Michael.[113] He also found that they practiced confession, used holy water, and performed certain ablutions which he thought represented Christian baptism.[114] Grueber observes that many Tibetan rituals and chants resemble those of the Catholic church, which similarities he ascribes to the devil's perverse cleverness.[115] He also thought he saw many vestiges of Prester John's rule in Lhasa, the most obvious among them the extreme reverence paid to the Dalai Lama.[116]

One measure of Tibetan piety was the esteem in which the people held

---

[108] Pereira (ed.), *op. cit.* (n. 89), pp. 67–71; Toscano, *op. cit.* (n. 85), pp. 68–71, 105.

[109] Pereira (ed.), *op.cit.* (n. 89), p. 80; Toscano, *op. cit.* (n. 85), p. 105.

[110] Hosten (ed.), *loc. cit.* (n. 86), pp. 64–65; Toscano, *op. cit.* (n. 85), pp. 150–51.

[111] Kircher, *op. cit.* (n. 65), pp. 102–3.

[112] Pereira (ed.), *op. cit.* (n. 89), pp. 71, 95–96; Toscano, *op. cit.* (n. 85), pp. 74, 122–23.

[113] Pereira (ed.), *op. cit.* (n. 89), p. 83; Toscano, *op. cit.* (n. 85), p. 110. The description suggests one or another of the protective deities.

[114] Pereira (ed.), *op. cit.* (n. 89), pp. 71–72; Toscano, *op. cit.* (n. 85), pp. 74–75.

[115] Kircher, *op. cit.* (n. 65), p. 100.

[116] *Ibid.*, p. 70. *Cf.* Andrew Athapilly, "An Indian Prototype for Prester John," *Terrae incognitae,* X (1978), 15–23.

their religious leaders, the lamas. Andrade describes people flocking around a lama asking him for a blessing as he walks through the streets. The lama, he reports, would lay his hand on the peoples' bared heads, which everyone believed pardoned them of sins. Lamas who had been to the southern province of U-Tsang, where there was a sort of university, were honored above the others.[117] Andrade does not describe the lamas as simple idolators or charlatans; he reports that they are celibate and live good lives. Some live in communities under a superior, some live privately in their own houses. They all profess poverty and live from charity, even those who might have been from rich families. They are kept busy studying their sacred books, handing down their legends, and praying—especially praying. Andrade reports that the lamas spend two hours each morning and two hours each evening in prayer.[118] Grueber describes and sketches a Tibetan prayer wheel, probably the first depicted in Western literature.[119]

The lamas dress in red woolen robes, similar to European cassocks, but without sleeves. They are tied around the waist with a long piece of cloth, the ends of which almost touch the ground. Their mantles vary in length and are either yellow or red. Ordinary monks wear hats like Capuchins; high lamas are distinguished by hats shaped like a bishop's mitre and closed at the top.[120] Ordination, Godinho reports, consists simply of investing the candidate with his lama robes.[121] There are many lamas. Andrade, for example, counts fifteen hundred of them in Toling where he accompanied the king on a pilgrimage.[122] Apparently some effort is taken to restrict their numbers; he reports that no man with two or more sons might become a lama. The king of Guge's brother is a lama.[123]

Grueber reports that the Grand Lama in Lhasa is called "eternal and heavenly father" and is adored like a god. All the kings of Tartary are his subjects; all bring him homage and rich gifts. No one but the lamas in the Potala Palace ever see him, but his statue stands at the entrance to the palace, always illuminated, and the people prostrate themselves before it as if he were

[117]Pereira (ed.), *op. cit.* (n. 89), pp. 86–87; Toscano, *op. cit.* (n. 85), pp. 115, 127n. Lamaseries were the universities and colleges, the only purveyors of higher education in the arts and sciences.

[118]Pereira (ed.), *op. cit.* (n. 89), pp. 70–71, 80–81; Toscano, *op. cit.* (n. 85), pp. 72–74, 105–6.

[119]Kircher, *op. cit.* (n. 65), p. 93; Zimmel, *loc. cit.* (n. 88), pp. 143–44. See our pl. 375.

[120]Pereira (ed.), *op. cit.* (n. 89), p. 81; Toscano, *op. cit.* (n. 85), p. 107. The yellow and red monks are respectively of the Gelukpa and non-Gelukpa sects, commonly but erroneously referred to as reformed and non-reformed. For depictions of the lamas' headgear see Tucci, *op. cit.* (n. 61), pp. 123, 124, 133, 136.

[121]Hosten (ed.), *loc. cit.* (n. 86), p. 69; Toscano, *op. cit.* (n. 85), p. 152. On ordination see Tucci, *op. cit.* (n. 61), pp. 17–18; on ceremonial robes see *ibid.*, pp. 140–41.

[122]Pereira (ed.), *op. cit.* (n. 89), pp. 83–84; Toscano, *op. cit.* (n. 85), pp. 111–12. Toling was the site of a famous temple in Guge.

[123]Pereira (ed.), *op. cit.* (n. 89), p. 71; Toscano, *op. cit.* (n. 85), pp. 72–74. On the large numbers of monasteries and monks see Stein, *op. cit.* (n. 61), pp. 139–40.

present. According to Grueber, even the Dalai Lama's urine and excrement are considered holy; people mix them with their food to ward off diseases. When the Dalai Lama dies, Grueber reports, the lamas search the kingdom for someone who resembles him and secretly put him on the throne.[124] Grueber sketched both the statue of the Dalai Lama and the Potala Palace, both of which were printed in Kircher's *China illustrata*. His picture of the Potala was reproduced in countless other European travel books; indeed it became the West's only picture of Lhasa and the Potala Palace until the beginning of the twentieth century.[125]

Andrade describes many Tibetan rituals and ceremonies in detail. He reports that the lamas fast two days per year. During the great fast called "Nhuna" (Tibetan, *nyung-ne,* the Indian Buddhist *posadha* fast), they eat only once during the day, drink no tea, and speak only by signs or through clenched teeth and unopened mouths. On the other, "ordinary," fast day they eat meat only once; tea and other foods are permitted.[126] Calls to prayer are sounded by trumpets, some of which are made of metal while others are made from human arm or leg bones. Lamas also use human skulls as crowns and as ritual vessels. The king's lama-brother explains to Andrade that the bones invoke thoughts of death and of the transitory nature of life and thus help the lamas live better.[127] According to Andrade, the temples are open to the public only twice a year, on which days the people walk around them three times, praying, before they enter to do reverence to all the images. The lamas, however, are always in the temples, even eating and sleeping there during the winter months.[128] Andrade also describes solemn disputations held by the lamas, after which the young lamas go to their rooms and dance, dressed in Chinese robes, crowns on their heads, tambourines or sticks in their hands. The king's brother explains to the astonished Andrade that the young lamas are imitating angels, observing that the Christian angels in Andrade's nativity scenes also danced.[129]

The Tibetans frequently talk about angels, called *lha,* which they depict in various ways, sometimes young and beautiful, sometimes savage or hor-

[124] Kircher, *op. cit.* (n. 65), pp. 97–100. Grueber has this wrong. They looked for a baby who was his reincarnation, not for one who resembled him. Nor was the new Dalai Lama's enthronement secret, although many searches and recognitions were. The fifth Dalai Lama (1617–82) was the first to assume political supremacy. See Tucci, *op. cit.* (n. 61), p. 41. The French physician Bernier also described the selection of the new Dalai Lama, although he never visited Tibet. See above, p. 734.

[125] Kircher, *op. cit.* (n. 65), p. 100. On the Potala see Zimmel, *loc. cit.* (n. 88), pp. 135–37. See our pl. 384.

[126] Pereira (ed.), *op. cit.* (n. 89), p. 89; Toscano, *op. cit.* (n. 85), pp. 107–8.

[127] Pereira (ed.), *op. cit.* (n. 89), p. 82; Toscano, *op. cit.* (n. 85), p. 108. On the role of bones in rituals see R. de Nebesky-Wojkowitz, *Oracles and Demons of Tibet* (The Hague, 1956), p. 345.

[128] Pereira (ed.), *op. cit.* (n. 89), p. 82; Toscano, *op. cit.* (n. 85), p. 108. On lay participation in religious festivals see Tucci, *op. cit.* (n. 61), pp. 150–51.

[129] Pereira (ed.), *op. cit.* (n. 89), pp. 82–83; Toscano, *op. cit.* (n. 85), p. 109. On the religious dances of Lamaism see Stein, *op. cit.* (n. 61), pp. 189–90. See also René de Nebesky-Wojkowitz, *Tibetan Religious Dances,* ed. Christoph von Fürer-Haimendorf (The Hague, 1976).

rible. Andrade perceptively notes that these pictures do not represent their essence but only their responses to malignant spirits or demons.[130] The Tibetan angels are divided into nine orders, which remind Andrade of the scriptural nine choirs of angels.[131]

Andrade describes a monthly procession intended to exorcize malignant spirits, during which the lamas wear masks over their mouths to prevent the spirits from entering.[132] Another ceremony invokes the *lha* of the city for help against enemies, and still another annual ceremony is held to consecrate holy water. According to Andrade, there is a ritual intended to prevent demons from entering into black animals, which they are thought to prefer.[133] To protect babies from demons or evil spirits Tibetans often give them despicable names such as Dog, Mouse, or Cold Wind.[134] Grueber describes a ritual in which a man is chosen by the lamas, armed, and sent out to kill people randomly in the streets. No one resists him, and the dead are consecrated to the god "Manipe."[135]

The lamas are consulted on all important matters. They divine for the king before battle, and they offer something to the *lha* of a mountain for travelers who must pass that way. They recite prayers through clenched teeth and closed mouths for sick animals, and physicians call on them to help cure the sick by praying and by blowing on the affected parts. According to Andrade, the Tibetans followed three ways of disposing of the dead. The lamas determine which is the appropriate method according to the star in ascendancy at the time of death. Some are buried with pyramid-shaped monuments marking their graves. Others are cremated, and their ashes, mixed with clay, are shaped into the little images used in swearing oaths. In the third and most desirable kind of funeral, the lamas carry the body to a distant place, where it is fed to a certain white bird about the size of a crane. All three varieties of funerals are intended for people whose lives have been good and without scandal. The remains of wicked or immoral people are cut into pieces and thrown to the dogs. Children mourn their parents for one year, during which time they wear their clothes inside out and go bareheaded with their hair untied.[136] Lamas, Andrade reports, are buried, sitting up, in large coffins. To remain sitting after death without falling is considered a sign of virtue. To increase the likelihood that they will die in that

[130] On pictorial representation as a religious act see Stein, *op. cit.* (n. 61), pp. 281–82.

[131] Pereira (ed.), *op. cit.* (n. 89), p. 83; Toscano, *op. cit.* (n. 85), pp. 109–10. On the various types of *lha* related to personal and household protection see Tucci, *op. cit.* (n. 61), p. 187.

[132] On masks (*'bag*) and their role in Lamaism see Stein, *op. cit.* (n. 61), pp. 189–90.

[133] Pereira (ed.), *op. cit.* (n. 89), pp. 84–86; Toscano, *op. cit.* (n. 85), pp. 112–15.

[134] Pereira (ed.), *op. cit.* (n. 89), p. 90; Toscano, *op. cit.* (n. 85), p. 119.

[135] Kircher, *op. cit.* (n. 65), pp. 94–95. Grueber's "Manipe" probably refers to *manipadme*, part of a mantra which Tibetans so frequently invoke that foreigners might think it to be a name. On murder as ritualistic exorcism see Tucci, *op. cit.* (n. 61), pp. 185–87, 205; on murder to end vendettas see Stein, *op. cit.* (n. 61), p. 135.

[136] Pereira (ed.), *op. cit.* (n. 89), pp. 87–89; Toscano, *op. cit.* (n. 85), pp. 115–18.

position the lamas sleep sitting up on small mats. Andrade suspects, however, that it is not virtue but the cold which enables them to remain sitting after death.[137]

Andrade also concludes that in addition to belief in God, some residual belief in the Trinity, belief in angels, and similarities between some lamaist rituals and chants and those of the Catholic church, the Tibetans believe in a heaven for those who die without sins and a hell for the wicked. Most people, however, are reincarnated after death, their form depending on their moral conduct while alive.[138] Andrade is also convinced that the Tibetans possess a sense of sin and of God's forgiveness. When he asked a lama how men, having sinned, could live at peace with God, the lama responds that the remedy lay in repeating "Om-mani-patmeonri" (*Om ma ni pad me hum hrih*). This repetition of the six or seven sacred syllables (the final *hrih* being optional) Andrade had heard thousands of times in Tibet. Although the lamas could not tell him exactly what it meant, Andrade concludes, after considerable discussion, that it means "Forgive me O Lord of my sins." In fact, he told the king's brother to think of that when he prayed, rather than simply to recite meaningless words like a parrot.[139] Grueber, however, probably because he frequently heard the formula repeated before images, decides it is a prayer to "Manipe," the Tibetans' chief idol.[140] He made two sketches of the figure he took to be "Manipe," one with nine heads arranged pyramidically.[141] (See pls. 386–87).

Andrade had high hopes for the mission in Tsaparang. Tibetan piety and the residual Christian elements in their religion he thought would make them easy to convert. He notes with satisfaction the reverence with which the king and queen and the people honor the crucifix and the Christian images during his first visit, and he describes the generosity of the king and even the lamas in the building of his church.[142] Nevertheless, the mission

[137] Pereira (ed.), *op. cit.* (n. 89), p. 91; Toscano, *op. cit.* (n. 85), pp. 119–20. On traditional practices of disposing of the dead see Stein, *op. cit.* (n. 61), pp. 201–2; and G. Bell, *The People of Tibet* (Oxford, 1928), chap. xxvii.

[138] Pereira (ed.), *op. cit.* (n. 89), pp. 97–98; Toscano, *op. cit.* (n. 85), pp. 126–27, 151; Hosten (ed.), *loc. cit.* (n. 86), p. 66.

[139] Pereira (ed.), *op. cit.* (n. 89), pp. 102–3; Toscano, *op. cit.* (n. 85), pp. 130–32. The prayer or incantation (mantra) is proper to Avalokitésvara, the bodhisattva of mercy, protector of Tibet, who is incarnate in the Dalai Lama. Literally it means "Om, o holder of jewel and lotus, hūm," *om* and *hūm* being untranslatable mantric syllables. Matthew Kapstein of the Department of South Asian Languages and Civilizations, the University of Chicago, contends that the common Western translation—"o, jewel in the lotus"—is a Western error (personal communication). For a discussion of its meaning see Toscano, *op. cit.* (n. 85), pp. 130–32n; and Zimmel, *loc. cit.* (n. 88), p. 143n. Also see C. Eliot, *Hinduism and Buddhism* (3 vols.; London, 1954), III, 395–96.

[140] Kircher, *op. cit.* (n. 65), pp. 95–96.

[141] *Ibid.*, p. 98. Zimmel, *loc. cit.* (n. 88), pp. 142–43, suggests that Grueber's sketch is of one of the so-called demon princes. More likely, however, it is the eleven-headed Avalokitésvara with the two backward-facing heads not showing. Also *cf.* Eliot, *op. cit.* (n. 139), III, 382–83.

[142] Pereira (ed.), *op. cit.* (n. 89), pp. 64–67, 107–16; Toscano, *op. cit.* (n. 85), pp. 66–68, 135–44.

practically ended in 1630 after the death of Andrade's protector and Ladhak's subjugation of Guge.[143] From this brief Jesuit mission, however, and from Grueber and D'Orville's later visit to Lhasa, came Europe's first significant glimpse into the land on the roof of the world. Much is missing. None of the seventeenth-century reports describe Tibet's political role, language, secular learning, money, economy, social structure, or family life. Nevertheless, the image of Tibet presented to seventeenth-century European readers by Andrade, Godinho, and Grueber, while incomplete, was perceptively and sympathetically drawn and for the most part accurate.

3

KOREA

Korea was known to sixteenth-century European readers through the reports of Jesuit missionaries in Japan and China. Father Gregorio de Cespedes was apparently the first European actually to visit Korea when he accompanied Hideyoshi's troops in 1593 during the Japanese invasion. Apart from reports about the fighting and complaints about the cold weather, however, neither he nor the other Japan Jesuits wrote much about Korea.[144] The Jesuits in China also reported Hideyoshi's invasion, primarily because the Chinese emperor's decision to aid his Korean vassal occasioned heavy new taxes and a wave of intense xenophobia in China, all of which hampered the Jesuit mission.[145] Trigault later reported on the general rejoicing in China at the news of the Japanese defeat, Hideyohsi's death, and the cancellation of the new war taxes.[146] Very little description of Korea accompanied these reports, however.

The Jesuit missionaries in Peking had occasional contacts with Korean envoys during the seventeenth century. Ricci's world map and other of his Chinese writings were taken back to Seoul by returning envoys in 1608.[147] More Western books followed. In 1630, for example, the Korean envoy Chŏng Tu-wŏn returned with books on astronomy, on the calendar, and on geography as well as a telescope, an alarm clock, and a cannon, which he presented to the king.[148] Crown Prince Sohyŏn, who had been taken as a

---

[143] See Maclagan, *op. cit.* (n. 84), pp. 348–62, and Toscano, *op. cit.* (n. 85), pp. 154–96.

[144] For sixteenth-century European information about Korea see *Asia*, I, 223–26, 308–9, 719–22. See also R. M. Cory, "Some Notes on Father Gregorio de Cespedes, Korea's First European Visitor," *JRAS, Korean Branch*, XXVII (1937), 1–55; and J. H. Grayson, *Early Buddhism and Christianity in Korea* (Leyden, 1985), pp. 70–71.

[145] For example, see Froes in *PP*, XII, 263–64; Longobardo in *PP*, XII, 318, 327–28; Pantoja in *PP*, XII, 403–4; Trigault in Gallagher (trans.), *op. cit.* (n. 4), pp. 260–99.

[146] Gallagher (trans.), *op. cit.* (n. 4), pp. 319–20.

[147] Woo-keun Han, *The History of Korea* (Honolulu, 1971), p. 318; Gari Ledyard, *The Dutch Come to Korea* (Seoul, 1971), p. 103; Ledyard's book also contains a reprint of the 1704 Churchill (*CV*) translation of Hamel's *Journael*.

[148] Han, *op. cit.* (n. 147), p. 318. Also see Grayson, *op. cit.* (n. 144), p. 65.

hostage by the Manchus during their 1636 Korean campaign, was brought to Peking in 1644, where he met Adam Schall. When Sohyŏn returned to Seoul later that year he carried with him scientific and religious books, maps, a globe, and several Christian Chinese servants—all gifts from Schall. Schall obviously hoped for an entrée into the Hermit Kingdom; however, he was frustrated by Sohyŏn's death shortly after the prince's return to Seoul. Subsequent Korean envoys nonetheless continued to visit the Jesuits in Peking.[149]

Brief notices about Korea appeared in other publications of the China Jesuits during the seventeenth century; those in Martino Martini's works were the most extensive.[150] In his *De bello tartarico* (1654) he reported the 1627 Manchu invasion of Korea.[151] Martini's *Novus atlas sinensis* (1655) contains a map and the most detailed Jesuit description of Korea to appear during the seventeenth century. It was obviously derived from Chinese sources.[152]

Martini's account of Korean geography is quite accurate. He plainly asserts that Korea is a peninsula, not an island, joined to "Niuche" (Manchuria) on the north and separated from it in the northwest by the river Yalu. He correctly names and locates the eight provinces of Yi dynasty Korea in almost recognizable romanizations, but he incorrectly calls P'yŏngyang the capital.[153] Martini also names what his Chinese sources considered to be several important mountains and rivers. The name Korea, Martini reports, came from the Japanese; the Chinese geographers called it "Chaosien" (Chao-hsien). He traces Korea's relationship to China all the way back to the founding of the Chou dynasty in 1121 B.C., when Wu Wang granted it in fief to "Kicius" (Korean, Ki-ja), a relative of the Shang emperors.[154] It was first called Chao-hsien (Chosŏn in Korean) by the Han emperors, who maintained a presence on the peninsula. Once having slipped out of Chinese control after the fall of the Han dynasty, it was reclaimed as a vassal state by the T'ang (A.D. 618–907). Martini reports nothing about the

---

[149] Ledyard, *op. cit.* (n. 147), pp. 103–4; Han, *op. cit.* (n. 147), pp. 318–19. See also Andreas Choi, *L'Érection du premier vicariat apostolique et les origines du Catholisme en Corée, 1592–1837* (Schöneck-Beckenried, 1961), pp. 1–14.

[150] For Martini's publications, see above, pp. 479–82, 525–27.

[151] Martini, *op. cit.* (n. 28), pp. 260–65.

[152] Martini, *op. cit.* (n. 17), pp. 207–9.

[153] P'yŏngyang had been the ancient seat of Chinese power in Korea, the capital of the Koguryŏ state (37 B.C.–A.D. 667), and a subordinate capital of Koryŏ (A.D. 918–1392). In 1392 the founder of the Yi dynasty moved the capital to Hanyang or Seoul. In 1413 the country was divided into eight provinces: Hamgil, P'yŏngan, Hwanghae, Kangwŏn, Kyŏnggi, Ch'ungch'ŏng, Kyŏngsang, and Chŏlla. These remained Korea's major administrative divisions until the late nineteenth century. For a map of the provinces and the regional military commands (fifteenth century) see Ki-Baik Lee, *A New History of Korea*, trans. E. M. Wagner and E. J. Shultz (Cambridge, Mass., 1984), p. 177.

[154] See Cornelius Osgood, *The Koreans and Their Culture* (New York, 1951), pp. 161–63, for the Ki-ja foundation myth. Also see W. E. Henthorn, *A History of Korea* (New York, 1971), p. 233.

fortunes of Korea during the Sung and Yüan dynasties (907–1368), but notes that its king voluntarily became a vassal of the Hung-wu emperor at the founding of the Ming dynasty (1368–1644) and consequently received a gold seal from the Chinese emperor. Since then, Korea remained a tributary state and its new kings were required to travel in person to Peking to render homage to the emperor.[155] Martini also mentions a Korean rebellion in 1651 over the Ch'ing requirement that they wear the queue and Manchu clothing.

Martini describes Korea as a fertile land which produces everything its people need. It especially abounds in rice and wheat, but Martini also lists fruits, especially pears, as well as ginseng and pearls. Koreans, he reports, make several kinds of paper, good writing brushes from wolf's hair, and unusually fine lacquer, all products much in demand by China. Gold and silver are to be found in Korea's mountains. According to Martini, Korea is heavily populated and boasts many large cities; he does not state exactly how many. Despite all this wealth and population, or possibly because of it, Korea has no relations with any people other than the Chinese and Japanese.

Korean cities, Martini writes, are built like Chinese cities. In fact, he reports that the structure and practice of Korea's government resembles China's, as does Korean clothing, language, writing, manners, ceremonies, and religion. Korean women, however, are not as secluded as their Chinese counterparts; Martini notes that they are frequently seen in public and in the company of men. Furthermore, he believes that Korean young people are able to choose marriage partners without the permission of their parents or relatives.[156] They can do so, he writes, because Korean women are more forthright than Chinese women, whose greater seclusion and sense of decorum might prevent them from refusing an undesirable proposal. Martini also reports some difference between Korean and Chinese funeral practices. Koreans keep the bodies of their dead relatives tightly sealed in beautifully decorated coffins for three years before burial.[157] Both Martini's account of the 1627 Manchu invasion and his general description of Korea were included in Johann Nieuhof's description of China.[158]

Although it contains some sound geographical and historical information, Martini's description is overgeneralized and in some places inaccurate; it betrays Martini's dependence on biased Chinese sources. In 1668, however, independent firsthand information about Korea finally became available to European readers through the account of Hendrik Hamel's shipwreck and his thirteen years of captivity in Korea. He and the other ship-

[155] Crown princes, not kings, were sent as hostages to Peking. They stayed there until they became kings.
[156] Very unlikely.
[157] Probably an error. See below, p. 1790.
[158] Johann Nieuhof, *Het gezantschap der Neerlandtsche Oost-Indische Compagnie aan den grooten Tartarischen cham, den tegenwoord keizer van China . . . sedert den jaaren 1655 tot 1657 . . .* (Amsterdam, 1665), II, 201–2, 206–8.

wrecked Dutch sailors were almost the only seventeenth-century Europeans to have visited Korea, and his *Journael* was the only eyewitness account of the Hermit Kingdom published during the century.[159] Unfortunately Hamel was not an urbane, cultured Jesuit: he was an ordinary, young, and largely uneducated Dutch sailor. His long residence in Korea afforded him marvelous opportunities to observe Korean society both in the capital and in the provinces, but his powers of critical perception and his literary abilities were severely limited. He knew very little about China and thus was unable to compare Korea with the empire. Nor did he gain a comprehensive view of, for example, Korean government or religion. He merely described—all too briefly in most cases—what he saw and experienced, whether or not he understood it. On the other hand, his account is honest and accurate; in many places it is supported by Korean sources. He did not try to relate what he saw to some preconceived ideal or bias. In fact, he displayed virtually no bitterness over his long captivity. His story, therefore, is a very useful and accurate description of Korea as seen by an outsider, from the bottom rather than the top of the social scale.[160]

Hamel's remarks about Korean geography complement Martini's. He, too, recognizes Korea as a peninsula, "Join'd to [Manchuria] on the north by a long and high mountain, which is all that hinders Corea's being an island." He does not mention the Yalu. Koreans, he writes, call their country "Tiozencouk" (Chosŏn) or "*Caoli*" and represent its shape as a "long square, like a playing card." It extends from 34° to 44° north latitude, about 150 leagues, and is about 75 leagues wide from east to west. Korea's coastline, Hamel reports, is rocky and dangerous, with some points of land running far out into the sea. He estimates only 25 leagues separate "Pousan" (Pusan) in the southeast from Japan, with the island of "Suissima" (Tsushima) in between. What he calls the Bay of Nanking—the Yellow Sea—divides Korea from China. Most travelers to China cross it in preference to the overland route. Hamel reports that fishermen on the northeast coast frequently catch whales with Dutch or French harpoons in them and that they regularly catch herring like those found in the North Sea, all of which argues, he believes, for an ocean passage north of Siberia.[161]

Korean winters are cold, especially in the north. The northern part of the Yellow Sea, for example, freezes solidly enough for it to become the winter

[159] For Hamel's experiences and the bibliographic details of his book see above, pp. 486–88.

[160] For evaluations see B. Hoetink (ed.), *Verhaal van het vergaan van het jacht "De Sperwer" en van het wedervaren der schipbreukelingen op het eiland Quelpaert en het vasteland van Korea (1653–1666) met eene beschrijving van dat rijk* ("WLV," XVIII; The Hague, 1920), pp. 119–32, and Ledyard, *op. cit.* (n. 147), pp. 121–27. Cf. Robert Knox's more sophisticated account of Ceylon as summarized above, pp. 958–93.

[161] Ledyard, *op. cit.* (n. 147), pp. 205–6. For a good brief discussion on Korea in European maps and atlases during the seventeenth century see Hermann Lautensach, *Korea: A Geography Based on the Author's Travels and Literature,* trans. and ed. by Katherine and Eckart Sege (New York, 1988), pp. 41–42.

route to China.[162] Even in "Sior" (Seoul) the river was frozen over so completely in late November, 1653, that three hundred heavily laden horses crossed it safely.[163] During a visit to a mountain monastery in 1662, the snow fell so deep that the monks dug tunnels between buildings and wore small boards as snowshoes to walk on its surface.[164]

Like Martini, Hamel reports that Korea is divided into eight provinces, but he does not name them. It includes 360 cities and towns, not counting forts and castles, all of which are in the mountains. He names all the cities and towns on the route between Cheju island and Seoul, about seventy-five leagues, but he describes none of them. Cheju, which the Dutch call Quelpaerts, is at 33°32' north latitude, about twelve or thirteen leagues south of Korea's southern tip. It is about fourteen or fifteen leagues in circumference and its coast is covered with rocks. There is a high, wooded mountain (probably Mt. Nalla, an extinct volcano) in the center of the island, with several smaller, treeless hills "embracing many vales, abounding in rice." The islanders also raise horses and cattle; they live poorly and are generally despised by mainland Koreans.[165]

Hamel reports that except for its northern provinces, "the Country is fruitful and produces all things necessary to support Life, especially Rice and other sorts of Grain." Hemp, cotton, silver, lead, tiger skins, ginseng root, horses, and cows he lists as other products of commercial value. He also mentions many wild animals and birds. He does not, however, mention gold, pearls, lacquer, paper, or writing brushes, and he reports that although the Koreans raised silkworms, "they know not how to work the silk."[166] No rice or cotton grows in the far north; the people there eat barley and make clothes from hemp and skins. Ginseng grows in the north, and constitutes a major article in Korea's trade with China and Japan. The Manchus also demand it as tribute.[167] According to Hamel, the Japanese taught the Koreans how to raise and use tobacco during the late sixteenth century, saying that it came from "Nampan Kouk" (Namp'an K'uk), the Japanese term for Portugal. Almost all Koreans smoke, even women and four- or five-year-old children.[168]

The Japanese at Pusan supply Korea with pepper, alum, buffalo horns, goatskins, and deerskins. Hamel knows there is also some trade between

---

[162] Ledyard, *op. cit.* (n. 147), p. 206. Korea, like north China, evidently was in a cold cycle. *Cf.* above, pp. 1574–75.

[163] Ledyard, *op. cit.* (n. 147), p. 188.

[164] *Ibid.*, p. 206.

[165] *Ibid.*, pp. 178, 184–85. Cheju island is also known to Koreans as *Samda-do,* a derogatory appellation which means an island abundant in three things: rocks, vermin, and wind.

[166] *Ibid.*, p. 207.

[167] *Ibid.*, pp. 206–7. Ginseng was considered to be a Korean state monopoly.

[168] *Ibid.*, p. 223. Today it is shameful for Korean women or youngsters to smoke. According to Henthorn, *op. cit.* (n. 154), p. 201, tobacco was introduced into Korea in 1621 through Pusan.

Korea and north China. But only rich merchants from Seoul trade directly with Peking, a commerce which he thought consisted chiefly of linen and cotton cloth. No other foreign trade is permitted. Nor does Hamel depict a robust domestic trade. Only the "great ones"—probably the learned aristocratic class called *yangban*—and wealthy merchants use money: copper cash is exchanged near the Chinese border and unminted silver elsewhere. Common people barter with rice and other commodities. Hamel does not describe Korean weights and measures, but observes that they are uniform for the entire kingdom. [169]

Despite his calling the land fruitful and productive, Hamel's image of the life of ordinary Koreans is one of hardship and poverty. During the drought and famine years from 1660 to 1662, for example, there is little to eat in Chŏlla Province. Many people survive solely on wild fruits and nuts, while others starve. Many turn to robbery, slaves revolt, and royal storehouses are looted. Early in 1663 the commander of Pyong'-yong distributes the remaining twenty-two Dutchmen to three separate villages because the local people can no longer provide rations for all of them. [170] Even before the famine, the Dutchmen found it impossible to survive on their rations and had obtained permission to beg in order to augment their income. Hamel thinks life in Korea was better before the Japanese and Manchu invasions. He judges the thrice-yearly tribute demanded by the Manchus to be particularly onerous, making it difficult for most people to survive during a poor year. [171]

The homes of the common people Hamel describes as "mean." They are small, one story and a garret high, and are "built with Wooden Posts or Pillars, with the intervals betwixt them fill'd up with stone up to the first Story, the rest of the Structure is all Wood daub'd without, and cover'd on the inside with White Paper glew'd on." [172] They are warm, however, having vaulted floors to permit fires underneath. He does not say what kind of fuel the Koreans use. Apparently there is some sort of sumptuary building code, since special permission is required for a tiled roof. Most houses, consequently, have thatched roofs. Hamel's description of nobles' houses is vague. They are "stately," he reports, having front apartments in which to entertain and lodge guests, gardens with covered walkways, fountains, fishponds, and secluded women's apartments. Merchants usually have storehouses attached to their living quarters. [173] Hamel also reports an abundance of "taverns and pleasure houses," but no hostels for travelers except the

---

[169] Ledyard, *op. cit.* (n. 147), pp. 223–24. On trade relations with Japan and Ch'ing China see Henthorn, *op. cit.* (n. 154), pp. 198–201; and K.-B. Lee, *op. cit.* (n. 153), pp. 229–30. On mediums of exchange see Henthorn, *op. cit.* (n. 154), pp. 168–69, 804.

[170] Ledyard, *op. cit.* (n. 147), pp. 193–94.

[171] *Ibid.*, p. 222.

[172] *Ibid.*, p. 216.

[173] *Ibid.*, pp. 216–17. Henthorn makes use of this description, *op. cit.* (n. 154), p. 198.

lodgings for officials on the great road to Seoul. Ordinary travelers sit down in front of the first house they come upon at nightfall, and its residents feel obliged to bring food out to them.[174]

Hamel reports virtually nothing about the appearance of the Koreans or their clothing. Concerning the first Koreans whom he met on Cheju island he merely notes that they are "clad after the Chinese fashion" except for hats made from horses' hair.[175] Although at first the castaways and the Koreans could not understand each other, the Koreans treated the Dutch well. The Koreans retrieved as much as they could from the wrecked ship and carefully sealed it in a tent while the Dutch looked on. Some Koreans caught stealing goods from the wreck were severely beaten. The governor of the island visited the Dutchmen each day and provided food and clothing for them.[176] In fact, the general impression conveyed by Hamel's narrative is that on the whole the Koreans were kind to the Dutch captives. Nevertheless in his general description of Koreans he presents them in an unattractive light:

The Coresians are very much addicted to stealing, and so apt to cheat and lye, that there is no trusting of them . . . Fraud is not infamous among them; . . . they are silly and credulous, and we might have made them believe any thing we would, because they are great lovers of Strangers, but chiefly the Religious Men. They are an effeminate People and shew very little Courage and Resolution . . . they are not asham'd of Cowardize, and lament the misfortune of those who must fight . . . They abhor Blood, and fly when they meet with any. They are much afraid of the Sick, and particularly those that have contagious Distempers.[177]

According to Hamel, the austerity imposed by Manchu tyranny had improved the morals of the Koreans: "Before the *Tartars* subdued this Kingdom, it was full of Luxury and Debauchery, the *Coresians'* whole business being eating and drinking, and giving themselves up to all *Leudness*."[178]

As Hamel describes them, Korean marriages were not as different from the Chinese practices as Martini had indicated. Children are married at eight or ten years of age, after which the couple live with the boy's parents until they are able to support themselves and maintain a home of their own; obviously these children did not choose their own mates.[179] Marriage ceremonies are simple. The groom, attended by his friends, rides on horseback to the bride's home, where he is received by her family; then he conveys the

---

[174] Ledyard, *op. cit.* (n. 147), p. 217.
[175] *Ibid.*, p. 177.
[176] *Ibid.*, pp. 178–79.
[177] *Ibid.*, pp. 221–22.
[178] *Ibid.*, p. 222.
[179] Early marriage was popular in Manchu times because married men were exempted from military service by the Manchus. Young boys were even married by older women to keep them out of service.

bride to his house. Men may divorce their wives at will; women may not divorce their husbands.[180] A man may keep as many concubines as he is able to afford, but only his wife may live at home with him. Noblemen, however, keep concubines in separate apartments in their houses; wives manage household affairs and exercise authority over the concubines. Hamel judges that Korean women are treated little better than slaves.[181] Nevertheless he reports that "there are virtuous Women among them, who are allow'd the liberty of seeing People, and going into Company, and to Feasts, but they sit by themselves, and opposite their Husbands."[182] This at least partially supports Martini's report.

"Parents are very indulgent to their children, and in return are much respected by them," Hamel observes. Among freemen and nobles, the concern for filial piety and funeral rites seem very much like those of the Chinese. Children mourn their parents for three years, during which time they live like monks: not holding any official position, wearing rough hempen mourning gowns, walking with a cane, never washing, and abstaining from sex. Hamel thinks mourners look like mulattoes from not washing, and he asserts that children born during the mourning period are considered illegitimate.[183] Like the Chinese, Koreans lavish great care on their coffins and on the selection of grave sites. Geomancers—Hamel calls them fortune-tellers—are called in. Burials are usually performed in the spring or autumn. Those who die during the summer are placed in a raised thatched hut until the harvest is in. Hamel, contrary to Martini, nowhere mentions keeping corpses in their coffins for three years prior to burial. He describes the funeral processions with their bearers and mourners, the offerings at the grave three days later, and the "merry" meal presented to friends and relatives. At every full moon Koreans cut down the grass over the graves and offer rice. When all the ceremonies are completed, the oldest son takes possession of the family house and its lands, dividing the rest of the estate among his brothers. Daughters appearently inherit nothing. Hamel also reports that at age sixty, Korean men typically retire, leaving the management of their affairs to their children, who maintain their parents and continue to show them great respect.[184]

Hamel seems to have decided that there was no hereditary nobility in Korea: "There are no Lords of peculiar places, that is, who are proprieters of Towns, Islands, or Villages, and all the Great Men's Revenues arise out of Estates they hold during [the king's] pleasure, . . . the Lands and Employ-

---

[180] Wives could be divorced for seven traditional reasons including adultery and failure to produce a son. Divorce for barrenness, however, was rare. That problem was solved by taking a second wife. See Kwang-Kyu Lee, *Kinship System in Korea* (2 vols.; New Haven, 1975), I, 61.

[181] Ledyard, *op. cit.* (n. 147), pp. 217–18.

[182] *Ibid.*, p. 217.

[183] *Ibid.*, p. 219. On mourning obligations, *cf.* K.-K. Lee, *op. cit.* (n. 180), II, 228.

[184] Ledyard, *op. cit.* (n. 147), pp. 220–21. On retirement of family heads *cf.* K.-K. Lee, *op. cit.* (n. 180), I, pp. 80–81.

ments the King bestows on any man, revert to him after his death."[185] Still,
he continually uses terms like Great Ones, nobility, freeman, commonality,
and slave, which suggest a rigid class structure. Half of the population, he
thinks, are freemen or slaves. The number of slaves seems enormous; great
officials often hold two or three hundred.[186] Furthermore, the lines between
social classes seem to be quite sharp. Hamel reports that children born of a
union between a slave and a freeman are always considered slaves and belong to the slave-parent's master.[187] Actually Hamel's picture of Yi dynasty
class structure, while unsystematic, is fairly accurate. Despite Confucian
theory, the examination system, and the dynasty's attempts to curb the
growth of hereditary private estates, the *yangban* class was still a hereditary aristocracy which monopolized government office-holding and was
sustained by landholding. The gulf between them and the freemen—the
sangmin—was great and rigidly enforced, as was the distinction between
freemen and slaves—*ch'onmin*. Children of *yangban* males and lower-class
concubines always became part of their mother's class. Marriage between
classes was not permitted.[188] On the other hand, Hamel's occasional incon-
sistent statements and his references to great merchants whose wealth and
prestige seemingly rival that of the *yangban* aristocrats may have accurately
reflected the actual erosion of the class structure during the seventeenth
century.[189]

Hamel provides his readers with no comprehensive picture of Korean
government; nevertheless, they could have gleaned from his account some
idea of its basic structure and a fairly accurate notion of how it worked. The
king is absolute throughout the land. His power is not limited by hereditary, fief-holding nobles. Nor is it limited by the royal council which, according to Hamel, meets every day to advise him. The council gives advice
only when the king asks for it, and manages only those affairs which the
king entrusts to it. It cannot initiate action or prevent any royal action.[190] For
example, after three of the Dutch captives had publicly approached the
Manchu ambassador in a desperate effort to gain their freedom, the royal
council advised that all the Dutchmen be killed. The king and his brother,
who was president of the council, ignored the advice and the Dutchmen
were instead exiled to Chŏlla Province.[191] Hamel thinks that members of the
royal council, as well as subordinate officials of the central government, are
appointed for life. Unless they die, are promoted, or are removed from

---

[185] Ledyard, *op. cit.* (n. 147), pp. 207–8. In the Yi dynasty the *yangban* literati virtually became an hereditary aristocracy. See K.-B. Lee, *op. cit.* (n. 153), p. 174.

[186] On slave numbers and their decline in the seventeenth century see K.-B. Lee, *op. cit.*
(n. 153), pp. 251–52.

[187] Ledyard, *op. cit.* (n. 147), pp. 208–9.

[188] See Han, *op. cit.* (n. 147), pp. 247–55.

[189] *Ibid.*, pp. 302, 313–14.

[190] Ledyard, *op. cit.* (n. 147), pp. 207–9.

[191] *Ibid.*, pp. 189–90.

office because of some crime, they serve until they become sixty years old, at which time they are usually retired. Provincial officials, however, serve only a term of three years. In fact, according to Hamel, few of them serve out their terms, because they are so frequently relieved of their duties for misdemeanors or maladministration. Their accusers Hamel calls the king's spies, whom the king keeps in every part of the kingdom—obviously the Censorate.[192] The experience of the Dutch captives in Chŏlla supports Hamel's generalizations about provincial government. Governors—Hamel calls all local and provincial officials governor—changed frequently, several because they had been accused by the censors of mismanagement. Each change of officials produced changes in the work, rations, and freedoms allowed the Dutchmen.

Nowhere does Hamel clearly describe how officials are appointed or promoted, although censorial reports seem to have been important in the promotion of some local officials to posts in the central government. He seems to have sensed that education and examinations played a part, but this is not clearly described. For example:

To perfect them in their learning there are Assemblies held yearly in two or three Towns of each Province, where Scholars appear to get their Employments, either by the Pen or by the Sword. The Governours of Towns send able Deputies thither to examine them, and choose the best qualified; and according to the report made of them, they write to the King.[193]

Others appear to have attended the examinations in hope of promotions. Hamel believes that the necessary gifts and entertainments often bring about the financial ruin of the candidates. According to Hamel, the examinations seem to have been open to both freemen and nobles.[194]

Hamel's description of Korean law and justice, while still not comprehensive, is more detailed than his account of administration, probably because he observed the functioning of justice more frequently than any other aspect of government. Punishments are harsh; Hamel lists many of them, often with concrete illustrations. For example, rebels against the king are destroyed along with their houses and their entire clan; officials who object to a royal decree are cruelly executed; women who kill their husbands are buried alive up to their shoulders near a busy road, with an axe placed nearby with which all passersby are required to strike her head until she dies. The officials of the town in which such a crime occurs are temporarily suspended and the town is subordinated to another jurisdiction. On the other hand, a

---

[192] *Ibid.*, pp. 209–10.
[193] *Ibid.*, p. 218.
[194] *Ibid.*, pp. 218–19. Literary examinations, the most prestigious, were open only to noblemen; military examinations were open to the sons of noblemen by concubines, to lower-ranking nobles, and to freemen; tests for administrative offices were taken exclusively by freemen. *Cf.* K.-B. Lee, *op. cit.* (n. 153), pp. 180–82.

man may kill his wife for cause—for example, adultery—and not be punished at all. Slaves who kill their masters are cruelly tortured to death, but it is no crime to kill a slave. Murderers and adulterers are condemned to particularly gruesome deaths, which Hamel describes in detail. Thieves are strangled, but that harsh punishment seems not to have prevented thievery. Death sentences require the approval of the provincial governor. A host of petty offenses are punished by beatings with canes or cudgels on the bared buttocks, calves of the legs, shins, or soles of the feet. Hamel carefully describes each kind of beating. Many people, he reports, die from them.[195] The Dutch castaways experienced this aspect of Korean justice a few days after their shipwreck, when six of them were beaten on the buttocks for trying to escape in a fishing boat.[196]

Hamel had a clearer grasp of Korea's military structure than of its political order. He reports that a large number of soldiers are maintained in the capital to guard the king and to accompany royal processions. Once every seven years each province is required to provide recruits for the royal guard, during which year each of the province's freemen serve for two months.[197] During most of 1654 and 1655 the Dutch captives are enrolled in the royal bodyguards. They parade and fire a musket volley on the first and fourth of each month. In addition to private exercises they are reviewed three times a month during the spring and autumn.[198]

Each province has a general, who has four or five colonels subordinate to him, each of whom in turn commands four or five captains, and so forth down to the corporals who command the militia in smaller villages. Military service seems to be a hereditary obligation, with officers being required to report the number of their soldiers annually. Men over sixty are discharged and their children enlisted in their place. Soldiers apparently are required to supply their own weapons and ammunition. Even monks perform military service.[199] In addition, each town is required to provide and maintain a warship—a two-masted galley able to carry three hundred men. The provincial admiral inspects each ship in his province once a year.[200] Hamel reports on many forts and castles in the mountains, where they can easily be defended. The most important of these is the royal fort about three hours from Seoul, which reportedly maintains a three-year supply of food and other necessities.[201] For all their numbers, Hamel observes that Korean soldiers are not very courageous. He was told that during the Manchu invasions more of them died fleeing into the woods than were killed by the

[195] Ledyard, *op. cit.* (n. 147), pp. 210–13.
[196] *Ibid.*, p. 184.
[197] Cf. K.-B. Lee, *op. cit.* (n. 153), p. 225.
[198] Ledyard, *op. cit.* (n. 147), pp. 186–87.
[199] *Ibid.*, p. 208.
[200] *Ibid.*, p. 210.
[201] *Ibid.*, p. 187.

enemy.[202] Martini, on the other hand, thought Korean soldiers were braver than the Chinese, although not as brave as the Japanese.[203]

The revenues to maintain the king, his armies, and his officials come from a tithe collected on all the produce of farms and fisheries. Royal storehouses in every town and village receive the tithe payments, and local administrative and military expenses are paid from them. The nobility live on the revenues from their estates. Each soldier is paid three pieces of cloth annually.[204]

Officials are treated with awe and reverence: the people prostrate themselves in their presence and address them only from their knees. Even more solemnity is observed when the king travels through the capital. All windows and doors are closed and absolute silence is maintained as the king is carried in a gold-canopied chair accompanied in procession by elaborately dressed court nobles, bodyguards, and many soldiers and horsemen. A secretary of state precedes the king, carrying a box into which he deposits the petitions from private citizens proferred at the ends of long poles or hung upon walls and fences.[205]

When the Manchu ambassador came to Seoul, however, the king and court met him outside the city. According to Hamel, the Koreans honor the Chinese envoy much as they do their own king. While he is in Seoul, the streets from his lodge to the royal palace are lined with soldiers: runners wait beneath his window to pick up the notes he throws out to them, which they rush to the king. Hamel reports that the ambassador from Peking comes to Seoul three times a year to collect tribute, and that the king is most anxious to please him. Korea's tributary relationship to the Ch'ing empire appears obvious.[206] Small wonder that some of the Dutchmen tried to make contact with the Manchu ambassador in hopes that he would obtain their release. The king's response—a heavy bribe for the ambassador, prison and death for the three Dutchmen involved, and exile to Chŏlla for the rest—is also not surprising. Hamel also reports that when the king died in 1658, "his son succeeded him, with the consent of the great Cham [Khan, or emperor of China]."[207] He does not say whether or not the new king went to Peking.

"As for Religion," writes Hamel, "the Coresians have scarce any."[208] In illustration he observes that the common people make "odd Grimaces" before idols, but pay them little respect; the nobility honors them even less. Still, much that he wrote suggests that Buddhism was still important and popular in seventeenth-century Korea. Priests preside at the funerals of

---

[202] *Ibid.*, p. 221.

[203] *Op. cit.* (n. 28), p. 261.

[204] Ledyard, *op. cit.* (n. 147), p. 210. On the cloth tax see K.-B. Lee, *op. cit.* (n. 153), pp. 225–26.

[205] Ledyard, *op. cit.* (n. 147), pp. 224–25.

[206] *Ibid.*, pp. 225–26.

[207] *Ibid.*, p. 193.

[208] *Ibid.*, p. 214.

nobles. People throng the temples on festival days to light sweetwood sticks and to bow before the images. Monks hold services offering incense twice each day and turn out in force during festivals. The kingdom swarms with monasteries and temples, most of which are located in the mountains, but which have been built by and so remain under the jurisdiction of the towns.[209] Some monasteries house five or six hundred monks, and some towns have as many as four thousand monks under their jurisdiction. The monks abstain from eating anything that has had life, shave their heads and beards, and live celibately. They work or beg for a living, pay taxes, and perform military service, for which reasons Hamel observes they are not much more respected than slaves.[210] Their superiors, however, especially if learned, are regarded as nobles. Anyone might become a monk, and it is also easy to leave the profession. Most of the monasteries are picturesquely situated in the mountains with beautiful views and gardens. Nobles frequently resort to them for parties and to entertain their women. Hamel thought they might better have been called houses of pleasure than temples. Many of the ordinary monks, he thinks, are hard drinkers as well.[211] The Dutch captives, who frequently visited monasteries on their begging tours, found the monks friendly and charitable and always eager to hear stories about far-away places and strange customs.[212] Hamel also reports on two nunneries in Seoul, one for noblewomen and one for commoners. The nuns observe the same rules as the monks. According to Hamel, however, the king had but recently given the nuns permission to marry.[213]

Hamel's comments on religion seem obviously to refer to Buddhism, although he mentions no Buddhist deities, texts, or sects. He seems to have learned almost nothing about Buddhist beliefs; he writes only two sentences about them.

For their Belief, they are of opinion, that he who lives well shall be rewarded, and he who lives ill shall be punished. Beyond this they know nothing of Preaching or of Mysteries, and therefore they have no Disputes of Religion, all believing and practising the same thing throughout the Kingdom.[214]

Nevertheless he mentions another sort of monks, who serve idols and abstain from eating what had life, but do not shave their heads and are permitted to marry. They were probably Taoists, but all that Hamel reports about

---

[209] Around the beginning of the sixteenth century the temples and monasteries in the capital and other cities were closed down by royal edict. That is why most Buddhist monasteries are still to be found in the mountains. See Eliot, *op. cit.* (n. 139), III, 338–39.

[210] Early in the Yi dynasty Buddhism kept its official sponsorship and its tax-exempt status.

[211] Ledyard, *op. cit.* (n. 147), pp. 214–16.

[212] *Ibid.*, p. 193.

[213] *Ibid.*, p. 216.

[214] *Ibid.*, p. 214.

their beliefs is that they thought all mankind once had a common language which became confused while they tried to build a tower that would reach heaven.[215] Korean popular religion, as inferred from Hamel's account, also includes fortune-tellers, geomancers, and magicians. The appearance of two comets in 1664, for example, threw both the court and the countryside into turmoil because, reports Hamel, the same signs had appeared just before the Japanese and the Manchu invasions. Hamel and his friends are of little comfort. When asked, they assure the Koreans that comets foretell some divine judgment, usually war, famine, or plague.[216]

Hamel is impressed with the Koreans' concern for education. Nobles and freemen, he reports, begin to teach their children to read and write when they are very young. Harsh discipline is never used. Students are encouraged to study by holding before them the example of those who had raised themselves to high honor and great fortune through diligent application. Hamel observes, "It is wonderful to see how they improve by these means, and how they expound the Writings they give them to read, wherein all their Learning consists."[217] He does not, however, name any "writing" or describe the content of their "learning." Neither Confucius nor Confucianism is mentioned anywhere in his account.

Hamel thought the Korean language was very difficult to learn. He complains that it has too many synonyms and that some people speak too rapidly. He apparently senses a difference between the Chinese characters and the *han'gŭl* syllabary, although his account of the various kinds of writing is not very clear:

> They have several sorts of Writing, the first and chiefly like that of *China* and *Japan,* which they use for printing their Books, and for all Publick Affairs. The Second is like the common writing among us. The great Men and Governours use it, to answer Petitions, and make notes on Letters of Advice, or the like, the Commonality cannot read this writing. The Third is more unpolish'd, and serves Women and the common sort. It is easier to write in this Character than the others, Names and Things never before heard of.[218]

---

[215] *Ibid.,* p. 215.

[216] *Ibid.,* pp. 196–97. On the comets of 1664–65 see G. W. Kronk, *Comets. A Descriptive Catalog* (Hillside, N.J., 1984), pp. 8–9.

[217] Ledyard, *op. cit.* (n. 147), p. 218.

[218] *Ibid.,* p. 224. See also Hoetink (ed.), *op. cit.* (n. 160), p. 50, for the original Dutch text, which justifies replacing the period after "others" in the last line with a comma to make sense of the sentence. As early as the late seventh century, a phonetic system called *idu* was evolved to adapt Chinese characters to the native Korean language. It was never very extensively used. In the fifteenth century a better phonetic system called *han'gŭl* (or Korean letters) was evolved, and in 1446 a royal decree proclaimed its adoption as the official syllabary. Works of scholarship and Confucian literature nonetheless continued generally to be written in Chinese characters. Until 1945 *han'gŭl* was used primarily in works designed for the lower classes and in correspondence carried on with people of limited education. At the end of Japanese rule, the Koreans liberated their own spoken language by generally transcribing it into *han'gŭl*. The invention of *han'gŭl* is still remembered and honored by a national holiday, "perhaps the only holiday in the world in honor of an alphabet" (Han, *op. cit.* [n. 147], p. 209).

Not surprisingly, Hamel writes very little about other aspects of Korean intellectual life. He mentions an "abundance of old Books" kept safe by the king's brother, who also had copies of them deposited in other towns.[219] About Korean printing he writes: "They print with Boards or Wooden Cuts, and lay one Cut to each side of the Paper, and so strike off a Leaf." He observes that almanacs are imported from China because the Koreans do not know how to make them. His account of arithmetic and bookkeeping also is too brief to be clearly understood: "They cast Accounts with little long sticks, as we do with Counters. They know not how to keep books of Accounts or Shop books, but when they buy anything, they set down the price under it, and write on it what they made of it, and so find what profit or loss."[220] Physicians, he implies, cure diseases with simple herbs; they are almost all employed by the nobility, leaving the common people to consult "Blind Men and Conjurers." Nevertheless, he describes how the Koreans quarantine houses and whole towns with contagious diseases by putting brambles on the rooftops or by blocking the roads with them.[221]

Although not comparable in quantity or quality with what was known about China, India, or Japan, some fairly reliable information about Korea became available through the reports of Martini and Hamel. From them, at least a shadowy image of the Hermit Kingdom emerged. It was clearer and sharper on geography, economics, and society than on government, religion, or intellectual life; clearer regarding the practice of government in the provinces than about the overall theory and structure of government; clearer regarding the life and persons of the monks than about Buddhist theology; clearer regarding the lives of ordinary Koreans than about *yangban* aristocrats. We might wish that it had been Martini or one of his fellow Jesuits rather than Hendrik Hamel who had lived in Korea for thirteen years and described it for his contemporaries. Nevertheless, apart from what Martini was able to learn from Chinese sources, Hamel provided the only peep into the mysterious Land of Morning Calm which Europeans would enjoy before the nineteenth century. Incomplete as it was, his *Journael* became the foundation for western knowledge of Korea.

4

FORMOSA (TAIWAN)

The European image of Formosa during the seventeenth century was based almost entirely on Dutch reports. Although the Portuguese named it Ilha

---

[219] Copies of the official annals of the dynasty were kept safe for posterity by being placed in four widely separated repositories. See K.-B. Lee, *op. cit.* (n. 153), p. 194.

[220] Ledyard, *op. cit.* (n. 147), p. 224.

[221] *Ibid.*, p. 222.

Formosa ("Beautiful island") and reputedly established a settlement on its northern coast in 1590, there are no early, published, Portuguese or Spanish descriptions of it. A settlement, if there actually was one, must have been quickly abandoned.[222] The Dutch came in 1624 after unsuccessfully trying to force the Chinese to trade with them in the Amoy area or on P'enghu. They built a fort, called Fort Zeelandia, on the small island of Tayouan off the southwest coast of Formosa near modern Tainan.[223] From this base they traded with Chinese merchants who came from the mainland. Gradually the Dutch extended their authority over the Formosan aborigines until by 1636 they controlled most of the western plain from the center of the island to its southern tip. Dutch domination of the western lowlands in the northern half of the island was completed in 1642 when they drove the Spanish from Fort Santo Domingo at Tamsui on the northern coast of the island where they had been established since 1626.[224]

Under Dutch control, Taiwan's products—mainly rice, deerskins, and sugar—were exported to China, Japan, and even Persia. Chinese were settled as tenants on VOC lands, greatly expanding agricultural productivity and the Chinese population. Immigration from mainland China increased still more rapidly after 1644 as Ch'ing armies pacified the south. By 1660 the Chinese population on Formosa numbered about twenty-five thousand armed men, and probably between forty and fifty thousand, counting women and children. The Dutch also sent missionaries to evangelize the Formosan aborigines and large numbers of them were converted to Reformed Christianity. But they did not attempt to evangelize the Chinese. The VOC taxed everyone and everything: there were export taxes, farm taxes, hunting taxes, and poll taxes.[225] The Dutch colony on Formosa

[222] Chiao-min Hsieh, *Taiwan-Ilha Formosa: A Geography in Perspective* (Washington, 1964), p. 140. See also *Asia*, I, 722–23. It should not be concluded that the Spanish, especially those in the Philippines, were unaware of Formosa. For example, a sketchy map of the Philippines, Formosa, and part of the south China coast by Hernando de los Riós Coronel, dated 1597, is preserved in the Archives of the Indies at Seville. It is reproduced in Rmo. P. Fr. José María Alvarez, O.P., *Formosa geografica e históricamente considera* (2 vols.; Barcelona, 1930), II, between pp. 34 and 35.

[223] The Chinese had derived the name of the island from the Tayouan (Paiwan?) tribe which lived on it. See Wen-hsiung Hsu, "From Aboriginal Island to Chinese Frontier: The Development of Taiwan before 1683," in Ronald G. Knapp (ed.), *China's Island Frontier* (Honolulu, 1980), p. 9. Silting has now joined the original Tayouan Island to the mainland of Formosa; now called An-p'ing, it has become part of Tainan city.

[224] On the Dutch consolidation of control over Taiwan see above, pp. 275–77. In 1626 the Spanish occupied the northeastern cape, which they called Santiago. Later that year they moved to Keelung where they built Fort San Salvador. In 1628 or 1629 they moved their headquarters to a new fort, Santo Domingo, at present-day Tamsui.

[225] For the general outlines of Dutch rule see Hsu, *loc. cit.* (n. 223), pp. 12–20, and Hsieh, *op. cit.* (n. 222), pp. 141–45. On the Dutch Reformed mission see above, pp. 275–79. For a fuller treatment see William Campbell, *Formosa under the Dutch* (London, 1903; reprinted Taipei, 1967); and J. J. A. M. Kuepers, *The Dutch Reformed Church in Formosa 1627–1662* ("Schriftenreihe der Neuen Zeitschrift für Missionswissenschaft," XXVII; Immensee, 1978). Part I of Campbell's book contains translations of selections from François Valentijn's *Oud en niew Oos-*

came to an end in 1662 when Fort Zeelandia finally capitulated after a long siege to Cheng Ch'eng-kung (Koxinga) and his Ming loyalist army.

The earliest Dutch descriptions of Formosa were the two inserts in Seyger van Rechteren's *Journael* (1635) which had been taken from a 1629 report written by Pieter Nuyts, the third governor of Formosa (1627–29).[226] The one insert, entitled "Kort verhael van Tayovang" is only a few pages long. It briefly describes Fort Zeelandia, the products of Formosa, the Taiwanese people, their livelihood, their marriage and family customs, and their religion. The other is a report concerning Dutch trade with China and Japan. It contains little description of Formosa, apart from Dutch trade at Fort Zeelandia, the Spanish settlement at Keelung, and the troubles between the Dutch and the Japanese in Taiwan. Nuyts thought Sino-Dutch trade at Taiwan was seriously hurting the trade between China and the Spanish in Manila, because many of the Chinese junks which used to go to Manila had begun trading at Taiwan instead. He worried that the new Spanish settlement at Keelung, however, might reverse the trend and recommended immediate forceful action against it. The Japanese, Nuyts reports, contend that they traded in Taiwan before the Dutch advent and refuse to pay taxes to the VOC for doing what they had done freely before. Nuyts recommended tact and patience in handling the Japanese. Although not mentioned in the published letter, relations between the Dutch and the Japanese merchants became very strained during the summer of 1628. The merchants appealed to the shogun for redress and at one point even held Governor Nuyts hostage.[227] Nuyts reminds his superiors that trade with China is the key to Dutch success in Formosa, Japan, and elsewhere in east Asia, and he sees the elimination of their Iberian rivals within grasp. Now that they have easy access to Chinese goods at Taiwan, the VOC lacks only sufficient capital to achieve its old goal of monopolizing the China trade.

Probably the best and by far the most influential description of Formosa during the seventeenth century was written by the pioneer missionary, George Candidius, who served in Formosa from 1627 to 1631 and from 1633 to 1637. Candidius wrote his "Discours ende cort verhael, van't eylant Formosa" already in 1628, although it was not published until its inclusion in the *Begin ende voortgangh* edition of Van Rechteren's *Journael* in 1646.[228] Almost all subsequent seventeenth-century descriptions of Formosa were based on it. For example, the descriptions of Formosa in Frederick Coyett's *'t Verwaerloosde Formosa* (1675), Wouter Schouten's *Oost-Indische voyagie* (1676), and Johann Nieuhof's *Zee- en lant-reize* (1682) were all taken almost

---

Indien (4 vols.; Dordrecht, 1724–26), and a translation of most of Candidius' account. Among the translations from Valentijn is Pieter Nuyts' 1629 account.

[226] For bibliography see above, pp. 453–55.

[227] See Campbell, *op. cit.* (n. 225), pp. 42–51.

[228] For bibliographical details see above, p. 454.

entirely from Candidius, as were large parts of that found in Olfert Dapper's *Gedenkwaerdig bedryf* (1670).[229]

A brief English report of the Dutch Reformed mission in Formosa appeared in 1650.[230] It is essentially a celebration of the success of Robertus Junius, a Dutch missionary on Formosa from 1629 to 1643, written by his friend Caspar Sibellius. Apart from listing some of their idolatrous and immoral traits, however, Sibellius does not describe the Formosans or their land. The Dutch missionaries worked both at teaching the aborigines to read Dutch and at developing a script for their own languages, into which parts of Christian scriptures and the Heidelberg Catechism could be translated. Several such translations were produced for the missionaries' use, and in 1650 Gilbertus Happart compiled a dictionary of the "Favorling" language. It did not appear in print during the seventeenth century, however.[231] Of the missionaries' translations only catechisms by Junius (1645) and Gravius (1661), and Gravius' Gospels of Saint Matthew and Saint John (1661) appear to have been published during the century.[232] From these an enterprising European reader might have gained some exposure to the sounds of an aboriginal Formosan language.

Martini includes a brief description of Formosa in his *Atlas,* which may have been derived in part from Spanish reports.[233] He thought, for example, that the Spanish named the island Formosa when they built their fort at Keelung, and he reports that the Spanish priests had repeatedly tried to evangelize the natives but with little success. The Chinese, he reports, call the island "Talieukieu," or "Grand Liu ch'iu." He thought they considered it to be part of Fukien Province, but notes that in fact it was not at all subject to Chinese authority. Martini's account of Formosa's people and products is very general but agrees with Dutch accounts. Almost a third of his description has to do with the importance of deerskins and antlers to the Chinese, who imported many of them from Formosa.[234]

---

[229] For bibliography see above, pp. 490–91. Apparently Candidius' reputation continued to be cherished by the aborigines of Formosa even into the twentieth century. Janet B. M. McGovern in her memoir, *Among the Head Hunters of Formosa* (London, 1922), claims (p. 91) that Candidius was remembered as the "Great White Chief" revered for his benevolence and sympathy. McGovern herself was presumably received in 1918 by the Atayal as an incarnation (pp. 83–84) of the beloved white rulers of old.

[230] Caspar Sibellius, *Of the Conversion of five thousand nine hundred East Indians In the Isle Formosa neere China* . . . (London). For bibliography see above, p. 573. For a modern reprint of Sibellius' tract see William Campbell, *An Account of Missionary Success on the Island of Formosa* (2 vols.; London, 1889).

[231] See *Dictionary of the Favorling Dialect of the Formosan Language, by Gilbertus Happart: Written in 1650* . . . , Trans. W. H. Medhurst (Batavia, 1840).

[232] Junius, *Soulat i A. B.* . . . *Katechismus in formosanischer Sprache* . . . (Delft, 1645); Gravius, *Patar ki Tna'-'msing an ki Christang. Formos. et Belge* (Amsterdam, 1661); *Het Heylige Evangelium Matthei en Johannis ofte Hagnau Ka d'llig Matiktik, ka na sasoulat ti Mattheus, ti Johannes appa* . . (Amsterdam, 1661). On these works see Kuepers, *op. cit.* (n. 225), pp. 32–33.

[233] *Op. cit.* (n. 17), pp. 158–60.

[234] Martini was wrong, however, about the Chinese name for Formosa. Ta Liu Ch'iu refers to

Albrecht Herport visited Formosa in 1661 and remained at Fort Zeelandia through Cheng Ch'eng-kung's attack and siege. His description of the island and its peoples is brief but it is based on personal observations. His journal also contains a description of the Chinese on Formosa. Most of Herport's account, however, is devoted to his experiences during the defense of Fort Zeelandia. Published in 1669, it is very detailed and solidly corroborates the account written later by Governor Frederick Coyett.[235]

Olfert Dapper's *Gedenkwaerdig bedryf* (1670) reproduces most of Candidius' description, but it also contains a lengthy account which Dapper says was taken from the papers of a certain Scotsman named David Wright, who lived on Formosa for several years just before Cheng's conquest of it.[236] While much of it agrees closely with Candidius' account, it contains a much fuller description of Formosan religious practices and considerable information about the changes in VOC government and in the lives of the aborigines subsequent to the writing of Candidius' account. Dapper's account also contains more information about the Chinese immigrants to Formosa and a detailed account of their religion.[237] The inveterate traveler Jan Janszoon Struys visited Formosa in 1650 and included a description of it in the account of his travels published in 1676.[238] Despite Struys' tendency towards the flamboyant and the bizarre, his description of Formosa is fairly sober and accurate and seems to have resulted from his own observations.

Seventeenth-century European writers all correctly locate Formosa between 21° and 25° north latitude with its center at 23°.[239] Candidius calculates that the island was 130 Dutch miles in circumference.[240] Herport reports that Formosa was about 200 miles from north to south and about 50 miles

Okinawa and the Liu ch'iu islands; they called Formosa Hsiao Liu Ch'iu (Little Liu Ch'iu). See Ludwig Riess, "Geschichte der Insul Formosa," *Mittheilungen der deutschen Gesellschaft für Natur-und Volkenkunst Ost-Asiens,* VI (1893–97), pp. 407–78, 415; and Michel Cartier, "La vision chinoise du monde: Taiwan dans la littérature géographique ancienne," *Actes du IIIe colloque international de sinologie* (Paris, 1983), p. 10.

[235] Albrecht Herport, *Reise nach Java, Formosa, Vorder-Indien und Ceylon, 1659–1668. Neu herausgegeben nach der zu Bern im Verlag von Georg Sonnleitner im Jahre 1669 erscheinenen original-Ausgabe* (NR, Vol. V; The Hague, 1930), pp. 38–86. For bibliography see above, pp. 532–33.

[236] *Gedenkwaerdig bedryf der Nederlandsche Oost-indische Maetschappye op de kuste en in het keizerrijk van Taising of China* (2 vols. in 1; Amsterdam, 1670), I, 10. Wright's description of Formosa is found on pp. 17–42. Campbell (*op. cit.* [n. 225], p. 551), after considerable effort, has not been able to trace Wright's notes or to learn more about Wright himself. Neither have we.

[237] See above, pp. 1740–41.

[238] Jan Janszoon Struys, *Drie aanmerkelijke en seer rampspoedige reysen* . . . (Amsterdam, 1676). For bibliography see above, pp. 497–98.

[239] Martini, *op. cit.* (n. 17), p. 159; Struys, *The Perilous and most unhappy Voyages of John Struys* . . . , trans. John Morrison (London, 1683), p. 55; Herport, *op. cit.* (n. 235), p. 39; George Candidius, "Discourse ende cort verhael, van't eylant Formosa," *BV,* IIb, 55; Campbell, *op. cit.* (n. 225), p. 9.

[240] Candidius, *loc. cit.* (n. 239), p. 55; Campbell, *op. cit.* (n. 225), p. 9. A Dutch mile in the seventeenth century was much longer than an English mile; estimates vary from three to six English miles to each Dutch mile. See chap. xvii, n. 343.

wide.²⁴¹ According to Martini, the little island of Taiwan was one mile from the main island of Formosa and fourteen from the Chinese mainland. Herport reports the distance between Taiwan and Formosa as a cannon shot and the distance to the mainland as twenty-four miles. Nuyts reports thirty-two miles separate Taiwan from Amoy on the Fukien coast.²⁴² Herport and Dapper also report that Formosa suffered from frequent earthquakes and typhoons. Dapper reports a severe earthquake and violent storms in 1654. Herport describes, in somewhat overly animated language, an earthquake which he experienced during January, 1661.²⁴³

All Western observers comment on Formosa's fruitfulness. The land is fertile, abounding in grains, fruits, and vegetables. It supports abundant wildlife; its rivers and coastal waters teem with fish. The lists of Formosa's flora and fauna are long—including rice, wheat, barley, millet, sugarcane, ginger, bananas, areca nuts, coconuts, oranges, lemons, pomegranates, muskmelons, cabbage, artichokes, pineapples, sweet potatoes, china root, taro, deer, wild boars, sheep, goats, cows, tigers, leopards, bears, apes, monkeys, rabbits, and many varieties of bird and fowl.²⁴⁴ Herport mentions buffaloes and wild horses, not listed by Candidius. Martini mentions muskdeer. Dapper and Struys describe in detail what they call the "Devil of Taiwan," obviously an anteater, which each asserts is found only on Formosa. Dapper also describes an awful plague of grasshoppers which destroyed most of the crops in 1655.²⁴⁵ Despite its fruitfulness, however, the land is little cultivated. The Formosans grow only what is necessary to stay alive. Martini guesses that the land would be very productive if cultivated in the Chinese fashion.²⁴⁶ Herport, writing about ten years later, attests to the industriousness of the thousands of Chinese settled on Formosa.²⁴⁷ Everyone comments on the numerous deer. Despite the large number that are killed each year, Struys reports, herds of two thousand to three thousand deer can still be seen.²⁴⁸ Most European writers also relay rumors about gold and

²⁴¹ Herport, *op. cit.* (n. 235), p. 39. Hsieh reports 240 miles from north to south and 98 miles across at its widest point, *op. cit.* (n. 222), p. 6.

²⁴² Martini, *op. cit.* (n. 17), p. 159; Herport, *op. cit.* (n. 235), p. 39; Nuyts in Campbell, *op. cit.* (n. 225), p. 52; Candidius, *loc. cit.* (n. 239), p. 53. According to Hsieh Formosa is one hundred English miles from the Chinese coast, *op. cit.* (n. 222), p. 3.

²⁴³ Dapper, *op. cit.* (n. 236), I, 18; Herport, *op. cit.* (n. 235), pp. 40–41.

²⁴⁴ See especially Candidius, *loc. cit.* (n. 239), pp. 56–57; Campbell, *op. cit.* (n. 225), pp. 9–10; Struys, *op. cit.* (n. 239), pp. 55–56; Herport, *op. cit.* (n. 235), pp. 81–82; Martini, *op. cit.* (n. 17), p. 159; Dapper, *op. cit.* (n. 236), I, 18–19.

²⁴⁵ Herport, *op. cit.* (n. 235), p. 82; Martini, *op. cit.* (n. 17), p. 159; Struys, *op. cit.* (n. 239), p. 56; Dapper, *op. cit.* (n. 236), I, 19. None of the seventeenth-century accounts lists dogs, although Candidius later mentions their use by the natives in hunting. See Candidius, *loc. cit.* (n. 239), p. 59; Campbell, *op. cit.* (n. 225), p. 12.

²⁴⁶ Martini, *op. cit.* (n. 17), p. 159.

²⁴⁷ Herport, *op. cit.* (n. 235), pp. 39 and 84.

²⁴⁸ Struys, *op. cit.* (n. 239), p. 56. Early Chinese reports also commented on the importance of deer hunting and the abundance of deer despite the hunting. See Cartier, *loc. cit.* (n. 234), p. 10.

silver mines on Formosa, although no one claims to have seen them.[249] Herport, however, describes a mountain tribe in the north which twice each year traded gold or gold dust for clothing and other products by leaving the gold in a certain place and returning after merchants left their wares alongside it, taking the goods and leaving the gold if they were satisfied with the exchange. Dapper also describes a gold-rich northern mountain from which gold washes down in its streams after the rainy season. The Dutch have frequently but unsuccessfully tried to subjugate the tribe which controls the area. He does not mention the silent trade.[250]

To Candidius the Formosans are "very barbarous and savage." The men, tall and robust, almost giants, have dark brown to black skin. The women, on the other hand, are much lighter skinned, between yellow and brown, much smaller and shorter, but fat and strong. Candidius thinks they are generally friendly and good-natured, hospitable to foreigners, faithful to their friends, and honest, except for those from the village of "Soulang" (Siau-lang), who are notorious thieves. In his judgment the Formosans are very intelligent, are quick to understand, and have good memories. They are also, however, impudent and persistent beggars, among the worst in the East Indies. In summer, Formosan men wear no clothing and apparently feel no shame. Women wear some clothes and seem to exhibit some modesty except when they bathe, which they do twice each day in plain view. Apparently cleanliness was also important to them.[251] Candidius, however, also describes a certain time during which no one may wear clothes, another during which they may not wear silk, and festivals for which the women wear their best clothing, all of which seems to imply that the Formosans were usually clothed.[252] Men over the age of seventeen, as well as women of any age, let their hair grow long like the Chinese. Boys under seventeen, however, keep it cut to just below the ears. Formosans, according to Candidius, dislike beards, which they remove along with hair on other parts of their bodies by plucking it out.[253]

Candidius admits that his description of the Formosans is drawn from those whose language and customs he knew, the Siraya, who lived in eight

---

[249] For other early reports of gold on Formosa see J. W. Davidson, *The Island of Formosa, Past and Present* (London and New York, 1903), pp. 462–64.

[250] Herport, *op. cit.* (n. 235), pp. 41–42; Dapper, *op. cit.* (n. 236), I, 19–20. Possibly Herport's is just another version of the oft-repeated tale of unseen exchanges.

[251] Candidius, *loc. cit.* (n. 239), pp. 56–57; Campbell, *op. cit.* (n. 225), pp. 9–10. Early seventeenth-century Chinese reports also noted that Formosan aborigines wore no clothing. See Cartier, *loc. cit.* (n. 234), p. 10.

[252] Candidius, *loc. cit.* (n. 239), pp. 62–63, 67; Campbell, *op. cit.* (n. 225), pp. 16, 21. For a full description of aboriginal clothing see Chen Chi-lu, *Material Culture of the Formosan Aborigines* (Taipei, 1968), pp. 163–204, and Tadao Kano and Kohichi Segawa, *The Illustrated Ethnography of Formosan Aborigines. The Yami Tribe* (Tokyo, 1945), Pt. iii.

[253] Candidius, *loc. cit.* (n. 239), p. 64; Campbell, *op. cit.* (n. 225), pp. 17–18. Cf. Chen, *op. cit.* (n. 252), pp. 257–58.

villages stretching from the sea to the mountains, all within one day's journey of Fort Zeelandia. He names the villages: "Sinkan" (Sin-kang, near today's Hsin-shih), "Mattau" (Ma-tou), "Soulang" (Siau-lang, near Chia-li), "Bakloan" (Backlauan, near Shan-hua), "Taffakan" (Tavakan), "Tifu-lukan" (?), "Teopan" (?), and "Tefurang" (Tevorang). The people in these villages all speak the same language.[254]

Struys' observations about Formosan dress, almost twenty-five years after Candidius', indicate some changes. Summer attire for Formosan men, he reports, is a long cotton sheath tied across the chest and girdled at the waist. Women wear a similar robe, except that it is also fastened around the legs. Sometimes they also wear a light outer coat which comes down to the knees. On their heads they wear black towels, knotted to resemble two horns. In winter, Struys notes, both men and women wear animal skins and furs. The people of "Soulang" reportedly dress like Europeans, while all the others dress like the Chinese. Struys reports that the natives went naked before the Europeans arrived, and that those who live in the mountains still wear only loin cloths. He also describes some men who are tattooed— "painted with a kind of colour which never goes out so long as they live"—on the back, chest, and arms.[255] Curiously, no earlier writer, including Candidius, mentions the tattoos which young men and women received at puberty in most Formosan tribes. Nor did any seventeenth-century European describe the practice of knocking out the upper lateral incisors of adolescents, although Dapper makes an indirect reference to the practice.[256] On festival days, Struys reports, some women hang large painted boards from their ears and others strings of shells. The men of one village fasten a long reed to their waistband in back which extends over their heads to which they attach silk streamers. They also wear cock feathers on their heads and bear tails on their arms and legs.[257]

Struys agrees with Candidius about the Formosans' intelligence as well as their hair and skin color. He did not think them beautiful:

Their men are mostly well-bodied and lusty, especially those in the Valleys and Champane Countrey; but those that keep themselves in the Hilly part of the Island, are not so big of stature. Their Women are short in Comparison of the Men, yet are staring beauties; having a Full Face, great Eies, a flat Nose, long Ears, with breasts hanging down like a flitch of Bacon, and would have handsome beards too, if they did not pull up the hair by the roots. The tips of their ears they bore through, and

---

[254] Candidius, *loc. cit.* (n. 239), p. 56; Campbell, *op. cit.* (n. 225), p. 9. On place names in Taiwan see Hsieh, *op. cit.* (n. 222), pp. 195–200; Kuepers, *op. cit.* (n. 225), p. 9; and Hsieh, "Sequent Occupance and Place Names," in Knapp (ed.), *op. cit.* (n. 223), pp. 107–14.

[255] Struys, *op. cit.* (n. 239), p. 58. Bing Lee, "Aborigines of Formosa," *Far Eastern Economic Review*, XII (1952), 605, reports that the Paiwan still tattoo their hands and upper bodies to show rank.

[256] See Hsieh, *op. cit.* (n. 222), p. 133; and Dapper, *op. cit.* (n. 236), I, 37.

[257] Struys, *op. cit.* (n. 239), pp. 57–58.

screw them flat with a horn, made for the purpose, which they think stands wondrous neat. Finally I hold it uncertain whether this Island has had the name Formosa, seriously from the Land it's self, or ironically from the monstrous People that inhabit it.[258]

Finally he "solemnly averred" that he saw a native from the south, condemned to be burned at the stake for killing a clergyman, who when his clothes were stripped off displayed a tail about a foot long, covered with hair. The Formosan indicated that most southerners had them.[259]

Herport, who came to Formosa in 1661, mentions wild people who live in the mountains, but he never saw them close at hand. Those who live in the lowlands, he reports, are all under Dutch jurisdiction and are more and more becoming Christianized. They wear long coats, like shirts, which extend to their feet and which are made from the inner bark of a certain tree which is as soft as silk. In the north, where it is colder, the coats are made from deerskins.[260] Unlike earlier observers, Herport includes more description of the Formosan Chinese than of the native Formosans.[261]

Dapper's description of the aborigines' appearance and clothing, based on Wright's notes, agrees closely with the others, except that it emphasizes their pierced and elongated ears, "very ugly to see, coming almost half-way down the chest." Dapper also describes the aborigines' bodily ornaments in greater detail: those mentioned by Struys, but also necklaces and bracelets made of shells, glass beads, iron, and even Dutch coins. Some mountain tribes, Dapper observes, still go entirely naked, as did all the aborigines before the Dutch arrived.[262] Candidius reports that there are no kings, governors, or chiefs, and no distinctions of rank among Formosans—not even words for master and servant in their languages.[263] Nevertheless, they treat each other with respect and courtesy, and age is honored. The oldest is served first at meals and speaks first in meetings, and younger people defer to their elders in the streets and roads. If an older person asks someone younger to do something, he dares not refuse regardless of the inconvenience involved.[264]

---

[258] *Ibid.*, p. 57.

[259] *Ibid.* Campbell, *op. cit.* (n. 225), p. 547, reports seeing a three-year-old child on Formosa with a two-inch tail. Hearsay reports about Dayak mountain people with tails were common in Borneo during the early twentieth century. See C. Snouck Hurgronje, *The Achehnese*, trans. A. W. S. O'Sullivan (2 vols.; Leyden, 1906), I, 18. B. Lee, *loc. cit.* (n. 255), p. 605, reports of the eastern-plain Ami aborigines that "many of the men have elongated spines which led the Chinese to scoff that they have tails."

[260] Herport, *op. cit.* (n. 235), pp. 43–44.

[261] *Ibid.*, pp. 82–86.

[262] Dapper, *op. cit.* (n. 236), I, 20–22.

[263] Candidius, *loc. cit.* (n. 239), pp. 55, 63; Campbell, *op. cit.* (n. 225), pp. 9 and 17.

[264] Candidius, *loc. cit.* (n. 239), p. 63; Campbell, *op. cit.* (n. 225), p. 17. Early seventeenth-century Chinese reports comment that Formosan aborigines, unlike Chinese, did not grant priority to age. See Cartier, *loc. cit.* (n. 234), p. 10.

Each village is independent, and without chiefs or headmen. Some villages, however, choose what Candidius calls a "nominal council": twelve men, over forty and all of the same age, who hold office for two years only. They seem to exercise little power. They enforce some of the religious taboos, such as not wearing clothing during a certain season of the year or silk clothing at another time. They levy small fines for infractions. More important matters are deliberated in an assembly of all the village's people. Candidius is amazed at the eloquence of the speeches and the orderliness of the deliberations. No one ever interrupts a speaker. Serious crimes—theft, murder, adultery, for example—are not punished by law. Those who are wronged simply revenge themselves, although sometimes the relatives and friends of the two parties adjudicate the matter.[265]

Between the villages there is almost constant war. The object of the wars seems not to be the annihilation of the enemy or the destruction of his villages, but rather the acquisition of one or two heads, scalps, or limbs. No pitched battles are fought; stealth and treachery are the usual means of acquiring enemy heads. Candidius describes several of the common strategems, the most common of which is simply to surprise an enemy farmer in his field or an enemy household at night, cut off the victim's head, and flee. If there is no time to take the enemy's head, his scalp, hand, foot, or even his spear will do, although heads are obviously preferred.

The return of a successful raiding party gives cause for the whole village to celebrate. The trophies being admired, the warriors are feasted and celebrated, usually for two weeks running. After the flesh is boiled off the head and bones of the trophy, the skull and bones are dried and placed in a conspicuous place in the warrior's house. Trophies are as highly regarded by the Formosans as are gold, silver, and precious gems by Europeans. In case of fire a householder's first concern is to save his trophies.[266] Candidius does not report, as many modern observers have, that head-hunting was not only a form of warfare among Formosan aborigines, but that the acquisition of an enemy's head was also part of a young man's initiation into adult society. In some tribes, apparently, a man had to bring in an enemy head before he was permitted to marry. Otherwise Candidius' account of Formosan tribal wars and head-hunting seems full and accurate.[267]

---

[265] Candidius, *loc. cit.* (n. 239), pp. 61–63; Campbell, *op. cit.* (n. 225), pp. 15–17. On egalitarian village organization, see Hsieh, *op. cit.* (n. 222), p. 133. Early seventeenth-century Chinese descriptions also note the absence of chiefs and of any central authority. See Cartier, *loc. cit.* (n. 234), pp. 8–9.

[266] Candidius, *loc. cit.* (n. 239), pp. 59–61; Campbell, *op. cit.* (n. 225), pp. 14–15. *Cf.* very similar third-century A.D. Chinese reports quoted in Chen-kang Chai, *Taiwan Aborigines: A Genetic Study of Tribal Variations* (Cambridge, Mass., 1967), p. 28.

[267] See, for example, Hsieh, *op. cit.* (n. 222), p. 133; Jose M. Alvarez, "The Aboriginal Inhabitants of Formosa," *Anthropology*, XXII (1927), 255–57; and W. H. H. Walton, "Among the Mountains and Headhunters of Formosa," *Geographic Journal*, LXXXI (1933), 486. The importance of head-hunting and the ritualistic nature of war was also stressed by early seventeenth-century Chinese reports. See Cartier, *loc. cit.* (n. 234), pp. 8–9.

Struys and Herport do not describe the wars and head-hunting except for Herport's account of a Dutch expedition against a mountain village in the south, whose inhabitants had been raiding villages under VOC control. In it he saw houses decorated with human skulls, and during the attack he watched the aborigines dismember a fallen Dutch soldier.[268] Struys mentions that the Formosans were "continually" at "warrs . . . and hate nothing worse than peace."[269] The Dutch apparently brought peace between the villages under their control. They invested elders from each village with robes and symbols of authority. The elders formed an advisory council to the Dutch governor.[270] Herport reports that young men in the villages practice long and rigorously with bows and arrows and spears—the same weapons Candidius describes—but he notes no warfare between the villages.[271]

Dapper, following Wright, reports that the lowlands of Formosa are divided into eleven dominions or lordships, each containing several cities and villages. In the mountains, however, are countless other lordships. The first of the eleven provinces is under the direct control of the VOC and contains the towns of "Sinkan, Tavakan, Baklawan, Soelang, Mattou, Tiverang, Faberlang, Takkais, Tornap, Terenip, and Assoek." The second province is called by the Dutch the Bay of "Kabelang." It contains seventy-two towns, each with its own government. The Dutch have never been able to conquer these towns but instead have made peace with them and trade with them. They often buy slaves from the "Kabelang" towns. A third province, lying northeast of Taiwan and south of the "Gedult" or "Patient" River, is ruled by the emperor of "Middag." It contains seventeen towns, the most important of which are "Middag, Sada, Boedor, Deredonsel, and Goema." The emperor permits no Christians to live in his domains. North of "Middag" and near the sea rises a steep square-shaped mountain called "Gedult." The "Gedult" River, named Rio Patientia by the Spanish, flows along its southern slope with a current so strong that no one dares ford it alone. "Pimaba," the fourth province, contains eight towns and several villages. Its warlike people are ruled by a brave king who was an ally of the VOC and served in its army. "Sapat," the fifth province, lies on Formosa's east coast, contains ten towns and is allied with "Pimaba." The sixth province, "Tokabolder," with eighteen towns and many villages, contains a very high mountain which is visible from the VOC fort at Taiwan. "Kardeman," the seventh province, is ruled by a woman whom the Dutch call "The Good Woman" because of her aid and kindness to them. She governs five villages. The eighth province is unnamed by Dapper, but he lists the most important villages as "Deredou, Arraro, Porraven, Barraba, Warrawarra, Tannatanna, and Kubeca." "Tokodekal," the ninth province, has seven towns and seven

---

[268] Herport, *op. cit.* (n. 235), pp. 44–48.
[269] Struys, *op. cit.* (n. 239), p. 59.
[270] See Hsieh, *op. cit.* (n. 222), pp. 141–42, and Campbell, *op. cit.* (n. 225), pp. 290–99.
[271] Herport, *op. cit.* (n. 235), p. 43.

villages; "Pukkal," the tenth, is usually at war with it and with "Percuzi and Pergunu," which two towns comprise the eleventh domain.[272]

Dapper's account still reports Formosan towns and villages as constantly at war with one another. Consequently they are heavily fortified, ringed not with walls but with dense groves of trees through which only a very narrow path gives access. The paths are always guarded and at night rigged with numerous sharp barbs to impale intruders. In "Middag" and "Pimaba," each village is also guarded by soldiers in three or four high bamboo towers. Before each battle villagers beat drums all night long. They observe the behavior of a small bird called the "Agdak" as an omen. If it flies toward them with a worm in its beak, victory is certain. The aborigines always make offerings to the gods before battles.

Dapper's account also describes head-hunting, and reports that the aborigines show no mercy towards defeated enemies. All, women and children as well as warriors, are killed and their heads taken as trophies. Offerings and celebrations continue for seven days after a victory and the dried skulls are used to decorate the victors' houses. Recently acquired skulls are taken into battle with rice stuffed in their mouths hoping they will help their new owners gain the day. When a warrior dies in battle and is taken by the enemy his comrades rush home in great sorrow to make a likeness of the fallen warrior out of cloth, which they bury as if it were a corpse, making offerings to persuade his spirit to remain with them and not go over to the enemy. Dapper also reports the use of spears with ropes attached to them so that warriors can pull slain or wounded enemies back towards them and take their heads. Sometimes instead of a battle, warring towns will select champions to fight a duel, the victor taking the head of the loser amidst great celebration.[273]

All seventeenth-century European observers thought Formosan men were lazy. They live in a fertile land but cultivate very little of it—no more than absolutely necessary. Even after the rice is harvested, for example, they store it unthreshed, drying and pounding only what is required for the day. Women do most of the hard work of farming: there are no horses, cows, or ploughs. Women's work also includes preparing meals, making the ubiquitous rice wine, and fishing.[274]

According to Candidius, most of Formosa's rice crop is used to make a wine, "an exceedingly strong and deliciously flavored beverage . . . which has the same effect as Spanish and Rhine wine in intoxicating a person." He

---

[272] Dapper, *op. cit.* (n. 236), I, 17–18. Present-day Formosan aborigines include ten tribal groups divided usually into six geographical areas.

[273] *Ibid.*, I, 26–27.

[274] Candidius, *loc. cit.* (n. 239), pp. 57–58; Campbell, *op. cit.* (n. 225), pp. 10–11. Hsieh, *op. cit.* (n. 222), p. 134, reports that in most aboriginal tribes women controlled hoe culture, the raising of animals, the manufacture of cloth, and the storehouses, but that men controlled hunting and fishing.

describes its preparation in some detail. Rice is simmered, then kneaded into dough. Then the women make a leaven by chewing rice flour. They spit this leaven into a pot until about a pint is collected. They mix the leaven with the rice dough, and put it into a large jar which they fill with water. After about two months it is ready to drink, although its strength increases with aging. Some of it is allowed to age for five, ten, twenty, or even thirty years. The liquor, Candidius reports, is crystal clear, strong, and delicious. Formosans sip it in small quantities. They also eat the mash at the bottom of the jar or mix it with water for drinking. Dapper's description of Formosan rice wine, which he reports is called "Masakhauw" or "Machiko," is slightly different. He says they tightly cover the large jars and bury them for a year before extracting the rice solids, and they keep pots which they wish to age buried underground. Some homes keep as many as two hundred to three hundred pots, digging them up to celebrate important events like the birth of a child, or a successful hunt. Another drink, a non-intoxicating one called "Kuthay," is made by squeezing the rice solids from the "Masakhauw" and mixing the juice with water. People in the northern part of the island make a strong drink from wood ashes which seems healthful to the aborigines but makes the Dutch ill.[275]

In addition to rice, millet, a kind of bean, and taro, fish and shellfish constitute an important part of the Formosans' diet. Fish are not eaten fresh; they are salted unscaled and uncleaned and eventually eaten in the same condition. Candidius notes that he had difficulty identifying the dried fish because of the worms and mites; nonetheless, Formosans prefer them to fresh fish. In fact he judges Formosan food generally to be "excessively filthy and stinking."[276] In addition to salted, uncooked, and dried meat (venison, pork, and fish), Dapper reports, steamed rice is a staple among the aborigines. They steam the rice by putting it in a pot with holes in the bottom, and hanging this over a pot of boiling water. In the south, rice is often cooked rather than steamed. Formosans use no utensils in eating; they simply grab handfuls of rice.[277]

Older men—those between forty and sixty—usually help their wives in the fields, often living in little huts on the fields and rarely appearing in the village. Younger men, however, rarely work in the fields. They spend their time hunting, fighting, or loafing.[278] Deer is their most common game and it is hunted with snares, spears, or bows and arrows. Candidius describes

[275] Candidius, *loc. cit.* (n. 239), pp. 57–58; Campbell, *op. cit.* (n. 225), p. 11; Dapper, *op. cit.* (n. 236), I, 23. *Cf.* Chen, *op. cit.* (n. 252), pp. 65–67.
[276] Candidius, *loc. cit.* (n. 239), pp. 58, 67; Campbell, *op. cit.* (n. 225), pp. 11 and 21. Third century and early seventeenth-century Chinese observers apparently agreed. See Chai, *op. cit.* (n. 266), p. 28, and Cartier, *loc. cit.* (n. 234), p. 10.
[277] Dapper, *op. cit.* (n. 236), I, 23.
[278] On labor division between the sexes and between young and old see Chen, *op. cit.* (n. 252), pp. 49–50.

some of the Formosans' ingenious snares, but he is most fascinated by their method of hunting with spears. All the men from a village, with their dogs, encircle a large area and drive the deer towards its center.[279] There they kill the prey using spears six feet long with bamboo shafts and barbed iron tips. The tip usually falls out of the shaft when it strikes a deer, but it is also fastened to the middle of the shaft with a long cord on which hangs a small bell. A wounded deer is thus slowed as it drags the bamboo shaft through the brush and trees while the bell betrays its location to the hunters. At other times, single hunters or small groups of hunters simply chase deer on foot until they are close enough to shoot them with bow and arrow. Candidius reports that Formosan men run almost as fast as deer. Some later writers contend that they can even outrun a deer. Dapper thinks they can outrun any men in the world and most horses as well.[280]

According to Candidius the deer is extremely useful, even though the Formosans eat very little venison. They frequently eat the entrails, sometimes salting them; they also eat deer embryos.[281] Under Dutch occupation deerskins become a major export. Usually they exchange the deer carcasses for Chinese goods. Formosans also use the skins for clothing, beds, and other household furnishings. Candidius reports that deerskins also function as money on Formosa.

Formosan houses he considers to be large and beautiful—the finest in all the Indies. Usually built of clay, they have bamboo floors, and four doors, one facing in each direction.[282]

Dapper's description of Formosan houses is quite different and much more detailed than Candidius'. They are all built of wood and bamboo, he reports, and since bamboo lasts only four or five years they are regularly destroyed and rebuilt. The houses are usually built on a six-foot-high pounded earth foundation rounded like a half-moon in front. Stairs lead to the street. Their straw roofs reach twenty or thirty feet high and extend about four feet outside the walls to form an ample eave. Each house is about sixty feet wide and two hundred feet long, one story high, with a single entrance. From the eaves hang all sorts of trinkets made from boars' teeth, glass, and shells, which emit a pleasant tinkling sound when rustled by a breeze.[283]

As reported by Dapper, building a house follows a prescribed ceremony. At every step certain offerings and prayers must be made to the gods, espe-

---

[279] See *ibid.*, p. 37, on team hunting.

[280] Candidius, *loc. cit.* (n. 239), pp. 58–59; Campbell, *op. cit.* (n. 225), pp. 11–12. Struys, *op. cit.* (n. 239), p. 59; Dapper, *op. cit.* (n. 236), I, 22. On aboriginal spears see Chen, *op. cit.* (n. 252), pp. 146–49.

[281] Candidius, *loc. cit.* (n. 239), p. 59; Campbell, *op. cit.* (n. 225), p. 12.

[282] Candidius, *loc. cit.* (n. 239), p. 67; Campbell, *op. cit.* (n. 225), p. 21. This is a reference to the ground-level, rectangular houses. See Chen, *op. cit.* (n. 252), p. 263.

[283] Dapper, *op. cit.* (n. 236), I, 23–24. *Cf.* the house-building practices of the Yami people in Kano and Segawa, *op. cit.* (n. 252), pls. 266–83.

cially the god of the east. Dapper, or Wright, describes each of them in detail, for example, that made when the bamboos are cut, when the old house is dismantled, when the walls are completed, and when the roof is raised. After the roof is raised, all the builders celebrate by drinking themselves into a stupor and the owner almost into poverty. After that follows an important ceremony which involves the sacrifice of a pig. Given the light materials of Formosan houses, fires are common. Responsiblity for a fire is laid on the first man found in the street after the fire. He must pay for the rebuilding of the destroyed house. If he is unwilling, his own house will be burned. If no one is found, all the villagers help rebuild the house.[284]

Apart from some festivals, Candidius reports that the Formosans keep no regular days of rest and no religious holidays. Few aspects of Formosan society seem stranger to Candidius than its marriage customs. Men do not marry until they are twenty or twenty-one years old; no age restrictions exist for the women. The marriage ceremony is exceedingly simple. A man proposes to a woman by sending his mother, sister, or some other female relative to her home with the gifts which become her dowry if she accepts the proposal. The gifts include dresses, girdles, Chinese garments, bracelets, rings made from antlers, deerskin stockings, and various ornaments made of dogs' hair. If the woman's family is satisfied with the proposal and the dowry, they keep the gifts and the couple are considered married. The husband spends the next night with his bride. The new couple does not, however, begin living together. The wife continues to live in her own house, the husband in his. They conduct entirely separate lives, rarely meeting during the daytime. Should they meet they do not speak to each other. At night the husband may steal into his wife's house like a thief and go directly to her bed, where she joins him after the family retires. He is expected to slip away again before daybreak. Only when a man reaches fifty years of age does he move in with his wife, who by then, Candidius observes, is old and ugly—"stricken in years." Until that time the men live in separate dormitories, one of which is maintained for each group of twelve or fourteen houses in the village. Even after age fifty, the men spend most of their time in the fields, where they sleep in small huts.[285]

Children, Candidius reports, remain with their mothers until adulthood, when sons move into the dormitories with their fathers.[286] During the first

---

[284] Dapper, *op. cit.* (n. 236), I, 24–26.

[285] Candidius, *loc. cit.* (n. 239), pp. 63–66; Campbell, *op. cit.* (n. 225), pp. 17–21.

[286] Candidius, *loc. cit.* (n. 239), p. 65; Campbell, *op. cit.* (n. 225), p. 19. Candidius' account is confusing on this subject. On p. 19, he writes that sons joined their fathers at age twenty-three. In other places he implies that they are younger and in *op. cit.* (n. 239), p. 66 (Campbell, *op. cit.* [n. 225], p. 21) he reports on children under four sleeping in the dormitories. This apparent confusion may result in part from a lack of uniformity in tribal social customs and in part from the variety of houses. What is referred to here is the House of Youth, which is different from the Public House and the House of Ancestor Spirits, both being religious centers where totems were kept. See Chiu Ming-chung, "Two Types of Folk Piety: A Comparative Study of Two

years of marriage, however, women bear no children; they are not permitted to do so until they are thirty-five, thirty-six, or thirty-seven years old. Children conceived before that time are crudely aborted by the *inibs* or priestesses. To bear children before the appropriate age is considered exceedingly shameful. Some women report they had suffered fifteen or sixteen painful abortions before they were finally allowed to give birth.[287]

Formosan marriages as described by Candidius appear to be monogamous. Although some men keep more than one wife, it is considered improper. Marriage is not permitted between near relatives until the fourth generation.[288] Fidelity in marriage is apparently rare. Candidius describes the Formosans as "great whoremongers," who regard adultery very lightly so long as their spouses do not discover it. A husband may divorce his wife for any reason, or simply because he tires of her. If he has a good reason for divorce her dowry is returned to him; if not she retains it. Candidius thought some men took a new wife almost every month. Women, he reports, might just as easily divorce their husbands.[289]

Candidius and the other Dutch missionaries were particularly eager for their Formosan converts to abandon their traditional marriage customs. Later, unpublished, reports from the Dutch Reformed mission on Formosa repeatedly refer to individual families or whole villages in which husbands and wives lived together and no longer practiced abortion.[290] Neither Struys nor Herport or Dapper describe marriage customs. Consequently it is difficult to determine the reliability of Candidius' description of them.[291]

Formosan funeral customs seemed almost as unusual to seventeenth-century Europeans as their marriages. They neither bury nor cremate their dead. Instead they dry their corpses by placing them on a raised platform next to a fire inside their homes. The drying takes nine days, according to Candidius, and each day the corpse is washed.[292] Meanwhile relatives and friends perform ceremonies in honor of the deceased. These include much eating and drinking and ritual dancing. The village women dance on top of

Folk Religions in Formosa" (Ph.D. diss., Divinity School, University of Chicago, 1970), pp. 39–40. See also Davidson, *op. cit.* (n. 249), p. 570.

[287] Candidius, *loc. cit.* (n. 239), pp. 65–66; Campbell, *op. cit.* (n. 225), pp. 19–20.

[288] *Cf.* Davidson, *op. cit.* (n. 249), p. 582.

[289] Candidius, *loc. cit.* (n. 239), p. 66; Campbell, *op. cit.* (n. 225), p. 20.

[290] See Campbell, *op. cit.* (n. 225), pp. 89–326.

[291] Hsieh contends that the bachelor-house system is one of the more enduring tribal customs in Formosa, but as he describes it, only unmarried men from about age fifteen or sixteen lived in the bachelors' dormitory or *khuva*. Its purpose, he points out, was to train warriors and to serve as a barrack where the warriors would always be kept on the ready (*op. cit.* [n. 222], p. 133). Early seventeenth-century Chinese reports, although different in details, support most of the general characteristics of aboriginal marriage customs described by Candidius. See Cartier, *loc. cit.* (n. 234), pp. 9–10. *Cf.* the bachelors' dormitories in the Marianas, above, p. 1550.

[292] *Cf.* McGovern, *op. cit.* (n. 229), pp. 170–71. Riess, *loc. cit.* (n. 234), p. 411, thinks Candidius is confused. He thinks it unlikely that anyone could tolerate drying corposes indoors for nine days in Formosa's heat and humidity. Furthermore, he contends no later reports mention the practice. Wright in Dapper, however, describes the drying just as Candidius does.

large troughs carved from huge tree trunks which are turned upside down in front of the dead person's house. Their feet on the drum-like platform produce what Candidius calls a hideous sound. After nine days the corpse is wrapped in a mat and placed on another platform, "a kind of pavilion," inside the house and another feast in honor of the dead is celebrated. The corpse remains there for three years, after which the skeleton is buried in the house, accompanied once more by a feast. In one village, death for a very sick person who suffers much pain is hastened, according to Candidius, by tying a cord around his neck by which to pull him up and let him fall. Their intention, he contends, is to deliver the poor wretch from his suffering.[293]

The description of Formosan funerals in Dapper is very similar to that of Candidius, but considerably more detailed with regard to offerings to the gods, the dressing of the corpse, the hired mourning-women and their sorrowful songs, the eulogies, and prayers. He, too, reports that they dry the corpse before a low fire for eight to ten days, which he observes subjects the entire town to an awful smell. According to Dapper, however, the dried corpse, after being kept in the house for several years, is buried not in the house but near a temple. During all the years a man's corpse is kept above ground his wife may not use a broom to sweep out her house.[294]

Dapper's account does not mention the method for hastening death described by Candidius. It describes, however, the treatment of sick people. The Formosans use no medicines, herbs, or cures. Nurses called "Tamatatah" treat the sick by offering wine or pinang to the gods. If the illness persists, exorcists are called in, first to determine whether the patient will live or die by communicating with his spirit, and later to drive out the demon which is causing the illness by incantations, offerings to the gods, and offerings and threats to the demon. Dapper includes ample details. When the patient is in his death throes they pour liquor down his throat until it runs out of his nose and mouth and he dies.[295]

Candidius also describes little huts which are always built for a person after his death. Inside they place a bowl of water and a bamboo ladle so that the soul of the deceased can return each day to wash. Candidius thinks the custom indicates belief in the immortality of the soul. Although this practice is strictly observed, not one person in a hundred knows why they build the little huts for the dead. Candidius learned about it from some very old people. His aged informers also retain a belief in rewards and punishments after death. They tell him about a narrow bamboo bridge spanning a broad river of filth over which the souls of the dead must pass before entering the delightful Land of Promise. Those who lived well in this life cross without difficulty, but when those who have lived badly attempt to cross, the bridge suddenly turns upside down, dumping them into the filthy stream where

[293] Candidius, *loc. cit.* (n. 239), p. 68; Campbell, *op. cit.* (n. 225), pp. 21–22.
[294] Dapper, *op. cit.* (n. 236), I, 29–30.
[295] *Ibid.*, I, 28–29.

they suffer great torment. Again, very few Formosans seemed to know this story.[296]

The reason for their ignorance of these teachings, Candidius thought, is the complete absence of religious books. Formosans have no books or writing; none of them can read or write. Their religious ideas were handed down orally from generation to generation.[297] In a report to Governor Nuyts, Candidius contends that the Formosan religion is decaying rapidly and would be entirely different in another sixty years even if there were no Christian mission. He judges the absence of books and the decay of the native religion to be of great advantage to the missionaries.[298]

The misdeeds for which Formosans thought people would be punished appear ridiculous to Candidius: wearing clothing during the season in which it is prohibited, wearing silk at the wrong time, bearing children before age thirty-six or thirty-seven, gathering oysters during a prohibited season, or failing to listen to the birds' songs before beginning some unusually important task. The list continues. On the other hand, some acts judged by Christians to be sinful are not considered wrong at all by the Formosans. Drunkenness, for example, they regard as a harmless pleasure, of which both men and women are very fond. Adultery and sexual activity outside of marriage are considered to be wrong only if done in public.[299] Even murder, theft, and lying do not seem to be punished very severely.[300]

Candidius reports that the Formosan natives know nothing about the creation of the world (they think it has always existed and always will) or the bodily resurrection. They worship not one but many gods. He describes only five, however. Their chief deity is called "Tamagisanhach" (Tamagisangak), who is supposed to live in the south. He created men and made them beautiful. His wife, "Taxankpada" (Takarupada), lives in the east. Thunder, they believe, is the sound of "Taxankpada" chiding her husband for not sending rain. He usually listens to her. Another deity, "Sariasingh" (Sariafey), is a demon who is supposed to live in the north and to be the cause of pockmarks and other disfigurations. They try to appease him and beg "Tamagisanhach" to protect them from him. Before they go to war the men call on two other gods, "Talafula" and "Tapaliape."[301]

Worship and sacrifices to the gods are generally conducted in their temples by priestesses called *inib*s. There are no male priests. Candidius de-

---

[296] Candidius, *loc. cit.* (n. 239), pp. 68–69; Campbell, *op. cit.* (n. 225), p. 23. See also Dapper, *op. cit.* (n. 236), I, 29. Cf. on life after death the Atayal story given in McGovern, *op. cit.* (n. 229), p. 147.

[297] Candidius, *loc. cit.* (n. 239), p. 68; Campbell, *op. cit.* (n. 225), p. 22.

[298] Candidius, *loc. cit.* (n. 239), p. 71; Campbell, *op. cit.* (n. 225), p. 90. See also Dapper, *op. cit.* (n. 236), I, 35.

[299] Candidius, *loc. cit.* (n. 239), p. 69; Campbell, *op. cit.* (n. 225), p. 24.

[300] Candidius, *loc. cit.* (n. 239), pp. 63, 69; Campbell, *op. cit.* (n. 225), pp. 23–24, and 15–17.

[301] Cf. Davidson, *op. cit.* (n. 249), p. 16; and Arundel del Re, *Creation Myths of the Formosan Natives* (Tokyo, 1951), pp. 57–58.

scribes a typical religious ceremony. After offering a sacrifice of meat, rice, areca nuts, wine, and the heads of boars or stags, one or two of the priestesses address the gods in a long oration or sermon, at the end of which they roll their eyes, fall to the ground, and scream. The gods are supposed to appear to them. While they lie on the ground, usually for about an hour, the people stand crying. After the priestesses recover consciousness, shivering and trembling as a sign that they have seen the gods, they climb to the roof of the temple, each in a corner, and again begin to address the gods. Finally they strip off their clothes and present themselves naked to the gods, striking their bodies and washing themselves in the gods' presence—and in the presence of the worshipping bystanders, of course. Candidius reports that most of the worshippers are women and that by the end of the service most of them have become so drunk they can scarcely stand. In addition to the temples, shrines stand in the people's houses and along the roads, where sacrifices can be made. The *inib*s also perform other religious services. They forecast the weather and many other matters, judge whether places are good or evil, chase away evil spirits or devils, and perform abortions.[302]

The description of Formosan religion found in Dapper's account is much more detailed and comprehensive than Candidius' account, although the two are in general agreement. Dapper's description of Tamagisangak and Takarupada, for example, is almost identical to that of Candidius. Dapper describes them, however, as the gods of agriculture, not as the Formosans' principal deities. The principal deity he calls "Tamagisangang," who lives in the west rather than the south; his wife's name as "Takaraenpada," who lives in the east. Dapper says nothing more about them, and their names seem almost identical to those of the agricultural deities. Altogether, Dapper lists thirteen Formosan gods: besides the four already named, there are two (husband and wife) who have power over sickness, two who control hunting, two ("Tapaliat" and "Tatawoeli") who control warfare, and two who preside over the seven festivals.[303] The thirteenth deity Dapper names "Farihhe, Fikarigo Gougosey" or "Fariche Fikri go Gon go Sey" (Sariafey) and like Candidius he attributes pockmarks and deformities to him. According to Dapper, however, Sariafey was once a man who lived in "Sinkan," a cruel and gruff man with an enormous nose. People in the town always made sport of him because of his nose. The distressed Sariafey therefore prayed that the gods would take him to heaven with them, and they eventually did. After a time Sariafey returned to earth and avenged himself by imposing twenty-seven prohibitions on the Formosan people to be observed each month for a ten-day period called "Karichang." Dapper lists

---

[302] Candidius, *loc. cit.* (n. 239), pp. 68–70; Campbell, *op. cit.* (n. 225), pp. 22–25.

[303] Dapper, *op. cit.* (n. 236), I, 33. For the Yami hierarchy of gods see Chiu, *op. cit.* (n. 286), pp. 82–85. In modern Taiwan there are more than three hundred deities in the folk pantheon. See A. F. Gates, *Christianity and Animism in Taiwan* (San Francisco, 1979), p. 131.

each prohibition and the consequence for disobeying it. For example, no one may build a house or erect the walls of a house during "Karichang," or Sariafey will cause it to burn; a baby born in "Karichang" may not be taken from its mother, or it will die; a young man may not take a wife and a married man may not sleep with his wife lest the married man die and the young couple live in chronic illness and bickering; parents may not extract their daughters' front teeth, as is customary, or pierce their daughters' ears during "Karichang."[304]

According to Dapper's account, seven solemn festivals were celebrated each year by the Formosan aborigines. In April the people gather on the seacoast to pray that the rain will come and the seeds will grow. They bring offerings of pigs, rice, liquor ("Masakhaw"), and pisang for the gods. The festival ends with all the old men sitting together, a white reed in one hand and a spear in the other, drinking and recounting old adventures: of heads they have taken, pranks played, and women seduced. This festival is called "Toepaupoe lakkang." In June they celebrate "Warabo Lang Varolbo," in which the aid of the two war gods is invoked by the men and everyone asks "Tamagisangak" and "Tekaroepada" to protect them from fire, poison, and wild animals. At this festival the priestesses or exorcists perform as described by Candidius. The evening ends, according to Dapper, in general drunkenness and debauchery. In July another feast implores the gods' aid in battle and their protection for the crops. This one, called "Sickariariang," is the most popular of all, because, as Dapper describes it, it is mainly a Bacchus and Venus festival. The September feast, "Lingout," is to pray for crops and protection from storms; "Piniangh" in October seems to honor parents and the elderly; at "Itaoungang" both young and old men do a ritual dance; and at "Karouloutaen" in November people paint white stripes on their heads and arms. Each festival involves prayers and the usual offerings to the gods. Priestesses play a leading role in some of them. For most of them the people wear no clothes; they all involve a great deal of drinking and they all end, according to Dapper's account, in gross immorality.[305]

Formosan religion as described in Dapper's account is not confined to the festivals. The mundane affairs of life, such as building a house, are accompanied by religious rituals.[306] So is agriculture. Offerings and prayers are made to the gods of agriculture, worshiped in two small houses, at every step of the agricultural year: before planting, whenever it rains, when the crops are ready to harvest, and when the harvest is brought in. A small plot near the temples is sowed for the gods and a ceremonial rice bowl stands on

---

[304] Dapper, *op. cit.* (n. 236), I, 33, 36–38. The last-mentioned prohibition contains the only reference to the practice of removing the lateral incisors at puberty that we have been able to find in published seventeenth-century European reports.

[305] *Ibid.*, I, 30–32.

[306] See above, pp. 1810–11. On agricultural and hunting rites and festivals see Chiu, *op. cit.* (n. 286), chap. vi.

the north side of the temples during the growing season. During seed time, especially, the people observe an astonishing number of prohibitions, some rather bizarre: they may not smoke tobacco, break wind, eat sugarcane, eat roasted meat, or sleep in the field, for example. Specific consequences attach to each of the prohibitions, and Dapper lists many of them.[307]

The annual hunt, ten to twelve days long, is similarly enveloped by religious ritual. Before the hunt begins, each hunter erects a small hut in the fields for his equipment and a small straw hut is built for the two gods of the hunt. The hunters beat drums all night before the first day of the hunt and they carefully read the omens given by the flight of the "Agdak" bird. Then they make an offering to the gods. Each hunter also offers pieces of his first kill, and still more offerings are proferred in each hunter's hut when the hunt is over. Then the huts are destroyed, the women come to help carry the game home, jars of the best liquor are opened, and the evening is spent in celebration. No wonder: according to Dapper the aborigines often bag seven hundred to one thousand, sometimes as many as two thousand deer during the annual hunt.[308]

Both Dapper and Herport include some description of the Chinese on Formosa. Herport's is very similar to the descriptions of the Chinese in Bantam, Batavia, and elsewhere written by European travelers throughout the century. He judges the Chinese to be "blind Heathen" despite their belief in a creator-god. He describes the beautifully carved images, the chief of which is called "Joossie," worshipped in their temples. Chinese marry only one wife, although they may also keep concubines. Only the children of the legitimate wife inherit their father's goods. They burn paper, sandalwood, and incense at their funerals; they are intelligent and very industrious, good merchants, astronomers, and mariners, but they are addicted to gambling for very high stakes. The Chinese wear long gowns; both men and women wear long hair coiled at the back of the head, and they let their fingernails grow very long. They eat a wide variety of foods with chopsticks from little porcelain dishes, and they drink a lot of tea. Herport mentions footbinding, but he reports that it is accomplished by forcing young girls to wear very small wooden shoes and never changing the size as the child grows. Herport's Chinese are not uniquely Formosan, and his detailed account of Koxinga's conquest contains almost no description of the Chinese conquerors.[309]

Neither are the Chinese described in Dapper's account in any way unique to Formosa. The author, David Wright, asserts:

The Chinese on both these islands, *Tayowan* and *Formosa,* maintain one and the same custom, manner, clothing, language and religion; the same speech and the same

[307] Dapper, *op. cit.* (n. 236), I, 33–35.
[308] *Ibid.,* I, 35.
[309] Herport, *op. cit.* (n. 235), pp. 82–86.

writing as those on the mainland of *China;* differing only in the wearing of their hair; which these islanders wear long after the old Chinese fashion.[310]

Wright's account of Chinese popular religion, however, is one of the most perceptive of the seventeenth century.[311]

Frederick Coyett's account of the loss of Formosa, published in 1675, contains some description of Formosa's inhabitants. His general information about the island and about the aborigines is taken entirely from Candidius' account.[312] Coyett's purpose is to demonstrate that the loss of Formosa to Koxinga (Cheng Ch'eng-kung) in 1662 resulted from neglect and the failure to heed warnings on the part of the governor-general and Council of the Indies in Batavia and not from mismanagement or any lack of concern on Coyett's part.[313] He was condemned to death in Batavia for the loss of Formosa, had his sentence commuted to exile, and was in 1666 banished to Pulau Ai in the Bandas. He was pardoned by the Prince of Orange in 1675.[314] To prove his innocence, Coyett provides a detailed description of the events leading up to Koxinga's invasion of the island and of the siege of Fort Zeelandia in 1661–62.

Part one of Coyett's apologia traces the background of Koxinga's invasion. Castle Zeelandia was built in 1624 when the Dutch evacuated their fort on "Pekou" (P'eng-hu). Chinese officials formally agreed to its founding and to the establishment of trade between Castle Zeelandia and China. About twenty-five thousand Chinese have settled on Formosa near the Dutch fort. They engage in trade and agriculture, growing mostly rice and sugarcane. Castle Zeelandia is built on a "small barren sandbank of about a mile in circumference, called Tayouan, separated from the mainland by the sea, which was at its broadest part about two cannon shots wide." The fort is erected on a high sand dune, its site "chosen to facilitate the landing as well as loading and unloading of the ships, rather than for its strategic position." While the rectangular fort is built with walls six feet thick and ramparts four feet thick, its other defenses are weak and its guns poorly placed. It has no moat or outer bulwarks, leaving it as "easily accessible as the commonest farmhouse upcountry." Outworks added later can neither be protected by the castle's guns nor defend themselves. One is commanded by a nearby sand dune. To rectify this problem an earlier governor built a

[310] Dapper, *op. cit.* (n. 236), I, 42.

[311] *Ibid.,* I, 42–51. See above, pp. 1740–41.

[312] Inez de Beauclair (ed.), *Neglected Formosa; A Translation from the Dutch of Frederic Coyett's 't Verwaerloosde Formosa* (San Franciso, 1975), pp. 1–14.

[313] Koxinga is the latinized form of the Amoy-area pronunciation of Kuo-hsing yeh, or "Master of the [imperial] surname." Cheng Ch'eng-kung had been given the Ming dynastic surname by the emperor as an honor to Ch'eng-kung's father, Cheng Chih-lung, known to Europeans as Nicholas Iquan. See A. W. Hummel, *Eminent Chinese of the Ch'ing Period (1644–1912)* (Washington, D.C., 1943), pp. 108–11.

[314] Beauclair (ed.), *op. cit.* (n. 312), p. xv.

strong fortification called "Uytrecht" on its top, but there are other dunes of equal height nearby.[315]

In 1646 rumors first come to Formosa, by way of Japan, that Koxinga, who is fighting a losing battle against Ch'ing armies in southeastern China, might retreat to Formosa with his troops. Fresh rumors about Koxinga's designs on Formosa in 1652 are accompanied by a revolt of Formosan Chinese against the Dutch, thought to have been instigated by Koxinga. In response, the VOC in 1653 builds a new fort, called Provintia, near the village of "Saccam" on the mainland across from Fort Zeelandia. It might be useful in quelling a local uprising, but it is too feebly built to withstand a siege or resist cannon fire. Rumors continue and governors continue to ask for more troops and for money to improve Fort Zeelandia's defenses. Coyett, who is appointed governor of Formosa in 1656, requests more troops and funds like his predecessors, but also tries to revive friendship with Koxinga. Letters and presents are exchanged and trade, which Koxinga had earlier cut off, is reopened. Still Coyett does not trust Koxinga, and by 1660 there seems to be ample evidence that the increasingly hard-pressed Koxinga is preparing for the invasion of Formosa. Coyett again pleads for reinforcements from Batavia while he resettles all of the Formosan Chinese in close proximity to the Dutch forts to prevent their being useful to Koxinga's army. Letters from Batavia, however, question the reality of the threat to Formosa, plead shortage of funds for reinforcements, and censure Coyett for repairing a crucially important wall without permission from the governor-general. In July, 1660, the VOC sends a fleet of twelve ships and six hundred men under Jan van der Laan to assist Coyett. But Van der Laan was ordered, in the event that Koxinga did not invade, to attack Macao on the return voyage. He is obviously much more interested in attacking Macao with its riches than in defending Formosa, although the presence of his fleet apparently leads Koxinga to postpone his invasion. Coyett sends Captain Thomas Pedel to Amoy to inquire about Koxinga's intentions and to observe the activities of his forces there. Koxinga cleverly admits that he creates rumors about an invasion of Formosa to throw the Manchus off guard. "How then," he asks, "is it possible to know my thoughts, and to proclaim intentions which are never breathed to anyone?" After months of bitter quarreling between Van der Laan and Coyett and his council, Van der Laan solicits a petition for Coyett's recall from members of the council and leaves in February, 1661, for Batavia. In recounting all this, Coyett overwhelms his readers with evidence of Koxinga's obviously hostile intentions, Batavia's penury and refusal to take them seriously, Van der Laan's greed and stupidity, and his own loyalty and determination.[316]

[315] *Ibid.*, pp. 14–15.
[316] *Ibid.*, pp. 16–41.

Van der Laan's departure, after his noisy condemnation of Governor Coyett, emboldens Koxinga. He knows that Taiwan will be isolated from Batavia and the Dutch on Formosa will not be able to send for help, if he waits until the end of the northerly monsoon before attacking. Koxinga's fleet of several hundred war junks carrying about twenty-five thousand soldiers appears in sight of Castle Zeelandia at dawn on April 31. In less than two hours he lands several thousand troops and places most of his ships inside the bay which separates Tayouan from Formosa, while the Dutch, with only two warships in the harbor, watch helplessly. Inside the castle are about eleven hundred people and forty fully equipped soldiers. Ammunition and skilled officers are also in short supply. Nevertheless the warships are ordered out; Captain Pedel with 240 men volunteers to confront the Chinese soldiers who landed at "Lakjemuyse" canal, about a mile from the fort; and Captain Aeldorp with 200 men crosses over to Fort Provintia to prevent a landing there. After sinking several junks one of the Dutch ships, the "Hector," blows up and sinks with all its crew. The other, the "'s Gravenlande," fights war junks, fire boats, and landing parties before escaping out to sea. Captain Pedel and his company, convinced that all Chinese soldiers are "cowardly and effeminate," expect Koxinga's troops to flee after the first musket volley. Instead they stand firm and discharge "so great a storm of arrows that they seemed to darken the sky," while another large contingent of Koxinga's army attacks the Dutch from the rear. The Dutch retreat in total disarray. Pedel and 118 of his troops are killed. Aeldorp fares little better: he is able to land only about 60 men to augment the garrison at Fort Provintia but is unable to prevent Koxinga from beseiging it. In only three or four hours after the failure of these Dutch offensives, Koxinga's army overruns the entire area and demands the surrender of both forts.[317]

After considerable deliberation Coyett and the Formosan Council decide to negotiate with Koxinga: first to offer him an indemnity if he will leave Formosa, and, should he refuse those terms, to offer him the Formosan mainland if he will agree to allow the Dutch to hold Fort Zeelandia and Tayouan. Two members of the council, Thomas van Iperen and a Mr. Leonardus, are sent to Koxinga's camp at "Sakkam" on May 2. After making them wait for some time, Koxinga receives them seated at a square table in a blue open-sided tent surrounded by aides in formal robes. The Dutch envoys present Coyett's letter which asks why, without provocation, Koxinga has attacked the VOC which has always maintained friendship with him. Koxinga impatiently responds that he knows all about VOC friendship with Asian rulers, that it means nothing unless it is to the Company's advantage. Formosa, he asserts, is Chinese territory, and he has seized it simply because he needs it as a base from which to fight the Manchus. If the Dutch will

[317] *Ibid.*, pp. 43–49.

surrender he will allow them to leave with all their goods; if they resist he will destroy them. He will wait until eight o'clock the following morning for the Dutch to signal their answer, but he will not negotiate.[318]

While in Sakkam, the Dutch envoys are careful to observe Koxinga's army. They estimate that about twelve thousand soldiers surround Provintia. The rest of his army has been sent to subdue the natives in other parts of Formosa. The troops are obviously well disciplined and armed, some with bows and arrows, some with swords and shields, and some with large battle swords which are wielded with both hands. The archers are Koxinga's best troops; their skill makes them comparable to riflemen. All the soldiers wear armor, "iron scales, fitting below one another like the slates of a roof," affording "complete protection from rifle bullets and yet . . . ample freedom to move." Lacking cavalry, Koxinga uses shield bearers. They "force themselves into the ranks of the enemy. With bent heads and their bodies hidden behind the shields, they try to break through the opposing ranks with such fury and dauntless courage, as if each one had still a spare body at home." Once the enemy's ranks are broken, "sword bearers follow . . . with fearful massacre amongst the fugitives." In addition Koxinga has cannons, ammunition, and "two companies of 'black boys,' many of whom had been Dutch slaves, and had learned the use of the rifle and musket-arms."[319]

The returning Dutch envoys are permitted by their Chinese escort to visit Fort Provintia before sailing across to Zeelandia. Provintia is crowded with townspeople who fled there for protection. It is virtually without water and very low on food and ammunition. The envoys instruct Provintia's commander to make his own surrender to Koxinga, trying to save the garrison and Dutch honor.[320]

Back at Zeelandia the governor's council meets. They have few options. If they do not surrender to Koxinga they can at best defend the fort until help arrives from Batavia in twelve or thirteen months—six months before the northerly monsoon allows them to send a message to Batavia and another six months before a relief fleet could sail north from Batavia. They have too few men to launch a counterattack; perhaps too few to resist a massive assault on the fort. They have too little food for a long siege, and while there are two wells inside the castle, the water in them is brackish and might make them sick. Ordinarily they bring water over from the Formosan mainland. Nevertheless they decide to defend Zeelandia until help arrives from Batavia. They also decide to take the inhabitants of the town on Tayouan into the castle since there is no way to defend the town. Provintia meanwhile surrenders, and during the following night Koxinga moves some troops to the south corner of Tayouan Island. Next morning the townsfolk hastily

[318] *Ibid.*, pp. 49–55.
[319] *Ibid.*, pp. 51, 55.
[320] *Ibid.*, pp. 55–56.

evacuate the city and attempt to set fire to it. Koxinga's soldiers, however, are able to extinguish it.[321]

Between the fifth and twenty-fifth of May, the Chinese make preparations for an attack on the castle, placing twenty-eight cannons in the city. The Dutch can do little to stop them. The early-morning assault on May 25, however, is poorly executed, and the Chinese retire to the town after losing over a thousand men and several cannons. After this the Chinese seem content to besiege the castle and to psychologically harass its defenders.[322]

Meanwhile, in Batavia, after hearing Van der Laan's report, the governor-general and the Council of the Indies officially remove Coyett from office and appoint Hermanus Clenk to replace him. Clenk leaves for Formosa on June 21, 1661. Two days after his departure a yacht which had escaped Tayouan harbor when Koxinga landed, and had sailed against the wind and around the Philippines, arrives at Batavia with the news of Koxinga's invasion. The governor-general immediately orders a yacht to overtake Clenk; it fails to do so. A fleet of ten ships and about seven hundred men is hastily put together, placed under the command of Jacob Caeuw, whom Coyett describes as utterly incompetent, and dispatched to Formosa on July 5. Clenk arrives at Fort Zeelandia on July 30. He sends the letter dismissing Coyett ashore but, pleading an impending storm, sails for Japan, seizing a licensed Chinese junk from Batavia as a prize on his way. Caeuw's fleet arrives on August 12. Storms prevent it from landing soldiers and supplies until early September.[323] In the weeks following, the Dutch use their newly acquired ships and soldiers to launch several counterattacks against the Chinese, but all of them fail. Early in November, Coyett receives an offer of assistance from "Simtangong" (Keng Chi-mao), the Ch'ing governor-general of Fukien Province. The Formosan Council decides to accept the offer and readies ships and soldiers to sail to Fukien for joint action against Koxinga with the Ch'ing forces. Caeuw, who some weeks earlier made the surprising proposal that he sail back to Batavia to request more help, now volunteers to command the new squadron. Instead of sailing to Fukien, however, he heads for Batavia, stopping in Siam on the way. December finds the Dutch in Fort Zeelandia quite demoralized. To save their lives, several soldiers defect, providing Koxinga with valuable information about the Dutch defenses.[324]

The end comes in January, 1662. Koxinga moves all his troops to the island of Tayouan, digs trenches, and builds fortifications in preparation for the final attack on the castle. Continual Dutch harassment impedes his work but ultimately cannot stop him. The bombardment begins on January 25.

[321] *Ibid.*, pp. 56–59.
[322] *Ibid.*, pp. 59–64.
[323] *Ibid.*, pp. 64–72.
[324] *Ibid.*, pp. 73–80.

Desperate measures undertaken by Zeelandia's defenders merely postpone the inevitable. In the end they negotiate a settlement by which they surrender the forts and most of the Company's money and goods to Koxinga, who permits them to return to Batavia with their ships and personal possessions.[325]

Appended to Coyett's account is a selection of letters, Formosan Council minutes, and other official papers intended to prove Coyett's innocence and Batavia's guilt for the loss of Formosa.[326] In addition there is a description of the atrocities committed by the Chinese against the Dutch citizens who fell into Koxinga's hands when he invaded Formosa.[327] The latter Coyett includes because "the fable (which is being divulged in the East Indies as well as in Europe) has originated that the Chinese have prosecuted [*sic*] the Christians on Formosa because of the Christian religion and murdered and tyrannized them and that the pastors, refusing to relinquish or foreswear their religion, have died as martyrs of the faith and therefore should have a red letter in the Almanac."[328] Twelve Netherlanders, he reports, had their noses, ears, and hands cut off by Koxinga's order after they unsuccessfully attempted to murder the Chinese crew of the junk which was transporting them from P'eng-hu to Formosa. Two others were crucified by Koxinga's men for trying to incite Formosan villagers against the Chinese. When Rev. Anthonius Hambroek, whom Koxinga sent to Zeelandia to persuade the Dutch to surrender, defiantly returned having urged his compatriots to resist rather than yield, Koxinga ordered a massacre that killed about five hundred Dutchmen. At this time Dutch women were given to Chinese officers as concubines. Some of these, however, were well treated according to Coyett, and had few complaints after their release. No, concludes Coyett, they were not martyrs: "Koxinga never troubled any of the Netherlanders because of religion, but only had them so grievously brought to death on political considerations and in order to bring about his progress."[329] He suspects that the same is true for many of those claimed as martyrs by the Catholics in Asia.

When the seventeenth century began, European readers could have known almost nothing about Formosa beyond its Portuguese name. When first introduced to European readers by the Dutch, it appeared as a large and indeed beautiful island, strategically near the Chinese coast but outside the empire's jurisdiction, frequented by Japanese and Chinese pirates and merchants, and inhabited by several tribes who lived in independent, continuously warring villages and whose languages and customs were different

[325] *Ibid.*, pp. 81–88. For the treaty see pp. 85–88.
[326] *Ibid.*, pp. 105–37.
[327] *Ibid.*, pp. 89–103.
[328] *Ibid.*, p. 93.
[329] *Ibid.*, p. 94.

from those of any people yet discovered by the Dutch and certainly different from those of the Chinese.

Except for Martini's description, which came primarily from earlier Chinese accounts, seventeenth-century Europe's new information about Formosa came entirely through Dutch reports. The most informative and influential of these were written by George Candidius and by Olfert Dapper, the latter's taken from David Wright's description. These accounts presented to European readers a surprising amount of information about the Formosan aborigines, about their livelihood, their incessant wars, their unusual family structure, their houses, their languages, and above all, their religion. Very perceptive readers might have been able to recognize some Formosan customs—ritual head-hunting, bachelor houses, their method of making rice wine—as being similar to those of the people on Borneo, the Moluccas, and the Pacific islands. Apart from the repetition of brief general statements about Formosa's beauty, however, none of the seventeenth-century European writers provided any details of the landscape beyond the immediate environs of Fort Zeelandia.

Candidius' account is crucial. On the one hand, he described the aborigines and their customs before he had learned a local language very well; on the other hand, he described them before Dutch occupation had appreciably changed their lives or driven them into the mountains. Later Dutch writers depicted some of the changes resulting from Dutch occupation and mission efforts, although Wright's account in Dapper displays considerable continuity with Candidius' observations.

One major change resulting from the VOC occupation was the increased immigration of mainland Chinese to the island. The VOC encouraged immigration, settling Chinese farmers on Company lands. The demographic and ecological consequences of this policy were apparent in some of the later Dutch reports: settled Chinese-style agriculture became common on the western plain; Chinese replaced aborigines in some areas; aborigines began to dress like Chinese; and later Dutch accounts often described the Chinese as well as the aborigines. In short the VOC had unwittingly extended the Chinese frontier in the southeast to include Formosa. What the Dutch began was greatly accelerated by Cheng Ch'eng-kung's conquest of the island in 1661, after which the stream of Chinese settlers became a flood. In 1683 Formosa was formally annexed to the Chinese empire.

During the seventeenth century, European readers received the first eyewitness reports about the lands beyond China's frontiers since those provided by Marco Polo and the other medieval travelers. The new reports were much more detailed and ranged over a much wider area than had the medieval notices, and they were generally more vivid and informative than descriptions of Chinese origin relayed to Europe by Jesuit missionaries. Although not as voluminous or as detailed as the seventeenth-century descriptions of India, China, Southeast Asia, and Japan (places already known to European readers in the sixteenth century), they nevertheless effectively introduced European readers to the hitherto least-known parts of Asia and thus considerably expanded Europe's image of Asia.

In these new seventeenth-century descriptions, European readers could have obtained glimpses of some of the world's most spectacular scenery, and from them they were able to envision more clearly vast areas of Asian geography. They were presented with an enormously varied landscape often vividly described. Beyond the Wall to China's north and northwest they encountered inhospitable deserts, craggy mountains, and treeless steppe lands which seemingly could support no settled populations but whose abandoned towns and fortresses bespoke earlier empires and movements of peoples. Nevertheless, Grueber and Verbiest's word pictures of Mongolia's open vistas and starry nights and the sparkling streams, high lakes, and clear air of the upper Yellow River valley convey something of the region's natural grandeur. Further north, European readers could have savored the vast Siberian forests crossed by long rivers whose banks were home to a multitude of Tungusic tribes interspersed by recently established Russian trading posts. With Ides, Brand, and Verbiest they could have marveled at Manchuria's varied landscape, from the intensely cultivated Chinese Pale in the south to the high mountains, dense forests, and pleasant valleys to the north and east. With Hamel they could have glimpsed Korea's mountainous but intensively cultivated landscape and understood something of the Korean peasants' hardship during the famine years. Andrade and Grueber provided vivid images of the rigorous climb over high mountains from the south and the northeast which brought them to Tibet's high plateau. Awesome peaks, thundering waterfalls, churning streams, blizzards, and reassuring mountain flowers were all part of the picture they painted. Their readers were the first Europeans to enjoy verbal sketches of Tibetan villages and the city of Lhasa, the first to see a picture of the Potala Palace. Presenting a sharp contrast to Tibet and Inner Asia, Formosa's majestic but tropically wooded mountains and its steamy western plain were introduced to European readers by Candidius, Wright, and Herport.

On China's periphery European readers met some peoples whom they may have heard about from Marco Polo and other medieval travelers. Much more frequently, however, the seventeenth-century reports introduced them to peoples and cultures entirely unknown to Europeans. They could have learned about a bewildering variety of Mongol and Tungusic tribes, some of whom were true nomads, some of whom were hunters, trappers, or fishers, and some of whom raised cattle and camels. They would have encountered some Manchu tribes who were hunters and fishers but also some who were farmers. In the reports from Korea they could have discovered an ancient and sophisticated civilization, supported by Chinese-style agriculture, governed by a complex bureaucracy, heavily influenced by Chinese culture but nevertheless displaying unique characteristics. In the descriptions of Formosa, European readers met aborigines of a seeming multitude of tribes and languages who both farmed and hunted. They lived in incessantly warring villages and had developed some of the most unusual familial and religious customs Europeans had ever observed. In Tibet, however, they encountered an apparently ancient and settled people whose society was heavily dominated by religion and priests.

Almost all European travelers, whether missionaries or merchants, commented extensively on the religions of the peoples they met. On China's periphery the spectrum of religious beliefs was exceedingly broad. Some religions were described in intimate detail, those of the Formosans and Tibetans, for example. The Jesuit descriptions of Tibetan Buddhism were uncharacteristically charitable, especially when compared with what their confreres wrote about Buddhism in China and elsewhere. While less detailed than the accounts of Formosan and Tibetan religion, seventeenth-century reports also included many descriptions of Lamaism and shamanism among the peoples of Mongolia, Inner Asia, and Manchuria, and of Korean Buddhism.

Seventeenth-century European descriptions of China's periphery quite clearly convey the fluid nature of political relationships and cultural influences in the regions beyond the empire's frontiers. They depict, for example, both Indian and Chinese influences in Tibetan Buddhism. They report Kalmuk political power in Lhasa, annual caravans from both India and China in Tsaparang, and Guge's subjugation by Ladakh after a brief period of independence. They describe the nervous reception of Ch'ing envoys in Seoul and the Koreans' fear of the Japanese; Japanese hostility towards the Dutch occupation of Formosa; and massive Chinese immigration to and eventual conquest of the island. They note abandoned towns and fortresses in Mongolia, the Ch'ing emperor's patronage of Lamaism among the Mongols, Chinese trade at Russian riverine outposts in Siberia, and Mongol chieftains switching allegiances from emperor to tsar and vice versa. In each case, seventeenth-century European reports provided information about the expansion of the Ch'ing empire and in some cases its confrontation with the expanding empire of the Russian tsars. Finally, they reported the reception of Russian embassies to the Ch'ing court and the establishment of a boundary between the two empires with the Treaty of Nerchinsk (1689). In each case, also, with the exceptions of Tibet and Korea, the European reports depicted cultures that were being changed or were about to be changed by the Chinese or the Russians, or in the case of Formosa, by the Europeans themselves. Not only did they introduce European readers to exotic peoples on China's periphery but they provided at the same time a last fleeting glimpse of peoples whose unique way of life was soon to disappear, for example that of the steppe nomads of Mongolia, the forest tribes of Manchuria, and the aborigines of Formosa. By the end of the century European readers learned that most of the aborigines wore clothes and lived in villages under VOC-appointed chiefs and that the K'ang-hsi emperor had divided Mongolia into provinces assigning specific pastures to each Mongol tribe. In some instances, therefore, seventeenth-century European descriptions of China's periphery have become important sources of information about peoples and ways of life that are no more.

CHAPTER XXIII

Japan

European visitors, beginning with the sixteenth-century Jesuit missionaries, witnessed and reported on one of the most dynamic periods of Japanese history—the unification of the island empire during the second half of the sixteenth century and the consolidation of Tokugawa rule during the seventeenth century. Francis Xavier, the Jesuit pioneer, landed at Kagoshima in 1549, the year in which Oda Nobunaga, the first of Japan's three great unifiers, inherited his father's domain. Xavier's successors were able to observe Oda's campaigns against rival lords (*daimyō*, or "great names") and the militant Buddhist establishment until he controlled all of central Japan. After Nobunaga's death in 1582 they watched Toyotomi Hideyoshi, Nobunaga's leading general, continue the unification until by 1590 he controlled all of Japan. The missionaries were joined by Dutch and English merchants at the beginning of the seventeenth century, in time to see Tokugawa Ieyasu win the contest for power which followed Hideyoshi's death and the establishment of the Tokugawa *bakufu* ("tent government" or shogunate).

Japan experienced profound changes during the seventeenth century as the Tokugawa shoguns consolidated their power. A central government was established and political devices for the control of the daimyos were developed. A new capital, Edo (Tokyo), was built and flourished. The role of the warrior class (*samurai*) was redefined as the almost continual warfare of the sixteenth century gave way to the final skirmishes of the seventeenth century and to the profound peace that followed. Openness to Europeans and their religion was replaced in the Tokugawa era by increasing suspicion and hostility towards foreigners and the persecution of Christianity, until by 1641 the country was effectively closed to all Westerners except the Dutch.

After 1641 fresh information about Japan decreased precipitously in Europe. Nevertheless occasional reports continued to appear during the second half of the century, filtered through the Dutch outpost in Nagasaki harbor.

I.

MISSIONARY REPORTS TO 1650

Probably no Asian land was so frequently and thoroughly described in sixteenth-century European reports as Japan. The earliest substantial accounts appeared in the late 1540's, and Saint Francis Xavier's principal letter from Japan was first published in 1562.[1] Thereafter "Japan letters," as they were called, were regularly published by Xavier's successors both in separate letterbooks and in general collections of Jesuit letters, finally finding their way into Jesuit histories of Japan and of the Jesuit mission there.[2] Europe's appetite for information was further whetted by Alessandro Valignano's Japanese mission to Europe (1584–86),[3] and Jesuit presses virtually inundated Europe with more and larger reports from the Japan missionaries, which were frequently republished and translated into most European languages.

The general purpose of the Jesuit letters was understandably to describe in edifying terms the exciting Jesuit mission to Japan and to elicit support for it. The story of the mission, therefore, dominates them, and some aspects of Japanese society may have been distorted or glossed over either by their authors or by more censorious editors in Europe in order to enhance the image of the mission's prospects. Nevertheless much information about Japanese customs, society, religions, geography, language, and politics appears in the letters. Also by the end of the sixteenth century more reflective and balanced histories of the Jesuit mission in Japan were appearing, of which the account in Luis de Guzman's *Historia de las missiones* (1601) was the most comprehensive.[4]

From this voluminous Jesuit literature a surprisingly accurate and detailed image of Japan emerged. In Guzman's sixteenth-century synthesis, Japan appears as a collection of islands, more mountainous and less fertile than Europe but nevertheless capable of producing enough food for its people if wars did not so regularly disrupt agriculture. Japan's farmers cultivate wheat, barley, millet, and rice, and raise sheep, dogs, oxen, and horses. Most fruits known to Europe grow in Japan, as well as some unknown to Europe. Wild boar,

---

[1] On Xavier's report and those which preceded it see *Asia*, I, 651–74.
[2] On the "Japan letters" of the sixteenth century see *ibid.*, pp. 674–88.
[3] See *ibid.*, pp. 688–706.
[4] *Ibid.*, pp. 706–19.

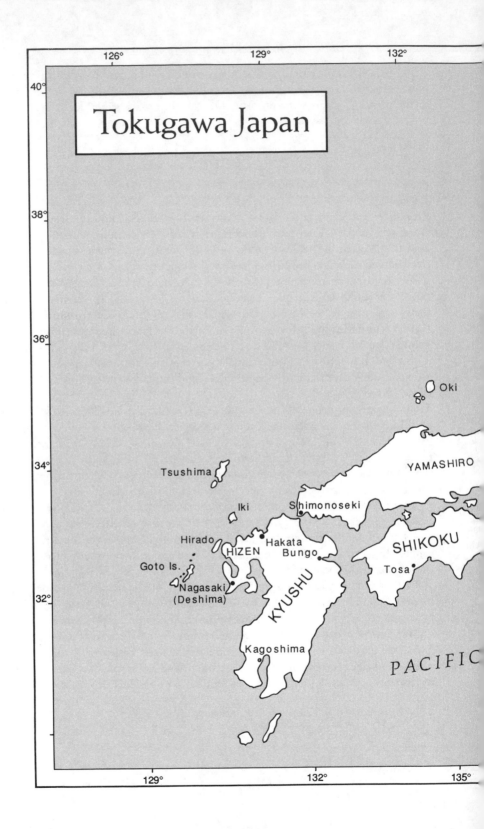

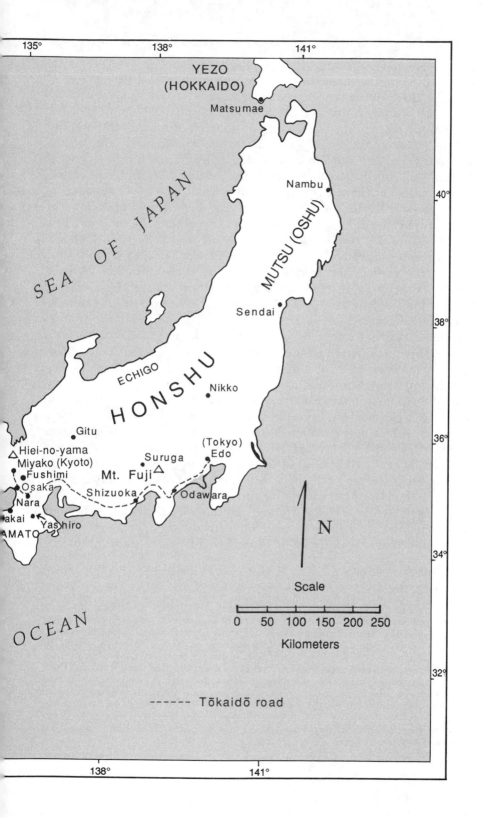

135° 138° 141°

YEZO
(HOKKAIDO)

• Matsumae

40°

SEA OF JAPAN

• Nambu

MUTSU (OSHU)

38°

• Sendai

ECHIGO

HONSHU

• Nikko

36°

• Gitu

△ Hiei-no-yama
• Miyako (Kyoto)
• Fushimi
• Osaka
• Nara
• akai
AMATO
↑ Yashiro

• Suruga
Mt. Fuji △

(Tokyo)
• Edo

• Shizuoka
• Odawara

N

Scale

├──┼──┼──┼──┼──┤
0 50 100 150 200 250
Kilometers

32°

34°

------ Tōkaidō road

OCEAN

138° 141°

deer, rabbits, pheasants, ducks, geese, chickens, doves, and other animals and fowl live in the mountains, forests, and fields. Good fishing can be found in Japan's streams and surrounding seas.[5]

Guzman accurately distinguishes the emperor from the shogun and makes a murky reference to the twelfth-century triumph of Minamoto Yoritomo and the establishment of the Kamakura *bakufu*. His account of sixteenth-century politics is much more detailed. He describes the major political divisions and lists the sixty-six "kingdoms" of Japan. The emperor (*dairi*), he observes, retains his ancient dignity and is held in high honor although he has no power. His chief function seems to be that of granting titles, some of which are purchased. Actual government is in the hands of "kings" and their vassals, "Conixus" (*kunshu*, lords or daimyos), and subvassals, "tonos." Guzman rather accurately describes what is often called Japanese feudalism, the granting of fiefs, the vassals' obligation to provide soldiers for their lords, and the lords' absolute authority over their vassals. He notes that Japanese lords usually turn over the government of their territories to their sons before they die.[6]

Following earlier Jesuit writers, Guzman provides several of the intriguing cultural contrasts between Japanese and Europeans which so fascinated sixteenth-century writers.[7] For example, the Japanese treasure antique swords and teacups rather than gold, they eat fish and rice but loathe beef, they build their houses of wood but their palaces and castles of stone. Despite such strange customs, however, Guzman, like most earlier Jesuits, considers the Japanese the finest, most intelligent, and most rational of all the Asian peoples. He describes in considerable detail their modesty and reserve, their disregard for physical discomfort, their resignation in the face of adversity, their hatred of theft and gambling, their respect and obedience towards superiors, and other aspects of their national character.

Guzman is fascinated by the Japanese language which he judges to be both difficult and rich, containing more synonyms and more expressions of propriety and elegance than Greek or Latin. It is difficult to learn because its

[5] What follows is based on Luis de Guzman, *Historia de las missiones . . .* , (2 vols.; Alcala, 1601), I, 305–14. On Guzman's account of Japan, see also *Asia*, I, 711–17.

[6] Guzman's sixty-six "kingdoms" refer to the old provinces (*kuni* or *koku*) of the *ritsuryō* system dating back to the beginning of the ninth century. While the boundaries of the larger seventeenth-century domains still corresponded to those of the old provinces, the provinces themselves had by then lost all administrative significance and their administrative offices (*kami* and *suke*) had disappeared. See *Kodansha Encyclopedia of Japan* (9 vols.; Tokyo, 1983), VI, 258–60. *Tono*, more accurately *tonosama*, is actually another expression for lord or daimyo.

Feudalism is a term used to describe medieval European political and social structure. There is considerable disagreement about whether or not it can accurately be applied to Japan. Still, while constantly changing and in some respects diverging widely from the medieval European model, Japanese society between the twelfth and the seventeenth centuries showed enough elements of European feudalism to make the term almost irresistible to those interested in comparative history. See, for example, Peter Duus, *Feudalism in Japan* (New York, 1969), or his article in *Kodansha Encyclopedia*, II, 263–67.

[7] Cf. Fróis' comparisons in *Asia*, I, 687–88.

appropriate vocabulary changes depending on whether one is speaking to a noble or a commoner, an old person or a young one, a man or a woman. Furthermore the Japanese employ two "alphabets" in writing it: one with single letters (kana), the other with characters like the Chinese. It is exceedingly economical. A whole European word can be signified by a single Japanese character, and there are fewer characters in a Japanese sentence than there are words in the same sentence translated into a European language.

While unsympathetic, Guzman's description of Japanese religion is detailed and fairly accurate. He identifies three principal sects: "Xenxi" (*Zenshū*), "Xodoxius" (*Jōdoshū*), and "Foguexus" (*Hokkeshū*). Zen bonzes (*bōzu*) or priests deny eternal life and stress meditation, although their temples also contain idols. *Jōdo* or Pure Land Buddhists worship an idol called Amida who saves all those who simply invoke the name. Followers of *Hokke,* or Nicheren Buddhism, worship "Iaca" (*Shaka* or *Shakyamuni*) and derive their beliefs from a single book called "Foque" (*Hokkekyō* or the *Lotus Sutra*) (see pl. 407). In addition Guzman mentions several other sects, among them "Icoxus" (*Shingon-shū*), which he erroneously thinks broke off from the principal sects. Some of the sects are extremely warlike, their armed monks terrorizing the people. There are many rich monasteries and temples, a very large number of which are concentrated on the mountains called "Frenoxama" (Hiei-no-yama or Hieizan) near Miyako (Kyoto). Although many of these buildings have been destroyed in the recent wars, over five hundred remain. Guzman also mentions Nara as an important religious center, and describes several great universities where the bonzes study, the largest of which is at "Bandou" (Bandō) in the northern part of the Kantō Plain, no doubt the Ashikaga Gakkō.[8]

The bonzes are many and varied, those of different sects wearing different robes, but they seem to be organized into a hierarchy headed by a supreme priest called the "Iaco" (*jaku*). Beneath him are "Tundos" (*hondō*) who are like bishops and archbishops and who approve those chosen to govern the monasteries. Ceremonies differ from sect to sect, but bonzes sing in choruses, read at prescribed times, preach, and officiate at funerals, tasks familiar to Christian priests. Guzman describes Japanese funerals and several identifiable festivals, among which are the Gion, the Hachiman, and the Bon festivals.[9]

Of particular interest is Guzman's account of a popular pilgrimage led by monks called "Xamabugis" (*yamabushi* or "soldiers of the mountains").[10]

[8] Bandō is an old name for the Kantō region. Although most of its students were monks, the Ashikaga Gakkō was not a Buddhist university. It specialized in Confucian learning. See *Kodansha Encyclopedia* (n. 6), I, 99–100.

[9] For the identifications of the "Iaco" and "Tundos" see S. R. Dalgado, *Glossário Luso-asiático* (2 vols.; Coimbra, 1921), II, 379, 436. For examples of several sorts of priests see our pls. 408, 409, and 411.

[10] Guzman, *op. cit.* (n. 5), I, 402–4. For an edited version of this section in German translation see G. Schurhammer, "Die Yamabushis," *ZMR*, XII (1922), 212–14. On earlier Jesuit

The *yamabushi* in the Jesuits' judgment are "entirely devoted to the service of Satan." Most of them live in the mountains and rarely descend. Some, however, travel from town to town practicing deceits and sorceries and encouraging believers to make a pilgrimage to "worship the devil in a certain temple." Guzman claims that his description of the pilgrimage comes from a bonze who had made seven such pilgrimages before he accepted Christian baptism. On a specified day twice each year more than two thousand pilgrims assemble in Nara to begin the journey.[11] Altogether the journey takes seventy-five days because the path is so difficult that the pilgrims can travel only one league per day. They carry all their provisions on their backs, and during the journey they may eat only a handful of fried rice in the morning and again in the evening. During the first eight days they endure extreme thirst because there is no water along the route. Many become ill and some die, but no one stops to take care of them. At "Ozin" (Yoshino),[12] eight days from Nara, at the foot of very high mountains, they are welcomed by bonzes called "Ienguis" (*zenki*), with ugly and terrifying faces and long, unkempt hair who accompany them to a place called "Ozaba" (Dorogawa-mura) where they are met by another group of *yamabushi* called "Guoguis" (*goki*), who guide them on the rest of the pilgrimage. The Japanese think these are devils in the form of men.[13] They lead the pilgrims over boulders and cliffs which they must climb using hands and feet and over which the *goki* leap like deer, all the while exhorting the pilgrims to worship "Iaca" (Shakyamuni) and keep the fast. Pilgrims who try to drop out or eat extra food are placed in trees hanging over cliffs to hold on with their hands until they tire and fall to their deaths. No one, not even a close relative, is allowed to stop or tend them. Upon reaching a field high in the mountains the pilgrims are detained for a day and a night and forced to sit with crossed arms and with their mouths pressed against their knees, contemplating their sins so that they will be able to confess them. The *yamabushi* roam through the meditating group beating any who change their posture. Finally they reach

---

references to the yamabushi see *Asia*, I, 661n, 662n, 716. The term *yamabushi* really means, in its earliest characters, "to 'lie down in the mountains', idealizing the earliest *yamabushi* career of solitary wandering and practices in the mountain groves. Later as *Shugendō* was organized from such loose activities, the word came to mean a practitioner or priest of this organized movement" (H. Byron Earhart, *A Religious Study of the Mount Haguro Sect of Shugendō: An Example of Japanese Mountain Religion* [Tokyo, 1970], p. 172).

[11] Most modern accounts call this an annual pilgrimage.

[12] Yoshino in the southern part of old Yamato is a pilgrimage center in the mountains directly south of Nara. The peaks in its vicinity vary from five thousand to six thousand feet in height. See B. H. Chamberlain and W. B. Mason, *A Handbook for Travellers in Japan* (5th, rev., ed.; London, 1899), pp. 321–24.

[13] The *zenki* and *goki* are demons who were subdued and have become the servants of En no Gyōja, revered as the founder of *Shugendō;* for details see the unabridged Japanese dictionary, *Nihon Kokugo Daijiten* (20 vols.; Tokyo, 1974), II, 311. For a drawing of a *yamabushi* see C. J. Dunn, *Everyday Life in Traditional Japan* (Tokyo, 1969), p. 80. On En no Gyōja see *Kodansha Encyclopedia* (n. 6), II, 219.

a high peak from which the monks have extended a huge iron bar at the end of which is a balance fitted with basins at either end. One by one the pilgrims are placed in one basin with counterweights in the other. Thus suspended over the abyss they must loudly confess the past year's sins so that all can hear. Should a pilgrim fail to satisfy the monks with his confession they trip the balance and he falls to his death. After each pilgrim has confessed, they descend the mountain to a temple containing a golden image of Shakyamuni which they all worship, each also giving three taels (*ryō* or *bu*) of silver to the monks. Then they travel to another temple where for seven or eight days they refresh themselves with banquets, dancing, plays, and other entertainments. They return home by a different route than the one by which they ascended.[14]

The Jesuits came to Japan in time to witness the last stages of the country at war (*sengoku jidai*) which eventually led to the establishment of the Tokugawa shogunate in 1603. Xavier arrived in the same year (1549) that Oda Nobunaga inherited his father's estates.[15] In their published letters, Xavier's successors reported countless details about the wars and the participants, traced the rise of Nobunaga to the position of *de facto* shogun in 1568, reported his assassination in 1582, and described Toyotomi Hideyoshi's subsequent rise to power. They described Hideyoshi's reforms, his administration, his wealth, his treatment of the daimyos, his foreign adventures, his personal character, and the effects of his government on the Jesuit missions and on the Japanese Christians. Through the Jesuit letters Europeans received regular and if not up-to-the-minute at least up-to-the-year news about the momentous events of this turbulent but crucial period in Japanese history. The Jesuit letters, in fact, are an indispensable aid in reconstructing the events of the *sengoku* era. Finally, in the last years of the sixteenth century the Jesuits reported Hideyoshi's sudden anti-Christian edict of 1587, the disruptive arrival of Franciscan missionaries from Manila in 1592 and 1593, and the shocking crucifixion of twenty-six Christians, including six Franciscan priests, in Nagasaki on February 5, 1597. Hideyoshi died during the following year. Guzman's *Historia* (1601) provides a systematic summary of these reports.[16]

In 1602 Marcelo de Ribadeneira, one of the Franciscans expelled from

[14] This is a description of a *Shugendō* pilgrimage to Mount Ōmine in Yamato. *Shugendō* is a distinctive religious practice which blends traditional Japanese rituals associated with sacred mountains with imported Buddhist and Taoist beliefs. For details see *The Encyclopedia of Religion*, ed. Mircea Eliade (15 vols.; New York, 1987), XIII, 302–5. Compare it to those pilgrimages conducted to Mount Atago by *yamabushi* confraternities; see Anne-Marie Bouchy, "The Cult of Mount Atago and the Atago Confraternities," *The Journal of Asian Studies*, XLVI (1987), 255–77. See also Harmut O. Rothermund, *Die Yamabushi: Aspekte ihres Glaubens, Lebens und ihre sozialen Function im japanischen Mittelalter* (Hamburg, 1968), especially pp. 52–54, 232–33, which describe the Ōmine pilgrimage.

[15] James Murdoch and Isoh Yamagata, *A History of Japan* (3 vols.; London, 1949), II, 121.

[16] *Asia*, I, 711, 717–19, 725–29. For an analysis of Hideyoshi's expulsion decree see George

Japan, published his *Historia de las islas del archipielago Filipino y reinos de la gran China, Tartaria, Cochin-China, Malaca, Siam, Cambodge y Japon,* the second volume of which is the first extended account of Japan by a non-Jesuit.[17] Most of Ribadeneira's account is devoted to the experiences of the Franciscan missionaries in Japan from their arrival in 1592 to the Nagasaki crucifixions of 1597, for which he depended heavily on Juan de Santa Maria's 1601 report.[18] A biography of each of the twenty-six martyrs is included.

Ribadeneira's description of the island kingdom is far less detailed than Guzman's and repetitious of it. Nevertheless there are some differences. Japan's climate, he reports, is extremely hot in summer and bitterly cold in winter. The land is covered with dense forests; there are many rivers and plenty of water in all seasons. The plains are fertile; he mentions many of the grains and animals reported by Guzman. Rice and fish, however, are the staples of the Japanese diet. Cattle are raised as draft animals, but never killed for food.[19]

The emperor, "called 'Vo' [Ō] but addressed as 'Dairi' [*dairi*]," is "believed to have been descended from the true God." He lives secluded in his palace, never appearing in public, and never speaking to any commoner. "From the very first," the kingdom was divided into sixty-six provinces, each governed by "captains of war," who represent the emperor and are absolute in their provinces. "Taicosama" (Taikōsama, Hideyoshi's title) became "lord of lords" because of his military power and acts in the name of the emperor.[20] Ribadeneira describes neither the contemporary complexity nor the historical development of Japanese feudalism.

Japanese nobles are much concerned about family genealogies and honor—"face-saving." When condemned they usually dispatch themselves by slashing their stomachs before they can be executed. They are violent, think little about cutting off their enemies' heads, and oppress the common people, who are very poor. The people generally are disciplined, obedient subjects and true to their word.

High-born women wear their hair long and loose; commoners wear it knotted at the top of their heads. Country landowners shave both their heads and beards. Other men cut their hair on the crown and tie what remains behind their necks (see pl. 419). They remove their straw sandals before they enter a house, as a sign of respect, according to Ribadeneira. Japanese people are very hospitable, always prepared to entertain visitors.

Elison, *Deus Destroyed: The Image of Christianity in Early Modern Japan* (Cambridge, Mass., 1973), pp. 115–33.

[17] For bibliography see above, pp. 321–22.

[18] See above, p. 315, n. 35.

[19] Marcelo Ribadeneira, *History of the Philippines and Other Kingdoms,* trans. Pacita Guevara Fernandez (2 vols.; Manila, 1970), II, 656, 657.

[20] *Ibid.,* pp. 657–58.

They sit at low tables and eat with chopsticks, never touching food with their fingers. A guest is always served first by the host. They eat mostly vegetables: radishes, turnips, eggplants, squash, and some fruits. They drink wine brewed from rice. Here Ribadeneira mentions neither rice nor fish.[21]

Ribadeneira is fascinated by Japanese medicine. The Japanese rely on Chinese medical books. Although they are generally a healthy people, they nevertheless employ many doctors, masseurs, and the like. Their medicines are quite simple, usually liquid concoctions made from herbs and sweetened with syrup. Most of them are purgatives. "For more serious illnesses of the stomach, the internal organs, especially earthworms in the intestines, they use . . . little buttons made of large grains of rice, and burnt, then applied externally to the parts of the body undergoing pains." They apply the "flaming balls" to open sores as well, and they cauterize open wounds. "Their theory about the cause of any kind of sickness is that all distempers of the body arise from cold; therefore heat, or the application of heat, presumably followed by perspiration or sweating will purge out illness."[22]

Ribadeneira's account of Japanese religion is hostile and not very perceptive. He judges the Japanese to be "idol-loving" people who worship a large number of gods, the most important of which are Amida and "the black god Xaca" (Shakyamuni). There are as many sects as there are idols, all run by priests called "Bonzos," who live in communities and are supported by alms and donations. Some are scholars, priding themselves on their mastery of Chinese characters and books. There are also some communities of nuns.[23] In later chapters Ribadeneira provides a more detailed but still confusing account of "the principal religious sects," those which worship Amida and "Xaca." Amida and "Xaca" are reputed to have been the first rulers of Siam and "Zamiro" (*Seiron,* Ceylon?) respectively. "Zamiro" is said to have been inhabited by black people. "Xaca," Ribadeneira reports, was supposedly Amida's disciple and biographer. Amida's followers hope to be reborn in a paradise somewhere in the West, where they will be "transformed into eighty-three different figures and creatures."[24] They also believe they will be reincarnated as animals or higher spirits to purify themselves before entering paradise. Those who follow "Xaca" forbid the killing or eating of any living creature. Ribadeneira's description of their practices, however—meditation and the discipline of mind and will—sounds like Zen. "Heaven," he reports, "is interior peace, while Hell is inquietude, anxiety, due to an un-

---

[21] *Ibid.,* pp. 658–59.

[22] *Ibid.,* pp. 659–660. The little buttons used in moxibustion (*kyū*) are not made from rice but from moxa leaves. On treating ills by cautery or *moxa* see B. H. Chamberlain, *Things Japanese* (London, 1905), p. 339; on general medicine see Dunn, *op. cit.* (n. 13), pp. 133–34.

[23] Ribadeneira, *op. cit.* (n. 19), II, 660.

[24] *Ibid.* Ribadeneira probably means thirty-three, referring to the thirty-three different incarnations of Kannon (Sanskrit, Avalokitesvara) depicted in the Lotus Sutra. See *Kodansha Encyclopedia* (n. 6), IV, 144–45. For depictions of Amida see our pls. 406 and 410.

disciplined mind and will, and a heart full of desires and afflicted by mundane cares." [25]

According to Ribadeneira, there are many other sects and two kinds of gods: "camis" (kami) and "fotoques" (Buddhas). The kami are the "source" of the Japanese military class and the chief kami is called "Fachiman" (Hachiman). The Buddhas are the "origin" of the Chinese. Priests cleverly induce wealthy Japanese to give liberally to the temples in the hope of being reincarnated as Buddhas. Some priests attribute a spiritual being and infinite power to Amida, calling him "Dainichi" (*Dainichi* or *Tai-jih* in Chinese; *Vairocana* in Sanskrit):

The belief proceeding from him is that at the beginning there was a globe, and like an egg, it burst forth, and broke itself in the center, creating the heavens out of the upper hemisphere and creating the earth out of the lower hemisphere. Out of the earth, emerged three men and three women predecessors of the Japanese race, with the sun moving around Mt. Fujiyama.

One sect worships a living bonze whom they believe to be a direct descendant of Amida. Ribadeneira reports that the "major idols gracing their principal temples number three thousand three hundred and thirty three, all of them having life-sized figures, lavishly decorated—each one having ten hands, and a head subdivided into five or six little heads." This is certainly a reference to the Sanjūsangendō temple of the Tendai sect in Kyoto. [26]

Ribadeneira's account of Japanese religious practices is obviously prejudiced. The author makes no effort to understand what he observed; nevertheless he portrays vivid images of what could be seen in the temples and on the streets of Kyoto. Believers, he reports, perform many kinds of penance: fasting, praying, living as hermits, standing without resting, and so forth. Some are buried alive, some throw themselves into the sea, or walk naked outdoors during the winter and die of the cold. They meet death with cheerful resignation, believing that Amida will reward them. Usually Amida is represented as a man, seated. "Xaca" is often represented with animals or birds. Some of the gods look like demons, ferocious and menacing. Some appear as monkeys. "A god of thunder and lightning [Raijin] is represented within an arch of kettledrums surrounding his head, where many candles

---

[25] Ribadeneira, *op. cit.* (n. 19), II, 686–87. For Shaka see our pl. 407.

[26] Ribadeneira, *op. cit.* (n. 19), II, 687–89. Sanjūsangendō is the main hall of the Rengeō-in Temple in the Shirakawa area of Kyoto. Founded in 1132 and rebuilt in 1266, it contains 1,001 images of the bodhisattva Kannon, goddess of mercy, each five feet tall with eleven faces and twenty-one pairs of arms. Since each arm can save twenty-five worlds, each image is considered to have one thousand arms, and because Kannon can transform herself into thirty-three different figures in order to save all mankind, the 1,001 images can be considered to be 33,033. See *Kodansha Encyclopedia* (n. 6), VII, 13; Chamberlain and Mason, *op. cit.* (n. 12), p. 368; and N. Tsuda, *Handbook of Japanese Art* (Tokyo, 1936), pp. 363–64. For a photograph of a number of the 1,001 individual figures see Japan Times, *Kyoto. An Essay in Photographs* (Tokyo, 1975), pp. 90–91. Also *cf.* our pl. 397.

are lighted, and gives the impression of a head on fire." The image of a "god of love" (probably Kannon) looks like the Madonna. The Japanese are fond of pilgrimages. At one shrine in Kyoto, pilgrims bathe naked in a fountain of clear water, after which they worship in a nearby temple.[27] Nara is a favorite pilgrimage site; its deer and doves are considered sacred. In the streets people can be seen telling enormous prayer beads, repeating "Amidabut" (*namu amida butsu*) with each bead. Worshippers beat the large brass gongs which stand at the temple doors before entering and after leaving the temples. Many of the bonzes beg for food, walking through the streets beating a small gong while people throw rice into their begging bowls. Some other, still more diabolical, bonzes have left Kyoto since Nobunaga destroyed four hundred of their temples during the recent wars. Burial services, Ribadeneira reports, are like those of the Chinese. The rich cremate their dead with much pomp and feasting, the festivity lasting for fifteen days. The poor often discard corpses in the rivers or the sea, or in a common burial ground.[28]

Finally Ribadeneira describes some public festivals, all of which he observes are "attended not with solemnity, but by debauchery and orgies." The fasts or vigils which they keep before holidays are not intended to be sacrifices but are observed to conserve food and drink for the feast. Every full moon is a feast, but the most important is on the first full moon of the New Year, some time in February. It is observed for fifteen days before and fifteen after the full moon. During this time people travel to visit relations or their lords. They eat rice cakes and drink sake. Commoners celebrate much like the nobles except for a shorter period, eight days before and eight days after the full moon. The poor, however, celebrate for only three days before and three days after. There is considerable noise and drunkenness in the streets. The Hachiman festival, in honor of the god of war, is celebrated by jousts, sword and dagger contests, "judo" contests, and wrestling. After the games the people go out to the countryside and march around a grove of large trees until a python emerges which they worship as an incarnation of the god. "Bo" (Bon) festival is held to honor the dead. For three or four days people visit temples, parade through the streets at night with lamps, bells, and drums, and set dishes with food outside their doors for the souls of the dead.[29]

Ribadeneira's brief account of the tea ceremony is more sensitive; perhaps even idealized:

[27] Possibly a reference to the Kiyomizudera, or "Temple of Pure Water," the object of pilgrimages since the ninth century. For a photograph see Japan Times, *op. cit.* (n. 26), p. 97.

[28] Ribadeneira, *op. cit.* (n. 19), II, 689–93. On cremation and interment see Dunn, *op. cit.* (n. 13), pp. 128–29.

[29] Ribadeneira, *op. cit.* (n. 19), II, 693–96. For a classical Western description of the Bon ceremonies see L. Hearn, *Glimpses of Unfamiliar Japan* (2 vols.; Boston, 1896), I, chaps. v–vi. See also Chamberlain, *op. cit.* (n. 22), p. 162.

Their houses stand in the midst of cool, green gardens where pine trees and weeping willows grow. They sit in their little rooms overlooking their gardens and drink tea, the tea ceremony being a vital ceremony in a Japanese house. They believe that tea refreshes the spirit, soothes the tired mind, and strengthens the body.[30]

The flow of Jesuit letters describing the progress of the now threatened mission, augmented by letters from missionaries of the other orders, continued unabated during the opening decades of the seventeenth century.[31] These letters also contain a wealth of detail about the rapidly changing political situation in Japan. Readers of the letterbooks learned about Hideyoshi's death in 1598 and the regency he established for his infant son Hideyori. They learned about the conspiracy of Ishida Mitsunari ("Ibonojo" in the Jesuit letters) and his allies against the regency's strongman, Tokugawa Ieyasu, and of the showdown at the battle of Sekigahara in 1600 which gave Ieyasu almost complete control of the country. The letters trace in detail Ieyasu's consolidation of power, his dealings with the daimyos, his assumption of the title of shogun in 1603, his formal retirement and the transfer of the title to his son Hidetada in 1605, and the siege and destruction of Osaka castle in 1614–15 during which Hideyori died.[32]

The missionaries' primary concern, however, was to describe the effect of these events on the Christian mission in Japan. Despite their initial fears, occasioned because some of the Christian daimyos had opposed Ieyasu at Sekigahara, the missionaries soon judged Ieyasu's triumph to have been good for the church in Japan. Francesco Pasio's Annual Letter of 1601, published in 1603, for example, is filled with details of Ieyasu's treatment of the defeated daimyos and of the missionaries' fears.[33] Valentim Carvalho's supplement to the Annual Letter of 1600, also published in 1603, reports Ieyasu's friendliness and favors towards the mission and judges that the mission is in as good a state as it was in 1586, before Hideyoshi's anti-Christian edict.[34] Although they occasionally report isolated instances of persecution in certain domains, the letterbooks published during the first decade of the century mainly describe conversions, miracles, the piety and progress of the converts, religious services, debates with bonzes, and the reception of the missionaries by the shogun and other great lords. Despite the sporadic persecutions, the image they project is of a confidently growing church.[35] Nowhere is this image

---

[30] Ribadeneira, *op. cit.* (n. 19), II, 696.

[31] For titles see above, pp. 331–33, 369–71, 373–75.

[32] For details of these events based in part on the missionaries' reports see Murdoch and Yamagata, *op. cit.* (n. 15), II, 387–553.

[33] *Lettera annua di Giappone scritta nel 1601* . . . (Rome, 1603). See above, pp. 369–70.

[34] *Sopplimento dell' annua del MDC* . . . (Rome, 1603). See above, p. 370.

[35] For the story of the Japan mission during the *Sengoku* period and the first years of the Tokugawa, see *Asia*, I, 86–93, 166–76, and C. R. Boxer, *The Christian Century in Japan* (Berkeley, 1951) pp. 137–247.

projected so clearly, even repetitiously, and in so much detail as in Fernão Guerreiro's five-volume *Relaçam* published between 1603 and 1611.[36]

Apart from particular events, political and ecclesiastical, Guerreiro and the letterbooks of the century's first decade contain relatively little description of Japan or its people, possibly because the authors thought Japan had been adequately described in earlier Jesuit accounts. Nevertheless a careful reader would occasionally be treated to fresh descriptions of things never before published. Among the specific events reported by Guerreiro are the grand procession of the daimyos to the emperor's palace in Miyako (Kyoto) when Ieyasu received the title of shogun from the emperor in 1603, and the 1604 "canonization" of Hideyoshi as the new Hachiman or "god of battles," "one of the principle kami of Japan." The new temple in Miyako in which the latter took place, Guerreiro reports, is the most elaborate in all Japan, and the canonization was celebrated in a grand festival which is intended to become an annual event. Guerreiro also reports the marriage of Ieyasu's granddaughter to Hideyori, Hideyoshi's son.[37]

Some interesting information can be gleaned from Guerreiro's brief notices about Japanese towns and cities. Nagasaki in 1600 is a fine city, well situated, with healthful air and about four or five thousand inhabitants.[38] Hakata, a port in Chikuzen, is a very important city, well situated with fine buildings, inhabited by rich merchants. Many Christians, both old and newly converted, live there.[39] Miyako and Osaka are the principal cities of Japan. Hideyoshi built magnificent castles in each of them. The castle near Miyako is called Fushimi. In these two castles live all the great lords of Japan, those from the west in Fushimi and those from the east in Osaka.[40] Miyako is very large, with over eighty thousand inhabitants. It is divided into two sections, one called Lower Miyako ("Miaco de baixo") and the other Miyako on the Hill ("Miaco de riba"). Lower Miyako borders on

[36] Modern edition by Artur Viegas, *Relação anual das coisas que fizeram padres da Companhia de Jesus nas suas missões* . . . (3 vols.; Coimbra, 1930–41), I, 55–234; II, 5–87, 217–89; III, 115–229. For bibliography and general contents see above, pp. 315–18.

[37] Viegas (ed.), *op. cit.* (n. 36), II, 5–7. The temple is probably Myōhō-in, the Buddhist edifice built in Kyoto by Hideyori which houses his father's relics. It was completed in 1614. See Chamberlin and Mason, *op. cit.* (n. 12), pp. 369–70. On these events also see Murdoch and Yamagata, *op. cit.* (n. 15), II, 448–49.

[38] Guerreiro in Viegas (ed.), *op. cit.* (n. 36), I, 81. In 1604 the population was 24,693, according to Japanese sources. See W. A. Wooley, "Historical Notes on Nagasaki," *Transactions of the Asiatic Society of Japan,* IX (1881), 134.

[39] Viegas (ed.), *op. cit.* (n. 36), I, 111. Hakata is now the commercial port of Fukuoka. For a Shinto shrine in Hakata, see our pls. 412 and 413.

[40] Viegas (ed.), *op. cit.* (n. 36), I, 114. Hideyoshi built his magnificent castle at Fushimi near the southern end of the Higashima Ridge in what is today the Momoyama district of Kyoto between 1592 and 1596. He lived there until his death in 1598. Tokugawa Ieyasu made it his residence in the central provinces from 1600 to 1615, when Osaka Castle fell to him. The third Tokugawa shogun, Iemitsu, was named shogun at Fushimi in 1623, after which he had the castle torn down. See *Kodansha Encyclopedia* (n. 6), II, 375.

Fushimi; Miyako and Fushimi form a continuous city extending for more than a league. The emperor and his "cungues" (*kuge* or court) live in Miyako on the Hill.[41] Gifu, the principle city of Mino, is the residence of "Chunu-gandono" (Chūnagon-dono), Nobunaga's grandson and the legitimate heir of the monarchy which the tyrant "Taicocama" (Hideyoshi) usurped from him.[42] Edo, in 1605 the seat of the new Tokugawa *bakufu,* is "large and beautiful in the Japanese fashion." Although it is at about 35° north latitude its climate is more temperate than Miyako's because it is so close to the sea. Several estuaries and canals, all man-made, permit even good-sized ships to load and unload their cargoes in various parts of the city. The shogun's castle, recently built by Ieyasu, is very large, more than a league in circumference, with very thick high walls all smoothly and evenly laid. Its broad and deep moat makes it almost unassailable. It is not quite completed, but when it is it will be one of the strongest and grandest in Japan. The shogun keeps a great many nobles at court, all of which makes it "seem much more populous and pleasant to see."[43] Guerreiro reports that some Englishmen and Dutchmen are living in and near Edo, having come on a ship several years earlier which Ieyasu had moved up to Edo. Its crewmen have been settled with houses and families. He worries about the damage these heretics may do to the church in Japan.[44] Guerreiro also includes a 1607 description of Edo castle in which the author, Francesco Pasio, marvels at its size, beauty, and neatness, at the beautiful paintings in it, and describes how 300,000 workers were used in building it, all provided and maintained by various daimyos in rotation, "the Cubo (Kubō-sama or shogun, Ieyasu) giving them only a little rice from time to time as extra rations."[45]

Guerreiro's *Relaçam* contains what may be the first published Western descriptions of the Tōkaidō, the "Eastern Sea Route," and of Mount Fuji. The Tōkaidō, the road between Miyako and Edo, he reports, is entirely man-made, sixty or more hands wide, smooth and evenly graded. From one end of the road to the other, it is planted with regularly spaced pine trees on either side, which cool and refresh travelers. Many towns and villages have grown up along it, and clean, well-provided inns (*honjin*) are located about one day's journey apart from one another. The larger towns have forts and military guards to make the road safer. At each league along the road is a signpost bearing the name of the place and something of its antiquity or

[41] Viegas (ed.), *op. cit.* (n. 36), I, 117–18. For a later view of the imperial palace see our pl. 395.

[42] Viegas (ed.), *op. cit.* (n. 36), I, 119. The Jesuits frequently refer to Hideyoshi as the tyrant or the usurper. Oda Nobunaga's grandson was named Hidenobu (1580–1605). *Chūnagon-dono* (middle councillor) is a powerless court rank.

[43] *Ibid.,* II, 232. On the early growth of the planned city of Edo see H. Magi, *A Historical Study of the Development of Edo* (Tokyo, 1966), pp. 42–44. See also our pls. 400 and 402.

[44] Viegas (ed.), *op. cit.* (n. 36), II, 233. The Englishmen and Dutchmen are obviously Will Adams and the crew of the "Liefde," who arrived in 1600. See below, p. 1848.

[45] Viegas (ed.), *op. cit.* (n. 36), III, 131–32. The castle was not completed until 1628. See Magi, *op. cit.* (n. 43), p. 45. For a later seventeenth-century view of the castle see our pl. 403.

importance. One such important place is the ruins of ancient Kamakura which had been the court of "Ioritono" (Yoritomo), the ancient lord of all Japan.[46]

Guerreiro's fine description of Mount Fuji comes from Vice-Provincial Francesco Pasio's 1607 visit to Ieyasu in Sumpu (present-day Shizuoka) and to the new shogun, Hidetada, in Edo:

The city of Yendo [Edo] lies to the east of the city of Fuchu [Sumpu], in the kingdom of Surunga [Suruga], four short days' journey away. On that road is that mountain greatly celebrated by writers and painters in Japan for its height and beauty, which is called Fuji or Fujican [Fujisan]. It is very tall, and exceeds by many degrees all of the highest mountains there, rising above them, so that it stands lording over all of them with its height, which is so great that the mountain appears three days before people reach it. This is that tall mountain which many leagues out to sea appears above the clouds to the Spaniards who sail from the Philippines to New Spain, who have called it a mountain of fire for the many times it spews forth through a frightening opening that is on its peak. This mountain is equally round on all sides, and with this form and figure rises gracefully to the top, like a pyramid. Continuing to the middle is a great and very thick forest, and from there upward it is completely open [*escampado*], without any trees, because of the deep snow with which it is covered much of the year. That therefore produces a beautiful and happy sight for those who view it as much for its very perfect figure as for the variety of things on it, such as trees, snow, fogs, and clouds which ordinarily surround its highest point. The circumference of this mountain is so great that it takes in with its slopes three or four kingdoms which abut them. There are at its skirts and base some temples to idols; and the principal one of them is that of a Cami [kami] to whom this mountain is dedicated, named Sengeum [Sengen].[47] Because this is held in Japan out of blind paganism for a sacred and holy mountain, large numbers of pilgrims from many kingdoms go to it once a year, in the month of August, for that is the hot season in which there are fewer snows and cold periods and which is therefore more suitable for climbing it and accomplishing their pilgrimage. Apart from the days of said month in which they climb this mountain, as determined and fixed by those who have done it, there is no one who dares to climb there because of the sharp and very cold winds, which immediately become so intense and harsh that no one can stand it.

The above-mentioned pilgrims, then, begin to climb this mountain at nightfall so that they will arrive at dawn, and return by day; and they climb at this time because they say it is such a high mountain and such an arduous and fearful climb, that were they to climb by day, the light of their eyes would be extinguished, seeing the great

---

[46] Guerreiro in Viegas (ed.), *op. cit.* (n. 36), II, 231. Minamoto no Yoritomo, the founder of the Kamakura shogunate, ruled from 1185 to 1199. The old Tōkaidō is today approximately paralleled by a modern highway and by the double-tracked Tōkaidō railway. For its route see our map 13 and pl. 401.

[47] The Sengen Jinja, located in the present-day city of Fujinomiya, Shizuoka prefecture, is dedicated to the Shinto goddess Konohana no Sakuyahime no Mikoto and two other deities. It is the central shrine of the cult which venerates Fujiyama as a sacred mountain. The shrine, established around A.D. 800, was restored by Tokugawa Ieyasu. See *Kodansha Encyclopedia* (n. 6), VII, 64.

peril in which they place themselves. Their pilgrimage finished, they return by various ways, tumbling down the mountain on top of loose sand or volcanic cinders which abound on top of that mountain, descending in this way in a few hours that which they had climbed in many.[48]

Almost no letterbooks from Japan were published between 1610 and 1615, after which descriptions of the renewed persecutions dominated missionary publications. In January, 1614, Ieyasu issued the famous edict proscribing Christianity in Japan and ordering the expulsion of all foreign priests.[49] Most of the missionaries left Japan in 1614, although some remained in hiding and tried surreptitiously to tend their flocks. The edict was not vigorously enforced until after Ieyasu's death in 1616. In that year Hidetada reissued the anti-Christian decree and the persecutions began anew, increasing in severity until the Shimabara rebellion of 1637–38 and the effective closure of Japan to all Europeans except the Dutch.[50] The many missionaries' reports after 1615 describe the plight of the missionaries and of the Japanese Christians in vivid detail: the fear, arrests, tortures, and executions. They praise the constancy of the Japanese Christians, although they also report some apostasies. They usually include biographies of the martyrs; some in fact are devoted to a single martyr. They are repetitious. Reports of new martyrdoms frequently begin with a brief history of the mission and of all the previous persecutions and martyrdoms. Few contain any description of Japan or of its people, and those which do provide little fresh information.[51]

The Annual Letter of 1609–10, written by João Rodrigues Girão and published in 1615, reports that Ieyasu becomes more devoted to Buddhism and Shinto as he becomes older, but that the state of the mission is still good.[52] Pedro Morejon's *Breve relacion de la persecucion,* published in Mexico one year later (1616), is a detailed account of the renewed persecutions of 1614.[53] Its preface, however, contains a brief general description of Japan and of Japanese Buddhism, a sketch of recent Japanese history, and a history of the Jesuit mission from Xavier to 1614. Giovanni Vremans' Annual Letter of 1615–16 on Japan (Naples, 1621) reports Ieyasu's 1614–15 assault on Osaka,

[48] Guerreiro in Viegas (ed.), *op. cit.* (n. 36), III, 128–29. Usually ten hours were allowed for the ascent and three for the descent. See Chamberlain and Mason, *op. cit.* (n. 12), p. 164.
[49] On the edict see Boxer, *op. cit.* (n. 35), pp. 317–19.
[50] On the persecutions see above, pp. 170–75, and Boxer, *op. cit.* (n. 35), pp. 308–97. The Tokugawa *bakufu* did not consciously decide to close Japan to the outside world. Rather a series of anti-Christian edicts and economic policy decisions effectively produced that result. See Derek Massarella, *A World Elsewhere: Europe's Encounter with Japan in the Sixteenth and Seventeenth Centuries* (New Haven and London, 1990), chap. 8, and esp. pp. 343–47.
[51] See above, n. 31. On the ideological opposition to Christianity and the other assumptions which guided the *bakufu*'s anti-Christian policies see Elison, *op. cit.* (n. 16). For illustrations of the tortures and executions see our plates 42–49.
[52] *Lettera annua del Giappone del 1609. e 1610. . . .* (Rome, 1615). See above, pp. 370–71. Under Ieyasu and his immediate successors Buddhism virtually became the state religion.
[53] See above, p. 332.

the burning of Sakai and of Osaka castle, and Hideyori's death.[54] The same information is reported in Nicolas Trigault's *De christianis apud Iapanios triumphis* (Mainz, 1623).[55] The Annual Letter of 1624, written by Rodrigues Girão in Macao (Rome, 1628) reports that Hidetada resigned the title of shogun in favor of his son (Iemitsu) in 1623, but observes that the new shogun is as anti-Christian as his father.[56] All the reports published after 1615, excepting Rodrigues Girão's letter of 1609–10, were written outside Japan, usually in Macao.

Scipione Amati's description of the embassy sent by Date Masamune to Mexico, Spain, and Rome, 1613 to 1620, contains what might be the earliest published European description of Date's domain in northern Honshu, called the "Kingdom of Voxu" (Oshu or Mutsu) in Amati's report.[57] Amati was the embassy's translator while it was in Italy and his information about Oshu must have come from conversations with Hasekura Rokuemon, the Japanese ambassador, and the Franciscan father, Luis Sotelo, who accompanied the embassy from Japan.

As described by Amati, Oshu is far and away the largest of Japan's sixty-six "kingdoms" (provinces), comprising about one-fourth of the main island (Honshu). It extends from the northeastern tip of the island southward for four hundred miles and is about three hundred miles from east to west at its widest.[58] Its climate is moderate in the south, but winters in the north are very severe, with the land blanketed in snow from November to April. It is a fruitful land, producing much wheat, barley, rice, and millet. Amati reports the same fruits, animals, birds, and fish as are found elsewhere in Japan. Oshu, however, produces the best horses in Japan. A particularly delicious fish called "Zuzuqui" (suzuki, or sea bass) is caught in its offshore waters. Mining—gold, silver, copper, lead, iron, and quartz—appears to be a major industry, and gold is also panned from the streams. Oshu's mountains supply wood for other parts of Japan as well. The land is densely populated and intensively cultivated. "The people are ingenious, frank, and sincere with those of a similar nature; however they are . . . astute and severe if they discover malice or duplicity of heart in those with whom they deal." They are courageous and warlike and "little inclined to study." Above all they are polite and ceremonious.[59]

[54] See above, p. 374. Hideyori committed suicide in Osaka castle in June, 1615.

[55] See above, p. 514.

[56] For bibliography see above, p. 376.

[57] Scipione Amati, *Historia del regno di Voxu del Giapone* (Rome, 1615). See above, pp. 370–71, for bibliography. Oshu is the Chinese name; Mutsu is the Japanese name now commonly used. For a fictional but perceptive and historically quite accurate account of Date's embassy see Shūsaku Endō, *The Samurai,* trans. Van C. Gessel (New York, 1982).

[58] In fact Oshu occupies about one-fifth of Honshu, comprising about 17,740 square miles, not 120,000. On the provinces see above, n. 6.

[59] Amati, *op. cit.* (n. 57), pp. 1–2.

According to Amati, Oshu had not been so large in ancient times when the Japanese emperors still governed the land. It became so about "five hundred and sixty years ago" when a court noble named "Findefira" (Fujiwara no Hidehira) rebelled and carved out the independent kingdom of Oshu in the north.[60] When Minamoto no Yoritomo became shogun, Hidehira supported him because, as Amati reports, Yoritomo's half brother Yoshitsune was Hidehira's adopted son.[61] Amati's account of the events after the death of Hidehira—Yoritomo's hostility, the defeat and death of Yoshitsune, Yoritomo's death, and the eventual establishment in Oshu of a branch of Hidehira's family which took the name Date—are greatly oversimplified and somewhat misleading. Nevertheless they are close enough to reality that personalities and events can be identified.[62]

Amati's description of Date Masamune (1566–1646) is extravagantly adulatory. He is virtuous, courageous, magnanimous, and generous. He has never been defeated or captured, although he always leads his soldiers into battle. He lives in great pomp and maintains a larger court than the shogun. He has built new palaces and he entertains lavishly. There are eighty thousand men in his army, and in an emergency he can call up another one hundred thousand. The shogun in Edo showers him with lands, revenues, and vassals in order to retain Date's good will. Indeed without Masamune's aid, Ieyasu would never have been able to gain control of the country. To cement their relationship Ieyasu has married one of his sons and one of his daughters with Masamune's daughter and son.[63]

The rest of Amati's book is devoted to Sotelo's missionary activities in Oshu, his friendship with Masamune, and the embassy to Mexico and Europe. As described by Amati—or by Sotelo—Sotelo was a courageous missionary who, after curing one of Masamune's concubines and preaching several sermons to him, convinced Masamune of the truth of Christianity. He told Sotelo that he would have accepted baptism except for his ambition to become shogun which he judged would be hampered by a public profession of Christianity. He therefore resolved to worship God privately, but ordered the gospel to be preached in his domains and encouraged his vassals and subjects to become Christians. According to Amati he would have made baptism mandatory had not Sotelo persuaded him that the sacrament

[60] *Ibid.*, pp. 2–3. He is obviously referring to the wars between the Minamoto and the Taira which ended in 1185 with the establishment of the Kamakura *bakufu* under Minamoto no Yoritomo. See Jeffrey P. Mass, "The Emergence of the Kamakura Bakufu," in John W. Hall and Jeffrey P. Mass (eds.), *Medieval Japan: Essays in Institutional History* (New Haven and London, 1974), pp. 127–56.

[61] Amati, *op. cit.* (n. 57), pp. 2–3. Hidehira did not adopt Yoshitsune, although he was Yoshitsune's protector for many years. See *Kodansha Encyclopedia* (n. 6), V, 182–83. On Yoshitsune see also G. B. Sansom, *Japan, a Short Cultural History* (rev. ed.; New York, 1943), pp. 293–96.

[62] Amati, *op. cit.* (n. 57), pp. 3–4. See Murdoch and Yamagata, *op. cit.* (n. 15), I, 374–412.

[63] Amati, *op. cit.* (n. 57), pp. 4–6. On the marriages see Murdoch and Yamagata, *op. cit.* (n. 15), II, 392, 494; on Masamune's role at Sekigehara see II, 401–3, 442. For a brief biography see E. Papinot, *Historical and Geographical Dictionary of Japan* (2 vols.; New York, 1968), I, 71.

must always be voluntary.[64] As evidence of his faith Masamune ordered the destruction of an important Buddhist temple in Sendai. So many people in Oshu wanted to become Christians that Sotelo and the other Franciscans could not keep up with the work. Therefore, according to Amati, Masamune decided to send an embassy to Mexico and Europe asking the king of Spain and the pope to send more missionaries.[65] Whatever Masamune's motives, Sotelo and Amati's optimism about the Christian mission in northern Japan was supported neither by events in Japan nor by any of the Jesuit reports about the state of Christianity in Japan.

Among the many martyrologies published after 1615 those of François Solier (1558–1628) and Bernardino Ginnaro (1577–1644) are large, comprehensive histories of the Japan mission and its latter-day troubles, each of which contains considerable description. Solier's two-volume *Histoire* is essentially a history of the Japanese Christian church, bishop by bishop, from its beginnings until 1624.[66] The first fifty-four pages, however, contain a general description of Japan, its people, and religions culled from earlier Jesuit reports, especially Guzman's history.

Concerning Japan's size and location Solier is more detailed but no more precise than Guzman. The island empire, he thought, ranged from about 30° to 38° north latitude, was six hundred leagues in circumference, two hundred leagues long, and varied between ten and thirty leagues in width.[67] Across the sea to the east lies America, to the north, Cathay, and to the west, China. He places the Japanese island of Goto only sixty leagues from "Liampo" (Ningpo) on the China coast and locates the city of Malacca over six hundred leagues away. He does not mention Japan's proximity to Korea.[68] Like Guzman, Solier names each of Japan's sixty-six "kingdoms," the islands on which they are found, and the major cities. Miyako (Kyoto) he reports is the "Paris of Japan."[69]

Solier describes Japan's natural resources in terms similar to Guzman's, although he provides more detail on particular plants and animals and on the harvest times for grains. Rice, of course, is the dietary staple, although the Japanese also grow wheat, barley, millet, and most fruits known in Europe. They often use barley bran instead of salt. They cultivate very few grapes. A sort of beer brewed from rice (obviously sake) is their principal drink. They make no butter, nor do they use olive oil since there are no olive trees in Japan. They use whale oil for both cooking and lighting. Sometimes they use pine torches. Japan's climate Solier thinks is healthful, because there are

[64] *Op. cit.* (n. 57), pp. 6–14.
[65] *Ibid.*, pp. 15–18.
[66] *Histoire ecclésiastique des isles et royaumes du Iapon* (Paris, 1627–29). For bibliography see above, p. 403.
[67] Solier, *op. cit.* (n. 66), I, 2. Thirty degrees is fairly accurate for Japan's southern extremity, but the northern tip of Honshu is at 41°30' and that of Hokkaido is at about 43°.
[68] *Ibid. Cf.* our pl. 390.
[69] *Op. cit.* (n. 66), I, 2–5.

few diseases and the people seem to live long. It has seasonal extremes of both hot and cold. Winters in some parts of Japan bring enough snow to completely cover the houses. There are frequent earthquakes.[70]

Solier praises Japanese character as highly as did Guzman and other Jesuit writers, but while he describes it in detail he adds nothing to what was written earlier.[71] He devotes an entire chapter, however, to the cultural contrasts between Japanese and Europeans which so fascinated sixteenth-century Jesuit writers: Europeans show respect by removing their hats while Japanese do so by removing their shoes; Europeans admire long hair, Japanese shave their heads; Europeans prefer blond hair and white teeth, while Japanese regard blond hair a deformity and blacken their teeth to make them beautiful; Europeans wear hats when dressed, Japanese go bareheaded; Japanese women go out of their houses leading their maids and servants and leaving their husbands behind, while Europeans do just the opposite; Japanese women, who ordinarily wear loose clothing, bind themselves tightly around the waist when pregnant, just the reverse of European practice; while newborn babies in Europe are pampered and protected, the Japanese bathe their newly born infants in cold streams even in winter; Europeans mount horses from the left, Japanese from the right; Europeans wear black for mourning, Japanese wear white; Europeans like cold drinks, Japanese like them hot; in contrast to Europeans, Japanese detest beef, mutton, and dairy products. The list continues, illustrated by stories from earlier Jesuit reports.[72] Solier also describes the advantages of lacquerware tables, the ritual of tea drinking, and the Japanese love for antique swords, cups, and vases. He devotes another chapter to "Japanese virtues": their patience, reserve, modesty, fortitude, insensitivity to physical discomfort, hatred of greed and theft, and the like, amply illustrated with anecdotes.[73]

The Japanese language is "very grave, copious, elegant, and appears to surpass Greek and Latin in the abundance of different words to signify the same thing, as in propriety and elegance."[74] Following Guzman, Solier comments on the two "alphabets," the brevity of written Japanese, and the diversity of styles used in speaking. Entirely different styles and words

---

[70] *Ibid.*, pp. 5–8.

[71] *Ibid.*, pp. 9–11.

[72] *Ibid.*, pp. 12–17. *Cf.* above, p. 1830. During the Edo period blackened teeth showed that a woman was married or pregnant. Blackening teeth had been an aristocratic custom sometimes practiced by men as well as women; see Yoshiaki Morisue and Suketaka Hinonishi (eds.), *Fūzoku Jiten* (Dictionary of Social Customs) (Tokyo, 1957), pp. 576–77. In modern Japan while the deceased is dressed in white the mourners wear black; see *Kodansha Encyclopedia* (n. 6), II, 369–70.

[73] Solier, *op. cit.* (n. 66), I, 17–19.

[74] *Ibid.*, p. 10. Guzman used almost the same words, but the common source of this observation appears to be a letter from Lourenço Mexia written on January 6, 1584, and published in the *Cartas* of 1598. See *Asia*, I, 714 n. 311. For a differing view by a modern scholar on the distinctiveness of the Japanese spoken language see R. A. Miller, *The Japanese Language* (Chicago, 1967), pp. ix–x.

are used depending on who is speaking, on the person spoken to, and on whether one is speaking in public as in a sermon, or privately with friends. Mastery of the language, both for foreigners and for Japanese students, is difficult and takes a long time.[75]

Solier's account of Minamoto no Yoritomo's usurpation of imperial power and of the emperor's current powerless honor and dignity is very similar to Guzman's, except that Solier includes more detail about the emperor's person and court. For example, the emperor wears a black tunic and a red robe, over which he wears a crepe-like veil, the fringes of which cover his hands. On his head he wears a bonnet decorated with various crests. He almost never leaves his palace and then only in a sedan chair. He rarely allows himself to be seen. He keeps 366 "idols" in his palace, one of which he takes to guard his bed each night. If he sleeps badly he has the idol beaten and banished from the palace for ten days. During the day he is carried in a chair. His feet never touch the ground. The emperor has only one wife. If she dies before he is thirty years old he may remarry; otherwise he will remain unmarried. Not only the emperor, "Dayri," but also the shogun, "Cubozama," and the chief Buddhist priest, "Iaco," live in Miyako, which explains the city's wealth and importance.[76]

Like Guzman's, Solier's description of Japan's government during the *sengoku* era is quite detailed and perceptive. He describes the current political system's origins, fiefholding and the obligations of feudal service, subinfeudation, and the redistribution of fiefs; and he describes it all as if it were normal: "like all other countries and kingdoms." He is amazed, however, by the dignified equanimity with which high Japanese nobles accept sudden drastic changes in fortune.[77] Solier notes also that Japanese lords have absolute power over their vassals and subjects. They judge and punish crimes without rendering account to anyone and without the accused having any legal means of defense or appeal. Punishments range from fines and beatings to banishment and death, usually by the sword. There are no jails. Nobles condemned to die are often allowed to commit suicide, thereby preserving their honor.[78] Solier's history of the Japanese church also rehearses the political history reported by earlier Jesuit writers.

Solier's description of Japanese Buddhism is quite lengthy and detailed, but closely follows Guzman's. He includes descriptions of specific shrines and idols, and a detailed account of the *Shugendō* pilgrimages also described by Guzman.[79] Finally, like Guzman, Solier describes funerals and the Bon festival.[80]

[75] Solier, *op. cit.* (n. 66), I, 10–11.
[76] *Ibid.*, pp. 20–23.
[77] *Ibid.*, pp. 24–28.
[78] *Ibid.*, pp. 28–30. For an example see our pl. 424.
[79] Solier, *op. cit.* (n. 66), I, 30–48.
[80] *Ibid.*, pp. 48–54.

Ginnaro's *Saverio orientale ò vero istorie de' Cristiani illustri dell' oriente* . . . (Naples, 1641) is also a massive composite of information taken from Jesuit letters and other reports about Japan. It is divided into four parts. About half of Part I describes Japan and the Japanese, and includes an important new map of Japan; the other half recounts the now familiar sixteenth- and seventeenth-century political history.[81] The remaining three books treat the history of the mission and the martyrs. Finally, among the martyrologies, the Jesuit Antonio Cardim (1596–1659) in 1643 published a report on the 1640 execution of four Portuguese envoys sent from Macao to Nagasaki in a last desperate attempt to reopen trade. In the same year the Portuguese captain Duarte Correa's letter describing the Shimabara rebellion of 1637–38 was published.[82]

2.

ENGLISH AND DUTCH DESCRIPTIONS BEFORE 1650

The first Dutch ship landed in Japan in 1600 with the English pilot Will Adams aboard. By 1609 the Dutch had established a factory at Hirado in northwestern Kyushu, and in 1613 the English were established there as well. By that time Adams had become one of Ieyasu's favorites and had replaced Father João Rodrigues as his interpreter.[83] Nevertheless, apart from some very brief notices in Dutch accounts, no substantial description of Japan by a non-Catholic northern European appeared before the publication of Samuel Purchas' *Pilgrimes* in 1625. The earliest Dutch report is found in the journal of Olivier van Noort's circumnavigation, published in 1601.[84] Van Noort met a Japanese ship as he sailed from the Philippines to Borneo and entertained its captain on board. The Japanese are all dressed in long robes, he reports, "almost like the Polish." The captain, "Iamasta Citissamundo," wears one of light silk with a leaf and flower pattern, artistically

---

[81] See above, p. 378, for bibliography. On the Ginnaro map see J. F. Schütte, "Japanese Cartography at the Court of Florence; Robert Dudley's Maps of Japan, 1606–1636," *Imago mundi*, XXIII (1969), 46–50. Cf. our pls. 11 and 390.

[82] See above, pp. 348–49, for bibliography.

[83] See Massarella, *op. cit.* (n. 50), pp. 71–266. See also Boxer, *op. cit.* (n. 35), pp. 285–307, and *The Affair of the Madre de Deus. A Chapter in the History of the Portuguese in Japan* (London, 1929). On the first Dutch ship in Japan see F. C. Wieder (ed.), *De reis van Mahu en de Cordes door de Straat van Magalhães naar Zuid-Amerika en Japan, 1598–1600* (3 vols.; "WLV," XXI, XXII, XXIV; The Hague, 1923–25). On the English in Japan see N. Murakami (ed.), *The Diary of Richard Cocks, Cape-Merchant in The English Factory in Japan, 1615–1622* (2 vols.; Tokyo, 1899), and E. M. Satow (ed.), *The Voyage of Captain John Saris to Japan* ("HS," 2d ser., V; London, 1900). The complete version of Cocks' diary has been published in English and Japanese by the Historical Institute, University of Tokyo, *Diary Kept by the Head of the English Factory in Japan* (3 vols.; Tokyo, 1978–80), in the series *Nihon kaigai kankei shiryo* (Records of Japanese Foreign Relations).

[84] See above, pp. 441–43, for bibliography.

made. They all have their heads shaved smooth except for the back of the head and neck where it grows long. They are tall and warlike people, and their weapons are the best in the East Indies. Japanese swords are so sharp they say they can cut through three men with a single stroke. Formerly the various Japanese "kings" were often at war with one another but now (1600) most of the country is subject to one "king." The Portuguese trade freely in Japan, making a great profit on one large ship per year. They bring Chinese goods to Japan because the Japanese are at war with China and cannot trade there. The Jesuits control most of the trade and have also converted many Japanese. They are greatly respected in Japan, "like little gods," and they allow no other order to preach there. Van Noort learns from a young Japanese sailor that the Chinese and Japanese use the same characters in writing and that while they cannot understand a single word of each other's spoken language they can read each other's writing.[85]

A brief note in Nicolaes van Wassenaer's *Historisch verhael* of June, 1624, reports that the VOC had been trading at Hirado for some years already. In 1620, the report continues, a Dutch ship brought to Japan a young Siamese elephant with which the governor of Hirado was quite fascinated. He asked its keeper, Daniel Dortsman, to bring it into his residence so that his wives and concubines could see it. While the women viewed the elephant, Dortsman viewed the women, over a hundred of them he thought, luxuriously dressed in long-sleeved silk robes with silk veils. They were, he reports, closely kept and never permitted to go out. Ordinary Japanese women, however, are often seen in the streets.[86]

Purchas' enormous collection of travel accounts contains several that pertain to Japan: two letters of Will Adams; the journal of Captain John Saris, who commanded the first English ship to visit Japan, in 1613; parts of the diary and some letters of Richard Cocks, whom Saris left in charge of the English factory at Hirado; the account of John Pring's second voyage, 1616–21, which touched on Japan; and a 1623 letter by Arthur Hatch which describes Japan.[87] None of these provide systematically organized descriptions of Japan as extensive or perceptive as those produced by the Jesuits. Pring's is essentially a rutter, limited to nautical details and relations with the Dutch. Nevertheless, they are all eyewitness reports and some, especially those of Saris and Cocks, contain fresh and interesting accounts of what these authors saw or heard in Japan.

Adams' letters recount the trip across the Pacific, the crew's reception in Japan, his first interviews with Ieyasu at Osaka, and his eventual favor and

[85]J. W. Ijzerman (ed.), *De reis om de wereld door Olivier van Noort, 1598–1601* (2 vols.; "WLV," XXVII, XXVIII; The Hague, 1926), I, 113–15.

[86]Wassenaer, *Historisch verhael,* VII (June, 1624), 67–68. For complete title and bibliography see above, pp. 449–50; for examples see our pls. 399, 417, 418, and 422.

[87]For Purchas bibliography see above, pp. 556–68. For the Japan accounts listed here see above, pp. 558, 560–61, 566–67.

service with the shogun. Ieyasu finally gave Adams a fief on which lived eighty to ninety husbandmen, something, Adams observes, never before done for a foreigner.[88] His description of Japan is confined to a brief account of its location and a few comments about the Japanese people: They are, he reports, "good of nature, courteous above measure . . . valiant in warre; their Justice is severely executed without any partiality. . . . They are governed in great civilitie, I thinke, no Land better governed in the world. . . . [They] are verie superstitious in their Religion, and are of divers opinions."[89]

Saris wrote brief but vivid descriptions of his first impressions upon anchoring at Hirado: his entertainment by the daimyo, Japanese clothes, greetings, banquets, and music. For example, he reports, when Japanese greet one another politely they first "put off their shoes (stockings they weare none) and then clapping their right hand within their left, they put them down towards their knees, and so wagging or moving of their hands a little to and fro, they stooping, step with small steps sideling from the partie saluted, and crie Augh, Augh."[90] The daimyo's women he describes as "attired in gownes of silke, clapt the one skirt over the other, and so girt to them, bare-legged, only a paire of halfe buskins bound with silke riband about their instep: their haire very blacke, and very long, tyed up in a knot upon the crowne in a comely manner: . . . They were well-faced, handed and footed; cleare skind and white, but wanting colour, which they amend by arte. Of stature low, but very fat; very courteous in behaviour."[91] Some of the women are Christians, and to Saris' amusement worship the "somewhat wantonly set out" painting of Venus and Cupid hanging in his cabin, obviously thinking it to be of the Virgin and the Christ-child.[92] The daimyo's women sing and play on a four-stringed "lute" (*biwa*) which Saris describes as "bellyed" like ours, "but longer in the necke, and fretted like ours, but [having] only foure gut-strings. Their fingering with the left hand like ours, very nimbly: but the right hand striketh with an Ivory bone." They keep "time with their hands, and playing and singing by booke, prickt on line and space, resembling much ours heere."[93] He describes companies of "common women" all "slaves of one man" who travel from town to town performing comedies and otherwise entertaining the nobles who hire them

[88] "William Adams his Voyage by the Magellan Straights to Japan, written in two Letters by himselfe, as followeth," *PP*, II, 337–38. Adams, Jan Joosten Lodensteyn, and Melchior van Santvoort were made *hatamoto* (bannermen) by Ieyasu and settled on small estates. Adams' at Hemi, near Edo on the Miura Peninsula, "was valued at 150 or 250 koku of rice." See Massarella, *op. cit.* (n. 50), pp. 80–81.

[89] Adams, *loc. cit.* (n. 88), pp. 338–39.

[90] John Saris, "The eighth voyage set forth by the East-Indian societie, wherein were employed three Ships, the Clove, the Hector, and the Thomas, under the command of Captaine John Saris: . . . ." *PP*, III, p. 443.

[91] *Ibid.*, p. 445. *Cf.* our pl. 422.

[92] *Loc. cit.* (n. 90), p. 445.

[93] *Ibid.*, pp. 445–46. On the *biwa* see F. Piggott, *The Music and Musical Instruments of Japan* (2d ed.; London, 1909), p. 136.

(*cf.* pl. 430). While in Hirado, Saris witnessed several executions. He describes a typical procession and notes that the condemned criminal marches resolutely through the streets showing no fear. Once the condemned has been decapitated by the executioner, anyone who wishes may test his sword on the corpse. Many do, reports Saris, and in one case three criminals were cut into pieces no larger than a man's hand.[94]

The journey from Hirado to Ieyasu's court in Sumpu and the shogun Hidetada's court in Edo provided many more scenes. Saris seems impressed with the size and vitality of Japanese cities, many of which he compares to London. "Fuccate (Hakata) he thinks is as large as London "within the walls, very well built, and even, so as you may see from one end of the street to the other." It is very populous, and the people are courteous, except that a gang of boys follows them crying "Coré, Coré, Cocoré, Waré, that is to say, You Coréans with false hearts."[95] Osaka also is as large as London within the walls and has many fine wooden bridges over a river as wide as the Thames at London. He admires the castle with its walls, six to seven yards thick, made from huge stones cut so exactly that no mortar was used to fit them. He observes that "Tiguasamma's" (Hideyoshi's) son lives there, married to Ieyasu's daughter, his power having been usurped by Ieyasu. At Fushimi castle, Saris watches the changing of the garrison which guards Osaka and Kyoto, over three thousand soldiers. He describes the horses, weapons, and uniforms, and marvels at the good order with which the change is accomplished. No traveler along the road was injured by them and those who ran eating-houses in the towns entertained the soldiers just like any other guests.[96] Saris describes the food and the price of food, commenting as most Europeans did, that the Japanese abhor milk, but drink warm water and a wine made from rice. He marvels at the Tōkaidō and the crowds of people traveling on it. He notes that outside each town crosses can be seen with the dead bodies of malefactors still on them. Near Sumpu they see a scaffold on which are displayed the heads of executed criminals, their mutilated bodies lying nearby. Sumpu, Saris estimates, is fully as large as London with all its suburbs.[97]

After his formal reception by Ieyasu, Saris went on to Edo. Of the sights on that journey he describes only a large copper Buddha at Kamakura, twenty to twenty-one feet high, hollow inside, that is much visited by trav-

---

[94] *Loc. cit.* (n. 90), pp. 450–51.

[95] *Ibid.*, p. 453. The gang of boys were probably not referring to Koreans, as the Japanese word for Koreans at that time was *chōsenjin*. What they were actually saying is difficult to determine; they were probably speaking Kyushu dialect. Massarella (*op. cit.* [n. 50], p. 113) suggests "something like 'Here, here? We're here!'" Michael Huissen of Bunkyo University, Tokyo, says "These are bad men" is a possible meaning. Harry Harootunian of the University of Chicago agrees that "cocorè" could be *kokoro* (heart) and "ware" a misunderstanding of *warui* (bad), but adds that "ware" could also mean we or us.

[96] *Loc. cit.* (n. 90), pp. 456–57.

[97] *Ibid.*, pp. 457–59.

elers. Some from their company go inside the Buddha, where they shout and make a lot of noise. Some, like countless earlier visitors, scratch their names on the statue.[98] Will Adams tells Saris about the nearby temple of "Tencheday" where each month a beautiful virgin is kept for the god's use.[99]

Edo is a much larger city than Sumpu and, thought Saris, much more beautiful. The shogun's castle, too, is more impressive than that of his father in Sumpu, and the shogun seems better guarded and attended than Ieyasu.[100]

On the way back to Hirado, Saris visits "Miaco" (Kyoto), "the greatest Citie in Japan, consisting most upon merchandizing." Of it, however, he briefly describes only the recently completed temple, begun by Hideyoshi, in which were buried the ears and noses of three thousand Koreans. It is, he reports, Japan's chief Buddhist temple and he estimates that it is as large as the west end of Saint Paul's in London.[101]

At the end of his account Saris adds a brief notice about "Yedzo" (Yezo or Hokkaido), allegedly from a Japanese who had been there. Yezo, he reports, is an island about ten leagues northwest of Japan's main island. Its people (the Ainu) are white, but hairy like monkeys. They defend themselves with poisoned bows and arrows. Those in the south trade with the Japanese: gold, silver, salmon, and other dried fish for such products as rice, cotton cloth, iron, and lead. The Japanese have a settlement in the south called "Matchma" (Matsumae). Those with whom the Japanese trade are about the same size as Japanese, but in the north of the island live "people of very low stature, like Dwarfes."[102]

Richard Cocks' diary, as published by Purchas, covers only the events of 1613 when Saris was traveling to and from Sumpu and Edo. Mostly it recounts events in the emporium of Hirado: his visits with the daimyo, attempts to sell his goods, fires, the misbehavior of English sailors in town, a typhoon, and his dealings with the Dutch. Some of the descriptions are quite interesting. He describes what appears to be the Bon festival, for example, which began on August 19 and lasted for three days. Like other residents of Hirado, Cocks sees to the graveling of the street in front of the English house and the hanging of paper lanterns. He heard about a man who was put to death for failing to do so. The Japanese, he reports, make merry all night by candlelight at the graves. The streets are full of people. Cocks, however, stays home each night ready with a banquet in case the

[98] *Ibid.*, p. 462. Saris is obviously describing the great Buddha at Kamakura.

[99] *Ibid.*, pp. 462–63. Apparently a reference to the custom of appeasing Tenshodaijin or Amaterasu Omikami at the Ise shrine. Until the reign of Go-Daigo (1318–39) an imperial princess was always chosen as the priestess at Ise. See *Kodansha Encyclopedia* (n. 6), III, 338–39.

[100] Saris, *loc. cit.* (n. 90), pp. 463–64. For the "privilege" supposedly obtained by Saris on his embassy see our pl. 432.

[101] *Loc. cit.* (n. 90), pp. 470–71. This is the Hiyoshi Jinja and the Buddhist temple of Myōhō-in. The Korean ear mound is opposite Hideyoshi's temple. *Cf.* Herbert E. Plutschow, *Historical Kyoto* (Tokyo, 1983), pp. 133–34.

[102] Saris, *loc. cit.* (n. 90), pp. 488–89. Ainu legend claims that Yezo was originally inhabited by dwarfs. See A. H. S. Landor, *Alone with the Hairy Ainu* (London, 1893), p. 251.

daimyo or some other high samurai official should call on him. The daimyo, despite rumors that he would, does not visit him, but some samurai do, and Cocks dutifully entertains them.[103]

Apparently the owners of houses in Hirado are responsible for maintaining the streets in front of their houses. They clean the streets, gravel them, and make channels covered with flat stones on either side to carry water away.[104] Officials appointed by the daimyo measure each house in the town, the English house included, to determine the amount of tax to be paid to the shogun for building fortresses, as Cocks understands it.[105]

During the typhoon, the "barbarous unruly" townspeople run up and down the street all night carrying firebrands. Cocks is more afraid of the firebrands than of the typhoon. The storm damage to the town is considerable, however: over one hundred houses destroyed and many others damaged, including the English house. Forty or fifty boats were sunk in the harbor.[106] Fires seem to be a constant problem. Cocks writes about them frequently. On October 2 the daimyo's house burns down, and on the nineteenth a more serious fire destroys forty homes. On October 23, the daimyo orders that each house should have a tank of water on its top to prevent the fire that "the devil" intended to set in the town that night. During this and subsequent nights people run up and down the streets warning everyone to watch for fires.[107] Also on October 23, Hirado celebrates the Hachiman festival. The streets are emptied, the daimyo and all the nobles meet at a summer house in front of the Pagoda (temple) to watch archers ride at full gallop shooting arrows at a target as they speed by.[108]

Cocks describes another great feast, held on October 31, during which the "king" and his nephew the "young king" personally serve their guests and personally act in a "comedy" for the entertainment of their guests. Cocks comments on the music:

Their acting Musique and singing (as also their Poetry) is very harsh to us, yet they keepe due time both hands and feet. Their Musique is little Tabers [drums], made great at both ends, and small in the middest, like to an Houre-glasse, they beating on the end with one hand, and straine the cords which goe about it, with the other, which maketh it to sound great or small as they list, according to their voices with it, one playing on a Phife or Flute; but all harsh, and not pleasant to our hearing.[109]

[103] Richard Cocks, "Relation of Master Richard Cocks Cape Merchant, . . ." *PP*, III, 520–21. The Buddhist festival of Bon is usually celebrated in mid-July. See Chamberlain, *op. cit.* (n. 22), p. 162.

[104] Cocks, *loc. cit.* (n. 103), p. 527.

[105] *Ibid.*, p. 523.

[106] *Ibid.*, pp. 523–24. Presumably the firebrands were intended to frighten off the typhoon, although Cocks does not say so.

[107] *Ibid.*, pp. 528, 537–38, 539–40.

[108] *Ibid.*, p. 539.

[109] *Ibid.*, pp. 542–43. Cocks probably saw *kyōgen* or *nō* drama. The hourglass-shaped drum is a type of *tsuzumi;* the flute, if end-blown, is probably the *shakuhachi;* if transverse, a type of *fue.* See Denis Arnold (ed.), *The New Oxford Companion to Music* (2 vols.; Oxford and New York,

Cocks is amused, when attending a dinner for the "king" at the Dutch house, to see the Dutch factor Hendrick Brouwer and his men on their knees, serving food and drink to their distinguished guests. After the dinner Brouwer explains that it is proper Japanese etiquette and that even the "king" does so for his own guests.[110]

The closest thing to a general description of Japan in the Purchas collection is the brief letter written by Arthur Hatch after he returned to England. It comments on Japan's geography, climate, natural resources, government, people, language, and customs in terms familiar to readers of the Jesuit accounts.[111] But his description is of Tokugawa Japan and some important characteristics of the new regime are visible in it. He describes, for example, the alternate year residence and hostage system of the new shoguns (*sankin kōtai*): "And each of those several Princes must alwayes bee either himselfe in person, or his Brother, eldest Sonne, or the chiefe Nobleman within his Realme at the Emperour's [shogun's] court."[112] He notes the many gifts and taxes the shogun receives from the "princes" (daimyos) without giving anything of value in return, and he suspects all of this is designed to prevent rebellion: "and that they may not grow rich, and of sufficient ability to make head against him, he suffers not their Fleeces to grow, but sheares them off, by raising taxes on them for the building of Castles, and the repairing of fortifications, and yet they are not suffered to repaire their owne, or any way to fortifie themselves."[113] Of the 66 "kings" in Japan, only five are in the "emperour's" privy council (senior council, *rōjū*). Hatch observes, too, that the shogun, unlike other Japanese noblemen, has only one wife, to whom he is reported to be faithful.[114]

Cocks' letter from Nagasaki in March, 1618, mentions the renewed persecution of Christians in Japan. He saw fifty-five people martyred in Kyoto, including small children burning in their mothers' arms. Later sixteen more were executed in Nagasaki.[115] The first separate, eyewitness account of the persecutions by a Protestant appeared in 1637—Reyer Gysbertszoon's *De*

1983), I, 970, 972. This may be the festival of Ebisu-kō, ordinarily held on October 20. On drums with braces see Piggott, *op. cit.* (n. 93), pp. 163–69. Matsūra Takanobu (d. 1637) was the daimyo; Matsūra Shigenobu (1549–1614) was his grandfather. See Massarella, *op. cit.* (n. 50), p. 107.

[110]Cocks, *loc. cit.* (n. 103), pp. 535–36.

[111]Arthur Hatch, "A Letter Touching Japon with the Government Affaires and later Occurrents there, . . . ," *PP*, X, 83–88.

[112]*Ibid.*, p. 85. See T. G. Tsukahira, *Feudal Control in Tokugawa Japan: The Sankin Kotai System* (Cambridge, Mass., 1966). The term *sankin kōtai* was not used until the time of the third shogun, Iemitsu (r. 1623–51), although the system had begun to take shape already in Ieyasu's day.

[113]Hatch, *loc. cit.* (n. 111), p. 85.

[114]*Ibid.*, p. 84. The 66 "kings" are the provincial governors in the old *ritsuryō* system. See above, n. 6. Hatch apparently did not know about the harem (*ōoku*); *cf.* Conrad Totman, *Politics in the Tokugawa Bakufu* (Cambridge, Mass., 1967), pp. 103–8.

[115]*PP*, III, 567–69.

tyrannie ende wreedtheden der Jappanen.[116] Gysbertszoon describes the persecutions which took place in Nagasaki between 1622 and 1629. He describes the details of the tortures used to make Christians recant and the methods of execution. He names the Japanese officials as well as many of the European victims. Most of the martyrs he names are also celebrated in the martyrologies written by the missionaries. Gysbertszoon's book is not a martyrology, however. He records recantations as well as martyrdoms, and indicates that a great many more Christians recanted than seems to be admitted in the martyrologies. Gysbertszoon, as harshly critical of the Catholic mission as any Dutch Protestant, nevertheless sees the recantations not as evidence of weak faith but as the inevitable, understandable result of the heinous tortures inflicted on the Japanese Christians. They would gladly die. For the most part Gysbertszoon's account strongly corroborates the story of the persecutions told by the Catholic missionaries. Some details about early Tokugawa government also emerge from Gysbertszoon's report, for example the use of a system of mutual responsibility to ferret out priests. If a Japanese family is discovered hiding a Christian priest, that family and those living in the two houses on either side of that family are executed, altogether five families.[117]

The first major description of Japan written by someone other than a Catholic missionary, François Caron's *Beschrijvinghe van het machtigh coninckrijck Iapan,* appeared in 1646 in the *Begin ende voortgangh* collection. It was also separately published in 1648 and reappeared in many subsequent editions and translations. It was surely the seventeenth century's single most popular and influential description of Japan.[118] It was also the first major description of Japan under the Tokugawa regime. Caron served the VOC in Japan from 1619 until 1641, although he was not continuously resident there for the entire period. He was involved in all the delicate negotiations resulting from the confrontation on Formosa between Japanese merchants and Governor Pieter Nuyts. He guided the VOC factory in Hirado through the dangerous years of the persecutions, finally supervising its removal to Deshima in 1640.[119] He was fluent in Japanese, although he apparently could not read it; he admired and understood Japanese culture. He had a Japanese wife, lived

[116] For bibliography see above, pp. 455–56.
[117] C. R. Boxer (ed.), *A True Description of the Mighty Kingdoms of Japan and Siam* (London, 1935), pp. 74, 76, 84. For a recent analysis of the persecutions, apostasies, and martyrdoms see Elison, *op. cit.* (n. 16), chap. 7. For a perceptive fictional portrayal see Endo Shusaku, *Silence* (Tokyo, [1969]). Both Elison and Endo discuss Christovão Ferreira, the best-known of the apostatized priests; on him see Itō Shuntarō, "The Introduction of Western Cosmology in Seventeenth Century Japan: The Case of Christovão Ferreira (1580–1652)," *The Japan Foundation Newsletter,* Vol. XIV, No. 1 (May, 1986), pp. 1–9. For illustrations of the tortures and executions see our pls. 42–49.
[118] For bibliography and for Caron's career see above, pp. 458–61.
[119] Boxer (ed.), *op. cit.* (n. 117), pp. 66–67. For the Dutch factory on Deshima see our pl. 27.

in a Japanese house, and seems even to have developed a liking for hot baths. Perhaps no secular European visitor to Japan during the seventeenth century was better qualified to write about it. His *Beschrijvinghe,* however, is quite brief, and it is not a balanced, comprehensive account. He wrote it in answer to a series of specific questions put to him by VOC Director-General Philips Lucaszoon in 1636, apparently with no thought of its possible publication. He wrote little or nothing, therefore, about matters unrelated to Lucaszoon's questions.[120]

Concerning Japan's geography and natural resources Caron provides less information than the earlier Jesuit writers. He reports that it is not entirely certain whether or not Japan is an island because the Japanese themselves have not explored the northern parts of the empire. The northernmost point of the main part of Japan, he reports, is a twenty-seven day journey from Edo. "Iezzo" (Hokkaido) lies across a long arm of the sea from that point and is a large, mountainous, but sparsely populated, land, rich in furs and skins. He seems to think Honshu and Hokkaido may be connected and that Hokkaido may be connected to the Asian mainland. Hokkaido's people are brutish and hairy, with long beards. Two large islands are also part of the empire: "Chirkock" (Shikoku) and "Saycock" (Kyushu).[121]

According to Caron Japan is divided into seven "provinces": "Saycock," "Chirkock," "Iamaysoirt" (Yamashiro), "Ietsengo" (Echigo), "Ietsengen" (Echizen), "Quanto" (Kanto), and "Ochio" (Oshu). He does not list the sixty-six old *ritsuryō*-system provinces usually mentioned by earlier writers.[122] He does, however, include a "Translation of the sealed accounts and specification of the revenue (except for the emperor's) of the Kings, Dukes, Princes, Counts, and Lords in Japan: together with the names of their Lands, Cities, and Castles," taken from the *Edo Kagami* (Edo Mirror), which was published twice each year during the Tokugawa period. One hundred forty-one daimyos are listed, together with the names and incomes of sixty-nine lesser lords and "imperial" counselors. Incomes are given in koku of rice (1 koku equals 4.96 bushels), which Caron equates with ten carolus guilders and which his English translator equates with twenty shillings. Caron's translation is apparently the oldest example of material from the *Edo Kagami* to be found anywhere; the original probably dates from 1629 or 1630.[123]

---

[120] Boxer (ed.), *op. cit.* (n. 117), pp. 69–74.

[121] François Caron, "Beschrijvinghe van het machtigh Coninckrijck Iapan," *BV,* IIb, 134; Boxer (ed.), *op. cit.* (n. 117), p. 13. *Cf.* our pls. 11 and 390.

[122] Caron, *loc. cit.* (n. 121), p. 134; Boxer (ed.), *op. cit.* (n. 117), p. 14. In what follows we cite both the *Begin ende voortgangh* 1646 edition and Boxer's edition of Roger Manley's 1663 English translation because there are some differences in content between the 1646 and 1661 Dutch editions and because Manley's translation of the 1661 edition is not all that good. The translations in the text are ours, from the *Begin ende voortgangh*.

[123] Caron, *BV,* IIb, 134–41; Boxer (ed.), *op. cit.* (n. 117), pp. 14–19. See especially Boxer's evaluation on p. 118. Harootunian observes that the term *kagami* (mirror) was often used "to

Caron asserts that "there is nothing for the use of man which Japan does not itself produce." His list of metals, textiles, manufactured goods, animals, and birds, however, is short and includes nothing not mentioned by earlier writers. He describes some hot springs and medicinal pools and fountains in some detail but does not specify their locations.[124]

Like most previous European writers, Caron knows that the *dairi* in Kyoto is the titular ruler of Japan and that the shogun is a usurper. His account of the wars between the Taira and the Minamoto which established the Kamakura *bakufu* and of the conflicts which elevated first the Hōjō regents, then the Ashikaga shoguns, and finally Hideyoshi, is, if anything, less precise than those of his predecessors. It conveys no sense of chronology; in fact, Caron seems to think that all this happened during the preceding century. Nevertheless, he correctly stresses that through it all the *dairi*'s prestige and religious importance continued, that all of the usurping "emperors" (shoguns), including "Taycko" (Hideyoshi) and his successors, were formally "crowned" by the *dairi,* and that the *dairi*'s court in "Miaco" (Kyoto) continues to function "wanting nothing, save that the land is governed by another."[125]

The *dairi,* Caron reports, is considered so holy that his feet never touch the ground, the sun and moon may never shine on him, nothing of his body—hair or nails, for example—may ever be cut, and all his food is served and cooked in new dishes. He has twelve wives, each of whom holds court in a separate palace and travels in a separate coach when the *dairi* goes out. Banquets with splendid entertainment are prepared in each of the twelve houses each evening, no one knowing with which of his wives the *dairi* will dine. When he enters one of the houses the food and entertainment of the other eleven are immediately brought there to help celebrate. When a son is born to the *dairi* a nurse is chosen for him from among eighty of the most beautiful and noble young women in Japan through a long series of elaborate entertainments and eliminations.[126] Caron also senses something of the isolation and the intellectual and cultural prestige of the imperial court (*kuge*):

The annals of the country are kept and continued by the Dayro [*dairi*] himself; all other books are written by the Dayro, his lords and nobles, which are at least eight hundred strong, or by their wives; for these people, both men and women, being mostly related and intermarried, do nothing but enjoy the pleasures of the world and

denote 'history' as a reflection unclouded by the 'dust' of moral error." The *Edo kagami* "was used to fix rankings, status, etc." (private communication).

[124] Caron, *BV,* IIb, 172–73; Boxer (ed.), *op. cit.* (n. 117), pp. 53–55.

[125] Caron, *BV,* IIb, 146–47; Boxer (ed.), *op. cit.* (n. 117), pp. 25–26.

[126] Caron, *BV,* IIb, 145–46; Boxer (ed.), *op. cit.* (n. 117), pp. 24–25. Caron's account here is generally accurate but contains several errors, such as the *dairi*'s feet never touching the ground, and the sun and moon not shining on him. See Boxer (ed.), *op. cit.* (n. 117), p. 122.

the study of wisdom; so that actually in that court men are respected and honored with titles according to the merit of their understanding rather than their birth, and again, the great are diminished by their folly and wickedness. Because their wisdom and dignified breeding are so proud and grand they respect no one but themselves, neither converse with anyone but their own companions; for their dwellings and streets are joined to each other, walled around and shut off from the rest of the world; their clothing is of a different fashion; they speak a higher language, a speech as earlier related in which all their learning is written. There are more than one hundred persons among them considered to be more noble than the emperor [shogun] and who are honored with higher and more esteemed titles.[127]

Caron's account of the events from Hideyoshi's triumph to the consolidation of Tokugawa rule is generally accurate, but probably familiar to those who had read any of the missionary accounts. He correctly surmises that Hideyoshi's Korean campaigns were primarily intended to divert the samurai and forestall possible rebellion at home. Hideyoshi's death he attributes to poison at the hands of the Korean ambassador, a story widely believed at the time but apparently not true. His sketch of Tokugawa Ieyasu's reign culminating in the Osaka campaign of 1614–15 and Hideyori's death lacks details but is generally accurate. Ieyasu—"Ongoschio" (*ōgosho,* or retired shogun) Caron calls him—did not enjoy his triumph for long. He died in 1616 and was succeeded by his son "Coubo or Coubosanna" (i.e., Hidetada; from *kubosama,* a popular title for shogun), the father of the present "Emperor Chiongon" (Shogun Iemitsu).[128]

Caron is at his best when describing the reigning shogun Iemitsu and the now comfortably established Tokugawa regime. Concerning the shogun's power Caron states simply: "He is sovereign lord and owner of the whole land, having power (as it happened several times during my residence there) to punish the great kings and lords, sometimes for small misdeeds, with banishment, confinement on an island, or with death, and to give their lands and treasures to others whom he judges more deserving."[129]

The shogun's palace in Edo is about a (Dutch) mile and a half around, surrounded by three deep moats, each bordered by a high stone wall.[130] The moats and walls are not symmetrical but intersect in odd ways. That and the multiplicity of points and fortifications make it impossible for a visitor to remember the plan of the castle. To enter, a visitor must pass through eight or nine fortified gates, irregularly placed, with large open spaces between them, each guarded by a company of soldiers. The gates are strong, covered on each side by crisscrossed iron bars one inch thick. At each gate there is

[127]Caron, *BV,* IIb, 174–75; Boxer (ed.), *op. cit.* (n. 117), p. 57. Caron's description of the *kuge* is in the main accurate. On the court during the Tokugawa period see Plutschow, *op. cit.* (n. 101), pp. 158–63, and our pls. 393 and 395; for a court lady, see pl. 399.

[128]Caron, *BV,* IIb, 147–48; Boxer (ed.), *op. cit.* (n. 117), pp. 27–28.

[129]Caron, *BV,* IIb, 141; Boxer (ed.), *op. cit.* (n. 117), p. 19.

[130]According to Totman, *op. cit.* (n. 114), p. 92, the circumference of the area inside the inner moat was about four present-day miles.

a barracks large enough for two hundred to three hundred soldiers. The streets within the castle grounds are broad and are lined with beautiful palaces belonging to the great lords of the realm. The shogun's palace, surrounded by woods, ponds, streams, and gardens, stands inside the innermost moat. The palaces of "princes of the blood" and members of the council are built inside the second moat. Between the second and outermost moats are the palaces of the "kings" and "dukes" (daimyos). Palaces of lesser nobles stand outside the outermost moat. The great lords compete with one another in the beauty and decoration of their residences. Gold is so lavishly used that from a distance the palace and its environs look like a golden mountain. In these courts and palaces live Japan's great lords (daimyos) or their wives and heirs, under the shogun's eye, as hostages.[131]

Despite its vast size the court always seems crowded, with the palanquins, horses, and entourages of the great nobles choking the streets. When the shogun goes out, either on his horse or in a palanquin, he is usually accompanied by nobles who are called "his majesty's companions": musicians, artists, physicians, writers, and the like. These enjoy high honors and salaries, but hold no fiefs. Following them comes the shogun's bodyguard composed of the natural sons and other relatives of the "kings and princes" who because they were born of concubines are not in the line of succession. The bodyguards are regularly examined and well trained. Garbed in black silk, they march in perfect order and absolute silence. The streets along which the shogun passes are freshly cleaned and sanded. No one dares look out of a window or door at the shogun, and those in the streets kneel with heads bowed while he passes. Preparations for the shogun's visit to the imperial court in "Miako" (Kyoto) take a whole year. Thousands of people are involved. Many of the great lords leave some days before the shogun and await him at various places along the Tōkaidō, each group accompanying him for a half day, the rest following behind. The distance between Edo and Kyoto is 125 Dutch miles and the shogun visits there once in every five to seven years. Caron observes that it is all accomplished smoothly and without confusion.[132]

Caron reports that the mausoleum for the shogun's father at "Niko" (Nikko) was completed in 1636. In it hangs a large copper candelabra which Caron presented to the shogun as a gift from the VOC in 1635. A large castle in which the shogun stays when he visits the shrine has been completed in five months, although the estimate had been that it would require three years.[133]

[131] Caron, *BV*, IIb, 141–42; Boxer (ed.), *op. cit.* (n. 117), pp. 20–21. For a modern description of Edo castle see Totman, *op. cit.* (n. 114), pp. 90–99. For a depiction of an audience with the shogun see our pl. 404.

[132] Caron, *BV*, IIb, 142–43; Boxer (ed.), *op. cit.* (n. 117), pp. 21–22. The distance from Edo (Tokyo) to Miyako (Kyoto) is actually 514 kilometers or 319 miles.

[133] Caron, *BV*, IIb, 143–44; Boxer (ed.), *op. cit.* (n. 117), p. 22. The mausoleum at Nikko was built for Ieyasu, Iemitsu's grandfather, not for Hidetada. Ieyasu's remains were taken there

The shogun's wealth in silver and gold is very large and continually grows, because his revenues for two months can pay an entire year's expenses. Caron also mentions other treasures and family heirlooms, and he lists those mentioned in Hidetada's will: several famous antique swords, a teapot, some paintings, and some pieces of calligraphy, most of which were bequeathed to Iemitsu, although some went to his three brothers. Caron estimates the value of these treasures at thirty million guilders.[134]

Caron's description of Iemitsu dwells on his marital affairs. Being "much given to sodomy," Iemitsu had no lawful wife or heir when his father died. According to Caron, the *dairi* persuaded him to marry a kinswoman, but Iemitsu showed no interest in her and finally had her shut up in a separate castle. Thereafter the shogun's old nurse kept searching out beautiful concubines for him in the hope that one would please him. When he finally favored a low-born woman—an armorer's daughter—the jealous court ladies had her child strangled as it was born.[135]

Caron quite accurately describes the military system of the Tokugawa. Each of the shogun's vassals is required to maintain soldiers in proportion to his income. The "Lord of Fiamor" (daimyo of Hirado in Hizen), for example, whose income is 60,000 koku of rice, must maintain 1,200 foot soldiers and 120 cavalry, together with the necessary servants. Altogether the shogun can command 368,000 foot soldiers and 36,800 horsemen maintained by the vassal daimyos, and another 100,000 foot soldiers and 20,000 horsemen paid for from his private domains. In their eagerness to please the shogun most of the daimyos maintain twice as many soldiers as are required. His armies are regularly organized—Caron supplies the details—and the shogun always knows exactly how many soldiers he has. In fact, he can as easily determine the entire population of the empire because all families are organized into groups of five and the head of each five-family group must report all births and deaths to the local lord, who reports it, in turn, to the daimyo, and he to two shogunal officials.[136]

Caron's account of Tokugawa government, especially of the shogun's methods for controlling the great daimyos, is very perceptive. Only four of the great lords regularly advise the shogun. These are chosen from among the nobles who have served the shogun well and who have grown up at

---

in 1617. Hidetada was buried at Zōjōji Temple in Shiba in Edo. Iemitsu was also buried at Nikko. For a photograph of the Dutch candelabra found at Nikko see G. Schurhammer, S. J., *Shinto, The Way of the Gods of Japan* (Bonn, 1923), p. 36, fig. 23. Also see our pl. 405.

[134] Caron, *BV*, IIb, 44; Boxer (ed.), *op. cit.* (n. 117), pp. 22–23. Boxer, pp. 120–21, identifies each piece reported by Caron to have been listed in Hidetata's will.

[135] Caron, *BV*, IIb, 144–45; Boxer (ed.), *op. cit.* (n. 117), pp. 23–24. While inaccurate in details—his first wife was not an imperial relative, although he did shut her away in a separate palace—Caron's account seems generally correct and probably reflects even in its errors what was popularly believed at the time. On Iemitsu's character see Boxer's note, pp. 121–22.

[136] Caron, *BV*, IIb, 148–49; Boxer (ed.), *op. cit.* (n. 117), pp. 28–29. The "five-man unit"

court with him (the *fudai daimyō*). They command high salaries but serve entirely at the shogun's pleasure. Contradicting him could easily result in banishment.[137]

Although the revenues of the great lords appear vast, Caron observes that their expenses were high enough to keep most of them continuously in debt. Each of them must spend half of each year in Edo, those from the north and east during one half of the year and those from the south and west during the other (*sankin kotai*). Banquets are held and gifts are exchanged at their coming and going. Moreover they travel in great state, some with as many as six thousand men. Even a minor lord like the daimyo of Hirado travels with three hundred retainers. He also maintains more than one thousand persons in his two Edo residences. Each lord builds as sumptuous a palace in Edo as he can afford—usually more than he can afford, Caron thinks. When a new palace is built, for example, a special and splendid entry, all lacquered, gilded, and decorated with fine carvings, is built in addition to the normal gates and doors, in anticipation of the shogun's visit. When completed it is covered with planks to protect it from the elements until the day of the shogun's visit, an event which usually takes about three years to arrange. Once the shogun has passed through the gate it is locked and never used again, no one else being worthy enough to enter it. Not only is entertaining the shogun an incredibly expensive affair, but after the shogun has dined in a daimyo's palace the daimyo feasts the shogun's relatives, councillors, and other daimyos for about three months. In addition to the continuous entertainments and gifts, the daimyo's servants, especially the women, must be elaborately clothed. Even a gift from the shogun, such as a hawk from one of his hunts, can prove ruinously expensive, because the recipient must entertain virtually the whole city in celebration. Caron estimates that such a bird costs its recipient half a year's income. Marriages arranged by the shogun have the same effect. A wife or concubine received from the shogun must be sumptuously housed and served by an extraordinary number of servants, sometimes more than a hundred. As if the expenses of *sankin kotai* are not enough, the shogun frequently orders the building of a castle, road, canal, or public building, the cost of which is divided among the daimyos.[138]

In addition to keeping them at court and impoverishing them, the shogun also controls his vassal daimyos by appointing officials to watch them. Caron calls them chancellors and suggests that the shogun appoints them as

---

(*gonin gumi*) was the device used to assure collective responsibility. *Cf.* the Chinese system of *li chia*, above, p. 1585.

[137] Caron, *BV*, IIb, 149–50; Boxer (ed.), *op. cit.* (n. 117), pp. 29–30. Caron is here describing the *rōjū* or senior council of the elders. *Cf.* Harold Bolitho, *Treasures among Men: The Fudai Daimyo in Tokugawa Japan* (New Haven and London, 1974), pp. 122–23.

[138] Caron, *BV*, IIb, 150–52; Boxer (ed.), *op. cit.* (n. 117), pp. 30–32.

part of a daimyo's staff to help govern his domain, while in fact they are spies for the shogun.[139]

Concerning law and justice in Tokugawa Japan, Caron reports that "every gentleman [*heer*], from the shogun to the least townsman [*burger*] exercises the right of justice over his subjects and servants."[140] Earlier writers understood this right to be reserved to the samurai, and most of what Caron writes also seems to assume that, except that he seems to think any husband, samurai or not, may kill his wife and any man found shut in a room with her. The shogun, he reports, maintains judges in all his cities and towns. All crimes, Caron asserts, are punished by death, although condemned samurai are allowed to ceremonially disembowel themselves (commit *seppuku*) and thus preserve their honor. Everyone suffers for his own crimes except in the case of treason, when all male family members are killed, their goods confiscated, and their women given away or sold as slaves. Caron lists several crimes: breaking the shogun's orders, pilfering royal revenues, forging coins, arson, rape, abuse of authority, lying. The means of execution include decapitation, roasting, burning, crucifixion, drawing and quartering, and boiling in oil or water. "Kings and great lords" (daimyos), Caron reports, are sometimes punished by banishing them to a small island, fourteen miles from Edo, called "Faitsnichina" (Hachijōjima). The island is only one mile around, with such steep and rocky shores that no boat can land there. The prisoners there are closely guarded, poorly housed and fed, and forced to raise silkworms and weave silk cloth.[141]

Caron illustrates his remarks about law and justice with several interesting stories: one about a poor samurai who hired an insolent commoner so that he could kill him for a minor infraction of duty; another of a daimyo who embezzled tax money and was ordered to commit *seppuku* along with his brothers and sons who were scattered about the country, entailing complex arrangements to ensure that they all would die at the same hour; and several gruesome stories about the punishment of adulteresses.[142]

According to Caron there is no crime or disorder in Japanese cities. The ends of each street are barricaded and guarded at night and no one is permitted to go out, even for emergencies, without a pass from the official on duty.[143]

Caron writes surprisingly little about trade and commerce in Japan, probably because he thought Director-General Lucaszoon, for whom he origi-

[139]Caron, *BV*, IIb, 154; Boxer (ed.), *op. cit.* (n. 117), p. 35. Here Caron is describing the *metsuke* (inspectors), but his description does not do them justice. See Murdoch and Yamagata, *op. cit.* (n. 15), III, 14, and Totman, *op. cit.* (n. 114), pp. 200–202.
[140]Caron, *BV*, IIb, 156; Boxer (ed.), *op. cit.* (n. 117), p. 37.
[141]Caron's description of Hachijōjima, like those of previous European writers, is quite inaccurate. The only notable person ever banished there was Ukida Hideiye in 1603. See Murdoch and Yamagata, *op. cit.* (n. 15), II, 432–33, and Boxer (ed.), *op. cit.* (n. 117), pp. 40–41, 125.
[142]Caron, *BV*, IIb, 156–61; Boxer (ed.), *op. cit.* (n. 117), pp. 36–41.
[143]Boxer (ed.), *op. cit.* (n. 117), p. 56.

nally wrote the book in 1636, would have adequate information about such things in VOC reports and correspondence. All Japan's foreign trade, he reports, is carried on by foreigners. The Japanese have been banned from China for many years because of disturbances they caused there. Recently the shogun has forbidden any of his subjects to trade abroad, partly because of problems like those with the Dutch in Taiwan and partly to prevent the importation of arms or Christianity. Japan maintains no embassies abroad. Foreign goods are transported to Japan primarily by the Chinese and the Dutch. The Spanish and Portuguese have traded in Japan for more than a century (but Hendrick Hagenaer notes in the *Begin ende voortgangh* edition that they were expelled in 1636). The Siamese and Cambodians rarely come any more, and the English have closed their factory. Caron lists some of the imported products: silk in great quantities, deerskins, "Roche vellen" or the skin of a ray much in demand for sword grips, hemp, cotton cloth, red wool, carpets, pewter, quicksilver, various drugs, spices, musk, sugar, porcelain, camphor, borax, ivory, and red coral. These, he reports, as well as domestic products, are primarily marketed in Kyoto, "which is the staple of the whole empire, merchants coming from every part of the country to trade there." [144]

The Japanese, asserts Caron, "have one language, one fashion of clothing, one mint, and one weight." His description of coinage, however, does not convey the impression of rigorous standardization. He describes three sorts of gold coins and their weights in taels. Their silver coins, of varying shapes, are "without certain weight, but by guess." Fifty taels worth of these are usually wrapped together in paper. In addition the Japanese use copper "cash," the value of which differs from one domain to another. The shogun has ordered all of these called in and is recoining them in a standard weight and value. [145] Measures of length, volume, and weight, however, are uniform throughout the empire. Commerce in Japan is entirely in the hands of the merchants; the shogun, daimyos, and samurai do not participate in it and gain no profit from it. Caron does not think profits for individual merchants are very great, however, because there are so many of them. [146] Japanese merchants do not use double-entry bookkeeping but nevertheless keep their accounts in a very orderly fashion. Caron is particularly impressed with how rapidly they can calculate with the *soroban* (abacus), which he describes as "a board with round pellets strung on little sticks, after the fashion of the Chinese." [147]

Houses are built of wood, thus making fires a major scourge of Japanese

---

[144] Caron, *BV*, IIb, 170–72; Boxer (ed.), *op. cit.* (n. 117), pp. 51–53. In fact, the Spanish were expelled in 1624, but the Portuguese were not officially expelled until 1639.

[145] Caron, *BV*, IIb, 173; Boxer (ed.), *op. cit.* (n. 117), pp. 53–54. On the intricate coinage system see Dunn, *op. cit.* (n. 13), pp. 97–99.

[146] Caron, *BV*, IIb, 172; Boxer (ed.), *op. cit.* (n. 117), p. 53.

[147] Caron, *BV*, IIb, 174; Boxer (ed.), *op. cit.* (n. 117), p. 57.

towns. Most houses, therefore, have a fireproof storehouse attached for the safekeeping of valuables. Houses are all built four feet above the ground, their floors covered with thick mats of uniform size, neatly fitted (*tatami*). The Japanese live on the lower floors of their houses; upper rooms seem to be used to store household goods. Rooms are divided with light "curtain doors" (*shōji,* or translucent sliding doors) which can be removed, thus enlarging the room. Decorations consist of figures painted on the walls and sliding doors, gilt paper, and a corner at one end of the room where a painting and a vase of flowers are displayed (the *tokonoma*). At one end of the room are steps leading to the garden, which is always green and placed so that it can be viewed from the main rooms of the house. Chests, cupboards, and the like are kept in storehouses or rooms in which no guests enter. The only furnishings a guest will see are paintings, specimens of fine calligraphy, lacquerware dishes, tea pots and cups, and swords.[148] Houses of the samurai are divided, one side being reserved for the women. The wives of merchants and other commoners live in the same rooms as their husbands, nevertheless very modestly and carefully avoiding any familiar discourse between them.[149]

Japanese are very hospitable. Guests are treated to tobacco, tea, and wine (sake) and entertained with music. They never quarrel during their entertainments and they visit with each other only in their private homes. There are no public houses or taverns in Japan.[150]

Marriages are arranged by parents or close relatives; there is no courtship. Each man has only one wife, but he may keep as many concubines as he wishes. He may also quite openly consort with prostitutes. His wife, on the other hand, may not so much as speak privately with another man. Divorce is easy for commoners, but not for the samurai. Caron thinks the freedom men enjoy regarding concubines and prostitutes makes their wives very submissive and continually concerned to serve and please their husbands. They never intrude in their husbands' affairs and are careful not to trouble them with unnecessary questions or requests. Caron seems to approve. He includes a few stories to illustrate the extreme modesty and fidelity of Japanese women.[151]

Children are raised permissively and rarely disciplined. They do not be-

[148] On the decorative art of Japan see H. Mizuo, *Edo Painting: Sotatsu and Korin* (New York, 1972), p. 9. *Cf.* Louis Fréderic, *Daily Life in Japan at the Time of the Samurai, 1185–1603,* trans. Eileen M. Lowe (New York and Washington, 1972), pp. 104–12, on houses and furnishings.

[149] Caron, *BV,* IIb, 166; Boxer (ed.), *op. cit.* (n. 117), pp. 46–47. *Cf.* Fréderic, *op. cit.* (n. 148), pp. 59–60.

[150] Caron, *BV,* IIb, 167; Boxer (ed.), *op. cit.* (n. 117), p. 47. Caron is surely wrong about taverns. Cocks, for example, reported constant problems resulting from English sailors drinking in Hirado's taverns and brothels.

[151] Caron, *BV,* IIb, 152–54, 167–68; Boxer (ed.), *op. cit.* (n. 117), pp. 32–34, 48. On marriage and the status of women see Fréderic, *op. cit.* (n. 148), pp. 45–51, 54–60.

gin school until age seven or eight and even then are induced to study by praise and competition with each other rather than by force. Caron openly admires the results. Seven- and eight-year-old children behave themselves better and converse more maturely than any children of that age in Europe.[152] Caron is also impressed with the devotion of Japanese towards their parents, which extends even beyond the grave. On the anniversary of their parents' death, they ceremoniously abstain from eating anything that had life.[153]

When a Japanese man grows old and his children are adults he usually retires from his office, business, or trade, turning responsibility over to his eldest son, who also inherits the greatest part of his estate. Younger sons are provided for, as well, but their portion of the inheritance reverts to the eldest should they die before him. Daughters receive nothing, unless it is a gift to their husbands at their marriage. Such gifts are usually declined, however.[154] A man's name changes with the stages of his life. He will be given a childish name when he is born, which he abandons for a more suitable name when he becomes an adult. When he is old and retires he takes still another personal name. His surname, however, is always pronounced first. The "lords" (daimyos) also have surnames and personal names but they are ordinarily called by that of their office or domain.[155]

Like many earlier European writers Caron praises the loyalty and faithfulness of the Japanese, especially that of the samurai. Nowhere is this better illustrated than by the willingness of vassals to accompany their lord in death. Caron describes vows expressing such willingness and the ceremonial *seppuku* which follows a great lord's death, frequently involving as many as thirty vassals. The 1661 edition of his work has a plate depicting such a ceremony.[156]

Among his observations about Japanese society, Caron makes one brief but accurate general statement about the Tokugawa class structure. The samurai, who are numerous, he reports, are much feared and honored. They do nothing, but are maintained by the merchants and peasants. Merchants, however rich, are despised, because people say they live by lying and by deceiving the people for the sake of gain. Artisans and laborers likewise

[152] Caron, *BV*, IIb, 168; Boxer (ed.), *op. cit.* (n. 117), pp. 48–49. It was a genial type of elementary education. See R. P. Dore, *Education in Tokugawa Japan* (2d ed.; London, 1984), p. 273. *Cf.* also Fréderic, *op. cit.* (n. 148), pp. 34–40.

[153] Caron, *BV*, IIb, 54; Boxer (ed.), *op. cit.* (n. 117), p. 34. On mourning customs see Dunn, *op. cit.* (n. 13), pp. 129–30, and Fréderic, *op. cit.* (n. 148), pp. 51–53.

[154] Caron, *BV*, IIb, 168–69; Boxer (ed.), *op. cit.* (n. 117), p. 49. On *inkyo* or retirement see Fréderic, *op. cit.* (n. 148), pp. 50–51.

[155] Caron, *BV*, IIb, 154–55; Boxer (ed.), *op. cit.* (n. 117), p. 35. On the complicated matter of names see Chamberlain, *op. cit.* (n. 22), pp. 344–48.

[156] Caron, *BV*, IIb, 155; Boxer (ed.), *op. cit.* (n. 117), pp. 35–36. The plate is embellished by the engraver beyond Caron's description of it, as are those found in Engelbert Kaempfer, *The History of Japan* . . . (London, 1727). See Beatrice M. Bodart Bailey, "Kaempher Restor'd," *Monumenta Nipponica*, Vol. XLIII, No. 1 (1988), pp. 1–33. See also our pl. 424.

are undervalued, because they are considered everyone's servants. Neither are the peasants respected, because they are so poor and miserable, working harder than anyone else for very little profit. "They lead a catfish life," says Caron.[157]

Caron contributes very little to Europe's understanding of Japanese religion. He describes no particular temples, deities, or teachings other than to say that some sects think the soul is immortal and will live in another world after death while others believe there is no separate soul. He says there are twelve sects in all but he names only one. Priests of the first eleven are celibate and avoid eating meat. The twelfth sect, called "Icko" or "Ickois" (*Ikkō,* "single-minded"; a formerly militant branch of the Jodō Shin sect of Buddhism), is the most respected, and has a high priest who is honored like a king and some temples that are endowed by the shogun. Its priests may marry and eat what they wish. Caron thinks the Japanese are not very religious. They seldom pray and seldom go to the temples. The priests do little but read before the idols and bury the dead, most of whom are first cremated. They never debate about theology or work to convert anyone to their sect. The priests are much given to sodomy, which, says Caron, is not judged a sin or even considered shameful among them. Many of their temples, which are sumptuous and built in pleasant gardens, are used for parties and entertainments frequently involving prostitution and other debaucheries.[158]

Despite Caron's apparent lack of interest in Japanese religion, he vividly describes the persecution of Japanese Christians and their European priests, including detailed descriptions of the tortures they endured. He too admires their constancy, judging it miraculous. He reports that in his time (1636) Christianity is almost completely stamped out. Nevertheless, the persecutions are renewed each year, with each person being asked to inscribe in the temple records that he renounces Christianity. Each year some Christians are discovered and tortured. Recently they have been pardoned only if they both apostatize and name other hidden Christians (*Kakure Kirishitan*).[159]

Of the various appendices published with Caron's description in most of its editions, only that of Coenraet Krammer (d. 1638) adds new, eyewitness information about Japan.[160] Krammer describes what could be seen in the streets of the famous meeting between the shogun Iemitsu, the ex-shogun

---

[157] Caron, *BV,* IIb, 156–57; Boxer (ed.), *op. cit.* (n. 117), p. 37. For peasant life during the Tokugawa era see Dunn, *op. cit.* (n. 13), pp. 50–83.

[158] Caron, *BV,* IIb, 161–63; Boxer (ed.), *op. cit.* (n. 117), pp. 42–43. On the *Ikkō* see Boxer, p. 125, and *Kodansha Encyclopedia* (n. 6), III, 269.

[159] Caron, *BV,* IIb, 163–66; Boxer (ed.), *op. cit.* (n. 117), pp. 44–47. "Hidden Christians" continued their secret worship throughout the Tokugawa era. See *Kodansha Encyclopedia* (n. 6), I, 308, and R. H. Drummond, *A History of Christianity in Japan* (Grand Rapids, 1971), pp. 109–17.

[160] For a brief biography of Krammer see W. Wijnaendts van Resant, *De gezaghebbers der Oost-Indische Compagnie . . . in Azië* (Amsterdam, 1944), p. 139.

Hidetada, and the emperor Go-Mizunō (r. 1611–29) in Kyoto on October 25, 1626. Krammer had audiences with both Iemitsu and Hidetada only four days earlier and he is invited to stay in Kyoto by the daimyo of Hirado and an official in the shogun's court. The Dutchmen secure a place along the processional route on the evening of the twenty-fourth and stay there all night long because of the expected crowds. Scaffolds are set up along the street for the spectators, the streets are cleaned and covered with white sand, the ditches are planked over, and guards dressed in white robes with black lacquer headpieces line both sides of the street. First come servants and porters carrying the emperor's baggage in large, square, lacquer chests, then sixty-four palanquins of bright white wood and copper carrying the empress' attendants. More elaborate sedan chairs follow, of black lacquer and gilded ornamentation, carrying members of the emperor's court; then a group of horsemen, each horse led by two footmen. Krammer describes each uniform and the decorations of the horses as well as the costumes of the numerous pages and servants. Gold, silver, fine silk, and black lacquerware are everywhere. The emperor's three principal wives are carried in three elaborate coaches four fathoms high, two long, and one wide, made of black lacquer with gold inlays and mother of pearl. Each coach is drawn by two huge black bulls covered with red silk netting and led by four footmen clothed in white. An army of pages and servants follows; then more horsemen, followed by porters carrying treasure, each piece of which Krammer lists. Finally there are the coaches of the shogun's father and the shogun himself, accompanied by foot soldiers, servants, parasol-carriers, and the like, after which come the shogun's brothers and all the 164 daimyos on horseback. Krammer names those who ride immediately behind the shogun, each of course with a large train of attendants and servants. The parade seems endless. Four hundred soldiers in white uniforms, then another six elegant ox-drawn coaches for the emperor's concubines, more nobles on horseback with slaves and servants, another coach for the emperor's secretary, several more elaborate coaches for court nobles, followed by the emperor's musicians, fifty-four of them. Following the musicians comes the emperor himself, sitting in a nine-foot-high portable palace with sliding doors and windows on each corner. Its roof is round, with a gilt ball in the center upon which stands a pure gold rooster with wings spread. The structure is elaborately and beautifully decorated with carved statues and gold-plated corners. The blue vault inside symbolizes the heavens with replicas of the sun, moon, and stars. It is carried by fifty of the shogun's nobles dressed in long white robes and black lacquer headpieces. Imperial bodyguards, more court nobles, thirteen more huge lacquered chests, and four hundred more soldiers in white marching six abreast complete the procession. As soon as the procession passes the crowd pours into the streets, quickly becoming uncontrollable. Purses are snatched, people are trampled to death, samurai are murdered with their own swords. The uproar lasts all night. In the morning, men, women, and children are found dead in the streets. Several young women are missing, to be discovered blindfolded and half-naked two weeks hence. The emperor and his wives are feasted in the shogun's palace for three days, each meal consisting of 140 courses. Before he leaves, the emperor receives costly presents from the shogun and his father. Krammer describes the gifts.[161]

Information about Japan can be found in two other pieces published in the *Begin ende voortgangh*. The more important of these is Hendrick Hagenaer's journal.[162] Hagenaer, a VOC senior merchant, visited Japan three times: in 1634, in 1635–36, and again in 1637, years in which Caron was resident there. While Hagenaer attempts no comprehensive description of Japan, his journal contains some interesting details about VOC trade in Japan, especially about the Dutch embassy in Edo in 1635–36, and some description of the sights and experiences along the way.

The account of Hagenaer's 1634 visit is brief. He notes the appearance of Hirado, its harbor and anchorage, and reports that a Japanese official came aboard the Dutch ship to register the name and age of each crew member. The Dutch also learn that they will not be permitted to leave Hirado until twenty days after the Portuguese leave Nagasaki. Efforts to change that rule prove unsuccessful. On October 17 thirty-seven Christians are martyred in Hirado; Hagenaer provides details. Twenty-three more Christians are arrested on October 31. On the next day Hagenaer sails to Nagasaki in a small boat, where he meets old Melchior van Santvoort, who had been an officer along with Adams on the first Dutch ship to come to Japan. When the Dutch are ready to sail, Japanese officials come aboard again to muster the crew.[163]

Back in Hirado on September 1, 1635, Hagenaer reports familiar routines: the crew is mustered and counted; he travels to Nagasaki to ask permission for some of his ships to leave before the Portuguese; the Japanese refuse to change the rule. Then Hagenaer becomes involved with Caron in

[161] *BV*, IIb, 189–94; Boxer (ed.), *op. cit.* (n. 117), pp. 65–72. The number of daimyos fluctuated during the seventeenth century. Bolitho (*op. cit.* [n. 137], pp. 45–46) reports that by the end of the Tokugawa period there were 265. J. W. Hall in the *Kodansha Encyclopedia* ([n. 6], II, 63) estimates "some 245 during the Tokugawa period" and counts 266 by the end of the eighteenth century. Tsukahira (*op. cit.* [n. 112], pp. 140–73) lists 265 as of 1853. In any case, Krammer's 164 seems very low for 1626. We have been unable to document the riot described by Krammer. The ten-volume history of Kyoto (Hayashiya Tatsusaburō [ed.], *Kyoto no Rekishi* [Kyoto, 1972], V, 56–72) reports Iemitsu and Hidetada's visit in detail, noting that there was a serious drought and water shortage at the time, that 3,327 samurai lined the main thoroughfare, and that another 1,200 patrolled the sidestreets. But it does not mention the riot. Perhaps such things were not so extraordinary. On the other appendices to Caron's account see above, pp. 460–61.

[162] Hagenaer, "Verhael van de reyz gedaen inde meeste deelen van de Oost-Indien, . . . ," *BV*, IIb, 1–133. Hagenaer's journal was never published apart from the 1645 and 1646 editions of the *Begin ende voortgangh*.

[163] *Ibid.*, pp. 76–78. For the Dutch factory at Hirado see our pl. 26.

negotiations for the release of Pieter Nuyts, the former governor of Formosa still held prisoner in Edo. On December 14 they leave for Edo. Most of Hagenaer's account deals with the negotiations and receptions. The gifts to the shogun and numerous other officials are carefully listed, including the thirty-armed copper chandelier which still hangs in Ieyasu's mausoleum at Nikko.[164] Occasionally, however, Hagenaer treats his readers to a glimpse of the scenery along the way. Houses are built close along the shore on either side of the narrow straits of "Camono Sicky" (Shimonoseki). "Acassie" (Nakatsu) has a large beautiful castle with stone walls; a little further west Hagenaer enjoys the splendid view of a pagoda on the shore of an island as the sun sets. Osaka is a populous city with a swift-running river spanned by heavy wooden bridges. Arriving in Edo on January 4, 1636, he finds the streets so crowded they can scarcely pass through them. The Dutch, as usual, are housed with a Buddhist priest.[165]

Hagenaer leaves Edo on February 4; Caron stays to continue the negotiations. He is in "Oudauwe" (Odawara) on February 6, where he finds a green bough erected in front of every door as part of the New Year celebrations. February 17 he spends sightseeing in Osaka. He visits seven or eight beautiful temples with many gilded images, and walks around the castle, which, with its moats and high walls, looks splendid and formidable. On February 26 he is back in Hirado.[166]

The negotiations all seem to be successful. There is a new trade agreement, Nuyts is freed, and they are given permission to leave without waiting for the Portuguese. All this good news calls for more entertainments and gifts, especially for the daimyo of Hirado and his regent, who have been very helpful. But during these days Hagenaer also reports on the *seppuku* of a samurai whose lord had died, on the arrest early in May of eight hundred Christians, on a trial by ordeal, on the Bon festival celebrations and decorations in Hirado (June 14), on a June 18 celebration of the capture of Osaka castle, on the Hachiman festival, October 18, and on the tearful departure of Portuguese "wives" and children for Macao. Hagenaer leaves Hirado on November 3.[167]

Hagenaer's last visit to Japan in 1637 produced little description. Trade is brisk: he reports six other Dutch and four English ships in port and six Portuguese galliots at Nagasaki. He hears about the martyrdom of a Portuguese priest and twenty-seven Japanese Christians at Nagasaki, and he witnesses the execution of a thief. He leaves optimistic about future Dutch trade in Japan.[168]

---

[164] Hagenaer, *loc. cit.* (n. 162), pp. 91–97. It is kept with other "tribute" from the "vassal states" of Korea and the Ryukyu Islands (Liu-ch'iu).

[165] *Ibid.*, pp. 86–88.

[166] *Ibid.*, p. 90. For one of the temples he may have seen, see our pl. 414.

[167] Hagenaer, *loc. cit.* (n. 162), pp. 91, 97–102.

[168] *Ibid.*, pp. 125–28. Hagenaer's report of English ships at Hirado is puzzling. While the

The *Begin ende voortgangh* also contains an account of Jacob Specx and Pieter Segerszoon's 1611 embassy to Ieyasu's court in Sumpu (Shizuoka). It is appended to Pieter Willemszoon Verhoeff's voyage.[169] Segerszoon's ship, the "Braeck," was the first Dutch ship to visit Japan after the establishment of the VOC residence at Hirado in 1609. The Japanese were displeased that no ship came in 1610, and the Portuguese happily assured them that the Dutch were not merchants but pirates. The voyage of the "Braeck" was intended to convince the Japanese otherwise. It carried little cargo, but upon arrival in Hirado Segerszoon and Specx, the VOC factor in Hirado, journeyed to Sumpu where they were graciously received by Ieyasu and reassured about their commercial position in Japan.[170] The *Begin ende voortgangh* piece is a very detailed account of the embassy and its negotiations in Hirado, Osaka, Kyoto, and Sumpu which throws some light on early Tokugawa politics and the beginnings of Dutch trade in Japan. Will Adams' role in the arrangements and negotiations looms very large; the Dutch are impressed with what they judge to be his growing influence with Ieyasu. In fact, João Rodriguez, the Jesuit interpreter whose function Adams had taken over, was exiled to Macao while Specx and Segerszoon were in Japan. The account of their embassy, however, contains very few descriptions of anything other than the negotiations and none that provides information not already available to European readers.

The year 1646 also saw the publication of what is probably the first European eyewitness account of Hokkaido, written by a participant in Martin Gerritszoon Vries' 1643 expedition and appended to Hendrick Brouwer's *Journael*.[171] Vries did not settle the questions outstanding regarding northern Japan's geography. He coasted the southern and eastern shores of Hokkaido and Sakhalin without discovering that they were not joined or that Hokkaido was an island. Vries' men landed on Hokkaido, however, and met the Ainu, all of which is described in the "Kort beschrijvinghe."[172]

The "Kort beschrijvinghe" first repeats what the author learned from a Japanese about "Eso" (Yezo or Hokkaido). It names "Matsmey" (Matsumae) as its chief city, and lists the names of several other places. The governor of Matsumae goes to Edo each year to pay his respects to the shogun. The Japanese trade there, and silver is to be found in the mountains.[173] The

---

Dutch worried that ships from John Weddel's fleet, outfitted by the Courteen Association, would come to Hirado in 1637, none appear to have done so. See Massarella, *op. cit.* (n. 50), pp. 342–43.

[169] *BV*, IIa, 72–98. For bibliography see above, pp. 470–72.

[170] See Boxer, *op. cit.* (n. 35), pp. 287–90, for details.

[171] See above, p. 475.

[172] The Ainu are the aboriginals of Hokkaido, southern Sakhalin, and the Kurile Islands.

[173] Hendrick Brouwer, *Journael ende historis verhael* . . . (Amsterdam, 1646), pp. 95–96. The Matsumae family established the Japanese presence in Hokkaido after 1514 and developed trade thereafter between northeast Honshu and southern Hokkaido. In 1604 the Matsumae clan re-

coast as seen by the Dutch themselves appears mountainous and wooded, with lots of birch, spruce, alder, and tall grass. In some places it reminds the author of the English coast. The waters offshore are unusually rich in fish, perhaps because whales chase the smaller fish towards the shore. In one small bay they catch a thousand pounds of salmon in four days. They find many oysters along the beaches.[174] The natives all look alike: short and stocky with long hair and beards, so that their faces seem covered with hair, although their foreheads are shaved. They have sharp features, yellow skin, black eyes, and noses that are short and fairly thick but not flat; they are hairy all over. The women are whiter than the men. Some women cut their hair; others let it grow long and tie it up as Javan women do. The women paint their lips blue. Everyone—man, woman, or child—has pierced ears and wears silver or other sorts of rings in them.[175]

The people seem to have no religion. They eat like barbarians, without any sort of ceremony. Still, whenever they sit around a fire and drink they first sprinkle a few drops in various places around the fire as if they were making some sort of offering. They keep firesticks and wood shavings in their houses and stuck into the ground in many other places. When someone is ill they cut long shavings and wind them around the patient's head and arms. They seem to have no government, no writing or books, and no one seems able to read or write. There appear to be bandits in some places who dominate the people. Most people have scars on their heads where they have been wounded.[176]

Each man has two wives, who make clothing and cook for him.[177] When they go out to cut wood the women row the boats. The men are very jealous of their wives and daughters and will kill anyone who tries to molest them. Both men and women like strong drink and very easily become drunken. They look wild, observes the author, but they are so sincere and straightforward in their dealings with strangers that they must be considered civilized. Whenever strangers come ashore they put on their best clothes and show every courtesy towards them, bowing with folded hands and singing with a quavering voice like the Japanese. However, whenever

ceived a decree of enfeoffment from the Tokugawa government and were proclaimed as over-lords of southern Hokkaido. See F. C. C. Peng and P. Geiser, *The Ainu: The Past in the Present* (Hiroshima, 1977), p. 10.

[174] Brouwer, *op. cit.* (n. 173), pp. 96–98. Salmon run in most of Hokkaido's rivers between May and October. For a description of Ainu catching salmon see Landor, *op. cit.* (n. 102), p. 64, and on oysters, p. 104.

[175] Brouwer, *op. cit.* (n. 173), pp. 98–99. Actually the women's lips were tattoed a blue color; see J. Batchelor, *Ainu Life and Lore* (Tokyo, n.d.), chap. vii. On earrings see Landor, *op. cit.* (n. 102), p. 249.

[176] Brouwer, *op. cit.* (n. 173), p. 99.

[177] The first wife was called the "great wife" and the second the "small wife." Normally the two wives lived apart. See Landor, *op. cit.* (n. 102), p. 294; also see N. G. Munro, *Ainu. Creed and Cult* (New York, 1963), p. 147, n. 1.

they receive a small gift from the strangers they quickly become familiar, showing friendly and happy faces.[178] After childbirth, women live in separate small huts for two or three weeks. Babies appear completely white. The women are very modest when feeding infants if the Dutch are present. In fact even small children, who often run naked in warm weather, quickly hide themselves when the Dutch approach.[179]

Their houses are built of boards, neatly fitted together, roofed over with bark. They leave an opening in the roof for the smoke from the fire which they build in the center of the house.[180] The floors are neatly covered with straw mats. The houses are low, not more than ten or twelve feet high. You must bend low to enter through the door. Inside are few furnishings; only mats on the floor, Japanese robes, and a few cushions on which to sit or sleep. Ordinarily only six to twelve houses are built close to each other, a half mile or more separating these small groups. Most of them appear empty and uninhabited. The winter this year was very cold and there was little food. Many people have died. In some places the people bury their dead, marking the grave with oyster shells. In other places coffins are placed in small huts on posts above the ground.[181]

The Ainu eat fish, whale blubber, greens, and red rose buds, which grow abundantly there. The buds are picked when they are the size of a mispel, dried, and kept as winter food. They eat from lacquer cups and square bowls with chopsticks like the Japanese, although in some places the people appear to eat with their fingers. Their clothing is like that of the Japanese, although they do not usually wear silk. Some clothing they buy from the Japanese and some they make for themselves. They also make some coats from animal skins.[182]

The Ainu are lazy and try to avoid hard work. They fish from dugout canoes, trap birds, and hunt with bows and arrows. They exchange whale blubber, smoked whale tongue, animal skins, and bird feathers with the Japanese for rice, sake, clothing (both silk and cotton), copper, tobacco pipes, tobacco boxes, lacquer cups and bowls, silver and pewter earrings, axes, and knives. The Japanese come to trade once a year. Japanese words have crept into their language. They are clever traders but not thievish. The "Kort beschrijvinghe" concludes with a detailed description of the Ainu's weapons—swords like those of the Japanese, bows and poisoned arrows like small harpoons—and of the way they execute captured foes by beating.[183]

---

[178] Brouwer, *op. cit.* (n. 173), pp. 99–100.

[179] *Ibid.*, p. 100.

[180] On the mythico-religious function of the opening see Mircea Eliade, *Shamanism: Archaic Techniques of Ecstasy* (New York, 1964), p. 262.

[181] Brouwer, *op. cit.* (n. 173), pp. 100–101.

[182] *Ibid.*, pp. 101–2.

[183] *Ibid.*, pp. 102–4.

3

POST-1650 REPORTS

Portuguese trade with Japan ceased in 1639, and in 1640 the Dutch factory in Hirado was dismantled and the Dutch were moved to the little island of Deshima in Nagasaki harbor (see pl. 27). Apart from the Dutch on Deshima no Europeans traded in Japan after 1640. Fresh information about Japan also soon dried up. Missionaries no longer wrote letters from Japan. Apart from an annual embassy to the shogun's court in Edo, the Dutch were virtually imprisoned on Deshima. Most of them had little opportunity or inclination to see or to learn much about Japan.[184] By mid-century the flood of information about Japan with which the century had begun was reduced to a trickle.

No new information about Japan appears to have been published between 1646 and 1669, between Vries' "Kort beschrijvinghe" and Arnoldus Montanus' *Gedenkwaerdige gesantschappen*. Bernhard Varen's *Descriptio regni Iaponiae* (1649) depends entirely on other published sources—Maffei, Xavier, and other Jesuit reports, but primarily on Hagenaer, Caron, and the appendices to their *Begin ende voortgangh* account.[185] Daniello Bartoli's *Giappone* (1660), part of his history of Jesuit missions, rehearses the story of the Jesuit mission in Japan and is based on earlier Jesuit letters and histories.[186] Athanasius Kircher (1667) tries to fit Japanese religion into his account of the spread of idolatry from ancient Egypt to India, China, and Japan, stressing the similarities between the religious traditions of these Asian lands. All of his information about Japanese religion, however, came from standard Jesuit sources, especially Guzman.[187]

Montanus' rambling, encyclopedic account, on the other hand, contains more firsthand information about Japan than any other post-1650 publication.[188] It is ostensibly an account of several VOC embassies to the shogun's court in Edo, beginning with that of Petrus Blokovius and Andreas Frisius in 1649–50. It is, however, chaotically organized. Montanus begins with a

---

[184] For these events see Murdoch and Yamagata, *op. cit.* (n. 15), II, 663–96, and Boxer, *op. cit.* (n. 35), pp. 362–97. On the Dutch at Deshima see Herbert E. Plutschow, *Historical Nagasaki* (Tokyo, 1983), pp. 45–71. See also Leonard Blussé, "Dancing to the Tune: How the Dutch Experienced Nagasaki, 1680–1730," paper delivered at Association for Asian Studies, Annual Meeting, Session 114, New Orleans, April 14, 1991.

[185] See above, p. 478.

[186] See above, p. 381.

[187] *La Chine illustrée* (Amsterdam, 1670), pp. 187–90, 206–11. For bibliography see above, pp. 485–86.

[188] For bibliography see above, pp. 488–89. There is a Japanese translation of and commentary on Ogilby's 1670 English version of Montanus by Wada Mankichi called *Montanusu Nihon shi* ["A. Montanus' *Atlas Japannensis*"] (Tokyo, [1925]). Wada also discusses Montanus' illustrations.

general description of the earth and its various parts, the origins of the various peoples of the world and especially that of the Japanese, a general history of explorations, and finally an account of Portuguese and Dutch overseas travels and their discovery of and trade with Japan.[189] His account of the Blokovius-Frisius embassy is repeatedly interrupted to describe the landscape, history, customs, and the like suggested by the experiences of the ambassadors. Frequently these descriptive digressions suggest to Montanus parallels with customs or events in other parts of the world or in classical and biblical history. His digressions have digressions. By the time his readers have completed the account of the 1649–50 embassy they have also read the story of Japan's original settlement by rebellious Chinese who were banished there, a description of Japan's location and the speculation about whether or not it is joined to Hokkaido and the mainland, general descriptions of Japan from several sources, several descriptions of Japanese religious sects and their priests, an account of the wars of unification, a history of the Christian mission and the persecutions, descriptions of specific towns, palaces, and the like taken from previously published materials, accounts of funeral practices, mourning, and the Bon festival, descriptions of the *dairi* and his court, and much more.[190] This descriptive information is drawn from a large number of Jesuit and Dutch sources. Montanus cites, for example, Xavier, Maffei, Galvão, Turrensis, Fróis, Martini, Hazart, Linschoten, Hagenaer, Caron, Krammer, Gysbertszoon, Specx, and Segerszoon. Still other sources can be readily identified. He reproduces some pieces almost totally: Caron's excerpt from the *Edo Kagami*, Krammer's description of the 1626 meeting of the shogun and emperor, Gysbertszoon's account of the persecutions, and the embassy of Specx and Segerszoon.[191] Some of Montanus' digressions have little to do with Japan. He includes, for example, descriptions of Batavia, Macao, Korea, the Philippines, Formosa, the Manchu conquest of China, and Koxinga's conquest of Formosa, all drawn from standard published sources.

Nevertheless, the account of the Blokovius-Frisius embassy and some of the accompanying descriptions come from heretofore unpublished materials produced by participants in the embassy. The route is given in detail, including the distances between towns. There are descriptions of several towns: Nagasaki, Hirado, Osaka, Sakai, Kyoto, Shizuoka, and Edo. All of them have been described by earlier visitors; nevertheless, these seem to be independent descriptions and contain some new observations. Montanus' description of Hirado, for example, contains a perplexing description of the

[189] Arnoldus Montanus, *Atlas Japannensis: Being Remarkable Addresses by Way of Embassy from the East India Company of the United Provinces to the Emperor of Japan,* trans. John Ogilby (London, 1670), pp. 1–35.

[190] The account of the Blokovius-Frisius embassy with its innumerable digressions is found in *ibid.,* pp. 36–311.

[191] *Ibid.,* pp. 81–86, 164–70, 253–69, 88–103.

governor's residence: "In stead of a Palace, the Governor keeps his Residence in a mean Shed built of Planks clenched together."[192] He attributes the Dutch removal to Nagasaki to their having built a new stone storehouse at Hirado which the Japanese feared could be used as a fort.[193] Montanus also describes a temple near Hirado where pregnant women go to pray for sons. Later he describes the castle at Hirado as an impressive structure on a hill in a pleasant meadow with a double-roofed gate and a seven-story tower.[194] Deshima, Montanus reports, is a small island joined to the mainland at Nagasaki by a forty-foot drawbridge. The island is surrounded by a wooden palisade. The governor's residence and VOC office are near the bridge gate and there are flower gardens across from it. The island has only two streets, which meet at right angles in the center. There is a second gate on the sea side.[195] Nagasaki presents a fine prospect to viewers on incoming ships because of its hills and many steeples and towers. Several streams flow through it, spanned by wooden bridges. The streets are unpaved and very muddy in rainy weather. Each street has a gate which is closed at night. There is no wall around the city. Most of the houses are built of wood, although some are of rice straw covered with clay. Montanus describes the houses, gardens, furnishings, and constant threat of fire in words similar to those of earlier descriptions.[196] His description of Osaka contains details on the images seen in two temples, one of a multi-armed Kannon rising from the jaws of a fish, the other of a "devil" with four arms and a boar's head.[197] "Surunga" (Sumpu or Shizuoka), Montanus reports, a large city, has become "desolate" since "Toxogunsama" (Ieyasu) died, many of its inhabitants having left.[198] Montanus' description of Edo and its palaces and temples is obviously a composite. Much of it comes from previously published accounts. But his description of the shogun's palace may be new. The palace has three square towers, each nine stories high with a wide roof over each story. Two gold-plated dolphins stand atop the middle tower. Opposite the shogun's residence is a large hall with a golden roof, where he holds audiences. The footpath around the moat of the shogun's castle is always crowded with people. Montanus' author goes on to describe and name some of the daimyos' palaces and some of Edo's temples.[199] On the road to Edo the Dutch ambassadors view Mount Fuji, which Montanus uses as the occasion to describe the

[192] *Ibid.*, p. 35.

[193] *Ibid.*, pp. 35–36. The Japanese indeed seem to have been concerned about the reconstructed stone Dutch buildings. See Massarella, *op. cit.* (n. 50), p. 345.

[194] Montanus, *op. cit.* (n. 189), p. 61. Today nothing of this castle stands except one wall. The rest is in ruins. See Chamberlain and Mason, *op. cit.* (n. 12), p. 419.

[195] Montanus, *op. cit.* (n. 189), p. 73. See our pl. 27.

[196] Montanus, *op. cit.* (n. 189), pp. 75–77.

[197] *Ibid.*, pp. 89–95. The first temple is Tennōji; the second may be the Higashi Hongwanji. Both are Buddhist temples. Also see our pl. 414; *cf.* these statues to the fish and boar avatars of Vishnu, pls. 158 and 160.

[198] Montanus, *op. cit.* (n. 189), p. 112. See our pl. 419 for an example of the people.

[199] Montanus, *op. cit.* (n. 189), pp. 134–48. The shogunal palace, after being rebuilt several

yamabushi who climb it once a year and stay on it for sixty days, fasting and beating themselves, after which they wear white knots around their necks and small black caps on their heads.[200] After describing the *dairi's* palace in Miyako, Montanus observes that the Japanese have good poets and actors, and many plays, which teach virtue. The plays, he reports, have choruses of musicians.[201] On other occasions he describes a race between a man and a horse[202] and Japanese wrestlers, who wear their hair in nets, tie their pants up between their legs, and wear nothing above the waist—obviously sumo wrestlers.[203] In Sakai near Osaka, the Dutch watch a local religious festival. The singing crowd parades through the streets carrying their "idol" on their shoulders. The author also describes his walk through the gardens of a beautiful temple near Sakai which was built by the *dairi*.[204]

The 1649 embassy pretended to be an official embassy from the Dutch government rather than from the VOC. It was intended to thank the shogun for releasing the crew of the yacht "Breskens," which had put in on the northeast coast in 1643, and to reassure the shogun that despite their aid to the Portuguese during the Portuguese revolt against Spain in 1640, and despite the peace treaty between the United Provinces and Spain in 1648, the Dutch still regarded the Iberians as their enemies. The ambassador, Blokovius, was consequently not a merchant or VOC official from Batavia, but the rector of a Latin School in Hoorn. He was so ill by the time he arrived in Batavia, however, that he was not expected to live. Nevertheless the embassy continued to Japan. Blokovius' second in command, Frisius, who was a VOC official, was instructed to have the ambassador embalmed and carried to Nagasaki should he die at sea. Indeed Blokovius died enroute, was embalmed and encoffined and given a sumptuous funeral in Nagasaki "to the Wonder and Admiration of the Natives."[205] The adventures of the crew of the "Breskens," the immediate occasion for the official embassy, are recounted in the second part of Montanus' book.

The "Breskens" was one of the two ships under Vries' command sent to explore the coast of Hokkaido in 1643. It was separated from Vries' ship, the "Castricum," during a severe storm off the coast of Kyushu. Continuing northward after the storm, it anchored in the "Bay of Namboe" (coast of the Nambu domain) on the northeast coast of Honshu hoping to obtain provisions. The captain of the "Breskens," Henry Corneliszoon Schaep,

---

times, was completely destroyed by fire in 1863. See our pls. 400, 402, 403, 404, 406, and 407.
    [200] Montanus, *op. cit.* (n. 189), pp. 118–19. On the *yamabushi* of Mount Fuji see Japan Times, *op. cit.* (n. 26), p. 100.
    [201] Montanus, *op. cit.* (n. 189), p. 161. He is obviously refering to *Nō* or *Kabuki* drama. For a view of the imperial palace see our pl. 395.
    [202] Montanus, *op. cit.* (n. 189), pp. 169–70.
    [203] *Ibid.,* p. 295.
    [204] *Ibid.,* pp. 302–3. Probably the Nicheren temple called Myōko-kugi.
    [205] *Ibid.,* p. 60. On the preparations and instructions for the mission see *ibid.,* pp. 394–98. On the mission see Murdoch and Yamagata, *op. cit.* (n. 15), III, 270–72.

and nine of his crewmen were invited ashore by local officials, where they were taken prisoner and conveyed to Edo for interrogation. The Japanese were apparently convinced that Schaep and his crew were not Dutchmen and feared that they may have been trying to smuggle priests into the country. Shortly before the "Breskens" arrived, five Jesuits from Manila had been arrested in Chikuzen. Schaep and his comrades were held for five months and released only after Jan van Elserack, the VOC director at Deshima, came to Edo to plead their cause.[206]

Montanus' relation of the experiences of the "Breskens" crew vividly illustrates the paranoia of Japanese officials regarding Christianity during the early closed-country period. From the first day after their arrest until their release the Japanese try to trick them into admitting that they are Catholic Christians. They are repeatedly shown crosses and pictures of the Virgin at unexpected times to test their reactions to them. Other Japanese, when alone with the Dutchmen, cross themselves or make crosses with their fingers. When the Dutch seem to abhor rather than worship these "papist" icons, the Japanese gleefully cry "Hollande, Hollande."[207] In Edo, Schaep and his colleagues are repeatedly interrogated by "Sicungodonne" (Inouye Chikugo no Kami Masashige, 1585–1661), the head of the commission for the suppression of Christianity in Japan and by an apostate Portuguese priest who seems to befriend them. On two occasions they witness the interrogation under torture of four Jesuits as they are being led to their own interrogation.[208] They are later told that all four apostatized because they could not endure the torture.[209] They are questioned in the rooms used to torture the priests, and on still another occasion they are present while the shogun and his council question the priests, who show signs of having been tortured.[210] The questions are repeated again and again to Schaep and his men, individually and collectively: where do you come from? where was your ship going? why did you fire guns in the Bay of Nambu? are you Christians? were you trying to put priests ashore there? is there a chaplain aboard your ship? who is governor-general in Batavia? who is the captain of the "Castricum"? do you know Elserack? will Caron return to Japan? and many more. After an interrogation before the shogun's council, they are given sake and asked to perform in ways that became part of the ritual of VOC embassies: the Dutch are asked to "shew them some antick Postures, to make wry Faces, and look asquint, to go splay-footed, and

---

[206] Murdoch and Yamagata, *op. cit.* (n. 15), III, 269–70.

[207] For example see Montanus, *op. cit.* (n. 189), p. 322.

[208] *Ibid.*, pp. 330–33. The Portuguese priest was Christovão Ferreira (1580–1652), who had apostatized under torture in 1633. See Ito, *loc. cit.* (n. 117), pp. 6–7.

[209] Montanus, *op. cit.* (n. 189), p. 334.

[210] *Ibid.*, pp. 351–54, 356. The four Jesuit priests—Pedro Marquez, Giuseppe Chiara, Francisco Cassola, and Alonzo de Arroya—were the second such group dispatched from Manila by Antonio Rubino. They had secretly landed in northern Kyushu with the intent of reconverting Christovão Ferreira. The shogun, Iemitsu, was present at some of the interrogations, and the priests apparently apostatized. See Itō, *loc. cit.* (n. 117), pp. 4–5.

swing their Arms to and again, which the Japan Lords took great delight to see."²¹¹ When Elserack finally arrives, he is questioned separately before being allowed to meet Schaep and the others. When they are at last released into Elserack's custody they must sign a promise never to land Catholic priests in Japan. They receive an audience with Shogun Iemitsu before leaving Edo.²¹²

Frightened as they were, Schaep or whoever actually wrote the account also included some rather good descriptive passages in his story. On the road to Edo, for example, they travel "through pleasant Valleys, by murmuring Streams, Rice-fields, and several Hamlets."²¹³ There are colorful descriptions of samurai dress: richly embroidered upper coats, underneath which hang others which display "their arms curiously wrought." Their long breeches drag the floor, swords hang at their sides, and their heads are shaven except for the nape of the neck and the topknot.²¹⁴ Later the author describes samurai armor.²¹⁵ On the road they meet and describe musicians who travel about to entertain at feasts and weddings, "being all Whores and Vagagonds."²¹⁶ Curious crowds gather to look at the Dutchmen wherever they go; they always ask the Dutchmen to sign their names on pieces of paper.²¹⁷ They experience an earthquake, which some of the Japanese explain results from the sea monster striking its tail against the shore, which elicits from Montanus a long digression about classical beliefs regarding earthquakes.²¹⁸ The Dutchmen marvel at Edo's costly palaces. The author describes an Edo prostitute sitting under the eave of her house with food and drink ready for clients. Her kimono is tied so loosely that her nipples show, she wears flowers in her elaborate "girdle" (obi), and her hair hangs loose except for one lock in the back which is tied with ribbons.²¹⁹ He also describes Japanese writing brushes, inkstones, and ink. The solid cakes of ink, red or black, all bear the shogun's seal. Brushes are held with the whole hand rather than with just three fingers.²²⁰ The author includes a list of Japa-

---

²¹¹Montanus, *op. cit.* (n. 189), p. 337.

²¹²The story of the "Breskens" crew in Japan is found in *ibid.*, pp. 319–94. *Cf.* Elison, *op. cit.* (n. 117), pp. 200–202. Montanus' account of the "Breskens" affair seems to differ appreciably from Schaep's manuscript journal. See article by Renier H. Hesselink in Arisaka Takamichi (ed.), *Nihon Yogakushi no kenkyu* (Studies in Japanese-Western Learning) (Osaka, 1991), X, 1–23.

²¹³Montanus, *op. cit.* (n. 189), p. 323.

²¹⁴*Ibid.*, pp. 325–26. See our pl. 423.

²¹⁵Montanus, *op. cit.* (n. 189), p. 332.

²¹⁶*Ibid.*, p. 329. See our pl. 430.

²¹⁷For example, see Montanus, *op. cit.* (n. 189), p. 328. For other people they may have met on the roads see our pls. 411, 431, and 433.

²¹⁸Montanus, *op. cit.* (n. 189), pp. 334–37.

²¹⁹*Ibid.*, pp. 350–51. On prostitution in Edo see Chamberlain, *op. cit.* (n. 22), pp. 524–26. Also *cf.* our pl. 429.

²²⁰Montanus, *op. cit.* (n. 189), pp. 363–66. *Cf.* Dunn, *op. cit.* (n. 13), pp. 94–95. See our pl. 427.

nese words and phrases, some of which are easily recognizable in spite of his archaic romanizations. Each city, he reports, has its distinctive seal and coat of arms; he describes several of them.[221] The people of "Tonsa" (Tosa?) dress differently from other Japanese. They wear long caps, the tops of which hang over their faces, "loose furr'd cotton coats about their shoulders," silk under-kimonos, and a broad embroidered "girdle" (obi), one end of which hangs almost to the ground. "Tonsa" women carry fans and wear over their shoulders a thin folded cotton cloth, fastened at the breasts, which hangs halfway down their kimonos.[222] Finally there is the audience with the shogun, surrounded by his councillors and guards, sitting under a golden canopy in which are carved heavenly bodies, beasts, fishes, dragons, and serpents. All are in terror of his power. Even daimyos bow with their faces to the floor in his presence, and none may have more than three servants with him in the shogun's palace.[223]

The remainder of Montanus' book contains the accounts of three annual VOC embassies to the shogun's court in Edo: those of Zacharias Wagenaer in 1657 and Henry Indyk in 1661, and a later one headed by a man named Zeldron. Each of these contains substantial description, much of it repetitious of earlier parts of the volume. Still, some interesting new material appears along with the familiar descriptions. Wagenaer's account contains a particularly vivid description of the gifts which must be carefully prepared for the shogun and for a host of arrogant officials. He is pleased to learn that the Dutch seeds sent to Inouye Chikugo are doing well in his Edo garden.[224] Alas, most of Wagenaer's carefully chosen gifts are burned in the great Edo fire of March 2, 1657. The Dutch house burns and even the valuables stored in the stone go-down are burned or melted. Over one hundred thousand houses, including the shogun's palace, are destroyed. The city is in chaos, many die in the fire, many more starve in the days after the fire. Everyone seems to flee the city, including several great nobles indebted to Wagenaer, who leave without paying him. Wagenaer also leaves.[225] In spite of the disaster, Wagenaer describes several cities which he visits enroute, a Japanese wedding, and the temple on an island near Sakai where many people offer themselves to Kannon by drowning themselves.[226] When he returns to Edo in April he has trouble finding a place to stay and to keep his presents. He is received by the shogun in a small palace west of the burned-out main palace. Despite its great cost, the embassy does not seem very successful. Some of

---

[221] Montanus, op. cit. (n. 189), pp. 374–75. See our pl. 426.

[222] Montanus, op. cit. (n. 189), p. 393. Tosa in southern Shikoku enjoys an exceptionally mild climate for Japan. Perhaps climate in this case accounts for costume differences.

[223] Ibid., pp. 384–86. See our pl. 404.

[224] Montanus, op. cit. (n. 189), pp. 400–401.

[225] Ibid., pp. 409–12. On the Meireki fire in Edo (March, 1657) and its consequences see Magi, op. cit. (n. 43), pp. 67–70.

[226] Montanus, op. cit. (n. 189), pp. 419–20. See n. 26, above, concerning Kannon.

Wagenaer's gifts to officials are returned and none of his noble debtors pay up.[227]

Wagenaer's account also contains many details about Dutch trade and about life on Deshima. When Dutch goods are ready for sale, Japanese merchants come to view the merchandise in the great gallery of the VOC storehouse. They do this on a Monday. On Tuesday they negotiate prices, and on Wednesday they deliver the money. After that the water gate is opened and the purchased goods are loaded into Japanese boats. Wagenaer also includes a brief description of the Nagasaki fair held each November. Japanese merchants set up booths, then drink sake and make merry while they sell their goods.[228]

Several stories illustrate the oppressive supervision and fear under which the Dutch on Deshima live. A Dutch employee pining for a Japanese prostitute leaves a suicide note and disappears. The Japanese immediately suspect that he is a Portuguese priest. Wagenaer has everyone on Deshima searching for the missing lover and is much relieved when he is found. Wagenaer explains that it would go hard indeed for both ship and crew if all those who arrive on a ship are not accounted for when it leaves. Another crisis arises when a drunken sailor on one of the Dutch ships removes the shogun's straw seal from one of the hatches. (All the hatches are sealed when the ships are in port.) An interpreter—most of them appear to be spies—informs the officials in Nagasaki. Twenty-one soldiers rush to the ship, search it, arrest the sailor, and take him ashore, where he is executed.[229] When a ship is ready for departure, its crew mustered, ammunition aboard, and its rudder hung in place, it must leave immediately regardless of the time of day or the weather.[230]

Wagenaer reports in 1659 that the Japanese have been making larger quantities of porcelain during recent years. The quality of the Japanese pieces improves each year. The best comes from "Fizen" (Hizen); it is finer and whiter than that made elsewhere because of the clay found there. Wagenaer buys 21,760 pieces, and observes that the Chinese are buying it as well.[231]

Of events in Nagasaki during 1659, Wagenaer reports the arguments with Japanese officials over the VOC seizure of Formosan Chinese junks, the arrival of a new governor and the attendant presents and receptions, the suicide of a young woman who was seduced by a Chinese ship captain, a great

[227] Montanus, *op. cit.* (n. 189), pp. 426–29.

[228] *Ibid.*, p. 432.

[229] *Ibid.*, pp. 432–33.

[230] *Ibid.*, p. 435.

[231] *Ibid.*, pp. 434–35. The Japanese porcelain (*jiki*) industry was founded by Korean potters in the late sixteenth century. They found kaolin in northwestern Kyushu, and concentrated their efforts in Hizen at Arita. Because they were sold at Imari, these porcelains became known as Imari ware. See Tsuda, *op. cit.* (n. 26), p. 250. In 1662 a bazaar was opened at Deshima for the sale of Imari porcelain. See Wooley, *loc. cit.* (n. 38), p. 138.

noble who cut down two young servants for a minor offense, a fire which burned one hundred houses in Nagasaki, a fire in Kyoto which burned even the emperor's palace, the torture of twenty-five Christians by hanging in the pit, and the decapitation of twenty-five others.[232]

The description of Henry Indyk's embassy to Edo in March, 1661, is unusually rich in details about the exchange of gifts, negotiations with officials, receptions, the formal audience with the shogun, the shogun's return gifts—"thirty imperial coats"—his instructions and admonitions to the Dutch, paying the landlord, and so forth. On his arrival in Edo, Indyk finds many empty streets despite the feverish rebuilding taking place all over the city. Many of the bridges are not yet repaired. He learns that Inouye Chikugo died only two days before his arrival. Inouye's secretary wants the gifts designated for Inouye to be delivered anyway. He tells Indyk that the shogun has been asking about the Dutch, which Indyk judges to be a good sign. A few days later, however, Indyk learns that the shogun is angry because the Dutch gifts are less valuable than in previous years. Indyk doesn't think they are. His official contacts are mostly with an interpreter named "Jossiesamma" (Yokoyama Yozaemon), who seems primarily concerned about his own presents. Nevertheless he invites Indyk to his home, makes a fuss over Indyk's six-and-one-half-year-old son, and even invites his wife to come out to see the Dutchmen.[233]

Indyk is enthralled with Japanese women, whom he judges to "exceed all other Females that are known in the World." They have broad faces and large heads. They wash their hair in egg whites each day to make it shine jet black. Single women wear a "coyfe" on their foreheads; married women a loose lock in front and in back. They usually go bareheaded, although some wear an embroidered cap. His description of the kimono is clearer than most: a large gown with silk images on it, folded over the breasts, the edges embroidered with gold. It hangs loose around the arms and upper body but is gathered around the waist under a "broad Tabby-Girdle on which they bestow great Charges" (the obi). Under the outer kimono are from eight to twelve more, all "party coloured" and embroidered with flowers. On their feet they sometimes wear "clogs" (geta), sometimes white "buskins" called "taepis" (*tabi*). Married women never go out except in sedan chairs or covered boats or for a walk in the evening with their husbands.[234]

During his formal audience with the shogun, Indyk is rapped on the back of the head by Yokoyama for raising his head too quickly. Nevertheless he thinks he is well received. Members of the shogun's council give Indyk's son a tour of the shogun's chambers. The shogun asks the Dutch to report any

[232] Montanus, *op. cit.* (n. 189), pp. 434, 438–440.

[233] *Ibid.*, p. 441.

[234] *Ibid.*, pp. 442–43. For examples of Japanese noblewomen's costumes see our pls. 399, 418, 420, and 422.

Portuguese plans to invade Japan and warns them not to molest Chinese junks. Indyk makes humble promises, and the audience is over.[235] On his return to Nagasaki, Indyk learns about the loss of Formosa to Cheng Ch'eng-kung (Koxinga). The Dutch have retaliated by seizing some of Cheng's trading junks. Japanese officials refuse to condone this seizure and there are difficult negotiations with them about it.[236] The account of Zeldron's embassy contains very little new description.

After the publication of Montanus' account in 1669, new information about Japan was almost entirely limited to brief reports in the published journals of people who sailed to Nagasaki on VOC ships. The German surgeon, Johann Jacob Merklein, for example, visited Nagasaki in 1651.[237] He is amazed at the mistrust of the Japanese for the Dutch, and describes the security precautions taken when a VOC ship enters the harbor: all money, small arms, books, images, and the like are confiscated, locked in chests, and carried ashore until the ship is ready to leave; the crew is mustered and the name and age of each person recorded; weapons, ammunition, sails, and rudder are removed; no chaplains or pastors may be aboard nor may worship services be held; and the Japanese keep constant watch from boats tied to the bow and stern of the ship. While Merklein's ship was in Nagasaki a sailor on a nearby ship fell overboard and drowned after drinking sake late one night. No one, not even the Japanese watch, realized it until he was missed in the morning. The Japanese immediately stopped all trade, doubled the guard, and permitted no one to go ashore or to travel from ship to ship. Three days later, when the poor sailor's body floated to the surface, trade was resumed and normal conditions restored. Merklein wonders what would have happened if the body had not been found.

Nothing is entirely bad. Because of Japanese suspicions and distrust, Dutch sailors have nothing to do in Nagasaki. Japanese workers, paid by the VOC, handle all the cargo, and the European crewmen while away the time with eating and drinking. Merklein describes two houses on Deshima maintained to entertain the sailors: one for their "pleasure [*lust*], conversation, and pastimes," the other for eating and drinking. Here a Japanese innkeeper sets out small pieces of cold meat (*sashimi*), which the Dutch rarely eat, and sweetmeats, which they like better.

Merklein describes the sale of VOC goods much as Wagenaer had described it, but he reports that when the Japanese merchants come to view the merchandise, the Dutch must keep a sharp watch to prevent theft. All the officers and men who can be spared from their ships are impressed into service. Still it is difficult to detect the thieves, Merklein wryly observes, because they dress exactly like the merchants. He wonders why there is so

[235] Montanus, *op. cit.* (n. 189), p. 444.
[236] *Ibid.*, pp. 451–52, 454–59.
[237] His *Journal* was published in 1663 and 1672. For details see above, pp. 530–31.

much theft at the sales if, as Caron reported, the Japanese are so honest and punish theft so severely.[238]

Merklein's amusing account of the Blokovius embassy probably reflects the attitude of those who organized it and the rather dark entertainment other VOC employees derived from it. As Merklein tells it, Inouye Chikugo had advised sending a noble ambassador because the Japanese had little regard for merchants, however rich. The VOC directors in Amsterdam tried to find one, but as Merklein observes, there were few nobles in VOC service and fewer still who could be induced to make so long and dangerous a journey. The directors therefore settled on the learned Blokovius. When Blokovius arrived in Batavia his health was so poor few thought he would survive the trip to Japan. The governor-general and his councillors, however, one of whom was Caron, were undeterred. Not only did they provide the Latin teacher with splendid gifts, costly clothing, servants, and attendants, but they took the precaution of sending an elegant coffin, black silk drapery, mourning clothes, and a tailor along with him when he sailed, all without poor Blokovius' knowledge. Blokovius, of course, died enroute. The funeral was magnificent, befitting a great noble. As Merklein reports, everyone thought Blokovius was more useful to the VOC in his coffin than when he had been alive.[239]

Although neither actually visited Japan, both Frederick Bolling (1678) and Johann Sigmund Wurffbain (1686) included brief descriptions of Japan in their published travel accounts.[240] Bolling's is actually only a list of VOC imports and exports to and from Japan and contains no actual description of Japan. Bolling regards the Japan trade as the VOC's most profitable, but he also notes that one of eight Japan-bound ships each year is lost to typhoons. For more information about Japan he refers his readers to Montanus.[241] The description of Japan in Wurffbain's account appears to have been inserted by the editor, but is not a standard description of the land and people. It describes the origin of the Japanese people, sketches the history of Portuguese trade and Jesuit missions, the persecutions and expulsion of the Iberians, and the conditions under which the Dutch trade in Nagasaki.[242]

A major description of Japan is included in Jean Crasset's two-volume *Histoire de l'eglise du Japon* first published in 1689.[243] Modeled on Solier's *Histoire ecclésiastique* (1627), it is essentially a history of the Jesuit mission in Japan. Solier had brought the story down to 1624; Crasset begins again with

---

[238] Merklein, *Reise nach Java, Vorder- und Hinter-Indien, China und Japan, 1644–1653* . . . , NR, III, 85–90.

[239] *Ibid.*, pp. 59–61.

[240] On Bolling see above, pp. 535–36; on Wurffbain see above, pp. 523–24.

[241] Bolling, *Oost-Indische resiboek* . . . , trans. J. Visscher, *BTLV*, LXVIII (1913), 350–51.

[242] Wurffbain, *Reise nach den Molukken und Vorder-Indien, 1632–1646*, NR, IX, 84–90.

[243] For bibliography see above, p. 427. For examples of the engravings in Crasset's book see our pls. 403, 415, 416, 418, and 421.

Xavier and continues the story to 1658. Crasset's account is much more readable than Solier's, which Crasset notes "is written in a somewhat old-fashioned style." [244] His history of the mission and of the persecutions is just as detailed as Solier's and, like it, contains considerable information about Japanese politics and the events of the *Sengoku* and early Tokugawa eras. For this information he depends heavily on Solier and on earlier Jesuit letter-books and histories. For the latter parts of the story he depends on the martyrologies and on the Dutch and English reports, especially on Caron and Montanus. These same sources enable him to update the general description of Japan found in the first fifty-four pages of volume one. While it closely parallels Solier's description in both organization and content, it also includes changes peculiar to the Tokugawa era gleaned from the more recent publications. In short, there was nothing new in Crasset's history for the European reader, although it provides a well-written compendium of European information about Japan with considerably more and better details about Japanese religion than could be found in Caron or Montanus.

During the last decade of the century a few brief notices about Japan appeared, usually in the published journals of those who sailed to Nagasaki in VOC ships. Christoph Frick, for example, visited Nagasaki in the 1680's; his travels were published in 1692. [245] While there is little description in his account, he reports three or four English ships anchored in Nagasaki harbor, which seems quite unlikely. He claims that the Japanese offered them women during their stay but that only the master and the bookkeeper accepted. [246]

Also published in 1692 was George Meister's *Der orientalish-indianische Kunst- und Lust-Gärtner,* the product of a "ten-year" experience (1677–88) in the East. [247] In Batavia the gardener Meister worked with Andreas Cleyer, the botanist. Meister superintended the fifty slaves who worked in Cleyer's garden and carried out experiments with trees and plants. He accompanied Cleyer on his two embassies to Japan undertaken from 1682 to 1684 and again in 1685 to 1687. Although Meister was confined to Deshima and Nagasaki, he learned and experienced as much as possible about Japan's language, products, customs, and flora. As a professional gardener, he was amazed by the variety of Japan's flora and by how different it was from that of Indonesia and Europe. He describes the characteristics of many Japanese trees and plants and gives their names in transliterated Japanese. [248]

[244] Crasset, *Historie de l'eglise du Japon* (Paris, 1689), I, i.

[245] For bibliography see above, pp. 541–42.

[246] Christoph Frick and Christoph Schweitzer, *Voyages to the East Indies,* C. Ernest Fayle (ed.) (London, 1929), pp. 98–100. The English attempted to reopen trade with Japan in 1673 but their request was refused because of Charles II's Portuguese marriage. See *ibid.,* pp. xxx–xxxi. For an evaluation of the 1673 mission see Massarella, *op. cit.* (n. 50), pp. 351–63.

[247] In what follows we refer to the second edition of 1710. For bibliographical data see above, pp. 542–43.

[248] Meister, *op. cit.* (n. 247), pp. 144–80. *Cf.* our pl. 428.

He is particularly enthralled by Japanese gardens and how their creators seek by art to imitate nature. The Japanese remove rocks and stones from the countryside, around which they build landscape gardens. They erect a hill of stone in the middle of the garden, around which they place smaller rocks. Over these artistically placed stones they grow moss to make it all look natural. Other rocks are formed into cliffs and sluices, from which water flows into round, oval, and square basins or ponds filled with gold-fish: if water is not available naturally, they pipe it into the garden and lead it over and through the stones. On the banks of the basins they plant grass which seems to grow there on its own. In the biggest stones they cut deep round or oblong holes which they fill with dirt, into which they set flower-ing and fruit trees as well as bulbous plants; when one stops blooming the other begins! Rocks are also hollowed out to be receptacles for figures out of whose heads grow shrubs and plants. In the round holes made in other rocks they place birds' nests poached from the forests into which sometimes are put genuine or porcelain birds' eggs. The borders of their gardens are decorated with stone chips as well as plants and trees whose foliage they trim so elegantly that no European can ever again assume conceitedly that we alone are clever.[249]

The Japanese, a thousand-year-old nation of adept people, cannot be taught anything by Europeans about the arts, sciences, or nature, accord-ing to Meister. In contrast to the Hottentots of southern Africa, they are as clever as any in government and business, as courageous in war, and as cultivated in the arts, as is illustrated by their incomparable shields and lacquer- and goldworks as well as by their admirable swords and beautiful porcelains. They comprise a proud and earnest nation who assume that they are wiser and richer than all others, so they trust no one else. Human life has little value for them, as can be seen from their ritual suicides and from the barbaric murders and systematic executions of innocent Christians. The Japanese divide the year into thirteen months each twenty-six days long.[250] The New Year in mid-February heralds the coming of spring and the re-quirement to pay all debts. To meet their obligations the Japanese will sell their homes and family members. Young girls are sometimes sold to be prostitutes. In Nagasaki there is a walled district called "Mariamma" (Maru-yama) of three hundred houses in which serve at least one hundred prosti-tutes.[251] Ordinarily, however, children are treated gently both at home and in school. To help Europeans understand Japanese customs and the pecu-liarities of the language, Meister provides a small German-Japanese vocabu-

[249] Meister, *op. cit.* (n. 247), pp. 181–84. On the Japanese art of gardening see Tsuda, *op. cit.* (n. 26), pp. 181–89.

[250] This refers to the lunar calendar. See Dunn, *op. cit.* (n. 13), p. 146.

[251] Meister, *op. cit.* (n. 247), pp. 138–39. Legal brothels were concentrated in most major cities in designated areas. See Dunn, *op. cit.* (n. 13), pp. 182–83. Meister gives the prices and conditions of a visit.

lary in Latin letters, a conversation between two Japanese men in German and romanized Japanese, and the characters for the Japanese alphabet (kana), numbers, and a few common words.[252]

Nikolaas de Graaf's *Reisen* was published in 1701 and contains a very brief notice of his 1640's visit to Nagasaki. Nothing in it would have seemed new to his readers.[253] In 1698 José Sicardo published still another history of the Christian mission and the persecutions. Its first five pages are a brief general description of Japan drawn from by then familiar sources.[254]

Finally, in 1701, the first published edition of Francesco Carletti's century-old *Ragionamenti* appeared.[255] Carletti (*ca.* 1573–1636), a Florentine merchant, visited Japan during 1597–98 as part of his voyage around the world between 1594 and 1606. His is one of the very few non-clerical descriptions of Japan during those crucial years. He witnessed the Nagasaki crucifixions of 1597 and he describes with detachment the arrival of the Manila Franciscans, the San Felipe affair, and the quarrels between the Jesuits and the other orders which led up to the crucifixions. For the most part, Carletti's description of Japan and its people corroborates that of the missionaries, although he pays more attention to trade, says almost nothing about religion, and writes more thorough descriptions of things like food, the way Japanese row boats without taking the oar out of the water, house construction, folding screens, tatami, geta, *tabi,* prostitution, and the temporary sale of daughters by poor families in order to raise money for their dowries. He includes a sizable discussion of the language, reproducing the kana and numbers in romanization.[256] Many of Carletti's descriptions are exceedingly clear and perceptive, frequently better than those written by most other seventeenth-century writers. Nevertheless his account must have seemed somewhat archaic to those who had already read the accounts of Japan produced during the second half of the century.

To European readers at the beginning of the seventeenth century, Japan was perhaps the most familiar place in Asia. Scores of Jesuit letterbooks and histories had described it repetitiously for them during the late sixteenth century, and this torrent of information continued during the first decades of the seventeenth century. Center stage in the missionaries' accounts was occupied by the exciting story of the Christian mission in Japan. Readers of the story, however, would have learned a great deal about the seemingly

---

[252] Meister, *op. cit.* (n. 247), pp. 136, 185–92, 193–95, and facing p. 310.

[253] J. C. M. Warnsink (ed.), *Reisen van Nicolaus de Graaf gedaan naer alle gewesten des werelds beginnende 1639 to 1687 inclus.* ("WLV," XXXIII; The Hague, 1930), p. 27. For bibliography see above, pp. 505–6.

[254] *Cristiandad del Japón, y dilatada persecución que padeció* . . . (Madrid, 1698). See above, p. 364.

[255] See above, p. 388, for details regarding its publication.

[256] Carletti, *My Voyage around the World,* trans. Herbert Weinstock (New York, 1964), pp. 99–135.

chaotic politics of the *sengoku* period and about Japan and its people. Such readers could have traced year by year the consolidation of Tokugawa power, the establishment of peace, the quarrels between the Jesuits and other missionaries, and the increasing hostility of the new government towards the Christian mission. As the persecutions increased, the missionaries' reports concentrated more exclusively on the tribulations of the Japanese church and on the martyrs. Amati's (1615) account of Date Masamune's embassy to Mexico and Europe and his description of Oshu was perhaps the last missionary publication to provide new information about Japan other than reports of persecutions and martyrdoms. By mid-century no more firsthand missionary reports from Japan were being published.

Fresh descriptions of Japan and news about Japanese politics continued to appear in Europe as the missionaries retreated; the new reports were written by the Dutch and the English who arrived in Japan soon after the turn of the century. The first of these were English, published in the Purchas collection, 1625; by mid-century Dutch accounts predominated. That of François Caron in 1646 was the most perceptive and the most popular. Although the new literature written by Protestant northern Europeans reported persecutions and martyrdoms and occasionally sketched the history of the Christian mission in Japan, its focus was on trade and politics and its tone was markedly secular. Even Japanese religion was treated more briefly and less perceptively than in the missionaries' accounts. And while the Protestant writers often sketched the history of the *sengoku* period and the founding of the Tokugawa *bakufu,* the politics they experienced and described were that of the established Tokugawa system.

During the latter half of the seventeenth century when Japan was closed to all Europeans except the Dutch, and the Dutch were virtually imprisoned on the minuscule island of Deshima in Nagasaki harbor, European notices of Japan became fewer and shorter. For example, none appears to have been published between 1650 and 1660 and only about a half-dozen firsthand reports, most of them brief, between 1660 and the end of the century, compared with about twenty firsthand missionary accounts during the first decade alone. One of these later reports, however, Arnoldus Montanus' huge *Gedenkwaerdige gesantschappen* (1669), is a major compilation of information about Japan drawn both from previously published accounts and from the eyewitness reports of several recent Dutch embassies to the shogun's court at Edo. Although overlong, repetitious, and clumsily organized, Montanus' work was translated into German, English, and French and was widely distributed. No better information about Japan became available in Europe until Engelbert Kaempfer's *History of Japan* (1727), and Kaempfer, himself an astute observer, also uses Caron and Montanus.

Reasonably diligent readers of the seventeenth-century European accounts of Japan could have become surprisingly knowledgeable about the island empire. Perhaps almost as much could be said for patient readers of

Montanus alone. They would have read accurate, perceptive descriptions of Japanese society, customs, dress, eating habits, language, aesthetic sensitivities, religions, and character. Although the problem of whether or not northern Japan was joined to the mainland was left unresolved, European readers could have learned a great deal about Japan's geography and climate. They would have encountered the names of hundreds of towns, mountains, islands, and rivers, and read descriptions of many of them. Some cities, like Nagasaki, Kyoto, Osaka, Sakai, Edo, Hirado, and Shizuoka, were described so frequently and in such detail that readers must have become familiar with them. Our readers would have known what Japanese houses and gardens looked like, would have read colorful descriptions of the Tōkaidō, Mount Fuji, numerous other mountains, and lakes. They would have vicariously sat in peaceful temple gardens, observed Buddhist meditations and worship services, and watched both religious and secular processions. Through Vries' account they would have met the hairy Ainu and seen their land and homes.

Our seventeenth-century readers would probably astonish us by their familiarity with the events and politics of the *sengoku* and the early Tokugawa. They would have read remarkably detailed accounts of the intrigues, battles, alliances, and accomplishments of Nobunaga, Hideyoshi, Hideyori and his mother, Ieyasu, Ishida, Date, Hidetada, and Iemitsu. They would have read fairly intimate character sketches of all these important people and of scores of other daimyos, samurai retainers, and Tokugawa councillors and commissioners. Perhaps more impressive still, they could have developed a sure grasp of the working of Japanese feudalism and the changes in it affected by the Tokugawa. They would surely have been aware of the changes; the Japan described by Caron and Montanus was very different from that of Guzman and Ribadeneira. Reading Crasset or Carletti at the end of the century would have sharpened the contrast. Although pre-Kamakura-era Japanese history was not as clearly presented to our European readers, they would have known something about it, would have read fuzzy accounts of the establishment of the Kamakura *bakufu* by Yoritomo in 1185, and would have read much clearer descriptions of the vestiges of imperial government in Kyoto. They would have been able, in short, to see the new Tokugawa regime in historical context. Even today it would be unwise for students of sixteenth- and seventeenth-century Japan to ignore these seventeenth-century European sources.

CHAPTER XXIV

Epilogue: A Composite Picture

The advance of the Europeans in the East during the seventeenth century was neither steady nor uninterrupted, although both traders and missionaries penetrated more deeply than previously into Asia's great states and insular reaches.[1] Intrepid individuals or small groups of Europeans reconnoitered the frontiers of northern India as well as the regions north and west of China; in the process they "discovered" Ladakh, Baltistan, Tibet, Mongolia, Manchuria, Korea, and eastern Siberia. From their coastal footholds in continental Southeast Asia they advanced inland into Arakan, northern Siam, Cambodia, and Laos. In the insular regions they surveyed from their ships or from land bases many archipelagoes and hundreds of islands that were previously known only by report or not at all: especially the Maldives, Laccadives, Nicobars, Bali, and Formosa. They crossed the frontiers of Insulindia to Australia, New Zealand, New Guinea, the Papuas, Marianas, and other islands of the south Pacific. On the larger islands, as on the continent, they explored many of the interiors, particularly on Sumatra, Java, Celebes, Borneo, Mindanao, Luzon, and Honshu. Within the known archipelagoes they also visited and reported on dozens of the smaller islands. Through their explorations of Asia's fringes and interiors they broadened the European definition of Asia and gave names to many places that previously had not appeared in European reports or on maps.

While extending their range of activities in Asia, the seventeenth-century Europeans also began to revise the earlier assessments of its great states. The

[1] Most of this generalized description was published in D. F. Lach and E. J. Van Kley, "Asia in the Eyes of Europe: The Seventeenth Century," *The Seventeenth Century* (Durham), Vol. V, No. 1 (Spring, 1990), pp. 93–109. © 1990 by The University of Chicago. All rights reserved.

sixteenth-century Europeans had considered Japan and China to be the great hopes of the future. The closure of Japan to the missionaries and to all European traders except the Dutch after 1640 forced reestimates of what might be expected from that quarter. The civil wars in China during the change from the Ming to the Ch'ing dynasty produced disturbances and uncertainties which were hardly to be expected from an empire which had been billed as a "model state." While the Dutch enjoyed a brief period of success in Formosa, they were ejected in the course of China's civil wars, and eventually the Ch'ing annexed the island. Over the course of the century the Europeans suffered their most severe setbacks in East Asia.

Not only did seventeenth-century Europeans discover more of Asia and become more knowledgeable about Asian societies than had their predecessors, but they also published much more information about Asia, which was more widely diffused and more profoundly affected European thought and culture than ever before. Hundreds of books about Asia, written by missionaries, merchants, sea-captains, physicians, sailors, soldiers, and independent travelers, appeared during the century. There were at least twenty-five major descriptions of South Asia alone, another fifteen devoted to mainland Southeast Asia, about twenty to the archipelagoes, and sixty or more to East Asia. Alongside these major independent contributions stood hundreds of Jesuit letterbooks, derivative accounts, travel accounts with brief descriptions of many Asian places, pamphlets, newssheets, and the like. The books were published in all European languages, frequently reprinted and translated, collected into the several large compilations of travel literature published during the century, and regularly pilfered by later writers or publishers.[2] Those who produced the literature sailed back to Europe with cargoes of Asian products which frequently included Asian books, clothing, dishes, plants, works of art or craftsmanship, and sometimes even Asian people. In short, the image of Asia sketched in these pages was channeled to Europe in a huge corpus of publications which was widely distributed in all European lands and languages. Few literate Europeans could have been completely untouched by it, and it would be surprising indeed if its effects could not be seen in contemporary European literature, art, learning, and culture.

India, always a source of puzzlement to European observers, appeared in the seventeenth century to possess in the Mughul Empire a more stable state than had earlier been appreciated. Most of the changes in the relations of the Europeans with India were brought about by the conflicts among the Europeans themselves over the control of coastal places. The rise of Sivaji and the downfall of Golconda and Bijapur, though serious disruptions in themselves, did not permanently threaten the European activities in India. Trade continued with but few interruptions as the markets of Europe gradually became overstocked with Indian textiles. In Ceylon, the source of

[2] For a more detailed summary of the publications see above, pp. 589–97.

cinnamon, trade continued despite domestic and foreign-inspired disturbances. The states around the Bay of Bengal—Coromandel, Arakan, and
Siam—often suffered from internal strife but nonetheless continued to function effectively enough to prevent commercial interruptions. When the
French sought to subordinate Siam, they were promptly ejected. In Insulindia the Dutch enjoyed relative peace and quiet despite the occasional forays
of Mataram against their positions in Java, and Makassar's persistent de-
fiance of their spice monopoly. Before the end of the century, Mataram,
Bantam, Makassar, and Acheh were all conquered by the VOC. In Vietnam, where war was almost constant between Tongking and Cochin-China,
the European traders and missionaries faced an uncertain future. The Spanish meanwhile consolidated their hold on the Philippines and the Marianas,
as they sought to maintain their shaky dominance in the Pacific. By century's end it appeared that future European empire-building would be centered in India, continental Southeast Asia, and Insulindia, rather than in
China and Japan.

From the Maldives in the west to the Marianas in the east, the European
traders and missionaries depended mainly on sea travel, although some
emissaries and missionaries followed overland routes in Asia to avoid the
dangers of ocean voyaging. Ships carried persons and goods on the round-
trip between Europe and Asia, as well as from place to place in the East.
Regular maritime travel stimulated the Europeans to learn more about the
monsoons, tides and currents, watering places, and meteorological phenomena of the East. Their armed vessels patrolled strategic waterways, such
as the Strait of Malacca, convoyed trading fleets, collected tolls, blockaded
ports, and chased down pirates. Unattached Europeans and able natives
where hired or impressed in areas where trained seamen and common soldiers and sailors were in short supply. The European navies mainly fought
one another, although over the century they were challenged by Malabar
Muslim fleets, by the Japanese, by Koxinga's Chinese ships, and, off west
India, by the naval forces of the Mughuls and Sivaji. However much the
Europeans professed to admire Asian ships and boats, the seas of Asia remained in the control of the servants of the great European chartered Companies. The French in their eagerness to break into the trade even sent royal
war armadas in the 1680's directly from Europe to the Bay of Bengal.

Although these French actions failed, the European servants of the Companies began at this point to lay the foundations for empire in South and
Southeast Asia. In eastern Asia, where the Philippines had long been the an-
chor of Spain's Pacific empire, the Dutch and other Europeans continued to
trade on terms set by the Japanese and Chinese. Because this regulated trade
was relatively unprofitable, the Europeans increasingly bought East Asian
goods at intermediary markets, particularly at Manila, Batavia, and Surat.
Bombay and Calcutta at opposite ends of the Mughul Empire were just
being readied around 1700 to be the twin pillars of England's later commer-

cial empire in India. The Dutch meanwhile continued to funnel as much of the inter-Asian trade as possible through the port of Batavia. In many instances the inter-Asian trade brought more profit to the VOC than the direct trade to Europe.

International commerce in eastern waters continued to be dominated by the Europeans and their ships, not only because the great nations of Asia had no navies able to challenge them effectively but in part because the Chinese and Japanese remained officially unconcerned about overseas commerce. Passivity about international trade likewise characterized the Mughul Empire and Siam. In fact, the greatest Asian empires—China, the Mughul Empire, and Japan—were all land empires, boasting powerful armies rather than navies. Their governments seemed more concerned to regulate seaborne commerce than to profit from it. Only some smaller states in insular Southeast Asia, such as Acheh, Ternate, and Makassar, appeared to be primarily naval powers. Nowhere, however, were Asian fleets or warships a match for the Europeans. Indeed it is striking that even after a passage of two centuries of direct maritime intercourse between Asia and Europe, no Asian nation had sent trading ships or fleets to Europe. All the Asians who appeared in Europe during the seventeenth century were carried there in European ships or were accompanied by Europeans across the land routes.

Throughout Asia the Europeans continued to be astonished, as they had been previously, by the huge populations and numerous great cities. With their penetration of the interiors they learned to know more at first hand about the court cities of Agra, Delhi, Golconda, Lahore, Ayut'ia, Hanoi, Phnom Penh, Luang Prabang, Nanking, Peking, Kyoto, and Edo (Tokyo). As they came to know them better, they were full of appreciation for other interior cities such as Madura, Ahmadabad, Srinagar, Mrauk-u, Mataram, Sukothai, Sian, Hangchow, Soochow, Osaka, Sendai, and Sumpu. They often made estimates of the extent of cities and of the numbers of urban dwellers, their population statistics being based sometimes on local records and censuses. They continued to provide fresh and up-to-date information on, and to put into a new perspective, the coastal cities that loomed so prominently in the writings of the previous century. Insulindia was correctly pictured as a series of coastal city-states more dependent upon foreign trade than upon their own mountainous and wild hinterlands. Where native cities did not exist or were not adequate at strategic commercial crossroads, the Europeans, with local help, built the new urban complexes of Manila, Tainan, Batavia, Surat, Bombay, and Calcutta. The old European entrepôts—Malacca, Macao, and Goa—faded in general importance with the rise of these new commercial cities.

While there were vast differences between, for example, the walled, grid-planned Chinese cities and the half-hidden Southeast Asian ports built up-river on stilts, the European visitors found common elements in many Asian cities. In most seaports they met the same groups of merchants:

Arabs, Gujaratis, Chinese, and Malays. In South and Southeast Asian ports they usually encountered similar officials, often with the same or similar titles, enforcing similar regulations. Most Asian cities were built of wood and consequently subject to frequent fires. The European reports contain numerous descriptions of fires and of the measures taken by local governments to prevent them. Europeans frequently observed that Asians usually built for only one generation rather than for posterity. Great palaces and monuments were the obvious exceptions to such European generalizations about Asian cities, and these were often described in careful detail. Some of them—the porcelain tower and the imperial palace in Nanking, for example—no longer exist. In fact, some of the cities described by seventeenth-century Europeans no longer exist or are mere ghosts of what they were in the seventeenth century. In addition, seventeenth-century European travelers described ruined cities in India, China, Southeast Asia, and Inner Asia which stood as mute testimony to the rise and fall of empires in the past. Inland, between the cities, the European travelers frequently described both convenient river transportation and excellent highways with inns and milestones.

Europeans made spectacular progress in their appreciation of the governments, languages, cultures, and religions of India, Siam, Vietnam, China, and Japan. India with its multitudinous diversities attracted much more attention than previously, as the Europeans learned more about Islam and Hinduism. They became aware of the philosophical and theological cleavages within Islam and of the hostilities between Sunnis and Shiites. They learned more about Islam's political power, its hierarchy and "heresies," and the relationships of Indian Muslims to their co-religionists in Arabia, Persia, Turkey, Southeast Asia, and the Philippines. While the Europeans enjoyed generally good relations with the dominant Muslims of the Mughul Empire, Bijapur, and Golconda, they mostly were at odds with the Muslims in south India and Southeast Asia. In the Philippines Islam, like Christianity, was still an expanding force. The Europeans, the southern Hindus, and certain Buddhist groups saw in Islam a common enemy, particularly the aggressive Malabar, Gujarati, and Malay Muslims. Always fearful of Islam, the Europeans conscientiously reported on the presence of Muslims on China's western frontiers and in the empire itself.

Penetration of India's interior, particularly Tamilnadu, produced reevaluations of Hinduism and its traditions. The Europeans noted, as they had not previously, the existence of Hindu seats of learning at Benares and Madura. They commented for the first time on hundreds of temples in south India, their dedication to particular gods, and their servitors. The writers were fascinated by the Hindu pilgrimages to the Ganges and other rivers, to Mathura, to Jagganath, and to Ramesvaram at the tip of the peninsula. Some Jesuits, such as Nobili, followed Hindu practices in an effort to insinuate Christian teachings; other Jesuits and some Protestant pastors—Lord,

Roger, Baldaeus—endeavored through informants to inquire into the tenets of Hindu thought. The Europeans soon came to realize that deep differences existed between the Hinduism of the north and the south and between the followers of Vishnu and Siva. Bernier, the French physician, was told by the pandits of Benares that Hinduism existed solely for Indians and had no universalistic or evangelistic aspirations. Nonetheless, the Europeans recognized that Hinduism had been exported to Bali and Cambodia and that Brahmans worked in many Southeast Asian courts as astrologers. They also knew that vestiges of Buddhism remained at Benares, that Buddhism was an offshoot of Hinduism, and that it had been rooted out of India by the Brahmans. The Buddhist cave temples in western India bore mute testimony to the former importance of Buddhism there, but the Europeans reported that Buddhism had all but vanished from the subcontinent.

From India, Buddhism had spread to Ceylon, continental Southeast Asia, Tibet, China, Korea, and Japan. In fact, the Europeans realized that it was the only doctrine that gave a degree of religious unity to the countries east of India. In Arakan, Siam, Tibet, Laos, and Japan, the dominant faith of Buddhism was supported and maintained by the ruler and the state. While tolerance ordinarily prevailed in these Buddhist states, neither the Muslims nor the Christians made many converts except for the Catholics in Japan. Buddhist rulers in Ceylon, Arakan, Siam, or Japan dealt promptly and severely with foreign threats to the state. In China, Korea, and Vietnam, where Buddhism had to compete with Confucianism and Taoism, it was mainly a popular faith that from time to time received official recognition and support. The European commentators usually reflected in their descriptions the attitude of the ruling class towards Buddhism and its works. Those who wrote about Siam admired the achievements of Buddhism, but those writing of China or Japan denigrated the Buddhists. The adverse experiences of the Catholics in Japan colored their descriptions of Buddhism throughout East Asia. They were also influenced in their dislike for Buddhism by the negative attitude of the Confucianists toward the alien faith born in India. Many of the European commentators, except for the French writers on Siam, remarked only on the externals of Buddhism while denouncing its teachings. In China, despite Confucian attitudes, a few of the Jesuits began to distinguish between the various forms of Buddhism. The Jesuits who visited Tibet described its Buddhism with remarkable sympathy, probably because they thought it to be a debased Christianity. To readers in Europe, Buddhism must have appeared as a rival Asian faith that resembled Christianity in its externals and in its missionary zeal. But most surprising to them was the tolerance that Buddhists everywhere exhibited for other faiths.

In Insulindia and the Philippines, the religions of India, China, and Japan no longer made much of an impression upon local peoples. Bali was the only island to remain faithful to the Hinduism that once had been widespread in western Indonesia. Like other exports from the great nearby cultures, Asian religions were brought into the islands by merchants and other foreigners who worked in urban centers. From the European records it clearly emerged that Islam continued to be carried throughout Insulindia and into the southern Philippines by Arab, Turkish, Persian, Malay, and Gujarati teachers, merchants, and middlemen. A number of the insular rulers followed Islam and some banded together to oppose the commercial and religious expansion of the Europeans based in Malacca, Batavia, and Manila. Christianity, the latest of the competing faiths to spread into the archipelagoes, made permanent conquests only in the Philippines, Amboina, Timor, and the Lesser Sundas. Elsewhere the European Christians and their converts lived in urban communities under the protection of European ships, guns, and soldiery, or in isolated places where they were sometimes enslaved or else were tolerated by peoples fearful of commercial or military reprisals.

From the European viewpoint, Asia was divided into four major regions: South Asia and its insular neighbors; continental Southeast Asia; Insulindia and the Philippines; and East Asia. India itself was divided into two separate but related parts, the Islamic north and the Hindu south. Politically the Mughul Empire had extended its authority eastward over Bengal and had even invaded Arakan. It had also pushed southward by its wars in the Deccan and by its overthrow of Bijapur-Golconda. The southward pressure exerted by these Muslim states was stubbornly resisted by the Hindu states of the south, especially Madura. Goa and the southwest coast remained free of Mughul incursions but suffered from the exploits of Sivaji. Calicut and Kanara on the Malabar coast were two Hindu states which remained relatively independent while the Portuguese and the Dutch overwhelmed their neighbors. The independence of the Maldives was periodically threatened by the Portuguese and by the Muslim corsairs of Cannanore who controlled their commerce. Buddhist Kandy in the interior of Ceylon managed to remain free of foreign control even while its northern and western coasts were overrun by Portuguese and Dutch invaders.

When writing of India, these European authors, like their predecessors of the sixteenth century, concentrated heavily on India's physical aspects and on related matters important to foreign visitors. In most provinces and states, the Europeans ordinarily were permitted to move about freely. Consequently they were able to provide information on internal land routes and the organization of overland travel in the Mughul Empire, in central India from Surat to Masulipatam, from Masulipatam to Golconda, and from the southern coastal cities inland to Vijayanagar, Gingee, Tanjore, and Madura. They commented on the dangers and discomforts of the roads and noted which ones required caravans, guides, and road guards, or charged tolls. They observed that in coastal southwest India, travel was safer and easier than elsewhere, and that in some places even free refreshment was offered. They were most specific about the tree-lined highway that linked the Mughul capitals of Agra, Delhi, and Lahore. And they noted in some cases the for-malities travelers had to observe when crossing internal frontiers. A few Europeans commented admiringly on how the roads were designed for night travel and how messages were conveyed by relays of runners. Natural impediments such as rains and floods, forays by bandits, and excessive exac-tions by greedy officials were the main general obstacles faced by European travelers. The roads from coastal Ceylon into the Kandyan highlands could not be traversed freely and were so well guarded that peaceful travel was virtually ruled out.

Most of the Mughul provinces, especially Bengal, were deemed to be productive and virtually self-sufficient in foodstuffs and cotton. Pasturage for the host of domesticated animals was generally thought to be in short supply during the dry season. Cultivation of north India's basically rich lands was hampered by the repressive land system maintained by the Mughuls. But particularly admirable was the control of water in the Mughul Empire and Golconda. In Golconda the land was controlled by the state, which farmed it out to the highest bidder; nonetheless, Golconda produced rice, indigo, opium, and elephants for export. Although the Europeans reported little about agriculture in the declining empire of Vijayanagar, they noted that famines repeatedly swept the Coromandel region. They also recorded the devastation produced by famine across central India in the 1630's. Agricul-ture in the south continued to produce foodstuffs enough to supply Goa and other European outposts and to provide pepper and other commodities for export. In Madura, as in Vijayanagar, agriculture suffered from incessant war. Ceylon and the Maldives continued to be relatively well off and to produce products for export.

Politically, India was seen to be a collection of rising and waning empires, enclaves, remnants of the former empire or nayakdoms, and coastal city-states. The Mughul state was divided into twenty provinces in which the emperor's authority was strong at the center, and weak and sometimes chal-lenged at the fringes. It was left to Aurangzib to pacify Bengal, Orissa, and the Deccan, to reassert periodically Mughul authority in Rajasthan, Qan-dahar, and Assam, to reduce Bijapur (1686) and Golconda (1688) to submis-sion, and to threaten in the 1690's the Portuguese and British positions on India's northwest coast. From Goa southward the western coastal tract to the peninsula's tip was divided politically into twenty-four identifiable small states. Of these, Kanara and Calicut were the most independent and viable entities. Inland they were bordered by nayakdoms or remnants of Vija-yanagar which struggled to maintain their independence from the south-ward advances of the Muslim states. Among the Hindu states of the south, Madura remained the most autonomous. The Europeans, who were subject to Mughul authority in the north, nibbled away at the coasts of south India, the Carnatic, and Ceylon to protect their commerce and the sea lanes run-ning from their bases at Cochin, San Thomé, Masulipatam, and Colombo.

Epilogue: A Composite Picture

When they moved inland away from their protective bases, the European merchants and missionaries conducted their affairs on terms set by the reigning Indian authorities.

The Mughul emperors, particularly Aurangzib, were considered to be among the richest and most powerful rulers in the world. The Europeans used the Mughul records to estimate the imperial and provincial revenues and the size of armies. From their own commercial activities they knew that the empire enjoyed a favorable balance of payments in international trade and was a "sink for silver." As sole owner of the land, the emperor garnered whatever revenues there were from agriculture and imposed extraordinary taxes at will. Gifts were expected by the emperors for every request and on every occasion. Some extravagant court ceremonies brought in additional revenues to the crown; others were lavish displays which cost the emperor. But it was the maintenance on a permanent basis of vast numbers of troops and fortresses which exhausted the financial resources of the empire. In times of war, which were frequent, this drain on the imperial exchequer became even greater. Since no power outside the subcontinent seriously threatened the Mughuls, these wars were mainly confined to India. Consequently they wrought widespread internal devastation and regular dislocations that interfered with agriculture and trade. Probably the least affected province was Gujarat, into which the Europeans steadily expanded their trade. In south India, wars were likewise endemic throughout most of the century and contributed to political instability and economic disorder.

The main stabilizing force in India derived from the tolerance that everywhere prevailed in social and religious relations. Throughout the Mughul Empire, as well as in the south, the Europeans were astounded by the forbearance shown by the Indians in dealing with diverse faiths and social practices. Although the empire was officially Sunni Muslim, its Hindu majority continued to follow without serious molestation the beliefs and customs of their ancestors. In Gujarat the Jains and the Parsees were not interfered with. Other groups such as Jews and Christian Armenians as well as newly arrived Christians from Europe freely practiced their faith. The practices of one group, the Europeans observed, rubbed off on the others. The caste system of the Hindus affected the beliefs and habits of Muslims, Jains, and St. Thomas Christians. The dominant Shiites of Golconda were less tolerant of Sunni Muslims than of Hindus or Christians. Hindus often participated in Muslim celebrations, perhaps just to have a holiday from work. Hindu yogis and Muslim fakirs lived side by side in relative peace, both groups enjoying the general respect of the public. Members of these communities were outwardly distinguished from one another by dress, by temples, mosques, or churches, and by ceremonies. While the Mughuls discouraged the practice of suttee, they did not outlaw it as the British later did. The Sinhalese Buddhists, perhaps because they were on the defensive, showed less tolerance than others of their faith for alien religious and social practices.

While the Europeans were generally hostile to Muslims and to Islamic customs, they never tired of trying to penetrate and understand the caste system of the Hindus. Serious efforts were undertaken to uncover and translate the sacred tracts of Hinduism, to differentiate Jainism from Hinduism, and to record the history of the Parsees. While some missionaries inveighed against the "superstitions" of the Indians, Nobili in Madura sought by adaptation to Hinduism to spread the Christian Gospel. Della Valle and other travelers sought to understand Hinduism by visiting Kanara, one of the coastal states not seriously affected by Islam or Christianity. Fenicio, a Jesuit, and Roger and Baldaeus, both Dutch Reformed preachers, sought to describe and to present in organized form the tenets of south Indian Hinduism. For them, as for other Europeans, Hinduism was the key to understanding south India. It alone explained caste, child marriages, suttee, temple prostitutes, and many of the hundreds of other practices which puzzled and perturbed the Europeans.

Although they were impressed by the stability and tolerance of Hindu society, the Europeans of the seventeenth century did not conclude that India was static or unchanging. Indeed they were impressed through their own experiences by the fluidity to be found in many aspects of Indian life. They studied Mughul and Kashmiri history and observed the monuments and remnants in north and south India left by past empires. They knew that the Mughul capital had moved from one city to the other and that Delhi had been the capital of several empires before the Mughuls built Shahjahanabad. They investigated the cave temples of Ellora, Elephanta, and Kanheri and learned of their antiquity. They watched with admiration the construction of Akbar's tomb and the Taj Mahal, the planned cities of Hyderabad and Shahjahanabad, and the great temples, tanks, and gardens scattered throughout the country. Indian artisans of many kinds were judged to be more skilled than Europeans in certain crafts and were quick to imitate European designs in shipbuilding and textiles. Indian creativity in the arts and crafts was hampered not by tradition or lack of individual ingenuity but by repressive economic and political conditions which discouraged and paid insufficient rewards for originality. The Indians were considered to be backward only in certain aspects of technology and science.

While some Europeans viewed the Brahmans as an arrogant and bigoted elite, others saw them as sincere teachers of moral doctrine and used them as informants on Hindu beliefs and customs. Caste was usually equated with occupations and not often with color, though the Europeans did emphasize the Mughul preference for white persons. Most Europeans appreciated the courtesy, modesty, and compassion of the Hindus. Others reviled the Indian merchants for their craftiness and the Bengalis for their sly servility, sentiments which were often shared by other Indians. Ordinary Muslims were considered to be less moral than Hindus, prostitution being legal in Golconda and other Muslim states. Still the Muslim authorities tried to limit suttee and the Hindus were castigated for their bad treatment of widows. Justice was seen to be severe but fair in the Mughul Empire; elsewhere it was considered to be a harsh and vindictive act by the ruler. Particularly repellent to Christian priests were the Hindu ceremonies designed to propitiate evil spirits and demons. Several Europeans wrote biographies of Sivaji in which he was hailed as a Hindu hero. From these few examples it can readily be seen that the Europeans possessed no single viewpoint on India, its customs, or its people, even though their judgments certainly reflected their European and Christian backgrounds. Despite their common Western background they were more diverse in outlook than those who described China. Those who wrote on India included merchants, physicians, and Protestant pastors as well as Catholic priests. For modern students who take into account these biases, the seventeenth-century European reports on India provide rich materials not found in the indigenous records, and descriptions of Indian life and activity which native observers would have dismissed as too commonplace for discussion.

Continental Southeast Asia and Insulindia displayed close historical associations with the neighboring great civilizations of India and China. The Lao and Thai peoples had emigrated from southern China, and most of Vietnam had once been a province of that empire. Buddhism was the general bequest of India and Ceylon, but the Buddhism of Vietnam came into that country by way of China and in its progress acquired Sinic attributes. Although the Pali language had emigrated along with Buddhism from India, most of the common languages of Southeast Asia exhibited strong relations to Chinese. The secular languages of Vietnam were written in Chinese characters; the Thai language, like Chinese, was seen to be monosyllabic and tonal although it was written in letters during the seventeenth century. Almanacs and calendars were borrowed from both India and China. The Chinese craft of printing was introduced into Vietnam but not into Siam. Siam, Laos, and Vietnam operated within and imitated the Chinese tribute system in the conduct of their international relations. The officialdom in Vietnam was Confucian and that of Siam and Arakan Buddhist.

The lesser states and city-states were much more open to Islamic and Christian influence than the larger countries of the continent. Their commerce was generally dominated by Chinese, Indian, Arabic, and European merchants, even when the ruler was a Muslim. In Malaya outside of Malacca, Patani and other cities on the eastern side of the peninsula paid tribute to Siam while the Portuguese and Dutch sought by war or intimidation to monopolize their trade. Malay Muslims were active in most Southeast Asian ports and entrepôts, particularly in Cambodia after mid-century. Malacca, occupied by the Dutch after 1641, declined in size and commercial importance during the rest of the century. The advance of the Dutch forced the Portuguese and their missionaries to flee Malacca and to seek refuge and employment in more tolerant centers. Mrauk-u, Ayut'ia, Phnom Penh, and

Makassar on Celebes consequently became hosts to displaced Portuguese and Muslims. The rulers of Arakan and Siam hired Japanese mercenaries, many of whom were Christians, for their armed forces. Turks and Iranians also conducted business in both the coastal ports and the interior markets.

Except for Malaya, all the countries of continental Southeast Asia were self-sufficient in food, according to the European writers. Their peoples lived on a diet of rice, fish, and fruits, and dwelled in bamboo and thatched houses built on stilts. The deltas of the great rivers were flooded annually, the inundations being particularly severe in Siam and Cambodia. By skillful management the waters were conserved for the paddy fields. Siam in particular had surplus rice for export to Malaya, India, and elsewhere. The Thai farmers in the mountains also raised wheat and began experimenting with maize around 1670. Wood and other forest products were exported from all of the larger states; deer hides were sold to Japan. The Malay peninsula, especially Kedah, was rich in tin, a metal much in demand throughout the trading world. Rumors that Siam had extensive gold resources were never substantiated.

Explorations of the interior of Southeast Asia by European merchants, diplomats, and missionaries revealed that travel was mostly by water. Mrauk-u and Ayut'ia were capital cities served almost exclusively by river and canal transport. The only way to investigate the interiors was to go upstream on the great rivers around which life centered. It was much easier, the Europeans found, to enter Laos by the Mekong River than to trek overland from Ayut'ia or Hanoi. It was speculated by some and denied by others that the great rivers originated in a mysterious lake in the mountains of Central Asia. French engineers prepared maps of Siam and of the Menam and its distributaries from Ayut'ia to the sea. The riverine explorations of the Europeans brought them up the Red River to Hanoi, up the Mekong to Phnom Penh and Lop Buri, up the Irrawaddy to Pegu, and up the river of Mrauk-u to the capital of Arakan. Since all these rivers ran generally from north to south, the Europeans relied on sea travel to take them east to west, thus avoiding the great mountain ranges that separated the river valleys.

The seventeenth-century Europeans frequented only the coastal regions of Burma, their investigations of the interior being limited to Arakan and the Pegu area. They knew the Tenasserim coast as a point of entry into Siam and they went up the Menam to Chiang Mai. From Phnom Penh they investigated other Cambodian cities and proceeded upriver to Laos. In Vietnam they knew the interiors of both Tongking and Cochin-China from the sea to the mountains. During these inland explorations they inspected the ancient ruins in Arakan and Pegu and were intrigued by the overgrown remains of Angkor. They learned that Cambodia was a center of pilgrimages for Buddhists from all over the region, even when wars were raging, and also that Laos was dominated by Buddhist priests. They mentioned in passing the Minangkabau Muslims of Malaya and the mountain peoples of Vietnam.

The wars in continental Southeast Asia were thought to be a constant threat to stability. The battles between Siam and Burma, and between Arakan and the Portuguese, were fought both on land and sea, as were the wars between Cochin-China and Tongking. Siam, living under the constant threat of war on its internal borders, maintained standing armies and striking forces. Nowhere did they build permanent forts, but relied on natural barriers. Walls of demarcation separated Tongking from Cochin-China, but only rudimentary and temporary fortifications were built. Massive land armies avoided pitched battles, as one general sought to outmaneuver the other. Elephants used as cavalry and shock forces became skittish under gunfire. One of the major objectives of war was not to kill but to capture masses of prisoners who were then held as slaves to labor in agriculture. Captured cities were usually burned, their populations carried off, and their valuables confiscated as loot. It was the constant need for firearms and ammunition in Vietnam that opened its doors to European and Japanese purveyors. Japanese, European, and Muslim mercenaries were everywhere in demand as gunners, for most other Asians except for the Vietnamese were considered to be inept in their use of artillery and muskets.

Siam, a politically, culturally, and religiously unified state, was the Southeast Asian nation best known to the Europeans. Its Buddhist king was the absolute ruler of both secular and religious affairs. He headed a complex hierarchical society of almost two million persons in which all registered adult males, except priests, slaves, and aliens, performed six months of state service annually. Women did most of the work on the farms and in the marketplaces. Many of the slaves were in bondage for debt or were war prisoners. Still much land was left idle because of labor shortages. Officials appointed by the king ran a bureaucracy divided into civil and military branches, while each of the provinces was administered by either a hereditary or an appointed governor. As final authority in legal matters, the king followed the ancient traditions and the law codes in rendering judgments and imposing punishments. But in matters closer to the court, the laws were not so carefully followed. Succession was often by usurpation, and the king, despite the strictures of law and religion, married his sister to preserve the purity of his line. He ruled with the aid of a "Second King" and kept his officials under close surveillance. All taxes were levied by the king; international trade as one aspect of foreign affairs was developed as a royal monopoly. Foreign embassies were treated as tribute missions except for those from China. Crafts, arts, and science did not flourish under the restraints of absolutism. Thais were thought to be natural poets, dancers, and musicians, and totally without interest in foreign arts.

Vietnam was seen as a single country divided by civil war into the states of Cochin-China in the south and Tongking in the north, with small principalities on both its northern and southern frontiers. Tongking was the largest and wealthiest of the states and the seat of the *vua,* or emperor, the recognized lord of the entire peninsula. Government in both states followed the Chinese model with a Confucian officialdom recruited through a system of civil service examinations. In Vietnam, as in Ming China, the rulers and the civil order were thought to be increasingly falling under the pernicious influence of court eunuchs. Persistent war forced both states to maintain permanent military forces and to open their doors to foreign suppliers of armaments, to alien merchants, and even to Christian missionaries. Nonetheless their rulers continued to regulate the economy in the hope of maintaining low and constant prices. Traditional customs and observations were strictly enforced by the state and the national heroes were worshipped regularly by the king and all elements of the population. Hanoi, the market of the Red River delta, and Fai-fo, the trading center in Cochin-China, were the points of entry for both the European merchants and missionaries. By century's end the Catholic missionaries had won substantial numbers of converts and a scattering of Christian communities existed throughout Vietnam.

The archipelagoes—Insulindia and the Philippines—south of the continent were seen differently by the Europeans. Here they confronted no great states impervious to their activities, but only small city-states and insular groupings that could be dealt with separately and definitively. While describing the insular reaches of Asia, the Europeans were also busily involved in transforming them. By century's end the Dutch had established a commercial hegemony over Insulindia and its eastern fringes; the Spanish controlled the northern Philippines from their base at Manila and were only halted in their progress southward by the Muslims in Sulu and Mindanao. While the Spaniards gradually conquered the Marianas, they were forced by the Dutch to withdraw from the Spiceries in 1662. Throughout the islands, except for the Marianas, the Europeans realized that they had been preceded as invaders and occupiers by Muslim merchants and mullahs. And they continued throughout the century to encounter hostility and resistance from both foreign Muslims and native converts, including rulers, to Islam. Gradually overcome elsewhere by the Europeans, the Muslims successfully maintained an independent base in the Sulu Islands between the Protestant Dutch and the Catholic Spanish empires. While Christianity spread in the Spanish Philippines, Islam continued to dominate Insulindia despite Dutch hegemony. European descriptions, however, disclose an Islam which varied considerably from that of India or the Near East. Europeans also noted the persistence of pre-Islamic beliefs and practices not only in the hinterlands of Insulindia, but also among the Muslim coast dwellers.

Despite their preoccupation with empire-building, the Europeans became acutely aware of the complexity of Insulindia. While its islands were physically separated one from the other, they were seen to be interrelated. A unity existed among the islanders of the coast in appearance and skin color that set these people apart from the aborigines in the mountains of the same islands and from the inhabitants of the Papuas and Australia. Malay was the *lingua franca* of commerce, and the islanders, including the Filipinos, were thought to have some sort of historical relationship to the peoples of the Malay Peninsula and India. The Europeans noted the similarities in commercial practices and ship construction from island to island. They saw that a commercial interdependence existed in island trade; for example, the Spiceries imported food and cloth from the other islanders who engaged in overseas trade. One international entrepôt was a city-state much like its neighbor with similar political and commercial organizations and officials. Trade was controlled by local princes who added other coastal places to their states rather than expanding into the interiors of the islands they already controlled. In all the city-states the command of manpower was the main basis of wealth; common institutions such as debt bondage were universally used as mechanisms for the control of society. The Europeans charted the rapidly changing fortunes of the major thalassocracies—Ternate, Tidore, Acheh, Makassar—and of the territorial empire of Mataram; indeed they participated decisively in the regional rivalries.

Chinese traders and settlements flourished in most commercial centers, while remaining subject to the local authorities of Insulindia. Although the Dutch broke up this earlier unity, they imposed one of their own creation. Peoples were forced by the VOC to move from their native islands, centers of production were shifted, new links of communication and trade were forged, and old power relationships were disrupted. The Chinese were tolerated as trading middlemen just as they had been before. Papua and other eastern peripheral places began to be integrated by the Dutch into the regional economy based on Batavia.

The Philippine archipelago with its thousands of islands, the Europeans recognized, had traditional, if tenuous, ties to Insulindia, the Malay Peninsula, and India. Both the Filipinos and the Chamorros of the Marianas had probably migrated from Malaya by way of Indonesia. In the Philippines the descendants of the Malays had occupied the coast and had driven the aboriginal negritos back into the mountains. Muslims from Borneo had captured slaves in the southern Philippines and had erected an outpost at Manila before the arrival of the Spanish. Other Muslims had occupied the Sulu Islands and Mindanao before the advent of Magellan. Chinese merchants from Fukien had long done business with the Muslims in the south and were quick to establish settlements in the Spanish north, particularly at Manila. The Japanese, who had watched with trepidation the advance of the Spanish in the Philippines, at first sought peaceful intercourse with the Christians who had crossed the broad Pacific Ocean. Like the Chinese, the Japanese were welcomed by the European traders and missionaries who sought closer relations with East Asia. Both Chinese and Japanese were feared in the

Philippines, however, as advance agents of their powerful native countries which were thought by the Spanish to have their own designs upon the Philippines.

Central governments, or even powerful city-states, did not exist in the Philippines before the coming of the Muslims and the Christians. Indeed a multitude of traditions, beliefs, and languages divided the Filipinos; even the Chamorros of the Marianas possessed a greater cultural unity. Divided by geography and culture, the Filipinos provided no unified resistance to the Muslims or the Christians. Authority resided in chieftains who made alliances or contended with one another over local issues. Protected by Spanish arms, the Christian priests learned the Filipino languages and traveled far and wide in the islands to make converts and to establish churches. The Christians, like the Muslims, tolerated indigenous mores and generally preferred peaceful to forceful pacification of the islanders. They were quick to recognize the superiority of native crafts for insular travel, to admire the inbred courtesy of the Filipinos in daily intercourse, and to approve their devotion to bathing and personal hygiene. While tolerating many native social practices, the missionaries denounced as superstitions the religious beliefs of the Filipinos and outlawed certain of their sacrifices and celebrations. Native languages and laws were studied and adopted by the Europeans wherever practicable. On their side, the Filipinos quickly adapted themselves to European mores and beliefs. This mutual accommodation led to a fusion of Filipino and Spanish culture and religion which persisted into the twentieth century. In the Marianas the native culture was rooted out by the Spanish as the Jesuits imposed the Christian system. The European sources relating this history are still the most available and the best of the materials necessary for its reconstruction.

China was the ultimate goal of most of the early seventeenth-century voyages, and it remained Asia's most impressive empire. A single, integrated culture within a single state, governed by a single ruler, it proved immensely attractive to European observers throughout the century. Other such states—Siam, Vietnam, Japan, and Korea—all within the Sinic world, were smaller and less powerful. More than fifty major, independent, eyewitness accounts of China or parts of it were published in Europe during the seventeenth century, exclusive of Jesuit letterbooks, derivative accounts, and general descriptions of Asia. Some of these were written toward the end of the century by Europeans who had journeyed overland rather than by sea and who described China's land frontiers to the north and west. Europeans knew more about China—its geography, government, history, and thought—than about any other part of Asia, despite their having no foothold in the empire apart from the Portuguese settlement at Macao.

During the seventeenth century, Europeans definitively identified China with medieval Cathay, and they developed accurate images of China's size, its varied landscape, its rivers, lakes, mountains, cities, villages, and frontier regions. Martini's *Atlas* provided individual maps and descriptions of each province, of the empire as a whole, and of the lands of its periphery. This and other publications contained accurate estimates of China's population, even of the population of hundreds of cities and towns. Few states anywhere in the seventeenth-century world were so thoroughly and accurately described. Europeans marveled endlessly over China's immense size and teeming population. Martini thought of it, enclosed by the Great Wall, as one enormous city. To pre-industrial European observers, China seemed richly supplied with all the resources necessary to maintain its enormous population and its prestigious place in the world. It needed very little from outside its borders, and like India, it was a "sink for silver." Goods and people continually moved across the vast empire on its many large navigable rivers. Where rivers failed, the Chinese had dug the Grand Canal, an engineering marvel almost as impressive to the Europeans as the Great Wall. On land a vast network of imperial post roads and regularly spaced inns united provincial cities to the capital.

What most fascinated Europeans was that this enormous empire was ruled by a single monarch who governed through a huge complex bureaucracy staffed not by hereditary aristocrats but by scholars who won their positions through written competitive examinations on the Confucian classics. European observers described China's government and its workings in intense detail, from the power and ritual of the imperial court through the metropolitan boards and bureaus to the provincial governors and district magistrates. They realized that the theoretically all-powerful emperor was significantly limited by the bureaucracy. They sensed frequently a disparity between the Confucian ideal of government and its less admirable practices. They understood the role of eunuchs in the imperial household and of factions in the bureaucracy. They understood the purpose of the censorate but also described the censors' frequent abuse of power. Despite deep familiarity with both the ideals and the defects of Chinese government and law, most seventeenth-century observers concluded that China was the best-governed land on earth.

Europeans were likewise impressed with Chinese learning and education. They described the examination system, the long years of study required to prepare for the examinations, and the scholarly, political, social, and economic rewards for those who succeeded in them. The Chinese language, so different from any European tongue, proved endlessly fascinating. During the century the Jesuits, who knew it best, described such things as the differences between written and spoken Chinese, the use of tones, the development of the characters, and the various calligraphic styles. They clearly conveyed, perhaps exaggerated, the literary nature of Chinese culture. Their descriptions of the language inspired some scholars in Europe to study it. The Jesuits and the Dutch commentators reported widespread literacy and the publication in China of innumerable books on such diverse subjects as philosophy, religion, history, law, government, natural science, military science, medicine, mathematics, agriculture, poetry, and drama. Although they were impressed with some aspects of Chinese medicine and other sciences, most European observers concluded that Chinese science lacked sound theoretical foundations. In the natural sciences at least, best exemplified by mathematics and astronomy, European accomplishments seemed superior. European observers were much more impressed with Confucian philosophy and with Chinese history. They produced perceptive and detailed descriptions of the classics, of pre–Han Confucianism, of the neo–Confucianism of the Sung dynasty philosophers, and of the various seventeenth–century schools of thought. By the end of the century several Confucian philosophical works were available in western language translations, as were some medical treatises. Equally impressive were Chinese historical writings. Voluminous official histories had been written for each Chinese dynasty in addition to several major "world" histories and innumerable local histories. Europeans soon concluded that the Chinese possessed the longest and most detailed historical record of any people on earth. Martini's *Sinicae historiae* (1658) and its continuation in Thévenot and by Couplet provided European readers with a detailed sketch of traditional Chinese history from the legendary sage emperors to the K'ang-hsi reign in the later seventeenth century. This chronological sketch was augmented and enriched in many other European publications.

China as a unified empire with its Confucian political ideals and its complex administration was so ancient that it may have appeared to foreigners, including Europeans, as indestructible. While European visitors learned quickly about the rise and fall of dynasties in the past, and about the thirteenth–century Mongol conquest, those who wrote about China in the first half of the century tended to emphasize its durability. The events of the Manchu Conquest, however, which were reported in close detail, seemed most disruptive. Some thought they were witnessing the fall of the Chinese empire and compared these events to the fourth-century barbarian invasions of Rome. As a consequence, therefore, China became for European readers a more dynamic state, subject to cataclysmic changes concerning which they awaited the latest news. By the end of the century, however, the continuity between Ming and Ch'ing seemed far weightier than the disjuncture, and most European reporters and chroniclers began adding the Ch'ing to the long list of Chinese dynasties.

While most scholar-officials espoused Confucianism, China was no religious monolith. Buddhism and Taoism were widely practiced, always tolerated, and sometimes patronized by emperors and officials. So were foreign religions such as Judaism, Islam, and, in the seventeenth century, Christianity. Usually the Chinese blended ideas from all three of their major traditions in their personal belief and practice. The Jesuits tried to accommodate Christianity with Confucianism and to distinguish Confucianism clearly from Buddhism and Taoism. In their descriptions, therefore, they lavished much more attention on Confucianism than on the other two, which they described unsympathetically. Nevertheless their readers could have learned much about Buddhist and Taoist beliefs, traditions, and practices, about the doctrinal differences between some of the Buddhist sects, and about syncretic popular religion. Some European observers, notably the mysterious David Wright, described Chinese popular religion in such detail that a very perceptive reader might have begun to see it as the pervasive faith.

European observers sensed the importance of the Chinese family and of the rites and customs related to it: filial piety, ancestor veneration, marriage, funerals, concubinage, inheritance, and divorce. All Chinese social relationships seemed excessively formal and ceremonious. The Jesuits understood the importance of *li* (ceremony) to Confucian ethics, and all observers seemed intrigued with the intricate details of social intercourse. They reported approvingly that Chinese women were generally secluded and chaste, and that unlike European fashions, clothing styles for both sexes did not change significantly, except for wearing the queue after the Manchu Conquest.

European observers admired the industry and frugality of Chinese peasants, but they generally shared the Confucians' disdain for merchants and soldiers. The observations of Dutch merchants, who found their Chinese counterparts crafty and frequently dishonest, did little to rehabilitate them in European eyes. Chinese artisans and their crafts, however, were highly regarded.

European penetration of China during the seventeenth century also revealed lands and peoples on the empire's periphery which had been totally unknown or but dimly perceived before. On the Tibetan plateau lived an old and settled people whose society was dominated by a distinctive form of Buddhism. Both Indian and Chinese influences could be clearly identified. To the west and north of the Great Wall lived numerous Mongol and Tungusic tribes, some herdsmen, some hunters and fishers, many of whom were nomadic. Some were allies of the Chinese, some had made treaties with the Russians, some were still free. In the Manchu homelands to the northeast of the empire lived both nomadic hunting and fishing tribes and settled agriculturalists. Many of these were allied with the Ch'ing emperor. The Koreans to the east possessed an ancient and sophisticated civilization supported by Chinese-style agriculture, heavily influenced by Chinese culture, but still in many ways unique. On Formosa, later to become China's island frontier, lived a large number of related but incessantly warring tribes who both hunted and farmed. Their religious and social customs were among the most unusual encountered by seventeenth-century Europeans. The descriptions of these peripheral areas also greatly improved Europe's grasp of Asian geography and introduced European readers to some of the world's most unusual and beautiful landscapes: the awesome Himalayas, the

Tibetan plateau, the deserts and steppes of central Asia, Manchurian forests and cultivated valleys, and Formosa's tropical plain and high verdant mountains.

In Japan, the *sengoku* era, in which powerful daimyos contended with one another for control of the country, gave way after 1600 to the unified state of the Tokugawa shoguns, who exercised tight control over their vassals and subjects and maintained a profound peace both within and without Japan's borders. Early seventeenth-century missionaries described the late sixteenth-century internal wars and the consolidation of Tokugawa power in exceedingly close detail. They also repeated earlier descriptions of Japan's geography, society, religion, and culture, and carefully charted the effects of the political changes on the impressively large Japanese Christian church. In the first decades of the century, Protestant Dutch and English observers also described Japan and the consolidation of Tokugawa rule, from a somewhat different perspective. As the century began no part of Asia was better known to European readers.

By 1640 all the missionaries were gone, the Christian church was largely persecuted out of existence, and Japan was closed to all Europeans except the Dutch, who traded at Deshima under prison-like limitations and supervision. During the remainder of the century Europe's only fresh information about Japan came from the Dutch and from those Germans who served in the Dutch East India Company. The Dutch in the two centuries which followed acted as Japan's narrow window to the West as well as Europe's window to Japan. Post-1640 reports were few, compared to those in the first decades of the century, but they enjoyed a wide distribution and contained surprisingly accurate information about Tokugawa Japan. Those of Caron, Montanus, and Meister were the most important. They described the regime's continued paranoia about Christianity and the harsh measures instituted to ferret out the remaining believers. They also accurately described the mature Tokugawa system of control: a system of hostages and alternate-year residence at the shogun's court in Edo for his vassal daimyos, roving censors (*metsuke*) to report on the loyalty of vassals, *bakufu* commissioners (*bugyo*) to supervise the towns and the Buddhist establishment, the registration of all Japanese at Buddhist temples, and the rigorous use of a mutual responsibility system. Daimyos were further weakened by the expenses involved in building and maintaining elaborate palaces in Edo, as it grew rapidly and became commercially as well as politically important. Like all Japanese cities, Edo frequently burned. Dutch reports also describe Edo castle, the ritual of their annual receptions there, the cities and countryside along the route between Nagasaki and Edo, law and justice, marriage customs, houses and gardens, trade and products. On many of these topics they are superior to earlier missionary reports. They say little about religion and learning, however.

Perceptive readers of many seventeenth-century European descriptions of

Asia could have detected elements common to many parts of Asia as well as startling contrasts between the various Asian societies. In many cases the authors explicitly commented on the similarities and differences. Sometimes these perceptions were distorted or limited by their authors' Christian, European bias. More frequently, however, they reflected Asian realities. For example, European visitors not only admired the architecture of Asia's great royal palaces, they seem to have been entranced with the pomp and power of Asian rulers as well. For even relatively minor princes they often used such phrases as "one of the most powerful in all of Asia," while lavishing disproportionate attention on the details of their wealth and power. They usually listed a ruler's vassals, the number of his soldiers, women, and servants; they estimated his wealth and annual revenue; and they described his court ritual. For the mightiest of Asia's emperors, the Chinese emperor and the Great Mughul, they pulled out all the stops. Still, both of these powerful monarchies were sometimes described as unstable. Most Asian rulers were deemed to be despotic, wielding absolute power over their subjects. Almost everywhere they were described as arbitrary and their laws as exceedingly harsh. The Europeans noted the existence in China and Japan of systems of collective and mutual responsibility, but without making condemnatory judgments as later writers were to do. Death seemed the most common punishment—and usually a tortuous form of death. Trials by ordeal were widely used; mutilation or dismemberment were common punishments, especially in Muslim lands. In the Mughul Empire, Siam, Mataram, and Japan, great nobles or members of their families were held hostage at court. Imperial spies or censors were used in India, China, Japan, Siam, and Mataram. European officials imitated Asian ostentatious display. While some imperious pomp might have been appropriate for the viceroys in Goa as great nobles representing the Portuguese crown, the common-born Dutch governors-general in Batavia also deemed it to be necessary in negotiating with Asian princes.

Political absolutism in Asia differed in many ways from the absolutism prevailing in contemporary Europe. The emperors of Mughul India and China, perhaps because of their geographical isolation, were not avid proponents of territorial and religious expansion as Louis XIV and other great European rulers were. Generally the Asians married their own kind and did not contract marriage alliances with foreign royal families. Foreign influence was uncommon in all Asian courts, except perhaps for sporadic periods when Persian power was exerted at Agra and in Golconda. Indeed, in Ceylon, Arakan, and Siam, the kings married their own sisters, and even daughters, to keep their lines pure. A powerful hereditary aristocracy based on land was not to be found anywhere in Asia except in Japan. Most Asian rulers, except possibly the Chinese emperor, paid little heed to the cultivation of the arts and sciences at a time when European rulers heavily patronized creativity in the arts and sponsored the establishment of scientific societies. In Asia itself the contrasts between absolutisms were equally marked. In Mughul India, the military aristocracy was more important than in China, where the civil bureaucracy predominated. Imperial favorites played a larger role in Agra than in Peking and Hanoi, where the court eunuchs created a buffer between the ruler and the working officialdom. In Japan and Vietnam the emperor, while enjoying official and public reverence, was thrust into the background politically by usurping shoguns and territorial kings. In Siam, Ceylon, and Laos, Buddhism was effectively the state religion, as Islam was in Mughul India; by way of contrast, the rulers of China, Vietnam, and Japan lived with several faiths while occasionally favoring one over the other. In Mughul India and Siam the ownership of the land itself was invested in the ruler, while in China and Japan much of it remained in private or corporate hands. Japan, unlike any other Asian state, possessed a large and powerful landed and hereditary aristocracy. In south India and Insulindia the absolutists ruled in conjunction with a powerful noble and merchant oligarchy. Similarly, the European governors in Batavia, Manila, Goa, and Macao ruled with the aid of merchants, soldiers, and Christian leaders from their homelands in a kind of bureaucratic absolutism.

Both India and China (at least for most of the century) lived under foreign rule. The Islamic Mughuls, unlike the Manchus, were never able to conquer and unite the whole of the country under their control. While the Manchus succeeded during the K'ang-hsi period in bringing all of China, Formosa, and nearby parts of Inner Asia under Peking's jurisdiction, their victory was achieved in large measure by compromise with and adaptation to traditional Chinese civilization and to its political system. The Mughuls, by contrast, increasingly repressed Hinduism, fought off the Hindu revival led by Sivaji, and remained mostly powerless in south India. The Europeans in the meanwhile expanded their coastal footholds in India into Coromandel and Bengal and penetrated Gujarat economically. In China, the Europeans remained confined to Macao as they had been in the sixteenth century, and they were ejected from Formosa by Koxinga. In sum, China remained united and almost impervious to the European advance, while India continued to be divided internally and more open to European trade and settlement—a harbinger of things to come!

Education and literacy were reported to be widespread in Asia by the standards of contemporary Europe. Reading, writing, and arithmetic were taught to male youngsters in the family, in village schools, in Buddhist monasteries, and by private tutors; upper-class females were taught, in Japan especially, within the family. The teachers of elementary subjects were Brahmans in Hindu India; monks in the Buddhist lands, Japan, and China; Confucian scholars in China, Korea, Vietnam, and Japan; mullahs in Mughul India, the Maldive Islands, and parts of Insulindia; Catholic priests in the Philippines; and Dutch Protestants in Java, Amboina, Banda, and Taiwan. Typically, young students were instructed in familial, civic, and religious virtues and ceremonies, as well as in academic subjects. The European writers noted repeatedly that discipline and education ranged from harsh to permissive, and observed that Asian children were better behaved and more mature than their contemporaries in Europe. Language and other subjects were learned in Asia by rote, sometimes individually and at other times in classes. Wherever a strong classical tradition existed, as in India and China, young students were required to memorize edifying passages from the classics.

Buddhist monasteries were often colleges where religion, philosophy, and the classics were taught to advanced students. At Benares and Madura, as well as elsewhere in India, Sanskrit universities trained students in the precepts and traditions of Hinduism. In Japan, Confucian learning was beginning to be emphasized in the universities. Advanced education in China, Korea, and Vietnam was given only by tutors and in study groups of students preparing for the state examinations. Both manuscript and printed books for students were produced in all the continental countries and Ceylon. Throughout Asia, learning and literacy were held in high esteem and thought to be necessities in government, business, and religion.

The social status and position of women in Asia was seen exclusively through male eyes. Of all the works consulted, not a single one was written by a woman. This was inevitable since only European men went to the East, except for the few women who accompanied their husbands or who were sent out to marry men of their own nation. From the European accounts consulted it appears that the women of Asia were universally cherished (except in some of the islands) for their chastity, fidelity, modesty, and motherhood. They were esteemed as mistresses of their households, but remained second in authority to their husbands and sometimes their sons. Daughters were generally regarded as household servants until they married, and ordinarily did not inherit from their own parents or from their husband's family. Women generally prepared the meals, but did not eat with their husbands. While most households consisted of the husband and one wife and their own children, polygamy and concubinage were to be found everywhere. Prostitution was often legal, but whether legal or not it was clearly in evidence throughout the East.

In Hindu India, widows either became suttees or experienced degradation for not following their husbands in death. Hindu women, like their husbands, were subject to caste regulations regarding marriage, divorce, and other social acts. The *devadāsi* (temple dancers and prostitutes) existed as a separate caste and were often individually wealthy and of high repute socially on the Coromandel Coast. Women were thought to be polluted during their menstrual periods and at childbirth in south India, Ceylon, and elsewhere. Devotees of Siva sometimes sacrificed the virginity of their daughters on the lingam. In Mughul India, women exerted a profound influence—sometimes described as baneful—on the emperor and his court, particularly the women of the harem. But it should also be remembered that Shah Jahan had the Taj Mahal erected as a memorial to his wife and empress.

Some of the city-states of south India and Southeast Asia were ruled by powerful queens and their consorts. Some Southeast Asian monarchs, the sultans of Acheh and Mataram, for example, were personally served and protected exclusively by women, who sometimes performed important governmental tasks and were highly trusted as messengers. In Malabar a matrilineal system of descent prevailed, especially among the Nayars, and women held property in their own right. A similar matrilineal system prevailed in the Marianas. In northern India, Malabar, Ceylon, and the Marianas, polyandry was practiced. The women of Siam, perhaps because their husbands were required to spend six months per year in state service, worked as farmers, money-changers, and merchants. Commerce and many agricultural tasks were considered women's work in Insulindia, as well, where women could also initiate divorce, remarry, and inherit property. The priestesses of the native religions in the Philippines and Formosa ranked high among the social arbiters of insular life. In Ceylon the farm women gathered the rice harvest and participated in other aspects of this communal activity. Nuns occupied a special place in Jain monachism and in both Siamese and Japanese Buddhism.

In East Asia, which was mainly reported on by celibate clergymen, the upper-class women of China and Japan were seen to be kept closely secluded and jealously guarded by their husbands. The European priests inveighed against the polygamy practiced by the emperors and the aristocrats of the Chinese court. Most European writers were intrigued by the vices of the harem and the beauty of its occupants, whether in India, China, or Japan. Chinese women of all classes suffered from foot-binding and but a few were literate. In Japan, literate women of the upper classes elevated some of the domestic graces to fine arts—as in flower arranging and the tea ceremony. In both China and Japan, ordinary women were seen on the streets, working in the fields, and performing publicly in dances, plays, and operas. Once the Manchus succeeded the Ming in China, the Manchu women were observed to be much less secluded and more open to social intercourse than their Han sisters.

Europeans were very conscious of Asian skin color which they carefully noted, although variations in the use of terms from one writer to another make precise shades of color impossible to establish. Asians were variously described as brown, yellow, yellow-brown, black, black-brown, and coal black or pitch black. The latter terms were usually reserved for Africans, frequently mentioned for comparison, and for Papuans, Philippine Negritos, and Australian aborigines. Northern Europeans occasionally compared the color of some Asian peoples to that of Iberians. Chinese and Japanese were sometimes described as "white like us," although many Europeans detected considerable variation in skin color among the Indians, the Chinese, and even among the Japanese. Some observed that most Asians did not admire white skin, occasionally comparing it to lepers' skin. There were exceptions, however; Mughuls thought fair skin beautiful, and the men of Brunei reportedly preferred Dayak women because of their very light skin.

European travelers frequently observed that styles of dress in Asia did not change. The major exception to that rule was the adoption of the queue and of Manchu gowns by Chinese men after the Manchu Conquest, a much-discussed change. In most Asian societies one's dress also denoted one's caste, rank, or office. The distinctions were sometimes exhaustively described.

Personal conduct in the high civilizations of Asia such as India, China, and Japan was frequently seen as superior to that of Europeans and sometimes held up for them to emulate. Still some reprehensible practices seemed ubiquitous. Sexual mores were frequently described as lax. Prostitution was found everywhere, although in some places Europeans may have confused it with concubinage. Sodomy was widely practiced, and in India and Insulindia European travelers met transvestites. Head-hunting was widely practiced by the aborigines of Insulindia, Formosa, and the Philippines. Cannibalism was frequently attributed to the most remote and savage tribes, although it was very rarely observed. Only two European writers claim to have actually witnessed it, each among Amboinese soldiers in VOC employ. Some less abhorrent customs such as communal bachelor quarters for young men, the piercing of earlobes and noses, and the filing and blackening of teeth at puberty seem to have been practiced in most of the archipelagoes and beyond. Indians, for example, pierced their ears and noses, and Japanese blackened their teeth. Filipinos, Tungus, and Japanese immersed newborn infants in cold water to make them hardy.

As described by seventeenth-century Europeans, slavery was institutionalized all over Asia, although some of the relationships which they understood to be slavery may have been quite different from what Europeans meant by that term. Some people became slaves because of debts which they could not pay; some slaves were captives from wars; some were hill people captured and sold by coastal merchants. Slavery contributed to the movement of peoples in Asia. Europeans met Chinese slaves in Burma and India, Indian slaves in Java, Papuan slaves in Bali, Filipino slaves in Celebes, Balinese and Bornean slaves everywhere. Since Europeans also kept slaves, which they procured in Africa as well as in Asia, they further contributed to the displacement of peoples.

While some missionaries and scholarly Europeans tried to understand Asian religions, most of the travelers described what they saw as confused and benighted idolatry. The propitiation of the devil, they believed, was a common aspect of popular religion all over Asia. Also widespread was the belief that the movements of heavenly bodies affected or forecast events on earth, a belief shared by many of the Europeans. Popular fear of eclipses was observed and recorded in Peking as well as in the Spiceries. Comets were recorded everywhere from Ceylon to Korea, a fact which has helped us to authenticate some accounts which were suspected of being spurious.

Asians do not appear to have been addicted to strong drink, although every people produced some alcoholic beverage. Arrack and palm wine seem to have been the most common. Many alcoholic drinks were made from rice. None was made from grapes; wine and brandy had to be imported by Europeans. Many European accounts report the use of opium and the dangers of addiction to it. Much of it was grown in Gujarat, Bengal, and Golconda, and it was frequently taken by soldiers in India and Southeast Asia, supposedly to give them more courage in battle. Betel chewing was universal in south and southeast Asia. Most European accounts described the making of the quid and its social importance. They also report on the cultivation of tobacco and its widespread use among Asians from northern India to the Philippines and Korea.

Asian craftsmen, whether Indian jewelers, Chinese porcelain-manufacturers, Sumatran kris-makers, or Makassarese boat-builders, were almost universally admired. Asian arts, especially music and painting, were less generally appreciated. Chinese painters, for example, did not paint with oils and did not understand the use of perspective, shading, and color. Chinese and Japanese music grated on European ears. Javan music they judged sweeter and more melodious.

Asian medicine was generally respected by European observers, especially for tropical diseases not known in Europe. Several books were written about it. Specific diseases and cures were described. Chinese techniques of diagnosis by feeling the pulse seemed particularly intriguing to European physicians. Evidently no schools existed in Asia specifically for the study of medicine. As a practical art it was learned from books of traditional treatments, by apprenticeship, and in hospitals. In some of the European centers, native and European physicians practiced side by side and learned from one another. Europeans in Asia also reported the spread of new diseases: smallpox and syphilis, although they frequently confused syphilis with yaws.

Not only were new diseases brought to Asia by the westerners, but new plants as well. Seventeenth-century European accounts contain references to several that had become acclimated in Asia, some very important. Maize, for example, was reported growing in Siam and China in the last third of the century, Spanish soldiers raised it on Ternate, and the people of Timor had "Indian corn" as their staple. European vegetables were grown first of all in the gardens of the European settlements. Chili peppers and pineapples grew in Java. Boym reported several plants of South American origin, including pineapples, which had become common in south China. Many American plants had been introduced into the Philippines as well. Wheat, however, did not grow well in the islands.

Europeans were very interested in Asian plants. Their works contain many descriptions and illustrations of them; several works were entirely devoted to them. The earliest Dutch voyagers, for example, were instructed to carry plants back to the Netherlands for study by Leyden botanists and physicians. Later, plants from all over Asia were taken to Batavia. In south India an international group of scholars studied Malabar flora and eventually produced the magnificent *Hortus indicus malabaricus* (1678–1703).

The Europeans commented extensively on rice cultivation in China, Siam, and Java. They reported areas of rice surplus, such as Siam, and areas dependent on imported rice, such as the eastern archipelago. Chinese farmers they described as industrious and resourceful; Indian farmers were lazy. The natives of the archipelagoes disliked farming and loved war. They raised very little rice, except in Mataram and Makassar, both of which were rice surplus areas. Everywhere in Asia, people ate mainly grains, vegetables, and fruits; meat was usually reserved for feasts or used as a garnish. Indians and Indonesians ate with their fingers; Chinese and Japanese with chopsticks.

Like travelers everywhere, seventeenth-century Europeans were most impressed by what was different from home; their accounts of Asia, therefore, sometimes contain detailed descriptions of customs about which native sources are silent, probably because they were too familiar to elicit comment. For some Asian societies, the European accounts are the only written sources and thus are indispensable for the history of the peoples they describe. In other instances they comment on conditions which were rapidly changing and could not be so described by later writers. In Japan, for example, they describe the last stages of the wars of unification and the consolidation of Tokugawa power. For Mongolia and Manchuria they provide a last glimpse of steppe nomadism as that way of life was being squeezed out of existence by the expanding Ch'ing and Tsarist empires. In some cases the Europeans themselves were radically changing what they described: for example in Ceylon, Formosa, the Spiceries, Banda, the Papuas, Celebes, and the Marianas. The image of Asia constructed by seventeenth-century European travelers and commentators, therefore, is important not only for the history of Europe and Europe's relationship to Asia but also for our understanding of Asia itself.

The Europeans in Asia also reported news—most frequently bad news, which seemed to them abundant. They described the numerous political dislocations of the first half of the century: the Mughul succession crises, the Deccan wars, the Manchu Conquest of China, the revolt of the Three Feudatories, the Tokugawa consolidation of power, and the persecution of Christians in Japan, to name only a few of the most dramatic disturbances. Nature, too, seemed disaster prone. The Europeans frequently reported on fires, floods, famines, earthquakes, and volcanic eruptions, sometimes remarking that these occurred more frequently or were more severe than before. The Banda Islands, for example, suffered three earthquakes and a major volcanic eruption between 1629 and 1631. The middle years of the century seemed exceptionally cold in northeast Asia. Ice on the river near

Seoul was thick enough in November, 1653, to allow three hundred pack-horses to cross it. Martini (1654) reports that rivers in north China remained frozen for four months of the year and that horses and chariots could safely cross them. Hamel writes that the northern Yellow Sea froze solidly enough each winter to become a winter route to China. He described snow so deep at the mountain monastery which he visited in the winter of 1662 that the monks dug tunnels between buildings and traveled on the surface with crude snowshoes. Vries reports that the winter of 1643 in Hokkaido was so cold that there was little food and many people died; over half of the Ainu's houses stood empty. Europeans may have given disproportionate space to earthquakes and volcanic eruptions, with which they had had little prior experience, although they surely knew something about cold winters and famines. It should be remembered, however, that many of the European reporters had lived long years in Asia and that all of them lived quite closely with native Asians as they traveled. Their reports, therefore, may reflect the perceptions of the local people to a much higher degree than is common among today's travelers. Whether there were fewer natural disasters in the last decades of the century is difficult to determine from the European sources. They do report, however, considerably more political stability than in earlier years: Tokugawa control brought peace to Japan. The VOC and the Spanish did so for the archipelagoes. The Ch'ing rulers were comfortably in control of China after the defeat of Koxinga and the Three Feudatories. The French were expelled from Siam, and Aurangzib faced fewer threats to his power after the death of Sivaji and the subjugation of Bijapur and Golconda.

Intemperate, uninformed, or hasty judgments of the Europeans frequently stereotyped Asians and their societies. Certain fixed formulations emerged from both the texts and the illustrations published in Europe, particularly from the great compendia which sought to put between two covers the opinions and reactions derived from observers in the field. Hindus were thought to be characterized by obsession with caste and a multitude of monstrous gods, Muslims by judicial severity and social rapacity, Chinese by undue attention to ceremony and convention, Japanese by a callous attitude towards suffering and death, Jains by a ridiculously excessive respect for lower forms of life, Buddhists by an irrational and uncritical tolerance of all religious persuasions and deviations, and all Asians by irritating and disgusting social habits and dietary customs. But while these and other hostile stereotypes reflected the prejudices of European and Christian commentators about a strange and foreign scene, they must not be considered in isolation. They were balanced, perhaps overbalanced, by expressions of sincere admiration for the achievements of Asia's great civilizations, for the stability of good government in China despite civil war and dynastic change, for the relatively peaceful coexistence in India of a plethora of peoples, social classes, and religions, and for the discipline of the Japanese in military and political affairs.

With the passage of time these European stereotypes, both the condemnatory and the adulatory, were modified by new and often conflicting data that forced finer distinctions and better-informed characterizations. And questions were certainly raised about Europe's superiority in the crafts by the flood of Indian textiles and Chinese porcelains that could not be successfully imitated on the looms or in the kilns of Europe. While most continued to condemn Asian religions as masses of "superstitions," the European writers of the latter half of the century, particularly the missionaries, assiduously and respectfully sought to learn about the fundamental tenets of Hinduism and Confucianism from native informants and texts. Admiration grew over the course of the century for the skill shown by continental Asians in water management and in the building of spectacular structures: Angkor, the Taj Mahal, and the Porcelain Pagoda of Nanking. While continuing to fear and detest Islam, the Europeans nonetheless admired grudgingly the business acumen of the Muslims as well as their mosques, tombs, and gardens. Most striking was the esteem generally expressed for the common Asians, for their courtesy, modesty, propriety, and devotion to family. Whatever their alien perversities and limitations, the Asians were recognized by century's end to be respectable, and, like the Europeans, to possess their own share of the weaknesses and strengths of humans everywhere.

General Bibliography

As a convenience to the reader, the bibliography is divided as follows:

General Bibliography

    Reference Materials

    Source Materials

    Jesuit Letterbooks

Chapter Bibliographies—twenty-three in number—each divided into books and articles.

The chapter bibliographies are limited, in general, to relevant secondary books and articles most important to individual chapters. Certain titles appear in more than one of the chapter bibliographies. The reference materials and sources for each chapter will be found in the general bibliography.

REFERENCE MATERIALS

Aa, Abraham Jacob van der. *Biographisch Woordenboeck der Nederlanden.* 21 vols. Haarlem, 1852–78.

Adams, Percy G. *Travelers and Travel Liars, 1660–1860.* Berkeley, 1962.

Adelung, Friedrich von. *Kritisch-Litterärische Uebersicht der Reisenden in Russland bis 1700.* . . . 2 vols. St. Petersburg and Leipzig, 1846.

Aernsbergen, A. J. van. *Chronologisch overzicht van de werkzaamheid der Jezuïeten in de missie van Nederlandsch Oost-Indië.* Amsterdam, 1934.

Aguado-Bleye, Pedro. *Manual de historia de España.* 8th ed. 3 vols. Madrid, 1958–59.

Ainslie, Whitelaw. *Materia Indica; or, Some Account of Those Articles Which Are Employed by the Hindoos and Other Eastern Nations in Their Medicine, Arts and Agriculture; Comprising also Formulae, with Practical Observations, Names of Diseases in*

General Bibliography

Various Eastern Languages and a Copious List of Oriental Books Immediately Connected with General Science, etc. 2 vols. London, 1826.

Alcocer y Martinez, Mariano. *Catálogo razonado de obras impresas en Valladolid, 1481–1800.* Valladolid, 1926.

Ali, Salim. *The Book of Indian Birds.* 7th rev. ed. Bombay, 1964.

Alkira, W. H. *An Introduction to the Peoples and Cultures of Micronesia.* New York, 1973.

Almagià, Roberto. *Monumenta cartographica Vaticana.* 4 vols. Vatican City, 1944–55.

Alpers, Antony. *Legends of the South Seas: The World of the Polynesians Seen through Their Myths and Legends, Poetry, and Art.* New York, 1970.

Amat di San Filippo, Pietro. *Gli illustri viaggiatori italiani, con una antologia dei loro scritte. . . .* Rome, 1885.

Ambrosius à S. Theresia, O.C.D. *Hierarchia Carmelitana.* Rome, 1939.

André-Marie, [Father], O.P. *Missions Dominicaines dans l'Extreme Orient.* 2 vols. Paris, 1865.

Anthiaume, Albert. *Cartes marines, constructions navales: voyages de découverte chez les Normands, 1500–1650.* 2 vols. Paris, 1916.

Arnold, Dennis. *The New Oxford Companion to Music.* 2 vols. Oxford and New York, 1983.

Arveiller, Raymond. *Contribution à l'étude des termes de voyage en français (1505–1722).* Paris, 1963.

Asher, A. *Bibliographical Essay on the Collection of Voyages and Travels Edited and Published by Levinus Hulsius and His Successors at Nuremburg and Francfort from Anno 1598 to 1660.* Berlin, 1839.

Attman, Artur. *The Bullion Flow between Europe and the East, 1000–1750.* Göteborg, 1981.

Backer, Augustin de; Backer, Aloys de; Sommervogel, Carlos; Carayon, Auguste; and Bilard, Pierre. *Bibliothèque de la Compagnie de Jésus.* 12 vols. Louvain, 1960.

Baginsky, Paul Ben. *German Works Relating to America, 1493–1800.* New York, 1942.

Bagrow, Leo (Castner, H. W., ed.). *A History of the Cartography of Russia Up to 1600 and a History of Russian Cartography to 1800.* Ontario, 1975.

Baker, George Pierce. *Calico Painting and Printing in the East Indies in the Seventeenth and Eighteenth Centuries.* London, 1921.

Ball, J. D. *Things Chinese.* 5th ed. London, 1926.

Bamboat, Zenobia. *Les voyageurs français aux Indes aux XVIIe et XVIIIe siècles.* Paris, 1933.

Bangert, W. V. *A History of the Society of Jesus.* St. Louis, Mo., 1972.

Baranowski, Bondan. *Znajomosc Wscnodu w dawnej Polsce do XVIII wieku.* ("Knowledge of the East in Old Poland up to the Eighteenth century.") Lodz, 1950.

Barbosa Machado, D. *Bibliotheca Lusitania.* 4 vols. Lisbon, 1741–59. Reprinted, Coimbra, 1966–67.

Barnett, Lionel David, and Pope, G. *A Catalogue of the Tamil Books in the Library of the British Museum.* London, 1909.

Baudet, Henri (Evenholt, Elizabeth, trans.). *Paradise on Earth*. New Haven, Conn., 1965.

Beauchamp, H. K. (trans. and ed.). *Hindu Manners, Customs, and Ceremonies by the Abbe J. A. Dubois*. 3d ed. Oxford, 1959.

Beckmann, Johann. *Litteratur der älteren Reisebeschreibungen*. 2 vols. Göttingen, 1808–9.

Bedini, S. A. "The Secret of Time: A Study of the Use of Fire and Incense for Time Measurement in Oriental Countries," *Transactions of the American Philosophical Society*, n.s., LIII (1963), 1–51.

Berlin, Japan-Institut. *Bibliographischer Alt-Japan-Katalog, 1542–1853*. Kyoto, 1940.

Bierens de Haan, David. *Bibliographie néerlandaise historique-scientifique des ouvrages importants dont les auteurs sont nés aux 16e, 17e et 18e siècles, sur les sciences mathématiques et physiques. . . .* Nieuwkoop, 1960.

Borchling, Conrad, and Claussen, Bruno. *Niederdeutsche Bibliographie; Gesamtverzeichnis der niederdeutschen Drucke bis zum Jahre 1800. . . .* 2 vols. Neumünster, 1931–36. (Vol. II, *1601–1800*.)

Boulnois, Luce. *The Silk Road*. (Translated from the French.) London, 1966.

Boxer, Charles R. "A Glimpse of the Goa Archives," *Bulletin of the School of Oriental and African Studies* (London), June, 1952, pp. 299–324.

――――. *Race Relations in the Portuguese Colonial Empire, 1415–1825*. Oxford, 1963.

――――. *The Dutch Seaborne Empire: 1600–1800*. New York, 1965.

――――. *The Portuguese Seaborne Empire, 1415–1825*. London, 1969.

――――. *Exotic Printing and the Expansion of Europe*. Bloomington, Ind., 1972.

――――. *The Church Militant and Iberian Expansion, 1440–1770*. Baltimore, Md., 1978.

Brébion, Antoine. *Bibliographie des voyages dans l'Indochine française du IXe au XIXe siècle*. Reprint of 1910 edition. New York, 1970.

Brown, C. J. *The Coins of India*. Calcutta, 1922.

Brown, Percy. *Indian Painting under the Mughals A.D. 1550 to A.D. 1750*. Oxford, 1924.

――――. *Indian Architecture (Buddhist and Hindu Periods)*. 5th ed. Bombay, 1965.

Bruijn, Caspar Adam Laurens van Troostenburg de. *Biographisch woordenboek van Oost-Indische predikanten*. Nijmegen, 1893.

Burkill, I. H. *A Dictionary of the Economic Products of the Malay Peninsula*. 2 vols. London, 1935.

Burney, J. *A Chronological History of the Discoveries in the South Seas or Pacific Ocean*. 5 vols. London, 1803–17.

Bushan, Jamila B. *The Costumes and Textiles of India*. Bombay, 1958.

Buzeta, Manuel, and Bravo, Felipe (eds.). *Diccionario geográfico, estádistico, histórico de las islas Filipinas*. 2 vols. Madrid, 1850–51.

Camara Manuel, Jeromynio P. A. *Missões dos Jesuitas no Oriente nos seculos XVI e XVII*. Lisbon, 1894.

The Cambridge History of Islam. Edited by P. M. Holt, Ann K. S. Lambton, and Bernard Lewis. 2 vols. Cambridge, 1970.

Camus, A. C. *Mémoire sur la collection des Grands et Petits Voyages et sur la collection des voyages de Melchisedec Thévenot.* Paris, 1802.

Castellani, Carlo (comp.). *Catalogo ragionato delle più rare o più importanti opere geografiche a stampa che si conservano nella Biblioteca del Collegio Romano.* Rome, 1876.

Castro, Augustin María de. *Misioneros augustinos en el extremo oriente, 1565–1780 (Osario venerable). Ed., introd. y notas por el P. Manuel Merino.* Madrid, 1954.

The Catholic Encyclopedia. 15 vols. New York, 1913–22.

Chakravarty, I. *Saga of Indian Food; A Historical and Cultural Survey.* New Delhi, 1972.

Chatterton, Edward R. *Sailing Ships, The Story of Their Development from the Earliest Times to the Present Day.* Philadelphia, 1909.

Chaudhuri, K. N. *Trade and Civilisation in the Indian Ocean.* Cambridge, 1985.

Chijs, J. A. van der. *Proeve eener Nederlandsch-Indische bibliographie (1659–1870).* Batavia, 1875.

Chulalongkorn University (Bangkok). *Bibliography of Material about Thailand in Western Languages.* Bangkok, 1960.

Cidade, Hernani; Baião, A.; and Murias, M. *História da expansão portuguesa no mundo.* 3 vols. Lisbon, 1937–40.

Cipolla, Carlo M. (ed.). *Guns, Sails, and Empire.* New York, 1965.

———. *Fontana Economic History of Europe.* Vol. II. *The Sixteenth and Seventeenth Centuries.* London, 1977.

Clair, Colin. *A History of European Printing.* London, 1976.

Coats, Alice M. *The Plant Hunters; Being a History of the Horticultural Pioneers, Their Quests, and Their Discoveries from the Renaissance to the Twentieth Century.* New York, 1970.

Coedès, G. *The Making of South East Asia.* Berkeley and Los Angeles, 1967.

Conlon, Pierre M. *Prélude au siècle des lumières en France. Répertoire chronologique de 1680 à 1715.* 6 vols. Geneva, 1970–75.

Coolhaas, W. Ph. *A Critical Survey of Studies on Dutch Colonial History.* The Hague, 1960.

Corbett, M., and Norton, M. *Engraving in England in the Sixteenth and Seventeenth Centuries.* Cambridge, 1964.

Cordier, Henri. *Bibliographie des ouvrages relatifs à l'île Formose.* Chartres, 1893.

———. *Bibliotheca indosinica; dictionnaire bibliographique des ouvrages relatifs à la péninsula indochinoise.* 5 vols. bound in 3. Paris, 1912–32.

———. *Bibliotheca japonica.* Paris, 1912.

———. *Bibliotheca sinica.* 2d ed. 6 vols. New York, 1968. Also see Yuan Tung-li for continuation.

Correia, Alberto Carlos German da Silva. *História da colonização portuguesa na India.* 5 vols. Lisbon, 1948–54.

Correia-Afonso, John, S.J. *Jesuit Letters and Indian History, 1542–1773.* 2d rev. ed. Oxford, 1969.

Cortazzi, Hugh. *Isles of Gold, Antique Maps of Japan.* New York and Tokyo, 1983.

Cortesão, Armando, and Teixeira da Mota, Avelino. *Portugaliae monumenta cartographica.* 5 vols. Lisbon, 1960–62.

Costantini, C. *et al. Le missioni cattoliche e la cultura dell'Oriente.* Rome, 1943.

Couling, Samuel. *The Encyclopedia Sinica.* London, 1917.

Cowan, C. D., and Wolters, O. W. (eds.). *Southeast Asian History and Historiography: Essays Presented to D. G. E. Hall.* Ithaca, N.Y., 1976.

Cox, Edward Godfrey. *A Reference Guide to the Literature of Travel, Including Voyages, Geographical Descriptions, Adventures, Shipwrecks and Expeditions.* 3 vols. Seattle, 1935–49.

Cox, Evan H. M. *Planthunting in China; A History of Botanical Exploration in China and the Tibetan Marches.* London, 1945.

Crawfurd, John. *History of the Indian Archipelago. . . .* 3 vols. Edinburgh, 1820.

———. *A Descriptive Dictionary of the Indian Islands and Adjacent Countries.* London, 1856. Reprinted, Varanasi, 1974.

Cunningham, Sir Alexander (ed.). *Archaeological Survey of India.* 23 vols. Calcutta, 1871–87.

Curtin, Philip D. *Cross-Cultural Trade in World History.* Cambridge, 1984.

Dalgado, S. R. *Glossário Luso-Asiático.* 2 vols. Coimbra, 1919, 1921.

———. *Portuguese Vocables in Asiatic Languages.* Translated, revised, and augmented by A. X. Soares. Baroda, 1936.

Dalyrymple, A. *An Historical Collection of the Several Voyages and Discoveries in the South Pacific Ocean.* 2 vols. London, 1770–71.

Dam, Pieter Van. *Beschryvinge van de Oostindische Compagnie.* 5 vols. The Hague, 1927–43.

Daniélou, A. *Hindu Polytheism.* New York, 1964.

Danvers, Frederick Charles. *The Portuguese in India, Being a History of the Rise and Decline of Their Eastern Empire.* 2 vols. London, 1894.

Das, P. K. *The Monsoons.* New Delhi, 1968.

De Backer; *see* Backer.

Dehergne, Joseph, S.J. *Répertoire des Jésuites de Chine de 1552 à 1800.* Rome and Paris, 1973.

Desgraves, Louis. *Bibliographie bordelaise: Bibliographie des ouvrages imprimés à Bordeaux au XVIIe siècle.* Geneva, 1971.

Díaz, José Simón. *Impresos del siglo XVII.* Madrid, 1972.

Diehl, Katherine S. *Printers and Printing in the East Indies to 1850.* Projected to be 9 vols; Volume I on Batavia was issued in 1990.

Djambatan Uitgeversbedrijf, N.V., Amsterdam. *Atlas of South-east Asia.* London, 1964.

Dobby, Ernest H. G. *Southeast Asia.* 9th ed. London, 1966.

Dowson, John. *A Classical Dictionary of Hindu Mythology and Religion.* 8th ed. London, 1953.

Draeger, Donn F. *Weapons and Fighting Arts of the Indonesian Archipelago.* New York, 1972.

Dymock, William. *Pharmacographia Indica. A History of the Principal Drugs of Vegetable Origin, Met with in British India.* 2 vols. London, 1890–93.

Edwardes, Michael. *East-West Passage. The Travel of Ideas, Arts and Inventions between Asia and the Western World.* New York, 1971.

Eliade, Mircea (ed.). *The Encyclopedia of Religion.* 15 vols. New York, 1987.

Eliot, Sir Charles. *Hinduism and Buddhism. An Historical Sketch.* 3 vols. London, 1921. Reprinted 1954.

Embree, John F., and Dotson, L. O. *Bibliography of the Peoples and Cultures of Mainland Southeast Asia.* New Haven, 1950.

Encyclopaedie van Nederlandsch-Indië. 2d ed. 4 vols. The Hague, 1917–21.

Encyclopedia of Islam. See Gibb, H. A. R., *et al.*

Encyclopedia of Religion. See Eliade, M. (ed.).

Febvre, L., and Martin, H. J. *The Coming of the Book. The Impact of Printing, 1450–1800.* London, 1979.

Fergusson, J. *History of Indian and Eastern Architecture.* New York, 1899.

Ferrando, Juan, O. P. *Historia de los PP. Domenicos en las Islas Filipinos y en sus misiones del Japón, China, Tungkin, y Formosa.* 6 vols. Madrid, 1871–72.

Ferrero, Manuel (ed.). *Historia de la provincia del Santo Rosario de la orden de predicadores en Filipinas, Japón, y China.* 2 vols. Madrid, 1962–63.

Fischel, Walter J. *The Jews of India: Their Contribution to the Economic and Political Life from the Sixteenth Century On.* Jerusalem, 1960.

Flückiger, F. A., and Hanbury, Daniel. *Pharmacographia. A History of the Principal Drugs of Vegetable Origin Met with in Great Britain and British India.* London, 1879.

Furber, Holden. *Rival Empires of Trade in the Orient, 1600–1800.* Minneapolis, 1976.

Gallardo, Bartolomé José. *Ensayo de una biblioteca española de libros raros y curiosos.* 4 vols. Madrid, 1863–89.

Gardiner, J. S. *The Fauna and Geography of the Maldive and Laccadive Archipelagos.* 2 vols. Cambridge, 1903.

Gensichen, Hans-Werner. *Missionengeschichte der neuern Zeit.* 3d rev. ed. Göttingen, 1976. In series: "Die Kirche in ihrer Geschichte," ed. by Bernd Moeller, Vol. IV.

Gibb, H. A. R.; Kramers, J. M.; *et al. The Encyclopaedia of Islam.* 5 vols. Leyden, 1960.

Goedertier, Joseph M. *A Dictionary of Japanese History.* Tokyo and New York, 1968.

Goldsmith, V. F. *A Short Title Catalogue of French Books 1601–1700 in the Library of the British Museum.* Folkestone and London, 1973.

———. *A Short-Title Catalogue of Spanish and Portuguese Books 1601–1700 in the Library of the British Museum.* London, 1974.

Gole, Susan (comp.). *Early Maps of India.* New Delhi, 1976.

———. *A Series of Early Printed Maps of India in Facsimile.* New Delhi, 1980.

Gonçalves, José Julio. *Bibliografia dos descobrimentos e navegações existenta na Sociedade de Geografia de Lisboa.* Lisbon, 1954.

Goodrich, L. Carrington (ed.). *Dictionary of Ming Biography, 1368–1644.* 2 vols. New York, 1976.

Greenslade, S. L. (ed.). *The Cambridge History of the Bible.* Cambridge, 1963.

Grist, D. H. *Rice.* 3d ed. London, 1959.

Grothe, J. A. (ed.). *Archief voor de geschiedenis der oude hollandsche zending.* 6 vols. Utrecht, 1884–91.

Habib, Irfan. *An Atlas of the Mughal Empire.* Delhi, 1982.

Hall, D. G. E. (ed.). *A History of South-East Asia.* New York, 1955; London, 1964.

———. *Historians of South East Asia.* London and New York, 1961.

Hambye, E. R. *A Bibliography on Christianity in India.* Serampore, 1976.

Hargrave, Catherine P. *A History of Playing Cards.* Boston and New York, 1930.

Hart, Clive. *Kites. An Historical Survey.* Rev. 2d ed. New York, 1982.

Heawood, Edward. *A History of Geographical Discovery in the Seventeenth and Eighteenth Centuries.* Cambridge, 1912. Reprinted, New York, 1969.

Henry, Blanche. *British Botanical and Horticultural Literature before 1800 . . .* Vol. I. London, 1975.

Henry, G. M. *A Guide to the Birds of Ceylon.* London, 1955.

Herrmann, Albert. *An Historical Atlas of China.* Edited and augmented by Norton S. Ginsburg. Chicago, 1966.

Hind, A. M. *Engraving in England in the Sixteenth and Seventeenth Centuries.* Cambridge, 1955.

Howard, Alexander L. *A Manual of the Timbers of the World.* 3d ed. London, 1948.

Huber, Raphael. *A Documented History of the Franciscan Order.* Milwaukee, 1944.

Hucker, Charles O. *A Dictionary of Official Titles in Imperial China.* Stanford, 1985.

Hummel, A. W. (ed.). *Eminent Chinese of the Ch'ing Period (1644–1912).* 2 vols. Washington, D.C., 1943–44.

Hunter, Sir William Wilson. *Imperial Gazetteer of India.* 2d ed., 14 vols., London, 1885–87. New ed., 26 vols., Oxford, 1908–31.

Hyams, Edward S. *Plants in the Service of Man: Ten Thousand Years of Domestication.* Philadelphia, 1972.

Imperial Gazetteer of India; see Hunter, Sir William Wilson.

Jal, Auguste. *Glossaire nautique. Répertoire polyglotte de termes de marine anciens et modernes.* Paris, 1850.

Jann, P. Adelheim, O.M.C. *Die katholischen Missionen in Indien, China, und Japan. Ihre Organisation und das portugiesische Patronat von 15. bis im 18. Jahrhundert.* Paderhorn, 1915.

Janson, H. W. *Apes and Ape Lore in the Middle Ages and the Renaissance.* London, 1952.

Jedin, H., Latourette, K. S., and Martin, J. (eds.). *Atlas zur Kirchengeschichte.* Freiburg, 1970.

Keith, A. Berriedale. *A History of Sanskrit Literature.* London, 1920; reprint 1961.

Kemp, Peter (ed.). *The Oxford Companion to Ships and the Sea.* London, New York, and Melbourne, 1976.

Kennedy, Raymond. *Bibliography of Indonesian Peoples and Cultures*. 2d rev. ed. New Haven, 1962.

Kern, H. *Manual of Indian Buddhism*. Varanasi, 1968.

Kloosterboer, W. *Bibliografie van nederlandse publikaties over Portugal en zijn overzeese gebiedsdelen: taal, literatuur, geschiedenis, land en volk. . . .* Utrecht, 1957.

Koeman, Cornelis (comp. and ed.). *Atlantes Neerlandici. Bibliography of Terrestrial, Maritime and Celestial Atlases and Pilot Books Published in the Netherlands up to 1880.* Amsterdam, 1969.

Kondansha Encyclopedia of Japan. 9 vols. Tokyo and New York, 1983.

Konvitz, Josef W. *Cities and the Sea*. Baltimore, 1978.

Kratz, E. U. "The Journey to the Far East. Seventeenth- and Eighteenth-Century German Travel Books as a Source Study," *JRAS, Malaysian Branch*, Vol. LIV, No. 239, Pt. 1 (1981), pp. 65–81.

Krishnaswami, S. *Musical Instruments of India*. Delhi, 1965.

Kronk, Gary W. *Comets. A Descriptive Catalog*. Hillside, N.J., 1984.

Latourette, K. S. *A History of the Expansion of Christianity*. Vol. III: *Three Centuries of Advance A.D. 1500–A.D. 1800*. New York, 1939.

Launay, Adrien. *Atlas des missions de la Société des Missions-Étrangères*. Lille, 1890.

Laures, Johannes, S. J. *Kirishitan Bunko; a Manual of Books and Documents on the Early Christian Mission in Japan*. 3d ed. Tokyo, 1957.

Law, B. C. (ed.). *Mountains and Rivers of India*. Calcutta, 1968.

Leggett, William Ferguson. *The Story of Silk*. New York, 1949.

Lehner, Ernst, and Lehner, Johanna. *Folklore and Odysseys of Food and Medicinal Plants*. New York, 1962.

Leitão, Humberto. *Dicionário de linguagem de marinha antiga e actual*. Lisbon, 1963.

Le May, Reginald. *The Culture of Southeast Asia. The Heritage of India*. London, 1954.

Lenox, James. *The Voyages of Thévenot*. New York, 1879.

Liebert, Gosta. *Iconographic Dictionary of the Indian Religions: Hinduism-Buddhism-Jainism*. Leyden, 1976.

Lopes, David. *A expansão da lingua portuguesa no Oriente durante os seculos XVI, XVII, e XVIII*. Barcelos, 1936.

Loureiro, Joannis de. *Flora Cochinchinensis. . . .* 2 vols. London, 1790.

Lubac, Henri de. *La rencontre du bouddhisme et de l'occident*. Paris, 1952.

MacKinnon, J., and MacKinnon, K. *Animals of Asia*. New York, 1974.

Macmillan, H. F. *Tropical Planting and Gardening with Special Reference to Ceylon*. 5th ed. London, 1962.

Magalhães Godinho, Vitorino. *Os descobrimentos e a economia mundial*. 2 vols. Lisbon, 1963, 1971.

A Manual of Netherlands India (Dutch East Indies). Compiled by the Geographical Section of the Naval Intelligence Division, Naval Staff, Admiralty. London, 1921.

Marazzi, Ugo (ed.). *La conoscenza dell'Asia e dell'Africa in Italia nel secoli XVIII e XIX*. 2 vols. Naples, 1984.

Marcellino da Civezza. *Storia universale delle missioni Francescani.* 9 vols. in 11. Rome, 1857–95.

Maroni, Gaetano (ed.). *Dizonario di erudizione storica-ecclesiastica.* 102 vols. Venice, 1840–61.

Mason, John Brown, and Parish, H. Carroll. *Thailand Bibliography.* Gainesville, Fla., 1958.

Masson, Joseph. *Missionaires belges sous l'ancien régime (1500–1800).* Brussels, 1947.

Medina, José T. *Bibliografia española de las Islas Filipinas (1523–1810).* Santiago, Chile, 1897.

———. *La imprenta en Manila desde sus origines hasta 1810.* Santiago, Chile, 1904.

Meilink Roelofz, M. A. P. *Sources to the General State Archives in The Hague Relating to the History of East Asia between c. 1600 and c. 1800.* In "Felicitation Volumes of Southeast Asian Studies." Pt. I, pp. 107–84. Bangkok, 1965.

Menachery, George (ed.). *The St. Thomas Christian Encyclopedia of India.* 2 vols. to date (anticipated 3 vols.). Trichur, 1982.

Menninger, Edwin A. *Fantastic Trees.* New York, 1967.

Merriman, R. B. *The Rise of the Spanish Empire in the Old World and the New.* 4 vols. New York, 1918–34.

Miller, Roy Andrew. *The Japanese Language.* Chicago, 1967.

Misra, S. D. *Rivers of India.* New Delhi, 1970.

Mitter, Partha. *Much Maligned Monsters.* Oxford, 1977.

Molhuysen, Philip Christiaan. *Nieuw nederlandsch biografisch woordenboeck.* 10 vols. Leyden, 1911–37.

Mollat, Michel (ed.). *Sociétés et compagnies de commerce en Orient et dans l'Océan Indien.* Paris, 1970.

Montalban, J. *Manual de historia de las misiones.* Bilbao, 1952.

Mooij, Jacob. *Atlas der Protestantsche Kerk in Nederlandsch Oost-Indië.* Weltevreden, 1925.

Morisue, Yoshiaki, and Hinonishi, Suketaka (eds.). *Fūzoku Jiten* [Dictionary of Social Customs]. Tokyo, 1957.

Mousnier, Roland. *Les européens hors d'Europe de 1492 jusqu'à la fin du XVIIe siècle.* Paris, 1957.

Müllbauer, Maximilian. *Geschichte der katholischen Missionen in Ostindien von der Zeit Vasco da Gama's bis zur Mitte des 18. Jahrhunderts.* Freiburg im Breisgau, 1852.

Murray, Hugh. *Historical Account of Discoveries and Travel in Asia from the Earliest Times to the Present.* 3 vols. Edinburgh, 1820.

Murray, John (publisher). *A Handbook for Travellers in India and Pakistan, Burma and Ceylon. . . .* 18th ed. London, 1959.

Nakayama, Shigero, and Sivin, Nathan (comps.). *Chinese Science, Explorations of an Ancient Tradition.* Cambridge, Mass., 1973.

Needham, Joseph. *Science and Civilization in China.* 5 vols. Cambridge, 1954–85.

Neill, Stephen. *Christian Missions.* Harmondsworth, 1964.

———. *A History of Christianity in India. The Beginning to A.D. 1707.* Cambridge, 1984.

New Catholic Encyclopedia. 18 vols. New York, 1967–89.

Nihon Koguyo Daijiten [Unabridged Japanese Dictionary]. 20 vols. Tokyo, 1974.

Nunn, Godfrey Raymond. *South and Southeast Asia: A Bibliography of Bibliographies.* Honolulu, 1966.

———. *East Asia: A Bibliography of Bibliographies.* Honolulu, 1967.

Papinot, E. *Historical and Geographical Dictionary of Japan.* 2 vols. New York, 1968.

Parker, John. *Books to Build an Empire: A Bibliographical History of English Overseas Interests to 1620.* Amsterdam, 1965.

Patterson, Maureen L. P., and Alspaugh, W. J. *South Asian Civilizations. A Bibliographic Synthesis.* Chicago, 1981.

Peeters-Fontainas, Jean. *Bibliographie des impressions espagnols des Pays-Bas.* Louvain and Antwerp, 1933. 2 vols. in 1965 3d ed.

Penrose, Boies. *Travel and Discovery in the Renaissance, 1420–1620.* Cambridge, Mass., 1965.

Perquin, W. *et al. Bibliotheca catholica neerlandica impressa, 1500–1727.* The Hague, 1954.

Perry, Frances. *Flowers of the World.* London, 1972.

Pfister, Louis. *Notices biographiques et bibliographiques sur les Jésuites de l'ancienne mission de Chine, 1552–1773.* 2 vols. Shanghai, 1932.

Philips, C. H. (ed.). *Handbook of Oriental History.* London, 1951.

———. *Historians of India, Pakistan and Ceylon.* London and New York, 1961.

Picart, Bernard (comp. and ed.). *The Ceremonies of Religious Customs of the Various Nations of the Known World.* . . . 7 vols. in 6. London, 1733–39. Translated from French.

Polgar, Ladislaus, S. J. *Bibliography of the History of the Society of Jesus.* Rome and St. Louis, Mo., 1967.

Prater, S. H. *The Book of Indian Animals.* 2d ed. Bombay, 1965.

Pratt, James B. *The Pilgrimage of Buddhism.* New York, 1928.

Pruthi, J. S. *Spices and Condiments.* New Delhi, 1976.

Pullapilly, C. K., and Van Kley, E. J. (eds.). *Asia and the West. Encounters and Exchanges from the Age of Explorations.* Notre Dame, 1986.

Qaisar, A. J. *The Indian Response to European Technology and Culture, A.D. 1498–1707.* Delhi, 1982.

Quinn, D. B. (ed.). *The Hakluyt Handbook.* 2 vols. London, 1974.

Ramunny, Murkot. *Laccadive, Minicoy and Amindivi Islands.* New Delhi, 1972.

Ray, Ram Kumar. *Encyclopedia of Yoga.* Varanasi, 1975.

Raychaudhuri, Tapan, and Habib, Irfan (eds.). *The Cambridge Economic History of India,* Vol. I, *c. 1200–c. 1750.* New York, 1982.

Reid, Anthony (ed.). *Slavery, Bondage, and Dependency in Southeast Asia.* New York, 1983.

————. *Southeast Asia in the Age of Commerce, 1450–1680.* Vol. I. *The Lands below the Winds.* New Haven, Conn., 1988.

Reis, Beatrice, and Batalha, Cinatti. *Useful Plants in Portuguese Timor.* Coimbra, 1964.

Répertoire de bibliographie française, Fasc. 1–10. Paris, 1937–41.

Retana, W. E. (comp.). *Aparato bibliográfico de la historia general de Filipinas.* 3 vols. Madrid, 1906. Reprinted, Manila, 1964.

Ridley, Henry N. *Spices.* London, 1912.

Rodrigues, Francisco, S. J. *História da Companhia de Jesus na assistencia de Portugal.* 4 vols. in 2 parts. Porto, 1931–50.

Rodríguez Moniño, A. "Bibliografía hispano-oriental," *Boletín de la Real Academia de la Historia,* XCVIII (1931), 417–75.

Rogers, Francis (ed.). *Europe Informed.* Cambridge, Mass., 1966.

Rosengarten, Frederic, Jr. *The Book of Spices.* Philadelphia, 1969.

Rosenthal, Franz. *A History of Muslim Historiography.* Leyden, 1968.

Ross, E. Denison. *An Alphabetical List of the Feasts and Holidays of the Hindus and Mohammedans.* Calcutta, 1914.

Ruinen, W. *Overzicht van de literatuur betreffende de Molukken.* 2 vols. Amsterdam, 1928–35.

Satyaprakash, A. *Kerala, a Select Bibliography.* "Indian States Bibliographical Series," IX. Gurgaon, 1979.

Savage, Victor R. *Western Impressions of Nature and Landscapes in Southeast Asia.* Singapore, 1984.

Schauensee, R. M. de. *The Birds of China.* Washington, D.C., 1984.

Schmid, M. *Végétation du Viet-Nam.* Paris, 1974.

Scholberg, Henry, et al. *Bibliography of Goa and the Portuguese in India.* New Delhi, 1982.

Scholberg, Henry, and Divien, Emmanuel. *Bibliographie des français dans l'Inde.* Pondicherry, 1973.

Schütte, Josef Franz, S. J. "Wiederentdeckung des Makao Archives wichtige Bestände des alten Fernost-Archivs der Jesuiten, heute in Madrid," *AHSI,* XXX (1961), 90–124.

————. *El "Archivo del Japon," vicistudines del Archivo Jesuitico del Extremo Oriente y descripción del fondo existente en la Real Academia de la Historia de Madrid.* Madrid, 1964.

Schwartzberg, J. E. (ed.). *A Historical Atlas of South Asia.* Chicago, 1978.

Scott, J. George. *Burma: A Handbook of Practical Information.* London, 1911.

Silva, Daya de. *The Portuguese in Asia. An Annotated Bibliography . . . , 1498–c. 1800.* Zug, Switzerland, 1987.

Silva, S. F. *A Regional Geography of Ceylon.* Colombo, 1954.

Silveira, Lúis. *Ensaio de iconografia das cidades portuguesas do ultramar.* Vol. III. *Ásia proxima e Ásia extrema.* Lisbon, n.d.

Singh, Gopal. *A Geography of India.* 2d ed. Delhi, 1976.

Sopher, David E. *The Sea Nomads. A Study Based on the Literature of the Maritime Boat People of Southeast Asia.* [Singapore], 1965.

Souza, G. B. "Portuguese Trade and Society in China and the South China Sea," *Itinerario,* Vol. III, No. 1 (1979), pp. 64–73.

Spate, O. H. K. *India and Pakistan: A General and Regional Geography.* London, 1954.

———. *The Spanish Lake.* Minneapolis, 1979.

Spiro, Melford E. *Buddhism and Society. A Great Tradition and Its Burmese Vicissitudes.* New York, 1970.

Srivastava, G. P. *History of Indian Pharmacy.* Calcutta, 1954.

Stephens, H. Morse, and Bolton, Herbert E. (eds.). *The Pacific Ocean in History.* New York, 1917.

Stoddard, T. L., *et al. Area Handbooks for the Indian Ocean Territories.* Washington, D.C., 1971.

Streit, Robert, *et al. Bibliotheca missionum.* 30 vols. Münster and Aachen, 1916–75.

Sudjatmoko (ed.). *An Introduction to Indonesian Historiography.* Ithaca, N.Y., 1965.

Szilas, L., S. J. *Xaveriana.* Lisbon, 1964.

Taylor, Clyde Romer Hughes. *A Pacific Bibliography.* Wellington, New Zealand, 1951.

Taylor, Norman. *Plant Drugs That Changed the World.* New York, 1965.

Tchemerzine, Avenir. *Bibliographie d'éditions originales et rares d'auteurs français des XVe, XVIe, et XVIIe siècles contenant environ 6,000 facsimiles de titres et du gravures.* 10 vols. Paris, 1927–33.

Ternaux-Compans, H. (comp.). *Bibliothèque asiatique et africaine, ou catalogue des ouvrages relatifs à l'Asie et à l'Afrique qui ont paru depuis la découverte de l'imprimerie jusqu'en 1700.* Reprint of Paris ed. of 1841: Amsterdam, 1968.

Tervanent, Guy de. *Attributes et symboles dans l'art profane, 1450–1600.* Geneva, 1958.

Thekkedath, Joseph. *History of Christianity in India.* 6 vols. Bangalore, 1982.

Thomas, Gertrude Z. *Richer than Spices.* New York, 1965.

Thrupp, G. A. *The History of Coaches.* London, 1877. Reprinted, Amsterdam, 1969.

Tiamson, Alfredo T. *Mindanao-Sulu Bibliography: A Preliminary Survey.* Davao City, 1970.

Tiele, Pieter Anton. *Bibliotheck van nederlandsche pamfletten . . . Eerste deel: 1500–1648.* Amsterdam, 1858.

———. *Mémoire bibliographique sur les journaux des navigateurs néerlandais réimprimés dans les collections de De Bry et de Hulsius, et dans les collections hollandaises du xviie siècle, et sur les anciennes éditions hollandaises des journaux de navigateurs étrangers; la plupart en la possession de Frederik Muller.* Amsterdam, 1960. (Reprint of 1869 edition; first published in 1867.)

———. *Nederlandsche bibliographie van land- en volkenkunde.* Amsterdam, 1884.

Tinto, Alberto. *Annali tipografici dei Tramezzino.* Venice, 1966.

Torres Lanzas, Pedro. *Relación description de los mapas, planos, etc., da Filipinas, existentes en el archivo general de Indias.* Madrid, 1897.

Trager, F. N. *Annotated Bibliography of Burma*. New Haven, 1956.

Tregear, T. R. *A Geography of China*. Chicago, 1965.

Trewartha, Glenn T. *The Earth's Problem Climates*. Madison, 1981.

Ukers, William H. *All about Tea*. 2 vols. New York, 1935.

Unger, Richard W. *Dutch Shipbuilding before 1800*. Assen, 1978.

Uphof, Johannes C. Th. *Dictionary of Economic Plants*. 2d ed. Brunswick, 1968.

Uriarte, José Eugenio de, S. J. *Catalogo razonado de obras anonimas y seudonimas de autores de la Compania de Jesus pertenecientes a la antigua asistencia española*. 5 vols. Madrid, 1904–1916.

Verwaltung der Staatlichen Schlösser und Gärten. *China und Europa: Chinaverständnis und Chinamode im 17. und 18. Jahrhundert*. (Catalog of the exhibition of 1973 held at the Schloss Charlottenburg, Berlin.)

Villiers, Alan. *The Indian Ocean*. London, 1952.

Vindel, Pedro. *Biblioteca oriental. Comprende 2.747 obras relativas à Filipinas, Japón, China y otras partes de Asia y Oceanía*. . . . 2 vols. in 1. Madrid, 1911–12.

Walckenaer, C. A. *Vies de plusieurs personnages célèbres des temps anciens et modernes*. 2 vols. Laon, 1830.

Walker, George Benjamin. *The Hindu World. An Encyclopedic Survey of Hinduism*. 2 vols. London, 1968.

Wall, Frank. *Ophidia Taprobanica, or the Snakes of Ceylon*. Colombo, 1921.

Waller, G. F. *Catalogus van nederlandsch en vlaamsch populaire boeken*. The Hague, 1936.

Wallerstein, Immanuel Maurice. *The Modern World System*. Vol. II. *Mercantilism and the Consolidation of the European World-Economy 1600–1750*. New York, 1980.

Walravens, H. *China illustrata. Das europäische Chinaverständnis im Spiegel des 16. bis 18. Jahrhunderts*. Wolfenbüttel, 1987.

Watt, Sir George. *A Dictionary of the Economic Products of India*. 7 vols. in 10. Calcutta, 1885–96; reprinted, Delhi, 1972.

Wernstedt, Frederick L., and Spencer, J. E. *The Philippine Island World. A Physical, Cultural, and Regional Geography*. Berkeley, 1967.

White, Thomas E. "Seventeenth-Century Spanish Sources on East Asia," unfinished Ph.D. diss., Dept. of History, Univ. of Chicago.

Whitfield, Danny J. *Historical and Cultural Dictionary of Vietnam*. Metuchen, N.J., 1976.

Wijnaendts van Resandt, Willem. *De gezaghebbers der Oost-Indische Compagnie op hare buiten-comptoiren in Azië*. Amsterdam, 1944.

Williams, L. F. R. *A Handbook for Travellers in India, Pakistan, Burma, and Ceylon*. 20th ed. London, 1965.

Wills, John E., Jr. "Advances and Archives in Early Sino-Western Relations: An Update," *Ch'ing-Shih Wen-T'i*, Vol. IV, No. 10 (1983), 87–105.

Winternitz, Moriz. *History of Sanskrit Literature*. Calcutta, 1927.

Wright, H. Nelson. *Catalogue of the Coins in the Indian Museum, Calcutta*. Vol. III, *Mughal Emperors of India*. Varanasi, 1972.

Yuan Tung-li. *China in Western Literature. A Continuation of Cordier's Bibliotheca Sinica.* New Haven, 1958.

Yule, Henry, and Burnell, A. C. *Hobson Jobson: A Glossary of Colloquial Anglo-Indian Words and Phrases, and of Kindred Terms, Etymological, Historical, Geographical, and Discursive.* New edition edited by William Crooke. Reprint of London, 1903 edition. New Delhi, 1968.

Zhou Xun and Gao Chunming. *Five Thousand Years of Chinese Costumes.* San Francisco, 1987.

Zimmer, Heinrich R. *Hindu Medicine.* Baltimore, 1948.

SOURCE MATERIALS

Abreu, Francisco de [pseudonym for Severim de Faria, Manuel]. *Relaçao universal do que sucedeu em Portugal e nas mais provincias do Ocidente e Oriente desde março de 625 até setembro de 625, desde março de 626 até agôsto de 627.* Evora, 1628.

Abreu Mousinho, Manuel de. *Breve discurso en que se cuento la conquista del Reyno de Pegu . . . hecha por los Portugueses desde el año de mil y seyscientos, hasta el de 1603. Siendo Capitan Salvador Ribera de Soza, natural de Guimaraés, a quien los naturales de Pegu eligieron por su Rey.* Lisbon, 1617.

———. *Breve discurso em que se conta a conquista do reino de Pegu.* Edited by M. Lopes d'Almeida. Barcelos, 1936.

Acta Audientiae Publicae. Rome, 1615.

Adams, William. "William Adams, His Voyage by the Magellan Straights to Japon, Written in Two Letters by Himselfe. . . ." *PP,* II, 326–47.

Aduarte, Diego. *Historia de la provincia del Santo Rosario de la orden de predicadores en Filipinas, Japon, y China.* Manila, 1640. (Ed. of 1693 reprinted in 2 vols., prepared by Manuel Ferrero, Madrid, 1962.)

———. *Relacion de los martires que ha hauido en Japon desde el año de 1626. hasta el de 28. en particular de seys de ellos de la religion de Sancto Domingo, dos sacerdotes Españoles, y quatro legos Iapones, collegida de algunas q han enuiado de alla a estas islas Philippinas algunos religiosos de differentes ordines. . . .* Manila, 1629.

Affair de la Chine. [Paris, 1700]. (Includes six different pamphlets on the Rites Controversy.)

Agostino, Francisco. *Breve racconti del viaggio di due religiosi Carmelitani scalzi al regno di Achien, nell' isole di Sumatra.* Rome, 1652.

Aguilar, Manuel Perusquets de (trans.); *see* Faria y Sousa, Manuel de.

Alegambe, Philippe. *Mortes illustres et gesta eorum de Societate Iesu. . . .* Rome, 1657.

Alexandre, Noel. *Apologie des Dominicains missionnaires de la Chine, ou Réponse au livre du Père Le Tellier Jésuite, intitulé, Défense des Nouveaux Chrétiens; Et l'éclaircissement du P. Le Gobien de la même Compagnie, sur les honneurs que les Chinois rendent à Confucius et aux morts.* Cologne, 1699.

———. *Conformité des ceremonies chinoises avec l'idolatrie Grecque et Romaine. Pour servir de confirmation à l'apologie des Dominicains missionnaires de la Chine. . . .* Cologne, 1700.

————. *Lettre d'un docteur de l'ordre de S. Dominique sur les ceremonies de la Chine.* Paris, 1700.

————. *Recueil des pièces des differens de Messieurs des Missions Etrangères et des religieux de l'Ordre de S. Dominique, touchant le culte qu'on rend à la Chine au philosophe Confucius.* Cologne, 1700.

Almeida, M. Lopes d' (ed.); *see* Abreu Mousinho, Manuel de.

Almeida, Manuel de. *Catéchisme, exemple et miracles, et trois volumes de sermons en langue concannique.* Goa, 1658.

Almeida, Miguel de. *Jardim dos Pastores.* 5 vols. Goa, 1658–59.

Amati, Scipione. *Historia del regno di Voxu del Giappone, dell' antichità, nobilità, e valore del suo re Idate Masamune.* Rome, 1615.

Les ambassades, et presents du Roy de Siam envoyez à l'excellence du prince Maurice. . . . Lyons 1608.

Amzalak, M. B. (ed.); *see* Gomez Solis, Duarte.

Andrade, Antonio de, S.J. *Novo descobrimento do Gram Cathayo ou reinos de Tibet.* Lisbon, 1626. (Modern Italian translation in Giuseppe M. Toscano, *La prima missione cattolica nel Tibet,* Parma, 1951.)

————. *O descobrimento do Tibet* . . . Ed. F. M. E. Pereira. Coimbra, 1921.

An Answer to the Committee of Seventeen; . . . London, n.d.

An Answer to the Hollanders Declaration Concerning the Occurents in the East India. London, 1622.

The Answer unto the Dutch Pamphlet made in Defense of the Unjust and Barbarous Proceedings against the English at Amboyna. London, 1624.

Anzi, Aurelio degli (pseudonym of Zani, Conte Valerio). *Il genio vagante.* Parma, 1691.

Apius, Martinus. "Verklaring van Martinus Apius van hetgeen hem en zijne medegevangenen van de vloot van Jacob van Neck in 1602 te Macao is overkomen." Edited by P. A. Tiele in *Bijdragen en mededeelingen van het Historisch Genootschap gevestigd te Utrecht,* VI (1883), 228–42.

Aranda, Gabriel de. *Vida y gloriosa muerta del V. padre Sebastian de Monroy . . . que murió dilatando la fe alanceado de los barbaros en las islas Mariannas.* Seville, 1690.

Archamone, Ignacio. *Ignacii Archamonis conciones per annum concannice composita.* Rachol, 1668.

Argensola, Bartolomé Leonardo de. *Conquista de las islas Malucas.* Madrid, 1609.

————. *The Discovery and Conquest of the Molucco and Philippine Islands.* Translated by John Stevens. London, 1708.

Arnold, Christoph (ed.); *see* Merklein, Johann Jacob.

Arthus, Gotthard. *Historia Indiae Orientalis ex variis auctoribus collecta.* . . . Cologne, 1608.

————. *Dialogues in the English and Malaiane Languages.* . . . Translated by Augustus Spalding. London, 1614.

Atáide, Dom António de (comp.). *Viagens do reino para a India e da India para o reino (1608–1612). Diarios de navecacão colligidos poro D. António de Ataíde no século*

XVII. With an introduction and notes by Humberto Leitão. 3 vols. Lisbon, 1957–58.

Avila, Francisco García de. *Para que se devan preferir todos los que huvieron servido en las Indias a su Majestad en conformidade de un decreto suyo*. Madrid, 1630.

Avisos del felix sucesso de las casas espirituales, y temporales en diversas provincias de la India, conquistas, y navegaciones de los Portugueses por los años 1620, y 1629. Lisbon, 1630.

Avity, Pierre d'. *Les estats, empires, et principautez du monde*. . . . Paris, 1614.

———. *Estates, Empires, and Principalities of the World*. . . . London, 1615.

Avril, Philippe, S. J. *Voyage en divers états d'Europe et d'Asie, entrepris pour découvrir un nouveau chemin à la Chine*. Paris, 1692.

Baeza, Pedro de. *Jesus Maria. Pedro de Baeza, vezino desta villa de Madrid. Dizo, q por V. Excel me mâdar hazer este memorial . . . de los Indias Orientales . . . y demas partes de la Mar del Sur*. n.p., 1608?

Baíkov, Fedor Isakovich. "Autre relation d'une ambassade du czar à l'empereur du Katay Bogdé l'an 1653, ecrite en Latin." In TR, Vol. V.

———. "Voyage d'un ambassadeur que le tzaar de Moscovie envoya à la Chine l'anée 1653. dont il est parlé dans la relation de voyage des ambassadeurs de la Compagnie Hollandoise à Pekin." In M. Thévenot, *Recueil de voyages*. . . . (English translation in *CV*, II, 547–51.)

Baldaeus, Philippus. *Naauwkeurige beschryvinge van Malabar en Choromandel, der zelver aangrenzende ryken, en het machtige eyland Ceylon*. . . . Amsterdam, 1672. (An abridged English translation first appeared in 1702.)

———. *A True and Exact Description of the Most Celebrated East India Coast of Malabar and Coromandel as also of the Isle of Ceylon*. . . . *CV* (1744–46 ed.), III, 509–793.

———. *Afgoderye der Oost-Indische heydenen door Philippus Baldaeus*. . . . Edited by A. J. de Jong. The Hague, 1917.

Baldinotti, Guiliano. "La relation sur le Tonkin du P. Baldinotti." *Bulletin de l'école française d'Extreme-Orient* (Hanoi), III (1903), 71–78. (Original published in 1629 in Jesuit letterbooks; see list, below.)

Ball, V., and Crooke, W. (eds.); *see* Tavernier, Jean Baptiste.

Bañuelos y Carrillo, Geronymo de. *Del estado de las Philippinas y conveniencias de ellas*. Mexico, 1638. (Original seems not to be extant. See TR (1696), Vol. I, Pt. 2. English translation of TR in BR, XXIX, 66–85.)

Barbosa, Duarte. *The Book of Duarte Barbosa*. Translated and edited by M. L. Dames. 2 vols. London, 1918, 1921.

Barbosa, Vicente. *Compêdio da relação, que veio da India o ano de 1691 a El-Rei Vosso Senhor D. Pedro II na nova missão dos clérigos regulares do Divina Providéncia na ilha de Borneu*. Lisbon, 1692.

Barbuda, Luys Coelho de. *Impresa militares de Lusitanos*. Lisbon, 1623.

Barreto, Francesco, S.J. *Relatione delle missione, e christianità che appartengono alla provincia di Malavar della Compagnia di Giesu*. . . . Rome, 1645.

Barrett, Ward (trans. and ed.). *Mission in the Marianas. An Account of Father Diego Luis de Sanvitores. 1669–1670*. Minneapolis, 1975.

Bartoli, Daniello. *Parte prima dell' historia della Compagnia di Giesu; L'Asia.* Rome, 1653.

——. *Giappone.* Rome, 1660.

——. *La Cina.* Rome, 1663.

Baudier, Michel. *Histoire de la cour du roy de la Chine.* Paris, 1624.

Beauchamp. *Relation du Sr. de Beauchamp.* Middelburg, 1689.

Beauclair, Inez de; *see* C. E. S.

Beaulieu, Augustin de. "Relation de l'estat présent du commerce des Hollandais et des Portugais dans les Indes Orientales. . . ." In TR (1666), Vol. II.

——. *Augustin de Beaulieu, sa navigation aux Indes orientales, 1616–1622.* Edited by Eugène Guénin. Paris, 1905.

Behr, Johann von der. *Diarium; oder Tage-Büch, über desjenige, so sich zeit einer neunjährigen Reise zu Wasser und Lande, meistentheils in Dienst der Vereinigten Geoctroyrten Niederländischen Ost Indischen Compagnie. . . .* Jena, 1668.

——. *Reise nach Java, Vorder-Indien, Persien und Ceylon 1641–1650. . . .* NR, Vol. IV. The Hague, 1930.

——; *see also* Raven-Hart, R.

Bergeron, Pierre. *Traicté de la navigation et des voyages de découvertes.* Paris, 1629.

——. *Relation des voyages en Tartarie.* Paris, 1634.

Bergeron, Pierre, and Coulon, Louis; *see* Le Blanc, Vincent.

Bernier, François. *Histoire de la dernière révolution des états du Gran Mogul.* 4 vols. Paris, 1670–71.

——. *Travels in the Mogul Empire, A.D. 1656–1668.* Edited by Archibald Constable. Rev. ed. Delhi, 1968. (This edition is based on the English translation of Irving Brock.)

Bernou, C. (ed.); *see* Magalhães, Gabriel de.

Berquen, Robert de. *Les merveilles des Indes Orientales et Occidentales. . . .* Paris, 1661.

Bertrand, Joseph. *La mission du Maduré, d'après des documents inédits.* 6 vols. Paris, 1847–54, 1865.

Best, Thomas. "A Journal of the Tenth Voyage to the East India, with Two Ships. . . ." PP, IV, 119–47.

——. *The Voyage of Thomas Best to the East Indies, 1612–1614.* Edited by Sir William Foster. "HS," 2d ser., LXXV. London, 1934.

Beyrlins, Jacob. *Reyss-Buch; das ist ein gantz schöne Beschreibung und Wegweyser etlicher Reysen durch gantz Teutschlandt, Polen, Siebenbürgen, Dennenmarck, Engeland, Hispanien, Frankreich, Italien, Sicilien, Egyptien, Indien, Ethiopien, und Türkey.* Strasbourg, 1606.

Biker, Judice, and Firmino, Julio (eds.). *Collecção de tratados e concertos de pazes que o Estado da India Portugueza fez com os Reis e Senhores com que teve relações nas partes da Asia e Africa Oriental.* 14 vols. Lisbon, 1881–87.

Blaeu, Johan. *Atlas major, sive cosmographia Blauiana, qua solum, salum, coelum, accuratissime describuntur.* 11 vols. Amsterdam, 1662.

——. *Le grand atlas. . . .* Amsterdam, 1663.

Blair, Emma H., and Robertson, James A. (eds.). *The Philippine Islands, 1493–1898.* 55 vols. Cleveland, 1903–9. Cited as BR.

Blanquet de La Haye, Jacob; *see* La Haye, Jacob Blanquet de.

B[loemaert], S[amuel]. "Discours ende ghelegentheyt van het eylandt Borneo, ende 't gene daer voor ghevallen is in 't Iaer 1609. . . ." *BV,* IIa. Appended to Verhoeff's voyage, pp. 98–107.

Bloody News of the East-Indies, Being a Relation and Perfect Abstract of the Barbarous Proceedings of the Dutch against the English at Amboyna. London, 1651.

Bobadilla, Diego De. *Relación de las gloriosas victorias de D. Sebastian Hurtado de Corcuera . . . en mar y tierra, contra Cuchil Curralat.* Mexico, 1638.

————. *Relations of the Glorious Victories against the Moros of Mindanao.* BR, XXIX, 86–101.

————. Spanish manuscript dealing with the Philippines, attributed to Bobadilla. Published in French translation in TR, Vol. I, Pt. 2 (1696), and in English in BR, XXIX, 277–311.

Bolling, Frederick. *Oost-Indiske Reise-bog hvor udi befattis hans Reise til Oost-Indien saa vel og endeel Platzers Beskrifvelse med en Andtall hedningers Ceremonier. . . .* Copenhagen, 1678.

————. "Friderici Bollingii, Oost-Indische reisboek . . . 1678, uit het Deensch vertaald door Mej. Joh. Visscher; met voorbericht en slotnoot van G. P. Rouffaer." *BTLV,* LXVIII (1913), 298–381.

Boncompagni-Ludovisi, Francesco. *Le prime due ambasciate dei Giapponesi a Roma, 1585–1615. Con nuovi documenti.* Rome, 1904.

Bontekoe, Willem Ysbrantszoon. *Journael ofte gedenckwaerdige beschrijvinghe vande Oost-Indische reyse van Willem Ysbrantsz. Bontekoe van Hoorn. . . .* Hoorn, 1646.

————. *Journalen van de gedenckwaerdige reijsen van Willem Ijsbrantsz. Bontekoe, 1618–1625.* Edited by G. J. Hoogewerff. "WLV," Vol. LIV. The Hague, 1952.

Bontius (Bondt), Jacob de. *Jac. Bontii, in indiis archiater, de medicina indorum libri IV.* Leyden, 1642.

————. "Historiae naturalis & medicae indiae orientalis, libri sex," appended to Willem Piso, *De indiae utriusque re naturali et medicae libri quatuordecim.* Amsterdam, 1658.

————. *An Account of the Diseases, Natural History and Medicines of the East Indies. . . .* London, 1769. (Reprinted in *Opuscula selecta Neerlandicorum de arte medica. . . ,* Vol. X, Amsterdam, 1931.)

Booy, Alfred de (ed.); *see* Caerden, Paulus van.

Bor, Levinus. *Amboinse oorlogen, door Arnold de Vlaming van Oudshoorn als superintendent, over d'oosterse gewesten oorlogaftig ten eind gebracht.* Delft, 1651.

Borges de Castro, Jose Ferreira, Visconde de. *Collecção dos tratados, convençoes, contratos e actos publicos celebrados entre a coroa de Portugal, e as mais potencias desde 1640 ate ao presente, . . .* 8 vols. Lisbon, 1856–58.

Borri, Cristoforo. *Relatione della nuova missione delle PP. della Compagnia di Giesu, al regno della Cocincina, scritta del Padre Christoforo Borri Milanese . . . che fù uno de primi ch' entrorone in detto Regno. . . .* Rome, 1631.

————. *Cochinchina, Containing Many Admirable Rarities and Singularities of That countrey,* . . . Translated by Robert Ashley. London, 1633. (Reprinted in 1970 by *Theatrum orbis terrarum* series, "The English Experience," No. CCXXIII.)

Bosmans, H. (ed.); *see* Rougement, François de.

Botero, Giovanni. *Delle relationi universali* . . . Rome, 1591–92.

————. *Relations of the Most Famous Kingdoms and Common-weales through the World.* . . . Translated by Robert Johnson. London, 1616.

Bourges, Jacques de. *Relation du voyage de M. l'Évêque de Beryte, par la Turquie, la Perse, les Indes, etc., jusqu'au royaume de Siam et autres lieux.* Paris, 1666.

Bourne, William. *A Regiment for the Sea, Containing Very Necessary Matters for All Sort of Seamen and Travellers . . . Whereunto is Added a Hidrographicall Discourse to go unto Cattay, Five Severall Wayes.* London, 1580.

Bouvet, Joachim. *L'estat présent de la Chine en figures.* Paris, 1697.

————. *Portrait historique de l'Empereur de la Chine.* Paris, 1697.

Boxer, C. R. (ed.). *Seventeenth Century Macao in Contemporary Documents and Illustrations.* Hong Kong, Kuala Lumpur, and Singapore, 1984.

———— (ed.); *see also* Caron, François, and Schouten, Joost.

Boym, Michael. *Sehr wehrte und angenehme newe Zeitung von der Bekehrung zum catholischen Glauben desz. jungen Königs in China und anderer furstl. Personen und von der Legation desz. Ehrw. P. Michaelis Bouyn der Societet Jesu priestern polnischer Nation zu ihrer Päbstl. Heyligkeit nach Rohm* . . . Augsburg, 1653.

————. *Briefe relation de la notable conversion des personnes royales & de l'estat de la religion Chrestienne en la Chine* . . . Paris, 1654.

————. *Flora sinensis, fructus floresque humillime porrigens.* . . . Vienna, 1656.

————. *Specimen medicinae sinicae, sive opuscula medica ad mentem sinensium,* . . . Edited by Andreas Cleyer. Frankfurt, 1682.

[————]. *Les secrets de la medécine des Chinois, consistant en la parfaite connoissance du pouls, envoyez de la Chine par un François, homme de grand mérite.* . . . Grenoble, 1671. (Apparently taken from Boym's manuscript "Medicus sinicus. . . .")

————. *Clavis medica ad chinarum doctrinam de pulsibus,* . . . in the *Miscellanea curiosa* . . . of the Academia Caesareo-Leopoldina Naturae Curiosorum. Nuremberg, 1686.

Brand, Adam. *Beschreibung der chinesischen Reise, welche vermittelst einer zaaris. Besandschaft durch dero Ambassadeur, Herrn Isbrand.* . . . Hamburg, 1698.

————. *A Journal of an Embassy from Their Majesties John and Peter Alexowitz, Emperors of Muscovy . . . into China.* . . . London, 1698.

Brandão, Lourenço. *Discurso sobre et susteno de las navegación de las armadas del reyno de Portugal.* . . . Madrid, 1622.

Bree, Jan Harmenszoon; *see* Warwijck, Wybrand van.

Brerewood, Edward. *Enquiries Touching the Diversity of Languages, and Religions through the Chiefe Parts of the World.* London, 1614.

Breve relazione del martyrio d'undeci religiosi dell' ordine de S. Domenico, sequato dell' Giappone nell' anno de 1618 e 1622. Rome, 1624.

Brewster, Francis. *Essays on Trade and Navigation.* London, 1695.

Broecke, Pieter van den. *Korte historiael ende journaelsche aenteyckeninghe . . . beneffens de beschrijvingh en afbeeldingh van verscheyden steden, op de custe van Indien, Persien, Arabien, en aen't Roode Meyr.* . . . Haarlem, 1634.

———. "Historische ende journaelsche aenteyckeningh. . . ." In *BV,* Vol. IIa.

———. *Pieter van den Broecke in Azië.* Edited by W. Ph. Coolhas. 2 vols. "WLV," LXII and LXIV. The Hague, 1962. (This is an edition of his manuscript journal, not published in the seventeenth century.)

———, and Pelsaert, Francisco. *A Contemporary Dutch Chronicle of Mughul India.* Edited by Brij Narain and Sri Ram Sharma. Calcutta, 1957.

Broekhuyzen, Gotfried (trans.); *see* Vairasse, Denis.

Brouwer, Hendrick. *Journael ende historis verhael van de reyse gedaen by oosten de Straet le Maire naer de custen van Chili.* . . . Amsterdam, 1646. (Includes a description of Hokkaido written by a participant in Martin Gerritszoon Vries' expedition of 1643.)

Brown, Arnold. "Briefe Extracts of a Journall of Arnold Brown, His Indian Voyage . . . in Five Yeeres Time to Bantam, Patanie, Japan, the Manillas, Macau, the Coast of China, With Other Indian Ports." *PP,* X, 499–507.

Brown, John. *A Brief Remonstrance of the Grand Grievances and Oppressions Suffered by Sir William Courten, and Sir Paul Pyndar, knts. Deceased.* . . . London, 1680.

Brune, Jean de la. *La morale de Confucius.* Amsterdam, 1688.

Brusoni, Girolamo. *Varie osservazioni sopra le Relazioni Universali de G. Botero.* [Venice, 1659].

Bruton, William. *Newes from the East Indies; or a Voyage to Bengalla.* . . . London, 1638.

Bry, Johann Theodor de, and Bry, Johann Israel de (comps.). *India orientalis.* 12 vols. Frankfurt, 1598–1628.

Burckhard, Christian. *Ost-Indianische Reisebeschreibung.* Halle und Leipzig, 1693.

[Burg, Pieter van der]. *Curieuse beschrijving van de gelegentheid, zeden, Godsdienst, en ommegang, van verscheyden Oost-Indische gewesten en machtige landschappen. En inzonderheid van Golconda en Pegu.* . . . Rotterdam, 1677.

B[urton], R[obert]. [Crouch, Nathaniel]. *A View of the English Acquisitions in Guiana and the East Indies.* . . . London, 1685.

C., *Histoire des ioyaux, et des . . . richesses de l'orient.* Genoa, 1667.

C. E. S. [Coyett, Frederick S.]. *'t Verwaerloosde Formosa, of waerachtig verhael, hoedanigh door verwaerloosinge der Nederlanders in Oost-Indien, het eylandt Formosa, van den Chinesen mandorijn ende zeerover Coxinga, overrompelt, vermeestert, ende ontweldight is geworden.* . . . Amsterdam, 1675.

———. *Neglected Formosa; A Translation from the Dutch of Frederick Coyett's 't Verwaerloosde Formosa.* Edited by Inez de Beauclair. San Francisco, 1975.

Cabaton, Antoine (ed.); *see* Quiroga de San Antonio, Gabriel.

——— (trans.); *see* Sevil, Pedro.

Cabreira, José. *Naufragio da não Belem.* Lisbon, 1636.

Caerden, Paulus van. "Kort verhael, ofte journael, . . ." In *BV,* Ib.

————. "Loffelijcke voyagie op Oost-Indien, met 8 schepen uyt Tessel gevaren int jaer 1606. . . ." In *BV*, IIa.

————. *De derde reis van de V. O. C. naar Oost-Indië onder het beleid van Admiraal Paulus van Caerden, uitgezeild in 1606*. Edited by A. de Booy. "WLV," LXX and LXXI. The Hague, 1968–70.

Caland, W. "Ziegenbalgs malabarisches Heidenthum herausgegeben und mit Indices versehen." *Verhandelingen der Koninklijke Akademie van Wetenschappen te Amsterdam*, Afd. Letterkunde. Nieuwe reeks, XXV, No. 3 (1926), pp. 1–291.

———— (ed.); *see* Roger, Abraham.

————, and Fokker, A. A. "Drie oude portugeesche verhandelingen over het hindoeisme." *Verhandelingen der Koninklijke Akademie van Wetenschappen te Amsterdam*, Afd. Letterkunde. Nieuwe reeks, XVI, No. 2 (1915), 1–216.

Cambut de Pontchateau, Sébastien J. *La morale pratique des Jésuites*. Paris, 1683.

Campbell, W. *Formosa under the Dutch*. London, 1903. (Includes translations of Candidius and of Pieter Nuyts' letter to the VOC.)

Candidius, George. "Discours ende cort verhael, van't eylant Formosa." *BV*, IIb. Appended to Van Rechteren's voyage, pp. 55–70.

Cannenburg, Willem Voorbeijtel (ed.); *see Journael vande nassausche vloot*. . . .

Capitoli della navigatione all' Indie orientale della Compagnia di Genova. Genoa, 1648.

Cardoso, Manoel Godinho. *Relaçam do naufrágio da Não Santiago e itinerario da gente que delle se salvou*. Lisbon, 1602.

Careri, Giovanni Francesco Gemelli. *Giro del mondo*. 6 vols. Naples, 1699–1700. (English translations in *CV*, Vol. IV, 1754, and in Sen, S. [ed].)

Carletti, Francesco. *Ragionamenti di Francesco Carletti Fiorentino sopra le cose da lui redute ne' suoi viaggi si dell' Indie Occidentali, e Orientali come d'altri paesi*. . . . Florence, 1701.

————. *My Voyage around the World by Francesco Carletti, a Sixteenth Century Florentine Merchant*. Translated by Herbert Weinstock. New York, 1964.

Carneiro, António de Mariz. *Regimento de pilotos e roteiro des navagçaoens da India oriental*. Lisbon, 1642.

Carneiro, Diego Gomes. *Historia da guerra dos Tartaros*. Lisbon, 1657.

Carolinus, D. Godefridus. *Het hedendaagsche heidendom, of beschrijving van de godtsdienst der heidenen*. Amsterdam, 1661.

Caron, François. *Beschrijvinghe van het machtigh coninckrijcke Japan vervattende den aert en eygenschappen van't landt, manieren der volckeren, als mede hare grouwelijcke wreedtheydt teghen de Roomsche Christenen gesteldt*. . . . Amsterdam, 1648.

————. "Beschrijvinghe van het machtigh coninckrijck Iapan, gestelt door Francoys Caron, directeur des compaignies negotie aldaer, ende met eenige aenteekeningen vermeerdert door Hendrik Hagenaer." *BV*, IIb. Appended to Hagenaer's voyage, pp. 134–75.

————. *Rechte beschryvinge van het machtigh koninghrijck van Iappan, bestaende in verscheyde vragen betreffende des selfs regiering, coophandel, maniere van leven, strenge justitie etc. voorgestelt door den Heer Philips Lucas, Directeur Generael wegens den Nederlandsen staet in India, ende door de Heer Francoys Caron, President over comp*.

ommeslach in Iappan, beantwoort inden Iare 1636. Welcke nu door den selven au-
theur oversien vermeerdert en uytgelaten is de fabuleuse aentekeningen van Hendrick
Hagenaer, soo dat nu alles met zijn voorige origineel komt te accorderen, en met kopere
figueren verrijckt. The Hague, 1661.

————, and Schouten, Joost. *A True Description of the Mighty Kingdoms of Japan and*
Siam. . . . Edited by C. R. Boxer. London, 1935.

Carré, Abbé. *Voyage aux Indes Orientales.* . . . 2 vols. Paris, 1699.

————. *The Travels of the Abbé Carré in India and the Near East, 1672 to 1674.* Translated and edited by Lady Fawcett and Sir Charles Fawcett. "HS," 2d ser.,
XCV–XCVII. London, 1947–48.

Cary, John. *A Discourse Concerning the East India Trade, Shewing it to be Unprofitable to*
the Kingdom of England. Being Taken out of an Essay on Trade; . . . To Which Are
Added Some Observations of Sir Jos. Child and of the Author of the Essay on Ways and
Means Relating to Trade. And Also a Copy of the French King's Decree, Concerning
Printed Callicoes. London, 1699. (First edition, without the appended essays,
London, 1696.)

Casteleyn, Pieter. *Vremde geschiedenissen in de konninckrijcken van Cambodia en*
Louwen-lant, in Oost-Indien, zedert den iare 1635. tot den iare 1644. aldaer voor-
gevallen. Mitsgaders de reyse der Nederlanders van Cambodia de Louse Rivier op, na
Wincjan, het hof van de Louse Majesteyt. . . . Haarlem, 1669. (Apparently based
on the journal of Geeraerd van Wusthof. Reprinted in H. P. N. Muller [ed.], *De*
Oost-Indische Compagnie in Cambodja en Laos ["WLV," XIII], The Hague, 1917,
pp. 1–54.)

Castro, Fernando Ulvia de. *Aphorismos y exemplos politicos, y militares. Sacados de la*
primera decada de Juan de Barros. Lisbon, 1621. (Extracts from the first of Barros'
Décadas da Ásia.)

Catalogue nouveau de toute sorte de livres françois . . . que se trouvent à Amsterdam.
Amsterdam, 1698.

Cayet, Pierre Victor Palma. *Chronologie septenaire de l'histoire de la paix entre les roys de*
France et d'Espagne . . . avec le succez de plusieurs navigations faicts aux Indes Orien-
tales. . . . Paris, 1605.

Cerqueira, Luis de. *Relatione delle gloriosa morte patita da sei Christiani Giaponesi.* . . .
Rome, 1607.

————. *Raccolta di relationi de' regni del Giappone.* . . . Venice, 1608.

[Chappuzeau, Samuel]. *Histoire des joyaux, et des principales richesses de l'orient & de*
l'occident. Geneva, 1665.

Chardin, Jean. *Journal du voyage du Chevalier Chardin en Pers et aux Indes Orientales.*
London, 1686.

Charmot, Nicolas (ed.). *Historia cultus Sinensium.* . . . Cologne, 1700.

Charpentier, François. *Discours d'un fidéle sujet du Roy touchant l'établissement d'une*
compagnie . . . pour le commerce des Indes Orientales. Paris, 1664.

Charpentier, Jarl (ed.); *see* Fenicio, Jacobo.

Chaumont, Alexandre de. *Relation de l'ambassade de Mr.* . . . *de Chaumont à la cour du*
Roi de Siam. Paris, 1686.

[Child, Sir Josiah]. *A Treatise; Wherein is Demonstrated I. That the East-India Trade is the Most National of all Foreign Trades* . . . *V. That the East India Trade is More Profitable and Necessary to the Kingdom of England, than to Any Other Kingdom or Nation in Europe.* London, 1681.

Chirino, Pedro. *Relación de las islas Filipinas i de lo que en ellas an trabaiado los padres de la Compañia de Jesús.* Rome, 1604.

[Choisy, François Timoléon, l'Abbé de]. *Journal ou suite du voyage de Siam. En forme des lettres familières fait en M.DC.LXXXV et M.DC.LXXXVI.* Amsterdam, 1687.

————. *Journal du voyage de Siam fait in 1685 et 1686.* Preface by Maurice Garçon. Paris, 1930.

Churchill, A., and Churchill, J. *A Collection of Voyages and Travels.* 4 vols., London, 1704; 6 vols., London, 1732. Cited as *CV* (1704 ed. unless otherwise specified).

Claeszoon, Cornelis. *Journael. ofte een Oost-Indische-reys-beschrijvinghe, ghedaen door Cornelis Claesz van Purmerendt.* . . . Amsterdam, 1651.

Clemens, Claudius (comp.). *Tablas chronologicos en que se contienen los sucessos eclesiasticos, y seculares de España, Africa, Indias Orientales, y Occidentales, desde . . . 1642, hasta . . . 1689 . . . por Vicente Joseph Miguel.* Valencia, 1689.

Cleyer, Andreas; *see* Boym, Michael.

Cocks, Richard. "Relation of Master Richard Cockes, Cape Merchant, of What Past in the Generals Absence Going to the Emperours Court. . . ." *PP*, III, 519–70.

————. *Diary of Richard Cocks, Cape Merchant in the English Factory in Japan, 1615–1622, With Correspondence.* Edited by Edward Maunde Thompson. 2 vols. "HS," 2d ser., LXVI–LXVII. London, 1883.

Colección de documentos inéditos para la historia de España. 113 vols. Madrid, 1842–1912. (See Vol. LII [1868] on the Moluccas.)

Colenbrander, H. T. (ed.); *see* Vries, David Pieterszoon de.

Colin, Francisco. *Labor evangélica, ministerios apostolicos de los obreros de la Compañia de Iesus, fundacion, y progressos de su provincia en las islas Filipinas . . . Parte primera. Sacada de los manuscriptos del Padre Chirino, el primero de la compañia que passó de los reynos de España e estas islas,* . . . Madrid, 1663.

————. *Labor evangélica, ministerios apostolicos de los obreros de la Compañia de Iesus, fundacion, y progressos de su provincia en las islas Filipinas. Historiados por el padre Francisco Colin . . . Nueva ed. ilustrada con copia de notas y documentos para la critica de la historia general de la soberania de España en Filipinas. . . .* Edited by Pablo Pastells. Barcelona, 1904. (Also in I.D.C. microcards.)

————. *India sacra, hoc est, suppetiae sacrae ex ultraque India in Europam, pro interpretatione facili ac genuina quorundam locorum ex veteri Testamento qui adhuc Europaeos morantur interpretes; opus posthumum.* Madrid, 1666.

Collado, Diego. *Ars grammaticae japonicae linguae.* Rome, 1631.

————. *Modus confitendi et examinandi penitentum japonensem, formula suam et lingua japonica.* Rome, 1631.

————. *Dictionarium sive thesauri japonicae linguae compendium.* Rome, 1632.

————. "Mémorial présenté à Philippe IV. . . ." In *Annales de la Société des soi-disans Jesuits. . . ,* III, 1764.

Combés, Francisco. *Historia de las islas de Mindanao, Iolo, y sus adyacentes.* Madrid, 1667. Critical edition by W. E. Retana, Madrid, 1897.

Commelin, Isaac (ed.). *Begin ende voortgangh van de Vereenighde Nederlantsche Geoctroyeerde Oost-Indische Compagnie.* 2 vols. Amsterdam, 1645. Cited as *BV.* (Facsimile of the 1646 edition, with a separate introduction by C. R. Boxer, published by Facsimile Uitgaven Nederland in Amsterdam, 1969. Facsimile edition has volumes numbered I, II, III, and IV, corresponding to volumes Ia, Ib, IIa, IIb of the 1646 edition.)

Commelin, Jan, and Commelin, Caspar. *Horti medici Amstelodamensis rariorum . . . plantarum . . . descriptio et icones.* 2 vols. Amsterdam, 1697, 1701.

Conceiçam, Manoel da. *Sermão funeral do arcebispo de Goa, D. Fr. Aleixo de Menezes.* Lisbon, 1617.

Conceiçam, Nuno da. *Relaçam, successo e viagem . . . da capitainia N. senhora do Bom Despacho . . . vindo da India.* Lisbon, 1631.

Constable, Archibald (ed.); *see* Bernier, François.

Constituicoens do Arcebispado de Goa. Goa, 1649.

La conversion du plus grand roy; des Indes orientales a present regnat a la foy catholique, Avec six milles habitans de son royaume. . . . Bordeaux and Paris, 1621. (Reproduced in Ternaux-Compans, *Archives des voyages* [Paris, 1852], I, 173–79.)

Coolhas, W. Ph. (ed.); *see* Broecke, Pieter van den.

Cooper, Michael, S.J. (comp.). *They Came to Japan. An Anthology of European Reports on Japan, 1543–1640.* London, 1965.

Copeland, Master; Bonner, Robert; and Withington, Nicholas. "Certaine Observations Written by Others Employed in the Same Voyage, Master Copland Minister, Robert Bonner Master, Nicholas Withington Merchant." *PP,* IV, 147–75. (Accounts of the tenth English voyage under Thomas Best.)

Copia de una carta, escrita al Padre Fray Alonso Sandin . . . Procurador General de . . . Santo Rosario de Philipinas. . . . Madrid, 1684.

Copie de la requête presentée au roi d'Espagne par le capitaine Ferdinand de Quir, sur la descouverte de la cinquième partie du monde. . . . Paris, 1617.

Corneliszoon, Reyer. "Schip-vaerdt by de Hollanders ghedaen naer Oost-Indien, onder 't beleydt van den Admirael Iacob Heemskerk, in den Iare 1601. . . ." In *BV,* Ib, 26–31 of Steven van der Hagen's voyage.

Coronel, Fernando. *Memorial y relacion para su magestad, del Procurador General de la Filipinas, de lo que conviene remediar, y de la requeza que ay en relas, y en las Islas del Maluco.* Madrid, 1621. (See BR, XIX, 189–297, for a partial summary and translation.)

Correia, Duarte. *Relaçam do alevantamento de Ximabara.* Lisbon, 1643; reprinted, Alemquer, 1901.

Correia-Afonso, John, S.J. (ed.). *Letters from the Mughal Court.* Bombay, 1980.

Cortereal, João Pereira. *Discursos sobre la navigation de las nãos de la India de Portugal.* Madrid, 1622.

Cortés Osorio, Juan. *Memorial apologético de los missioneros de la China al conde de Villa Hombrosa.* Madrid, 1676.

————. *Reparos historiales apologéticos.* . . . Pamplona, 1677.

Coryate, Thomas. *Thomas Coriate Traveller for the English Wits: Greetings from the Court of the Great Mogul, Resident at the Towne of Asmere in Eastern India.* London, 1616.

————. *Mr. Thomas Coriat to his Friends in England Sendeth Greetings.* London, 1618.

————. "A Letter of Mr. Thomas Coryat, . . ." *PP*, IV, 469–94.

Couplet, Philippe. *Catalogus patrum Societatis Jesu, qui post obitum S. Francisci Xaverii primo saeculo sive ab anno 1581 usque ad 1681, in imperio sinarum Jesu Christi fidem propagarunt.* . . . Paris, 1686.

————. *Tabula chronologica monarchiae Sinicae* . . . *ad annum post Christum 1683.* Paris 1686.

————. *Histoire d'une dame chrétienne de la Chine, où par occasion les usages de ces peuples, l'etablissement de la religion, les manières des missionaires, & les exercises de pieté des nouveaux chrétiens sont expliquez.* Paris, 1688.

————, et al. *Confucius Sinarum philosophus, sive scientia sinensis latine exposita.* Paris, 1687.

Courten, Sir William. *Catastrophe and Adieu to the East-Indies, or a General and Particular protest Framed there at Goa in the Year 1644.* n.p., 1652.

Couto, Diogo do. *Da Ásia, Década IV.* Madrid, 1615.

————. *Da Ásia, Década VIII.* Revised by João Baptista Lavanha. Lisbon, 1673.

————. *The Tragic History of the Sea, 1589–1622.* Translated by C. R. Boxer ("HS," 2d ser., CXII), 53–104. Cambridge, 1959.

Coverte, Robert. *A True and Almost Incredible Report of an Englishman, that . . . Travelled by Land through Many Unknowne Kingdomes, and Great Cities; . . .* London, 1612.

Cowley, Ambrose. "Voyage Round the Globe." In William Hacke, *A Collection of Original Voyages.* . . . London, 1699.

Coyett, Frederick S.; *see* C. E. S.

Cramer, Mattys. *Borts voyagie naer de kuste van China en Formosa.* . . . Amsterdam, 1670.

Crasset, Jean. *Histoire de l'église du Japon.* 2 vols. Paris, 1689.

Crawther, John; *see* Steele, Richard.

Crocker, T. Croften; *see* La Boullaye Le Gouz, François de.

Crooke, W. (ed.); *see* Fryer, John.

Crouch, Nathaniel; *see* B[urton], R[obert].

Crus, Manoel de. *Fala, que fes O. P. Manoel de Crus* . . . *no acto solemne, emque o conde, Ioam de Silva, Tello y Meneses, Visorey* . . . *da India.* Goa, 1641.

Cruz, Extêvão da. *Discursos sobre a vida do apostolo s. Pedro em que se refutão os principaes errores do oriente compostos em verso, em lengua bramana.* . . . 2 vols. Goa, 1634.

Cruz, Miguel de (ed.); *see* Pereyra, Antonio Pinto.

Cubero, Sebastián Pedro. *Breve relacion, de la peregrinación que ha hecho de la mayor parte del mundo* . . . *con el viage por tierra desde España, hasta las Indias orientales.* . . . Madrid, 1680.

Cummins, J. S. (ed.); *see* Morga, Antonio de; Navarrete, Domingo Fernandez.

Dalquié, F. S. (trans.); *see* Kircher, Athanasius.

Dam, Pieter van. *Beschrijving van de Oostindische Compagnie.* Edited by F. W. Stapel. 3 vols. The Hague, 1927–43.

Dames, M. L. (trans. and ed.); *see* Barbosa, Duarte.

Dampier, William. *A New Voyage Round the World.* London, 1697.

———. *A New Voyage Round the World. With an Introduction by Sir Albert Gray.* Edited by Norman Mosley Penzer. London, 1927.

———. *Voyages and Descriptions.* London, 1699.

———. *Dampier's Voyages.* Edited by John Masefield. 2 vols. London, 1906.

———. *Voyages and Discoveries.* Edited by Clennell Wilkinson. London, 1931.

———. *A Voyage to New Holland, &c. in the Year, 1699.* London, 1703.

———. *A Voyage to New Holland, &c. in the Year, 1699; A Continuation of a Voyage to New Holland &c. in the Year 1699. . . .* London, 1709.

———. *A Voyage to New Holland; the English Voyage of Discovery to the South Seas in 1699.* Edited by James Spencer. Gloucester, 1981.

Dan, Pierre. *Le trésor des merveilles de la maison royale de Fontainebleau.* Paris, 1642.

Danckaerts, Sebastiaen. *Historische ende grondich verhael van de standt des Christendoms int quartier van Amboina. . . .* The Hague, 1621. (Reprinted in *BTLV*, n.s., Vol. VI, Pt. 2 [1859], pp. 105–36.)

Dapper, Olfert. *Gedenkwaerdig bedryf der Nederlandsche Oost-indische Maetschappye op de kuste en in het keizerrijk van Taising of China: . . .* 2 vols. Amsterdam, 1670.

———. *Asia, of naukeurige beschrijving van het rijk des grooten Mogols en de groot gedeelt van Indien: . . .* Amsterdam, 1672.

———. *Asia, oder: ausführliche Beschreibung des Reichs des Grossen Mogols und eines grossen Theils von Indien.* Nuremberg, 1681.

———; *see also* Montanus, Arnoldus.

D[arell], J. *Strange News from the Indies; or East India Passages Further Discovered. . . .* London, 1652.

———. *A True and Compendious Narration; or (Second Part of Amboyna) of Sundry Notorious or Remarkable Injuries, Insolences, and Acts of Hostility which the Hollanders have Exercised from Time to Time against the English Nation in the East Indies, &c. And Particularly of the Totall Plundering and Sinking of the Dragon & Catherine Both Ships and Men. . . .* London, 1665.

Dassié, F. *L'architecture navale, avec le routier des Indes orientales et occidentales.* Paris, 1677.

D'Avalo, Marcus. "Beschryvinge van de stadt Maccaon, ofte Maccauw, met haer fortressen, geschut, commercien, ende zeeden der inwoonderen, . . ." *BV*, IIb. In Van Rechteren's journal, pp. 78–86. English translation in C. R. Boxer (ed.), *Seventeenth Century Macao in Contemporary Documents and Illustrations.* Hong Kong, Kuala Lumpur, and Singapore, 1984, pp. 69–80.

Davies, John (trans.); *see* Olearius, Adam.

Davis, John. "The Voyage of Captain John Davis to Easterne India, Pilot in Dutch Ship, written by himself." *PP*, II, 305–26.

————. "The Second Voyage of John Davis with Sir Edward Michelbourne. . . ." *PP*, II, 347–66.

Davys, John. "The Ninth Voyage of the Indian Companie to the East Indies, in the James, whereof Was Captaine, Master Edmund Marlowe of Bristoll, and the Master, John Davy, Which Wrote This Journall." *PP*, IV, 77–87.

————. "A Rutter, or Briefe Direction for Readie Sayling into the East India. . . ." *PP*, IV, 88–119.

Decker, Adolph. *Diurnal der nassawischen Flotta oder Tagregister und historische ordentliche Beschreibung einer gewaltigen mächtigen Schiffarht umb die gantze Erd-Kugel rund umbher. . . .* Strasbourg, 1629.

De Feynes; *see* Feynes.

De Jong, A. J. (ed.); *see* Baldaeus, Philippus.

De Laet, Joannes (comp.); *see* Laet, Joannes de (comp.).

De La Haye, Jacob Blanquet; *see* Blanquet de La Haye, Jacob.

De l'Isle, Claude; *see* L'Isle, Claude de.

Della Valle, Pietro; *see* Valle, Pietro della.

Dellon, Gabriel. *Relation d'un voyage fait aux Indes Orientales.* 2 vols. Paris, 1685.

————. *Relation de l'Inquisition de Goa.* Leyden, 1687; Paris, 1688.

[Desfarges, Pierre]. *Relation des révolutions arrivées à Siam dans l'année 1688.* Paris and Amsterdam, 1691.

De Villiers, J. A. J. (trans.); *see* Spilbergen, Joris van.

De Vlamingh, Willem Hesselszoon; *see* Vlamingh, Willem Hesselszoon de.

De Vries, David Pieterszoon; *see* Vries, David Pieterszoon de.

Dharampal, Gita (trans.). "Heinrich von Poser's Travelogue of the Deccan," *Quarterly Journal of the Mythic Society*, LXXIII (1982), 103–14.

Diamper, Synod of. *Synodo diocesano da igreia e bispado de Anzamale dos antigos Christaõs de Sam Thome das serras do Malavar . . . da India Oriental.* 2 pts. Coimbra, 1606.

Dias, Manuel, the Younger. *Lettera del padre vicareo provinciale dell' ordine di Santo Agostino dell' India Orientale.* Rome, 1629.

Dichiaratione di una pietra antica scritta e scolpita con l'infrascritte lettere, ritrovata nel regno della Cina. Rome, 1631. (Probably the first notice about the discovery of the Nestorian Monument published in Europe.)

Dieckszoon, Reynier; *see* Dirckszoon, Reynier.

Diogo de Santa Anna. *Relaçam verdadeira do milagroso portento e portentoso milagre q aconteceo na India no santo Crucifixo, q esta no coro do observantissimo mosteiro das Freiras de S. Monica da Cidade de Goa, em oito de Fevereiro de 1636. & continuou por muitos dias. . . .* Lisbon, 1640.

Dirckszoon, Reynier. "Aenteeckeninghe uyt het journael ghehouden by Reynier Diecksz [*sic*] van Nimmegen, alias Kreijsman, voor stuerman gevaren hebbende op het jacht *de Leeuw met de Pijlen* naar Jappan, ende van daer weder t' huys, onder de vloote van den Admirael Pieter Willemsz Verhoef." *BV*, IIa. Appended to Verhoeff's voyage, pp. 68–72.

Dodsworth, Edward; *see* Elkington, Thomas.

Donneau de Visé, Jean. *Voyage des ambassadeurs de Siam en France.* 4 pts. Paris, 1686–87.

D'Orleans, Pierre Joseph. *Histoire des deux conquerans Tartares, qui ont subjugué la Chine.* . . . Paris, 1688. (Includes a copy of Ferdinand Verbiest's letters.)

————. *History of the Two Tartar Conquerors of China.* . . . Translated and edited by the Earl of Ellesmere. "HS," o.s., XVII. London, 1854.

————. *Histoire de M. Constance, premier ministre du roy de Siam et de la dernière revolution de cet état, dediée à N. S. P. le Pape Alexandre VIII.* Paris, 1690.

Downton, Nicholas. "Extracts of the Journall of Captaine Nicholas Downton, Who Was Employed Chiefe Commander in the Second Voyage Set Forth for the Joyned Stockes in the East Indies. . . ." *PP,* IV, 214–51. (Voyage of 1614–15.)

————. "Nicholas Downtaine Captaine of the Pepper-Corne . . . Sixth Voyage . . . His Journall, or Certaine Extracts Thereof." *PP,* III, 194–304.

————. *The Voyage of Nicholas Downton to the East Indies, 1614–1615.* Edited by Sir William Foster. "HS," 2d ser., LXXXII. London, 1939.

————; *see also* Pring, Martin.

Dryden, John. *Amboyna: A Tragedy As it is Acted by their Majesties Servants.* London, 1691.

Dudley, Robert. *Dell' Arcano del Mare.* 6 vols. Florence, 1646–47.

Du Jarric, Pierre, S.J. *Histoire des choses plus memorables advenues tant ez Indes Orientales.* . . . 3 vols. Bordeaux, 1608, 1610, 1614.

Duquesne-Guiton, Abraham. *Journal du voyage de Duquesne aux Indes Orientales, par un garde-marine servant sur son escadre.* Brussels, 1692.

E. G. *The Civil Wars of Bantam:* . . . London, 1683.

East Indian Trade, Selected Works, Seventeenth Century. London, 1968. (Facsimile reprints of pamphlets, including Thomas Mun and Charles Davenant.)

Elia, Pasquale M. d'. *Fonti Ricciane; documenti originali concernenti Matteo Ricci e la storia delle prime relazioni tra l'Europa e la Cina (1579–1615).* . . . 3 vols. Rome, 1942–49.

Elkington, Thomas, and Dodsworth, Edward. "Relations of Master Elkington and Master Dodsworth Touching the Former Voyage." *PP,* IV, 251–66. (Downton's voyage of 1614–15. See also Foster, Sir William [ed.].)

Ellesmere, Earl of; *see* D'Orléans, Pierre Joseph.

Encarnação, António da. *Relaçam de alguns serviços que fizerão a Deos e a estes reynos de Portugal, nas partes do oriente os religiosos da ordem dos prégadores:* . . . . In Encarnação and Rangel, *Relaçoes summárias.*

————. *Relaçam do principio da Christandade das ilhas de Solor, e da segunda restauração della, feita pellos religiosos da ordem dos prégadores.* In *Relaçoes summárias.*

————, and Rangel, Miguel. *Relaçoes summárias de alguns serviços que fizerão a Deos, e a estes reynos, os religiosos Dominicos nas partes da India Oriental nestes annos proximos passados.* Lisbon, 1635. (For a modern edition see Sá, Artur Basilio de [ed.], *Documentaçao,* V, 279–347.)

Engelbrecht, W. A., and Herwerden, P. J. (eds.); *see* Le Maire, Jacob.

Espinola, Juan de (trans.); *see* Suarez, Joseph, S.J.

Ezquerra, Domingo. *Arte de la lengua bisaya de la provincia de Leyte.* Manila, 1663.

F[arewell], C[hristopher]. *An East-India Colation, or a Discourse of Travels;* . . . London, 1633.

Fargeon, Jean. *Catalogue des marchandises rares, curieuses, et particulières . . . qui se font et debitent à Montpelier.* Pezenas, 1665.

Faria, Manuel Severim. *Discursos varios politicos.* Evora, 1624.

Faria y Sousa (also Faria e Souza), Manuel de. *Epitome de las historias portuguesas.* Madrid, 1628.

———. *Asia portuguesa.* 3 vols. Lisbon, 1666–75.

———. *The Portuguese Asia: Or, the History of the Discovery and Conquest of India by the Portuguese;* . . . Translated into an English abridgment by John Stevens. 2 vols. London, 1694–95.

———. *Asia portuguesa por Manuel de Faria e Sousa.* Translated by Manuel Perusquets de Aguilar. 6 vols. Porto, 1945–47.

——— (ed.); *see* Semedo, Alvarez.

Favery, Luc Fermanel de. *Relation des missions des evesques françois aux royaumes de Siam, de la Cochinchina, de Cambodge, et du Tonkin.* Paris, 1674.

Fawcett, Sir Charles, *et al.* (eds.); *see* Carré, Abbé.

Fayle, C. Ernest (ed.). *Voyages to the East Indies: Christopher Fryke and Christopher Schweitzer.* . . . London, 1929. (Translation of 1700 by S. L.)

Fenicio, Jacobo, S.J. *The Livro da seita dos Indios Orientais (Brit. Mus. Ms. Sloane 1820).* Ed. Jarl Charpentier. Uppsala, 1933.

Ferguson, D. (ed.); *see* Vennip, Cornelis Janszoon.

Fernandez, Pacita Guevara (trans.); *see* Ribadeneira, Marcelo de.

Fernandez Navarrete; *see* Navarrete, Domingo Fernandez.

Ferreira, Antonio Fialho. *Relaçam da viagem, que . . . [A.F.F.] fez . . . , deste Reyno à Cidade de Macao na China* . . . Lisbon, 1643. English translation in C. R. Boxer (ed.), *Seventeenth Century Macau in Contemporary Documents and Illustrations* (Hong Kong, Kuala Lumpur, and Singapore, 1984), pp. 87–126.

Ferreira, Manoel, S.J. *Noticias summárias das perseguições da missam de Cochinchina principiada & continuada pelos padres da companhia de Jesu.* . . . Lisbon, 1700.

Ferrero, Manuel (ed.); *see* Aduarte, Diego.

Ferro, Bartolomeo. *Istoria delle missioni de' cherici regolari Teatine.* 2 vols. Rome, 1705.

Feynes, Henri de. *An Exact and Curious Survey of the East Indies . . . by Monsier de Monfart.* Translated from the French manuscript into English. London, 1615.

———. *Voyage faict par terre depuis Paris iusques a la Chine. . . . Avec son retour par mer.* Paris, 1630.

Finch, William. "Observations of William Finch, Merchant, Taken out of His Large Journall." *PP,* IV, 1–77.

Fitzherbert, Humphrey. "A Pithy Description of the Chiefe Ilands of Banda and Moluccas. . . ." *PP,* V, 174–81.

Floris, Pieter. "Extracts of Peter Williamson Floris, His Journal for the Seventh Voyage. . . ." *PP*, III, 319–43.

———. *Peter Floris, His Voyage to the East Indies in the Globe, 1611–1615; the Contemporary Translation of His Journal.* . . . Edited by W. H. Moreland. "HS," 2d ser., LXXIV. London, 1934.

Fonseca, Henrique Quirino da. *Diários da navegação de Carreira da India nos annos de 1595, 1596, 1597, 1600, e 1603.* Lisbon, 1938. (Includes a collection of Portuguese rutters.)

Foster, William (ed.). *The Voyages of Sir James Lancaster to Brazil and the East Indies, 1591–1603.* "HS," 2d ser., Vol. LXXXV. London, 1940.

——— (ed.); *see also* Best, Thomas; Downton, Nicholas; Herbert, Thomas; Middleton, Henry; and Roe, Thomas.

France, Compagnie des Indes Orientales. *Articles et conditions sur lesquelles les marchands negotions du royaume supplient . . . le Roy . . . por l'établissement d'une compagnie . . . pour le commerce des Indes Orientales.* Paris, 1664.

Freire de Andrade, Jacinto. *Vida de dom João de Castro, quarto visorey da India.* Lisbon, 1651.

———. *Life of Dom John de Castro, Fourth Viceroy of India.* Translated by Sir Peter Wycke. London, 1664.

Freitas, Serafim de. *De iusto imperio lusitanorum asiatico.* Valladolid, 1625.

Freyre, Antonio. *Elogio do livro "primor e honra da vida soldatisca no estado da India."* Lisbon, 1630.

Frick, Christoph. *Ost-Indienische Räysen und Krieges-Dienste, oder eine ausführliche Beschreibung was sich zeit solcher nemlich von A. 1680 bis A. 1685 so zur See also zu Land, in öffentlichen Treffen und Scharmüzeln, in Belagerungen . . . mit ihme . . . hin und wieder begeben, Da den insonderheit der Bantamische Krieg auf Gross-Java un Anfang bis zu Ende Wahrhafftig vorgestellt und entworffen.* . . . Ulm, 1692. (English translation of 1700 in Fayle, C. Ernest [ed.].)

———; *see also* Raven-Hart, R.

Froger, François. *Relation du premier voyage des François à la Chine fait en 1698, 1699, et 1700 sur le vaisseau "l'Amphitrite."* Edited by E. A. Voretzsch. Leipzig, 1926.

Froideveaux, Henri (ed.). *Documents inédits relatifs à la constitution de la Compagnie des Indes Orientales de 1642.* Paris, 1898.

Fryer, John. *A New Account of East India and Persia, in Eight Letters, Being Nine Years Travels, Begun 1672, and Finished 1681.* . . . London, 1698.

———. *A New Account of East India and Persia* . . . Ed. W. Crooke. 3 vols. "HS," 2d ser., XIX, XX, and XXXIX. London, 1909–15.

A Full and True Relation of the Great and Wonderful Revolution that Happened Lately in the Kingdom of Siam in the East Indies. . . . London, 1690. (Reprinted in *CV*, VIII.)

G. M. A. W. L.; *see* Lodewyckszoon, Willem.

Gali, Francisco. *Viaje y descubrimientos y observaciones desde Acapulco a Filipinas.* . . . Amsterdam, 1638.

Gallagher, Louis J. (trans.); *see* Trigault, Nicolas.

García, Francisco. *Persecucion que movieron los Tartaros en el imperio de la China contra la ley de Iesu Christo, y sus predicadores; y lo sucedido desde el año de 1664 hasta el fin del año de 1668.* Alcalà, 1671.

————. *Vida del venerable P. Louis de Medina, muerto por la fe en las islas Marianas.* Madrid, 1673.

————. *Historia de la conversion de las Marianas que se llamaban de los Ladrones.* Madrid, 1683.

————. *Vida y martirio de el venerable padre Diego Luis de Sanvitores . . . apostol de las islas Marianas, y successos . . . desde . . . [1668] hasta [1681].* Madrid, 1683.

————. *Relacion de los successos de los missiones Marianas, desde el 25 de abril 1684 hasta el primeiro de mayo de 1685.* s.l., 1685.

Garcia, Juan. *Aviso que se ha embiado do . . . Manila, del estado que tiena la religion . . . en las Philipinas, Japon y . . . China.* Seville, 1633.

Gaspar dos Reys, Frey. *Commentarios do Grande Capitão Ruy Freyre de Andrade.* Lisbon, 1647.

Geddes, Michael. *The History of the Church of Malabar, from the Time of its being First Discovered by the Portuguese in the Year 1501 . . . Together with the Synod of Diamper . . . 1599. With Some Remarks upon the Faith and Doctrine of the Christians of St. Thomas of the Indies, Agreeing with the Church of England, in Opposition to that of Rome. . . .* London, 1694. (Includes the English translation of Antonio de Gouveia's *Synodo diocesam. . . .*)

Gemelli Careri, Giovanni Francesco; *see* Careri, Giovanni Francesco Gemelli.

Gerritszoon, Hessel (ed.). *Beschryvinghe vander Samoyeden landt in Tartarien. . . .* Amsterdam, 1612. (Contains the first publication of Massa's treatises.)

Gervaise, Nicolas. *Description historique du royaume de Macaçar.* Paris, 1688.

————. *Histoire naturelle et politique du royaume de Siam. . . .* Paris, 1688.

————. *An Historical Description of the Kingdom of Macassar in the East Indies.* London, 1701.

————. *The Natural and Political History of the Kingdom of Siam, A.D. 1688.* Translated by H. S. O'Neill. Bangkok, 1928.

Ghirardini, Giovanni. *Relation du voyage fait à la Chine sur le vaisseau l'Amphitrite en l'année 1698. . . .* Paris, 1700.

Ginnaro, Bernardino. *Saverio orientale ò vero istorie de' Cristiani illustri dell' oriente li quali nelle parti orientali sono stati chiari per vertù, e pietà cristiana, dall' anno 1542. . . .* Naples, 1641.

Glen, Jean Baptiste de (trans.). *La messe des anciens Chrestiens dicts de S. Thomas. . . .* Antwerp, 1609.

Godinho, Manoel, S.J. *Relação do novo caminho que fez por terra, e mar vindo da India para Portugal, no anno 1663. o padre Manoel Godinho. . . .* Lisbon, 1665.

————. *Relação do novo caminho que fêz por terra e mar, vindo da India para Portugal, no ano de 1663, o padre Manuel Godinho da Companhia de Jesus.* 2d ed., Lisbon, 1842. (Reprinted with an introduction by Augusto Reis Machado. Lisbon, 1944.)

Goens, Rijcklof Volckertszoon van. *Javaense reijse gedaen van Batavia over Samarangh na de koninncklijcke hoofdplaets Mataram, . . .* Dordrecht, 1666.

————. "Reijs beschrijving van den weg uit Samarangh nae de konincklijke hoofplaets Mataram. . . ." Edited by P. A. Leupe. *BTLV,* IV (1856), pp. 307–67.

————. *De vijf gezantschapsreizen van Rijkloff van Goens naar het hof van Mataram, 1648–1654.* Edited by H. J. de Graaf. "WLV," Vol. LIX. The Hague, 1956.

Gomes de Brito, Bernardo. *História tragico-maritima.* . . . 2 vols. Lisbon, 1735–36.

Gomez Solis, Duarte. *Discursos sobre los comercios de las dos Indias, donde se tratan materias importantes de estado, y guerra.* . . . [Madrid?], 1622.

————. *Discursos sobre los comercios de las dos Indias.* Edited by Moses Bensabat Amzalak. Lisbon, 1930.

————. *Alegación en favor de la Compañia de la India Oriental y comercios ultramarinos, que de nuevo se instituyó en el Reyno de Portugal.* [Lisbon], 1628. (Modern edition, edited by M. B. Amzalak, Lisbon, 1955.)

Gonçalves, Diogo, S.J. *Historia do Malavar.* Edited by Josef Wicki. Munster, 1955.

González, Domingo. *Relación del martirio del B. P. F. Alonso Navrrete, del la orden de predicadores, y de su compañero el B. P. F. Hernando de S. Joseph, de la orden de S. Agustin, en Japon. Año 1617.* . . . Manila, 1618.

González de Mendoza, Juan. *Historia de las cosas mas notables, ritos y costumbres del gran reyno de la China.* Rome, 1585.

————. *The History of the Great and Mighty Kingdom of China.* . . . Reprinted from the translation of R. Parke. Edited by Sir George T. Staunton. "HS," o.s., Vols. XIV–XV. 2 vols. London, 1853–54.

Gouvea, António de, O.S.A. *Iornada do Arcebispo de Goa Dom Frey Aleixo de Menezes primaz da India Oriental, . . . Quando foy as Serras do Malavar, & lugares em que morão os antigos Christãos de S. Thome, & os tirou de muytos erros & heregias em que estavão, & reduzio à nossa Sancta Fè Catholica, & obediencia da Santa Igrega Romana, da qual passava de mil annos que estavão apartados.* Coimbra, 1606.

————. *Synodo diocesam da igrega e bispado de Angamale dos antigos Christãos de Sam Thome.* Coimbra, 1606. (For English translation see Geddes, Michael.)

————. *Relaçam em que se tratem as guerras e grandes victorias que alcançou o grãde rey da Persia X'a Abbas do grão Turco Mahometto.* Lisbon, 1611.

Gouvea, António de, S.J. *Innocentia victrix.* . . . Canton, 1671.

Gouye (or Gouge), [Thomas], S.J. *Observations physiques et mathematiques à l'histoire naturelle et à la perfection de l'astronomie et de la géographie: Envoyées de Siam à l'Academie Royale des Sciences à Paris par les Pères Jésuites François qui vont à la Chine en qualité de Mathematiciens du Roy.* . . . Paris, 1688.

Graaf, H. J. de (ed.); see Goens, Ryckloff Volckertszoon van.

Graaf, Nikolaas de. *Oost-Indise spiegel, behelsende een beschrijving van de stad Batavia, en wijse van leven der hollandse vrouwen in Oost-Indien, een net verhaal der bysondere handelaars; alsmede de gewone wijse van de scheepsbevelhebberen, mitsgaders een generale beschrijvinge van gants Oost-Indien.* . . . Hoorn, 1701.

————. *Reisen van Nicolaus de Graaff na de vier gedeeltens des werelds, als Asia, Africa, America en Europa. Behelsende een beschryving van sijn 48 jarige reise . . . Als ook een nette, dog korte beschryvinge van China . . . Hier agter is by gevoegd d'Oost-Indise spiegel.* . . . Hoorn, 1701.

————. *Reisen van Nicolaus de Graaff, gedaan naar alle gewesten des werelds beginnende 1639 tot 1687 incluis.* . . . Edited by J. C. M. Warnsinck. "WLV," Vol. XXXIII. The Hague, 1930.

Grau y Monfalcón, Juan. *Memorial informatorio al rey nuestro señor en su real supremo Conseio de las Indias.* . . . Madrid, 1637.

————. *Justificación de la conservación, y comercio de las islas Filipinas.* Madrid, 1640?

Graves, Edward, *et al. A Brief Narrative and Deduction of the Several Remarkable Cases of Sir William Courten and Sir Paul Pyndar,* . . . *and William Courten,* . . . *Deceased: Together With Their Surviving Partners and Adventurers With Them to the East Indies, China, and Japan, and Divers other Parts of Asia, Europe, and Africa, and America;* . . . [London], 1679.

Gravius, Daniel. *Patar ki Tna'-'msing an ki Christang. Formos et Belge.* Amsterdam, 1661.

Gray, Albert; *see* Dampier, William.

Gray, Albert (trans. and ed.); *see* Pyrard, François.

Greslon, Adrien. *Histoire de la Chine sous la domination des Tartares.* . . . Paris, 1671.

Grey, Edward (ed.); *see* Valle, Pietro della.

Grueber, Johann. "Voyage à la Chine des P. P. Grueber & d'Orville, avec la relation du voyage par terre de ces meme peres depuis Pekin jusqu' en Europe, où il se trouve aussi des remarques curieuses sur la langue chinoise." TR, Vol. II, pt. iv, pp. 1–23. (Also included in Athanasius Kircher, *China illustrata.*)

Guénin, Eugène (ed.); *see* Beaulieu, Augustin de.

Guerreiro, Fernão. *Relaçam annual das cousas que fizeram os padres da Companhia de Jesus.* . . . 5 vols. Evora and Lisbon, 1603–11. (Title varies with each volume.) Complete Spanish translation, Madrid, 1613.

————. *Relação anual das coisas que fizeram os padres da Companhia de Jesus nas suas missões do Japão, China, Cataio, Tidore, Ternate, Amboino, Malaca, Pegu, Bengala, Bisnagá, Maduré, Costa da Rescaria, Manar, Ceilão. Travancor, Malabar, Sodomala, Goa, Salcete, Lahor, Diu, Etiopia.* . . . Edited by Artur Viegas. 3 vols. Coimbra, 1930–42. (This is a modern edition of *Relaçam annual.*)

————; *see also* Payne, C. H.

Guzman, Luis de. *Historia de las missiones* . . . *en la India Oriental y en los reynos de la China y Iapón.* 2 vols. Alcalá de Henares, 1601.

Gysbertszoon, Reyer. *De tyrannie ende wreedtheden der Jappanen.* . . . Amsterdam, 1637.

————. "Historie der martelaeren, die in Iapan om de Roomsche Catolijcke Religie schrickelijcke ende onverdraghelycke pynen geleeden hebben, ofte gedoodt zyn." *BV,* IIb. Appended to Hagenaer's voyage, pp. 176–88. (Included as an appendix to almost all editions and translations of Caron and Schouten.)

Hacke, William (ed.). *A Collection of Original Voyages: Containing I. Capt. Cowley's Voyage Around the Globe. II. Captain Sharp's Journey over the Isthmus of Darien, and Expedition into the South Seas, Written by Himself. III. Capt. Wood's Voyage thro' the Streights of Magellan. IV. Mr. Roberts's Adventures among the Corsairs of the Levant.* . . . London, 1699.

Haelbos, Hendrick. "Onbekende Zuid-land. . . ." In *De nieuwe en onbekende weer-eld . . .* , compiled by Arnoldus Montanus, pp. 577–85. Amsterdam, 1671. (The first published report of Tasman's discoveries.)

Haex, David. *Dictionarium Malaico-Latinum et Latino-Malaicum cum aliis quamplurimus quae quarta pagina edocebit. . . .* Rome, 1631.

Hagen, Steven van der. *Kort ende warachtich verhael vande heerlicke victorie te weghe gebracht. . . .* Rotterdam, 1606.

———. "Beschryvinge van de tweede voyagie, ghedaen met 12 schepen naer d'Oost-Indien onder den Heer Admirael Steven vander Hagen. . . ." *BV,* IIa.

———; *see also* Sas, Jan.

Hagenaer, Hendrick. "Verhael vande reysze gedaen inde meeste deelen van de Oost-Indien. . . ." *BV,* IIb.

Hakluyt, Richard. *The Principall Navigations, Voiages and Discoveries of the English Nation, Made by Sea and Overland.* 3 vols. London, 1598–1600.

Hamel, Hendrick. *Journael van de ongeluckige voyagie van't jacht de Sperwer. . . .* Amsterdam, 1668.

———. *The Dutch Come to Korea,* by Gari Ledyard. Seoul, 1971. (Contains a reprint of the Churchill translation of Hamel's *Journael.*)

———. *Verhaal van het vergaan van het jacht "De Sperwer" en van het wedervaren der schipbreukelingen op het eiland Quelpaert en het vasteland van Korea (1653–1666) met eene beschijving van dat rijk.* Edited by B. Hoetink. "WLV," Vol. XVIII. The Hague, 1920.

Happart, Gilbertus. *Dictionary of the Favorling Dialect of the Formosan Language, . . . Written in 1650.* Translated by W. H. Medhurst. Batavia, 1840.

Harmenszoon, Wolfert. "Journael, ofte dach-register vande voyagie, ghedaen onder het beleydt van den Admirael Wolfhart Harmansen. Naer de Oost-Indien, in-den iaren 1601. 1602. ende 1603. . . ." *BV,* Ib, 1–15.

Hartgers, Joost (comp.). *Oost-Indische voyagien door dien begin en voortgangh, van de Vereenighde Nederlandtsche Geoctroyeerde Oost-Indische Compagnie. . . .* Amsterdam, 1648.

Hatch, Arthur. "Letter Touching Japon with the Government, Affaires and Later Occurrents There. . . ." *PP,* X, 83–88.

Hatch, John. "Relations and Remembrances. . . ." *PP,* IV, 535–47.

Havart, Daniel. *Op- en ondergang van Cormandel . . . als mede de handel der Hollanders op Coromandel, met een beschrijving aller logien van de Compagnie op die landstreek; ook op- en ondergang der koningen, die zedert weynige jaren in Galconda . . . geregeerd hebben. . . .* 3 vols. Amsterdam, 1693.

Hawes, Roger. "Memorials Taken out of the Journall of Roger Hawes Touching . . . the Factorie at Cranganor. . . ." *PP,* IV, 495–502.

Hawkins, William. "Capt. William Hawkins His Relations of the Occurrents Which Happened in the Time of His Residence in India, in the Countrie of the Great Mogol. . . ." *PP,* III, 1–51.

Heemskerk, Jacob van; *see* Corneliszoon, Reyer; and West-Zanen, Willem Pieters-zoon van.

Heiden, Franz Janszoon van der. *Vervarlyke schip-breuk van't Oost-Indische jacht Ter Schelling onder het landt van Bengale; . . .* Amsterdam, 1675.

Herbert, Thomas. *A Relation of Some Yeares Travaile, Begunne Anno 1626. Into Afrique and the Greater Asia, Especially the Territories of the Persian Monarchie and Some Parts of the Oriental Indies and Isles Adjacent.* London, 1634.

————. *Thomas Herbert. Travels in Persia, 1627–1629.* Edited by Sir William Foster. New York, 1929.

Heredia, Manuel Godinho de. *Declaracam de Malaca e India meridional com o Cathay.* Goa, 1613. (English translation by J. V. Mills in *JRAS, Malay Branch,* VIII [1930], 1–227.)

Herport, Albrecht. *Eine kurtze ost-indianische Reiss-Beschreibung, . . .* Bern, 1669.

————. *Reise nach Java, Formosa, Vorder-Indien und Ceylon, 1659–1668. . . .* NR, Vol. V. The Hague, 1930.

————; *see also* Raven-Hart, R.

Herrera, Pedro de. *Confessionario en laengua Tagala.* Manila, 1636.

Herrera Maldonado, Francisco de. *Epitome historial del Reyno de la China, muerte de su Reyna, madre de este Rey que oy vive, que sucedio a treinta de Março, del ano de mil y seiscientos y diez y siete. . . .* Madrid 1620.

———— (trans.); *see* Pinto, Fernão Mendes.

Herrera y Tordesillas, Antonio de. *Descripcion de las Indias Occidentales. . . .* Madrid, 1601.

————. *Historia general de los hechos de los Castellanos en las islas i tierra firma del mar oceano.* 3 vols. Madrid, 1601–15.

Hertz, Solange (ed. and trans.); *see* Rhodes, Alexandre de.

Hesse, Elias. *Ost-Indische Reise-Beschreibung oder Diarium, was bey der Reise des chur-fürstl. Sächs. Raths und Berg-Comisarii D. Benjamin Olizschens im Jahr 1680 von Dresden aus biss in Asien auff die Insul Sumatra denckwürdiges vorgegangen auffge-zeichnet von Elias Hessen. . . .* 2d rev. ed., Leipzig, 1690.

————. *Gold-Bergwerke in Sumatra, 1680–1683. . . .* NR, Vol. X. The Hague, 1931.

Heurnius, Justus (ed.). *De vier Heylighe Evangelien . . . in de Maleysche tale ghe-steldt. . . .* [Amsterdam], 1651. (Translations by A. C. Ruyl, J. van Hasel, and J. Heurnius.)

————. *Jang ampat Evangelia derri Tuan kita Jesu Christi, Jang ampat Evangelia derri Tuan kita Jesu Christi, daan Berboatan derri jang apostoli bersacti bersalin dallam Bassa Malayo. That Is, The Four Gospels of our Lord Jesus Christ, and the Acts of the Holy Apostles, Translated into the Malayan Tongue.* Oxford, 1677.

Histoire de la persécution de deux saints évêques, par les Jésuites, l'un D. Bernardim de Car-dinas, l'autre D. Philippe Pardo, archévêque de Manille. n.p., 1691.

L'histoire de la vie et de la mort du Grand Mogor. [Paris, 1640?].

Hoetink, B. (ed.); *see* Hamel, Hendrick.

Hoffman, Johann Christian. *Oost-indianische Voyage; oder eigentliches Verzeichnüs worin nicht nur einige merckwürdige Vorfälle die sich Theils auff einer indische See-Reise, Theils in India selbst begeben und zugetragen. . . .* Cassel, 1680.

————. *Reise nach Kaplande, nach Mauritius, und nach Java, 1671–1676.* . . . NR, Vol. VII. The Hague, 1931.

Holland, J. *A Short Discourse on the Present Temper of the Nation with Respect to the Indian and African Company.* . . . Edinburgh, 1696.

The Hollanders Declaration of the Affairs of the East Indies, or a True Relation of that which Passed in the Islands of Banda. . . . Amsterdam, 1622.

Hollandtsche mercurius, verhalende de voornaemste saken van staet, en andere voorvallen, die in en omtrent de Vereenigde Nederlanden, en elders in Europe . . . zijn geschiet. 41 vols. Haarlem, 1678–91.

Hooge, Romein de. *Les Indes Orientales et Occidentales, et autres lieux; representée en très belles figures.* Leyden, 1680?

Hoogewerff, G. J. (ed.); *see* Bontekoe, Willem Ysbrantszoon.

Hore, William. "William Hores Discourse of His Voyage in the Dragon and Expedition, from Surat to Achen, Tico, and Bantam. . . ." *PP*, V, 64–86.

Houtman, Cornelis de; *see* Lodewyckszoon, Willem; and *Verhael vande reyse.*

Houtman, Frederick. *Spraeck ende woord-boeck, Maleysche ende Madagaskarsche.* . . . Amsterdam, 1603.

Hoyland, J. S. (trans.); *see* Laet, Joannes de.

Hulsius, Levinus (comp.). [*Sammlung von sechs und zwanzig Schiffahrten in verschiedene fremde Länder durch Levinus Hulsium und einige andere aus dem Holländischen ins Deutsche übersetzt und mit allerhand Anmerkungen versehen*]. 26 vols. Nuremberg, Frankfurt, and Hannover, 1598–1660. (There is no general title page for this work; it is usually catalogued under the above factitious title.)

Hussey, G. *Memorabilia Mundi; or Choice Memoirs of the History and Description of the World.* London, 1670.

Hyde, Thomas. *Epistola de mensures et ponderibus Serum seu Sinensium.* Oxford, 1688.

Ides, Evert Ysbrandszoon. *Driejaarige reize naar China, te lande gedaan door den Moscovischen afgezant. E. Ysbrants Ides . . . hier is bygevoegt eene beknopte beschryvinge van China, door eenen Chineeschen schryver t'zamengestelt; . . .* Amsterdam, 1704.

————. *Three Years Travels from Moscow Overland to China.* . . . London, 1706.

Ijzerman, J. W. *Dirck Gerritsz. Pomp alias Dirck Gerritz. China, de eerste Nederlander die China en Japan bezocht, 1544–1604.* "WLV," Vol. IX. The Hague, 1915.

———— (ed.); *see* Noort, Olivier van.

An Impartial Vindication of the English East India Company, from the Unjust and Slanderous Imputations Cast upon them in a Treatise Intituled, a Justification of the Directors of the Netherlands East India Company. . . . London, 1688.

Intorcetta, Prospero. *Compendiosa narratione dello stato della missione Cinese, cominciádo dall' anno 1581, fino al 1669.* Rome, 1672.

————. *Sinarum scientia politico-moralis, sive scientiae sinicae liber inter Confucii libros secundus.* . . . Paris, 1672.

————. *La science des Chinois ou le livre de Cum fu çu traduit mot pour mot de la langue Chinoise.* . . . Paris, 1673.

————. *Testimonium de cultu sinensi datum anno 1668.* Paris, 1700.

Iwao Seiichi (ed.); *see* Vliet, Jeremias van.

Jacobs, Hubert, S.J. (ed.). *Documenta Molucensia.* 3 vols. "Monumenta missionum Societatis Iesu," XXXII, XXXIX, XLIII. Rome, 1974, 1980, 1984.

Jacque de los Rios de Mancaned, Christoval de. *Voyages aux Indes orientales et occidentales.* . . . [Valladolid], 1606. (Reprinted in Ternaux-Compans (ed.), *Archives des voyages* . . . [Paris, 1840–44], Vol. I, pp. 241–350.)

Jang ampat Evangelia . . .; *see* Heurnius, Justus (ed.).

Janszoon, M. Barent. *Wijdtloopigh verhael van 'tgene de vijf schepen.* . . . Amsterdam, 1600. (Sebald de Weert's voyage.)

Jesuits. *Letters from Missions (The East); see* list below.

Jones, Thomas. "Relations of the Said Voyage. . . ." *PP,* III, 61–72. (Written by a survivor of the "Ascension," wrecked off Surat in 1609.)

Jong, Albert Johannes de (ed.); *see* Baldaeus, Philippus.

Journael vande nassausche vloot ofte beschryvingh vande voyagie om den gantschen aerdtkloot ghedaen met elf schepen: onder 't beleydt vanden Admirael Jaques l'Hermite, ende Vice-Admirael Geen Huygen Schapenham, inde jaeren 1623, 1624, 1625, en 1626. Amsterdam, 1626. (Also *BV,* IIb, 1–79. Modern edition: *De reis om de wereld van de nassausche vloot 1623–26,* edited by Willem Voorbeijtel Cannenburg [The Hague, 1964].)

Journael vande reyse der hollandtsche schepen ghedaen. . . . Middelburg, 1598.

Jovet, Jean. *L'histoire des religions de tous les royaumes.* 3 vols. Paris, 1676.

Junius, Robert. *Soulat i A.B.* . . . *Katechismus in formosanischer Sprache.* . . . Delft, 1645.

Keeling, William. "A Journal of the Third Voyage to the East India, Set out by the Company of Merchants Trading in Those Parts: in Which Voyage Were Employed Three Ships, viz. the Dragon, the Hector, and the Consent, . . ." *PP,* II, 502–49.

Kelly, Celsus (ed. and trans.). *Calendar of Documents: Spanish Voyages in the South Pacific* . . . *1517–1794.* Madrid, 1965.

————; *see* Quiros, Pedro Fernandes de.

Kerkhove, Iudocus van. *Nouvelles des choses qui se passent en diverses et loingtaines parties du monde.* Paris, 1607.

Kerr, Robert (ed.). *A General History and Collection of Voyages and Travels.* 2 vols. London, 1824.

Keuning, J. (ed.); *see* Neck, Jacob Corneliszoon van, and Warwijck, Wybrant van.

Khan, Sharfaat Ahmed (ed.). *John Marshall in India. Notes and Observations in Bengal, 1668–1672.* London, 1927.

Kircher, Athanasius. *Oedipus Aegyptiacus.* 3 vols. Rome, 1653.

————. *China monumentis, qua sacris qua profanis, nec non variis naturae & artis spectaculis, aliarumque rerum memorabilium argumentis illustrata.* . . . Amsterdam, 1667.

————. *La Chine illustrée de plusieurs monuments tant sacrés que profanes, et de quantité de recherches de la nature & de l'art.* . . . Translated by F. S. Dalquié. Amsterdam, 1670.

————. *China Illustrata by Kircher. Translated by Dr. Charles D. Van Tuyl from the 1677* [*sic*] *Original Latin Edition.* Muskogee, Okla., 1987.

Kirwitzer, Wenceslaus. *Observationes cometarum anni 1618 factae in India Orientale a quibusdam Soc. Jesu mathematicis in Sinense regnum navigantibus.* Aschaffenburg, 1621. (*Cf.* the description in G. W. Kronks, *Comets. A Descriptive Catalog* [Hillside, N.J., 1984], pp. 9–10.)

Knowlton, E. C., Jr.; *see* Sá de Meneses, Francisco de.

Knox, Robert. *An Historical Relation of the Island Ceylon in the East Indies: Together with an Account of the Detaining in Captivity of the Author and Divers other Englishmen Now Living There, and of the Author's Miraculous Escape.* London, 1681. (Modern critical edition of S. D. Saparamadu is in *The Ceylon Historical Journal,* Vol. VI [1956–57].)

"Kort beschrijvinghe van het eylandt by de Japanders Eso genaemt . . ." (written by a participant in Martin Gerritszoon Vries' expedition). Appended to Hendrick Brouwer's *Journael ende historis verhael* . . . (Amsterdam, 1646), pp. 95–104.

Krammer, Coenraet. "Verhael van de groote pracht die daer geschiedt, ende ghebruyckt is, op den feest gehouden inde stadt van Meaco, alwaer den Dayro, zijn keyserlijcke mayst. van Jappan quam besoecken, voor gevallen op den 20 October 1626. . . ." *BV,* IIb, 189–94. (Appended to almost all editions and translations of Caron's description of Japan.)

La Boullaye Le Gouz, François de. *Les voyages et observations . . . où sont décrites les religions, gouvernemens & situations des estats & royaumes d'Italie, Grece, Natolie, Syrie, Palestine, Karamenie, Kaldée, Assyrie, grand Mogol, Bijapour, Indes Orientales des Portugais, Arabie, Egypte, Hollande, grande Bretagne, Irlande, Dannemark, Pologne, isles & autres lieux d'Europe, Asie & Affrique, où il a séjourné. . . .* Paris, 1653.

————. *The Tour of the French Traveller M. de la Boullaye le Gouz in Ireland, A.D. 1644.* Ed. T. Croften Crocker. London, 1837.

Laet, Joannes de (comp.). *De imperio magni mogolis sive India vera commentarius e varijs auctoribus congestus.* Leyden, 1631.

————. *The Empire of the Great Mogol: a Translation of de Laet's "Description of India and a Fragment of Indian History."* Translated by J. S. Hoyland. Bombay, 1928.

La Haye, Jacob Blanquet de. *Journal du voyage des grandes Indes.* . . . Orleans, 1697.

La Loubère, Simon de. *Du royaume de Siam.* 2 vols. Paris, 1691.

————. *The Kingdom of Siam.* Introduction by David K. Wyatt. Kuala Lumpur, 1969. A reprint of the English translation published in 1693.

Lancaster, Sir James; *see A True and Large Discourse* . . . ; and *A Letter Written to the Right Worshipfull the Governours.* . . . *See also* Foster, William (ed.), *The Voyages of Sir James Lancaster.* . . .

Laneau, Louis. *Lettre de M. L'evesque de Metellopolis, Vicaire Apostolique de Siam au Supérieur et aux Directeurs du Séminaire des Missions-Etrangères étably à Paris.* . . . Paris, 1690.

The Last East-Indian Voyage . . . ; *see* Middleton, Sir Henry.

Le Blanc, Marcel, S.J. *Histoire de la révolution du royaume de Siam arrivée en l'année 1688.* . . . Lyon, 1692.

Le Blanc, Vincent. *Les voyages fameux du Sieur Vincent le Blanc, Marseillois.* . . . Edited by Pierre Bergeron and Louis Coulon. Paris, 1648.

―――. *The World Surveyed; or the Famous Voyages.* . . . Translated by F. B. London, 1660.

Le Comte, Louis, S.J. *Nouveaux mémoires sur l'état present de la Chine.* Paris, 1696.

―――. *Memoirs and Remarks . . . Made in Above Ten Years Travels through the Empire of China.* . . . London, 1738.

Ledyard, Gari; *see* Hamel, Hendrick.

Le Gobien, Charles, S.J. *Histoire de l'édit de l'empereur de la Chine en faveur de la religion chrestienne. Avec un éclairissement sur les honneurs que les Chinois rendent à Confucius & aux morts.* Paris, 1698.

―――. *Histoire des isles Marianas nouvellement converties à la religion chrestienne.* . . . Paris, 1700.

―――. *Lettre sur les progrez de la religion à la Chine.* n.p., [1697].

Le Gouz, Francois de la Boullaye; *see* La Boullaye Le Gouz, François de.

Le Maire, Jacob. *Spieghel der australische navigatie door den wijt vermaerden ende cloeck-moedighen zee-heldt, Iacob le Maire.* . . . Amsterdam, 1622.

―――. *De ontdekkingsreis van Jacob le Maire en Willem Cornelisz. Schouten in de jaren 1615–1617.* . . . Edited by W. A. Engelbrecht and P. J. Herwerden. "WLV," XLIX. 2 vols. The Hague, 1945.

Leon, Miguel de. *Breve relacion de la estampa en que estava pintada su santidad con los Cardenales y demas personages que asistieron a las ceremonias de la canonización de los Santos Isidro de Madrid, Ignacio de Loyola, Francisco Xavier, Teresa de Jesús y Felipe Neri.* Madrid, 1622.

―――. *Fiestas de Madrid, celebrados a XIX de Junio de 1622 años, en la canonización de San Isidro, S. Ignacio, S. Francisco Xavier.* . . . Madrid, 1622.

Leonardo y (or de) Argensola, B.; *see* Argensola.

Leon Pinelo, Antonio de. *Epitome de la biblioteca oriental i occidental, náutica i geografica.* Madrid, 1629.

L'Estra, François. *Relation ou journal d'un voyage fait aux Indes Orientales. Contenant l'état des affaires du pais et les établissements de plusieurs nations que s'y sont faits depuis quelques années.* Paris, 1677.

Le Tellier, Jean. *Voyage faict aux Indes Orientales.* . . . 3 pts. Dieppe, 1631.

Le Tellier, Michel. *Defense des nouveaux chrestiens et des missionaires de la Chine, du Japon, & des Indes. Contre deux livres intitulez La morale pratique des Jesuites et l'esprit de M. Arnauld.* Paris, 1687.

―――. *Lettre à monsieur docteur de Sorbonne, au sujet de la Révocation faite par m. l'abbé de Brisacier de son approbation donnée en 1687 au livre intitulé Defense des nouveaux chrestiens.* . . . [n.p.] 1700.

Letona, Bartolomé de, O.F.M. *Descripción de las islas Filippinas.* La Puebla, Mexico, 1662.

A Letter Written to the Right Worshipfull the Governours and Assistants of the East Indian Merchants in London. London, 1603. (On the first English East India Company voyage under Sir James Lancaster. *See also* Foster, William [ed.], *The Voyages of Sir James Lancaster.* . . .)

Lettre à monseigneur le duc de Mayne sur les cérémonies de la Chine. Paris, 1700.

Lettre écrite de la province de Fokien, dans la Chine, où l'on rapporte le cruel traitement que les chrétiens des jesuites ont fait souffrir à Maigrot et au R. P. Croquet. [n.p.], 1700.

Leupe, P. A. (ed.); *see* Goens, Rijklof Volkertszoon van.

L'Hermite, Jacques; *see Journal vande nassausche vloot.* . . .

L'Honoré Naber, Samuel Pierre (ed.). *Reisebeschreibungen von deutschen Beamten und Kriegsleuten im Dienst der Niederländischen West- und Ost-Indischen Kompagnien, 1602–1797.* 13 vols. The Hague, 1930–32. Cited as NR.

Libertinus, Karl. *Divus Franciscus Xaverius Indiarum apostolus elogiis illustratus.* Prague, 1673.

Linschoten, Jan Huygen van. *Reysgheschrift vande navigatien der Portugaloysers in orienten.* . . . Amsterdam, 1595.

———. *Itinerario, voyage ofte schipvaert.* . . . Amsterdam, 1596.

———. *Itinerario, voyage ofte schipvaert van Jan Huygen van Linschoten naer Oost ofte Portugaels Indien, 1579–1592.* Edited by H. Terpstra. 2d ed., 3 vols. "WLV," Vols. LVII, LVIII, and LX. The Hague, 1955–57.

———. *The Voyage of John Huyghen van Linschoten to the East Indies. From the Old English Translation of 1598.* Edited by Arthur Coke Burnell and P. A. Tiele. "HS," Vols. LXX and LXXI; 2 vols. London, 1885.

L'Isle, Claude de. *Relation historique du royaume de Siam.* Paris, 1684.

Liste de livres nouvellement imprimés en Hollande. . . . n.p., 1693.

Lodewyckszoon, Willem. *D'eerste boeck. Historie van Indien, waer inne verhaelt is de avontueren die de hollandtsche schepen bejeghent zijn.* . . . Amsterdam, 1598.

——— (G. M. A. W. L.). *Premier livre de la navigation aux Indes Orientales par les Hollandois . . . ; Le second livre, Iournal, ou Comptoir,* . . . Amsterdam, 1609. (2 books in one volume, separately paginated and with an appendix of Javan and Malay words with their French equivalents.)

———, *et al. De eerste schipvaart der Nederlanders naar Oost-Indië onder Cornelis de Houtman, 1595–1597.* Edited by G. P. Rouffaer, and J. W. Ijzerman, 3 vols. "WLV," VII, XXV, and XXXII. The Hague, 1915, 1925, 1929.

Logan, Josias. "The Voyage of Master Josias Logan to Pechora, and His Wintering There, with Master William Pursglove, and Marmaduke Wilson. Anno 1611." *PP,* XIII, 122–38.

Lord, Henry. *A Display of Two Forraigne Sects in the East Indies vizt: the Sect of the Banians the Ancient Natives of India and the Sect of the Persees the Ancient Inhabitants of Persia. Together with the Religion and Manners of Each Sect.* London, 1630.

Lualdi, Michelangelo. *L'India orientale, suggettata al vangelo.* . . . Rome, 1653.

Luard, C. E., and Hosten, H. (trans. and eds.); *see* Manrique, Sebastião.

Magalhães, Diego de. *La conversion de trois grands rois infidèles de la secte de Mahomet.* Rouen, 1608.

Magalhães, Gabriel de. *Nouvelle relation de la Chine, contenant la description des particularitez le plus considerables de ce grand empire.* Edited and translated from Portuguese into French by C. Bernou. Paris, 1688. (The Portuguese original was never published.)

―――. *A New History of China, Containing a Description of the Most Considerable Particulars of that Vast Empire.* . . . Translated from French by John Ogilby. London, 1688.

Magalhães, Sebastian de (trans.); *see* Rougemont, François de.

Magalotti, Lorenzo. *Notizie varie dell'imperio della China, e di qualche altro paese adiacente con la vita di Confucio, il gran savio della China, e un saggio della sua morale.* . . . Florence, 1697. *Also see* Couplet *et al., Confucius Sinarum.* . . .

Magdalena, Augustín de la. *Arte de la lengua Tagala, sacado de diversos artes.* Mexico, 1679.

Magistris, Giacinto de, S.J. *Relatione della Christianità di Maduré.* Rome, 1661.

―――. *Relation dernière de ce qui s'est passé dans les royaumes de Maduré, de Tangeor, et autres lieux voisins du Malabar aux Indes Orientales.* Paris, 1663.

Magnino, Leo (ed.). *Pontificia Nipponica. Le relazioni tra la Santa Sede e il Giappone attraverso i documenti pontifici.* Rome, 1947.

Maldonado, Francisco de Herrera; *see* Herrera Maldonado, Francisco de.

Maldonado, Miguel Rodriquez (comp.). *Relacion del levantamiento de los Sangleyes, nacion gentil, habitadores en las Islas Filipinas.* . . . Seville, 1606.

Maldonde, J. B. *Prodigieux événements de notre temps arrivés à des Portugais dans un voyage extremement dangereux du côté de la Chine.* Mons, 1693.

Mandelslo, Johann Albrecht von. *Schreiben von seiner ostindischen Reise an Ad. Olearius . . . mit etlichen Anmerkungen Ad. Olearii.* . . . Schleswig, 1645. *Also see* Olearius.

Manrique, Sebastião. *Itinerario de las missiones.* Rome, 1649.

―――. *Itinerário de Sebastião Manrique.* Edited by Luis Silveira. Lisbon 1946. (Reissue of the 1653 edition.)

―――. *Travels of Fray Sebastian Manrique, 1629–1643.* Translated with an introduction and notes by C. E. Luard and H. Hosten. "HS," 2d ser., LIX and LXI. Oxford, 1926–27.

Marini, Gian Filippo de, S.J. *Delle missioni de' padri della Compagnia di Giesu nella provincia del Giappone, e particolarmente di quella di Tumkinó, libri cinque.* Rome, 1663.

Markham, Clements (ed.); *see* Torquemada, Fray Juan de, O.F.M.; and Quiros, Pedro Fernandes de.

Marshall, John; *see* Khan, Sharfaat Ahmed.

Martin, Nathaniel. "The Seventh voyage . . . in the Globe . . . under Captain Anthonie Hippon. . . ." *PP,* III, 304–19.

Martin de Vitré, François. *Description du premier voyage faict aux Indes Orientales par les François en l'an 1603.* . . . Paris, 1604.

Martinello, Cechino. *Ragionamenti . . . sopra l'amomo et calamo aromatico novamente, l'anno 1604, havuto di Malaca, città d'India.* Venice, 1604.

Martinez de la Puente, Jose. *Compendio de las historias de los descubrimientos, conquistas, y guerras de la India Oriental y sus islas.* Madrid, 1681.

Martini, Martino, S.J. *De bello tartarico historia; in quâ, quo pacto Tartari hac nostrâ aetate sinicum imperium invaserint, ac ferè totum occuparint, narratur; eorumque mores breviter describuntur.* Antwerp, 1654. French translation by Gilbert Girault, Paris, 1654.

———. *Bellum Tartaricum, or the Conquest of the Great and Most Renouwned Empire of China, by the Invasion of the Tartars.* . . . London, 1654.

———. *Brevis relatio de numero, & qualitate christianorum apud Sinas.* Rome, 1654.

———. *Novus atlas sinensis.* . . . Amsterdam, 1655. (Became part of Johan Blaeu's *Atlas major.* . . , Amsterdam, 1662. Blaeu version reprinted at Trent in 1981, by its Museum of Natural Sciences.)

———. . . . *Sinicae historiae decas prima res à gentis origine ad Christum natum in extremâ Asia, sive magno sinarum imperio gestas complexa.* Munich, 1658.

[———?]. "Synopsis chronologica monarchiae sinicae. . . ." TR, Vol. II, Pt. IV.

Masefield, John (ed.). *Dampier's Voyages.* 2 vols. London, 1906.

[Massa, Isaac]. "Copie vande beschryvinge der landen Siberia, Samoieda ende Tingoesa, met oock de weghen uyt Moscovia derwaert. . . ." In Gerritszoon, Hessel (ed.), *Beschryvinghe vander Samoyeden landt in Tartarien* . . . , pp. 1–8. (English translation in *PP*, XIII, 172–79.)

———. "Een cort verhael van de wegen ende rivieren uyt Moscovia oostwaerts en oost ten noorden aen to landewaert. . . ." In Gerritszoon, Hessel (ed.), *Beschryvinghe vander Samoyeden landt in Tartarien* . . . , pp. 9–22. (English translation in *PP*, XIII, 180–93.)

Mastrilli, Marcello Francesco. *Relación de un prodigiosos milagro que San Francisco Xavier Apostel de la India ha hecho en la ciudad de Napoles este año de 1634.* Madrid, 1634.

Matelief, Cornelius. *Breeder verhael ende klare beschrijvinge.* . . . Rotterdam, 1608.

———. *Historiale ende ware beschrijvinge.* . . . Rotterdam, 1608.

———. "Historische verhael vande treffelijcke reyse gedaen naer de Oost-Indien ende China, met elf schepen. . . ." *BV*, IIa, 1–139.

Mayor, T. *Simbolo de la fe en langue y letra China.* Briondoc en Philippinos, 1607.

Medhurst, W. H. (trans.); *see* Happart, Gilbertus.

Medina, Baltasar de. *Vida, martyrio y beatification del protomartyr del Japon San Felipe de Jesus.* . . . Mexico City, 1683.

Megiser, Hieronymus (ed.). *Septentrio novantiquus, oder die newe nort Welt. Das ist: Gründliche und warhaffte Beschreibung aller der mitternächtigen und nortwerts gelegenen Landen und insulen, so . . . von etlichen berühmten . . . Adelspersonen, Schiffern, Befelchshabern . . . seynd erfunden worden . . . Sampt angehengter Relation, welcher gestalt in dem . . . 1612. Jahr, beydes, eine newe kurtze Schiffart nach der China gegen nortwerts, und dann auch ein unsegliche grosse und reiche Landschafft sudwerts im füfften Theil der Welt Magellanica erfunden worden.* . . . Leipzig, 1613.

Meister, George. *Der orientalisch-indianische Kunst- und Lust-Gärtner. Das ist: Eine aufrichtige Beschreibung der meisten indianischen als auf Java Major, Malacca und Jappon, wachsenden Gewürtz- Frucht- und Blumen-Bäume.* . . . Dresden, 1692.

Memoria de lo que an de advertír los pilotos de la carrera de las Indias, a cerca de la reforma-

ción del padron de las cartas de marear, y los demas instrumentos de que usan, para saber las alturas y derrotas de sus viages. [Madrid?, 1630?]

Memorial que os Mandarins ou Governadores do Reyno da China mandarão ao seu Rey, em que ehe davão côta das grandes guerras que tinhão com os Tartaros; et dos admiraveis sinaes qua apparecarão no mesmo Reyno o anno de 1618 etc. Lisbon, 1620.

Mendes da Luz, F. P. (ed.). *Livro das cidadas, e fortalezas que a coroa de Portugal tem nas partas da India.* . . . n.p., n.d. Reproduced in *Studia* (Lisbon), VI (1960).

Mendoza, Juan Gonzáles de; *see* Gonzáles de Mendoza, Juan.

Menezes, Alexis de. *La messe des anciens Chrestiens dicts de S. Thomas, en l'Evesché d'Angamal, 'es Indes Orientales: repurgée des erreurs et blasphèmes du Nestorianisme.* . . . Translated and preface by Jean Baptiste de Glen, Liegsois. Antwerp, 1609.

Mentrida, Alonso de. *Diccionario de lingua Bisaya, Heligueyna y Haraia de la isla de Panai y Sugbu y para las demas islas.* Manila, 1637.

Mentzel, Christian. *Kurtze chinesische Chronologia oder Zeit-Register aller chinesischen Käyser.* . . . Berlin, 1696.

Le Mercure Galant. Paris, 1684–88.

Mericke, John. "A Note of the Travels of the Russes over Land, and by Water from Mezen, Neere the Bay of Saint Nicholas to Pechora, to Obi, to Yenisse, and to the River Geta, Even unto the Frontiers of Cataia. . . ." *PP*, XIII, 193–94.

Merklein, Johann Jacob. *Journal, oder Beschreibung alles dess jenigen was sich auf währendder unserer neunjährigen Reise im Dienst der Vereinigten Geoctroyrten Niederländischen Ost-Indischen Compagnie, besonders in denselbigen Ländern täglich begeben und zugetragen.* . . . In Arnold, Christoph (ed.), *Wahrhaftige Beschreibungen dreyer mächtigen Königreiche, Japan, Siam und Corea.* . . . Nuremburg, 1663.

———. *Reise nach Java, Vorder- und Hinter-Indien, China und Japan, 1644–1653.* NR, Vol. III. The Hague, 1930.

Mesquita, Manoel Iacome de. *Relacam do que socedeo na cidade de Goa, e em todas as mais cidades e fortalezas do estado da India.* Goa, 1643.

Methwold, William. "Relations of the Kingdome of Golchonda, and Other Neighbouring Nations within the Gulf of Bengala. . . ." In *Purchas His Pilgrimage,* 4th ed. revised, London, 1626. (Also see Moreland, W. H. [ed.], *Relations of Golconda.* . . .)

Middleton, David. "The Voyage of Master David Middleton in the Consent, a Ship of an Hundred and Fifteen Tunnes, Which Set Forth from Tilburie Hope on the Twelfth of March 1606." *PP*, III, 51–61.

———. "The Voyage of Master David Middleton to Java and Banda . . . This Being the Fifth Voyage. . . ." *PP*, III, 90–115.

Middleton, Henry. *The Last East-Indian Voyage. Containing Much Varietie of the State of the Severall Kingdomes where they have traded;* . . . London, 1606. (Anonymous account of Sir Henry Middleton's voyage, 1604–6.)

———. "The Sixth Voyage. . . ." *PP*, III, 115–94.

———. *The Voyage of Sir Henry Middleton to the Moluccas, 1604–1606.* Edited by Sir William Foster. "HS," 2d ser., LXXXVIII. London, 1943.

Mildenhall, John. "The Travailles of John Mildenhall into the Indies, and in the Countries of Persia, and of the Great Mogor or Mogul. . . ." *PP*, II, 299–304.

Mills, J. V. (trans.); *see* Heredia, Manuel Godinho de.

Missions étrangères; see Paris. Séminaire des Missions Etrangères.

Mocquet, Jean. *Voyages en Afrique, Asie, Indes orientales et occidentales.* . . . Paris, 1616.

Moelre, Johan de, and Febvere, Jacques le. "Journael ende verhael, van alle het gene dat ghesien ende voor-ghevallen is op de reyse, gedaen door den E. ende gestrengen Pieter Willemsz. Verhoeven, Admirael Generael over 13. schepen, gaende naer de Oost-Indien, China, Philipines, ende byleggende rijcken, in den Iare 1607. ende volgende. . . ." *BV*, IIa.

Moetjens, Adriaan. *Catalogue des livres de Hollande, de France, et des autres pays . . . qui se trouvent à present dans la boutique.* The Hague, 1700.

A Momento for Holland, or a True and Exact History of the Cruelties Used on the English Merchants Residing in Amboyna. London, 1653.

Monfalcón, Juan Grau y; *see* Grau y Monfalcón, Juan.

Monforte y Herrera, Fernando de. *Relacion de las fiestas que ha hecho el Colegio Imperial de la Compañia de Jesus de Madrid en la canonizacion de San Ignacio de Loyola, y S. Francisco Xavier.* Madrid, 1622.

Montanus, Arnoldus [Dapper, Olfert]. *Atlas Chinensis: Being a Second Part of Relation of Remarkable Passages, in Two Embassies, from the East India Company of the United Provinces, to the Vice-Roy Singlamong and General Taising Lipovi and to Konchi, Emperor of China and East-Tartary.* . . . Translated by John Ogilby. London, 1671. (A translation of Dapper's *Gedenkwaerdige bedryf,* erroneously attributed to Montanus.)

―――. *Atlas Japannensis, Being Remarkable Addresses by Way of Embassy from the East India Company of the United Provinces, to the Emperor of Japan.* . . . Translated by John Ogilby. London, 1670.

――― (comp.). *De nieuwe en onbekende weereld; of beschrijving van America en 't Zuidland.* Amsterdam, 1671. (Contains the first published reports of Abel Tasman's Australian discoveries, pp. 577–85.)

―――. *Gedenkwaerdige gesantschappen der Oost-Indische maatschappy in't Vereenigde Nederland, aan de kaisaren van Japan.* Amsterdam, 1669.

―――. *Denckwürdige Gesandtschafften.* Amsterdam, 1669.

Moraga, Hernando de, O.F.M. *De las cosas, y costumbres de los Chinos, Japones, Turcos y otras naciones del Asia.* Madrid, 1619.

―――. *Relación breve de la embaxada . . . hijo a . . . Persia . . . el año passado de 1618 . . . ; aviendo venido de Manila, a Malaca.* . . . Seville, 1619.

Moreira, João Marquez. *Relação da magestosa, misteriosa, e notavel acclamaçam, que se fez a magestade d'El Rey Dom Ioam o IV nosso senhor na cidade do nome de Deos do grande imperio da China.* . . . Lisbon, 1644. English translation in C. R. Boxer (ed.), *Seventeenth Century Macau in Contemporary Documents and Illustrations* (Hong Kong, Kuala Lumpur, and Singapore, 1984), pp. 147–73.

Morejon, Pedro, S.J., *Breve relacion de la persecucion que huvo estos años contra la iglesia de Iapon.* . . . Mexico, 1616.

————. *A Briefe Relation of the Persecution Lately Made Against the Catholike Christians in the Kingdome of Iaponia.* . . . (Translated by W. W.) Saint-Omer, 1619.

Moreland, W. H. (ed.). *Relations of Golconda in the Early Seventeenth Century.* "HS," 2d ser., LXVI. London, 1931.

———— (ed.); *see also* Floris, Pieter.

————, and Geyl, Pieter (trans.); *see* Pelsaert.

Morga, Antonio de. *Sucesos de las islas Filipinas.* . . . Mexico, 1609.

————. *Sucesos de las islas Filipinas.* Translated into English and edited by J. S. Cummins. "HS," 2d ser., CXL. Cambridge, 1971.

Morrison, John (trans.); *see* Struys, Jan Janszoon.

Motta, Alexio da. "Le routier d'Alexio da Motta, traduit du Portugais." TR, Pt. II. (Reprint in Pereira, F. [ed.], *Roteiros portuguezes.* . . .)

Müller, Andreas. *Abdullae beid avaei historia sinensis persicè e gemino manuscripto edita, latine quoque reddita ab Andrea Mullero Greiffenhagio, Berolini MDCLXXVII expressa, nunc vera una cum additamentis edita ab auctoris filio Quodvultdeo Abraham Mullero.* Jena, 1698.

Muller, Hendrik P. N. (ed.). *De Oost-Indische Compagnie in Cambodja en Laos.* "WLV," Vol. XIII. The Hague, 1917.

Mun, Thomas. *A Discourse of Trade from England into the East Indies.* [London], 1621.

Mundy, Peter; *see* Temple, Richard Carnac.

Murakami, N.; *see* Cocks, Richard.

Murchio, Vincenzo Maria; *see* Vincenzo Maria di Santa Caterina da Siena.

Narain, Brij, and Sharma, Sri Ram (eds.); *see* Broecke, Pieter van den.

Naufragio, que fizeramos duas naos de India: O Sacramento, nosso Senhora da Atalya, no cabo de Boa Esperança. Lisbon, 1648? (Also included in Bernardo Gomes de Brito's *História tragico-maritima.*)

Navarrete, Domingo Fernandez. *Tratados historicos, politicos, ethicos y religiosos de la monarchia de China:* . . . Madrid, 1676. (English translation in *CV*, Vol. I.)

————. *The Travels and Controversies of Friar Domingo Navarrete, 1618–1686.* Edited by J. S. Cummins. 2 vols. "HS," 2d ser., CXVIII, CXIX. Cambridge, 1962.

Neck, Jacob Corneliszoon van, and Warwijck, Wybrant van. *Journael ofte dagh-register, inhoudende een waerachtigh verhael ende historische vertellinghe vande reyse, ghedan door acht shepen van Amsterdamme onder't beleydt van Jacob Cornelisz, van Neck als Admirael ende Wybrandt van Warwijck, als Vice-admirael, van Amsterdam gheseylt in den jare 1598.* . . . Amsterdam, 1600.

————. *Het tweede boeck, journael oft dagh-register inhoudende een warachtich verhael.* . . . Amsterdam, 1601.

————. *De tweede schipvaart der Nederlanders naar Oost-Indië onder Jacob Cornelisz. van Neck en Wybrant Warwijck, 1598–1600.* Edited by J. Keuning. 5 vols. "WLV," Vols. XLII, XLIV, XLVI, XLVIII, and L. The Hague, 1938–51.

————. *Waarachtige beschryving.* Amsterdam, 1599.

————. "Waerachtigh verhael van de schipvaerd op Oost-Indien ghedaen by de acht schepen in den jare 1598 van Amsterdam uyt-ghezeylt. . . ." *BV*, Ia, 1–56.

Neuville, Foy de la. *Relation curieuse et nouvelle de Moscovie.* The Hague, 1698.

Newe und grundlich Relation von der mercklichen Victori oder Sig welchen Herr Joannes de Sylva . . . den 24 Aprill des 1610 Jars wider etliche hollendsche Raubschiff. . . . Augsburg, [1611].

Nicolai, Eliud. *Newe und warhaffte Relation, von deme was sich in beederley, das ist in den West- und Ost-Indien, von der Zeit an zugetragen, dass sich die Navigationes der hollunnd engelländischen Compagnien daselbsthin angefangen abzuschneiden . . . Alles auss gewissen castiglianischen unnd portugesischen Relationen colligiert. . . .* Munich, 1619.

Nicols, William. "The Report of William Nicols . . . Which Traveled from Branpert by Land to Masulipatam. . . ." *PP,* III, 72–74. (Written by a survivor of the *Ascension,* wrecked off Surat in 1609.)

Nierop, Dirck Rembrantsz van. *Eenige oefeningen in god-lijcke, wis-konstige en natuerlijcke dingen.* 2 vols. Amsterdam, 1674. (Includes a version of Abel Tasman's journal.)

Nieuhof, Johann. *Het gezantschap der Neêrlandtsche Oost-Indische Compagnie aan den grooten tartarischen cham, den tegenwoordigen kiezer van China. . . .* Amsterdam, 1665.

———. *Die Gesantschaft der Ost-Indischen Geselschaft in den Vereinigten Niederländern an den tartarischen Cham und nunmehr auch sinischen Keiser. . . .* Amsterdam, 1666.

———. *Gedenkwaerdige zee- en lant-reize door de voornaemste landschappen van West en Oostindien.* Amsterdam, 1682.

Nijhoff, Wouter; L'Honoré Naber, S. P.; Stapel, F. W.; and Wieder, F. C. (eds.); *see* Vennip, Cornelis Janszoon.

Nispen, Adriaen. *Voyagien ende beschryvinge van't koninckrijck von Siam, Moscovien ofte Russ-landt, Ys-landt ende Groene-landt. Yder vertoonde in 't bysonder de gelegenheyt, religie, macht, regeringe, costumen, koopmanschappen, ende andere aenmerckensweerdige saken derselver landen.* Dordrecht, 1652.

Noort, Olivier van. *Beschryvinghe vande voyagie om de geheelen werelt cloot, ghedaen door Olivier Van Noort van Utrecht. . . .* Rotterdam [and Amsterdam, 1601].

———. *Extract oft kort verhael wt het groote journael vande wonderlijcke ende groote reyse ghedaen door de strate Magellana en andere vremde konincrijcken en landen byden E. Olivier Van Noort, Admirael en Generael vande vier schepen toegerust tot Rotterdam A°. 1598.* Rotterdam, 1601.

———. *De reis om de wereld door Olivier van Noort, 1598–1601.* Edited by J. W. Ijzerman. 2 vols. "WLV," XXVII, XXVIII. The Hague, 1926.

Novoa, Matiás de. *Memorias.* In *Colleccion de documentos inéditos para la historia de España. . . .* LX, 300–49, Madrid, 1875.

Ogilby, John (trans.); *see* Magalhães, Gabriel de; Montanus, Arnoldus.

O'Kane, John (trans.). *The Ship of Sulaiman.* New York, 1972. (A translation of Safinah-i Sulaymani, a seventeenth-century Persian manuscript in the British Library.)

Olearius, Adam. *Des hoch edelgebornen Johan Albrechts von Mandelslo morgenländische Reyse-Beschreibung. Worinnen zugleich die gelegenheit und heutiger Zustand etlicher fürnehemen indianischen Länder, Provincien, Städte und Insulen, sampt deren Ein-*

wohner Leben, Sitten, Glauben und Handthierung: . . . *Herausgegeben durch Adam Olearium.* . . . Schleswig, 1658.

―――. *Muskowitische offt begehrte Beschreibung der newen orientalischen Reise so durch Gelegenheit einer holsteinischen Legation an den König in Persien geschehen* . . . *Item ein Schreiben des woledeln* . . . *Johan Albrecht von Mandelslo worinnen dessen ostindianische Reise über den Oceanum enthalten.* . . . Schleswig, 1647.

―――― (ed.). *Orientalische Reise-Beschreibungen Jürgen Andersen aus Schlesswig der An. Christi 1644 aussgezogen und 1650. wieder kommen. Und Volquard Jversen aus Holstein so An. 1655 aussgezogen und 1668 wider angelanget.* . . . Schleswig, 1669.

―――. *Reise Beschreibungen bestehend in der nach Musskau und Persien. Wie auch Johann Albrechts von Mandelslo morgenländischen und Jürg. Andersens und Volq. Yversens orientalischen Reise: mit angehängter chinesischen Revolution,* . . . *Auch: wie der flüchtende Chinesische Mandarin und See-Räuber Coxinga, die von den Hollandern besetzten Insul Formosa angefallen und erobert: Nebenst beygefügtem Persianischen Rosen-Thal und Baum-Garten.* Hamburg, 1696.

―――. *The Voyages and Travels of the Ambassadors sent by Frederick Duke of Holstein to the Great Duke of Muscovy, and the King of Persia* . . . *Whereto are added the Travels of Johan Albert de Mandelslo.* . . . Translated by John Davies. London, 1662.

O'Neill, H. S. (trans.); *see* Gervaise, Nicolas.

Opstall, M. E. van (ed.); *see* Verhoeff, Pieter Willemszoon.

Or, Marque d'. *Furieuse et sanglante bataille donnée entre les Portugois et les Hollandois (auprès de Malacca).* . . . Paris, 1621.

Ordóñez y Cevallos, Pedro. *Historia y viages del mundo.* Madrid, 1614.

―――. *Tratado da las relaciones verdaderas de los reynos de la China, Cochinchina, y Champas.* Jaen, 1628.

Orfanel, Jacinto. *Historia ecclesiastica de los sucessos de la christiandad en Japon, desde* . . . *1602* . . . *hasta* . . . *1622.* Madrid, 1633.

Orléans, Pierre Joseph d', S.J.; *see* D'Orleans, Pierre Joseph.

Ortiz, Ambrosio (trans.). *Istoria della conversione* . . . *dell'Isole Mariane.* . . . Naples, 1686. (See also Tinelli, Francesco.)

Osborne, Thomas. *Collection of Voyages and Travels.* London, 1745.

Ovington, John. *A Voyage to Suratt in the Year, 1689.* . . . London, 1696.

―――. *A Voyage to Surat in the Year 1689.* Edited by H. G. Rawlinson. London, 1929.

Palafox y Mendoza, Juan de. *Historia de la conquista de la China por el Tartaro.* Paris, 1670.

―――. *Histoire de la conqueste de la Chine par les Tartares.* . . . Amsterdam, 1723.

Pallu, François. *Relation abregée des missions et voyages des evesques françois, envoyez aux royaumes de la Chine, Cochinchine, Tonquin, et Siam.* . . . Paris, 1668.

―――. *Mémoires sur l'état présent des missions et des evesques français vicaires apostoliques dans la Chine et dans les royaumes de l'Orient.* n.p., 1677.

―――. *Relation des missions et des voyages des evesques* . . . *ès années 1676 et 1677.* Paris, 1680.

―――. *Relation des missions et voyages des evesques Vicaires Apostoliques, et leurs éccle-*

siastiques ès années 1672, 1673, 1674, et 1675. Paris, 1680.

The Palme of Christian Fortitude or the Glorious Combats of Christians in Iaponia. Taken out of the Letters of the Society of Iesus from thence, Anno 1624. St. Omer, 1630.

Pantoja, Diego de, S.J. "A Letter of Father Diego de Pantoia, One of the Company of Jesus, to Father Luys de Guzman, Provincall in the Province of Toledo: Written in Panquin, Which is the Court of the King of China, the Ninth of March, the Yeere 1602." *PP*, XII, 331–410.

——. *Relación de la entrada de algunos padres de la Compania de Iesus en la China y particulares sucessos que tuvieron.* . . . Seville, 1605.

Paris. Séminaire des Missions Etrangères. *Lettre . . . au Pape, sur les idolatries et les superstitions chinoises*. Brussels, 1700.

Parthey, Daniel. . . . *ost-indische und persianische neun-jährige Kriegs-Dienste und wahrhafftige Beschreibung*. Nuremberg, 1697.

Pastells, Pablo (ed.); *see* Colin, Francisco.

Payne, C. H. (trans. and ed.). *Akbar and the Jesuits*. London, 1926. (Translations from Fernão Guerreiro's *Relaçam*.)

——. *Jahangir and the Jesuits*. New York, 1930. (Translations from Fernão Guerreiro's *Relaçam*.)

Payton, Walter. "The Second Voyage of Captaine Walter Peyton into the East Indies. . . ." *PP*, IV, 289–310.

Pedroche, Cristóbal de. *Breve, y compendiosa relacion de la estrañez, y destierro de el señor arçobispo, Don Fray Phelipe Pardo, por la gracia de Dios, y de la santa sede apostolica, arçobispo de Manila, metropolitano de estas islas, de el consejo de su Magestad Catholica, . . .* Seville, 1683.

Pelsaert, Francisco. *Jahangir's India; the Remonstrance of Francisco Pelsaert*. Translated by W. H. Moreland and Pieter Geyl. Cambridge, 1925.

——. *Ongeluckige voyagie, van't schip "Batavia" nae Oost-Indien. Uyt-gevaren onder de E. Francois Pelsaert.* . . . Amsterdam, 1647.

——. "La terre australe descovverte, par le capitaine Pelsart, qui y fait naufrage." TR (1696), Vol. I, pp. 50–56.

——. "Très-humble remonstrance . . . sur le sujet de leur commerce en ces quartiers là. . . ." TR (1696), Vol. I, pp. 1–20.

Penzer, N. M. (ed.); *see* Dampier, William.

Perara, S. G.; *see* Queyroz, Fernão.

Percheron, I. Bellefleur. *Nouvelle histoire de la Chine*. . . . Paris, 1622.

Pereira, F. (ed.). *Roteiros portuguezes da viagem de Lisboa á India nos séculos XVI e XVII*. Lisbon, 1898. (Contains a reprint of Vicente Rodriguez' and Alexio da Motta's *Roteiros*.)

Pereira, F. M. E. (ed.); *see* Andrade, Antonio de, S.J.

Pereira, Francisco (ed.). *Relatione autentica mandata da prelati, vicere', cancelliere maggiore, e secretario dello stato dell' Indie. Alla maestà catholica intorno alli maomettani orientali, che per misericordia di Nostro Signor' iddio col mezo de' frati dell' ordine Eremitano di Sant' Agostino del regno di Portugallo, riceverono l'acqua del Santo Battesimo nell' anno, M.DC.II*. Rome, 1606.

Pereyra, Antonio Pinto. *Historia da India no tempo en que a governovo visorey dom Luis de Ataide.* Edited by Miguel da Cruz. Coimbra, 1616–17.

Pérez, Juan. *Relación muy verdadera de un caso nuevamente sucedido en la India de Portugal, en que se cuenta como un cavallero Portugues llamado Felipe Brito, que es governador, y Capitan general en aquellas partes por su Magestad vencio a un Rey gentil del Pegú.* Cuença, 1614.

Perusquets de Aguilar, Manuel; *see* Faria y Sousa.

Petech, Luciano (ed.). *I missionari italiani nel Tibet e nel Nepal.* 7 vols. Rome, 1952–56.

[Petlin, Ivan]. "A Relation of Two Russe Cossacks Travailes, out of Siberia to Catay, and Other Countries Adjoyning Thereunto. . . ." *PP*, XIV, 272–85.

Philippe de Sainte-Trinité, O.C.D. *Itinerarium orientale . . . In quo varii successus itineris, plures orientis regiones, earum montes, maria & flumina, series principum, qui in eis dominati sunt, incolae tam christiani, quam infideles populi, animali, arbores, planta & fructus; religiosorum in oriente missiones ac varii celebres eventus describuntur.* Leyden, 1649.

———. *Voyage d'Orient.* Lyons, 1652.

———. *Orientalische Reisebeschreibung, warinnen unterschiedliche Begebenheiten seiner Reise vielerley orientalische Landschaften . . . , so darinnen geherzschet. . . .* Frankfurt, 1671.

Philosophical Transactions; see Royal Society of London.

Pieris, P. E. (trans. and ed.); *see* Ribeiro, João.

Pieterszoon van West-Zanen, Willem; *see* West-Zanen, Willem Pieterszoon van.

Pinelo, Antonio de Leon; *see* Leon Pinelo, Antonio de.

Pinkerton, John. *A General Collection of the Best and Most Interesting Voyages and Travels in All Parts of the World. . . .* 17 vols. London, 1808–14.

Pinpin, Tomas, and Magourha, J. *Vocabulario de Japon declarado primero en Portugues. . . .* Manila, 1630.

Pinto, Fernão Mendes. *Peregrinação.* Lisbon and Madrid, 1614.

———. *Historia oriental de las peregrinaciones de Fernan Mendez Pinto. . . .* Translated by Francisco de Herrera Maldonado. Madrid, 1664.

———. *The Travels of Mendes Pinto.* Ed. and trans. Rebecca D. Catz. Chicago, 1989.

Pinto Pereyra, Antonio. *Historia da India no tempo en que a governovo visorey dom Luis de Ataide.* 2 pts. Coimbra, 1616 [and 1617].

Piso, Willem. *De indiae utriusque re naturali et medica libri quatuordecim.* Amsterdam, 1658.

Pomp, Dirck Gerritszoon; *see* Ijzerman, J. W.

Poser und Gross Nedlitz, Heinrich von. . . . *Lebens und Todes Geschichte, worinnen das Tage Buch seiner Reise von Constantinople aus durch die Bulgarey, Armenien, Persien, und Indien aus Liecht gestellet. . . .* Jena, 1675.

———; *see also* Dharampal (trans.).

Posthumus Meyjes, R.; *see* Wurffbain, Johann Sigmund.

Pouchot de Chantassin, Claude-Michel. *Relation du voyage et retour des Indes Orien-*

tales, par un garde de la marine, servant à bord du vaisseau de M. Duquesnes. Paris, 1692.

[Powell, Thomas]. *Humane Industry; or a History of Most Manual Arts, Deducing the Original Progress, and Improvement of Them.* . . . London, 1661.

Prévost, Antoine François. *Histoire générale des voyages.* 16 vols. Paris, 1764–91.

Priezac, Salomon de. *Histoire des éléphants.* Paris, 1650.

Pring, Martin. "Briefe Notes of Two Voyages of Master Martin Pring into the East Indies, the First with Captain Nicholas Downton. . . ." *PP,* IV, 567–71. (Downton's voyage of 1614–15. *See also* Downton, Nicholas, *The Voyage of Nicholas Downton* . . . , ed. Sir William Foster.)

————. "The Second Voyage of Captain Pring into the East Indies. . . ." *PP,* V, 1–64. (Voyage of 1616–21.)

Puente, José Martinez de la. *Compendio de las historias de los descubrimientos, conquistas, y guerras de la India Oriental y sus islas.* Madrid, 1681.

Purchas, Samuel (ed.). *Hakluytus Posthumus or Purchas his Pilgrimes.* 4 vols. London, 1625.

————. *Hakluytus Posthumus, or Purchas His Pilgrimes.* 20 vols. Glasgow, 1905–7. Cited as *PP.*

————. *Purchas His Pilgrimage. Or, Relations of the World and of Religions Observed in all Ages and Places Discovered, from the Creation unto this Present.* London, 1613. 4th rev. ed., 1626.

Purificação, Miguel de. *Relação defensiva dos filhos da India.* . . . Barcelona, 1640.

————. *Vida evangelica de los frayles menores en Oriente.* Barcelona, 1641.

Pursglove, William. "A Briefe Relation of a Voyage to Pechora, and Wintering There, Began in the Yeere 1611. . . ." *PP,* XIII, 239–55.

Pyrard, François. *Discours du voyage des françois aux Indes Orientales.* . . . Paris, 1611.

————. *Voyage de François Pyrard.* 2 vols. Paris, 1615.

————. *The Voyage of François Pyrard of Laval to the East Indies, the Maldives, the Moluccas, and Brazil.* Translated and edited by Albert Gray, assisted by H. C. P. Bell. 2 vols. in 3. "HS," o.s., LXXVI, LXXVII, and LXXX. London, 1887, 1888, and 1890.

Quarles, John. *The Tyranny of the Dutch against the English.* . . . London, 1653.

Queyroz, Fernão. *The Temporal and Spiritual Conquest of Ceylon.* Translated by S. G. Perara. 3 vols. Colombo, 1930.

Quiroga de San Antonio, Gabriel. *Breve y verdadera relacion de los sucesos del Reyno de Camboxa.* Valladolid, 1604.

————. *Brève et véridique relation des événements du Cambodge.* Translated and edited by A. Cabaton. Paris, 1914.

Quiros, Pedro Fernandes de. *La Austrialia del Espiritu Santo.* Translated and edited by Celsus Kelly. "HS," 2d ser., CXXVI and CXXVII. 2 vols. London, 1966.

————. *El Capitan Pedro Fernandes de Quiros con este son ocho los memoriales.* [Seville?], 1610.

————. *Relacion de un memorial que presentado a su Magestad el Capitan Pedro Fernandez de Quir. sobre la población y describrimiento do la quarto parto del mundo, Austrialia incognita*. . . . Pamplona, 1610.

———. *The Voyages of Pedro Fernandez de Quiros, 1595–1606*. Translated and edited by Sir Clements Markham. "HS," 2d ser., XIV and XV. 2 vols. London, 1904.

Rangel, Miguel. *Relaçam das Christandades, e Ihas de Solor, em particular da fortaleza que para amparo dellas foi feita*. . . . In Encarnação and Rangel, *Relaçoẽs summarias*. (For a modern edition see Sá, Artur Basilio de (ed.), *Documentaçao*, V, 318–47.)

Raven-Hart, R. (trans. and ed.). *Germans in Dutch Ceylon*. Colombo, [1953]. (Translations from Behr, Herport, Schweitzer, and Fryke [Frick].)

Rawlinson, H. G. (ed.); *see* Ovington, John.

Rebello, Amador (comp.), *Compendio de algumas cartas que este anno de 97 vierao dos Padres da Companhia de Jesu*. Lisbon, 1598.

Rechteren, Seyger van. *Journael gehouden door . . . op zyne gedane voyagie naer Oost-Indien*. Zwolle, 1635.

———. "Journael ghehouden op de reyse ende weder-komste van Oost-Indien. . . ." *BV*, IIb. Appended to the voyage of Wybrant Schram, pp. 19–89.

Récit de ce qui s'est passé entre les Portugois et les Hollandois au delà de la ligne équinoxiale avec la copie de la cargaison de trois navires chargés aux Indes pour venir en Hollande et en Zélande, en 1616. Amsterdam, 1616.

Reede tot Drakestein; *see* Rheede tot Drakestein.

Reflexions générales sur la lettre que paraît sous le nom de messieurs des missions étrangères au pape, touchant les cérémonies chinoises. Paris, 1700.

Regni chinensis descriptio ex variis authoribus. Leyden, 1629.

Reimão, Gaspar Ferreira. *Roteiro de navagacām carreira da India*. . . . Lisbon, 1612.

Relacion breve, y sumaria del edito que mandó publicar en todo su Reyno del Bojõ, uno de las mas poderosos del Iapon, el Rey Idate Masamune, publicando la fé de Cristo, y del embaxador que embio a España, en compañia del reverendo padre Fr. Luys Sotelo . . . que viene eo embaxada del Emperador del Iapon, hijo de Sevilla, y lo que en el viage le sucedio. Seville, 1614.

Relacion cierta y verdadera de la feliz vitoria y prosperos sucessos que en la India Oriental han conseguido los Portugueses, contra armados muy ponderosas de Olanda y Persia este año de 1624. . . . Madrid, 1624.

Relacion de la batalla, que Nuno Alvarez Botello . . . tuvo con los armadas de Olanda y Inglaterra en el estrecho de Ormuz. Seville, 1626.

Relacion de un prodigiosos milagro que San Francisco Xavier de la India ha hecho en la ciudad de Napoles este ano de 1634. Madrid, 1634.

Relacion escrita por uno de los padres de la mission, Mariana, remitada Mexico. Seville, 1674. (On the death of Diego Luis de Sanvitores.)

Relacion verdadera del Levantamiento que les Sangleyes o Chinos hizieron en las Filipinas y de las vitorias que tuvo contra ellos el Governador Don Sebastian Hurtado de Corcuero, el ano passado de 1640 y 1641. Madrid, 1643.

Relation de deux caravelles envoyées en 1618 . . . sous la conduite de D. Juan de More, pour decouvrir le détroit de Lemaire. Amsterdam, 1622.

Relatione della solenne entrata fatta in Roma da D. Filippo Francesco Faricura [Hasekura] con il Reverendiss Padre Luis Sotel. Rome, 1615.

Relatione delle missioni di vescovi vicarii apostolici mandati dalla S. Sede Apostolica alli regni de Siam, Cocinchina, Camboia, e Tunkino. Rome, 1677.

Relation succincte de tout ce qui s'est passé . . . en la guerre que la compagnie hollandoise . . . a euë contre le roy et . . . regens de Macassar, depuis . . . 1666 . . . à 1669. [Amsterdam?], 1670.

Relation véritable de huict navires, venus des Indes orientales et occidentales. . . . Paris, 1628. (Reports the return of ships from Cornelis Matelief's fleet.)

A Remonstrance of the Directors of the Netherlands East-India Company Presented to the General States in Defence of the Said Company, Touching the Bloody Proceedings against the British Merchants Executed at Amboyna, together with Acts of Process against the Said English, and the Reply of the English East India Company to the Said Remonstrance and Defence. London, 1632.

Rennefort, Urbain Souchu de. *Mémoires pour servir à l'histoire des Indes orientales.* Paris, 1688.

Rheede tot Drakestein, Hendrik Adriaan van, and Casearius, Joannes. *Hortus indicus malabaricus continens regni malabarici apud indos celeberrimi omnis generis plantas rariores, latinis, malabaricis, arabicis, & bramanum characteribus nominibusque expressas, unà cum floribus, fructibus, & seminibus, naturali magnitudine à pertissimis pictoribus delineatas, & ad vivum exhibitas. . . .* 12 vols. Amsterdam, 1678–1703.

Rhodes, Alexandre de, S.J. *Relazione de' felici successi della santa fede predicata da' padri della Compagnia di Giesu nel regno di Tunchino. . . .* Rome, 1650.

———. *Catechismus pro ijs, qui volunt suscipere baptismum, in octo dies divisus. . . .* Rome, 1651. (Catechism in Latin and Annamese.)

———. *Dictionarium annamiticum, lusitanum, et latinum. . . .* Rome, 1651.

———. *Relatione della morte di Andrea Catechista che primo de Christiani nel regno di Cocincina è stato ucciso da gl'infedeli in odio della fede, alli 26. di Luglio, 1644.* Rome, 1652.

———. *Divers voyages et missions . . . en la Chine, & autres royaumes de l'orient, avec son retour en Europe par la Perse et l'Armenie. . . .* Paris, 1653.

———. *Sommaire des divers voyages et missions apostoliques . . . à la Chine, & autres royaumes de l'Orient, avec son retour de la Chine à Rome. Depuis l'année 1618, jusques à l'année 1653.* Paris, 1653.

———. *Relation de ce qui s'est passé en l'annee 1649 dans les royaumes . . . du Iapon.* Paris, 1655.

———. *Rhodes of Vietnam.* Edited and trans. by Solange Hertz. Westminster, Md., 1966. Translation of *Divers voyages.*

Ribadeneira, Marcelo de, O.F.M. *Historia de las islas del archipiélago Filipino y reinos de la gran China, Tartaria, Cochin-China, Malaca, Siam, Cambodge y Japon.* Barcelona, 1601.

———. *History of the Philippines and Other Kingdoms.* Translated by Pacita Guevara Fernandez. 2 vols. Manila, 1970.

Ribadeneyra, Antonio San Román de; *Historia general de la Yndia Oriental . . . desde sus principios hast' el año de 1557.* Valladolid, 1603.

Ribeiro, Diego (trans.). *Declaraçam de doutrina christam collegida do cardinal Roberto Belarmino da Cõmpanhia de Iesu e outros autores composta em lingoa Bramana vulgar.* . . . Rachol, 1632.

Ribeiro, João. *Ribeiro's History of Ceilão.* . . . Edited and translated by P. E. Pieris. 2d ed., Colombo, 1909.

Rios Coronel, Hernando de. *Memorial, y relacion para su magestad, del Procurador General de la Filipinas, de lo que conviene remediar, y de la requeza que ay en ellas, y en las Islas del Maluco.* Madrid, 1621.

Rodriguez, João. *Arte de lingoa de Iapon.* . . . Nagasaki, 1604–8.

Rodriguez de Saa y Menezes, Juan (also Sá de Meneses, Sao y Menezes). *Rebelion de Ceylan, y los progressos de su conquista en el gobierno de Constantino de Saa y Moronha.* Lisbon, 1681. (English translation by J. J. St. George in *JRAS, Ceylon Branch,* Vol. XI.)

Roe, Thomas. *The Embassy of Sir Thomas Roe to the Court of the Great Mogul, 1615–1619, as Narrated in His Journal and Correspondence.* Edited by Sir William Foster. "HS," 2d ser., I and II. 2 vols. London, 1899.

———. *The Embassy of Sir Thomas Roe to India, 1615–1619, as Narrated in his Journal and Correspondence.* Edited by Sir William Foster. Rev. ed. London, 1926.

———. "Observations Collected Out of the Journall of Sir Thomas Roe. . . ." *PP,* IV, 310–468.

Roelofszoon, Roelof. "Kort ende waerachtigh verhael van de tweede schipvaerd by de Hollanders op Oost-Indien gedaen, onder den Heer Admirael Iacob van Neck, getogen uyt het journael van Roelof Roelofsz, vermaender op 't schip Amsterdam, ende doorgaens uyt andere schrijvers vermeerdert." In *BV,* Ib. (The account of Van Neck's second voyage.)

Roger (Rogerius), Abraham. *De open-deure tot het verborgen heydendom.* Leyden, 1651.

———. *Le theatre de l'idolatrie, ou la porte ouverte pour parvenir à la connaissance du paganisme caché,* . . . Trans. Thomas le Grue. Amsterdam, 1670.

———. *De open-deure tot het verborgen heydendom.* Edited by W. Caland. "WLV," Vol. X. The Hague, 1915.

Röslin, Helisaeus. *Mitternächtige Schiffarth, von der herrn Staden inn Niderlanden vor XV. Jaren vergebenlich fürgenommen, wie dieselbige anzustellen, dass man daselbst herumb in Orient und Chinam kommen möge.* . . . Oppenheim, 1611.

Rosnel, Pierre de. *Le mercure indien ou le trésor des Indes.* Paris, 1667.

Rotman, Paul Alofszoon. *Kort verhael van d'avonteurlicke voyagien en reysen.* . . . Amsterdam, 1657.

Rouffaer, G. P., and Ijzerman, J. W. (eds.); *see* Lodewyckszoon, Willem.

Rougemont, François de, S.J. *Relaçam do estado politico e espiritual do imperio da China, pellos annos de 1659 até o de 1666.* Translated from Latin by S. de Magalhães. Lisbon, 1672.

———. *Historia Tartaro-Sinica nova.* Louvain, 1673.

———. *Lettres inédites de Francois de Rougemont.* Edited by H. Bosmans. Louvain, 1913.

Roy, Jacob Janssen de. *Voyagie gedaan door Jacob Janssen de Roy na Borneo en Atchen, in't jaar 1691 en vervolgens: . . . Gedrukt volgens de copy van Batavia. . . .* n.p., n.d.

Royal Society of London. *Philosophical Transactions. . . .* London, 1666–1700. (Especially Vol. XVI [1686–87].)

Sá, Artur Basilio de (ed.). *Documentaçao para a história das missões do padroado português do oriente. Insulindia.* Vol. V. Lisbon, 1958.

Saar, Johann Jacob. *Ost-Indianische fünfzehen-jährige Kriegs-Dienst, und wahrhafftige Beschreibung. . . .* Nuremberg, 1662.

———. *Johann Jacob Saars Ost-indianische fünfzehen-jährige Kriegs-Dienste und wahrhafftige Beschreibung . . . zum anderen Mahl heraus gegeben. . . .* Edited by Daniel Wülfer. Nuremberg, 1672.

———. *Reise nach Java, Banda, Ceylon, und Persien, 1644–1660. . . .* NR, Vol. VI. The Hague, 1930.

Saa y Menezes, Juan Rodriguez de; *see* Rodriguez de Saa y Menezes, Juan.

Sá de Meneses, Francisco de. *Malacca conquista.* Lisbon, 1634.

———. *The Conquest of Malacca. Francisco de Sa de Meneses.* Translated by E. C. Knowlton, Jr. Kuala Lumpur, 1970.

Sá de Meneses, Juan Rodriguez de; *see* Rodriguez de Saa y Menezes, Juan.

Sainte-Trinité, Philippe de; *see* Philippe de Sainte-Trinité.

Salbranche, Joseph. "The Voyage of Master Joseph Salbranch through India, Persia, . . ." *PP,* III, 82–90. (An account by a survivor of the *Ascension,* wrecked off Surat in 1609.)

Salgueiro, Diego Marques de. *Relaçam das festas que a religiam de Companhia de Jesu fez em . . . Lisboa, na beatificaçam do beato P. Francisco de Xavier.* Lisbon, 1621.

Sampayo, Salvador do Coreto de. *Relaçam dos succesos victoriosos que na barra de Goa ouve dos Olandeses Antonio Tellez de Menezes, capitano geral do mar da India, nos annos de 1637 à 1638.* Coimbra, 1639.

———. *Relacion de los succesos de las armas españolas por mar y tierra en las islas Filippinas, y victorias contra Mindanao y con los Olandeses de Terrenate.* Madrid, 1639.

San Agustín, Gaspar de. *Conquista de las islas Philipinas.* Madrid, 1698.

San Antonio de Quiroga, Gabriel; *see* Quiroga de San Antonio, Gabriel.

San Bernardino, Gaspar de. *Itinerario da India por terra ate este reino de Portugal. . . .* Lisbon, 1611.

San Román de Ribadeneyra, Antonio. *see* Ribadeneyra, Antonio San Román de.

Sanson d'Abbeville, Nicolas. *L'Asie en plusieurs cartes nouvelles et en plusieurs traités.* Paris, 1652.

Santa Caterina da Siena, Vincenzo Maria di; *see* Vincenzo Maria di Santa Caterina da Siena.

Santa Mariá, Juan de. *Relación del martirio que seys padres descalços Franciscõs, tres hermanos de la Compañia de Jesus, y decisiete Japones podecieron.* Madrid, 1601.

Santiago, Pedro de. *Relacion de lo que hicieron los religiosos augustinos en el transito a las Indias.* n.p., 1605.

Santos, Joam dos. *Ethiopia oriental, e varia historia de cousas notaveis do Oriente, e da christiandade que os religiosos da ordem de prègadores nelle fizerão.* Evora, 1609.

Sanvitores, Diego Luis de; *see* Barrett, Ward (trans. and ed.).

Sao y Menezes, Rodriguez de; *see* Rodriguez de Saa y Menezes, Juan.

Saparamadu, S. D. (ed.); *see* Knox, Robert.

Sardinha, João Mimosa. *Relació de la real tragicomédia con los padres . . . , recibie- ron . . . Felipe II de Portugal, y de su entrada in este reino. . . .* Lisbon, 1620.

Saris, John. "The Eighth Voyage Set Forth by the East-Indian Societie. . . ." *PP*, III, 357–490.

———. "Observations of the Said . . . Saris, of Occurents which Happened in the East Indies During His Abode at Bantam from October 1605. till October 1609. . . ." *PP*, III, 490–519.

———. *The Voyage of Captain John Saris to Japan, 1613.* Edited by Ernest M. Satow. "HS," 2d ser., V. London, 1900.

———. *Saris Nihon tokōki Wilman Nihon taizaiki* [*The Voyage of Captain John Saris to Japan, 1613, and Wilman's Stay in Japan*], trans. Murakawa Kengo *et al.* Tokyo, 1970.

Sas, Jan. "Historisch verhael van de voyagie der Hollanderen met dry schepen ge- daen naer de Oost-Indien, onder het beleydt van den Admirael Steven vander Hagen. In den Iare 1599 ende volghende . . . Daer by ghevoecht is de voyagie van twee Achins-vaerders, onder het beleyt van Cornelis Pietersz, ende Guiljam Senecal. Gedaen inden Jaere 1600 ende 1601. Item: Extract uyt het iournael van den Admirael Jacob Heemskerckx voyagie, ghedaen inden jaere 1601 &c. ghe- houden by Reyer Cornelisz stierman op den vice-admirael. Alles waerdich om te lesen." In *BV*, Ib.

Satow, Ernest M. (ed.); *see* Saris, John.

Schall von Bell, Johann Adam. *Historica narratio de initio et progressu missionis Societatis Jesu apud Chinenses, ac praesertim in regia Pequinensi, . . .* Vienna, 1665.

———. *Historica relatio de ortu et progressu fidei orthodoxae in regno chinensi per mis- sionarios Societatis Jesu ab anno 1581. usque ad annum 1669. . . .* Ratisbon, 1672. (A second edition of *Historica narratio.*)

Schilder, G. G. (ed.); *see* Vlamingh, Willem Hesselszoon de.

Schleusing, Georg Adam. *Neu-entdecktes Sibyrien oder Siewerien, wie es anitzo mit allen Städten und Flecken angebauet ist nebst dessen . . . gräntzen so wohl bisz an Kara Ka- thaya und Chinesische Mauer. . . .* Jena, 1690.

Schott, Andreas. *Hispania illustrata seu rerum urbiumque Hispaniae, Lusitaniae, Aethio- piae et Indiae scriptores varii.* 4 vols. Frankfurt, 1603–8.

Schotte, Appolonius. "Corte beschrijvinge van het ghetal ende ghelegent vande for- ten, . . ." *BV*, IIa. Appended to Verhoeff's voyage, pp. 125–28.

———. "Discours van . . . aengaende de Moluques." *BV*, IIa. Appended to Ver- hoeff's voyage, pp. 107–16.

———. ". . . verhael, wegens sijn voyagie gedaen van Bantam, nae Botton, Solor ende Tymor. . . ." *BV*, IIa. Appended to Verhoeff's voyage, pp. 116–25.

Schouten, Joost. "Beschrijvinge van de regeeringe, macht, religie, costuymen, traf- frijcken, ende andere remarquable saecken des coningkrijcks Siam." *BV*, IIb. Appended to Hagenaer's voyage, pp. 203–17.

————. *Notitie vande situatie, regeeringe, macht, religie, costuymen, trafficquen ende andere remarcquable saecken des Coningkrijcks Siam.* The Hague, 1638.

————; *see also* Caron, François.

Schouten, Willem Corneliszoon. *Journal ofte beschryvinghe van de wonderlicke reyse, ghedaen door Willem Corneliszoon Schouten van Hoorn, in de jaren 1615, 1616, en 1617. . . .* Amsterdam, 1618.

————; *see also* Le Maire, Jacob.

Schouten, Wouter. *Oost-Indische voyagie, vervattende veel voorname voorvallen en ongeneeme vreemde geschiedenissen, bloedige zee- en landt-gerechten. . . .* 2 vols. in 1; Amsterdam, 1676.

————. *Reys-togten naar en door Oost-Indien.* 3d ed. Amsterdam, 1740.

Schreyer, Johann. *Neue ost-indianische Reise-Beschreibung, von Anno 1669 biss 1677. Handelnde von unterschiedenen africanischen und barbarischen Völckern, sonderlich derer an dem vor Gebürge Caput Bonae Spei. . . .* Salfeld, 1679.

————. *Reise nach dem Kaplande und Beschreibung der Hottentotten 1669–1677. . . .* NR, Vol. VII. The Hague, 1931.

Schweitzer, Christoph. *Journal- und Tage-Buch seiner sechs-jährigen Ost-Indianischen Reise. Angefangen den 1. Decembr. Anno 1675 und vollendet den 2. Septemb. Anno 1682. . . .* Tübingen, 1688. (English translation of 1700 in Fayle, C. Ernest [ed.].)

————. *Reise nach Java und Ceylon, 1675–1682.* NR, Vol. XI. The Hague, 1931.

————; *see also* Raven-Hart, R.

Scott, Edmund. *An Exact Discourse of the Subtilties, Fashishions, Pollicies, Religion, and Ceremonies of the East Indians, as well Chyneses as Javans. . . .* London, 1606.

Sebastiani, Giuseppe Maria. *Prima speditione all' Indie Orientali. . . .* Rome, 1666.

————. *Seconda speditione all' Indie Orientali. . . .* Rome, 1672.

Les secrets de la médecine des Chinois . . . ; see Boym, Michael.

Semedo, Alvarez. *Imperio de la China. I cultura evangélica en él, por los religiosos de la Compañía de Iesus.* Translated and edited by Manuel de Faria y Sousa. Madrid, 1642.

————. *The History of that Great and Renowned Monarchy of China . . . to Which is Added the History of the Late Invasion and Conquest of that Flourishing Kingdom by the Tartars. With an Exact Account of the other Affairs of China till these Present Times.* London, 1655.

Sen, Surendranath (ed.). *Indian Travels of Thevenot and Careri, Being the Third Part of the Travels of M. de Thevenot into the Levant and the Third Part of a Voyage Round the World by Dr. John Francis Gemelli Careri.* New Delhi, 1949.

Settle, Elkanah. *Insigniae Batavia: or the Dutch Trophies Displayed; Being Exact Relations of the Unjust Horrid, and Most Barbarous Proceedings of the Dutch against the English in the East Indies. . . .* London, 1688.

Severim de Faria, Manuel; *see* Abreu, Francisco de.

Sevil, Pedro. *Conquista de Champan, Camboja, Siam, Cochinchina y otros paises de Oriente.* [Valladolid], 1603.

————. "Le Memorial de Pedro Sevil [de Guarga] à Philippe III . . . (1603)." Translated from Sevil's *Conquista* by Antoine Cabaton in *Bulletin de la commission archéologique de l'Indochine* (1914–16), 1–102, Paris.

Seys, Gillis. "Verhael vande Mollucs eylanden, hoe ende in wat manieren de selvige in 't jaer 1627 bevonden hebben, onder de regeringhe van de Heer Gouverneur Jacques le Febvres, . . ." *BV*, IIa appended to Verhoeff's voyage, pp. 162–87.

————. "Verhael van de tegenwoordigen [1627] staet inde quartieren van Amboyna, ende omleggende plaetsen. . . ." *BV*, IIa. Appended to Verhoeff's voyage, pp. 130–51.

A Short Account of the Siege of Bantam: and His Surrender to the Rebels, Who Were Assisted by the Dutch, and Their Fleet in the East Indies. London, 1683.

Sibellius, Caspar. *Of the Conversion of five thousand nine hundred East Indians In the Isle Formosa neere China, to the Profession of the True God in Jesus Christ; by Means of M. Ro. Junius, a Minister Lately in Delph in Holland. . . .* London, 1650.

Sicardo, José. *Cristiandad del Japón, y dilatada persecución que padeció. Memorias sacras, de los martyres de las ilustres religiones de Santo Domingo, San Francisco, Compañia de Jesus; y crecido numero de seglares: y con especialidad, de los religiosos del Orden de N. P. S. Augustin.* Madrid, 1698.

Silva, Fernando da. *Verissima relación en que se da quenta en el estado en que estan las guerras en las Filipinas, y reynos de el Japon, contra los Olandeses. . . .* Seville, 1626.

Silveira, Luis (ed.); *see* Manrique, Sebastião.

Sinclair, William F. (trans.); *see* Teixeira, Pedro.

Skelton, R. A. (ed.); *see* Waghenaer, Lucas Janszoon.

Solá, Magino. *Informe al Rey . . . Felipe quarto, en su real y supremo Consejo de las Indias, del estado eclesiástico y seglar de las islas Filipinas.* Mexico, 1658.

Solier, François. *Histoire ecclésiastique des isles et royaumes du Iapon.* 2 vols. Paris, 1627–29.

Solis, Duarte Gomez; *see* Gomez Solis, Duarte.

Solt, Paulus van. "Verhael ende journael vande voyagie gedaen van Bantam naer de cust van Choromandel ende andere quartieren van Indien . . . inden jaere 1605. 1606. 1607. 1608." *BV*, IIa. Appended to Van der Hagen's second voyage, pp. 40–91.

Sommaire recueil des raisons plus importantes, qui doyvent mouvoir Messieurs des Estats des Provinces Unies du Pays-bas, de ne quitter point les Indes. Traduit de Flamand en François. La Rochelle, 1608.

Sotelo, Luys; *see Relacion breve, y sumaria . . .* ; *see also* Amati, Scipione.

Specx, Jacob, and Siegerszoon, Pieter. "[Reisjournaal van] Jacob Specx ende Pieter Siergertsz met het jacht *den Brack* van Patane naar Japan." *BV*, IIa. Appended to Verhoeff's voyage, pp. 72–98.

Speerway, Thomas. "A Letter of Thomas Spurway, Merchant Touching the Wrongs Done at Banda to the English by the Hollanders. . . ." *PP*, IV, 508–35.

Spencer, James (ed.); *see* Dampier, William.

Spilbergen, Joris van. *Oost ende West-Indische spiegel der 2 leste navigatien, ghedaen in de jaeren 1614. 15. 16. 17. ende 18. daer in vertoont wort, in wat gestalt Ioris van Speilbergen door de Magellanes de werelt rontom geseylt heeft . . . Met de australische navigatien, van Jacob le Maire, die int suyden door een nieuwe straet ghepasseert is.* . . . Leyden, 1619.

————. "Historisch journael van de voyagie ghedaen met ses schepen. . . ." *BV,* IIa.

————. *The East and West Indian Mirror, Being an Account of Joris van Speilbergen's Voyage Round the World (1614–1617), and the Australian Navigations of Jacob Le Maire.* . . . Translated and edited by J. A. J. de Villiers. "HS," 2d ser., XVIII. London, 1906.

————. *De reis om de wereld van Joris van Spilbergen, 1614–1617.* Edited by J. C. M. Warnsinck. "WLV," Vol. XLVII. 2 vols. The Hague, 1943.

————; *see also* Vennip, Cornelius Janszoon.

Spon, Jacob [?]. *De l'usage du caphé, du thé, et du chocolate.* Lyons, 1671.

————. *Traitez nouveaux et curieux du café, du thé, et du chocolate.* Lyons, 1685.

Staunton, Sir George T. (ed.); *see* González de Mendoza, Juan.

Steele, Richard. "A Journey of Richard Steel, and John Crawther, from Azmere in Endia . . . to Spahan . . . Persia, in the Affairs of the East Indian Society. Anno 1615. 1616." *PP,* IV, 266–80.

Stevens, John (trans.); *see* Argensola, Bartolomé Leonardo de.

Stokram, Andries. *Korte beschryvinge van de ongeluckige weer-om-reys, van het schip Aernhem, nevens noch zes andere schepen, onder 't gebiedt van den Heer Arnout de Vlaming van Outshoorn, van Batavia na het vaderlandt afgevaren, op den 23. December 1661.* . . . Amsterdam, 1663.

Struys, Jan Janszoon. *Drie aanmerkelijke en seer rampspoedige reysen door Italien, Griekenlandt, Lijflandt, Moscovien, Tartarijen, Meden, Persien, Oost-Indien, Japan, en verscheyden andere gewesten.* . . . Amsterdam, 1676.

————. *The Perillous and Most Unhappy Voyages of John Struys through Italy, Greece, Lifeland, Moscovia, Tartary, Media, Persia, East-India, Japan, and other Places in Europe, Africa, and Asia.* . . . Translated by John Morrison. London, 1683.

Suarez, Joseph, S.J. *La libertad de la ley de Dios en el imperio de la China.* . . . Translated by D. Juan de Espinola. Lisbon, 1696.

Summaria relaçam dos prodigiosos feitos que as armas portuguesas obrasão na ilha Ceylão contra os Olandeses e Chingalas, no anno passado de 1655. Lisbon, 1656.

Tacchi-Venturi, Pietro, S.J. (ed.). *Opera storiche del P. Matteo Ricci.* 2 vols. Macerata, 1913.

Tachard, Guy, S.J. *Voyage de Siam des pères jésuites, envoyéz par le roy aux Indes et a la Chine.* . . . Paris, 1686.

————. *Second voyage du Père Tachard et des Jésuites envoyés par le roy au royaume de Siam.* . . . Amsterdam, 1689.

Tanner, Mathias. *Societas Jesu usque ad sanguinis et vitae profusionem militans, in Europe, Africa, Asia, et America, contra gentiles, Mohametanos, Judaeos, haereticos, impios, pro Deo, fide, ecclesia, pietate;* . . . Prague, 1675.

Tappen, David. *Fünffzehen-jährige curiöse und denkwürdige auch sehr gefährliche ost-indianische Reise-Beschreibung.* . . . Hanover and Wolfenbüttel, 1704.

Tasman, Abel Janszoon. "Een Kort verhael uyt het journael van den Kommander

Abel Jansen Tasman. . . . ." In *Eenige oefeningen in godlycke, wiskonstige en nateur-lycke dingen,* by Dirck Rembrantszoon van Nierop (2 vols.; Amsterdam, 1674), II, 56–64. (Based on Tasman's original journal.)

———. "The Voyage of Captain Abel Jansen Tasman For the Discovery of Southern Countries by Direction of the Dutch East India Company." In *A General Collection of the Best and Most Interesting Voyages and Travels in All Parts of the World. . . ,* by John Pinkerton (17 vols. London, 1808–14), XI, 441–42.

———. *Journal of His Discovery of van Dieman's Land and New Zealand in 1642.* Edited by J. E. Heeres and W. van Bemmelen. Amsterdam, 1898.

———. *De reizen van Abel Janszoon Tasman en Franchoys Jacobszoon Visscher ter nadere ontdekking van het zuidland in 1642/3 en 1644.* Edited by R. Posthumus-Meyjes. "WLV," Vol. XVII. The Hague, 1919.

———; *see also* Haelbos, Hendrik; Montanus, Arnoldus.

Tavernier, Jean Baptiste. *Les six voyages . . . , qu'il a fait in Turquie, en Perse, et aux Indes. . . .* 2 vols. Paris, 1676–77.

———. *Recueil de plusieurs relations et traitez singuliers et curieux . . . qui n'ont point esté mise dans ses six premiers voyages, devisé en cinq parties.* Paris, 1679.

———. *Travels in India. . . .* Edited by V. Ball and W. Crooke. 2 vols. London, 1925.

Teixeira, Pedro. *Relaciones de Pedro Teixeira d'el origen descendencia y succession de los reyes de Persia y de Hormuz, y de un viage hecho por el mismo autor desde la India Oriental hasta Italia por tierra.* 2 pts. Antwerp. 1610.

———. *The Travels of Pedro Teixeira with His "Kings of Hormuz," and Extracts from His "Kings of Persia."* Translated and edited by William F. Sinclair with notes by Donald Ferguson. "HS," 2d ser., IX. London, 1902.

Tellier, Michel le; *see* Le Tellier, Michel.

Tello de Guzmán, Francisco. *Relación que embio de seys frayles españoles dela orden de San Francisco que crucificaron los del Iapon, este año próximo passado de 1597.* Seville, 1598.

Temple, Richard Carnac (ed.). *The Travels of Peter Mundy in Europe and Asia, 1608–1667.* 5 vols. "HS," 2d ser., XVII, XXXV, XLV, XLVI, LV, and LXXVIII. Cambridge, 1907–36.

Ternaux-Compans, H. (ed.). *Archives des voyages, ou collection d'anciennes relations in-édites ou très-rares de lettres, mémoires, itinéraires et autres documents relatifs a la géographie et aux voyages. . . .* 2 vols. Paris, 1840–44.

Terpstra, H. (ed.); *see* Linschoten, Jan Huygen van.

Terry, Edward. "A Relation of a Voyage to the Eastern India. . . ." *PP,* IX, 1–55.

———. *A Voyage to East India. Wherein Some Things Are Taken Notice of in Our Passage Thither, but Many More in Our Abode There, Within that Rich and Spacious Empire of the Great Mogul.* London, 1655.

Thévenot, Jean de. *Relation d'un voyage fait au Levant. . . .* 3 pts. Paris, 1664–84. (English translation in Sen, S. [ed.].)

Thévenot, Melchisédech (comp.). *Relations de divers voyages curieux, qui n'ont point esté publiées ou qui ont esté traduites d'Hacluyt, de Purchas, & d'autres voyageurs Anglois, Hollandois, Portugais, Alemands, Espagnols; et de quelques Persans, Arabes & autres auteurs orienteaux. . . .* 4 vols. Paris, 1663–96. Cited as TR.

—— (comp.). *Recueil de voyages.* . . . Paris, 1681.

Thompson, Edward Maunde (ed.); *see* Cocks, Richard.

Tiele, P. S. (ed.); *see* Apius, Martinus.

Tinelli, Francesco. *Compendio della* . . . *Sanvitores.* Brescia, 1695. (Epitomizes Ortiz' *Istoria.* . . .)

Tissanier, Joseph. *Relation du voyage* . . . *depuis la France jusq'u au royaume de Tunquin, avec ce qui s'est passé* . . . *dans cette mission durant les années 1658–1660.* Paris, 1663.

Torquemada, Fray Juan de, O.F.M. *Monarquia Indiana.* Seville, 1615. (Contains a narrative of the Quiros expedition, extracts of which are also to be found in C. Markham [ed.], *The Voyages of Pedro Fernandez de Quiros, 1595–1606;* 2 vols.; "HS," 2d ser., XIV–XV; London, 1904, II, 405–51.)

Toscano, Giuseppe M.; *see* Andrade, Antonio de, S.J.

Tosi, Clemente. *Dell' India orientale descrittione geografica et historica.* . . . Rome, 1669.

"Translaet van een Japansche brief, van Siragemondonnae, burgermeester in Nanga-sacqui, aen den gouverneur-generael etc. door den opperkoopmen Jan van Elzerach overgesonden dato den 28 Oct. 1642." *BV,* IIb. Appended to Caron's account, pp. 195–97.

Trigault, Nicolas. *De christiana expeditione apud Sinas suscepta, ab Societate Jesu. Ex P. Matthaei Ricci* . . . *commentariis. libri V* . . . *in quibus sinensis regni, mores, leges atque instituta & nova illius ecclesiae difficillima primordia* . . . *describuntur.* Augsburg, 1615.

——. *De christianis apud Iaponios triumphis, sive de gravissima ibidem contra Christi fidem persecutione exorta anno MDC XII usq. ad annum MDCXX. Libri quinq.* . . . Munich, 1623.

——. *China in the Sixteenth Century: The Journals of Matthew Ricci: 1583–1610.* Translated by Louis J. Gallagher. New York, 1953.

A True Account of the Burning and Sad Condition of Bantam, in the East Indies. . . . London, 1682.

A True and Large Discourse of the Voyage of the Whole Fleete of Ships Set Forth the 20. of Aprill 1601. by the Gouvernours and Assistants of the East-Indian Merchants in London, to the East Indies. . . . London, 1603. (The first published report of the first English East India Company voyage under Sir James Lancaster. *See* also Lancaster, Sir James.)

A True Declaration of the News Concerning a Conspiracy Discovered in the Island of Amboyna and the Punishment that Followed thereof. London, 1628.

A True Declaration of the News that Came Out of the East Indies with the Pinnace Called the Hare. . . . London, 1624.

A True Relation of the Unjust, Cruell, and Barbarous Proceedings against the English at Amboyna. . . . London, 1624.

A True Relation Without All Exceptions of Strange and Admirable Accidents which Lately Happened in the Kingdom of the Great Magor or Mugul, Who is the Greatest Monarch in the East Indies, as also with a True Report of the Manners of the Country. . . . London, 1632.

Twist, Jonathan van. "Generale beschrijvinghe van Indien. Ende in't besonder van't coninckrijck van Guseratten. . . ." *BV*, IIb, 1–112. (Reproduced in separate publications, Amsterdam, 1647 and 1648.)

Vairasse, Denis. *Historie des Sevarambes, volkeren die een gedeelte van het derde vast-land bewoonen, gemeenlyk Zuid-land genaamd . . . mitsgaders een zeer naauwkeurig journaal wegens de voyagie derwaarts gedaan in de jaaren 1696 en 1697 op ordre door der Hollandsche Oost-Indische Maatschappy door de schepen de Nyptang, de Geelvink, en de Wezel*. Translated by Gotfried Broekhuyzen. Amsterdam, 1701. (Contains the only seventeenth-century edition of Vlamingh's journal.)

Valentijn, François. *Oud en nieuw Oost-Indien*. . . . 8 vols. Dordrecht, 1724–26.

———. *François Valentijn's Description of Ceylon*. Trans. and ed. S. Arasaratuam. "HS," 2d ser., Vol. CXLIX. London, 1978.

Valle, Pietro della. *Viaggi di Pietro della Valle il Pellegrino . . . descritti da lui medesimo in 54. lettere familiari . . . all'erudito . . . suo amico Mario Schipano, divissi in tre parti, cioè la Turchia, la Persia, e l'India*. . . . Rome, 1650.

———. *The Travels of Pietro Della Valle in India from the Old English Translation of 1664 by G. Havers*. Edited by Edward Grey. "HS," o.s., LXXXIV, LXXXV. 2 vols. London, 1891–92.

Van Dam, Pieter; *see* Dam, Pieter van.

Van den Broecke, Pieter; *see* Broecke, Pieter van den.

Van der Hagen, Steven; *see* Hagen, Steven van der.

Vandrille, De St. *Relation des révolutions arrivées dans le royaume de Siam*. Paris, 1690.

Van Goens, Rijcklof Volckertszoon; *see* Goens, Rijcklof Volckertszoon van.

Van Vliet, Jeremias; *see* Vliet, Jeremias van.

Van Zeyst, Gillis; *see* Seys, Gillis.

Varen, Bernhard. *Descriptio regni Iaponiae cum quibusdam affinis materiae, ex variis auctoribus collecta*. . . . Amsterdam, 1649.

Veen, Cornelis van. "Kort verhael van de twee-jaerige voyagie ghedaen door Cornelis van Veen, in de Oost-Indien." *BV*, Ib. Appended to Wolfert Harmenszoon's voyage, pp. 26–27.

Veer, Gerrit de. "Kort verhael van d' eerste schipvaerd der Hollandsche ende Zeeusche schepen by noorden Noorwegen, Moscovien ende Tartarien om, nae de coningrijcken van Cathay ende China." In *BV*, Ia. (Isaac Massa's treatises are appended to this edition.)

Veiga, Manoel da. *Relaçam geral do estado da christandade de Ethiopia . . . e do que de novo socedeo no descobrimento do Thybet, a que chamam gram Catayo*. Lisbon, 1628. (Contains an extract from Andrade's description of Tibet.)

Velloso, Gonçalo de S. José. *Iornada que Francisco de Souza de Castro . . . fez ao Achem*. Goa, 1642. (See facsimile in C. R. Boxer, "Uma obra rarissima impressa em Goa no século XVII," *Boletim internacional de bibliografia Luso-Brasileiro*, VIII, No. 33 [1967], 431–528.)

[Vennip, Cornelis Janszoon]. *'t Historiael journael van tghene ghepasseert is van weghen dry schepen, den Ram, Schaep, ende't Lam . . . onder t' beleyt van Ioris van Spilberghen, generael*. [Delft, Floris Balthazar, 1604].

———. " 't Historiael journael vande voyagie ghedaén met drie schepen, ghenaemt den Ram, Schaep, ende het Lam . . . onder 't beleyt van den Heer Admirael Joris van Spilbergen, gedaen in de Jaren 1601, 1602, 1603, ende 1604." *BV,* Ib.

———. "The Visit of Spilbergen to Ceylon, Translated from Admiral Joris van Spilbergen's 'Relation.'" Translated and edited from Vennip's *'t Historiael journale* by D. Ferguson. *JRAS, Ceylon Branch,* XXX (1927), 127–79, 361–409.

———. *De reis van Joris van Spilbergen naar Ceylon, Atjeh en Bantam, 1601–1604.* Edited by Wouter Nijhoff, S. P. L'Honoré Naber, F. W. Stapel, and F. C. Wieder. "WLV," Vol. XXXVIII. The Hague, 1933.

Verbiest, Ferdinand, S.J. *Astronomia europaea sub imperatore tartaro sinico Cám Hy appellato ex umbra in lucem revocata.* . . . Dillingen, 1687.

———. "A Voyage of the Emperor of China into Eastern Tartary, Anno 1682," *Philosophical Transactions,* XVI (1686–87), pp. 35–78.

———. *Voyages de l'empereur de la Chine dans la Tartarie.* Translated by D. D. Paris, 1685. (English translation in D'Orléans, Pierre Joseph, *History of the Two Tartar Conquerors of China.*)

Verhael vande reyse by de hollandtsche schepen gedaen naer Oost-Indien. . . . Middelborgh, 1597. (The earliest account of Houtman's voyage. See also Lodewyckszoon, Willem.)

Verhoeff, Pieter Willemszoon; *see* Moelre, Johan de, and Febvre, Jacques le; *also* Dirckszoon, Reynier.

———. *De reis van de vloot van Pieter Willemsz. Verhoeff . . . 1607–1612.* Edited by M. E. van Opstall. 2 vols. "WLV," Vols. LXXIII, LXXIV. The Hague, 1974.

Verken, Johann. *Johann Verken, Molukken-Reise, 1607–1612. Neu herausgegeben nach der zu Franckfurt am Main im Verlag Joh. Th. De Bry im Jahre 1612 erschienenen Original-Ausgabe.* NR, Vol. II. The Hague, 1930. (First edition in Theodore de Bry [ed.], *India orientalis,* Part IX. Frankfurt, 1612.)

Vermeulen, Gerret. *De gedenkwaerdige voyagie . . . naar Oost-Indien in't jaer 1668 aangevangen, en in't jaer 1674 voltrokken: Daarin onder veel andere toevallen de vermaarde oorlog tegen de koning van Macassar beknoptelijk verhaalt.* . . . Amsterdam, 1677.

Verquains, Vollant des; *see* Vollant des Verquains.

Viegas, Artur (ed.); *see* Guerreiro, Fernão.

Villacastin, Thomas de. *Apostolica vida, virtudes y milagros del santo padre y maestro Francisco Xavier.* Valladolid, 1602.

Villiers, J. A. J. de (trans.); *see* Spilbergen, Joris van.

Vincenzo Maria di Santa Caterina da Siena. *Il viaggio all' Indie Orientali.* . . . Rome, 1672.

Vlamingh, Willem Hesselszoon de. *Journael wegens een voyagie, gedaan op order der Hollandsche Oost-Indische Maatschappy in de jaaren 1696 en 1697 . . . na het onbekende Zuid-land, en wijders na Batavia.* Amsterdam, 1701. (Bound with a Dutch translation of Denis Vairesse, *Histoire des Sevarambes.*)

———. *De ontdekkingsreis van Willem Hesselsz. de Vlamingh in de jaren 1696–1697.* Edited by G. G. Schilder. 2 vols. "WLV," Vols. LXXVIII, LXXIX. The Hague, 1976.

Vliet, Jeremias van. *Beschrijving van het koningryk Siam.* . . . Leyden, 1692.

——. *Historiael verhael der sieckte, ende doot van Pra Interra-Tsia 22en coninck in Siam ende den regherenden coninck Pra Ongh Srij,* . . . *1640; with French Translation of Part thereof, Taken from Les revolutions arrivées au royaume de Siam, Paris, 1663.* Transcribed and edited by Seiichi Iwao. "The Toyo Bunko Publications," Ser. D, No. 5. Tokyo, 1958.

Vogel, Johann Wilhelm. *Diarium oder Journal seiner gethanen Reise aus Teutschland nach Holland und Ost-Indien.* Nuremberg, 1690.

Vollant (or Volant) des Verquains, [Jean]. *Histoire de la révolution de Siam. Arrivée en l'année 1688.* Lille, 1691.

Vondel, Joost van. *Volledige dichtwerken.* Ed. A. Verwey. Amsterdam, 1937.

Voretzsch, E. A. (ed.); *see* Froger, François.

Vries, David Pieterszoon de. *Korte historiael, ende journaels aenteyckeninge van verscheyden voyagiens in de vier deelen des wereldts-ronde, als Europe, Africa, Asia, ende Amerika gedaen.* Hoorn, 1655.

——. *Korte historiael ende journaels aenteyckeninge van versheyden voyagiens in de vier deelen des wereldtsronde.* . . . Edited by H. T. Colenbrander. "WLV," Vol. III. The Hague, 1911.

Vries, Martin Gerritszoon; *see* Brouwer, Hendrick.

Waerachtich verhael van't geene inde eylanden van Banda, in Oost-Indien, inden jaere sestien-hondert eenentwintich, ende to vooren is ghepassert. [Amsterdam], 1622.

Waghenaer, Lucas Janszoon. *Thresoor der zeevaert.* Leyden, 1592.

——. *Thresoor der zeevaert, Leyden, 1592.* . . . Edited with an introduction by R. A. Skelton. Amsterdam, 1965.

Wagner, Johann Christophe. *Interiora orientis detecta, oder grundrichtige und eigentliche Beschreibung aller heut zu Tag bekandten grossen und herrlichen Reiche des Orients* . . . Augsburg, 1687.

——. *Das mächtige Kayser-Reich Sina und die asiatische Tartarey vor Augen gestellet.* Augsburg, 1688.

Warnsinck, J. C. M. (ed.); *see* Graaf, Nikolaas de; Spilbergen, Joris van.

Warwijck, Wybrant van. "Historisch verhael vande reyse gedaen inde Oost-Indien, . . ." *BV,* Ia. (Part of this account was written by Jan Harmenszoon Bree.)

——. *See also* Neck, Jacob Corneliszoon van.

Wassenaer, Nicolaes van. *Historisch verhael alder ghedenck-weerdichste geschiedenisse.* . . . Amsterdam, 1621–1632.

Webb, John. *An Historical Essay Endeavoring a Probability that the Language of the Empire of China is the Primitive Language.* London, 1669.

Weinstock, Herbert (trans.); *see* Carletti, Francesco.

West-Zanen, Willem Pieterszoon van. *Derde voornaemste zee-getocht (der verbondene vrye Nederlanden) na de Oost-Indien: Gedaan met de Achinsche en Moluksche vloten, onder de ammiralen Iacob Heemskerk, en Wolphert Harmansz. in den Jare 1601. 1602. 1603.* . . . Amsterdam, 1648.

White, Samuel. *A Letter from Mr. Samuel White to His Brother in London.* . . . *Giving a*

Full Account of the Late Rebellion Made by the People of Macassar, Inhabiting in that Country, Which Ended in the Death of all the Rebells, Who Were Totally Destroyed by the King's Forces, Assisted by Some Europeans, of Several Nations, Amongst Whom Capt. Henry Udall, and Some Others of our Countrymen Most Unhappily Lost their Lives. London, 1687.

Wicki, Josef, S.J. (ed.); *see* Gonçalves, Diogo.

Wieder, F. C. (ed.). *De reis van Mahu en de Cordes door de Straat van Magalhães naar Zuid-Amerika en Japan.* 3 vols. "WLV," Vols. XXI, XXII, XXIV. The Hague, 1923–25.

Wilkinson, C. (ed.); *see* Dampier, William.

Willman, Olof Eriksson. . . . *Reesa till Ostindien, jempte een kort berättelese om konungerijket Japan och thess keysare.* . . . In *Een kort beskrffning vppä trenne reesor.* . . . Wijsindzborg, 1674.

Willson, David Harris. *A Royal Request for Trade. A Letter of King James I to the Emperor of Japan.* . . . Minneapolis, 1965.

Wilson, Ralph. "The Eleventh Voyage to the East Indies in the Salomon, Begun in the Yeere of Our Lord 1611. . . ." *PP,* IV, 175–80.

Withington, Nicholas. "Extracts of a Tractate, . . ." *PP,* IV, 162–75.

Witsen, Nicolaas. *Noord en Oost Tartarye.* . . . Amsterdam, 1692.

Wood, Benjamin. "The Voyage of Master Benjamin Wood, . . ." *PP,* II, 288–97.

Wurffbain, Johann Sigmund. *Reisebeschreibung welche er wegen der in Niederland angeordneten Ost-Indianische Compagnie, 1632 dahin fürgenommen und 1646 vollendet hat.* Nuremberg, 1646.

————. *Reise nach den Molukken und Vorder-Indien, 1632–1646. Neu herausgegeben nach der zu Nürnberg im Verlag von Johann Georg Endter im Jahre 1686 erscheinenen Original-Ausgabe.* Edited by R. Posthumus Meyjes. NR, Vol. VIII. The Hague, 1931.

————. *Joh. Sigmund Wurffbains vierzehen jährige Ost-Indianische Krieg- und Ober-Kauffmanns-Dienste. In einem richtig geführten Journal- und Tage-Buch. In welchem viel denckwürdige Begebenheiten, wohlbeglaubte Erzehlungen, fern entlegener Länder und dero Einwohner annehmliche Beschreibungen ausländischer Gewächse und Thiere deutliche Erklärungen sambt vielen in Handlungs-Sachen dienlichen wichtigkeiten vorgestellet werden.* . . . Nuremburg, 1686.

Wusthof, Geeraerd van; *see* Casteleyn, Pieter.

Wytfliet, Cornelius. *Histoire universelle des Indes Orientales et Occidentales.* . . . Douay, 1605. Translated from Latin into French.

Xavier, Manoel, S.J. *Vitorias do governador da India Nuno Alvarez Botelho.* Lisbon, 1633.

Ximenez, C. *Doctrina cristiana in lengua Bisaya.* Manila, 1610.

Zani, Conte Valerio; *see* Anzi, Aurelio degli.

Zeitung auss der newen Welt oder chinesischen Königreichen. . . . Augsburg, 1654.

Jesuit Letterbooks

TENTATIVE LIST OF THE
PRINCIPAL EDITIONS OF SEVENTEENTH-CENTURY
PUBLISHED JESUIT LETTERBOOKS.

The following list is highly selective. For the most part it includes only the first editions of published Jesuit letterbooks. Translations are included only in the case of (1) collections of important translated letters published together for the first time, and (2) letterbooks better known in translation than in the originals. Although the distinction between a book published by a Jesuit missionary and a Jesuit letterbook is sometimes difficult to make, we have tried not to include major books written by Jesuit missionaries which more properly belong in the general bibliography. Only a few of the more important martyrologies are included here, and almost none of the Rites Controversy literature which dominated the last decades of the century. For a list of Jesuit letterbooks from India see John Correia-Afonso, S.J., *Jesuit Letters and Indian History, 1542–1773* (2d ed.; Bombay, 1969), Appendix D. The most complete bibliography of both published and unpublished seventeenth-century missionary reports is Robert Streit, *Bibliotheca missionum,* Vols. IV and V (Aachen, 1928, 1929).

The publication of Jesuit letterbooks from Asian mission fields declined during the course of the seventeenth century. Probably twice as many of them were published during the first three decades than were published during the century's remainder. This does not mean that Jesuit contributions to Europe's information about Asia declined; but many Jesuit publications of the latter half of the century cannot properly be called letterbooks. Many were histories or descriptions written by a single author, and during the last decades of the century, Rites Controversy polemics dominated mission publications. Nevertheless, some Jesuit letterbooks continued to appear down to the end of the century.

While many of the earlier letterbooks contained letters from several of the Society's Asian fields, some specifically reported on a single mission, on Japan or on China, for example. The Japan letters were by far the most numerous during the first three decades. After 1615, however, these were usually written in Macao and contained letters from Siam, Indochina, and China, as well as from the exiled Japan missionaries. In fact, they contained very little about Japan beyond the reports of persecutions and martyrdoms. China became relatively more important than either Japan or India in the latter half of the century. If descriptive books and Rites Controversy polemics—neither included in this list—are counted in with the letterbooks, China overwhelmingly dominated the reports from Jesuit missions by the century's end.

For most of the century, more first-edition letterbooks were published in Italy than elsewhere, although in the first decades many were also published in Iberian centers. Translations and subsequent editions were abundant, however. Many letters first published in Rome had been translated from unpublished Portuguese or Spanish originals. Published Iberian letterbooks were quickly translated into Italian. Most of the letterbooks also appeared in Latin translations, published not only by Italian printers but also in Mainz, Dillingen, Augsburg, Douai, and Antwerp by printers who seemed to specialize in Jesuit letterbooks. Some were also translated into German, French, and Flemish; a few even into English. Several letterbooks were first published in Latin, French, or German. Whatever the language of the first editions, the Jesuit letterbooks were usually available in Latin and in most European vernaculars within eighteen months after their original publication and between two and three years after the letters were written. Early in the century two major compilations of Jesuit letterbooks appeared: Fernão Guerreiro's *Relaçam annual* was published in five volumes between 1603 and 1611; Pierre Du Jarric's *Histoire des choses plus memorable* appeared in three volumes between 1608 and 1614.

In the beginning of the century, French Jesuits published very few letterbooks. They were not themselves involved in the eastern missions, and their political troubles at home during the first decade sometimes made it difficult for them even to publish translated reports. Still, even during the first decade, some of the most important letterbooks were translated into French, and the first volume of Du Jarric's compilation appeared in 1608. Subsequently translations of letterbooks into French proceeded apace. Beginning in 1625 many of the most important of them appeared in a series whose titles begin with *Histoire de ce qui s'est passé,* most of which were published by Sebastien Cramoisy of Paris. By the end of the century French publications dominated mission reports. Most of them, however, were separate books or Rites Controversy polemics rather than letterbooks. In 1702 there appeared at Paris the first volume of *Lettres édifantes et curieuses écrites des missions étrangères,* perhaps the greatest collection of Jesuit letters, reaching thirty-four volumes when it was completed in 1778.

The following list is organized chronologically by date of publication. We cite the titles as they appear on the title pages, making only minor orthographic changes.

1596

Francisci Xaverii Epistolarum libri quatuor, ab Horatio Tursellino e Societate Jesu in Latinum conversi ex Hispano. Ad Franciscum Toletum S. R. E. Cardinalem. Roma, 1596. (Correia-Afonso, p. 181. Many subsequent editions.)

1598

Cartas Que os Padres e Irmãos da Companhia de Iesus escreverão dos Reynos de Iapão & China aos da mesma Companhia da India, & Europa, desde anno de 1549 atè o de 1580. Primeiro Tomo. Nellas se conta o principio, socesso, & bondade da Christandade da quellas partes, & varios costumes, & falsos ritos da gentilidade. . . . Em Evora por Manoel de Lyra. Anno de M.D.XCVIII. (Streit, IV, 500–503. Contains a large number of Japan letters.)

Compendio de algunas cartas que este anno de 97. vierão dos Padres da Companhia de Iesu, que residem na India, & corte do Grão Mogor, & nos Reinos da China, & Iapão, & no Brasil, em que se contem varia cousos. Lisboa. Colligidas por o Padre Amador Rebello da mesma companhia. 1598. (Correia-Afonso, p. 181.)

Nova Relatio Historica de Statu Rei Christianae in Japonia et de Quabacundoni: Hoc Est, Monarchae Japonici trucidatione, binis Epistolis a R. P. Aloysio Frois Soc. Jesu, Anno M DXCV datis, comprehensa. Nunc ex Italico Idiomate in latinum traducta. Moguntiae [Mainz] ex Officina Typ. Joannis Albini, Anno M.D.XCVIII. (Streit, IV, 498. Contains two 1595 letters by Frois.)

Ragguaglio della Morte di Quabacondono, Scritta dal P. Luigi Frois della Compagnia di Giesù, dal Giappone nel Mese d'Ottobre del 1595. Et dalla Portoghesa nella lingua Italiana tradotta dal P. Gasparo Spitilli di Campli, della Compagnia medesima. In Roma, Appresso Luigi Zannetti, 1598. . . . (Streit, IV, 498.)

1599

De Rebus Iaponicis Historica Relatio, Eaque Triplex: I. De gloriosa morte 26. cruci-
fixorum. II. De Legatione Regis Chinensium ad Regem Iaponiae, & de Prodigijs
legationem antegressis. III. De rebus per Iaponiam anno 1596. a PP. Soc. Iesu
durante persecutione gestis. A. R. P. Ludovico Frois . . . Et ex Italico Idiomate
Moguntiae in Latinam linguam translata. Moguntiae [Mainz], ex officina Ty-
pographica Ioannis Albini, M.D.XCIX. (Streit, IV, 505–6. Contains translations of three letters of Luis Frois: March 15, 1597; Dec. 28, 1596; and Dec. 13,
1596.)

Historica relatio de magno rege Mogor et de Japoniae regnis. Moguntiae [Mainz],
1599.

Lettera Annua del Giappone, dell' Anno M.D.XCVI. Scritta dal P. Luigi Frois . . .
Tradotta in Italiano dal P. Francesco Mercati . . . In Roma, Appresso Luigi Zannetti 1599. (Streit, IV, 506. Letter dated Dec. 13, 1596.)

Relatione della Gloriosa Morte di XXVI Posti in Croce per commandamento del Re
di Giappone, alli 5. di Febraio 1597. de quali sei furono Religiosi di S. Francesco, tre della Compagnia di Giesù & dicesette Christiani Giapponesi. Mandata
dal P. Luigi Frois alli 15. di Marzo . . . Et fatta in Italiano dal P. Gasparo Spitilli . . . In Roma, Appresso Luigi Zannetti 1599. . . . (Streit, IV, 506. Letter
dated March 15, 1597.)

Trattato d'Alcuni Prodigii Occorsi l'Anno M.D.XCVI. Nel Giappone. Mandato dal
P. Luigi Frois . . . Tradotto in Italiano dal P. Francesco Mercati . . . In Roma,
Appresso Luigi Zannetti. M.D.XCIX. . . . (Streit, IV, 507. Letter dated
Dec. 28, 1596.)

1601

Breve relatione del Regno della Cina. Nella quale si dà particolar conto dello stato
presente di quel Regno, della dispositione di quei popoli alla Fede Christiana, &
de'loro costumi, studij, & dottrina. Scritta di là dal R. P. Nicolo Longobardi
della Compagnia di Giesu. In Mātova, Per Francesco Osanna Stampator
Ducale. 1601. (Streit, V, 684.)

Copia d'una Breve Relatione della Christianità di Giappone, del mese di Marzo del
M.D.XCVIII. insino ad Ottob. del medisimo anno, et della morte di Taicosama
Signore di detto Regno. Scritta del P. Francesco Pasio, . . . et dalla Portoghese
tradotta nella lingua Italiana dal P. Gasparo Spitilli, di Campli della Compagnia
medesima. In Roma, Appresso Luigi Zannetti M.DCI. . . . (Streit, V, 7. Contains Pasio's 1598 letter from Japan, Pedro Gomez' 1598 letter, Longobardo's
1598 letter from China, and the 1589 and 1599 letters of "Gerolamo Sciavier"
[Jerome Xavier] and Emanuel Pigneiro [Manuel do Pinheiro] from the Mughul
Empire.)

Epistola Patris Nicolai Pimentae Visitatoris Societatis Jesu in India Orientali. . . .
Goae VIII. Kal. Januarij 1599. Romae, Apud Aloysium Zannettum. MDCI. . .
(Streit, V, 8.)

Lettera del P. Nicolo Pimenta Visitatore della Compagnia di Giesù nell' India Orientale. . . . Da Goa, li 25. di Decembre. 1598. [*sic*] In Roma. Appresso Luigi Zannetti. M.DC.I. . . . (Streit, V, 9. In the text, the letter is dated 1599, not 1598.)

Newe Historische Relation und sehr gute fröliche und lustige Bottschaft was sich in vilen gewaltigen Königreichen der Orientalischen Indien. . . . Dilingen durch Johannes Mayer. 1601. (Streit, V, 10. Contains Pasio's 1598 letter from Japan, and Nicolas Pimenta's of 1598 and 1599.)

1602

Cartas Que o Padre Nicolao Pimenta da Companhia de Iesu, Visitador nas Partes do Oriente, escreveo ao Geral della mesma Companhia à 26 de Novẽbro [*sic*] do ano de 1599 et ao 1. de Dezembre de 1600. nas quaes entre agũas cousas notaveis et curiosas q conta de diversos reinos, relata o sucesso da insigne Victoria q Andre Furtado de Mendoça alcaçou do Cunhale grande perseguidor da Fee et Christãdade da India et cruel inimigo daquelle estado. Em Lisboa, por Pedro Crasbeeck 1602. (Streit, V, 15–16. Portuguese translation of the *Epistola* [Rome, 1600] and of the *Copia* [Rome, 1602]. Translated into English and edited by H. Hosten, S.J., in the *JRAS, Bengal Branch*, XXIII [1927], 95–97.)

Copia d'Una del P. Nicolo Pimenta, Visitatore Della Provincia d'India Orientale. . . . del primo di Decembre 1600. In Roma, Appresso Luigi Zannetti 1602. . . . (Streit, V, 12. Contains letters from Corsi, Soares, Cotigno, Fernandez, Fonseca, Boves, Brito.)

Relations des Peres Loys Froes, et Nicolas Pimenta de la Compagnie de Iesus. . . . Concernant l'accroissement de la foy Chrestienne au Iappon & autres contrées des Indes Orientales és années 1596 & 1599. Traduittes du Latin imprimé à Rome. A Lyon, Par Iean Pillehotte, . . . M.DCII. (Streit, V, 12. The two letters were each published before, but not together.)

1603

Lettera Annua di Giappone Scritta nel 1601. e mandata dal P. Francesco Pasio V. Provinciale . . . In Roma, Appresso Luigi Zannetti M DC III. . . . (Streit, V, 367–72.)

Lettera del P. Alessandro Valignano, Visitatore della Compagnia di Giesù nel Giappone, e nella Cina de' 10 d' Ottobre del 1599. . . . In Roma, Appresso Luigi Zanetti. 1603 . . . . (Streit, V, 372. Bound with *Sopplimento dell'Annua del MDC*, published 1603.)

Lettera della Cina dell' Anno 1601. Mandata dal P. Valentino Carvaglio Rettore del Collegio di Macao, . . . In Roma nella Stamperia di Luigi Zannetti, 1603. . . . (Streit, V, 689.)

Relaçam Annual das Cousas Que Fizeram os Padres da Companhia de Iesus na India & Iapão nos Annos de 600. & 601. & do processo da conversão, & Christandade daquellas partes: tirada das cartas gêraes que de lâ vierão pello Padre Fernão Guerreiro da Companhia de Jesus. Vai dividada em dous livros, hum das cousas da India & outro da Japam. Impressa com licença do S. Officio, & Ordinario. Em Evora, por Manoel de Lyra. Anno 1603. (Streit, V, 16–17. This work, which contains a great many Jesuit letters, was published in five volumes at Evora and Lisbon, 1603–11; the title varies with each volume.)

Relatione Breve del P. Diego de Torres della Compagnia di Giesù. Procuratore della Provincia del Perù circa i frutto che si raccoglie con gli Indiani di quel Regno. . . . Al fine s'aggiunge la lettera annua dell' Isole Filippine del 1600. In Roma, Appresso Luigi Zannetti. M.DC III. . . . (Streit, V, 243. Contains Francesco Vaez's *Lettera Annua dell'Isole Filippine,* dated 10, VI, 1601; see Streit, V, 240.)

Sopplimento dell'Annua del MDC. nel Qual Si da Raguaglio di quel chè è socceduto alla Christianità di Giappone, dal mese d'Ottobre di detto anno, insino à Febraio del 1601. . . . dal P. Valentino Carvaglio della medesima Compagnia. In Roma, Apresso Luigi Zannetti. 1603. (Streit, V, 372. Bound with *Lettera del P. Aless. Valignano, Ottobre 1599,* above.)

1604

Japponiensis Imperii Admirabilis Commutatio Exposita Litteris ad Reverendum admodum P. Claudium Aquavivam Praepositum Generalem Soc. Jesu, quas ex Italis latinas fecit. Io. Hayus Dalgattiensis Scotus de eadem Societate. Antverpiae Sumptibus Viduae & Heredum Io: Belleri, sub Insigni Aquilae aureae. Anno M.DC.IV. (Streit, V, 376. A translation of Valentim Carvalho's letter of 1601 in *Sopplimento dell'Annua del MDC,* published 1603; the first of John Hay of Dalgetty's many letterbook translations.)

Litterae Annuae Insularum Philippinarum Scriptae a P. Francisco Vaez . . . X. Die Junij, anno M.DCI. Moguntiae [Mainz], Excudebat Balthasarus Lippius. Anno M.DCIV. (Streit, V, 247. A translation of Vaez's letter first published in D. de Torres' *Relatione breve,* Rome, 1603. This appears to be the first time it was published separately.)

Litterae societatis Jesu, duorum annorum 1594 et 1595. Naples, 1604.

Nouveaux Advis du Royaume de la Chine, du Jappon et de l'Estat du Roy de Mogor, successeur du grand Tamburlā & d'autres Royaumes des Indes à luy subiects. Tirez de plusieurs Lettres, memoires & Advis envoyez à Rome: Et nouvellement traduits d'Italien en François. A Paris, Chez Claude Chappelet, rüe S. Jacques à la Licorne, M.DCIIII. (Streit, V, 21. Contains Longobardo's letter of 1598, Valignano's Japan letter of 1599, Carvalho's Japan letter of 1601, and three letters from the Mughul Empire.)

1605

De Rebus Iaponicis, Indicis, et Peruanis Epistolae Recentiores. A Joanne Hayo Dalgattiensi Scoto Societatis Iesu in librum unum coacervatae. Antverpiae. Ex Officina Martini Nutij, ad insigne duarum Ciconiarum, Anno M.DC.V. (Streit, V, 28–29. A compilation of Jesuit letters from 1577 to 1601.)

Lettera Annua della V. Provincia delle Filippine dal Giugno del 1602. al seguente Giugno del 1603. Scritta dal P. Gio. de Ribera della Compagnia di Giesu . . . In Roma, Appresso Luigi Zannetti, M DC V. (Streit, V, 247.)

Lettera Annua di Giappone del M.DC.III. Scritta da P. Gabriel de Matos . . . Con una della Cina e delle Molucche. In Roma, Appresso Luigi Zannetti. M.DC.V. . . . (Streit, V, 31–33. Contains Matos' letter from Japan, 1603; Luigi Fernandez' letter from the Moluccas, 1603; Lorenzo Masonio's letter from Amboina, 1603; and Diego Antunez' letter from the college of Macao, 1603.)

Relacion de la Entrada de Algunos Padres de la Cōpañia de Iesus en la China, y particulares successos q tuvieron, y de cosas muy notables que vieron en el mismo Reyno. . . . En Sevilla. Por Alonso Rodriguez Gamarra. Año de 1605. (Streit, V, 692. Written by Diego de Pantoja; many subsequent editions and translations.)

1606

Relacion del Martyrio Que Seis Christianos nobles padecieron en el Iapō, en el Reyno de Fingo, por causa de nuestra Sancta Fee Catholica. Sacada de unas que Dō Luis Sequeyra Obispo del Iapon escrivio desde Nangasaqui, su fecha a 25. de Enero del año de 1604. las quales se recibieron en España este de 1606. Por Iuan Mosquera Religioso de la Compañia de Iesus. Dirigida al Conde de Haro, &c. En Valladolid Año de 1606. . . . En casa de Andres de Merchan. (Streit, V, 381. The Portuguese original of this frequently translated work was supposedly printed in China; see Streit, V, 376.)

1608

Tre Lettere Annue del Giappone de gli Anni 1603. 1604. 1605. e parte del 1606. Mandate dal P. Francesco Pasio V. Provinciale di quelle parti. . . . In Roma, Appresso Bartholomeo Zannetti. 1608. . . . (Streit, V, 385–86. Letters by Matteo Couros, 1603; João Rodrigues Girão, 1604 and 1605/1606; frequently translated and reissued.)

Histoire des Choses Plus Memorables Advenues tant ez Indes Orientales, que autres païs de la descouverte des Portugais, en l'establissement & progrez de la Foy Chrestienne, & Catholique: & principalement de ce que les Religieux de la Compagnie de Iesus y ont faict, & enduré pour la mesme fin; Depuis qu'ils y sont entrez jusques à l'an 1600. Le tout recueilly des lettres, & autres Histoires, qui en ont esté escriptes cy devant, et mis en ordre par le P. Pierre du Iarric Tolosain, de la mesme Compagnie. A Bourdeaus, Par S. Millanges, Imprimeur ordinaire du Roy M. DC.VIII. Avec Privilege de sa Majesté. (Streit, V, 44. 3 vols., 1608, 1610, 1614.)

1609

Coppie de la Lettre du R. P. Nicolas Trigault Douysien de la Compagnie de Iesus, Contenant l'accroissement de la Foy Catholique aux Indes, Chines, & lieux voisins. Ensemble, L'assiegement de Mozambic, Malaca, Amboin &c. par la Flotte Hollandoise. Escrite Au R. P. François Fleron, Provincial de la mesme Compagnie, en la Province des Pays-pas, datée de Goa en l'Inde Orientale, la veille de Noël. 1607. En Anvers, Chez Daniel Vervliet, à l'Escu d'Artois. 1609. . . . (Streit, V, 49.)

1610

Annua della Cina del M.DC.VI. e M.DC.VII. del Padre Matteo Ricci della Compagnia di Giesu. . . . In Roma, Nella Stamparia di Bartolomeo Zannetti. Anno, M.DC.X. . . . (Streit, V, 702.)

Lettera di Giappone dell'Anno M.DC.VI del P. Giovanni Rodriguez della Compagnia di Giesu. . . . In Roma, Nella Stamparia di Bartolomeo Zannetti. Anno, M.DC.X. . . . (Streit, V, 389.)

1611

Drey merkliche Relationes. Erste von der Victori Sigismundi III. desz Groszmäch-
tigen Königs in Polen und Schweden so jhr May. uber der Moscuwiter ver-
mainten unüberwindtliche Vestung Smolenzko erhalten und mit stirmender
Hand erobert den 13. Junij desz 1611. Jars. Andere von bekörung und Tauff
dreyer Junger Herren und Vettern desz mächtigen Königs Mogor in Indien den
27. Sept. Anno 1610. Dritte Wie die Insul und Königreich Ternate in jhr Mag.
Königs in Spanien Namen den Moren und Holländern widerumb sighafft
abgetrungen. Gedruckt zu Augspurg bey Chrysostomo Dabertzhofer. 1611.
(Streit, V, 62).

Historicher Bericht Was sich in dem grossen unnd nun je lenger je mehr bekandten
Königreich China in verkündigung desz H. Evangelij und fortpflantzung des
Catholischen Glaubens von 1604. und volgenden Jaren Denkwürdigs zugetragen. Ausz Portugesischen zu Lisabona gedruckten Exemplaren ins Teutsch
gebracht. M.DC.XI. Gedruckt zu Augspurg bey Chrysostomo Dabertzhofer.
(Streit, V, 704. Translations from Guerreiro's *Relaçam* and from Ricci's letter
of 1607.)

Indianische Relation was sich in den Königreichen Pegu, Bengala, Bisznaga, und
etliche andern Ländern der gegen Auffgang gelegen Indien von 1604. und etlich
volgenden Jahren, so wol in geist- als weltlichen Sachen zugetragen. Ausz Portugesischen zu Liszbona getruckten Exemplaren ins Teutsch gebracht. Augsburg: Chrysostomus Dabertzhofer, 1611.

Lettera Annua della Provincia delle Filippine dell' Anno M.DC.VIII. Scritta dal P.
Gregorio Lopez Provinciale in quell' Isole. . . . In Roma, Per Bartolomeo Zannetti, 1611. . . . (Streit, V, 253–54.)

Relationi della Gloriosa Morte di Nove Christiani Giaponesi, Martirizzati per la Fede
Cattolica nei Regni di Fingo, Sassuma, e Firando; Mandate dal P. Provinciale
della Compagnia di Giesu in Giapone, nel Marzo del 1609 e 1610. . . . In Roma,
Appresso Bartolomeo Zannetti. M.DC.XI. . . . (Streit, V, 391–92.)

1614

Deux Lettres, l'une envoyée des isles Philippines par le P. Gregoire Lopez, et l'autre
de la Chine par le P. Matthieu Ricci au Reverend Pere Claude Aquaviva General
de la Compagnie de Jesus à Rome. A Lille, De l'Imprimerie de Pierre de Rache,
1614. (Streit, V, 258. Ricci's letter of Aug. 22, 1608, does not appear to have
been previously published.)

Indianische Newe Relation Erster Theil. Was sich in der Goanischen Provintz unnd
in der Mission Monomatapa Mogor auch in der Provintz Cochin, Malabaria,
Chinna, Pegu, unnd Maluco, so wol in Geistlichen als Weltlichen Sachen von
1607. 1608. und folgenden zugetragen. Vom R. Patre Fernando Guerreiro, der
Societet Jesu, in Portugesischer Sprach beschriben. Nachmals ausz dem zu
Liszbona getruckten Exemplaren ins Teutsch gebracht. Gedruckt zu Augspurg
bey Chrysostomo Dabertzhofer. Anno M.DC.XIIII. (Streit, V, 70. A partial
translation of Guerreiro's 1611 volume.)

1615

Due Lettere Annue della Cina del 1610. e del 1611. . . . Dal Padre Nicolò Trigaut della medesima Compagnia di Giesu. In Roma, Per Bartolomeo Zannetti, MDCXV. . . . (Streit, V, 715.)

Lettera Annua del Giappone del 1609. e 1610. . . . Dal P. Giovan Rodriguez Girano. In Roma, Appresso Bartolomeo Zannetti. 1615. . . . (Streit, V, 401–5.)

Raguagli d'alcune Missioni Fatte dalli Padri della Compagnia di Giesu nell' Indie Orientale, cioè nelle Provincie di Goa, e Coccinno, e nell' Africa in capo verde. In Roma, Appresso Bartolomeo Zannetti. M.DC.XV. . . . (Streit, V, 75.)

Rei Christianae apud Japonios Commentarius. Ex litteris annuis Societatis Jesu annorum 1609. 1610. 1611. 1612. collectus. Auctore P. Nicolao Trigautio Eiusdem Societatis. Augustae Vindelicorum apud Christophorum Mangium M DC XV. (Streit, V, 406.)

1616

Breve Relacion de la Persecution Que huvo estos años contra la Iglesia de Iapon, y los ministros della. Dividida en dos Partes, la primera de lo sucedido, antes del destierro de los padres. Y la segunda de lo que huvo despues de su partida. Sacada de la carta anua, y de otras informaciones autenticas que truxo el Padre Pedro Morejon de la Compañia de Iesus, Procurador de la Provincia de Iapon. En Mexico, en casa de Iuan Ruiz, año de 1616. Con licencia de los Superioes. (Streit, V, 408. Frequently translated and reissued.)

1617

Lettera Annua del Giappone dell' Anno M.DC.XIII. Nella quale si raccontano molte cose d'edificatione, e martirij occorsi nella persecutione di questo Anno. Scritta dal P. Sebastiano Vieira della Compagnia di Giesu. . . . In Roma, Per Bartolomeo Zannetti, 1617. . . . (Streit, V, 429.)

Lettera Annua del Giappone del M.DCXIV. . . . Scritta dal Padre Gabriel de Mattos della medesima Compagnia di Giesu. In Roma. Appresso Bartolomeo Zannetti. M.DCXVII. . . . (Streit, V, 419–27.)

Relacion del Sucesso Que Tuvo Nuestra Santa Fe en los Reynos del Iapon, desde el año de seyscientos y doze hasta el de seyscientos y quinze, Imperando Cubosama. Dirigida a la Magestad Catolica del Rey Filippo Tercero nuestro Señor. Compuesta por el Padre Luys Piñeyro de la Compañia de Iesus. Año 1617. Con Privilegio. En Madrid, Por la viuda de Alonso Martin de Balbao. (Streit, V, 428.)

1618

Annuae Litterae Societatis Iesu. Anni M.DC.IV. Ad Patres & Fratres eiusdem Societatis. Duaci [Douay]. Ex Officina Viduae Laurentii Kellami, & Thomae filij. . . M.DC.XVIII. (Pages 332–61 are on the Philippines.)

Annuae Litterae Societatis Iesu. Anni M.DC.V. Ad Patres & Fratres eiusdem Societatis. Duaci [Douay], Ex Officina Viduae Laurentii Kellami, & Thomae filij . . . M.DC.XVIII. (Pages 442–515 are on the Philippines.)

Annuae Litterae Societatis Iesu, Anni M.DC.IX. Ad Patres et Fratres Eiusdem Societatis. Dilingae, Apud Viduam Ioannis Mayer . . . M.DC.XVIII. (Pages 545–90 are on the Philippines.)

Litterae Annuae Societatis Iesu, Anni MDCII. Antverpiae. Apud Heredes Martini Nutij. Anno MDCXVIII. (Pages 284–94 are on the Philippines.)

Lettres Annales du Jappon, des Annees M.DC.XIII. et M DC.XIV. Où plusieurs choses d'edification sont racontees fidelement, et les Martyres arrivez durant la persecution desdictes Annees, . . . par le P. Sebastien Vieira, de la mesme Compagnie. Mises d'Italien en François, au Collège de Lyon, par le Pere Michel Coyssard. A Lyon, Par Claude Morillon, Libraire et Imprimeur de Madame la Duchesse de Montpensier. M.DC.XVIII. . . . (Streit, V, 437. Vieira's letter of 1613, and Matos' of 1614.)

1619

Litterae Societatis Iesu, Annorum Duorum, MDCXIII, et MDCXIV, ad Patres, et Fratres eiusdem Societatis. Lugduni [Lyons], apud Claudium Cayne typographum, MDCXIX. (Pages 713–31 are on the Philippines.)

1620

Epistola R. P. Nicolai Trigautii e Societate Iesu de Felici sua in Indiam navigatione: itemque de Statu rei Christianae apud Sinas & Iaponios. Coloniae Agrippinae [Cologne], Apud Ioannem Kinchium Anno M.DC.XX. (Streit, V, 82.)

Histoire du Massacre de Plusieurs Religieux de S. Dominique, de S. François, et de la Compagnie de Iesus, et d'autres Chresticns, advenu en la rebellion de quelques Indois de l'Occident contre les Espagnols . . . A Valencienne, de l'Imprimerie de Ian Vervliet, l'An M.DC.XX. (Streit, V, 82–83. Contains letters from P. Elie Philippe Trigault, 1618; Nicolas Trigault, Goa, 1618; and Pierre Spira, Macao, 1612.)

Lettere del P. Giacomo Ro, della Compagnia di Giesù, doppò la sua partenza di Lisbona per la Cina, che fù alli 6. d'Aprile 1618. Scritta al Signor Alessandro Ro I. C. suo Padre, in mezo al Oceano, et poi da Goa capo delle Indie orientali al Signor Paolo suo fratello hora Vicario di Provisione, et Regio Fiscale in Milano, et ad altri suoi di casa. In Milano, Appresso Gio. Battista Bidelli. M.DC.XX. (Streit, V, 81.)

Narré Veritable de la Persecution Excitée Contre les Chrestiens au Royaume de la Chine, Extrait des Lettres du P. Alvares Semede de la Compagnie de Jesus, captif au mesme lieu, l'An 1619. A Paris, Chez Sebastien Chappelet, ruë S. Jacques, à l'Olivier. M.DCXX. (Streit, V, 737. Also contains W. Kirwitzer's letter of Jan. 9, 1619.)

1621

Estado, i Sucesso de las Cosas de Iapon, China, i Filipinas. Dase cuenta de la cruel persecucion que padece la Cristiandad de aquellas partes, i del numero de martyres que en ellas â avido de diferentes Religiones. . . . Escrito por un Religioso de la Cõpañia, q̃ assiste en las Filipinas, a otro de Mexico, i de alli enbiado en el aviso a los desta ciudad de Sevilla. Con licencia impresso en Sevilla, por Francisco de Lyra. Año 1621. (Streit, V, 262. Written by Diego de Bobadilla.)

Historia y Relacion de lo Sucedido en los Reinos de Japon y China, en la qual se continua la gran persecucion que ha avido en aq̃lla Iglesia, desde el año de 615. hasta el de 19. Por el Padre Pedro Morejon de la Compañia de Jesus, Procurador de la Provincia de Japon, natural de Medina del Campo. Anno 1621. Con licẽcia en Lisboa por Iuan Rodriguez. (Streit, V, 456. Includes B. de Torres' Japan letter of 1615; contains letters from other parts of Asia and Ethiopia as well.)

Kurtze Relation, was inn den Königreichen Iapon unnd China, in den Jahren 1618. 1619. und 1620. mit auszbreittung desz Christlichen Glaubens sich begeben Auch was massen vil Christen so wohl Geistliche als Weltliche darüber ihr Blut vergossen und die Marter Cron erlangt. Darbey auch etwas Berichts was in den Insuln Filippinen sich begeben Alles ausz glaubwürdigen Hispanischen schreiben und Relationen in die Teutsche Sprach ubergesetzt. Gedruckt zu Augspurg bey Sara Mangin Wittib. M.DC.XXI. (Streit, V, 456.)

Lettere Annue del Giappone, China, Goa, et Ethiopia. . . . da Padri dell' istessa Compagnia ne gli anni 1615. 1616. 1617. 1618. 1619. Volgarizati dal P. Lorenzo delle Pozze della medesima Compagnia. In Napoli per Lazaro Scorriggio. M.DC.XXI. (Streit, V, 87. Contains a great many important letters by, for example, Johannes Vreman, Gaspar Luis, Pedro Paez, Michele della Pace, Francesco Vieira, Camillo di Costanzo, Alphonso Vagnone, Matteo de Couros, Francesco Pacco, Luis Martínez de Fiqueiredo, and Francesco Eugenio.)

1622

Copia de unas cartas de los padres . . . en que se da cuentas de lo sucedido en las canonizaciones de los cinco santos, Isidro, Ignacio, Francisco, Teresa y Filipo. Madrid: Luis Sanchez, 1622.

1623

Relation-Schreiben Ausz Japon vom M.DC.XXII. Jahr . . . Vom P. Jeronimus Maiorica zu Macao in Japon den 30. Septembris im Jahr 1623 datiret . . . Ausz dem Spanischen ins Teutsch versetzt. Gedruckt zu Augspurg durch Andream Aperger auff unser Lieben Frawen Thor im Jahr 1623. (Streit, V, 463.)

Relatione Sommaria delle Nuove che son venute dal Giappone, China, Cochinchina, India, & Etiopia, l'anno 1622. Cavate d'alcune lettere di persone degne di fede. Stampata in Milano, nella Stampa Regia Camerale. Adi primo Giugno MDCXXIII. Et Ristampata in Bologna, Per gl'Heredi del Cochi, al Pozzo rosso, da S. Damiano. 1623. . . . (Streit, V, 96.)

1624

Relacion Breve de los Grandes y Rigurosos Martirios que el año passado de 1622. dieron en el Iapon, a ciẽto y diez y ocho ilustrissimos Martyres, sacada principalmente de las cartas de los Padres de la Compañia de Iesus que alli residẽ: y de que han referido muchas personas de aquel Reyno, que en dos Navios llegaron a la Ciudad de Manila a 12. de Agosto de 1623. Impresso con licencia, en Madrid por Andres de Parra año 1624. (Streit, V, 476.)

Relatione delle Cose Piu Notabili Scritte ne gli anni 1619, 1620, e 1621 dalla Cina. . . . In Roma, Per l'Erede di Bartolomeo Zannetti. M.DC.XXIV. (Streit,

V, 755. Letters by Manuel Dias the Elder, 1619; Pantaleone [Kirwitzer], 1620; Trigault, 1621; etc.)

Relatione di Alcune Cose Cavate dalle lettere scritte ne gli anni 1619. 1620. & 1621. Dal Giappone. . . . In Roma, Per l'Erede di Bartolomeo Zannetti. M.DC.XXIV. . . . (Streit, V, 477.)

1625

Carta Nuevamente embiada a los Padres de la Compañia de Iesus, en que da quenta de los grandes martirios q̄ en el Iapon, an padecido muchos padres de muchas Religiones. Y las grandes novelas y revolucion que ay en aquellas Provincias. . . . En Sevilla por Iuan de Cabrera, año de 1625. (Streit, V, 482–83).

Histoire de ce qui s'est passé à la Chine. Tirée des lettres escrites és années 1619. 1620. & 1621. . . . Traduicte de l'Italien en François par le P. Pierre Morin de la mesme Compagnie. A. Paris, Chez Sebastien Cramoisy, ruë sainct Iacques aux Cicognes. M.DC.XXV. . . . (Streit, V, 755. A translation of *Relatione delle cose piu notabili* [Rome, 1624]; it is the first of a long series of French translations from Italian originals with titles that begin with *Histoire de ce qui s'est passé*.)

1626

Novo Descobrimento do Gram Cathayo, ou Reinos de Tibet. Pello Padre Antonio de Andrade da Companhia de Jesu, Portuguez, no Anno de 1624. Com todas as licenças necessarias. Em Lisboa, Por Mattheus Pinheiro. Anno de 1626. (Streit, V, 107. Many subsequent editions and translations.)

1627

Lettere Annue d'Etiopia, Malabar, Brasil, e Goa. Dall' Anno 1620. fin' al 1624. . . . In Roma, Per Francesco Corbelletti M DC XXVII. . . . (Streit, V, 111.)

Lettere Annue del Giappone dell' Anno MDCXXII. e della Cina del 1621. & 1622. . . . In Roma, Per Francesco Corbelletti. MDCXXVII. . . . (Streit, V, 497. Maiorica's Japan letters of 1621 and 1622; Trigault's China letter of 1621; Semedo's of 1622.)

1628

Advis certain, d'une plus ample descoverte du royaume de Cataï. avec quelques autres particularitez notables de la coste de Cocincina, & de l'antiquité de la Foy Chrestienne dans la Chine. Tirées des lettres des PP. de la Compagnie de Iesus, de l'année 1626. A Paris, Chez Sebastien Chappelet, rue Sainct Iacques, au Chapelet, M. DC. XXVIII. (Streit, V, 116. Contains Francisco Godinho's letter of August 16, 1626, from Tibet.)

Breve Relatione della gloriosa morte di Paolo Michi, Giovanni Goto, e Giacomo Ghisai Martiri Giapponese della Compagnie di Giesù, Seguita in Nangasachi alli 5. di Febraro 1597. Cavata da una lettera del P. Pietro Gomez Viceprovinciale . . . l'anno 1597. In Roma. Per l'Erede del Zannetti. 1628. . . . (Streit, V, 511.)

Extrait des Lettres Addressées au R. P. General de la Compagnie de Jesus, contenant ce qui s'est passé de plus memorable depuis 1621. iusques à 1626. ès Indes au grand Mogor, et principalement en Ethiopie, au Royaume de Tibet et en la Chine. Au Pont-a-Mousson, Par François Gaunault, M. DC. XXVIII. (Streit, V, 116.)

Lettere Annua del Giappone dell' Anno 1624. . . . In Roma, Per l'Erede di Bartolomeo Zannetti. M.DC.XXVIII. . . . (Streit, V, 515. Written by João Rodrigues Girão.)

Lettere Annue del Tibet del M.DC.XXVI. e della Cina del MDCXXIV. . . . In Roma, Appresso Francesco Corbelletti. 1628. Con Licenza de' Superiori. (Streit, V, 117. Contains letters from Antonio de Andrade, Aug. 15, 1626, and Kirwitzer in Macao, Oct. 27, 1625.)

Vita del P. Carlo Spinola della Compagnia di Giesù, morto per la Santa Fede nel Giappone dal P. Fabio Ambrosio Spinola dell' istessa Compagnia. In Roma, Appresso Francesco Corbelletti, M.DC.XXVIII. (Streit, V, 513.)

1629

Lettere dell' Etiopia dell' Anno 1626. fino al Marzo del 1627. e della Cina dell' Anno 1625. fino al Febraro del 1626. Con una breve Relatione del viaggio al Regno di Tunquim, nuovamente scoperto. . . . In Roma, Appresso l'Erede di Bartolomeo Zannetti 1629. . . . (Streit, V, 589. Letters of Manuel de Almeida, Apr. 17, 1627; Dias the Younger, Mar. 1, 1626; and Baldinotti, Jul. 3, 1626.)

1630

Relacion de Alguna de las cosas tocantes a la vide y glorioso martyrio que con su Provincial y otros siete Religiosos de la Compañia de Jesus, padecio el S. P. Baltasar de Torres; sacada de las cartas autenticas, que han venido del Japon, de lo sucedido el año de seisciētos y veinte y seis en la cruel persecucion, que en aquel Imperio padece la Christiandad. [Salamanca, 1630.] (Streit, V, 528. The author is Antonio de Torres y Quesada.)

1632

Lettere Annue del Giappone de gl' Anni MDCXXV. MDCXXVI. MDCXXVII. . . . In Roma, Appresso Francesco Corbelletti. MDCXXXII. . . . (Streit, V, 533. Contains letters by G. B. Bonelli, Morejon, Rodrigues Girão, and Christovão Ferreira.)

1633

Compendio de lo Sucedido en el Iapon desde la Fundacion de Aquella Christiandad. Y relacion de los Martires Que Padecieron estos años de 1629. y 30. Sacada de las cartas Que Escrivieron los Padres de la Compañia que alli assisten. . . . En Madrid en la Imprenta del Reyno, año 1633. (Streit, V, 538. Written by Matias de Sousa.)

1635

Catalogo de los Religiosos de la Compañia de Iesus, que fuerō atormentados, y muertos en Iapon por la Fé de Christo, año de 1632 y 1633. Sacado de las cartas annuas que llegaron este año de 1635 a Lisboa, con la Nave Capitana de la India

Oriental. . . . Por el P. Francisco Rodriguez de la Compañia de Jesus . . . Con licencia en Madrid por Andres de Parra. Año de 1635. (Streit, V, 543.)

Relatione Delle Persecutioni Mosse Contro La Fede Di Christo In Varii Regni Del Giappone Ne gl'Anni MDCXXVIII. MDCXXIX. e MDCXXX. . . . In Roma. Appresso Francesco Corbelletti. MDCXXXV. . . . (Streit, V, 542. Written by Christovão Ferreira.)

1637

R. P. Marcelli Mastrilli e Societate Iesu et XXXII. Sociorum, ac XVI. Aliorum Religiosorum. Iter in Indiam S. P. Francisci Xaverii Patrocinio Feliciter Peractum. Ab eodem Marcello descriptū, atque ad Catholicam Hispaniarum Reginam transmissum. Antverpiae, Typis Joannis Meursi. M.DC.XXXVII. Superiorum Permissu. (Streit, V, 124. This appears to be the first published edition; Meurs published a Dutch translation in the same year.)

1638

Breve Relacion del Martirio del Padre Francisco Marcelo Mastrillo de la Compañia de Iesus, martirizado en Nangasaqui, Ciudad del Xapon, en 17. de Octubre de 1637. embiada por el Padre Nicolás de Acosta, Procurador del Xapon, al Padre Francisco Manso, Procurador general de las Provincias de Portugal de la dicha Compañia en Madrid. [Madrid, 1638.] (Streit, V, 547.)

Relación del Insigne Martyrio, Que padecio por la Fe de Christo el Milagroso P. Marcelo Francisco Mastrilli de la Compañia de Jesus en la Ciudad de Nangasaqui de los Reynos dcl Japõ a 17. dias del mes de Octubre deste año pasado de 1637. [Manila, 1638.] (Streit, V, 549.)

1639

Historia de la celestial Vocacion, Missiones apostolicas, y gloriosa Muerte; del Padre, Marcello Fran. Mastrilli, Hijo del Marques de S. Marsano, Indiatico felicissimo de la Compañia de IHS a Antonio Telles de Silva. Por el P. Ignacio Stafford de la Compañia de Jesus . . . En Lisboa Por Antonio Alvarez. Ano de 1639. (Streit, V, 551.)

1640

Paciecidos Libri XII. Decantatur P. Franciscus Paciecus Lusitanus S. J., Japponiae Provincialis, ibique vivus pro Christi fide lento igne concrematus, anno 1626. Auctore Bartholomeo Pereira S. J. Conimbriae, Expensis Emmanuelis de Carvalho, 1640. (Streit, V, 552.)

1642

Breve Recopilação dos principios, continuação e estado de christandande da China. Pelo P. Alvaro Semedo S. J. Em Lisboa, Por Paulo Craesbeeck 1642. (Streit, V, 778.)

1643

Relação da Gloriosa Morte de Quatro Embaixadores Portuguezes, da Cidade de Macao, con sincoenta, & sete Christaõs de sua companhia, degolados todos pella fee de Christo em Nangassaqui, Cidade de Iappaõ, a tres de Agosto de 1640 . . . Pello Padre Antonio Francisco Cardim da Companhia de Iesu Procurador geral da Provincia de Iappaõ. Em Lisboa . . . Na Officina de Lourenço de Anveres Anno de 1643. . . . (Streit, V, 556–57.)

1645

Relatione della Provincia del Giappone Scritta dal Padre Antonio Francesco Cardim della Compagnia di Giesu, Procuratore di quella Provincia. . . . In Roma, Nella Stamperia di Andrea Fei. M.DC.XLV. . . . (Streit, V, 558.)

Relatione delle Missioni, e Christianità che appartengono alla Provincia di Malavar della Compagnia di Giesu. Scritta dal P. Francesco Barreto dell' istessa Compag. Procuratore di quella Provincia. En Roma, Appresso Francesco Cavalli. 1645. Con licenza de' Superiori. (Streit, V, 135.)

Relation de ce qui s'est passé depuis quelques années iusques a l'an 1644. au Iapon, à la Cochinchina, au Malabar, et en plusieurs autres isles et royaumes de l'orient compris sous le nom des provinces du Iapon et du Malabar, de la Compagnie de Iesus. (Published in 2 pts., Paris, 1645–46. Pt. 1 is by Cardim.)

1646

Fasciculus e Iapponicis Floribus, Suo Adhue Madentibus Sanguine, Compositus a P. Antonio Francisco Cardim è Societate Iesu Provinciae Iapponiae ad Urbem Procuratore. . . . Romae, Typis Heredum Corbelletti. 1646. Superiorum Permissu. (Streit, V, 560.)

1650

Relação da conversão a nossa Sancta Fè da Rainha, & Principe da China, & de outras pessoas da casa Real que se baptizarão o anno de 1648 . . . Em Lisboa, . . . Na Officina Craesbeeckiana, anno 1650. . . . (Streit, V, 790. Author is Matias de Maya.)

1651

Relation de Ce Qui S'est Passé dans les Indes Orientales en Ses Trois Provinces de Goa, de Malabar, du Iapon, de la Chine, & autres païs nouvellement descouverts . . . Par le P. Iean Maracci Procureur de la Province de Goa, au mois d'Avril 1649. A Paris, Chez Sebastien Cramoisy, . . . M.DC.LI. Avec Privilege du Roy. (Streit, V, 142–43.)

1652

Breve Relazione della China, e della Memorabile Conversione di Persone Regali di quella corte alla Religione Christiana. Per il P. Michele Boym S. J. Roma, 1652. (Streit, V, 793.)

1653

Relation des Progrez de la Foy au Royaume de la Cochinchine Ès Années 1646. & 1647. Envoiée au R. P. General de la Compagnie de Iesus. Par le P. Mettelle Saccano, . . . A Paris, Chez Sebastien Cramoisy, . . . M.DC.LIII. . . . (Streit, V, 598.)

1659

Relation des Missions des Pères de la Compagnie de Iesus dans les Indes Orientales où l'on verra l'estat present de la Religion Chrestienne, et plusieurs belles curiositez de ces Contrées. . . . A Paris, Chez Iean Henault . . . M.DC.LIX. Avec Privilege du Roy. (Streit, V, 153. Editor is P. Machault.)

1661

El Apostel de las Indias y Nuevas Gentes San Francisco Xavier de la Compañia de Iesus. Epitome de Sus Apostolicos Hechos, Virtudes, Enseñança y Prodigios Antiguos, y Nuevos. . . . Impresso en Mexico: En la Imprenta de Augustin de Santistevan, y Francisco Lupercio. Año de 1661. (Streit, V, 157. Author is Luis de Sanvitores.)

1662

Extract Schreibens, So ausz dem Weitberühmten gegen Aufgang gelegenem Königreich China. . . . 6. Feb. 1659, in Europa 1662 angelangt. München, Wagener 1662. (Streit, V, 821.)

Lettre du R. P. Iacques le Favre . . . Sur Son Arrivée à la Chine, & l'estat present de ce Royaume. A Paris, Chez Edme Martin, ruë S. Iacques au Soleil d'or. M. DC. LXII. Avec permission. (Streit, V, 821.)

1663

Relation du Voyage du P. Joseph Tissanier de la Compagnie de Iesus. Depuis la France, jusqu'au Royaume de Tunquin. Avec ce qui s'est passé de plus memorable dans cette Mission, depuis les années 1658. 1659. et 1660. A Paris, Chez Edme Martin, M.DC.LXIII. (Streit, V, 607.)

1665

Estat Sommaire des Missions de la Chine, et l'envoy de trois Evesques dans les nouvelles Eglises de cet Empire. [1665] (Streit, V, 609. Written by Vincent de Meur.)

Metodo Della dottrina che i Padri della Compagnia di Giesù insegnano a' Neofiti, nelle missioni della Cina. Con la risposta alle obiettioni di alcuni Moderni che la impugnano. Opera del Padre Antonio Rubino della Compagnia di Giesù, Visitatore della Provincia di Giappone e Cina. Tradotta dal Portoghese in Italiano, dal Padre Gio: Filippo de Marini, della medesima Compagnia. . . . In Lione Appresso Horatio Boissat, E Georgio Remeus. M.DC.LXV. . . . (Streit, V, 825–26.)

Relação do Novo Caminho Que Fez por Terra, e Mar, Vindo da India Para Portugal, no anno 1663. O Padre Manoel Godinho. . . . Em Lisboa: Com Licença Na Officina de Henrique Valente de Oliveira, . . . 1665. (Streit, V, 161.)

Relatio Rerum Notabilium Regni Mogor in Asia: ex R. P. Henrici Roht Dilingani Soc. Iesu, . . . Complectitur Imperij Mogor Religionem Regionem Regimen: Tum Ritus varios & inaudita de Regno Cabul Christianorum, Potente Ethnicorum incognito hactenus: de Christianitatis statu in Iaponia, China: . . . Aschaffenburgi Typis Joannis Michaelis Straub M DC LXV. (Streit, V, 163.)

Abrege d'une Lettre du P. Ioseph Zanzini, appellé Sanchés, escrite des Philippines à Rome, . . . Touchant la Persecution qui s'est eslevée contre les Chrestiens de la Cochinchine; Et la mort glorieuse de trente-sept Martyrs qui y ont repandu leur sang pour la deffense de nostre sainte Foy, depuis le mois de Decembre 1664. iusqu'au mois de Février 1665. [s.l., s.a.] (Streit, V, 614.)

1668

Les Dernieres Nouvelles de la Chrestienté de la Chine, Tirées des Lettres receuës par le Procureur des Missions de ce pays-là. A Paris, Chez Denys Bechet, . . . M.DC.LXVIII. . . . (Streit, V, 832–33. Edited by P. Chaignon.)

Lettres des Pays Estrangers, où il y a plusieurs choses curieuses d'édification. Envoyées des Missions de ces pays-là. A Paris, Chez Denys Bechet . . . M.DC.LXVIII. . . . (Streit, V, 168. Edited by P. Chaignon.)

1672

Compendiosa Narratione Dello Stato della Missione Cinese, cominciãdo dall' Anno 1581. fino al 1669. . . . Dal Prospero Intorcetta della Compagnia di Giesù . . . In Roma Per Francesco Tizzoni. MDCLXXII, . . . (Streit, V, 849.)

1673

Vida del venerable P. Louis de Medina, muerto por la fe in las islas Marianas. . . . Madrid, . . . 1673. (Written by Francisco García.)

1681

Le Progrèz de la Religion Catholique dans la Chine. Avec le Bref de N. S. P. le Pape Jnnocent XI. Au Père Ferdinand Verbiest, Jésuite, du 3. Decembre 1681. Jouxte la copie imprimée à Paris. A Toulouse, Par J. Boude, 1681. (Streit, V, 873.)

1682

La Vie de Saint François Xavier de la Compagnie de Jesus Apostre des Indes et du Japon. A Paris, Chez Sebastien Mabre-Cramoisy, Imprimeur du Roy, ruë Saint Iacques, aux Cicognes. M.DC.LXXXII. . . . (Streit, V, 184.)

1683

Vita del venerabile P. Girolamo Lopez missionario apostolico della Compagnia di Giesù, scritta dal P. Giovanni Marini e tradotta dallo spagniceolo da un sacerdote della medesima Compagnia. Rome, 1683.

Vida y martirio de el venerable padre Diego Luis de Sanvitores . . . apostol de las islas Marianas, y successos . . . Madrid, . . . 1683.

1684

Lettre du P. Ferdinand Verbiest de la Compagnie de Jesus. Ecrite de la Cour de Pekin sur un voyage que l'Empereur de la Chine a fait l'an 1683 dans la Tartarie Occidentale. A Paris, Chez la Veuve P. Bouillerot, M.DC.LXXXIV. . . . (Streit, V, 880.)

1685

Relacion de los successos de los missiones Marianas, desde el 25 de abril 1684 hasta el primeiro de mayo de 1685. . . . 1685. (Written by Francisco García.)

1687

Breve Ragguaglio delle cose più notabili spettanti al grand' imperio della Cina. . . . P. Filippo Couplet della Compagnia di Giesù 1687. (Streit, V 896.)

1696

La Libertad de la Ley de Dios en el Imperio de la China. Compuesta por el Rmo. P. Joseph Suarez . . . De la Lengua Portuguesa à la Castellana, por Don Juan de Espinola, . . . Lisboa. En la Oficina de Miguel Deslandes, Impressor de su Magestad. Año de 1696. . . . (Streit, V, 934.)

1698

Annua do Collegio de Pekim desde o fim do anno 1694 atè o fim de Mayo de 1697 e d'algunas outras Residencias, e Christandades da Missão da China, escrita em Pekim 30 de julio 1697. Valencia 1698. (Streit, V, 945. Written by Joseph Suarez.)

1699

Relacion de las Missiones de la Gran China, Copiada de una Carta, Que Escriviò de Aquel Reyno un Ministro Evangelico. . . . Com licencia en Cadiz, por Cristoval de Requena, ano 1699. (Streit, V, 953–54. Written by Juan de Irigoyen.)

Chapter Bibliographies

I. EMPIRE AND TRADE

BOOKS

Abeyasinghe, Tikiri. *Portuguese Rule in Ceylon, 1594–1612.* Colombo, 1966.

Alexandrowicz, Charles Henry. *An Introduction to the History of the Law of Nations in the East Indies (Sixteenth, Seventeenth, and Eighteenth Centuries).* Oxford, 1967.

Andaya, Leonard Y. *The Kingdom of Johor, 1641–1728.* Kuala Lumpur, 1975.

———. *The Heritage of Arung Palakka: A History of South Sulawesi (Celebes) in the Seventeenth Century.* The Hague, 1981.

Arasaratnam, Jimmappah. *Dutch Power in Ceylon, 1658–1687.* Amsterdam, 1958.

Attman, Artur. *The Bullion Flow between Europe and the East, 1000–1750.* Göteborg, 1981.

Azevedo, J. L. *Epocas de Portugal economico.* 2d ed., Lisbon, 1947.

Barbour, Violet. *Capitalism in Amsterdam in the Seventeenth Century.* Ann Arbor, 1966.

Barrett, Ward (trans. and ed.). *Mission in the Marianas. An Account of Father Diego Luís de Sanvítores and His Companions, 1669–70.* Minneapolis, 1975.

Blussé, L., and Gaastra, F. (eds.). *Companies and Trade. Essays on Overseas Trading Companies during the Ancien Régime.* Leyden, 1981.

Borah, W. *Early Colonial Trade and Navigation between Mexico and Peru.* Berkeley, 1954.

Boxer, Charles Ralph. *Fidalgos in the Far East, 1550–1770; Fact and Fancy in the History of Macao.* The Hague, 1948.

———. *The Christian Century in Japan, 1549–1650.* Berkeley, 1951.

Chapter Bibliographies

————. *The Great Ship from Amacon; Annals of Macao and the Old Japan Trade, 1555–1640*. Lisbon, 1959.

————. *The Dutch Seaborne Empire, 1600–1800*. London, 1965.

————. *The Portuguese Seaborne Empire, 1415–1825*. London, 1969.

————. *The Anglo-Dutch Wars of the Seventeenth Century, 1652–1674*. London, 1974.

Boyajian, James C. *Portuguese Bankers at the Court of Spain, 1626–1650*. New Brunswick, N.J., 1983.

Braudel, Fernand. *Civilization and Capitalism, 15th–18th Centuries*. Trans. by Sian Reynolds. 3 vols. New York, 1981–84.

Bruijn, J. R.; Gaastra, F.; and Schöffer, S. (eds.). *Dutch Asiatic Shipping in the Seventeenth and Eighteenth Centuries*. 3 vols. The Hague, 1979.

Burke, Peter. *Venice and Amsterdam: A Study of Seventeenth-Century Elites*. London, 1974.

Carvalho, T. A. de. *As companhias portuguesas de colonização*. Lisbon, 1902.

Chang T'ien-tsê. *Sino-Portuguese Trade from 1514 to 1644. A Synthesis of Portuguese and Chinese Sources*. Leyden, 1934.

Chaudhuri, K. N. *The English East India Company: The Study of an Early Joint-Stock Company, 1600–1640*. London, 1965.

————. *The Trading World of Asia and the English East India Company, 1660–1760*. Cambridge, 1978.

————. *Trade and Civilisation in the Indian Ocean*. Cambridge, 1985.

Chaunu, Pierre. *Les Philippines et le Pacifique des Ibériques (XVIe, XVIIe, XVIIIe siècles)*. Paris, 1960.

Clark, G. W., and Van Eysinga, W. J. M. *The Colonial Conferences between England and the Netherlands in 1613 and 1615*. Pt. 1, Leyden, 1940; Pt. 2, Leyden, 1951.

Clark, Peter (ed.). *The Early Modern Town. A Reader*. London, 1976.

Coolhaas, W. Ph. *A Critical Survey of Studies on Dutch Colonial History*. The Hague, 1960.

Cottineau de Kloquen, Denis L. *An Historical Sketch of Goa. . . .* Madras, 1831.

Dahlgren, E. W. *Les relations commerciales et maritimes entre la France et les côtes de l'océan Pacifique*. Paris, 1909.

Das Gupta, J. *India in the Seventeenth Century as Depicted by European Travellers*. Calcutta, 1916.

Davies, D. W. *A Primer of Dutch Seventeenth-Century Overseas Trade*. The Hague, 1961.

De la Costa, Horacio, S.J. *The Jesuits in the Philippines, 1581–1768*. Cambridge, Mass., 1961.

De Vries, Jan. *The Economy of Europe in an Age of Crisis, 1600–1750*. Cambridge, 1976.

————. *European Urbanization, 1500–1800*. Cambridge, Mass., 1984.

Delumeau, J., et al. *Le mouvement du port de Saint-Malo (1681–1720)*. Paris, 1966.

Disney, A. R. *Twilight of the Pepper Empire. Portuguese Trade in Southwest India in the Early Seventeenth Century*. Cambridge, Mass., 1978.

Duncan, T. Bentley. "The Portuguese Enterprise in Asia, 1500–1750." Unpublished typescript.

Eames, J. B. *The English in China*. London, 1909.

Flinn, Michael W. *The European Demographic System, 1500–1820*. Baltimore, 1981.

Foster, William. *England's Quest of Eastern Trade*. London, 1933.

Furber, Holden. *Rival Empires of Trade in the Orient, 1600–1800*. Minneapolis, 1976.

Glamann, Kristof. *Dutch Asiatic Trade, 1620–1740*. Copenhagen, 1955.

Gokhale, B. G. *Surat in the Seventeenth Century*. London, 1978.

Haan, Hans den. *Modernegotie en grote vaart, een studie over de expansie van het hollandse handelskapitaal in de 16 en 17 eeuw*. Amsterdam, 1977.

Hamilton, Earl J. *War and Prices in Spain, 1651–1800*. Cambridge, Mass., 1947.

Hutchinson, E. W. *Adventurers in Siam in the Seventeenth Century*. London, 1940.

Jack-Hinton, Colin. *The Search for the Islands of Solomon, 1567–1838*. Oxford, 1969.

Kaeppelin, Paul. *La compagnie des Indes orientales et François Martin*. Paris, 1908. Reprinted at New York in 1967.

Khan, S. A. *The East India Trade in the Seventeenth Century*. New Delhi, 1975.

Kiers, L. *Coen op Banda, de conqueste getoest aan het recht van den tijd*. Utrecht, 1943.

Konvitz, Josef W. *Cities and the Sea. Port City Planning in Early Modern Europe*. Baltimore, 1978.

Krause, G. *Tagebuch Christians des Jüngeren, Fürst zu Anhalt. . . .* Leipzig, 1858.

Larsen, Kay. *De dansk-ostindische koloniers historie I–II*. Copenhagen, 1907–8.

Leitão, Humberto. *Os portugueses em Solor e Timor de 1515 a 1702*. Lisbon, 1948.

Léon, P. (ed.). *Histoire économique et sociale du monde*. 6 vols. Paris, 1978.

Leroy, Charles. *La compagnie royale des Indes orientales au Havre de 1664 à 1670*. Rouen, 1936.

Macau, Jacques. *L'Inde danoise: la première compagnie (1616–1670)*. Aix-en-Provence: Institut d'histoire des pays d'Outre-Mer; Etudes et documents, no. 3, Université de Provence, 1972.

Madrolle, Claudius. *Les premiers voyages français à la Chine. La compagnie de la Chine, 1698–1719*. Paris, 1901.

Mansvelt, W. M. F. *Rechtsform en geldelijk beheer bij de Oost-Indische Compagnie*. Amsterdam, 1922.

Massarella, Derek. *A World Elsewhere: Europe's Encounter with Japan in the Sixteenth and Seventeenth Centuries*. New Haven, Conn., 1990.

Masselman, George. *The Cradle of Colonialism*. New Haven, 1963.

Mauro, Frédéric. *Le Portugal et l'Atlantique au XVIIe siècle, 1570–1670*. Ecole pratique des hautes études, Centre de recherches historiques, ser. 6: Ports, routes, traffics, Vol. X. Paris, 1960.

Mazumdar, Sucheta. "A History of the Sugar Industry in China: The Political Economy of a Cash Crop in Guangdong, 1644–1834." Ph.D. diss., Dept. of History, University of California of Los Angeles, 1984.

Meilinck-Roelofsz, M. A. P. *Asian Trade and European Influence in the Indonesian Archipelago between 1500 and about 1630*. The Hague, 1962.

Chapter Bibliographies

Mendes da Luz, F. P. *O consehlo da India.* Lisbon, 1952.

Mollat, Michel (ed.). *Sociétés et compagnies de commerce en Orient et dans l'Océan Indien.* Paris, 1970.

Mukerji, Chandra. *From Graven Images. Patterns of Modern Materialism.* New York, 1983.

Norton, Luiz. *Os portugueses no Japão, 1543–1640. Notas e documentos.* Agencia Geral do Ultramar, Divisão de publicações e biblioteca. [Lisbon] 1952.

Oliveira-Marques, A. H. de. *History of Portugal.* 2d ed. New York, 1976.

Olsen, Gunnar. *Dansk Ostindien, 1616–1732.* Copenhagen, 1952.

Pearson, M. N. *Merchants and Rulers in Gujarat.* Berkeley, 1976.

Penrose, Boise. *Sea Fights in the East Indies, 1602–1639.* Cambridge, Mass., 1931.

Peres, Damião (ed.). *Regimento das Cazas das Indias e Mina.* Coimbra, 1947.

Pissurlencar, Panduronga S. S. *Agentes da diplomacia portuguesa na India (Hindus, Muçulmanos, Judeus e Parses), Documentos coordenados, anotados e prefaciados.* Goa, 1952.

Poonen, T. I. *A Survey of the Rise of Dutch Power in Malabar.* Trichinopoly, 1943.

Quiason, S. D. *English "Country Trade" with the Philippines.* Quezon City, 1966.

Rabb, Theodore K. *Enterprise and Empire: Merchant and Gentry Investment in the Expansion of England.* Cambridge, Mass., 1967.

Raychaudhuri, T. *Jan Company in Coromandel, 1605–90.* The Hague, 1962.

Ricklefs, M. C. *A History of Modern Indonesia.* Bloomington, Ind., 1981.

Rostow, W. *The Stages of Economic Growth.* Cambridge, 1960.

Rothermund, Dietmar. *Europa und Asien im Zeitalter des Merkantilismus.* "Erträge der Forschung," LXXX. Darmstadt, 1978.

Schilder, Günter. *Australia Unveiled. The Share of the Dutch Navigators in the Discovery of Australia.* Translated from German by O. Richter. Amsterdam, 1976.

Schurz, W. L. *The Manila Galleon.* New York, 1959.

Sharp, Andrew. *The Discovery of the Pacific Islands.* Oxford, 1960.

Singh, O. P. *Surat and Its Trade in the Second Half of the Seventeenth Century.* Delhi, 1977.

Spate, O. H. K. *The Spanish Lake.* Minneapolis, 1979.

Stapel, F. W. *Geschiedenis van Nederlandsch Indië.* 5 vols. Amsterdam, 1938–40.

Steensgaard, Niels. *The Asian Trade Revolution of the Seventeenth Century.* Chicago, 1974.

Thomas, Parakunnel Joseph. *Mercantilism and the East India Trade.* London, 1926.

Trend, J. B. *Portugal.* London, 1957.

Unger, E. W. *Dutch Shipbuilding before 1800.* Assen, 1978.

Van Kley, Edwin. "China in the Eyes of the Dutch, 1592–1685." Ph.D. diss., Dept. of History, Univ. of Chicago, 1964.

Vixeboxse, J. *Een hollandsch gezantschap naar China . . . (1685–87).* Vol. V of *Sinica Leidensia.* Leyden, 1946.

Vlekke, Bernard H. M. *Nusantara. A History of the East Indian Archipelago.* Cambridge, Mass., 1945.

Wallerstein, Immanuel Maurice. *The Modern World System. II. Mercantilism and the Consolidation of the European World-Economy 1600–1750.* New York, 1980.

White, Thomas E. "Seventeenth-Century Spanish Sources on East Asia." Unfinished doctoral dissertation.

Wills, John E., Jr. *Embassies and Illusions: Dutch and Portuguese Envoys to K'ang-hsi 1666–87.* Cambridge, Mass., 1984.

———. *Pepper, Guns, and Parleys. The Dutch East India Company and China, 1622–81.* Cambridge, Mass., 1974.

Willson, David Harris. *A Royal Request for Trade: A Letter of King James I to the Emperor of Japan Placed in Its Historical Setting.* Minneapolis, 1965.

Wilson, Charles Henry. *England's Apprenticeship, 1603–1763.* New York, 1965.

Winius, G. O. *The Fatal History of Portuguese Ceylon. Transition to Dutch Rule.* Cambridge, Mass., 1971.

ARTICLES

Alam, Shah Manzoar. "Masulipatam, a Metropolitan Port in the Seventeenth Century A.D." *The Indian Geographical Journal,* XXXIV (1959), 33–42.

Alvarez, J. L. "Don Rodrigo de Vivero et la destruction de la Não Madre de Deus, 1609." *Monumenta Nipponica,* II (1939), 479–511.

Andres, Gregorio. "Juan Bautista Gesio, cosmógrafo de Felipe II y postador de documentos geográficos desde Lisboa para la Biblioteca de El Escorial en 1573." *Boletín de la Real Sociedad Geografica* (Madrid), CIII (1967), 365–74.

Atwell, William S. "International Bullion Flows and the Chinese Economy circa 1530–1650." *Past and Present,* XCV (1982), 68–90.

Bangs, Carl. "Dutch Theology, Trade, and War, 1590–1610." *Church History,* XXXIX (1970), 470–82.

Barassin, J. "Compagnies de navigation et expéditions françaises dans l'Océan Indien au XVIIᵉ siècle." *Studia* (Lisbon), No. 11 (Jan. 11, 1963), 373–89.

Bassett, D. K. "The Trade of the English East India Company in the Far East, 1623–84." *JRAS,* 1960, pp. 32–47, 145–57.

———. "The Amboina Massacre of 1623." *Journal of Southeast Asian History,* Vol. I, No. 2 (1960), pp. 1–19.

———. "The Trade of the English East India Company with Cambodia." *JRAS,* 1962, pp. 35–61.

Bonaparte, Roland Prince. "Les premiers voyages des Néerlandais dans l'Insulinde 1595–1602." *Revue de géographie,* Vol. XIV (1884), Pt. 1, pp. 446–55; Pt. 2, pp. 46–55.

Boxer, Charles Ralph. "Spaniards in Cambodia." *History Today,* XXI (1971), 280–87.

———. "A Note on the Triangular Trade between Macao, Manila, and Nagasaki." *Terrae Incognitae,* XVII (1985), 51–60.

———. "*Plata es Sangre:* Sidelights on the Drain of Spanish-American Silver in the Far East, 1550–1700." *Philippine Studies,* Vol. XVIII, No. 3 (July, 1970), 29–40.

————. "Portuguese and Spanish Projects for the Conquest of Southeast Asia, 1580–1600." *Journal of Asian History,* III (1969), 118–36.

————. "Manila Galleon, 1565–1815." *History Today,* VIII (1958), 538–47.

Brand, Donald. "Geographical Exploration by the Spanish." In Herman R. Friis (ed.), *The Pacific Basin: A History of Its Exploration,* pp. 109–44. New York, 1967.

Braudel, F., and Spooner, F. "Prices in Europe from 1450 to 1750." In E. E. Rich and C. H. Wilson (eds.), *The Cambridge Economic History of Europe,* IV, 378–486. Cambridge, 1977.

Brennig, J. J. "Chief Merchants and the European Enclaves of Seventeenth-Century Coromandel." *Modern Asian Studies,* XI (1977), 321–40.

Briggs, L. P. "Spanish Intervention in Cambodia, 1593–1603." *T'oung Pao,* XXXIX (1949), 132–60.

Brugmans, I. J. "De Oost-Indische Compagnie en de welvaart in de republick." *Tijdschrift voor geschiedenis,* LXI (1948), 225–31. Reprinted in *Welvaart en Historie. Tien studien,* pp. 28–37. The Hague, 1950.

Bruijn, J. R. "Between Batavia and the Cape: Shipping Patterns of the Dutch East India Company." *Journal of Southeast Asian Studies,* XI (1980), 251–65.

Carter, Charles H. "The Nature of Spanish Government after Philip II." *The Historian,* XXVI (1963), 1–18.

Castillo, A. "Dans la monarchie espagnole du XVIIe siècle; les banquiers portugais et le circuit d'Amsterdam." *Annales. E.S.C.,* XIX (1964), 311–16.

Chaudhuri, K. N. "The English East India Company in the Seventeenth and Eighteenth Centuries: A Pre-Modern Multinational Organization." In Leonard Blussé and F. Gaastra (eds.), *Companies and Trade,* pp. 29–46. The Hague, 1981.

————. "Treasure and Trade Balances: The East India Company's Export Trade, 1660–1720." *The Economic History Review,* 2d ser., XXI (1968), 480–502.

Chaunu, Pierre. "Le galion de Manile, grandeur et décadence d'une route de la soie." *Annales. E.S.C.,* VI (1951), 447–62.

Davis, Ralph. "English Foreign Trade, 1660–1700." In W. E. Minchinton (ed.), *The Growth of English Overseas Trade in the Seventeenth and Eighteenth Centuries,* pp. 78–98. London, 1969.

————. "The Rise of Protectionism in England, 1689–1786." *The Economic History Review,* 2d Ser., XIX (1966), 306–17.

Dermigny, L. "L'organization et le rôle des compagnies." In M. Mollat (ed.), *Sociétés et compagnies de commerce en Orient et dans l'Océan Indién,* pp. 443–51. Paris, 1970.

Duncan, T. Bentley. "Navigation between Portugal and Asia in the Sixteenth and Seventeenth Centuries." In C. K. Pullapilly and E. J. Van Kley (eds.), *Asia and the West,* pp. 3–25. Notre Dame, 1986.

————. "Niels Steensgaard and the Europe-Asia Trade of the Early Seventeenth Century." *Journal of Modern History,* XLVII (1975), 512–18.

Duyvendak, J. J. L. "The First Siamese Embassy to Holland." *T'oung Pao,* XXXII (1936), 286–92.

Feldbaek, Ole. "The Organization and Structure of the Danish East India, West India and Guinea Companies in the Seventeenth and Eighteenth Centuries." In L. Blussé and F. Gaastra (eds.), *Companies and Trade*, pp. 135–58. The Hague, 1981.

Fisher, F. J. "London's Export Trade in the Early Seventeenth Century." *The Economic History Review*, 2d ser., Vol. III, No. 2 (1950), pp. 151–61.

———. "London as an 'Engine' of Economic Growth." In J. S. Bromley and E. H. Kossman (eds.), *Britain and the Netherlands*, IV, 3–46. The Hague, 1971.

Fruin-Mees, Willemine. "Een bantamsch gezantschap naar Engeland en 1682." *Tijdschrift voor indische taal land en volkenkunde*, LXIV (1924), 207–26.

Fu Lo-shu. "The Two Portuguese Embassies to China during the K'ang-hsi Period." *T'oung Pao*, XLIII (1955), 75–94.

Gaastra, Femme. "The Shifting Balance of Trade of the Dutch East India Company." In L. Blussé and F. Gaastra (eds.), *Companies and Trade*, pp. 44–70. The Hague, 1981.

Gentil da Silva, Jose. "Portugal and Overseas Expansion from the Fifteenth to the Eighteenth Centuries." *Journal of European Economic History*, VIII (1979), 681–87.

Glamann, Kristof. "The Changing Patterns of Trade." In E. Rich and C. Wilson (eds.), *The Cambridge Economic History of Europe*, V, 42–68. Cambridge, 1978.

———. "The Danish East India Company." In M. Mollat (ed.), *Sociétés et compagnies de commerce en Orient et dans l'Océan Indien*, pp. 471–77. Paris, 1970.

Gould, J. D. "The Trade Depression of the Early 1620's." *The Economic History Review*, 2d ser., VII (1954), 81–90.

Hazan, Aziza. "The Silver Currency Output of the Mughal Empire and Prices in India during the Sixteenth and Seventeenth Centuries." *Indian Economic and Social History Review*, VI (1969), 85–116.

Heras, Henry, S.J. "The Portuguese Alliance with the Muhammadan Kingdoms of the Deccan." *JRAS, Bombay Branch*, n.s., I (1925), 122–25.

Hugo-Brunt, Michael. "The Portuguese Settlement at Goa in India." *Plan* (Toronto), IX (1968), 72–86, 108–22.

Hutchinson, E. W. "Four French State Manuscripts Relating to Embassies between France and Siam in the Seventeenth Century." *Selected Articles from the Siam Society Journal*, VIII (1959), 90–98.

———. "The Retirement of the French Garrison from Bangkok in the Year 1688." *Ibid.*, 159–99.

Irwin, G. W. "The Dutch and the Tin Trade of Malaya in the Seventeenth Century." In Jerome Ch'en and N. Terling (eds.), *Studies in the Social History of China and South-East Asia*, pp. 267–87. Cambridge, Mass., 1970.

Iwao, Seiichi. "Japanese Foreign Trade in the Sixteenth and Seventeenth Centuries." *Acta Asiatica*, XXX (1976), 1–18.

Joshi, P. M. "Muhammad Adil Shah (1627–1656) and the Portuguese." *Journal of Indian History*, XXXIII (April 1955), 1–10.

Kato, Eiichi. "The Japan-Dutch Trade in the Formative Period of the Seclusion Policy—Particularly on the Raw Silk Trade by the Dutch Factory at Hirado, 1620–1640." *Acta Asiatica*, XXX (1976), 34–84.

———. "Unification and Adaptation, the Early Shogunate and Dutch Trade Policies." In L. Blussé and F. Gaastra (eds.), *Companies and Trade*, pp. 207–30. The Hague, 1981.

Kesivani, D. G. "Western Commercial Enterprises in the East. Some Oriental Archival Sources." In M. Mollat (ed.), *Sociétés et compagnies de commerce en Orient et dans l'Océan Indien*, pp. 12–20. Paris, 1970.

Keuning, J. "Sixteenth-Century Cartography in the Netherlands." *Imago Mundi*, IX (1952), 59–61.

Klein, E. "De zeventiende eeuw, 1585–1700." In J. H. van Stuijvenberg (ed.), *De economishche geschiedenis van Nederland*, pp. 106–15. Groningen, 1977.

Leuilliot, Paul. "Influence du commerce oriental sur l'économie occidentale." In M. Mollat (ed.), *Sociétés et compagnies de commerce en Orient et dans l'Océan Indien*, pp. 611–27. Paris, 1970.

Lombard, Denis. "Questions on the Contact between European Companies and Asian Societies." In L. Blussé and F. Gaastra (eds.), *Companies and Trade*, pp. 179–88. The Hague, 1981.

Mirkovich, Nicholas. "Ragusa and the Portuguese Spice Trade." *Slavonic and East European Review*, XXI (1943), 174–87.

Mols, Roger, S.J. "Population in Europe, 1500–1700." In C. M. Cippola (ed.), *The Sixteenth and Seventeenth Centuries*, Vol. II of *The Fontana Economic History of Europe*, pp. 15–181. New York, 1977.

Morineau, M. "Quelques remarques sur l'abondance monétaire aux Provinces-Unies." *Annales. E.S.C.*, XXIX (1974), 767–76.

Murakami, N. "Japan's Early Attempts to Establish Commercial Relations with Mexico." In H. M. Stephens and H. E. Bolton (eds.), *The Pacific Ocean in History*, pp. 467–80. New York, 1917.

Ortega, A. N. "Noticia entre Mexico y el Japon, durante el siglo XVII." *Archivo histórico diplomático Mexicano*, No. 2 (1923), 26–42.

Parker, Geoffrey. "The Emergence of Modern Finance in Europe, 1500–1730." In C. M. Cipolla (ed.), *The Fontana Economic History of Europe*, II, 527–94. New York, 1977.

Parry, John H. "Transport and Trade Routes." In E. E. Rich and C. H. Wilson (eds.), *The Cambridge Economic History of Europe*, IV, 155–219. Cambridge, 1967.

Pearson, Michael N. "Indigenous Dominance in a Colonial Economy, the Goa Rendas, 1600–1700." In Jean Aubin (ed.), *Mare Luso-Indicum* (2 vols.), II, 61–73. Paris, 1972.

Pelliot, Paul. "Les relations du Siam et de la Hollande en 1608." *T'oung Pao*, XXXII (1936), 223–29.

Pérez, Lorenzo, O.F.M. "Las relaciónes diplomáticas entre España y el Japon." *Archivo Ibero-Americano*, XXXI (1929), 79–114.

Perez, R. Ferrando. "Felipe III y la política española en el Mar del Sur." *Revista de Indias*, Vol. XIII, No. 54 (1953), pp. 539–58.

Petech, Luciano. "Some Remarks on the Portuguese Embassies to China in the K'ang-hsi period." *T'oung Pao,* XLIV (1956), 227–41.

Prakash, O. "The European Trading Companies and the Merchants of Bengal, 1650–1725." *Indian Economic and Social History Review,* Vol. I, No. 3 (1964), pp. 37–63.

Ptak, Roderick. "The Demography of Old Macao, 1555–1640." *Ming Studies,* XV (1982), 27–35.

Rau, Virginia. "Les portugais et la route terrestre des Indes à la Méditerranée aux XVIe et XVIIe siècles." In M. Cortelazzo (ed.), *Mediterraneo e Oceano Indiano,* pp. 91–98. Florence, 1970.

Ray, Indrani. "The French Company and the Merchants of Bengal, 1680–1730." *Indian Economic and Social History Review,* VIII (1971), 41–55.

Regla, Juan. "Spain and Her Empire." In *The New Cambridge Modern History,* V, 369–83. Cambridge, 1961.

Rodríguez-Moñino, A. "Bibliografía hispano-oriental." *Boletín de la Real Academia de la Historia* (Madrid), XCVIII (1931), 418–19.

Romano, Ruggiero. "Una crisi economica, 1619–22." *Rivista storica italiana,* Vol. LXXIV, No. 3 (1962), pp. 480–531.

———. "Encore la crise de 1619–22." *Annales. E.S.C.,* XIX (1964), 31–37.

Ronall, Joachim O. "Spain and Japan—Early Diplomatic Relations." *Eastern World,* Vol. XI, No. 12 (1957), pp. 38–39; Vol. XII, No. 1 (1958), pp. 24–25.

Seidenfaden, E., and His Highness Prince Dhani Nivat. "Early Trade Relations between Denmark and Siam." In *Selected Articles from the Siam Society Journal,* VIII (1959), 271–88.

Sen, Anjali. "Murshid Quli Khan's Relations with the European Merchants." *Indian Historical Quarterly,* XXXV (1959), 16–42.

Sola, Emilio. "Notas sobre el comercio Hispano-Japonés en los siglos XVI y XVII." *Hispania,* XXXIII (1973), 265–83.

Souza, G. B. "Portuguese Trade and Society in China and the South China Sea." *Itinerario,* III (1979), 64–73.

Stols, E. "The Southern Netherlands and the Foundation of the Dutch East India and West India Companies." *Acta Historiae Neerlandicae, Studies on the History of the Netherlands,* IX (1976), 30–47.

Tamaskar, B. G. "Malik Ambar and the Portuguese." *Journal of the Bihar Research Society,* XXXIII (1947), 25–44.

Teague, Michael. "The Portuguese in Japan." *Geographica,* I (1965), 80–94.

Unger, R. W. "Dutch Ship Design in the Fifteenth and Sixteenth Centuries." *Viator,* IV (1973), 403–11.

Usher, A. P. "Spanish Ships and Shipping in the Sixteenth and Seventeenth Centuries." In A. P. Usher (ed.), *Facts and Factors in Economic History,* pp. 189–213. Cambridge, Mass., 1932.

Van Dillen, J. G. "Economic Fluctuations and Trade in the Netherlands, 1650–1750." In E. Earle (ed.), *Essays in European Economic History, 1500–1800,* pp. 199–211. Oxford, 1974.

Chapter Bibliographies

Van Eeghen, I. H. "Arnoldus Montanus's Book on Japan." *Quaerendo*, II (1972), 250–72.

Van Gelder, H. E. "Oud-Nederlandsch Aardewerk." *De Gids*, LXXXVIII (1924), 1–18.

Van Kley, E. J. "The Effect of the Discoveries on Seventeenth-Century Dutch Popular Culture." *Terrae Incognitae*, VIII (1976), 34–42.

Vinaver, V. "Mercanti e bastimenti di Ragusa in India: una leggenda." In M. Cortelazzo (ed.), *Mediterraneo e oceano Indiano*, pp. 177–90. Florence, 1970.

Wake, C. H. H. "The Changing Pattern of Europe's Pepper and Spices Imports, *ca.* 1400–1700." *Journal of European Economic History*, VIII (1979), 361–403.

Wilson, Charles. "The British Isles." In C. Wilson and G. Parker (eds.), *An Introduction to the Sources of European Economic History*, pp. 115–54. Ithaca, N.Y., 1977.

——. "Transport as a Factor in the History of Economic Development." *Journal of European Economic History*, II (1973), 320–37.

II. THE CHRISTIAN MISSION

BOOKS

Allan, Charles Wilfred. *Jesuits at the Court of Peking*. Shanghai, 1935.

Allen, William Osborn Bird, and M'Clure, Edmund. *Two Hundred Years. The History of the Society for Promoting Christian Knowledge, 1698–1898*. London, 1898.

Almeida, Fortunato de. *História de igreja em Portugal*. 4 vols. Coimbra, 1910–24. New ed., Barcelos, 1968.

André-Marie, R. P. F., O.P. *Missions dominicaines dans l'Extrême Orient*. Paris, 1865.

Arasaratnam, Sinnappah. *Dutch Power in Ceylon, 1658–1687*. 2 vols. Amsterdam, 1958.

Ashley-Brown, William. *On the Bombay Coast and Deccan. The Origin and History of the Bombay Diocese, a Record of Three Hundred Years' Work for Christ in Western India*. London, 1937.

Ausejo, Luz. "The Philippines in the Sixteenth Century." Ph.D. diss., Dept. of History, Univ. of Chicago, 1972.

Bachmann, Peter R. *Roberto Nobili, 1577–1656. Ein missiongeschichtlicher Beitrag zum Christlichen Dialog mit Hinduismus*. Rome, 1972.

Bangert, W. V. *A History of the Society of Jesus*. St. Louis, 1972.

Barrett, Ward (trans. and ed.). *Mission in the Marianas, An Account of Father Diego Luis de Sanvitores and His Companions, 1669–70*. Minneapolis, 1975.

Bernard, Henri, S.J. *Les îles Philippines du grand archipel de la Chine: un essai de conquête spirituelle de l'Extrême Orient, 1571–1641*. Tientsin, 1936.

Biermann, Benno Maria, O.P. *Die Anfänge der neueren Dominikanermission in China*. Münster, 1927.

Birch, T. T. (ed.). *Robert Boyle, The Works*. Hildesheim, 1965.

Boetzelaer van Asperen en Dubbeldam, Carel Wessel Theodorus Baron van (ed.). *De protestantsche kerk in Nederlandsch-Indië, 1620–1939*. The Hague, 1947.

Chapter Bibliographies

Bolton, Herbert E. *Rim of Christendom. A Biography of Eusebio Francisco Kino, Pacific Coast Pioneer*. New York, 1936.

Bontinck, François. *La lutte autour de la liturgie chinoise aux XVIIe et XVIIIe siècles*. Louvain and Paris, 1962.

Boudens, Robrecht, O.M.I. *The Catholic Church in Ceylon under Dutch Rule*. Rome, 1957.

Boxer, Charles Ralph. *Fidalgos in the Far East 1550–1770*. The Hague, 1948.

———. *The Christian Century in Japan*. Berkeley, 1951.

———. *The Great Ship from Amacon. Annals of Macao and the Old Japan Trade, 1555–1640*. Lisbon, 1959.

———. *Race Relations in the Portuguese Colonial Empire, 1415–1825*. Oxford, 1963.

———. *The Dutch Seaborne Empire, 1600–1800*. London, 1965.

Bruijn, Caspar Adam Laurens van Troostenburg de. *De Hervormde Kerk in Nederlandsch Oost-Indië onder de Oost-Indische Compagnie, 1602–1795*. Arnhem, 1884.

Burrus, E. J. *Father Kino Writes to the Duchess*. Rome, 1965.

Callenbach, J. R. *Justus Heurnius, eene Bijdrage tot de Geschiedenis des Christendoms in Nederlandsch Oost-Indië*. Nijkerk, 1897.

Campbell, William. *An Account of Missionary Success in the Island of Formosa Published in London in 1650 and Now Reprinted with Copious Appendices*. London, 1889.

———. *Formosa under the Dutch, Described from Contemporary Records with Explanatory Notes and a Bibliography of the Island*. London, 1903. Reprinted Taipei, 1967.

Cácegas, Luís de. *História de São Domingos particular de reyno, e conquistas de Portugal*. 4 vols. Lisbon, 1623, 1662, 1678, 1733.

Chappoulie, H. *Aux origines d'une église. Rome et les missions d'Indochine au XVIIe siècle*. 2 vols. Paris, 1943.

Chatterton, Eyre. *The History of the Church of England in India*. London, 1924.

Clarke, J. (trans.). *The Truth of the Christian Religion by Hugo Grotius. . . .* Cambridge, 1860.

Collis, Maurice. *The Land of the Great Image, Being Experiences of Friar Manrique in Arakan*. New York, 1943.

Coolhas, W. Ph. *A Critical Survey of Studies on Dutch Colonial History*. The Hague, 1960.

Cooper, Michael, S.J. *Rodrigues the Interpreter. An Early Jesuit in Japan and China*. New York, 1974.

Correia-Afonso, John, S.J. *Jesuit Letters and Indian History: A Study of the Nature and Development of the Jesuit Letters from India (1542–1773) and Their Value for Indian Historiography*. Bombay, 1955; 2d rev. ed., Bombay, 1969.

Coutinho, Fortunato. *Le régime paroissial des diocèses de rite latin de l'Inde des origines (XVIe siècle) à nos jours*. Louvain and Paris, 1958.

Croizier, Ralph C. *Koxinga and Chinese Nationalism: History, Myth, and the Hero*. Cambridge, Mass., 1977.

Cronin, Vincent. *A Pearl to India: The Life of Roberto de Nobili*. London, 1959.

———. *The Wise Man from the West*. London, 1955.

Chapter Bibliographies

Dai Nippon Shiryo (*Japanese Historical Materials*). Vol. XII, Pt. 12. Tokyo, 1909.

Dehaisnes, Chretien Abbe. *Vie du Père Nicolas Trigault de la Compagnie de Jésus.* Tournai, 1861.

Dehergne, Joseph, S.J. *Répertoire des Jésuites de Chine de 1552 à 1800.* Rome and Paris, 1973.

De la Costa, H., S.J. *The Jesuits in the Philippines, 1581–1768.* Cambridge, Mass., 1967.

D'Sousa, Herman. *In the Steps of St. Thomas.* San Thomé, 1952.

Duncan, T. Bentley. *The Portuguese Enterprise in Asia.* Unpublished typescript.

Dunne, George, S.J. *Generation of Giants. The Story of the Jesuits in China in the Last Decades of the Ming Dynasty.* Notre Dame, 1962.

Elia, Pasquale M. d', S.J. (ed.). *Fonti Ricciane; documenti originali concernenti Matteo Ricci e la storia delle prime relazioni tra l'Europa e la Cina (1579–1615) . . . sotto il patrocinio della Reale Accademia d'Italia.* 3 vols. Rome, 1942–49.

———. *Galileo in China: Relations through the Roman College between Galileo and the Jesuit Scientist-Missionaries.* Cambridge, Mass., 1960.

Fenger, J. Fred. *History of the Tranquebar Mission.* Madras, 1906.

Ferrando, Juan. *Historia de los PP. Dominicos en las Islas Filipinas y en sus misiones del Japon, China, Tung-kin, y Formosa.* In Wm. Campbell (trans.), *Formosa under the Dutch Described from Contemporary Records.* Taipei, 1967.

Ferroli, Domenco, S.J. *The Jesuits in Malabar.* 2 vols. Bangalore, 1939, 1951.

Fu Lo-shu. *A Documentary Chronicle of Sino-Western Relations (1644–1820).* 2 vols. Tucson, 1966.

Gensichen, Hans-Werner. *Missionsgeschichte der neuern Zeit.* 3d rev. ed. In B. Moeller (ed.), *Die Kirche in ihrer Geschichte.* Göttingen, 1976.

Gernet, Jacques. *China and the Christian Impact: A Conflict of Cultures.* Translated from French by Janet Lloyd. Cambridge, 1985.

Gesquiére, Th. *Mathieu de Castro, premier Vicaire Apostolique aux Indes. Une création de la Propagande à ses débuts.* Bruges, 1937.

Gibbs, M. E. *The Anglican Church in India.* New Delhi, 1972.

Grayson, James Huntley. *Early Buddhism and Christianity in Korea. A Study in the Emplantation of Religion.* Leyden, 1985.

Guennou, Jean. *Les Missions Etrangères.* Paris, 1963.

Hartmann, Arnulf, O.S.A. *The Augustinians in Seventeenth-Century Japan.* Marylake, Ontario, 1965.

Havret, Henri. *La stèle chrétienne de Si-ngan-fou.* "Variétès sinologiques," No. XII. Shanghai, 1897.

Hay, Malcolm. *Failure in the Far East. Why and How the Breach between the Western World and China First Began.* Wettoren, Belgium, 1956.

Heras, Henry, S.J. *The Aravidu Dynasty of Vijayanagar.* 2 vols. Madras, 1927.

———. *The Conversion Policy of the Jesuits in India.* "Studies in Indian History of the Indian Historical Research Institute, St. Xavier's College, Bombay," No. XVIII. Bombay, 1933.

Hertz, Solange (ed. and trans.). *Rhodes of Viet Nam*. Westminster, Md., 1966.

Hull, Ernest, S.J. *Bombay Mission-History with a Special Study of the Padroado Question*. 2 vols. Bombay, 1927–30.

Hummel, A. W. (ed.). *Eminent Chinese of the Ch'ing Period (1644–1912)*. Washington, D.C., 1943.

Hutchinson, E. W. (ed. and trans.). *1688. Revolution in Siam. The Memoir of Father de Bèze, S.J.* Hong Kong, 1968.

Jack-Hinton, Colin. *The Search for the Islands of Solomon, 1567–1838*. Oxford, 1969.

Jann, P. Adelhelm, O.M.C. *Die katholischen Missionen in Indien, China und Japan. Ihre Organisation und das portugiesische Patronat von 15. bis ins 18. Jahrhundert*. Paderborn, 1915.

Janson, H. W. *Apes and Ape Lore in the Middle Ages and the Renaissance*. London, 1952.

[Kroot, Antonius]. *History of the Telugu Christians by a Father of the Mill Hill St. Joseph's Society*. Trichinopoly, 1910.

Kuepers, J. J. A. M. *The Dutch Reformed Church in Formosa, 1627–1662. Mission in a Colonial Context*. "Schriftenreihe der Neuen Zeitschrift für Missionswissenschaft," Vol. XXVII. Immensee, 1978.

Lach, D. F. *The Preface to Leibniz' Novissima Sinica*. Honolulu, 1957.

Latourette, K. S. *A History of the Expansion of Christianity*. 7 vols. New York, 1937–45.

———. *A History of Christian Missions in China*. New York, 1929.

Launay, Adrien. *Histoire de la mission de Cochinchine, 1658–1823. Documents historiques, 1658–1728*. Paris, 1923.

Laures, John. *The Catholic Church in Japan: A Short History*. Revised by Joseph P. Ryan. Rutland, Vt., 1954.

Lemmens, Leonhard, O.F.M. *Geschichte der Franziskanermissionen*. Münster, 1929.

Lind van Wijngaarden, Jan Daniel de. *Antonius Waleus*. Leyden, 1891.

Lopez, Teofilo Aparicio, O.S.A. *La Orden de San Agustin en la India (1572–1622)*. Valladolid, 1977.

Maclagan, Edward Douglas. *The Jesuits and the Great Mogul*. London, 1932.

Maras, Raymond J. *Innocent XI, Pope of Christian Unity*. Notre Dame, 1984.

Margiotti, Fortunato, O.F.M. *Il cattolicismo nello Shansi dalle origini al 1738*. Rome, 1958.

Meersman, A., O.F.M. (ed.). *Historia missionum ordinis Fratrum Minorum. I. Asia centro-orientalis et Oceania*. Rome, 1967.

———. *The Franciscans in Tamilnad*. Supplementa XVII of the *Neue Zeitshcrift für Missionswissenschaft*. Fribourg, Switzerland, 1962.

Merino, Manuel, O.S.A. *Misioneros Agustinos en el Extremo Oriente, 1565–1780. Obra inédita que con el titulo "Osario Venerable," compuso el Agustino P. Agustin Maria de Castro, Año de 1780*. Madrid, 1954.

Metzler, Josef. *Die Synoden in China, Japan, und Korea, 1570–1931*. Paderborn, 1980.

Michael, Franz. *The Origin of Manchu Rule in China*. Baltimore, 1942.

Montalbán, Francisco J., S.J. *Das spanische Patronat und die Eroberung der Philippinen.* Freiburg im Breisgau, 1930.

Mousnier, R. *The Institutions of France under the Absolute Monarchy, 1598–1789.* Trans. by Brian Pearce. Chicago, 1979.

Mulders, A. *Missionsgeschichte. Die Ausbreitung des katholischen Glaubens.* Translated from Dutch into German by J. Madey. Regensburg, 1960.

Müllbauer, Maximilian. *Geschichte der katholischen Missionen in Ostindien von der Zeit Vasco da Gamas bis zur Mitte des 18. Jahrhunderts.* Freiburg im Breisgau, 1852.

Neill, Stephen. *A History of Christianity in India, The Beginnings to A.D. 1707.* Cambridge, 1984.

———. *Christian Missions.* Harmonsworth, 1964.

Nevett, Albert M., S.J. *John de Britto and His Times.* Anand, 1980.

Nicholl, R. (ed.). *European Sources for the History of the Sultanate of Brunei.* Brunei, 1975.

Nilakanta Sastri, K. A. *A History of South India from Prehistoric Times to the Fall of Vijayanagar.* 3d ed. Madras, 1966.

Nobbs, Douglas. *Theocracy and Toleration.* Cambridge, 1938.

O Chronista de Tissuary. Nova Goa, 1867.

Oxnam, R. B. *Ruling from Horseback. Manchu Politics in the Oboi Regency, 1661–69.* Chicago, 1975.

Pachtler, G. M., S.J. *Das Christenthum in Tonkin und Cochinchina, dem heutigen Annamreiche von seiner Einführung bis auf die Gegenwart.* Paderborn, 1861.

Pastor, L. von. *The History of the Popes from the Close of the Middle Ages.* Vol. XXIX. Translated by Dom Ernest Graf, O.S.B. London, 1938.

Payne, C. H. (ed. and trans.). *Akbar and the Jesuits. An Account of the Jesuit Missions at the Court of Akbar by Father Pierre du Jarric, S.J.* New York, 1926.

———. *Jahangir and the Jesuits.* New York, 1930.

Pedot, Lino M., O.S.M. *La S. C. de Propaganda Fide e le missioni del Giappone, 1622–1838. . . .* Vicenza, 1946.

Penny, Frank. *The Church in Madras, Being the History of the Ecclesiastical and Missionary Action of the East India Company in the Presidency of Madras in the Seventeenth and Eighteenth Centuries.* 3 vols. London, 1904.

Phelan, John Leddy. *The Hispanization of the Philippines; Spanish Aims and Filipino Responses, 1565–1700.* Madison, Wis., 1959.

Pieris, P. E. (ed. and trans.). *Ribeiro's History of Ceilão.* Colombo, 1909.

Pinot, Virgile. *La Chine et la formation de l'ésprit philosophique en France, 1640–1740.* Paris, 1932.

Pinto da Franca, Antonio. *Portuguese Influence in Indonesia.* Djakarta, 1970.

Piskaty, P. Kurt. *Die katholische Missionsschule in Nusa Tenggara (Südost-Indonesien)— ihre geschichtliche Entfaltung und ihre Bedeutung für die Missionsarbeit.* "Studia. Instituti Missiologici Societatis Verbi Divini," V. Steyr, 1964.

Richter, Julius. *Die evangelische Mission in Niederlandische-Indien, Fern- und Südost-Asien, Australia, Amerika.* Vol. V of his *Allgemeine evangelische Missionsgeschichte.* Gütersloh, 1931.

Chapter Bibliographies

Rosso, Antonio S., O.F.M. *Apostolic Legations to China of the Eighteenth Century.* South Pasadena, Cal., 1948.

Rowbotham, Arnold H. *Missionary and Mandarin. The Jesuits at the Court of China.* Berkeley, 1942.

Saeki, P. Y. *The Nestorian Documents and Relics in China.* Tokyo, 1937. 2d rev. ed., Tokyo, 1951.

Sánchez, Victor, and Fuertes, C. S. (eds.). *España en Extremo Oriente. Filipinas, China, Japon. Presencia Franciscana, 1578–1978.* Madrid, 1979.

Saulière, Augustin, S.J. *Red Sand. A Life of St. John de Britto, S.J., Martyr of the Madura Mission.* Madura, 1947.

Scherer, James A. (trans. and ed.). *Justinian Welz. Essays by an Early Prophet of Missions.* Grand Rapids, Mich., 1969.

Sebes, Joseph, S.J. *The Jesuits and the Sino-Russian Treaty of Nerchinsk (1689): The Diary of Thomas Pereira, S.J.* Rome, 1961.

Shield, W. E., S.J. *King and Church. The Rise and Fall of the Patronato Real.* Chicago, 1961.

Sitsayamkan, Luang. *The Greek Favourite of the King of Siam.* Singapore, 1967.

Spence, Jonathan D. *Ts'ao Yin and the K'ang-hsi Emperor, Bondservant and Master.* New Haven, 1966.

———. *Emperor of China. Self-Portrait of K'ang-hsi.* New York, 1974.

———. *The Memory Palace of Matteo Ricci.* New York, 1984.

Stegmaier, Ortrud, S.Sp.S. *Der missionarische Einsatz der Schwestern auf den Inseln Flores und Timor (Südost-Indonesien).* No. 15, Studia Istituti Missiologici Societatis Verbi Divini. St. Augustin, 1974.

Teixeira, Manuel. *The Portuguese Missions in Malacca and Singapore, 1511–1698.* 3 vols. Lisbon, 1961–63.

Thekedathu, Joseph, S.D.B. *The Troubled Days of Francis Garcia S.J., Archbishop of Cranganore (1641–59).* Rome, 1972.

Thomaz de Bassierre, Yves de. *Un belge mandarin à la cour de Chine aux XVIIe et XVIIIe siècles. Antoine Thomas, 1644–1709.* Paris, 1977.

Tisserant, Eugène, Cardinal. *Eastern Christianity in India; a History of the Syro-Malabar Church from the Earliest Time to the Present Day.* Bombay, [1957].

Toscano, G. M. *La prima missione cattolica nel Tibet.* Parma, 1951.

Van den Berg, Johannes. *Constrained by Jesus' Love: An Inquiry into the Motives of the Missionary Awakening in Great Britain in the Period between 1698 and 1815.* Kampen, 1956.

Väth, Alfons. *Johann Adam Schall von Bell S.J., Missionar in China, Kaiserlicher Astronom und Ratgeber am Hofe von Peking, 1592–1666.* Cologne, 1933.

Vaumas, G. de. *L'éveil missionnaire de la France d'Henri IV à la fondation du Séminaire des Missions Etrangères.* Lyon, 1942.

Warneck, G. *Outline of a History of Protestant Missions.* Translated from 7th German ed. by George Robson. Chicago, 1901.

Wessels, Cornelius. *Histoire de la mission d'Amboine depuis sa fondation par saint François Xavier . . . à 1605.* Translated from the Dutch by J. Roebroek. Louvain, 1934.

Widmer, Eric. *The Russian Ecclesiastical Mission in Peking during the Eighteenth Century.* Cambridge, Mass., 1976.

Wills, John E., Jr. *Pepper, Guns, and Parleys.* Cambridge, Mass., 1974.

Young, John D. *Confucianism and Christianity.* Hong Kong, 1983.

ARTICLES

Abad, Antolín. "El P. Alonso Muñoz." *Archivo Ibero-Americano* (Madrid), XIX (1959), 126–31.

———. "Los Franciscanos en Filipinas, 1578–1898." *Revista de Indias,* Vol. XXIV, Nos. 97–98 (Jul.–Dec., 1964), pp. 411–44.

Alonso, Carlos, O.S.A. "Agustinos en la India. Relaciónes y listas de religiosos inéditas (1624–42)." *Analecta Augustiniana,* XXXVII (1974), 243–96.

———. "Primer projecto de Propaganda Fide para la creación de un obispado en Bengala (1624–25)." *Augustinianum,* VI (1966), 77–90.

Ambruzzi, Luigi, S.J. "Il contributo dei missionari cattolici alla conoscenza delle religioni, dei costumi e della geografia dell' India dalla seconda metà del '500 alla metà del secolo XVIII." In C. Costantini *et al., Le missioni cattoliche e la cultura dell' Oriente,* pp. 261–92. Rome, 1943.

Besse, L., S.J., and Hosten, H., S.J. "List of Portuguese Jesuit Missionaries in Bengal and Burma (1576–1642)." *Journal of the Asiatic Society of Bengal,* n.s., VII (1911), 15–23.

———. "Father Manoel da Fonseca, S.J., in Ava (Burma), 1613–52." *Ibid.,* n.s., XXI (1925), 12–19.

Biermann, Benno M. "Frei Luis de Andrada und die Solormission." *ZMR,* XLIII (1959), 176–87.

———. "Die Mission der portugiesischen Dominikaner in Hinterindien." *ZMR,* XXI (1931), 305–27.

Bocarro, Antonio. "Decada 13 da Historia da India." In P. E. Pieris (ed. and trans.), *Ribeiro's History of Celão.* Colombo, 1909.

Bot, J. "Mission History Sketch of the Lesser Sunda Islands." *Mission Bulletin* (Hong Kong), 1955, pp. 573–78.

Boudens, Robrecht, D.M.I. "Attempts of Catholic Missionaries to Enter Ceylon in 1661–83." *JRAS, Ceylon Branch,* n.s., IV (1955), 35–44.

Boxer, C. R. "Macao as a Religious and Commercial Entrepôt in the Sixteenth and Seventeenth Centuries." *Acta Asiatica,* XXVI (1974), 64–74.

———. "Portuguese Military Expeditions in Aid of the Mings against the Manchus, 1621–1647." *T'ien Hsia Monthly,* Vol. VII, No. 1 (Aug. 1938), pp. 24–36.

———. "The Portuguese Padroado in East Asia and the Problem of the Chinese Rites, 1576–1773." *Instituto Português de Hongkong. Boletim,* No. 1 (July 1948), pp. 199–216.

———. "The Problem of the Native Clergy in Portuguese India, 1518–1787." *History Today,* XVII (1967), 772–80.

Boxer, C. R., and Cummins, J. S. "The Dominican Mission in Japan (1602–1622) and Lope de Vega." *Archivum fratrum predicatorum,* XXXIII (1963), 1–88.

Brouwer, A. M. "De Zending onder de Oost-Indische Compagnie." In H. D. J. Boissevain (ed.), *De Zending in Oost en West* (2 vols.), I, 27–69. The Hague, 1934.

Burnay, J. "Notes chronologiques sur les missions Jésuites du Siam au XVIIᵉ siècle." *AHSI,* XXII (1953), 170–202.

Carretto, P. "Vatican Papers of the Seventeenth Century." *Journal of the Thailand Research Society,* Vol. XXXV (1944), Pt. 2, pp. 173–89. Reprinted in *Selected Articles from the Siam Society Journal,* VII (1959), 177–94.

Chalumeau, Raymond, C.M. "Saint Vincent de Paul, et le Saint-Siège." *Archivum historiae pontificiae,* V (1967), 263–88.

Chen Min-Sun. "Hsü Kuang-ch'i (1562–1633) and His Image of the West." In C. Pullapilly and E. Van Kley, *Asia and the West,* pp. 27–44. Notre Dame, 1986.

Cummins, J. G. "Two Missionary Methods in China: Mendicants and Jesuits." In V. Sánchez and C. S. Fuertes (eds.), *España in extremo oriente,* pp. 33–108. Madrid, 1979.

De la Costa, H., S.J. "Philippines." *New Catholic Encyclopedia,* XI, 280–84.

Fernandes, Lagrange Romeo. "Uma descripção e relação 'Di Sasatana Peninsula' (1664) do Padre Inacio Arcamone." *AHSI,* L (1981), 76–120.

Gibbin, R. W. "The Abbe de Choisy." In *Selected Articles from the Siam Society Journal,* VIII (1959), 1–16.

Gonçalves, José Júlio. "Os Portugueses no Sião." *Boletim da sociedade de geografia de Lisboa,* LXXV (1957), 435–62.

Gordon, Amy Glassner. "The First Protestant Missionary Effort: Why Did It Fail?" *International Bulletin of Missionary Research,* Vol. VIII, No. 1 (Jan., 1984), pp. 12–18.

Grisar, Josef, S.J. "Francesco Ingoli über die Aufgaben des kommenden Päpstes nach dem Tode Urbans VIII (1644)." *Archivum historiae pontificae,* V (1967), 289–324.

Gschaedler, Andre. "Religious Aspects of the Spanish Voyages in the Pacific during the Sixteenth Century and the Early Part of the Seventeenth." *The Americas,* IV (1948), 302–15.

Guennou, J. "Paris Foreign Mission Society." *New Catholic Encyclopedia,* X, 1016–17.

Hartmann, Arnulf, O.S.A. "The Augustinians in Golden Goa. . . ." *Analecta Augustiniana,* XXX (1967), 5–147.

———. "The Augustinian Mission of Bengal (1599–1834)." *Ibid.,* XLI (1978), 159–213.

Henkel, Willy. "The Polyglot Printing-office of the Congregation." *SCPFMR,* Vol. I/1, pp. 335–50. Freiburg im Breisgau, 1971.

Hoàng Xuân-hãn. "Girolamo Maiorica, ses oeuvres en langue Vietnamienne conservées à la Bibliothèque Nationale de Paris." *AHSI,* XXII (1953), 203–14.

Hoffman, R. "Propagation of the Faith, Congregation for the." *New Catholic Encyclopedia,* XI, 840–44.

Hoffmann, Karl. "Das erste päpstliche Missionsinstitut." *Zeitschrift für Missionswissenschaft,* XII (1922), 76–82.

Hogg, W. R. "The Rise of Protestant Missionary Concern, 1517–1914." In G. H. Anderson (ed.), *The Theology of the Christian Mission*, pp. 95–111. New York, 1961.

Hosten, H. "Saint Thomas and San Thomé, Mylapore." *Journal of the Asiatic Society of Bengal*, n.s., XIX (1923), 153–235.

Hutchinson, E. W. "The French Foreign Mission in Siam during the XVIIth Century." In *Selected Articles from the Siam Society Journal*, VIII (1959), 17–90.

———. "Journal of Mgr. Lambert, Bishop of Beritus, from Tenasserim to Siam in 1662." *Ibid.*, pp. 91–94.

———. "The Retirement of the French Garrison from Bangkok in the Year 1688." *Ibid.*, pp. 159–99.

Kaung, Maung. "The Beginnings of Christian Missionary Education in Burma, 1600–1824." *Journal of the Burma Research Society*, XX (1930), 59–75.

Kelly, Celsus, O.F.M. "The Franciscan Missionary Plan for the Conversion to Christianity of the Natives of the Austral Lands as Proposed in the Memorials of Fray Juan de Silva O.F.M." *The Americas*, XVII (1961), 277–91.

Kilger, Laurentz. "Die ersten Jahre Propaganda—eine Wendezeit der Missionsgeschichte." *Zeitschrift für Missionswissenschaft*, XII (1922), 1–20.

Kowalsky, Nikolaus, O.M.I. "Die Errichtung des Apostolischen Vikariates Madras nach den Akten des Propagandaarchivs." *NZM*, VIII (1952), 36–48.

Lamalle, Edmond, S.J. "La propaganda du P. Nicolas Trigault en faveur des missions de Chine, 1616." *AHSI*, IX (1940), 49–120.

Lancashire, Douglas. "Anti-Christian Polemics in Seventeenth-Century China." *Church History*, XXXVIII (1969), 218–41.

Littell, F. H. "The Free Church View of Missions." In G. H. Anderson (ed.), *The Theology of the Christian Mission*, pp. 112–21. New York, 1961.

Maas, Otto. "Zum Konflikt der spanischen Missionäre mit den französischen Bischöfen in der chinesischen Mission des 17. Jahrhunderts." In H. Finke *et al.*, *Gesammelte Aufsätze zur Kulturgeschichte Spaniens*, II, 165–95. Münster, 1930.

Margiotti, Fortunato. "La Cina, ginepraio di questioni secolari." *SCPFMR*, Vol. I/2, pp. 597–631. Freiburg im Breisgau, 1971.

Maybon, Charles B. "Notice sur Cristoforo Borri et sur les éditions de sa 'Relation.'" *Bulletin des amis du Vieux Hué*, XXXVIII (1931), 270–75.

Meriwether, C. "A Sketch of the Life of Date Masamune and an Account of His Embassy to Rome." *Transactions of the Asiatic Society of Japan*, XXI (1894), 1–105.

Merkel, Franz R. "The Missionary Attitude of the Philosopher G. W. von Leibniz." *The International Review of Missions*, IX (1920), 399–410.

Metzler, Josef. "Foundation of the Congregation 'de Propaganda Fide' by Gregory XV." *SCPFMR*, Vol. I/1, pp. 79–111. Freiburg im Breisgau, 1971.

———. "Francesco Ingoli, der erste Sekretär der Kongregation." *Ibid.*, pp. 197–243.

———. "Die Kongregation in der zweiten Hälfte des 17. Jahrhunderts." *Ibid.*, pp. 244–305.

———. "Wegbereiter und Vorläufer der Kongregation." *Ibid.*, pp. 38–78.

Mungello, D. E. "The Jesuits' Use of Chang Chü-cheng's Commentary in Their Translation of the Confucian Four Books (1687)." *China Mission Studies (1550–1800) Bulletin,* III (1981), 12–22.

Pacheco, Diego, S.J. "The Europeans in Japan, 1543–1640." In M. Cooper (ed.), *The Southern Barbarians: The First Europeans in Japan,* pp. 35–98. Tokyo, 1971.

Perera, Simon G., S.J. "The Jesuits in Ceylon in the Sixteenth and Seventeenth Centuries." *Ceylon Antiquarian and Literary Register,* II (1916–1917), 1–11.

Peréz, Lorenzo. "Historia de las misiones de los Franciscanos en las islas Malucas y Celebes." *Archivum Franciscanum Historicum,* VI (1913), 45–60; VII (1914), 198–226, 424–46, 621–53.

Peri, Noel. "Essai sur les relations du Japon et de l'Indochine aux XVIe et XVIIe siècles." *Bulletin de l'Ecole Française d'Extreme-orient* (Hanoi), XXIII (1923), 1–136.

Phelan, John Leddy. "Pre-Baptismal Instructions and the Administration of Baptism in the Philippines during the Sixteenth Century." *The Americas,* XII (1955–56), 3–23.

Ptak, Roderick. "The Demography of Old Macao, 1555–1640." *Ming Studies,* XIV (1982), 27–35.

Pullapilly, C. K. "Religious Impact of the Discovery of the Sea Route to India." In C. K. Pullapilly and E. Van Kley (eds.), *Asia and the West,* pp. 173–94. Notre Dame, 1986.

Rouleau, F. A., S.J. "Chinese Rites Controversy." *New Catholic Encyclopedia,* III, 612.

Schilling, P. Doroteo. "Il contributo dei missionari cattolici nei secoli XVI e XVII alla conoscenza dell'isola di Ezo e degli Ainu." In C. Costantini *et al., Le missioni cattoliche e la cultura dell'Oriente,* pp. 139–214. Rome, 1943.

Schmidlin, J. "Die Gründung der Propaganda Kongregation." *Zeitschrift für Missionswissenschaft,* XII (1922), 1–2.

Schütte, Joseph F., S.J. "Die Wirksamkeit der Päpste für Japan im ersten Jahrhundert der japanischen Kirchengeschichte (1549–1650)." *Archivum historiae pontificiae,* V (1967), 175–261.

———. "Japan, Martyrs of." *New Catholic Encyclopedia,* VII, 835–45.

Schwade, A. "Japan." *New Catholic Encyclopedia,* VII, 828–35.

Silva Rego, A. da. "Padroado." *New Catholic Encyclopedia,* X, 1114–16.

Stokman, Sigfridus, O.F.M. "De eerste Missionarissen van Borneo." *Historisch Tijdschrift,* VII (1928), 347–60.

Taladriz, José Luis Alvarez. "Notas para la historia de la entrada en Japon de los Franciscanos." In V. Sánchez and C. S. Fuertes (eds.), *España en Extremo Oriente . . . ,* pp. 3–32. Madrid, 1979.

Teixeira, Manuel. "Os Franciscanos em Macau." *Ibid.,* pp. 309–75.

Trindade, Paulo da. "Conquista espiritual do Oriente. . . ." In R. Boudens (ed.), *The Catholic Church in Ceylon under Dutch Rule.* Rome, 1957.

Van Kley, E. J. "Some Seventeenth-Century European Protestant Responses to Matteo Ricci and His Mission in China." In C. K. Pullapilly and E. J. Van Kley (eds.), *Asia and the West*, pp. 195–203. Notre Dame, 1986.

Väth, Alfons. "P. F. Antonio Caballero de Santa Maria über die Mission der Jesuiten und anderen Orden in China." *AHSI*, I (1932), 291–302.

Wessels, Cornelius, S.J. "Catalogus patrum et fratrum e Societate Iesu qui in missione Moluccana ab A. 1546 ad A. 1677 adlaboraverunt." *AHSI*, I (1932), 237–53.

———. "De Katholieke missie in het Sultanaat Batjan (Molukken) 1557–1609." *Historisch Tijdschrift*, VIII (1929), 115–148, 221–245.

———. "De Augustijen in de Molukken, 1544–46, 1601–25." *Ibid.*, XIII (1934), 44–59.

Wicki, Josef. "Auszüge aus den Briefen der Jesuitengenerale an die Obern in Indien, 1549–1613." *AHSI*, XXII (1953), 114–69.

———. "India." *New Catholic Encyclopedia*, VII, 435–44.

Willeke, Bernward. "Die Ankunft der ersten Franziskaner in Japan." *ZMR*, XLIII (1959), 166–76.

Winckworth, E. P. T. "A New Interpretation of the Pahlavi Cross-Inscriptions of Southern India." *Journal of Theological Studies*, XXX (1929), 237–44.

Winslow, F. J. "Vicar Apostolic." *New Catholic Encyclopedia*, XIV, 638–39.

Wyngaert, Anastase van den, O.F.M. "Mgr. Fr. Pallu et Mgr. Bernardin Della Chiesa." *Archivum Franciscanum Historicum*, XXI (1938), 17–47.

———. "Le patronat portugais et Mgr. Bernardin della Chiesa (1690–1714)." *Ibid.*, XXXV (1942), 3–34.

Zürcher, E. "The First Anti-Christian Movement in China. Nanking (1616–1621)." In P. W. Pestman (ed.), *Acta Orientalia Neerlandica*, pp. 187–97. Leyden, 1971.

Zwemer, S. M. "Calvinism and the Missionary Enterprise." *Theology Today*, VII (1950), 206–16.

III. THE IBERIAN LITERATURE

BOOKS

Alexandrowicz, Charles Henry. *An Introduction to the History of the Law of Nations in the East Indies (Sixteenth, Seventeenth, and Eighteenth Centuries)*. Oxford, 1967.

Amzalak, Moses Beneabat. *Anciens économistes portugais*. Lisbon, 1940.

Aquarone, J. B. *D. João de Castro. Gouvernour et Vice-Roi des Indes Orientales*. 2 vols. Paris, 1968.

Ausejo, Luz. "The Philippines in the Sixteenth Century," Ph.D. diss., Dept. of History, Univ. of Chicago, 1972.

Barbosa Machado, Diogo. *Bibliotheca Lusitana, historica, critica, e cronologica*. . . . 4 vols. Lisbon, 1741–59.

Barrett, Ward (trans. and ed.). *Mission in the Marianas. An Account of Father Diego Luis de Sanvitores and His Companions, 1669–1670*. Minneapolis, 1975.

Chapter Bibliographies

Bell, Aubrey F. G. *Diogo do Couto*. London, 1924.

Boxer, Charles R. *A Portuguese Embassy to Japan (1644–47). Translated from Unpublished Portuguese Ms., and Other Contemporary Sources, with Commentary and Appendices*. London, 1928.

———— (trans. and ed.). *Commentaries of Ruy Freyre de Andrada*. . . . London, 1930.

————. *A aclamação del Rei D. João IV em Goa e em Macau*. . . . Lisbon, 1932.

————. *Macau na época da restauração. Macau Three Hundred Years Ago*. Macao, 1942. Revised ed., *Seventeenth-Century Macau in Contemporary Documents and Illustrations*. Hong Kong, 1984.

————. *The Christian Century in Japan, 1549–1650*. Berkeley and Los Angeles, 1951.

———— (ed. and trans.). *The Tragic History of the Sea, 1589–1622, and Further Selections from the Tragic History of the Sea, 1559–1565*. "HS," 2d ser., CXII, CXXXII. Cambridge, 1959, 1968.

————. *Exotic Printing and the Expansion of Europe*. Bloomington, Ind., 1972.

Boxer, Charles R., and Vasconcelos, Frazâo de. *André Furtado de Mendoça (1558–1610)*. Lisbon, 1955.

Brosses, C. de. *Histoire des navigations aux terres australes*. Paris, 1756.

Chen Min-sun. "Three Contemporary Western Sources on the History of Late Ming and the Manchu Conquest of China." Ph.D. diss., Dept. of History, Univ. of Chicago, 1971.

Clair, C. *A History of European Printing*. London, 1976.

Collis, Maurice. *The Land of the Great Image, Being Experiences of Friar Manrique in Arakan*. New York, 1943.

Cooper, Michael, S.J. *Rodrigues the Interpreter. An Early Jesuit in Japan and China*. New York, 1974.

Cortesão, A., and Teixeira da Mota, A. *Portugaliae monumenta cartographica*. 5 vols. Lisbon, 1960.

Cummins, J. S. (ed.). *Lope Felix de Vega Carpio. Triunfo de la fee en los reynos del Japon*. London, 1965; also London, 1967.

————. *The Travels and Controversies of Friar Domingo Navarrete, 1618–86*. "HS," 2d ser., CXVIII, CXIX. Cambridge, 1962.

Dai Nippon Shiryo (Japanese Historical Materials). Tokyo, 1909.

Dalrymple, A. *An Historical Collection of the Several Voyages and Discoveries in the South Pacific Ocean*. 2 vols. London, 1770–71.

Davies, David. *The World of the Elseviers, 1580–1712*. The Hague, 1954.

De la Costa, H. *The Jesuits in the Philippines, 1581–1768*. Cambridge, Mass., 1961.

Diehl, Katherine S. *Printers and Printing in the East Indies to 1850*. (Projected to be 7 vols.; Volume I on Batavia was issued in 1990 at New Rochelle, N.Y. The others have not yet appeared.)

Disney, A. R. *Twilight of the Pepper Empire. Portuguese Trade in Southwest India in the Early Seventeenth Century*. Cambridge, Mass., 1978.

Eisenstein, Elizabeth. *The Printing Press as an Agent of Change*. 2 vols. Cambridge, 1979.

Chapter Bibliographies

Endo, Shusaku. *The Samurai.* Translated by Van C. Gessel. New York, 1982.

Febvre, L., and Martin, H. J. *The Coming of the Book. The Impact of Printing, 1450–1800.* London, 1979.

Ferrero, Manuel. *Historia de la provincia del Santo Rosario de la orden de predicadores en Filipinas, Japon, y China.* 2 vols. Madrid, 1962–63.

Fonseca, Henrique Quirino da. *Diários da navegação de carreira da India nos anos de 1595, 1596, 1597, 1600 e 1603.* Lisbon, 1938.

González Sánchez, José María. *Un misionero diplomatico. Vida del J. Victorio Ricci en el tercer centenario de su primer entrada en China, 1655.* Madrid, 1955.

Gordon, Michael. "Morality and Politics in Seventeenth-Century Spain: The Arbitrista Pedro Fernandez Navarrette." Ph.D. diss., Dept. of History, Univ. of Chicago, 1972.

Graff, H. J. *The Legacies of Literacy.* Bloomington, Ind., 1987.

Greenslade, S. L. (ed.). *The Cambridge History of the Bible.* Cambridge, 1963.

Groslier, B. P. (with C. R. Boxer). *Angkor et le Cambodge au XVIe siècle, d'après les sources portugaises et espagnoles.* Paris, 1958.

Haley, K. H. D. *The Dutch in the Seventeenth Century.* London, 1972.

Heras, H. *The Aravidu Dynasty of Vijayanagar.* Madras, 1927.

Kagan, Richard. *Students and Society in Early Modern Spain.* Baltimore, 1974.

Kelly, Celsus (ed.). *La Austrialia del Espiritu Santo.* "HS," 2d ser., CXXVI–CXXVII. Cambridge, 1966.

Leitão, Humberto (ed.). *Viagens do reino para a India e da India para o reino.* 2 vols. Lisbon, 1957–58.

Ley, C. D. *Portuguese Voyages, 1498–1663.* London, 1948.

Luard, C. E. (ed.). *Travels of Sebastian Manrique, 1629–43.* "HS," 2d ser., LIX, LXI. Oxford, 1926–27.

Maclagan, Edward D. *The Jesuits and the Great Mogul.* London, 1932.

Magalhães, José Calvet de. *História do pensamento económico em Portugal. Da idade-média ao mercantilismo.* Coimbra, 1967.

Markham, Sir Clements (trans.). *The Voyages of Pedro Fernandez de Quiros, 1595–1606.* "HS," 2d ser., XIV, XV. London, 1904.

Martin, Henri-Jean. *Livre pouvoirs et société à Paris au XVIIe siècle (1598–1701).* 2 vols. Geneva, 1969.

Meersman, A. *The Franciscans in the Indonesian Archipelago.* Louvain, 1967.

Merino, Manuel. *Misioneros Agustinos en el extreme oriente, 1565–1780. Obra inédita que con el titulo "Osorio Venerable," compuso el Agustino P. Agustin Maria de Castro, Año de 1780.* Madrid, 1954.

Müllbauer, Maximilian. *Geschichte der katholischen Missionen in Ostindien.* Freiburg im Breisgau, 1852.

Murdoch, James, and Yamagata, Isoh. *A History of Japan during the Century of Early Foreign Intercourse (1542–1651).* Vol. II. Kobe, Japan, 1903.

Murray, Hugh. *Historical Account of Discoveries and Travel in Asia from the Earliest Times to the Present.* 3 vols. Edinburgh, 1820.

Parker, John. *Books to Build an Empire: A Bibliographical History of English Overseas Interests to 1620.* Amsterdam, 1965.

Payne, C. H. (ed. and trans.). *Akbar and the Jesuits. An Account of the Jesuit Missions at the Court of Akbar by Father Pierre du Jarric, S.J.* London, 1926.

————. *Jahangir and the Jesuits.* New York, 1930.

Peddie, R. A. (ed.). *Printing: A Short History of the Art.* London, 1927.

Peeters-Fontainas, J. F. *Bibliographie des impressions espagnols des Pays-Bas.* Antwerp, 1933.

Penrose, Boies. *Travel and Discovery in the Renaissance, 1420–1620.* Cambridge, Mass., 1965.

Pereira, F. *Roteiros portuguezes da viagem de Lisboa à India nos seculos XVI e XVII.* Lisbon, 1898.

Pérez, Lorenzo. *Apostolado y martirio del Beato Luis Sotelo en el Japón.* Madrid, 1924.

Pieris, P. E. *Ribeiro's History of Ceilão; With a Summary of de Barros, de Couto, Antonio Bocarro and the documentos remettidos, with the Parangi Hatane and Kostantinu Hatane, Translated from the Original Portuguese and Sinhalese.* 2d ed. Colombo, 1909.

Pottinger, David. *The French Book Trade in the Ancien Regime, 1500–1791.* Cambridge, Mass., 1958.

Priolkar, Anant Kakba. *The Printing Press in India; Its Beginnings and Early Development, Being a Quatercentenary Commemoration Study of the Advent of Printing in India (in 1556). With . . . an Historical Essay on the Konkani Language of J. H. da Cunha Rivara. . . .* Translated from the Portuguese by Theophilus Lobo. Bombay, 1958.

Rogers, Francis M. (ed.). *Europe Informed: An Exhibition of Early Books Which Acquainted Europe with the East.* Sixth International Colloquium on Luzo-Brazilian Studies. Cambridge, Mass., and New York, 1966.

Saraiva, António José. *História da cultura em Portugal.* 3 vols. Lisbon, 1950–62.

Schilder, Günther. *Australia Unveiled.* Amsterdam, 1976.

Schurz, W. L. *The Manila Galleon.* New York, 1959.

Schütte, Josef Franz, S.J. *El "Archivo del Japon," vicistudines del Archivo Jesuitico del Extremo Oriente y descripción del fondo existente en la Real Academia de la Historia de Madrid.* Madrid, 1964.

Sinclair, William Frederick, and Ferguson, D. (eds.). *The Travels of Pedro Teixeira, with His "Kings of Hormuz," and Extracts from His "Kings of Persia."* "HS," 2d ser., IX. London, 1902.

Steinberg, S. H. *Five Hundred Years of Printing.* 3d ed. Harmondsworth, 1974.

Stephens, M., and Bolton, H. E. (eds.). *The Pacific Ocean in History.* New York, 1917.

Struve, Lynn A. *The Southern Ming, 1644–1662.* New Haven, 1984.

Szilas, L. *Xaveriana.* Lisbon, 1964.

Ternaux-Compans, Henri. *Bibliothèque asiatique et africaine; ou, catalogue des ouvrages relatifs à l'Asie et à l'Afrique qui ont paru depuis la découverte de l'imprimerie jusqu'en 1700.* 2 vols. Paris, 1841–42. Reprinted, Amsterdam, 1968.

Chapter Bibliographies

Thaliath, Jonas. *The Synod of Diamper.* "Orientalia Christiana analecta," No. CLII. Rome, 1958.

Tiele, Pieter Anton. *Mémoire bibliographique sur les journaux des navigateurs néerlandais réimprimés dans les collections de De Bry et Hulsius . . . avec tables des voyages, des éditions et des matières.* Amsterdam, 1867.

Toscano, Giuseppe M. *La prima missione cattolica nel Tibet.* Parma, 1951.

Wessels, Cornelius. *Early Jesuit Travellers in Central Asia, 1603–1721.* The Hague, 1924.

White, Thomas E. "Seventeenth-Century Spanish Sources on East Asia," unfinished Ph.D. diss., Dept. of History, Univ. of Chicago.

Wicki, Josef (ed.). *Diogo Gonçalves S.J. Historia do Malavar.* Münster, 1955.

ARTICLES

Alonso, Carlos. "Documentación inédita para una biografía de Fr. Alejo de Meneses, O.S.A., Arzobispo de Goa, 1595–1612." *Analecta Augustiniana,* XXVII (1964), 263–333.

Bosmans, H. "Lettres inédites de François de Rougement. Missionnaire belge de la Compagnie de Jesus au XVIIe siècle." *Analecta Bollandiana,* XXXIII (1914), 174–293.

Boxer, Charles R. "Portuguese Roteiros, 1500–1700." *Mariner's Mirror,* XX (1934), 171–86.

———. "Three Historians of Portuguese Asia (Barros, Couto, and Bocarro)." *Instituto Português de Hongkong. Boletim,* No. 1 (July, 1948), 15–44.

———. "An Introduction to João Ribeiró's 'Historical Tragedy of the Island of Ceylon, 1685.'" *Ceylon Historical Journal,* III (1953), 234–55.

———. "An Introduction to the História Tragico-Marítima." *Revista da Faculdada de Letras* (Lisbon), 3d ser., Vol. XXIII, Pt. 1 (1957), pp. 48–99.

———. "Uma obra raríssima impressa em Goa no século XVII: A jornada que Francisco de Souza de Castro fez ao Achem no anno de 1638." *Boletim internacional de bibliografia Luso-Brasileira,* Vol. VIII, No. 3 (1967), pp. 431–528.

———. "Portuguese and Spanish Projects for the Conquest of Southeast Asia, 1580–1600." *Journal of Asian History,* III (1969), 118–36.

———. "A Tentative Check-List of Indo-Portuguese Imprints." *Arquivos do cêntro cultural português,* IX (1975), 567–600.

Briggs, L. P. "Spanish Intervention in Cambodia, 1593–1603." *T'oung Pao,* XXXIX (1949), 132–60.

Cabaton, A. (ed.). "Le Memorial de Pedro Sevil [de Guarga] à Philippe III. . . ." *Bulletin de la commission archéologique de l'Indochine,* 1914–16, pp. 1–102.

Chen Min-sun. "Philippine Sources of Palafox y Mendoxa's 'History of the Conquest of China by the Tartars.'" *Annals of the Philippine-Chinese Historical Association,* V (1975), 51–62.

D'Silva, J. A. "On the Rebellion of Khusrū." *Journal of Indian History,* V (1926), 267–81.

Fenn, Eric. "The Bible and the Missionary." In S. L. Greenslade (ed.), *The Cambridge History of the Bible*, pp. 383–407. Cambridge, 1963.

Ferguson, Donald (trans. and ed.). "The History of Ceylon from the Earliest Times to 1600 A.D., as Related by João de Barros and Diogo do Couto." *JRAS, Ceylon Branch*, Vol. XX, No. 60 (1908), 1–445.

Ferrando Pérez, Roberto. "Zeichnungen von Südsee-Eingeborenen aus dem frühen 17. Jahrhundert." *Zeitschrift für Ethnologie*, LXXIX (1954), 75–81.

Heras, Henry, S.J. "The Siege and Conquest of the Fort of Asirgarh by the Emperor Akbar, Described by an Eye-witness [Fr. Jerome Xavier, a Spanish Jesuit]." *Indian Antiquary*, LIII (1924), 33–41.

———. "The Jesuit Influence in the Court of Vijayanagar." *Quarterly Journal of the Mythic Society*, XIV (Oct. 1923), 130–40.

Hosten, Henry, S.J. "Fr. Fernão Guerreiro's Annual *Relation* of 1602–03 on the Mogor Mission." *Examiner* (Bombay), Nov. 22, 1919, pp. 469–70; Nov. 29, 1919, pp. 478–80.

——— (trans.). "Fr. N. Pimenta's Annual of Margão, Dec. 1, 1601." *Journal of the Asiatic Society of Bengal*, XXII (1927), 83–107.

———. "The Annual Relation of Father Fernão Guerreiro, S.J., for 1607–1608." *Journal of the Panjab Historical Society*, VII (1918), 50–73.

———. "A Letter of Father Francisco Godinho, S.J., from Western Tibet (Tsaparang, August 16, 1626)." *Journal of the Asiatic Society of Bengal*, XXI (1925), 49–73.

Knowlton, E. C. "South East Asia in the Travel Book by Pedro Ordóñez de Ceballos." *Proceedings of the Second International Symposium on Asian Studies* (Hong Kong, 1980), pp. 499–510.

Kömmering-Fitzler, H. M. A. "Fünf Jahrhunderte portugiesischer Kolonialgeschichtsschreibung." *Die Welt als Geschichte*, Vol. VIII, Pt. 2 (1942), pp. 104–17.

MacGregor, A. (trans.). "A Brief Account of the Kingdom of Pegu, Translated from the Portuguese." *Journal of the Burma Research Society*, XVI (1926), 99–138.

Meriwether, C. "A Sketch of the Life of Date Masamune and an Account of His Embassy to Rome." *Transactions of the Asiatic Society of Japan*, 1st ser., XXI (1893–94), 1–105.

Mills, J. A. (trans.). "Eredia's Description of Malacca, Meridional India, and Cathay." *JRAS, Malay Branch*, VIII (1930), 1–288.

Murakami, N. "Japan's Early Attempts to Establish Commercial Relations with Mexico." In H. M. Stephens and H. E. Bolton (eds.), *The Pacific Ocean in History*, pp. 467–80. New York, 1917.

Pérez, P. Lorenzo. "Fr. Francesco de Jesús Escalona y su Relacion de China." *Extractum ex Periodico Archivum Franciscanum Historicum*, Vols. VIII–IX (1915–1916), 558–91, 184–218.

———. "De Filipinas a España, Naufragio de una armada en el siglo XVII." *Archivo Ibero-Americano*, IX (1922), 289–320.

Rehatsek, E. "Journal of Padre Manuel Godinho, S.J., from India to Portugal, in the Year 1663, by Way of Mesopotamia." *Calcutta Review*, XCIII, 63–97.

Chapter Bibliographies

Retana, W. E. "La literatura histórica de Filipinas de los siglos XVI y XVII." *Revue hispanique*, LX (1924), 293–325.

Rodríguez Moñino, A. R. "Bibliografía hispano-oriental." *Boletín de la Academia de la Historia* (Madrid), XCVIII (1931), 417–75.

Schurhammer, Georg, S.J. "Historical Research into the Life of Francis Xavier in the Sixteenth Century." In L. Szilas (ed.), *Xavieriana*, pp. 90–114. Lisbon, 1964.

Tamaskar, B. G. "Malik Ambar and the Portuguese." *Journal of the Bihar Research Society*, XXXIII (1947), 25–44.

Teixeira, Manuel. "Diogo Veloso e a gesta lusíada em Cambodja." *Actas da Congresso Internaciónal de História dos Descobrimentos* (Lisbon), Vol. V, Pt. 1 (1961), pp. 339–77.

Van Kley, E. J. "News from China. Seventeenth-Century European Notices of the Manchu Conquest." *Journal of Modern History*, XLV (1973), 561–82.

Wills, John E., Jr. "The Hazardous Missions of a Dominican: Victorio Riccio, O.P., in Amoy, Taiwan, and Manila." *Actes du IIe Colloque International de Sinologie* (Chantilly), IV (1980), 243–57.

Zürcher, E. "The First Anti-Christian Movement in China, Nanking (1616–21)." In P. W. Pestman (ed.), *Acta Orientalia Neerlandica* (Leyden, 1971), pp. 188–95.

IV. THE ITALIAN LITERATURE

BOOKS

Bietenholz, Peter G. *Pietro della Valle (1586–1652); Studien zur Geschichte der Orientkenntnis und des Orientbildes im Abendlande.* Basel and Stuttgart, 1962.

Blunt, Wilfrid. *Pietro's Pilgrimage.* London, 1953.

Cooper, Michael, S.J. *Rodrigues, The Interpreter. An Early Jesuit in Japan and China.* New York, 1974.

———. *They Came to Japan. An Anthology of European Reports on Japan, 1543–1640.* London, 1965.

Correia-Afonso, John. *Jesuit Letters and Indian History.* Bombay, 1955; 2d rev. ed., Bombay, 1969.

Costantini, C., et al. *Le missioni cattoliche e la cultura dell' oriente.* Rome, 1943.

Cronin, Vincent. *A Pearl to India. The Life of Roberto de Nobili.* London, 1959.

Degel, Gustav Germann. "Die Erforschung des Festlandes von Hinterindien durch die Jesuiten am Eingang und Ausgang des 17. Jahrhunderts." Ph.D. diss., Univ. of Würzburg, 1905.

De la Costa, H. *The Jesuits in the Philippines, 1581–1768.* Cambridge, Mass., 1967.

Ferroli, D. *The Jesuits in Malabar.* 2 vols. Bangalore, 1951, 1959.

Guglielminetti, Marziano (ed.). *Viaggiatori del Seicento.* Turin, 1967.

Hängü, Anton. *Der Kirchenhistoriker Natalis Alexander (1639–1724).* Freiburg, 1955.

Maclagan, Edward Douglas. *The Jesuits and the Great Mogul.* London, 1932.

Magnaghi, Alberto. *Il viaggiatore Gemelli Careri (secolo XVII.) e il suo "Giro del Mondo."* Bergamo, 1900.

Chapter Bibliographies

Müllbauer, Maximilian. *Geschichte der katholischen Missionen in Ostindien.* Freiburg im Breisgau, 1852.

Oxnam, Robert B. *Ruling from Horseback: Manchu Politics in the Oboi Regency, 1661–69.* Chicago, 1975.

Renaldo, John J. *Daniello Bartoli. A Letterato of the Seicento.* Naples, 1979.

Sen, Surindranath (ed.). *The Indian Travels of Thevenot and Careri.* New Delhi, 1949.

Toscano, Giuseppe M. *La prima missione cattolica nel Tibet.* Parma, 1951.

Tragella, G. B. *L' impero di Cristo, Le missioni cattoliche nel mondo.* Florence, 1941.

Weinstock, Herbert (trans.) *My Voyage around the World by Francesco Carletti, a Sixteenth-Century Florentine Merchant.* New York, 1964.

ARTICLES

Ambruzzi, Luigi, S.J. "Il contributo dei missionari cattolici alla conoscenza delle religioni, dei costumi e della geografia dell' India." In C. Costantini *et al., Le missioni cattoliche e la cultura dell' oriente,* pp. 261–92. Rome, 1943.

Baldinotti, Guiliano. "La Relation sur le Tonkin du P. Baldinotti." *Bulletin de l'Ecole Française d'Extrême-Orient* (Hanoi), III (1903), 71–74.

———. "Relation du Royaume de Tunquim, 'Nouvellement Découvert.'" *Ibid.,* pp. 75–78.

Berchet, Guglielmo. "Un ambasciatore della Cina a Venezia nel 1652." *Archivio veneto,* n.s., Vol. XXIX, Pt. 1 (1885), pp. 369–80.

Lamalle, Edmond. "La propaganda du P. Nicolas Trigault en faveur des missions de Chine, 1616." *AHSI,* IX (1940), 59–60.

Maybon, C. B. "Notice biographique et bibliographique sur G. F. de Marini, auteur d'une relation du royaume de Lao." *Revue indochinoise,* July, 1910, pp. 15–25; August, 1910, pp. 152–82; Sept., 1910, pp. 257–71; Oct., 1910, pp. 358–65.

Schütte, J. F. "Japanese Cartography at the Court of Florence: Robert Dudley's Maps of Japan, 1606–1636." *Imago Mundi,* XXIII (1969), 29–58.

Trollope, M. N. (trans.). "The Carletti Discourse: A Contemporary Italian Account of a Visit to Japan in 1597–98." *Transactions of the Asiatic Society of Japan,* 2d ser., IX (1932), 1–35.

Vargas, Philippe de. "Le 'Giro del Mondo' de Gemelli Careri, en particulier le récit du séjour en Chine. Roman ou verité?" *Schweizerische Zeitschrift für Geschichte,* V (1955), 417–51.

Vigielmo, V. "The Preface and First Ten Chapters of Amati's *Historia del regno di Voxu* . . . Translated and Annotated." *Harvard Journal of Asiatic Studies,* XX (1957), 619–43.

V. THE FRENCH LITERATURE

BOOKS

Anderson, John. *English Intercourse with Siam in the Seventeenth Century.* London, 1890.

Atkinson, Geoffroy. *La littérature géographique française de la Renaissance. Répertoire bibliographique.* Paris, 1927. *Supplément.* Paris, 1936.

Baddeley, John F. *Russia, Mongolia, China.* 2 vols. London, 1919.

Bamboat, Zenobia. *Les voyageurs français aux Indes aux XVIIe et XVIIIe siècles.* Paris, 1933.

Brébion, Antoine. *Bibliographie des voyages dans l'Indochine française du IXe au XIXe siècle.* Paris, 1910.

Camus, A. G. *Mémoire sur la collection des grands et petits voyages de De Bry, et sur la collection des voyages de M. Thévenot.* Paris, 1802.

Chappoulie, Henri. *Aux origines d'une église. Rome et les missions d'Indochine au XVIIe siècle.* . . . 2 vols. Paris, 1943.

[Crawford, James Ludovic Lindsay]. *Bibliotheca Lindesiana . . . Catalogue of the Printed Books Preserved at Haigh Hall.* 4 vols. Aberdeen, 1910. See especially Vol. IV.

Desmarquets, J. A. S. *Mémoires chronologiques pour servir à l'histoire de Dieppe, et à celle de la navigation française.* 2 vols. Paris, 1785.

Fargeon, Jean. *Catalogue des marchandises rares, curieuses . . . qui se font et debitent à Montpelier.* Pezenan, 1665.

Fouqueray, Henri, S.J. *Histoire de la Compagnie de Jésus en France.* 5 vols. Paris, 1910–25.

Froidereaux, H. (ed.). *Documents inédites relatifs à la constitution de la Compagnie des Indes Orientales de 1642.* Paris, n.d.

Gatty, J. Collet (ed.). *Voiage de Siam du Père Bouvet.* Leyden, 1963.

Hertz, Solange. *Rhodes of Viet Nam.* Westminster, Md., 1966.

Hutchinson, E. W. *1688. Revolution in Siam.* Hong Kong, 1968.

———. *Adventurers in Siam in the Seventeenth Century.* London, 1940.

Jal, A. *Abraham du Quesne et la marine de son temps.* 2 vols. Paris, 1873.

Joret, Charles. *J. B. Tavernier.* Paris, 1886.

Lach, D. F. *The Preface to Leibniz' Novissima Sinica.* Honolulu, 1957.

La Roncière, Charles Germaine Marie Bourel de. *Histoire de la marine française.* 6 vols. Paris, 1899–1932.

Madrolle, Claudius. *Les premiers voyages français à la Chine. La Compagnie de la Chine, 1698–1719.* Paris, 1901.

Marchand, P. (ed.). *Dictionnaire historique et critique par M. Pierre Bayle.* . . . 4 vols. Rev. ed. 1730.

Martin, Henri-Jean. *Livre pouvoirs et société à Paris au XVIIe siècle (1598–1701).* 2 vols. Geneva, 1969.

Masson, Joseph. *Missionnaires belges sous l'ancien régime (1500–1800).* Brussels, 1947.

Mousnier, Roland. *The Assassination of Henry IV.* New York, 1973.

Mungello, David E. *Curious Land: Jesuit Accommodation and the Origins of Sinology.* Stuttgart, 1985.

Oxnam, R. B. *Ruling from Horseback.* Chicago, 1968.

Chapter Bibliographies

Payne, C. H. (ed. and trans.). *Abkar and the Jesuits. An Account of the Jesuit Missions to the Court of Akbar by Father Pierre du Jarric, S.J.* London, 1926.

Priolkar, A. K. *The Goa Inquisition.* Bombay, 1961.

Rivière, Ernest M. *Supplément* (Vol. XII) to A. and A. de Backer and E. Sommervogel, *Bibliothèque de la Compagnie de Jésus.* Louvain, 1960.

Rosso, A. S. *Apostolic Legations to China of the Eighteenth Century.* South Pasadena, Cal., 1948.

Sottas, Jules. *Histoire de la compagnie royale des Indes Orientales, 1664–1719.* Paris, 1905.

Voretzsch, E. A. (ed.). *François Froger, Relation du premier voyage des François à la Chine, fait en 1698, 1699, et 1700.* . . . Leipzig, 1926.

ARTICLES

Barassin, J. "Compagnies de navigation et expéditions françaises dans l'Océan Indien au XVIIe siècle." *Studia* (Lisbon), XI (1963), 373–89.

Fitzler, M. A. H. "Die Maldiven im 16. und 17. Jahrhundert; ein Kapitel portugiesischer Kolonialeschichte." *Zeitschrift für Indologie und Iranistik,* X (1935–36), 215–56.

Flaumenhaft, Eugene, and Flaumenhaft, Carol. "Asian Medicinal Plants in Seventeenth-Century French Literature." *Economic Botany,* XXXVI (1982), 147–62.

Joret, Charles. "Le voyage de Tavernier (1670–89). Un manuscrit des 'Voyages'; relations de Tavernier avec le Grand Electeur; le lieu de sa mort et de sa sépulture." *Revue de géographie,* XII (1889), 161–74, 267–75, 328–41.

Kajdański, Edward. "Michael Boym's *Medicus Sinicus.*" *T'oung Pao,* LXXIII (1987), 161–89.

Lamalle, E. "La propagande du P. Nicolas Trigault en faveur des missions de Chine, 1616." *AHSI,* IX (1940), 49–120.

Lindsay, R. O. "Pierre Bergeron: A Forgotten Editor of French Travel Literature." *Terrae Incognitae,* VII (1976), 31–38.

"Review of *Historia Cultus Sinensium.*" In *History of the Works of the Learned, or an Impartial Account of Books Lately Printed in All Parts of Europe,* II (1700), 466–72.

Van Kley, E. J. "News from China. Seventeenth-Century European Notices of the Manchu Conquest." *Journal of Modern History,* LXXVI (1973), 561–82.

VI. THE NETHERLANDISH LITERATURE

BOOKS

Abeyashinge, T. *Portuguese Rule in Ceylon, 1594–1612.* Colombo, 1966.

Arnold, Thomas I. *Bibliographie de l'oeuvre de Lucas Jansz. Waghenaer.* Amsterdam, 1961.

Baddeley, John F. *Russia, Mongolia, China.* 2 vols. London, 1919.

Batchelor, J. *Ainu Life and Lore.* Tokyo, n.d.

Chapter Bibliographies

Blussé, Leonard, and Falkenburg, R. *Johan Nieuhofs beelden van een chinareis 1655–1657.* Middleburg, 1987.

Boxer, C. R. (ed.). *A Description of the Mighty Kingdoms of Japan and Siam by François Caron and Joost Schouten.* London, 1935.

———. *Isaac Commelin's "Begin ende Voortgangh." Introduction to the Facsimile Edition.* Amsterdam, 1969.

Briels, J. G. C. A. *Zuidnederlandse boekdrukkers en boekverkopers in de der Vereenigde Nederlanden omstreeks 1570–1630.* Nieuwkoop, 1974.

Campbell, W. *Formosa under the Dutch.* London, 1903.

Charpentier, Jarl (ed.). *The Livro da Seita dos Indios Orientais.* Uppsala, 1933.

Drake-Brockman, H. *Voyage to Disaster.* London, 1964.

Ferdon, E. N. *Early Tonga as the Explorers Saw It, 1616–1810.* Tucson, 1987.

Gebhard, Johan Fredrik. *Het leven van Mr. Nicolaas Cornelisz. Witsen (1641–1717).* 2 vols. Utrecht, 1881.

Groeneveldt, W. P. *De Nederlanders in China. BTLV,* Vol. XLVIII, 1898.

Heawood, Edward. *A History of Geographical Discovery in the Seventeenth and Eighteenth Centuries.* Cambridge, 1912. Reprinted in New York, 1969.

Heeres, J. E. *The Part Borne by the Dutch in the Discovery of Australia, 1606–1765.* London, 1899.

Ijzerman, J. W. (ed.). *Dirck Gerritsz. Pomp alias Dirck Gerritz. China, de eerste Nederlander die China en Japan bezocht 1544–1604.* "WLV," Vol. IX. The Hague, 1915.

Koeman, Cornelis. *Joan Blau and His Grand Atlas.* Amsterdam, 1970.

Ledyard, Gari. *The Dutch Come to Korea.* Seoul, 1971.

Leupe, P. A. *Voyage de M. Gerritsz. Vries vers le nord et l'est du Japon. . . .* Amsterdam, 1858.

Locher, J. G., and Bucks, P. de (eds.). *Moscoviche reyse, 1664–1665.* "WLV," Vols. LXVI, LXVII, LXVIII. The Hague, 1966–67.

Mungello, David. *Curious Land: Jesuit Accommodation and the Origins of Sinology.* Stuttgart, 1985.

Nachod, O. *Die Beziehungen der Niederländichen Ostindischen Kompagnie zu Japan im siebzehnten Jahrhundert.* Leipzig, 1897.

Ottow, Willem Martin. *Rijckloff Volckertsz. van Goens; de carrière van een diplomaat, 1619–1655.* Utrecht, 1954.

Phillips, George. *Dutch Trade in Formosa in 1629.* Shanghai, 1878.

Pott, P. H. *Naar wijder horizon.* The Hague, 1962.

Rouffaer, G. P., and Juynboll, H. H. *De Batik-Kunst in Nederlandsch-Indië en haar geschiedenis.* Utrecht, 1914.

Schilder, Günter. *Australia Unveiled: The Share of Dutch Navigators in the Discovery of Australia.* Amsterdam, 1976.

Schiltmeijer, J. R. (ed.). *Amsterdam in 17e eeuwse prent.* 3d ed. Amsterdam, 1968.

Schotel, G. D. J. *Vaderlandsche volksboeken en volksprookjes van den vroegste tijden tot einde der 18e eeuw.* Haarlem, 1875.

Smith, George Vinal. *The Dutch in Seventeenth Century Thailand.* Special Report No. 16 of the Center for Southeast Asian Studies, Northern Illinois University. De Kalb, Ill., 1977.

Sullivan, Michael. *The Meeting of Eastern and Western Art.* Greenwich, Conn., 1973.

Terpstra, H. *De Nederlanders in Voor-Indië.* Amsterdam, 1947.

Unger, W. S. (ed.). *De oudste reizen van de Zeeuwen naar Oost-Indië, 1598–1604.* "WLV," Vol. LI. The Hague, 1948.

Wieder, Frederik Caspar (ed.). *De reis van Mahu en de Cordes door de Straat van Magalhães naar Zuid-Amerika en Japan 1598–1600; scheepsjournaal, rapporten, brieven, zeilaanwijzingen, kaarten, enz.,* . . . The Hague, 1923–25.

Wills, John E., Jr. *Pepper, Guns, and Parleys. The Dutch East India Company and China, 1627–1681.* Cambridge, Mass., 1974.

ARTICLES

Blink, H. "Bernhard Varenius, de grondlegger der wetenschappelijke geographie." *Tijdscrift van het Nederlandsch Aardrijkskundig Genootschap gevestigd te Amsterdam,* ser. II, pt. 3 (1887).

Bodel Nijenhuis, J. T. "Johan Nieuhof." *Bijdragen van geschiedenis en oudheidkunde,* n.s., pt. 2 (1862), pp. 32–51.

Duyvendak, J. J. L. "Early Chinese Studies in Holland." *T'oung Pao,* XXXII (1936), 293–344.

Ferguson, D. (trans. and ed.). "The Visit of Spilbergen to Ceylon, Translated from Admiral Joris van Spilbergen's 'Relation.'" *JRAS, Ceylon Branch,* XXX (1927), 127–79, 361–409.

Goetz, H. "Notes on a Collection of Historical Portraits from Golconda." *Indian Arts and Letters,* X (1936), 10–21.

Ijzerman, J. W. "Over de belegering van het fort Jacatra (22 Dec. 1618–1 Febr. 1619)." *BTLV,* LXXIII (1917), 558–679.

Leupe, P. A. (ed.). "Reysbeschryving van het weg uit Samarangh nae de koninck-lijke hoofplaets Mataram. . . ." *BTLV,* IV (1856), 307–47.

———. "Het gezandtschap naar Bali . . . en 1633." *Ibid.,* V (1856), 1–71.

———. "Verhael van de belegeringhe der stadt Batavia . . . anno 1628. . . ." *Ibid.,* III (1855), 289–312.

Pott, P. H. "The Orient Reflected Our Views on the East throughout the Ages." In *Acta orientalia Neerlandica,* ed. P. W. Pestman (Leyden, 1971), 8–10.

Ronkel, Philippus Samuel van. "De eerste europeesche Tamilspraakkunst en het eerst malabarsche glossarium." *Mededeelingen der Nederlandsche Akademie van Wetenschappen, afdeeling letterkunde,* n.s., V (1942), 543–98.

Tiele, P. A. (ed.). "Verklaring van Martinus Apius van hetgeen hem en zijne mede-gevangen van de vloot van Jacob van Neck in 1602 te Macao is overkomen." *Bijdragen en mededeelingen van het Historisch Genootschap gevestigd te Utrecht,* VI (1883), 228–42.

Van Eeghen, Isabella H. "Arnoldus Montanus's Book on Japan." *Quaerendo,* II (1972), 250–72.

Chapter Bibliographies

VII. THE GERMAN AND DANISH LITERATURE

BOOKS

Asher, Adolph. *Bibliographical Essay on the Collection of Voyages and Travels Edited and Published by Levinus Hulsius and His Successors at Nuremburg and Francfurt from Anno 1598 to 1660.* Berlin, 1839.

Benzing, J. *Die Buchdrucker des 16. und 17. Jahrhunderts im deutschen Sprachgebiet.* 2d rev. ed. Wiesbaden, 1982.

Camus, A. C. *Mémoire sur la collection des grands et petits voyages de De Bry.* . . . Paris, 1802.

Chabrié, Robert. *Michel Boym. Jésuite Polonais et la fin des Ming en Chine (1646–1662).* Paris, 1933.

Chen Min-sun. "Three Contemporary Western Sources on the History of Late Ming and the Manchu Conquest of China." Ph.D. diss., Dept. of History, Univ. of Chicago, 1971.

Commissariat, Manekshah Sorābshah. *Mandelslo's Travels in Western India (A.D. 1638–9).* London, 1931.

Kronk, G. W. *Comets. A Descriptive Catalog.* Hillside, N.J., 1984.

Lach, D. F. *The Preface to Leibniz' Novissima Sinica.* Honolulu, 1957.

Maclagan, Edward Douglas. *The Jesuits and the Great Mogul.* London, 1932.

Raven-Hart, R. (trans.). *Germans in Dutch Ceylon.* Colombo, n.d. (ca. 1953).

Väth, Alfons. *Johann Adam Schall von Bell, S.J., Missionar in China, kaiserlicher Astronom und Ratgeber am Hofe von Peking, 1592–1666.* Cologne, 1933.

Weigel, Theodor O. *Bibliographische Mittheilungen über die deutschen Ausgaben von de Bry's Sammlungen der Reisen.* . . . Leipzig, 1854.

Wessels, C. *Early Jesuit Travellers in Central Asia, 1603–1721.* The Hague, 1924.

Wills, John E., Jr. *Pepper, Guns, and Parleys.* Cambridge, Mass., 1974.

ARTICLES

Dharampal, Ghita (trans.). "Heinrich von Poser's Travelogue of the Deccan (1622)." *Quarterly Journal of the Mythic Society,* LXXIII (1982), 103–14.

Foss, Theodore N. "Nicholas Trigault S.J.—Amanuensis or Propagandist?" *International Symposium on Chinese-Western Cultural Relations,* Supplement (Taipei, 1983), pp. 1–94.

Kajdánski, Edward. "Michael Boym's *Medicus Sinicus.*" *T'oung Pao,* LXXIII (1987), 161–89.

Knox, Robert. "An Historical Relation of Ceylon." *The Ceylon Historical Journal,* VI (1956–57), Nos. 1–4.

Rouffaer, J. S. "Een curieus Duitsch boekje over onze oost uit 1646." *BTLV,* LXIX (1914), 127–29.

Spence, J. "Reflections on Matteo Ricci." *China and Europe, Sixteenth to Eighteenth Centuries,* International Symposium, Hong Kong, 1987.

Szczesniak, Boleslaw. "The Writings of Michael Boym." *Monumenta Serica,* XIV (1949–55), 481–538.

Van Kley, E. "News from China. Seventeenth-Century Notices of the Manchu Conquest." *Journal of Modern History,* XLV (1973), 561–582.

———. "Europe's 'Discovery' of China and the Writing of World History." *American Historical Review,* LXXVI (1971), 358–85.

Widman, Hans. "Geschichte des deutschen Buchhandels." In H. Hiller and W. Strauss (eds.), *Der deutsche Buchhandel,* pp. 13–48. Munich, 1961.

Zimmel, Bruno. "Der erste Bericht über Tibets Hauptstadt Lhasa aus dem Jahre 1661." *Biblos,* II (Vienna, 1953), 127–45.

VIII. THE ENGLISH LITERATURE

BOOKS

Clair, Colin. *A History of European Printing.* London, 1976.

Collis, Maurice. *Siamese White.* Rev. ed. London, 1951.

Foster, William. *England's Quest of Eastern Trade.* London, 1933.

Lloyd, C. C. *William Dampier.* London, 1966.

Parker, John. *Books to Build an Empire: A Bibliographical History of English Overseas Interests to 1620.* Amsterdam, 1965.

Parks, George B. *Richard Hakluyt and the English Voyages.* New York, 1928.

Pennington, L. E. (ed.). *The Purchas Handbook.* Forthcoming.

Penrose, Boies. *Tudor and Early Stuart Voyages.* Washington, 1962.

———. *Urbaine Travelers, 1591–1635.* Philadelphia, 1942.

Prasad, Ram Chandra. *Early English Travellers in India. A Study in the Travel Literature of the Elizabethan and Jacobean Periods, with Particular Reference to India.* Delhi, Patna, and Varanasi, 1965.

Ramsay, George Daniel. *English Overseas Trade during the Centuries of Emergence.* London, 1957.

Rawlinson, H. G. *British Beginnings in Western India, 1579–1657.* Oxford, 1920.

Satow, Ernest M. (ed.). *The Voyage of Captain John Saris to Japan, 1613.* "HS," 2d ser., V. London, 1900.

Shipman, Joseph. *William Dampier, Seaman Scientist.* Lawrence, Kansas, 1962.

Strahan, Michael. *The Life and Adventures of Thomas Coryate.* London, 1962.

Tragen, Cecil. *Elizabethan Venture.* London, 1953.

ARTICLES

Foster, William. "Samuel Purchas." In Edward Lynam (ed.), *Richard Hakluyt and His Successors,* pp. 47–61. "HS," 2d ser., XCIII. London, 1946.

Lach, D. F. "The Far East." In D. B. Quinn (ed.), *The Hakluyt Handbook.* "HS," 2d ser., CXLIV, pp. 214–22. London, 1974.

Pennington, L. E. "Hakluytus Posthumus: Samuel Purchas and the Promotion of English Overseas Expansion." *The Emporia State Research Studies* (Emporia, Kansas), Vol. XIV, No. 3 (1966).

Strachan, M. F. "India." In D. B. Quinn (ed.), *The Hakluyt Handbook*. "HS," 2d ser., CXLIV, pp. 208–13. London, 1974.

Williamson, J. A. "Richard Hakluyt." In Edward Lynam (ed.), *Richard Hakluyt and His Successors,* "HS," 2d ser., XCIII, pp. 20–40. London, 1946.

IX. THE MUGHUL EMPIRE BEFORE AURANGZIB

BOOKS

Ansari, M. A. *Social Life of the Mughal Emperors (1526–1707)*. Allahabad, 1974.

———. *European Travellers under the Mughals, 1580–1627*. Delhi, 1975.

Aziz, Abdul. *The Mansabdari System and the Mughul Army*. Delhi, 1972.

Banerji, R. D. *History of Orissa from the Earliest Times to the British Period*. 2 vols. Delhi, 1980.

Beauchamp, H. K. (ed.). *Hindu Manners, Customs and Ceremonies by the Abbé J. A. Dubois*. 3d ed. Oxford, 1959.

Bietenholz, Peter G. *Pietro della Valle (1586–1652); Studien zur Geschichte der Orientkenntnis und des Orientbildes im Abendlande*. Basel and Stuttgart, 1962.

Brown, Perry. *Indian Architecture (Buddhist and Hindu Periods)*. 5th ed. Bombay, 1965.

Burgess, James, and Cousens, Henry. *The Architectural Antiquities of Northern Gujarat. . . .* London and Calcutta, 1903.

Caland, W. (ed.). *De Remonstrantie van W. Geleynessen de Jongh*. Amsterdam, 1929.

Cambridge History of India; see Dodwell, H. H. (ed.).

Camps, Arnulf. *Jerome Xavier and the Muslims of the Mogul Empire; Controversial Works and Missionary Activity*. Schöneck-Beckenried, 1957.

Commissariat, M. S. *Studies in the History of Gujarat*. Bombay, 1935.

———. *A History of Gujarat with a Survey of Its Monuments and Inscriptions*. 2 vols. Bombay, 1938, 1957.

———. *Mandelslo's Travels in Western India (A.D. 1638–9)*. London, 1931.

Daniélou, A. *Hindu Polytheism*. New York, 1964.

Das, A. K. *Mughul Painting during Jahangir's Time*. Calcutta, 1978.

Day, C. R. *The Music and Musical Instruments of Southern India and the Deccan*. Delhi, 1974. Reprint of the 1891 edition.

Deo, S. B. *History of Jaina Monachism from Inscriptions and Literature*. Poona, 1956.

Dodwell, H. H. (ed.). *The Cambridge History of India*. 6 vols. Cambridge, 1922–53.

D'Souza, V. S. *The Navayats of Kanara*. Dharwar, 1955.

Glasenapp, H. von. *Der Jainismus. Eine indische Erlösungsreligion*. Berlin, 1925.

Gokhale, B. G. *Surat in the Seventeenth Century: A Study in Urban History of Pre-Modern India*. London, 1979.

Chapter Bibliographies

Grist, D. H. *Rice.* 3d ed. London, 1959.

Habib, Irfan. *The Agrarian System of Mughal India (1556–1707).* Bombay, 1963.

Harvey, G. P. *Outline of Burmese History.* Bombay, 1947.

Hopkins, Thomas. *The Hindu Religious Traditions.* Encino, Cal., 1971.

Hutton, J. H. *Caste in India.* 4th ed. Bombay, 1963.

Jaini, Padmanabh S. *The Jaina Path of Purification.* Berkeley, 1979.

Katrak, S. K. H. *Who Are the Parsees?* Karachi, 1965.

Khan, Y. M. *The Deccan Policy of the Mughuls.* Lahore, 1971.

Maclagan, Edward Douglas. *The Jesuits and the Great Mogul.* London, 1932.

Mahapatra, K. *The Jaganatha Temples in Eastern India.* Bhubaneswar, 1977.

Majumdar, M. R. *Cultural History of Gujarat.* Bombay, 1965.

Mazumdar, K. C. *Imperial Agra of the Mughuls.* Agra, 1939.

Mehta, B. S., and Mehta, J. S. *Pratap the Patriot.* Udaipur, 1971.

Modi, Jivanji Jamshedji. *The Religious Ceremonies and Customs of the Parsees.* 2d ed. Bombay, 1937.

Moreland, W. H. *From Akbar to Aurangzeb. A Study in Indian Economic History.* London, 1972. Reprint of the 1923 original.

———. *India at the Death of Akbar: An Economic Study.* London, 1920.

Murray, John (publ.). *A Handbook for Travellers in India, Pakistan, Burma and Ceylon.* . . . 18th ed. London, 1959.

Neill, Stephen. *A History of Christianity in India. The Beginnings to A.D. 1707.* Cambridge, 1984.

Ojha, P. N. *North Indian Social Life during the Mughal Period.* Delhi, 1975.

Pant, C. *Nur Jahan and Her Family.* Allahabad, 1978.

Payne, C. H. (ed. and trans.). *Akbar and the Jesuits. An Account of the Jesuit Missions at the Court of Akbar by Father Pierre du Jarric.* London, 1926.

———. *Jahangir and the Jesuits.* New York, 1930.

Penrose, B. (ed.). *The Travels of Captain Robert Coverte.* Philadelphia, 1931.

Phul, R. K. *Armies of the Great Mughals, 1526–1707.* New Delhi, 1978.

Prasad, Ishwari. *The Mughal Empire.* Allahabad, 1974.

Prasad, R. C. *Early English Travellers in India.* Delhi, 1965.

Prater, S. H. *The Book of Indian Animals.* 2d rev. ed. Bombay, 1965.

Qaisar, A. J. *The Indian Response to European Technology and Culture, A.D. 1498–1707.* Delhi, 1982.

Ravenshaw, J. *Gaur: Its Ruins and Inscriptions.* London, 1878.

Rawlinson, Hugh George. *British Beginnings in Western India, 1579–1657.* Oxford, 1920.

Rizvi, Athar Abbas. *Fatehpur Sikri.* New Delhi, 1972.

Roy, A. C. *A History of Mughal Navy and Naval Warfares.* Calcutta, 1972.

———. *History of Bengal; Mughal Period, 1526–1765 A.D.* Calcutta, 1968.

Sarkar, Jadunath. *A Short History of Aurangzib, 1618–1707.* 3d ed. Calcutta, 1962.

Shah, P. G. *Ethnic History of Gujarat.* Bombay, 1968.

Sherwani, H. K. *History of the Qutb Shāhī Dynasty.* New Delhi, 1974.

Strachan, Michael. *The Life and Adventures of Thomas Coryate.* London, 1962.

———. *Sir Thomas Roe: A Life.* Salisbury, 1989.

Thompson, Edward John. *Suttee. A Historical and Philosophical Enquiry into the Hindu Rite of Widow Burning.* Boston and New York, 1928.

Thoothi, Nasarvan Ardshur. *The Vaishnavas of Gujarat, Being a Study in Methods of Investigation of Social Phenomena.* Calcutta, 1935.

Wijnaendts van Resandt, Willem. *De Gezaghebbers der Oost-Indische Compagnie op hare buiten-comptoiren in Azië.* Amsterdam, 1944.

Yasin, Mohammad. *A Social History of Islamic India, 1605–1748.* 2d rev. ed. New Delhi, 1974.

ARTICLES

Acharya, S. P. (ed.). "Bruton's Account of Cuttack and Puri." *Orissa Historical Journal,* X (1961), 25–50.

Gokhale, B. G. "Ahmadabad in the Seventeenth Century." *Journal of the Economic and Social History of the Orient* (Leyden), XII (1969), 187–97.

———. "Burhanpur. Notes on the History of an Indian City in the Seventeenth Century." *Ibid.,* XV (1972), 316–23.

Goysal, S. "Gujarati Shipping in the Seventeenth Century." *Indian Economic and Social History Review,* VIII (1971), 31–40.

Heras, Henry, S.J. "The Siege and Conquest of the Fort of Asirgarh by the Emperor Akbar." *Indian Antiquary,* LXXXIII (1924), 33–41.

Irwin, John. "Indian Textile Trade in the Seventeenth Century: Western India." *Journal of Indian Textile History,* I (1955), 4–24.

Moreland, W. H. "Johan van Twist's Description of India." *Journal of Indian History,* XVI (1937), 63–77.

Pradash, O. "The Dutch East Indies Company in Bengal; Trade Privileges and Problems, 1633–1712." *Indian Economic and Social History Review,* Vol. IX, Pt. 3 (1972), 258–87.

Randle, H. N. "Henry Lord and His Discoverie of the Banians." In *Jhā Commemoration Volume. Essays on Oriental Subjects,* "Poona Oriental Series," XXXIX, pp. 277–96. Poona, 1937.

Smith, Vincent A. "The Credit Due to the Book Entitled 'The Voyages and Travels of J. Albert de Mandelslo into the East Indies,'" *JRAS,* 1915, pp. 245–54.

Stein, Aurel. "Note on the Routes from the Panjab to Turkestan and China Recorded by William Finch (1611)." *Journal of the Panjab Historical Society,* Vol. VI, No. 2 (1917), pp. 144–48.

X. THE EMPIRE OF AURANGZIB

BOOKS

Ahmad, Aziz. *Studies in Islamic Culture in the Indian Environment.* Oxford, 1964.

Ali, Solim. *The Book of Indian Birds.* 7th rev. ed. Bombay, 1964.

Chapter Bibliographies

Ansari, M. A. *Social Life of the Mughal Emperors (1526–1707)*. Allahabad, 1974.

Athar Ali, M. *The Mughal Nobility under Aurangzeb*. Bombay, 1966.

Aziz, Abdul. *The Mansabdari System and the Mughul Army*. Delhi, 1972.

Banerji, Rakhal Das. *History of Orissa from the Earliest Times to the British Period*. 2 vols. Delhi, 1980.

Burgess, J. *Elura Cave Temples*. Varanasi, 1972.

———. *Report on the Elura Cave Temples and the Brahmanical and Jaina Caves in Western India*. Vol. V of the *Archaeological Survey of Western India*. Varanasi, 1970. (Reprint of 1882 ed.)

———. *The Muhammedan Architecture of India*. 2 pts. London, 1900, 1905.

Chaube, J. *History of Gujarat Kingdom*. New Delhi, 1975.

Chopra, P. N. *Ladakh*. New Delhi, 1980.

Commissariat, M. S. *A History of Gujarat, with a Survey of Its Monuments and Inscriptions*. 2 vols. Bombay, 1938, 1957.

———. *Studies in the History of Gujarat*. Bombay, 1935.

Crooke, William. *The Tribes and Castes of the North-Western Provinces and Oudh*. 4 vols. Calcutta, 1896.

Da Cunha, J. Gerson. *Notes on the History and Antiquities of Chaul and Bassein*. Bombay, 1876.

Daniélou, A. *Hindu Polytheism*. New York, 1964.

David, M. D. *History of Bombay, 1661–1708*. Bombay, 1973.

Dehejia, V. *Early Buddhist Rock Temples. A Chronology*. Ithaca, N.Y., 1972.

Deo, S. B. *A History of Jaina Monachism. . . .* Poona, 1956.

Drury, Heber. *The Useful Plants of India: With Notices of Their Chief Value in Commerce, Medicine, and the Arts*. London, 1873.

Ferguson, J. P. *Kashmir. An Historical Introduction*. London, 1961.

Fergusson, James, and Burgess, James. *The Cave Temples of India*. London, 1880.

Gherwal, R. S. *Lives and Teachings of the Yogis of India. Miracles and Occult Mysticism of India*. 2 vols. Santa Barbara, Cal., 1939.

Gokhale, B. G. *Surat in the Seventeenth Century*. London, 1979.

Habib, Irfan. *The Agrarian System of Mughal India (1556–1707)*. Bombay, 1963.

Hallissey, Robert C. *The Rajput Rebellion against Aurangzib*. Columbia, Missouri, 1977.

Hambly, Gavin, *et al. Central Asia*. New York, 1969.

———. *Cities of Mughal India; Delhi, Agra, and Fatehpur Sikri*. New York, 1968.

Herklots, G. A., and Crooke, W. (trans. and eds.). *Islam in India or the Oānūn-i-Islām . . . by Ja' Far Sharif*. New Delhi, 1972. (Reprint of 1921 ed.)

Hutton, J. H. *Caste in India*. 4th ed. Oxford, 1963.

Irvine, William. *Army of the Indian Moghuls: Its Organization and Administration*. London, 1903.

Katrak, S. K. H. *Who Are the Parsees?* Karachi, 1965.

Chapter Bibliographies

Kempers, A. J. B. (ed.). *Journaal van Dircq van Adrichem's Hofreis naar den Groot-mogol Aurangzeb, 1662.* "WLV," Vol. XLV. The Hague, 1941.

Khan, Y. M. *The Deccan Policy of the Mughuls.* Lahore, 1971.

Kitts, Eustace John. *A Compendium of the Castes and Tribes Found in India. . . .* Bombay, 1885.

Koul, S. C. *Srinigar and Its Environs.* 3d ed. Srinigar, 1962.

Krishnaswami, S. *Musical Instruments of India.* Delhi, 1965.

Kulkarnee, N. H. (ed.). *Chhatrapati Shivaji, Architect of Freedom.* Delhi, 1975.

Lall, R. Manohar. *Among the Hindus. A Study of Hindu Festivals.* Cawnpore, 1933.

Law, B. C. (ed.). *Mountains and Rivers of India.* Calcutta, 1968.

Levine, Nancy E. *The Dynamics of Polyandry.* Chicago, 1988.

Liebert, Gosta. *Iconographic Dictionary of the Indian Religions: Hinduism-Buddhism-Jainism.* Leyden, 1976.

Magnaghi, Alberto. *Il viaggiatore Gemelli Careri (secólo XVII) e il suo "Giro del Mondo."* Bergamo, 1900.

Modi, J. J. *The Religious Ceremonies and Customs of the Parsees.* 2d ed. Bombay, 1937.

Moreland, W. H. *From Akbar to Aurangzeb, A Study in Indian Economic History.* London, 1923.

Murray, John (publ.). *A Handbook for Travellers in India, Pakistan, Burma and Ceylon.* 18th ed. London, 1959.

Nath, R. *Monuments of Delhi, Historical Study.* New Delhi, 1979.

Nayeem, M. A. *External Relations of the Bijapur Kingdom, 1489–1686.* Hyderabad, 1974.

O'Flaherty, W. D.; Mitchell, George; and Berkson, Carmel. *Elephanta, The Cave of Shiva.* Princeton, 1983.

Ojha, P. N. *North Indian Social Life during Mughal Period.* Delhi, 1975.

Pandey, R. B. *Varanasi, The Heart of Hinduism.* Varanasi, 1969.

Parker, Richard Neville. *A Forest Flora for the Punjab with Hazara and Delhi.* New Delhi, 1973.

Puhl, R. R. *Armies of the Great Mughals.* New Delhi, 1978.

Qaisar, J. *The Indian Response to European Technology and Culture (A.D.1498–1707).* Delhi, 1982.

Rizvi, S. A. A. *A History of Sufism in India.* 2 vols. New Delhi, 1983.

Roy, A. C. *A History of Mughal Navy and Naval Warfares.* Calcutta, 1972.

Saran, P. *The Provincial Government of the Mughals, 1526–1658.* 2d ed. New York, 1973.

Sarkar, J. *History of Aurangzib, Mainly Based on Persian Sources.* 2d rev. ed. Calcutta, 1921.

———. *A Short History of Aurangzib.* 3d ed. Calcutta, 1962.

———. *House of Shivaji.* 3d ed. Calcutta, 1955.

———. *Mughal Administration.* 3d ed. Calcutta, 1972.

Schierlitz, E. *Die bildlichen Darstellungen der indischen Göttertrinität in der älteren ethnographischen Literatur.* Munich, 1927.

Sen, S. N. (trans. and ed.). *Foreign Biographies of Shivaji.* 2d rev. ed. Calcutta, 1977.

Sharma, G. N. *Mewar and the Mughal Emperors.* Agra, 1954.

Sharma, Y. D. *Delhi and Its Neighbourhood.* New Delhi, 1944.

Sherwani, H. K. *History of the Qutb Shāhī Dynasty.* New Delhi, 1974.

Srinivas, M. N. *Caste in Modern India and Other Essays.* Bombay, 1962.

Thomas, Edward. *The Revenue Resources of the Mughal Empire in India from A.D. 1593 to A.D. 1707.* London, 1871.

Thomas, P. *Hindu Religion, Customs, and Manners.* 4th rev. ed. Bombay, 1960.

Thootl, N. A. *The Vaishnavas of Gujarat.* Calcutta, 1935.

Toy, S. *The Strongholds of India.* London, 1957.

Watt, Sir George. *The Commercial Products of India.* London, 1908.

Wauchope, R. S. *The Buddhist Cave Temples of India.* New Delhi, 1981.

Wessels, Cornelius, S.J. *Early Jesuit Travellers in Central Asia, 1603–1721.* The Hague, 1924.

Wijnaendts van Resandt, Willem. *De gezaghebbers der Oost-Indische Compagnie op hare buiten-comptoiren in Azië.* Amsterdam, 1944.

Yasin, Mohammed. *A Social History of Islamic India.* 2d rev. ed. New Delhi, 1974.

Yazdani, G. *Bidar. Its History and Monuments.* Oxford, 1947.

ARTICLES

Devra, G. L. "Manucci's Comments on Indian Social Customs and Traditions." In U. Marazzi (ed.), *La conoscenza dell'Asia . . . in Italia nei secoli XVIII e XIX* (2 vols.), I, 351–71. Naples, 1984.

Gokhale, B. G. "Ahmadabad in the XVIIth Century." *Journal of the Economic and Social History of the Orient,* XII (1969), 187–97.

Guah, Amalendu. "Appendix." In *Cambridge Economic History of India,* I, 478–86.

Hatalkar, V. G. "French Sources for the History of Shivaji." In N. H. Kulkarnee (ed.), *Chhatrapati Shivaji, Architect of Freedom,* pp. 199–205. Delhi, 1975.

Keswané, D. G. "Shivaji through Foreign Eyes." In *ibid.,* pp. 182–98.

Lach, Alma. "Dining on the Rim of the Pacific Plate." *The World and I* (March, 1988), pp. 321–27.

Moraes, G. M. (trans.). "Surat in 1663 as Described by Manoel Godinho." *JRAS, Bombay Branch,* XXVI (1952), 121–33.

Refai, G. Z. "Foreign Embassies to Aurengzeb's Court at Delhi." In R. E. Frykenberg (ed.), *Delhi through the Ages: Essays in Urban History, Culture, and Society,* pp. 192–204. Delhi, 1986.

Zimmel, B. "Die erste Sanskrit-Grammatik." *Biblos,* V (1956), 48–63.

———. "Die erste Sanskrit-Grammatik wiederentdeckt." *Ibid.,* XVI (1967), 219–22.

Chapter Bibliographies

XI. FROM GOA TO CAPE COMORIN

BOOKS

Anantha Krishna Iyir, L. K. *The Tribes and Castes of Cochin.* 3 vols. Madras, 1909–12; reprinted in New Delhi, 1981.

Aubin, J. (ed.). *Mare Luso-Indicum.* 2 vols. Paris, 1972.

Basham, A. L. *The Wonder That Was India.* 3d rev. ed. London, 1967.

Battacharji, S. *The Indian Theogony.* Cambridge, 1970.

Bhardwaj, S. M. *Hindu Places of Pilgrimage in India; A Study in Cultural Geography.* Berkeley, 1973.

Bietenholz, Pieter G. *Pietro Della Valle (1586–1652): Studien zur Geschichte der Orientkenntnis und des Orientbildes im Abendlande.* Basel and Stuttgart, 1962.

Bobroff, Sara Ann. "Exotic Plants in Carl Linnaeus' *Species Plantarum* (1753)." Ph.D. diss., Dept. of History, Univ. of Chicago, 1973.

Brown, C. J. *The Coins of India.* Calcutta, 1922.

Caland, W. (ed.). *Ziegenbalgs Malabarisches Heidenthum heraus gegeben und mit Indices versehen.* "Verhandelingen der Koninklijke Akademie van Wetenschappen," Vol. XXV, Pt. 3. Amsterdam, 1926.

Caland, W., and Fokker, A. A. *Drie oude Portugeische Verhandelingen over het Hindoeisme.* In "Verhandelingen der Koninklijke Akademie van Wetenschappen te Amsterdam," Afdeeling Letterkunde, n.s., Vol. XVI, No. 2, pp. 166–175, 211. Amsterdam, 1915.

Charpentier, Jarl (ed.). *The Livro da seita dos Indios Orientais.* Uppsala, 1933.

Chatelain, H. A. *Atlas historique.* Paris, 1719.

Cousens, Henry. *Bijapur. The Old Capital of the Adil Shahi Kings. A Guide to Its Ruins with Historical Outline.* 3d ed. Poona, 1923.

Dale, Stephen Frederic. *Islamic Society on the South Asian Frontier: The Māppilas of Malabar, 1498–1922.* Oxford, 1980.

Daniélou, A. *Hindu Polytheism.* New York, 1964.

Danvers, Frederick Charles. *The Portuguese in India, Being a History of the Rise and Decline of Their Eastern Empire.* 2 vols. London, 1894.

Day, F. *The Land of the Perumals, or Cochin; Its Past and Its Present.* Madras, 1863.

Edgerton, F. *Vikrama's Adventures, or the Thirty-Two Tales of the Throne.* Edited by C. R. Lanman in *Harvard Oriental Series,* Vol. XXVI. Cambridge, Mass., 1926.

Elliot, Sir Walter. *Coins of Southern India.* London, 1886.

Ferroli, Domemco, S.J. *The Jesuits in Malabar.* 2 vols. Bangalore, 1939, 1951.

Fonseca, José Nicolau da. *An Historical and Archaeological Sketch of the City of Goa, Preceded by a Short Statistical Account of the Territory of Goa Written by the Authorization of the Government.* Bombay, 1878.

Ghose, R. L. M., *et al. Rice in India.* Rev. ed. New Delhi, 1960.

Gupta, Shakti M. *Vishnu and His Incarnations.* Bombay, 1974.

Chapter Bibliographies

Hough, James. *The History of Christianity in India from the Commencement of the Christian Era.* 2 vols. London, 1839.

Hutton, J. H. *Caste in India.* 4th ed. Bombay, 1963.

Jagadisa Ayyar, P. V. *South Indian Festivities.* Madras, 1921.

Koshy, Ninan. *Caste in the Kerala Churches.* Bangalore, 1968.

Krishna Ayyar, K. V. *A Short History of Kerala.* Ernakulam, 1966.

Krishna Iyer, L. A. *Social History of Kerala.* 2 vols. Madras, 1968.

Kuriakose, M. K. (comp.). *History of Christianity in India: Source Materials.* Madras, 1982.

Kurup, K. K. N. *The Ali Rajas of Cannanore.* Trivandrum, 1975.

Logan, William. *Malabar.* 3 vols. Madras, 1951.

Luiz, A. A. D. *Tribes of Kerala.* New Delhi, 1962.

Meena, V. *Temples of South India.* Kanyakumari, n.d.

Menachery, George (ed.). *The St. Thomas Christian Encyclopedia of India.* 3 vols. Madras, 1982.

Misra, S. D. *Rivers of India.* New Delhi, 1970.

Mitter, Partha. *Much Maligned Monsters.* Oxford, 1977.

Nayeem, M. A. *External Relations of the Bijapur Kingdom, 1489–1686.* Hyderabad, 1974.

Padmanabha Menon, K. P. *A History of Kerala, Written in the Form of Notes on Visscher's Letters from Malabar.* 3 vols. New Delhi, 1982. (Reprint of 1924 edition.)

Padmanabhan, S. *Temples of South India.* Napercoil, 1977.

Panikkar, K. M. *Malabar and the Portuguese.* Bombay, 1929.

Pereira, Rui Gomes. *Goa. Hindu Temples and Deities.* Translated from the Portuguese by Antonio Victor Couto. 2 vols. Panaji, 1978.

Poonen, T. I. *Dutch Hegemony in Malabar and Its Collapse (A.D. 1663–1795).* Trivandrum, 1978.

Priolkar, A. K. *The Goa Inquisition.* Bombay, 1961.

Radwan, Ann Bos. *The Dutch in Western India, 1601–32.* Calcutta, 1978.

Rajā, P. K. S. *Mediaeval Kerala.* Chidambaram, 1953.

Sen, S. P. *The French in India—First Establishment and Struggle.* Calcutta, 1947.

Silva, Severine. *History of Christianity in Canara.* 2 vols. Kumta, 1957–61.

Swaminathan, K. D. *The Nāyakas of Ikkēri.* Madras, 1957.

Terpstra, H. *De Nederlanders in Voor-Indië.* Amsterdam, 1947.

Thaliath, Jonas, T.O.C.D. *The Synod of Diamper.* No. 152 in *Orientalia Christiana analecta.* Rome, 1958.

Thekedathu, Joseph, S.D.B. *History of Christianity in India.* 6 vols. Bangalore, 1982.

———. *The Troubled Days of Francis Garcia, S.J., Archbishop of Cranganore (1641–59).* Rome, 1972.

Thompson, Edward. *Suttee.* Boston, 1928.

Thurston, E. *Castes and Tribes of Southern India.* 7 vols. Madras, 1909.

————. *Ethnographic Notes in Southern India.* 2 pts. Reprint of 1906 edition. New Delhi, 1975.

Tisserant, Eugène, Cardinal. *Eastern Christianity in India; a History of the Syro-Malabar Church from the Earliest Time to the Present Day.* Bombay, 1957.

Toy, Sidney. *The Strongholds of India.* London, 1957.

Verma, D. C. *History of Bijapur.* New Delhi, 1974.

Wheeler, J. Talboys (ed.). *Early Travels in India.* Delhi, 1975.

Wicki, Josef, S.J. (ed.). *O homem das trinta e duas perfeicões e outras histórias.* Lisbon, 1958.

ARTICLES

Da Cunha, J. Gerson. "The Portuguese in South Kanara." *JRAS, Bombay Branch,* XIX (1895–97), 249–62.

De Souza, T. R., S.J. "Glimpses of Hindu Dominance of Goan Economy in the Seventeenth Century." *Indica,* XII (1975), 27–35.

Dharampal, Gita (trans.). "Heinrich von Poser's Travelogue of the Deccan (1622)." *Quarterly Journal of the Mythic Society.* LXXIII (1982), 103–14.

————— (trans.). "On Kanarese Language and Literature [written by Reverend Weigle of Tübingen]." *Quarterly Journal of the Mythic Society,* LXXII (1981), 1–34.

Figueìredo, Manuel Pacheco de. "The Practice of Indian Medicine in Goa during the Portuguese Rule, 1510–1699." *The Luso-Brazilian Review,* IV (1967), 51–60.

Joshi, P. M. "Johan van Twist's Mission to Bijapur, 1637." *Journal of Indian History,* XXXIV (1956), 111–37.

Koshy, M. O. "Dutch Impact on Kerala Society and Culture." *Journal of Kerala Studies,* IV (1977), 559–70.

Mundadan, A. M. "History of St. Thomas Christianity in India to the Present Day." In George Menachery (ed.), *The St. Thomas Christian Encyclopedia of India.* 3 vols. Madras, 1982.

Pearson, Michael N. "Indigenous Dominance in a Colonial Economy, the Goa Rendas, 1600–1700." In Jean Aubin (ed.), *Mare Luso-Indicum,* II, 61–73. 2 vols. Paris, 1972.

Vasanth Madhava, K. G. "Kēladi Nāyakas in Malabar (1669–1763), Part II." *Journal of Kerala Studies,* I (1974), 429–39.

Warner, Marjorie F. "The Dates of Rheede's Hortus Malabaricus." *The Journal of Botany British and Foreign,* LVIII (1920), 291–92.

Wicki, Joseph, S.J. "Portuguese Works of Frs. J. Fenicio and Diogo Gonçalves on Malabar (1609–1615)." *Journal of Kerala Studies,* IV (1977), 543–58.

XII. INSULAR SOUTH ASIA

BOOKS

Abeyashinge, Tikiri. *Portuguese Rule in Ceylon, 1594–1612.* Colombo, 1966.

Alexander, P. C. *The Dutch in Malabar.* Annamalainager, 1946.

Arasaratnam, Sinnappah (trans. and ed.). *Francois Valentijn's Description of Ceylon.* "HS," 2d ser., CIL (London, 1978).

Bachmann, P. R. *Roberto Nobili, 1577–1656. Ein missionsgeschichtlicher Beitrag zum Christlichen Dialog mit Hinduismus.* Rome, 1972.

Cartman, J. *Hinduism in Ceylon.* Colombo, 1957.

Danvers, Frederick Charles. *The Portuguese in India, Being a History of the Rise and Decline of Their Eastern Empire.* 2 vols. London, 1894.

De Silva, C. R. *The Portuguese in Ceylon 1617–1638.* London, 1968.

De Silva, S. F. *A Regional Geography of Ceylon.* Colombo, 1954.

Farmer, B. H. *Pioneer Peasant Colonization in Ceylon.* London, 1957.

Gardiner, J. S. *The Fauna and Geography of the Maldive and Laccadive Archipelago.* 2 vols. Cambridge, 1903.

Geiger, Wilhelm. *A Grammar of the Sinhalese Language.* Colombo, 1938.

Glamann, Kristof. *Dutch-Asiatic Trade, 1620–1740.* Copenhagen, 1958.

Goonewardena, K. W. *The Foundations of Dutch Power in Ceylon 1638–1658.* Amsterdam, 1958.

Grist, Donald Henry. *Rice.* 3d ed. London, 1959.

Harper, E. B. (ed.). *Religion in South Asia.* Seattle, 1964.

Hayley, F. A. *A Treatise on the Laws and Customs of the Sinhalese, Including the Portions Still Surviving under the Name Kandyan Law.* Colombo, 1923.

Henry, G. M. *A Guide to the Birds of Ceylon.* London, 1955.

Kern, Hendrik. *Manual of Indian Buddhism.* Varanasi, 1968.

Kronk, Gary W. *Comets. A Descriptive Catalog.* Hillside, N.J., 1984.

Le Grand, Joachim, Abbé. *Histoire de L'Isle Ceylan.* . . . Paris-Amsterdam, 1701.

Ludowyk, E. F. C. (ed.). *The Story of Ceylon.* London, 1962.

Macmillan, H. F. *Tropical Planting and Gardening with Special Reference to Ceylon.* 5th ed. London, 1962.

Perera, S. G., S.J. (trans. and ed.). *The Temporal and Spiritual Conquest of Ceylon.* Colombo, 1930.

Prater, S. H. *The Book of Indian Animals.* 2d rev. ed., Bombay, 1965.

Ramunny, [Murkot]. *Laccadive, Minicoy, and Amindivi Islands.* New Delhi, 1972.

Raychaudhuri, Tapan. *Jan Company in Coromandel, 1605–1690. A Study in the Interrelations of European Commerce and Traditional Economies.* The Hague, 1962.

Rouffaer, G. P. *Batik-Kunst in Nederlandsch Indië.* Utrecht, 1914.

Ryan, Bryce. *Caste in Modern Ceylon.* New Brunswick, N.J., 1953.

Silva, C. R. de; *see* De Silva.

Stoddard, T. L., et al. *Area Handbook for the Indian Ocean Territories.* Washington, D.C., 1971.

Wait, W. E. *Manual of the Birds of Ceylon.* 2d ed. London, 1931.

Wall, Frank. *Ophidia Taprobanica, or the Snakes of Ceylon.* Colombo, 1921.

Wijesekara, N. *Veddas in Transition.* Colombo, 1964.

Winius, George Davison. *The Fatal History of Portuguese Ceylon. Transition to Dutch Rule.* Cambridge, Mass., 1971.

Yalman, Nur. *Under the Bo Tree. Studies in Caste, Kinship, and Marriage in the Interior of Ceylon.* Berkeley, 1967.

ARTICLES

Ames, M. M. "Magical-Animism and Buddhism: A Structural Analysis of the Sinhalese Religious System." In E. B. Harper (ed.), *Religion in South Asia,* pp. 21–52. Seattle, 1964.

Charpentier, Jarl. "Preliminary Report on the *Livro da seita dos Indios Orientais* (Brit. Mus. Ms. Sloane, 1820)." *Bulletin of the School of Oriental Studies* (London), II (1922–23), 731–54.

———. "The Brit. Mus. Ms. Sloane 3290, the Common Source of Baldaeus and Dapper." *Bulletin of the School of Oriental Studies* (London), III (1923–25), 413–20.

Chicago Tribune. March 14, 1983. Article on Maldive culture in the atolls in 2000 B.C.

Ferguson, Donald W. (trans. and ed.). "Captain João Ribeiro: His Work on Ceylon and the French Translation Thereof by the Abbé (Joachim) le Grand." *JRAS, Ceylon Branch,* X (1887–88), 243–70.

———. "The Reverend Phillipus Baldaeus and His Book on Ceylon." *Monthly Literary Register* (Colombo), III (1895), 144–48.

———. "Robert Knox's Sinhalese Vocabulary." *JRAS, Ceylon Branch,* XIV (1896), 155–99.

———. "The History of Ceylon, from the Earliest Times to 1600 as Related by João de Barros and Diogo do Couto." *JRAS, Ceylon Branch,* Vol. XX, No. 60 (1908–9), 1–445.

———. "The Visit of Spilbergen to Ceylon, Translated from Admiral Joris van Spilbergen's 'Relation.'" *JRAS, Ceylon Branch,* XXX (1927), 127–79, 361–409.

Fitzler, M. A. H. "Die Maldiven im 16 und 17 Jahrhundert." *Zeitschrift für Indologie und Iranistik,* X (1935–36), 215–56.

Freudenberg, P. (trans. and ed.). "Wouter Schouten's Account of Ceylon." *JRAS, Ceylon Branch,* XI (1889–90), 315–54.

Gaspard, E., S.J. (trans. and ed.). "Ceylon according to Du Jarric." *Ceylon Antiquarian and Literary Register,* III (1917–18), 163–73; IV (1918), 5–18; V (1919), 49–57.

Godahumba, G. E. "Historical Writing in Sinhalese." In C. H. Philips (ed.), *Historians of India, Pakistan, and Ceylon,* pp. 72–86. London, 1961.

Ronkel, Ph. S. van. "De eerste europeesche Tamilspraakkunst en het eerste Mala-baarsche Glossarium." *Mededeelingen der Nederlandsche Akademie van Wetenschap-pen,* n.s., V (1942), 543–98.

St. George, H. H. *Rebelion de Ceylan* of Sa de Meneses (English summary)." *JRAS, Ceylon Branch,* XI (1890), 427–45.

Saparamadu, Sumana D. (ed. and trans.). "A True and Exact Description of the Great Island of Ceylon by Phillipus Baldaeus." *Ceylon Historical Journal,* Vol. VIII, Nos. 1–4 (July, 1958–April, 1959).

Van Buitenen, J. A. B., and Ganeshsundaram, P. C. "A Seventeenth-Century Dutch Grammar of Tamil." *Bulletin of the Deccan College Research Institute* (Poona), XIV (1952–53), 168–82.

XIII. COROMANDEL

BOOKS

Bachmann, P. R. *Roberto Nobili, 1577–1656. Ein missionsgeschichtlicher Beitrag zum Christlichen Dialog mit Hinduismus.* Rome, 1972.

Basham, A. L. *The Wonder That Was India.* 3d rev. ed. London, 1967.

Beauchamp, Henry K. (trans. and ed.); *see* Du Bois.

Bertrand, Joseph, S.J. *La mission du Maduré d'après des documents inédits.* 4 vols. Paris, 1847–54 and 1865.

Bilgrami, Syed Ali Asgar. *Landmarks of the Deccan.* Hyderabad, 1927.

Buck, C. H. *Faiths, Fairs, and Festivals of India.* Reprint of 1917 ed. New Delhi, 1977.

Bühler, Georg (trans.). *Laws of Manu.* Vol. XXV of *The Sacred Books of the East.* Delhi, 1967.

Cronin, Vincent. *A Pearl to India; the Life of Roberto de Nobili.* London, 1959.

Daniélou, A. *Hindu Polytheism.* New York, 1964.

Devakunjari, D. *Madurai through the Ages.* Madras, 1957.

Diehl, Carl Gustav. *Instrument and Purpose. Studies on Rites and Rituals in South India.* Lund, 1956.

Drury, Heber. *The Useful Plants of India: with Notice of Their Chief Value in Com-merce, Medicine, and the Arts.* 2d ed. London, 1873.

Du Bois, Abbé J. A. *Hindu Manners, Customs, and Ceremonies.* Translated and edited by H. K. Beauchamp. 3d ed. Oxford, 1959.

Dupuis, Jacques. *Madras et le nord du Coromandel. Etude des conditions de la vie indienne dans un cadre géographique.* Paris, 1960.

Edgerton, Franklin (trans. and ed.). *Vikrama's Adventures.* 2 vols. Cambridge, Mass., 1926.

Farquhar, J. N. *A Primer of Hinduism.* 2d ed. London, 1912.

Ferroli, D., S.J. *The Jesuits in Mysore.* Kozhikode, 1955.

Furber, Holden. *Rival Empires of Trade in the Orient, 1600–1800.* Minneapolis, 1976.

Goetz, Hermann. *Indian and Persian Miniature Paintings in the Rijksprentenkabinet Rijksmuseum.* Amsterdam, 1958.

Chapter Bibliographies

Gonda, Jan. *Aspects of Early Visnuism*. Utrecht, 1954.

Hari Rav, V. N. *History of the Srirangam Temple*. Tirupati, 1976.

Heras, H., S.J. *The Aravidu Dynasty of Vijayanagar*. Madras, 1927.

Imperial Gazetteer of India. Provincial Series. Hyderābad State. Calcutta, 1909.

Jagadisa Ayyar, P. V. *South Indian Festivities*. Madras, 1921.

Krishnaswami, A. *The Tamil Country under Vijayanagar*. Annamalainagar, 1964.

Krishnaswami Aiyangar, S. *Sources of Vijayanagara History*. Madras, 1919.

Lal, K. *Holy Cities of India*. Delhi, 1961.

Majumdar, R. C. (ed.). *The History and Culture of the Indian People. The Classical Age*. Bombay, 1954.

Manual of the Administration of Madras Presidency. Madras, 1893.

Meena, V. *The Temples of South India*. Kanyakumari, n.d.

Meersman, Achilles, O.F.M. *The Franciscans in Tamilnad*. Supplement XII of the *NZM*. Schöneck-Beckenried, Switzerland, 1962.

Miller, Barbara S. (trans.). *Bhartrihari: Poems*. New York, 1967.

Mitter, Partha. *Much Maligned Monsters*. Oxford, 1977.

Moreland, W. H. *From Akbar to Aurangzeb, A Study in Indian Economic History*. London, 1923. Reprinted in New Delhi, 1972.

Muthia, S. *Madras Discovered*. New Delhi, 1987.

Natarajan, B. *The City of the Cosmic Dance. Chidambaram*. New Delhi, 1974.

Nilakanta Sastri, K. A. *Sources of Indian History with Special Reference to South India*. New York, 1964.

Padmanabhan, S. *Temples of South India*. Nagercoil, 1977.

Palaniappan, K. *The Great Temple of Madurai*. Madurai, 1963. Reprint 1970.

Parr, Charles McKew. *The Voyages of David de Vries, Navigator and Adventurer*. New York, 1969.

Pillay, K. P. K. *The Caste System in Tamil Nadu*. Madras, 1977.

Qaisar, J. *The Indian Response to European Technology and Culture (A.D. 1498–1707)*. Delhi, 1982.

Rajayyan, K. *Rise and Fall of the Poligars of Tamilnadu*. Madras, 1974.

Rav; *see* Hari Rav.

Raychaudhuri, T. *Jan Company in Coromandel, 1605–1690*. The Hague, 1962.

Richards, J. F. *Mughal Administration in Golconda*. Oxford, 1975.

Saletore, B. A. *Social and Political Life in the Vijayanagara Empire, A.D. 1346–A.D. 1646*. 2 vols. Madras, 1934.

Sathyanatha Aiyar, R. *History of the Nayaks of Madura*. . . . "Madras University Historical Series," II. Madras, 1924.

Schaeder, H. H. *Goethes Erlebnis des Ostens*. Leipzig, 1938.

Schwab, Raymond. *La renaissance orientale*. Paris, 1950.

Sen, S. P. *The French in India. First Establishment and Struggle*. Calcutta, 1947.

Sewell, Robert, and Dikshit, Sankara Balkrishna. *The Indian Calendar*. London, 1896.

Sherwani, H. K. *History of the Qutb Shāhī Dynasty.* New Delhi, 1974.

Singh, Gopal. *A Geography of India.* 2d ed. Delhi, 1976.

Srinivasachari, C. S. *A History of Gingee and Its Rulers.* Annamalainagar, 1943.

Terpstra, H. *De Nederlanders in Voor-Indië.* Amsterdam, 1947.

Thani Nayagam, Xavier S. *Antão de Proença's Tamil-Portuguese Dictionary, A.D. 1679.* Kuala Lumpur, 1966.

Thekedathu, Joseph, S.D.B. *The Troubled Days of Francis Garcia, S.J., Archbishop of Cranganore (1641–59).* Rome, 1972.

Thompson, Edward. *Suttee. A Historical and Philosophical Enquiry into the Hindu Rite of Widow-Burning.* Boston and New York, 1928.

Thurston, E. *Castes and Tribes of Southern India.* 7 vols. Madras, 1909.

Toy, Sidney. *The Strongholds of India.* London, 1957.

Trewartha, Glenn T. *An Introduction to Climate.* New York, 1954.

Viraraghavacharya, T. K. T. *History of Tirupati: The Thiruvengadam Temple.* 3 vols. 2d ed. Tirupati, 1977.

Vriddhagirisan, V. *The Nayaks of Tanjore.* Annamalainagar, 1942.

Williams, L. F. R. *A Handbook for Travellers in India, Pakistan, Burma, and Ceylon.* 20th ed. London, 1965.

Willson, A. L. *A Mythical Image: The Ideal of India in German Romanticism.* Durham, N.C., 1964.

Wilson, H. H. *Sketch of the Religious Sects of the Hindus.* 2 vols. in 1. London, 1861.

Yasdani, G. (ed.). *The Early History of the Deccan.* 2 vols. London, 1960.

Ziegenbalg, B. *Genealogie der malabarischen Götter.* Madras, 1867.

ARTICLES

Arasaratnam, S. "François Valentijn's Description of Coromandel." In *Professor K. A. Nilakantra Sastri Felicitation Volume,* pp. 1–10. Madras, 1971.

Balusubramanyan, T. B. "Chidambaram in Vijayanagar Days." *Journal of the Bombay Historical Society,* IV (1931), 40–53.

Elliot, Sir Walter. "The Edifice Formerly Known as the Chinese or Jaina Pagoda at Negapatam." *Indian Antiquary,* VII (1878), 224–27.

Ghauri, Iftikhar Ahmad. "Kingship in the Sultanates of Bijapur and Golconda." *Islamic Culture,* XLVI (1972), 39–52, 137–51.

Goetz, Hermann. "Notes on a Collection of Historical Portraits from Golconda." *Indian Arts and Letters,* Vol. X, No. 1 (1936), pp. 10–34.

Goonewardena, K. W. "Dutch Historical Writing on South Asia." In C. H. Philips (ed.), *Historians of India, Pakistan and Ceylon,* pp. 170–82. London, 1961.

Heras, H., S.J. "The City of Jinji at the End of the Sixteenth Century." *Indian Antiquary,* LIV (1925), 41–43.

Irwin, John. "Indian Textile Trade in the Seventeenth Century, II: Coromandel Coast." *Journal of Indian Textile History,* II (1956), 24–42.

Krishnaswami Aiyangar, S. "Mysore and the Decline of the Vijayanagar Empire." *Quarterly Journal of the Mythic Society,* XIII (1922), 621–27, 742–54.

Long, J. Bruce. "Mahāśwarātri: The Saiva Festival of Repentance." In G. R. Welbon and G. E. Yocum (eds.), *Religious Festivals in South India and Sri Lanka,* pp. 189–217. New Delhi, 1982.

Narain, Brij (trans.), and Sharma, Sri Ram (ed.). "Schorer's Account of the Coromandel Coast." *The Indian Historical Quarterly,* XVI (1940), 827–37.

Rahim, M. Abdul. "Nagapattinam Region and the Portuguese." *Journal of Indian History,* LIII (1975), 483–96.

Raychaudhuri, H. "Geography of the Deccan." In G. Yazdani (ed.), *The Early History of the Deccan,* I, 40–42. 2 vols. London, 1960.

Richards, J. F. "The Seventeenth-Century Concentration of Power at Hyderabad." *Journal of the Pakistan Historical Society,* XXIII (1975), 33–34.

Saulière, A., S.J. "The Revolt of the Southern Nayaks." *Journal of Indian History,* XLII (1964), 89–105; XLIV (1966), 163–80.

Sharma, Arvind. "Suttee: A Study in Western Reaction." In *Thresholds in Hindu-Buddhist Studies,* pp. 83–111. Calcutta, 1979.

Sherwani, H. K. "The Reign of Abdu'l-lah Qutb Shah (1626–1672), Economic Aspects." *Journal of Indian History,* XLII (1964), 443–70.

Subbarayappa, B. V. "The Indian Doctrine of Five Elements." *Indian Journal of the History of Science,* I (1966), 60–67.

Terpstra, H. "Daniel Havart en zijn 'Op- en Ondergang van Cormondel.'" *Tjidschrift voor Geschiedenis,* LXVII (1954), 165–89.

Thani Nayagam, Xavier S. "Antāo de Proença's Tamil-Portuguese Dictionary, 1679. An Introduction." *Tamil Culture,* XI (1964), 117–27.

Van Buitenen, J. A. B., and Ganeshsundaram, P. C. "A Seventeenth-Century Dutch Grammar of Tamil." *Bulletin of the Deccan College Research Institute,* XIV (1952–53), 168–82.

Wicki, J., S.J. "Ein vorbildlicher Missionar Indiens, P. Henriques (1520–1600)." *Studia missionalia,* XIII (1963), 113–68.

XIV. CONTINENTAL SOUTHEAST ASIA

BOOKS

Andaya, Barbara W. *Perak, the Abode of Grace. A Study of an Eighteenth-Century Malay State.* Kuala Lumpur, 1979.

Andaya, Leonard Y. *The Kingdom of Johor, 1641–1728.* Kuala Lumpur, 1975.

Anderson, John. *English Intercourse with Siam in the Seventeenth Century.* London, 1890.

Aymonier, E. *Le Cambodge.* 3 vols. Paris, 1900–1904.

Bastin, John, and Roolvink, R. *Malayan and Indonesian Studies.* Oxford, 1964.

Berval, René de (ed.). *Kingdom of Laos. The Land of the Million Elephants and of the White Parasol.* Saigon, 1959.

Boxer, C. R., and Vasconcelos, Frazão de. *André Furtado de Mendoça (1558–1610).* Lisbon, 1955.

Chapter Bibliographies

Burkhill, I. H., *et al.* *A Dictionary of the Economic Products of the Malay Peninsula.* 2 vols. London, 1935.

Chandler, David P. *A History of Cambodia.* Boulder, Co., 1983.

Chappoulie, Henri. *Aux origines d'une église. Rome et les missions d'Indochine au XVIIe siècle.* . . . 2 vols. Paris, 1943.

Coedès, G. *The Making of South-East Asia.* Trans. by H. M. Wright. Berkeley and Los Angeles, 1967.

Collis, Maurice. *The Land of the Great Image, Being Experiences of Friar Manrique in Arakan.* New York, 1943.

Dobby, Ernest H. G. *Southeast Asia.* 9th ed. New York, 1966.

Groslier, B. P., and Boxer, C. R. *Angkor et le Cambodge au XVIe siècle d'après les sources portugaises et espagnoles.* Paris, 1958.

Hale, A. *The Adventures of John Smith in Malaya, 1600–1605.* Leyden, 1909.

Hall, D. G. E. *A History of South-East Asia.* New York, 1955. 2d ed. London, 1964.

———. *Early English Intercourse with Burma, 1587–1743.* London, 1928. 2d ed. New York, 1968.

———. *Europe and Burma: A Study of European Relations with Burma to the Annexation of Thibaw's Kingdom, 1886.* London, 1945.

Harvey, Godfrey Eric. *History of Burma from the Earliest Times to 10 March 1824, the Beginning of the English Conquest.* London, 1925.

Hertz, Solange. *Rhodes of Vietnam.* Westminster, Md., 1966.

Htin Aung, Maung. *A History of Burma.* New York, 1967.

Kunstadter, Peter (ed.). *Southeast Asian Tribes, Minorities, and Nations.* 2 vols. Princeton, 1967.

LeBar, Frank M., and Suddard, A. (eds.). *Laos: Its People, Its Society, Its Culture.* New Haven, 1963.

Lieberman, Victor B. *Burmese Administrative Cycles: Anarchy and Conquest, c. 1580–1760.* Princeton, 1984.

Lombard, Denys. *Le Sultanat d'Atjéh au temps d'Iskandar Muda, 1607–1636.* Paris, 1967.

——— *et al. Le "Spraeck ende woord-boek" de Frederick de Houtman. Première méthode de malais parlé (fin du XVIe siècle).* "Bulletin de l'école française d'Extrême-Orient," LXXIV. Paris, 1970.

Long, Ly Kim. *An Outline of Cambodian Architecture.* Varanasi, 1967.

Luard, C. E., and Hosten, H., S.J. *Travels of Fray Sebastien Manrique, 1629–43.* "HS," 2d ser., LIX. Oxford, 1927.

Manguin, Pierre Yves. *Les Portugais sur les côtes du Viêt-Nam et du Campā; étude sur les routes maritimes et les relations commerciales, d'après les sources portugaises (XVIe, XVIIe, XVIIIe siècles).* Paris, 1972.

Maring, Joel M., and Maring, E. G. *Historical and Cultural Dictionary of Burma.* Metuchen, N.J., 1973.

Muller, Hendrik P. N. (ed.). *De Oost-Indische Compagnie in Cambodja en Laos.* The Hague, 1917.

Chapter Bibliographies

Osborne, Milton. *River Road to China. The Mekong River Expedition, 1866–1873.* New York, 1975.

Payne, C. H. (ed. and trans.). *Jahangir and the Jesuits.* New York, 1930.

Reid, Anthony. *Southeast Asia in the Age of Commerce, 1450–1680.* Vol. I, *The Lands below the Winds.* New Haven, Conn., 1988.

Scott, J. George. *Burma: A Handbook of Practical Information.* London, 1911.

Singh Sandhu, K., and Wheatley, Paul (eds.). *Melaka.* 2 vols. Kuala Lumpur, 1983.

Spiro, Melford E. *Buddhism and Society: A Great Tradition and Its Burmese Vicissitudes.* New York, 1970.

Teixeira, Manuel. *The Portuguese Missions in Malacca and Singapore, 1511–1598.* 3 vols. Lisbon, 1961–63.

Wallace, Alfred R. *The Malay Archipelago . . . with an Introduction by John Bastin.* Singapore, 1986.

Wheatley, Paul. *Nagara and Commandery. Origins of the Southeast Asia Urban Traditions.* Chicago, 1983.

Wijnaendts van Resandt, Willem. *De gezaghebbers der Oost-Indische Compagnie op hare buiten-comptoiren in Azië.* Amsterdam, 1944.

Yoe, S. *The Burman, His Life and Notions.* London, 1910.

ARTICLES

Andaya, Barbara Watson, "Melaka under the Dutch, 1641–1795." In K. Singh Sandhu and P. Wheatley (eds.), *Melaka,* I, pp. 195–241. 2 vols., Kuala Lumpur, 1983.

Bassett, D. K. "The Trade of the English East India Company in Cambodia, 1651–1656." *JRAS* (1962), 35–61; (1963), 145–57.

Boxer, C. R. "The Spaniards in Cambodia." *History Today,* XXI (1971), 280–87.

———. "The Achinese Attack on Malacca in 1629 as Described in Contemporary Portuguese Sources." In J. Bastin and R. Roolvink (eds.), *Malayan and Indonesian Studies,* pp. 105–21. Oxford, 1964.

Briggs, L. P. "Les missionnaires portugais et espagnols au Cambodge, 1555–1603." *Bulletin de la société des études indochinoises,* n.s., XXV (1950), 7–29.

Buch, W. J. M. "La Compagnie des Indes Neérlandaises et l'Indochine." *Bulletin de l'école française d'Extrême-Orient,* XXXVI (1936), 97–196; XXXVII (1937), 121–237.

Collis, M. S., and San Shwe Bu. "Dom Martin, 1606–1643, the First Burman to Visit Europe." *Journal of the Burma Research Society,* Vol. XVI, Pt. 1 (1926), pp. 11–23.

———. "The City of Golden Mrauk-U," *ibid.,* Vol. XIII, Pt. 3 (1923), pp. 244–56.

Coolhaas, W. Ph. "Malacca under Jan van Riesbeeck." *JRAS, Malaysian Branch,* Vol. XXXVIII, Pt. 2 (1965), pp. 173–82.

Duyvendak, J. J. L. "The First Siamese Embassy to Holland." *T'oung Pao,* XXXII (1936), 255–92.

Garnier, Francis. "Voyage lointain aux royaumes de Cambodge et Laowen par les

Néerlandais et ce qui s'y est passé jusqu'en 1644." *Bulletin de la société de géographie de Paris*, 6th ser., II (1871), 249–89.

Hall, D. G. E. "Studies in Dutch Relations with Arakan." *Journal of the Burma Research Society*, Vol. XXVI, Pt. 1 (1936), pp. 1–31.

Heine-Geldern, R. "Concepts of State and Kingship in Southeast Asia." *Far Eastern Quarterly*, II (1942–43), 15–30.

Hoffman, J. E. "Early Policies in the Malacca Jurisdiction of the United East India Company: The Malay Peninsula and the Netherlands East Indies Attachment." *Journal of Southeast Asian Studies*, III (1972), 1–38.

Hosten, Henry, S.J. (trans. and ed.). "Fr. N. Pimenta's Annual of Margão, Dec. 1, 1601." *JRAS, Bengal Branch*, XXIII (1927), 83–107.

Irwin, Graham W. "The Dutch and the Tin Trade of Malaya in the Seventeenth Century." In Jerome Ch'en and Nicholas Tarling (eds.), *Studies in the Social History of China and South-East Asia, Essays in Memory of Victor Purcell* (Cambridge, 1970), pp. 267–87.

Kratz, E. U. "The Journey to the Far East. Seventeenth and Eighteenth Century German Travel Books as a Source Study." *JRAS, Malaysian Branch*, Vol. LIV, Pt. 1, No. 239 (1981), 65–81.

Lévy, Paul. "Two Accounts of Travels in Laos in the Seventeenth Century." In René de Berval (ed.), *Kingdom of Laos. The Land of the Million Elephants and of the White Parasol*, pp. 50–67. Saigon, 1959.

Lieberman, Victor B. "The Political Significance of Religious Wealth in Burmese History: Some Further Thoughts." *Journal of Asian Studies*, XXXIX (1980), 753–69.

———. "Europeans, Trade, and the Unification of Burma, c. 1540–1620." *Oriens Extremus*, Vol. XXVII, Pt. 2 (1980), pp. 203–26.

Linehan, W. "The Earliest Word-lists and Dictionaries of the Malay Language." *JRAS, Malay Branch*, Vol. XXII, Pt. 1 (1949), pp. 183–87.

Macgregor, I. A. (trans.). "A Brief Account of the Kingdoms of Pegu." *Journal of the Burma Research Society*, Vol. XVI, Pt. 2 (1926), pp. 99–138.

———. "Notes on the Portuguese in Malaya." *JRAS, Malayan Branch*, Vol. XXVIII, Pt. 2 (1955), pp. 1–47.

Maxwell, W. G. "Barretto de Resendes' Account of Malacca." *JRAS, Straits Branch*, LX (1911), 1–24.

Pelliot, Paul. "Les relations du Siam et de la Hollande en 1608." *T'oung Pao*, XXXII (1936), 223–29.

Saulière, A., S.J. "The Jesuits in Pegu at the End of the Sixteenth Century." *Bengal Past and Present*, XIX (1919), 64–80.

Sheehan, J. J. "Seventeenth Century Visitors to the Malay Peninsula." *JRAS, Malay Branch*, Vol. XII, Pt. 2 (1934), pp. 71–107.

Smith, W. H. C. "The Portuguese in Malacca during the Dutch Period." *Studia* (Lisbon), VII (January, 1961), 87–106.

Teixeira, Manuel. "Diogo Veloso e a Gesta Lusiada em Camboja." *Actas*, Congresso Internacional de História dos Descobrimentos, Vol. V, Pt. 1 (1961), pp. 339–77.

XV. SIAM

BOOKS

Alabaster, Henry. *The Wheel of the Law: Buddhism Illustrated from the Siamese Sources.* London, 1871; reprinted Varanasi, 1972.

Andaya, Barbara W. *Perak, the Abode of Grace, A Study of an Eighteenth-Century Malay State.* Kuala Lumpur, 1979.

Andaya, Barbara W., and Andaya, Leonard Y. *A History of Malaysia.* London, 1982.

Andaya, Leonard Y. *The Kingdom of Johor, 1641–1728.* Kuala Lumpur, 1975.

Anderson, John. *English Intercourse with Siam in the Seventeenth Century.* London, 1890.

Basche, J. *Thailand: Land of the Free.* New York, 1971.

Blanchard, Wendell, *et al. Thailand, Its People, Its Society, Its Culture.* New Haven, 1958.

Boxer, Charles Ralph (ed. and intro.). *A True Description of the Mighty Kingdoms of Japan and Siam by François Caron and Joost Schouten.* London, 1935.

Boxer, Charles Ralph, and Vasconcelos, Frazão de. *André Furtado de Mendoça (1558–1610).* Lisbon, 1955.

Brandon, J. R. *Theatre in Southeast Asia.* Cambridge, Mass., 1967.

Buribhand, Luang Baribal. *Thai Images of the Buddha.* "Thailand Culture Series," No. 9, Bangkok, 1955.

Burkhill, I. H., *et al. A Dictionary of the Economic Products of the Malay Peninsula.* 2 vols. London, 1935.

Campbell, Stuart, and Shaweevongse, Chuan. *The Fundamentals of the Thai Language.* 4th ed. Kent, 1957.

Chandler, David P. *A History of Cambodia.* Boulder, 1983.

Chappoulie, Henri. *Aux origines d'une église. Rome et les missions d'Indochine au XVIIe siècle.* . . . 2 vols. Paris, 1943.

Coedès, Georges. *The Making of South-East Asia.* Translated by H. M. Wright. Berkeley and Los Angeles, 1967.

Collis, Maurice. *Siamese White.* London, 1936.

―――. *The Land of the Great Image, Being Experiences of Friar Manrique in Arakan.* New York, 1943.

Dobby, Ernest H. G. *Southeast Asia.* 9th ed. London, 1966.

Duriyanga, Phra Chen. *Thai music.* "Thailand Culture Series," No. 8, 3d ed. Bangkok, 1955.

Gatty, J. Coullet (ed.). *Voiage de Siam du Père Bouvet. Précédé d'une introduction, avec une biographie de son auteur.* Leyden, 1963.

Graham, Walter A. *Siam.* 2 vols. London, 1924.

Groslier, B. P., and Boxer, C. R. *Angkor et le Cambodge au XVIe siècle, d'après les sources portugaises et espagnoles.* Paris, 1958.

Hale, A. *The Adventures of John Smith in Malaya, 1600–1605.* Leyden, 1909.

Chapter Bibliographies

Hall, D. G. E. *Europe and Burma: A Study of European Relations with Burma to the Annexation of Thibaw's Kingdom, 1886*. London, 1945.

———. *A History of South-East Asia*. New York, 1955. 2d ed., London, 1964.

Hart, C. *Kites. An Historical Survey*. Rev. ed., New York, 1982.

Hutchinson, E. W. *Adventurers in Siam in the Seventeenth Century*. London, 1940.

——— (ed. and trans.). *1688. Revolution in Siam. The Memoir of Father de Bèze, S.J.* Hong Kong, 1968.

Ishii, Yoneo (ed.). *Thailand: A Rice-Growing Society*. Trans. by Peter and Stephanie Hawkes. Honolulu, 1978.

Iwao, Seeichi (ed.). *Historiael verhael der sieckte ende doot van Pra Interra-Tsia 22en coninck in Siam, ende den regherenden coninck Pra Ongh Srij door Jeremias van Vliet, 1640*. Tokyo, 1958.

Kasetsiri, C. *The Rise of Ayudhya*. Kuala Lumpur, 1976.

Kern, H. *Manual of Indian Buddhism*. Varanasi, 1968.

Kunstadter, Peter (ed.). *Southeast Asian Tribes, Minorities, and Nations*. 2 vols. Princeton, 1967.

Landon, Kenneth P. *Southeast Asia, Crossroads of Religions*. Chicago, 1949.

Lanier, Lucien. *Etude historique sur les relations de la France et du royaume de Siam de 1662 à 1703*. Versailles, 1883.

Librairie Larousse (publ.). *Le Thaïlande*. Paris, 1983.

Lieberman, Victor B. *Burmese Administrative Cycles: Anarchy and Conquest, c. 1580–1760*. Princeton, 1984.

Lombard, Denys. *Le Sultanat d'Atjéh au temps d'Iskandar Muda, 1607–1636*. Paris, 1967.

———. *et al. Le "Spraeck ende woord-boek" de Frederick de Houtman. Première méthode de malais parlé (fin du XVI siècle)*. "Bulletin de l'école française d'Etrême-Orient," LXXIV. Paris, 1970.

Manguin, Pierre-Yves. *Les portugais sur les côtes du Viêt-nam et du Campā: étude sur les routes maritimes et les relations commerciales d'après les sources portugaises (XVIe, XVIIe, XVIIIe siècles)*. Paris, 1972.

Martignan, L. R. *La monarchie absolue Siamoise de 1350 à 1926*. n.p., n.d.

Nimit Co. (publ.). *Thailand in Colour*. Bangkok, n.d.

O'Kane, John. *The Ship of Sulaiman*. New York, 1972.

Osborne, Milton. *River Road to China. The Mekong River Expedition, 1866–1873*. New York, 1975.

Osman, M. T. (ed.). *Traditional Drama and Music of Southeast Asia*. Kuala Lumpur, 1974.

Pratt, James B. *The Pilgrimage of Buddhism*. New York, 1928.

Rabibhadana, Akin. *The Organization of Thai Society in the Early Bangkok Period*. Data Paper No. 74, Cornell University Southeast Asia Program. Ithaca, N.Y., 1969.

Rajadhon, Phya Anuman. *The Nature and Development of the Thai Language*. "Thai Culture," n.s., No. 10, 2d ed. Bangkok, 1963.

Chapter Bibliographies

——. *Thai Traditional Salutations.* "Thai Culture," n.s., No. 14. Bangkok, 1963.

Reid, Anthony. *Southeast Asia in the Age of Commerce, 1450–1680.* Vol. I, *The Lands below the Winds.* New Haven, Conn., 1988.

——— (ed.). *Slavery, Bondage, and Dependency in Southeast Asia.* New York, 1983.

Sitsayamkan, Luang. *The Greek Favourite of the King of Siam.* Singapore, 1967.

Smith, George Vinal. *The Dutch in Seventeenth-Century Thailand.* Special Report No. 16, Northern Illinois University Center for Southeast Asian Studies. De Kalb, Ill., 1977.

Smithies, Michael (ed. and trans.). *The Discourses at Versailles of the First Siamese Ambassadors to France, 1686–87.* Bangkok, 1985.

Sopher, D. E. *The Sea Nomads.* Singapore, 1965.

Spiro, M. E. *Buddhism and Society: A Great Tradition and Its Burmese Vicissitudes.* New York, 1970.

Tambiah, S. J. *World Conqueror and World Renouncer: A Study of Buddhism and Polity in Thailand against a Historical Background.* Cambridge, 1976.

Teeuw, A., and Wyatt, D. K. *Hikayat Patani, The Story of Patani.* 2 pts. The Hague, 1970.

Terwiel, B. J. *Monks and Magic.* Bangkok, 1975.

Viraphol, Sarasin. *Tribute and Profit: Sino-Siamese Trade 1652–1853.* Cambridge, Mass., 1977.

Wales, Horace Geoffrey Quaritch. *Ancient Siamese Government and Administration.* London, 1934.

——. *Siamese State Ceremonies, Their History and Function.* London, 1931.

Wallace, Irving, and Wallace, Amy. *The Two.* New York, 1978.

Welbon, Guy Richard. *The Buddhist Nirvana and Its Western Interpreters.* Chicago, 1967.

Wells, Kenneth E. *Thai Buddhism, Its Rites and Activities.* Bangkok, 1939.

Wenk, K. *Studien zur Literatur der Thai. Texte und Interpretationen.* Hamburg, 1982.

Wheatley, Paul. *Nagara and Commandery. Origins of the Southeast Asia Urban Traditions.* Chicago, 1983.

Wijnaendts van Resandt, Willem. *De gezaghebbers der Oost-Indische Compagnie op hare buiten-comptoiren in Azië.* Amsterdam, 1944.

Wyatt, David K. *Thailand: A Short History.* New Haven, 1984.

——. *The Politics of Reform in Thailand: Education in the Reign of King Chulalongkorn.* New Haven, 1969.

Yoe, S. *The Burman, His Life and Notions.* London, 1910.

ARTICLES

Bassett, D. K. "English Relations with Siam in the Seventeenth Century." *JRAS, Malaysian Branch,* Vol. XXXIV, Pt. 2 (1961), pp. 90–105.

Briggs, Laurence P. "Les missionnaires portugais et espagnols au Cambodge, 1555–1603." *Bulletin de la Société des études indochinoises,* n.s., XXV (1950), 7–29.

Chapter Bibliographies

Burnay, J. "Notes chronologiques sur les missions Jésuites du Siam au XVIIe siècle." *AHSI*, XXII (1953), 170–202.

Chorin, L. A. C. "From Paris to Ayuthia Three Hundred Years Ago, June 18th 1660 to August 22nd 1662." *Journal of the Siam Society*, L (1962), 23–33.

Damrong, Prince. "The Foundations of Ayuthia." *Selected Articles from the Siam Society Journal*, III, 199–202. Bangkok, 1959.

Dhani, Prince. "The Old Siamese Conception of Monarchy." *The Siam Society Fiftieth Anniversary Commemorative Publication*, II, 160–75. Bangkok, 1954.

Duyvendak, J. J. L. "The First Siamese Embassy to Holland." *T'oung Pao*, XXXII (1936), 255–92.

Fournereau, Lucien. "Le Siam ancien: archéologie, épigraphie, géographie, première partie." *Annales du Musée Guimet*, XXVII (1895), 1–321.

Garnier, Francis. "Voyage lointain aux royaumes de Cambodge et Laowen par les Néerlandais et ce qui s'y est passé jusqu'en 1644." *Bulletin de la société de géographie de Paris*, 6th ser., II (1871), 249–89.

Giblin, R. W. "The Abbe de Choisy." *Selected Articles from the Siam Society Journal*, VIII, 1–16. Bangkok, 1959.

———. "Lopburi Past and Present." *Ibid.*, IV, 113–31. Bangkok, 1959.

Giles, Frances H. "A Critical Analysis of Van Vliet's Historical Account of Siam in the Seventeenth Century." *Selected Articles from the Siam Society Journal*, VII, 91–158. Bangkok, 1959.

Heine-Geldern, R. "Concepts of State and Kingship in Southeast Asia." *The Far Eastern Quarterly*, II (1942–43), 15–30.

Hoffman, J. E. "Early Policies in the Malacca Jurisdiction of the United East India Company: The Malay Peninsula and Netherlands East Indies Attachment." *Journal of Southeast Asian Studies*, III (1972), 1–38.

Hutchinson, E. W. "Journey of Mgr. Lambert, Bishop of Beritus, from Tenasserim to Siam in 1662." *Selected Articles from the Siam Society Journal*, VIII, 91–4. Bangkok, 1959.

Irwin, Graham W. "The Dutch and the Tin Trade of Malaya in the Seventeenth Century." In Jerome Ch'en and Nicholas Tarling (eds.), *Studies in the Social History of China and South-East Asia, Essays in Memory of Victor Purcell*, pp. 267–87. Cambridge, 1970.

Ishii, Yoneo. "History and Rice Growing." In Y. Ishii (ed.), *Thailand: A Rice Growing Society*, trans. by Peter and Stephanie Hawkes, pp. 27–29. Honolulu, 1978.

———. "Seventeenth-Century Japanese Documents about Siam." *Journal of the Siam Society*, Vol. LIX, Pt. 2 (1971), pp. 161–74.

Jacq-Hergoualc'h, M. "Les ambassadeurs siamois à Versailles." *Journal of the Siam Society*, LXXII (1984), 19–36.

Kratz, E. U. "The Journey to the Far East. Seventeenth and Eighteenth Century German Travel Books as a Source Study." *JRAS, Malaysian Branch*, Vol. LIV, Pt. 1, No. 239 (1981), pp. 65–81.

Lévy, Paul. "Two Accounts of Travels in Laos in the Seventeenth Century." In René de Berval (ed.), *Kingdom of Laos. The Land of the Million Elephants and of the White Parasol*, pp. 50–67. Saigon, 1959.

Linehan, W. "The Earliest Word-Lists and Dictionaries of the Malay Language." *JRAS, Malay Branch,* Vol. XXII, Pt. 1 (1949), pp. 183–87.

Pelliot, Paul. "Les relations du Siam et de la Hollande en 1608." *T'oung Pao,* XXXII (1936), 223–29.

Sariman, Chua. "Traditional Dance Drama in Thailand." In M. T. Osman (ed.), *Traditional Drama and Music of Southeast Asia,* pp. 165–71. Kuala Lumpur, 1974.

Satow, E. M. "Notes on the Intercourse between Japan and Siam in the Seventeenth Century." *Transactions of the Asiatic Society of Japan,* Vol. XIII, Pt. 2 (1885), pp. 139–210.

Sternstein, Larry. "An Historical Atlas of Thailand." *Journal of the Siam Society,* Vol. LII, Pt. 1 (1964), pp. 7–20.

———. "Krung Kao, the Old Capital of Ayutthaya." *Ibid.,* Vol. LIII, Pt. 1 (1965), pp. 83–132.

Unno, K. "The Asian Lake Chiamay in the Early European Cartography." In C. C. Marzoli *et al., Imago et mensura mundi. Atti del IX Congresso internazionale di Storia della Cartografia* (1985).

XVI. VIETNAM

BOOKS

Bernard, Henri, S.J. *Pour la compréhension de l'Indochine et de l'Occident.* Paris, 1950.

Bezacier, L. *L'art Vietnamien.* 2d ed. Paris, 1954.

Cadière, Leopold. *Croyances et pratiques religieuses des Vietnamiens.* Saigon, 1958.

Chappoulie, Henri. *Aux origines d'une église. Rome et les missions d'Indochine au XVIIe siècle.* . . . 2 vols. Paris, 1943.

Coedès, G. *The Making of South-East Asia.* Translated by H. M. Wright. Berkeley and Los Angeles, 1967.

Devéria, Gabriel (ed. and trans.). *Histoire des relations de la Chine avec l'Annam-Vietnam du XVIe au XIXe siècle; d'après des documents chinois traduits pour la première fois.* Paris, 1880.

Diguet, Edouard J. *Les Annamites: société, coutumes, religions.* Paris, 1906.

Dobby, E. H. G. *Southeast Asia.* 9th rev. ed. London, 1966.

Giran, Paul. *Magie et religion annamites.* Paris, 1912.

Hall, D. G. E. *A History of South-East Asia.* New York, 1955. 2d ed. London, 1964.

Hejzlar, J. *The Art of Vietnam.* London, 1973.

Hertz, Solange (ed. and trans.). *Rhodes of Vietnam.* Westminster, Md., 1966.

Kronk, Gary W. *Comets. A Descriptive Catalog.* Hillside, N.J., 1984.

Lê Thânh Khôi. *Histoire du Vietnam des origines à 1858.* Paris, 1981.

Maybon, Charles B. *Histoire moderne du pays d'Annam (1592–1820). Etude sur les premiers rapports des Européens et des Annamites.* . . . Paris, 1919.

Pachtler, G. M. *Das Christenthum in Tonkin und Cochinchina.* Paderborn, 1861.

Pasquier, Pierre. *L'Annam d'autrefois.* Paris, 1929.

Petit, R. *La monarchie annamite.* Paris, 1931.

Chapter Bibliographies

Reid, Anthony. *Southeast Asia in the Age of Commerce, 1450–1680.* Vol. I, *The Lands below the Winds.* New Haven, Conn., 1988.

Schreiner, A. *Les institutions annamites en Basse-Cochinchine avant la conquête français.* 3 vols. Saigon, 1900–1902.

Taboulet, Georges. *La geste française en Indochine. Histoire par les textes de la France en Indochine des origines à 1914.* 2 vols. Paris, 1955–56.

Viraphol, Sarasin. *Tribute and Profit: Sino-Siamese Trade 1652–1853.* Cambridge, Mass., 1977.

Watt, Sir George. *A Dictionary of the Economic Products of India.* 7 vols. in 10. Calcutta, 1885–96.

Whitfield, Danny J. *Historical and Cultural Dictionary of Vietnam.* Metuchen, N.J., 1976.

ARTICLES

Baldinotti, Guiliano. "La relation sur le Tonkin du P. Baldinotti." *Bulletin de l'école française d'Extrême-Orient* (Hanoi), III (1903), 71–78.

Boxer, C. R. "Asian Potentates and European Artillery in the 16th–18th Centuries: A Footnote to Gibson-Hill." *JRAS, Malaysian Branch,* Vol. XXXVIII, Pt. 2 (1966), pp. 156–72.

Deloustal, Raymond. "La justice dans l'ancien Annam, traduction et commentaire du Code des Lê." *Bulletin de l'école française d'Extrême-Orient* (Hanoi), VIII (1908), 117–220; IX (1909), 91–122, 471–91, 765–96; X (1910), 1–60, 349–92, 461–505; XI (1911), 25–66, 313–37; XII (1912), No. 6, pp. 1–33; XIII (1913), No. 5, pp. 1–59; XXII (1922), 1–40.

Knowlton, E. C., Jr. "South East Asia in the Travel Book by Pedro Ordóñez de Ceballos." In *Proceedings of the Second International Symposium on Asian Studies,* pp. 499–510. Hong Kong, 1980.

Lamb, Alastair (ed.). "British Missions to Cochin China, 1778–1822." *JRAS, Malaysian Branch,* Vol. XXXIV, Pt. 3 (1961), pp. 1–98.

XVII. INSULINDIA: THE WESTERN ARCHIPELAGO

BOOKS

Andaya, L. Y. *The Kingdom of Johore, 1641–1728.* Kuala Lumpur, 1975.

Ball, J. D. *Things Chinese.* 5th ed. London, 1926.

Bock, Carl. *The Head Hunters of Borneo.* London, 1881.

Boxer, Charles Ralph. *The Dutch Seaborne Empire, 1600–1800.* London, 1965.

Chijs, J. A. van der (ed.). *Nederlandsche-Indisch plakaatboek, 1602–1811.* 17 vols. Batavia, 1885–1900.

Clarke, T. H. *The Rhinoceros from Dürer to Stubbs, 1515–1799.* London, 1986.

Covarrubias, Miquel. *Island of Bali.* New York, 1937.

Crawfurd, John. *A Descriptive Dictionary of the Indian Islands and Adjacent Countries.* Varanasi, 1947.

Chapter Bibliographies

——. *History of the Indian Archipelago*. 3 vols. Edinburgh, 1820.

De Graaf, H. J. *Islamic States in Java, 1500–1700. Eight Dutch Books and Articles Summarized by T. G. Th. Pigeaud*. The Hague, 1976.

Dobby, E. H. G. *Southeast Asia*. 9th ed. London, 1966.

Draeger, Donn F. *Weapons and Fighting Arts of the Indonesian Archipelago*. New York, 1972.

Eikman, A. J., and Stapel, F. W. *Leerboek der geschiedenis van Nederlandsch Oost-Indië*. Groningen, 1928.

Ferro, Bartolomeo. *Istoria delle missioni de' clerici regolari Teatine*. 2 vols. Rome, 1705.

Fisch, Jörg. *Holland's Ruhm in Asien; Francois Valentyns Vision des niederländischen Imperiums im 18. Jahrhundert*. Stuttgart, 1986.

Foster, William (ed.). *The Voyage of Sir Henry Middleton to the Moluccas, 1604–1606*. "HS," 2d ser., LXXXVIII (1943).

Freeman, D. *Report on the Iban*. New York, 1970.

Furber, Holden. *Rival Empires of Trade in the Orient, 1600–1800*. Minneapolis, Minn., 1976.

Furnivall, J. S. *Netherlands India*. Cambridge, 1944.

Geertz, Clifford. *Islam Observed: Religious Development in Morocco and Indonesia*. New Haven, 1968.

——. *The Religion of Java*. Chicago, 1960.

Haan, F. de. *Oude Batavia*. Bandoeng, 1935.

Hesse, Elias. *Gold-Bergwerke in Sumatra, 1680–1683. NR,* Vol. X. The Hague, 1931.

Howard, Alexander L. *A Manual of the Timbers of the World*. 3d ed. London, 1948.

Jonge, J. K. J. de, and Deventer, M. L. van (eds.). *De opkomst van het Nederlandsch gezag in Oost-Indië*. 20 vols. Amsterdam and The Hague, 1862–95.

Klerck, E. S. de. *History of the Netherlands East Indies*. 2 vols. Rotterdam, 1938.

Koentjaraningrat, R. M. *Javanese Culture*. Singapore, 1985.

Lasker, Bruno. *Human Bondage in Southeast Asia*. Chapel Hill, N.C., 1950.

Lauts, U. G. *Geschiedenis van der veroveringen der Nederlanders in Indië*. 2 vols. Kampen, n.d.

Lombard, Denys. *Le sultanat d'Ajtéh au temps d'Iskandar Muda, 1607–1636*. Paris, 1967.

Marsden, William. *The History of Sumatra*. Reprint of 3d ed. Kuala Lumpur, 1966.

McVey, Ruth T. (ed.). *Indonesia*. New Haven, 1963.

Müllbauer, Maximillian. *Geschichte der katholischen Missionen in Ostindien*. Freiburg, 1852.

Nicholl, R. *European Sources for the History of the Sultanate of Brunei in the Sixteenth Century*. Brunei, 1975.

Nothofer, B. *The Reconstruction of Proto-Malayo-Javanic*. The Hague, 1975.

Osman, M. T. (ed.). *Traditional Drama and Music of Southeast Asia*. Kuala Lumpur, 1974.

Oud Batavia. Gedenkboek uitgegeven door het Bataviaasch Genootschap van Kunsten en Wetenschappen. 2 pts. Batavia, 1922.

Chapter Bibliographies

Purcell, Victor. *The Chinese in Southeast Asia*. London, 1965.

Pruthi, J. S. *Spices and Condiments*. New Delhi, 1926.

Raffles, Sir Thomas Stamford. *History of Java*. 2 vols. London, 1817; 2d ed., 1830.

Reid, Anthony. *Southeast Asia in the Age of Commerce, 1450–1680*. Vol. I, *The Lands below the Winds*. New Haven, 1988.

———. (ed.). *Slavery, Bondage, and Dependency in Southeast Asia*. New York, 1983.

Reid, Anthony, and Castles, Lance (eds.). *Pre-Colonial State Systems in Southeast Asia; The Malay Peninsula, Sumatra, Bali-Lombok, South Celebes.* "Monographs of the Malaysian Branch of the Royal Asiatic Society," VI (Kuala Lumpur, 1975).

Sanford, W. R., and Green, C. R. *Gone Forever. The Dodo*. New York, 1989.

Savage, Victor R. *Western Impressions of Nature and Landscape in Southeast Asia*. Singapore, 1984.

Schärer, Hans. *Ngaju Religion. The Conception of God among a South Borneo People.* Translated by R. Needham. The Hague, 1963.

Simons, R. D. G. Ph. (ed.). *Handbook of Tropical Dermatology*. Amsterdam, 1952.

Snouk Hurgronje, C. *The Achehnese*. 2 vols. Leyden, 1906.

Sopher, David E. *The Sea Nomads. A Study Based on the Literature of the Maritime Boat People of Southeast Asia.* In *Memoirs of the National Museum* [Singapore], No. 5, 1965.

Taylor, Jean Gelman. *The Social World of Batavia; European and Eurasian in Dutch Asia*. Madison, Wis., 1983.

Unger, W. S. (ed.). *De oudste reizen van de Zeeuwen naar Oost-Indië, 1598–1604.* "WLV," LI. The Hague, 1948.

Van Dijk, Ludovicus Carolus D. *Nederland's vroegste betrekkingen met Borneo, den Solo-Archipel, Cambodja, Siam en Cochin-China; een nagelaten werk van Mr. L. C. D. van Dijk; met eene levensschets en inleiding van Mr. G. W. Vreede.* Amsterdam, 1862.

Vlekke, Bernard H. M. *Nusantara, A History of Indonesia*. Rev. ed. Chicago, 1960.

Von Grünebaum, G. E. (ed.). *Unity and Variety in Muslim Civilization*. Chicago, 1956.

Vreeland, Nena; Just, Peter; et al. *Area Handbook for Indonesia*. Washington, D.C., 1975.

ARTICLES

Armstrong, Patrick. "The Dodo and the Tree." *Geographical Magazine,* Vol. LVII, No. 10 (October, 1985), 541–43.

Ashworth, William B., Jr. "The Persistent Beast: Recurring Images in Early Zoölogical Illustration." In *The Natural Sciences and the Arts. An International Symposium* ("Acta Universitatis Upsaliensis," n.s., XXII; Uppsala, 1985), 46–66.

Banks, Edward. "A Note on Iban Omen Birds." *The Brunei Museum Journal,* Vol. V, No. 3 (1983), pp. 104–7.

Berg, C. C. "The Islamization of Java." *Studia Islamica,* IV (1955), 111–42.

Blumentritt, F. "Spain and the Island of Borneo." *The Brunei Museum Journal,* Vol. IV, No. 1 (1977), pp. 82–96.

Blussé, Leonard. "Batavia, 1619–1740. The Rise and Fall of a Chinese Colonial Town." *Journal of Southeast Asian Studies,* Vol. XII, No. 1 (March, 1981), pp. 159–78.

———. "The Caryatids of Batavia: Reproduction, Religion, and Acculturation under the V.O.C.," *Itinerario,* Vol. VII, No. 1 (1983), pp. 57–85.

Broek, Jan O. M. "Place Names in Sixteenth- and Seventeenth-Century Borneo." *Imago Mundi,* XVI (1962), 129–48.

Brummund, J. F. G. "Bijdragen tot de geschiedenis der kerk te Batavia." *Tijdschrift voor indische taal-, land-, en volkenkunde,* III (1864), 1–190.

Cole, F. J. "The History of Albrecht Dürer's Rhinoceros in Zoölogical Literature." In *Science, Medicine, and History: Essays . . . in Honour of Charles Singer,* ed. E. A. Underwood (London and New York, 1953), I, 337–56.

Drewes, G. W. J. "Indonesia: Mysticism and Activism." In G. E. von Grünebaum (ed.), *Unity and Variety in Muslim Civilization* (Chicago, 1956), pp. 284–310.

———. "New Light on the Coming of Islam to Indonesia." *BTLV,* CXXIV (1968), 433–59.

Fruin-Mees, W. "Een Bantamsch gezantschap naar Engeland in 1682." *Tijdschrift voor indische taal-, land-, en volkenkunde,* LXIV (1923), 207–27.

Fung Yee Pong, and Konawa. "Blowpipes." *Sabah Society Journal,* III (1968), 294–96.

Hall, Kenneth R. "Trade and Statecraft in the Western Archipelago at the Dawn of the European Age." *JRAS, Malay Branch,* LIV (1981), 21–47.

Hoetink, B. "Chineesche officieren te Batavia onder de compagnie." *BTLV,* LXXVIII (1922), 1–136.

———. "So Bing Bong. Het eerste hoofd der Chineezen te Batavia, 1619–1636." *Ibid.,* LXXIII (1917), 311–43.

Hood, Mantle. "The Enduring Tradition: Music and Theater in Java and Bali." In Ruth T. McVey (ed.), *Indonesia.* New Haven, 1963, pp. 438–71.

Krom, N. J. "De naam Sumatra." *BTLV,* (1941), pp. 5–25.

Leupe, P. A. (ed.). "Het gezandtschap naar Bali, onder den Gouverneur-Generaal Hendrik Brouwer in 1633." *Ibid.,* V (1856), 1–71.

———. "Schriftelijck rapport gedaen door den predicant Justus Heurnius, aengaende de gelegentheijt van't eijlandt ende tot het voorplanten van de Christelijcke religie, en van wegen de gelegentheit van Bali, 1638." *Ibid.,* III (1855), 250–62.

———. "Verhael van de belegeringhe der stadt Batavia in't coninckrijck van Jaccatra, anno 1628, den 22 Agustij. (door en oogetuige)." *Ibid.,* 289–312.

Manguin, Pierre-Yves. "The Southeast Asian Ship; an Historical Approach." *Journal of Southeast Asian Studies,* XI (1980), 266–76.

Nicholl, R. "Brunei and Camphor." *The Brunei Museum Journal,* Vol. IV, No. 3 (1979), pp. 52–74.

———— (ed.). "Relations of the East Indies Company with Borneo (Brunei), the Sulu Archipelago, Mindanao, etc." *Ibid.*, Vol. V, No. 3 (1983), pp. 61–80; Vol. V, No. 4 (1984), pp. 6–34.

————. "Relation between Brunei and Manila, A.D. 1682–1690." *Ibid.*, Vol. IV, No. 1 (1977), pp. 129–75.

————. "The Mission of Father Antonio Ventimiglia to Borneo." *Ibid.*, Vol. II, No. 4 (1972), pp. 183–205.

Reid, Anthony. "The Structure of Cities in Southeast Asia, Fifteenth to Seventeenth Centuries." *Journal of Southeast Asian Studies*, XI (1980), 235–50.

————. "Trade and State Power in Sixteenth- and Seventeenth-Century Southeast Asia." In *Proceedings of the International Association of Historians of Asia. Seventh Conference, Bangkok, 1977* (2 vols.; Bangkok, 1977), Vol. I, pp. 391–419.

————. "Trade and the Problem of Royal Power in Aceh. Three Stages: c. 1550–1700." In Anthony Reid and Lance Castles (eds.), *Pre-Colonial State Systems in Southeast Asia; The Malay Peninsula, Sumatra, Bali-Lombok, South Celebes*, "Monographs of the Malaysian Branch of the Royal Asiatic Society," No. 6, pp. 45–55. Kuala Lumpur, 1975.

Suwandono. "Gamelan Orchestra in Wayang Kulit." In M. T. Osman (ed.), *Traditional Drama and Music of Southeast Asia*, pp. 290–97. Kuala Lumpur, 1974.

Umemoto, Diane L. "The World's Most Civilized Chew." *Asia*, VI (1983), 25–27, 48.

XVIII. INSULINDIA: THE EASTERN ARCHIPELAGO AND THE AUSTRAL LANDS

BOOKS

Andaya, Leonard K. *The Heritage of Arung Palakka: A History of South Sulawesi (Celebes) in the Seventeenth Century.* "Verhandelingen van het Koninklijk Instituut voor Taal-, Land-, en Volkenkunde," Vol. XCI. The Hague, 1981.

Arndt, P. P. *Gesellschaftliche Verhältnisse im Sikagebiet (Mittleflores).* Ende, Flores, s.d.

Austin, Robert F. *A Historical Gazetteer of Southeast Asia.* Dept of Geography, University of Missouri, Columbia, April, 1983.

Beekman, E. M. (ed.). *The Poison Tree. Selected Writings of Rumphius.* Amherst, Mass., 1981.

Bellwood, P. *Man's Conquest of the Pacific.* New York, 1979.

Boxer, Charles Ralph. *Francisco Viera de Figueiredo: A Portuguese Merchant-Adventurer in South East Asia, 1624–1667.* The Hague, 1967.

Boxer, Charles Ralph, and Vasconcelos, Frazão de. *André Furtado de Mendoça (1558–1610).* Lisbon, 1955.

Cobley, L. S. *An Introduction to the Botany of Tropical Crops.* London, 1956.

Collins, T. "The Historical Relationship of the Languages of Central Maluku, Indonesia," Ph.D. diss., Dept. of Linguistics, The University of Chicago, 1980.

Crawfurd, John. *History of the Indian Archipelago.* 3 vols. Edinburgh, 1820.

Chapter Bibliographies

Eliade, Mircea. *Shamanism: Archaic Techniques of Ecstasy.* New York, 1964.

Ferdon, E. N. *Early Tonga.* Tucson, 1987.

Fisch, Jörg. *Holland's Ruhm in Asien; François Valentyns Vision des niederländischen Imperiums im 18. Jahrhundert.* Stuttgart, 1986.

Gibbs, W. M. *Spices and How to Know Them.* Buffalo, N.Y., 1909.

Guppy, H. B. *The Solomon Islands and Their Natives.* London, 1887.

Hall, Kenneth R. *Maritime Trade and State Development in Early Southeast Asia.* Honolulu, 1955.

Hanna, Willard E. *Indonesian Banda; Colonialism and Its Aftermath in the Nutmeg Islands.* Philadelphia, 1978.

Hart, Clive. *Kites. An Historical Survey.* Rev. ed. Mt Vernon, New York, 1982.

Jack-Hinton, C. *The Search for the Islands of Solomon, 1567–1838.* Oxford, 1969.

Jacobs, H., S.J. (ed.). *Documenta Malucensia.* 3 vols. Rome, 1974, 1980, 1984.

Kiers, Luc. *Coen op Banda; de conqueste getoetst aan het recht van den tijd.* Utrecht, 1943.

Klerck, E. S. de. *History of the Netherlands East Indies.* 2 vols. Rotterdam, 1938.

Leitão, Humberto. *Os Portugueses em Solor e Timor de 1515 a 1702.* Lisbon, 1948.

Matos, A. T. de. *Timor português, 1515–1769.* Lisbon, 1974.

Oliver, W. H., and Williams, B. R. (eds.). *The Oxford History of New Zealand.* Oxford, 1981.

Prins, J. *The South Moluccas.* Leyden, 1960.

Reid, Anthony. *Southeast Asia in the Age of Commerce, 1450–1680.* Vol. I, *The Lands below the Winds.* New Haven, 1988.

—— (ed.). *Slavery, Bondage and Dependency in Southeast Asia.* New York, 1983.

Reid, Anthony, and Castles, Lance (eds.). *Pre-Colonial State Systems in Southeast Asia; The Malay Peninsula, Sumatra, Bali-Lombok, South Celebes.* "Monographs of the Malaysian Branch of the Royal Asiatic Society," VI. Kuala Lumpur, 1975.

Reid, Anthony, and Marr, David (eds.). *Perceptions of the Past in Southeast Asia.* Singapore, Kuala Lumpur, and Hong Kong, 1979.

Savage, Victor R. *Western Impressions of Nature and Landscape in Southeast Asia.* Singapore, 1984.

Schilder, Günter. *Australia Unveiled.* Amsterdam, 1976.

Sharp, A. *The Discovery of the Pacific Islands.* Oxford, 1960.

Shipman, Joseph. *William Dampier, Seaman-Scientist.* Lawrence, Kansas, 1962.

Simons, R. D. G. Ph. (ed.). *Handbook of Tropical Dermatology and Medical Mycology.* Amsterdam, 1952.

Skeat, W. W. *Malay Magic.* London, 1900.

Sopher, D. E. *The Sea Nomads.* Singapore, 1964.

Tauern, Odo D. *Patasiwa und Patalima vom Molukkeneiland Seran und seinen Bewohnern.* Leipzig, 1918.

Verwey, A. (ed.). *Vondels volledige dichtwerken.* Amsterdam, 1937.

Vlekke, Bernard H. M. *Nusantura: A History of Indonesia.* Rev. ed. Chicago, 1960.

Chapter Bibliographies

Wallace, Alfred R. *The Malay Archipelago.* New York, 1962. First published in 1869.

Wessels, Cornelius J., S.J. *De geschiedenis de R. K. Missie in Amboina, 1546–1605.* Nijmegen-Utrecht, 1926.

Wichmann, Arthur. *Entdeckungsgeschichte von Neu-Guinea.* 2 vols. Leyden, 1909–12.

Wilken, G. A. *Het animisme bij de volken van den Indischen Archipel.* 2 pts. Amsterdam, 1881.

ARTICLES

Andaya, L. K. "The Nature of Kingship in Bone." In Anthony Reid and Lance Castles (eds.), *Pre-Colonial State Systems in Southeast Asia; The Malay Peninsula, Sumatra, Bali-Lombok, South Celebes,* "Monographs of the Malaysian Branch of the Royal Asiatic Society," VI, pp. 114–25. Kuala Lumpur, 1975.

———. "A Village Perception of Arung Palakka and the Makassar War of 1666–1669." In Anthony Reid and David Marr (eds.), *Perceptions of the Past in Southeast Asia,* pp. 360–78. Singapore, Kuala Lumpur, and Hong Kong, 1979.

Boxer, Charles Ralph. "Portuguese Timor." *History Today,* X (1960), 351–52.

Bronson, B. "Exchange at the Upstream and Downstream Ends: Notes toward a Functional Model of the Coastal State in Southeast Asia." In Karl L. Hutterer (ed.), *Economic Exchange and Social Interaction in Southeast Asia,* pp. 39–52. Ann Arbor, 1977.

Bruijn, Jaap R. "Between Batavia and the Cape; Shipping Patterns of the Dutch East India Company." *Journal of Southeast Asian Studies,* IX (1980), 251–65.

Davidson, J. M. "The Polynesian Foundation." In W. H. Oliver and B. R. Williams (eds.), *The Oxford History of New Zealand,* pp. 3–25. Oxford, 1981.

Hamonic, Gilbert. "Travestissement et bisexualité chez les 'Bissu' du pays Bugis." *Archipel,* X (1975), 121–34.

Howells, W. "Physical Anthropology." In J. D. Jennings (ed.), *The Prehistory of Polynesia.* Cambridge, Mass., 1979.

Leupe, P. A. "De reizen der Nederlanders naar Nieuw-Guinea en de Papoesche eilanden in de 17e en 18e eeuw." *BTLV,* XXII (1875), 175–79.

Manguin, Pierre-Yves. "The Southeast Asian Ship: An Historical Approach." *Journal of Southeast Asian Studies,* Vol. XI, No. 2 (Sept., 1980), pp. 266–76.

Reid, A. "The Structure of Cities in Southeast Asia, Fifteenth to Seventeenth Centuries." *Journal of Southeast Asian Studies,* Vol. XI, No. 2 (Sept., 1980), pp. 235–50.

———. "Trade and State Power in Sixteenth- and Seventeenth-Century Southeast Asia." *Proceedings, Seventh IAHA Conference,* I, 391–419. Bangkok, 1979.

Sukanto, M. "Climate of Indonesia." In H. Arakawa (ed.), *Climates of Northern and Eastern Asia,* Vol. VIII of *World Survey of Climatology,* pp. 215–29. Amsterdam, 1969.

Van Dam van Isselt, W. E. "Mr. Johan van Dam en zijne tuchtiging van Makassar in 1660." *BTLV,* LX (1908), 1–44.

Chapter Bibliographies

XIX. THE PHILIPPINES AND THE MARIANAS

BOOKS

Alip, E. M. *Philippine-Japanese Relations*. Manila, 1959.

Alkire, W. H. *An Introduction to the Peoples and Culture of Micronesia*. n.p., 1973.

Ausejo, Luz. "The Philippines in the Sixteenth Century." Ph.D. diss., Dept. of History, Univ. of Chicago, 1972.

Barrett, Ward (trans. and ed.). *Mission in the Marianas: An Account of Father Diego Luis de Sanvitores and His Companions, 1669–70*. Minneapolis, 1975.

Boxer, C. R. *South China in the Sixteenth Century*. "HS," 2d ser., CVI. London, 1953.

Burney, James. *A Chronological History of the Discoveries in the South Sea or Pacific Ocean*. . . . 5 vols. London, 1803–17. Reprinted at Amsterdam, 1967, in 4 vols.

Burrus, E. J., S.J. *Father Kino Writes to the Duchess*. Rome, 1965.

Carano, Paul, and Sanchez, P. C. *A Complete History of Guam*. Rutland, Vt., and Tokyo, 1964.

Cushner, Nicholas P., S.J. *Spain in the Philippines from Conquest to Revolution*. Quezon City, 1971.

De la Costa, H., S.J. *The Jesuits in the Philippines, 1581–1768*. Cambridge, Mass., 1967.

Dobby, Ernest H. G. *Southeast Asia*. 9th ed. London, 1966.

Dudley, Robert. *Dell'Arcano del Mare*. 6 vols. Florence, 1646–47.

Felix, Alfonso, Jr. (ed.). *The Chinese in the Philippines, 1550–1770*. 2 vols. Manila, 1966, 1969.

Foss, Theodore N. "A Jesuit Encyclopedia for China." Ph.D. diss., Committee on the History of Culture, Univ. of Chicago, 1979.

Garcia, Mauro (ed.). *A Voyage to the Philippines by Giovanni Francesco Gemelli Careri*. Manila, 1963.

Garvan, John M. *The Manóbos of Mindanáo*. "Memoirs of the National Academy of Science," Vol. XXIII. Washington, D.C., 1941.

———. *The Negritos of the Philippines*. In B. Hochegger (ed.), *Wiener Beiträge zur Kulturgeschichte und Linguistik*, Vol. XIV (1963).

Gowing, P. G. *Muslim Filipinos—Heritage and Horizon*. Quezon City, 1979.

Griffin, A. P. C. *et al. Bibliography of the Philippine Islands*. 2 vols. Washington, D.C., 1903.

Grist, D. H. *Rice*. 3d ed. London, 1959.

Hachisuka, the Marquess. *The Birds of the Philippine Islands*. 2 vols. London, 1931–35.

Hargrave, Catherine P. *A History of Playing Cards*. Boston and New York, 1930.

Hezel, Francis X., S.J. *The First Taint of Civilization: A History of the Caroline and Marshall Islands in Pre-Colonial Days, 1521–1885*. Honolulu, 1983.

Huke, R. E. *Shadows on the Land: An Economic Geography of the Philippines*. Manila, 1963.

Jack-Hinton, Colin. *The Search for the Islands of Solomon, 1567–1838.* Oxford, 1969.

Keesing, Felix M. *The Ethnohistory of Northern Luzon.* Stanford, 1962.

Lardizabal, A. S., and Tensuan-Leogardo, F. (eds.). *Readings on Philippine Culture and Social Life.* Manila, 1970.

Larkin, John A. *The Pampangans. Colonial Society in a Philippine Province.* Berkeley, 1972.

Lebar, Frank M. (ed.). *Ethnic Groups of Insular Southeast Asia.* 2 vols. New Haven, 1975.

Lopez-Gonzaga, Violeta B. *The Mangyans of Mindoro: An Ethnohistory.* Manila, 1975.

————. *Peasants in the Hills.* Quezon City, 1983.

Menninger, Edwin A. *Fantastic Trees.* New York, 1967.

Merrill, Edwin D. *An Enumeration of Philippine Flowering Plants.* 4 vols. Manila, 1922.

Montero y Vidal, José. *El archipielago filipino y las islas Marianas, Carolinas, y Palaos. Su historia, geografia y estadistica.* Madrid, 1886.

Murdock, G. F. (ed.). *Social Structure in Southeast Asia.* Chicago, 1960.

Pardo de Tavera, T. H. *The Medicinal Plants of the Philippines.* Philadelphia, 1901.

Phelan, John Leddy. *The Hispanization of the Philippines. Spanish Aims and Filipino Responses, 1565–1700.* Madison, Wis., 1959.

Plants of the Philippines. Prepared under the direction of C. V. Asis and D. F. Hernandez for the Science Education Center of the University of the Philippines. Quezon City, 1971.

Quirino, Carlos. *Philippine Cartography (1320–1899).* 2d rev. ed. Amsterdam, 1963.

Reid, Anthony (ed.). *Slavery, Bondage, and Dependency in Southeast Asia.* New York, 1983.

Retana, W. E. (comp.). *Aparato bibliográfico de la historia general de Filipinas.* 3 vols. Madrid, 1906; reprint, 1964, Manila.

Roger, Juan. *Estudio etnológico comparativo de las formas religiosas primitivas de las tribus salvajes de Filipinas.* Madrid, 1949.

Safford, W. E. *The Useful Plants of the Island of Guam with an Introductory Account of the Physical Features and Natural History of the Island, of the Character and History of Its People, and of Their Agriculture.* "Contributions from the United States National Herbarium," IX. Washington, D.C., 1905.

Tantuico, F. S., Jr. *Leyte, the Historic Islands.* Tacloban City, Philippines, 1964.

Thompson, Laura. *Guam and Its People.* New York, 1941.

————. *The Native Culture of the Mariana Islands.* Bernice P. Bishop Museum publication No. 185. Honolulu, 1945.

Topping, D. M.; Ogo, P. M.; and Gungca, B. C. *Chamorro-English Dictionary.* Honolulu, 1975.

U.S. Department of the Navy. *Civil Affairs Handbook, Mandated Marianas Islands.* Washington, D. C., 1944.

Chapter Bibliographies

Wernstedt, Frederick L., and Spencer, J. E. *The Philippine Island World. A Physical, Cultural, and Regional Geography.* Berkeley, 1967.

Zaide, G. F. *The Pageant of Philippine History.* 2 vols. Manila, 1979.

ARTICLES

Boxer, C. R. "A Late Sixteenth Century Manila MS." *JRAS,* April, 1950, pp. 37–49.

———. "The Mother of the Missions." *History Today,* XXIII (1973), 733–39.

———. "Two Jesuit Letters on the Marianas Mission, Written to the Duchess of Aveiro (1676 and 1689)." *Philippine Studies,* XXVI (1978), 35–50.

Burnes, E. J. "Sanvitores' Grammar and Catechism in the Mariana (or Chamorro) Language (1668)." *Anthropos,* XLIX (1954), 934–60.

Chan, Albert. "Chinese-Philippine Relations in the Late Sixteenth Century and to 1603." *Philippine Studies,* XXVI (1978), 51–82.

Chang, Y. Z. "Sangley, the Merchant-Traveller." *Modern Language Notes,* III (1937), 189–90.

Churchill, M. H. "Indian Penetration of Pre-Spanish Philippines: A New Look at the Evidence." *Asian Studies,* XV (1977), 21–45.

Frake, Charles O. "The Eastern Subanun of Mindanao." In G. F. Murdock (ed.), *Social Structure in Southeast Asia,* pp. 51–64. Chicago, 1960.

Harrisson, Tom. "The 'Palang.' Its History and Proto-history in West Borneo and the Philippines." *JRAS,* Vol. XXXVI, Pt. 2 (1964), pp. 162–74.

Hester, E. D. "Alzina's *Historia de Visayas,* a Bibliographical Note." *Philippine Studies,* X (1962), 331–65.

Hewitt, John. "Head Pressing amongst the Milanos of Sarawak." *JRAS,* Straits Branch, LX (Dec. 1911), pp. 69–72.

Jacobs, H., S.J. "*The Discurso Politico del Gobierno Maluco* of Fr. Francisco Combes and Its Historical Impact." *Philippine Studies,* XXIX (1981), 309–44.

Jurado, M. R., S.J. "Pedro Chirino, S.J., and Philippine Historiography." *Philippine Studies,* XXIX (1981), 345–59.

Manguin, Pierre-Yves. "The Southeast Asian Ship: An Historical Approach." *Journal of Southeast Asian Studies,* Vol. XI, No. 3 (Sept. 1980), pp. 266–76.

Murakami, Naojiro. "Japan's Early Attempts to Establish Commercial Relations with Mexico." In H. Morse Stephens and H. E. Bolton (eds.), *The Pacific Ocean in History,* pp. 467–80. New York, 1917.

Pardo de Tavera, T. H. "Biblioteca Filipina." In A. P. C. Griffin, *et al., Bibliography of the Philippine Islands* (2 vols.), Pt. 2, pp. 414–15. Washington, D.C., 1903.

Phelan, J. H. "Philippine Linguistics and Spanish Missionaries, 1565–1700." *Mid-America,* XXXVII (1955), 153–70.

Quirino, Carlos, and Garcia, Mauro (eds.). "The Manners, Customs, and Beliefs of the Philippine Inhabitants of Long Ago; Being Chapters of a Late Sixteenth Century Manila Manuscript, Transcribed, Translated, and Annotated." *The Philippine Journal of Science,* LXXXVII (1958), 325–453.

Radilla de Leon, Felipe. "Philippine Music." In A. S. Lardizabal and F. Tensuan-Leogardo (eds.), *Readings in Philippine Culture and Social Life,* pp. 357–63. Manila, 1970.

Santamaria, A., O.P. "The Chinese Parian (El Parian de los Sangleyes)." In A. Felix, Jr. (ed.), *The Chinese in the Philippines, 1550–1770,* pp. 67–118. Manila, 1966.

Santamaria, M. G. "The Religion of the Filipinos." In A. S. Lardizabal, and F. Tensuan-Leogardo (eds.), *Readings in Philippine Culture and Social Life,* pp. 126–34. Manila, 1970.

Scott, William H. "*Oripun* and *Alipin* in the Sixteenth-Century Philippines." In A. Reid (ed.), *Slavery, Bondage, and Dependency in Southeast Asia,* pp. 138–55. New York, 1983.

Thompson, Laura. "The Function of *Latte* in the Marianas." *Journal of the Polynesian Society,* XLIX (1940), 447–65.

Villa, R. L., Jr. "Filipino Identity in Folk Dances." In A. S. Lardizabal, and F. Tensuan-Leogardo (eds.), *Readings on Philippine Culture and Social Life,* pp. 164–69. Manila, 1970.

XX. CHINA: THE LATE MING DYNASTY

BOOKS

Ball, J. D. *Things Chinese, or, Notes Connected with China.* 5th rev. ed. London, 1926.

Boxer, C. R. *The Great Ship from Amacon; Annals of Macao and the Old Japan Trade, 1555–1640.* Lisbon, 1959.

———. *Fidalgos in the Far East, 1550–1770.* The Hague, 1948.

——— (ed.). *Seventeenth Century Macau in Contemporary Documents and Illustrations.* Hong Kong, Kuala Lumpur, and Singapore, 1984.

Carter, T. C., and Goodrich, L. F. *The Invention of Printing in China and Its Spread Westward.* New York, 1955.

Chaffee, John W. *The Thorny Gates of Learning in Sung China: A Social History of Examinations.* Cambridge, 1985.

Chan, Albert, S.J. *The Glory and Fall of the Ming Dynasty.* Norman, Okla., 1982.

Ch'en, Kenneth K. S. *Buddhism in China: A Historical Survey.* Princeton, 1974.

———. *Buddhism: The Light of Asia.* Woodbury, New York, 1968.

Chen Min-sun. "Geographical Works by Jesuits in Chinese, 1584–1672." M.A. diss., Univ. of Chicago, 1959.

———. "Three Contemporary Western Sources on the History of Late Ming and the Manchu Conquest of China." Ph.D. diss., Univ. of Chicago, 1971.

Ch'ien Mu. *Traditional Government in Imperial China.* Trans. by Chün-tu Hsüeh and George O. Totten. Hong Kong, 1982.

Ch'ü, T. T. *Law and Society in Traditional China.* Paris, 1961.

Cormack, J. G. *Chinese Birthday, Wedding, Funeral, and Other Customs.* Peking, 1923.

Costa, A. *Macau, imagens e numeros.* 2 vols. Lisbon, 1981–82.

Couling, Samuel. *The Encyclopedia Sinica.* London, 1917.

Chapter Bibliographies

Creel, H. G. *Confucius and the Chinese Way*. New York, 1960.

———, et al. *Literary Chinese by the Inductive Method*. 3 vols. Chicago, 1948.

De Bary, William T. *Neo-Confucian Orthodoxy and the Learning of the Mind-and-Heart*. New York, 1981.

Dehergne, Joseph, and Leslie, D. D. *Juifs de Chine à travers la correspondance inédite des Jésuite du dix-huitième siècle*. Rome and Paris, 1980.

Doolittle, J. *Social Life of the Chinese*. 2 vols. New York, 1867.

Eliot, Charles. *Hinduism and Buddhism*. 3 vols. London, 1954.

Elvin, Mark. *The Pattern of the Chinese Past*. Stanford, 1973.

Farmer, E. L. *Early Ming Government: The Evolution of Dual Capitals*. Cambridge, Mass., 1976.

Foss, T. N. "A Jesuit Encyclopedia for China. A Guide to Jean-Baptiste Du Halde's *Description . . . de la Chine* (1735)." Ph.D. diss., 2 vols.; Committee on History of Culture, Univ. of Chicago, 1979.

Fuchs, Walter. *The "Mongol Atlas" of Chu Ssu-pen and the Kuang-yü t'ü*. "Monumenta Serica," Monograph VIII. Peiping, 1946.

Fung Yu-lan. *A History of Chinese Philosophy*. Trans. Derk Bodde. 2 vols. Princeton, 1952.

Groeneveldt, W. P. *De Nederlanders in China*. BTLV, Vol. XLVIII, Pt. 4 (1898), pp. 1–598.

Ho Ping-ti. *The Ladder of Success in Imperial China*. New York, 1962.

———. *Studies on the Population of China, 1368–1953*. Cambridge, Mass., 1959.

Huang, Ray. *1587, A Year of No Significance: The Ming Dynasty in Decline*. New Haven, 1981.

Hucker, Charles O. *The Censorial System of Ming China*. Stanford, 1966.

———. *A Dictionary of Official Titles in Imperial China*. Stanford, 1985.

———. *The Traditional Chinese State in Ming Times, 1368–1644*. Tucson, 1961.

Jordan, David K. *Gods, Ghosts, and Ancestors: Folk Religion in a Taiwanese Village*. Berkeley and Los Angeles, 1972.

Levy, Howard S. *Chinese Footbinding: The History of a Curious Erotic Custom*. New York, 1966.

Lubac, H. de. *La rencontre du Bouddhisme et de l'Occident*. Paris, 1954.

Lu Guei-djen and Needham, Joseph. *Celestial Lancets. A History and Rationale of Acupuncture and Moxa*. Cambridge, 1980.

Lundbaek, Knud. *The Traditional History of the Chinese Script from a Seventeenth-Century Jesuit Manuscript*. Aarhus, 1986.

MacSherry, C. W. "Impairment of the Ming Tribute System as Exhibited in Trade through Fukien." Ph.D. diss., Univ. of California, Berkeley, 1956.

Malm, William P. *Music Cultures of the Pacific, the Near East, and Asia*. 2d ed. Englewood Cliffs, N.J., 1977.

Miyazaki, Ichisada. *China's Examination Hell*. Trans. by C. Shirokauer. New York and Tokyo, 1976.

Chapter Bibliographies

Mote, R. W., and Twitchett, D. (eds.). *The Cambridge History of China*, Vol. VIII. Cambridge, 1988.

Mungello, David E. *Curious Land: Jesuit Accommodation and the Origins of Sinology.* Stuttgart, 1985.

Needham, Joseph. *Science and Civilization in China.* 6 vols. Cambridge, 1955–85.

Olschki, L. *Marco Polo's Asia.* Berkeley, 1960.

Overmeyer, Daniel L. *Folk Buddhist Religion: Dissenting Sects in Late Traditional China.* Stanford, 1976.

Rawski, Evelyn S. *Education and Popular Literacy in Ch'ing China.* Ann Arbor, 1979.

Renaldo, John J. *Daniello Bartoli. A Letterato of the Seicento.* Naples, 1979.

Spence, Jonathan D., and Wills, John E., Jr. (eds.). *From Ming to Ch'ing. Conquest, Religion, and Continuity in Seventeenth-Century China.* New Haven, 1979.

Struve, Lynn. *The Southern Ming, 1644–1662.* New Haven, 1984.

Sullivan, Michael. *The Meeting of Eastern and Western Art.* London, 1973.

Sung Ying-hsing. *T'ien-kung K'ai-wu. Chinese Technology in the Seventeenth Century.* Trans. by E-tu Zen Sun and Shiou-huan Sun. University Park, Pa., 1966.

Thompson, Laurence G. *Chinese Religion, An Introduction.* Belmont, Cal., 1979.

Till, Barry. *In Search of Old Nanking.* Hong Kong, 1982.

Torbert, P. M. "The Ch'ing Imperial Household Department: A Study of Its Organization and Principal Functions." Ph.D. diss., Univ. of Chicago, 1973.

Tsien Tsuen-hsuin. *Written on Bamboo and Silk.* Chicago, 1962.

———. *Paper and Printing.* Vol. V, Pt. 1, of J. Needham, *Science and Civilization in China.* Cambridge, 1985.

Wakeman, Frederic, Jr. *The Great Enterprise. The Manchu Reconstruction of Imperial Order in Seventeenth-Century China.* 2 vols. Berkeley, 1985.

Wills, John E., Jr. *Embassies and Illusions: Dutch and Portuguese Envoys to K'ang-hsi, 1666–1687.* Cambridge, Mass., 1985.

———. *Pepper, Guns, and Parleys: The Dutch East India Company and China, 1662–1681.* Cambridge, Mass., 1974.

Wolf, Arthur P. (ed.). *Religion and Ritual in Chinese Society.* Stanford, 1974.

Yang, C. K. *Religion and Chinese Society.* Berkeley and Los Angeles, 1961.

Zhou Xun, and Gao Chunming. *Five Thousand Years of Chinese Costumes.* San Francisco, 1987.

ARTICLES

Bertuccioli, Giuliano. "Matteo Ricci and Taoism." *International Symposium on Chinese-Western Cultural Interchange in Commemoration of the 400th Anniversary of the Arrival of Matteo Ricci, S.J., in China.* Taipei, 1983.

Bürke, Alois, S.M.B. "Das Nestorianer-Denkmal von Si-an-fu. Versuch einer Neuübersetzung." *NZM,* Supplementa XVII (1971), 125–41.

Dehergne, Joseph, S.J. "Les historiens jésuites du Taoisme." *Actes du Colloque International de Sinologie. La mission française de Pékin aux XVIIe et XVIIIe siècles.* Paris, 1976.

Ho Ping-ti. "The Introduction of the American Food Plants into China." *American Anthropologist*, Vol. LVII, No. 2, Pt. 1 (April, 1955), pp. 191–201.

Leslie, D. D. "Assimilation and Survival of Muslims in China." *Actes du IIIe Colloque International de Sinologie. Appréciation par Europe de la tradition Chinois a partir du XVIIe siècle*, pp. 116–26. Paris, 1983.

Lundbaek, K. "Notes sur l'image de Néo-Confucianisme dans la littérature européenne du XVIIe à la fin de XIXe siècle." *Actes du IIIe Colloque International de Sinologie. Appréciation par Europe de la tradition Chinois a partir du XVIIe siècle*, pp. 127–35. Paris, 1983.

McDermott, J. "Bondservants in the T'ai-hu Basin during the Late Ming: A Case of Mistaken Identities." *Journal of Asian Studies*, XL (1981), 675–701.

Nishijima Sadao. "The Formation of the Early Chinese Cotton Industry." In *State and Society in China: Japanese Perspectives on Ming-Qing Social and Economic History*, ed. Linda Grove and Christian Daniels, pp. 17–77. Tokyo, 1984.

Shen Wen-hsiung. "Changes in China's Climate." *Bulletin of the American Meteorological Society*, LV (1974), 1348–52.

Szcześniak, B. "The Seventeenth-Century Maps of China. An Inquiry into the Compilations of European Cartographers." *Imago Mundi*, XIII (1956), 116–36.

Van Kley, Edwin J. "Europe's 'Discovery' of China and the Writing of World History." *American Historical Review*, LXXVI (1971), 358–85.

Waldron, A. "The Great Wall Myth: Its Origins and Role in Modern China." *The Yale Journal of Criticism*, Vol. II, No. 1 (1988), pp. 67–98.

Wolf, Arthur P. "Gods, Ghosts and Ancestors." In Arthur P. Wolf (ed.), *Religion and Ritual in Chinese Society*, pp. 131–82. Stanford, 1974.

Young, John D. "Original Confucianism versus Neo-Confucianism: Matteo Ricci's Chinese Writings." *Actes du XXIXe Congrés International des Orientalistes. Chine ancienne*, pp. 371–77. Paris, 1977.

XXI. CHINA: THE EARLY CH'ING DYNASTY

BOOKS

Audemare, L. *Les jongues chinoises*. "Publicaties van het Museum voor Land- en Volkenkunde," No. 4 (Rotterdam, 1962), and No. 6 (Rotterdam, 1965).

Ball, J. D. *Things Chinese*. 5th rev. ed. London, 1926.

Blussé, L., and Falkenburg, R. *Johan Nieuhofs beelden van een Chinareis, 1655–1657*. Middelburg, 1987.

Boxer, Charles R. *Fidalgos in the Far East 1550–1770; Fact and Fancy in the History of Macao*. The Hague, 1948.

———. *Francisco de Figueiredo: A Portuguese Merchant-Adventurer in South East Asia, 1624–1667*. "Verhandelingen van het Koninklijk Instituut voor Taal-, Land-, en Volkenkunde," *LII*. The Hague, 1967.

Boyd, Andrew. *Chinese Architecture and Town Planning, 1500 B.C.–A.D. 1911*. Chicago, 1962.

Cameron, Nigel, and Blake, Brian. *Peking: A Tale of Three Cities*. New York, 1965.

Chapter Bibliographies

Cammann, S. *China's Dragon Robes.* New York, 1952.

Campbell, William. *Formosa under the Dutch.* London, 1903; reprinted Taipei, 1967.

Chabrié, Robert. *Michel Boym. Jésuite Polonais et la fin des Ming en Chine (1646–1662).* Paris, 1933.

Chan Wing-tsit. *Religious Trends in Modern China.* New York, 1953.

Ch'en, Kenneth. *Buddhism in China: A Historical Survey.* Princeton, 1974.

Chen Min-sun. "Three Contemporary Western Sources on the History of Late Ming and the Manchu Conquest of China." Ph.D. diss., Dept. of History, Univ. of Chicago, 1971.

Collani, Claudia von. *P. Joachim Bouvet, S.J., sein Leben und sein Werk.* Nettetal, 1985.

Cormack, J. G. *Chinese Birthday, Wedding, Funeral, and Other Customs.* Peking, 1923.

Creel, H. G. *Confucius and the Chinese Way.* New York, 1960.

De Bary, Wm. Theodore, *et al.* (eds.). *Sources of Chinese Tradition,* Vol. I. New York, 1965.

Dennerline, J. *The Chia-ting Loyalists: Confucian Leadership and Social Change in Seventeenth-Century China.* New Haven, 1981.

Doolittle, J. *Social Life of the Chinese.* 2 vols. New York, 1867.

Dunne, George, S.J. *Generation of Giants; The Story of the Jesuits in China in the Late Decades of the Ming Dynasty.* Notre Dame, 1962.

Eliot, Sir Charles. *Hinduism and Buddhism.* 3 vols. London, 1954.

Fung Yu-lan. *A Short History of Chinese Philosophy.* New York, 1959.

Henry, B. O. *Ling-Nam or Interior Views of Southern China.* London, 1886.

Ho Ping-ti. *The Ladder of Success in Imperial China.* New York, 1967.

Hummel, Arthur W. (ed.). *Eminent Chinese of the Ch'ing Period (1644–1912).* Washington, D.C., 1943.

Kessler, Lawrence D. *K'ang-Hsi and the Consolidation of Ch'ing Rule, 1661–1684.* Chicago, 1976.

Mungello, David E. *Curious Land: Jesuit Accommodation and the Origins of Sinology.* Stuttgart, 1985.

Needham, Joseph. *Science and Civilization in China.* 6 vols. Cambridge, 1954–84.

Pachow, W. *Chinese Buddhism: Aspects of Interaction and Reinterpretation.* Lanham, Maryland, 1980.

Parsons, J. B. *The Peasant Rebellion of the Late Ming Dynasty.* Tucson, 1976.

Rawski, Evelyn S. *Education and Popular Literacy in Ch'ing China.* Ann Arbor, 1979.

Reichelt, Karl L. *Religion in Chinese Garment.* Trans. J. Tetlie. London, 1951.

————. *Truth and Tradition in Chinese Buddhism. A Study of Chinese Mahayana Buddhism.* Shanghai, 1928.

Rosenthal, Franz. *A History of Muslim Historiography.* Leyden, 1968.

Skinner, G. W. (ed.). *The City in Late Imperial China.* Stanford, 1977.

Spence, Jonathan. *Emperor of China: Self Portrait of K'ang-hsi.* New York, 1974.

Struve, Lynn A. *The Southern Ming.* New Haven, 1984.

Sullivan, Michael. *The Meeting of Eastern and Western Art.* New York, 1973.

Chapter Bibliographies

Sung Ying-hsing. *T'ien-kung k'ai-wu. Chinese Technology in the Seventeenth Century.* Trans. by E-tu Zen Sun and Shiou-chuan Sun. University Park, Pa., 1966.

Thompson, Laurence G. *Chinese Religion: An Introduction.* Encino, Cal., and Belmont, Cal., 1975.

Till, Barry. *In Search of Old Nanking.* Hong Kong, 1982.

Torbert, Preston M. "The Ch'ing Imperial Household Department: A Study of Its Organization and Principal Functions, 1662–1796." Ph.D. diss., Dept. of History, Univ. of Chicago, 1973.

Tsien Tsuen-hsuin. *Paper and Printing.* Vol. V, Pt. 1 of J. Needham, *Science and Civilization in China.* Cambridge, 1985.

———. *Written on Bamboo and Silk.* Chicago, 1962.

Wakeman, Frederic, Jr. *The Great Enterprise. The Manchu Reconstruction of Imperial Order in Seventeenth-Century China.* 2 vols. Berkeley, 1985.

Wills, John E., Jr. *Embassies and Illusions: Dutch and Portuguese Envoys to K'ang-hsi, 1666–1687.* Cambridge, Mass., 1984.

Worcester, G. R. G. *The Junks and Sampans of the Yangtze.* Annapolis, Md., 1971.

Zhou Xun and Gao Chunming. *Five Thousand Years of Chinese Costumes.* San Francisco, 1987.

ARTICLES

Bürke, Alois. "Das Nestorianer-Denkmal von Si-an-fu. Versuch einer Neuübersetzung." *NZM,* Supplementa XVII (1971).

Chan, Albert. "Chinese-Philippine Relations in the Late Sixteenth Century and to 1603." *Philippine Studies,* XXVI (1978), 51–82.

Destombes, M. "A Rare Chinese Atlas," *Quaerendo,* IV (1974), 336–37.

Heeren, J. J. "Father Bouvet's Picture of Emperor K'ang-hsi (with Appendices)." *Asia Major,* VII (1932), 556–72.

Ho Ping-ti. "The Significance of the Ch'ing Period in Chinese History." *Journal of Asian Studies,* XXVI (1967), 189–95.

Huart, C. Imbault. "Le voyage de l'ambassade hollandaise de 1656 à travers la province de Canton." *JRAS (North China Branch),* n.s., Vol. XXX, No. 1 (1895–96), pp. 1–73.

Hucker, Charles O. "Governmental Organization of the Ming Dynasty." *Harvard Journal of Asiatic Studies,* XXI (1958), 1–66.

Lundbaek, K. "The First Translation from the Confucian Classics in Europe." *China Mission Studies (1550–1800) Bulletin,* I (1979), 2–11.

———. "The Image of Neo-Confucianism in *Confucius sinarum philosophus.*" *Journal of the History of Ideas,* XLIV (1983), 19–30.

Merkel, Franz R. "Deutsche Chinaforscher." *Archiv für Kulturgeschichte,* XXXIV (1951–52), 81–106.

Mungello, David. "Unearthing the Manuscripts of Bouvet's *Gujin* after Nearly Three Centuries." *China Mission Studies (1550–1800) Bulletin,* X (1988), 34–61.

———. "The Jesuits' Use of Chang Chü-cheng's Commentary in Their Translation of the Confucian Four Books (1687)." *Ibid.,* III (1981), 12–22.

Petech, L. "L'ambasciata olandese del 1655–57 nei documenti cinesi." *Rivista degli studi orientali,* XXV (1950), 77–87.

———. "La pretesa ambascita di Shah Jahan alla Cina." *Ibid.,* XXVI (1951), 124–27.

Rao Sahib, C. S. K. "Shah Jehan's Embassy to China, 1656 A.D." *Quarterly Journal of the Mythic Society,* Silver Jubilee Number XXV (1934–35), 117–21.

Szczesniak, Boleslaw. "The Writings of Michael Boym." *Monumenta Serica,* XIV (1949–55), 481–538.

Van Kley, E. "An Alternative Muse: The Manchu Conquest of China in the Literature of Seventeenth-Century Northern Europe." *European Studies Review,* VI (1976), 21–43.

———. "Europe's 'Discovery' of China and the Writing of World History." *American Historical Review,* LXXVI (1971), 358–85.

———. "News from China: Seventeenth-Century European Notices of the Manchu Conquest." *Journal of Modern History,* XLV (1973), 561–82.

Vargas, Philippe de. "Le 'Giro del Mondo' de Gemelli Careri, en particulier le récit du séjour en Chine. Roman ou verité?" *Schweizerische Zeitschrift für Geschichte,* V (1955), 417–51.

Wallis, H. "Missionary Cartographers to China." *Geographical Magazine,* XLVII (1975), 751–59.

Walravens, Hartmut. "Eine Anmerkung zu Michael Boyms Flora Sinensis (1656)— einer wichtigen naturhistorischen Quelle." *China Mission Studies (1550–1800) Bulletin,* I (1979), 16–20.

Wolf, Arthur P. "Gods, Ghosts, and Ancestors." In A. P. Wolf (ed.), *Religion and Ritual in Chinese Society,* pp. 131–82. Stanford, 1974.

XXII. CHINA'S PERIPHERY

BOOKS

Ahmad, Z. *Sino-Tibetan Relations in the Seventeenth Century.* Rome, 1970.

Armstrong, T. (ed.). *Yermak's Campaign in Siberia.* "HS," 2d ser., CXLVI. London, 1975.

Baddeley, John Frederick (ed.). *Russia, Mongolia, China . . . Being Some Record of the Relations between Them from the Beginning of the Seventeenth Century to the Death of the Tsar Alexei Milhailovitch A.D. 1602–1676. . . .* 2 vols. London, 1919.

Bell, G. *The People of Tibet.* Oxford, 1928.

Cammann, Schuyler. *The Land of the Camel. Tents and Temples in Inner Mongolia.* New York, 1951.

Campbell, William. *An Account of Missionary Success in the Island of Formosa.* London, 1899.

———. *Formosa under the Dutch.* London, 1903; reprinted Taipei, 1967.

Chai Chen-kang. *Taiwan Aborigines: A Genetic Study of Tribal Variations.* Cambridge, Mass., 1967.

Chen Chi-lu. *Material Culture of the Formosan Aborigines.* Taipei, 1968.

Chapter Bibliographies

Choi, Andreus. *L'Erection du première vicariat apostolique et les origines du Catholicisme en Corée, 1592–1837.* Schöneck-Beckenried, 1961.

Chopra, P. N. *Ladakh.* New Delhi, 1980.

Czaplicka, M. A. *Aboriginal Siberia. A Study in Social Anthropology.* Oxford, 1914.

Davidson, J. W. *The Island of Formosa, Past and Present.* London and New York, 1903.

Deny, Jean, et al. (eds.). *Philologiae turciae fundamenta.* 2 vols. Wiesbaden, 1959.

Dmytryshyn, Basil; Crownhart-Vaughan, E. A. P.; and Vaughan, Thomas (eds. and trans.). *Russia's Conquest of Siberia, 1558–1700.* Vol. I. Portland, Oregon, 1985.

Eliade, Mircea. *Shamanism: Archaic Techniques of Ecstasy.* New York, 1964.

Eliot, Sir Charles. *Hinduism and Buddhism.* 3 vols. London, 1954.

Gates, A. F. *Christianity and Animism in Taiwan.* San Francisco, 1979.

Grayson, J. H. *Early Buddhism and Christianity in Korea.* Leyden, 1985.

Grousset, René. *The Empire of the Steppes.* Trans. from French by N. Walford. New Brunswick, N.J., 1970.

Han Woo-keun. *The History of Korea.* Seoul, 1971; reprinted Honolulu, 1971.

Henthorn, William E. *A History of Korea.* New York, 1971.

Hsieh Chiao-min. *Taiwan-Ilha Formosa; Geography in Perspective.* Washington, D.C., 1964.

Hummel, Arthur W. (ed.). *Eminent Chinese of the Ch'ing Period (1644–1912).* Washington, D.C., 1943.

Kano, Tadao, and Segawa, Koichi. *The Illustrated Ethnography of Formosan Aborigines. The Yami Tribe.* Tokyo, 1945.

Knapp, Ronald G. (ed.). *China's Island Frontier.* Honolulu, 1980.

Kronk, Gary W. *Comets. A Descriptive Catalog.* Hillside, N.J., 1984.

Kuepers, J. J. S. M. *The Dutch Reformed Church in Formosa, 1627–1662.* "Schriftenreihe der Neuen Zeitschrift für Missionswissenschaft," XXVII. Immensee, 1978.

Kwanten, Luc. *Imperial Nomads.* Philadelphia, 1979.

Lattimore, Owen. *Inner Asian Frontiers of China.* Boston, 1962.

———. *Manchuria, Cradle of Conflict.* New York, 1932.

Lee, R. H. G. *The Manchurian Frontier in Ch'ing History.* Cambridge, Mass., 1970.

Lee Ki-Baik. *A New History of Korea.* Trans. by E. M. Wagner and E. J. Schultz. Cambridge, Mass., 1984.

Lee Kwang-Kyu. *Kinship System in Korea.* 2 vols. New Haven, 1975.

Levin, M. G., and Potapov, L. P. (eds.). *The Peoples of Siberia.* Trans. from Russian by Stephen Dunn. Chicago, 1964.

MacGregor, J. *Tibet. A Chronicle of Exploration.* New York, 1970.

Maclagan, Edward Douglas. *The Jesuits and the Great Mogul.* London, 1932; New York, 1972.

Mancall, Mark. *Russia and China: Their Diplomatic Relations to 1728.* Cambridge, Mass., 1971.

McGovern, Janet B. M. *Among the Headhunters of Formosa.* London, 1922.

Michael, Franz. *The Origin of Manchu Rule in China.* New York, 1972.

Murzaev, E. M. *Die mongolische Völkerrepublik, physisch-geographische Beschreibung.* Trans. Tutenberg. Gotha, 1954.

Nebesky-Wojkowitz, René de. *Oracles and Demons of Tibet.* The Hague, 1956.

———. *Tibetan Religious Dances.* Ed. Christoph von Fürer-Haimendorf. The Hague, 1976.

Osgood, Cornelius. *The Koreans and Their Culture.* New York, 1951.

Oxnam, R. B. *Ruling from Horseback. Manchu Politics in the Oboi Regency, 1661–69.* Chicago, 1975.

Petech, Luciano (ed.). *I missionari italiani nel Tibet e nel Nepal.* 7 vols. Rome, 1952–56.

———. *The Kingdom of Ladakh, c. 950–1842 A.D.* Rome, 1977. Vol. LI of G. Tucci (ed.), *Serie orientale Roma* of the Istituto Italiano per il Medio ed Estremo Oriente.

Re, Arundel del. *Creation Myths of the Formosan Natives.* Tokyo, 1951.

Rossabi, M. *China and Inner Asia from 1368 to the Present Day.* London, 1975.

Schauensee, Rodolphe M. de. *The Birds of China.* Washington, D.C., 1984.

Schwartzberg, J. E. (ed.). *A Historical Atlas of South Asia.* Chicago, 1978.

Sebes, Joseph, S.J. *The Jesuits and the Sino-Russian Treaty of Nerchinsk (1689); The Diary of Thomas Pereira, S.J.* Rome, 1961.

Sinor, Denis. *Inner Asia and Its Contacts with Medieval Europe.* London, 1977.

Stein, R. A. *Tibetan Civilization.* Trans. from French by J. C. Stapleton Driver. Stanford, 1972.

Su Chung (Davis, Lucille). *Court Dishes of China. The Cuisine of the Ch'ing Dynasty.* Rutland, Vt., 1970.

Toscano, Giuseppe M. *La prima missione cattolica nel Tibet.* Parma, 1951; reprinted, The Hague, 1953.

Tregear, T. R. *A Geography of China.* Chicago, 1965.

Tucci, G. *The Religions of Tibet.* Trans. from German and Italian by G. Samuel. Berkeley, 1980.

Wakeman, Frederic, Jr. *The Great Enterprise. The Manchu Reconstruction of Imperial Order in Seventeenth-Century China.* 2 vols. Berkeley, 1985.

Wessels, Cornelius. *Early Jesuit Travellers in Central Asia 1603–1721.* The Hague, 1924.

Widmer, Eric. *The Russian Ecclesiastical Mission in Peking.* Cambridge, Mass., 1976.

ARTICLES

Alvarez, Jose M. "The Aboriginal Inhabitants of Formosa." *Anthropology,* XXII (1927), 255–67.

Athapilly, Andrew. "An Indian Prototype for Prester John." *Terrae Incognitae,* X (1978), 15–23.

Cartier, Michel. "La vision chinoise du monde: Taiwan dans la littérature géographique ancienne." *Actes du IIIe Colloque International de Sinologie. Apprécia-tion par Europe de la tradition chinois a partir du XVIIe siècle.* Paris, 1983.

Corbett, M. "The Dutch Mission to Peking in 1655." *Quaerendo,* Vol. XVI, No. 2 (Spring, 1986), pp. 131–36.

Cory, Ralph M. "Some Notes on Father Gregorio de Cespedes, Korea's First Euro-pean Visitor." *JRAS, Korea,* XXVII (1937), 1–55.

Hosten, H., S.J. (trans. and ed.). "A Letter of Father Francisco Godinho, S.J., from Western Tibet (Tsaparang, August 16, 1626)." *Journal of the Asiatic Society of Bengal,* n.s., XXI (1925), 49–73.

Hsieh Chao-min. "Sequent Occupance and Place Names." In Ronald G. Knapp (ed.), *China's Island Frontier,* pp. 107–14. Honolulu, 1980.

Hsu Wen-hsiung. "From Aboriginal Island to Chinese Frontier: The Development of Taiwan before 1683." In Ronald G. Knapp (ed.), *China's Island Frontier,* pp. 3–28. Honolulu, 1980.

Jochelson, Woldemar. "The Yakut." In *Anthropological Papers of the American Museum of Natural History,* Vol. XXXIII, Pt. 2 (1933), pp. 35–225.

Lee Bing. "Aborigines of Formosa." *Far Eastern Economic Review,* XII (1952), 605.

Riess, Ludwig. "Geschichte der Insul Formosa." *Mittheilungen der deutschen Gesell-schaft für Natur- und Volkenkunst Ost-Asiens,* Vol. VI, Pt. 59 (1893–97), pp. 405–15.

Roux, Jean-Paul. "Le chaman altaïque d'après les voyageurs européens des XVIIe et XVIIIe siècles." *Anthropos,* LVI (1961), 438–58.

Walton, W. H. H. "Among the Mountains and Headhunters of Formosa." *Geo-graphical Journal,* LXXXI (1933), 481–500.

Wessels, C. "New Documents Relating to the Journey of Fr. John Grueber." *AHSI,* IX (1940), 281–302.

Widmer, Eric. "'Kitai' and the Ch'ing Empire in Seventeenth-Century Russian Documents on China." *Ch'ing-shih Wen-t'i,* Vol. II, No. 4 (Nov. 1970), pp. 21–39.

Zimmel, Bruno. "Der erste Bericht über Tibets Hauptstadt Lhasa aus dem Jahre 1661." *Biblos,* II (Vienna, 1953), 127–45.

XXIII. JAPAN

BOOKS

Arnold, Denis (ed.). *The New Oxford Companion to Music.* 2 vols. Oxford and New York, 1983.

Batchelor, J. *Ainu Life and Lore.* Tokyo, n.d.

Boxer, C. R. *The Christian Century in Japan, 1549–1650.* Berkeley, 1951.

———. *Jan Compagnie in Japan.* The Hague, 1950.

———. (ed.). *The Affair of the Madre de Deus. A Chapter in the History of the Por-tuguese in Japan.* London, 1929.

Chamberlain, Basil Hall. *Things Japanese.* London, 1905.

———, and Mason, W. B. *A Handbook for Travellers in Japan.* 5th rev. ed. London, 1899.

Dore, R. P. *Education in Tokugawa Japan.* 2d ed. London, 1984.

Drummond, R. H. *A History of Christianity in Japan.* Grand Rapids, Mich., 1971.

Dunn, Charles J. *Everyday Life in Traditional Japan.* Tokyo, 1969.

Duus, Peter. *Feudalism in Japan.* New York, 1969.

Earhart, H. Byron. *A Religious Study of the Mount Haguro Sect of Shugendo: An Example of Japanese Mountain Religion.* Tokyo, 1970.

Eliade, Mircea. *Shamanism: Archaic Techniques of Ecstasy.* New York, 1964.

Eliot, Sir Charles. *Japanese Buddhism.* London, 1935.

Elison, George. *Deus Destroyed: The Image of Christianity in Early Modern Japan.* Cambridge, Mass., 1973.

Endo, Shusaku. *The Samurai.* Translated by Van C. Gessel. New York, 1982.

———. *Silence.* Tokyo, [1969].

Fredéric, Louis. *Daily Life in Japan at the Time of the Samurai, 1185–1603.* Trans. by Eileen M. Lowe. New York and Washington, D.C., 1972.

Geiser, P., and Peng, F. C. C. *The Ainu: The Past in the Present.* Hiroshima, 1977.

Hayashiya, Tatsusaburō (ed.). *Kyoto no rekishi* [History of Kyoto]. 10 vols. Kyoto, 1972.

Hearn, Lafcadio. *Glimpses of Unfamiliar Japan.* 2 vols. Boston, 1896.

Japan *Times. Kyoto. An Essay in Photographs.* Tokyo, 1975.

———. *Mt. Fuji.* Tokyo, 1970.

Kodansha Encyclopedia of Japan. 9 vols. Tokyo, 1983.

Landor, A. H. S. *Alone with the Hairy Ainu.* London, 1893.

Massarella, Derek. *A World Elsewhere: Europe's Encounter with Japan in the Sixteenth and Seventeenth Centuries.* New Haven and London, 1990.

Miller, Roy Andrew. *The Japanese Language.* Chicago, 1967.

Minnich, H. B. *Japanese Costume and the Makers of Its Elegant Tradition.* Tokyo, 1964.

Mizuo, Hiroshi. *Edo Painting: Sotatsu and Korin.* New York, 1972.

Mogi, Hitoshi. *A Historical Study of the Development of Edo.* Tokyo, 1966.

Morisue, Yoshiaki, and Hinonishi, Suketaka (eds.). *Fuzoku Jiten* [Dictionary of Social Customs]. Tokyo, 1957.

Munro, Neil Gordon. *Ainu. Creed and Cult.* New York, 1963.

Murdoch, James, and Yamagata, Isoh. *A History of Japan.* 3 vols. London, 1949.

Nihon Kokugo Daijiten [Unabridged Japanese Dictionary]. 20 vols. Tokyo, 1974.

Papinot, E. *Historical and Geographical Dictionary of Japan.* 2 vols. New York, 1968.

Peng, F. C. C., and Geiser, P. *The Ainu: The Past in the Present.* Hiroshima, 1977.

Piggot, F. *The Music and Musical Instruments of Japan.* 2d ed. London, 1909.

Plutschow, Herbert E. *Historical Kyoto.* Tokyo, 1983.

———. *Historical Nagasaki.* Tokyo, 1983.

Rothermund, Harmut O. *Die Yamabushi. Aspekte ihres Glaubens, Lebens und ihrer sozialen Funktion im japanischen Mittelalter.* "Monographien zur Völkerkunde, herausgegeben vom Hamburgischen Museum für Völkerkunde," V. Hamburg, 1968.

Sansom, George B. *Japan, a Short Cultural History.* Rev. ed. New York, 1943.

Schurhammer, George, S.J. *Shinto. The Way of the Gods of Japan. According to Printed and Unprinted Reports of the Japanese Jesuit Missionaries in the Sixteenth and Seventeenth Centuries.* Bonn, 1923.

Statler, Oliver. *Japanese Inn.* New York, 1961.

Szilas, László, S.J. (ed.). *Orientalia.* Lisbon, 1963.

Totman, Conrad. *Politics in the Tokugawa Bakufu.* Cambridge, Mass., 1967.

Tsuda, N. *Handbook of Japanese Art.* Tokyo, 1936.

Tsukahira, T. G. *Feudal Control in Tokugawa Japan: The Sankin Kotai System.* Cambridge, Mass., 1966.

Wijnaendts van Resandt, W. *De gezaghebbers der Oost-Indische Compagnie . . . in Azië.* Amsterdam, 1944.

ARTICLES

Bodart Bailey, Beatrice M. "Kaempher Restor'd." *Monumenta Nipponica,* Vol. XLIII, No. 1 (1988), pp. 1–33.

Bouchy, Ann-Marie. "The Cult of Mount Atago Confraternities." *Journal of Asian Studies,* XLVI (1987), 255–77.

Ito, Shuntaro. "The Introduction of Western Cosmology in Seventeenth-Century Japan: The Case of Christovão Ferreira (1580–1652)." *The Japan Foundation Newsletter,* Vol. XIV, No. 1 (May, 1986), pp. 1–9.

Mass, Jeffrey. "The Emergence of the Kamakura Bakufu." In John W. Hall and Jeffrey Mass (eds.), *Medieval Japan: Essays in Institutional History,* pp. 127–56. New Haven and London, 1974.

Nakamura, Hirosi. "The Japanese Portolanos of Portuguese Origin of the Sixteenth and Seventeenth Centuries." *Imago Mundi,* XVIII (1964), 24–44.

Schurhammer, Georg, S.J. "Die Yamabushis." In László Szilas, S.J. (ed.), *Orientalia.* Lisbon, 1963, pp. 705–30.

Schütte, J. F. "Japanese Cartography at the Court of Florence; Robert Dudley's Maps of Japan, 1606–1636." *Imago Mundi,* XXIII (1969), 46–50.

Van Eeghen, I. H. "Arnoldus Montanus's Book on Japan." *Quaerendo,* Vol. II, No. 4 (1972), pp. 250–72.

Wooley, M. A. "Historical Notes on Nagasaki." *Transactions of the Asiatic Society of Japan,* IX (1881), 125–51.

Cumulative Index

Index

Ibabao (or East Samar), 1499, 1516

Ibatan (in the Bisayan islands), 1516

Iberia, 23; exclusive rights of empire in Asia, 106, 340–41; fiscal administration of, 25; printing in, 303–4, 589; reading public, 306; union, 9. *See also* Portugal; Spain

Ibn Batuta, 933, 939n

Ibrahim, ruler of the Maldives, 935

Ibrahim 'Adil Shah II, 855–56

Ibrahim of Cambodia, 1154

I Ching, 1733–34; China's oldest book, 1719

Ides, Evert Ysbrandszoon, 503–4, 543, 1701; embassy to China (1692–95), 1686, 1690, 1759; on Manchuria, 1762–67

Iemitsu. *See* Tokugawa Iemitsu

Ieyasu. *See* Tokugawa Ieyasu

Ikkeri, 20, 863, 865–66; Della Valle on, 863–69; and Gersoppa, 864; and the Portuguese, 874; and Ulla, 867

Ilahbas or Allahabad, 702

Ilocos, 1518; costume, 1524; and gold, 1498; Igorots, 1514; tattooing, 1523–24

Imam Shah, 619n

Indalvai (in the Deccan), 769

India, 3, 10, 228, 581, 609, 625, 645, 747, 838–40, 893, 927, 1061, 1126; agriculture, 607, 808, 822, 826, 1896; ancient texts in translation, 900; arithmetic, 810; Armenians in, 711; arts and crafts, 625, 716–17, 812, 834, 836, 1898; astronomy, 624, 782; atheists, 874; beverages, 608; books, 810–11, 898; brass industry, 1697; and Buddhism, 782, 1653; calendar, 1040–41; the Carnatic (Karnatak) missions, 258–59; carnelian rings, 812; cave temples, 773n, 796–98, 834; childbirth, 611, 814, 817; child marriages, 816–17; child naming ceremony, 817, 1025–26, 1037; children, 717, 814; chronology, 783, 1046; civil wars, 81, 562, 697, 759, 1064n, 1897; climate, 581, 607, 639–40, 668, 702, 762, 776, 811, 1021; coastal trade, 20, 29; coffee, 815; coins, 580, 696n; color line, 610, 814, 894, 917n, 1015; comets, 776; compared to China, 1564; coracles, 1070; cos, 612, 621; costumes, 610–11, 653, 661, 681–82, 709, 721, 729, 812, 835, 868–69, 883, 885, 895, 1001, 1026; and the cow, 606, 624, 780, 787–88, 864–65; customs, 610–11, 746, 813–14, 818, 823; descriptions, 414, 416–17, 451–52, 493–95, 497, 558–59; diet, 682, 745, 814–15, 835–36;

diseases, 624, 752–53, 755, 836, 841, 885, 1060; education, 781, 819, 834, 864, 871, 878, 898, 930, 1058; elephants, 608, 720, 778n, 820–21, 1083; emblems, 771; entertainments, 623, 814, 819; European records on, 1898–99; exports, 609, 799; fakirs, 581, 680, 790, 881; famine in, 78, 81, 663, 668; fauna, 608, 611, 624, 656, 670, 677–78, 737, 762, 819, 821–23, 868, 873; festivals, 691, 762, 788, 791, 1040; flora, 612, 621, 652–53, 656, 751–52, 772, 774, 792, 822–23, 1071; the flying fox, 670, 821n; foods, 625, 674n, 682, 690, 693, 716, 822; fortresses, 1023; Fort St. George, 257, 286, 1078; and the French, 96, 418, 748–49; fruits, 607, 621, 716, 815; gardens, 608, 622, 637, 670, 689–90, 692, 714, 721–22, 731–33, 737, 746–47, 751, 761, 772–73, 802, 804–5, 1073; gems, 1068; geography, 782, 799, 1072; ghee (clarified butter), 682; gold, 27, 752, 799; guides, 624, 805, 811; history, 1898; Holi, 777, 788, 874; holy men, 784, 786–87; horses, 608, 624, 743, 820; housing, 608–9, 625–26, 745, 818, 835, 864–65; hunting, 562, 623, 804, 819–21; hygiene, 716, 813, 818; imports, 610, 799, 823; inns, 611, 622, 685, 1084–85, 1088; iron, 769–70, 1088; Jesuits in, 4, 145–46, 258–59, 373, 379–80, 557–58; lac, 669–70; languages, 356, 375, 809–10, 873, 899, 1060; lime, 1064; literature, 809, 822n, 899, 916; Manila-Madras trade, 39; medicine, 753, 755, 762, 782, 788, 809–10, 814, 823, 834–36, 841, 899; morality, 755, 837, 884; music, 624, 659, 669, 674, 693, 718, 803, 809–10; Muslims of, 610, 789, 803, 869, 874, 886, 925, 931, 1008, 1060–61; narcotics, 670–71, 751; native clergy, 199, 293; natural philosophy, 809, 899; Navarrete in, 359; occupational mobility, 718; ornaments, 813, 1026; overland routes, 502, 696, 910, 924, 1070–71; oxen, 821–22; paintings, 716–17; paper, 775, 810–11; pests, 822, 824; pilgrimages, 610, 624; pirates, 880–81, 917; planned cities, 1072; political entities, 1896–97; polyandry, 555; polygamy, 817, 1039–40; Portuguese in, 20, 494, 564; and printing, 307, 344, 356; prostitution, 615, 653, 694–95, 885; religions, 86, 415, 493, 1897–98; religious toleration, 885, 929–31, 1897; salutations,